Mrs. Beeton's
Family Cookery

Mrs. Beeton's Family Cookery

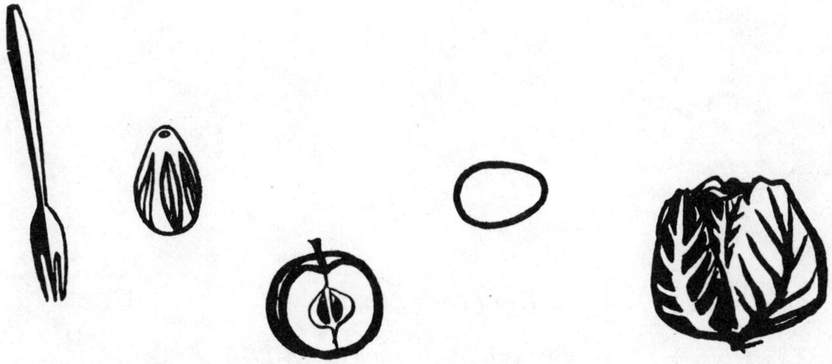

WARD LOCK LIMITED · LONDON

Acknowledgments

THE illustrations both in colour and black and white have always been a feature of earlier editions of this work, and many photographs were taken by Ward Lock staff to illustrate this volume. In addition we should like to thank the following firms and authorities for kindly supplying plates:

MacFisheries Ltd.; Lincolnshire Canners Ltd.; Alfred Bird & Sons Ltd.; Spry Kitchen; Tate & Lyle; MacDougalls Ltd.; Nestlé Company Limited.

We should also like to thank the following firms for offering facilities to take photographs or for providing material for photographs:

Froy's Ltd., Hammersmith; Staines Kitchen Equipment Co. Ltd., S.W.1; National Federation of Meat Traders' Associations; The Fatstock Marketing Corporation Ltd.

The following firms have also rendered valuable assistance:

The Flour Advisory Bureau; The White Fish Authority; the Superintendent, Billingsgate Fish Market; the Coffee Publicity Association Ltd.; Australia House; New Zealand House; South Africa House; Bird's Eye Foods Ltd.; Walls Ice Cream Ltd.; Young & Rubicam Ltd.

Revised edition first published 1976
Second impression 1978

ISBN 0 7063 1431 X

Published in Great Britain by Ward Lock Limited
116 Baker Street, London W1M 2BB, a member of the Pentos Group

Printed in Great Britain by
William Clowes & Sons Limited, London, Beccles and Colchester

Contents

CONTENTS

Plates

HOME MANAGEMENT

RUNNING A HOME requires as much skill in management as it does manual skill. Whoever takes the responsibility for running the household has to manage time and money and other people. The tasks involved in running a house are both endless and ever-recurring and time has to be allocated carefully so that the most important jobs are done first and nothing vital has been forgotten at the end. The family budget has to balance and everyone has to do a fair share of the work, so somebody has to be the organiser.

The manager of the household has traditionally been the wife. While the husband worked outside the home to provide an income, the wife worked inside to manage the house. More frequently now both work outside the home, so both have to work inside it as well. However, the actual management, the decisions about who does which jobs and when, about how much should be spent on food and how much on equipment or clothes, often remains with the woman. Even with the labour-saving equipment now available, the job of keeping house is no less demanding.

SHOPPING

Capital expenditure is these days usually a family decision. When to buy furniture, a new television, a washing machine and so on depends on everybody agreeing certain priorities. Food shopping, though, is expected to happen without any major thought or discussion—which leaves the person responsible, usually the housewife, very much on her own. It is up to her to see that the weekly or monthly budget stretches to cover everything needed.

One of the best ways to ensure that you keep within your budget is to shop with a written list of requirements. It is not always possible these days to forecast in advance the cost of everything you are going to buy, as prices change too quickly. Try dividing the list into two. In one section have all the essential items such as eggs, cheese, meat and washing up liquid, the lack of which will cause justifiable complaints. When you have covered these, make a list of extras in case there is some of the budgeted allowance left over; include small luxuries such as a pot of cream or some prawns, or something for the store cupboard such as tinned foods that you don't require immediately but would be glad to have as a standby.

In any new locality, spend a little time initially shopping around to decide which stores give best value for the type of goods you buy, and which carry the best stocks. Then stick to those shops. Going from one to another to find which supermarket has a penny off this and which has a penny off that each week is far too time consuming to be economical. With specialist shops such as the butcher's and greengrocer's it will pay you to be a regular customer, for regular customers can always expect the best service and the best advice.

If you have suitable storage facilities, and particularly if you have a freezer, do not neglect the savings that can be made by buying in bulk. In many areas there are "Cash and Carry" stores that give considerable discounts for bulk sales, and freezer centres specialize in bulk packs of meat and vegetables. If you do not trust the quality of bulk-packed meat your regular butcher may be able to supply you with, say, half a lamb at a price that shows a considerable saving over what you would have to pay to buy it in joints.

Buying in bulk requires careful planning, though. First you must be sure that you like the particular brand that is offered; however cheaply you get it it is no saving to buy large quantities of something the family won't eat. Then you must be able to gauge roughly how much you use of a particular product over a given period; you may know that you buy three tins of baked beans each week, but do you know how often you buy washing up liquid? Finally you must have suitable storage conditions and space for the bulk supplies, plus enough containers into which to transfer smaller quantities for economical use in the kitchen.

When it comes to buying the kind of thing that is not acquired every day—equipment, kitchen utensils, bedding and so on—a reliable shop can often give the most valuable guidance. Better still, go to several good shops and compare the advice they give you. There are also several quite unbiased agencies that exist to help purchasers choose sound merchandise, suited to individual requirements. These include:

Consumers' Association Ltd.,
14, Buckingham Street,
London WC2N 6DS.

The British Standards Institution,
2, Park Street,
London W1.

The Consumers' Association publishes the monthly *Which*, examining different types of product each month and giving guidance on standards of performance, safety and value for money.

THE HOUSEWORK ROUTINE

Many people enjoy shopping; there is a certain challenge in getting the best value for your money and the interest of seeing what is around, comparing new products and fashions. Housework is more of a challenge, and can seem a dreary part of life, an endless struggle against muddle and cobwebs. But tackled in a more positive frame of mind it can be made rewarding and creative.

The secret is to work to daily, weekly and annual routines. The daily routine involves the endless small chores like getting everybody up and off to work or school in time, with breakfast inside them; it involves washing the dishes, planning and cooking the meals, tidying rooms, making beds, throwing out old newspapers, vacuuming carpets. These are things that keep the house looking cheerful and help the surface life of a family to run smoothly. Weekly routines are for longer jobs like washing and ironing, turning out a room for thorough cleaning, washing the kitchen floor and so on. These are all tasks that certainly do not need doing every day but if they are neglected they can soon make a house dirty and unpleasant to live in. The annual routine involves major upheavals like turning out cupboards, washing curtains and chair covers, shampooing carpets and cleaning paintwork.

There are regular seasonal events that upset the routine of a house, the most obvious of these being Christmas, which requires planning and shopping for presents, cooking the traditional festive foods, possibly preparing for family or friends to come and stay for a few days and probably involvement in those school plays, pantomimes and carol services that are such a drain on time and energy. Once again, planning is the secret. Those who start shopping, wrapping presents and cooking early enough will survive to enjoy the festivities, those who don't will be exhausted and irritable when the day finally arrives.

Other seasonal activities include jamming and bottling in the summer when the soft fruits are plentiful, and making chutneys, pickles and more jams in the autumn when the hard fruits are harvested. When the fruit is ripe for picking, or has been carried home from the shop, there can be no time wasted before you start the necessary preparation and preserving. But the ordinary household routines must still go on all the time.

This is the moment to rope in all the family to help; usually they will be keen to participate, especially in picking the fruit and eating the end product. Advance planning ensures that the necessary jam jars and covers, bottling jars, rings and caps are available and in good condition and takes a lot of the rush out of the work when the time comes.

Few houses are small enough for one person to be able to cope with all this work single-handed. In some households paid part-time help offers a partial solution, but whether or not this is possible the whole family should still normally be expected to take a share in the work. Small children will obviously not be given more than a token task—though it must be done regularly—but bigger ones will automatically fall into a routine if each has his own responsibility; laying the table for breakfast, making beds, cleaning the bath are all the sort of task that children readily see the point of and can carry out efficiently. It is probably better for a husband with long working hours to undertake responsibility for weekly rather than daily tasks. It is absolutely essential that all the members of the family do their share if the wife has a job outside the home; even if she doesn't, running a house and family is still a mammoth task for one person.

Most stains respond to home treatment and it is sensible to keep a "first-aid" kit which should include cleaning fluids, grease solvents and bleaches. The method used depends largely on the type of fabric that is being treated; for instance some man-made fibres are marked by water and need to be treated with spirit; others are dissolved by spirit and need only soap and water; others will rot or discolour if bleaches are used. In general soap and water should be tried first, and any article that has been treated, and will stand water on it, must be washed after the stain has been removed.

GENERAL HINTS

When spirit cleaners are used, the area around the stain must be wetted with the spirit first to prevent "ringing". Most spirit cleaners are highly inflammable, and must be kept away from a naked fire or flame; it is best to use them out of doors if possible. They should be clearly marked and stored where they cannot be reached by children.

Strong bleaches are very corrosive, and the hands and other clothes should be protected while they are being used.

Stains should always be dealt with as soon as they happen if possible, and, if not, at the first available minute. This is to prevent them "setting" into the fabric and being very much more difficult to remove as a result. In general most stains will give way to plain soap and water, but where chemicals are being used the stained part should be laid on a clean cloth and sponged with a clean pad.

There are so many things which may stain fabrics that it is not possible to give them all, but the following will help with the more common stains which have to be dealt with in the home wash:

Acids: Use a weak alkaline solution such as 1 teasp. washing soda or borax in 1 pint water or 1 part household ammonia to 4 parts water. Wash and rinse.

Ball-point pen ink: Sponge with methylated spirit. Test rayons before using.

Blood: Soak in cold salted water at once. If already set and stiff, stains need special dry-cleaning treatment.

Cocoa, Coffee, Tea, Fruit juice, Wine: Sprinkle stain with borax and pour hot water through it, leaving the stained part to soak in the solution. Sponge coloured fabrics with a weak solution of borax ($\frac{1}{2}$ oz. to $\frac{1}{2}$ pint warm water). For old or difficult stains, apply 1 part of glycerine to 1 part of water and leave for a few minutes before rinsing.

Cod-liver oil: This must be attended to at once. Wash with hot water and if necessary bleach with dilute hydrogen peroxide.

Creosote, Tar: Scrape off excess, then sponge with benzine, cleaning fluid or eucalyptus oil. Wash well.

Egg: Soak in cold water and then wash well.

STAIN REMOVAL

Grass: Sponge with methylated spirits and wash well.

Grease and oil: Scrape off excess. Wash with soapy water and ammonia; if stain persists, remove it with cleaning fluid. If the material is not suitable for this, apply pads of blotting paper or thick brown paper on either side of the stain and press with a warm iron to melt the grease, which is then absorbed by the paper. Where suitable, complete all cleaning with a wash, or sponge with cleaning fluid or spirit.

Ink: Rinse at once in cold water or in a little milk, then wash well. On white fabrics use a bleach of oxalic acid; on coloured fabrics apply a mixture of permanganate of potash (¼ teasp. to ½ pint water), and then remove the brown stain of the permanganate by using a solution of hydrogen peroxide and a dash of vinegar.

Iodine: When fresh wash well or boil. Otherwise soak in a solution of washing soda or well-diluted starch for about 20 minutes. If the stain persists, wash and then give a mild bleach.

Iron mould: On white linen or cotton, sponge with a solution of oxalic acid (½ teasp. to ½ pint water) and wash well.

Lipstick: Wash well, boiling if the material can stand it. If not, use cleaning fluid. If the stain is very persistent, apply a little glycerine, rub well in and leave to soak for an hour, then wash.

Mildew: When it is quite dry, brush off the surface spores, then sponge with permanganate of potash (¼ teasp. to ½ pint water) followed by 20 vol. peroxide of hydrogen (1 part to 5 parts of water) with a few drops of vinegar.

Nail Varnish: Sponge with acetone and wash to remove traces of dye. N.B. Test rayons before using acetone; for acetate rayons use amyl acetate.

Perspiration: Soak in a mild solution of ammonia or vinegar and water.

Paint: If the paint is of the usual kind, rub with turpentine or white spirit. Cellulose paint must be treated with acetone, but this will damage rayons.

Scorch marks: Apply a paste of borax and glycerine, leave for a few minutes and then sponge off. A bad scorch can never be satisfactorily removed.

Shoe polish: Sponge with turpentine followed by methylated spirit.

Yellowing linen: Linen that is old or that has been stored, goes yellow; this can be removed by placing the articles in a mild bleach for ½ hour, then laundering well, boiling and blueing.

Suits: First turn out and brush the pockets, mend them if necessary, then brush the suit well and remove specific stains. Make a good lather with a detergent and apply the lather only, not the water, to the suit with a clean cloth, working quickly and lightly. Then rub again with another cloth wrung out of clean water, keeping it as dry as possible. Then press the suit, using a pressing cloth, keeping trouser creases in the right place and not over-flattening lapels and shoulders. Finally hang the suit to air in a warm, airy place.

Coats: Treat these in the same way as suits. If black material has become greenish or a bad colour, sponging with a mixture of vinegar and water will often help to restore the original colour.

Gloves: Washable gloves should be washed on the hands in soapy water and well rinsed; while still wet they should be blown into to keep their shape, and then hung to dry away from direct heat. Gloves that are not washable may, if the leather is not too delicate, be cleaned by shaking them vigorously in a jar containing cleaning fluid. White sheepskin may be cleaned by rubbing powdered borax into it and then beating it all out again.

Furs: Furs should be given an occasional brush with a soft brush; for more complete cleaning warm bran may be rubbed into them, left for a while and then brushed out, or they may be gently rubbed with methylated spirit and hung out in the air. White furs should always be kept away from the light, preferably in black tissue paper as well as an outer moth-proof container.

Shoes: Shoes should always be cleaned after being worn, and should be kept in a good state of repair. Wet shoes should be loosely stuffed with newspaper to absorb the damp and left in a warm (not hot) airy place to dry out. Gold and silver kid should be kept wrapped in black tissue paper to preserve the colour. Natural leather can be cleaned with cleaning fluid or, better, with saddle soap, before polishing. Suede shoes should be brushed well with a suede brush to remove all traces of dust before being cleaned with one of the special suede cleaners available for the purpose.

Hats: All hats, even those made of straw, should be kept well brushed. The inside of men's hats can be cleaned with cleaning fluid, and if necessary the ribbon can be removed, washed and replaced. Very dirty hats of felt or straw can be sponged with a cloth wrung out of a good soapy lather, and then wiped clean and dried away from strong heat.

Rainwear: Raincoats may be sponged with warm suds and dried in a cool place, but cleaning fluid should never be used on them as it may effect the waterproofing. Many modern mackintoshes can be washed.

NUTRITION

A BALANCED DIET

All kinds of food should normally be included in the family menus, as with variety it is unlikely that any of the essential substances will be missed and the danger of monotonous meal planning will be avoided. The daily menus should contain a selection of foods from all sections of Table I (p. 15) chosen with due regard to flavour, appearance, season, and suitability to those who are taking the meals. The menus should contain:

(*a*) At least one helping of meat or bacon, poultry, fish, cheese or eggs at each of the main meals (breakfast, midday and evening meals) and at least one pint of milk daily. Children and expectant and nursing mothers need even more than one pint of milk daily.

(*b*) Fats, starches and sugars enough to satisfy the appetite, to allow normal growth in children and to maintain the recommended body weight of adults.

(*c*) At least one serving of fresh vegetables, or salad or fruit to assure an adequate amount of vitamin C. The best sources of vitamin C can be selected from Table I.

MENU SUGGESTIONS

Meal patterns vary widely, from community to community, and even from family to family. In most cases, the type of meal and the hour at which it is eaten depend for the most part on the occupations of the individual members of the family. In general, most families are accustomed each day to taking the three set meals—breakfast, lunch and dinner or supper, with one or more subsidiary snacks.

Breakfast: The breakfast of porridge, other cereal dish, or fruit with cereal, followed by tomato, egg, bacon or fish, or a combination of any two of these and toast, butter and marmalade with tea or coffee, is an adequately balanced meal with which to start the day. A hasty bite of toast and black coffee taken on the run is not at all a good nutritional beginning as numerous advertisements remind us.

Main meal: The main meal of the day, whether midday or evening, should contain meat or fish or an equivalent source of protein served with several vegetables. This is usually followed by a second course planned to give extra energy with a light first course or to avoid heaviness after, for example, a meal of roast meat and Yorkshire pudding.

Third meal: The third meal should again, if possible, contain either meat, fish, cheese or egg. It is at most times of a simpler form than the main meal and it usually has a less defined pattern. This meal is often the opportunity for introducing fresh fruit or salad into the menu and for putting in a junket or similar dish which increases the milk consumption without offering too much liquid milk.

Snacks: The content of these snacks can make very important contributions when it is necessary to raise the nutritional value of the diet. Conversely it is often these snacks that provide the unnecessary food that puts extra weight on people who fatten easily. The snack meals should therefore be watched as carefully as the main meals by those who guard the family health.

Season: Although the general principles of menu planning always remain the same, a menu made out for summer often differs in composition of actual foods from that made out for winter. This is because:

(*a*) foods which are in season are used, in order to reduce costs,

(*b*) in the cold weather the requirement for heat and energy is increased, with the result that heavier meals containing more carbohydrate and fat are often provided.

TABLE I

Table of Food Values for a Balanced Diet

PROTEIN OR BODY BUILDING FOODS	FATS AND CARBOHYDRATES OR ENERGY FOODS	
Meat	Butter	Dried peas
Offal	Margarine	Haricot beans
Poultry	Lard	Rice
Game	Cooking fats	Sago
Fish	Bread	Macaroni
Eggs	Potatoes	Spaghetti
Cheese	Oatmeal	Wholemeal bread
Milk	Biscuits	
Beans	Cakes	
Peas	Honey	
Nuts	Jam	
	Sugar	

FOODS THAT GIVE CALCIUM	FOODS THAT GIVE IRON	
Cheese	Lean meat	Wholemeal bread
Milk	Liver	Black treacle
Sardines	Kidney	Raisins
Herrings	Eggs	Currants
Eggs	Watercress	Dried Apricots
Green vegetables	Spinach	
Bread—white	Oatmeal	
Black treacle	Bread—white	

FOODS THAT CONTAIN VITAMIN A		FOODS THAT CONTAIN VITAMIN D
Butter	Carrots	Butter
Margarine	Halibut liver oil	Margarine
Eggs	Cod-liver oil	Eggs
Milk		Milk
Liver		Halibut liver oil
Green vegetables		Cod-liver oil

DAILY CALORIE ALLOWANCE

FOODS THAT CONTAIN THE VITAMIN B GROUP	FOODS THAT CONTAIN VITAMIN C	
Liver	Blackcurrants	Parsnips
Meat	Rosehip syrup	Swedes
Yeast	Oranges	Tomatoes
Yeast extracts	Lemons	Potatoes
Eggs	Grapefruit	Lettuce
Milk	Green vegetables	
Cheese	Watercress	
Oatmeal	Parsley	
Wholemeal bread	Cauliflower	

Many of the foods listed in the preceding groups contain more than one of the essential elements of nutrition. The *Manual of Nutrition* issued by H.M. Stationery Office covers the subject in much greater detail than is possible here.

TABLE II

Recommended Daily Calorie Allowances

AGE AND SEX		CALORIES	AGE AND SEX		CALORIES
Children under	1 yr.	100 per kg. (2.205 lb.)	Women	light activity	2000
	1–6	1000 to 1500		moderate activity	2500
	7–10	2000		pregnant	2500
Boys	11–14	2750		nursing	3000
	15–19	3500	Men	light activity	2250
Girls	11–14	2750		moderate activity	3000
	15–19	2500		heavy work	3500

Note: Recently these figures have been slightly modified.

Portions of Common Foods which Yield 100 Calories

FOOD	WT.	MEASURE	FOOD	WT.	MEASURE
Bread	1½ oz.	1 slice	Banana	5 oz.	1 large
Rice	1 ,,	4 tablesp.	Orange	10½ ,,	2 large
Sweet biscuits	¾ ,,	2 small	Cabbage	13½ ,,	½
Bacon	¾ ,,	1 rasher	Carrots	16 ,,	5–6 medium
Cheese (Cheddar)	¾ ,,	1 in. cube	Onion	16 ,,	4 medium
Egg	2¼ ,,	1 extra large	Potato	4¾ ,,	1 medium
Steak	1 ,,	¼ helping	Potato chips	1½ ,,	1 packet
Butter	½ ,,	1 tablesp.	Tomato	25 ,,	10 medium
Cream, thick	1 ,,	1¾ tablesp.	Marmalade	1½ ,,	3 tablesp.

PORTIONS OF COMMON FOODS WHICH YIELD 100 CALORIES (*cont'd.*)

Margarine	½	,,	1 tablesp.	Toffee	¾	,,	3
Milk	6	,,	1 teacup	Sherry	2½	,,	1 medium glass
Apples, cooking	10	,,	2	Sugar	1	,,	2 tablesp.

NOTE: Weights given are edible portion. Spoon measures are level measuring spoons.

COOKING METHODS

In order that good food may be used to the best advantage it must be cooked well, and served attractively. This is of particular importance with an invalid, as usually the appetite needs to be tempted to encourage an adequate intake of food. The methods of cooking and serving food not only influence the flavour, colour and texture, but also the nutritive value. Some of the essential vitamins are easily destroyed by heat or by exposure to light or air. Some are also soluble in water and are lost if the cooking water used in preparation is discarded. Liquid left after cooking vegetables should be used for sauces, gravies or soups where possible. Vitamin A may be damaged by prolonged heating but generally more than enough is present so that the losses are unimportant. Vitamin B_1 is destroyed if it is heated with alkaline substances such as baking soda. It has been observed for instance that bread made from flour and yeast contained most of the B_1 in the original flour, while soda bread lost nearly all its vitamin B_1 in the process of baking. The vitamin most liable to destruction during cooking is vitamin C, and much of the value of fruits or vegetables may be lost if they are not carefully cooked. Vitamin C is also destroyed by cooking with baking soda, which should not be added to green vegetables. See section on Vegetables, p. 320.

For salads, avoid shredding lettuce—preferably tear or break the leaves.

Some of the minerals are also soluble in water, another reason for not soaking foods in water and for using up the water in which they are cooked.

SERVICE OF FOOD

At any time, the way in which food is served and presented either adds to, or detracts considerably from the enjoyment of a meal.

Although the food may have been cooked carefully to contain the maximum amount of vitamins and minerals, if it is allowed to stand about for some time before it is eaten more than half the nutritive value is often lost. Unpleasant flavours and colours sometimes are developed in waiting about in a warm oven, or on a hot plate. It is best, therefore, to serve food as soon after it is cooked as is possible.

The way in which food is presented on the plate, and the table or tray appointments are important especially when dealing with a finicky appetite, which is often found in young children and sick people. A gay cloth, simple china and perhaps a flower on the tray help to create an interest in food. Small helpings arranged with an "eye for colour" are also aids to poor appetites. Some times a "surprise" dish will work wonders with children. In all cases, a quiet and restful atmosphere where there is no sense of urgency, worry or irritation has a good effect on either a patient or a child who seems to have no appetite.

HYGIENE IN FOOD HANDLING

Food poisoning is caused by the contamination of foodstuffs with large numbers of certain micro-organisms which can cause abdominal pain, diarrhœa, vomiting and sometimes fever, 2 to 24 hours after eating the contaminated food. The three main sources of these food-poisoning bacteria are given below:

(*a*) The *human carrier*, where the organisms

may be present in the stool, the nose, septic injuries, boils and carbuncles; from these sources they can be transferred to foodstuffs by the hands.

(*b*) The *animal carrier*. A small proportion of most domestic animals and birds are known to carry organisms capable of causing food-poisoning in human beings, therefore their presence in kitchens is inadvisable, and separate dishes should be provided for feeding pets.

(*c*) Certain foodstuffs may reach the kitchen already contaminated with small numbers of food-poisoning bacteria. Raw meat, ducks' eggs, dried and frozen egg products, both imported and home produced, should be handled with care; receptacles used for their storage or for mixing should be well cleaned and scalded after use. Every effort must be made to keep these foods cold both before and after cooking. If they are not to be eaten immediately it is essential that meats bought already cooked, and perhaps semi-preserved, should be kept cold during storage. The large majority of bacteria cannot multiply in the cold, and the risk of food poisoning will be reduced if there are only small numbers present. Most bacteria are killed by cooking, but one group causing food-poisoning survives boiling and may cause trouble when boiled, steamed or stewed meat is allowed to cool slowly overnight through the temperatures which encourage maximum bacterial growth; slow gentle reheating may also encourage multiplication of bacteria. It is wise, therefore, to eat meats hot and freshly cooked, otherwise they should be cooled quickly and kept cold until required. To reheat, foods should be rapidly brought to the boil and kept boiling for some minutes before eating hot.

Canned goods freshly opened are safe, but if food is stored for long, either in opened tins or taken out of the tin, contamination may occur in the same way.

To cut down the risk of cross-contamination from one food to another in the kitchen, all surfaces and washing-up sinks should be capable of being easily cleaned. Plastic brushes with nylon bristles and the use of paper instead of cloths will minimize the spread of infection.

To summarize, remember to keep personal bacteria out of food; make sure your hands are clean before touching or cooking anything. Keep animals away from exposed foodstuffs and design and equip the kitchen so that all surfaces can be quickly and thoroughly cleaned.

The main preventive measures are summarized below:

1. Wash the hands frequently, always after using the toilet, and always before handling food.
2. Do not touch food with the hands more than necessary.
3. Cover cuts, burns, spots with waterproof dressing.
4. Keep food stored in the cold if it is not eaten immediately after preparation.
5. Cook thoroughly all foods likely to harbour micro-organisms which cause food-poisoning (i.e. meat, meat preparations, ducks' eggs).
6. Protect food from flies, rats, mice and other animals and pests.
7. Clean all pots, pans, dishes, cutlery and glasses with a good detergent and rinse in very hot water; drain dry if possible. A good dishwasher with a "bio" wash can do this better than anything.
8. Keep a patient's dishes separate from those of the remainder of the family. This is essential with infectious diseases, but even with non-infectious cases it is a wise precaution.

THE KITCHEN

PLANNING THE KITCHEN

It is difficult to lay down hard-and-fast rules about how to plan kitchens that meet the ever-changing patterns of modern living. Social requirements as well as the design of domestic equipment are altering all the time, and if the kitchen is to remain the "hub of the house" it must adapt itself with them. It is not difficult, however, to plan a workable and labour-saving kitchen at any time if observation and common sense are used. Although it is more difficult to adapt and modernize a kitchen which is already in existence the following notes will help in re-planning to make the most of the facilities available, and also serve as a guide if structural alterations can be made.

What is going into the kitchen?

The equipment found in a kitchen varies with every individual family; ideally it should be tailored to the person who is going to use it, but this is often difficult if standard units are installed. Although in general a working height of 36 in. is standard for all domestic fitments and appliances, there is a growing feeling that this is too high for the average housewife, who stands 5 ft. 4 in. in her low-heeled working shoes. This is realized by cooker manufacturers, who supply some models with their hotplates at lower heights than 36 in., but where the cooker is incorporated into the "continuous worktop" arrangement with standard kitchen fitments everything has to be at this standard height. If this is done there should be one working surface somewhere in the room at 32–34 in. high. If the units are tailored to the women, her best working height is found by making her stand with her arms straight down from her shoulders, but held fairly loosely; the working surfaces should come where her palms, held flat at right angles to her arms, can rest on it.

Sinks: Great advances have been made recently in the materials of which sinks are made: plastic and nylon ones are available, and there is an application of plastic on steel, as well as vitreous enamel or stainless steel. Most modern sinks are made in one with the draining board; where space is not restricted a double sink with a draining board at either end is ideal, but often one sink with a single or double draining board is all that can be fitted into the space available. For general use, which may include a certain amount of clothes washing, the sink should be not less than 10 in. deep, with 15 in. between the bottom of the sink and the spout of the taps, in order that full buckets may be removed with their contents intact.

Worktables: These may be built-in to the other fitments or free-standing, according to the available space. Smooth, hard, washable laminate or melamine surfaces are ideal for all kitchen purposes.

Cookers: The choice of a cooker is purely personal, but its size and number of hotplate burners should bear some relation to the amount and complexity of the cooking done.

Refrigerators: A refrigerator is a necessity in most households, and space should be made for one which will be large enough for the family requirements.

Larders: Nowadays the larder is often nothing more than a ventilated food cupboard, especially in towns where food can be bought as required; some kind of ventilated storage is needed, even if the kitchen includes a refrigerator, as there are some foods which should not be refrigerated.

Laundry equipment: Most households do at least some of the weekly wash at home, and provision must be made for such things as washing machines, drying cupboards, spin dryers, ironing and airing.

Storage: The amount of storage space depends very much on the individual needs of the family, but room must be found for dry goods, vegetables, bread, cooking tools and utensils, cutlery, glass and crockery, cleaning equipment and miscellaneous articles.

Rubbish: Most people still rely on the small bin under the sink which feeds the big dustbin placed conveniently near the back door, but waste disposal units where the refuse is ground to sludge under the sink and washed away with the washing-up water, are becoming increasingly common.

What will make the kitchen a pleasant place to work in?

Ventilation: Good ventilation all the year round is important. The various processes which are carried out in the kitchen invariably produce condensation, and although modern semi-porous surfaces cut this down considerably, something further is still needed. Windows alone are not enough, because people shut them in cold weather; a flued appliance in the room gives adequate air changes for comfort, but where no such appliance exists some form of extraction is necessary. This may take the form of airbricks, window ventilators or mechanical extraction.

Lighting: Both normal and artificial lighting must be carefully studied so that they are, if anything, more than adequate and the housewife is never in her own light as she works. Windows should be large and as high in the wall as possible, so that the light is thrown right across the room.

Artificial lighting is even more important, because the housewife has to spend so much of her time under it. Where possible, lights should always be flush to ceilings or walls; if pendant lights are unavoidable the flex should be surrounded by a piece of piping which can easily be cleaned. Centre lights should be avoided, but if they are inescapable, they should be totally enclosed in opaque glass shades, giving a diffused light which eliminates sharp shadows. Where there are two entrances to the room the main lights should be controlled by two-way switches.

Finishes: Modern finishes are so varied that no definite advice on the kind to choose can be given; generally, the pocket is the best guide. Walls and ceilings should be easy to clean and should not reflect glare, and if possible should be semi-porous to cut down condensation. Floors should be easy to clean, quiet and resilient.

Heating: Very often the kitchen is left unheated in the assumption that the cooking and laundry processes which are carried out there will provide the heat that is required. Many jobs that are done in the kitchen, however, do not generate heat, and unless there is a solid-fuel cooker or boiler there, some other form of background heating should be considered.

Outlook: It is becoming generally recognized that the housewife who spends a large amount of her working day in one room suffers from boredom of which she may not consciously be aware. To prevent this, modern kitchens are being built with their windows looking either on to the garden or the road outside. Where there is more than one window, that with the most attractive view should light the sink.

GETTING DOWN TO PLANNING

First consideration will be the way in which the work should flow.

This should always follow a logical sequence, which is the same for the domestic kitchen as it is for the largest industrial or hotel kitchen. Briefly, food should come in to be stored, go from the storage centres to the preparation centres, be made up, cooked, served, eaten, the remains cleared away, washed up, and put away. In the domestic kitchen, therefore, the sequence is as follows:

Back door → larder and refrigerator → worktable → cooker → serving table → dining-room → sink → dustbin → cupboards.

It is obviously impossible in any but the largest domestic kitchens to follow this exactly, and the whole art of planning is to adapt the arrangement of the equipment to make the best of such things as the physical and structural limitations of the room. Even if it is practical it may not necessarily be the best way to arrange things, as the units are interdependent. One cannot use the worktable, for instance, or the cooker, without the sink; and indeed the sink is the most important article of equipment in the whole kitchen. It is better to take what might be called the "big three" and to place them in a convenient relationship with each other and then to fit in the rest of the equipment in its logical sequence as far as possible.

The cooking sequence should always be fixed before anything else, because cooking is carried out several times a day every day of the year, and all the other kitchen processes only once or twice a week. It is better, for instance, to have only one step between cooker, sink and worktable, and to have to move a washing machine into position on washdays, than to reverse the process, and only be really comfortable when doing the weekly wash.

Cooker, sink and worktable: These three, therefore, should be as near to each other as possible, either in a straight line or forming a triangular relationship. Under the window or at right angles to it are the best positions for them; the sink, having regard to plumbing considerations, should be fixed first. In no case should the housewife have to work in her own light.

Food storage: Storage for food should be as near as possible to the point of entry into the room, so that purchases may be put away as they are brought in. It must also be near to the worktable, and condiments and flavourings near the cooker. Ventilated food cupboards should be well away from any heat source, and vegetable racks in an airy position near the sink or worktable.

Utensils and kitchen cutlery: There are two suitable positions for these; either near the sink, so that they are easy to put away after washing-up, or with utensils and pots and pans near the cooker and cutlery near the worktable. Dining-room cutlery, crockery, and glass may either be kept in the kitchen near the sink or in the dining-room near the table.

Cleaning materials and appliances: Many of these need to be kept near the sink, where they will be used, but mops, brushes, cleaners, etc., should if possible be kept just outside the kitchen proper, well away from the food.

Miscellaneous considerations

Other things which might be considered at this point are:

Shelves: Shelves can form a decorative feature of the kitchen, and are often desirable to break up the monotony of too many cupboards, but they should hold only articles in constant use, so that these are kept clean, and greasy cooking vapours will not collect on them.

Stools: Most housewives do not sit down enough to work. A small stool at a convenient height with a backrest which will fit into the small of the sitter's back may be scorned at first, but will generally become popular, and take a lot of the hard work off her feet.

Hatches: A service hatch is often the answer to the problem of taking meals from the kitchen to the dining-room. Where meals are eaten in the kitchen the dining area may be divided from the cooking area by free standing cupboards with work surfaces.

EQUIPMENT IN THE KITCHEN

Probably the most important item in your kitchen is the cooker. Your choice of cooker will depend first of all on your choice of fuel, the most common being electricity and gas; in areas where mains gas is not supplied, a cooker can be run off bottled gas. Both electric and gas cookers give instantly controllable heat for hob, oven and grill. Alternatively the cooker can be run on solid fuel or oil; in these cases the cooker is often also a source of room heat, supplies hot water or provides a central heating system.

The type of fuel and the cooker you choose will depend on your way of living, the size of your family and the type of cooking you normally do. For instance, there is no point in buying a large cooker if you are catering for a small family of two or three and do not often entertain. If you have a large family or entertain frequently you will need a cooker with a large oven and the maximum number of hot plates—in fact the biggest you can afford. If you enjoy grilled food or spit-roasted joints, you will want a cooker with a large grill and spit-roasting attachment—if not you may prefer to settle for a small grill, which may leave more space for warming plates and dishes. Devices such as automatic ignition or simmer control on a gas cooker are useful to most people but features such as automatic timing for the oven, an extra oven or a built in griddle are only an advantage if you are going to use them. Look around and think carefully before you buy what is a major piece of equipment that will be expected to last you a good many years.

Keep your cooker clean by wiping it down thoroughly immediately after use—both the top and the oven. The finishes used for oven interiors vary widely as manufacturers develop new easy-to-clean surfaces. Thorough cleaning will be necessary from time to time, but do follow the manufacturer's instructions carefully as many of the new finishes can be damaged by strong chemical cleaners.

OTHER APPLIANCES

Refrigerator: Most modern homes contain a refrigerator for food storage. This maintains a temperature of usually approximately 45° F., sufficient to slow down bacterial growth on fresh and cooked foods, enabling them to be stored for periods varying from a few days to a few weeks. The size of refrigerator you choose will depend on the size of your family, how frequently you wish to shop, what alternative cool storage you have such as larder or store cupboards; and the space available in the kitchen. The minimum capacity suggested is usually 1 cu. ft. per person, plus more if you entertain regularly; in fact this will rarely be enough for someone who likes to shop once a week instead of every day.

Defrost a refrigerator regularly, as soon as the frost on the frozen storage compartment reaches about $\frac{1}{4}$ in. thick. This may mean defrosting as often as every two or three weeks but it does ensure that the refrigerator works at maximum efficiency.

Freezer: Many refrigerators are now combined with a small freezer cabinet, suitable for deep freezing your own foods as well as for storing commercially frozen products. This is a valuable addition in many households, though it may absorb more kitchen space than you can afford. Alternatively you can buy a separate freezer, which need not be kept in the kitchen. A freezer is a great help if you have a large family or do a lot of entertaining, as it enables you to schedule cooking to a time that is convenient to you, reheating the food when it is needed. You can also store a variety of uncooked foods such as meat, fish, poultry and vegetables, which may be a particular advantage if you live far from a good shopping centre or if your time is limited by a job outside the home.

A freezer needs defrosting only two or three times a year.

Electric Kettle: Electric kettles boil water so quickly and economically that they are now generally regarded as a normal part of kitchen equipment even if you have a gas cooker.

Electric Toaster: A toaster is usually a more economical method of toasting bread than using the grill on the cooker; it takes next to no time to heat up, no heated areas are wasted and most toasters have an automatic time control setting that "pops up" the toast as soon as it is cooked, switching off the heat.

Electric Mixer or Blender: There is a wide range of mixers and blenders available, varying from the large tabletop models which consist of a powerful motor with a wide range of accessories for cake and pastry making, blending, grinding and chopping, shredding, slicing, mincing and extracting juice, to smaller hand-held models. Most people find a small hand-held electric mixer helpful for making cakes, whipping cream and so on; the more ambitious will enjoy the labour-saving devices offered on the large models. Even if you don't have a large mixer, a large blender is often useful for making soups and pâtés, and for a variety of chopping, grinding and puréeing operations.

Rotisseries, Infra-red Grills, Electric Frying Pans: These are all appliances that can extend the available cooking possibilities in your kitchen. Operated independently from the cooker, they may serve either as additional cooking space or as alternatives. It may often be more economical to cook a casserole in an electric frying pan than to heat up the oven, or you might wish to spit-roast a large joint while using the oven for some slower baking.

An infra-red grill cooks extremely quickly, and is excellent for expensive cuts of meat such as steak or chops, and makes tasty snacks such as toasted sandwiches.

Warming Plate or Hostess Trolley: These are a boon if you are entertaining, making it simple to heat plates and dishes before the meal and to keep vegetables or meat hot during the meal, ready for second servings. The largest are very expensive and suitable only if you entertain a lot, but a small hot plate is useful at the most modest dinner party, and can sit conveniently on a nearby table or sideboard.

Washing up Machines: These are designed to wash, rinse and dry crockery, cutlery and utensils. To make good use of a dish washer you need to have sufficient crockery to enable you to wait until it is full before switching on —this will be no problem in a large family but a small family might only fill it once a day.

Pressure Cooker: A pressure cooker offers a most convenient method of cooking to save both time and fuel and to conserve food values. Any food that is normally boiled, steamed or stewed can be cooked in a pressure cooker. The principle is that the higher the atmospheric pressure, the higher the temperature at which water boils; and the higher the temperature of the water, the shorter the cooking time. At a pressure of 15 lb. per sq. in. above normal atmospheric pressure, a meat stew will cook in 20 minutes instead of 2 hours. Most pressure cookers offer variable pressures and precise instructions for use are supplied by the manufacturers. These instructions may seem complicated at first but it is well worth mastering them, to take advantage of the savings. Several foods can be cooked at the same time if you wish.

To clean a pressure cooker you simply wash the pan as an ordinary saucepan but take particular care that the rubber sealing ring and the safety vent in the lid are completely clean. Store it with the lid placed loosely on top, or inverted into the pan, so that air can circulate freely.

THE BASIC WELL-EQUIPPED KITCHEN

There is now an almost unlimited choice of kitchen utensils on the market, and the housewife's choice of what is included in her kitchen is governed largely by the amount of cupboard space available in the kitchen, and the amount of money she can afford to spend.

We list here the utensils a young couple setting up home would require, together with suggestions of what to buy later. Much will depend, of course, on the couple's way of life, the amount of entertaining they do, and the amount of cooking done in the home.

COOKING UTENSILS

Pots and Pans

TO START WITH:

1 pt. milk saucepan with pouring lip
3 saucepans with lids—6 in., 8 in. and 9 in. diameter.
1 frying-pan
1 kettle
1 coffee percolator

TO BUY LATER:

1 omelette pan
1 double saucepan
1 egg saucepan
1 steamer
1 fish kettle

Cooking Utensils

TO START WITH:

1 colander
2 casseroles with lids
2 pie-dishes—1 and $1\frac{1}{2}$ pt. sizes
1 set of oven-to-table dishes
3 pudding basins—small, medium and large
1 sieve
1 pastry board (if you have no suitable wipe-clean working surface)
1 rolling pin
1 chopping board
1 mincer
1 strainer
1 funnel
1 measuring jug
2 7-in. sandwich tins
1 7-in. cake tin
1 bun tin to hold 12 buns
1 meat tin } unless supplied
1 baking-sheet } with cooker
2 wire cooling trays

TO BUY LATER:

Fruit juice extractor
Mixer
Blender
Flan rings
Pressure cooker
Individual moulds
1 coffee grinder
1 pepper-mill
Other cooking tins
Oven glass plates

Kitchen Cutlery

TO START WITH:

2 wooden spoons
1 whisk
1 grater
1 large cook's knife
1 small cook's knife
1 serrated knife
1 vegetable knife
1 fork
1 potato peeler
1 palette knife or spatula
1 wide flat lifter or slice
1 solid metal spoon
1 perforated metal spoon
1 can opener
1 bread knife
1 set measuring cups
1 set measuring spoons
Lemon squeezer

TO BUY LATER:

1 pair kitchen scissors
1 corkscrew
Pastry cutters
1 bean slicer
1 tomato and egg slicer
1 vegetable masher
1 apple corer

General

TO START WITH:

1 bread bin
2 tins for cakes and biscuits
1 bread board
1 pair of scales
1 washing-up bowl
1 garbage bin
Set of storage containers
Vegetable rack

Tableware, Glass and Cutlery

TO START WITH:
6 dinner plates
6 soup bowls
6 sweet plates
6 side or tea plates
2 meat dishes
2 vegetable dishes
6 bowls for fruit or cereals
1 large bowl
6 cups
6 saucers
Coffee cups
Coffee jug
1 teapot
1 milk jug
1 gravy boat
1 sauceboat
1 sugar bowl
1 cruet
6 glasses and 1 water jug
6 all-purpose wineglasses
1 hot-water jug
6 large knives
6 small knives
6 tablespoons
6 dessertspoons
6 soupspoons
6 large forks
6 small forks
6 teaspoons
1 carving knife and fork
1 steel or knife sharpener
1 butter knife
1 butter dish
1 cheese dish

TO BUY LATER:
6 fish knives
6 fish forks
6 tea knives
Extra plates and cups
Large breakfast cups
Salad servers
Salad bowl
Hors d'œuvre set
Other serving dishes
6 pastry forks

COOKING UTENSILS

There is such a wide variety of cooking utensils on the market today that it is impossible to give more than the most general advice on choice. The old axiom that it pays to buy the best still holds good, but the best is not always the most expensive; many of the lower-priced ranges of kitchen equipment are well designed and give excellent service.

The materials used for cooking utensils today are mainly aluminium, stainless steel, mild steel finished with vitreous enamel, enamelled cast iron or heatproof glass. Some of the utensils are so attractive that they do double duty, and can be used for serving as well as cooking. Many accessories to the cooking process, such as bowls, colanders, juice squeezers, etc., are made from what is loosely called "plastic". This material has many good points, and reputable makes have a long life, providing that they are not allowed to come into contact with excessive heat.

The design of the utensils is largely a matter of personal choice, but there are certain general points which should be considered when buying new equipment. Surfaces should be smooth, and there should be no sharp corners or protuberances either inside or out; the whole utensil should be well balanced whether full or empty; handles should be comfortable to hold, and should stay cool. The question of balance is extremely important. Good balance means good stability; utensils should always stand steady on a flat surface and should never tilt towards the handle when they are empty.

The base of pans to be used on cooker hotplates should also be considered. Solid electric hot plates and the hobs of solid-fuel cookers need pans with machined bases so that good contact can be obtained and the heat will not be wasted; radiant electric hotplates and all gas hotplates will take any kind of pan, but utensils with re-entrant bases, where there is a rim below the actual base of the utensil, should be avoided, as they will waste heat.

Saucepans: Many modern saucepans are

made from aluminium; this is light and durable. Aluminium has a natural film of oxide protecting the surface, which can be increased by anodizing, a process which also allows the introduction of colour to the outside of the pan. Non-stick surfaces make cleaning very easy. Stainless steel is increasingly popular.

Saucepans should be neither too light nor too heavy. If they are very light they will dent and bend out of shape, and may cause the food in them to burn, while if they are very heavy they will be difficult to lift. The correct pan, therefore, should be of medium weight, strong enough to withstand being knocked or dropped, and light enough to be easy to use. Large pans should always have a knob or boss opposite the handle, so that they may be carried comfortably in both hands when they are full. Any material used for handles should be heat-resisting, in case the pans are ever used in the oven. Lids should fit well, and be of the same thickness as the pan.

Special care should be taken when buying milk saucepans. Cheap ones are often top-heavy, and rely on the liquid itself to balance them; the popular shape where the base is narrower than the top is particularly apt to be unsteady. Pouring lips should be deep, and should pour positively in a well-defined stream

The actual shape of the pan is not important, provided that any corners are widely rounded for easy cleaning, and there are no corners and joins which may be grease-traps.

Frying-pans: Most frying-pans are made from aluminium, and the chief requirement for a good one is that it should be reasonably weighted so that heat is evenly distributed over the whole base. Very light pans tend to give local hot-spots, and may warp in use. Non-stick surfaces prevent food sticking, a fault which sometimes occurs with pans made from aluminium. Non-stick pans need care, however; scratches or scrapes damage the surface, so wooden or nylon implements should be used.

Frying-pans should have sides which slope outwards so that food can be easily removed. Generally an oval shape is best, but omelette pans should always be round; if omelettes are popular in the family, it is best to keep one pan exclusively for them.

Casseroles and **Oven-ware:** As well as the traditional casseroles made in earthenware there are also casseroles in steel or cast iron finished in vitreous enamel, or in heatproof glass. The metal ones can be used either in the oven or on the hotplate, but most of the glass ones are only suitable for the oven. Before using a glass utensil on the hotplate check that it is intended to be used on direct heat or flame.

THE STORE-CUPBOARD

With modern methods of packing, preservation and refrigeration of food, and its ready availability from day to day even in the more remote parts of the country, the appearance of the kitchen store-cupboard has altered considerably. The store-cupboard now holds only the staple cooking materials, and a few "emergency" rations for the unexpected happening.

Although the refrigerator has become a familiar part of the kitchen it has not, and never will, entirely replace the larder; some foods are best kept away from extreme cold. The larder must be kept cool and airy, as far away as possible from heat and steam; it must be fly-proof, and easily kept clean, as hygiene is the most important consideration in food storage.

Other things which have to be stored are vegetables, which should be kept in wire containers or on racks so that the air can circulate round them, and soaps, detergents, and cleaning materials, which must be kept well away from the food, so that it will not be tainted by the scent they emit.

PERISHABLE FOODS

Under this heading come meat, fish, and dairy produce of all sorts, which are kept either in a refrigerator or in the larder. They should be covered with greaseproof paper or aluminium foil or put in polythene bags or plastic boxes. Meat and fish should not be stored raw for any length of time, and cooked left-overs should be put on clean plates and dishes and covered before storing. Milk is sometimes a problem in the summer if there is no refrigerator; the earthenware milk-cooler is probably the best answer to this. Milk should never be left in bright sunlight or a strong light, as this will quickly destroy most of its food value. Cheese keeps well in a polythene bag in a cool place; butter, margarine and lard also need to be kept cool and covered.

GROCERIES

Most groceries are sold in pre-packed cartons and containers and may be stored in these until they are opened, after which some foods should be put into air-tight tins.

Coffee is bought ready ground either in a vacuum pack or loose, when it should be put immediately into a tin or air-tight jar; or as beans, which are ground in a mill as required. For the emergency cupboard a jar of instant coffee is a useful stand-by.

Tea keeps best in a tin or a caddy. The right blend to buy depends partly on personal taste and partly on the composition of the water in the locality; this can have a considerable effect on the flavour in some districts.

Sugar needs to be kept in a dry place away from steam or moisture.

Flour should be kept in a dry bin, and not in the packet, once it has been opened. Do not add fresh flour to that which has been stored.

Rice comes in many varieties; Patna is best for curries, Italian for risottos and pilaffs, and Carolina for sweet dishes.

Salt must be kept very dry. Table salt can be used for cooking, but ideally common salt is better for this purpose.

Dried fruit is either sold already cleaned and ready for use, or sometimes at a slightly cheaper price in its original state. Uncleaned fruit must be washed well, dried *slowly* and picked over before use.

Breakfast cereals should be kept in a dry, warm place. If they become soft, they can be quickly crisped up again by placing them in a hot oven for a few minutes.

Canned foods are useful stand-bys in the store-cupboard. Most canned foods keep well for up to 1 year.

Herbs. For those with gardens fresh herbs are easily obtainable but the dried varieties can be used with good results. Store away from the light in air-tight jars.

Flavourings and **seasonings** should also be kept in small quantities in the store-cupboard in air-tight containers.

WASHING-UP

The most essential requirement for washing-up is a constant supply of hot water; this should be as hot as the hand can bear for the actual washing, and very hot indeed for rinsing, so that as well as sterilizing the articles the heat can help to dry them.

The various agents used for washing-up are largely a matter of personal choice; synthetic detergents are perhaps better for this than soap, because of their greater grease-removing properties. If the hands are especially sensitive, the use of rubber gloves is recommended. Mops, cloths, scrapers, sponges and other means for removing particles of food from the articles being washed are all useful; those made from plastic or nylon are best, as they have a long life, and do not get greasy or slimy easily.

Food should be scraped off plates, dishes and pans, and any that have very stubborn particles should be put to soak in lukewarm water. Cups, glasses, jugs and teapots should be emptied, and if the glasses have contained milk, they should be given an initial rinse in cold water. After this, everything should be stacked in an orderly way beside the sink.

Washing, rinsing, and draining are continuous operations; the temperature of the wash and rinse waters must be maintained throughout and both waters should be changed if they become dirty. The articles should be washed and then transferred immediately to the rinse water, and then put straight on to the draining board or into a drainer. The order in which the articles are washed is important: glasses, cutlery, crockery, and finally pots, pans and other utensils.

If the rinse water is really hot, as it should be, most articles will be almost dry in a minute or so, and will need only a final polish with a clean soft cloth before they are put away. Cloths should be boiled regularly, and many people prefer to dry with soft kitchen paper, so that any possibility of germs being transferred to the clean utensils is eliminated.

A FEW HELPFUL HINTS

Glass: A polish with a soft cloth will bring up the lustre on glass very well, but if the glass is dull a little vinegar should be added to the rinse water. Stained decanters should be half filled with cold tea or with water and detergent, and well shaken; finally several good rinses must be given to remove any chance of a taste remaining.

Knives: Those with bone handles should never be completely immersed in hot water or the cement which holds the blade to the handle may become loosened, and the handles discoloured. Some people prefer to rinse them by immersing them in very hot water in a jug, in such a way that the handles are kept out of the water.

Cake-tins: Unless they are badly stained these should never be washed at all, as this will destroy the "seasoning" of the tin and cause the next cake to stick to it. They should be rubbed clean with kitchen paper as soon as they have come out of the oven and the cake has been removed, while they are still hot. Omelette pans should also be rubbed clean with paper and never washed. A sprinkling of salt acts as a good scouring agent if this is necessary.

Breakages: These can be kept to a minimum by having a plastic mat in the bottom of the sink, and by using a plastic rinsing bowl and drainer. Very delicate china should be washed separately, and should be rinsed at the same temperature as it is washed.

Care of the sink: A sink trap should be put over the drain so that it will catch everything that is emptied into it. At least once a week some disinfectant or antiseptic should be poured gently into the waste, left for five minutes, and then flushed away with boiling water.

Sinks fitted with mechanical disposal units are becoming popular; all the rubbish is emptied into the drain, and is then ground away through it. The instructions for caring for these disposal units must be very carefully followed, especially those on cleaning, as it is extremely important to keep them very fresh and clean at all times to prevent the possibility of germs being encouraged and smells developing.

KITCHEN CRAFT

THE COOKING OF FOOD

THERE are three basic methods of cooking food:

(*a*) in water,

(*b*) in fat; either of which may be actually constituent in the food, or supplied as a cooking medium.

(*c*) by dry heat.

The water methods include boiling, poaching and stewing, where liquid is supplied as a cooking fluid in varying quantities, according to whether it is to be consumed or not, and heated to temperatures suitable for rendering the food palatable and digestible. Steaming is also a wet method as the food is cooked either by its own juices or by steam at ordinary atmospheric or compressed pressure, being served in a moist state whatever the process.

Cooking in fat aims at producing a crisp dry-surfaced food, and is therefore usually described as cooking by "dry" methods. "Dry" frying is used to describe the use of a hot pan to extract melted fat from those foods rich in fat, such as bacon rashers, pork chops and sausages. Shallow and Deep (French) frying merely denote the difference in the depth of fat, and therefore the essential difference in temperature between the two methods. Roasting and grilling make use of the natural fat in the food, though present-day adaptations of oven-roasting require extra fat on cut surfaces, as does grilling.

Cooking in fat gives a more highly flavoured surface to food and for this reason less tender cuts of meat are often cooked by moisture but browned in hot fat, as in braising, where the food is cooked by steaming and roasting.

Baking is a dry method of cooking food, usually in an enclosed oven.

(*a*) COOKING IN WATER

BOILING

This means ebullition or "bubbling", and actual boiling is used only on rare occasions, such as for the deliberate evaporation of sugar syrups; meat stock when making a fumet, or glaze; chutneys and sauces. Also when cooking rice and Italian pasta to be served whole and well drained, when plenty of water should be used to allow for evaporation and absorption. Green vegetables should also be cooked as quickly as possible, but in only sufficient depth of water to provide steam, and with a lid firmly in place.

All foods should be put into water at 212° F., with perhaps the possible exception of old potatoes, which tend to cook too quickly on the outside. The use of hot water shortens cooking time, saves fuel and helps to impart stronger colour and flavour to food as heat coagulates the surface proteins of meat and fish and gelatinizes the surface starch of vegetables and cereals, so preventing early losses of extractives in the water. Conversely, when making soup, food should be cut up finely to expose as much surface as possible to the water, which is used cold, and heated gently so that flavours may be drawn into the liquid.

The rate of boiling must be adjusted to the structure of the food.

STEWING

This term is used when food is cooked slowly in a small quantity of water or liquor either in the oven or on top of the cooker. "Casserole" cookery involves the use of a sauce as the liquid, as it is not practical to thicken the contents of a casserole after cooking unless it is truly fireproof. Stewing is a very economical method of cooking as all the flavours are retained and the lengthy process renders the toughest food digestible. Thick pans or casseroles with tight lids are essential to prevent evaporation, and seasoning must be done at the beginning. Food which is to be stewed should be cut into pieces to expose more surface to the moderate heat of the liquor. Birds and rabbits should be jointed, meat cut *across* the fibres, fruit quartered or, if small, left whole. The consistency of the liquor at the completion of the stew should be just thick enough to coat the solid ingredients and so keep them moist in the serving dish, where they should be visible and not completely submerged in an excessive amount of liquid. Thickening is achieved by the use of blended flour, etc., or by the inclusion of potatoes which fall during cooking.

Approximate proportion of ingredients: 1 lb. meat to ¾ pt. water.

A stew should never be boiled.

STEAMING

Here food is cooked in steam from boiling water or from the food itself, in which case it is enclosed in a container surrounded by steam or boiling water. For example, small pieces of food (fish) wrapped in buttered paper may be steamed between two plates over a pan of boiling water, as for invalids. Foods cooked in steam must be covered to protect them from condensing steam, which would make them sodden, and they will require longer cooking than if boiled; usually half as long again. Water providing the steam must be kept boiling and replenished with *boiling* water when necessary, especially for puddings, otherwise they will be heavy. *See also* p. 410.

For pressure cooking *see* p. 688.

POACHING

The process of poaching is similar to that of boiling, except that the liquid must not bubble and the food is only just submerged, the temperature being just below boiling-point.

(*b*) COOKING IN FAT

ROASTING

Roasting and grilling are similar methods applied to large and small pieces of food respectively when a quick, fierce heat is used. These methods are suitable only for top-quality flesh foods, as these are composed of thin muscle-fibres and even-graining of fine fat, which is quickly released by heat.

The ideal weight of a joint for high-temperature roasting is approximately 4 lb. The oven must be hot when the food is put in. Joints which require to be cooked through, such as joints of pork, veal and mutton, will need a reduced temperature after the first hour. Tender joints of beef and lamb should be cooked quickly so that the interior is served pink.

The oven should be pre-heated to 450° F., Gas 8, and the joint should be placed on a trivet in a tin in the middle of the oven. The trivet is necessary to raise the joint from the fat and thus prevent spitting fat splashing the inside of the oven.

Joints lacking in fat, such as veal, and poultry, may be kept moist by occasional basting or barding, *see* p. 33.

SLOW ROASTING OR POT ROASTING

This method is used for joints of poor-quality meat, when the temperature should not exceed 360° F., Gas 4. The meat is cooked on a trivet in a roasting tin in the oven or on a trivet in a saucepan with a little fat and a very small quantity of liquid—either stock or water. It should be covered with a lid or aluminium foil to retain the steam. If the meat is cooked in a pan it may be browned first in hot fat to give it a good colour and flavour. If cooked in the oven, uncover the joint for the last ½ hour. As these joints are cooked at a lower temperature there is less evaporation and therefore more moisture is retained in the tissues of the meat and this helps to soften the coarser muscle-fibres. The inclusion of such vegetables as onions flavours the steam, and the use of strips of green bacon placed over the top of the joint will moisten the flesh, and help to brown the surface.

BRAISING

The method is the same as for slow roasting but the cover is removed half an hour before serving and the heat of the oven increased to allow the top to brown. Alternatively the meat may be fried to brown the surface before being placed in the cooking container. The meat is cooked on a bed of roughly sliced vegetables in a little stock. The layer of vegetables, chosen for flavour, should be sufficiently thick to support the joint above the level of the stock so that the meat is steamed. Bacon rinds, bones, mushroom trimmings and a bouquet garni are utilized for flavouring, especially immature meat such as veal. After dishing, a suitable accompanying sauce may quickly be produced from the strained vegetable liquor, diluted with water, thickened with blended flour or cornflour and made piquant with tomato purée, wine, cider, etc.

GRILLING (OR BROILING)

This involves the use of a well-heated radiant; charcoal imparts the finest flavour and is used extensively for portable grills and rotisseries in America where barbecue cooking is so popular. For indoors, the electrically operated infra-red grill and rotisserie is considered to be the best equipment yet designed to produce meat of the finest flavour by searing and crisping the outside while retaining all the juices inside. As the food being grilled is spitted, it is essential that it is carefully arranged on the spit so that turning is smooth. If not, the food will not cook evenly and the machine will be strained. Gas and electrically heated fixed grills must be preheated to an even, glowing heat before food is placed under them. Grill-cuts should not be less than 1 inch thick and should be seasoned and brushed with fat before being cooked. Both sides of the food are exposed to the heat to coagulate the surface protein and sear the flesh. This forms a seal on the outside which retains the juices. Further cooking may entail placing the food farther away from the heat to allow it to penetrate more slowly. Food must not be pierced after the seal has formed (two spoons should be used to turn the meat if tongs are not available). Delicate-skinned food, such as fish, may be grilled successfully if wrapped in thickly greased foil or parchment and placed in the bottom of the grill-pan. This prevents charring of the skin and retains all the juices.

FRYING

Frying resembles grilling in that only small pieces of food are cooked and the process is quick. In fact, the "pan-broiling" of America is comparable to dry-frying, when the hot pan is used to draw fat from the food. Fats chosen for frying must be capable of being heated to a temperature of 400° F. approximately, without burning or disintegrating. Commercially prepared frying fats, clarified dripping and some vegetable oils are all suitable. ALL fats must be heated slowly so that the heat may spread throughout the depth of fat evenly, otherwise the fat at the bottom of the pan will burn before the frying temperature of the whole fat has been reached. ALL food must be dried before being placed in the hot fat, either by shaking in a towel, as for chipped potatoes, or by dusting with seasoned flour, oatmeal, etc., as for oily fish, or by coating with a suitable medium which will dry on contact with hot fat, such as egg and breadcrumbs, batter or pastry. Wet foods, like fish fillets, need to be dried with flour before being coated, otherwise the coating may be dislodged by the steam forming underneath it. The choice of coating depends on the nature of the food and the method of frying. All foods fried in deep fat should be coated unless they are of a starchy nature, such as potatoes and doughnuts, to prevent any flavour of them escaping into the fat, so making it unfit for further use. A pan of deep fat is considerably hotter than shallow fat and food is consequently cooked at a higher temperature. Immediate sealing should prevent adulteration of the fat so that it may be used for many differently-flavoured foods at a time: e.g. fish, apple fritters, cutlets. A frying basket facilitates the removal of food from deep fat. It should be a very easy fit in the pan, and must be heated with the fat so that food does not stick to it when put in, and does not cool the fat by being cold when lowered into the pan. Never overload the basket; only sufficient food to cover the bottom should be fried at once to avoid cooling the fat too much. Draining after frying is essential, first over the pan, then on absorbent paper, before dishing on a dish-paper.

The temperature of the fat can be tested simply, by frying a cube of day-old bread. If it becomes golden brown in 1 minute, the fat is approximately 360° F., in ½ minute the fat is approximately 380° F. *N.B.* If a fat thermometer is used, it must be remembered that it must be heated gradually in the fat and cooled slowly after use.

Generally speaking, raw foods are fried at the lower temperature to ensure thorough cooking, and re-heated foods at the higher one, as they are merely heated and only the coating needs to be cooked. Potato crisps are cooked at the higher temperature; but thicker slices, such as are used for soufflé potatoes, need the lower temperature for cooking, followed by immersion in fat at the higher temperature for "puffing" them out.

All fat must be kept clean, otherwise food will taste of the impurities, as a little fat is always absorbed. Strain through a fine mesh after each use, and clarify occasionally (*see* p. 36).

Foods fried in shallow fat must be thin enough for complete cooking merely by being turned over during frying. Turn with spoons to avoid piercing the seal and drain well when lifting from the pan.

SAUTÉING

Sautéing is a French term applied to the practice of shaking food in fat while it is frying. It may be used as a preliminary method of developing the flavour of vegetables for sauces and soups, or as a method of cooking complete in itself, as in the cooking of kidneys. A well-flavoured fat must be used, as it is absorbed: butter, chicken fat rendered down, etc. A lid is used to keep in the steam to assist with the cooking of raw food, but cooked food such as sliced potatoes is usually turned in the melted fat with a fork.

(*c*) BY DRY HEAT

Baking in an oven subjects food to the heat radiated from the walls and top, to convection currents of hot air, and to heat conducted along shelves, baking-sheets and tins, steel skewers, etc., which is a very dry heat. There are occasions when a water bath is included for the purpose of providing insulation against this, as in baked custard.

AUTOMATIC TIME-CONTROLLED MEALS

It is possible to obtain surprisingly good results by placing food in an oven and leaving the auto-controls to switch the oven ON and OFF. Generally speaking, dishes which require approximately the same temperature and the same length of time to cook are suitable. For example, when planning a breakfast menu which will include any or all of the following: bacon, sausages, tomatoes, mushrooms, kippers (whole or filleted), porridge (made from the quick-type rolled oats), the bacon should be rolled so that it will be cooked ready for serving with the other dishes. Alternatively, the bacon could be rolled around the chipolata sausages. The kippers and porridge should be placed in dishes with lids or covered well with aluminium foil.

Various types of casserole dishes, any root vegetables, stewed fruit and milk puddings always produce good results cooked by this method from cold. Pies, etc., made from shortcrust pastry; sponge and batter puddings

LAMB

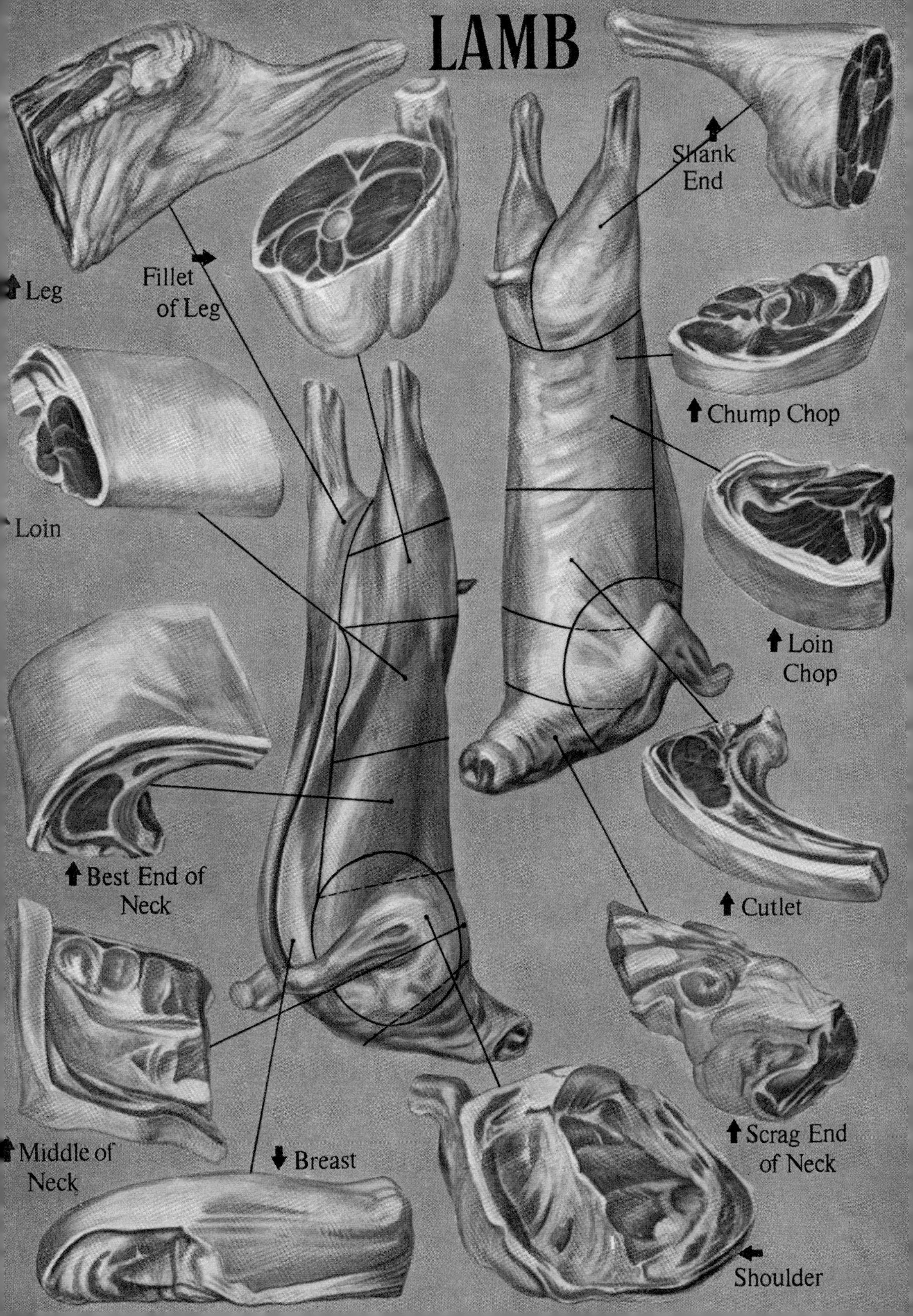
Leg
Fillet of Leg
Shank End
Chump Chop
Loin
Loin Chop
Best End of Neck
Cutlet
Middle of Neck
Breast
Scrag End of Neck
Shoulder

PLATE 2

Making a Raised Pie

1 Pour the boiling lard and water or milk on to the sifted flour and salt, mixing well with a wooden spoon or a palette knife.

2 When the mixture is cool enough, knead it thoroughly with the hands.

3 Cut off ¼ of the dough and keep covered in warm place till needed.

4 Roll out the remaining dough to a round and line greased tin, working the dough up the sides of tin.

5 Roll the chopped meat in seasoned flour, put half into lined tin with the shelled eggs, fill with the remaining meat. Damp edge of the pastry lining the tin and cover with the remaining rolled out pastry.

6 When the pie is baked fill up with stock poured through a funnel made of clean greaseproof paper.

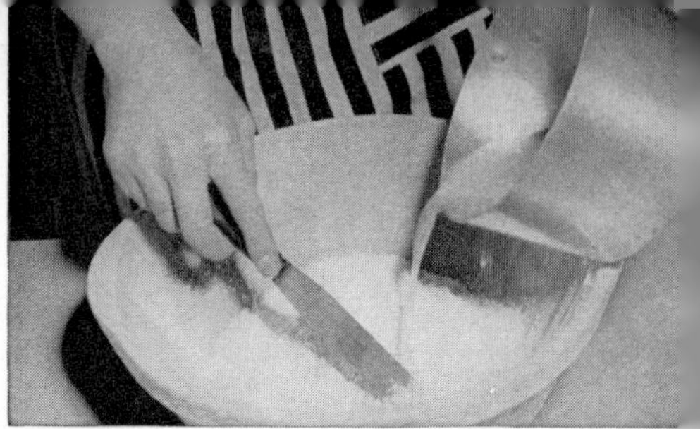
1

2

3

4

6

5

are also a success. Cakes requiring a very short cooking time (e.g. buns and scones, Swiss rolls, etc.) are not very satisfactory when placed in a cold oven.

Victoria sandwich, fruit cakes and gingerbread, etc., which require a comparatively longer time to cook, are all quite successful. With the exception of the Victoria sandwich (which will take approximately 10 minutes longer than the cooking time given in the normal recipe) they will require cooking for the same length of time as when placed in an oven at the correct temperature. The auto-timer can be used merely to switch off the oven at the end of the cooking period, which is an added convenience.

PREPARATION TERMS EXPLAINED

TO BARD

To place very thinly cut rashers of fat, green (or plain) bacon on the breasts of poultry and game to prevent them from drying up when roasting, the reason being that the legs take longer to cook. Very thinly cut rashers should be tied on with string and only removed just before completion of cooking, so that the poultry or game can brown. Certain joints of butcher's meats, such as veal and lean beef are barded for roasting. This does not obviate basting from time to time.

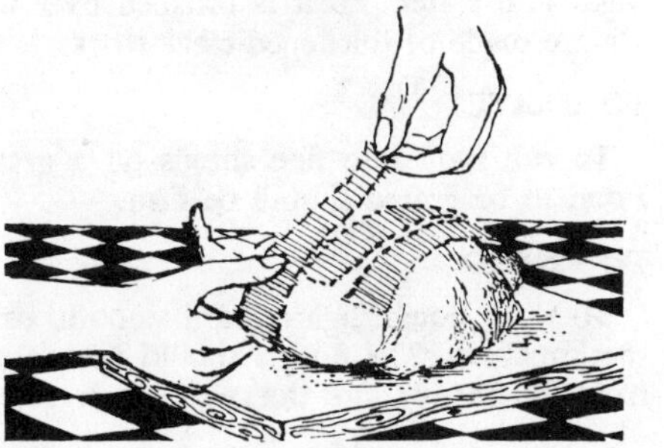

Barding

TO BASTE

To pour liquid or melted fat over food during cooking to keep the food moist.

TO BEAT

To turn cake mixtures, batters, etc., over and over with a circular motion to mix in the maximum amount of air.

TO BLANCH

Some foods are blanched to improve their colour, others to remove some strong, undesirable flavour, and nuts such as almonds are blanched to facilitate removal of their skins. In all cases, the method is the same: immerse the article to be blanched in a saucepan of cold water (without a lid) bring to the boil, then strain the water off.

TO BLEND

To mix smoothly. When referring to thickening liquids with flour, it means mixing the flour to a smooth paste with a little cold liquid before adding the hot liquid.

TO COAT

To cover completely with a thin layer of sauce, icing, etc.

TO CREAM

To mix fat and sugar with a wooden spoon or with the hand until light and fluffy and white in colour. To mix to the consistency of whipped cream.

TO DEVIL

To rub a highly-flavoured paste—mustard, cayenne pepper, etc., into the legs of game, poultry, etc., before grilling.

TO DICE

To cut (food) into small cubes. A simple method is to slice the food first, cut the slices into strips, then holding the strips together, cut into dice by cutting across them.

TO DOT

To put small bits (e.g. butter) over the surface of food.

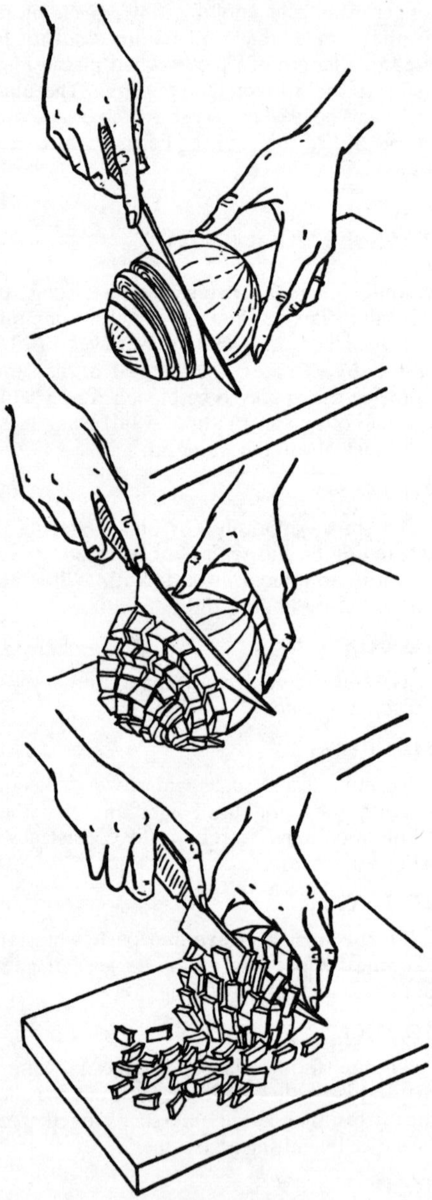

Dicing

TO DREDGE

To sprinkle lightly with flour or sugar.

TO FOLD IN

This means the combining of an aerated ingredient with other ingredients so that the air entrapped is retained. It is used when combining sifted flour with other ingredients or to combine two whisked mixtures. Place the ingredient to be folded in, on top of the whisked mixture or other ingredients. With a spoon, cut a line vertically through the centre of the mixture, take the spoon round the half of the bowl, spoon up half the mixture and lay it lightly on the other half, thus trapping the dry ingredient between two layers of whisked mixture. Repeat this process until all the dry ingredient has been folded in.

TO GLAZE

To brush over the tops of pies, galantines, etc., with some preparation to improve their appearance. Fruit pies and buns are usually brushed over with egg and water, or milk or sugar and water. Meat is brushed over with a glaze made of thickened clear stock.

TO GRATE

To rub food into fine shreds on a grater. Food to be grated should be firm.

TO KNEAD

To work dough lightly until smooth, using the knuckles. The dough should be brought from the outside into the centre each time.

Larding

TO LARD

To insert strips of fat bacon into the breasts of poultry, game or into pieces of meat, to prevent them drying up when roasting. The fat bacon should be cut into short pieces about 2 in. long and ¼ in. thick, chilled well to harden them and make them firm, then inserted into the bird or meat with a larding needle. The ends should be left protruding, but they can be trimmed with scissors if they look ragged or uneven.

TO MASK

To cover with a thin layer—of sauce, icing, etc.

TO PARBOIL

To partly-boil. The food is boiled by the normal method, but for only half the normal time, and finished by some other cooking method.

TO REDUCE

To boil (mixtures) quickly in an open pan to reduce the amount and thus strengthen the flavour and make a thicker consistency.

TO RUB IN

To combine fat and flour for shortcrust pastry, plain cakes, etc. First cut the fat into small pieces with a knife, then using the tips of the fingers, rub the fat into the flour, lifting the fat above the bowl so that, in falling back between the fingers, the mixture becomes aerated. When all the lumps of fat have been worked down the mixture should resemble breadcrumbs.

TO SCALD

To heat a liquid to just below boiling-point; to pour boiling water on to an article of food.

TO SCORE

To make gashes or cut narrow grooves, to make incisions in the surface of food.

TO SEAR

To brown or form a hard surface on meat to seal in the juices by exposing to fierce heat, after which the heat is reduced and cooking continued.

TO SIEVE

To rub or pass through a sieve to reduce the food to a fine consistency and to introduce air into the food. The back of the bowl of a wooden spoon is usually used to rub or press most substances through a sieve, but the palm of the hand is better when sieving bread-crumbs. Sieving some purées is not an easy process, but it may be facilitated by moistening the purée with any liquid ingredients included in the recipe.

TO SIFT

This is the same as "to sieve".

TO SIMMER

To cook at just below boiling-point, only an occasional bubble should rise to the surface when a liquid is simmering.

TO STEEP

To soak in liquid, which may be hot or cold.

TO TAMMY

To pass sauces or soups through a tammy cloth (a cloth made of fine wool) to produce a smooth, glossy finish.

CULINARY HINTS

TO CLARIFY BUTTER

Put the butter into a saucepan, heat it slowly, removing the scum as it rises, and when quite clear, pour it carefully into clean and dry jars, leaving the sediment behind.

Clarified butter, or as it is sometimes called, oiled or melted butter, is often served instead of sauce with fish, meat and vegetables; it is also used to moisten the surface of many things grilled or cooked "au gratin"; for oiling moulds and baking-tins; and for sealing potted meats.

To de-salt butter: Put into a bowl and pour over boiling water. Leave until cold. The butter will then have risen to the top of the water and can be lifted off. The water will have washed out the salt.

TO CLARIFY FAT

To clean fat, put the fat in a saucepan and cover with cold water. Bring slowly to the boil, removing the scum as it rises. Strain into a bowl and leave to cool. When the fat has formed a solid cake, remove from bowl, and scrape off the impurities which will have settled at the bottom of the cake. Finally, put in a pan and heat *slowly* to drive off any water.

Clarifying fat

TO CLARIFY MARGARINE FOR GREASING PURPOSES

Heat the margarine in a saucepan until the sizzling sound has ceased—this means that the water has been driven off and the salt has fallen to the bottom of the pan. Carefully pour the fat which is left, through muslin into a bowl. The resulting clear oil is suitable for greasing purposes and should be kept liquid over a pan of warm water.

TO RENDER FAT OR SUET

Cut the fat into small pieces, put into a saucepan and cover with cold water. Bring to the boil and continue boiling until nearly all the water has evaporated, then cook more slowly, stirring occasionally. When the fat is ready it should be clear, and any piece of skin shrivelled and light brown in colour. Allow to cool slightly before straining through a fine strainer into a clean basin.

Fat may also be rendered in the oven. Cut it into pieces, place in a roasting tin in a warm oven until the fat has melted, and any piece of skin shrivelled. Strain into a clean basin, pressing the pieces of skin and tissue against the strainer to extract all the fat.

Do not have the heat too fierce for either method or the fat will burn and be spoiled.

TO MAKE BAKING POWDER

Mix well together 2 oz. ground rice, 2 oz. bicarbonate of soda and 4½ oz. cream of tartar *or* 2 oz. tartaric acid, and pass them through a fine sieve. Keep in an air-tight tin.

TO MAKE BREADCRUMBS

Fresh white breadcrumbs: Remove the crusts from some bread that is at least 1 day old and either rub the bread through a fine wire sieve, or grate it; or rub between the palms of the hand until fine crumbs are obtained; the crusts are not used. Note: Fresh crumbs will not keep.

Dried white breadcrumbs are fresh white breadcrumbs which have been dried slowly. They may be dried in a very cool oven, or left in a warm place until thoroughly dry. They will keep for several weeks if kept in an air-tight tin or jar.

Any crumbs left over from egging and crumbing should be dried in the oven, passed through a sieve, and kept in an air-tight tin or jar for future use.

Browned breadcrumbs or raspings: Put the crusts or any pieces of stale bread in a moderate oven (**350° F., Gas 4**) and bake them until golden and crisp. Then crush them with a rolling-pin or put them through the mincer. Store in an air-tight tin or jar. Use for coating croquettes, fish cakes, rissoles, or for covering au gratin dishes.

Fried Breadcrumbs: Put some fresh, fine white breadcrumbs in a frying-pan or baking-tin, with a little butter; season with salt and pepper, and either fry or bake until well browned. Drain well on kitchen paper and serve hot with roast game.

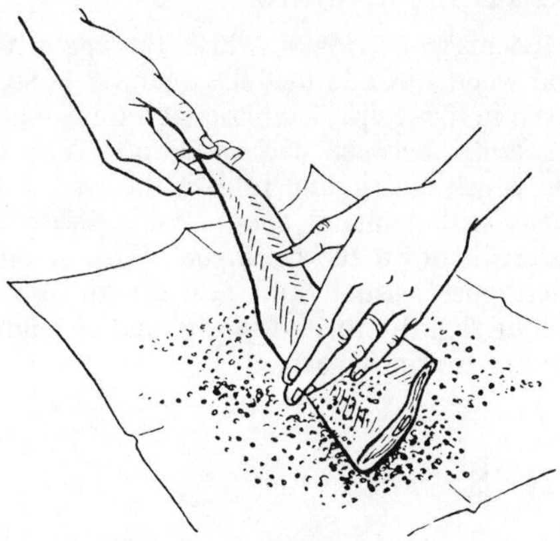

Egg and crumbing fish before frying

Egging and crumbing: Food is often given a protective coating of egg and breadcrumbs before frying.

An egg, slightly beaten, is often used, but better results may be obtained by adding 1 teasp. salad oil, 1 dessertsp. milk and a little salt and pepper. Mix these together in a deep plate. Lightly flour the food to dry it, dip each piece individually in the egg coating and then toss lightly in plenty of crumbs held in a piece of kitchen paper, pressing them on firmly with the hand or knife blade. Shake off the loose crumbs. Use fine crumbs as they will adhere more firmly than coarse ones.

White breadcrumbs should be used for coating uncooked food and browned breadcrumbs (raspings) for coating food which is already cooked and only requires heating.

TO MAKE EGG WASH

Lightly beat together ½ teasp. salt and 1 egg with a fork. Use for glazing.

TO MIX MUSTARD

Mustard is usually prepared for use by simply mixing it smoothly with cold water, and it is generally considered of the right consistency when sufficiently moist *to drop slowly* from the spoon. A milder flavoured mustard may be obtained by mixing with cream or milk instead of water.

A more pungent mustard may be obtained by mixing a little chilli vinegar and cayenne with the mustard; add a good pinch of sugar to soften the flavour.

Mustard should only be mixed in small quantities, as it quickly loses its flavour and fresh appearance.

TO MAKE PANADA

Put ½ pt. water, 1 oz. butter and a good pinch of salt into a small pan. When boiling, gradually stir in 4 oz. sifted flour and work vigorously with a wooden spoon over heat until the panada leaves the sides of the pan clear. Spread on a plate, and when cool, use as directed.

Panada is used to bind together ingredients which possess no adhesive properties themselves.

TO MAKE QUENELLES

Use 2 dessertspoons. Dip one spoon into boiling water, shake off the surplus water, then fill it with quenelle mixture. Press the mixture from the sides and shape it into an oval shape with a knife dipped in hot water. Dip the second spoon into hot water and scoop the mixture carefully from the first spoon into the second, and place the quenelle in the pan.

TO PREPARE RICE FOR CURRY

Put ½ lb. Patna rice in a saucepan with sufficient cold water to cover. Bring to the boil, then strain, and hold the strainer under running cold water until the rice is thoroughly washed. Have ready 3–4 pt. boiling salted water, put in the rice, and cook for 12–15 min., then turn into a colander. Rinse with hot water, cover with a clean dry cloth, and leave in a warm place until dry (½–¾ hr.) stirring occasionally with a fork.

The above is the better method of boiling rice for curry, but if time is short the following method cuts out the first boiling. Drop the dry rice into sufficient fast boiling salted water to keep it moving in the pan, boil for 7–10 min. Drain and dry as above.

TO WHISK EGG WHITE

All utensils must be perfectly clean and free from grease, and once the process has been started it must be carried through without a break. Separate the egg whites from the yolks so that the whites are perfectly clean and free from egg yolk.

Put the whites into a basin with a pinch of salt, then whisk until they stand up in firm peaks.

TO MAKE MERINGUE

To make meringue, whisk the egg whites and when stiff add half the quantity of sugar given in the recipe, 1 tablesp. at a time, whisking stiffly between each addition. Take out the whisk and lightly fold in the rest of the sugar with a metal spoon, taking care not to break down the meringue. Use at once. Meringue is usually put into a cool oven to colour slightly, to set the egg, and to slightly caramelize the sugar.

GARNISHES

WITH ALL THE gadgets and equipment now on the market, preparing garnishes is a relatively simple matter. One important point to remember is that the garnish should be prepared beforehand so that it can be arranged before the dish gets cold—work quickly.

ALMONDS

To prepare almonds *see* p. 512 .

To make almond acorns: Dip the rounded ends of 8 blanched almonds into raspberry jam so that half is covered with jam; then dip the jammed ends into chocolate nibs.

TO MAKE CELERY CURLS

Cut 2–3 pieces of celery about 2 in. long. Cut lengthwise in very fine shreds or shred by drawing the pieces lengthwise over a coarse grater. Put the shreds into very cold water (iced if possible) and leave for ½ hr. Drain the curls well.

CROÛTES AND CROÛTONS

To make croûtes: Croûtes, used as bases for entrees, are usually cut to the size of the dish in which they are to be served. Cut them from stale bread, discard the crusts, and fry or toast.

To make croûtons: Small croûtons for garnish or savouries should be cut from slices of stale bread about ½ in. thick, in round, oval, square, triangle or heart shapes. Fry in clarified fat (preferably butter) until lightly brown, drain well and keep hot and crisp until required. They can be toasted if liked.

To make croûtons to serve with soup, remove the crusts from stale bread and cut into ¼ in. dice, fry in hot butter or fat (deep or shallow) then drain on kitchen paper until quite free from grease. Alternatively butter a ¼ in. thick slice of bread, cut it into cubes, arrange on a tin butter-side down and bake in a moderate oven (**350° F., Gas 4**) till crisp and golden.

DECORATIVE ICE CUBES

If you have a refrigerator and wish to add interest to fruit or alcoholic drinks, colour the water for ice cubes with a little vegetable colouring or make the cubes with diluted fruit juice. Alternatively, half-fill the ice trays with cold water; chill, and when nearly frozen place a cherry, a piece of angelica or shred of orange or lemon rind in each section; chill; almost fill with cold water, and complete the freezing.

TO MAKE GHERKIN FANS

Make about 6 cuts from the top almost to the base of the gherkins, taking care not to cut right through, thus cutting the gherkins into slices. Spread out the gherkins into fan shapes.

TO MAKE GLAZE

Strictly speaking, glaze should be made by reducing 4 quarts of stock to about ¼ pt. As this is extravagant, gelatine is often used.

Demi-glaze is made by reducing stock until it is slightly thick and syrupy.

IMITATION GLAZE—ECONOMICAL

Add 1½ oz. gelatine to ¼ pt. cold water; at once warm it gently, stirring with a metal spoon until dissolved. Do not allow the solution to boil but while hot add 1 level teasp. meat extract, 1 level teasp. yeast extract and sufficient gravy browning to colour.

Use the glaze hot for glazing galantines, etc.

Note: This glaze can only be kept for a few days.

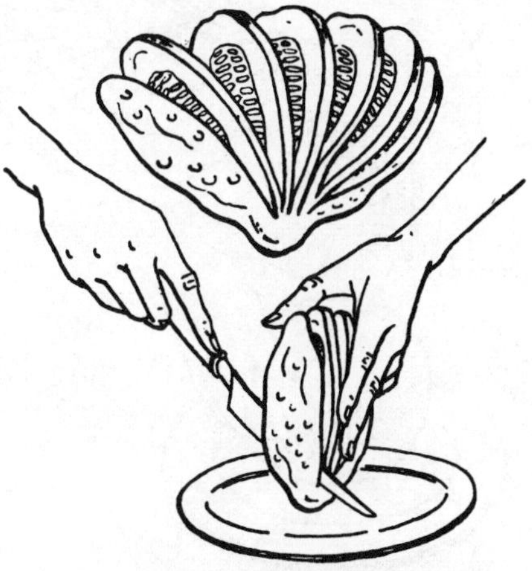

Making gherkin fans

TO SKIN HAZELNUTS AND PEANUTS

Heat the nuts under a slow grill or in a cool oven. Rub in a cloth to remove papery skins.

TO MAKE LEMON OR ORANGE BASKETS

Take a clean lemon or orange and with a sharp stainless steel knife remove almost a whole quarter segment. Leaving a strip of rind wide enough for the handle remove the corresponding segment. Remove the pulp from the lower half.

Making lemon or orange baskets

TO MAKE LEMON BUTTERFLIES

Wash and dry a lemon. Cut thin slices from the widest part of the lemon and remove the pips. Cut the slices either in halves or quarters, depending on the width of "wings" required. Cut through the rind in the middle of each piece and gently pull into 2 wings without breaking into 2 pieces. A piece of parsley may be placed in the centre to represent the butterfly's body.

Making lemon butterflies

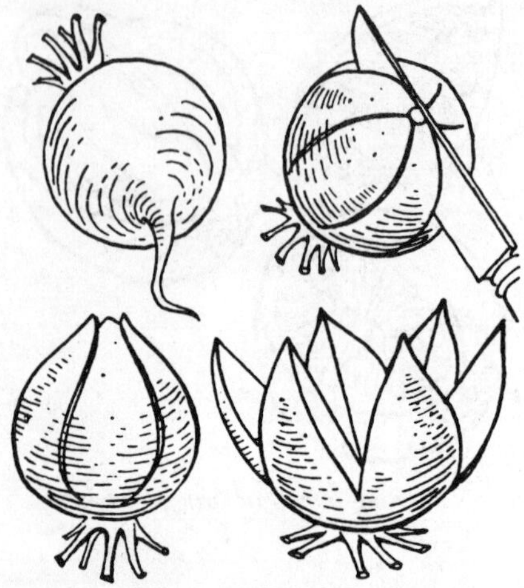

Making radish roses

PARSLEY

To chop parsley: If parsley is chopped by the following method, it is bright green in colour, retains most of its Vitamin C and is chopped quickly, without leaving a stain on the chopping board. (1) Hold a bunch of parsley by the stalks and plunge the leaves into boiling water. Leave for 1 min. in the water. (2) Shake the parsley well and wring it tightly in the corner of a cloth. (3) Cut off the stalks and chop the parsley.

PISTACHIO NUTS

To prepare pistachio nuts *see* p. 512.

TO MAKE A POTATO BORDER

White border: Allow 3 medium-sized potatoes for a border. Boil or steam the potatoes, then sieve them. Add 1 raw egg yolk, ½ oz. butter, season to taste and beat well over heat. When smooth and creamy, allow to cool sufficiently to handle, then shape mixture into a long, narrow roll, using as little flour as possible. Arrange the roll on the serving dish in a ring or oval form, re-heat in the oven and use. Alternatively put the potato mixture into a forcing bag and pipe a round or oval shaped border.

Brown border: Prepare a border as directed above, place on a greased baking-sheet, brush over with beaten egg, bake until nicely browned, then transfer to a hot dish.

TO MAKE RADISH ROSES

Cut off the roots of the radishes, make 4–6 cuts down almost to the base, taking care not to cut right through, thus cutting the radishes in pieces. Put into cold water, preferably iced, and leave until the radishes open like roses.

TO MAKE TOMATO LILIES

Using a stainless steel knife, make zigzag cuts into the centre of the tomato and pull the two halves apart. Alternatively use a potato peeler to make the zigzag cuts.

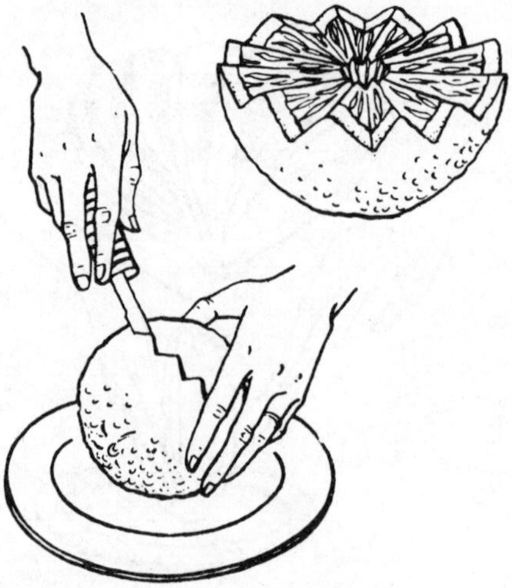

Making tomato lilies

ASPIC JELLY

Gelée d'Aspic

1 qt. jellied veal stock (p. 78)
1 oz. gelatine
Bouquet garni (parsley, thyme, bay leaf)
2 sticks of celery
2 egg whites and shells
1 glass sherry (optional)
¼ pt. vinegar

Let the stock become quite cold, and remove every particle of fat. Put it into a stewpan with the gelatine, herbs, celery cut into large pieces, the egg whites previously slightly beaten and the shells previously washed and dried. Whisk over heat until nearly boiling, then add the wine and vinegar. Continue the whisking until quite boiling, then reduce the heat and simmer for about 10 min., strain till clear, and use as required.

ASPIC JELLY (from gelatine)

2 egg whites and shells	**1 onion**
1 lemon	**1 carrot**
2 chicken *or* veal bouillon cubes	**2–3 sticks of celery**
1 qt. water	**Bouquet garni (parsley, thyme, bay leaf)**
2½ oz. gelatine	**10 peppercorns**
¼ pt. malt vinegar	**1 teasp. salt**
1 tablesp. tarragon vinegar	

Whisk the egg whites slightly, wash the shells; peel the lemon rind as thinly as possible, and strain the juice; crumble the cubes. Put them with the rest of the ingredients into a pan, whisk over heat until boiling, then simmer very gently for about 20 min. Strain through a jelly bag.

NOTE: This jelly is used principally for lining and garnishing moulds. If too stiff it may be diluted with a little water, or sherry, when additional flavour is desired.

ASPIC CREAM

1 gill double cream	**Pinch of white pepper**
1½ gills aspic jelly	**Pinch of castor sugar**
1 teasp. lemon juice	

Put the cream into a basin, stir it with a whisk, and gradually add the aspic, which must be liquid. Add the lemon juice and seasoning and pass through a tammy cloth or fine strainer.

Use for masking entrees, chicken, etc.

TOMATO ASPIC

½ oz. gelatine	**½ gill aspic**
2 tablesp. water	**1 tablesp. meat glaze**
½ pt. tomato pulp	**Salt and cayenne pepper to taste**

Soak the gelatine in the water. Put all the ingredients in a saucepan over heat, stir until boiling, season to taste with salt and a pinch of cayenne pepper. Strain through a cloth or fine sieve.

Use for masking and decorating purposes.

SPUN SUGAR

1 lb. loaf sugar	**½ saltsp. cream of tartar**
½ pt. water	

Dissolve the sugar in the water in a sugar boiler or pan, and boil to the "large crack" degree (312° F.). Add the cream of tartar, reduce the heat, repeatedly test the consistency of the syrup with a tablespoon, and use as soon as it runs in a fine thread from the spoon to the pan.

To spin sugar: Take in the left hand a large knife previously oiled, hold it in a horizontal position, take a spoonful of syrup and spin the sugar into fine threads by moving the spoon to and fro over the flat blade of the knife.

To spin sugar successfully it must be done in a dry atmosphere, and the worker must avoid standing in a draught.

GLOSSARY OF CULINARY TERMS

Absinthe (Fr.) Name of an aromatic plant; also of a liqueur prepared from this plant, formerly used in France and Switzerland as a beverage to stimulate the appetite; sometimes used for flavouring purposes.

À la carte (Fr.) A list of dishes with the prices attached to each dish.

À la mode de (Fr.) After the style or fashion of, e.g. *à la Francaise* French style, *à la Reine* Queen style, *à la Russe* Russian style, etc.

Albumine (Fr.) **Albumen** (Eng.) Egg white.

Anglaise, à l' (Fr.) English style.

Apéritif (Fr.) Drink taken before meals.

Appetissants (Fr.) **Appetizers** (Am.) Small titbits or savouries.

Aquavit A potent, colourless, unsweetened Scandinavian liqueur. Often flavoured with caraway seeds.

Aromates (Fr.) Aromatic herbs used for flavouring, such as thyme, bay leaves, tarragon, chervil, etc.

Aspic (Fr.) A savoury jelly used for garnishing, etc.

Au bleu (Fr.) Term applied to fish boiled in salted water, seasoned with vegetables, herbs, and white wine or vinegar.

Au four (Fr.) Baked in the oven.

Au gratin (Fr.) A term, derived from the French verb *gratiner*, to brown, applied to certain dishes prepared with sauce, garnish and breadcrumbs, baked brown in the oven or under the grill; and served in the dish in which they are baked. The term does not necessarily imply that cheese is an ingredient although it often is.

Au jus (Fr.) A term for dishes of meat dressed with their juice or gravy.

Au maigre (Fr.) Dishes prepared without meat, Lenten dishes.

Au naturel (Fr.) Food served without cooking or cooked plainly and simply.

Baba (Polish *babka*) A very light yeast cake. A substitute for tipsy cake.

Bain-marie (Fr.) The culinary water bath. It is a large open vessel, half filled with hot water, in which saucepans containing sauces, etc., are placed so that their contents are kept nearly at boiling-point without burning or reducing.

Barbecue (Fr.) Originally the method of cooking (roasting) an animal whole; to dress and roast whole; a social entertainment where the food is cooked outside in the open.

Bavarois (Fr.) Bavarian cream. A term applied to creams, but incorrectly used, unless custard forms their base.

Béchamel (Fr.) French white sauce. One of the four foundation sauces.

Beignets (Fr.) Fritters. Also a kind of pancake, fried in deep fat.

Bisque (Fr.) Fish soups of a thick, creamy consistency usually made from molluscs or crustaceans.

Blanquette (Fr.) A white fricassée or stew, usually made of veal or fowl, with a white sauce enriched with cream or egg yolks.

Bombay duck A small East Indian fish, which when salted and cured is eaten as a relish.

Bombe (Fr.) An iced pudding which is shaped like a bomb and filled with a rich custard of fruit cream.

Bouchées (Fr.) Literally "A mouthful". Small patties of puff pastry (petits pâtés) with savoury or sweet fillings.

Bouillabaisse (Fr.) A kind of fish stew, very popular in France.

Bouquet garni (Fr.) A small bunch of herbs tied together and used to impart a rich flavour to stews, sauces, etc. Often called a faggot or fagot. In its most simple form it consists of a sprig of parsley, thyme and bay leaf, but a small quantity of chervil, chives, celery leaf, basil and tarragon may be added.

Brioche (Fr.) A light French yeast cake, similar to a Bath bun.

Callipash The fatty gelatinous substance close to the upper shell of a turtle.

Callipée The glutinous meat found in the under part of a turtle's undershell.

Canapés Small shapes of fried bread, toast or pastry on which savouries, etc., are served.

Caramel (Fr.) A colouring substance made by boiling sugar.

Carmine Crimson colouring used in confectionery, etc.

Carte du Jour (Fr.) The bill of fare for the day.

Casserole (Fr.) Originally a copper stewpan, now a fireproof earthenware or glass cooking dish with a lid, used especially for stews. The food is served in the dish. When used in menus it indicates a case of rice, baked pastry crust, or macaroni, filled with minced meat, game purée, etc.

Cassolette (Fr.) A very small case filled with a savoury filling, served as hot hors d'œuvres or savoury. The case may be made from fried bread, butter, pastry, egg and breadcrumbs, etc.

Caviar (Fr.) **Caviare** (Eng.) The salted roe of the sturgeon or sterlet fish.

Cereals All grains such as rice, wheat, oats, oatmeal, barley and semolina.

Charlotte (Fr.) A corruption of the old English word Charlyt, "a dish of custard".

Chartreuse A mixture of fruit, or meat, or vegetables, served as an entrée. A French liqueur, there are two well known kinds—yellow and green.

Chaudfroid (Fr.) A cold entrée; a sauce for masking cold fish, game, etc.

Chianti (It.) Wine from the region of the Chianti Mountains, Tuscany, especially a dry red variety; also wine of the same type made elsewhere.

Chipolata (It.) Small Italian sausages. Also dishes which contain Italian sausages, or a kind of mixed minced meat with which they are served.

Chowder (Eng.) A dish of American origin, consisting of boiled pickled pork cut in slices, fried onions, slices of turbot or other fish, and mashed potatoes, all placed alternately in a stewpan, seasoned with spices and herbs, claret and ketchup, and simmered.

Citronné (Fr.) Anything which has the taste or flavour of lemon.

Clam A bivalve shell-fish, several kinds of which are edible, popular in N. America.

Cochenille (Fr.) Cochineal. A liquid pink colouring substance, used for colouring creams, sauces, icing, etc.

Cocottes Small fireproof cooking and serving dishes which hold one portion.

Compôte (Fr.) Fruit stewed with sugar. A stew of small birds.

Condé Name of an old French family. Several soups, entrées and sweets, of which rice forms an essential part, are styled "â la Condé".

Condiments Highly-flavoured seasoning spices, etc.

Cordon Bleu (Fr.) An ancient culinary distinction bestowed on skilful female cooks in France since the time of Louis XV. It consists of a rosette made of dark blue ribbon.

Coulibriac Name of a Russian dish—a kind of fish-cake mixture wrapped up in Brioche paste and baked.

Court Bouillon (Fr.) Name given to a liquid in which fish is poached; a highly-seasoned fish stock and stew.

Crécy, Potage à la (Fr.) Crécy or carrot soup (Eng.) Dishes named "à la Crécy" are generally connected with carrots in the form of a purée.

Crêpes (Fr.) Pancakes.

Croissants (Fr.) Crescent-shaped bread rolls.

Croquettes (Fr.) Savoury mince of fowl, meat, fish or potatoes mixed with a binding ingredient, and formed into various shapes. They are usually coated with egg and breadcrumbs and fried crisp.

Croustades (Fr.) Shapes of fried bread, rice or pastry, in which various mixtures are served.

Croûtes Blocks or shapes of fried bread on which salmis, whole birds, etc. are served.

Croûtons (Fr.) Sippets of fried bread or toast cut into dice shapes and fried, used for garnishing dishes.

Cuillères de cuisine (Fr.) Wooden spoons, the use of which is strongly recommended instead of metal spoons, especially for stirring sauces.

Cuisine (Fr.) Kitchen, cookery. *Faire la cuisine*, to cook or to dress foods.

Culinaire (Fr.) Anything connected with the kitchen or the art of cooking.

Curaçao (Fr.) A liqueur prepared from the yellow part of the rind of a peculiar kind of bitter orange. Used for flavouring jellies, ices, etc.

Dariole (Fr.) A small tin mould. A kind of small entrée mixture, composed of a compound of forcemeat or mince, baked or steamed in these small moulds.

Dhâll or **Dholl** A kind of pulse much used in India for kedgeree, or as a kind of porridge. In England it is best represented by split peas or lentils.

Diable (Fr.) "Devil". Applied to numerous dishes with sharp and hot seasoning.

Drageés (Fr.) **Sugar plums** (Eng.) A kind of sweetmeat made of fruits, small pieces of rinds or aromatic roots, or nuts, covered with a coating of sugar icing.

Dripping The fat obtained from cooked meat or from rendering down pieces of fat.

Dunelm A dish of braised mutton or veal, originating from Durham.

Éclair (Fr.) A French pastry made from choux pastry filled with cream or custard.

En casserole (Fr.) A dish cooked and served in an earthenware or glass casserole.

Entrée (Fr.) A course of dishes, or corner dish for the first course; the conventional term for hot or cold side dishes. Also defined as dishes generally served with a sauce.

Entremets (Fr.) Dainty dishes of vegetables, or hot and cold sweets, and after-dinner savouries, served as second course.

Epigrammes (Fr.) Used as a culinary term for breast of lamb or mutton braised and divided into small portions, egged, crumbed and fried. Also defined as a dish of alternate cutlets of the neck and breast.

Escalopes (Fr.) Thin round steaks of veal called "collops". Also thin slices of any kind of meat, usually egged, crumbed and fried. Fish, meat, etc., served in escallop shells.

Escargot (Fr.) The edible vineyard snail.

Espagnole (Fr.) A rich brown sauce, one of the four foundation sauces.

Farce (Fr.) Forcemeat or stuffing.

Farinaceous Consisting or made of meal or flour.

Feuilletage (Fr.) Puff pastry; leafy, flaky.

Filet (Fr.) Fillet. The under-cut of a loin of beef, mutton, veal, pork and game. Boned breasts of poultry, birds, and the boned sides of fish are also called fillets.

Fines herbes (Fr.) A combination of finely-chopped fresh herbs, such as parsley, tarragon, chervil and other kitchen herbs; mostly used in omelets and sauces.

Flamber (Fr.) To singe poultry or game. To cover a pudding or omelet with spirit and set it alight.

Flan (Fr.) An open tart.

Flapjack A griddle cake.

Fleurons (Fr.) Small half-moon shapes of puff pastry, baked, used for garnishing.

Flummery (Eng.) Cold sweet dish, mainly of cereals, originally of oatmeal set in a mould and turned out. To be eaten with wine, cider, milk or a compound sauce.

Foie de veau (Fr.) Calf's liver.

Foie gras (Fr.) Fat goose liver.

Fondant (Fr.) Melting. A soft kind of icing; dessert bonbons.

Fondue (Fr.) A preparation of melted cheese. A savoury.

Forcemeat Stuffing.

Fouetté (Fr.) Whipped with a whisk.

Frangipane A substitute for custards made of eggs, milk, some flour, with lemon peel, rum, brandy, vanilla, etc., to flavour.

Frappé (Fr.) Iced (champagne etc.). *Frapper*: To place on ice; ice (used when cooling champagne).

Fricassée (Fr.) **Fricasséed** A white stew of chicken or veal.

Frit (Fr.) Fried in shallow or deep fat.

Frittata (It.) An Italian dish; a kind of rolled pancake, crumbed and fried in fat.

Frosting (Am.) Icing.

Fumet (Fr.) The flavour or essence of game, fish, or any highly flavoured concentrated substance used to impart a rich flavour to certain dishes.

Galantine (Fr.) A dish of white meat, rolled, glazed and served cold. A fowl or breast of veal, boned and stuffed with farce, tongue, ham, etc.

Garnish The decorations added to a dish to improve its appearance.

Gâteau (Fr.) A cake, usually implies a rich, elaborate, decorated cake.

Gaufre (Fr.) A thin biscuit wafer; baked or fried in specially constructed gaufre moulds.

Gelatine A manufactured substance for giving solidity to liquids.

Genièvre (Fr.) Juniper berry. A blue-black berry, possessing a peculiar aromatic flavour, used as a flavouring condiment in mirepoix, marinades, etc.; also used in syrups and liqueurs.

Ghee An Indian word for clarified butter.

Glacé (Fr.) Frozen, iced or glazed; coated or masked with glaze.

Glaze (Eng.) Stock or gravy reduced to the thickness of jelly; used for glazing meats, etc., to improve their appearance. Well-made glaze adheres firmly to the meat. Used also for strengthening soups and sauces.

Gnocchi (It.) Dumplings; a light savoury dough, boiled and served with tomato sauce and grated Parmesan cheese. Also fancy-shaped pieces of semolina paste used for garnishing soups and savoury dishes.

Goulash Hungarian dish. A rich meat stew.

Gourmet (Fr.) An epicure; a judge of good living; one who values and enjoys good eating; a connoisseur of wine.

Gramolata (It.) A kind of half-frozen lemon. Water-ice served in glasses.

Grenadin (Fr.) Small fillets of veal or fowl larded and braised.

Guinée pepper (Eng.) **Poivre de guinee** (Fr.) A kind of cayenne, prepared from the seeds of the ripe chilli or capsicum annum. Also called chilli pepper. The name of Guinée pepper is also given to the ground seeds of dried fruit of certain plants of the same kind as capsicums, all of which are of a pungent character.

Gumbo The American term for okra soup, or other preparations from okra, gumbo being the name by which okra is chiefly known in South America.

Hominy A farinaceous food made of maize.

Hors d'œuvre (Fr.) Small side dishes, served cold, generally before the soup, in order to create an appetite. They consist of anchovies, sardines, cheese and other dainty relishes. Large hors d'œuvres may be served as a main course.

Icing or **Glaze** Covering for cakes, etc.

Irlandaise, à l' (Fr.) Irish style. This term is applied to dishes containing potatoes in some form.

Isinglass Egg preservative.

Jardinière (Fr.) A garnish of mixed spring vegetables; vegetables stewed down in their own sauce.

Julep Ancient Arabian name for a cooling drink containing mucilage, opium, etc. An American drink.

Julienne (Fr.) Name of a vegetable clear soup (*see* p. 87) named after the 18th century French chef, Jean Julien; also a garnish consisting of fine strips of mixed vegetables.

Junket (Eng.) A dessert made of sweetened and flavoured curds.

Jus (Fr.) Juice, broth, gravy. The juice of cooked meats seasoned, but without any thickening.

Kebabs, Kabobs, Khubab Originally name of a dish served in India and Turkey, consisting of small slices of mutton run on skewers, and either grilled or braised; now term given to any savoury items, e.g. tomatoes, sausages, slices of kidney, etc., run on skewers and grilled.

Kedgeree, Kadgiori, Kitchri, or **Kegeree** An Indian dish of fish and rice often curried.

Kirsch A colourless liqueur distilled from black cherries. It comes from Germany and Switzerland and is often added to trifles.

Kromeskis A Polish word, having the same meaning as croquette in French.

Liaison (Fr.) The mixture of egg yolks, cream, etc., used for thickening or binding white soups and sauces.

Liquor Any liquid or juice produced by cooking, as meat liquor.

Lyonnaise, à la (Fr.) Lyonese style. As a garnish it generally signifies that shredded onion (fried) has been introduced.

Macaroni (It.) A paste prepared from wheat flour dried in various shapes and forms but usually made into long tubes.

Macaroons Sweet biscuits made of almonds, sugar and egg whites.

Macédoine (Fr.) A mixture of various kinds

of vegetables or fruits, cut in even-shaped dice. The name is also applied to a collection of fruit embedded in jelly and set in a mould, or a fruit salad flavoured with liqueurs and syrup.

Madeleine (Fr.) Small cakes baked in a dariole mould, often coated with jam and sprinkled with coconut. Also the name of a pear.

Madère (Fr.) Madeira wine. A Spanish wine very often used in cooking.

Maintenon Name of the Marchioness Françoise d'Aubigné. Louis XIV's favourite; a great patroness of cooks. Several dishes are called "à la Maintenon", usually signifying something grilled in a paper case.

Maître d'Hôtel, à la (Fr.) Hotel stewards' fashion. The name of a butter (*see* recipe, p. 676) served on grilled meats. Dishes named Maître d'Hôtel are usually composed of food quickly and plainly prepared, parsley being the principal flavouring.

Maraschino, Marasquin (Fr.) A delicately flavoured white liqueur, distilled from a species of cherry used for flavouring jellies and ices.

Marinade (Fr.) A mixture of oil, herbs, vinegar, etc., in which fish or meat is soused or pickled.

Marsala (It.) A wine similar to Madeira.

Marzipan (Ger.) Delicate dessert dainties made from almond paste.

Mayonnaise (Fr.) A kind of salad of fish or poultry, with a thick cold sauce made of egg yolks, oil and vinegar. A salad sauce or dressing.

Mazarines (Fr.) Turbans. Forcemeat decorations of fish, poultry or game. Entrées consisting of combined fillets of meat and forcemeat.

Médallion (Fr.) Round fillets, meat mixtures, etc. in a round form.

Medlar Roundish fruit about ½–1 in. long; reddish-brown in colour. The Japanese Medlar is the Loquat.

Menu (Fr.) The bill of fare. Literally, the word means minute detail of courses.

Meringue (Fr.) A light pastry, made of egg whites and sugar, filled with cream; a topping for a pie or pudding.

Mignonette Pepper Coarsely-ground white peppercorns. A form of comminuted pepper, which resembles mignonette seed when sifted.

Minute, à la (Fr.) A surname given to dishes which are hurriedly prepared or anything cooked in the quickest possible way.

Mirepoix (Fr.) The foundation bed of mixed vegetables, herbs and bacon on which meat and vegetables are braised; also a mixture of diced carrots, onions, ham sautéed in fat then added to brown soups and sauces for flavouring.

Miroton (Fr.) Thin round slices of meat, about 2 in. in diameter, braised, stewed, and dished up in a circle.

Muscat (Fr.) **Muscadine** (Eng.) A wine, also the grape producing it.

Napolitaine, à la (Fr.) Naples or Neapolitan style.

Navarin (Fr.) A stew of mutton or lamb. A kind of haricot mutton.

Neat's Foot The foot of a calf or ox.

Nepaul pepper A red pepper of the same character as cayenne and Guinée pepper, being a species of capsicum with a sweet pungent flavour.

Noisettes Neatly trimmed, round or oval shapes of lamb, mutton, or beef not less than ½ in. thick.

Normande, à la (Fr.) Normandy style, with the exception of a dish known as *Filets de soles à la Normande*, and other fish entrées. The application of this name implies that the flavour of apple has in some form or other been introduced into the composition of the dish.

Nougat (Fr.) A sweetmeat made with sugar, honey, almonds, pistachios, etc.

Nouilles (Fr.) **Noodles.** A German preparation *Nudeln.* It consists of a stiff paste made with flour and eggs, rolled out very thinly, cut up in thin strips and boiled, and served as garnish or main dish.

Noyau (Fr.) The stone of a fruit; a liqueur flavoured with peach or nectarine kernels.

Okra Name of a vegetable extensively used in South America. Used as a vegetable and also for soup.

Orly Name given to dishes prepared in a certain style. Usually slices of fish or meat dipped in rich batter and fried in fat.

Pain d'épice (Fr.) Spiced bread; a kind of gingerbread.

Panada Culinary paste of flour and water or soaked bread, used for preparing forcemeat or stuffing.

Papillotes (Fr.) Paper cases in which food is cooked and served.

Paprica The fleshy fruit of the green and red mild capsicum, grown in the south of Europe, and used as spice for ragoûts or salads.

Paprika Hungarian red pepper. A kind of sweet capsicum of a brilliant scarlet colour; it is less pungent than the Spanish pepper.

Parson's nose The extreme end portion of the carcass of a bird.

Passer (Fr.) **Pass** (Eng.) To pass a sauce, soup, vegetable or meat, means to run it through a tammy-cloth, sieve or strainer.

Pâte feuilletée (Fr.) Puff pastry.

Pâte frisée (Fr.) Short pastry.

Pâté (Fr.) A pie, pastry; a savoury meat paste or a raised pie.

Pâté de foie gras (Fr.) A well-known delicacy prepared from the livers of fat geese.

Pâtisserie (Fr.) Pastry. A pastry-cook's business.

Perry (Eng.) Name of a beverage made of pears, similar to cider made of apples.

Petits Fours (Fr.) Small fancy cakes highly decorated with fancy icing, crystallized fruits, etc.

Pilaf, Pilloff, Pillau, Pilaw Fish or meat with savoury rice, i.e. rice flavoured with spices and cooked in stock.

Pitcaithly Bannock Name of a kind of Scottish shortbread.

Pimiento A red Spanish pepper pod used in salads, and as garnish.

Pistaches (Fr.) **Pistachios** Kernels of the nut of the turpentine tree, used for flavouring and garnishing galantines, sweets, etc.

Pizza (It.) Pie; a large flat tart spread with tomatoes, cheese and often meat, anchovies, etc.

Polenta (It.) A standard Italian dish made of Indian cornflour.

Pot-au-feu (Fr.) is an economical and wholesome beef broth. It is the standard dish of all classes in France, and the origin of beef stock.

Praline (Fr.) Burnt almond.

Praliné (Fr.) Flavoured with burnt almonds.

Provençale, à la (Fr.) A surname for certain French dishes, indicating generally that garlic or onion, and olive oil has been used.

Pulses Term used for peas, beans, lentils and split peas.

Pumpernickel (Ger.) Westphalian brown bread.

Purée (Fr.) A smooth pulp; mashed vegetables or fruit; thick soup. The name is also given to meat or fish which is cooked, pounded, then passed through a sieve.

Quenelles (Fr.) Forcemeat of different kinds, composed of fish, poultry or meat, eggs, etc., shaped in various forms—balls, ovals, etc., poached, and served as an entrée or garnish to soup, etc.

Quoorma Name of a very mild Indian curry.

Ragoût (Fr.) A rich stew of meat, highly seasoned.

Ramequin (Fr.) **Ramakin** Cheese fritter; small fondues served in china or paper cases.

Raspings Very fine crumbs made from baked bread, used with beaten egg to coat foods for frying, and for au gratin dishes.

Ratafie or **Ratafia** A culinary essence; the essence of bitter almonds. A special kind of almond biscuit. The name is also given to a liqueur flavoured with almonds.

Réchauffé (Fr.) Warmed-up food, left-over food re-cooked or re-dressed.

Rennet The name given to the prepared inner membrane of a calf's, pig's, hare's or fowl's stomach; used for curdling or coagulating milk.

Rissoles (Fr.) A mixture of minced fish or meat, enclosed in pastry half-moon shapes, and fried in deep fat. The name is now given to meat mixtures which are shaped into rolls and coated with egg and bread-crumbs before frying.

Roe Fish eggs.

Roulade (Fr.) Roll, rolling. Rolled meat, cooked.

Roux (Fr.) A mixture of equal quantities of fat and flour cooked together and used for thickening soups and sauces. There are 3 kinds—"white", "blond" and "brown", depending on the length of time of the preliminary cooking.

Royal Name of an egg custard used for garnishing clear soups. Also the name applied to an icing (glacé royale) made with egg whites and icing sugar, and used for coating and decoration.

Sabayon (Fr.) **Zabaglione** (It.) A sauce served with puddings, composed of cream or milk, sugar, white wine and eggs. Also served in glasses as a cold sweet.

Saccharometer A device for measuring the amount of sugar in a solution, especially a hydrometer with a special scale.

Salami (It.) A kind of uncooked sausage that is smoked or air-dried and keeps indefinitely in a dry atmosphere.

Sally Luns or **Lunn** Name of a kind of tea-cake, slightly sweetened and raised with yeast.

Salmi or **Salmis** A hash made of half-roasted game.

Salpicon A mince of poultry or game with ham, tongue, and mushrooms, used for croquettes, rissoles, etc. or for filling bouchées, patty cases, etc.

Salsify or **Salsifis** An edible plant; sometimes called oyster-plant.

Sauerkraut (Ger.) **Choucroute** (Fr.) A kind of pickled cabbage, cabbage preserved in brine. A national dish of Germany. Served hot with bacon or sausages.

Sauté-pan, Sautoire (Fr.) A shallow cooking pan.

Sauterne (Fr.) A French white wine much used in cookery.

Savarin A light pudding made from a yeast mixture.

Seasoned flour Flour mixed with salt and pepper usually in the proportion of 1 tablesp. flour, 1 teasp. salt and ½ teasp. pepper.

Sippets Bread cut into crescents and triangles, then fried, used as a garnish.

Skewer A metal or wooden pin used for fastening pieces of meat together, also used for trussing poultry.

Sorbet (Fr.) An iced Turkish drink. Also the name of a water ice with fruit or liqueur flavour, usually served in goblets.

Soubise (Fr.) A smooth onion pulp served with various kinds of meat entrées. As a surname to dishes, *à la Soubise* is generally applied when onions enter largely into the composition of a dish.

Soufflé (Fr.) A light, fluffy, very lightly-baked or steamed pudding. Also applied to light sweet or savoury creams set with gelatine and served cold, similar to mousses.

Soy A dark-brown condiment sauce, originally made in Japan; there are many English relishes in which soy is employed as an ingredient.

Spaghetti (It.) An Italian paste made into long tubes, intermediate in size between macaroni and vermicelli.

Stirabout Name of an Irish dish similar to Scotch porridge.

Syllabub A kind of milk punch flavoured with liqueurs and spices. A cold sweet made from brandy or wine and milk, flavoured and sweetened.

Table d'Hôte (Fr.) A general title for a meal of several courses at a fixed price. Table at which meals at an hotel or restaurant are served; common table for guests.

Tamis (Fr.) **Tammy** (Eng.) Woollen canvas cloth which is used for straining soups and sauces.

Tepid Almost blood heat, the temperature of a mixture of 2 parts cold water and 1 part boiling water.

Terrapin South American fresh-water and tidal turtle.

Timbale (Fr.) Literally "kettle-drum". A kind of crusted hash baked in a mould.

Toddy A punch. The fundamental juice of various palms of the East Indies; a mixture of whisky, sugar and hot water.

Tournedos (Fr.) Small thin fillets of beef served as entrées.

Tourte (Fr.) An open tart; also a flat dough case in which ragoûts are served.

Tutti frutti (It.) Various kinds of fruits, or fruit ice.

Vermicelle (Fr.) **Vermicelli** (It.) Very fine strings of paste, made from a wheat flour dough, forced through cylinders or pipes till it takes a slender, worm-like form, when dried; used in soups, puddings, and (crushed) for coating.

Vitamins Vital food elements; especially found in or just under the husk of rice, wheat, barley, etc.

Vol-au-vent (Fr.) A light round puff-pastry case, filled with delicately flavoured ragoûts of chicken, sweetbread, etc.

Zabaglione *See* Sabayon.

Zephire (Fr.) Name of a small oval-shaped forcemeat dumpling, poached and served with a rich sauce; anything shaped in a Zéphire mould.

Zest The coloured, oily, outer skin of citrus fruits added to cookery for flavouring. It should be very finely cut, grated, or rubbed off with lumps of sugar.

SPICES AND FLAVOURINGS

Allspice: This is the popular name given to pimento or Jamaica pepper. It is the berry of a tree growing in the West Indies, Mexico and parts of South America. It is called "allspice" because its smell and flavour very closely resembles that of a combination of cloves, cinnamon and nutmeg. It may be used whole or ground.

Capsicums: Several varieties of this plant are cultivated in the East and West Indies and in America. The red chilli, which invariably forms part of mixed pickles, is the pod of the capsicum, and chilli vinegar is made by infusing capsicum pods in vinegar until some of their pungency and strength is extracted. From the same source comes cayenne pepper, obtained from the pods and the seeds, which are well dried and then ground to a fine powder.

Cayenne: This is an acrid and stimulating spice. It is a powder prepared from several varieties of the capsicum.

Cinnamon: The cinnamon tree is a valuable and beautiful species of the laurel family. When the branches are three years old they are stripped of their outer bark, the inner bark is dried, causing it to shrivel up. The bark is sold in stick form and in powdered form. Besides being used extensively for culinary purposes—flavouring cakes, buns and puddings, cinnamon is used as a powerful stimulant.

Cloves: The clove contains about 20 per cent of volatile aromatic oil, to which is attributed its peculiar pungent flavour, its other parts being composed of woody fibre, water, gum and resin. They form a well-known spice, and are much used in cookery, both in sweet and savoury dishes.

Curry: Curry is composed of various condiments and spices, which include cardamom seed, coriander seed, cumin seed, dried cassia leaves, dried chillies, cayenne, ginger, mustard seed, turmeric, cinnamon, mace and cloves. It owes its peculiar smell and bright colour to the presence of turmeric, a variety of ginger largely cultivated in the East Indies. Thorough cooking is absolutely necessary to develop the full flavour of the various ingredients.

Garlic: This is a pungent, strong-scented bulb, composed of smaller bulbs called "cloves".

Ginger: Ginger is the tuber of a perennial plant called *Zingiber officinale*. It is sold in root or ground form. Ginger is much used in culinary operations; grated green ginger is considered by epicures to be an important item in a dish of curry.

Krona Pepper: This well-known condiment is made from the Hungarian *paprika*, capsicum pod, etc. It is bright red in colour, with a pleasant flavour, and is less pungent than cayenne. Consequently it may be regarded as an exceedingly useful combination of flavouring and seasoning ingredients.

Mace: Mace is the outer shell or husk of the nutmeg, and naturally resembles it in flavour. Its general qualities are the same as those of nutmeg, producing a pleasant aromatic odour. It is sold in "blade" or ground form.

Mustard: There are two varieties of mustard seeds: *Sinapis nigra* (the common), and *Sinapis alba* (the white). Commercial mustard is composed of the seeds of both varieties ground and mixed together. Mustard taken in small quantities is said to stimulate the appetite and aid digestion. The pungency of mustard is not fully developed until moistened with water; its flavour is best when freshly prepared. A pinch of salt added to mixed mustard will prevent it from becoming dry, and will, in some slight degree, preserve its aroma.

Nutmeg: Nutmegs are the seeds of the nutmeg tree. There are two kinds of nutmegs—one wild, and long and oval shaped, the other cultivated and nearly round: the husk which surrounds the shell of the nutmeg when growing is known as mace. Nutmeg is largely used as a flavouring: but it should be added sparingly to cereal dishes, for its strong aromatic flavour is disliked by many. It is sold whole or in ground form.

Pepper: This valuable condiment is produced from the seed of the berries of the plant *Piper nigrum*. The plant produces both white pepper and black pepper. The berries, when ripe, are bright in colour, and each contains a single seed of globular form and brownish colour, which changes to nearly black when dried. This is the commercial black pepper, white peppercorns being produced by further treatment, and subjecting them to certain rubbing processes, by which their dark husks are removed. It is sold as whole peppercorns or ground pepper.

Owing to the high cost of peppercorns most of the so-called "pepper" now on the market is a mixture of other highly flavoured spices.

Salt: The importance of salt as a condiment, as an antiseptic, and as food cannot be overestimated. In cookery its uses are apparently contradictory, for it helps to soften certain substances when applied through the medium of cold water, and assists in hardening them when the medium is boiling water. It increases the specific gravity of water, and consequently raises the boiling-point, a matter of considerable importance in boiling rice, when it is necessary to keep the water in a state of ebullition to prevent the rice coalescing. Every other condiment, no matter how desirable, may be dispensed with, or one condiment may be substituted for another, but salt is indispensable, for it makes palatable food that would otherwise be uneatable. Salt, like all other seasonings, must be used with judgment.

It is sold as common or table salt or as sea salt. Common salt and sea salt are purer and therefore better for cooking as table salt contains other ingredients to make it run freely.

Turmeric: Turmeric is the tuber of the *Curcuma longa*, a branch of the ginger family, extensively cultivated in the East Indies. The tubers are dried and then ground to a fine powder. It is a main component of curry powder, and is responsible for its peculiar odour and characteristic bright yellow colour.

Vanilla: Vanilla is the fruit of a tropical orchid plant. The dried, aromatic, sheath-like pod has a delicious fragrance. It is extensively used as a flavouring for cakes, custards, puddings, chocolate, liqueurs, etc.

A vanilla pod should be stored in the sugar jar. It may be used for custard, etc., in a pan of heating milk as an infusion (dried after use and returned to the sugar jar), but if the sugar is flavoured then anything the sugar is used for is also flavoured.

Vinegar: Vinegar serves many useful purposes in cookery: it is an ingredient in many sauces, and helps to soften the fibres of tough meat. Vinegar is also an antiseptic: and taken in small quantities it promotes digestion, by stimulating the digestive organs into greater activity; but, if taken to excess, it is highly injurious. Malt vinegar is generally used in pickles and chutneys. Wine vinegar (red or white) is more delicate and preferable for salad dressings. Cider vinegar is also delicately flavoured, less expensive than wine vinegar and said to have additional health-giving qualities.

A LIST OF CULINARY HERBS AND THEIR USES

Herb	*Part Used*	*Purpose*
Angelica	Leaf stalks	These can be candied and used for flavouring and decorating cakes and fruit
	Midribs	As a vegetable
Anise	Leaves	Flavouring soups and sweets
	Seeds	Flavouring drinks
Balm	Leaves	Flavouring soups, stews, sauces and dressings
Basil	Leaves	In salads or for flavouring soups and sauces
Bay	Leaves	Flavouring stock, sauces, puddings and custard
Borage	Leaves	In salads
	Leaves and shoots	Flavouring fruit cups and other drinks
Caraway	Seeds	Flavouring cakes, soups and sauces
Chervil	Leaves	As a garnish, in salads or for flavouring soups, entrees and sauces
Chives	Leaves	In salads or for flavouring soups, omelettes and entrees
Coriander	Seeds	In pickles or for flavouring cakes, sauces and drinks
Dill	Leaves	Flavouring soups and sauces
	Seeds	In preserves or pickles
Fennel	Leaves	As a garnish or for flavouring sauces
Garlic	"Clove" (bulb)	In salads or for flavouring soups and stews
Horseradish	Root	Flavouring sauces
Hyssop	Leaves	Flavouring soups
Marjoram	Leaves	In stuffings or for flavouring soups, stews or sauces
Mint	Leaves	As a garnish or for flavouring sauces, soups or vegetables
Parsley	Leaves	As a garnish, in salads or for flavouring soups and sauces
Purslane	Leaves	In salads or for flavouring soups and sauces
Rosemary	Leaves and shoots	In salads or for flavouring stews, sauces and fruit cups
Rue	Leaves	Flavouring fruit cups—use sparingly
Sage	Leaves	In stuffings or for flavouring soups, sauces and stews
Savory	Leaves	As a garnish, in stuffings or for flavouring stews, sauces and vegetables
Sorrel	Leaves	In salads, as a vegetable or for flavouring soups
Southernwood	Leaves	Flavouring cakes
Tansy	Leaves	As a garnish, in salads or for flavouring cakes, puddings and stews

Tarragon	Leaves	In salads, for making Tarragon vinegar or flavouring omelettes, sauces and stews
Thyme	Leaves	In stuffings or for flavouring soups and stews

EQUIVALENT WEIGHTS AND MEASURES

AVOIRDUPOIS WEIGHTS

(*British and American*)	*Metric* (*approximate*)
1 ounce (oz.)	28 grams (g.)
1 pound (lb.)	454 g.
2.2 lb.	1 kilogram (kg.)

LINEAR MEASURES

British and American	*Metric* (*approximate*)
1 inch (in.)	2·5 centimetres (cm.)
1 foot (ft.)	30 cm.
39 ins.	1 metre (m.)

LIQUID MEASURES

British Standard	*Metric* (*approximate*)	*American*
1 pint (pt.) = 20 fluid ounces (fl. oz.)	600 millilitres (ml.)	1¼ pints
8 fl. oz.	200 ml.	½ pt. (1 cup)
1¾ pts. (35 fl. oz.)	1 litre (1.)	2.2 pts.
1 quart (qt.) (2 pts.)	1.2 1.	2½ pts.

In addition to the above, the following abbreviations are used throughout the book:

sp.	spoonful
teasp.	teaspoonful
dessertsp.	dessertspoonful
tablesp.	tablespoonful
hr.	hour

Where spoonfuls are referred to, level spoons are meant unless otherwise stated.

If metric standard measures are used, a 15 ml. spoon is approximately the equivalent of a tablespoon and a 5 ml. spoon approximately the equivalent of a teaspoon.

American tablespoons and teaspoons are smaller than the standard British ones, holding only about four-fifths of the same ingredient.

WEIGHTS AND MEASURES

SOME HANDY MEASURES USED IN BAKING

INGREDIENT	STANDARD MEASURING SPOONS (LEVEL)			
	BRITISH	(WEIGHT)	AMERICAN	(WEIGHT)
Sifted flour	3 tablesp.	1 oz.	4 tablesp.	1 oz.
Granulated, castor, or superfine sugar	2 tablesp.	1¼ oz.	2 tablesp.	1 oz
Sifted icing or confectioner's sugar	3 tablesp.	1 oz.	4 tablesp.	1 oz.
Margarine or butter	2 tablesp.	1¼ oz.	2 tablesp.	1 oz.
Rice, whole	2 tablesp.	1¼ oz.	2 tablesp.	1 oz.
Cornflour or cornstarch	2 tablesp.	1 oz.	3 tablesp.	1 oz.
Syrup, treacle, molasses (warmed)	1 tablesp.	1 oz.	1 tablesp.	¾ oz.
Granulated or powdered gelatine	4 teasp.	½ oz.	5 teasp.	½ oz.

OVEN CHART

	ELECTRICITY	GAS MARK
Very cool	240° F. (116° C.) 265° F. (129° C.) 290° F. (143° C.)	¼, ½, 1
Cool	310° F. (154° C.)	2
Warm	335° F. (168° C.)	3
Moderate	356° F. (179° C.)	4
Fairly hot	380° F. (193° C.) 400° F. (204° C.)	5, 6
Hot	425° F. (218° C.)	7
Very hot	445° F. (229° C.) 470° F. (243° C.)	8, 9

METRIC WEIGHTS OF BRITISH AND AMERICAN MEASURES

	1 BRITISH STANDARD CUP (10 FL. OZ. CAPACITY)		1 AMERICAN CUP (8 FL. OZ. CAPACITY)	
	WEIGHT IN OZ.	WEIGHT IN GRAMS	WEIGHT IN OZ.	WEIGHT IN GRAMS
Butter, margarine, lard	9½	270	8	227
Suet, shredded	5	140	4½	120
Oil	8½	241	8	227
Cheddar cheese, grated	5	140	4	113
Cream, double	9	255	8⅓	236
Milk—condensed	12	340	10¾	304
evaporated	10½	297	9	255
Breadcrumbs—dry	5¾	162	4	113
fresh	1½	42	1	28
Cornflour	5¾	162	4½	128
Rice—Patna	7¾	219	6½	182
pudding	8½	241	7	198
Flour—plain, self-raising	6	170	4	113
cake	5½	154	3⅓	95
Currants	7	198	5	140
Raisins—seedless	7½	212	5¾	162
stoned	7	198	5	140
Dates, stoned	7¾	219	6⅓	178
Cherries, glacé	9	255	7	198
Candied peel, chopped	9½	270	6½	182
Almonds, whole, blanched	6½	182	5½	154
Walnuts—halved	4	113	3½	100
chopped	5	140	4½	128
Peanut butter	10	284	8	227
Gelatine, powdered	7	198	5⅓	159
Sugar—brown (packed down),				
granulated, caster	8½	241	7	198
icing	6	170	4½	128
Syrup—corn, molasses	16	453	11½	326
maple	14	397	11	312
Honey	15	414	12	340

CARVING

GOOD carving is neither an art nor a science, but an acquired skill. Many who would sometimes carve at table on festive occasions are deterred from doing so by lack of confidence. Any who consult the literature on the subject are further put off by directions which make it appear necessary to possess the knowledge and skill of a surgeon and the speed of a sawmill.

A knife is essentially a very finely toothed saw and it should be used in the same way, that is, drawn back and forth through the meat it is cutting. Never try to push even a sharp knife through meat without this sawing action. If the knife is sharp, the backward and forward motions can be long and light. In this way less-jagged slices are removed. Try to keep the knife at the same angle all the way through the joint and try to take a slice of equal thickness. This is not always possible, as with the first cuts from a roast joint of beef.

Try always to cut across or away from yourself. Protect the left hand by using a fork, preferably a proper carving fork with a stout thumb-piece.

BEEF

When carving rolled joints of beef, leave the string and skewers in position until you have carved down to them and then if there are many, only remove those which impede the progress of further carving. Joints on the bone are carved from the outside fat towards the bone. When this is reached the knife is turned upwards and the slices gently detached. With sirloin and ribs try to carve the outside rib muscles first as these are better eaten hot. Save the central, least-cooked meat to be eaten cold for it will have a better flavour. As with most butchers' meat carve across the grain or run of the muscle. Generally this means cutting parallel to the rib bone. With boneless joints the obvious way to carve is usually the correct way.

Aitchbone of Beef: Set the joint on the wide, flat base. Take small slices towards the bone parallel to the base until a thick slice is being cut across the whole joint. At the end of each slice turn the knife blade upwards to separate the meat from the bone.

Beef Tongue: *Unpressed*, cut nearly through across the tongue at the thick part, and then serve a fairly thick slice. The carving may be continued in this way towards the point until the best portions of the upper side are served. The fat which lies about the root of the tongue can be served by turning it over. If *pressed*, carve thinly across the top, parallel to the round base.

Brisket of Beef (*see* Fig. I): The joint should be cut evenly and firmly across the bones (1)–(2), in slices the whole width of the joint.

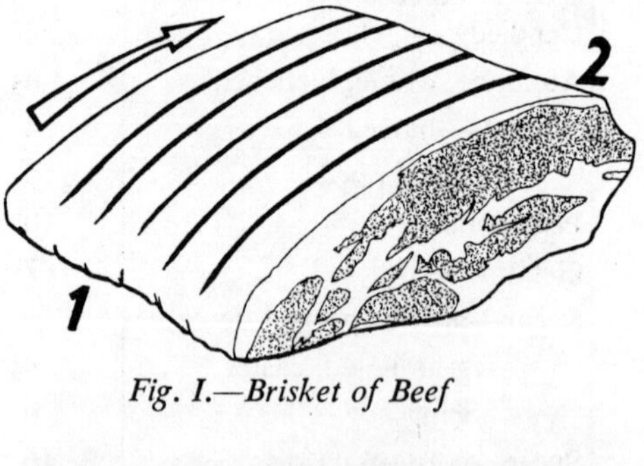

Fig. I.—Brisket of Beef

Ribs of Beef (*see* Fig. II): Cut slices off the sides, starting at the thick end (3) and through

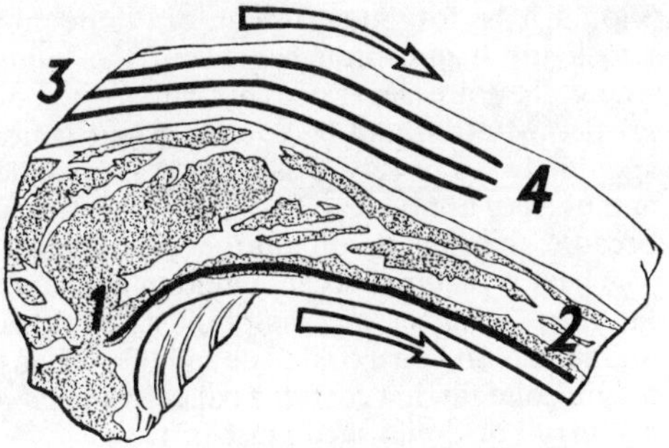

Fig. II.—Ribs of Beef

to the other (4). The joint will be more easily cut if, before commencing to carve, the knife is slipped between the meat and the bone from (1) to (2).

Round of Beef (*see* Fig. III): A round of beef, or ribs rolled, are not so easily carved as some joints. A thin-bladed and very sharp knife should be used. Off the outside of the joint, at its top, cut a thick slice first, leaving the surface smooth; then thin and even slices should be carved to leave a level-topped joint.

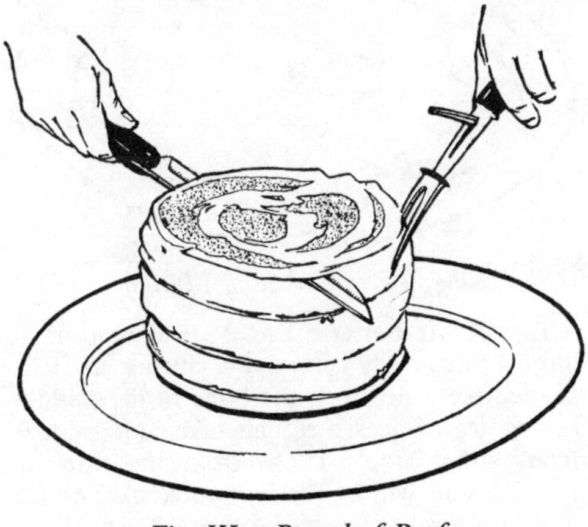

Fig. III.—Round of Beef

Sirloin of Beef (*see* Fig. IV): Sirloin is seldom carved "on the bone" today. If it is, the carver should first slice the fillet or under-cut into a suitable number of pieces (1–2). It is best eaten hot (being rather flavourless cold). When the fillet has been used, turn the joint over, loosen the meat from the backbone (3) and carve down towards the blade of the bone (4).

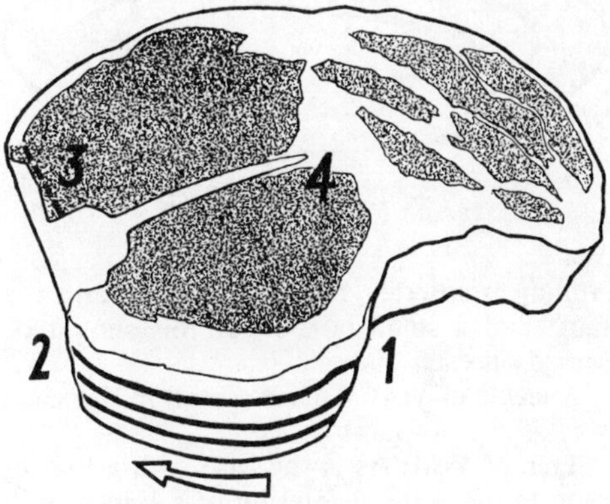

Fig. IV.—Sirloin of Beef

VEAL

Breast of Veal: The breast of veal consists of two parts—the rib-bones and the gristly brisket. These two parts should first be separated by sharply passing the knife through the centre of the joint; when they are entirely divided, the rib-bones should each be detached separately and served. The brisket can be helped by cutting pieces from the centre part of the joint. If boned and stuffed, carve by cutting downwards across the end of the rolled joint.

Calf's Head: A calf's head is nearly always boned before serving, and is then cut into slices like any other boned and rolled joint. If the bones have not been removed, cut strips from the ear to the nose (*see* Fig. V); with each of these should be helped a piece of what is called the throat sweetbread, cut in semicircular form from the throat part. The tongue and brains should be served on a separate dish.

Fillet of Veal: The carving of this joint is similar to that of a round or roll of beef. The

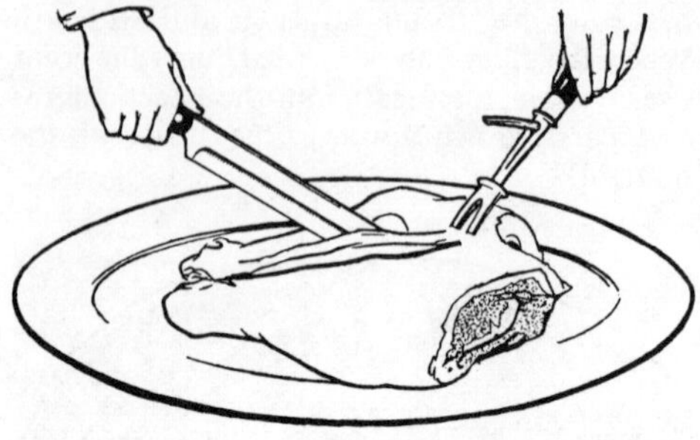

Fig. V.—Calf's Head

stuffing is inserted between the flap and the meat and a small portion of this should be served on each plate.

Knuckle of Veal: This is carved in the same way as a leg of lamb.

Loin of Veal: As is the case with a loin of mutton, the careful jointing of a loin of veal is more than half the battle in carving it. The butcher should be asked to do this. When properly jointed there is little difficulty in separating each chop. Each should carry a piece of the kidney and kidney fat.

MUTTON AND LAMB

Legs are cut perpendicularly to the bones inside the leg. Once one has been attempted the remainder will be easy. In the case of loins ask the butcher to "chine" them or saw across the blade parts of the bone or ask him to chop it through the joints for serving in cutlets.

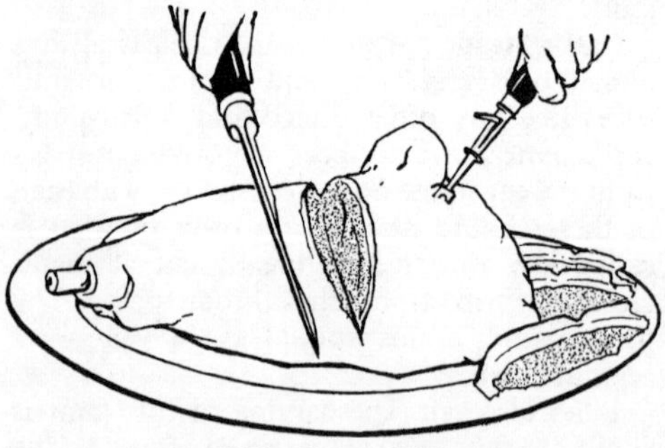

Fig. VI.—Leg of Mutton

Should it be forgotten, use an old knife and knock the blade through between the joints where they are separated by white discs of gristle. Mutton, and to a lesser extent lamb, should always be served as quickly as possible and on very hot plates. The speed is necessary because the flavour of mutton is soon lost. The heat is required because mutton and lamb fat have a higher melting-point than other animal fats and on a cold plate solidify, leaving a semi-solid fat that coats the palate, producing a "furry" or diminished sense of taste.

Forequarter of Lamb: In carving a forequarter of lamb, separate the shoulder from the breast by raising the shoulder, into which the fork should be firmly fixed. It will come away easily by cutting round the outline of the shoulder and slipping the knife beneath it. The shoulder should be served cold. The remainder of the joint is then ready to be served as cutlets carved from the ribs.

Fig. VII.—Saddle of Mutton

Leg of Mutton (*see* Fig. VI): This joint is almost invariably carved by cutting a "V"-shaped piece down to the bone in the middle of the leg. Slices are then taken alternately from either side. Those from the thin or knuckle end will be the best-cooked. The fat will be found near the bottom corner of the thick end.

Loin of Mutton: Loin, and other similar joints, should be well jointed. Examine the loin before cooking it, and carefully joint any part that has been neglected. The knife should be inserted in the white gristle of the joint, and tapped between the bones with a steel or small hammer.

Saddle of Mutton (*see* Fig. VII): This consists of two loins connected by the spinal bone. The method adopted in carving this joint, contrary to the general rule of cutting meat across the grain, is carved across the ribs, in slices running parallel with the backbone and the fibres or grain of the meat. Each long slice should be cut across into two or three pieces, according to its length; and with each portion is usually served a small piece of fat cut from the bottom of the ribs where the joint rests on the dish, and some good gravy. Red-currant jelly or mint sauce is served separately.

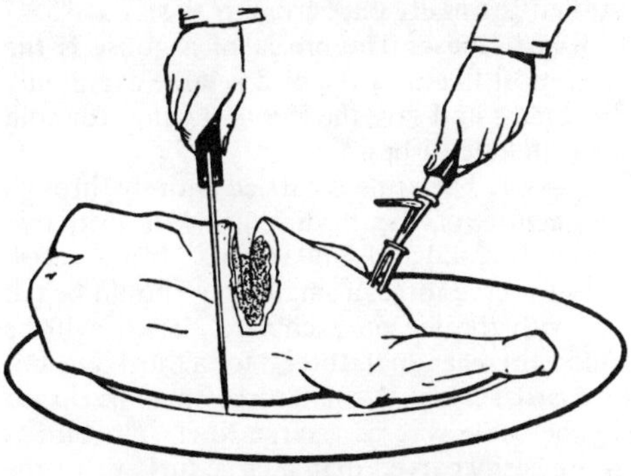

Fig. VIII.—Shoulder of Mutton

Shoulder of Mutton: The joint should be raised from the dish and slices cut parallel to the face of the meat (*see* Fig. VIII). Lay the joint down and carve the meat lying on either side of the bladebone from the knuckle end. (Fig. IX).

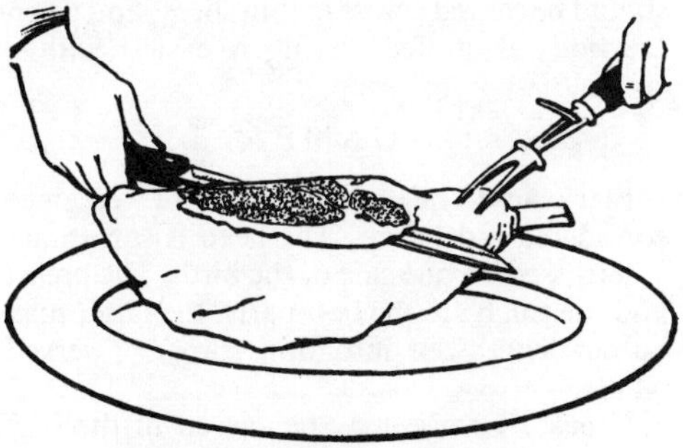

Fig. IX.—Shoulder of Mutton

PORK

The remarks made about jointing loins of lamb are true of loins of pork. When carving a joint with crackling, remove a section of crackling first. Only remove as much as will expose that part of the joint to be carved hot.

Ham: In cutting a ham the carver must be guided by economy, or the desire to have at once fine slices out of the prime part. To be economical commence at the knuckle end, and cut off thin slices towards the thick part of the ham, slanting the knife from the thick part to the knuckle. To reach the choicer parts, the knife, which must be very sharp and thin, should be carried quite down to the bone, at the centre of the ham.

Leg of Pork: This joint, which is such a favourite one with many people, is easy to carve. The knife should be carried sharply down to the bone, clean through the crackling, in exactly the same way as that described for leg of mutton. Carving is easier if a section of the crackling is removed.

Loin of Pork: As with a loin of mutton, it is essential that a loin of pork should be properly jointed before cooking, and the crackling must be scored. Divide into neat, even chops.

Sucking Pig: A sucking pig seems, at first sight, an elaborate dish, or rather animal, to carve; like small poultry it is mainly jointed rather than sliced. It is usually prepared by splitting in half, and the head is separated from the body. Separate the shoulder from the carcase, in the same way that the shoulder of a forequarter of lamb is raised. Then take off the hind leg; the ribs are then open to the knife and may be served as two or three helpings.

POULTRY

Larger birds are usually jointed at the wings and legs, which are served as portions or carved into slices. This is made easier if before the bird is placed on the table a small, pointed knife is worked between each joint. The joints occur at the natural bends of the limb and are quite easy to discover. When all else fails at a first attempt they are quite easily broken open, but the carving is rather more dignified if this is done out of sight in, say, the kitchen.

Roast Duck: A young duck or duckling is carved in the same way as a chicken. First remove the wings, then the breast should be cut off the bone in one slice, or several slices if very plump. The legs are next removed and divided at the joints. The foot, and the bone to which it is attached, is today rarely left on the dressed bird.

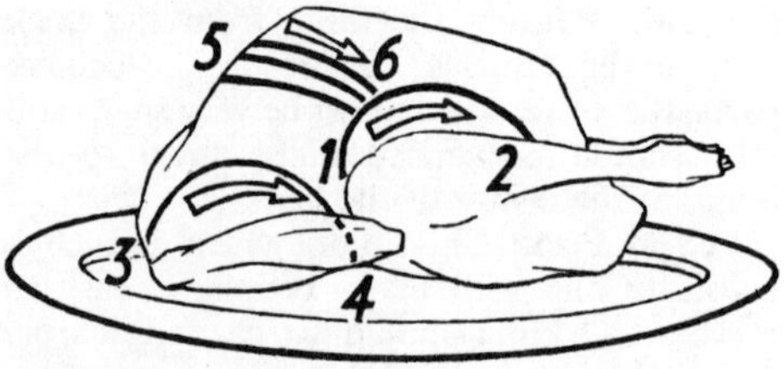

Fig. X.—Roast Fowl

Boiled or **Roast Fowl** (*see* Fig. X): Though the legs of a boiled fowl may be hidden beneath the skin, the method of carving is not affected, and the following directions may be applied to birds either roasted or boiled. The fork should be inserted firmly in the breast of the bird (1)–(2) and with a sharp knife a downward cut made between the thigh and the body, after which an outward turn of the blade of the knife usually detaches the leg sufficiently to allow the joint connecting it to the body to be easily severed. Some carvers "open" the joint with a small knife before the bird is sent to table. With the fork still inserted in the breast, the next step should be to remove the wings (3)–(4). In doing this a good carver will contrive, by cutting widely, but not too deeply, over the adjacent part of the breast, to give to the wing the desired shape without depriving the breast of much of its flesh. When carving a large fowl the breast may be sliced (5)–(6), otherwise it should be separated from the back by cutting through the rib-bones near the neck. The breast should be cut across in half, thus providing two portions, to which may be added, when a larger helping is desired, a slice off the thigh. Cut lengthwise into rather thin slices, the legs may be served as several portions or part-portions. To conclude the carving, the back should be turned over with the cut side to the dish, and if the knife is pressed firmly across the centre of it, and the neck raised at the same time with the fork, the back is easily dislocated about the middle. To remove the sockets of the thigh-joints (the side-bones to which are attached choice morsels of dark-coloured flesh), unless the joints have previously been opened, the tail part of the back must be stood on end, and held firmly with the fork, while the bones are cut off on either side. A fowl when boned and stuffed is usually cut across in slices.

Roast Goose: The breast of a goose is the part most liked. If the bird is large carve only the breast and save the legs and wings for cold or rechauffé dishes.

Pigeon: The knife is carried entirely through the centre of the bird, cutting it into two precisely equal and similar parts. If it is necessary to serve three, a small wing should be cut off with the leg on each side. There will be sufficient meat on the breast for a third portion.

Roast Turkey: A small turkey may be carved in the same way as a large fowl. No bird is more easily carved than a large turkey, for the breast alone may, when properly carved, supply several helpings. If more meat is required than the breast provides, the upper part of the wing should be served. When it is necessary for the legs to be carved, they should be severed from the body and then cut into slices. The forcemeat in the crop of the bird should be carved across in thin slices; and when the body is stuffed serving is easiest with a spoon.

GAME

Blackcock: The brains of this bird were once considered a delicacy. The head is sometimes still trussed on one side of the bird. The breast and the thigh are the best parts, the latter may be cut lengthwise into thin slices, or served whole.

Grouse: Grouse may be carved in the way first described in carving partridge. The backbone of the grouse, as of many game birds, is considered to possess the finest flavour.

Roast Hare (*see* Fig. XI): Place the hare on the dish with the head at the left hand. Cut along the spinal bone from about the centre of the back to the end (1)–(2). Then cut through the side and middle, and remove this portion. Cut off the hind leg (3)–(4) and afterwards the foreleg or wing. It is usual not to serve any bone and the flesh should be sliced from the legs and placed alone on the plate. Plenty of gravy should accompany each helping; otherwise this dish, which is naturally dry, will lose half its flavour.

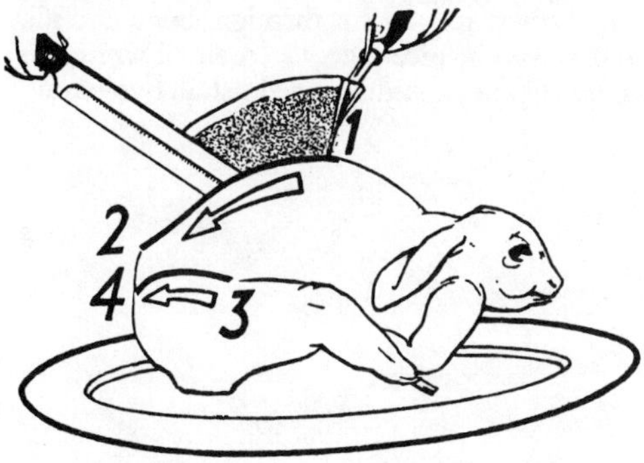

Fig. XI.—Roast Hare

Ortolans, *see* Snipe.

Partridges: There are several ways of carving this bird. The usual method is to carry the knife sharply along the top of the breast-bone and cut it through, dividing the bird into two equal parts. When smaller portions are desired the legs and wings may be easily severed from the body in the way described for boiled fowl, while the breast, if removed intact, will provide a third helping. Another easy and expeditious way of carving birds of this description is to cut them through the bones lengthwise and across, thus forming four portions. A piece of toast should accompany each portion of bird.

Pheasant: The choice parts of a pheasant are the breast and wings. The various joints of the bird are cut in exactly the same way as those of a roast fowl.

Plover: Plover may be carved like woodcock, being trussed and served in the same way as woodcock.

Ptarmigan, *see* Partridge.

Rabbits: In carving a boiled rabbit, the knife should be drawn on each side of the backbone, the whole length of the rabbit, thus separating the rabbit into three parts. Now divide the back into two equal parts, then cut off the leg and next the shoulder.

A roast rabbit is rather differently trussed from one that is meant to be boiled; but the carving is nearly similar. The back should be divided into as many pieces as it will yield, and the legs and shoulders can then be separated.

Snipe: One of these small but delicious birds may be served whole or cut through the centre into two portions.

Teal and **Widgeon,** *see* Wild Duck.

Haunch of Venison: The thick end of the joint should be turned towards the carver and slices taken parallel to the dish on which the joint rests. Venison, like mutton, should be cut and served quickly.

Wild Duck: The breast alone is considered by epicures worth eating, and slices are cut; if necessary, the leg and wing can be taken off as for a fowl.

Woodcock: *see* Partridge.

FISH

Brill and **John Dory,** *see* Turbot.

Cod: Cut in fairly thick slices through to the centre bone and detach just above it. The parts about the backbone and shoulders are the firmest.

Crab, *see* p. 187.

Eel and all flat fish: The thickest parts of the eel are considered the best.

Lobster, *see* p. 190.

Mackerel: First cut along the backbone of the fish. Then insert the fish-knife at this part and cut through, separating the upper half of the fish, which may be divided; when the fish is of moderate size serve for two helpings only. Next remove the backbone, tail and head, and divide the lower half.

CARVING FISH

Plaice: First run the knife down the centre of the fish. Then cut downwards to the bone and remove " fillets " from each side. Next take away the backbone and head of the fish, and divide the lower half in the same way.

Salmon: First run the knife down the centre of the back and along the whole length of the fish. Then cut downwards from the backbone to the middle of the fish, cut through the centre and remove the piece from the back. Next cut the lower part of the fish in the same way. A slice of the thick part should always be accompanied by a smaller piece of the thin from the belly, where the fat of the fish lies.

Sole: The usual way of serving this fish is to cut quite through, bone and all, distributing it in nice and not-too-large pieces. The middle part is generally thought better than either head or tail. The head should be cut off and not laid on a plate.

Turbot: First slice down the thickest part of the fish, quite through to the bone, and then cut slices out towards the sides of the fish. When the carver has removed all the meat from the upper side of the fish, the backbone should be raised, and the under side served in portions.

Whiting, Haddock, etc.: Whiting, pike, haddock and similar fish, when sufficiently large, may be carved in slices from each side of the backbone in the same way as salmon; each fish serving for four or more slices. When small, they may be cut through, bone and all, and served in nice pieces. A small whiting is served whole; a middle-sized fish in two pieces.

HORS D'ŒUVRES

THE HORS D'ŒUVRES of a meal today can either be an appetizer, grapefruit, melon, smoked salmon—or one of the dishes suggested in this chapter—or it can be a selection of these dishes, augmented by simple but colourful salads—diced beetroot, sliced tomato, Russian salad, etc. Hors d'œuvres present one of the best opportunities for the cook to show her skill and originality in combination and garnish.

When a large hors d'œuvres dish is used the ingredients should be arranged in their sections and each person left to help themselves. If, however, the proper dish is not available, then arrange the selection of ingredients on individual plates.

Generally salads are "dressed" in oil and vinegar or mayonnaise, so there is no need to serve these separately.

A cold hors d'œuvres is not only an attractive, but also a very practical, first course to a meal when entertaining with little domestic help—for it can be prepared and set on the dining-table beforehand.

SIMPLE HORS D'ŒUVRES

ANCHOVIES

Lift the rolled or filleted anchovies out of the can—put on to crisp lettuce leaves. If wished coat with chopped parsley, chopped chives and a little cayenne pepper.

Allow about 3 anchovy fillets *or* rolled anchovies per person.

RÉMOULADE OF ARTICHOKE BOTTOMS

12 small cooked artichoke bottoms
2–3 gherkins
1 tablesp. capers
½ pt. macedoine cooked vegetables
¼ pt. mayonnaise (approx.)
1 pimento
4–6 stuffed olives

Trim the artichokes neatly, mix the finely-chopped gherkins, the capers, the vegetables and enough mayonnaise to moisten, and fill in the hollow part of the artichoke with the mixture. Mask the surface carefully with stiff mayonnaise, and decorate with strips of red pimento and sliced stuffed olives.

12 savouries

ASPARAGUS SALAD WITH SHRIMPS

Salade d'Asperges aux Crevettes

1 small *or* ½ a large bundle of green asparagus *or* can of asparagus
½ pt. shrimps (picked)
Mayonnaise sauce
4 hard-boiled eggs

Prepare and cook the asparagus or drain canned asparagus. When cold, cut the tender portions into small pieces and put them into a bowl with the shrimps. Mix lightly with enough mayonnaise sauce to moisten. Serve on a dish in the centre of a border of sliced hard-boiled egg.

4 helpings

AVOCADO PEARS

These make an unusual ingredient for hors d'œuvres. Halve the pears and remove the stone, then cover the pear halves with oil, vinegar and seasoning. Allow to stand for a while. Alternatively try them filled with prawns as in the next recipe.

AVOCADO PEARS AND PRAWNS

2 large Avocado pears
2 tablesp. olive oil
2 tablesp. vinegar
Good pinch of salt
Good pinch of pepper
A little mixed mustard
2 teacups (about ½ pt.) shelled prawns
Crisp lettuce leaves
Lemon
Pinch of sugar (optional)
¼ crushed clove of garlic (optional)

Halve the pears. Blend the oil, vinegar and seasonings together. Toss the prawns in this, and then spoon into the pear halves. Put on to crisp lettuce leaves and garnish with wedges of lemon.

A pinch of sugar can be added to the dressing if wished, also a little garlic.

4 helpings

DEVILLED CRAB

Crabe à la Diable

1 medium-sized crab
1 teacup of breadcrumbs
1 teasp. mixed mustard
1 teasp. Worcester sauce
1 tablesp. oiled butter
Cayenne pepper
Salt to taste
Cream *or* milk
2 tablesp. breadcrumbs
Extra butter

Remove the crab meat from the shell and claws, clean the shell and put it aside. Chop the meat of the crab, add the breadcrumbs, mustard, sauce, butter and a very liberal seasoning of cayenne pepper and salt, mix well. If necessary, moisten with a little milk or cream, then turn the whole into the prepared shell. Cover lightly with breadcrumbs, add a few small pieces of butter, and brown in a fairly hot oven **(375° F., Gas 5).**

3 helpings
Cooking time—15 min.

CRAYFISH

Écrevisses

Crayfish, which must not be confused with crawfish, are similar to lobsters, only much smaller. The flesh is most delicate in flavour. They are extremely useful for hors d'œuvres as well as for serving in salads. There are several kinds, the best being those which are quite red under the claws. Shell and serve on crisp lettuce, garnished with lemon or tossed in mayonnaise.

FOIE GRAS as Hors d'œuvre

Foie gras or goose liver, either in the form of pâté or sausage, is frequently served as hors d'œuvre. A pâté or terrine may be served plain after removing the fat on its surface, or scooped out with a dessertspoon previously dipped in hot water, and then dressed neatly on a dish and garnished with parsley. Foie gras sausage must be cut into thin slices, dished up and similarly garnished. In all cases, foie gras must be served very cold.

FOIE GRAS DARIOLES

Foie gras
Aspic jelly
Beetroot
Hard-boiled egg white
Cucumber

Thinly coat some small plain dariole moulds with a little aspic jelly; fill up with potted foie gras cut into convenient slices. Put into a refrigerator or place on ice for 1 hr., then turn out on to glass dishes. Decorate with chopped beetroot, hard-boiled egg white and slices of cucumber.

GRAPEFRUIT

Select sound, ripe fruit, wipe carefully, cut them in halves. Take out the pips and core

PLATE 3

Jointing a Hare or Rabbit

Before starting the following set of operations the hare or rabbit should be thoroughly washed in salt water.

1 *With a sharp knife cut off the side flaps, then the hind legs.*

2 *Cut off front legs at the joint.*

3 *Chop the back sharply once or twice (depending on size of the animal), and separate the body into fairly even parts as shown.*

4 *This photograph shows nine separate joints which can be cut from a hare or rabbit. In foreground are the liver and kidneys.*

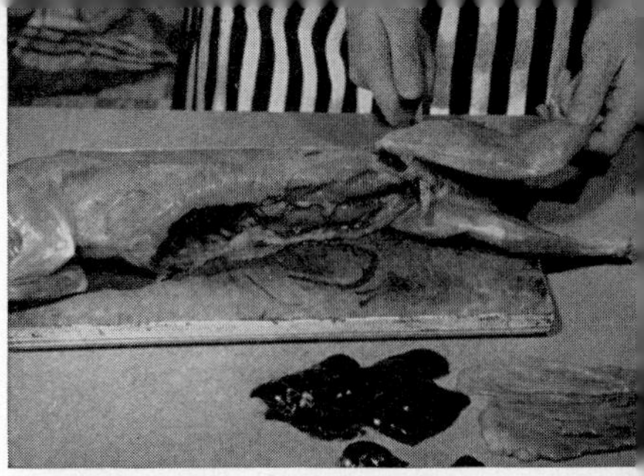

1

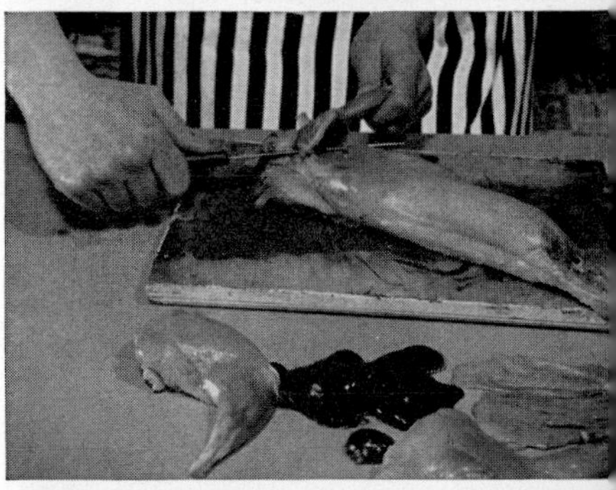

2

3

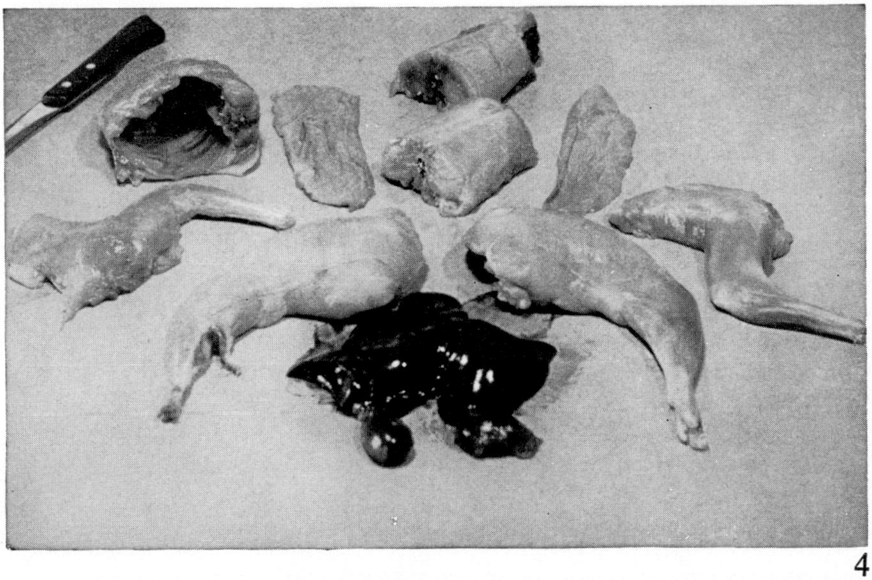

4

BEEF

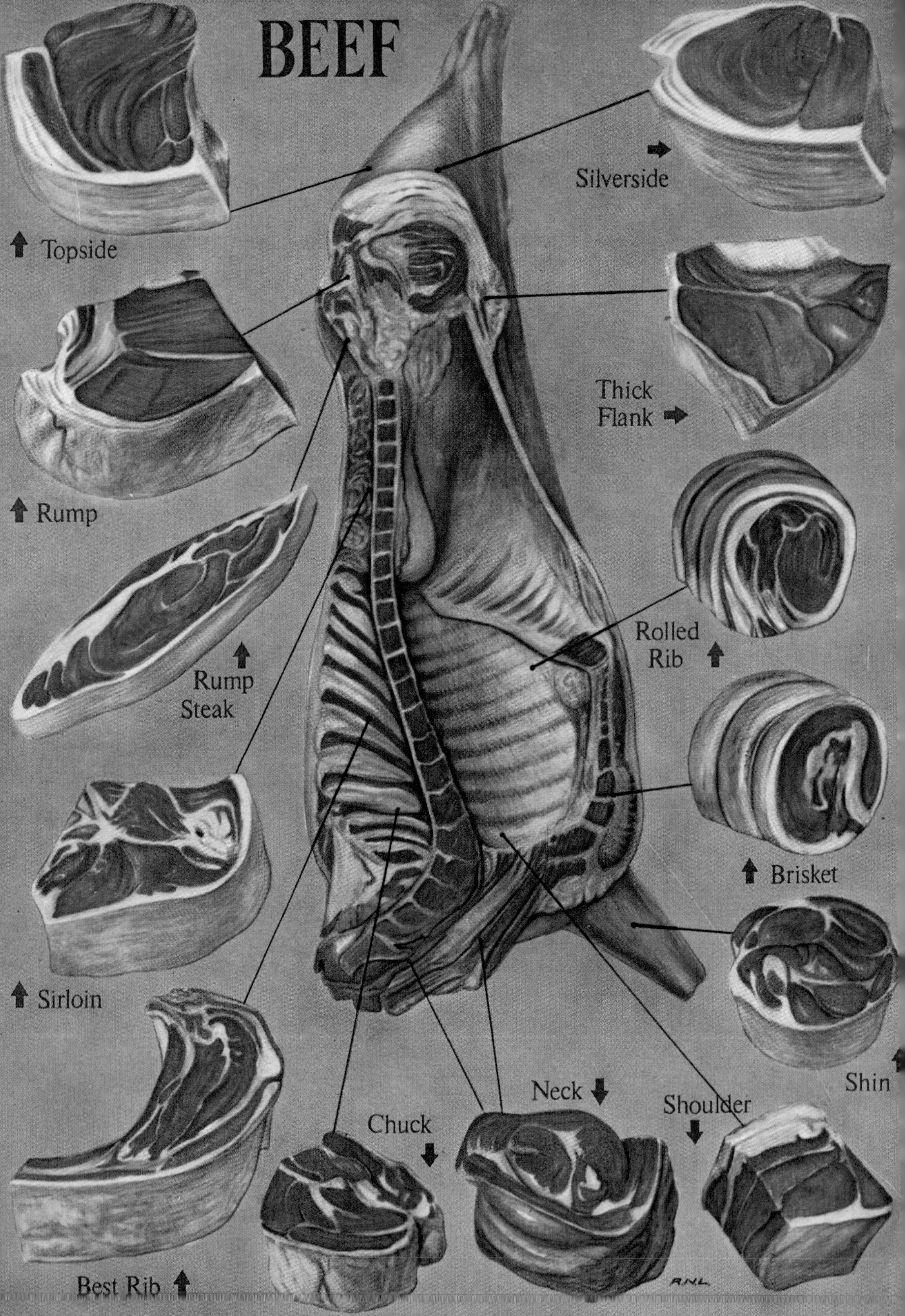

Topside
Silverside
Rump
Thick Flank
Rump Steak
Rolled Rib
Brisket
Sirloin
Shin
Neck
Shoulder
Chuck
Best Rib
RNL

and loosen the fruit from the skin. Cut the fruit into suitable small pieces but leave the pieces as if uncut in the halved skin. Sweeten to taste and, if liked, flavour with sherry poured over the fruit.

Serve in glass dishes and decorate with angelica. Keep in the refrigerator or on ice until required, if possible.

GRAPEFRUIT BASKETS

Remove grapefruit sections as described in previous recipe—mix with diced melon, diced pineapple, pieces of orange and Maraschino cherries but do not make too sweet. Add sugar to taste. Replace in grapefruit halves. Serve in glasses topped with sprigs of mint.

SPICED GRAPEFRUIT

2 large grapefruit
1 oz. butter
1–2 oz. brown sugar
½–1 teasp. mixed spice
Cherries—glacé *or* Maraschino to decorate

Halve the grapefruit and loosen the pulp from the skins, discarding pips and pith. Spread with the softened butter and sprinkle sugar and spice over the top. Put for about 4 min. under a hot grill *or* for 10 min. in a fairly hot oven (**400° F., Gas 6**). Decorate with cherries and serve at once.

4 helpings

BAKED HERRING ROES

Laitance de Harengs au gratin

1½ oz. butter *or* margarine
4 small mushrooms
1 small shallot *or* onion
½ teasp. chopped parsley
Lemon juice
Few drops anchovy essence
Seasoning
½ gill thick white sauce
8 fresh soft roes
2 tablesp. breadcrumbs

Brush the inside of 8 small ramekin dishes or individual scallop shells with a little butter. Chop the mushrooms coarsely; chop the shallot or onion finely. Heat 1 oz. butter in a saucepan, put in the mushrooms, shallot and parsley and cook gently. When tender, remove from the pan, leaving any surplus butter in the pan, and put the mixture into the dishes or shells. Add a little lemon juice, anchovy essence and seasoning to the white sauce and pour a little over the mushroom mixture. Re-heat the butter in the pan and cook the roes until tender. Put on top of the mixture in the cases and top with breadcrumbs and tiny knobs of butter. Bake in a hot oven for 7 min. or under a hot grill for about 3–7 min. until the crumbs are brown.

8 savouries

HERRING ROLLS

Paupiettes de Harengs

4 salt or rollmop herrings
8 anchovy fillets
2 hard-boiled eggs
1 oz. butter
Cayenne pepper
Lemon
4–6 gherkins
1 small beetroot
Parsley

If using salt herrings soak in cold water for several hours, fillet—removing all bones. If using rollmop herrings divide into 2 fillets. Mix chopped anchovy fillets with egg yolks, butter, pepper and little lemon juice. Put on to the herring fillets and roll firmly. Dip each end in finely chopped egg white. Sprinkle with lemon juice. Garnish with slices of lemon, sliced gherkin, diced beetroot and parsley.

8 savouries

CREAMED KIPPER FILLETS

One 8 oz. packet kipper fillets
½ oz. butter
1 level tablesp. finely-chopped onion
¼ pt. single cream
Pepper
Chopped parsley

Melt the butter in a frying-pan and sauté the onion until soft but not browned. Add the cream, bring to the boil and then add the kipper fillets and simmer for 5 min. Season with pepper and serve sprinkled with chopped parsley.

NOTE: Kipper fillets served in this way are very rich and a small serving only is sufficient for an hors d'œuvre.

3–4 helpings

LIVER PÂTÉ

1 lb. calf's *or* pig's liver *or* the livers from poultry
4 oz. very lean ham *or* bacon
1 small onion
3 oz. butter
Seasoning
Pinch of mixed herbs
A few gherkins (optional)
1–2 hard-boiled eggs (optional)
A little cream (optional)
Extra butter

Cut the liver, ham and onion into small pieces. Heat the butter in a pan and cook the liver, ham and onion for about 6 min.—no longer. Put through a very fine mincer twice to give a very smooth mixture. Add the seasoning, herbs and chopped gherkins or chopped hard-boiled eggs too if wished. For a very soft pâté also add a little cream. Put into a dish and cook for about ½ hr. in a moderate oven (**350° F., Gas 4**), covering with buttered paper and standing in a dish of cold water to prevent the mixture becoming dry. When the pâté is cooked, cover with a layer of melted butter.

Serve cut in slices on a bed of crisp lettuce and accompanied with hot toast and butter.

4–6 helpings

LOBSTER COCKTAIL

As for Prawn Cocktail, but use a small lobster instead of the prawns.

Garnish with the tiny lobster claws.

CREAMED LOBSTER

Homard à la Newbury

1 small cooked lobster
1 oz. butter
2 egg yolks
½ gill cream *or* creamy white sauce
Good pinch of salt
Pinch of pepper
Pinch of grated nutmeg
8–10 small rounds of fried bread *or* toast; *or* 2–3 slices of toast
Parsley

Remove the flesh of the lobster from the body and claws, and cut this into flakes. Cook in the butter for about 5 min. only—no longer as this toughens the lobster meat. Add the beaten egg yolks and cream or white sauce, the seasonings and nutmeg, and heat gently until the mixture thickens. Put on to the rounds of bread and garnish with parsley.

NOTE: Canned lobster could be used for this dish.

SCALLOPED LOBSTER

Escalopes de Homard

1 cooked hen lobster (*see* note below)
¼ pt. white sauce
½ teasp. anchovy essence
Pinch of cayenne pepper
Pinch of pepper
Pinch of salt
1–2 egg yolks
2 tablesp. breadcrumbs
½–1 oz. butter

GARNISH

Lemon
Parsley

NOTE: A hen lobster can be recognized by its broad back—it gives a better colour to this dish to use the hen, since the red coral gives a delicious flavour as well as tinting the dish pale pink.

Remove the coral from the lobster meat, and pound this well until very smooth. Remove all the lobster flesh from the body and claws and mix with the white sauce, together with the coral, anchovy essence and seasonings. Put into a saucepan and heat gently for several minutes, then add the egg yolk or yolks and continue cooking, *without* letting the mixture boil, for 2–3 min. Put into 4 small scallop shells—or into the 2 halves of the lobster shell, top with breadcrumbs and knobs of butter and brown under a hot grill.

Garnish with the small lobster claws, lemon and parsley.

NOTE: Canned lobster could be used in this dish, in which case increase the amount of anchovy essence slightly.

2 helpings or 4 small savouries
Cooking time—10 min. (approx.)

MELON

There are various kinds of melon served as hors d'œuvres, the cantaloup and rock melon being the most favoured. They must not be over-ripe, and should be served as fresh as possible and above all, very cold.

During the summer put crushed ice round the dish on which the slices of melon are served. Serve with powdered ginger and castor sugar.

MELON CANTALOUP AU MARASQUIN

1 *or* more cantaloup *or* rock melons | **Maraschino liqueur**

Cut the fruit in half, and put it into a glass bowl or deep dish, place it on another (flat) dish surrounded with crushed ice. Pour about 1 tablesp. of Maraschino liqueur in each half melon, then serve as hors d'œuvres with castor sugar.

If small melons are used allow ½ per person but otherwise slice in the usual way.

OYSTERS

Huîtres

English oysters are in season from September to the end of April and the best oysters to obtain to eat "*au naturel*" are the natives from Whitstable or Colchester—although during the close season in this country Continental oysters are imported.

All the oysters need, after being opened, is to be placed on the upper shell with a little of the liquor; they are then arranged on a dish, garnished with sprigs of fresh parsley, and, if possible, surrounded with ice. Thin slices of buttered brown bread, and quarters of lemon are handed round at the same time; also cayenne pepper and vinegar.

It is advisable to ask the fishmonger to open the shells for you.

In the savoury dishes with oysters it is often possible to obtain small imported oysters which are ideal for this purpose and are not too expensive.

FRIED OYSTERS

Fritot d'Huîtres

10 small oysters
5 large rashers of bacon
Lemon juice
Cayenne pepper
4 oz. flour
Seasoning
1 egg
¼ pt. milk
½ teasp. chopped shallot *or* onion
2 teasp. chopped parsley
Fat for frying
Slices of lemon

Beard the oysters and dry them gently before using. Divide each rasher of bacon into 4 pieces, season each oyster with lemon juice and cayenne pepper, and place each oyster between 2 pieces of bacon, pressing the edges together very firmly. Make a batter by sifting the flour with a good pinch of salt, adding the egg then the milk gradually, beating until a very smooth thick batter. Add the shallot and ½ teasp. of parsley, dip each bacon and oyster round into the batter then fry steadily until crisp and golden brown. Do *not* fry too quickly, otherwise the batter will be brown, but the bacon and oysters inside not cooked or even hot. Drain well on kitchen or crumpled tissue paper. Garnish with the rest of the chopped parsley and slices of lemon.

If wished, serve on crisp rounds of toast or fried bread.

10 savouries

JELLIED OYSTERS

Huîtres en Gelée

6 oysters (natives if possible)
1 gill aspic jelly
Lemon
Parsley

Open the oysters and beard them. Put them on a plate or pie-dish to marinade in semi-liquid aspic, well flavoured with oyster liquor, lemon juice and chopped parsley. Clean the lower (deep) shell of each oyster, put in ½ teasp. of aspic jelly: place a marinaded oyster on top, and pour over a little aspic to mask it nicely. Keep cold until required, then dish up. Garnish with slices of lemon and parsley, and serve.

This should be made some time before wanted.

6 helpings.—If this is the only hors d'œuvre allow 4-6 to each person

OYSTERS IN CASES

Huîtres en Caisses à la Diable

10-12 small *or* 8 large oysters
½ gill white sauce
2 oz. grated cheese
Salt and cayenne pepper
1 oz. butter (approx.)
1 tablesp. breadcrumbs
Lemon

Beard the oysters and cut each into 4 pieces. Strain the liquid into the white sauce, then mix with the oysters, ½ the cheese, add a good pinch of cayenne pepper and salt. Grease 4 individual scallop shells or small dishes and put in the oyster mixture. Mix the remainder of the cheese with the breadcrumbs, spread over the top of the oyster mixture, cover with tiny knobs of butter. Bake for about 10 min. only, in a hot oven (**425° F., Gas 7**), until crisp and brown on top and very hot. Garnish with wedges of lemon.

4 helpings
Cooking time—10 min.

PACIFIC PRAWNS

These make an unusual hors d'œuvre. If they are not already boiled when bought, put into cold water, bring to the boil and simmer for not more than 8 min. They have a slightly sweet flavour but are not very interesting plain, they need either to be fried or served boiled with a sauce. See Scampi.

PRAWNS

Crevettes

These make an excellent hors d'œuvre—either by themselves or with a selection of some of the other small savouries in this section. Large Mediterranean prawns should be served in their shells, garnished with lettuce and lemon slices. Put finger bowls on the table in this case.

If preferred shell the prawns, arrange on crisp lettuce, garnished with lemon. Serve with brown bread and butter and cayenne pepper.

Shrimps can be served in the same way.

PRAWN COCKTAIL

Heart of a small lettuce
½ pt. picked prawns
½ gill mayonnaise
1 tablesp. tomato purée (*see below*) *or* tomato ketchup
1 teasp. chilli vinegar—if available
1 teasp. tarragon vinegar
Good pinch of salt
Good pinch of cayenne pepper
Lemon

Wash and dry the lettuce very well—pick out the tiny leaves and break into very small pieces. Arrange in cocktail glasses. Put the prawns on top. Mix the mayonnaise with the tomato ketchup or purée—to obtain this rub one large tomato through a fine sieve. Add the vinegars and seasoning. Put over the prawns and garnish with a piece of lemon and a dusting of cayenne pepper.

Serve very cold.

4 helpings

PRAWNS IN SAVOURY JELLY

Écrevisses en Aspic

1 pt. aspic jelly
3–4 chopped gherkins *or* 4–6 stuffed olives
30 prawns (shelled) (approx.)
10–12 rounds of fried bread

PARSLEY BUTTER

2 oz. butter
2 teasp. chopped parsley
Lemon juice
Seasoning

Line some small dariole moulds with a thin layer of aspic jelly and when nearly set arrange chopped gherkins or stuffed olives on this. Place 2–3 picked prawns in each mould and fill up with aspic jelly. Allow to set. Prepare as many fried bread croûtes as there are moulds, cover 1 side of each with parsley butter. Turn out the moulds and place 1 on the centre of each croûte.

To make parsley butter cream the butter with the parsley, add lemon juice and seasoning to taste.

To make approximately 10

SCAMPI

These large prawns have become a very popular hors d'œuvres. If you wish to buy fresh prawns then ask the fishmonger for Dublin Bay prawns, shell them and cook as individual recipes. If preferred, packets of quick frozen Scampi can be bought; these are uncooked, and need cooking as individual recipes. The ordinary boiled prawns are NOT suitable for these recipes.

FRIED SCAMPI

8 oz. frozen *or* fresh Dublin bay prawns (weight when peeled)
Fat for frying
Tartare sauce
Lemon wedges

BATTER

2 oz. flour
1 egg
½ teacup milk
Salt and pepper

Separate the frozen prawns or dry the fresh prawns. To make the batter sift the flour, add the egg and milk gradually, giving a smooth thick batter. Season well. Dip each prawn in the batter and lower into really hot fat. Cook fairly quickly until golden brown. Drain on crumpled tissue or kitchen paper.

Serve on a hot dish with Tartare sauce and garnish with wedges of lemon or serve with spinach.

SCAMPI MEUNIERE

8 oz. frozen *or* fresh Dublin Bay prawns (weight when peeled)	**2–3 oz. butter**
	Seasoning
	Lemon juice

Separate the frozen prawns. Heat the butter and cook the prawns steadily for about 5 min. only. Lift on to a hot dish. Add seasoning and lemon juice to the hot butter and cook gently until brown. Take care not to overcook the butter and turn it too dark. Pour over the prawns and garnish with lemon and parsley.

Serve with brown bread and butter.

2–3 helpings

SCAMPI PROVENCALE

8 oz. frozen *or* fresh Dublin Bay prawns (weight when peeled)	**2 tomatoes**
1 oz. butter	**2–3 large mushrooms**
1–2 tablesp. olive oil	**Seasoning**
1 small onion	**2 teasp. chopped parsley**
½ clove garlic	**Lemon juice**

Separate the frozen scampi. Heat the butter and oil together, then fry the thinly-sliced onion, crushed clove of garlic (½ clove is sufficient for most people). Skin and slice the tomatoes, slice the mushrooms and add to the onion with the scampi and fry together until just tender. Season well, then add the parsley and lemon juice and serve at once.

For a more substantial dish serve on a bed of boiled rice.

2–3 helpings Cooking time—10 min. (approx.)

SMOKED SALMON

1. Serve this with cayenne pepper, wedges of lemon and thin slices of brown bread and butter.

2. For an unusual hors d'œuvre, serve thin slices of smoked salmon with tiny crisp pastry cases filled with very hot and very creamy spinach.

3. Serve a mixture of smoked salmon and potted shrimp on a bed of crisp lettuce.

SMOKED SALMON WITH CUCUMBER

1 large cucumber	**Butter**
Olive oil	**4–6 oz. smoked salmon**
White *or* malt vinegar	**Salt and pepper**
Chopped parsley	**Mustard and cress**
Bread	**Watercress**

Cut the cucumber into 1-in. pieces as near as possible of the same size. Cut the rind so as to form stripes of green and white (crinkled). Scoop out some of the centre and round off the bottom of each to give them the appearance of cups. Chop the pulp scooped out of the centre and put it in a basin with the oil, vinegar and parsley. Stamp out some rounds of bread with a 1½-in. cutter, butter them on one side, cover the buttered side with thin slices of smoked salmon; cut some of the salmon into fine strips and mix with the cucumber pulp; season with salt and pepper. Put the cucumber cups on the prepared rounds of bread, and fill the cavities with the above mixture. Arrange on a dish in the shape of a crown, garnish with mustard and cress and watercress.

10–12 savouries

SOUSED SALMON

Saumon mariné

¾ lb. boiled salmon	**1 lump *or* 1 teasp. sugar**
1½ gills vinegar	**Good pinch of salt**
2 bay leaves	**Mayonnaise *or* Vinaigrette sauce**
4 cloves	**Lettuce**
6 peppercorns	

Place the boiled salmon in a deep dish; boil the vinegar, add 2 small bay leaves, cloves, peppercorns, sugar and salt. Pour the boiling vinegar over the fish. Serve, when cold with mayonnaise or vinaigrette sauce on a bed of lettuce.

4–6 helpings as hors d'œuvre

CURRIED SHRIMPS

Crevettes au Kari

½ pt. shrimps—*unshelled*	**1 teasp. flour**
¼ pt. water	**1 tablesp. cream *or* top of milk**
1 oz. butter *or* margarine	**1 teasp. lemon juice**
	Parsley
1 shallot *or* tiny onion	**Toast**
1 teasp. curry powder	

Shell the shrimps and put the shells into a saucepan with the water and simmer for about 10 min. to get the flavour from the shells. Meanwhile melt the butter in another saucepan, add the finely-chopped shallot or onion and fry gently until tender. Work in the curry powder and flour and cook for several minutes, then add the strained shrimp stock. Bring to the boil and cook until slightly thickened, then put in the shrimps and heat for a few minutes. Remove from the heat and when no longer boiling whisk in the cream and lemon juice. Pour into 4 small dishes, garnish with chopped parsley and serve with crisp toast.

This makes an excellent hot hors d'œuvre.

4 helpings
Cooking time—15–20 min.

POTTED SHRIMPS

1 pt. shrimps—measure when picked	**Pinch of salt**
	Grating of nutmeg
2–3 oz. butter	**Lettuce**
Good pinch of cayenne pepper	**Lemon**

Heat the butter and turn the shrimps in this until they are well coated, but do not cook them. Add the seasonings and nutmeg. Pour into small moulds or dishes and leave until the butter is set. Turn out on to a bed of crisp lettuce and garnish with lemon.

Serve with cayenne pepper and crisp toast.

SHRIMP MOULDS

Petits Pains de Crevettes

½ pt. picked shrimps	**Pinch of cayenne pepper**
3–4 Spanish olives	
2 gherkins	**Pinch of salt**
1 tablesp. chutney	**2 tablesp. cream**
2 eggs	**Knob of butter**
¼ pt. milk	

Chop the shrimps, olives and gherkins very finely. Mix with the chutney, the beaten eggs and milk and season well. Lastly stir in the cream. Coat 4 dariole moulds with butter and put in the mixture. Stand these moulds in a dish of cold water—to prevent the mixture curdling—and cook for about 25 min. in the centre of a moderate oven **(350° F., Gas 4)** until firm. Cool for a minute or two then turn out and serve.

These are a delicious start to a meal.

4 helpings

SOUSED FISH

Poissons marinés

1¼ lb. boiled fish *or* other fish left over	**2 bay leaves**
	2 cloves
½ gill fish stock	**1 dozen peppercorns**
½ gill vinegar	**2 slices of lemon**
A few leaves of fennel (if obtainable)	**Salt**
	Chopped parsley

Place the neatest pieces of fish in a deep dish. Boil up the fish stock with an equal quantity of vinegar, and the herbs, cloves, peppercorns, lemon and seasoning. Pour over the fish, turn fish over gently from time to time so that the seasoning gets thoroughly saturated. Serve in a little of the vinegar liquid—garnished with chopped parsley.

4 helpings

SMOKED TROUT

This makes a delicious hors d'œuvre. Buy the trout already smoked and remove the bones if possible. Serve with horseradish sauce, lemon, cayenne pepper and brown bread and butter.

TUNA SALAD IN GRAPEFRUIT

Allow one grapefruit for two helpings. Cut across in half and remove the pulp. Add to it an equal amount of drained canned peas and half this amount in flaked tuna fish moistened with mayonnaise. Cut out the core and skinny bits of the grapefruit and squeeze their juice into the grapefruit shells. Line the inside of the shells with shredded lettuce, heap the mixture into them and sprinkle with paprika.

SUGGESTIONS FOR SELECTION OF HORS D'ŒUVRES

ANCHOVY ROLLS

Paupiettes d'Anchois

1 large thin *or* 2 small thin cucumbers
Oil
Vinegar
Seasoning
1 teacup crab *or* lobster meat
Mayonnaise
Small can anchovy fillets
Stuffed olives
Parsley

Peel the cucumbers and cut them into 1-in. thick slices. Cut out the centre portion, place rings on a dish, and pour over a little oil and vinegar; season well. Pound the crab or lobster meat, and mix with mayonnaise. Drain the cucumber shapes and fill the cavity with this mixture. Twist a whole anchovy fillet round each, and place a slice of stuffed olive on top. Garnish with parsley.

About 10 savouries

BEETROOT CASSOLETTES

Cassolettes de Betterave

1 large cooked beetroot
Vinegar
Oil
Seasoning

FILLING

Small can anchovy fillets (well drained)
3–4 gherkins
1 hard-boiled egg
Salt and pepper
1 teasp. chopped parsley
1 teasp. chopped chives if available
Pinch of mixed herbs

Cut 8 or so small cassolette shapes from the cooked beetroot, and cover them in vinegar, oil and seasoning. Prepare the filling by cutting the ingredients into thin strips, retaining the egg yolk for garnish. Season with a pinch of salt and pepper, oil and vinegar, and mix with the parsley and other herbs. Drain the cassolettes and fill them with the anchovy mixture. Dish up, garnish with egg yolk.

8–9 savouries

CELERY À LA GRECQUE

The heart portion of 2 heads of white celery
Vinaigrette sauce
1 dessertsp. finely-chopped chives *or* parsley

Clean the celery and shred finely. Put into a pie-dish and pour over the Vinaigrette sauce. Sprinkle the chopped chives or parsley over and allow to stand for 2 hr. Arrange on a hors d'œuvre dish and serve.

About 6 helpings

CELERY À LA RIVAZ

The white part of 2 heads of celery
1 good-sized pickled beetroot
Tartare sauce

Wash, trim and cook the celery till tender, cut into fine strips or shreds. Peel the beetroot and cut it into strips. Mix both together with enough tartare sauce to season the salad well, then arrange on a hors d'œuvre dish, and serve.

About 6 helpings

CUCUMBER

Concombre

1 large cucumber
Salt
Salad oil
Vinegar *or* white wine vinegar
Chopped parsley

Peel the cucumber thinly if wished and cut into thin slices. Place the slices on a dish, and sprinkle with salt, cover, and let them remain for 1–2 hr. Drain well, dish up on small glass dishes, season with a little salad oil and vinegar. Sprinkle parsley over and serve.

10–12 helpings

CUCUMBER BARQUETTES

Barquettes de Concombre

1 large cucumber
Salad oil
Vinegar
4–6 oz. smoked salmon *or* fresh *or* canned salmon
2 tablesp. capers
3–4 gherkins
Salad dressing

Cut the cucumber into boat-shapes, peel if wished, and scoop out the centre part of each. Soak for about 1 hr. in a marinade of oil and vinegar. Mix together the salmon, capers, and gherkins, and season with salad dressing. Fill the little boats with the mixture, dish up, garnish and serve.

8–10 savouries

STUFFED CUCUMBER À LA JOSEPHINE

1 large *or* 2 small cucumbers	**½ gill thick white sauce**
3 oz. cooked chicken, veal *or* rabbit	**½ gill aspic jelly**
6 small cooked mushrooms	**½ gill whipped cream**
1 oz. cooked ham	**Brown *or* white bread**
Salt and pepper	**Butter**
Grated nutmeg	**Parsley**
	Lemon juice

Cut the cucumber into 1-in. thick slices, peel thinly, and stamp out the inside with a tiny pastry-cutter or knife. Blanch the pieces in salted water and drain on a cloth. Pound the meat, mushrooms and ham together or rub through a fine sieve. Season with pepper, a little salt and a pinch of grated nutmeg. Warm up the sauce and aspic together, cool until it begins to set, then add the whipped cream. Cut out some rounds of bread a little larger than the cucumber shapes, spread over a little of the chicken purée, then place a round of cucumber on each and fill up the centre of each with the purée (pile up high). Decorate with some creamed butter and parsley well mixed together and seasoned with lemon juice, salt and pepper.

About 10 savouries

EGG À LA DIJON

4 hard-boiled eggs	**Tomato garnish**

FILLING

4 oz. cooked ham	**Seasoning**
2 oz. cooked mushrooms	

Cut the eggs in halves, remove the yolk and cut small thin slices off the bottom to make them stand properly. Make a purée of the minced or chopped ham, and mix with the egg yolks and chopped mushrooms and season. Fill the egg whites with the mixture. Garnish with tiny pieces of tomato and serve.

8 savouries

ROLLMOP HERRINGS

These make a most economical hors d'œuvre by themselves, and add flavour to a mixed hors d'œuvres.

6 large herrings	**2 bay leaves**
2 oz. kitchen salt	**4–6 small gherkins**
1 pt. water	**Chillies**
1 pt. malt vinegar	**1 tablesp. pickling spice**
2 large onions	

Clean, bone and fillet the herrings. Mix the salt and water together and put the herrings to soak in this for 2 hr. Lift out of the brine, drain and put into a shallow dish, covering with the vinegar and leaving for several hours. Shred the onions finely. Drain the herring fillets, reserving the vinegar, put 1 tablesp. of onion on to each fillet and roll firmly. Secure with small wooden cocktail sticks if possible. Put into jars with bay leaves, gherkins and chillies (use 1 per jar). Pour the vinegar from the dish into a saucepan and boil for a few minutes with the pickling spice. Cool and strain over the herrings. Cover the jars and store in a cool place. They will keep for 2–3 weeks prepared in this way. Note that the herrings are NOT cooked for this dish.

6–12 helpings—or fillets can be divided into halves for part of a mixed hors d'œuvres

OLIVES

Both Spanish and French olives are suitable for hors d'œuvres, the Spanish being considered better. Choose them large and firm and a nice green colour. Toss in a little oil and vinegar if wished but this is not essential. Those left over from a meal should be rebottled at once otherwise they will turn black.

OLIVES À LA MADRAS

12 Spanish olives	**Cayenne pepper**
1 oz. butter	**12 rounds fried bread *or* crisp biscuits**
1 tablesp. anchovy paste	**12 anchovy fillets**
2 hard-boiled eggs	**Parsley**
1 teasp. chutney	

Stone the olives. Mix together the butter, anchovy paste, yolks of the eggs, chutney and seasoning. Spread a little of the purée on each croûte, and put a stoned olive filled with the rest of the mixture on each. Decorate with chopped egg white. Curl an anchovy fillet round the base of each olive, garnish with parsley.

12 savouries

OLIVES À LA TARTARE

12 slices of brown bread	**12 Spanish olives**
½ gill aspic jelly	**12 shrimps *or* prawns**
1 gill stiff Tartare sauce	**Parsley**

Stamp out 12 rounds of stale brown bread with a 1½ in. cutter. Thoroughly mix the aspic jelly with the tartare sauce. Dip each round of bread in the sauce to mask completely. If not satisfactory at first, coat for a second or third time. Stone the olives, fill each with tartare sauce, and place in the centre of each croûte. Put a shrimp or small prawn in each olive, garnish with parsley.

12 savouries

INDIAN PINEAPPLE SALAD

Salade d'Ananas à l'Indienne

1 small pineapple	**Mayonnaise sauce**
1 sour apple	**Pimento *or* red pepper (capsicum)**
2 heads of celery	

Peel the pineapple and cut into slices. Peel and core the apple, cut into fine shreds, also prepare the celery and cut it into fine strips. Mix these 3 together and add enough mayonnaise sauce to moisten. Place in a glass bowl and garnish the top with thinly cut slices of pimento, and fine sprigs of white celery. Keep the salad as cold as possible.

6 or more helpings

RADISHES

Radis

Choose small, round and firm radishes of a light red and white colour. Trim and wash them in plenty of water. Dish up in little glass dishes. Keep in a refrigerator if possible until ready to serve.

RICE SALAD

3 oz. Patna rice	**Small red *or* green pepper (capsicum)**
1–2 tablesp. olive oil	**2–3 gherkins**
1–2 tablesp. vinegar	**Seasoning**
½ teacup cooked peas	**1 teasp. chopped chives *or* onion**
½ teacup cooked diced carrots	**Watercress**

Cook the rice in boiling salted water, drain and mix with the oil and vinegar while still hot. The smaller quantity of oil and vinegar gives a fairly dry salad. Add the peas, carrots, finely-chopped uncooked red or green pepper, chopped gherkins, seasoning and chives or onion. Put into a dish and garnish with watercress.

5–6 helpings
Cooking time—12 min. (approx.)

SALADS TO SERVE IN AN HORS D'ŒUVRE

As well as Rice Salad the following are suitable for serving in an Hors d'œuvre: Potato Salad, Russian Salad, Tomato Salad, Cucumber Salad and Beetroot Salad.

Recipes for these will be found in the Salad section, pages 362-378.

SARDINES IN ASPIC

Sardines en Gelée

8 sardines	**½ pt. aspic jelly**
2 oz. very thinly sliced tongue *or* smoked salmon	**2 tomatoes**
	Sliced cucumber
	Sliced beetroot

Roll up each sardine in a thin slice of cooked tongue or smoked salmon. Place them in a shallow dish containing a layer of previously set aspic jelly, pour over sufficient half-set aspic to cover the sardine rolls and allow to set. Cut out the shapes as neatly as possible and arrange them on a dish. Garnish the dish with slices of tomatoes, cucumber and beetroot.

8 savourles

SOUPS

"SOUP HAS BEEN AND STILL IS, a mode of preparing food much neglected in this country. It forms the first course of all dinners with any pretension to fashion, but it has not yet come to be an everyday diet of the multitude. And yet it may fairly be said that no food is more digestible and wholesome, and that none offers the same opportunities of utilizing material that must otherwise be wasted." So wrote the original author of this book.

It is unfortunately still true that soup-making is neglected in British domestic cookery, if not by those with "pretension to fashion" yet certainly by "the multitude". In fact today to serve soup, more often than not, means to open a can and reheat its contents. Now, excellent as canned soups are, they do not "offer the same opportunities of utilizing material that must otherwise be wasted" as do the home-made kind.

SOUP IN THE MENU

Soup may be served at the beginning of a dinner in which two or more other courses are to follow or it may be the main course of a simpler meal—a peasant-style lunch, a light supper or a snack meal. The soup that is the forerunner of the meal must stimulate the appetite and by the excellence of its flavour excite the gastric juices so that the following courses may be the better enjoyed and digested. The soup that forms the main course should contain a large proportion of solid foods, in fact it must be as much a stew as a soup, for example Scots Broth or French Pot au Feu.

A soup served at the beginning of a meal should provide a contrast in flavour, colour and texture to the dishes which follow it. Soups are generally served hot so that they may give a feeling of warmth and well-being, but in hot weather certain varieties may be served very cold or iced, so that they may be cooling and refreshing.

The amount of soup to be served varies between quarter of a pint before a generous meal to over half a pint as a main course.

The food value of thin or clear soups is very slight; they contain meat extractives or essences, vitamins of the B group, mineral elements and a little gelatine from the meat and bones used. Their fuel and body-building value is negligible. Meat soups in which all the meat used is served, may contribute a reasonably large proportion of fat and body-building food to the meal. Vegetable soups have the great value of conserving all the mineral elements and—provided they are not over-cooked—the vitamins of the original vegetable ingredients; they are, in fact, the most economical ways of serving vegetables.

Soups of the soup-cum-stew variety usually provide a well-balanced meal of meat or other protein food, vegetables, fat and often starchy foods. The addition of eggs and milk or cream to any soup will further increase the food value by adding protein, fat, vitamins A and D and traces of calcium and iron.

STOCK FOR SOUP-MAKING

Although it is not absolutely essential to the making of good soup, stock made from meat, bones and vegetables and, for certain recipes, from fish, provides a good basis of flavour for most soups and many sauces. An economical substitute for stock is the water in which any vegetables have been cooked.

For consommé, stock made from raw meat is essential, but for all other soups and sauces a household stock will suffice and in this stock the inedible skin and gristle of raw meat, scraps and trimmings of cooked meat and raw or cooked bones may all be utilized.

In the making of stock (pp.78–79) most of the flavour will be extracted from the meat in the first two or three hours of cooking. Subsequent simmering will not greatly improve the flavour of the stock although it may become more concentrated, but more gelatine and finally more calcium will be extracted, particularly if lemon juice or vinegar is added.

CLASSIFICATION OF SOUPS

Although there are hundreds of different soups they can be divided into a few distinct classes. The two main groups of thin and thick soups may be subdivided—thin soups into broths and clear soups; thick soups into purées and thickened soups.

SOUP-MAKING

There remains quite a large group of soups which fit into no one group; these may be termed "mixed" or "national" soups.

BROTHS are the uncleared liquids in which mutton, beef, veal, rabbit, sheep's head or chicken have been cooked. They are not thickened but may have such a large proportion of small pieces of meat, vegetables and pearl barley or rice that they may be confused with thick soups.

CLEAR SOUPS are made from good first stock and if cleared with egg white are known as consommés. Consommés must be sparkling clear; they may vary in colour from pale fawn to deep golden-brown according to the kind of meat used and they are always garnished. They take their distinguishing names from the different garnishes, of which there is an enormous variety.

PUREÉS are soups in which the main ingredients are sieved to make them thick. They may often have an additional thickening, as have thickened soups. Purées are not garnished but are usually served with an accompaniment of croûtons of fried or toasted bread, or some form of rusked bread handed separately.

THICKENED SOUPS. These are thickened by various added ingredients, the chief of which are:

Cereal foods, such as flour, cornflour, arrowroot, barley or rice flour, semolina or fine tapioca.
White or brown roux.
Kneaded butter and flour.
Egg yolk mixed with milk or cream.
Cream.
Blood, almost exclusively for hare soup.

Thickened soups may or may not be garnished.

CREAM SOUP: Any thick soup, whether purée or thickened soup, may be termed a cream soup if cream has been added.

PROPORTIONS USED IN SOUP-MAKING

Meat: For first stock and meat purées and broths: 1 lb. meat to 1 quart water.
Vegetables: 2 lb. vegetables to 1 quart stock *or* water.
Pulses: 4 oz. dry pulse to 1 quart stock *or* water.
Thickening: 1 oz. starchy ingredient to 1 quart of finished soup.

Approximately 2 egg yolks and $\frac{1}{8}$ pint cream to each quart, but this may vary widely according to personal taste and economy.

2 oz. roux or kneaded butter and flour to each quart.

There are on the market several labour-saving devices to make the preparation of soup easy and rapid. For sieving soups stainless metal and nylon replace the older hair sieves; they are easier to clean, they do not become stained and having a harder mesh they make sieving more rapid.

Various vegetable mills are available which will grate, shred or sieve vegetables with very little labour. Many powered mixers have an attachment for liquidizing foods, while both large and small blenders chop and purée vegetables successfully.

Pressure cookers make it possible to produce well-cooked and well-flavoured soups in $\frac{1}{3}$ to $\frac{1}{4}$ of the normal time. Recipes supplied by the makers show the necessary modifications to the standard proportions and times.

ACCOMPANIMENTS FOR SOUPS

Accompaniments are usually handed separately.

Forcemeat Balls are served with meat purées, notably with hare soup.

Croûtons of Bread: Tiny cubes of bread, fried in deep or shallow fat, served hot, golden brown. Or baked croûtons made by buttering a $\frac{1}{4}$-in. thick slice of bread, cutting it into cubes, arranging these, butter side up, on a tin and baking them in a moderate oven till golden and crisp.

Sippets or Croûtons of Toast: The toast to be fairly thin, crisp and golden, cut into fingers or tiny cubes.

Fairy Toast: Bread cut into very thin slices, baked in a slow oven till golden and very crisp.

Melba Toast: Bread toasted golden on both sides, then carefully split into two thicknesses and slowly dried till crisp.

Pulled Bread: The inside of a French loaf pulled with a fork out of the crust, torn into rough pieces which are then dried in a slow oven until pale golden and very crisp. The crusts cut into fingers and dried make delicious rusks.

Grated Cheese: Handed with Minestrone and other mixed vegetable soups.

Sour Cream: Handed with Bortsch and with other Polish, Russian or Hungarian soups.

AUXILIARY RECIPES FOR SOUPS

BOUQUET-GARNI or BUNCH OF FRESH HERBS or FAGGOT OF HERBS

1 sprig of thyme	**1 small bay leaf**
1 sprig of marjoram	**A few stalks of parsley**
1 small sage leaf (optional)	**A few chives (optional)**
1 strip of lemon rind (optional)	**Sprig of chervil (optional)**

Tie all the herbs into a bunch with thick cotton or fine string, leaving a long piece free, which may be used to tie the bunch to the handle of the pan. Alternatively the herbs may be tied in a small square of muslin and fastened with string or cotton, as before.

BROWNING

¼ lb. sugar	**¼ pt. water (approx.)**

Dissolve the sugar very slowly in 1 tablesp. water, then boil it quickly till it is a dark brown. Add a little water and warm this gently till the caramel dissolves, then add enough water to make a thin syrup. Bring this to boiling point, cool and bottle it. Use for colouring brown soups, sauces or gravies.

A better method of producing a brown colour and a good flavour is to fry the vegetables and meat, and often the flour, until all are of a pleasant nut-brown colour.

ESSENCES

This term means natural juices of meat and vegetables extracted by simmering in wine and then reducing them until the flavour is concentrated and the liquid slightly thick.

FUMETS

These are the same as essences but made from fish and vegetables instead of meat.

STOCKS FOR SOUP

BONE STOCK or HOUSEHOLD STOCK
(Also called Second Stock)

Cooked *or* raw bones of any kind of meat or poultry	**Salt**
Cooked or raw skin, gristle and trimmings of lean meat	**1 outside stick of celery**
Clean peelings of carrots, turnip, mushrooms	**1 onion**
	1 bay leaf
	Peppercorns

Break or chop the bones to 3-in. pieces and put them with the skin and trimmings into a strong pan. Cover with cold water and add ½ teasp. salt to each quart of water. Bring slowly to simmering point. Add the vegetables, including a piece of outer brown skin of onion, if a brown stock is required. Simmer for at least 3 hr., without a lid on top heat, or covered in a slow oven. Bones may be cooked until they are porous and so soft that they crumble when crushed, but they should be strained and cooled at the end of each day, the vegetables removed at once, and fresh water added next day. If the stock is not required at once it must be cooled quickly, kept cold—preferably in a refrigerator; and used within 24 hr. even in cool weather or within 3 days if kept in a refrigerator.

In warm weather it must be made as required and used at once. These precautions are necessary because stock provides an excellent medium for the growth of bacteria which can cause food-poisoning. Before use, skim the fat from the top of the stock. This fat may be clarified with other meat fat, or used as needed in meat cookery.

Quantity—1½ pt. from each 1 lb. bones, etc.

FIRST BROWN STOCK
(Suitable for Consommé)

2 lb. veal and beef bones, mixed	**1½ teasp. salt**
1 lb. shin beef (lean only)	**1 carrot**
3 qt. cold water	**1 stick of celery**
	1 onion
	½ teasp. peppercorns

Scrape the bones, remove fat and marrow and wash the bones in hot water. Wipe the meat with a damp cloth and cut it into small pieces, removing any fat. Put all into a pan and add the cold water and salt. Soak for ½ hr. Bring very slowly to simmering point and simmer 1 hr. Add the vegetables whole, including a piece of outer, brown skin of onion, and simmer for a further 3 hr. Strain the stock through a metal sieve and cool it. The remaining meat may be used in any dish requiring cooked meat. The bones should be used for household stock.

Quantity—5 pt. Cooking time—at least 4 hr.

WHITE STOCK

2 lb. knuckle of veal
2 qt. cold water
1 teasp. salt
1 dessertsp. white vinegar *or* lemon juice
1 onion
1 stick of celery
½ teasp. white peppercorns
Small strip of lemon rind
1 bay leaf

Make as for Brown Stock.

Quantity—about 3 pt. Cooking time—at least 3 hr.

CHICKEN STOCK or GAME STOCK

Carcase of chicken *or* game bird
Cleaned feet of bird
Giblets
Salt
Cold water to cover
1 onion
White peppercorns

Make as for Brown Stock.

HARE or RABBIT STOCK

Bones of rabbit *or* hare
Head, heart and liver
"Helmet" and flaps
Salt
1 onion
1 bay leaf
1 blade of mace
Peppercorns

Make as for Brown stock.

VEGETABLE STOCK

2 large carrots
½ lb. onions
3 sticks of celery
2 tomatoes
Outer leaves of 1 lettuce *or* ¼ small cabbage
1 oz. butter *or* margarine
2 qt. boiling water
½ teasp. vegetable extract
Bouquet garni
1 teasp. salt
½ teasp. peppercorns
1 blade of mace
1 bay leaf

Clean the vegetables in the usual way. Thinly slice the roots, cut up the tomatoes and shred the lettuce or cabbage. Fry the roots gently in the fat until golden brown, add the tomatoes and fry slightly. Add the boiling water, the extract, bouquet garni, salt, peppercorns, mace and bay leaf and simmer for 1 hr. Add the lettuce or cabbage and simmer 20 min. longer. Strain and use as soon as possible.

NOTE: Water in which fresh vegetables or pulses have been boiled should always be utilized for soups, sauces or gravy.

Quantity—4 pt. Cooking time—1½ hr.

FISH STOCK

Bones, skin and heads from fish which have been filleted *or* fish trimmings *or* cod's *or* other fish heads
Salt
Peppercorns
1 onion
1 stick of celery
1 blade of mace
1 bay leaf
Bouquet garni

Wash the fish trimmings and break up the bones. Cover them with cold water, add salt and bring slowly to simmering point. Add the other ingredients and simmer gently for no longer than 40 min. Strain and use the same day, if possible.

NOTE: If cooked for longer than 40 min. the fish stock will taste bitter. Fish stock will not keep and should be made as required.

Cooking time—50 min. altogether

BROTHS

BEEF BROTH

Croûte-au-pot

1 carrot
1 turnip (small)
1 onion
1 clove of garlic (optional)
1 oz. butter *or* margarine
1 qt. brown stock *or* bone stock
Salt and pepper
½ small cabbage
A sprig of parsley
A few chives
Grated nutmeg
6 thin slices of French roll

Scrub and peel the carrot and turnip, peel the onion and crush the garlic (if used). Slice the vegetables in thin rounds. Melt the fat and in it cook the vegetables gently for 10 min with a lid on the pan. Add the stock (boiling) and ½ teasp. salt. Simmer the whole for 30 min.

Meanwhile wash the cabbage, shred it finely and chop the parsley and chives. Add the cabbage to the broth and simmer for 20 min. longer; then add seasoning, a little grated nutmeg, and the chopped parsley and chives. Toast or bake the slices of roll till golden and put one in each soup plate or cup; pour the hot soup over them. If liked, grated cheese may be handed with this soup.

4–6 helpings **Cooking time—50 min.**

BOUILLON EN TASSES

This is any good, well-flavoured beef stock, or strong broth, served in soup cups, without vegetables of the broth. Usually served with fingers of toast, Melba toast, or "pulled" bread.

CHICKEN BROTH

Bouillon de Volaille

1 small old fowl
3–4 pt. water to cover
Salt and pepper
1 onion
1 blade of mace
A bunch fresh herbs (thyme, marjoram, parsley stalks)
Lemon rind
1 bay leaf
1 tablesp. rice (optional)
1 tablesp finely-chopped parsley

Wash and joint the fowl, break the carcase bones, scald and skin the feet and wash the giblets. Put the pieces of fowl and the giblets into a pan and cover them with cold water. Add ½ teasp. salt to each quart of water and bring the whole very slowly to simmering point. Add the onion, peeled whole, the mace, herbs, lemon rind and bay leaf, and simmer very gently for 3–4 hr. Strain the broth through a colander, return it to the pan and sprinkle into it the washed rice, if used. Simmer for a further 20 min.

Meanwhile, the meat may be removed from the chicken bones and cut into small cubes, to be returned to the broth before serving, or the chicken may be finished and served as a separate dish. Just before serving the broth, season to taste and add the chopped parsley.

8 helpings **Cooking time—3–4 hr.**

CHICKEN BROTH CHIFFONADE

Consommé de Volaille à la Chiffonade

3 pt. chicken broth (made as above but omitting rice)
1 leek
1 oz. butter *or* margarine
1 cos lettuce
A handful of sorrel *or* spinach leaves
A few chervil *or* tarragon leaves

When the broth has simmered for 2 hr., add the leek (well washed and sliced in thin rings) and simmer for another hour. In a separate pan, melt the fat. Wash the lettuce, sorrel and chervil. Shred them very fine and cook them very gently in the melted fat (with the lid on) for 10 min. Add a little of the boiling broth and simmer for 15 min. Strain the remainder of the broth into this. Cut some of the chicken into small cubes and return these, the pieces of leek and the shredded leaves to the broth. Reheat all and season to taste.

6–8 helpings **Cooking time—3–4 hr.**

COCK-A-LEEKIE or COCKIE-LEEKIE

1 small boiling fowl
¼ lb. prunes
Salt and pepper
1 lb. leeks

Soak the prunes 12 hr. in ½ pt. water. Clean the fowl and truss it, wash the giblets, scald and skin the feet. Put the fowl, giblets and sufficient cold water to cover them in a pan, bring very slowly to simmering point, add 2 teasp. salt. Wash and trim the leeks thoroughly and cut them into thin rings. Add the leeks to the broth after 1 hr. cooking and simmer for 2–3 hr. more. Half an hour before serving add the soaked prunes; simmer till they are just tender but not broken. Lift out the fowl and the giblets and feet. Cut some of the flesh of the fowl into small cubes and return these to the broth. (The rest of the bird may be served with a suitable sauce as a separate course). Season the broth carefully and serve it with the prunes.

Cooking time—3 hr.

FRENCH CABBAGE SOUP

2 oz. French *or* runner beans
½ small cabbage
4 small onions
2 oz. streaky bacon rashers
Clove of garlic, if liked
2 pt. vegetable stock *or* water
4–6 slices of French bread
Salt and pepper
Grated cheese

Wash the vegetables, peel the onions and cut the bacon into small pieces. Warm the bacon gradually in a large saucepan until the fat runs freely. Chop the onions fine and cook them in the bacon fat, with garlic (if used) for 10 min., until soft. Add the stock or water and bring it to boiling point. Shred the cabbage and add it to the liquid and simmer for 20 min. String and shred the beans; add them to the soup and simmer for another 20 min. Toast or bake the bread till golden and put one slice into each soup plate or cup. Season the soup and serve it with the toast floating in it. Hand grated cheese separately.

4–6 helpings **Cooking time—50–60 min.**

HOTCH POTCH

2 lb. neck mutton (scrag and middle neck)
2 qt. water
Salt and pepper
Bunch of fresh herbs
1 carrot
1 small turnip
1 very small cauliflower
1 small lettuce
6 spring onions
¼ pt. young shelled broad beans *or* ¼ lb. runner beans
½ pt. shelled peas
Chopped parsley

Wash the mutton, remove all fat and cut the lean meat into small pieces. Put bone and meat into a pan, add the cold water and bring very slowly to simmering point. Add 2 teasp. salt and the herbs, and simmer very gently for ½ hr.

Meanwhile, scrub and peel roots, wash cauliflower and lettuce. Cut the carrot and turnip into ¼-in. dice and the onions into thin rings; add them to the pan and simmer for 1½ hr. Break the cauliflower into small sprigs, shred the lettuce finely and shred the runner beans, if used. Add all these with the shelled beans and peas to the soup and simmer for ½ hr. longer. Season the broth, skim off the fat and remove the bunch of herbs and the bones. Add 1 tablesp. chopped parsley just before serving.

NOTE: The mixture of vegetables may be varied with the season. This soup may well be cooked in a cool oven (300°–310°F., Gas 1-2).

8 helpings as soup; or 4 as a thin stew with extra stock for other soups
Cooking time—2½ hr.

LEEK BROTH

Bouillon de Poireaux

1 qt. broth from sheep's head *or* bone stock
1 tablesp. medium *or* coarse oatmeal
Salt and pepper
6 large leeks

Have the cooked broth free from fat and at boiling point. Stir in the oatmeal and add salt to taste. Shred the leeks finely. Add the leeks to the broth and simmer them gently till quite soft. Season to taste, and serve while hot.

4–6 helpings
Cooking time—50 min.

MAJORCAN or CATALAN COUNTRY BROTH

2 Spanish onions
2 cloves of garlic
1 leek
1 red pepper (pimento)
½ lb. tomatoes
2 tablesp. olive oil
1 qt. boiling water
¼ cabbage
Sprig of thyme
1 bay leaf
1 clove
Small piece of mace
Salt and pepper
4 thin slices brown bread

Clean all the vegetables, scald and skin the tomatoes. Chop all the vegetables, keeping the cabbage separate. Warm the oil in a saucepan, add the onions, garlic and leek and cook them very gently for 10 min. Add the pimento and the tomatoes and cook for 10 more min. Add the boiling water and the spices and herbs tied together in a scrap of muslin. When the broth boils, add the chopped cabbage and simmer for 1½ hr.

Remove the herbs, season carefully and pour the hot soup over the slices of bread in the tureen or soup cups.

4–6 helpings
Cooking time—1 hr. 50 min.

MESLIN KAIL or GREENKAIL or SCOTS PANKAIL

2 lb. curly kail
1 leek (optional)
1 qt. water
½ oz. butter *or* margarine
Salt and pepper
1 heaped tablesp. medium *or* coarse oatmeal

Wash the kail and the leek. Shred the leek finely. Boil the water; add to it the leek, the fat and 1 teasp. salt.

Meanwhile strip the green kail from the "ribs", and shred it finely. Add the stalks or "ribs" and the shredded kail to the pan, then sprinkle the oatmeal into the boiling broth. The oatmeal will absorb the fat which floats on the broth. Simmer the whole for about 15 min. or until the kail is cooked. Season to taste and serve, removing the "ribs" of kail before serving.

4–6 helpings
Cooking time—about 20 min.

MUTTON BROTH

1½ lb. neck of mutton *or* 1 lb. knuckle of mutton
1 qt. water
1 teasp. salt and pepper
1 tablesp. pearl barley
1 carrot
1 onion *or* leek
1 small turnip
1 stick of celery
Chopped parsley

Wash the meat and remove all fat. Put the meat with the bones, water and salt into a stew pan and bring very slowly to simmering point. Blanch the barley by covering it with cold water in a small pan, bringing it just to boiling point, straining and rinsing it. Add barley to the pan and simmer all for 2 hr. Lift meat from broth, remove bones, cut meat into ¼-in. cubes and return to broth. If possible, let the broth cool and remove the fat from the top; otherwise skim very thoroughly and draw pieces of absorbent paper over the top till it is free from fat. Scrub, peel and cut the vegetables into ¼ in. dice. Add them to the simmering broth and cook for 1 hr. longer.

Season the broth to taste and add 1 tablesp. chopped parsley before serving.

4–6 helpings **Cooking time—3 hr.**

NETTLE BROTH

Bouillon d'Ortie

1 qt. young nettle tops
1 qt. stock
1 heaped tablesp. medium oatmeal
Salt and pepper

Wash the nettles thoroughly. Chop the nettles finely, discarding the fibrous main stems. (Rubber gloves make this process painless.) Have the stock boiling, sprinkle in the oatmeal and add the nettles. Simmer till the nettles are quite tender, about 15 min. if they are really young.

Season to taste and serve.

4–6 helpings
Cooking time—15–20 min.

POT-AU-FEU

(2 dishes, a broth and a meat dish)

2 lb. brisket, topside *or* boned, top ribs of beef
½ lb. broken beef bones
2 teasp. salt
2 qt. water
Bunch of fresh herbs—parsley stalks, chervil, thyme, garlic, bay leaf
4 carrots
2 turnips
1 small parsnip
2 leeks
4 onions stuck with one clove each
6 peppercorns
¼ cabbage
2 tomatoes
Potatoes (optional)
6 toasted slices of French roll

Wipe the meat with a damp cloth and remove some of the outside fat if this is excessive, tie the meat into shape. Wash the bones. Put meat and bones in a large strong pan, add the salt and the cold water, and soak for ½ hr. Bring very slowly to simmering point, add the herbs and simmer very gently for 1 hr.

Meanwhile, scrub and peel the root vegetables; keep the onions whole but cut the others into large pieces and add these to the broth after the first hour's simmering. Put on the lid but leave it slightly tilted to allow steam to escape, and simmer very gently for another 2½ hr. Soak, wash and finely shred the cabbage, scald and skin the tomatoes and cut them into small pieces. Add these to the broth and, if liked, sufficient medium-sized peeled potatoes to serve with the meat. Continue gentle simmering for ½ hr.

To serve: strain the broth through a colander, return it to the pan and keep it hot. Dish the meat with the potatoes, some of the large pieces of vegetable round it and a little of the broth to moisten; keep this covered and hot. Remove the bones and herbs from the broth, cut 1 tablesp. of ¼-in. cubes from the carrot, leek, parsnip and turnip and add these to 1 qt. of the broth and reheat. Serve the broth with the toasted bread floating in it. There will be some broth left to use as stock, and the bones can be reboiled for stock.

Broth—6 helpings
A meat dish—6 helpings
Stock—about 1½ pt.
Cooking time—4 hr.

RABBIT BROTH

Bouillon de Lapin

1 rabbit
½ lb. streaky bacon *or* pickled pork
3 pt. water
Bunch of herbs—parsley stalks, thyme, marjoram, bay leaf
A strip of lemon rind
4 peppercorns
1 clove
1 small piece blade mace
2 onions *or* leeks
1 carrot
1 very small turnip
1 stick of celery
1 tablesp. rice
½ teasp. salt
1 teasp. lemon juice
Chopped parsley

Soak the rabbit in salt water for ½ hr., then rinse it well, or blanch it by covering with cold water in a saucepan (with a lid), bringing to boiling point and rinsing. The best pieces of meat may be filleted from back and legs to be used for another dish, or the jointed rabbit may be cooked in the broth and served with a sauce made from ½ pt. of the broth.

Split the head, divide the backbone in sections, cut off the flaps and keep them, discard the internal organs unless their rather strong flavour is liked, and have the rabbit neatly jointed or the bones separated into small units. Put the bones and as much of the meat as is to be used into a strong pan; scrape and wash bacon or pork and add it whole, with rind, to the pan; cover all with the cold water and bring very slowly to simmering point. Add the bunch of herbs, the lemon rind, the peppercorns, clove and mace and simmer very gently for 1 hr. Meanwhile cut the vegetables into ¼-in. dice, blanch the rice and add these to the broth at the end of the hour. Simmer for a further 1½ hr. If the rabbit joints are being cooked in the broth, remove them to serve separately. If only bones have been used, drain the broth through a colander or metal sieve. Return the broth to the pan and keep it hot. Remove bones, herbs, rind and spices and cut small any scraps of meat that cling to the bones; return these pieces of meat to the pan. Cut the bacon into ½-in. cubes and return it to the broth. Reheat; season carefully, being cautious not to over-salt it if the bacon is already salt; add the lemon juice and parsley.

6 helpings
Cooking time—2½ hr.

SCOTS or "SCOTCH" BROTH

Bouillon Écossais

1 lb. scrag neck of mutton
1 teasp. salt
1 qt. cold water
1½ oz. pearl barley
2 carrots
2 leeks
1 small turnip
1 stick of celery
Pepper
1 dessertsp. chopped parsley

Scrape and wipe the meat, remove outside fat and skin. Cut the lean meat into ½-in. cubes. Put the meat, bones and salt into a pan with the cold water; bring slowly to simmering point. Blanch the barley (*see* p. 33), and add it to the broth. Simmer very gently for 1 hr.

Scrub and peel the vegetables and cut them into ¼-in. dice, except 1 carrot, which is grated and added later. Simmer for a further 2 hr., adding the grated carrot 20 min. before serving. Skim the fat from the surface and remove the bones. Season; add the chopped parsley and serve.

NOTE: To remove fat more completely, *see Mutton Broth.*

4-6 helpings
Cooking time—3 hr.

SCOTS KAIL BROSE or BROTH

Potage au choux Écossais

2 lb. shin of beef *or* "hough" *or* half an ox head *or* 2 cow heels
2 qt. water
2 teasp. salt
2 leeks
2 lb. kail *or* 1 medium cabbage
2 oz. toasted oatmeal *or* 2 oz. pearl barley
Pepper

Have the ox head thoroughly cleaned and blanched, or the cow heels scraped, cleaned and blanched. If shin of beef is used, keep it whole. Put the meat whole into a strong pan, add water, salt and the leeks, cut in 1 in. pieces, bringing slowly to simmering point and simmer gently till the meat is tender 3–4 hr. for shin or cow heel, 2–3 hr. for ox head. If barley is used, blanch it and simmer it in the broth for the last 2 hr. Strip the green from the ribs of the kail or cabbage, shred it finely and simmer it in the broth for 20 min. If oatmeal is added it should be toasted till golden-brown and cooked in the broth for 2–3 min. before serving. To serve, lift out tne meat, dice some of the lean and return it to the broth. Season the broth and serve. The remainder of the meat may be used for another dish or served separately with a little of the broth.

6–8 helpings

Cooking time—3–4 hr.

SHEEP'S HEAD BROTH

1 sheep's head split in two
3 qt. water
3 teasp. salt
2 oz. pearl barley
2 leeks
1 turnip
2 carrots
1 tablesp. chopped parsley
Pepper

Remove the brains and soak them in vinegar and water (these may be used for Brain Cakes to be served with Dressed Sheep's Head). Soak the head in salt water for 1 hr. Scrape the small bones and centre cartilage from the nostril and scour with salt. Scrape and scour the teeth. Blanch the head and rinse it (*see* p. 33). Tie the head with string, put it into a large pan with the water and 3 teasp. salt; bring very slowly to boiling point and simmer gently. Blanch the barley and add it to the broth. Cut the leeks, turnip and 1 carrot into ¼-in. dice and add them. Simmer the broth 3–4 hr. Half an hour before serving, grate and add the other carrot. When the head is tender lift it out and serve it as Dressed Sheep's Head (*see* p. 242). To serve the broth, skim off the fat, add the chopped parsley and season carefully. Some broth may be strained off for stock.

6–8 helpings, keeping 2–3 pt. of broth for stock
Cooking time—3–4 hr.

SPRING BROTH

12 spring onions
4 young carrots
1 young, small turnip
A few head of "sprue" asparagus
¾ oz. butter *or* 2 small tablesp. olive oil
½ pt. shelled green peas
1 qt. stock, preferably white
Salt and pepper
2 teasp. chopped parsley

Cut the onions and carrots into thin rings and the turnip into ¼-in. dice. Remove the tips of the asparagus, to be added later, and cut the stalks into ¼-in. lengths, using only the tender part. Melt the butter and in it cook the vegetables over very gentle heat. Keep the pan covered, shake it vigorously every few minutes and continue cooking without browning for about 10 min. Add the stock, boiling, and simmer all for ½ hr., add the asparagus and cook for a further ¼ hr. Season and add the chopped parsley just before serving.

4–6 helpings **Cooking time—55 min.**

VEAL BROTH

Bouillon de Veau

1½ lb. knuckle of veal
3 pt. water
2 teasp. lemon juice
1½ teasp. salt
1 oz. pearl barley *or* rice
1 carrot
1 small turnip
1 leek
1 stick of celery
A bunch of herbs: parsley stalks, thyme, bay leaf
Strip of lemon rind
Peppercorns
1 dessertsp. chopped parsley

Scrape and wash the knuckle, put it into a pan with cold water. Bring slowly to simmering point, add lemon juice and salt. Blanch barley (*see* p. 33), and add it to the pan. Simmer gently 2 hr. Scrub and peel the vegetables and cut them in ¼-in. dice. Add them to the broth with the herbs (tied in a bundle), lemon rind and spice and simmer for a further 1 hr. before serving. When the meat is quite tender lift it out. Remove the meat from the bones and cut it into ½-in. cubes. Strain the broth through a colander, return it to the pan to keep hot and remove bones, spice and herbs from the vegetables. Return meat and vegetables to the pan, add parsley, season and reheat. Use the bone again for stock.

4–5 helpings **Cooking time—3–4 hr.**

WELSH MUTTON BROTH or CAWL

1½ lb. neck of mutton	**1–1½ lb. potatoes**
1 qt. water	**6 small leeks**
1 teasp. salt	**Pepper**
2 oz. pearl barley	**1 tablesp. chopped parsley**
1 carrot	
1 turnip	

Scrape and wash the meat, remove outside fat and joint it. Put the joints in a saucepan with the cold water and salt and bring slowly to simmering point. Blanch the barley (*see* p. 33), and add it to the pan. Dice the carrot and turnip, add them to the broth and simmer for 1½ hr. Add the potatoes whole and the leeks cut into thin rings and simmer for another ½ hr. Season, skim fat from the top and strain the broth through a colander. Serve the mutton, potatoes and a little of the broth and vegetables separately, and keep it hot. Serve the broth with the leeks barely tender and with the chopped parsley added.

4–6 helpings
Cooking time—2 hr.

CONSOMMÉS OR CLEAR SOUPS

For consommé it is essential to use stock made from raw meat, i.e. First Brown Stock; this is cleared by either of the two following methods except where otherwise stated in the recipes. The albumen in the egg whites coagulates at 160° F., and as the hardened particles rise to the surface they carry with them all the insoluble substances with which they come in contact, forming a thick "crust" of foam. The soup is then strained through a finely-woven linen cloth, the foam "crust" covers the bottom of the cloth and acts as a filter.

TO CLEAR FIRST BROWN STOCK

1 qt. stock (cold and free from fat)	**¼ pt. water**
	1 egg white
1 small onion, scalded	**⅛ teasp. salt**
1 small carrot	**4 peppercorns**
1 small stick of celery	**Small piece of blade mace**
¼ lb. lean shin of beef	

Method 1. Scrub and peel vegetables and rinse them thoroughly. Scrape the lean beef into fine shreds with a sharp knife, discarding every scrap of fat, soak the beef in the water for ¼ hr. Put all the ingredients into a deep pan with the stock and whisk over moderate heat till almost boiling. Remove the whisk and let the stock boil till the froth rises to the top of the pan, then cover the pan and infuse the contents for ½ hr. Strain very slowly through a dry, finely-woven linen cloth.

6 helpings (with garnish)
Cooking time—about 35 min.

Method 2. Using the recipe above, prepare vegetables, shred and soak the beef as directed, beat the egg white. Put all the ingredients into a pan and bring them very slowly to simmering point. Simmer, without stirring or whisking, very gently for 1 hr. Strain as above.

NOTE: This method gives a better flavour and is almost as clear as the first.

Cooking time—1 hr.

CONSOMMÉ AUX BETTERAVES

Clear Beetroot Soup

1 qt. first white stock	**4 peppercorns**
1 small raw beetroot	**Salt**
1 small onion, scalded	**½ glass sherry**
1 stick of celery	**A few drops of carmine**
1 egg white	

GARNISH

1 steamed egg white

Prepare the vegetables as usual, peeling the beetroot and cutting it into thick slices. Put all ingredients except sherry and carmine into a pan and clear as for consommé (p. 85). Steam the egg white for garnish in a small greased basin till just firm, cut it into tiny dice or fancy shapes, rinse these in hot water. Tint the soup clear pink, add the sherry and the garnish and serve. Hand separately sour cream or yoghourt.

4–6 helpings
Cooking time as for consommé

CONSOMMÉ À LA BRUNOISE

Clear Soup—Brunoise style

1 qt. consommé

GARNISH

1 tablesp. ⅛ in. dice of carrot	**1 tablesp. ⅛ in. dice of green leek**
1 tablesp. ⅛ in. dice of turnip	**½ teasp. lemon juice**
	1 tablesp. sherry
1 tablesp. ⅛ in. dice of celery	**⅛ teasp. sugar**

Cook the diced vegetables very carefully in a little boiling salted water till just tender. Have the cleared consommé at boiling point then add lemon juice and sherry. Strain the vegetables, add to them the sugar, add them to the consommé.

6 helpings

CONSOMMÉ BRUNOISE AU RIZ

Clear Soup—Brunoise style with Rice

As for Brunoise with the addition of 1 oz. Patna rice. Wash and blanch the rice, cook in boiling salted water for 10 min. or until just tender. Rinse in boiling water and add with the vegetables to the consommé.

6 helpings

CONSOMMÉ A LA CARMEN

Clear Soup with Pimento

1 qt. consommé with 2 large tomatoes

GARNISH

1 tablesp. each of: fine shreds of pimento, fine strips of steamed egg white and boiled Patna rice	**1 teasp. each of: shredded tarragon leaves and shredded chervil**
	Chopped parsley
	½ glass sherry

When clearing the stock add 2 large ripe tomatoes roughly cut up. Steam the egg white in a small basin till firm, cut it in fine shreds, rinse in boiling water. Scald and skin the pimento and cut it in $\frac{1}{16}$-in. thick shreds, cover these with boiling water and keep hot. Blanch and boil the rice for 10 min. Shred and chop the herbs, have the consommé boiling, add the sherry and garnishes.

6 helpings

CONSOMMÉ À LA CELESTINE

Clear Soup with Cheese Pancakes

1 qt. consommé

CHEESE PANCAKE BATTER

½ oz. flour	**1 teasp. chopped parsley**
½ teasp. melted butter	**½ beaten egg**
½ teasp. grated Parmesan cheese	**⅛ pt. milk**
	Salt and pepper

Make a pancake batter with the ingredients. Fry very thin pancakes in the usual way and rinse them in hot water. Cut them in short strips ¼ in. wide, and serve them in the hot consommé.

6 helpings

CONSOMMÉ À LA DUBARRY

Clear Soup Dubarry style

1 qt. consommé made from first chicken stock

GARNISH

4 chopped Jordan almonds	**Salt and pepper**
	1 tablesp. tiny sprigs cauliflower
Royal custard (see p. 89)	**½ oz. Patna rice**

Add the blanched and finely-chopped almonds to the royal custard; season carefully. Steam the custard, cut it into ⅛-in. dice. Boil the cauliflower sprigs in salted water till just done. Wash, blanch and boil rice; drain it. Add all garnishes to the boiling consommé and serve.

6 helpings

CONSOMMÉ FRAPPÉ

Iced clear soup

Iced consommé may be made from either beef or chicken stock, in either case veal bones added to the stock will give a better jellied result. To serve it iced, the stock is cleared in the usual way and must be most carefully seasoned, it is then allowed to cool, sherry is added and finally it should be put in a refrigerator or packed into a colander with ice for 1–2 hr. before serving. It should be a soft jelly.

SUITABLE GARNISHES:

Chopped parsley, chives and tarragon *or* chervil to taste
***or* tiny dice of raw cucumber**
***or* chopped hard-boiled egg white**
***or* small squares of the fleshy part of scalded tomato**

To serve consommé frappé the jelly should be lightly whipped so that it is not quite solid, and served with its garnish in soup cups.

See also consommé aux Betteraves, Consommé Carmen (without the rice) and Consommé Madrilène which are very refreshing iced.

CONSOMMÉ À LA JARDINIÈRE

Clear soup Jardinière style

1 qt. consommé

GARNISH

1 tablesp. turnip cut in pea shapes
1 tablesp. carrot cut in pea shapes
1 tablesp. small green peas
1 tablesp. tiny cauliflower sprigs *or* 1 tablesp. ⅛-in. cubes cucumber

Scrub and peel the turnip and carrot, wash the cauliflower. Cut the vegetables into pea shapes with a scoop cutter. Boil them separately in salted water, taking care that they are only just cooked. Drain well, add the vegetables to the boiling soup, simmer for a few minutes, then serve.

6 helpings

CONSOMMÉ À LA JULIENNE

1 qt. consommé

GARNISH

1 tablesp. shreds of carrot
1 tablesp. shreds of turnip
1 tablesp. shreds of green leek

Cut the shreds $\frac{1}{16}$ in. thick and 1–1¼ in. long. Boil them separately for a few minutes till just tender, drain them and put them into the soup tureen, pour on to them the hot consommé.

6 helpings

CONSOMMÉ À LA MADRILÈNE

1 qt. first brown stock (p. 78)
1 lb. tomatoes
1 green pepper
1 clove of garlic
Parsley stalks
Thyme
1 bay leaf
¼–½ lb. lean beef
1 egg white
1 carrot
1 onion
1 stick of celery

Cut up the tomatoes and green pepper. Tie the herbs together in a small piece of muslin. Shred and soak the beef in ¼ pt. water. Whip the egg white slightly. Put all ingredients into a pan and simmer very gently for 1 hr. Strain as usual. To garnish cut tiny dice from the firm flesh of skinned tomato, 2 tablesp. to the quart.

Serve the consommé hot or iced; if iced it should be almost liquid and may therefore need whisking a little.

6 helpings

CONSOMMÉ À L'INDIENNE
CONSOMMÉ À LA MULLIGATAWNY

Clear Mulligatawny soup

1 qt. first brown stock (p. 78)
2 level tablesp. curry powder
1 small onion
1 small apple
1 egg white
Juice of ½ lemon
Salt

GARNISH

2 oz. cubes of cooked chicken

Mix the curry powder with a little of the stock. Add the peeled, chopped onion and apple with the curry paste and egg white to the stock. Clear the stock without whisking

(p. 85). Flavour the consommé to taste with lemon juice and salt. It is as well to make certain that the curry flavour is strong enough during the clearing process as no curry powder can be added later. Heat the dice of chicken for a few minutes in the consommé before serving.

6 helpings

CONSOMMÉ DE QUEUE DE BOEUF

Clear Oxtail soup

1 ox tail
1 lb. shin of beef
3 qt. water
1 carrot
1 onion
1 stick of celery
1 blade of mace
6 peppercorns
3 teasp. salt
1 egg white
Sherry (optional)

GARNISH

Small rounds from the thin end of the tail
1 tablesp. tiny dice of carrot

Joint the tail, remove solid fat, cover the tail with cold water, bring to the boil, drain and rinse it. Make the stock with the water and vegetables in the usual way (p. 79). Take the required amount of stock and a few pieces of the thin end of the tail for the soup; keep the rest of the tail and stock for other dishes. Clear the measured stock with the egg white, *see* p. 85. Add sherry to taste. Cook the diced carrot separately and add with the pieces of tail to the boiling consommé.

CONSOMMÉ AUX PATÉS ITALIENNES or CONSOMMÉ À L'ITALIENNE or CONSOMMÉ AUX NOUILLES

Clear soup with Italian paste, Noodles, Spaghetti or Vermicelli

1 qt. consommé
1 tablesp. Italienne paste: bought in tiny fancy shapes *or* **as fancy shaped macaroni;** *or* **macaroni** *or* **spaghetti** *or* **vermicelli** *or* **home made noodles** (*see below*)

Sprinkle the paste into the boiling consommé to allow it to cook before serving. Italian paste requires 3 min. boiling. Macaroni should be cut with scissors in ½-in. rings after boiling for 20–30 min. in the consommé. Spaghetti should be cooked for 15–20 min. then cut into ¾-in. lengths. Break vermicelli into 1-in. pieces and sprinkle into the consommé 5 min. before serving.

NOODLE OR NOUILLE PASTE

4 oz. flour
Pinch of salt
¼ oz. butter
½ egg
Water, if needed

Make a firm, smooth dough as for short pastry with the above ingredients and knead it very well. Roll it so thinly that it is almost transparent, flour lightly and roll it up as for Swiss roll. Cut slices under ¼ in. wide from the roll, unroll them and leave them to dry for at least ½ hr. If dried completely they may be kept as macaroni. Cook the noodles for 15 min. in boiling salted water; cut in convenient lengths with scissors before adding to the consommé.

CONSOMMÉ À LA PORTUGUAISE

1 qt. consommé

GARNISH

12 small French plums
1 large tomato
1 small leek
Pinch of cayenne

Wash the plums, soak them overnight in a little stock then stew them till barely tender. Scald and skin the tomato and cut ¼-in. dice from the firm flesh. Wash and clean the leek, cut it into fine shreds or Julienne strips about 1 in. long, wash well in cold water, drain, and cook in a little of the stock for a few minutes till just tender. Add the cayenne pepper and all the garnishes to the consommé.

CONSOMMÉ AU PRINCE or AUX NAVETS

1 qt. consommé

GARNISH

1 piece raw turnip
2 tablesp. green peas
1 dessertsp. shreds of truffle *or* **pickled walnut**

Scoop the turnip into pea shapes with a pea-scoop cutter. Cook the turnip shapes and peas in boiling salted water till just tender. Drain and add them with the fine shreds of truffle or walnut to the boiling consommé.

6 helpings

CONSOMMÉ À LA PRINCESSE

1 qt. consommé made from stock which contained some raw chicken bones

GARNISH

1 tablesp. pearl barley
2 tablesp. dice of cooked chicken
2 tablesp. asparagus tips

Wash and blanch the barley (*see* p. 33), cook it in some of the stock till quite soft. Cook the asparagus tips till just soft in a little boiling stock *or* water. Cut the white meat of chicken into ¼-in. dice and allow it to become hot in the boiling consommé. Add the barley and asparagus with the stock in which they were cooked.

CONSOMMÉ PRINTANIÈRE

Clear Spring soup

1 qt. consommé

GARNISH

1 tablesp. each of: green peas; diamond shapes of french beans; pea shapes of young carrot and shreds of outer lettuce leaves

Cut the french beans in diamond shapes less than ½ in. long. Scoop out pea shapes of carrot with a pea-scoop cutter. Shred outer leaves of lettuce into shreds ⅛ in. thick and 1½ in. long. Cook each vegetable separately until just tender in a little of the consommé. Each will take a different length of time. Add all garnishes and stock in which they were cooked to the boiling consommé. Serve at once.

4–6 helpings

CONSOMMÉ ROSÉ

Pink clear soup

4 raw beetroots
Sugar
1 qt. water *or* stock
3 carrots
1 stick of celery
1½ lb. tomatoes *or* 1 large can of tomatoes
1 onion
1 bay leaf
1 clove garlic
1 clove
1 egg white
Salt and pepper

Scrub and peel the beetroots, slice and sugar them and cook in the water or stock till soft, then lift them out to be used in salad. Cool the stock, add the other vegetables and spices. Beat the egg white and add to the stock. Bring slowly to simmering point and simmer very gently for 1 hr. Strain through a linen cloth. Season and reheat.

This soup may be served hot or cold. If cold, ¼ oz. gelatine should be dissolved in a little stock and added to the whole before cooling.

6 helpings

CONSOMMÉ ROYALE

Royal clear soup

1 qt. consommé

ROYAL CUSTARD

1 egg yolk
Salt and pepper
1 tablesp. milk *or* stock

To make the custard: mix the egg yolk with the seasoning and milk or stock. Strain it into a small greased basin. Stand the basin in hot water and steam the custard until it is firm. Turn out the custard, cut it into thin slices and from these cut tiny fancy shapes with a "brilliant" cutter. Rinse the custard shapes with hot water, drain and add them to the hot consommé.

6 helpings

CONSOMMÉ SOLFERINO

1 qt. consommé

GARNISH

1 tablesp. of raw choux pastry
Salt and pepper
Deep frying fat

Put the choux pastry into a bag with a ¼-in. meringue pipe and force it into the hot frying fat, cutting off each ½ in. of paste with a sharp knife and dropping the little cylinders into the fat. Drain the fried choux when they are crisp and golden brown. Add the choux to the hot consommé immediately before serving.

6 helpings

CONSOMMÉS

CONSOMME AUX TOMATES

Clear tomato soup

1 qt. consommé (p. 85) **with 2 large tomatoes added during clearing**

GARNISH

Tiny dice of vegetable, if liked

The brown stock is cleared in the usual way with the addition of the tomatoes cut in small pieces. The long method of clearing the stock should be used for greater flavour. Add the vegetables to the boiling consommé.

6 helpings

CONSOMMÉ À LA TORTUE

Clear Turtle soup

¼ lb. sun-dried turtle
1 lb. shin of beef
2 lb. knuckle of veal
3 qt. water
Lemon juice
1 onion
1 carrot
1 piece of celery
A bunch of herbs: parsley, thyme, marjoram, basil, bay leaf
1 strip of lemon rind
3 teasp. salt
6 peppercorns
1 clove
1 blade of mace
1 egg white
1 glass sherry

Wash the turtle and soak it in cold water for 3 days, changing the water daily, or twice a day in warm weather; throw away the water. Prepare the beef and veal as usual for stock, and put them together with the soaked turtle into a large pan with the water. Bring slowly to simmering point, add 1 tablesp. of lemon juice and simmer gently for 4 hr. Add the prepared vegetables, the bunch of herbs, strip of lemon rind, salt and the spices, tied in muslin, to the simmering stock, continue simmering for a further 4 hours. Strain, cool and skim the fat from the stock. Lift out the turtle, cut it in ½-in. cubes and keep it for garnishing the finished soup. Clear 1 qt. of the stock with egg white as for consommé, p. 85. Add lemon juice to taste, sherry and pieces of turtle to the boiling consommé and allow to simmer for 15 min.

Serve immediately.

6 helpings turtle soup (also 3 pt. first stock)

CONSOMMÉ VERT

Clear Green soup

1 qt. white *or* **chicken stock**
2 tomatoes
A bunch of green herbs: marjoram, thyme, basil
1 egg white

GARNISH

1 tablesp. shreds of lettuce
1 tablesp. shreds of spinach *or* **sorrel**
1 tablesp. small green peas
1 dessertsp. shreds of cucumber rind
6 leaves of mint
6 leaves of chives
Lemon juice
½ glass dry white wine (optional)
A few leaves of chervil

Skin and dice the flesh of the tomatoes. Add with the herbs to the boiling stock. Clear as for consommé with the egg white (p. 85). Cook each of the shredded vegetables and the green peas separately in a little boiling stock till just tender. Chop the mint and the chives. Have the consommé boiling and to it add the cooked shredded leaves and peas with the stock in which they were cooked. Reheat for 1 min. only. Immediately before serving add a little lemon juice, the wine and the mint and chives. Float on the top of each portion of consommé one leaf of chervil.

6–8 helpings
Time—to cook garnish, about 20 min.

CLEAR VEAL SOUP WITH ALMONDS

2 lb. veal bones
2 oz. blanched almonds
2 qt. water
1 blade of mace
1 bay leaf
6 peppercorns
1 oz. seed tapioca to each qt. soup
1 teasp. lemon juice
½ glass sherry *or.* **white wine** (optional)

Chop the blanched almonds finely. Make white stock (p. 79), add the almonds and herbs tied in muslin. Simmer about 3 hr. Remove herbs, strain stock, allowing the chopped almonds to pass through the strainer. Cool and remove fat from the stock. Bring to the boil sufficient of the stock with all the chopped almonds, and sprinkle into it the tapioca. Cook till the grain is quite clear and soft. Add the lemon juice and wine and season to taste.

4–6 helpings for each qt.

THICK SOUPS

MEAT PURÉES

CHICKEN PURÉE

Potage à la Princesse

For the stock:

1 boiling fowl *or* **carcase, giblets, skin and legs of a fowl**	**A bunch of herbs: parsley, thyme, marjoram**
¼ lb. lean bacon	**1 bay leaf**
2 onions	**1 blade of mace**
1 carrot	**6 peppercorns**
3 qt. water	**Lemon juice**
Salt and pepper	**A strip of lemon rind**

For each quart of chicken stock:

1 oz. butter *or* **margarine**	**Lemon juice**
	Nutmeg
1 oz. flour	**½ gill cream** *or* **milk**

Prepare the fowl, chop the bacon, peel and slice the vegetables; put into a large pan with the water, salt, herbs, spice, lemon juice and rind. Cook until the flesh of the chicken is absolutely white; the addition of lemon juice makes the flesh tender more quickly. Cool the stock and skim off all fat. Mince 4 oz. of the cooked chicken and moisten it with a little stock. Rub it through a coarse wire sieve. Melt the fat, stir into it the flour then the stock a little at a time; boil well. Stir the hot soup gradually into the chicken purée. Season lightly with lemon juice, salt, pepper and a trace of nutmeg. Add the cream or milk and reheat without boiling.

4–6 helpings
Cooking time—stock 3–4 hr.; soup 10 min.

CHICKEN PURÉE WITH ALMONDS

1 oz. almonds	**Salt and pepper**
1 oz. soft white bread	**Nutmeg**
1 qt. chicken stock	**2 egg yolks**
4 oz. cooked chicken	**½ gill milk**
Lemon juice	**½ gill cream**

Blanch, dry and pass the almonds through a nutmill. Simmer the almonds and bread in the stock for a few minutes, then pass them through a wire sieve. Return them to the stock and reheat. Mince the chicken flesh and moisten it with a little stock. Rub it through a coarse wire sieve, and add to the soup with the lemon juice. Season and add a trace of nutmeg. Beat the egg yolks with milk, stir in the cream and strain this mixture into the hot soup. Thicken without boiling.

4–6 helpings
Cooking time—about 20 min.

GAME PURÉE

1 qt. second stock and remains of 1 cold roast pheasant *or* **2–3 smaller game birds;** *or* **1 pheasant** *or* **2–3 smaller game birds too old and tough for roasting made into game stock**	**Bunch of herbs**
	1 onion
	1 carrot
	1 bay leaf
	1 blade of mace
	1 chicken's liver or 2 oz. calf's liver
	Salt and pepper
	1 oz. flour
2 oz. lean bacon	**½ glass port** *or* **sherry (optional)**
1 oz. butter *or* **margarine**	

Lightly fry the pieces of game and diced bacon in the fat. Drain off the fat and keep it for thickening. Add the stock to the bones, and bring to boiling point, add the vegetables, herbs and spices, and simmer all for 2–2½ hr. Add the liver and simmer for a further 15 min. Strain the soup. Lift out the liver, lift out the meat, separate all meat from bones and mince it. Melt the fat again, add to it the flour and brown very slowly. Sieve the meat through a wire sieve. Stir the stock into the browned flour, boil well, then stir this soup gradually into the meat purée. Add wine, season and reheat.

4–6 helpings **Cooking time—2½–3 hr.**

GAME AND LENTIL PURÉE

Potage à la St. Hubert

Remains of cooked game as for Game Purée	**1 leek**
	A bunch of herbs
	1 bay leaf
1 qt. water	**1 blade of mace**
¼ lb. lentils	**Salt and pepper**
1 onion	**½ gill cream**

Remove any scraps of meat from the carcase, break the bones, cover them with the water and simmer for 2–3 hr. Strain this stock and in it cook the lentils, with the vegetables, herbs and spices, for 1 hr. Mince the scraps of meat. When the lentils etc. are quite soft strain them, mix them with the meat and sieve the mixture through a wire sieve. Stir the stock into this purée, bring to boil; season. Remove from the heat and stir in the cream, reheat without boiling.

4–6 helpings
Cooking time—for the stock 2–3 hr.; for the soup 1 hr.

GAME PURÉE WITH MUSHROOMS

Potage de gibier aux champignons

As for Game Purée with the addition of ¼ lb. mushrooms. Fry and simmer the mushrooms with the game. Sieve half of them, cut the others into shreds and add them at the end.

HARE PURÉE

Purée de lievre

The bones and inferior pieces of a hare, raw	**A bunch of herbs**
3 qt. second stock	**1 bay leaf**
2 oz. lean bacon	**1 blade of mace**
1 onion	**Flour**
1 carrot	**1 glass port**
1½ oz. butter *or* **margarine**	**Salt**
	Cayenne pepper

Paunch the hare and save the blood; (a few drops of vinegar will prevent clotting.) The best of the flesh and ½ the blood will be used for jugged hare. Break the bones, cover them and the scraps of flesh with the stock and simmer very gently. Fry the bacon, onion and carrot in the butter till brown; add them with the herbs and spices to the simmering stock and simmer for 3–4 hr. Strain, remove the meat from the bones and mince it. Moisten the meat with stock and pass it through a wire sieve. Stir the soup into the purée. For each quart of finished soup blend 1 oz. flour with a little stock or water, add it to the soup, bring to the boil, stirring well. Mix the wine and blood and stir them into the soup; cook them carefully without boiling but until they thicken and the blood does not taste raw. Season carefully.

6–8 helpings

Cooking time—3–4 hr.

KIDNEY PURÉE

Purée de Rognons

½ lb. ox kidney	**1 qt. second stock**
1 oz. dripping	**A bunch of herbs**
1 onion	**1 bay leaf**
1 carrot	**1 blade of mace**
1 stick of celery	**6 peppercorns**
1 small turnip	**Salt**
1 oz. flour	

Skin and wash the kidney; cut it in small pieces, removing the core. Melt the fat in a saucepan and when the fat hazes, lightly fry the kidney till just brown. Remove kidney and fry the vegetables, sliced. When the vegetables begin to brown, add the flour and carefully brown it without allowing it to become bitter. Add the stock and the pieces of kidney, herbs and spices, bring to simmering point and simmer for 3 hr. Remove herbs and spices, strain the soup, keep a few pieces of kidney for garnish, pass the rest through a wire sieve. Stir the soup into the purée and reheat it. Season carefully.

4–6 helpings **Cooking time—3½ hr.**

LIVER PURÉE

Purée de foie de veau, de boeuf, d'Agneau

½ lb. calf's, ox, or lamb's liver	**1 qt. stock**
1 carrot	**1 blade of mace**
1 onion	**¼ teasp. yeast** *or* **meat extract**
1 oz. butter *or* **margarine**	**Salt and pepper**
1 oz. flour	**2 tomatoes**
	Lemon juice

Slice the carrot and onion, put the slices in a saucepan and fry them in the fat until beginning to brown; add the flour and brown it. Stir in the stock, bring to boil, stirring well. Add the mace, yeast or meat extract and salt and simmer the soup for 1 hr. Scald, skin and cut up the tomatoes and add. Simmer for another ½ hr. Pass the soup through a nylon sieve, pressing through all the tomato. Mince the liver or chop it finely and whisk it into the soup with the lemon juice. Simmer the soup until the liver just loses its red colour. Season.

4–6 helpings **Cooking time—1¼ hr.**

RABBIT PURÉE WITH SORREL

Purée de lapin à l'oseille

The bones and inferior pieces of 1 rabbit
3 pt. second stock *or* water
2 oz. lean bacon
1 onion
1 carrot
1 oz. butter
A bunch of herbs
1 bay leaf
1 blade of mace
6 peppercorns
1 oz. flour
1 teasp. lemon juice
Salt
A few leaves of sorrel or spinach

As for Hare Purée, omitting the blood and cooking the shredded leaves of sorrel for 10 min. in the soup before serving.

6–8 helpings **Cooking time—3 hr.**

THICKENED MEAT SOUPS

BARLEY SOUP

Potage au crème d'orge

1½ oz. cream of barley *or* patent barley
½ pt. milk
1 qt. well flavoured stock
1 oz. butter *or* margarine
½ teasp. yeast *or* meat extract (if needed)
Salt and pepper
Grated nutmeg

Blend the barley with the milk. Boil the stock with the fat and the yeast or meat extract, stir it into the barley and milk, return all to the pan and simmer until the barley thickens and becomes clear. Stir all the time as the barley easily forms lumps. Season very carefully, adding the merest trace of nutmeg.

Serve with croûtons of fried bread, handed separately.

6 helpings **Cooking time—20–30 min.**

BARLEY CREAM SOUP

1½ oz. cream of barley *or* patent barley
½ pt. milk
1 qt. well flavoured stock
1 oz. butter *or* margarine
½ teasp. yeast *or* meat extract (if needed)
Salt and pepper
Grated nutmeg
2 egg yolks
½ gill cream

As for Barley Soup but add the egg yolks and cream mixed with ½ gill of the milk, at the end of cooking; reheat without boiling.

NOTE: Cream of Rice, Minute Tapioca, Oat Flour, Fine Sago and Farola may all be used for this recipe instead of Patent Barley.

BREAD SOUP, WELSH "BRYWAS" or LANCASHIRE "BREWIS"

1 qt. stock *or* broth *or* liquor from any boiled meat
½ lb. crusts of bread
Salt and pepper

Boil ½ pt. of the stock and add to it the bread crusts, cover the pan and keep the mixture hot for ½ hr. or until the bread is soft enough to mash. Mash the bread with a potato masher or sieve it. Stir into the bread purée the rest of the stock, simmer for 20 min. Season well and sieve. Success depends on the flavour of the stock.

6 helpings
Cooking time—50 min.

CALF'S TAIL SOUP

See Oxtail Soup (p. 96).

CHICKEN CREAM SOUP

Potage à la crème de volaille

1 oz. cream of rice
¼ pt. milk
1 qt. chicken stock
A few pieces of cooked chicken
Salt and pepper
1 teasp. lemon juice
Grated nutmeg
2 egg yolks
2 tablesp. cream

Blend the "cream of rice" with ½ the milk and a little stock. Boil the stock and into it stir the blended rice and milk. Simmer the mixture for 20 min. or until the mixture has thickened. Cut the chicken into ¼-in. dice and heat these in the soup. Season and add lemon juice and a trace of nutmeg. Mix the egg yolks with the rest of the milk and the cream. Strain this mixture into the soup and thicken without boiling.

4–6 helpings
Cooking time—30 min.

COW HEEL SOUP

1 cow heel
3 pt. water
1 onion
1 carrot
1 piece of celery
A bunch of herbs
Salt and pepper
1 oz. fine tapioca *or* sago
Lemon juice
Grated nutmeg
Chopped parsley

Scrape, clean and blanch the cow heel; divide it into convenient pieces. Put it in a pan with the water, bring to boiling point, add the vegetables (cut in ¼-in. dice) and herbs, and simmer for 3–4 hr. Strain, remove some of the meat from the bone and cut into ¼-in. dice. Season the soup, reboil it and sprinkle in the sago or tapioca. Cook till the grain is quite clear and soft. Add the pieces of meat, a little lemon juice, nutmeg and parsley, and serve.

4–6 helpings
Cooking time—4 hr.

EGG SOUP

Potage aux œufs

1 pt. very full-flavoured stock
½ teasp. yeast *or* malt extract
Salt and pepper
⅛ pt. cream *or* milk
2 egg yolks
Chopped parsley, chives, chervil *or* tarragon (optional)

Heat the stock, add the yeast or meat extract, and season well. Mix the egg yolks with the cream or milk and stir this mixture into the stock, well below boiling point. Stir the soup over gentle heat until the egg yolks thicken, but do not allow to boil or the eggs may curdle. Add chopped herbs if liked.

4 helpings
Cooking time—5–10 min.

GAME SOUP or HUNTER'S SOUP

Potage au chasseur

Carcases and trimmings of 2 partridges *or* equivalent amount of any game
1 oz. lean bacon
1 oz. butter *or* margarine
1 onion
1 carrot
½ parsnip
1 stick of celery
1 oz. flour
1 qt. stock
A bunch of herbs
1 clove
Some neat pieces of breast of bird
Salt and pepper

Put the pieces of carcase, the trimmings, and the bacon, with the fat in a saucepan and fry them till brown. Remove the game and fry the sliced vegetables till brown. Add the flour and fry it till golden-brown. Stir in the stock, bring to the boil, add the herbs, return the game to the pan and simmer for 1½–2 hr. Meanwhile cut the pieces of breast meat into ¼-in. dice. Strain the soup, in it reheat the diced game, season carefully and serve.

4–6 helpings
Cooking time—about 2 hr.

GIBLET SOUP

Potage aux abatis

2–3 sets chicken giblets *or* 1 set turkey *or* goose giblets
1 qt. water
1 onion
1 carrot
1 stick of celery
A bunch of herbs
1 clove
Small blade of mace
6 peppercorns
1 teasp. salt
1 oz. flour
1 oz. butter *or* margarine

Prepare the giblets in the usual way then cover them with cold water, bring to simmering point very slowly. Add the whole vegetables, herbs, spice, peppercorns and salt, simmer for 2–3 hr. Strain this stock. In a saucepan, fry the flour in the fat till nut brown without being bitter, stir in the stock, bring to the boil and boil for 5 min. Cut tiny dice from the best pieces of giblets, reheat these in the soup. Season well and serve.

4–6 helpings
Cooking time—2½–3¼ hr.

GRAVY SOUP or SHIN OF BEEF SOUP

Potage au jus

1 lb. lean shin of beef
1 oz. beef dripping
1 onion
1 carrot
1 piece of turnip
1 stick of celery
1 qt. second stock *or* water (p. 78)
1 teasp. salt
A bunch of herbs
6 peppercorns
1 oz. flour

Cut the shin of beef in very thin slices across the fibres. Make the dripping smoking hot and in it fry ½ the meat till brown then remove it. Slice the vegetables and fry them till golden brown, then remove them. Put the fried and raw meat and the fried vegetables into a deep pan, cover with the liquid, bring very slowly to boiling point. Add the salt, herbs and peppercorns and simmer very gently for 3–4 hr. Meanwhile fry the flour in the dripping until golden brown. Strain the soup, return to the soup some of the pieces of meat cut very small, and whisk in the browned flour. Whisk till boiling, season and serve. The remainder of the meat may be minced and served with another dish.

6 helpings
Cooking time—4½ hr.

HARE SOUP, THICKENED

Potage de lièvre

Bones and trimmings of a hare	**1½ oz. dripping**
3 pt. second stock *or* **water**	**A bunch of herbs**
1 onion	**1 bay leaf**
1 carrot	**1½ teasp. salt**
½ turnip	**8 peppercorns**
Small parsnip	**1½ oz. flour**
1 stick of celery	**½ glass port**

Collect the blood from the hare by piercing the diaphragm. Carefully fillet the meat from the back and legs to be used for Jugged Hare (*see* p. 313). The head, flaps and bones of the hare, with the blood may be used for the soup. Split the head, separate the bones, cover them with the cold liquid, add the blood and soak for 1 hr. Fry the sliced vegetables in the dripping then lift them out. Bring the panful of bones and liquid very slowly to simmering point; add the vegetables, herbs, salt and peppercorns and simmer very gently for 3–4 hr. Meanwhile fry the flour till golden brown in the dripping. Strain the soup. Remove from the bones any trimmings of meat, cut these neatly and return them to the soup. Whisk in the fried flour, whisk till boiling, add the port and season the soup.

See also Hare Purée.

8 helpings
Cooking time—4½ hr.

IMITATION HARE SOUP

Shin of Beef Soup (*see* p. 94) **with the addition of:**

1 teasp. red currant jelly	**½ glass port**
1 dessertsp. Worcester sauce	**Veal forcemeat balls (optional)**

After thickening the Shin of Beef soup add the jelly, Worcester sauce and port and cook for 10 min. Garnish, if liked, with tiny balls of veal forcemeat (*see* p. 144), poached in a little of the soup for 20 min.

HUNTER'S SOUP

See Game Soup.

KIDNEY SOUP, THICKENED

Potage aux rognons

1 lb. ox kidney	**1 teasp. salt**
1 oz. dripping	**A bunch of herbs**
1 carrot	**1 bay leaf**
1 onion	**6 peppercorns**
½ turnip	**1 blade of mace**
1 stick of celery	**1 oz. flour**
1 qt. bone stock *or* **water**	

Cut the kidney in very thin slices. Make the dripping hot and in it fry ½ the meat till brown, then remove it. Slice the vegetables and fry them till golden brown; remove them. Put the fried and raw meat and the fried vegetables into a deep pan, cover with the liquid, bring very slowly to boiling point. Add the salt, herbs, spice and peppercorns and simmer very gently for 2–3 hr. Meanwhile fry the flour in the dripping until golden brown. Strain the soup, return to the soup the finely-chopped kidney and whisk in the browned flour. Whisk till boiling, season and serve the soup.

4–6 helpings **Cooking time—2½–3 hr.**

MACARONI SOUP

Potage au pâte d'Italie

1 qt. good stock	**Salt and pepper**
¾ oz. flour	**A little powdered mace** *or* **nutmeg**
¾ oz. butter *or* **margarine**	**2 tablesp. grated cheese (optional)**
1½ oz. macaroni	
1 teasp. yeast *or* **meat extract**	

Boil the stock. Knead the flour and fat together. Cook the macaroni in a little of the stock until quite tender—about 20 min., then cut it into ¼-in. lengths. Whisk the kneaded flour and fat into the boiling soup, whisk until it thickens. Add the meat or yeast extract and dissolve it, season carefully, add the mace or nutmeg. Add the cooked macaroni and serve the soup. Grated cheese may be handed separately.

4–6 helpings **Cooking time—30 min.**

MOCK TURTLE SOUP

Potage de tortue fausse

½ calf's head	**1 bay leaf**
2 oz. lean bacon	**A bunch of herbs**
1 onion	**2 qt. water**
1 carrot	**2 teasp. salt**
1 stick of celery	**Flour *or* cornflour**
3 cloves	**Salt and pepper**
1 blade of mace	**Lemon juice**
6 peppercorns	**Sherry (optional)**

Prepare the head (*see Sheep's Head Broth*, p. 84). Simmer the head, bacon, vegetables and flavouring in the water with the salt for 3–4 hr. Strain the soup. Cut some of the meat from the head into ½-in. dice. To each quart of soup blend 1 oz. flour or cornflour with a little milk or water and with it thicken the broth, season, add lemon juice to taste and ½ glass sherry, if liked. Return the pieces of meat to the soup and reheat them.

8–12 helpings
Cooking time—4¼ hr.

MULLIGATAWNY SOUP

Potage à l'Indienne

1 lb. lean mutton *or* rabbit *or* stewing veal *or* shin of beef *or* ox tail	**1 qt. bone stock *or* water**
	Salt
	1 carrot
1 onion	**½ small parsnip**
1 small cooking apple	**A bunch of herbs**
1 oz. butter *or* margarine	**Lemon juice**
	¼ teasp. black treacle
½ oz. curry powder	**2 oz. boiled rice**
1 oz. flour	

Cut the meat in small pieces. Chop finely the onion and the apple. Heat the butter in a deep pan and in it quickly fry the onion, then the curry powder. Add the apple and cook it gently for a few minutes, then stir in the flour. Add the liquid, meat and salt, and bring slowly to simmering point, stirring all the time. Add the other vegetables, the herbs tied in muslin and a few drops of lemon juice. Simmer until the meat is very tender. This will take between 2 hr. for rabbit to 4 hr. for shin of beef. Taste the soup and add more lemon juice or add black treacle to obtain a flavour that is neither predominatingly sweet nor acid. Strain the soup, cut some of the meat in neat cubes and reheat them in the soup. Boil, drain and partly dry the rice as for curry (p. 37) and hand it with the soup.

NOTE: The amount of curry powder may be varied to taste; the quantity given is for a mild-flavoured soup.

4–6 helpings
Cooking time—from 2–4 hr. according to the meat used.

OX CHEEK SOUP

Potage de Moufle de Bœuf

½ ox head and 4 qt. water; *or* 1 ox cheek and 2 qt. Bone stock *or* water	**1 stick of celery**
	1½ oz. dripping
	A bunch of herbs
	1 bay leaf
1 onion	**1½ teasp. salt**
1 carrot	**8 peppercorns**
½ turnip	**1½ oz. flour**
Small parsnip	**½ glass port**

Cleanse the head as for sheep's head. Split the head, separate the bones, cover them with the cold liquid, add the blood and soak for 1 hr. Fry the sliced vegetables in the dripping then lift them out. Bring the panful of bones and liquid very slowly to simmering point; add the vegetables, herbs, salt and peppercorns and simmer very gently for 3–4 hr. Meanwhile fry the flour till golden brown in the dripping. Strain the soup. Remove from the bones any trimmings of meat, cut these neatly and return them to the soup. Whisk in the fried flour, whisk till boiling, add the port and season the soup.

8 helpings
Cooking time—4½ hr.

OXTAIL SOUP

Potage de Queue de Bœuf

1 ox tail	**1 qt. water *or* bone stock**
1 oz. beef dripping	
1 onion	**1 teasp. salt**
1 carrot	**A bunch of herbs**
1 piece of turnip	**6 peppercorns**
1 stick of celery	**1 oz. flour**

Cleanse the ox tail, remove outside fat and joint the tail. Make the dripping hot and in it fry ½ the meat till brown, then remove it.

Slice the vegetables and fry them till golden brown, then remove them. Put the fried and raw meat and the fried vegetables into a deep pan, cover with the liquid, bring very slowly to boiling point. Add the salt, herbs and peppercorns and simmer very gently for 3–4 hr. Meanwhile fry the flour in the dripping until golden brown. Strain the soup, return to the soup some of the thinner pieces of meat and small rounds of carrot. Whisk in the browned flour. Whisk till boiling, season and serve. The thicker pieces of meat may be served as stewed ox tail.

6 helpings
Cooking time—4½ hr.

RABBIT SOUP—WHITE

Potage blanc de lapin

1 rabbit	**1 blade of mace**
3 pt. bone stock *or* water	**¼ lb. lean bacon *or* pickled pork**
2 onions stuck with 2 cloves	**1½ oz. flour**
1 small turnip	**¼ pt. milk *or* ½ gill milk and ½ gill cream**
2 sticks of celery	**Salt and pepper**
A bunch of herbs	**Lemon juice**
1 bay leaf	

Cleanse and joint the rabbit; blanch it. Make a broth with the rabbit, the liquid, the vegetables (cut into dice) and spices (*see* p. 83). Strain the broth, cut some neat ½-in. dice of rabbit and lean bacon or pork (the rest of the meat can be used for a fricassée, etc.). Blend the flour with cold milk and stir this into the broth; boil till the soup is thickened. Season and add lemon juice to taste. If cream is used add it to the boiling soup, off the heat, and serve at once.

NOTE: The internal organs of rabbit, having a strong flavour may be used or omitted as liked.

6–8 helpings
Cooking time—2½–3 hr.

SHEEP'S HEAD SOUP
also called Mock Turtle Soup

Make as for Mock Turtle Soup (p. 96), substituting a whole sheep's head for half a calf's head.

TURKEY SOUP

Potage de dinde

Carcase and trimmings of 1 turkey	**1 oz. flour**
1 oz. lean bacon	**1 qt. water to each 1 lb. cooked turkey remains**
1 oz. butter *or* margarine	**A bunch of herbs**
1 onion	**1 clove**
1 carrot	**Some neat pieces of breast of bird**
½ parsnip	**Salt and pepper**
1 stick of celery	

Put the pieces of carcase, the trimmings, and the bacon, with the fat in a saucepan and fry them till brown. Remove the turkey and fry the sliced vegetables till brown. Add the flour and fry it till golden-brown, stir in the stock, bring to the boil, add the herbs, return the turkey to the pan and simmer for 1½–2 hr. Meanwhile cut the pieces of breast meat into ¼-in. dice. Strain the soup, in it reheat the diced meat, season carefully and serve.

NOTE: Scraps of forcemeat improve the flavour and help to thicken.

4–6 helpings
Cooking time—about 2 hr.

FISH SOUPS AND BISQUES

BISQUES

Bisques are fish soups of a thick, creamy consistency usually made from molluscs or crustaceans, the flesh of which is pounded and sieved to form a purée.

BISQUE AUX HUÎTRES

Oyster soup

1 doz. oysters, fresh *or* canned	**½ glass white wine**
1 qt. fish stock	**Salt and pepper**
¼ pt. cream	**Lemon juice**
1 oz. butter	**Grated nutmeg**
1 oz. flour	**1 egg yolk**

Add the beards, buttons and liquor of the oysters (fresh or canned) to the simmering fish stock. Cut the oysters into halves and cover them with the cream. Melt the butter in a deep pan, stir in the flour, then the fish stock and oyster liquor and the wine. Simmer the liquid for ½ hr. Season carefully, adding a little lemon juice and nutmeg to taste. Strain the soup through a fine sieve. Mix the egg yolk with the cream. Boil the soup, remove it from the heat and stir in the egg yolk, cream and halved oysters. Cook the egg without boiling.

6 helpings
Cooking time—40 min. for fish stock
40 min. for bisque

BISQUE DE CREVETTES

Shrimp soup

- **1½ pt. fish stock (p. 79) in which the shells of the shrimps have been cooked**
- **3 tablesp. fresh bread-crumbs**
- **2 oz. butter**
- **1 pt. cooked shrimps**
- **1 teasp. lemon juice**
- **Grated nutmeg**
- **1 glass white wine *or* cider**
- **1 egg yolk**
- **¼ pt. cream *or* milk, *or* ½ cream and ½ milk**
- **Salt and pepper**

Heat ½ pt. of the fish stock and in it soak the breadcrumbs. Melt ½ oz. butter in a deep pan and in it toss the shrimps over gentle heat for 5 min. Add lemon juice, nutmeg, bread-crumbs and ½ pt. stock, heat gently for 5 min., beat in the rest of the butter. Pound this paste and rub it through a wire sieve. Gradually add the wine and the rest of the fish stock and bring to boiling point. Mix the egg yolk with the milk or cream. Season the soup carefully, remove it from the heat, stir in the egg and cream mixture and cook this without allowing the soup to boil.

4–6 helpings
Cooking time—40 min. for fish stock
15–20 min. for the bisque

BISQUE DE GROSSES CREVETTES

Prawn soup

- **4 oz. butter**
- **1 pt. cooked prawns**
- **1 oz. flour**
- **1¾ pt. fish stock (p. 79) in which prawn shells have been cooked**
- **¼ pt. white wine *or* cider**
- **1 egg yolk**
- **¼ pt. cream *or* milk; *or* ½ cream and ½ milk**
- **Salt and pepper**
- **Lemon juice**
- **Nutmeg**

Melt ½ oz. butter; in it toss the prawns over gentle heat for 5 min. Pound the prawns, gradually working in 2½ oz. of the butter. Rub the prawns and butter through a wire sieve. Melt the remaining 1 oz. of butter in a sauce-pan and stir into it first the flour, then the fish stock and wine, bringing to boiling point. Mix the egg yolk and milk or cream. Season the soup carefully adding lemon juice and a trace of nutmeg to taste. Add to the soup, just below boiling point, first the prawn butter, whisking it in a pat at a time, then the egg yolk and cream, stirring the soup till the egg thickens without boiling.

NOTE: The preceding recipes are inter-changeable, and may be used for either crus-tacean.

4–6 helpings
Cooking time—40 min. for fish stock
15 min. for the bisque

BISQUE D'ECREVISSES

Crayfish soup

As for Bisque de Crevettes; allowing 12 cray-fish and 2 boned, bottled or canned anchovies to each quart of bisque.

Either of the two preceding recipe methods is suitable.

BISQUE D'HOMARD

Lobster soup

- **The shell, trimmings and a little of the flesh of a medium-sized lobster**
- **1 onion**
- **1 carrot**
- **1 clove of garlic**
- **1 bay leaf**
- **1 blade of mace**
- **Lemon juice**
- **1 teasp. anchovy essence**
- **¼ pt. white wine**
- **1¾ pt. fish stock**
- **Salt and pepper**
- **1 tablesp. cooked lobster coral**
- **2 oz. butter**
- **1 oz. flour**
- **¼ pt. cream**
- **A few drops carmine if needed**

Crush the shell; flake the rough pieces of flesh as finely as possible, keeping neat pieces of the better parts for garnish. Slice the vegetables finely, put them into a pan with the spices, flavouring, shell, flaked lobster and the wine. Heat all quickly and cook briskly for a few minutes. The alcohol in the wine should extract much of the flavour from the lobster and vegetables. Add the stock, and salt, bring to boiling point; simmer 1 hr. Strain through a wire sieve, and rub through the sieve any of the scraps of lobster that are still firm. Pound the lobster coral with 1 oz. butter and rub through a nylon sieve. Melt the other 1 oz. butter, stir into it the flour, then the strained stock, bring to boiling point. Whisk in, just at boiling point, the lobster butter, then stir in the cream, off the heat. Season carefully, colour if necessary to obtain a deep orange-pink, reheat without boiling, adding any neat pieces of lobster.

NOTE: Live lobster may be used, *see* p. 190 for the methods of killing lobsters.

4-6 helpings Cooking time—40 min. for fish stock
1 hr. 20 min. for bisque

FISH SOUPS

BOUILLABAISSE

NOTE: This, the most famous of all fish soups is made chiefly in the South of France, different districts having particular recipes. It is a kind of thick stew of fish which should include a very wide mixture of different kinds of fish. The original French recipes use many fish not available in Great Britain. The following recipe is adapted to use the available fish. In order to get a wide enough variety a large quantity must be made.

A mixture of 8 *to* 10 *different kinds of fish, e.g.:*

Whiting	**John Dory**
Red mullet	**Monk fish**
Crawfish *or* **lobster**	**Crab**
Conger eel *or* **eel**	**Bass**
Gurnet	**Sole**

To every 2 *lb. fish allow:*

1 large onion	**A sprig of fennel** *or* **tarragon**
1 leek	**1/8 teasp. saffron**
1 clove of garlic	**Salt and pepper**
2 tomatoes	**1/4 pt. olive oil**
1 bay leaf	**1/4 pt. white wine**
A sprig of parsley	
A sprig of savory	

To each portion of bouillabaisse allow:
1 thick slice of French roll

Clean the fish, cut them into thick slices and sort them into 2 groups, the firm-fleshed kind and the soft kind. Chop the onion; slice the leek; crush the garlic; scald, skin and slice the tomatoes. In a deep pan make a bed of the sliced vegetables and the herbs, season this layer. Arrange on top the pieces of firm-fleshed fish; season them and pour the oil over them. Add to the pan the wine and enough cold water or fish stock barely to cover the top layer of fish. Heat as quickly as possible to boiling point and boil briskly for 8 min. Now add the soft pieces of fish, forming a fresh layer. Boil for a further 5 min. Meanwhile toast the slices of bread and arrange them in the bottom of the soup tureen or individual bowls. Pour the liquid over the bread and serve it as a fish bouillon. Serve the mixture of fish separately.

NOTE: The vegetables and herbs are for flavour only, and need not be served, the olive oil should be distributed over the pieces of fish if cooking has been brisk enough.

The mixture suggested would probably weigh 4 lb.

Sufficient for 8-10 helpings
Cooking time—15-20 min.

CRAB or CRAWFISH SOUP

Soupe au Crabe ou Langousie

1 medium-sized cooked fresh *or* **canned crab** *or* **crawfish**	**1/8 teasp. saffron**
1/2 lb. onions	**1 clove of garlic**
1 1/2 lb. tomatoes *or* **1 large can of tomatoes**	**Lemon rind**
1 oz. butter	**Lemon juice**
A bunch of herbs: parsley, basil, fennel *or* **tarragon**	**Grated nutmeg**
	Salt and pepper
	1/2 glass dry white wine
	1 qt. water
	1/4 pt. cream

Slice the onions and tomatoes. Melt the butter in a deep pan and cook the onions for 10 min. over gentle heat; add the tomatoes, the herbs, flavourings and seasoning. (If canned tomatoes are used, drain off the juice and use it instead of some of the water.) Simmer the vegetables for another 20 min., add the wine and boil for 2 min. Add the soft meat from the crab, or ½ the flesh of the crawfish, finely-chopped. Add the water and simmer for 20 min. Press the soup through a wire sieve, season and reheat it. Stir in the cream just below boiling point, reheat without boiling.

5-6 helpings
Cooking time—1 hr.

EEL SOUP

Soupe aux Anguilles

1 lb. eel	**1 strip of lemon rind**
1 onion	**1 teasp. lemon juice**
1 oz. butter	**1 oz. flour**
1 qt. water	**Salt and pepper**
A bunch of herbs	**¼ pt. cream *or* milk**
1 blade of mace	

Clean and cut the eels into small pieces. Slice the onion. Melt the butter in a saucepan and gently fry the onion and eel for 10 min. without browning them. Add the water, bring to simmering point; add herbs, mace, lemon rind and juice, and seasoning. Simmer very gently till the eel is tender. Strain the soup and keep the pieces of eel warm. Blend the flour with a little milk and stir into the soup, reheat and boil till the flour thickens the soup. Season carefully, and stir in the cream just at boiling point, reheat without boiling. Add the pieces of eel and serve the soup.

5-6 helpings
Cooking time—about 1 hr.

FISH CHOWDER

This American dish is something between a soup and a fish stew.

2 lb. filleted fresh cod *or* haddock, the head, bones and skin of the fish	**1 blade of mace**
¾ pt. water	**2 onions**
Salt and pepper	**1 lb. potatoes**
Lemon rind	**¼ lb. salt pork**
A bunch of herbs	**1 oz. flour**
	1 pt. milk
	1 oz. butter

Skin the filleted fish. Make a fish stock with the water, bones, head and skin of the fish, salt, lemon rind, herbs and mace, simmer gently for ½ hr. Cut the fillets into 2-in. strips, slice the onions thinly and dice the potatoes. Cut the pork in tiny cubes and heat it gently in a deep pan until the fat flows freely. In the pork fat cook the onion without browning for 10 min., then add the potatoes and shake them well in the fat for a few minutes. Sprinkle in the flour. Gradually add the hot, strained stock, then put in the pieces of fish and season the soup. Cook very gently for ½ hr. Heat the milk and butter and add them to the soup when the fish and potatoes are soft. Do not reboil. Serve at once.

4-6 helpings
Cooking time—1¼ hr.

FISH SOUP—HADDOCK, COD or SKATE

Soupe au Merluche, Morue ou Raie

1½ lb. haddock, cod, skate *or* any available white fish	**1 teasp. curry powder**
2 large onions	**1½ pt. boiling water**
1 carrot	**A bunch of herbs**
2 sticks of celery	**Salt and pepper**
½ lb. potatoes	**½ glass white wine (optional)**
1 oz. butter	**1 oz. flour**
1 tablesp. olive oil	**¼ pt. milk**
	⅛ pt. cream

Slice the onions, carrot and celery into thin rounds. Cut the potatoes into thick fingers. Heat the butter and olive oil together in a deep pan and in this toss all the vegetables over gentle heat for 10 min. Add the curry powder and stir the mixture over the heat for a few more minutes. Add the boiling water, the herbs, salt and pepper. Cut the fish into neat pieces and add to the soup. Simmer until the fish is tender. Lift the best pieces of fish from the soup and keep them hot with a little of the liquid. Reduce the remaining liquid for 15 min.—pour it through a sieve and press through the potatoes and scraps of fish. Add the wine, if used, and reheat the soup. Blend the flour and milk, stir this into the soup and boil it. Return the pieces of fish and add the cream to the soup, just at boiling point.

4-6 helpings
Cooking time—¾-1 hr.

MUSSEL SOUP

Soupe aux Moules

1 qt. mussels
¼ pt. white wine
Lemon juice
1½ pt. fish stock (p. 79)
1 oz. butter
¾ oz. flour
Salt and pepper
Chopped parsley
1 egg yolk
⅛ pt. cream

Wash and scrub the mussels; put them into a pan with the wine, lemon juice and ½ pt. of fish stock. Heat them in the liquid until they open. Strain the liquid through muslin into the remaining 1 pt. stock. Shell the mussels and remove the beards. Melt the butter in a deep pan, stir in the flour, then the fish stock. Bring to boiling point, boil till the flour thickens. Season the soup carefully; add the chopped parsley. Mix the egg yolk and cream and add them and the mussels to the soup, just below boiling point. Cook the egg without allowing it to boil.

NOTE: Other shell fish may be treated in the same way.

4–6 helpings
Cooking time—25–30 min.

SHELL FISH AND TOMATO SOUP

1 lb. cooked *or* 1 can of crawfish, crayfish *or* prawns
2 raw potatoes
1½ pt. fish stock (p. 79)
A bunch of herbs: fennel *or* tarragon, parsley, basil
1 bay leaf
Lemon juice
Lemon rind
1 lb. tomatoes *or* 1 medium-sized can
1 onion
2 oz. rice
¼ pt. white wine *or* cider
Chopped parsley
Paprika pepper
½ gill cream

Slice the potatoes thickly, and boil them till soft in ½ pt. fish stock with the herbs, lemon juice and a piece of lemon rind. Meanwhile cut up the tomatoes and chop the onion. Cook the tomatoes and onion without any other additions till they are quite soft. Sieve the potatoes and to them add all the stock. Bring the stock and potatoes to the boil, add the rice and cook till quite soft. Sieve the tomatoes and onion and add this purée to the thickened fish stock. Add the wine and the chopped fish and bring the soup to boiling point. Grate in a little lemon rind, add the chopped parsley and season well. Off the heat, stir in the cream.

Serve at once.

4–6 helpings
Cooking time—30 min.

VEGETABLE PURÉES AND CREAM SOUPS

VEGETABLE PURÉE

Basic Recipe (1)

1 lb. vegetable
Flavouring vegetable
½–1 oz. butter, margarine *or* other suitable fat
1 pt. stock—white for white and pale green vegetables; brown for dark-coloured vegetables; *or* water; *or* vegetable boilings
Flavouring herbs (optional)
¼ pt. milk *or* ⅛ pt. milk and ⅛ pt. cream for light-coloured soups
½ oz. starchy thickening, e.g. flour, cornflour, ground rice, tapioca *or* potato to each pint of sieved soup
Salt and pepper
Other flavouring *or* colouring if required

For a Cream Soup add:

⅛–¼ pt. cream (this may replace some of the milk), sometimes also 1 egg yolk

Slice or chop the main and flavouring vegetables. Melt the fat in a deep pan and in it cook the vegetables over gentle heat for 10 min. Keep the lid on the pan and shake it vigorously from time to time. Boil the stock, add it to the vegetables with the herbs and other flavouring (if used) and simmer the whole until the vegetables are quite soft. This cooking time should be as short as possible but will vary with the kind and age of the vegetables used. Remove the herbs, rub or press the vegetables through a sieve (wire for soft, pulpy or very firm vegetables; nylon if a very smooth purée is needed). Mix the liquid with the purée and measure the soup. Weigh or measure the thickening in the proportion given above. Blend the starch powder with cold milk, stock or water and stir it into the soup. Cook the soup until the starch is thickened and no longer tastes raw. Season carefully to taste.

For a Cream soup:

After the starch thickening has been cooked, remove the pan from the heat. Mix the egg yolk and cream together, stir them into the soup, which should be well below boiling point. Stir over gentle heat till the egg yolk thickens, but do not boil. Serve the soup at once; cream and eggs cannot be kept hot. Cream when used alone may be stirred into the soup just at boiling point, as it is removed from the heat. It must not be allowed to boil.

Serve separately with any vegetable purée, fried croûtons of bread, pulled bread, Melba toast or "fairy" toast.

Basic Recipe (2)

1 lb. vegetable	**1 pt. thin sauce, i.e. 1 oz. fat and flour to 1 pt. Béchamel** (p. 128) **for light-coloured purées,** *or* **Velouté** (p. 133) **for dark-coloured purées**
½–1 oz. butter, margarine *or* **fat and/or ⅛ pt. boiling stock** *or* **water**	

(Flavouring vegetables are included in the recipes for the foundation sauces.)

Cook the vegetable as in Basic Recipe (1), adding only sufficient boiling liquid to moisten it. Cook very carefully without allowing it to evaporate or burn. Rub this concentrated purée through a sieve and whisk it into the hot sauce. Boil the soup and if required convert it to a cream soup as in the previous recipe.

ARTICHOKE (JERUSALEM) PURÉE, also called "PALESTINE" SOUP

Purée aux Topinambours

1 lb. Jerusalem artichokes	**Lemon juice**
Vinegar	**¼ pt. milk**
1 onion	**½ oz. cornflour to each pint of sieved soup**
¾ oz. butter *or* **margarine**	**Salt and pepper**
1 pt. white stock	**⅛ pt. cream (optional)**

Scrape the artichokes under water to which has been added a little vinegar, preferably white vinegar. Keep the scraped artichokes in vinegar water till all are done, then quickly rinse and dry them. Proceed as in Basic Recipe (1), p. 101. Lemon juice improves the flavour and whiteness of the soup.

4 helpings
Cooking time—about 1 hr.

ASPARAGUS CREAM SOUP

Crème d'asperges

1 bundle (25 heads) of "sprue" *or* **thin asparagus**	**1 onion**
1 pt. white stock	**Lemon juice**
1 oz. butter	**Pinch of sugar**
1 oz. flour	**Salt and pepper**
	⅛ pt. cream

Cut off the tips of the asparagus and cook them till just tender in a little of the stock—about 10 min.; keep them for garnish. Melt the butter, stir into it the flour, then the stock, and bring to boiling point. Slice the onion and cut the asparagus in short lengths. Add the onion and asparagus sticks to the boiling stock and simmer them very gently till quite tender—30–40 min. Press through a hair or nylon sieve. Add lemon juice and sugar to taste, season. Reheat. Stir in the cream, add the asparagus tips last.

4 helpings
Cooking time—about 50 min.

BROAD BEAN PURÉE

Purée de Fèves

1 pt. shelled broad beans *or* **if very young, 1 pt. beans in the pod**	**1 sprig of savory**
1 oz. lean bacon scraps and rinds	**¼ pt. milk**
½ oz. butter	**Cornflour to thicken**
1 onion	**Salt and pepper**
1 pt. stock	**Sugar**
	Lemon juice
	1 teasp. chopped parsley

Unless the beans are young, boil them for 10 min. in salted water and remove the skins. In a deep pan fry the bacon, butter and onion together for 10 min., add the stock and savory and when boiling add the beans. Simmer until the beans are soft, about 20 min. unless very old. Rub through a sieve, stir the milk into the purée and measure the soup. For each 1 pt. of soup blend ½ oz. cornflour with a little cold milk, stock or water, and stir into the soup. Cook until the soup is thickened. Season, add sugar and lemon juice to taste. Sprinkle the parsley over.

Decorate with piped double cream or a few cooked beans, if liked.

4 helpings **Cooking time—45–50 min.**

BRUSSELS SPROUT SOUP

Purée de Choux de Bruxelles

½ lb. prepared sprouts
A few bacon rinds *or* a bacon bone
1 onion
½ oz. butter *or* margarine
1 pt. white *or* bone stock
¼ pt. milk
Cornflour to thicken
Salt and pepper
⅛ pt. cream (optional)
Green colouring, if needed

Fry the bacon rinds and onion in the fat for 10 min. without browning. Add the stock and bring to the boil. Add the sprouts and simmer them till tender, 15–20 min. Sieve the sprouts, stir the milk into the purée and measure the soup. For each 1 pt. of soup blend ½ oz. cornflour with a little cold milk, stock or water and stir into the soup. Cook until the soup is thickened, season carefully. Remove from heat and stir in the cream (if used), add colouring if required.

4 helpings **Cooking time—½ hr.**

CARROT SOUP

Purée à la Crécy

1 lb. carrots
1 onion
2 sticks of celery
½ small turnip *or* swede
A few bacon rinds, bones *or* scraps
½ oz. butter *or* margarine
1 pt. brown stock
1 blade of mace
1 bay leaf
A bunch of herbs
Peppercorns
A little yeast *or* meat extract
Lemon juice
¼ pt. milk
Cornflour to thicken
Salt

Proceed as for Basic Recipe (p. 101).

CAULIFLOWER CREAM SOUP

Purée de Choufleur or *Crème de Choufleur*

1 medium-sized cauliflower about ¾–1 lb. after trimming
1 onion
1 oz. butter *or* margarine
1 pt. white stock
Lemon juice
1 blade of mace
1 bay leaf
¼ pt. milk
Cornflour to thicken
Salt and pepper
1 egg yolk
⅛ pt. cream

Remove the green leaf from the cauliflower but keep all the stalk. Continue as for Basic Recipe (p. 101). The cauliflower should be cooked for the shortest time possible or its flavour will be spoilt.

CELERIAC PURÉE

¾ lb. celeriac
1 onion
1 oz. butter *or* margarine
1 pt. white stock
Lemon juice
¼ pt. milk
Cornflour to thicken
Salt and pepper
⅛ pt. cream (optional)

Method as for Basic Recipe (p. 101). The celeriac will require ¾–1 hr. to cook.

4 helpings
Cooking time—1 hr.

CELERY SOUP or CELERY CREAM SOUP

Crème de Céleri

1 lb. outer sticks of celery
1 onion
¾ oz. butter *or* margarine
1 pt. white stock (p. 79)
Lemon juice
¼ pt. milk
Cornflour to thicken
Salt and pepper
⅛ pt. cream (optional)

Proceed as in Basic Recipe (p. 101). Cook the celery without boiling or it will become stringy and difficult to sieve. If cut in ½-in. lengths it is easy to sieve.

4 helpings
Cooking time—1 hr.

CHESTNUT PURÉE

Purée de Marrons

1 lb. chestnuts after peeling (about 1½ lb. in shells)
1 onion
1 oz. butter
1 qt. stock
Lemon juice
Salt and pepper
A little yeast *or* meat extract
A pinch of sugar
A pinch of cinnamon
Grated nutmeg
¼ pt. cream (optional)

Make an incision in the rounded sides of the chestnuts then drop them into fast boiling water and boil for 15 min. Drain them and while still warm remove shells and brown skins. Proceed as for Basic Recipe (p. 101). Add the spices so sparingly that they cannot be recognized but merely enhance the chestnut flavour. No added thickening is required except the cream which is optional.

CHICORY SOUP

2 large heads of chicory (Witloof) also called Belgian Endive
1 oz. butter
1 onion
1 pt. white stock
½ oz. flour
A bunch of herbs
1 blade of mace
Salt and pepper
Lemon juice
¼ pt. milk *or* cream; *or* ½ milk and ½ cream
1 egg yolk

Cut the chicory in ¼-in. slices and cook it with the onion gently in the butter for 10 min. Continue as for asparagus soup, reserving a few shreds of cooked chicory for garnish. Lemon juice added with the stock improves the flavour. The chicory must not be allowed to boil or it will become tough and stringy.

4 helpings

CORN SOUP

3 young cobs sweet corn *or* 1 medium can of sweet corn
½ oz. butter
1 pt. white stock
Salt and pepper
Ground nutmeg
⅛ pt. cream (optional)

(The corn must be picked while still soft and juicy.) Scrape the corn from the cobs, discarding the leaves, silk and tassel. Melt the butter in a deep pan and cook the corn and scraped cobs over very gentle heat for 10 min. Add the stock, bring to simmering point and simmer the soup for 1–1½ hr. until the corn is quite soft. Sieve and season. If cream is used, reheat the soup to boiling point, remove from heat and stir in the cream. Do not allow the cream to boil.

4 helpings
Cooking time—1½–2 hr.

CRÈME VICHYSSOISE

½ lb. white leeks
½ lb. potatoes
1 oz. butter
1 pt. stock
¼ pt. milk
¼–⅛ pt. cream
Salt and pepper

Proceed as for Basic Recipe (p. 101).

NOTE: This soup may be served iced.

4 helpings

CUCUMBER CREAM SOUP

Crème de Concombre

1 lb. cucumber
1 oz. butter
6 spring onions
1 oz. flour
1 pt. white stock
Salt and pepper
Lemon juice
Green colouring
A sprig of mint
A sprig of parsley
⅛ pt. cream

Peel the cucumber, reserve a 2-in. length for garnish, slice the rest. Melt the butter in a deep pan and cook the onions gently, without browning for 10 min. Stir in the flour, then the stock and bring to boiling point. Add the sliced cucumber and cook till tender. Sieve through a nylon sieve. Season and add lemon juice to taste. Cut the 2-in. piece of cucumber into ¼-in. dice and boil these in a little stock or water till just tender and add them to the finished soup. Five minutes before serving the soup add the mint and parsley. Tint the soup pale green. Stir the cream into the hot soup immediately before serving.

4 helpings **Cooking time—20–30 min.**

CUCUMBER AND POTATO SOUP

2 ridge cucumbers *or* 1 long cucumber
1 lb. potatoes
1 onion
1 oz. butter
1 pt. stock *or* water
¼ pt. milk
Salt and pepper
1 pickled cucumber
Chives
Mint
Parsley

Slice or chop the potatoes and onion. Melt the fat in a deep pan and cook the potatoes and onion over gentle heat for 10 min. Keep the lid on the pan and shake the pan vigorously from time to time. Boil the stock or water, add it to the vegetables and simmer till the vegetables are soft. Sieve and into the purée stir the milk and grate the raw, peeled cucumbers. Season and reheat. Five minutes before serving stir in the pickled cucumber, chives, mint and parsley, all finely chopped.

4–6 helpings **Cooking time—40–60 min.**

FLEMISH SOUP

1 lb. potatoes
2 leeks *or* onions
3–4 outer sticks of celery
1½ oz. bacon *or* pork fat *or* fat from pork sausages
1 qt. stock *or* water
A bunch of herbs
¼ pt. milk
Salt and pepper
Nutmeg

Slice the potatoes, leeks and celery. Melt the fat in a deep pan and lightly fry the vegetables over a gentle heat for 10 min. Keep the lid on the pan and shake it vigorously from time to time. Boil the stock or water, add it with the herbs to the vegetables and simmer until the vegetables are quite soft. Remove the herbs, sieve the vegetables, add the milk to the purée. Season to taste and add a little grated nutmeg. Reheat.

6 helpings
Cooking time—1½ hr.

FRENCH or RUNNER BEAN SOUP

Potage aux Haricots Verts

1 lb. young beans
¼ lb. potatoes
1 onion
1 oz. butter
1 pt. water *or* stock
Parsley stalks
A sprig of savory
Salt and pepper
¼ pt. milk

Proceed as for Basic Recipe (p. 101), cooking the beans, onion and potatoes in the stock for 30 min. at the longest, before sieving. Serve with diamond-shaped sections of beans cooked separately then added to the soup at the end.

4 helpings
Cooking time—40 min.

GREEN PEA SOUP

Purée de Petits Pois

1½ lb. green peas in the pod
1 onion
½ oz. butter
1 pt. white stock
A few leaves of spinach
A sprig of mint
A few parsley stalks
Cornflour
Salt and pepper
Sugar to taste
Green colouring, if needed
⅛ pt. cream *or* ⅛ pt. milk

Shell the peas, wash ½ the shells, slice the onion. Melt the butter in a deep pan and cook the washed pods and onion very gently for 10 min. Add the stock and bring to boiling point, add the spinach leaves, the peas and the herbs. Simmer only long enough to cook the peas, from 10–20 min. Sieve and measure the soup. For every 1 pt. of soup blend ½ oz. cornflour with a little cold milk, stock or water and stir into the soup. Cook until the soup is thickened, season carefully, add sugar to taste and colouring, if required. If cream is used stir in at boiling point off the heat. A few small cooked peas and a few blobs of cream may be added to the cooked soup.

4 helpings
Cooking time—30 min.

GUMBO SOUP (AMERICAN OKRA SOUP)

1 pt. *or* 1 medium can okra
2 large tomatoes
A few scraps of bacon *or* bacon bone
Parsley stalks
¼ pt. Lima *or* fresh haricot beans
1½ pt. brown stock
Salt and pepper
Chopped parsley

Slice the okra pods and cook them with the sliced tomatoes, bacon, parsley stalks and the beans in boiling stock until tender. Rub through a hair or nylon sieve; reheat and season. Sprinkle with chopped parsley.

NOTE: See Okra in Vegetable section.

4 helpings
Cooking time—½ hr.

LEEK SOUP

Potage aux Poireaux

1 lb. thick white leeks
¾ lb. potatoes
½ oz. butter *or* margarine
1 pt. stock *or* water
½ pt. milk
Salt and pepper
⅛ pt. cream (optional)
1 egg yolk (optional)

Proceed as for Basic Recipe (p. 101). The potatoes provide sufficient starch thickening. The leeks should be cut into ½-in. lengths to make sieving easier.

4–5 helpings
Cooking time—¾–1 hr.

LETTUCE SOUP

Purée de Laitue

1 lb. lettuce
1 onion
½ lb. potatoes
1 clove of garlic
1 pt. white stock (p. 79)
½ oz. butter
1 bay leaf
1 blade of mace
1 clove
Salt and pepper
Sugar
¼ pt. milk *or* ¼ pt. cream and 1 egg yolk

Shred the lettuce, slice the onion and potatoes, crush the garlic. Pour boiling stock on to the lettuce. Cook the onion, potato and garlic, gently in the butter for 10 min. Add the stock, lettuce, spices and salt and simmer till the lettuce is tender. Sieve, stir the milk (if used) into the purée; reheat, season carefully and add sugar to taste. If cream and egg yolk are used, mix them together, stir into the soup which should be below boiling point. Stir over gentle heat till the egg yolk thickens—but do not boil. Serve immediately.

4 helpings
Cooking time—20–40 min.

MUSHROOM CREAM SOUP

Crème aux Champignons

½ lb. mushrooms
1 onion
1 clove of garlic
2 oz. butter
¾ pt. water *or* white stock
A little yeast *or* meat extract
¾ pt. milk
1 oz. flour
Salt and pepper
¼ pt. cream (optional)
1 egg yolk (optional)

Proceed as for Basic Recipe (p. 101), cooking the whole mushrooms till tender then chopping them and returning them to the soup before thickening it.

6 helpings
Cooking time—30–45 min.

NETTLE SOUP

1 lb. nettle tops
A few leaves of sorrel *or* spinach
1 onion
1 oz. butter
1½ pt. stock
Salt and pepper
Lemon juice
¼ pt. milk *or* cream

Proceed as for Basic Recipe (p. 101).

4–6 helpings
Cooking time—½ hr.

ONION SOUP

Purée aux Oignons

3 large Spanish onions (about 2 lb.)
1 oz. butter *or* margarine *or* dripping
1 qt. white stock *or* 1 pt. stock and 1 pt. milk
1 clove
1 bay leaf
1 blade of mace
Flour to thicken
Salt and pepper
¼ pt. milk *or* cream

Peel and slice the onions. Melt the fat in a deep pan and lightly fry the onions for 10 min., cook slowly to prevent the onions colouring. Boil the stock, add it to the onions with the spices, and simmer until the onions are tender. Rub through a fine sieve, return the purée to the pan and add milk if used. To each 1 pt. of soup allow ½ oz. flour, blend the flour with a little cold milk, water or stock and stir into the soup. Cook until the soup thickens, season to taste. If cream is used, add it to the soup before serving.

NOTE: For Brown Onion soup use brown stock and brown the onions very slowly in the fat (about 20 min.) before adding the stock.

6 helpings
Cooking time—1–1½ hr.

PARSNIP SOUP

Purée de Panais

2 lb. parsnips
2 onions
2 sticks of celery
1 oz. butter *or* margarine *or* dripping
1 qt. white stock
1 bay leaf
1 blade of mace
Lemon juice
¼ pt. milk
Cornflour to thicken
Salt and pepper

Proceed as for Basic Recipe (p. 101).

6 helpings
Cooking time—1¼ hr.

PEA POD SOUP

2 lb. pea pods
1 sliced onion
A few sprigs of mint and parsley
1½ pt. white stock *or* water
¾ oz. flour
¾ oz. butter *or* margarine
Salt and pepper
Sugar to taste
4 tablesp. small, cooked peas
Chopped mint

Wash the pods, and boil them with the onion, mint and parsley in the stock until the outer flesh of the pods is soft. Cook the flour in the butter for 2–3 min. without browning it. Sieve the pulp from the pea-pods. Stir the purée into the butter and flour and bring to boiling point. Season and sugar to taste. Just before serving, add the cooked peas and the chopped mint.

4 helpings
Cooking time—20 min.

PIMENTO SOUP

3–4 sweet red peppers
1 qt. stock
1 onion
1–2 tomatoes
Salt
Cayenne pepper
Cornflour
Sugar

Simmer the peppers in the stock with the sliced onion and tomatoes till soft. Rub them through a hair or nylon sieve. Season, thicken with ½ oz. cornflour to each 1 pt. of soup blended with a little cold milk, stock or water. Stir the cornflour paste into the soup, reheat and add sugar to taste.

4–6 helpings
Cooking time—20 min.

POTATO SOUP

2 lb. potatoes
2 onions *or* the white of 2 leeks
2 sticks of celery
2 oz. dripping, bacon fat *or* margarine
1 qt. white stock *or* water
A bunch of herbs
¼ pt. milk
Salt and pepper
Grated nutmeg

Proceed as for Basic Recipe (p. 101). No added starch thickening is needed.

4–6 helpings
Cooking time—¾–1 hr.

ST. GERMAIN SOUP

As for Green Pea Soup (p. 105). Add 1 clove of garlic, 1 diced carrot and 1 diced small potato with the peas and herbs. Thicken with cream and cornflour.

SAUERKRAUT SOUP

Purée de Chou Croute

1 lb. sauerkraut (or medium-sized can)
1 qt. stock *or* water
½ lb. potatoes
A few scraps of fat bacon and bacon rinds
1 oz. mushrooms *or* left-over mushroom stalks and peelings from another dish
1 bay leaf
1 blade of mace
Salt and pepper
A pinch of sugar
2 sausages—preferably Frankfurter
⅛ pt. cream (optional)
Grated cheese

Boil the stock, and add to it the sauerkraut, sliced potatoes, bacon, mushrooms, spices and salt. Simmer for ¾ hr. or until the sauerkraut is quite soft. Rub through a sieve. Reheat, adding the sugar and seasoning and the sausages cut into ¼-in. thick rounds. Simmer the soup 15–20 min. until the sausage is cooked. Add the cream if liked. Sprinkle cheese on top or serve separately.

6 helpings **Cooking time—1 hr. 20 min.**

SORREL SOUP

Purée d'Oscille

½ lb. sorrel leaves
¼ lb. lettuce *or* spinach leaves *or* turnip tops
1 onion
½ lb. potatoes
1 oz. butter
1 qt. stock *or* water
Salt and pepper
⅛–¼ pt. cream (optional)

Shred the leaves; chop the onion; slice the potatoes. Melt the butter in a deep pan and gently fry the leaves, onion and potatoes for 10 min. (*see* p. 101). Boil the stock and pour over the vegetables; simmer for 10–15 min. Rub through a hair or nylon sieve, season to taste and reheat. If cream is used, stir in just before serving.

4–6 helpings **Cooking time—20–25 min.**

SPINACH SOUP

Purée d'Épinards

2 lb. spinach
1 small onion
1 oz. butter
1 qt. white *or* bone stock
¼ pt. milk
Cornflour to thicken
Salt and pepper
Green colouring
¼ pt. cream (optional)
1 egg yolk (optional)

Shred the spinach, chop the onion, and fry lightly in the melted butter (*see* p. 101) for 10 min. Boil the stock and pour over the spinach and onion; simmer for 10 min. Rub through a hair or nylon sieve, add the milk to the purée. Measure the soup and thicken with ½ oz. cornflour to each 1 pt. of soup, blended with a little cold milk, stock or water. Stir the cornflour paste into the soup, reheat and season to taste, colour if liked. If either cream or egg yolk is used, stir in below boiling point, reheat until egg is cooked but do not allow to boil.

4–6 helpings
Cooking time—25 min.

SPRING PURÉE

Purée Printanière

1 pt. shelled green peas
Pea pods from above
A few heads of asparagus
A few leaves of lettuce, of spinach and watercress
½ lb. potatoes
6 young spring onions
6 young carrots
½ oz. butter *or* margarine
1 qt. stock
¼ pt. milk
Salt and pepper
⅛ pt. cream (optional)
1 egg yolk (optional)

GARNISH

Chopped parsley
Chopped chives

As for Basic Recipe (p. 101). Add the stock boiling and cook the vegetables in it for 20 min. at most. Add chopped parsley and chives to the finished soup.

4–6 helpings
Cooking time—30 min.

TOMATO SOUP

Purée de Tomate

1 lb. tomatoes fresh *or* canned
1 onion
1 carrot
½ oz. margarine
1 oz. bacon scraps, rind *or* bone
1 pt. white stock *or* juice from canned tomatoes
Grated nutmeg
Lemon juice
A bunch of herbs
Minute tapioca *or* cornflour
Salt and pepper
Sugar
Red colouring, if needed

Slice the tomatoes, onion and carrot. If canned tomatoes are used, strain them and make the juice up to 1 pt. with stock. Melt the margarine in a deep pan and lightly fry the sliced vegetables and chopped bacon for 10 min. Boil the stock or tomato juice and add to the vegetables with the nutmeg, lemon juice and herbs and cook for ¾–1 hr. Sieve and thicken the soup with ½ oz. cornflour or minute tapioca to each 1 pt. soup, blended with a little cold milk, stock or water. Stir into the soup, cook till clear, season, add sugar to taste and colouring if needed.

4 helpings
Cooking time—¾–1 hr.

TURNIP SOUP

Purée de Navets

1 lb. turnips *or* swedes
1 onion
1 oz. butter *or* margarine *or* dripping
1 pt. stock
Bunch of herbs
¼ pt. milk
Flour
Salt and pepper
Nutmeg

Proceed as for Basic Recipe (p. 101).

4 helpings
Cooking time—1 hr.

VEGETABLE CREAM SOUP

Crème de Légumes

2 lb. mixed vegetables: onions, carrots, turnip, leeks, 1 tomato, 2 medium potatoes
1 oz. butter, margarine *or* dripping
1 qt. stock *or* water
1 teasp. yeast *or* meat extract if water is used
A bunch of herbs
¼ pt. milk
1 oz. flour to each qt. of sieved soup
Salt and pepper
¼ pt. cream (optional)
2 egg yolks (optional)

Proceed as for Basic Recipe (p. 101).

6–8 helpings
Cooking time—1 hr.

VEGETABLE MARROW SOUP

Purée de Courge

1 lb. marrow after peeling and removing seeds	**1 pt. white stock**
2 onions	**A bunch of herbs**
1 stick of celery	**1 blade of mace**
1 oz. margarine	**¼ pt. milk**
	Cornflour to thicken
	Salt and pepper

Proceed as for Basic Recipe (p. 101).

4–6 helpings **Cooking time—30 min.**

WATERCRESS CREAM SOUP

Potage Cressonnière

½ lb. watercress	**¼ pt. milk**
1 oz. butter *or* margarine	**Salt**
1 pt. white stock	**Cayenne pepper**
½ oz. cornflour	**⅛ pt. cream**

Plunge the cress into boiling water, drain and chop it. Melt the fat and in it cook the watercress very gently for 2–3 min., then rub it through a nylon sieve. Thicken the stock with the cornflour blended with the milk, into this whisk the watercress and butter purée. Season, reheat and add the cream.

4 helpings **Cooking time—10 min.**

PULSE PURÉES

BUTTER BEAN PURÉE

6 oz. butter beans	**1 medium-sized potato**
1 qt. water *or* bone stock	**½ oz. bacon fat**
A few scraps of bacon *or* a bacon bone *or* a few bacon rinds	**A bunch of herbs**
1 onion	**1 blade of mace**
2 sticks of celery	**½ pt. milk**
½ small turnip	**Salt and pepper**

Wash the beans, boil the stock or water. Soak the beans in the stock or water all night. Chop the bacon and slice the vegetables. Melt the fat in a deep pan and fry the bacon, onion, celery, turnip and potato very gently for 10 min. Add the water or stock, beans, herbs and mace; bring all to boiling point and simmer for 2 hr. or until the beans are quite soft. Remove the herbs, sieve the vegetables and stir the milk into the purée. No starch thickening, other than the potato, should be needed. Reheat and season carefully.

6 helpings **Cooking time—2½ hr.**

GROUND-NUT or PEA-NUT SOUP

1 lb. shelled peanuts	**¼ pt. unsweetened evaporated milk *or* ¼ pt. milk and 1 egg yolk *or* ¼ pt. cream**
1 pt. white *or* chicken stock	**A little yeast extract**
	Salt and pepper

Roast the peanuts sprinkled with a little salt until golden brown and crisp. Pound, crush or pass them through a nut or vegetable mill. Boil the stock and in it simmer the milled nuts for ½ hr. Rub through a wire sieve. Add the evaporated milk or milk and egg and reheat, adding yeast extract and seasoning. If cream is used add it at boiling point, off the heat.

4–6 helpings

Cooking time—35 min.

HARICOT BEAN SOUP

See Butter Bean Purée.

HARICOT BEAN AND TOMATO SOUP

6 oz. haricot beans	**½ oz. butter *or* margarine *or* bacon fat**
1½ pt. water *or* ½ water and ½ stock	**Salt and pepper**
½ lb. tomatoes	**A bunch of herbs**
1 onion	**1 bay leaf**
1 carrot	**1 blade of mace**
1 medium-sized potato	

Wash the beans and soak them in water overnight. Drain, and put them in a pan with the 1½ pt. water, bring to boil and simmer for 1 hr. Meanwhile slice the tomatoes, onion, carrot and potato. Melt the fat and gently fry the sliced vegetables for 10 min. Add the fried vegetables to the beans with the herbs, bay leaf and mace, and simmer until the beans are quite soft. Remove the herbs, rub soup through a fine wire sieve; reheat and season.

6 helpings

Cooking time—2–2½ hr.

LENTIL SOUP

Purée de Lentilles

As for Butter Bean Purée (p. 109), substituting red Egyptian or brown lentils, and including carrot with the flavouring vegetables.

Cooking time—Egyptian lentils 1½ hr.
Brown lentils 2½ hr.

PEA SOUP

Purée de Pois Secs

As for Butter Bean Puree (p. 109), using dried, whole or split peas and adding a sprig of mint or a little dried mint.

Cooking time—2 hr. (after 12 hr. soaking)

THICKENED SOUPS

ALMOND CREAM SOUP

Potage à la Crème D'Amandes

2 oz. almonds *or* ground almonds
1 pt. white stock (p. 79)
2 tablesp. breadcrumbs
½ oz. butter
½ oz. flour
Salt and pepper *or* cayenne
Lemon juice
3 drops almond essence
2 tablesp. cream

Blanch the almonds, dry and toast them until light golden brown. Put them through a nut mill. If ground almonds are used, toast them as for whole almonds. Stew the milled or ground almonds in the stock until soft, add the crumbs and stew for 10 min. Rub the soup through a wire sieve. Melt the fat, stir in the flour, then the almond and crumb purée. Add the stock and stir the soup till it boils. Season and flavour carefully. Add the cream just at boiling point.

Serve the soup at once.

4 helpings **Cooking time—about 1 hr.**

BONNE FEMME SOUP

Potage Bonne Femme

½ lettuce, a few leaves of sorrel, chervil, watercress *or* tarragon *or* a mixture of these, 1½ in. length cucumber; to make ¼ pt. in all
½ oz. butter
1 qt. white stock
½ oz. flour
¼ pt. milk
Salt and pepper
Lemon juice
2 egg yolks
⅛ pt. cream

Shred the lettuce and other leaves finely. Cut the cucumber into match-like strips. Melt the butter in a deep pan and fry the vegetables very gently for 3 min. Add the stock, boiling, to the vegetables and simmer for 10 min. Blend the flour with ½ the milk, stir this into the soup and cook till the flour thickens. Season very carefully, add lemon juice to taste and cook slightly. Mix the remaining milk with the egg yolks and cream, add these to the cooked soup and cook till the egg yolks thicken, but do not allow to boil.

Serve at once.

6 helpings
Cooking time—20 min.

CABBAGE SOUP

Potage aux Choux

1 lb. young cabbage with a good heart
1 onion
2 oz. fat bacon rashers
1 clove of garlic (optional)
1 large tomato
1½ pt. stock *or* vegetable boilings *or* water in which mild pickled pork *or* bacon has been cooked
A few caraway or dill seeds (optional)
1 oz. minute tapioca
Salt and pepper
A very little grated horseradish
½ pt. milk *or* 1 bottle yoghourt

Wash, dry and shred the cabbage; chop the onion and the bacon; crush the garlic, skin and chop the tomato. In a deep pan fry the bacon slowly until the fat runs freely, add the shredded vegetables and shake them over gentle heat for 5 min. Add the stock, boiling, caraway seeds if used, and simmer until the cabbage is very soft. Sprinkle and stir in the tapioca and cook it till clear and soft. Season and flavour to taste. Stir in the milk *or* yoghourt and reheat without boiling.

Serve with grated cheese handed separately.

6 helpings
Cooking time—about 40 min.

EGG SOUP

Potage à la Royale

1 oz. macaroni
¾ oz. butter
¾ oz. flour
1½ pt. stock
Trace of nutmeg
1 bay leaf
A little yeast *or* meat extract
Salt and cayenne pepper
2 egg yolks
⅛ pt. milk
⅛ pt. cream

Boil the macaroni until very soft, cut it into ¼-in. lengths. Melt the butter, stir in the flour, then the stock and bring to the boil. Add the spices, yeast or meat extract and the macaroni and season the soup. Mix the egg yolks, milk and cream and add to the soup well below boiling point. Cook the egg yolks without allowing the soup to boil.

Serve with grated cheese.

6 helpings

HOLLANDAISE SOUP

Potage Hollandaise

Carrot
Cucumber
2 tablesp. small green peas
¾ oz. butter
¾ oz. flour
1½ pt. white stock
2 egg yolks
⅛ pt. milk
⅛ pt. cream
Salt and pepper
Chopped tarragon

Cut out 2 tablesp. each of pea shapes of carrot and cucumber. Cook the vegetables in a little boiling stock till just tender. Melt the fat in a deep pan and stir in the flour, then the stock. Boil the stock till the flour is completely cooked, then cool it. Mix the egg yolks, milk and cream and stir them into the hot soup. Cook the egg yolks without boiling. Season and add the chopped tarragon and the cooked vegetables.

6 helpings
Cooking time—about 20 min.

MILK SOUP WITH ONION

1 Spanish onion *or* 3 medium-sized onions
¾ oz. butter *or* other fat
¾ oz. flour *or* rice
1 pt. milk
1 bay leaf
1 clove
1 blade of mace
A little grated lemon rind
Salt and pepper
2 tablesp. sherry (optional)

Melt the fat in a deep pan and cook the finely-chopped onion gently for 10 min. Sprinkle and stir in the flour, add the milk and boil. Add the spices and lemon rind; simmer till the onion is just tender. Season and add sherry (if used) before serving.

NOTE: If rice is used add it instead of the flour and cook it in the soup.

4 helpings
Cooking time—about ¾ hr.

VELVET SOUP

1 rounded teasp. curry powder
1 oz. flour
1 oz. butter
1 pt. milk
2 tablesp. boiled Patna rice
Salt and pepper
2 tablesp. cream

In a saucepan fry the curry powder and flour in the butter for a few minutes. Add the milk and boil the soup; stir and simmer for 5 min. Cook the rice separately and add it to the hot soup; season to taste. Remove soup from heat and stir in the cream.

4 helpings
Cooking time—10 min.

WHITE VEGETABLE SOUP

½ pt. fine shreds of carrot, turnip and green leek
¾ oz. butter *or* margarine
1 pt. stock *or* water
Salt and pepper
Lemon rind
Lemon juice
¾ oz. flour
½ pt. milk
1 egg yolk
⅛ pt. cream

Cut the vegetables into match-like strips not more than 1½ in. long. Melt the fat in a deep pan and cook the shreds of vegetable very gently for 5 min. Add the stock or water (boiling) and simmer very gently for 5 min. Season, and add a trace of grated lemon rind and a few drops of juice. Blend the flour with ½ the milk, stir this into the soup and simmer for a minute or two then cool the soup. Mix the egg yolk, cream and remaining milk, stir these into the cooled soup and cook the egg yolk without boiling it. Serve the soup at once.

4–6 helpings
Cooking time—15 min.

WINTER SOUP

1 onion
1 leek
1 oz. dripping *or* bacon fat
1 carrot
½ turnip
½ good cabbage
A bunch of herbs
A trace of nutmeg
A little yeast- *or* meat extract
1 pt. stock *or* water
1 oz. rice
1 pt. milk
Salt and pepper

Chop the onion and leek; melt the dripping in a deep pan and cook them with the grated carrot and turnip until they begin to brown. Lower the heat, add the cabbage (shredded) the herbs, nutmeg, yeast- or meat-extract and cook gently for 3 min. Add the stock (boiling) and the rice and simmer till the vegetables are soft. Remove the herbs, add the milk and reheat the soup. Season carefully and serve.

Serve with grated cheese handed separately.

6 helpings **Cooking time—about ¾ hr.**

UNCLASSIFIED, NATIONAL OR REGIONAL SOUPS

BASQUE CABBAGE AND BEAN SOUP

¼ lb. haricot beans
2 onions
½ lb. white cabbage
1 oz. pork *or* bacon fat
1 clove of garlic
1 qt. water
Salt and pepper
A few drops of vinegar

Soak the beans overnight in the water. Slice the onion, shred the cabbage. In a deep pan fry the onions very slowly till brown, in the fat, add the cabbage and shake the pan over gentle heat for a few minutes. Add the crushed garlic, the beans and water. Simmer the soup for 3-4 hr. until the beans are quite soft. Season and add a few drops of vinegar.

4-6 helpings **Cooking time—3-4 hr.**

BORTSCH, POLISH or RUSSIAN BEETROOT SOUP

4 raw beetroots
1 qt. brown stock
1 onion stuck with 1 clove
Bunch of herbs
A few caraway seeds
1 oz. goose fat *or* bacon fat
Shredded white leek, cabbage, beetroot, celery to make ½ pt. in all
Salt and pepper
Grated nutmeg
¼ pt. sour cream *or* 1 bottle yoghourt

Slice 3 of the beetroots and simmer them in the stock with the onion, clove, herbs and caraway seeds for about 1 hr. or until the colour has run into the soup and the flavour is no longer raw. Melt the fat and in it cook the shreds of vegetable and the finely-grated 4th beetroot very gently for 10–15 min. Strain the stock and press the juice out of the beetroots into it. Add the shreds of vegetable and finish cooking them in the soup. Season, add a trace of nutmeg to the soup. Beat the sour cream or yoghourt into the hot soup but do not allow it to boil; *or* put a spoonful of yoghourt or sour cream into each soup plate before pouring in the soup.

6 helpings
Cooking time—1½ hr.

CARAWAY SOUP—HUNGARIAN

1 oz. bacon *or* pork fat
1 teasp. caraway seeds
1 oz. flour
Salt
1 pt. brown stock

Melt the fat in a deep pan, add the caraway seeds and fry them for a few minutes. Add the flour and a pinch of salt and fry very gently till brown. Add the stock, stir till boiling, then simmer the soup for ½ hr. Strain it and re-season to taste.

3-4 helpings
Cooking time—¾ hr.

CATALAN SOUP

2 oz. bacon
2 Spanish onions
1 sweet pepper
1 stick of celery
2 large potatoes
2 large tomatoes
1 qt. stock
1 glass white wine
Thyme
Parsley
Salt and pepper
Nutmeg
2 egg yolks
⅛ pt. milk

Chop the bacon, slice the onions very thinly. Melt the fat of the bacon in a deep pan and fry the onions and bacon together till golden brown. Slice the pepper and celery very thin, cut the potatoes and skinned tomatoes into thick slices, add them to the pan, shake over gentle heat for 5 min. Add the stock, wine and herbs and boil the soup, then simmer gently for ½–¾ hr. until all the vegetables are soft. Season, add a trace of grated nutmeg, and cook the soup slightly. Mix the egg yolks and milk and stir them into the soup. Cook the egg yolks without boiling.

4–6 helpings
Cooking time—1½ hr.

FRENCH ONION SOUP

2 oz. fat bacon	**¼ pt. white wine *or* cider**
6 medium-sized onions	**6 small slices of bread**
½ oz. flour	**2 oz. cheese: Gruyère *or* Parmesan**
Salt and pepper	**A little butter**
½ teasp. French mustard	
1½ pt. stock	

Chop the bacon and heat it gently in a deep pan till the fat runs freely. Slice the onions thinly and fry them slowly in the bacon fat till golden. Add the flour, salt and pepper to taste and continue frying for a few minutes. Stir in the mustard, the stock and the wine or cider. Simmer till the onions are quite soft. Toast the bread, grate the cheese. Butter the toast and spread the slices with grated cheese. Pour the soup into individual fireproof soup-bowls, float a round of toast on each and brown it in a very hot oven or under the grill.

6 helpings
Cooking time—about 1½ hr.

GOULASH SOUP—HUNGARIAN

1 oz. dripping	**A few bacon rinds**
1 onion	**¼ teasp. caraway seeds**
1 carrot	**1½ pt. water**
1 small parsnip	**Salt and pepper**
8 oz. meat (shin of beef)	**2 potatoes**
1 teasp. paprika	**¼ pt. sour milk *or* yoghourt**
1 tomato	

Melt the fat in a deep pan and fry the sliced onion, carrot and parsnip until they begin to brown. Add the meat in ½ in. cubes, the paprika, the tomato roughly cut up, the bacon rinds and caraway seeds. Heat gently, stirring for a few minutes. Add the water and a pinch of salt and bring very slowly to simmering point. Simmer for 2 hr. Dice the potatoes and add them to the soup; continue simmering for another hour. Remove the bacon rinds. Season soup to taste and stir in the sour milk or yoghourt.

4–6 helpings **Cooking time—3½ hr.**

PISTOU—SOUTH OF FRANCE, GENOA

1 qt. water	**½ lb. vegetable marrow**
1 lb. French beans	**3 cloves of garlic**
2 medium-sized potatoes	**1 dessertsp. olive oil**
2 tomatoes	**A sprig of basil**
4 onions	**Salt and pepper**
2 sweet green peppers	**2 oz. vermicelli**

Boil the water and in it simmer briskly the vegetables cut in neat dice. Meanwhile pound together the garlic, oil and basil. When the vegetables have simmered for 20 min., season the soup and stir in the vermicelli, simmer for 10 more min. Ladle a little of the hot soup on to the garlic, oil and basil and return this mixture to the pan of soup.

Stir until well mixed.

Serve with grated Gruyère cheese handed separately.

6 helpings **Cooking time—½–¾ hr.**

SOUR CHERRY SOUP—SCANDINAVIA

1 lb. morello *or* other acid variety of cherry	**3–4 oz. sugar to taste**
Pinch of cinnamon	**¼ pt. white *or* red wine (optional)**
1 pt. water	**A little lemon rind**
To each pint of sieved soup: ½ oz. cornflour, arrowroot *or* minute tapioca	**Whipped cream (optional)**

Halve the cherries and crack some of the stones. Put the cherries, stones, cinnamon and water into a pan and simmer till the cherries are soft. Rub the fruit through a hair or nylon sieve. Blend the cornflour with a little wine or water and stir it into the soup. Reboil and stir the soup till it thickens. Sweeten, add the wine (if used) and grated lemon rind. The soup may be served hot or iced.

Whipped cream (served separately) makes a delicious accompaniment.

NOTE: Other suitable fruits are **damsons, cranberries**, white or red **currants, apples** *or* **rosehips.**

4 helpings **Cooking time—about 20 min.**

SAUCES, GRAVIES AND FORCEMEATS

THE FRENCH JOKE, now more than a hundred and fifty years old, that the English "are a nation of only one sauce" is as true or untrue now as ever it was. Today, a solitary sauce is more often than not bought ready-made and poured out of a bottle indiscriminately on to hot and cold meat and fish. Perhaps this is better than using the other sauce that makes a good joke—this time an English joke—the sauce likened to "paper-hanger's paste". Both these single sauces are, however, really bad because they make food monotonous, which is exactly what sauces are intended to prevent.

In the days before refrigeration, when meat and fish could not always be obtained fresh, it was frequently necessary to disguise "tainted" or "high" flavours in these foods, and sauces were therefore often hot, vinegary and highly spiced, in fact greatly resembling pickles. Nevertheless, many of the traditional sauces of British cookery are dietetically and gastronomically excellent by modern standards. Mint sauce with lamb, apple sauce with pork and horseradish sauce with beef, to quote only three examples, all provide delightful contrasts without overpowering the flavour of the meats they accompany. Moreover the acids they contain make the digestion of meat proteins easier. These sauces have stood the test of time, as has much of the best of our national cookery, and are still popular today.

The main tendency of modern British cookery is to conserve as much as possible of the natural quality and flavour of foods. It is today therefore held that a sauce should enhance and add to—but never overpower or disguise the flavour of the food with which it is served. Sauces should make the food they accompany both look and taste more delicious and they should if possible add to its food value or make it more digestible.

There is such a large number of sauces to choose from that there is plenty of scope for variety and for originality in the choice of sauce to serve with any food.

GRAVIES

Gravy is really meat essence, usually diluted by washing and stirring round the cooking vessel with a little water, as in the making of gravy to serve with roast meat. Gravy may or may not be thickened according to custom in the accompaniments for different kinds of meat.

In the making of gravy for roast meat it is an excellent modern practice to use the water in which green vegetables have been cooked, the only other addition that is permissible is of a good meat or yeast extract.

FOUNDATION SAUCES—SAVOURY

From the following foundation sauces many variations in flavour, texture and colour can be evolved. In the later alphabetical list of recipes the foundation sauces will be referred to constantly.

1. ENGLISH FOUNDATION SAUCE

WHITE SAUCE

Sauce Blanche

For a coating sauce:

2 oz. butter *or* margarine
2 oz. flour
1 pt. milk *or* fish stock *or* white stock *or* a mixture of stock and milk
Salt and pepper to taste

For a pouring sauce:

1½ oz. butter *or* margarine
1½ oz. flour
1 pt. of liquid as for coating sauce
Salt and pepper to taste

(1) *Roux Method*

Melt the fat in a deep saucepan, large enough to hold the amount of liquid with just enough room to spare for beating the sauce. Stir the flour into the fat and over gentle heat allow it to bubble for 2—3 min. On no account allow it to change colour; this is a White Roux. Remove from heat and stir in ½ the liquid. Return to moderate heat and stir the sauce briskly till it thickens, then beat it vigorously for a minute or two. Stir in the rest of the liquid, always adding the last portion with due regard to the required thickness of the sauce. Boil the sauce for 3 min., beating vigorously. Season and use the sauce at once. If a sauce must be kept hot cover it with wet greaseproof paper and a lid and before use beat it again in case skin or lumps should have formed.

A coating sauce should coat the back of the wooden spoon used for stirring, and should only just settle to its own level in the pan.

A pouring sauce should barely mask the spoon, flow freely, and easily settle to its own level in the pan.

Cooking time—15 min.

(2) *Kneaded Butter and Flour or Beurre Manié*

Knead the butter and flour, or work them together with a fork or spoon until they are quite smoothly mixed.

Heat the liquid, and when just below boiling point, gradually whisk in the kneaded butter and flour. Whisk the sauce until it boils by which time all the thickening must be smoothly blended into the whole. Season and use.

NOTE: Both White Roux and Beurre Manie may be prepared in advance and stored for weeks, if necessary, in a refrigerator or cold larder. To use: allow 4 oz. to 1 pt. for a coating sauce, 3 oz. to 1 pt. for a pouring sauce.

SAUCES MADE FROM WHITE SAUCE FOUNDATION

ANCHOVY SAUCE

Sauce d'Anchois

To ½ pt. white sauce made from fish stock *or* water *or* ½ milk and ½ water add 1 *or* 2 teasp. anchovy essence to taste and a few drops of lemon juice and a few drops of carmine to tint the sauce a dull pink.

Serve with fish.

BRAIN SAUCE

½ pt. white sauce (p. 115) made with the liquid in which sheep's head has been cooked
1–2 cooked onions
1 set of sheep's brains
A little vinegar *or* lemon juice
1 dessertsp. chopped parsley

To cook the brains, soak them in vinegar and water for 1 hr., then simmer them very gently in a little of the stock in which the head is being cooked, for 20–30 min. Chop the onion and brains and add them to the finished sauce with the vinegar and parsley.

CAPER SAUCE

Sauce aux Câpres

To ½ pt. white sauce made with broth from boiled mutton *or* ½ broth and ½ milk, add 1 tablesp. capers and 1 teasp. vinegar in which the capers were pickled.

Serve with boiled mutton or fish.

CELERY SAUCE

Sauce Céléri

6 outside sticks of celery, leaves and all
½ pt. water
Butter
Flour
Seasoning
1–2 tablesp. cream (optional)
1–2 drops lemon juice

Cut the celery in very short lengths, simmer the pieces in the water till quite soft. Rub the celery through a sieve. Make a white sauce (*see* p. 115) with the celery purée for liquid. Cream is an excellent addition, stirred in at boiling point, off the heat.

Serve with mutton or rabbit.

CHEESE SAUCE

To ½ pt. white sauce (p. 115) made with vegetable boilings *or* milk *or* ½ milk and ½ vegetable liquid, add 2 heaped tablesp. grated cheese, seasoning, mixed English *or* French mustard and a grain or two of cayenne pepper.

Add the cheese to the cooked, seasoned sauce at boiling point. Do not reboil the sauce, use at once.

CRAB SAUCE

Sauce de Crabe

½ pt. white sauce made from fish stock in which crabshell, claws and legs have been simmered
Meat from a small cooked crab
Cayenne pepper
Salt
A few drops of lemon juice

Stir the soft crab meat and the chopped white meat into the hot sauce, season, add lemon juice and simmer for 5 min.

DUTCH SAUCE

Sauce Hollandaise

½ pt. white sauce made with milk
1 egg yolk
Lemon juice *or* vinegar

Cool the finished sauce slightly. Stir 1 tablesp. of the cooled sauce into the egg yolk, then beat this mixture into the sauce. Reheat the sauce without allowing it to boil. Add a few drops of lemon juice *or* vinegar.

EGG SAUCE

Sauce aux œufs durs

½ pt. white sauce made with milk
1 hard-boiled egg
1 teasp. chopped chives, if liked

Chop the hard-boiled egg, stir it, with the chives, into the hot, well-seasoned sauce. Reheat the whole.

FENNEL SAUCE

Sauce Fenouil

½ pt. white sauce made with milk *or* fish stock
1 tablesp. chopped green fennel
Lemon juice

Plunge the fennel into boiling water, drain, squeeze dry, chop and add it to the sauce. Add a few drops of lemon juice.

Serve with fish, notably mackerel.

FISH SAUCE

Make a white sauce (p. 115) using concentrated fish stock. A few drops of lemon juice improve the flavour.

FLEMISH SAUCE

½ pt. white sauce made with ½ fish stock and ½ milk
1–2 egg yolks
½ teasp. English mustard *or* 1 dessertsp. French mustard
Lemon juice

Stir a little of the cooled sauce into the egg yolks; beat this mixture with the mixed mustard into the sauce, and cook the egg yolk without boiling. Add lemon juice to taste.

Serve with fish.

HERB SAUCE

½ pt. white sauce
1–2 tablesp. mixed chopped herbs: parsley, chives, tarragon, sorrel, very little thyme, marjoram and savory

Add the chopped herbs to the hot sauce and simmer them for a few minutes.

HOT HORSERADISH SAUCE

Sauce de Raifort Chaude

To ½ pt. white sauce add 1 rounded tablesp. grated horseradish, 1 teasp. vinegar and ½ teasp. sugar.

LEMON SAUCE—SAVOURY

½ pt. white sauce made with chicken *or* fish stock, *or* milk and stock
1 lemon
1–2 tablesp. cream (optional)
1 tablesp. chopped parsley (optional)
½ teasp. sugar (optional)

Peel the rind from the lemon very thinly and simmer it in the milk or stock for 10 min. Strain the liquid and with it make the white sauce. Carefully stir the juice of the lemon and then the cream into the hot sauce but do not boil it again. Sweeten if liked.

Serve with fish, chicken or rabbit.

LIVER SAUCE

½ pt. white sauce made with chicken stock *or* ½ milk and ½ stock
1 chicken liver
Juice and rind of ½ lemon
1 tablesp. chopped parsley

Cook the liver for 20 min. in the pan with the boiling fowl. Remove and chop the liver. Add to the white sauce with the finely grated lemon rind and simmer the sauce for a few minutes. Just before serving add the lemon juice and parsley.

Serve with boiled chicken.

MAÎTRE D'HÔTEL SAUCE

½ pt. white sauce made with milk *or* fish stock
1 rounded tablesp. very finely-chopped parsley
Juice of ½ lemon
1 oz. butter

Add the lemon juice and chopped parsley to the hot sauce. Whisk the extra butter into the sauce just below boiling point, adding it a small pat at a time.

Serve mainly with fish or with poultry.

MELTED BUTTER SAUCE

Sauce au Beurre

To ½ pt. white sauce (which may be savoury or sweet) made with milk or water, add flavouring as desired. Whisk an extra ounce of butter into the sauce just below boiling point, a small pat at a time.

Serve with fish, poultry, rabbit and certain vegetables.

MUSHROOM SAUCE—WHITE

Sauce aux Champignons

½ pt. white sauce
2–4 oz. mushrooms
½–1 oz. butter

Cook the thinly sliced mushrooms very gently in the butter for 15–20 min. Stir the mushrooms with the butter and their juice into the hot sauce.

Serve with fish and meat entrées, poultry etc.

MUSTARD SAUCE

Sauce Moutarde

½ pt. sauce made with meat *or* fish stock, milk *or* milk and stock
1 teasp. dry English mustard *or* 1 tablesp. French mustard
1 teasp. tarragon vinegar
1 teasp. sugar
½–1 oz. butter

Mix the dry mustard with the vinegar. Whisk the mixed mustard and sugar into the hot sauce. Whisk the butter into the sauce just below boiling point, adding it a small pat at a time.

Serve with boiled beef, herring or mackerel.

ONION SAUCE—WHITE

Sauce aux Oignons

To ½ pt. white sauce made from ½ milk and ½ liquor in which onions were boiled, add 2 chopped, cooked onions and a few drops of lemon juice.

Serve with mutton, rabbit or tripe.

OYSTER SAUCE

Sauce aux Huîtres

½ pt. white sauce made with fish stock
6 oysters, fresh *or* canned
Liquor from the oysters
Salt and pepper
Lemon juice

For fresh oysters: strain the liquor from the deep shell, beard the oysters, drop them into the boiling fish stock and simmer them with the lid on the pan very gently 20–30 min., do not allow to boil. Strain the stock and with it make the white sauce. Cut the oysters into 3–4 pieces each and return them to the sauce. Season and add lemon juice. For canned oysters: cut the oysters in 3–4 pieces and add them, together with the liquid from the can, to very thick white sauce. Season and add lemon juice.

Serve with fish.

PARSLEY SAUCE

Sauce de Persil

½ pt. white sauce made with stock, fish stock *or* water
1 heaped tablesp. finely-chopped parsley
1 oz. butter

Add the chopped parsley to the boiling sauce, then whisk in the butter, a small pat at a time, at just below boiling point.

Serve with fish, white meat or vegetables.

ROE SAUCE

Sauce Laitence

½ pt. white sauce made with ½ fish stock and ½ milk
½ lb. cod's roe
½ teasp. mixed mustard
1 teasp. anchovy essence
1 dessertsp. vinegar *or* lemon juice

Poach the roe in a very little salted water. This water may be used in the sauce. Skin the roe and crush it with the back of a wooden spoon, working into it the mustard, anchovy essence and vinegar or juice and finally the white sauce. Reheat and simmer the sauce for 10 min.

Serve with fish.

SHRIMP SAUCE

Sauce aux Crevettes

To ½ pt. white sauce made with ½ fish stock and ½ milk, add ¼ pt. picked *or* canned shrimps and a few drops of anchovy essence and lemon juice to taste. Season with cayenne pepper.

Serve with fish.

SORREL SAUCE—WHITE

Sauce à l'Oseille

½ pt. white sauce made with ½ stock and ½ milk
A good handful of sorrel leaves
½ oz. butter
Salt and pepper
Nutmeg
2 tablesp. cream (optional)

Cut the sorrel into shreds, gently cook it in the butter and rub it through a hair or nylon sieve. Whisk this purée into the finished sauce at boiling point, season and add a trace of ground nutmeg. Stir in the cream, do not re-boil.

Serve with fish or poultry; without cream serve it with goose.

SOYER SAUCE

½ pt. white sauce made with fish stock	**Lemon juice**
2 shallots	**1–2 egg yolks**
½ oz. butter	**2 tablesp. cream**
1 tablesp. finely-chopped herbs: thyme, marjoram, tarragon, fennel, sorrel, parsley	

Finely chop the shallots and cook them gently in the butter till soft; add these to the sauce. Add herbs and lemon juice to the sauce and reheat for 2–3 min. Cool the sauce; mix a little cool sauce with the egg yolks and cream; stir into the sauce.

VENETIAN SAUCE

½ pt. white wine sauce (*see* below)	**1 teasp. chopped chervil**
6 tablesp. tarragon vinegar	**1 teasp. chopped tarragon**
2 shallots	

Reduce the tarragon vinegar with the finely-chopped shallots to ½ its volume, strain it. Add this flavoured vinegar, then the herbs, to the hot white wine sauce.

Serve with chicken, veal *or* fish.

NOTE: This sauce may also be made with Béchamel foundation.

WHITE WINE SAUCE

Sauce au Vin Blanc

½ pt. white stock *or* fish stock	**⅛ pt. white wine**
2 oz. butter	**1–2 egg yolks**
1 oz. flour	**Juice of ½ lemon**
	Salt and pepper

Make a white sauce with the stock, ½ the butter and the flour. To this add the wine and simmer it for 10 min. Whisk in the remaining butter just below boiling point, then stir in the egg yolks mixed with lemon juice; season. Thicken the egg yolks without boiling.

Serve with fish or white meat.

XAVIER SAUCE

½ pt. white sauce made from fish stock	**A few leaves of fennel *or* tarragon**
½ bunch of watercress	**A few drops of lemon juice**

Plunge the watercress and leaves into boiling water, drain, dry and chop them. Stir the chopped leaves into the hot sauce and simmer for a minute or two. Add lemon juice to taste.

Serve with fish.

2. ENGLISH FOUNDATION SAUCE

BROWN SAUCE

Sauce Brune

1 small carrot	**1 oz. flour**
1 onion	**1 pt. household stock**
1 oz. dripping	**Salt and pepper**

Thinly slice the carrot and onion. Melt the dripping and in it slowly fry the onion and carrot until they are golden brown. Stir in the flour and fry it even more slowly till it is also golden brown. Stir in the stock, bring to simmering point, season then simmer for ½ hr. Strain the sauce before use. As the frying of the flour is a long process extra colour may be given to the sauce by adding a piece of brown onion skin, or a little gravy browning or a little meat or vegetable extract which will also add to the flavour.

Cooking time—40 min.–1 hr.

SAUCES MADE FROM BROWN SAUCE FOUNDATION

CHRISTOPHER NORTH'S SAUCE

¼ pt. brown sauce in which mushroom trimmings have been cooked	**½ glass port**
2–3 tablesp. juices from roast game	**Castor sugar to taste**
1 dessertsp. mushroom ketchup	**Cayenne pepper to taste**
	1 tablesp. lemon juice
	¼ teasp. salt

Heat all these ingredients together in a double saucepan. The sauce must on no account boil.

Serve with meat or game.

CIDER SAUCE

Sauce au Cidre

½ pt. brown sauce
¼ pt. cider
½ bay leaf
½ clove
Salt and pepper

Mix all the ingredients and simmer the sauce to reduce it to the required thickness. Strain the sauce.

Serve with braised ham, pork or duck.

GENEVA SAUCE

Sauce Génevoise

½ pt. brown sauce made with fish stock
2 oz. mushrooms
½ glass sherry *or* **Madeira**
1 teasp. lemon juice
1 teasp. anchovy essence

Wash, peel if necessary, and slice the mushrooms. Add them with the stock when making the brown sauce. After straining the sauce, chop the mushrooms and return them to the sauce. Simmer the wine with the sauce for 10 min. Add the other flavourings.

Serve with fish.

GHERKIN SAUCE

Sauce aux Cornichons

To ½ pt. brown sauce add 1 tablesp. chopped gherkins, 1 tablesp. gherkin vinegar and sugar to taste.

Serve with meat and poultry entrées or grills.

HAM SAUCE

Sauce au Jambon

½ pt. brown sauce
2 oz. lean cooked ham
3 shallots *or* **1 tablesp. chopped chives**
½ oz. butter
Juice of ½ lemon
Pepper
1 tablesp. chopped parsley

Melt the butter and in it gently cook the onions or chives (chopped finely) for 10 min. Add the ham and heat for a few minutes. Stir in the brown sauce, lemon juice, pepper to taste and when boiling add the parsley.

Serve with fried or grilled meat.

KIDNEY SAUCE

Sauce aux Rognons

2–4 oz. ox kidney
½ pt. brown sauce

Remove any fat and skin, cut the kidney in small pieces and fry it for a few minutes before frying the vegetables and flour for the brown sauce. Remove the kidney from the fat as soon as it is brown. Return it to the sauce when the liquid has been added and simmer it with the other ingredients.

MUSHROOM SAUCE—BROWN

Sauce aux Champignons

½ pt. brown sauce
2–4 oz. mushrooms

Fry the mushroom stalks with the other vegetables when making the brown sauce (p. 119). Add the mushroom skins and the sliced mushrooms with the stock when making the sauce, and simmer them for ½ hr. Strain the sauce, lift out and chop the mushrooms and return them to the sauce.

NOTE: This sauce may also be made with Espagnole sauce foundation.

ONION SAUCE—BROWN

Sauce Miroton

½ pt. brown sauce (p. 119) using 2 medium-sized onions (chopped) and omitting the carrot
Nutmeg
Salt and pepper
1 teasp. wine vinegar
½ teasp. French *or* **mixed mustard**

Make the sauce in the usual way. Do not strain it. Add nutmeg, vinegar and mustard at the end of cooking. Season to taste.

PARISIAN SAUCE

Sauce Parisienne

½ pt. brown sauce
2 shallots
½ oz. butter
1 teasp. meat glaze *or* **good meat extract**
1 teasp. lemon juice
1 dessertsp. chopped parsley

Chop the shallots and cook them gently in the butter until quite soft. Add the sauce, glaze and lemon juice, and reheat. Stir in the chopped parsley and serve the sauce.

Serve with fried steak or chops.

PIQUANT SAUCE

Sauce Piquante

½ pt. brown sauce
1 onion *or* 2 shallots
1 oz. mushrooms
1 bay leaf
1 blade of mace
2 tablesp. vinegar
1 tablesp. halved capers
1 tablesp. chopped gherkins
1 dessertsp. mushroom ketchup
½ teasp. sugar (optional)

Finely chop the onion or shallots, chop the mushrooms coarsely. Simmer the onion or shallots, the bay leaf and mace in the vinegar for 10 min. Add this mixture and the chopped mushrooms to the brown sauce and simmer till the mushrooms are soft. Add all the other ingredients. Do not strain the sauce but lift out bay leaf and mace.

Serve with pork, mutton or vegetables.

NOTE: This sauce may also be made with Espagnole foundation.

ROBERT SAUCE

Sauce Robert

½ pt. brown sauce
1 small onion
½ oz. butter
¼ teasp. mixed mustard
½ teasp. sugar
⅛ pt. white wine

Chop the onion and fry it till golden brown in the butter. Add the mustard, sugar and wine and simmer for 10 min. Add the sauce and cook it for 10 min. more.

Serve with roast or grilled beef, mutton, pork or goose.

NOTE: This sauce may also be made from Espagnole foundation.

SAGE AND ONION SAUCE

Sauce au Sauge

½ pt. brown sauce
2 onions
1 oz. butter *or* pork *or* goose dripping
½ teasp. chopped fresh sage
1 tablesp. fresh crumbs

The onions may either be boiled till tender and then chopped, or chopped fine and cooked very gently till quite tender, but not brown, in the fat. Add onion, sage and crumbs to the brown sauce and cook it gently for a further 10 min.

Serve with pork, goose or duck.

SORREL SAUCE—BROWN

Sauce l'Oseille

½ pt. brown sauce
1 qt. sorrel leaves
½ oz. butter
Salt and pepper
Lemon juice to taste
Sugar to taste

Chop the sorrel, cook it with the butter and a few spoonfuls of water until tender. Rub the sorrel through a hair or nylon sieve. Add the sieved sorrel and its juice to the hot brown sauce, reheat and season the sauce, add sugar and lemon juice to taste. Serve at once.

Serve with goose.

WALNUT SAUCE

Sauce aux Noix

To ½ pt. brown sauce add 4 pickled walnuts, 1 tablesp. walnut vinegar and sugar to taste (optional).

MISCELLANEOUS, UNCLASSIFIED SAUCES

AGRO-DOLCE

Bitter-sweet Sauce

1 onion
1 carrot
1 clove of garlic (optional)
1 bay leaf
6 peppercorns
1 tablesp. olive oil
¼ pt. red wine
⅛ pt. wine vinegar
2 oz. sugar
2 tablesp. water
¼ pt. good meat gravy

SWEETENING

Any one or any mixture of the following to taste: 1 teasp. chopped mint; 1 teasp. finely-shredded candied orange peel; 1 dessertsp. chopped nuts; 1 dessertsp. sultanas; 1 tablesp. grated bitter chocolate

Chop the onion and carrot, crush the garlic. Cook them with the bay leaf and peppercorns very gently in the oil for 15–20 min. Drain off the oil and add the wine and vinegar. Simmer gently ½ hr. In a separate pan boil the sugar, dissolved in the water until it turns golden brown. Add to this the wine mixture. Add the gravy and any one or any mixture of the sweetening ingredients to taste.

Serve with braised meat.

MISCELLANEOUS SAUCES

AÏOLI

4–6 cloves of garlic *or* 4 shallots	**Lemon juice *or* wine vinegar**
1 egg yolk	**1 medium-sized cooked potato**
Salt	**Cayenne pepper**
¼ pt. olive oil	

Crush and pound the garlic to a smooth pulp. Mix with it the egg yolk and salt. Proceed as for mayonnaise (p. 135). Finally work the sauce gradually into the sieved, cold potato. Season to taste.

Serve with salads, vegetables, fish or meat.

BÂTARDE SAUCE (Quickly made)

¾ oz. butter	**A little milk *or* cream**
¾ oz. flour	**2 oz. butter**
½ pt. boiling water	**Lemon juice**
2 egg yolks	**Salt**

Melt the butter, add the flour, pour in all the boiling water and whisk briskly. Mix the egg yolks and milk or cream, stir these into the sauce, below boiling point, and thicken without boiling. Whisk in the butter, flavour and season the sauce.

Serve at once.

BOAR'S HEAD SAUCE

Rind of 2 large oranges	**1 oz. sugar**
1 shallot	**¼ teasp. mixed mustard**
½ lb. redcurrant jelly	**Cayenne pepper**
½ glass port	**Juice of 1 orange**

Grate the rind of the oranges, carefully avoiding any pith. Chop the shallot. Put the jelly, port, rind and shallot in a small pan; heat slowly to simmering point, cover, and infuse for ½ hr. over a very gentle heat. Add sugar, mustard, cayenne and orange juice, strain the sauce and cool it. This sauce may be bottled and stored for future use.

Serve with game, venison or mutton.

BREAD SAUCE

Sauce au Pain

1 large onion	**2 oz. dry white bread-crumbs**
2 cloves	**½ oz. butter**
1 blade of mace	**Salt and pepper**
1 bay leaf	**2 tablesp. cream (optional)**
4 peppercorns	
1 allspice berry	
½ pt. milk	

Put the onion and spices into the milk, bring them very slowly to boiling point. Cover the pan and infuse over a gentle heat for ½–1 hr. Strain the liquid. To it add the crumbs and butter, and season to taste. Keep the mixture just below simmering point for 20 min. Stir in the cream if used, serve the sauce at once.

Serve with roast chicken or turkey.

CAMBRIDGE SAUCE (Cold)

3 hard-boiled egg yolks	**1 teasp. chopped parsley**
¼ pt. olive oil	**½ teasp. chopped tarragon**
Vinegar to taste	**½ teasp. chopped chives**
½ teasp. French mustard	**Salt**
½ teasp. chopped capers	**Cayenne pepper**
1–2 chopped anchovies	
1 teasp. chopped chervil	

Pound the egg yolks until they are quite smooth. Beat into them (as for Mayonnaise, *see* p. 135) the olive oil and enough vinegar to make a thin cream. Work all the other ingredients into this creamy mixture.

Serve with salads, fish and cold meat.

CHESTNUT SAUCE

Sauce aux Marrons

½ lb. chestnuts	**A small strip of lemon rind**
¾ pt. stock	**Salt and pepper**
1 oz. butter	**⅛ pt. cream (optional)**
A trace of ground cinnamon	

Score the rounded side of the shells of the chestnuts and bake or boil them for 15–20 min. Remove shells and skins. Simmer the chestnuts until soft in the stock, about ½ hr. Rub them through a fine wire sieve. Reheat the sauce with the butter and flavourings, season to taste. Add the cream just below boiling point. Serve at once.

Serve with roast chicken or turkey.

CUMBERLAND SAUCE

1 orange	**¼ teasp. mixed mustard**
1 lemon	**Salt**
⅛ pt. water	**Cayenne pepper**
⅛ pt. port wine	**6–8 glacé cherries**
2 tablesp. vinegar	
¼ lb. redcurrant jelly	

Grate the rind of the orange and lemon, carefully avoiding the pith. Simmer the rinds in the water for 10 min. Add the wine, vinegar, jelly and mustard and simmer them together until the jelly is completely melted. Add the juice of the orange and lemon, season to taste and cool. Chop the glacé cherries and add them to the sauce.

Serve with roast game or mutton.

CURRY SAUCE

Sauce Indienne

1 medium-sized onion	**½ pt. white stock, coconut infusion (see below) *or* water**
1 oz. butter *or* margarine	**½ teasp. black treacle**
1 small cooking apple	**1–2 teasp. lemon juice**
½ oz. curry powder	**1 dessertsp. chutney**
½ oz. rice flour *or* flour	**Salt**

Chop the onion, put it into a saucepan and fry it very gently in the butter for 10 min. Chop the apple and cook it in the butter with the onion for a further 10 min. Stir in the curry powder and heat it for a few minutes. Add the flour and then stir in the liquid. When boiling, add all the other ingredients and simmer the sauce for at least ½ hr., or better 1½ hr.

To make the coconut infusion: Soak 1 oz. dessicated *or* fresh grated coconut in ½ pt. water for a few minutes, bring slowly to boiling point and infuse it for 10 min. Wring the coconut in a piece of muslin to extract all the liquid.

DEVIL SAUCE

Sauce Diable

1 oz. butter, margarine *or* beef dripping	**1 teasp. mixed mustard**
1 oz. flour	**¼ teasp. pepper**
½ pt. good meat gravy	**½ teasp. grated lemon rind**
1–2 tablesp. Worcester or other commercial sauce	**½ teasp. chopped shallot**
2 teasp. lemon juice	**1 teasp. chopped capers**
¼ teasp. anchovy essence	**½ teasp. chilli vinegar**
	A very little cayenne pepper

Make a brown sauce with the fat, flour and gravy (*see* p. 119). Add all the other ingredients to taste and simmer them together for 5–10 min.

Serve with fried or grilled beef, or mutton.

CHAUDFROID SAUCES

WHITE CHAUDFROID SAUCE

Sauce Chaudfroid Blanche

½ pt. Béchamel sauce	**1 teasp. wine vinegar *or* lemon juice**
¼ pt. aspic jelly	**1 tablesp. thick cream**
¼ oz. powdered gelatine	
Salt and pepper	

Have the sauce just warm. Heat the jelly over hot water and in it dissolve the gelatine. Cool the jelly until it also is just warm. Fold the jelly into the sauce and season the mixture, add the vinegar or juice. Wring the sauce through muslin, fold in the cream.

Use the sauce for masking fish, poultry or veal served en chaudfroid, using it when cold but liquid.

BROWN CHAUDFROID SAUCE

Sauce Chaudfroid Brune

As above substituting Espagnole sauce for Béchamel sauce.

Use for masking beef, mutton or game.

FAWN CHAUDFROID SAUCE

Sauce Chaudfroid Faune

As for White Chaudfroid Sauce, using Velouté sauce in place of Béchamel sauce.

Use for lamb, veal, poultry instead of white chaudfroid.

GREEN CHAUDFROID SAUCE

Sauce Chaudfroid Grune

As for White Chaudfroid Sauce, using 1 tablesp. of spinach purée or green colouring with the Béchamel sauce.

TOMATO CHAUDFROID SAUCE

Sauce Chaudfroid Tomate

As for White Chaudfroid Sauce, substituting Tomato Sauce for Béchamel Sauce.

FRUIT SAUCES TO SERVE WITH MEAT

APPLE SAUCE

Sauce aux Pommes

1 lb. apples
2 tablesp. water
½ oz. butter *or* margarine
Rind and juice of ½ lemon
Sugar to taste

Stew the apples very gently with the water, butter and lemon rind until they are pulpy. Beat them quite smooth or rub them through a hair or nylon sieve. Reheat the sauce with the lemon juice and sweeten to taste.

Serve with roast pork, roast goose or pork sausages. Excellent also as a sweet sauce with ginger pudding.

APPLE SAUCE WITH HORSERADISH

As for apple sauce with the addition of 1–2 tablesp. grated horseradish.

Serve with pork or beef.

CHERRY SAUCE

Sauce aux Cerises

½ lb. freshly-stewed *or* bottled cherries, morellos for preference
¼ pt. juice in which cherries were cooked *or* bottled
Sugar to taste
2 tablesp. redcurrant jelly
Pepper
1–2 teasp. vinegar
2 tablesp. red wine
½ teasp. arrowroot (optional)

Stone the cherries. Heat all the ingredients together and simmer the sauce till the juice is slightly syrupy, or blend the arrowroot with 1 teasp. cold water and add it to thicken the liquid.

Serve with braised game or rabbit.

CRANBERRY SAUCE

½ lb. cranberries
¼–½ pt water
Sugar to taste

Stew the cranberries till soft, using ¼ pt. water and adding more if needed. Rub the fruit through a hair or nylon sieve. Sweeten to taste. For economy, half cranberries and half sour cooking apples make an excellent sauce.

Serve with roast turkey, chicken or game.

CURRANT SAUCE

2 oz. washed, dried currants
1 oz. flour
1 oz. butter *or* margarine
½ pt. water
Sugar to taste
⅛ pt. red *or* white wine
A little grated lemon rind
Juice of ½ lemon
A pinch of powdered nutmeg
A pinch of cloves
A pinch of ginger

Fry the flour in the butter until golden-brown. Stir in the water, bring the sauce to boiling point, add all the other ingredients and simmer for 10 min.

Serve with roast pork, hare or venison.

GOOSEBERRY SAUCE

Sauce aux Groseilles

½ lb. green gooseberries
¼ pt. water
½ oz. butter
1 oz. sugar
Lemon juice
Nutmeg
Salt and pepper
½ teasp. chopped chives (optional)
A few chopped leaves of sorrel (optional)

Stew the gooseberries very gently with the water and butter until they are pulpy. Beat them quite smooth or rub them through a hair or nylon sieve. Reheat the sauce, stir in the sugar, add lemon juice and grated nutmeg to taste, season. Stir in the chives and sorrel if used.

Serve with mackerel.

PRUNE SAUCE

½ lb. prunes
½ pt. water
1 strip of lemon rind
1 oz. sugar
Pinch of ground cinnamon
1 tablesp. rum *or* brandy (optional)
Lemon juice

Soak the prunes overnight in the water. Stew them with the lemon rind till quite soft. Rub them through a hair, nylon or fine wire sieve. Add the other ingredients to taste.

Serve with roast pork, goose, venison or mutton. It is also good with some hot puddings.

QUINCE SAUCE

½ lb. quinces	**Sugar**
½ pt. water *or* water in which carrots have been cooked	**Ground clove**
Ground nutmeg	**Lemon juice**
	⅛ pt. red wine (optional)

Stew the quinces very gently in the water until pulpy. Beat them quite smooth or rub them through a hair or nylon sieve. Reheat the sauce, add nutmeg, sugar, clove and lemon juice to taste. Stir in the red wine if used.

REDCURRANT SAUCE

Sauce aux Groseilles Rouges

¼ lb. redcurrant jelly	**⅛ pt. port *or* other red wine**

Heat the two ingredients together gently until the jelly is melted.

Serve with game, venison *or* as a sweet sauce with puddings.

SULTANA SAUCE

As for Currant Sauce (p. 124), substituting sultanas for currants.

GRAVIES

GRAVY—
for any Roast Joint except Pork

Jus de Viande

Meat dripping from the roasting tin	**Water in which vegetables have been boiled *or* stock**
Flour	**Salt and pepper**
Essences from the joint	

Drain the fat from the roasting tin, carefully saving any sediment and meat juices. Dredge into the thin film of dripping sufficient flour to absorb it all. Brown this flour slowly till of a nut brown colour. Stir in water in which green vegetables or potatoes have been cooked, or stock, allowing ½ pt. for 6 persons. Boil the gravy and season it to taste.

To obtain a brown colour without browning the flour add a few drips of gravy browning from the end of a skewer. To improve the flavour add a good meat or yeast extract.

GRAVY (thickened)
(for a Stuffed Joint or for Roast Pork)

Bones and trimmings from the joint	**Cold water**
	Salt

To each pint of gravy:

1 oz. dripping	**1 oz. flour**

Make a stock from the bones, allowing at least 2 hr. simmering—much longer if possible (*see* p. 78). Melt the dripping and sprinkle in the flour. Brown the flour slowly until a nut brown colour. Stir in the stock, boil up and season to taste.

GIBLET GRAVY for Poultry

Jus de Gibier

1 set of giblets	**Flour**
1 onion (optional)	**Salt and pepper**
Cold water to cover	

Simmer the giblets very gently in the water with the onion (if liked) for at least 2 hr.—much longer if possible. Drain the fat from the tin in which the bird has been roasted, carefully saving the sediment. Dredge into the thin film of dripping only sufficient flour to absorb it all. Brown this flour until a nut brown colour. Stir in the liquid from the giblets, boil up and season to taste.

GRAVY MADE FROM SHIN OF BEEF

½ lb. shin of beef	**Dripping**
1 pt. water	**Flour**
½ teasp. salt	

Cut the shin of beef across the grain into very thin slices. Soak it in the water with the salt for ½ hr. Bring very slowly to simmering point and simmer very gently for at least 2 hr. Melt the dripping, brown the flour slowly, then stir in the strained liquid from the shin of beef. Boil up and season to taste.

GRAVY for Game

Bones, giblets *or* trimmings of game	**1 clove**
Cold water to cover	**6 peppercorns and 1 piece of onion to each pt. of water**
1 bay leaf	**Salt**
Thyme	

Make stock from the above ingredients.

GRAVIES

Drain all the fat from the roasting-tin and rinse the tin with the game stock, using no flour. Boil the gravy and skim it.

GRAVY for Hare—JUGGED GRAVY

½ lb. shin of beef
1 pt. water
Small piece of lean ham *or* bacon bone and rinds
½ carrot
2 in. of celery
1 blade of mace
4 peppercorns
A bunch of herbs
1 clove
Dripping
Flour
Salt
2 tablesp. redcurrant jelly
1–2 tablesp. port wine

Make stock with the beef, water, ham or bone, vegetables, spices and herbs (*see* p. 78). Make a thickened brown gravy (p. 125) and add to it the jelly and port.

Use also for venison.

HOLLANDAISE SAUCE

See also Mock Hollandaise

2 tablesp. wine vinegar
2 egg yolks
2–4 oz. butter
Salt and pepper
Lemon juice

Boil the vinegar till it is reduced by half; allow to cool. Mix the cool vinegar with the egg yolks in a basin and place this over hot water. Whisk the egg yolks till they begin to thicken, then whisk in the butter gradually until all is absorbed. Season, add lemon juice to taste and serve immediately.

Serve with fish or vegetables.

HORSERADISH CREAM (COLD)

Sauce Raifort Froide

2 tablesp. grated horse-radish
1 tablesp. wine vinegar *or* lemon juice
2 teasp. castor sugar
Salt and pepper to taste
Mixed mustard to taste
¼ pt. cream

Mix all ingredients except the cream. Half-whip the cream, i.e. until the trail of the whisk just shows on the surface. Lightly fold the horseradish mixture into the cream. Serve the sauce very cold. It may be chilled in a refrigerator and served semi-solid.

Serve with beef.

NOTE: See also Hot Horseradish Sauce.

MINT SAUCE

Sauce à la Menthe

3 heaped tablesp. finely-chopped mint
A pinch of salt
2 teasp. sugar
2 tablesp. boiling water
¼ pt. vinegar

The mint should be young and freshly gathered if possible. Wash well, pick the leaves from the stalks and chop the leaves finely.

Mix the mint, salt and sugar in the sauce-boat. Pour on to them the boiling water and leave the mixture to cool. Add the vinegar and if possible leave the sauce for 1 hr. to infuse the flavour of mint into the vinegar.

Serve with roast lamb.

MOUSSELINE SAUCE—SAVOURY, HOT

Sauce Mousseline chaude

2 egg yolks
⅛ pt. cream
1 tablesp. stock
Grated nutmeg
Cayenne pepper
Salt
½ oz. butter
Lemon juice
1 whipped egg white

Put all the ingredients except butter, lemon juice and egg white into a china basin. Place the basin over boiling water and whisk the mixture briskly till it thickens. Remove from heat and whisk in the butter and lemon juice. Fold in the egg white. Serve at once.

Serve with fish, poultry or vegetables.

PORT WINE SAUCE

Sauce au Vin d'Oporto

1 tablesp. redcurrant jelly
¼ pt. good mutton *or* venison gravy
⅛ pt. port wine

Heat all the ingredients together until the jelly is melted.

Serve with roast mutton or venison.

SHALLOT SAUCE

Sauce Échalote

6 shallots
½ oz. dripping *or* butter
½ oz. flour
½ pt. good brown stock
Salt and pepper
Lemon juice
1 heaped teasp. chopped parsley

Chop the shallots finely, put them in a

saucepan and fry them in the fat till golden. Add the flour then the stock, boiling. Simmer the sauce for ½ hr., season and add lemon juice to taste, stir in the parsley.

Serve with meat, fish, ham or game.

SHARP SAUCE—HOT or COLD

Sauce Piquante

1 shallot
2 hard-boiled egg yolks
4 anchovies
½ teasp. mixed mustard
2 teasp. vinegar
1 teasp. chopped capers
Salt and pepper
Sugar to taste
For a cold sauce: **¼ pt. thin cream**
For a hot sauce: **¼ pt. good meat gravy**

Chop the shallot finely. Crush and pound the hard-boiled egg yolks, anchovies and shallot together. Add the other ingredients to this paste. For a cold sauce, half-whip the cream and fold it carefully into the other ingredients. For a hot sauce, add the gravy (boiling) and reheat the sauce.

Serve with meat, fish or vegetables.

SOUR-SWEET SAUCE

2 onions
1½ oz. butter *or* **margarine**
1½ oz. flour
¾ pt. water *or* **stock**
4 tablesp. vinegar
1–2 teasp. any good commercial bottled sauce
2 tablesp. sugar
1 level teasp. French mustard
1 level teasp. yeast *or* **meat extract**
Salt and pepper

Chop the onions, put into a saucepan and fry them till tender and golden-brown in the butter. Add the flour and brown it a very little. Stir in the liquid, bring to the boil, stirring all the time. Add the other ingredients and simmer the sauce for 15–20 min.

Serve with boiled beef or other meat, fish or vegetables.

SUCHET SAUCE

½ lb. carrots
2 oz. butter
¾ oz. flour
⅜ pt. fish stock *or* **liquid in which fish has been cooked**
⅛ pt. milk
Salt and pepper
Lemon juice
2 tablesp. cream

Cut the carrots in shreds about 1½ in. long and the thickness of a match. Melt 1 oz. of the butter and gently cook the carrots (with the saucepan lid on) for 10–15 min. or until they are soft but not brown. Stir in the flour, then the fish stock and milk; stir till the sauce boils. Season and add lemon juice to taste. Just below boiling point whisk in the other 1 oz. butter in small pats and stir in the cream. Serve at once.

Serve with fish.

SWEDISH SAUCE

1 hard-boiled egg yolk
1 raw egg yolk
¼ teasp. mustard
⅛ teasp. salt
Pepper
2 teasp. sugar
1 tablesp. wine vinegar
¼ pt. thin cream *or* **evaporated milk**

Crush the hard-boiled egg yolk with a wooden spoon, and work into it the raw egg yolk, the mustard, salt, pepper and sugar. Thin the paste with vinegar. Whip the cream or evaporated milk till thick and fold it carefully into the vinegar mixture.

Serve with hot fish, fish or other salads.

TEXAS SAUCE

½ pt. curry sauce (p. 123)
1 teasp. lemon juice
⅛ teasp. saffron
½–1 oz. butter
1 heaped teasp. chopped parsley

Add the lemon juice and saffron to the hot curry sauce. With the sauce just below boiling point, whisk in the butter a small pat at a time. Stir in the parsley and serve the sauce.

Serve with curried fish and meat.

TOMATO SAUCE

1 onion
1 small carrot
1 oz. bacon scraps *or* **bacon bone** *or* **rinds**
½ oz. butter *or* **margarine**
4 medium-sized tomatoes, fresh, bottled *or* **canned**
½ oz. rice flour
½ pt. white second stock *or* **liquid from canned** *or* **bottled tomatoes**
Salt and pepper
Lemon juice
Sugar
Grated nutmeg

Slice the onion and carrot. Put them into a saucepan with the bacon and fry them in the fat without browning them for 10 min. Slice and add the tomatoes and cook them for 5 min. Sprinkle in the rice flour, add the stock or juice, stir till the sauce boils. Simmer the sauce for 45 min. Rub the sauce through a hair or nylon sieve. Reheat, season and add lemon juice, sugar and nutmeg to taste.

TOMATO SAUCE—CLEAR (Quick Method)

½ pt. canned tomato juice	**Salt and pepper**
1 heaped teasp. arrowroot	**Grated nutmeg**
1 onion *or* shallot	**Lemon juice**
	Sugar

Blend the arrowroot with a little cold juice. Slice the onion and simmer it for 10 min. in the juice. Stir in the blended arrowroot and boil it for a minute. Season the sauce, add nutmeg, a few drops of lemon juice and sugar to taste. Strain the sauce.

THE FRENCH FOUNDATION SAUCES (GRANDES SAUCES)

These important sauces are internationally famous. The white Béchamel, the brown Espagnole and the fawn Velouté form the bases of hundreds of more complex sauces; while Mayonnaise, though not lending itself to so many additions still has a number of variations. A representative selection of the sauces derived from each is given here under the foundation or "parent" sauce.

1. BÉCHAMEL SAUCE

French White sauce

1 pt. milk	**Salt**
1 small onion	**6 peppercorns**
1 small carrot	**A small bunch of herbs**
2 in. celery stick	**2 oz. butter**
1 bay leaf	**2 oz. flour**
1 clove	**⅛ pt. cream (optional)**
1 blade of mace	

Warm the milk with the vegetables, herbs, salt and spices, and bring it slowly to simmering point. Put a lid on the pan and stand it in a warm place on the cooker to infuse for ½ hr. Strain the milk, melt the butter, add the flour, cook this roux for a few minutes without browning it. Stir the flavoured milk gradually into the roux. Bring the sauce to boiling point, stirring vigorously. For an extra smooth result, wring the sauce through damp muslin. If cream is used, add it to the sauce just at boiling point and do not reboil it.

Serve with chicken, veal, fish or white vegetables.

NOTE: Béchamel sauce may be made with ½ white stock and ½ milk, the result will have a good flavour but will not be so creamy in texture.

Cooking time—40 min.

SAUCES MADE FROM BÉCHAMEL FOUNDATION

AURORA SAUCE

Sauce Aurore

½ pt. Béchamel sauce	**2 tablesp. concentrated tomato purée *or* 1 tablesp. purée of canned pimento (sweet red pepper)**
Paprika pepper to taste	

Add the purée carefully to the hot sauce, reheat without boiling and serve the sauce at once. The sauce should be a deep pink colour.

NOTE: Aurora sauce may also be made with Velouté sauce (p. 133) made with fish stock, and with tomato puree added.

Serve Béchamel Aurore with chicken or fish; Velouté Aurore with fish.

BEARNAISE SAUCE

¼ pt. Béchamel sauce	**⅛ pt. white wine *or* wine vinegar**
2 shallots	**2–3 egg yolks**
Sprig of tarragon	**4 oz. butter**
Sprig of chervil	**2 teasp. lemon juice**
6 peppercorns	**Salt and pepper**

Chop shallots and herbs. Put wine in a very

small pan with the shallots, herbs and peppercorns and simmer gently till reduced by ½, then strain. Mix egg yolks and sauce and heat them in a double boiler or in a basin over a pan of hot water. Add the wine and whisk in the butter, a pat at a time, until all is absorbed. The water must not be allowed to boil or the sauce will curdle. Season sauce and add lemon juice, add a little chopped tarragon and chervil and use sauce at once. Serve with grilled meat.

CARDINAL SAUCE

¼ pt. Béchamel sauce	**⅛ pt. cream**
¼ pt. well-reduced fish stock	**1 dessertsp. lemon juice**
Cayenne pepper	**1–2 oz. lobster butter** (p. 676)
Salt	

Heat sauce and stock together and season to taste. Just below boiling point stir in cream and lemon juice and whisk in the lobster butter, a small pat at a time. Do not allow sauce to boil. This sauce should be bright scarlet. Serve with lobster or other fish.

NOTE: Cardinal sauce may be made with Velouté sauce made from fish stock, instead of the Béchamel sauce and stock.

CREAM SAUCE

½ pt. Béchamel sauce	**Lemon juice to taste**
Cayenne pepper	**⅛ pt. cream**
Salt	

Heat the sauce; add cayenne, salt and lemon juice. Stir cream into seasoned sauce, just below boiling point. On no account allow sauce to boil or it will curdle. Serve at once, with chicken, veal, fish or delicately-flavoured vegetables.

CUCUMBER SAUCE

½ oz. butter	**Lemon juice**
½ a cucumber	**Sugar**
1 tablesp. stock	**Nutmeg**
¼ pt. Béchamel sauce	**Green colouring**
Salt and pepper	**2 tablesp. cream**

Melt the butter in a saucepan, slice the cucumber and slowly cook the slices in the butter for 10 min. Add the stock and continue cooking until the cucumber is soft. Rub the cucumber through a hair or nylon sieve. Return the purée to the saucepan and simmer with any of the butter and liquid remaining, until reduced a little. Stir the hot Béchamel sauce and the cucumber purée together; season and flavour to taste; colour the sauce. Lastly stir in the cream at boiling point, do not reboil. Use the sauce at once.

Serve with salmon and other fish, veal or poultry.

HOLLANDAISE SAUCE—ECONOMICAL or "MOCK" HOLLANDAISE

Sauce Hollandaise

½ pt. Béchamel sauce	**1 dessertsp. lemon juice *or* wine vinegar**
1–2 egg yolks	**Cayenne pepper**
2 tablesp. cream	**Salt**

Mix the egg yolks and cream, stir them into the hot sauce—well below boiling point and cook the egg yolk without boiling it. Add the lemon juice and seasoning to taste. Use the sauce at once.

Serve with salmon or other fish, or with delicately flavoured vegetables such as asparagus and seakale.

LOBSTER SAUCE

½ pt. Béchamel sauce	**½ oz. butter**
2 oz. finely-chopped lobster	

Mix ingredients together, season and add a little paprika, if wished.

MORNAY SAUCE

½ pt. Béchamel sauce	**¾ oz. Gruyère *or* Cheddar cheese**
1 egg yolk	**⅛ pt. cream (optional)**
¾ oz. Parmesan cheese	**Cayenne pepper**

For a fish dish:

¼ pt. fish stock reduced to 2 tablesp. *or* 2 tablesp. fish fumet

Add the egg yolk mixed with a little cooled sauce to the Béchamel sauce well below boiling point. Cook the egg yolk without boiling it. Stir in the grated cheese and the cream, season and serve the sauce at once. If fish fumet is used add it hot, before the cream.

Serve with fish or vegetables.

POULETTE SAUCE *Sauce Poulette*

½ pt. Béchamel sauce (p. 128)
1 egg yolk
1 tablesp. cream
1 tablesp. chopped parsley
1 dessertsp. lemon juice
Salt and pepper

Mix the egg yolk and cream; stir them into the hot sauce—well below boiling point and cook the egg yolk without boiling it. Add the parsley and lemon juice, season to taste. Use at once.

SOUBISE SAUCE *Sauce Soubise*

½ pt. Béchamel sauce
½ lb. onions
1½ oz. butter
1–2 tablesp. stock
Salt and pepper
Sugar
Nutmeg

Peel and slice the onions and cook them gently in ½ oz. of the butter and just enough stock to moisten them. When they are tender, sieve them. Have the sauce very thick, add to it the onion purée, reheat, season and add sugar and nutmeg to taste. Whisk the remaining 1 oz. butter into the sauce at boiling point, adding a small pat at a time. Do not allow the sauce to boil. Serve at once.

TARTARE SAUCE—ECONOMICAL (HOT)

½ pt. Béchamel sauce
1–2 egg yolks
1 tablesp. cream
1 heaped teasp. chopped gherkin
1 heaped teasp. chopped capers
1 dessertsp. chopped parsley
Lemon juice *or* wine vinegar

Mix the egg yolks and cream, stir them into the hot sauce well below boiling point. Cook the egg yolk without boiling it. Add the gherkin, capers and parsley and flavour with lemon juice or vinegar. Serve at once.

Serve with salmon and other fish.

WHITE ITALIAN SAUCE

½ pt. Béchamel sauce
2 shallots
2 oz. button mushrooms
½ oz. butter
¼ pt. good stock (veal *or* chicken)
½ glass dry white wine (optional)
Salt and pepper
Lemon juice to taste
1 dessertsp. chopped parsley
2 tablesp. cream

Chop the shallots and mushrooms very fine. Melt the butter and in it cook the mushrooms and shallots very gently for 10 min. Add the sauce, the stock and wine if used. Stir all well together and simmer the sauce steadily until mushrooms are soft and the whole is reduced to a creamy texture. Season, add the lemon juice and chopped parsley and just before serving stir in the cream.

Serve with chicken, fish, etc.

2. ESPAGNOLE SAUCE

1 onion
1 carrot
2 oz. mushrooms *or* mushroom trimmings
2 oz. lean raw ham *or* bacon
2 oz. butter *or* dripping
2 oz. flour
1 pt. brown stock
Bouquet garni
6 peppercorns
1 bay leaf
¼ pt. tomato pulp
Salt
⅛ pt. sherry (optional)

Slice the vegetables, chop the ham. Melt the fat and fry the ham for a few minutes and then, very slowly, the vegetables until they are golden brown. Add the flour and continue frying very slowly till all is a rich brown. Add the stock, herbs and spices and stir till the sauce simmers; simmer for ½ hr. Add the tomato pulp and simmer the sauce for a further ½ hr. Wring the sauce through a tammy cloth or rub it through a fine hair or nylon sieve. Season, add the sherry, if used, and reheat the sauce.

SAUCES MADE FROM ESPAGNOLE FOUNDATION

BIGARADE SAUCE *Sauce Bigarade*

½ pt. Espagnole sauce
½ Seville orange
½ lemon
⅛ pt. red wine (optional)
Salt
Cayenne pepper
Pinch of sugar

Remove the outer orange rind, avoiding the pith, and cut the rind in neat, thin strips. Cover it with a little cold water; stew till just tender; then strain. Squeeze the orange and lemon juice into the sauce, add the orange rind, reheat, add the wine, if used, season and add sugar to taste.

Serve with roast duck, goose, wild duck, pork or ham.

BORDELAISE SAUCE *Sauce Bordelaise*

½ pt. Espagnole sauce
1 carrot
2 onions *or* shallots
1 clove of garlic
¼ pt. good stock
6 peppercorns
1 bay leaf
Sprig of thyme
Parsley stalks
Sprig of tarragon
¼ pt. red *or* white wine
Lemon juice
Cayenne pepper
1 teasp. chopped chervil
1 teasp. chopped parsley

Chop the vegetables, crush the garlic. Put stock, vegetables, spices and herbs into a small saucepan, bring slowly to simmering point and simmer until the liquid is reduced to a sticky consistency. Add the wine and again reduce the liquid slightly. Add the Espagnole sauce, boil then strain the sauce. Add lemon juice to taste, season and just before serving add the chopped chervil and parsley.

Serve with beef, pork, ham or duck.

BRITTANY SAUCE *Sauce Brétonne*

½ pt. Espagnole sauce
2 onions
½ oz. butter
2 tablesp. sieved, cooked haricot beans

Chop the onions and cook gently in butter until quite soft, without browning them. Add this mixture with the beans to the Espagnole sauce and reheat. Serve with meat.

NOTE: This sauce may also be made with a foundation of Normandy sauce to serve with fish.

BROWN CAPER SAUCE

Sauce aux Câpres Brunes

½ pt. Espagnole sauce *or* Brown sauce (p. 119)
1 onion *or* shallot
1 tablesp. halved capers
1 teasp. caper vinegar
1 teasp. anchovy essence
Cayenne pepper
Lemon juice to taste

Chop the onion or shallot and simmer it in the sauce for 10 min. then strain. Add the other ingredients, reheat the sauce.

Serve with steak, kidneys or fish.

CREOLE SAUCE

½ pt. Espagnole sauce
1 onion
4 mushrooms
1 green sweet pepper
½ red sweet pepper
1 oz. butter
Salt and pepper
1 tablesp. chopped parsley

Finely chop the onion and mushrooms, cut the peppers into fine shreds. Cook them in the butter, very gently, for 10 min. Add the sauce and simmer very gently for 1 hr. Season to taste and add the chopped parsley. Do not strain the sauce. Serve with grilled steak.

DEMI-GLACE SAUCE Half glaze

½ pt. Espagnole sauce
¼ pt. juices from roast meat *or* ¼ pt. stock and 1 teasp. good beef extract *or* meat glaze

Boil the sauce and meat juices together until well reduced. Skim off any fat before serving the sauce.

Serve with meat, poultry, game etc.

GAME SAUCE *Sauce Gibier*

½ pt. Espagnole sauce
Trimmings and carcase of strong-flavoured roast game
1 onion
2 shallots
1 blade of mace
4 peppercorns
½ clove
Parsley stalks
Sprig of thyme
1 bay leaf
¼ pt. sherry *or* stock

Break the game carcase into small pieces, chop the onion and shallots. Put the vegetables, game scraps, spices and herbs into a pan with the sherry or stock and simmer very slowly for ½ hr. Strain the liquid into the hot Espagnole sauce and reduce it slightly.

GENOESE SAUCE *Sauce Génoise*

½ pt. Espagnole sauce
1 onion
2 shallots
1 clove of garlic
1 pt. fish stock
¼ pt. dry red wine (optional)
Peppercorns
1 clove
1 bay leaf
Sprig of thyme
A few parsley stalks
Sugar to taste
1 dessertsp. anchovy essence

Chop the onion and shallots; crush the garlic. Put the stock into a saucepan with the wine (if used), vegetables, spices and herbs, cover, and cook until reduced to about ¼ pt. Strain this liquid into the hot Espagnole sauce, reheat, add a pinch of sugar, stir in the anchovy essence and serve.

Serve separately with poached fish, or pour over braised fish.

ITALIAN SAUCE—BROWN

Sauce Italienne, Brune

½ pt. Espagnole sauce	**⅛ pt. white wine (optional)**
4 shallots	**Parsley stalks**
6 mushrooms	**Sprig of thyme**
1 tablesp. olive oil	**1 bay leaf**
⅛ pt. stock	**Salt and pepper**

Chop the shallots and mushrooms and very gently cook them for 10 min. in the olive oil. Add the stock, wine (if used), herbs and spices and simmer gently until reduced by half. Add the Espagnole sauce and cook gently for 20 min. Season and lift out the herbs.

Serve with fish and meat.

MADEIRA SAUCE

Sauce Madère

½ pt. demi-glace sauce	**1 teasp. meat glaze *or* good beef extract**
⅛ pt. Madeira wine	**Salt and pepper**

Simmer the sauce, wine and extract (if used) together until well reduced. Season to taste, put in the meat glaze (if used), stir until dissolved; strain and use as required.

Serve with meat, poultry and game.

MATELOTE SAUCE

Sauce Matelote

½ pt. Espagnole sauce	**⅛ pt. red wine**
1 onion	**A bunch of herbs**
1 carrot	**4 peppercorns**
4 mushrooms *or* mushroom trimmings	**Lemon juice**
¼ pt. fish stock	**Salt and pepper**
	¾ oz. butter

Chop the onion, carrot and mushrooms. Simmer the stock and wine with the vegetables, herbs and peppercorns until reduced by half. Add the Espagnole sauce and simmer for 10 min. Strain the sauce, add the lemon juice, salt and pepper to taste, and reheat. Whisk in the butter, just at boiling point; serve at once.

Serve with poached or braised fish.

MUSHROOM SAUCE—BROWN

See p. 120.

OLIVE SAUCE

Sauce aux Olives

½ pt. Espagnole sauce	**Lemon juice to taste**
12 French olives	

Rinse the whole olives to remove the preserving vinegar, stone them. Heat the olives carefully in the Espagnole sauce for 10 min. Add lemon juice to taste.

ORANGE SAUCE—SAVOURY

Sauce au Jus d'Orange

½ pt. Espagnole sauce	**2 tablesp. redcurrant jelly**
½ orange	**Salt**
½ lemon	**Cayenne pepper**
⅛ pt. red wine (optional)	**Pinch of sugar**

Remove the outer orange rind without the pith, and cut it in neat, thin strips. Cover the orange rind with a little cold water; stew till just tender; then strain. Squeeze the orange and lemon juice into the sauce, add the orange rind. Reheat, add the wine (if used), the redcurrant jelly, season with salt, pepper and sugar to taste.

Serve with roast duck, goose or wild duck.

PIQUANT SAUCE—ESPAGNOLE

See p. 121.

POIVRADE SAUCE (PEPPER SAUCE)

½ pt. Espagnole sauce	**12 peppercorns**
2 shallots	**½ glass red wine**
1 sprig of thyme	**2 tablesp. wine vinegar**
1 bay leaf	**Ground pepper to taste**

Finely chop the shallots and simmer them with the herbs and spices in the wine and vinegar until reduced by half. Strain the liquid into the hot Espagnole sauce and add extra ground pepper to taste.

REFORM SAUCE

Sauce Réforme

½ pt. Poivrade sauce	**1 dessertsp. shredded cooked mushroom**
½ small glass port	**1 dessertsp. shredded cooked tongue**
1 tablesp. redcurrant jelly	**1 dessertsp. shredded hard-boiled egg white**
1 dessertsp. shredded gherkin	

Gently heat all the ingredients in the hot Poivrade sauce.

Serve with cutlets.

SALMI SAUCE

Sauce Salmis

½ pt. Espagnole sauce	**⅛ pt. red wine (optional)**
2 shallots	**Sprig of thyme**
A few mushroom trimmings	**1 bay leaf**
1 tablesp. olive oil	**1 dessertsp. redcurrant jelly**
¼ pt. game stock	

Chop the shallots, put them in a saucepan and fry them with the mushrooms in the olive oil until they are golden brown. Add the stock and wine (if used) with the herbs. Simmer till reduced by half. Add the Espagnole sauce and simmer very gently for 10 min. Strain, add the redcurrant jelly and serve.

Serve with game or duck "en casserole".

VENISON SAUCE

Sauce Chevreuil

½ pt. Espagnole sauce	**1 bay leaf**
1 shallot	**½ glass port (optional)**
12 peppercorns	**2 tablesp. vinegar**
Sprig of thyme	**1 dessertsp. redcurrant jelly**
A few parsley stalks	

Chop the shallot, crush the peppercorns. Simmer the herbs and spices in the wine (if used) and vinegar for 20 min. Add the Espagnole sauce and simmer for 10 min. Strain the sauce, reheat it with the jelly.

Serve with venison or mutton.

3. VELOUTÉ SAUCE

French Fawn sauce

2 oz. butter	**1 pt. good white stock (p. 79)**
6 button mushrooms *or* mushroom trimmings	**Salt and pepper**
12 peppercorns	**Lemon juice**
A few parsley stalks	**⅛–¼ pt. cream**
2 oz. flour	

Melt the butter in a saucepan and gently cook the mushrooms, peppercorns and parsley for 10 min. Add the flour and cook for a few minutes without browning it. Stir in the stock, bring the sauce to simmering point and simmer for 1 hr. Wring the sauce through a tammy cloth or damp muslin. Season, add lemon juice, and reheat. Just at boiling point stir in the cream. The mushrooms may be rinsed and used as garnish for the dish.

Serve with chicken, veal, sweetbreads, fish or vegetables.

SAUCES MADE FROM VELOUTÉ FOUNDATION

ALLEMANDE SAUCE

Sauce Allemande

½ pt. Velouté sauce	**Salt and pepper**
1 egg yolk	**Nutmeg**
1 tablesp. cream	**Lemon juice**
½ oz. butter	

Heat the Velouté sauce, preferably in a double boiler. Mix the egg yolk and cream, and stir into the sauce, cook without boiling till the egg yolk thickens. Whisk in the butter, a small pat at a time. Add a pinch of nutmeg, a few drops of lemon juice, season and use the sauce at once.

Serve with any meat, poultry, fish or vegetables.

BERCY SAUCE

Sauce Bercy

½ pt. Velouté sauce made with *fish stock* for fish dishes *or* with *veal stock* for meat dishes	**2 shallots**
	⅛ pt. white wine
	1 oz. butter
	1 dessertsp. chopped parsley

Chop the shallots and cook them gently in the wine until reduced by half. Add to this the sauce and reheat it. Whisk in the butter just at boiling point and add the chopped parsley.

NORMANDY SAUCE

Sauce Normande

½ pt. Velouté sauce made with fish stock	**½–1 oz. butter**
1 egg yolk	**Lemon juice to taste**

VELOUTÉ FOUNDATION SAUCES

The Velouté sauce should be made with fish stock containing liquor from oysters or mussels to give the correct flavour. Heat the sauce—in a double boiler, if possible. Stir in the egg yolk and cook without boiling, till the egg yolk thickens. Whisk in the butter, a small pat at a time. Add a few drops of lemon juice. Use at once.

Serve with sole or other white fish.

PAPRIKA SAUCE

½ pt. Velouté sauce (p. 133)
1 small red pimento *or* sweet pepper, fresh *or* canned
Paprika pepper to taste
2 tablesp.–⅛ pt. cream

Shred the pimento into neat, equal-length strips. If raw pimento is used it may be necessary to simmer it for 10 min. and to remove the skin before shredding it. Add paprika pepper to the sauce to give it a pink colour and desired flavour. Carefully reheat the pimento strips in the sauce. Stir in the cream when the sauce is below boiling point.

Serve with veal or beef.

POLONAISE SAUCE

½ pt. Velouté sauce (p. 133)
⅛ pt. sour cream *or* yoghourt
1 teasp. grated horse-radish
1 teasp. finely-chopped fennel
1 teasp. lemon juice

Blend all the other ingredients with the hot Velouté sauce. Reheat without boiling.

Serve with grilled cutlets or steaks.

RAVIGOTE SAUCE—HOT

½ pt. Velouté sauce (p. 133)
1 tablesp. Ravigote butter
1 tablesp. wine vinegar
Nutmeg
Sugar
Salt and pepper

RAVIGOTE BUTTER

1 heaped tablesp. of a mixture of picked parsley, chervil leaves, chopped shallot, tarragon leaves, chopped chives, crushed garlic
½ oz. butter

To make the Ravigote butter, scald the herbs, shallot and garlic in a little boiling water; drain them and wring dry in muslin. Pound the herbs and butter together, then rub through a fine sieve. Heat the Velouté sauce, add to it the vinegar, nutmeg, sugar and seasoning. Whisk the Ravigote butter into the sauce, adding a small pat at a time, keeping the sauce almost at boiling point but not allowing it to boil. Serve the sauce at once.

REGENCY SAUCE

½ pt. Normandy sauce
1 dessertsp. shredded truffle
1 tablesp. shredded cooked mushroom
1 tablesp. liquor in which the mushrooms were cooked
White wine to taste

Blend all the other ingredients with the hot Normandy sauce. Serve with fish.

To serve with chicken or veal use Suprême sauce instead of Normandy sauce.

SUPRÊME SAUCE

Sauce Suprême

½ pt. Velouté sauce
2 tablesp.–⅛ pt. cream
1 egg yolk
½–1 oz. butter
Nutmeg to taste
Lemon juice
Salt and pepper

Heat the Velouté sauce, preferably in a double boiler. Mix the egg yolk and cream, and stir into the sauce, cook without boiling, till the egg yolk thickens. Whisk in the butter, a small pat at a time. Add a pinch of nutmeg, a few drops of lemon juice, season and use the sauce at once.

Serve with any meat, poultry, fish or vegetables.

TOURNÉE SAUCE

½ pt. Velouté sauce (p. 133)
6 spring onions—white parts only
4 small mushrooms
A bunch of herbs
Chopped parsley

Chop the onions and mushrooms and simmer them with the bunch of herbs in the Velouté sauce until they are quite tender. Remove the herbs, add the chopped parsley and serve the sauce.

Serve with meat or fish.

4. MAYONNAISE

1–2 egg yolks (new laid)	**Mixed vinegars to taste—4 parts wine vinegar *or* lemon juice, 2 parts tarragon and 1 part chilli vinegar**
Salt and pepper	
Mustard	
¼–½ pt. best olive oil	

The eggs and oil should be at the same temperature and that not too cold. In summer it is easier to make a good mayonnaise beginning with 2 egg yolks.

Remove every trace of egg white from the yolks. Put the yolks in a thick basin which will stand steady in spite of vigorous beating. Add to the egg yolks the pepper, salt and mustard to taste. Drop by drop add the olive oil, beating or whisking vigorously all the time. As the mayonnaise thickens the olive oil can be poured in a thin, steady stream but whisking must never slacken. When the mixture is really thick a few drops of vinegar or lemon juice stirred in will thin it again. Continue whisking in the oil, alternately with a little vinegar until the whole amount is added.

To store the mayonnaise cover it with damp muslin and store in a cool larder or refrigerator.

To use after storing, whisk it again and add a drop or two more vinegar.

If the mayonnaise should curdle, break fresh egg yolk and beat into this the curdled mixture just as the oil was added originally.

COLD SAUCES MADE FROM MAYONNAISE

ANDALUSIAN SAUCE

Sauce Andalouse

¼ pt. mayonnaise	**1 small, sweet, red pepper (pimento)**
2 tablesp. concentrated tomato purée	

Cut the pimento in thin strips and stir into the mayonnaise with the tomato purée.

ASPIC MAYONNAISE

¼ pt. mayonnaise	**¼–½ pt. aspic jelly**

Have the mayonnaise really stiff and the jelly liquid but cold. Fold the jelly carefully into the mayonnaise. Use the aspic mayonnaise when it is beginning to thicken.

NOTE: The smaller proportion of jelly gives a mixture which may be piped through a forcing tube and bag; the higher proportion of jelly gives a mixture for coating cold foods served with salad.

COLD GREEN MOUSSELINE SAUCE

¼ pt. mayonnaise	**2 tablesp. whipped cream**
1 tablesp. cooked spinach purée	

Fold the cold purée and then the whipped cream into the mayonnaise.

Serve with fish.

EPICUREAN SAUCE

¼ pt. mayonnaise	**1 teasp. anchovy essence**
½ cucumber	**1 dessertsp. chopped gherkin**
⅛ pt. aspic jelly *or* ⅛ pt. good stock and ½ level teasp. powdered gelatine	**1 dessertsp. chopped chutney**
1 tablesp. tarragon vinegar	**Salt and pepper**
⅛ pt. cream	**Sugar**

Peel, dice and cook the cucumber in a very little salted water. When tender sieve the cucumber. Have the aspic jelly liquid but cool. Mix the cucumber purée, the liquid jelly and vinegar together. Carefully fold the cream into the mayonnaise then fold in the anchovy essence, the gherkins and chutney and lastly the aspic jelly and cucumber mixture. Season and add sugar to taste.

Serve with fish salads or with asparagus or globe artichokes.

ESCOFFIER SAUCE (MAYONNAISE)

¼ pt. mayonnaise	**1 teasp. chopped parsley**
½ teasp. horseradish cream	**1 teasp. chopped chervil**

Fold the horseradish cream into the mayonnaise, then the parsley and chervil.

MAYONNAISE SAUCES

GLOUCESTER SAUCE

¼ pt. mayonnaise (p. 135).
1 tablesp. sour cream *or* yoghourt
A little Worcester sauce
½ teasp. chopped chives
Lemon juice
Cayenne pepper

Fold the cream and sauce into the mayonnaise, add the chives and lemon juice and pepper to taste.

Serve with meat salads.

GREEN SAUCE (MAYONNAISE)

Sauce Verte

¼ pt. mayonnaise
About 1 oz. mixed leaves of watercress, spinach, chervil, tarragon, parsley and chives

Plunge the leaves into boiling water. Drain and wring them dry in a cloth. Pound and sieve them. Add this green purée to the seasoned mayonnaise.

Serve with fish and fish salads.

INDIAN MAYONNAISE

¼ pt. mayonnaise
1 clove of garlic
½ teasp. curry powder

Crush the garlic and with it rub the bowl in which the mayonnaise is to be mixed. Add the curry powder to the egg yolks when making the mayonnaise.

RED MAYONNAISE

¼ pt. mayonnaise
The coral from a small lobster
A little juice squeezed from raw grated beetroot *or* red colouring

Pound the lobster coral and fold it into the mayonnaise. Add a few drops of colouring.

RÉMOULADE SAUCE

¼ pt. mayonnaise
1 teasp. French mustard
A few drops of anchovy essence
1 dessertsp. mixed chopped: gherkins, capers, parsley, tarragon, chervil

Stir the mustard, essence and herbs into the mayonnaise.

TARTARE SAUCE—COLD

¼ pt. mayonnaise (p. 135)
1 teasp. each of chopped gherkin, chopped olives, chopped capers, chopped parsley, chopped chives
A little French mustard
1 dessertsp. wine vinegar
A little dry white wine (optional)

Mix the chopped ingredients into the mayonnaise, add the mustard. Thin to the required consistency with vinegar and wine.

Serve with fried and grilled fish and meat.

TOMATO MAYONNAISE

¼ pt. thick mayonnaise
⅛ pt. tomato purée, canned *or* fresh, *or* ⅛ pt. cold tomato sauce *or* bottled tomato sauce

Fold the tomato purée carefully into the mayonnaise.

NOTE: If fresh tomatoes are used some of the juice must be pressed out and kept apart from the firm flesh before sieving.

SWEET SAUCES TO SERVE WITH PUDDINGS

APPLE SAUCE

Sauce aux Pommes

See p. 124.

Serve with hot gingerbread or steamed ginger pudding.

APRICOT SAUCE

Sauce à l'Abricot

½ lb. apricots, fresh *or* canned
¼ pt. water *or* syrup from can
1–2 oz. brown sugar
Lemon juice
1 teasp. Maraschino (optional)
1 level teasp. arrowroot

Stone the apricots and stew them till soft in the water. When soft rub them through a hair or nylon sieve. Meanwhile crack the stones, scald and skin the kernels. Add sugar, lemon juice, liqueur (if used) and kernels to the sauce. Reheat the sauce, stirring in the arrowroot blended with a little cold water. Bring to the boil and serve the sauce.

See also Jam Sauce (p. 139).

ARROWROOT SAUCE—CLEAR

1 rounded teasp. arrowroot	**Lemon rind**
½ pt. fruit juice *or* white wine and fruit juice *or* cider	**Sugar**
	Lemon juice

Blend the arrowroot with a little cold liquid. Boil the rest of the liquid with lemon juice and rind to taste. Remove rind and stir the boiling liquid into the blended arrowroot, return the mixture to the pan and bring it just to boiling point. Sweeten to taste.

BRANDY BUTTER (Hard Sauce)

See p. 677.

BRANDY SAUCE (1)

Sauce au Cognac

1 level teasp. arrowroot *or* cornflour	**⅛ pt. good brandy**
¼ pt. milk	**1 teasp. sugar, Barbados if possible**
1 egg yolk	

Blend the arrowroot with a little cold milk. Heat the rest of the milk and when boiling stir it into the blended arrowroot. Return mixture to pan and bring to boiling point. Mix together the egg yolk, brandy and sugar. Cool the arrowroot sauce a little, then stir into it the egg mixture. Cook without boiling until the egg yolk thickens.

BRANDY SAUCE (2)—RICH

¼ pt. thin cream	**1 dessertsp. light Barbados sugar**
2 egg yolks	**⅛ pt. good brandy**

Mix all the ingredients in a basin. Set the basin over a saucepan of boiling water and whisk steadily until the mixture thickens.

BUTTERSCOTCH SAUCE

4 oz. moist, dark brown sugar	**1 teasp. arrowroot**
¼ pt. water	**A few drops of vanilla essence**
1 oz. butter	**A few drops of lemon juice**
1 strip of lemon rind	

Dissolve the sugar in the ¼ pt. water, add the butter and lemon rind and boil for 5 min. Remove lemon rind. Blend the arrowroot with 2 teasp. water; thicken the sauce with the blended arrowroot. Add vanilla and lemon juice to taste.

CARAMEL SAUCE

Sauce au Caramel

2 oz. sugar *or* golden syrup	**½ pt. custard sauce**
⅛ pt. water	**Lemon juice *or* vanilla essence**

Put the sugar and 2 tablesp. water in a small pan; dissolve the sugar over gentle heat, then boil the syrup so made until it is a deep golden brown. Add to the caramel the rest of the water and leave it in a warm place to dissolve. If golden syrup is used heat it without water until of a golden-brown colour, then dissolve it in the water. Add the dissolved caramel to the custard sauce and flavour to taste.

CHANTILLY SAUCE—COLD

1 lb. cooking apples	**1 oz. butter**
1½ oz. sugar	**¼ pt. cream**

Peel, core and slice the apples, put them in a saucepan with 2–3 tablesp. cold water. Add the butter and sugar, cook gently until tender, then rub through a nylon sieve. Whip the cream stiffly, stir it into the apple purée, use as required.

CHOCOLATE SAUCE (1)—PLAIN

Sauce au Chocolat

3 oz. bitter chocolate *or* cooking chocolate *or* 1 heaped tablesp. cocoa	**Sugar if required**
½ pt. water	**Vanilla essence**
¼ oz. cornflour *or* custard powder	**1 teasp. rum (optional)**
	A few drops of coffee essence (optional)

Break the chocolate in rough pieces and warm them gently with a very little water. When melted, beat the chocolate mixture till smooth, adding the rest of the water gradually. Thicken the sauce with the cornflour or custard powder blended with a little cold water. Flavour and sweeten to taste.

If cocoa is used, mix it with the dry cornflour before blending with water.

CHOCOLATE SAUCE (2)—RICH

¼ lb. chocolate
½ pt. milk
2–3 egg yolks
Vanilla essence
1 teasp. rum
Sugar, if required
1 egg white (optional)

Dissolve the chocolate in the milk. Make a custard with the egg yolks and the chocolate-flavoured milk—*see Custard Sauce*. Flavour and sweeten to taste. If liked one egg white may be whipped to a stiff froth and folded into the finished sauce.

CHRISTMAS PUDDING SAUCE

2 eggs
⅛ pt. rum *or* brandy
1½ oz. castor sugar
⅛ pt. water

Whisk all the ingredients in a basin placed over a pan of boiling water. Whisk vigorously all the time until the sauce is thick and frothy. Serve at once.

COFFEE SAUCE

Sauce au Café

¼ pt. very strong coffee
¼ pt. milk
1 heaped teasp. cornflour *or* custard powder
1 egg yolk
Sugar to taste
Vanilla essence (optional)
1 teasp. rum (optional)

Thicken the coffee and milk with the cornflour or custard powder (*see Cornflour Sauce*). Cool the sauce, add the egg yolk and cook it without boiling. Sweeten and flavour to taste.

CORNFLOUR CUSTARD

½ oz. lightweight cornflour *or* custard powder
½ pt. milk
1 dessertsp. sugar
Flavouring
1 egg yolk

Blend the cornflour with a little of the cold milk. Boil the rest of the milk with thinly cut lemon rind if used for flavouring. Remove rind and stir the boiling liquid into the blended cornflour. Rinse the pan and return the sauce to it. Just bring it to boiling point for custard powder; boil for 3 min. for cornflour. Sweeten and flavour the sauce unless lemon rind has been used. Cool the sauce, add the egg yolk and sugar and cook gently until the egg thickens without boiling. At once pour out of the pan into a basin or the sauceboat. Flavour and add extra sweetening if required.

CORNFLOUR SAUCE

½ pt. milk
½ oz. cornflour
1 dessertsp. sugar
Lemon rind *or* any flavour to blend with the flavour of pudding which it accompanies

Blend the cornflour with a little of the cold milk. Boil the rest of the milk with the thinly cut lemon rind if used. Remove rind and stir the boiling liquid into the blended cornflour. Rinse the pan and return the sauce to it. Bring to boiling point and boil for 3 min. Sweeten and flavour the sauce, unless lemon rind has been used for flavouring.

CUSTARD SAUCE

1 dessertsp. sugar
2 egg yolks *or* 1 whole egg
½ pt. milk
Flavouring

Mix together the sugar and egg yolks *or* whole egg. Warm the milk until about at blood heat. Stir the milk into the egg, return the whole to the rinsed pan and cook gently until the egg thickens, without boiling or the egg will curdle. At once pour out of the pan into a basin or the sauceboat. Flavour and add extra sweetening if required. If the custard should curdle, whisk it vigorously just before serving.

FROTHY SAUCE

Crème fouettée

¼ pt. milk
1 tablesp. sugar
2 eggs
⅛ pt. sherry *or* white wine
Flavouring of lemon rind *or* any spice, if liked

Heat the milk. Dissolve the sugar in the milk; then allow to cool a little. Whisk the eggs and sherry together, add the warm milk. In a basin, placed over boiling water, whisk all the ingredients until the sauce is thick and frothy. Serve at once.

FRUIT SAUCE

Fruits suitable are: Damsons, Plums, Raspberries, Redcurrants, Blackberries.

1 lb. bottled *or* fresh fruit	**Lemon juice, if liked**
A very little water to stew	**1 teasp. (rounded) arrowroot to each ½ pt. purée**
Sugar to sweeten	

Stew the fruit in the water till soft, sieve it. Sweeten, flavour and thicken the sauce with arrowroot blended with a little cold water or fruit juice.

FRUIT AND YOGHOURT SAUCE—COLD

½ pt. fruit purée	**Sugar to sweeten**
1 bottle plain yoghourt	

Carefully mix the cold fruit purée and yoghourt together. Sweeten well as the mixture will be very sour.

See also Fruit Sauces to Serve with Meat: also Apple and Apricot Sauces in this section.

GINGER SAUCE

Sauce au Gingembre

½ pt. cornflour *or* custard sauce	**Golden syrup to sweeten**
1 level teasp. ground ginger	**Lemon juice**
	½ teasp. grated lemon rind (optional)

Stir the ginger into the sauce, sweeten and flavour with lemon juice and rind if liked.

NOTE: Caramel sauce with the addition of ginger is also good.

GINGER SYRUP SAUCE

Sirop du Gingembre

4 oz. brown sugar	**1 teasp. arrowroot**
½ pt. water *or* ¼ pt. syrup from preserved ginger and ¼ pt. water	**½ teasp. ground ginger**
Piece of root ginger	**1 teasp. lemon juice**
Strip of lemon rind	**1 tablesp. chopped preserved ginger**

Dissolve the sugar in the water, add the root ginger and lemon rind and simmer for 15 min. Blend the arrowroot and ground ginger with a little cold water and the lemon juice, and with this thicken the sauce. Add the preserved ginger and simmer the sauce for 2–3 min.

NOTE: Golden syrup or honey may be used instead of sugar.

JAM SAUCE

4 good tablesp. jam	**1 heaped teasp. arrowroot**
½ pt. water	**Colouring, if needed**
Sugar	
Lemon juice	

Boil the jam and water together, add sugar and lemon juice to taste, and thicken with the arrowroot blended with a little cold water. Strain the sauce if the jam has pips. Colour if necessary.

MARMALADE SAUCE (1)

Sauce Marmelade

As for Jam Sauce above substituting marmalade for jam. Do not strain the sauce.

MARMALADE SAUCE (2)

4 tablesp. stiff marmalade	**⅛ pt. white wine**

Heat the marmalade and wine together.

LEMON SAUCE (1)

Sauce Citron

½ pt. milk	**Rind of 1 lemon**
½ oz. cornflour *or* custard powder	**Sugar *or* golden syrup**
	Juice of ½ lemon

Blend the cornflour with a little cold milk. Boil the rest of the milk with the thinly cut lemon rind. Strain the boiling milk on to the blended cornflour and stir well. Rinse the pan and return the sauce to it. Just bring to boil for custard powder, boil 3 min for cornflour, then add the lemon rind, sugar or golden syrup to taste, stir in the lemon juice.

LEMON SAUCE (2)

Rind of ½ lemon	**Juice of 2 lemons**
½ pt. water	**1 heaped teasp. arrowroot**
4 oz. sugar *or* golden syrup to sweeten	

Infuse the thinly cut lemon rind in the water for 15 min., then remove it. Add sugar or syrup to flavoured water and boil for 5 min. Add the lemon juice and thicken the sauce with the arrowroot blended with a little cold water.

SWEET SAUCES

NOTE: If desired richer, a small glass of sherry and an egg yolk may be added to the above a few minutes before serving, but the sauce must not be allowed to boil again once the egg yolk has been added.

MOUSSELINE SAUCE—SWEET

1 egg	**1/8 pt. cream**
1 egg yolk	**1 tablesp. sherry *or* fruit juice**
1½ oz. castor sugar	

Separate the egg white from the yolk and whip it to a stiff froth. Put all the other ingredients into a basin placed over a pan of hot water and whisk until creamy and thick. Fold the egg white into the hot sauce. Serve at once.

ORANGE SAUCE

Sauce à l'Orange

As for Lemon sauce (1) or (2) but use much less sugar.

RUM BUTTER

See p. 677.

SABAYON SAUCE—HOT or COLD

2 egg yolks	**¼ pt. Marsala wine *or* Madeira**
1 oz. castor sugar	

In a saucepan whisk the egg yolks and sugar till very light and frothy. Stir in the wine and over very gentle heat continue whisking briskly until the sauce rises; it must not boil. Serve at once.

SWEET MELTED BUTTER SAUCE

Sauce au Beurre Sucrée

To ½ pt. white sauce (p. 115) add 1 oz. butter extra, sweeten to taste and add any sweet flavouring desired.

SWEET SAUCE—RICH

4 egg yolks *or* 2 whole eggs	**¼ pt. milk**
	Grated rind of 1 orange
4 oz. castor sugar	**¼ pt. cream**

Beat the egg yolks or whole eggs with the sugar and milk until well mixed. Add the orange rind and cream and cook over very gentle heat or in a double boiler until the sauce thickens. It must not boil.

SWEET WHIPPED EGG SAUCE

2 egg yolks	**1/8 pt. sherry *or* fruit juice *or* water and suitable flavouring**
½ oz. castor sugar	

Put all the ingredients in a china bowl, whisk them till well mixed. Place the bowl over boiling water and continue whisking until the sauce thickens. Serve at once.

SWEET WINE SAUCE

Sauce au Vin Sucré

1/8 pt. water	**Sugar to taste**
1/8 pt. sherry	**Lemon juice to taste**
2 tablesp. any jam *or* jelly	

Boil all the ingredients together for 5 min. Rub through a hair or nylon sieve or strain the sauce. Adjust the flavour, reheat if necessary. If liked this sauce may be thickened as Jam sauce.

SAVOURY VINEGARS AND STORE SAUCES

BENTON SAUCE

¼ pt. vinegar, preferably wine	**1 teasp. mixed mustard**
2 tablesp. grated horseradish	**1–2 teasp. castor sugar**

Mix all the ingredients well together. This sauce will keep for a month.

Serve with beef.

CARRACK SAUCE

1 clove of garlic	**1 tablesp. chopped pickled walnuts**
4 anchovies	
½ pt. vinegar	**1 dessertsp. good chutney, chopped**
1 dessertsp. mushroom ketchup	
1 dessertsp. any good commercial savoury sauce	

Crush and pound the garlic; crush and sieve the anchovies. Mix all the ingredients well together; bottle the sauce. Shake it frequently. Store 1 month before use.

Serve with cold meat.

CELERY VINEGAR

½ lb. celery *or* ½ oz. celery seed	**1 pt. vinegar, wine *or* white**
	½ teasp. salt

Chop the celery if used. Boil the vinegar with the salt. Pour the hot vinegar on to the chopped celery or seed, cover and leave till cold. Bottle and leave the vinegar for 3 weeks, then strain and re-bottle. Cork securely.

Use in salad dressings.

CHILLI VINEGAR

6 fresh chillies (small red peppers)	**1 pt. vinegar**

Chop the chillies roughly. Boil the vinegar, pour it hot on to the chillies, cover and allow to cool. Bottle the vinegar for 3 weeks, strain and rebottle.

Use in salad dressings.

CRESS VINEGAR

½ oz. crushed cress seed	**1 pt. vinegar**

Proceed as for chilli vinegar.

CUCUMBER VINEGAR

6 cucumbers	**2 teasp. white peppercorns**
1 qt. vinegar	**4 shallots**
2 teasp. salt	**2 cloves of garlic**

Boil the vinegar, salt and peppercorns together for 20 min., then allow the mixture to become quite cold. Slice the cucumbers without peeling them into a wide-necked bottle or jar, add the shallots and garlic, and the vinegar when cold. Cover closely and leave for 14 days, then carefully strain off into smaller bottles. Cork tightly, and store in a cool, dry place.

ESCAVEEKE SAUCE

1 pt. wine vinegar	**½ teasp. ground ginger**
Rind of 1 lemon, grated	**½ teasp. salt**
6 shallots	**⅛ teasp. cayenne pepper**
1 clove of garlic	
1 tablesp. coriander seed	

Pound all the dry ingredients well together. Boil the vinegar and pour it boiling on to the pounded mixture. Bottle when cold. Store for 1 month before use.

HERB VINEGAR

1 pt. malt vinegar	**2 cloves**
2 oz. grated horseradish	**A sprig each of thyme, basil, savory, marjoram, tarragon**
1 teasp. chopped shallot	**1 bay leaf**
Rind and juice of ½ lemon	

Simmer all the ingredients for 20 min. Cool and then strain the vinegar. Bottle when cold.

Use a very little with other vinegar in salad dressings.

HORSERADISH VINEGAR

1 pt. vinegar	**½ teasp. salt**
2 oz. grated horseradish	**$\frac{1}{16}$ teasp. cayenne**
½ oz. chopped shallot	**1 oz. sugar**

Boil the vinegar; mix together the other ingredients. Pour the boiling vinegar on to the mixture, cover. When cool bottle the mixture and store for 10 days. It may now be used unstrained as horseradish sauce. To store the vinegar, strain, boil it and bottle it in hot, dry sauce bottles. Screw them down at once.

MINT VINEGAR or BOTTLED MINT SAUCE

1 pt. wine vinegar	**1 oz. sugar**
¼ pt. chopped mint	

Make this exactly like mint sauce, omitting any water and drying the mint leaves completely before chopping them. The mint should be young and fresh. The vinegar may be strained and used for salad dressings, the mint in vinegar will keep through the winter months.

RASPBERRY VINEGAR

Raspberries	**Sugar**
Malt, wine *or* cider vinegar	

To each pound of ripe fruit allow 1 pt. wine or malt vinegar. Pick over the raspberries, cover them with vinegar, and allow to stand for 4 days. Strain through a fine hair or nylon sieve (do not press the fruit). To each pint of strained vinegar add 4–5 oz. sugar. Simmer gently for 10 min.; bottle.

SHALLOT VINEGAR

1 pt. vinegar *or* ½ pt. vinegar and ½ pt. white wine	**2 oz. shallots, chopped**

Mix the ingredients, store them in an air-tight bottle for 2 weeks. Strain the vinegar and rebottle it.

SOY

This sauce is usually bought ready prepared. It is imported from China and Japan, where it is made from small beans which are subjected to long fermentation and then long digestion in brine.

TARRAGON VINEGAR

1 pt. vinegar	**2 oz. tarragon leaves**

Bruise the tarragon leaves slightly. Put them into a bottling jar, pour in the vinegar and screw down the cap. Store the vinegar for 6 weeks, then strain and rebottle it. Store in a cool dry place.

NOTE: If using home-grown tarragon, the leaves should be gathered on a dry day about the end of July, just before the plant begins to bloom.

WORCESTER SAUCE

4 shallots	**5 tablesp. anchovy essence**
1 qt. best brown vinegar	**4 tablesp. soy**
6 tablesp. walnut ketchup	**½ teasp. cayenne pepper**
	Salt to taste

Chop the shallots very finely. Put with all the other ingredients into a large bottle, and cork it closely. Shake well 3 or 4 times daily for about 14 days, then strain the sauce into small bottles, cork tightly, and store in a cool, dry place.

FORCEMEATS OR STUFFINGS

Forcemeat, or **Farcemeat** as it was originally called, derives its name from the French verb *farcie*, to stuff.

The excellence of forcemeat depends on flavouring and seasoning. The flavouring should enhance the flavour of the dish with which the stuffing is to be used, e.g. lemon flavouring with sweet dishes, anchovy flavouring with white fish, etc.

Many forcemeats may be made into balls the size of a walnut and baked, fried or poached to serve with roast, braised or stewed meats. For this purpose the mixture must be bound with egg and should be stiff enough to shape into balls. The balls may be coated with egg and crumbs before frying or baking.

APPLE AND CELERY STUFFING

2 oz. chopped salt pork *or* bacon diced *or* pork sausage meat	**3 oz. stale breadcrumbs**
2 onions	**2 tablesp. chopped parsley**
4 tablesp. chopped celery	**Sugar to taste**
4 medium cooking apples	**Salt and pepper**

Brown the pork, bacon or sausage in its own fat, lift it out of the pan. Chop the onion. In the pork fat cook the onion and celery for 5 min., then remove them. Dice the apples and in the same fat fry them till tender and brown. Mix all the ingredients together.

Use with duck, goose or pork.

APPLE AND WALNUT STUFFING

1 onion	**2 oz. breadcrumbs**
½ oz. butter	**½ teasp. powdered, mixed herbs**
1 large, sour apple	**Salt and pepper**
12 walnuts	**1 egg**
2 oz. pork sausage meat	**Milk if needed to mix**

Finely chop the onion. Fry it very gently till soft and light golden in the butter. Peel, core, chop the apple, peel and chop the walnuts. Mix all the ingredients together and bind them with beaten egg and as much milk as necessary.

Use for stuffing roast goose or duck.

CHESTNUT STUFFING

2 lb. chestnuts	**A trace of powdered cinnamon**
$1/4$–$1/2$ pt. stock	**$1/2$ teasp. sugar**
2 oz. butter	
Salt and pepper	

Slit the chestnuts and bake or boil them for 20 min. Remove shells and skins. Stew the chestnuts till tender in sufficient stock barely to cover them. Rub them through a fine wire sieve. Add the butter, seasoning, flavouring, sugar and sufficient stock to make a soft dough.

Use for roast turkey, also good with chicken.

FISH FORCEMEAT

$1/2$ lb. raw white fish without bone or skin	**1–2 eggs**
1 oz. butter	**Salt and pepper**
1 oz. flour	**Grated lemon rind**
$1/4$ pt. fish stock *or* milk	**Lemon juice**

Melt the butter in a saucepan, stir in the flour then the stock and beat the mixture over heat till it forms a stiff ball. Cool this panada, then beat into it the beaten eggs and seasoning. Flake the fish, removing all small bones. Beat the fish into the egg mixture. Add grated lemon rind and lemon juice to taste.

GIBLET STUFFING

Cooked giblets	**1 teasp. mixed fresh herbs *or* $1/2$ teasp. dried herbs**
1 onion, cooked	**1 tablesp. chopped parsley**
2–4 oz. breadcrumbs	**A little grated lemon rind (if liked)**
$1/8$–$1/4$ pt. boiling stock	**Salt and pepper**
1–2 oz. butter	
1 egg	

The giblets are stewed for $1\frac{1}{2}$ hr. or until tender, with the onion. The liquid in which they are cooked makes the gravy for the roast bird. Remove all bones from the neck and the lining of the gizzard and chop or mince the flesh of the giblets. Soak the crumbs in sufficient boiling stock to moisten them. Melt the fat. Beat the egg. Mix all the ingredients together and season the mixture to taste.

Use for chicken or turkey.

HAM STUFFING or FORCEMEAT

4 oz. lean ham *or* bacon	**Grated rind of 1 lemon**
2 oz. suet *or* margarine	**A little grated nutmeg**
4 oz. breadcrumbs	**$1/16$ teasp. powdered allspice**
1 tablesp. chopped parsley	**1 egg**
1 teasp. mixed fresh herbs *or* $1/2$ teasp. dried herbs	**A little milk *or* stock**
	Salt and pepper

Chop or mince the ham and chop or grate the suet. Mix all the dry ingredients and bind with the egg and stock or milk. Season well.

When the mixture is intended for balls, the consistency should be tested by poaching a small quantity in boiling water.

Use for veal, poultry or hare.

LIVER FARCE or STUFFING

$1/2$ lb. calf's *or* chicken's liver	**$1/2$ beaten egg**
$1/4$ lb. bacon *or* pork sausage meat	**$1/2$ teasp. chopped fresh herbs**
1 very small onion	**1 teasp. chopped parsley**
1 oz. butter	**Salt and pepper**

Cut the liver and bacon into $\frac{1}{4}$-in. dice. Chop the onion. Melt the butter and in it cook the bacon, liver and onion gently for 10 min. Chop them still more finely and add the other ingredients.

Use for poultry or game.

MUSHROOM STUFFING

4 oz. mushrooms	**Salt and pepper**
1 oz. bacon	**Nutmeg**
4 oz. breadcrumbs	**1 egg**
$1/2$ oz. butter	

Skin and chop the mushrooms (including the stalks). Chop the bacon. Fry the bacon for a few minutes then add the mushrooms and fry them very slowly for 5 min. Mix all the ingredients and season to taste.

Use for pigeons and other small birds, for fish or vegetables.

FORCEMEATS OR STUFFINGS

OATMEAL STUFFING

½ lb. medium oatmeal
¼ lb. suet
2 medium onions, cooked
Salt and pepper
Nutmeg

Toast the oatmeal a light golden colour. Shred and chop the suet and the onions. Mix all the ingredients together and season them.

Use for boiled fowl.

OYSTER FORCEMEAT

6 canned *or* fresh oysters
¼ lb. breadcrumbs
2 oz. suet *or* butter
1 teasp. fresh mixed herbs
1 egg
A little oyster liquor
Salt and pepper
A very little nutmeg

Beard fresh oysters and simmer them very gently in their own liquid for 10 min. Canned oysters need no further cooking. Cut the oysters into small pieces. Mix all the dry ingredients and bind them with beaten egg and oyster liquor. Season carefully.

Use for roast turkey.

RICE STUFFING for chicken

2 oz. rice
1 chicken liver
1 small onion
2 oz. raisins
2 oz. ground *or* chopped almonds
2 tablesp. chopped parsley
1 oz. butter
1 sprig of thyme
Salt and pepper
1 egg (optional)

Boil the rice till just tender. Chop the liver and the onion. Mix all the ingredients, mashing the butter into the mixture with a fork. Season and bind them well together.

Use also for other meat, fish or vegetables.

SAGE AND ONION STUFFING

¼ lb. onions
4 young sage leaves *or* ½ teasp. powdered sage
2 oz. breadcrumbs
1 oz. butter
Salt and pepper
½ egg (optional)

Slice the onions thickly, parboil them 10 min. in very little water. Scald the sage leaves. Chop the onions and sage. Mash and work all the ingredients together and season to taste.

Use for pork, goose or duck.

SAUSAGE STUFFING—HOME-MADE

½ lb. lean pork
2 oz. breadcrumbs
½ teasp. mixed fresh herbs *or* ¼ teasp. dried herbs
2 small sage leaves
Salt and pepper
Grated nutmeg to taste
The liver of the bird to be stuffed
Stock

Mince the pork. Chop the liver. Mix all the ingredients, using enough stock to bind the mixture. Season to taste.

Use for turkey or chicken.

NOTE: A good bought pork sausage meat mixed with the liver of the bird makes a quick stuffing for poultry.

SOYER'S STUFFING

2 cooking apples
2 small leaves of sage
4 leaves of thyme
2 onions
½ lb. dry, mashed potatoes
Salt and pepper

Chop the apples and herbs. Parboil and chop the onion. Mix all ingredients together and season to taste.

Use for roast goose.

TOMATO STUFFING

1 large ripe tomato
½ sweet, red pepper *or* pimento
½ clove of garlic
2 tablesp. breadcrumbs
Salt and pepper

Scald, skin and chop the tomato. Remove the seeds from the pimento and chop it. Crush and chop the garlic. Mix the ingredients, using enough crumbs to absorb the juice of the tomato. Season to taste.

Use with pigeon or other small birds.

VEAL STUFFING or FORCEMEAT

4 oz. breadcrumbs
2 oz. chopped suet *or* margarine
1 tablesp. chopped parsley
½ teasp. chopped mixed herbs
Nutmeg
Grated rind of ½ lemon
Salt and pepper
1 beaten egg

Mix together all the ingredients and season to taste.

Use for veal and poultry, fish or vegetables.

FISH

PERHAPS IT IS BECAUSE fish must be handled and cooked with care that it does not figure on the menu as often as it might. Yet fish is as rich in protein—one of the best body-building foods—as meat. Oily fish, such as salmon, grilse (young salmon), herring, mackerel and sprats, where the fat is distributed throughout the flesh, provide valuable quantities of vitamins A and D. The flesh of white fish, such as cod, haddock and whiting, contains very little fat, most of the oil being stored in the liver. Canned fish are often packed in oil, thus adding extra fat, and as the bones are usually sufficiently soft to be eaten, they also provide calcium and phosphorus—both bone- and teeth-building materials.

The cost of the different varieties of fish gives little indication of their value as food. Herrings are one of the cheapest varieties and yet have a high nutritive value.

Most varieties of white fish (particularly whiting), because of their lack of fat have less flavour than oily fish but are easily digested, and it is for this reason that white fish figures in the diet of invalids and convalescents.

Fish can be served in many varied ways at almost any meal, and provides an economical and wholesome dish.

SEA AND FRESH WATER FISH

CHOOSING FISH—POINTS TO LOOK FOR

1. Fish should first of all be fresh. The flesh should be firm not flabby.
2. There should be no stale smell.
3. The gills of most varieties should be bright red.
4. The eyes should be bright and not sunken in the head.
5. A "slimy" skin is a sure sign of freshness, providing it is not a decomposed yellowish slime.

BUYING FISH

When about to buy fish, the housewife should not set out with the fixed intention of buying a certain kind of fish, but be guided in her selection by the state of the market.

Many circumstances combine to make the variations in the price of fish greater than in the case of any other food commodity. The fact that fish is a most perishable article of food and is usually caught while travelling in shoals results in alternate scarcity and over-supply of a particular kind. More often than not the housewife will find that some particular fish is scarce, and that in consequence it is priced far beyond its worth, and quite out of comparison with the price of other kinds of fish which are plentiful in the market. The cheaper varieties of fish can be a much better buy than the more fashionable varieties and vice versa.

Smaller, younger fish are to be preferred. A flat fish should be thick in proportion to its size. In buying a slice of fish it is better to choose a thick slice from a small fish than a thin slice from a large one. Avoid cuts of fish with too much bone or waste tissue.

All fresh fish should be cooked the day it is bought as it quickly loses its freshness and flavour. If fish is put into a refrigerator it must be covered to prevent the fish smell tainting other foods. Quick frozen fish should be stored in the "freezer" compartment; it can be kept for 48 hr. and once it has thawed out it must not be re-frozen. If you have a deep freezer (0° F.) it can be kept for 2–3 months, 2 months for oily fish and 3 for lean fish.

PREPARING FISH

Fishmongers are only too glad to prepare fish ready for the housewife to cook, but if for some reason that is impracticable here are the simple ways of doing it.

TO CLEAN WHOLE FISH

Scrape off any scales on both sides of the fish with the back of a knife. Hold the fish by the tail and scrape from the tail towards the head. Rinse often whilst working to remove loose scales.

Round fish: With a pair of kitchen scissors or sharp knife slit the belly from just below the head to half-way to the tail, remove and discard the entrails, reserve the roe. Wash well. Rub with a little salt to remove any black tissues. If the head is to be left on take out the eyes, if the head is to be removed cut across behind the gills.

Flat fish: Cut off the fins, remove the gills. Cut open the belly which is just under the head, on the dark side, and remove and discard the entrails. Wash with cold water. To remove the head make a semi-circular cut below the head.

TO SKIN WHOLE FLAT FISH

The dark skin of sole is always removed but not necessarily the white. The skin of turbot is usually cut off after filleting.

To skin any fish it must be kept wet. With whole flat fish begin at the tail. Cut the skin across, but do not cut into the flesh, and loosen the skin along the fins on either side with the fingers. Then tear off the skin with the left hand, keeping the thumb of the right hand well pressed over the backbone to prevent the removal of the flesh with the skin.

TO SKIN WHOLE ROUND FISH

Cut off a narrow strip of skin over and along the backbone near the tail. Make another cut just below the head and loosen the skin below the head with the point of a sharp knife. Dip the fingers in salt to give a better grip and gently pull off the skin, working towards the tail. Keep the thumb of the right hand well pressed over the backbone to prevent the removal of the flesh with the skin. Remove the skin from the other side in the same way.

FILLETING

A fillet is virtually a whole piece of fish taken from shoulder to tail; if a fillet is cut up then the resulting pieces are, correctly speaking, called "pieces" or "portions". Four fillets are obtained from flat fish and two from round fish.

Flat Fish: Place the fish flat on a board or table, and with the point of a sharp, flexible knife cut the flesh from head to tail down the backbone. Next insert the knife in the slit made, and carefully separate the flesh from the bone, keeping the knife pressed lightly against the bone meanwhile. Remove the fillet, turn the fish round, remove the second fillet from tail to head, then turn the fish over and remove the other two fillets in the same way.

Round Fish: With a sharp knife slit the fish down the centre back to the bone. Working from head end to tail, cut along the belly, cutting the flesh cleanly from the bones by keeping the knife pressed against the bones. Remove the fillet from the other side in the same way.

TO SKIN FILLETS

Place the fillets on a board skin side down. Rub a little salt on the fingers of the left hand, take a firm hold of the tail in the left hand, and with a knife in the right hand, and using a "sawing" movement, peel the flesh away from the skin, working from tail to head.

Always use the skin and bones for making fish stock.

COOKING FISH

It is a common error to wash fish too much, as by doing so the flavour is diminished. Usually whole fish are washed and dried, but portions of cut fish are wiped with a clean damp cloth.

COOKING FISH

As fish can so easily be spoiled by over or under cooking, it is essential to know when it is sufficiently cooked. Test for readiness by pressing gently in the thickest part. The flesh will readily separate from the bones when fully cooked. When cooking fillets or cutlets the presence of a white "curd" like substance between the flakes is an indication that the fish is cooked.

Of the various ways in which fish may be cooked, boiling or poaching is the least recommended as more flavour is lost by these methods.

BOILING OR POACHING—suitable for whole fish or cuts of large fish, e.g. cod and haddock.

The term "boiled" fish is really a misnomer, strictly speaking fish should *never be boiled*, the water should just simmer gently *below boiling* point.

The ideal way to poach fish is to use a fish-kettle, i.e. a large pan fitted with a strainer so that the fish can be gently lifted out without breaking. If no fish-kettle is available, use a large saucepan, tie the fish loosely in clean muslin (for easy removal) and place on a plate on the bottom of the pan.

Salmon and salmon trout should be put into boiling salted water, to preserve their colour; but other kinds of fish should be placed in warm water, because boiling water has a tendency to break the skin, and cold water extracts much of the flavour.

Cook the fish in just sufficient water to cover the fish (this should afterwards be used as a basis for fish soup or fish sauce) as soluble nutrients diffuse out into the cooking water. For each quart of water add 1 tablesp. vinegar and 2 level teasp. salt. Lemon juice added to the water when cooking white fish tends to increase its whiteness.

When boiling point is reached, reduce heat immediately and allow fish to simmer gently in water just off the boil. The time required for cooking depends more on the thickness than on the weight of the fish, allow 10–15 min. per lb.

FRYING—suitable for fillets, steaks and small whole fish.

Fish to be fried should be well dried after washing or wiping, and should first be coated to prevent the fat from soaking into the fish. It may be coated with egg and breadcrumbs, milk or beaten egg and seasoned flour; or if to be fried in deep fat, coated with batter. See also notes on frying p. 47.

Shallow frying is better for thick slices or steaks, which require longer cooking to ensure that they are cooked through.

There should be enough fat in the pan to come half-way up the fish. Heat the fat, put in the coated fish and fry until golden brown on one side, then turn and brown the other side. Allow 6–8 min. for fillets and 8–12 min. for larger pieces.

Deep frying requires a deep frying-pan with a frying basket or deep heavy pan with a perforated spoon to remove the fish from the hot fat. The fat should be very hot, but its temperature must be slightly lower when frying fish fillets than when frying croquettes, rissoles, etc., which are usually composed of cooked fish. When the surface of a small piece of bread immediately hardens and slightly changes its colour on being immersed in the fat, the temperature is correct for raw food or anything thickly coated with batter, but when frying anything of which the exterior only has to be cooked, it is better to have the fat sufficiently hot to brown at once whatever is immersed in it. Heat the fish basket, if used, in the fat, but gently drop the coated fish into the fat—do not place directly on the fish basket or the coating will stick to the wires of the basket.

Do not try to fry too much fish at a time as this reduces the temperature of the fat and the result will be pale, greasy fish.

Anything fried should afterwards be well drained on kitchen paper. Fish is usually garnished with lemon and parsley; croquettes with parsley alone.

GRILLING—suitable for steaks, cutlets or fillets and small whole fish, e.g. herring, plaice and sole.

This method of cooking is an extremely simple one. The fish should be thoroughly dried, then liberally brushed over with a little oil or melted fat and seasoned with salt and pepper. Score deep gashes across whole fish to allow the heat to penetrate, or the outside may dry up before the fish is cooked.

Heat the grill and grease the grill rack to prevent the fish sticking. Cook the fish rather slowly, turning carefully until done. Allow 7–8 min. for thin fillets and 10–15 min. for steaks and thicker fish.

STEAMING—suitable for fillets or thin slices.

This is a very favourite and excellent way of cooking fish, as although it is a rather slower process than boiling, the flavour is better preserved, and the danger of the fish being broken is eliminated. If using a steamer a piece of greased greaseproof paper placed in the bottom will facilitate removal of the fish after cooking. Season the prepared fish and sprinkle with lemon juice.

When a small quantity of fish has to be steamed the following method is exceedingly easy and gives excellent results: Place the fish on a well-greased soup plate. Sprinkle lightly with salt, pepper and lemon juice, and cover with a piece of greased greaseproof paper. Place the plate over a saucepan of boiling water (or over the pan of potatoes if serving potatoes with the fish) and cover with another plate or the lid of the saucepan. Steam for 10–25 min., depending on the thickness of the fish. Turn the fish once during cooking. Serve with the fish liquor or a fish sauce made from the liquor.

STEWING—suitable for steaks, fillets and small pieces of cod.

In stewing, a gentle simmering in a small quantity of fish stock made from bone and fish trimmings, or in milk and water, until the flesh comes easily away from the bones, is all that is required. This is one of the most economical and tasty ways of cooking fish. Cook slowly. Fish should invariably be stewed in a fireproof glass or an earthenware dish. The liquid in which the fish has been simmered may be flavoured and thickened and used as a sauce.

BAKING—This is a very satisfactory method of cooking almost any whole round white fish or a middle cut from a large fish, or steaks or fillets.

Place the prepared fish in a well-greased baking-tin or fireproof dish with a very little fat, cover with greased greaseproof paper. Bake in a fairly hot oven **(375° F., Gas 5)**. Cooking time will vary according to thickness and weight, but average times are 10–20 min. for fillets, depending on thickness; allow about 10 min. per lb. and 10 min. over for whole fish weighing up to 4 lb.

BARBEL

BARBEL

Barbeau

1–2 barbel, according to size
1 tablesp. salt
2 small onions, sliced
2 anchovies
2 tablesp. vinegar
Juice of 1 lemon
Bouquet garni
Grated nutmeg to taste
Pinch of mace

Soak the fish in slightly salted water for 2–3 hr. Put into a fish-kettle or saucepan with warm water and the salt, and poach gently until done. Take 1 pt. of the water in which the fish was cooked and add to it the other ingredients. Simmer gently for about 15 min., then strain, and return to the saucepan. Put in the fish and let it heat gradually in the flavoured liquor.

4 helpings

BLOATERS

GRILLED BLOATERS

Break off the head, split the back, remove the roe and take out the backbone. Rub over with a little fat, place the fish, inside down, on a grill pan grid. Cook until nicely browned, turn over and cook the back. If preferred place 2 bloaters with the insides together, and cook as above. The roes should be cooked and served with the bloaters.

Cooking time—7 min.

BREAM

Brème

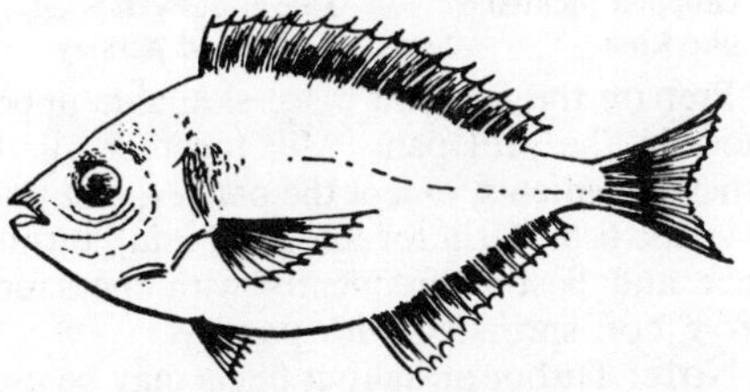

Sea Bream is available all the year but best from June to December. Fresh-water Bream is in season July–February. Bream can be baked or grilled. It is often sold ready filleted.

BAKED SEA BREAM

Brème de Mer rôtie

1 bream about 2 lb. weight
Salt and pepper
Cayenne pepper
2 oz. butter *or* cooking fat (approx.)

Thoroughly wash the bream, but do not remove the scales, dry thoroughly with a clean cloth. Season inside and out with salt and pepper and place in a well-greased baking-dish. Place the butter in small pieces on the fish and bake in a fairly hot oven (**375° F., Gas 5**) for a little more than 30 min.

4 helpings

BAKED STUFFED SEA BREAM

Brème de Mer farcie cuite au Four

One 3–4 lb. sea bream (cleaned)
3 rashers streaky bacon

STUFFING

2 oz. margarine
1 medium sized onion
2 sticks celery
4 oz. cooked rice
¼ level teasp. sage
¼ level teasp. thyme
1½ oz. chopped stuffed olives (optional)
Seasoning to taste

GARNISH

Parsley *or* watercress

Scale the fish and trim the fins and tail. Leave the head on, but remove the eyes. To make the stuffing, melt the margarine in a pan, add the chopped onion and celery and fry gently for about 3 min. Add the rice and remaining ingredients and mix thoroughly over the heat for 2–3 min. Stuff fish with some of the mixture and spread the remainder over the bottom of a shallow fireproof dish. Place the fish on top and cover with the bacon, cut in long thin strips, arranged in a criss-cross pattern. Bake in a fairly hot oven (**375° F., Gas 5**) for 30–40 min. (allowing 10 min. per lb.). Serve in the same dish, garnished with parsley or watercress.

4 helpings **Cooking time—30–40 min.**

SAVOURY GRILLED SEA BREAM

Brème de Mer grillée aux fines Herbes

1 lb. fillet of sea bream (approx.)
2 tablesp. salad oil
1 tablesp. vinegar
1 level dessertsp. chopped pickled gherkins
1 level dessertsp. chopped pickled capers
Salt and pepper
1 level dessertsp. chopped parsley

Remove the rack of the grill pan. Wipe the fish and place skin side uppermost in the bottom of the grill pan. Mix together all the other ingredients, except the parsley, and pour over the fish. Grill steadily for about 15 min., turning once and basting frequently with the sauce. Serve hot sprinkled with parsley.

4 helpings **Cooking time—15 min. (approx.)**

SEA BREAM MAYONNAISE

Mayonnaise de Brème de Mer

1–1½ lb. fillets of sea bream (approx.)
A little lemon juice
Seasoning
¼ pt. mayonnaise
1 tablesp. chopped parsley
1 hard-boiled egg
Lettuce

Skin the fillets and place in a greased fireproof dish, sprinkle with lemon juice and seasoning. Cover with greaseproof paper and bake in a fairly hot oven (**375° F., Gas 5**) for about 20 min. When cooked, flake with a fork, remove any bones and leave to become cold. Just before serving mix the fish with mayonnaise, parsley and chopped egg and serve on a bed of lettuce.

4 helpings

BRILL

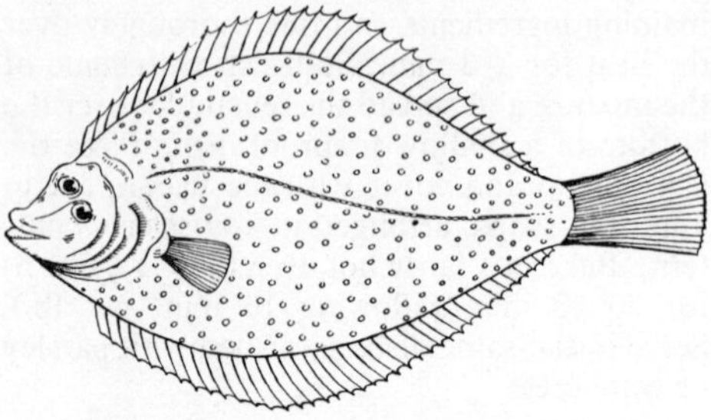

In season practically all the year, but only small quantities landed.

BRILL

Barbue

1 small brill	Salt
Lemon juice	Vinegar

Clean the brill, cut off the fins, and rub a little lemon juice over it to preserve its whiteness. Barely cover the fish with warm water, add salt and vinegar to taste and simmer gently until done (allow about 10 min. per lb.). Garnish with cut lemon and parsley, and serve with either lobster, shrimp, Hollandaise or melted butter sauce.

NOTE: This fish is also nice baked or grilled.

Allow 4–6 oz. per helping

BRILL À LA CONTI

Barbue à la Conti

1 brill weighing about 2½ lb.	Salt and pepper
1 glass white wine (optional)	1½ pt. stock
	1 teasp. finely-chopped parsley

Clean and skin the fish and cut some slits down the back. Add the wine (if used) and salt and pepper to the stock; when warm, put in the fish and simmer gently until done. Remove the fish and keep it hot; boil the stock rapidly until reduced to half its original quantity; then add the parsley and pour over the fish.

6 helpings
Cooking time—20 min.

SAVOURY GRILLED BRILL

Barbue grillée aux fines Herbes

1 lb. fillets of brill	1 level dessertsp. chopped pickled capers
2 tablesp. salad oil	Salt and pepper
1 tablesp. vinegar	1 level dessertsp. chopped parsley
1 level dessertsp. chopped pickled gherkins	

Prepare the fish and place skin side uppermost in the grill pan. Mix together all the other ingredients, except the parsley, and pour over the fish. Grill for about 15 min., turning once and basting frequently with the sauce. Serve hot, sprinkled with parsley.

NOTE: Turbot or halibut fillets may be used instead of brill.

4 helpings

CARP

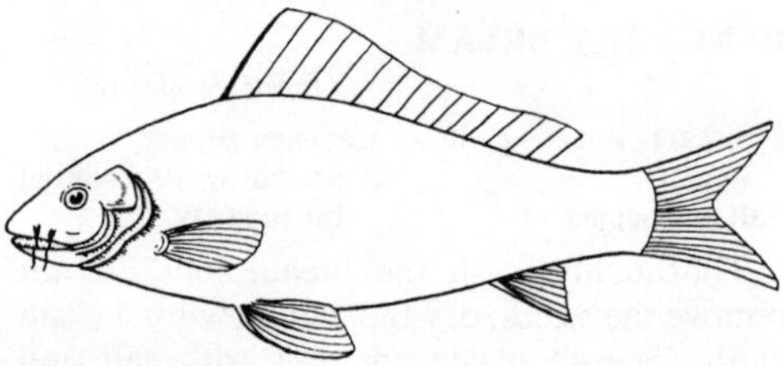

BAKED CARP

Carpe farcie

1 carp	Butter for basting
Egg and breadcrumbs	

FORCEMEAT

8 sauce oysters	1 shallot
3 anchovies, boned	Salt
2 tablesp. breadcrumbs	Cayenne pepper
1 teasp. finely-chopped parsley	1 egg yolk

SAUCE

1 oz. butter	1 tablesp. lemon juice
1 tablesp. flour	½ tablesp. Worcester sauce
¾ pt. good stock	
1 teasp. mixed mustard	

Clean and scale the fish. Remove the beards of the oysters and simmer for 15 min. in a little fish stock or water. Cut the oysters into small pieces, but do not cook them; also cut the anchovies into small pieces. Mix together the breadcrumbs, oysters, anchovies, parsley, finely-chopped shallot and seasoning; add the egg yolk, the liquor of the oysters and the stock in which the oysterbeards were simmered. Put the forcemeat inside the fish and sew up the opening; brush over with egg and coat with breadcrumbs. Place in a baking-dish and cook gently for about 1 hr., basting frequently with hot butter. To make the sauce: melt the butter in a saucepan, stir in the flour, add the stock and stir until the sauce boils. Simmer for 2–3 min. then add the mustard, lemon juice, Worcester sauce and the liquor (strained) in which the fish was cooked. Garnish the fish with cut lemon and parsley, and serve the sauce in a sauceboat.

NOTE: The fish may be stuffed with veal forcemeat instead of oyster forcemeat if liked.

4–5 helpings
Cooking time—1¼–1½ hr.

FRIED CARP

Carpe frite

1 small to medium-size carp	**Salt and cayenne pepper**
	Flour
	Fat for frying

Clean, scale, and soak the fish 1 hr. in salt water, then split open and lay it flat. Dry well, sprinkle with salt and cayenne, dredge with flour and fry in hot butter or fat until nicely browned. Garnish with cut lemon and the roe fried. Serve with anchovy sauce.

2–3 helpings
Cooking time—20–30 min.

STEWED CARP

Carpe en Ragoût

1 large carp	**Bouquet garni**
Vinegar	**A good pinch of grated nutmeg**
2–3 small onions	**Salt and pepper**
2 oz. butter	**1 tablesp. flour**
1 pt. stock	**Toasted bread**
12 small button mushrooms	

Wash the fish in vinegar and water and cut it into thick slices. Slice the onions. Melt 1½ oz. of the butter in a saucepan, fry the onion until brown, then add the stock, mushrooms, herbs, nutmeg and seasoning. When warm, add the fish and simmer gently for 30–40 min. Meanwhile knead together the flour and remaining butter. Take out the fish and keep it hot. Add the butter and flour to the contents of the saucepan, simmer and stir until the sauce is cooked smoothly. Place the fish on a hot dish, strain the sauce over and garnish with the mushrooms and sippets of toasted bread.

5–6 helpings

CATFISH

See Rockfish

COALFISH

See Saithe

COD

Cabillaud

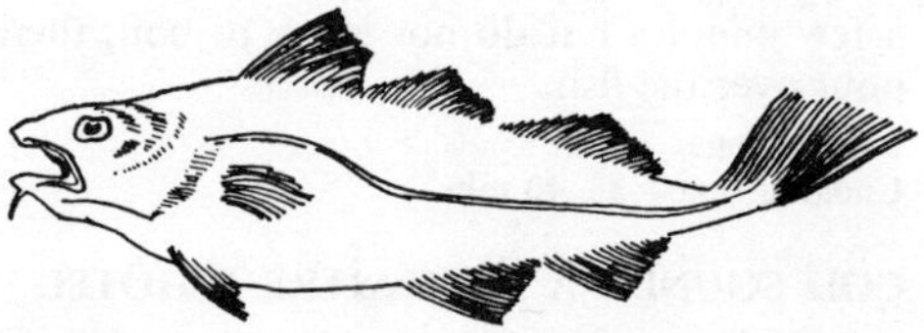

Cod is available all the year; best from October to February. It is suitable for all methods of cooking, and is good cold with salad. Also smoked and sold as Smoked Cod Fillet.

COD À LA MAÎTRE D'HÔTEL

Cabillaud à la Maître d'Hôtel

2 lb. cod (cold remains can be used)	**1 teasp. finely-chopped parsley**
4 oz. butter	**Juice of ½ lemon**
1 teasp. finely-chopped onion	**Pepper and salt**

Poach the cod, and afterwards remove skin and bone and separate the flesh into large flakes. Melt the butter in a saucepan, add the onion, and fry for 2–3 min. without browning. Add the parsley, lemon juice, a good pinch of pepper, salt and the fish. Heat until quite hot, shaking gently all the time, then serve.

5–6 helpings
Cooking time 30–40 min.

COD À LA PROVENÇALE

2 lb. middle cut cod (approx.)
Salt and pepper
½ pt. Velouté *or* other rich white sauce
1 gill white stock
2 small shallots
A small bunch of parsley
Bouquet garni
1 egg yolk
2 oz. butter
1 teasp. anchovy paste
1 teasp. chopped parsley
2 teasp. capers

Wash and wipe the fish well and place in a saucepan. Season with pepper and salt, and add the sauce, stock, finely-chopped shallots, bunch of parsley and the bouquet garni. Simmer slowly until the fish is done, basting occasionally. Remove the fish to a hot dish, and keep it warm. Reduce the sauce until the desired consistency is obtained. Remove the herbs, add the egg yolk, work in the butter, and pass through a strainer. Return to a smaller saucepan, add the anchovy paste, chopped parsley and capers, stir over heat for a few minutes but do not allow to boil, then pour over the fish.

5–6 helpings
Cooking time—35–40 min.

COD SOUNDS À LA MAÎTRE D'HÔTEL

2 lb. cod sounds
1–2 oz. butter
1 teasp. finely-chopped onion
1 tablesp. lemon juice
1 dessertsp. finely-chopped parsley
Pepper

Soak and boil the sounds and cut them into small pieces. Melt the butter, fry the onion for 2–3 min. without browning, then put in the lemon juice, parsley, a good sprinkling of pepper and the fish. Allow to get hot then serve.

6–7 helpings
Cooking time—about 1 hr.

COD STEAKS

Tranches de Cabillaud

Four 4–6 oz. cod steaks
Flour
Salt and pepper
Fat for frying
Parsley

Make a rather thin batter of flour and water, season well with salt and pepper. Melt sufficient clarified fat or dripping in a frying-pan to form a layer about ½ in. deep. Wipe the fish, dip each piece separately in the batter, place these at once in the hot fat, and fry until light-brown, turning once during the process. Drain well, and serve garnished with crisply-fried parsley. If preferred, the fish may be coated with egg and breadcrumbs and fried in deep fat.

Serve with anchovy or tomato sauce.

4 helpings

COD STEAKS—CARDINAL STYLE

Tranches de Cabillaud à la Cardinal

2 cod steaks 1¼–1½ in. thick
Salt and pepper
1½ oz. butter
1 oz. flour
¼ pt. milk
2 tomatoes
A few drops carmine *or* cochineal
A little finely-chopped parsley

Wipe the cod steaks with a clean damp cloth, place them in a baking-dish and sprinkle with salt and pepper. Place ½ oz. of butter in small pieces on the top of the fish, cover with greased paper and bake for 20–25 min. in a moderate oven (**350° F., Gas 4**). Meanwhile melt the remaining 1 oz. of butter in a saucepan, stir in the flour, add the milk and boil well. Sieve the tomatoes and add the purée to the contents of the saucepan. When the fish is done, remove it to a hot dish, strain the liquor from it and add it to the sauce. Season to taste, add carmine or cochineal until a bright-red colour is obtained and pour it over the fish. Sprinkle on a little parsley and serve.

3–4 helpings

COD WITH CREAM SAUCE

Cabillaud à la Crême

2 lb. cod
2 oz. butter
½ pt. white stock *or* milk
1 oz. flour
2 tablesp. cream
1 teasp. lemon juice
Salt and pepper

Wash and dry the fish thoroughly. Melt 1½ oz. butter in a saucepan, put in the cod and fry quickly on both sides without browning. Add the stock or milk, cover closely and simmer gently for about 20 min. Drain the fish then place on a hot dish. Melt the remaining ½ oz. butter, stir in the flour, add the stock in which the fish was cooked and enough milk to make up the original quantity (½ pt.), boil up and simmer for about 4 min. to cook the flour. Add the cream and lemon juice, season to taste and strain over the fish.

5–6 helpings

CURRIED COD

Cabillaud au Kari

2 lb. cod	**1 pt. white stock (fish *or* bone)**
2 oz. butter	**1 tablesp. lemon juice**
1 medium-sized onion	**Salt and pepper**
1 tablesp. flour	**Cayenne pepper**
1 dessertsp. curry powder	

Wash and dry the cod, and cut into pieces about $1\frac{1}{2}$ in. square. Melt the butter in a saucepan, fry the cod slightly, then take out and put aside. Add the sliced onion, flour and curry powder to the butter in the saucepan and fry 15 min., stirring constantly to prevent the onion becoming too brown, then pour in the stock. Stir until boiling then simmer gently for 20 min. Strain and return to the saucepan, add lemon juice and seasoning to taste, bring nearly to boiling-point, then put in the fish. Cover closely, and heat gently until the fish becomes thoroughly impregnated with the flavour of the sauce. An occasional stir must be given to prevent the fish sticking to the bottom of the saucepan.

NOTE: Remains of cold fish may be used for this dish in which case the preliminary frying may be omitted.

5–6 helpings

GOLDEN GRILLED COD

4 cutlets *or* steaks of cod about 1 in. thick	**1–2 oz. grated cheese**
1 oz. margarine	**2 tablesp. milk (optional)**
	Salt and pepper

Place the prepared fish in a greased fireproof dish and grill quickly for 2–3 min. on one side. Meanwhile soften the margarine and cream the cheese and margarine together, then work in the milk if used and season to taste. Turn the fish over and spread the cheese mixture over the uncooked side and return to the grill. Reduce the heat slightly and cook gently for a further 10–12 min. until the coating is brown and the fish cooked through. Serve at once.

NOTE: Cod fillet can be used instead of cutlets. Allow $1\text{–}1\frac{1}{4}$ lb. and cut into 4 portions before cooking.

4 helpings

The topping can be varied as follows:

Devilled Grill

1 oz. margarine	**1 teasp. anchovy essence (optional)**
1 level teasp. chutney	**Salt and pepper to taste**
1 level teasp. curry powder	
1 level teasp. dry mustard	

Surprise Grill

1 oz. margarine	**3 level tablesp. grated onion**
2 teasp. lemon juice	**Salt and pepper**

HASHED COD

Cabillaud en Hachis

2 lb. cooked cod	**$\frac{1}{4}$ pt. picked shrimps**
$1\frac{1}{2}$ oz. butter	**Salt and pepper**
$1\frac{1}{2}$ oz. flour	**Mashed potatoes**
1 pt. milk	**Chopped parsley**

Remove skin and bone and flake the fish into small pieces. Blend the butter and flour in a saucepan, and fry for a few minutes without browning. Add the milk and stir until boiling. Then put in the cod and the shrimps. Cook until thoroughly hot and season carefully. Make a deep border of mashed potatoes on a hot dish, pour the hash in the centre and sprinkle a little chopped parsley over the top.

4–5 helpings **Cooking time—$\frac{1}{2}$ hr.**

COD'S ROE

Laitance de Cabillaud

1 lb. cod's roe	**Melted butter sauce *or* other white sauce**
Salt	**A little milk *or* cream**
Vinegar	**Brown breadcrumbs**

Wash and wipe the cod's roe and poach for 10 min. in water with a little salt and vinegar. Dice the roe and put into melted butter sauce or other white sauce diluted with a little cream or milk. Butter 3–4 scallop shells, put in the roe, cover with brown breadcrumbs and brown in the oven, or serve on hot buttered toast.

3–4 helpings

FRIED COD'S ROE

Laitance de Cabillaud, frite

1 lb. cod's roe
Egg and breadcrumbs
Fat for frying

Poach the roe for 15 min. then drain and cut into slices. When cold, brush over with egg, roll in breadcrumbs and fry until nicely browned, in hot fat.

3–4 helpings

SALT COD AND PARSNIPS

Morue aux Panais

2 lb. salt cod
12 young parsnips
Egg sauce

Wash the fish and soak it in cold water for 12 hr. or longer if very salty, changing the water every 3 or 4 hr. Cover the fish with cold water and bring slowly to simmering point, then reduce heat and cook very gently for 20 min., or until the fish leaves the bones. Meanwhile boil the parsnips, if small cut them lengthwise into 2, or if large into 4 pieces. Drain the fish well, place it on a hot dish, pour the egg sauce over and garnish with parsnips.

4–5 helpings

CONGER EEL

Congre or Anguille de Mer

This forms the basis of the well-known soup of the Channel Islands, and is made into pies in the West of England. Like a tough steak, it always needs long stewing or cooking, as the flesh is remarkably firm and hard. It can be cooked like a fresh-water eel. Available all the year; best from March to October.

BAKED CONGER EEL

Congre cuit au Four

2 lb. conger eel
Suet forcemeat *see* **Baked Stuffed Plaice**
Butter *or* **fat**
Flour

Wash and dry the fish thoroughly, skin and stuff with forcemeat and bind it with tape. Melt the butter or fat in a baking-dish or tin, put in the fish and baste well. Bake gently for 1 hr., basting occasionally with fat and dredging the surface with flour.

Serve with the gravy poured round, or if preferred with tomato, brown caper, or a suitable fish sauce.

4–5 helpings

CONGER EEL PIE

Pâté de Congre

1 small conger eel
Salt and pepper
1 teasp. finely-chopped onion
1 teasp. powdered mixed herbs
1 teasp. finely-chopped parsley
1 tablesp. vinegar
Rough puff *or* **puff pastry, using 4 oz. flour, etc.**

Wash and dry the fish thoroughly, remove all skin and bones and cut into neat pieces. Place in layers in a pie-dish, sprinkling each layer with salt, pepper, onion, herbs and parsley. Add water to $\frac{3}{4}$ fill the dish and mix with it the vinegar. Cover the pie-dish with pastry and bake in a very hot oven (**450° F., Gas 8**) until pastry is set then reduce heat to moderate (**350° F., Gas 4**).

Serve either hot or cold.

6–8 helpings **Cooking time—about $\frac{3}{4}$–1 hr.**

STEWED CONGER EEL

Fricassée de Congre

3 slices from a medium-sized (skinned) conger
½ pt. water
1 onion
Bouquet garni
1 blade of mace
2 cloves
Salt and pepper
1 oz. butter
1 oz. flour
¼ pt. milk

Heat the water, put in the fish, sliced onion, herbs, mace, cloves and a little salt and pepper, and simmer gently for 20 min. Meanwhile melt the butter in a saucepan, add the flour, stir and cook slowly for 3–4 min. without browning. Strain the liquor from the fish on to the prepared butter and flour, stir until boiling, then add the milk. Season to taste, boil up, pour over the fish and serve.

3 helpings **Cooking time—about ½ hr.**

DABS

Dabs are available all the year; best from June to February. They are suitable for frying, steaming or poaching.

DOGFISH

See Flake

EELS

Anguilles

Eels are available practically all the year; least seasonable in winter. Suitable for baking, frying, poaching or serving cold jellied.

COLLARED EEL

Anguille en Galantine

1 large eel
Salt and pepper
3–4 oz. veal forcemeat
A good pinch each: ground cloves, mace, allspice, mixed herbs and sage
Vinegar

Cut off the head and tail of the eel and remove the skin and backbone. Simmer the backbone, head and tail in water well seasoned with salt. Mix the forcemeat with the herbs and spices, spread the eel flat on the table and cover its inner side with the mixture. Roll up the eel, beginning with the broad end, and bind it in shape with strong tape. Add 1 tablesp. vinegar to the simmering bones, head, etc., put in the eel and simmer gently for about 40 min. Remove the eel and press between 2 dishes until cold. Meanwhile add a pinch of allspice and a little more vinegar to the liquor in which the eel was cooked, simmer gently for ½ hr., then strain. When the eel is cold, put it into the liquor and let it remain until required. The eel should be glazed before serving.

4–5 helpings

EELS À LA MATELOTE

Anguille en Matelote

2 lb. eels
Flour
Salt and pepper
2½ oz. butter
¾ pt. good stock
1 glass claret
12 preserved mushrooms

Wash, dry and skin the eels, cut into pieces 3 in. long. Roll them in flour seasoned with a little salt and pepper. Melt 1 oz. of butter in a saucepan, fry the eels until lightly browned, then drain off any butter that remains. Put in the stock and wine, bring to the boil, and simmer gently for ½ hr. Meanwhile melt the remaining butter in another saucepan, stir in 1½ oz. flour, cook gently until nut-brown, then put it aside. Drain the pieces of eel from the stock, and keep them hot. Strain the stock, add to the browned flour, and stir until boiling. Have ready the mushrooms cooked, heat them up in a little stock, and add them to the sauce, season to taste, and boil gently for 3–4 min. Pour the sauce over the fish and serve.

4–5 helpings
Cooking time—about 45 min.

FRIED EELS

Anguilles frites

1–2 medium-sized eels
1 tablesp. flour
½ teasp. salt
⅛ teasp. pepper
Egg and breadcrumbs
Fat for frying
Fried parsley for garnish

Wash, skin and thoroughly dry the eels. Divide them into pieces 2½–3 in. long. Mix the flour, salt and pepper together, and roll the pieces of eel separately in the mixture. Coat carefully with egg and breadcrumbs, fry in hot fat until crisp and lightly-browned, drain well.

Allow 2 lb. for 5–6 helpings
Cooking time—about 20 min.

JELLIED EELS

Anguilles en Gelée

Live eels are usually purchased. The fishmonger will prepare them for you, but if you prefer to do it at home, this is the method: Prepare by half-severing the head and slitting down the stomach. Scrape away the gut, etc., and cut off with the head. Cut into 2-in.

lengths. Put in a pan with sufficient water to just cover, boil for about ½ hr., turn into a bowl and leave to set. If the liquor does not look thick enough, add a little gelatine, but normally it will "jell" on its own.

STEWED EELS

Fricassée d'Anguilles

2 lb. eels
1 pt. good stock
1 small glass port wine *or* claret
1 onion
2 cloves
Strip of lemon rind
Salt
Cayenne pepper
1 oz. butter
1 oz. flour
2 tablesp. cream
1 teasp. lemon juice

Wash and skin the eels. Cut into pieces about 3 in. long. Put into a saucepan, add the stock, wine, finely-chopped onion, cloves, lemon rind and seasoning. Simmer gently for ½ hr., or until tender, then lift carefully on to a hot dish. Meanwhile knead together the butter and flour, add it to the stock in small portions, stir until smoothly mixed with the stock. Boil for 10 min., then add the cream and lemon juice and a little more hot stock if the sauce is too thick. Season and strain over the fish.

5–6 helpings **Cooking time—¾ hr.**

FLAKE

(sometimes called DOGFISH)

Available all the year; best from October to June. Suitable for frying, poaching, steaming and for made-up dishes.

FLOUNDERS

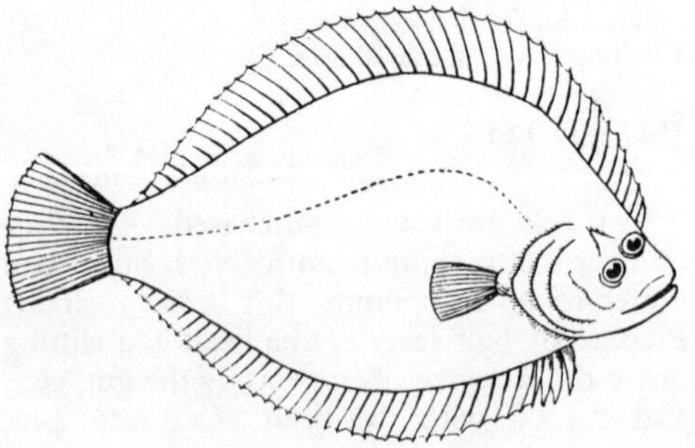

Flounders are available in small quantities most of the year, but are not at their best in March and April. Suitable for frying, steaming and poaching.

FLOUNDERS

Carrelets

3–4 flounders
½ carrot
½ turnip
1 slice parsnip
Water *or* fish stock
1 small onion
1 small bunch herbs
6 peppercorns
Salt
Parsley

Cut the carrot, turnip and parsnip into very fine strips and cook till tender in slightly-salted water or fish stock. Trim the fish and place in a deep sauté-pan, with the onion cut up in slices, the bunch of herbs and peppercorns. Add a little salt and pour on sufficient water to cover the fish well. Bring to the boil and cook gently for about 10 min. Lift out the fish and place in a deep entrée dish, sprinkle over the shredded cooked vegetables and some finely-chopped parsley, add a little of the fish liquor and serve.

3–4 helpings

FRIED FLOUNDERS

Carrelets frits

Flounders
Salt
Egg and breadcrumbs
Fat for frying
Fried parsley

Clean the fish and 2 hr. before required rub them inside and out with salt, to make them firm. Wash and dry them thoroughly, dip into beaten egg and coat with breadcrumbs. Fry in hot fat. Serve garnished with parsley.

6 oz.–7 oz. per helping for breakfast; rather less when served in the fish course of a dinner
Cooking time—10–15 min. according to size

POACHED FLOUNDERS

Carrelets bouillis

1 medium-sized flounder
Salt
Vinegar

Wash the fish, put into a pan with just sufficient water to cover, and add salt and vinegar to taste. Bring gently to the boil and simmer for 5–10 min., according to thickness of fish.

Allow 6 oz.–8 oz. per helping

GARFISH

STEWED GARFISH

2 medium-sized garfish	**2 cloves**
1 pt. stock *or* water	**Salt and pepper**
1 onion	**1½ oz. butter**
Bouquet garni	**1½ oz. flour**
1 blade of mace	

Remove the skin, which would impart a disagreeable oily taste to the dish, and cut the fish into pieces 1½ in. long. Bring the stock or water to simmering-point, put in the fish, onion (sliced), herbs, mace, cloves, a little salt and pepper and simmer gently for 20 min. Meanwhile melt the butter in a saucepan, add the flour, stir and cook slowly for 3 min., without browning. Strain on the liquor from the fish, stir until boiling, boil for 5 min. then season to taste. Strain over the fish and serve.

4 helpings

GRAYLING

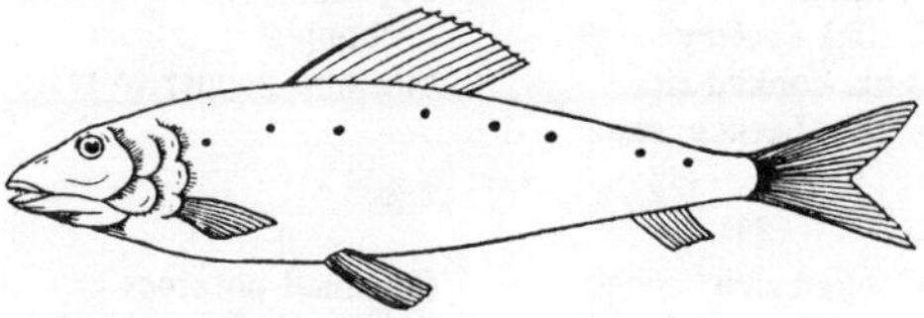

BAKED GRAYLING

Ombre rôti

2 medium-sized grayling	**Salt and pepper**
Butter for basting	**⅓ pt. melted butter sauce**

Empty, wash and scale the fish. Dry well, place in a baking-dish in which a little butter has been previously melted and baste well. Season with salt and pepper, cover with a greased paper and bake gently for 25–35 min., basting occasionally. Make the melted butter sauce very thick and a few minutes before serving strain and add the liquor from the fish. Place the fish on a hot dish, strain the sauce over and serve.

4 helpings

FRIED GRAYLING

Ombre frit

4 small grayling	**Egg and breadcrumbs**
Flour	**Fat for frying**
Salt and pepper	**Parsley sauce**

Empty, scale, wash and dry the fish, remove the gills and fins, but leave the heads. Roll in flour seasoned with salt and pepper, coat carefully with egg and breadcrumbs and fry in hot fat until nicely browned. Serve with parsley sauce, or any other sauce preferred.

4 helpings
Cooking time—8–9 min.

GRILLED GRAYLING

Ombre grillé

4 small grayling	**Salt and pepper**
Salad oil	**Lemon**

Empty, scale, wash and thoroughly dry the fish. Brush over with salad oil, sprinkle with salt and pepper and grill on both sides until sufficiently cooked and nicely browned. Serve garnished with quarters of lemon.

4 helpings
Cooking time—about 10 min.

GUDGEON

GUDGEON

Goujons frits

Gudgeon	**Frying-fat**
Egg and breadcrumbs	

Clean the fish, remove the inside and gills, but do not scrap off the scales. Dry well, dip in egg and breadcrumbs and fry in hot fat until nicely browned.

Cooking time 4–6 min.

GURNET or GURNARD

Grondin

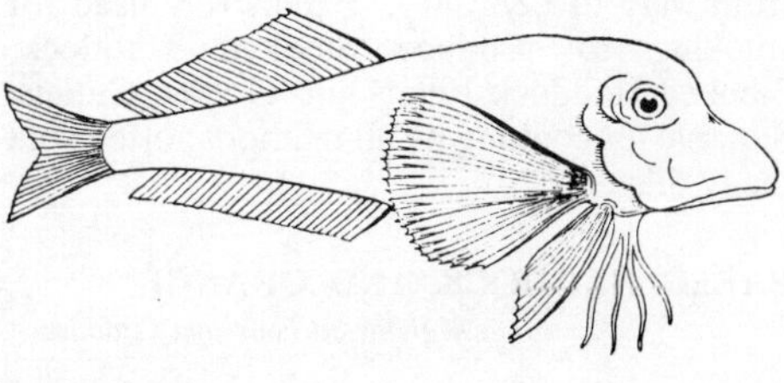

Gurnet are available all the year. Out of condition April to June. Suitable for baking, frying and poaching. Excellent cold with salad.

BAKED GURNET

Grondin cuit au Four

1 medium-sized gurnet	**Butter *or* fat for basting**
Veal forcemeat	**2–3 rashers bacon**

Empty and wash the fish, cut off the fins and remove the gills. Leave the head on. Put the forcemeat inside the fish and sew up the opening. Fasten the tail in the mouth of the fish, place in a pie-dish or baking-dish, baste well with hot fat or butter. Cover with bacon and bake in a moderate oven (**350° F., Gas 4**) for 30–45 min. Serve with either parsley or anchovy sauce.

2–3 helpings

POACHED GURNET

Grondin bouilli

1 medium-sized gurnet	**Salt**

Clean and wash the fish and cut off the fins and gills. Have ready just enough warm water to cover it, add salt to taste, put in the fish. Bring slowly to near boiling-point and cook gently for 20–30 min. Serve with anchovy or parsley sauce.

2–3 helpings

HADDOCK

Aiglefin, Aigrefin or Égrefin

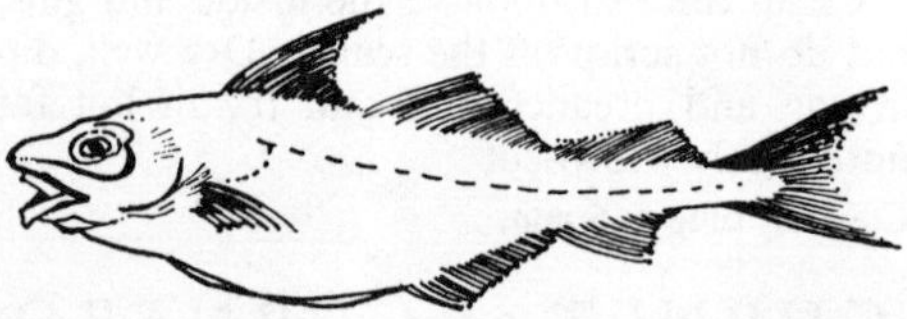

Haddock are available all the year; best from May to February. Extensively used for smoking to produce Smoked Haddock, Smoked Haddock Fillets and Golden Cutlets. Suitable for cooking by all methods; often sold ready filleted.

BAKED HADDOCK AND ORANGE

Aiglefin au Four aux Oranges

1 orange	**Juice of 1 lemon**
1½ lb. fillet of haddock	**2 level teasp. cornflour**
Salt	**½ level teasp. sugar**

Grate the rind from the orange, remove pith and cut pulp across into slices. Cut the fish into convenient portions for serving and arrange in a greased dish. Sprinkle with a little salt, add the lemon juice and arrange the slices of orange over the top. Cover with greased paper and cook in a fairly hot oven (**400° F., Gas 6**) for 15–20 min. Strain off the liquor and make up to ¼ pt. with water. Blend the cornflour with this, add the grated orange rind and sugar and bring to the boil, stirring constantly. Boil gently for 3 min., correct the seasoning and serve with the fish.

4 helpings

BAKED HADDOCK WITH RICE AND OLIVE STUFFING

Aiglefin au Four farci au Riz et aux Olives

One 2–3 lb. fresh haddock—cleaned

STUFFING

2 oz. butter	**¼ level teasp. thyme**
1 onion	**1½ oz. stuffed olives, chopped**
2 sticks celery	**Salt and pepper to taste**
4 oz. cooked rice	
¼ level teasp. sage	

GARNISH

Cooked rice	**Creamed potatoes**
Tomatoes	**Parsley**
Lemon	

Scale the haddock and trim the fins and tail. Leave the head on, but remove the eyes. To make the stuffing, melt the butter in a pan, add the finely-chopped onion and celery and sauté for about 3 min. Add the rice and the remaining ingredients and cook gently for a further 3 min. Stuff the fish with this mixture then place the fish, with the tail curled inwards, in a well-greased baking-tin. Cover with greased paper and bake in a fairly hot oven (**375° F., Gas 5**) for 30–40 min. Serve on a bed of rice garnished with quarters of tomatoes, lemon wedges, creamed potatoes and parsley.

4–6 helpings

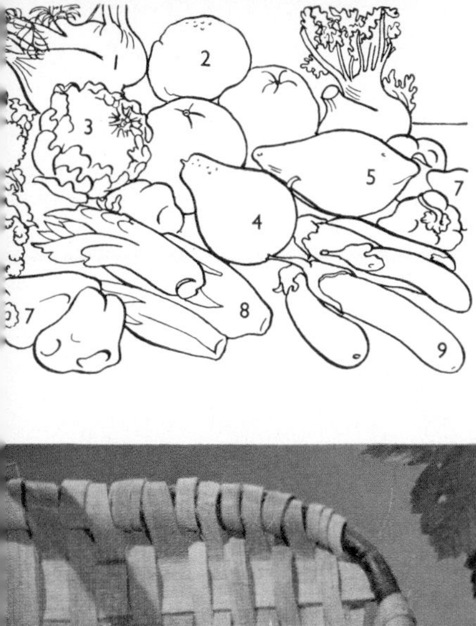

PLATE 5
Vegetables and Fruits

Above: 1 fennel, 2 uglies, 3 globe artichokes, 4 avocado pear, 5 sweet potato, 6 broccoli, 7 peppers, 8 chicory, 9 aubergines. Below: a selection of fruits for preserves.

PLATE 6

Jointing a Chicken

1 Pull the leg away from body, cut through skin. Break leg from body at joint and cut through joint.

2 Cut thigh from the drum stick at the joint. Repeat with the other leg. Turn the carcase so that neck end is towards you. Cut off extreme wing tips and cook with the giblets.

3 Cut the breast meat straight down to the wing joint. Break joint and cut so that the wing and the piece of breast meat are all in one piece.

4 With a heavy knife, cut down back of carcase, cut from vent to neck end.

5 Cut breast into 2 or 4 pieces, according to size. For dishes where joints are to be coated they should be skinned. Remove all small bones.

6 Eight separate joints of chicken.

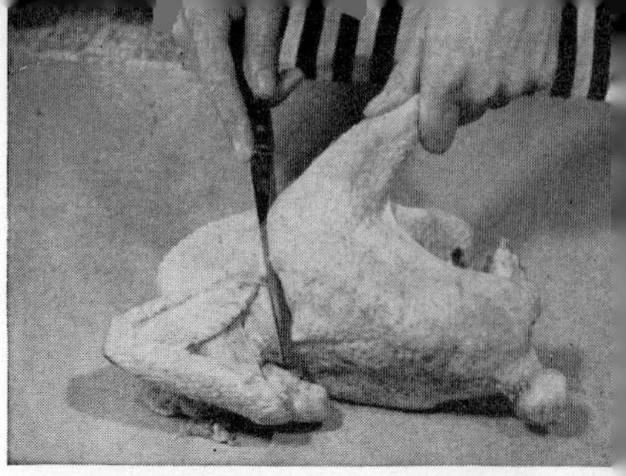
1

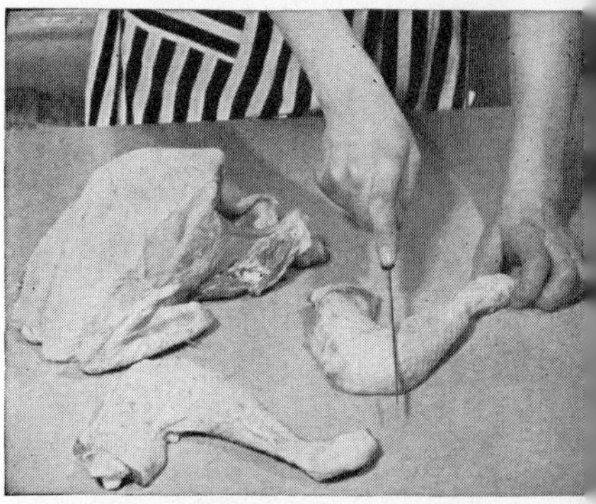
2

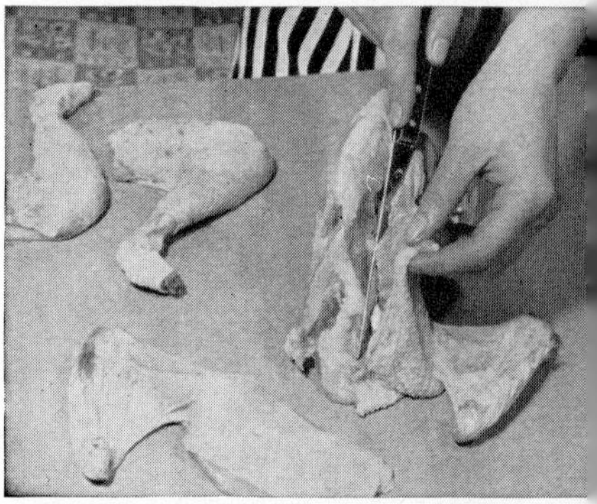
3

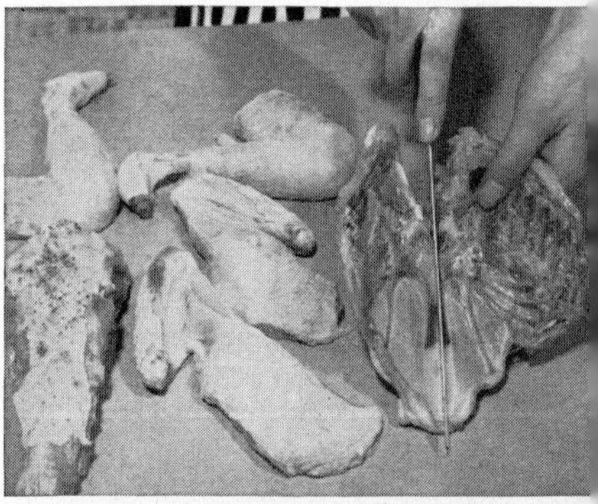
4

5
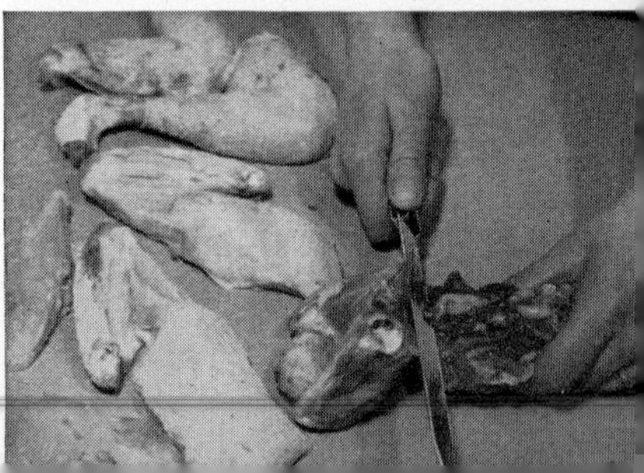

6
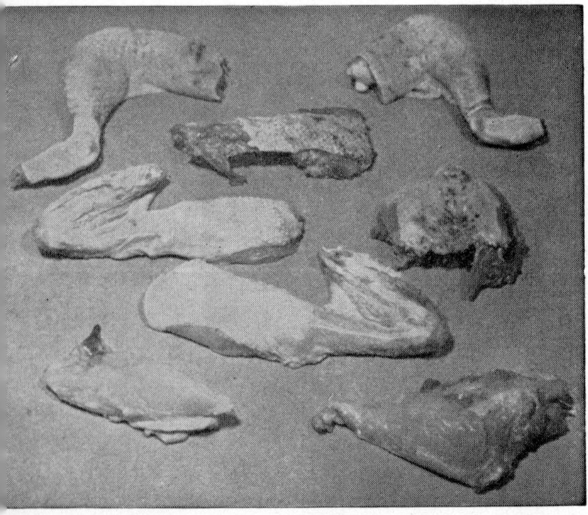

BAKED HADDOCK WITH VEAL FORCEMEAT STUFFING

Aiglefin au Four

1 medium-sized fresh haddock	**1 egg**
Veal forcemeat	**Browned breadcrumbs**
	Fat for basting

Wash, clean and scale the fish. Stuff the forcemeat inside the haddock and sew up the opening. Skewer the fish into the shape of the letter S and brush over with beaten egg, coat lightly with browned breadcrumbs and bake in a moderate oven (**350°–375° F., Gas 4–5**) for 30–40 min., basting occasionally with hot fat. Serve with anchovy or melted butter sauce.

4 helpings

SMOKED HADDOCKS

Aiglefins fumés

Smoked haddocks are best cooked either in the oven or on the top of the cooker in a dish with a little water to create steam, to prevent the surface of the fish becoming hardened. Medium-sized haddocks should be cooked whole, and before serving an incision should be made from head to tail and the backbone removed. The fish should be liberally spread with butter, sprinkled with pepper and served as hot as possible.

SMOKED HADDOCK AND TOMATOES

Aiglefins fumés aux Tomates

1 small smoked haddock	**½ teasp. finely-chopped parsley**
2–3 small tomatoes	**Salt and pepper**
1 oz. butter	**Boiled rice**
1 teasp. finely-chopped onion	

Place the haddock in a dish with a little water and bake for 10 min. Remove skin and bones and separate the fish into large flakes. Slice the tomatoes. Melt the butter in a saucepan, fry the onion slightly, add the tomatoes and cook until soft. Put in the fish and parsley, season to taste, and stir gently over a low heat until the fish is thoroughly hot. Arrange the boiled rice in a circle on a hot dish and serve the fish in the centre.

2–3 helpings
Cooking time—25–30 min.

HAKE

Merluche

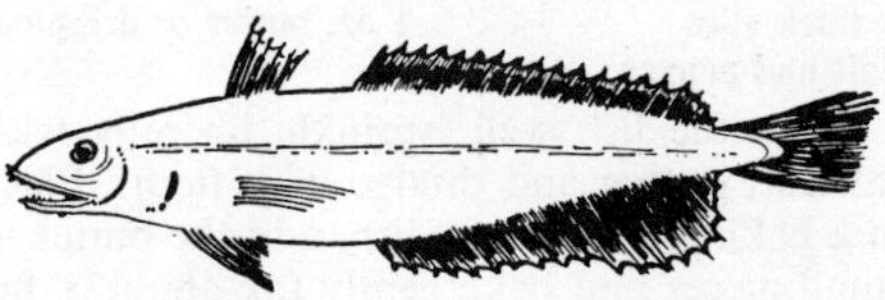

Available all the year; best from June to January. Suitable for baking, frying and steaming. It is often sold ready filleted, or cut into steaks or cutlets.

BAKED HAKE STEAKS

Darnes de Merluche cuites au Four

4 medium-sized hake steaks	**1 teasp. finely-chopped parsley**
Flour	**1 teasp. finely-chopped onion**
Salt and pepper	**1 oz. butter**

Wipe the steaks and place them side by side in a greased baking-dish. Dredge well with flour, season with salt and pepper, sprinkle over the parsley and onion and add the butter in small pieces. Bake gently for ½ hr., basting occasionally, then place the fish on a hot dish, strain the liquor over it and serve.

4 helpings

HALIBUT

Flétan

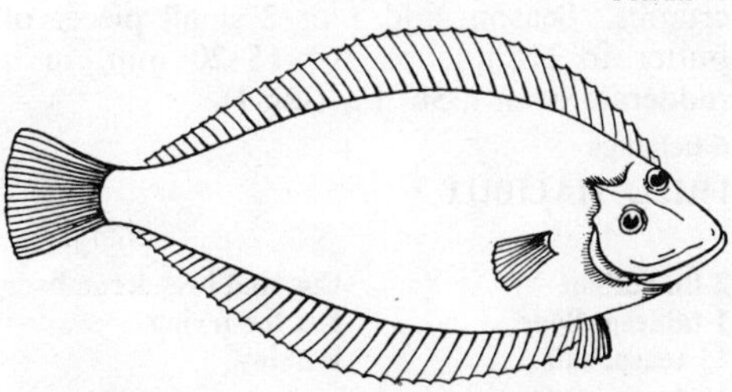

Available all the year; best from July to March. Suitable for cooking by all methods. Excellent cold with salad.

BAKED HALIBUT

Flétan rôti

2 lb. halibut, cut in one thick slice
Salt and pepper
Flour
1 oz. butter *or* dripping

Wipe the fish well, sprinkle liberally with salt and pepper and dredge with flour. Place in a baking-dish or pie-dish, add the butter in small pieces and bake gently for about 1 hr. Serve on a hot dish with the liquid from the fish strained and poured round.

4–5 helpings **Cooking time—30–40 min.**

BOILED HALIBUT

Flétan bouilli

3–4 lb. halibut
Salt
1 lemon
Parsley
½ pt. anchovy *or* shrimp sauce

Add salt to hot water in the proportion of 1 oz. to 1 qt., and put in the fish. Bring slowly to boiling-point and simmer very gently for 30–40 min., or until the fish comes away easily from the bone. Drain well, arrange on a hot dish garnished with slices of lemon and parsley, and serve the sauce separately.

8–12 helpings (*or* 3 helpings per lb.)
Cooking time—30–40 min.

COQUILLES or ESCALLOPS OF HALIBUT

Flétan en Coquilles

¾ lb. cooked halibut
½ pt. white sauce
Grated cheese
Browned breadcrumbs
Salt and pepper
Butter

Flavour the sauce with grated cheese to taste. Divide the fish into large flakes, put into 6 buttered scallop shells, cover with sauce and sprinkle thickly with browned bread-crumbs. Season, add 1 or 2 small pieces of butter to each, cook for 15–20 min. in a moderate oven (**350° F., Gas 4**).

6 helpings

FRIED HALIBUT

Flétan frit

2 lb. halibut
1 tablesp. flour
½ teasp. salt
⅛ teasp. pepper
Egg and breadcrumbs
Fat for frying
Parsley

Divide the fish into small thin slices. Mix the flour, salt and pepper together, coat the pieces of fish lightly with the seasoned flour, brush over with beaten egg and toss in breadcrumbs. Fry in a deep pan of hot fat until crisp and lightly-browned, or, if more convenient, in a smaller amount of hot fat in a frying-pan. Serve garnished with crisply-fried parsley. Serve with anchovy or shrimp sauce.

4–6 helpings **Cooking time—6–7 min.**

GRILLED HALIBUT

Flétan grillé

Six 6 oz. slices halibut
Oiled butter
Salt and pepper

Brush the fish with oiled butter and sprinkle with salt and pepper. Grill for 10–12 min., turning them 2 or 3 times during the process. Serve with lemon or fish sauce.

6 helpings

HALIBUT BRISTOL

Flétan Bristol

1 lb. halibut (centre cut)
Salt and pepper
¼ pt. milk and water
½ oz. butter *or* margarine
½ oz. flour
1½ oz. grated cheese
12 mussels (fresh-cooked)

Place the halibut in a greased fireproof dish, sprinkle with a little seasoning and add the liquid. Cover with greased paper and cook for 20 min. in a fairly hot oven (**375° F., Gas 5**). Remove from the oven, strain off the liquid and remove the centre bone from the fish. Use the liquid to make a creamy sauce with the fat and flour, add 1 oz. cheese and seasoning if necessary. Arrange the mussels round the halibut, cover all with the sauce and sprinkle over the remaining cheese. Return the dish to a very hot oven (**450° F., Gas 8**) for a further 10 min. to brown.

NOTE: Turbot may be used if halibut is not available.

4 helpings

HALIBUT WITH ORANGE AND WATER-CRESS SALAD

Flétan à l'Orange et au Cresson

Four 5–6 oz. pieces of halibut
Seasoning
1 lettuce
Mayonnaise
1 bunch watercress (¼ lb.)
2 small oranges

Prepare the fillets, season, fold in half and steam for 10–15 min. between 2 plates; allow to cool. Shred the outer leaves of lettuce and arrange on a salad dish. Place the cooked fillets on this and coat them evenly with mayonnaise. Garnish with the remaining lettuce, fairly large sprigs of watercress and slices of orange.

NOTE: Turbot may be substituted for halibut.

4 helpings

HERRINGS

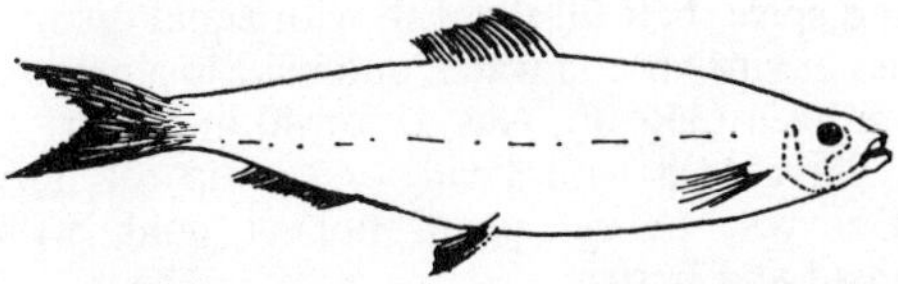

Supplies of herring are difficult in early January, late March and April, September and late December. Herrings are extensively used for smoking into Kippers, Bloaters, Buckling, etc. Suitable for cooking by all methods, including sousing and serving cold with salad.

BAKED STUFFED FRESH HERRINGS

Harengs frais farcis et cuits au Four

6 herrings
2 tablesp. breadcrumbs
1 tablesp. finely-chopped suet
1 teasp. chopped parsley
¼ teasp. grated lemon rind
Salt and pepper
Milk

Wash and split the herrings and remove the backbone. Mix together the breadcrumbs, suet, parsley and lemon rind, season to taste and add enough milk to moisten. Season each herring with salt and pepper, spread on a thin layer of the forcemeat and roll up tightly, beginning with the neck. Pack closely in a greased pie-dish, cover with greased paper and bake 30–40 min. in a moderate oven (**350° F., Gas 4**). Serve hot.

5 helpings

GRILLED HERRING WITH MUSTARD SAUCE

Harengs au Naturel, Sauce Moutarde

4 fresh herrings
1 onion
1 oz. butter
½ oz. flour
1 teasp. dry mustard
⅛ pt. vinegar

Chop the onion finely and fry in the butter until lightly browned. Put in the flour and mustard, add the vinegar and ¼ pt. water. Stir until boiling and simmer gently for 15 min. Wipe and dry the herrings, remove the heads and score across the back and sides, but avoid cutting the roe. Sprinkle with salt and pepper and grill for 10–15 min. Place on a hot dish and serve the sauce separately.

3–4 helpings

HERRINGS AND HORSERADISH

Harengs au Raifort

4 herrings
½ pt. water
⅛ pt. vinegar
1 small onion
½ level teasp. mixed herbs
1 bay leaf
½ level teasp. salt
2 large cooking apples
1 level tablesp. horseradish sauce
Chopped parsley

Scale, clean and fillet the herrings. Simmer the fish bones, water, vinegar, sliced onion, herbs, bay leaf and salt together for 20 min. Strain and return the liquid to the saucepan. Roll the filleted herrings from tail to head and place side by side in the liquid. Simmer for 10 min., remove from heat and allow to remain in the liquid until cold. Just before serving, grate the raw apples, mix with the horseradish sauce and arrange on a shallow dish. Serve the herrings neatly on top, sprinkle with chopped parsley.

4 helpings

HERRINGS STUFFED WITH SHRIMPS

Harengs farcis aux Crevettes

4 fresh herrings
1 tablesp. white breadcrumbs
Milk
2 tablesp. picked shrimps
Salt and pepper
Cayenne pepper
Anchovy essence
1 egg
Brown breadcrumbs
Butter

Wash and dry the herrings. Remove the heads, split them open, remove the backbone and wipe the insides with soft paper. Soak the white breadcrumbs in a little milk, chop the shrimps finely, mix with the breadcrumbs, season with salt and pepper and add a few drops of anchovy essence. Spread the filling on the inside of the herrings, roll them up tightly, beginning at the head end, and fasten them with skewers. Brush over with beaten egg, coat lightly with brown breadcrumbs, add a few small pieces of butter and bake gently for 30–35 min. Serve hot.

4 helpings

HERRINGS—TAILS IN AIR

4 herrings	**1 level tablesp. chopped parsley**
2 oz. fresh breadcrumbs	**Salt and pepper to taste**
1 small onion	**A little milk if required**
1 tomato	**1 tomato**

Scale the herrings and remove the heads, then clean and bone but leave the tails on; reserve the roes, if any. Trim the tails and cut off the fins with kitchen scissors. Chop the roes and mix with the crumbs, grated onion, chopped tomato, parsley and seasoning and, if necessary, bind with a little milk. Lay the herrings flat on a board, put 1 tablesp. stuffing on the head end of each and roll up towards the tail. Place tightly in a fireproof dish, with the tails uppermost, and garnish with slices of tomato. Cook in a fairly hot oven (**400° F., Gas 6**) for ½ hr.

4 helpings

HERRINGS WITH TOMATOES

Harengs aux Tomates

4 fresh herrings	**A few drops of vinegar *or* lemon juice**
3–4 ripe tomatoes	**¼ lb. boiled rice**
Salt and pepper	**½ oz. dripping**

Wipe, fillet and skin the herrings. Cut each fillet in two, crossways, and put a layer of fish in a fireproof dish. Dip the tomatoes into boiling water, skin and cut them into slices. Place a layer of tomato slices over the fish. Sprinkle over enough salt and pepper to season, as well as vinegar or lemon juice to flavour. Cover with the remainder of the fish, then place over the cooked rice, and lastly the remaining slices of tomatoes. Distribute the dripping in little bits on top. Bake in a moderate oven (**350° F., Gas 4**) for about ¾ hr. Serve hot.

4 helpings

SOUSED HERRINGS

Harengs marinés

8 fresh herrings	**1 level dessertsp. mixed pickling spice**
1 Spanish onion	**Vinegar**
Salt and pepper	
1 bay leaf	

Wash and scale the herrings, cut off the heads, split the herrings open and remove the gut and backbone. Put a slice of onion in the centre of each fish, roll up tightly, beginning with the neck. Pack the herrings closely in a pie-dish, sprinkle with salt, pepper, bay leaf and spice, half fill the dish with equal quantities of vinegar and water, and bake in a moderate oven (**350° F., Gas 4**) for 40 min.

Serve cold with salad, or cut up for hors d'œuvres; or eat plain, hot or cold, with bread and butter.

6 helpings

STUFFED HERRINGS WITH MUSTARD BUTTER

Harengs farcis à la Moutarde

4 fresh herrings	**1 teasp. anchovy essence *or* paste**
1½ tablesp. white breadcrumbs	**½ teasp. finely-chopped shallot *or* onion**
1 tablesp. oiled butter	**Salt and pepper**

MUSTARD BUTTER

1 oz. butter	**1 teasp. lemon juice**
½ teasp. dry mustard	

To make the mustard butter: mix the butter, mustard and lemon juice on a plate, form the mixture into a pat and put it in a cool place until firm. Wash and dry the herrings. Remove the heads, split them open and discard the backbone. Put the roes into boiling water, cook gently for 10–15 min., then chop coarsely. Mix them with the breadcrumbs, butter, anchovy essence and shallot; season rather highly with salt and pepper and stuff the herrings with the mixture. Form the fish back into shape, brush over with warm butter and bake for about 20 min. in a moderate oven (**350° F., Gas 4**). Place a pat of mustard butter on top of each herring and serve.

3–4 helpings

RED HERRINGS

Harengs Saurs

Red herrings
Milk *or* water
Oil
Vinegar
Egg yolk and gherkins *or* diced boiled potatoes

Cover the herrings with boiled water and after several minutes, drain. Soak in milk or water for 1 hr. Skin and fillet, then cut into pieces and dress with oil and vinegar. The herrings can be garnished with sieved egg yolk and chopped gherkins. Alternatively mix the herring pieces with diced boiled potatoes and dress the whole with oil and vinegar.

JOHN DORY

John Dory is best from January to April, but landings are light and erratic.

JOHN DORY

St. Pierre

This fish is dressed in the same way as turbot, which it resembles in firmness but not in richness. Wash it thoroughly, cut off the fins but not the head, place in a pan and cover with warm water, adding salt to taste. Bring gradually to near boiling-point and simmer gently for 20–30 min. for a 2–3 lb. fish.

Serve garnished with cut lemon and parsley. Lobster, anchovy or shrimp paste sauce, and plain melted butter, should be served with it.

NOTE: Small John Dorys are excellent baked.

6–7 helpings

STUFFED FILLETS OF JOHN DORY

Filets de Saint Pierre farcis

One 2–3 lb. dory
2 smelts
1 gill picked shrimps
2 oz. panada (approx.)
1 teasp. anchovy essence
1 egg
Salt and pepper
1 oz. butter
1 tablesp. Chablis *or* cider
Few drops of lemon juice
Génoise sauce

Wash the fish, wipe it and remove the fillets (the bones etc., may be used for stock for the Génoise sauce). Trim the fillets neatly, and cut them into oblong pieces. Remove the bones and heads, then mix the smelts together with the shrimps until they are quite smooth, then add the panada and anchovy essence and moisten with beaten egg. Mix thoroughly, season to taste then rub through a sieve. Spread each piece of fillet with this farce, fold over and place in a well-buttered sauté-pan. Season, lightly moisten with the wine or cider and lemon juice, cover and cook in the oven for about 15 min. or longer, according to the thickness of the fillets. Remove carefully and dish up on a hot dish. Pour some Génoise sauce into the pan in which the fish was cooked, boil up and strain over the fillets. Serve hot.

5 helpings

LING

BAKED LING

Lingue rôtie

2 lb. ling
3 oz. butter
Ground mace
Salt and pepper
1 oz. flour
¾ pt. milk

Wash and dry the fish, cut it into slices ¾ in. thick. Put into a fireproof dish with 2 oz. butter, a good pinch of mace and a liberal seasoning of salt and pepper. Cover and cook gently for 1 hr., basting occasionally. When the fish is rather more than half cooked, melt the remaining butter in a saucepan and add the flour. Cook for 2–3 min., put in the milk and stir until boiling. Pour the sauce over the fish and continue to cook gently until done.

4–6 helpings

FRIED LING

Lingue frite

2 lb. ling
Salt and pepper
Flour
Egg and breadcrumbs
Fat for frying

Wash and dry the fish and cut it into slices. Sprinkle with salt and pepper, dredge well with flour, brush over with beaten egg and coat with breadcrumbs (when well coated with flour the fish browns nicely without the addition of egg and breadcrumbs). Fry in hot fat, drain well and serve with a suitable fish sauce.

4–6 helpings **Cooking time—about 20 min.**

MACKEREL

Maquereau

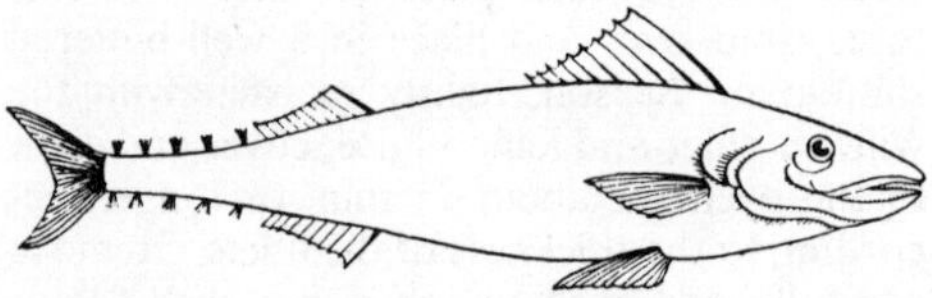

Mackerel is most seasonable in winter and spring. Suitable for all methods of cooking.

BAKED MACKEREL

Maquereau au Four

2 large-sized mackerel
Veal forcemeat
1 oz. butter *or* sweet dripping
Flour
Salt and pepper

Clean the fish and take out the roes. Stuff with the forcemeat and sew up the opening. Put them with the roes into a fireproof dish. Add the butter or dripping, dredge with flour, sprinkle well with salt and pepper and bake for 30–40 min., basting occasionally.

Serve with parsley sauce, or melted butter to which a little lemon juice has been added, and finely-chopped parsley.

3–4 helpings

BOILED MACKEREL WITH PARSLEY SAUCE

Maquereau bouilli au Persil

2 large mackerel
Salt
Parsley sauce

Remove the roes, wash the fish, put them into the pan with just sufficient hot water to cover and add salt to taste. Bring the water gently to near boiling-point, then reduce heat and cook very gently for about 10 min. If cooked too quickly, or too long, the skin is liable to crack and spoil the appearance of the fish. The fish is sufficiently cooked when the skin becomes loose from the flesh. Drain well, place the mackerel on a hot dish, pour a little parsley sauce over and serve the remainder of the sauce separately.

Fennel and anchovy sauces may also be served with boiled mackerel.

4 helpings **Cooking time—10–15 min.**

GRILLED MACKEREL WITH GOOSEBERRY SAUCE

Maquereau grillé à la Sauce de Groseilles

2 large mackerel
1 tablesp. seasoned flour
1 oz. margarine
Tomatoes
½ lb. gooseberries *or* a small bottle *or* can of gooseberries
¼ level teasp. grated nutmeg

Trim, clean and fillet the mackerel. Dip each fillet in seasoned flour. Melt the margarine in the bottom of the grill pan, add the fillets, brush them with the melted fat and grill for 8–10 min., turning once. Cut the tomatoes in half and grill at the same time, for garnish. Meanwhile prepare the gooseberries, stew in a very little water, or in their own juice if bottled or canned. Sweeten slightly if necessary, rub through a sieve and return the purée to the pan. Stir in the grated nutmeg and reheat (reduce by rapid boiling if necessary). Serve the fillets on a hot dish, garnished with the tomatoes and serve the sauce separately.

NOTE: Grilled mackerel may be served with Maître d'Hôtel butter or Maître d'Hôtel sauce if preferred to gooseberry sauce.

4 helpings **Cooking time—8–10 min.**

MACKEREL À LA BÉCHAMEL

Maquereau à la Béchamel

2 large-sized mackerel
1½ oz. butter
¾ pt. Béchamel sauce
1 teasp. lemon juice
Salt and pepper

Wash, dry and fillet the fish. Melt the butter in a sauté-pan and fry the fillets without browning them. Remove the fish and keep it hot, put in the Béchamel sauce and bring nearly to boiling point. Return the fish to the sauté-pan, cover closely and simmer gently for 10 min. Remove the fish carefully to a hot dish, add the lemon juice to the sauce, season if necessary and strain over the fish.

4 helpings

MACKEREL EN PAPILLOTES

Maquereaux en Papillotes

4 mackerel, about ½–¾ lb. each
2 oz. margarine
1 small onion *or* 2–3 shallots
1 level tablesp. chopped parsley
1 tablesp. lemon juice
Salt and pepper

GARNISH

Lemon wedges
Parsley

Clean and wipe the mackerel, removing the tails, fins and eyes, but leaving the heads on. Finely chop the onion or shallots. Cream the margarine and beat in the onion, parsley, lemon juice, plenty of salt and a little pepper. Divide into 4, then spread a ¼ of the mixture into the belly cavity of each fish. Wrap each fish separately in a piece of well greased greaseproof paper and twist the ends of the paper tightly to keep all the juices inside. Bake in a fairly hot oven (**375° F., Gas 5**) for approximately 30 min. Serve with the liquid from the cases poured over the fish and garnish with lemon wedges and sprigs of parsley.

4 helpings

MACKEREL MAYONNAISE

Mayonnaise de Maquereaux

2 large mackerel
Mayonnaise
Sprigs of tarragon, chervil *or* parsley

GARNISH

Tomato lilies
Watercress

Clean and fillet the fish, and poach gently for about 15 min. in salted water. Drain and allow to cool. To serve, arrange on a flat dish and coat each fillet with mayonnaise. Decorate with sprigs of tarragon, chervil or parsley and garnish with tomato lilies and watercress.

PICKLED MACKEREL

Maquereaux marinés

2–3 small mackerel
Salt and pepper
2 bay leaves
Allspiee
12 peppercorns
½ pt. vinegar

Clean and wash the fish and take out the roes. Place the mackerel in a fireproof dish with the roes (mackerel are best in that part of the season when the roes are not full grown). Sprinkle well with salt and pepper, add the bay leaves, allspice, peppercorns, vinegar and about ¼ pt. of water. Cover with a greased paper and bake in a cool oven (**310° F., Gas 2**) for nearly 1 hr.

Leave them in the liquor until required.

2–3 helpings

MEGRIM

This is a flat fish which can be cooked by any of the methods given for sole. See pp. 177–180.

MULLET

GREY MULLET

Surmulet

4 grey mullet

Clean and scale the fish. If very large, place them in warm salted water; if small, they may be put into hot water and cooked gently for 15–20 min. Serve with anchovy or melted butter sauce.

NOTE: Grey mullet may also be grilled or baked.

4 helpings
Cooking time—15–20 min.

MULLET EN PAPILLOTES

Mulet en Papillotes

4 mullet **1 tablesp. lemon juice**
Salt and pepper

GARNISH

Slices of lemon **Parsley**

Prepare the fish, sprinkle the insides with salt and pepper and wrap carefully in well oiled greaseproof paper or aluminium foil, twisting the ends securely. Place on a baking-sheet and bake for about 15–20 min. in a fairly hot oven (**375° F., Gas 5**). When cooked, loosen the paper carefully and place the fish on a hot dish. Add the lemon juice to the liquid which has collected in the paper, pour this over the fish and serve. Garnish with lemon and parsley.

NOTE: If liked, the mullet may be stuffed with a mixture of 1 oz. fresh breadcrumbs, 1 level tablesp. grated onion, 1 level dessertsp. chopped parsley, salt and pepper to taste, moistened with a little milk. Allow a little longer cooking time.

4 helpings

MULLET-FRIED À LA MEUNIÈRE

Mulet frit à la Meunière

4 mullet **Lemon juice**
Seasoned flour **Parsley**
Butter

Prepare the fish then coat with seasoned flour. Fry them gently in the melted butter, turning until cooked on either side, about 12–15 min. Arrange on a hot flat dish, sprinkle with lemon juice and chopped parsley. Add a large nut of fresh butter to the pan, heat until nut brown in colour then pour over the fish and serve.

4 helpings

GRILLED RED MULLET

Rouget grillé

4 small red mullet **Olive oil**
Salt and pepper **Parsley**

Scrape the scales from the fish, cut off the fins and remove the eyes, but leave the head and tail on. Gut the fish if necessary and keep the liver. Wash well. Season the inside of each fish and replace the liver. Brush the fish with olive oil and put a little oil in the grill-pan before putting in the fish. Grill quickly for 3 min., then turn the fish over and baste well. Reduce the heat and continue grilling until the mullet are cooked, about a further 15 min. Serve on a hot dish with the remaining oil poured over. Garnish with parsley.

4 helpings

RED MULLET À LA NIÇOISE

Rouget à la Niçoise

4 small red mullet **Olive oil for frying**
Salt and pepper

SAUCE

2 shallots **1 lb. ripe tomatoes**
1 clove of garlic **Salt and pepper**
1 tablesp. olive oil

GARNISH

Anchovy fillets **A few stoned olives**

Prepare the fish and season the insides with salt and pepper. Grill or fry the fish in olive oil, turning to cook and brown evenly on both sides. Meanwhile make the sauce: chop the shallots, crush the garlic and fry for several minutes in the oil. Peel and roughly chop the tomatoes, add to the shallots and cook rapidly until reduced to a thick sauce consistency; season to taste. Place the fish in a shallow dish, pour the hot sauce over and leave to get cold.

Serve garnished with olives and with a lattice pattern of thin strips of anchovy.

4 helpings

PERCH

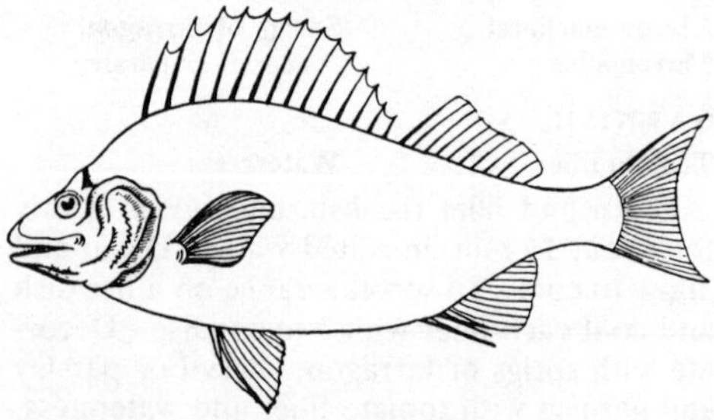

BOILED PERCH

Perche bouillie

4 perch	**Salt**

The scales of perch are rather difficult to remove; the fish can either be boiled and the scales removed afterwards, or a better method is to plunge the fish into boiling water for 2–3 min. then scale.

Before cooking, the fish must be washed in warm water, cleaned, and the gills and fins removed. Have ready boiling water to cover the fish, add salt to taste, put in the fish, reduce heat and simmer gently for 10–20 min., according to size. Serve with Hollandaise or melted butter sauce.

NOTE: Tench may be cooked the same way, and served with the same sauces.

4–5 helpings

FRIED PERCH

Perche frite

4 small perch 6–8 oz. each	**Flour**
Salt and pepper	**Egg and breadcrumbs**
	Frying-fat

Scale, clean, wash and dry the fish thoroughly. Sprinkle with salt and pepper, dredge well with flour, brush over with beaten egg and coat with breadcrumbs. Fry the fish in hot fat until nicely browned. Drain well, and serve with anchovy, shrimp or melted butter sauce.

4 helpings

STEWED PERCH

Perche au Vin blanc

4 small perch about 8 oz. each	**1 bay leaf**
2 oz. butter	**Bouquet garni**
1 dessertsp. finely-chopped onion	**1 clove**
½ pt. good stock	**1 oz. flour**
1 tablesp. vinegar	**1 dessertsp. finely-chopped parsley**
½ teasp. anchovy essence	**Lemon juice**
	Salt and pepper

Scale, clean and wash the fish; remove the fins and gills. Melt half the butter in a saucepan and fry the onion without browning. Then add the stock, vinegar, anchovy essence, bay leaf, bouquet garni and clove, and simmer for 10 min. Put in the fish and cook gently for 10 min., then lift them out carefully on to a hot dish and keep them warm. Melt the remaining butter in a saucepan, stir in the flour and cook for 2–3 min., then add the liquor (strained) in which the fish was cooked and stir until it boils. Add the parsley and lemon juice, season to taste and pour over the fish.

4 helpings

PIKE

BAKED PIKE

Brochet farci

1 medium-sized pike (about 4 lb.)	**1 egg**
4 oz. veal forcemeat	**Brown breadcrumbs**
	Butter *or* fat for basting

Wash, clean and scale the fish and remove the fins and gills. Fill the inside with forcemeat, sew up the opening, brush over with beaten egg and coat with breadcrumbs. Sometimes the fish is trussed in a round shape, the tail being fastened in the mouth with a skewer. Before putting the fish in the oven it should be well basted with hot fat or butter, and as this fish is naturally dry it must be frequently basted and kept covered with greased paper while cooking. Bake gently for 40–45 min.

8–10 helpings

BOILED PIKE

Brochet bouilli

1 pike (about 3 lb.)	**Vinegar**
Salt	

Pour boiling water over the fish until the scales look dull, then plunge it into cold water and remove the scales at once with the back of a knife. Empty the fish, remove the gills and fins and wash well. Have ready a pan or fish kettle of warm water, add salt and vinegar to taste, put in the fish and simmer gently until the fish separates easily from the bone (one weighing 3 lb. would require about 30–40 min.). Serve with Hollandaise, anchovy or melted butter sauce.

8 helpings

FRIED PIKE

Brochet frit

1 pike (about 3–4 lb.)	**Egg and breadcrumbs**
Flour	**Frying-fat**
Salt and pepper	**Fried parsley**

Scale and clean the fish thoroughly, remove head and tail. Cut the fish into ½-in. slices and cover with very cold water. Let them remain until the fish becomes sufficiently firm, then dry well and rub lightly with flour seasoned with salt and pepper. Brush over with beaten egg, coat carefully with breadcrumbs and afterwards fry in hot fat until lightly browned. Drain well and garnish with crisply-fried parsley. Serve with anchovy or brown caper sauce.

8–10 helpings
Cooking time—½ hr.

STEWED PIKE

Brochet à l'Anglaise

1 small pike (2–3 lb.)	**1 teasp. lemon juice** *or*
½ oz. butter	**1 tablesp. vinegar**
Rashers of bacon	**Salt and pepper**
½ pt. stock *or* **water**	

Wash, clean and dry the pike. Melt the butter in a saucepan, put in the pike and cover with rashers of bacon. Put on a close-fitting lid, let the fish cook gently in the steam for 15 min., then add the stock, lemon juice or vinegar and season to taste. Simmer very gently for about ¼ hr., then serve on a hot dish with the liquor strained round.

6 helpings

PILCHARDS

Pilchards

The taste of pilchards is very similar to that of herrings, but more oily. They may be dressed according to the directions given for cooking herrings. Pilchards are very often canned in either oil or tomato sauce and may be served cold with salad, or as hors d'œuvre, or on toast as a savoury.

PLAICE

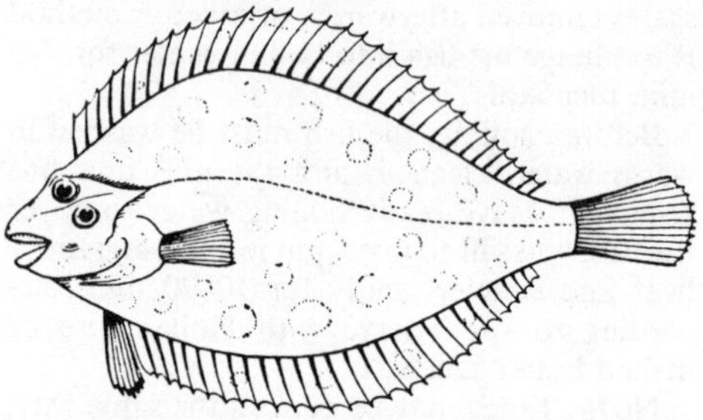

Plaice is available all the year; best from May to January. Most plentiful of the flat fish varieties. Suitable for all methods of cooking, including serving cold.

BAKED STUFFED PLAICE

Plie farcie

1 medium-sized plaice	**¼ teasp. mixed herbs**
2 tablesp. white breadcrumbs	**A pinch of nutmeg**
	Salt and pepper
1 tablesp. finely-chopped suet	**1 egg**
	Milk
1 dessertsp. finely-chopped parsley	**Pale brown breadcrumbs**
	A little butter *or* **fat**

Mix the white breadcrumbs, suet, parsley, herbs and nutmeg together, season well with salt and pepper, add ½ the egg and enough milk to moisten thoroughly. Make an incision down the centre of the fish as for filleting, raise the flesh each side as far as possible and fill with forcemeat. Instead of drawing the sides of the fish close together, fill up the gap with forcemeat and flatten the surface to the level of the fish with a knife. Brush over with the remaining egg, coat lightly with pale brown breadcrumbs, put into a fireproof dish and dot a few small pieces of butter on top. Bake for 20–30 min. in a moderate oven (**350° F., Gas 4**).

NOTE: The forcemeat may be varied by using shrimps or oysters.

3–4 helpings

FILLETS OF PLAICE WITH LEMON DRESSING

Filets de Plies au Citron

4 fillets of plaice (4 oz. each approx.)
Seasoning
1 oz. butter *or* margarine
Juice of ½ lemon
Chopped parsley

Season the fish. Melt the fat in the grill pan and place the fish skin side uppermost in the pan. Cook for 1 min., then turn with flesh side up and grill steadily until golden brown and cooked, about 5–8 min., depending on thickness of fillets. Remove to a hot serving dish, keep hot. Add the lemon juice to the remaining fat in the pan, reheat and pour over the fish. Sprinkle liberally with chopped parsley.

4 helpings

FRIED PLAICE

Plie frite

Four 4 oz. fillets of plaice
1 tablesp. flour
Salt and pepper
A little milk *or* water
Egg and breadcrumbs
Frying-fat
Parsley

Wipe the fillets with a clean damp cloth. Season the flour with salt and pepper to taste and dip each fillet in it. Beat the egg, mix with a little milk or water and brush over each fillet. Coat the fillets with breadcrumbs, press on firmly and fry in hot fat until nicely browned. Garnish with fresh or fried parsley, and serve plain with cut lemon or with anchovy, shrimp or melted butter sauce.

4 helpings

PAUPIETTES OF PLAICE

Paupiettes de Plie

1 medium-sized plaice
1 gill milk
1 gill water
1 bay leaf
Parsley
2 cloves
½ shallot
Salt and pepper
Lemon juice
1 oz. butter
1 oz. flour

Fillet the plaice. Put the bones into a saucepan with the milk and water, bay leaf, parsley stalks, cloves and sliced shallot, and simmer for 20 min. Season the fillets with salt, pepper and lemon juice. Roll them, put in a greased fireproof dish and cover with greased paper. Bake for about 10 min., or until sufficiently cooked, and season to taste. Melt the butter in another saucepan, add the flour and cook for a few minutes, then add the strained fish stock and stir until it boils. Place the fish on a hot dish, strain the sauce over, sprinkle a little chopped parsley on top and serve very hot.

3–4 helpings

PLAICE MORNAY

Plie Mornay

Four 4 oz. fillets of plaice

SAUCE

1 oz. butter *or* margarine
1 rounded tablesp. flour
Salt and pepper
½ pt. milk and fish stock mixed
2 tablesp. grated cheese
Mustard
Grated nutmeg

Fold the fillets in half and steam between 2 plates. Meanwhile make the sauce by melting the fat in a small saucepan, adding the flour, a pinch of salt and pepper, and cooking for 2–3 min. without browning. Remove from heat and stir in the liquid gradually, mixing well to prevent lumpiness. Bring to the boil, still stirring, and cook for 5 min. Add most of the cheese and season with mustard and nutmeg. Arrange the cooked fish in a shallow fireproof dish, coat with sauce and sprinkle with the remaining cheese. Place under a hot grill until golden brown.

Serve with grilled half tomatoes and mashed potatoes.

4 helpings

ROCK SALMON

See Saithe.

ROCKFISH

(sometimes called CATFISH)

Rockfish are available all the year; best from February to July. Suitable for frying, steaming, poaching and for made-up dishes. Usually sold skinned.

SAITHE

(sometimes called ROCK SALMON or COALFISH)

Saithe is available all the year; best September to February. Suitable for all methods of cooking.

SALMON

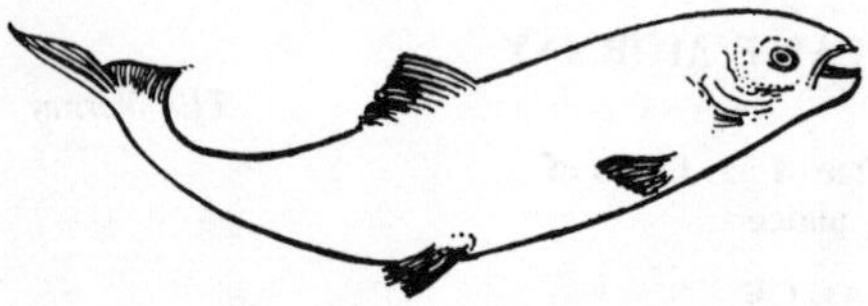

Seasons: English and Scottish, February to August; Irish, January to September. Suitable for poaching, grilling, baking; excellent served cold.

BAKED SALMON

Saumon à l'Italienne

2 lb. salmon (middle) (approx.)	**1 teasp. chopped parsley**
Salt and pepper	**A little butter**
Grated nutmeg	**1 small glass claret *or* cider (optional)**
2 small shallots	**Génoise *or* tomato sauce**

Cut the fish into 2–3 even-sized slices and place in a well-buttered fireproof dish. Season with salt, pepper and a little grated nutmeg. Chop the shallots and sprinkle over with the parsley. Dot a little butter on top of the fish. Moisten with the wine or cider (if used), and bake for about 15 min. in a fairly hot oven (**375° F., Gas 5**), basting the fish frequently. When done, dish up and pour some Génoise or tomato sauce over the slices of salmon. Use the essence left in the dish in which the fish was baked to flavour the sauce.

6-8 helpings

BOILED SALMON

Saumon bouilli

Salmon	**Boiling water**
Salt	

Scale and clean the fish, and put into a saucepan or fish-kettle with sufficient *boiling* water to just cover, adding salt to taste. The boiling water is necessary to preserve the colour of the fish. Simmer gently until the fish can be easily separated from the bone. Drain well. Dish, garnished with cut lemon and parsley. Serve with lobster, shrimp or other suitable sauce, and a dish of thinly-sliced cucumber.

Allow 4–6 oz. per helping
Cooking time—allow 10 min. per lb.

BOILED SALMON—in Court Bouillon

Salmon

COURT BOUILLON

To each quart of water allow:

1 dessertsp. salt	**1 strip of celery**
1 small turnip	**6 peppercorns**
1 small onion	**Bouquet garni**
½ leek	

Put into the pan just enough water to cover the fish, and when boiling add the prepared vegetables and cook gently for 30 min. In the meantime, wash, clean, and scale the fish and tie it loosely in a piece of muslin. Remove any scum there may be on the court bouillon, then put in the fish and boil gently until sufficiently cooked (the time required depends more on the thickness of the fish than the weight; allow 10 min. for each lb. when cooking a thick piece, and 7 min. for the tail end). Drain well, dish, garnished with parsley.

Serve with sliced cucumber, and Hollandaise, caper, shrimp or anchovy sauce.

Allow 4–6 oz. per helping

CUTLETS OF SALMON À LA MORNAY

Filets de Saumon à la Mornay

2 slices of salmon ¾–1 in. thick	**Salt and pepper**
1 onion	**1 oz. flour**
2½ oz. butter	**¼ pt. cream**
½ pt. fish stock	**1 tablesp. grated Parmesan cheese**
Bouquet garni	**1 dessertsp. lemon juice**

Chop the onion coarsely. Melt half the butter in a shallow saucepan, fry the onion and the salmon quickly on both sides, then add the stock (boiling), the bouquet garni and salt and pepper. Cover closely, and simmer gently for 20 min. Meanwhile, melt the remainder of the butter in another saucepan, add the flour and cook for 4 min. When the fish is done, transfer it to a hot dish and keep warm. Strain the stock on to the flour and butter and stir until boiling. Simmer for 5 min., then add the cream, cheese, lemon juice and seasoning to taste. Pour the mixture over the fish and serve.

5–6 helpings

GRILLED SALMON

Saumon grillé

2–3 slices of salmon (middle cut) about ¾ in. thick	**Salt and pepper**
2 tablesp. olive oil *or* oiled butter (approx.)	**1 tablesp. (about 1 oz.) Maître d'Hôtel *or* anchovy butter**
	Parsley
	Lemon (optional)

Wipe the fish with a damp cloth, then brush over with oil or oiled butter. Season to taste with salt and pepper and place the slices on a well-greased grill rack. Grill each side for 6–8 min., according to thickness of slices. When done, place the fish on a flat oval dish, spread a little Maître d'Hôtel or anchovy butter over each. Garnish with sprigs of fresh parsley, and if liked with quarters of lemon.

Serve hot.

4–6 helpings
Cooking time—about 15 min.

POTTED SALMON

Terrine de Saumon

Cold salmon	**Ground mace**
Salt and pepper	**Anchovy essence**
Cayenne pepper	**Clarified butter**

Free the fish from skin and bone, and pound it thoroughly. Add the seasoning by degrees, add anchovy essence to taste and clarified butter a few drops at a time, until the right consistency and flavour is obtained. Rub the ingredients through a fine sieve, press into small pots and cover with a good layer of clarified butter.

Fresh salmon may also be potted.

SALMON CUTLETS EN PAPILLOTES

Côtelettes de Saumon en Papillotes

Slices of salmon, about ¾–1 in. thick	**Butter**
Salt and pepper	**Anchovy *or* caper sauce**

Season the slices with salt and pepper. Butter some pieces of greaseproof paper or aluminium foil. Enclose a slice of fish in each, secure the ends of the paper case by twisting tightly, and bake for 15–20 min. in a moderate oven (**350° F., Gas 4**). Serve with anchovy or caper sauce.

Allow 4–5 oz. per helping

SALMON DARIOLES

Darioles de Saumon

¾ lb. cooked salmon	**1 truffle (optional)**
1 gill plain aspic jelly for lining	**½ pt. Mayonnaise sauce stiffened with ¾ gill well-reduced aspic jelly**
Tarragon leaves	
Chervil leaves	

Line 6–8 small dariole moulds with cold, liquid aspic jelly. When set decorate with the herb leaves and slices of truffle (if used). Set the decoration with another thin layer of aspic jelly. When set, coat with a layer of mayonnaise. Remove all skin and bone and flake the fish, season with mayonnaise and add the remainder of the truffle, chopped coarsely. Threequarters fill the moulds with dressed salmon, and finish filling with some mayonnaise and aspic. Chill the moulds; when set turn out on to a serving dish, garnish with small green salad and chopped aspic.

SALMON MAYONNAISE

Mayonnaise de Saumon

Cold boiled salmon	**Beetroot**
Lettuce	**Gherkins**
Mayonnaise sauce	**Capers**
Aspic jelly (optional)	**Boned anchovies**
Cucumber	**Hard-boiled eggs**

A mayonnaise of salmon may consist of a large centre-cut, a thick slice, or the remains of cold salmon cut into pieces convenient for serving. Arrange a bed of shredded lettuce in the bottom of a salad bowl. Remove the skin and bone from the fish. Flake the fish and place on the lettuce. Mask the fish completely with thick mayonnaise sauce. The sauce may be made stiffer by adding a little liquid, but nearly cold, aspic jelly. When obtainable, a little endive should be mixed with the lettuce, for although the somewhat bitter flavour of this salad plant is disliked by many, its delicate, feathery leaves greatly improve the appearance of a dish. Garnish with the suggested ingredients or many other garnishings, in addition to those given above, may be used; tarragon and chervil leaves and fancily-cut thin slices of truffle are particularly effective when used to decorate the surface of Mayonnaise sauce.

Allow 5–6 oz. salmon per helping

SALMON MOUSSE

Saumon en Gelée

1 lb. cooked salmon (approx.) *or* one 16 oz. can	**1 pt. clear fish stock**
1 oz. gelatine	**Salt and pepper**
	2 egg whites

Dissolve the gelatine in the stock and season to taste. Cook the egg whites in a dariole mould or small cup until firm; when cold cut into thin slices and cut out into fancy shapes. Drain the oil from the salmon and remove all skin and bones. Cover the bottom of a mould with the jellied stock, let it set, and then decorate with egg white shapes. Set the garnish with a little jelly, allow to set. Add a layer of salmon, cover with jelly and put aside until set. Repeat until the mould is full. Keep in the refrigerator or in a cool place until wanted, then turn out and serve.

NOTE: 1 tablesp. sherry or Marsala can be added to the jelly to give it additional flavour.

6–8 helpings

SALMON WITH SAUCE GÉNEVOISE

Saumon à la Sauce Génevoise

2 slices salmon ¾–1 lb. each	**1 carrot**
2 oz. butter	**Bouquet garni**
1 dessertsp. finely-chopped onion	**1 blade of mace**
½ pt. good stock	**1 teasp. anchovy essence**
½ gill white wine	**Salt and pepper**
1 dessertsp. finely-chopped parsley	**Cayenne pepper**
	1 oz. flour
	Juice of 1 lemon

Melt 1 oz. of the butter in a saucepan and fry the onion until slightly browned. Add the stock, wine, parsley, sliced carrot, bouquet garni, mace, anchovy essence and seasoning, and boil gently for a few minutes. Strain and return to the saucepan. Bring the stock to boiling-point, put in the slices of fish and let them simmer gently for about 20 min., or until the fish separates easily from the bone. Meanwhile melt the remaining 1 oz. of butter in another saucepan, add the flour, stir and cook for about 5 min. When the fish is cooked, transfer it carefully on to a hot dish. Pour the liquid in which the fish was cooked on to the butter and flour, stir until smooth, then simmer for about 6 min. Add the lemon juice, season the sauce to taste, strain over the fish and serve.

6 helpings

DEVILLED SMOKED SALMON

½ lb. smoked salmon (approx.)	**1 oz. fresh butter**
3–4 slices toasted bread	**Salt and pepper**
	Curry butter

Trim the slices of toast, cut each into 3 even-sized pieces and butter one side of each. Sprinkle with salt and pepper, cover with thin slices of smoked salmon, then spread with curry butter. Place in a hot oven for a few minutes. Dish up neatly, garnish with sprigs of parsley and serve hot.

5–6 helpings

SALMON TROUT

Salmon trout is of the same species as river trout and is related to the salmon; it is very similar in appearance to grilse. It is in season March to August, its average weight being 2–4 lb., and its average length 1 ft. 6 in.–2 ft. 6 in.

POACHED SALMON TROUT

Clean the fish, removing the gills, intestines and eyes but leaving on the head and tail. If a fish kettle with drainer is not available, cradle the fish in muslin and cook in a large saucepan or preserving pan. Lower the fish into simmering, lightly salted water (1 teasp. per qt.) and poach, allowing 10 min. per lb. and 10 min. over. As soon as cooked, lift carefully from the water and drain. To serve cold, cool a little and then neatly remove the skin from one side. When serving hot skinning is optional.

To serve hot: Arrange on a flat dish, garnish with sliced cucumber, parsley, lemon and new potatoes. Serve with melted butter or Hollandaise sauce.

To serve cold: 1. Serve quite plain, garnished with salad and accompanied by mayonnaise.

2. Glaze the cold fish with aspic jelly made with the liquor in which the fish was cooked, garnish with chopped aspic, stuffed tomatoes and sliced cucumber.

SHAD

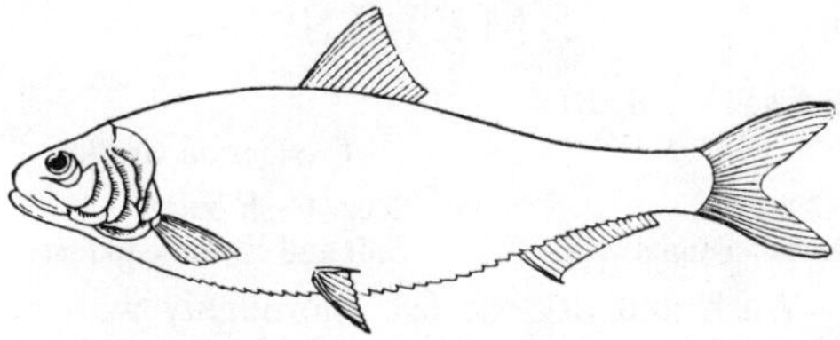

BAKED SHAD

Alose rôtie au four

One 2–3 lb. shad — **2–3 rashers bacon**
3–4 oz. veal forcemeat

Wash, clean, scale and dry the fish. Stuff the fish with forcemeat and sew up the opening. Place in a fireproof dish or baking-tin, lay the slices of bacon on top and bake gently in a moderate oven (**350° F., Gas 4**) for 25–30 min.

4 helpings

FRIED SHAD

Alose frite

1 medium-sized shad — **Egg and breadcrumbs**
Seasoned flour — **Frying-fat**

Wash and scale the fish, separate it from the backbone and divide into neat fillets. Add a little salt and pepper to 1 tablesp. flour, dip in the fillets, then coat them carefully with egg and breadcrumbs. Have ready a deep pan of hot fat, fry the fish until lightly browned, then drain well. Garnish with crisply-fried parsley, and the roe, previously fried.

Serve with anchovy, tomato or piquant sauce.

4–5 helpings — **Cooking time—10 min.**

GRILLED SHAD

Alose grillée

One 2 lb. shad — **1 teasp. finely-chopped parsley**
4 tablesp. salad oil — **Salt and pepper**
1 dessertsp. finely-chopped onion

Wash, empty and thoroughly dry the fish, place it in a deep dish and add the salad oil, onion, parsley and a good seasoning of salt and pepper. Baste frequently, let the fish remain in the marinade for 2 hr., then drain and dry well. Grill under a medium-hot grill for about 20 min., according to size, turn the fish frequently and brush over occasionally with some of the oil in which the fish was soaked.

Serve with sorrel, caper or piquant sauce.

4–5 helpings

SKATE

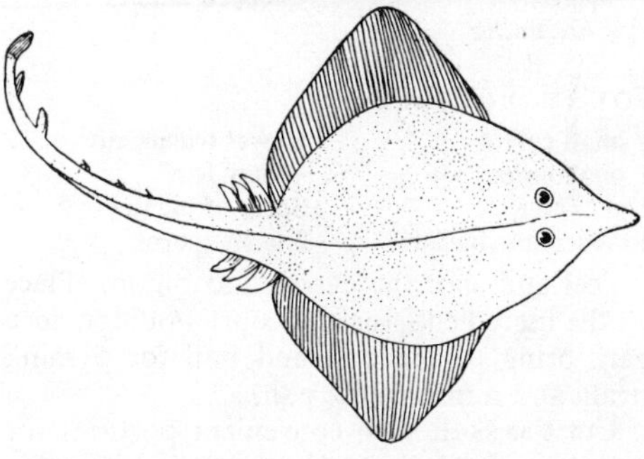

Skate is available all the year; spawns in March and April. Excellent for poaching or frying, or cold with salad. Only the "wings" are eaten.

BOILED SKATE

Raie au Naturel

One 5–8 oz. piece of skate wing — **Salt**

Wash the skate, put into a saucepan containing sufficient salted warm water to just cover, and simmer gently for about 15 min. or until the fish separates easily from the bone. Drain well, dish and serve with shrimp, lobster or caper sauce.

1 helping

FRIED SKATE WITH TOMATO SAUCE

Raie frite à la Sauce Tomate

1½ lb. wing of skate	**Fat for frying**
Egg *or* thin batter and white crumbs for coating	**¼ pt. tomato sauce**

Cut the skate into neat pieces and simmer in salted water for 5 min. Drain and dry, then coat each piece with egg or batter and white breadcrumbs, pressing the coating on firmly with a knife. Fry the skate slowly in hot fat until golden brown, turning once during cooking. Drain the fish well and arrange in the centre of a hot dish. Pour the sauce round and serve at once.

4 helpings

SKATE AU BEURRE NOIR

Raie au Beurre noir

1¼ lb. skate wing (approx.)	**1 tablesp. vinegar**
1½ oz. butter	**Chopped parsley**

COURT BOUILLON

1 small carrot	**1 level teasp. salt**
1 small onion	**½ bay leaf**
1 pt. water	**Sprig of parsley**
1 dessertsp. vinegar	**2 peppercorns**

Peel and slice the carrot and onion. Place all the ingredients for the court bouillon in a pan, bring to the boil and boil for 5 min., strain and return to the pan.

Cut the skate into convenient portions for serving and poach in the court bouillon for 10–15 min. Remove the pieces of fish carefully, drain and place on a hot dish. Heat the butter in a small, strong pan until it begins to turn brown, remove from the heat and add the vinegar very gradually to prevent spluttering. Pour over the fish, sprinkle with a little chopped parsley and serve.

4 helpings

SKATE WITH CAPER SAUCE

Raie, Sauce aux Câpres

4 small slices of skate	**2 bay leaves**
¼ pt. vinegar	**2–3 sprigs of thyme**
1 tablesp. salt	**½ pt. caper sauce**
½ teasp. pepper	
1 sliced onion	
1 small bunch of parsley	

Put all the ingredients except the caper sauce into a saucepan with just sufficient warm water to cover the fish, and simmer for about 15 min. until tender. When the fish is cooked, drain well, put on a hot dish, pour over a little caper sauce and serve the remainder separately.

NOTE: Skate may also be served with onion sauce, or parsley and butter.

4 helpings

SMELTS

BAKED SMELTS

Éperlans au Gratin

12 smelts	**2 oz. fresh butter**
Breadcrumbs	**Salt and cayenne to taste**

Wash and dry the fish thoroughly with a cloth; arrange them in a flat baking-dish. Cover with fine breadcrumbs and place dabs of butter over them. Season and bake for 15 min. Just before serving, add a squeeze of lemon juice and garnish with fried parsley and cut lemon.

4 helpings

FRIED SMELTS

Éperlans frits

12 smelts	**Egg and breadcrumbs**
A little flour	**Fat *or* oil for frying**

Smelts should be very fresh and not washed more than is necessary to clean them. Dry in a cloth, flour lightly, dip them in egg and coat with very fine breadcrumbs. Put them into hot fat or oil and fry until pale brown. Drain well and serve with plain melted butter. This fish is often used as a garnish.

4 helpings **Cooking time—5 min.**

SNAILS

SNAILS WITH PIQUANT SAUCE

Escargots, Sauce piquante

2 doz. snails	**Salt and pepper**
½ oz. butter	**Maître d'Hôtel butter**
2 shallots	
2–3 tablesp. piquant sauce	

Clean the snails thoroughly by brushing them under running water or in several changes of water, cover with salt and water and let them remain in it for 12 hr., then wash and drain well to remove the slime. Put the snails into a saucepan containing sufficient boiling water to cover, cook gently for about 20 min., then drain, and when cool take them out of their shells and remove the black end from each. Meanwhile, melt the butter, fry the finely-chopped shallots without browning, add the piquant sauce and snails and season to taste. Wash, drain and dry the shells. When the snail mixture is thoroughly hot, replace the snails in their shells, cover with Maître d'Hôtel butter and serve.

SOLE

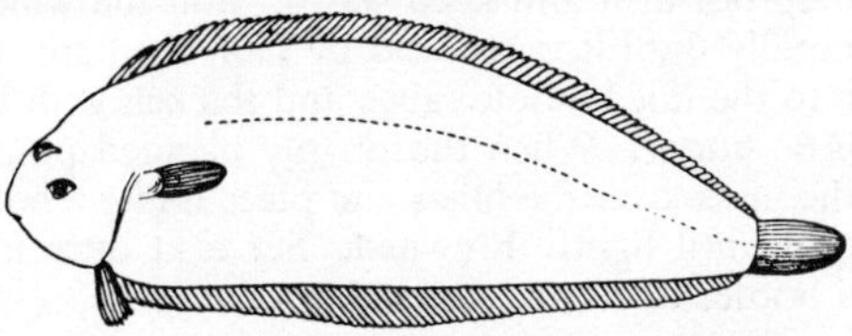

The true sole is the Dover Sole, the so-called Lemon Sole is a different species but can be cooked by the same methods.

Sole is seasonable all the year; it spawns February to May, sole without roe are superior. Sole is suitable for all methods of cooking.

Allow one 3–4 oz. fillet per helping when served as the fish course of a 4-course menu and 2 fillets when a main dish.

BAKED FILLETS OF SOLE WITH FORCE-MEAT

Filets de Sole farcis

4 fillets of sole	**¼ teasp. mixed herbs**
2 tablesp. breadcrumbs	**1 egg**
1 tablesp. finely-chopped suet	**Salt and pepper**
1 dessertsp. finely-chopped parsley	**Pale-brown bread-crumbs**
	Butter

Wipe fillets with a clean damp cloth. Mix the other ingredients together with sufficient beaten egg to moisten. Spread a thin layer of forcemeat on each fillet and fold in two. Place the fillets in a fireproof baking-dish and fill up the spaces between with the rest of the force-meat. Sprinkle lightly with pale-brown bread-crumbs, add a few small pieces of butter and bake for about 30 min. in a moderate oven (350° F., Gas 4). Serve in the cooking dish.

4 helpings

BAKED SOLE WITH SHRIMPS

Sole aux Crevettes

1 medium-sized sole	**1 teasp. anchovy essence**
¼ pt. picked shrimps	**1 egg**
1 dessertsp. white bread-crumbs	**A little white sauce *or* milk**
Cayenne pepper	**Brown breadcrumbs**
Salt	**A little butter**

Remove the skin from the sole, make an incision down the centre as for filleting, and raise as far as possible the flesh on each side. Chop the shrimps coarsely, add the bread-crumbs, cayenne, salt (if necessary), anchovy essence, half the egg and sufficient white sauce or milk to moisten. Press the mixture lightly inside the fish, and instead of drawing the two sides together, fill the gap between them with forcemeat and flatten the surface of it to the level of the fish. Brush over with the remainder of the egg, coat lightly with pale-brown bread-crumbs. Place in a fireproof dish, dot with a few small pieces of butter and bake for about 20–25 min. in a fairly hot oven (**375° F., Gas 5**).

2–3 helpings

FILLETS OF SOLE À LA NORMANDE

Filets de Soles à la Normande

Eight 4 oz. fillets of sole	**Butter**
Salt and pepper	**½ pt. Normandy sauce**
1 gill white wine	
1 shallot	

GARNISH

Poached oysters	**Fried button mushrooms**
Cooked mussels	**Croûtes *or* fleurons**

Wipe the fillets with a damp cloth, fold them in two and place in a buttered sauté-pan or fireproof dish. Season with salt and pepper, moisten with the white wine, sprinkle with finely-chopped shallot, place a few pieces of butter over, cover and cook in a fairly hot oven (**375° F., Gas 5**) for about 10 min. Have the garnish ready, put the fillets on a dish, arrange the oysters, mussels and mushrooms neatly and strain over some of the Normandy sauce made with the liquor in which the oysters were cooked. Garnish the sides with croûtes of bread (buttered slices of French rolls browned in the oven) or with fleurons (little half-moon shapes of puff pastry). Serve the remaining sauce separately in a sauce boat.

NOTE: If smelts are in season, this dish should be garnished with a few fried smelts in addition to the other garnish.

8 helpings

FILLETS OF SOLE À LA ORLY

Filets de Soles à la Orly

Six 4 oz. fillets of sole	**Fried parsley**
Deep fat for frying	

MARINADE

1 tablesp. lemon juice	**1 teasp. chopped onion *or* shallots**
1 tablesp. salad oil	**Salt and pepper**
1 teasp. finely-chopped parsley	

BATTER

2 oz. flour	**1 tablesp. salad oil *or* melted butter**
Pinch of salt	**1 egg white**
½ gill tepid water	

Wipe the fillets with a clean damp cloth and place in a deep dish with the marinade. Soak for 1 hr., then drain well. Meanwhile mix the batter; blend the flour and salt smoothly with the water and oil, then add the stiffly-whisked egg white. Dip the fillets in the batter, drop them carefully into a deep pan of hot fat and fry until golden-brown. Serve garnished with fried parsley. Serve with tomato sauce.

6 helpings

FILLETS OF SOLE AUX FINES HERBES

Filets de Soles aux fines Herbes

Eight 2 oz. fillets of sole	**½ pt. white wine sauce** (p. 119)
Salt and pepper	**1 tablesp. finely-chopped fresh herbs**
4 tablesp. fish stock	

Wipe the fillets with a clean, damp cloth, season with salt and pepper and fold them in 3. Place in a greased fireproof dish, add the fish stock, cover, and cook in a fairly hot oven (**375° F., Gas 5**) for 15–20 min. Drain the fillets well and place on a dish, coat with white wine sauce and sprinkle with the finely-chopped fresh herbs.

4 helpings

FILLETS OF SOLE BONNE FEMME

Filets de Sole a la bonne Femme

4 fillets of sole	**Salt and pepper**
4 oz. mushrooms	**¼ pt. white wine**
1 shallot	**¼ pt. fish Velouté sauce**
1 teasp. chopped parsley	**A little butter**

Wipe the fillets with a clean damp cloth. Put them flat in a shallow pan with the sliced mushrooms, sliced shallot, parsley and seasoning. Add the wine, cover and poach for 10–15 min. Drain the fish from the wine, place on a fireproof dish and keep warm. Boil the wine rapidly until it is reduced by half, then stir it into the hot Velouté sauce and thicken with a little butter. When thoroughly blended pour the sauce over the fillets and place under a hot grill until lightly browned. Serve at once in a border of sliced, steamed potatoes.

4 helpings

FILLETS OF SOLE CAPRICE

Filets de Sole Caprice

4 large fillets of sole	**2 oz. butter *or* margarine**
A little lemon juice	**2 bananas**
Egg and breadcrumbs	**Chopped parsley**

Sprinkle each fillet with a little lemon juice, then coat with egg and breadcrumbs. Fry in the hot fat until golden brown and cooked through—about 7 min. Drain and keep hot. Peel and cut the bananas in ½ lengthwise, rub with lemon juice and sauté in the remainder of the fat until soft but not broken. Place half a banana on each fillet, sprinkle with parsley and serve at once.

4 helpings

FILLETS OF SOLE MEUNIÈRE

Filets de Sole à la Meunière

4 large *or* 8 small fillets of sole	**1 level tablesp. chopped parsley**
A little seasoned flour	**Lemon "butterflies"** (see p. 39)
3 oz. butter	
1 tablesp. lemon juice	

Dredge the fillets lightly, but thoroughly, with seasoned flour. Heat the butter in a frying-pan and when hot fry the fillets until golden brown and cooked through—about 7 min. Arrange the fillets on a hot dish. Reheat the fat until it is nut brown in colour and then pour it over the fish. Sprinkle the lemon juice and parsley over the fillets, garnish with lemon "butterflies" and serve at once.

4 helpings

FILLETS OF SOLE WITH CREAM SAUCE

Sole à la Creme

1 large sole	**1 pt. milk *or* milk and fish stock**
Salt and pepper	**2 oz. butter**
Lemon juice	**1½ oz. flour**
1 small piece of onion	
1 blade of mace	

Wash, skin and fillet the sole, and divide each fillet lengthwise into two. Tie each strip loosely in a knot, or fold the ends over each other. Place in a greased tin, season with salt and pepper, sprinkle with lemon juice, cover with a greased paper and bake for 10–15 min. in a moderate oven (**350° F., Gas 4**). Simmer the bones of the fish, the onion and mace in the milk for about 15 min., then strain and season to taste. Melt the butter in a saucepan, add the flour, cook for 3–4 min., then pour in the flavoured milk and stir until boiling. Let the sauce simmer 10 min. at least; then arrange the fish on a hot dish, either in a circle or forming 2 rows, and strain the sauce over. Decorate with a little chopped parsley or lobster coral.

4 helpings

FILLETS OF SOLE WITH MUSHROOMS

Filets de Sole aux Champignons

Eight 2 oz. fillets of sole	**6 oz. button mushrooms**
Salt and pepper	**1 oz. butter *or* margarine**
Lemon juice	**¾ oz. flour**
2 tablesp. white wine	**⅛ pt. creamy milk**
2 tablesp. fish stock *or* water	**1 teasp. chopped parsley**

Wipe the fillets with a clean damp cloth, season with salt, pepper and lemon juice to taste, then fold them in three. Place in a greased fireproof dish, add the wine and fish stock, cover and cook in a fairly hot oven (**375° F., Gas 5**) for 15–20 min. Cook the mushrooms at the same time, placing them in a covered casserole with a very little water, salt and lemon juice. Shortly before serving make a sauce with the butter or margarine, flour and milk, adding the cooking liquor drained from the mushrooms and sufficient of the fish poaching liquor to give a coating consistency; season to taste and if necessary whisk until smooth. Arrange the well-drained fillets round the outer edge of a flat serving dish and coat with the sauce. Pile the mushrooms in the centre and sprinkle with chopped parsley.

4 helpings

FRIED SOLE

Sole frite

1–2 medium-sized soles	**Egg and breadcrumbs**
Salt and pepper	**Deep fat for frying**
1 tablesp. flour	

Wash and skin the soles, cut off the fins, and dry well. Add a liberal seasoning of salt and pepper to the flour. Coat the fish with seasoned flour then brush over with egg, and coat with fine breadcrumbs. Lower the fish carefully into the hot fat and fry until golden-brown.

Soles may also be fried, though less easily, and sometimes less satisfactorily, in a large frying-pan. The oval form is preferable for the purpose; and in frying, care should be taken to cook first the side of the sole intended to be served uppermost, otherwise breadcrumbs that have become detached from the side first fried may adhere to the side next cooked, and spoil its appearance. Drain well on kitchen paper and serve garnished with fried parsley.

1–2 helpings Cooking time—about 10 min.

SOLE À LA MAÎTRE D'HÔTEL

As for Sole with Cream Sauce, but stir 1 dessertsp. finely-chopped parsley and 1 teasp. lemon juice into the sauce just before serving.

SOLE À LA PORTUGAISE

1 medium-sized sole	**1 onion**
1 oz. butter	**2–3 tomatoes**
1 shallot	**1 dessertsp. grated Parmesan cheese**
1 teasp. finely-chopped parsley	**1 dessertsp. brown breadcrumbs**
½ teasp. anchovy essence	**Extra butter**
Salt and pepper	

Skin the sole and make an incision down the centre as for filleting; raise the flesh from the bone on each side as far as possible. Mix the butter, finely-chopped shallot, parsley and anchovy essence well together, and stuff the mixture inside the sole. Place the fish in a buttered fireproof dish, season. Arrange slices of onion and tomato alternately and overlapping each other, on top of the fish; or if less onion is preferred, surround each slice of tomato with a single ring of onion. Mix together the cheese and breadcrumbs and sprinkle over the fish. Place small pieces of butter on top, cover with a lid or greased paper and bake for about 20 min. in a moderate oven (**350° F., Gas 4**).

Serve with tomato or brown sauce.

2 helpings

SOLE AU GRATIN

3 fillets *or* 1 large sole	**Preserved mushrooms, sliced**
Salt and pepper	**Italian sauce** (pp. 130, 132)
½ glass white wine	**Lemon juice**
Mushroom liquor	**Brown breadcrumbs**
1 teasp. chopped parsley	**Butter**

If using a whole sole, skin both sides, cut off the head and fins and make several incisions with a knife across one side of the fish. Place fish on a well-buttered fireproof dish (if using whole fish place cut side uppermost), season with pepper and salt, add the white wine, a few drops of lemon juice, a little mushroom liquor and some chopped parsley. Slice the mushrooms and place in a row down the centre of the fish; cover with a rich Italian sauce. Sprinkle with brown breadcrumbs, dot a few tiny bits of butter on top of the fish and bake in a moderate oven (**350° F., Gas 4**) for 20–30 min., according to size of sole.

2–3 helpings

SPRATS

Melettes or Harenguets

Choose sprats with a silvery appearance, brightness being a sign of freshness. They are best from November to March. Supplies are rather erratic, as they are affected by weather.

Sprats should be cooked very fresh. Wipe dry; fasten in rows by a skewer run through the eyes; dredge with flour and grill under a red-hot grill. The grill rack should first be rubbed with suet. Serve very hot, with cut lemon and brown bread and butter.

Allow 1 lb. for 3 helpings
Cooking time—3–4 min.

FRIED SPRATS

Melettes frits

3 doz. sprats (approx.)	**Salt and pepper**
2 tablesp. flour	**½ oz. cooking fat**
	Lemon wedges

Wash and dry the sprats thoroughly, mix the flour with the salt and pepper to season. Dip the sprats in the seasoned flour and fry them in the hot fat. Serve as quickly as possible on a hot dish with a wedge of lemon per helping.

5 helpings Cooking time—20 min.

SPRAT PASTE

Pâte de Melettes

Sprats	**Cayenne**
Butter	**Ground mace**
Salt and pepper	**Anchovy essence**

To make sprat paste, which is similar to anchovy paste, bake the sprats with a little butter in a fireproof dish. Remove the heads, tails, backbone and skin, pound the fish well and rub through a fine sieve. Season well with salt, cayenne and pepper, add a good pinch of ground mace and anchovy essence to taste. Press into small pots and cover with clarified butter.

STURGEON

BAKED STURGEON

Esturgeon rôti au Vin blanc

2 lb. sturgeon	**Juice of ½ lemon**
Salt and pepper	**½ pt. white wine**
1 small bunch of herbs	**¼ lb. butter**

Clean the fish thoroughly and skin it. Lay the fish in a large fireproof dish, sprinkle over the seasoning and herbs very finely minced, and moisten with the lemon juice and wine. Place the butter in small pieces over the whole of the fish, put into a moderate oven (**350° F., Gas 4**) for about 30–40 min., and baste frequently. Bake until brown, then serve with its own gravy.

5–6 helpings

STURGEON CUTLETS

Côtelettes d'Esturgeon

1½ lb. sturgeon	**Egg and breadcrumbs**
½ teasp. finely-chopped parsley	**Salt and pepper**
¼ teasp. finely-grated lemon rind	**Fat for frying**

Cut the fish into thin slices, flatten them with a heavy knife, and trim them into shape. Add the parsley and lemon rind to the breadcrumbs, and season with salt and pepper. Brush over with beaten egg, coat carefully with the seasoned breadcrumbs, and fry in hot fat until cooked and lightly browned on both sides. Drain free from fat, and serve with piquant or tomato sauce.

6–8 helpings **Cooking time—about 10 min.**

TENCH

BAKED TENCH

Tanche rôtie

1 tench	**2 shallots**
Juice of 2 lemons	**1 tablesp. coarsely-chopped gherkin**
2 oz. butter *or* fat	**½ pt. white sauce**
Salt and pepper	

Scale and clean the fish thoroughly, remove the gills, which are always muddy, sprinkle the fish liberally with lemon juice, reserving 1 tablesp. of juice, put the fish aside for 1 hr. Then melt the butter in a baking-dish, put in the fish and baste it well, sprinkle with salt and pepper and add the finely-chopped shallots. Cover with greased paper and bake gently for 25–35 min, according to taste. Add the gherkin and 1 tablesp. lemon juice to the sauce and season to taste. Serve the fish with the sauce poured over.

2–3 helpings

TENCH-MARINADED AND GRILLED

Tanche grillée

3 small tench	**¼ teasp. powdered mixed herbs**
Salt and pepper	**2–3 tablesp. salad oil**
1 small onion	**Piquant sauce**
2 shallots	
1 dessertsp. finely-chopped parsley	

Wash and clean the fish thoroughly, remove the gills and completely cover the fish with boiling water. Let them remain for 5 min., then dry and scale them carefully. Place in a deep dish, add a good seasoning of salt and pepper, and the finely chopped onion and shallots, parsley, herbs and salad oil. Allow the tench to lie for 2 hr., meanwhile basting frequently with the marinade, then drain well. Enclose each fish in a piece of well-greased greaseproof paper or aluminium foil and grill under a medium-hot grill for 10–15 min., according to size. When ready, remove the papers and serve the fish with the piquant sauce poured over.

3 helpings

TROUT

River Trout are available all the year. Serve grilled, baked, fried or cold with salad.

BAKED STUFFED TROUT

Truite rôtie au Four

2 large trout	**1 teasp. lemon juice**
Veal forcemeat	**½ teasp. anchovy essence**
3 oz. butter	**Salt and pepper**
1 oz. flour	
1 dessertsp. capers	

Clean, scale, empty and dry the fish. Make the forcemeat stiff. Stuff the trout with forcemeat, and sew up or skewer the openings. Place in a baking-tin or dish with 2 oz. of butter and bake in a moderate oven (**350° F., Gas 4**) for about ½ hr., basting frequently. Fry the flour and the rest of the butter together. When the fish is ready, remove it to a hot dish and strain the liquor in the baking-dish on to the flour and butter. Stir until boiling and smooth, then add the capers, lemon juice, anchovy essence and season to taste. Simmer for 2–3 min., then pour over the fish and serve.

5–6 helpings

STEWED TROUT

Truite au Vin Rouge

2 good-sized trout	**A little thyme**
½ onion, thinly sliced	**Salt and pepper**
A little parsley	**1 pt. fish stock**
2 cloves	**1 glass claret**
1 blade of mace	**1 oz. butter**
2 bay leaves	**1 oz. flour**

Wash the fish well, then wipe dry. Place in a pan with all the ingredients except the butter and flour, and simmer gently for ½ hr. While the fish is cooking, melt the butter in another pan, stir in the flour, and cook for 3–4 min. When ready, place the fish on a hot dish, strain the liquor over the flour and butter, and stir until it boils and becomes smooth. Season to taste, pour over the fish, and serve.

5–6 helpings
Cooking time—40 min.

TRUITES AU BLEU

One 6–8 oz. trout	**Salt**
Vinegar	**Parsley**

The essential factor of this famous dish is that the trout should be alive until just before cooking. In continental restaurants they are often kept in a tank from which the customer selects his fish, which is then stunned, cleaned and cooked immediately.

The fish should be stunned, cleaned (gutted) and immediately plunged into a pan of boiling salted water to which a little vinegar has been added. (The fish are not scaled or washed as this would spoil the blue colour.) Draw the pan aside or reduce the heat and poach the fish for about 10–12 min. Drain and serve garnished with parsley and accompanied by melted butter, Hollandaise sauce and small boiled potatoes.

TRUITES À LA MEUNIÈRE

As for Mullet à la Meunière (p. 168) substituting trout for mullet.

TURBOT

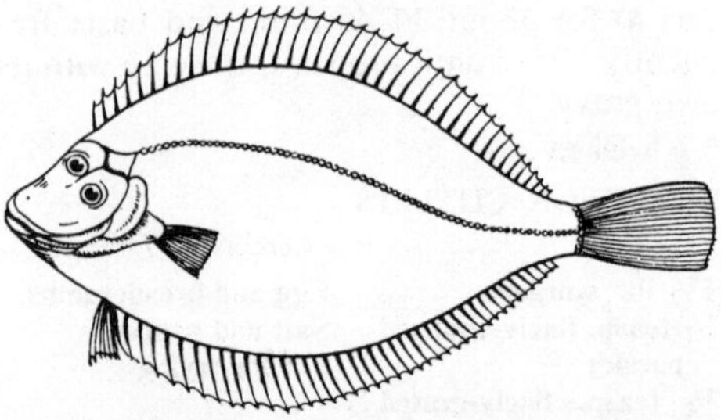

Turbot is considered by many to be the finest of the flat fish. It is notable for the small bony tubercles on the dark skin surface and for the complete absence of scales. Turbot often grow to considerable size—25 lb. is not unusual—and are usually sold cut in thick slices or cutlets.

Young turbot are referred to as Chicken Turbots and they are cut entirely into fillets.

Turbot is seasonable most of the year; normally cheapest when salmon is in season. It can be cooked by any method, and is excellent cold with salad. It must be noted that if cooking a whole turbot, a turbot kettle (shaped) will be required.

POACHED TURBOT

Turbot poché

1 chicken turbot *or* a cut 1½–2 lb. in weight	**Lemon**
	Salt

Wipe the fish thoroughly and trim the fins.

Make an incision down the middle of the back, to lessen the possibility of the skin cracking; and rub the white side of the fish with a cut lemon to retain its whiteness. Have ready a pan containing sufficient warm water to cover the fish, add salt to taste, put in the fish, bring gradually to near boiling-point, then simmer very gently for 15–20 min. Drain the fish and dish up neatly.

Garnish with lobster coral, parsley and cut lemon, and serve with Hollandaise, anchovy, shrimp *or* lobster sauce.

5–6 helpings

TURBOT À LA DUGLÉRÉ

Turbot Dugléré

Four 5–6 oz. pieces of turbot (skinned)	**¼ pt. dry white wine**
½ lb. tomatoes	**Salt and pepper**
1 small onion	**1 oz. butter *or* margarine**
1 level tablesp. chopped parsley (optional)	**1 oz. flour**

Place the fish in a greased casserole. Skin and chop the tomatoes, peel and finely chop the onion. Mix the tomatoes, onion, parsley (if used) and wine together, season and pour over the fish. Cover the casserole and cook in a fairly hot oven (**400° F., Gas 6**) for 30–35 min. Remove from the oven, lift the fish on to a hot dish and keep hot while making the sauce. Measure the tomato mixture and make up to ½ pt. with water if necessary. Melt the fat, add the flour and cook for 1–2 min. Add the tomato mixture, bring to the boil, stirring all the time and boil gently for 5 min. Season to taste, then pour over the fish and serve at once.

4 helpings

TURBOT À L'ITALIENNE

Turbot à l'Italienne

Remains of cold turbot	**Italian sauce**

Remove the bone and black skin carefully from the fish. Heat the sauce in a flat saucepan and when hot place in the fish to warm through, but do not let it boil. Serve on a hot dish garnished with fried bread croûtons.

Cooking time—5 min.

TURBOT AU GRATIN

Turbot au Gratin

Remains of cold turbot	**Seasoning**
Béchamel *or* other white sauce	**Breadcrumbs**
	Butter

Divide the flesh of the turbot into small pieces, carefully freeing it from all bone and black skin. Put the fish into a saucepan, moisten with sufficient white sauce to cover well. Season to taste with salt and pepper and let it get thoroughly hot, but do not allow to boil. Arrange the fish and sauce in a baking-dish, cover with white or brown breadcrumbs and place a few very small pieces of butter over the top. Brown in the oven or under the grill.

Cooking time—altogether ½ hr.

TURBOT WITH AUBERGINES

Turbot aux Aubergines

2 lb. of turbot (middle cut)	**3 aubergines**
	Olive oil
Salt and pepper	**Clarified butter**
Milk	**Juice of ½ lemon**
Flour	**1 tablesp. finely-chopped parsley**
2 oz. butter	

Remove the dark skin from the fish, free it from bones. Cut the fish into 6 even-sized slices. Trim the slices neatly, season with salt and pepper, dip them into milk and then into flour. Melt about 1½ oz. of butter in a sauté pan, place in the fillets, cover with greased greaseproof paper, and cook in the oven for 15 min., or longer if required, basting occasionally. Meanwhile remove the skin from the aubergines, cut them into slices, dip in flour and fry in a mixture of olive oil and clarified butter in equal proportions, until golden-brown. Drain and season with salt. Serve the turbot on an oblong dish, sprinkle with a little lemon juice, then the parsley and lastly some nut-brown clarified butter. Garnish with the fried aubergines.

6 helpings

TURBOT WITH CREAM SAUCE

Turbot à la Crème

¾ lb. cold cooked turbot (approx.)	**1 teasp. lemon juice**
1½ oz. butter	**3 tablesp. cream**
1 oz. flour	**Pinch of ground mace**
½ pt. milk	**Salt and pepper**

Remove the bones and skin from the fish, and separate the flesh into large flakes. Melt the butter in a saucepan, add the flour and cook for 3 min. Pour in the milk, stir until it boils and then simmer gently for 10 min. Put in the fish and let it become thoroughly hot, then add the lemon juice, cream and seasoning to taste and serve.

3–4 helpings **Cooking time—about 20 min.**

WHITEBAIT

Whitebait is most seasonable from February to July. Best deep fried.

WHITEBAIT

Blanchailles

Whitebait	**Cayenne *or* black pepper**
Ice	**Salt**
Flour	**Lemon**
Deep fat for frying	

Frying whitebait is a difficult task for inexperienced cooks. The following is a well-tried method which, if carefully followed, never fails to produce satisfactory results. Put the whitebait with a piece of ice in a basin, which must be kept cool. When required for cooking, spread the fish on a cloth to dry, dredge well with flour, place in a wire basket and shake off the superfluous flour. Plunge the basket into a pan of clean, very hot lard and fry rapidly for 3–4 min. Keep moving the basket all the time whilst frying. Lift the basket, shake it to strain off the fat, and turn the fish on to greaseproof paper. Place on a warm dish and repeat until all the whitebait are fried. Season with cayenne or black pepper and fine salt. Serve garnished with quarters of lemon.

Cooking time—3–4 min.

WHITING

Merlan

Whiting is available all the year; best in winter months. It is the traditional fish for invalids. It can be served poached, steamed, baked or fried.

BAKED WHITING

Merlan au Gratin

As for Sole au Gratin (p. 180), substituting skinned whiting for sole.

BAKED WHITING AUX FINES HERBES

Merlan aux fines Herbes

As for Sole aux Fines Herbes (p. 178).

FRIED WHITING

Merlan frit

3–4 whiting	**Egg and breadcrumbs**
1 tablesp. flour	**Deep fat *or* oil for frying**
Salt and pepper	**Parsley**

Wash, clean and dry the fish. Remove their skins and fasten the tail in the mouth with a small skewer. (The fishmonger will usually do this for you.) Season the flour with salt and pepper and coat the fish with it. Brush them over with egg, coat with breadcrumbs and fry in hot fat until nicely browned. Serve on a fish paper, garnished with sprigs of fresh or crisply-fried parsley.

3–4 helpings
Cooking time – 6–7 min.

WITCH

Available all the year; best from August to April. Suitable for all methods of cooking. *See also* recipes for cooking sole (pp. 177–180).

MISCELLANEOUS FISH DISHES

CAPKIN GRILL

Four 4–5 oz. portions sea bream, turbot halibut, brill *or* cod	**1 level dessertsp. chopped pickled capers**
2 tablesp. salad oil	**1 level dessertsp. chopped parsley**
1 tablesp. vinegar	
Salt and pepper to taste	
1 level dessertsp. chopped pickled gherkins	

Prepare the fish and place skin side uppermost in the grill pan. Mix together all the other ingredients, except the parsley, and pour over the fish. Grill for about 12–15 min., turning once and basting frequently with the sauce. Serve hot, sprinkled with parsley.

4 helpings

FISH AND OYSTER PIE

Pâté de Poisson et d'Huîtres

1 lb. cold cooked fish	**Breadcrumbs** *or* **puff-pastry**
1 doz. oysters	**Melted butter sauce** *or* **white sauce**
Salt and pepper	
½ teasp. grated nutmeg	
1 teasp. finely-chopped parsley	

Remove the skin and bones and put a layer of fish in a pie-dish, add a few oysters, with seasoning and chopped parsley. Repeat the layers until dish is quite full. Cover with browned breadcrumbs or puff-pastry. If using puff-pastry, cut it into long strips, lay a strip round the edge of the dish and lay the other strips in lattice pattern over the fish. Pour in some melted butter sauce or a little thin white sauce, and the oyster-liquor, then bake.

6 helpings
Cooking time: If made of cooked fish and browned crumbs—¼ hr.
If made of fresh fish and puff-pastry —¾ hr.

FISH PUDDING

1 lb. any kind of white fish	**Salt and pepper**
4 oz. finely-chopped suet	**A few drops of anchovy essence**
2 oz. breadcrumbs	**2 eggs**
1 teasp. finely-chopped parsley	**¼ pt. milk** *or* **stock made from fish bones**

Grease well a plain mould or basin. Free the fish from skin and bones, chop the fish finely and rub through a fine sieve. Add to the suet with the breadcrumbs, parsley, salt, pepper and anchovy essence, and mix well. Beat the eggs slightly, add the milk or fish stock and stir into the mixture. Put into the mould or basin, cover with greased paper, and steam gently for nearly 1½ hr.

4-5 helpings

FRICASSÉE OF FISH

1 lb. white fish	**A small piece of mace**
½ pt. milk	**A pinch of nutmeg**
¼ pt. water	**1 oz. butter**
Salt and pepper	**1 oz. flour**
½ bay leaf	**Lemon juice**

Divide the fish into pieces about 1½ in. square. Put the milk, water, salt and pepper, bay leaf, mace and nutmeg into a saucepan, and when warm add the fish. Bring to the boil and simmer for 10 min., then remove the bay leaf and mace. Meanwhile knead together the butter and flour, add in small portions to the contents of the saucepan and stir gently until the flour is mixed smoothly with the liquor. Simmer for 10 min., then add lemon juice, season to taste and serve.

2–3 helpings

IRISH BAKE

1 lb. potatoes	**2 oz. mushrooms (optional)**
1 lb. cod *or* **fresh haddock fillet**	**Salt and pepper**
1 small onion	**1 small can tomato soup**

Peel the potatoes and slice them thinly. Cook for 10 min. in boiling, salted water, then drain well. Meanwhile, skin and bone the fish and cut into small cubes. Grate the onion and mix with the fish and chopped mushroom stalks (if used) and season well. Place the fish in a shallow fireproof dish, cover evenly with potato and pour the soup over the top. Bake in a fairly hot oven **(400° F., Gas 6)** for 35 min. Garnish with fried mushrooms and parsley.

4 helpings

SEA-FOOD CHOWDER

1 smoked haddock (1–1¼ lb.)	**1 tablesp. flour**
1–2 sliced onions	**3–4 tablesp. cream**
1 breakfastcup diced raw potatoes	**Salt and pepper**
2–3 skinned tomatoes	**½ pt. shelled prawns** *or* **shrimps**
1–1½ oz. butter *or* **margarine**	**½ A1 can peas**
	1 dessertsp. freshly-chopped parsley

Cover the well-washed haddock with cold water, bring slowly to boil then remove and wash again. Skim off scum from the stock. Cook onions in a little of the stock until almost soft. Add potatoes and cook until soft. Cut tomatoes into eighths, discard seeds; simmer in remaining stock. Add tomatoes to other vegetables and cook a little. Meanwhile, free the haddock flesh of skin and bones. Melt the fat, add flour and cook for a few min. without browning. Remove from heat. Slowly stir the strained remaining stock into this roux. Cook gently for a few min., while stirring. Stir in the cream and season to taste. Add the vegetable mixture, then the haddock and prawns or shrimps, reserving a few. Add the drained peas. Heat through but do not boil. Sprinkle in the parsley, turn into a serving dish and garnish with the reserved shellfish.

4–5 helpings

SOMERSET CASSEROLE

1 lb. fillet of cod *or* haddock	**A little margarine**
Salt and pepper	**¾ oz. butter *or* margarine**
2 oz. mushrooms	**¾ oz. flour**
1 medium sized tomato	**1 lb. creamed potatoes**
¼ pt. cider	**A little grated cheese**

GARNISH

Tomato **Parsley**

Cut the prepared fish into small cubes and place in a shallow casserole with seasoning to taste. Add the sliced mushrooms, sliced tomato and cider and dot with shavings of margarine. Cover the casserole and bake for about 25 min. in a fairly hot oven (**375° F., Gas 5**). Strain off the liquor and use it to make a sauce with the ¾ oz. fat and flour. Pour the sauce over the fish. Pipe a border of creamed potatoes round the edge of the dish, sprinkle grated cheese in the centre and garnish with slices of tomato. Return to a very hot oven (**450° F., Gas 8**) to brown; alternatively, brown under the grill. Garnish with parsley and serve hot.

4 helpings

WATER SOUCHET

Souchet

Flounders, plaice, soles, perch *or* tench	**Salt**
Parsley	**Carrot**

Any of the above-named fish will be suitable. Wash and clean the fish, put into a saucepan with just sufficient cold water to cover, add a small bunch of parsley and salt to taste. Cook gently until done, then transfer the fish carefully to a serving dish. Sprinkle over some finely-chopped parsley and finely-shredded cooked carrot. Strain and add the liquor, then serve. Serve with thinly cut brown bread and butter.

SHELLFISH

The shellfish commonly eaten are the lobster, crab, crayfish, oyster, cockle, mussel, escallop, shrimp and prawn. Prawns are much sought after for garnishing.

COCKLES

Cockles are available all the year and are normally sold cooked. Serve cold with vinegar or hot in sauces, pies, etc.

CRABS

Crabs are on sale all the year round, but are at their best from May to October. It is usual to buy crabs which have been boiled by the fishmonger. Choose crabs which are heavy for their size and which are not "watering" or sound "watery" when shaken. Avoid crabs which are attracting flies, especially around the mouth, as this is a sign of deterioration; choose a crab which looks and smells fresh. A crab should look clean and wholesome—if the shell is dark the meat will invariably be dark. The hen crab may be distinguished from the cock crab by its broader tail flap. Normally the flesh of the cock crab is more reliable for quality than the hen, the cock crab usually yields more meat for its size and is therefore a more economical buy. Avoid crabs that are less than 4½ inches across the shell. An average crab about 6 inches across should weigh 2½–3 lb., this will be found sufficient for 4 people. It is illegal to sell "berried" or "rush" crab.

Crabs are normally served in salads or in hot made-up dishes.

TO PREPARE A CRAB

After wiping well with a damp cloth, place the crab on its back with tail facing, and remove claws and legs by twisting them in the opposite way to which they lie. Place the thumbs under flap at tail and push upwards, pull flap away upwards so that the stomach contents are not drawn over the meat, and lift off. (The fishmonger will always do this on request.) Reverse the crab so that the head is facing, then press on the mouth with the thumbs, pushing down and forward, so that the mouth and stomach will then come away in one piece. Remove the meat from the shell by easing round the inside edge of the shell to loosen the tissues with the handle of a plastic teaspoon, and the meat will then come away easily. Keep the dark and the white meat separate. With the handle of a knife, tap sharply over the false line around the shell cavity, press down and it will come away neatly. Scrub and dry the shell, then rub over with a little oil. Remove the "dead-men's fingers" (the lungs) and discard, then scoop out the meat from the claw sockets. Scoop out as much as possible but keep it free of bone. Twist off first joint of large claws and scoop out meat. Tap sharply round the broad shell with back of knife until halves fall apart. Cut the cartilage between the pincers, open pincers and meat will come away in one piece. See plate 14.

CURRIED CRAB

Kari de Crabe

1 good-sized crab
Mustard
1 shallot *or* onion
½ apple
1 oz. butter *or* other good cooking fat
½ pt. curry sauce
4 oz. well-boiled rice

Remove the meat from the crab, including the claws, flake it up and sprinkle a little dry mustard over it. Peel and finely chop the shallot or onion; peel, core and chop the apple. Melt the butter in a saucepan and lightly fry the shallot and apple. Fry for a few minutes only, then add the curry sauce and lastly the crab meat. Re-heat and serve on a hot dish in the centre of a border of rice.

3–4 helpings

DRESSED CRAB

Crabe froid

One 2½–3 lb. crab
Salt and pepper
Fresh breadcrumbs (optional)
A little lemon juice (optional)
French dressing

GARNISH

1 hard-boiled egg
Parsley

Pick the crab meat from the shells (see p. 186). Mix the dark crab meat with salt and pepper, fresh breadcrumbs and a little lemon juice if liked. The breadcrumbs are optional but they lessen the richness and give a firmer texture. Press the mixture lightly against the sides of the previously cleaned shell. Flake up the white meat, mix with French dressing and pile in the centre of the shell. Garnish with sieved egg yolk, chopped egg white, chopped parsley, sieved coral if any, and decorate with small claws. Make a necklace with the small claws, place on a dish and rest the crab on this. Surround with salad.

4 helpings

HOT CRAB

Crabe au Gratin

1 medium-sized crab
Salt and pepper
Nutmeg
2 oz. butter
3 tablesp. white sauce
1 tablesp. vinegar
2 oz. breadcrumbs
Browned breadcrumbs

Pick the crab meat from the shell, season well with salt and pepper, add a little grated nutmeg, the butter slightly warmed, white sauce, vinegar and 2 oz. breadcrumbs and mix well together. Wash and dry the shell, put in the mixture, cover with a thin layer of browned breadcrumbs, add 3–4 small pieces of butter and bake for 10–15 min. in a fairly hot oven (375° F., Gas 5).

3–4 helpings

POTTED CRAB

Terrine de Crabe

2 crabs
Salt
Cayenne pepper
Powdered mace
About 4 oz. clarified butter

Pick the crab meat from the shells, mix with salt, cayenne and mace to taste, rub through a fine sieve. Press into small pots, cover with melted butter and bake in a moderate oven (350° F., Gas 4) for ½ hr. When cold, cover each pot with clarified butter.

SCALLOPED CRAB

Crabe en Coquille

1 medium-sized crab	**Vinegar**
Fine breadcrumbs	**A little white sauce**
Salt and pepper	**Butter**
Mustard	

Remove the meat from the claws and body of the crab. Add about half its bulk in breadcrumbs, season with salt, pepper and mustard, and stir in a few drops of vinegar. Add white sauce to moisten, then turn into buttered escallop shells and sprinkle the surface lightly with breadcrumbs. Place small pieces of butter on top and bake in a moderate oven (**350° F., Gas 4**) until nicely browned—about 15 min.

4–5 helpings
Cooking time—15 min.

CRAYFISH

Écrevisse

Crayfish are freshwater shellfish closely resembling lobsters but much smaller in size. They are greenish-brown above and yellowish-brown beneath when alive, and bright red when boiled. They are in season June–March.

TO BOIL CRAYFISH

Wash thoroughly, remove the intestinal cord, then throw the fish into fast boiling salted water. Keep boiling for about 10 min.

POTTED CRAYFISH

Écrevisses en Terrine

4 doz. live crayfish	**¼ lb. butter (approx.)**
Salt and pepper	**Ground mace**
A little vinegar	**Clarified butter**

Put the crayfish into boiling water to which has been added a good seasoning of salt and a little vinegar. Cook for about 15 min., then drain and dry. Pick the meat from the shells, pound to a fine paste, adding gradually the butter and mace, salt and pepper to taste. Press into small pots, cover with clarified butter and use when cold.

ESCALLOPS OR SCALLOPS

Escalopes or *Coquilles St. Jacques*

Escallops are usually opened by the fishmonger and displayed in their flat shells. If the escallops are to be served in their shells ask the fishmonger for the *deep* shells. If however it is necessary to open escallops they should be put over a gentle heat to allow the shells to open. When they have opened, remove from the shells, trim away the beard and remove the black parts. Wash the escallops well, drain and dry. Wash and dry the shells; keep the deep shells for serving dishes.

Escallops are in season from November to March. They can be served baked, fried, poached or grilled.

BAKED ESCALLOPS

Escalopes cuites au Four

4 large escallops	**A little lemon juice**
Cider (optional)	**Salt and pepper**
2½ oz. bacon fat *or* **margarine**	**Grating of nutmeg**
2 oz. breadcrumbs (approx.)	**Sprigs of watercress** *or* **parsley**
1 teasp. finely-grated onion	

Prepare the escallops. Separate the roes (orange tongue) and place in a casserole with just enough cider or water to prevent sticking and a shaving of fat on top; cover. Melt the rest of the fat, add sufficient breadcrumbs to give a moist texture then add onion, lemon juice and seasoning. Cut the escallops in half horizontally; season. Cover the bottom of each shell with a thin coating of the breadcrumb mixture and place the fish on top. Coat with the remaining breadcrumb mixture. Bake shells and roes in a fairly hot oven **(375° F., Gas 5)** for 25–30 min. Serve each fish garnished with a roe and a sprig of watercress or parsley.

4 helpings

ESCALLOPS AND MUSHROOMS

Coquilles St. Jacques aux Champignons

6 escallops	**1–2 tablesp. white sauce**
Milk	**6 large flat mushrooms**
Salt and pepper	**1 oz. butter**

Put the prepared escallops in a saucepan with just sufficient milk to cover, add a little salt and pepper and simmer gently for about 15 min. Drain well, reserve the orange roe for garnish and chop the white parts, moisten with a little white sauce and season to taste. While the escallops are cooking remove the stalks of the mushrooms. Peel the tops of the mushrooms and fry in hot butter. Place an equal portion of the white part of the escallops on each mushroom and garnish with the orange roe.

Serve hot.

3–6 helpings, depending on size of scallops

ESCALLOPS AU GRATIN

6 escallops	**6 tablesp. top of milk**
5 tablesp. dry cider *or* **dry white wine**	**Seasoning**
2 oz. mushrooms *or* **1 small onion**	**A little finely-grated cheese** *or* **browned breadcrumbs**
1 oz. margarine	**Creamed potatoes (optional)**
¾ oz. flour	

Put the prepared escallops in a small pan with the cider or white wine. Simmer until tender, approximately 6–8 min.—do not allow to boil. Meanwhile chop the mushrooms or onion finely. Melt the margarine in another small saucepan and fry the mushrooms or onion. When soft add the flour and cook for 2–3 min. Stir in the liquid from the escallops, and the milk. Stir and boil for a few minutes, then season to taste. Cut the escallops into pieces and add to the contents of the saucepan. Put the mixture into 4 deep escallop shells. Sprinkle with grated cheese or breadcrumbs, and if liked, pipe a border of creamed potatoes round the edge and brown lightly under the grill.

Serve at once.

4 helpings

ESCALLOPS EN BROCHETTE

Coquilles St. Jacques en Brochette

4 large escallops	**8 small rashers streaky bacon**
6 oz. rice	**4 thick slices pineapple**

Cook the rice in fast boiling salted water until just tender. Wash the escallops and cut in half, then roll each half in a rasher of bacon. Impale on a skewer with a half slice of pineapple between each. Grill under a moderate heat, turning once, for 8–10 min. Drain the rice when cooked, rinse under running cold water, then spread out on a sieve and reheat. Pile up on a dish and lay the 4 skewers on the rice. Serve hot.

4 helpings

ESCALLOPS IN SHELLS

1½ doz. small escallops	**A little chopped parsley**
1 oz. butter	**A little lemon juice**
1 cup fresh breadcrumbs	**Salt and pepper**
Cayenne pepper	**1 gill white sauce**

Prepare the escallops and 6 shells. Butter the shells and sprinkle in a few breadcrumbs. Put 3 escallops in each and season with cayenne, chopped parsley and a drop or two of lemon juice. Mix a little pepper and salt with the remaining breadcrumbs. Cover the escallops with white sauce, sprinkle with breadcrumbs, place bits of butter on top and bake for about 20 min. in a fairly hot oven **(375° F., Gas 5)**.

6 helpings

LOBSTERS

Homards

Lobsters can be obtained all the year round, but are scarce from December to March. They are cheapest during the summer months. Lobsters are usually bought already boiled, but live lobsters can be obtained to order if a few days' notice is given to the fishmonger. Choose one of medium size and heavy in weight, it is illegal to sell lobsters less than 9 inches in length, or to offer "berried" or "spawny" fish, i.e. when the coral is visible outside the shell. If fresh, the tail of a cooked lobster will be stiff, and if gently raised, will return with a spring. The narrowness of the back part of the tail and the stiffness of the two uppermost fins (swimmerettes) in the tail distinguish the cock lobster from the hen.

TO BOIL LOBSTERS

There are two methods of boiling lobsters, each method having points in its favour.

Method 1: Wash the lobster well before boiling, tie the claws securely. Have ready a saucepan of boiling water, salted in the proportion of $\frac{1}{4}$ lb. salt to 1 gallon water. Throw the lobster head first into the water (this instantly destroys life), keep it boiling for 20–45 min., according to size, and skim well. Allow 20 min.–$\frac{1}{2}$ hr. for small lobsters and $\frac{1}{2}$–$\frac{3}{4}$ hr. for large lobsters. If boiled too long the meat becomes thready, and if not done enough, the coral is not red. Rub the shells over with a little salad oil to brighten the colour.

Method 2: Put the lobsters into warm water, bring the water gradually to the boil and boil as above. This is believed by many to be a more humane method of killing, as the lobster is lulled to sleep and does not realise it is being killed.

TO PREPARE A LOBSTER

Wipe the lobster well with a clean damp cloth and twist off claws and legs. Place lobster on a board parallel to the edge with back uppermost and head to left. Cut along the centre of back, from junction of head with body to tail, using a sharp, stainless knife. Reverse so that tail is to left and cut along head; the stomach, which lies just behind the mouth, is not cut until last. Remove intestinal cord, remove stomach and coral (if any) and keep for garnish. Meat may be left in shell or removed and used as required. Knock off the tips of the claws with the back of a knife and drain away any water. Tap sharply round broadest part of each claw and shell should fall apart. Cut cartilage between pincers, open pincers and meat can be removed in one piece. Remove meat from smaller joints of claws.

BAKED LOBSTER

Homard au Gratin

1 boiled lobster
1½ oz. butter
½ teasp. finely-chopped shallot
2–3 tablesp. white sauce
1 dessertsp. finely-chopped parsley
Juice of ½ lemon
Pinch of nutmeg
Salt and pepper
1 egg
Browned breadcrumbs

Remove the lobster meat from the shells (*see* above) and mince or chop it coarsely. Clean the two halves of the large shell. Melt the butter in a saucepan, fry the shallot for 2–3 min. without browning, then add the lobster meat, white sauce, parsley, lemon juice, nutmeg and salt and pepper to taste. Stir and heat until thoroughly hot. Beat the egg slightly, add it to the mixture and cook until it begins to bind. Put the mixture into the shells, cover lightly with brown breadcrumbs, put 3–4 very small pieces of butter on top and bake for 10–15 min. in a moderate oven (**350° F., Gas 4**).

4–5 helpings **Cooking time—½ hr.**

COQUILLES OF LOBSTER

1 boiled *or* canned lobster
Mushrooms
Butter
White sauce
Salt and pepper
Nutmeg
Cayenne pepper
8 baked shell-shaped pastry cases
Fried breadcrumbs
Parsley

Dice the meat of the lobster and put it in a saucepan with some chopped mushrooms and butter, allowing 8 mushrooms and ½ oz. butter to every ½ lb. of lobster. Heat, stirring all the time, until thoroughly hot, then moisten with white sauce. Season with salt, pepper, a little grated nutmeg and a pinch of cayenne. Keep the mixture hot so that it is ready for use when required. Warm the baked shells in the oven, fill them with the mixture and sprinkle over some fried breadcrumbs. Dish up on small plates and garnish with parsley.

NOTE: A little anchovy essence added to the mixture will improve the flavour considerably.

8 helpings

DEVILLED LOBSTER

Homard à la Diable

1 boiled lobster
Butter
3 tablesp. white breadcrumbs
2 tablesp. white sauce *or* cream
Cayenne
A few browned breadcrumbs

Cut the lobster in two lengthwise, remove the meat carefully, as the ½ shells must be kept whole, and chop the meat finely. Melt 1½ oz. butter and pour it on the lobster. Add the white breadcrumbs, and the sauce, season rather highly with cayenne and mix well. Press the mixture lightly into the shells, cover with browned breadcrumbs, put 3 or 4 pieces of butter on top and bake for about 20 min. in a moderate oven (**350° F., Gas 4**). Serve hot or cold.

DRESSED LOBSTER

Homard froid

Prepare the boiled lobster (*see* p. 190). Leave the meat in the shell and arrange the two halves on a bed of salad. Garnish with the claws. Serve with oil and vinegar handed separately. Piped lobster butter may be used to garnish the shell, if wished (p. 676).

LOBSTER CAPRICE

Homard Caprice

6 oz. lobster meat
1 hard-boiled egg
4 tablesp. mayonnaise
Paprika pepper *or* sieved coral if available
A few salted almonds
Watercress
Tomatoes
Cucumber

Slice the lobster meat and mix with the chopped hard-boiled egg. Pile in the centre of a round dish and coat with mayonnaise. Sprinkle with paprika or coral and stud with the shredded salted almonds. Surround with watercress and alternate slices of tomato and cucumber.

3 helpings

LOBSTER CROQUETTES

Croquettes de Homard

1 large boiled lobster
1½ oz. butter
1 oz. flour
¼ pt. milk *or* water
1 tablesp. cream
Cayenne pepper
Salt
Egg and breadcrumbs
Fat for frying

Remove the flesh from the lobster and chop it into small pieces. Beat the coral (if any) together with ½ oz. of butter, then sieve. Melt the remaining 1 oz. of butter in a small saucepan, stir in the flour, add the milk and boil well. Add to it the lobster, cream, coral, cayenne and salt. Mix well together and turn on to a plate to cool. When the mixture is firm enough to mould, form into balls or oval shapes. Brush with beaten egg, roll in breadcrumbs and fry in hot fat until nicely browned.

Serve immediately.

9–10 small croquettes

LOBSTER IN ASPIC

Homard en Aspic

1 large *or* 2 small boiled lobsters
1 pt. aspic jelly
A few tarragon leaves
Capers
1 large lettuce
Oil and vinegar
Salt and pepper
Mayonnaise sauce (p. 135)
3 hard-boiled eggs
Truffle (optional)
Stoned olives

Put into a quart border mould enough cold, liquid aspic jelly to cover it thinly. Cut the lobster meat from the body and claws into neat pieces. When the jelly begins to set, arrange in it some of the lobster meat with a few tarragon leaves and capers, filling up the mould with jelly. Well wash, dry and shred the lettuce. Mix it with the remainder of the lobster, the oil and vinegar, salt and pepper. When the mould is firmly set, turn it out and pile the salad in the centre and round it as a border, masking it smoothly with thick mayonnaise sauce. Garnish with the eggs cut up, the coral and the little claws of the lobster, capers, truffle (if used) and olives.

6 helpings

LOBSTER MAYONNAISE

Mayonnaise de Homard

1 boiled lobster
Mayonnaise
Salad

Lobster Mayonnaise may be served in any of the following ways:

(*a*) Serve as dressed lobster (*see* p. 191) but with mayonnaise instead of oil and vinegar.

(*b*) Cut the lobster in half lengthways, scoop out the meat from the body, mix with a little mayonnaise and return. Carefully remove the meat from the tail, slice and return to the shell, arranging it in overlapping slices with the red part uppermost. Serve on a bed of salad, garnished with the claws. Serve mayonnaise separately.

(*c*) Remove all the meat from the shell and claws. Arrange on a bed of salad, either cut into slices or roughly flaked and coat with mayonnaise.

The coral can be used, sieved, as a garnish or for making butter.

LOBSTER MORNAY

Homard Mornay

2 small boiled lobsters
½ pt. cheese sauce
2–3 tablesp. grated cheese

Cut the lobsters in half lengthwise. Remove the meat from the tail and cut into slices, keeping the knife on the slant. Place a little of the sauce at the bottom of each shell and arrange the meat on top, overlapping the slices slightly. Pour a little sauce over the top and sprinkle with grated cheese. Brown in a hot oven (450° F., Gas 8) for about 10 min.

4 helpings

LOBSTER PATTIES

Bouchées de Homard

1 small boiled lobster
1½ oz. butter
½ oz. flour
¼ pt. fish stock *or* milk (approx.)
½ gill cream
3 egg yolks
½ teasp. lemon juice
A few drops of anchovy essence
Cayenne pepper
Salt
8–9 patty cases about 2 in. diameter
Parsley

Melt the butter in a saucepan, stir in the flour and cook for a few minutes. Then pour in the fish stock or milk and stir until the sauce boils. Simmer for 10 min., then add the cream, egg yolks, lemon juice, anchovy essence and seasoning to taste. Simmer gently until the egg yolks thicken, then sieve. Return the sauce to the saucepan, cut the lobster into dice and add to the sauce. When thoroughly hot put into the cases, put on the covers, garnish with parsley and serve.

8–9 patties

LOBSTER THERMIDOR

Homard Thermidor

2 small boiled lobsters
1 shallot
1 wine glass white wine
1½ oz. butter
¼ pt. Béchamel sauce
1 level teasp. mixed mustard
Pinch of cayenne pepper
A little grated cheese

Cut the lobsters in half lengthwise and remove the stomach and the intestinal cord. Remove the meat from the shell and cut into slices, keeping the knife on the slant. Chop the shallot very finely. Put the white wine in a small saucepan and cook the shallot until it is tender and the wine reduced to half. Meanwhile, melt the butter and heat the meat very carefully in this. Add the shallot and wine mixture to the lobster meat with the sauce, mustard and pepper, mix and return to the shells. Sprinkle with grated cheese and brown under a hot grill.

4 helpings

POTTED LOBSTER

Terrine de Homard

2 boiled lobsters
2 oz. butter
Salt and pepper
Cayenne pepper
¼ pt. cream
Clarified butter

PLATE 7

Cleaning and Filleting Plaice

1 Cut off the fins of the plaice with a pair of kitchen scissors.

2 Cut open the belly, and remove and discard entrails. Remove the head with a semi-circular cut.

3 Slit the flesh from head to tail down the line of the backbone.

4 Insert the knife in the slit and separate the flesh from the bone, keeping the knife pressed against the bone. Remove second fillet.

5 Turn the fish over and remove the other two fillets as described above.

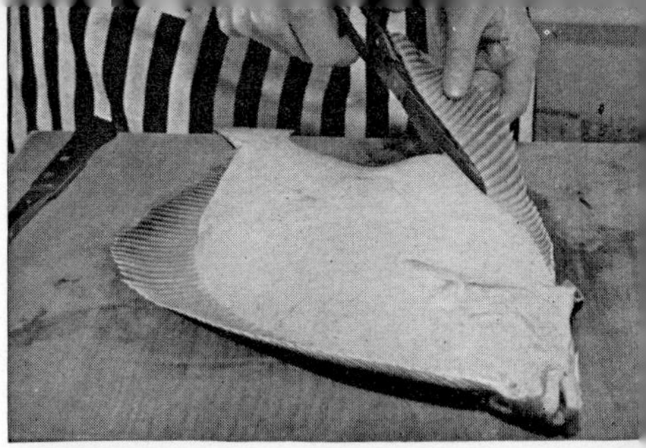

1

2

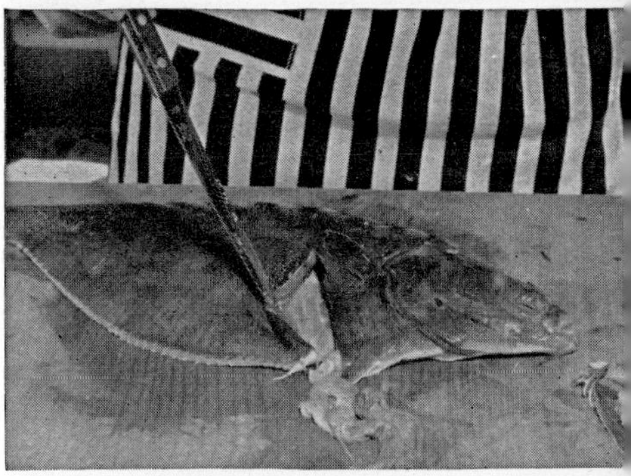

3

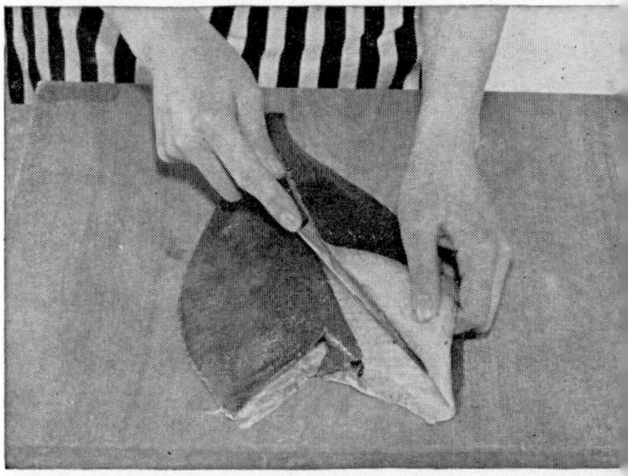

4

5

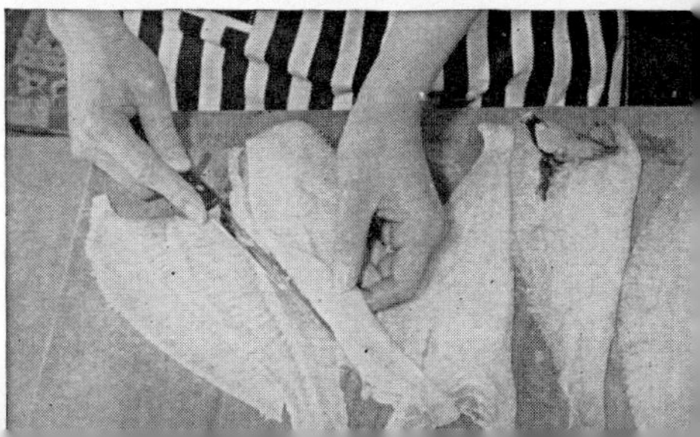

6

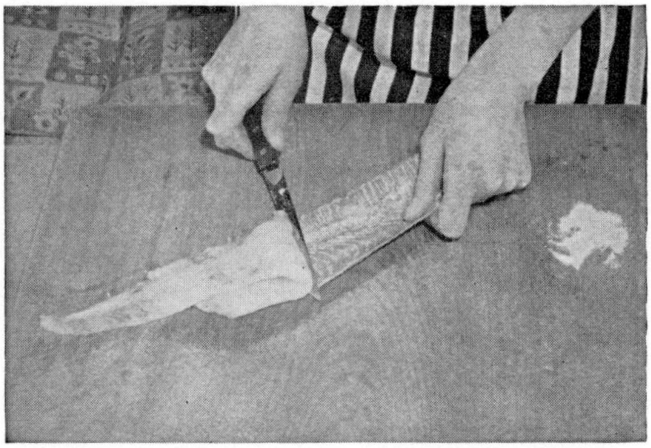

6 To skin the fillets, dip the fingers of the left hand in salt, take a firm hold of the tail, and with the knife peel the flesh away from the skin, keeping the edge of the knife pressed hard against the skin.

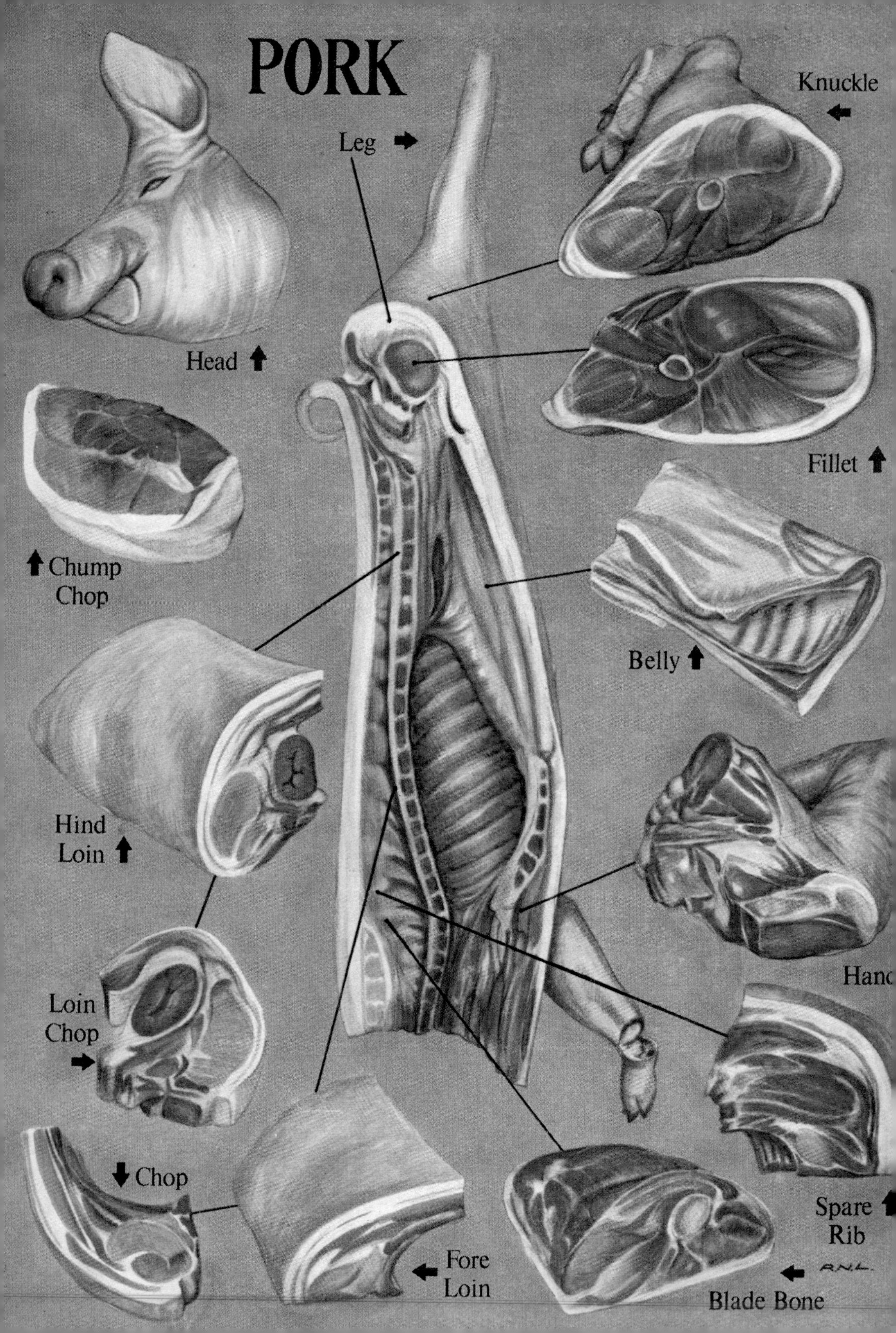
PORK
Leg
Knuckle
Head
Fillet
Chump Chop
Belly
Hind Loin
Hand
Loin Chop
Chop
Spare Rib
Fore Loin
Blade Bone
R.N.L.

Pick the meat from the shells, chop finely and put into a saucepan with the butter and seasoning. Cook slowly for 20 min. Add the cream, stir, and cook gently until the mixture has the consistency of a smooth and fairly thick paste. Rub through a fine sieve, press into pots, and when cold cover with clarified butter. It will keep for several days in a refrigerator.

RAGOÛT OF LOBSTER

Ragoût de Homard

1 large boiled lobster
1 oz. butter
Mace
Salt and pepper
1 gill white sauce
½ gill fish stock *or* water
2 egg yolks

Remove the flesh from the shell of the lobster, keeping it as whole as possible, and divide into pieces 1 in. square. Beat the coral together with the butter, add a pinch of mace and salt and pepper to taste, and sieve the mixture. Put the sauce and stock into a saucepan, boil up, season to taste, then add the egg yolks, butter and lobster. Cook gently for a few minutes to remove the raw taste of the eggs, then serve.

5–6 helpings

MUSSELS

Moules

Mussels are bought while still alive and their shells should be tightly shut. Discard any that do not shut immediately when given a sharp tap, as they are probably dead. Mussels are in season from September to March. They can be served cold with vinegar or hot in soups, sauces or pies.

TO PREPARE MUSSELS

Allow 1–1½ pt. mussels per person. Scrape and clean the shells thoroughly in several lots of cold water. Mussels are not opened with a knife like oysters, but open themselves during cooking. The only part of a mussel which needs to be removed is the breathing apparatus which is found in the form of a black strip known as the "beard". This is removed after the shells have been opened.

TO OPEN

There are two simple methods of opening mussels:

English method—For a small quantity of 1–2 pt., place the mussels (after cleaning) in a rinsed wide pan and cover them closely with a folded damp teacloth. Heat quickly, shaking the pan at intervals, and at the end of 5–7 min. the shells will open. Remove from the heat promptly as overcooking toughens them.

French method—To 3½ pt. of cleaned mussels in a wide pan, add 1 shallot, finely chopped, 5–6 stalks of parsley, a sprig of thyme, ⅓ of a bay leaf, a pinch of pepper and ¼ pt. dry white wine (½ water and ½ dry cider could be used) Cover the pan tightly and cook over a sharp heat for 5–6 min. shaking the pan from time to time. Remove from the heat as soon as the shells open.

MOULES MARINIÈRES

3½ pt. mussels
1 shallot, chopped finely
5–6 stalks of parsley
⅓ of a bay leaf
Sprig of thyme
Pinch of pepper
¼ pt. dry white wine (½ water and ½ dry cider can be used)
1 oz. butter
Chopped parsley

Open the mussels by the French method. Strain the liquid through muslin, to remove any traces of sand, then return the liquid to the pan with the butter and boil rapidly until reduced by half. Meanwhile, remove the beards from the mussels, and return the mussels to their half shell, discard empty shells, Arrange in soup plates, pour the reduced liquor over the mussels and sprinkle with chopped parsley.

MUSSELS

Moules

1 qt. mussels
1 oz. butter
½ oz. flour
2 egg yolks
1 tablesp. vinegar
1 teasp. chopped parsley
Salt and pepper

Open the mussels by the English method. Take them out of the shells and strain the liquor into a basin. Carefully remove the beards. Melt the butter, add the flour and cook for 3–4 min., then pour in the mussel liquor and stir until boiling. Cool slightly, then add the egg yolks, vinegar, and parsley, season to taste and stir over a low heat until the egg yolks thicken. Put in the mussels to re-heat and serve in the sauce.

2–3 helpings **Cooking time—about ½ hr.**

OYSTERS

Huîtres

Oysters have the best reputation of the bivalve shellfish, for flavour and digestibility, and are for that reason given to invalids. They are in season from September to April, and can be served raw or baked, stewed, or in sauces, pies, etc. Oysters should be opened as near as possible to the time of eating. Do not try to open them yourself unless you are an expert: ask your fishmonger either to loosen the shell for you or to open them completely and put the oyster with its liquor in the deep shell.

DEVILLED OYSTERS

Huîtres à la Diable

1 dozen oysters	**Cayenne pepper**
Salt	**1 oz. butter**

Open the oysters carefully so as to preserve as much of the liquor as possible, or ask your fishmonger to open them for you and leave them in their shells. Sprinkle lightly with salt, and more liberally with cayenne, and put a small piece of butter on top of each one. Place the oysters on a baking sheet and put in a hot oven until thoroughly heated.

Serve with sliced lemon and thin brown bread and butter.

3–4 helpings **Cooking time—4 min.**

FRICASSÉED OYSTERS

Fricassée d'Huîtres

18 large oysters	**¼ gill cream**
2½ oz. butter	**3 egg yolks**
Salt and white pepper	**1 teasp. lemon juice**
Nutmeg	**10 small heart-shaped slices of fried bread**
¾ oz. flour	**Parsley**
1 gill white stock	

Open the oysters, preserving the liquor. Remove the beards, and put the oysters in a saucepan with 1 oz. of butter and a little oyster liquor. Season with a pinch of salt and pepper and a grating of nutmeg. Heat and stir for 2 min., then strain. Melt the remaining 1½ oz. butter in a saucepan, stir in the flour, cook slightly without browning then dilute with the liquor from the oysters, the remainder of the oyster liquor and the stock. Stir until boiling, simmer for about 10 min., then add the cream, egg yolks and lemon juice. Stir the mixture over heat a few seconds longer to bind the yolks. Pass the sauce through a fine strainer, put in a saucepan with the oysters, heat thoroughly, but on no account allow to boil. Serve on a hot dish, garnished with croûtes of fried bread and a few sprigs of parsley.

6 helpings

OYSTER FLORENTINE

Huîtres à la Florentine

12 oysters	**½ pt. milk**
12 oz. spinach	**Seasoning**
1½ oz. butter	**A little grated cheese**
1 oz. flour	

Cook the spinach. Put the oysters in a small saucepan and add their liquor, previously strained through muslin. Poach for 2–3 min. until the edges just begin to ruffle slightly, then remove from the heat. Melt the butter in a saucepan, stir in the flour and cook for 2 min. Add the milk, stir until boiling and boil for 3 min. Cool slightly, then add the oysters and their liquor. Drain the spinach and spread over the bottom of a fireproof dish, pour the oyster sauce on top, sprinkle with finely-grated cheese and brown lightly under the grill. Serve immediately.

2–3 helpings

OYSTER FRITTERS

Beignets aux Huîtres

12 large oysters
$\frac{1}{4}$ pt. tepid water
1 tablesp. salad oil *or* oiled butter
3 oz. flour
Salt
2 egg whites
Frying fat

Make a batter by stirring the water and salad oil gradually into the flour; when perfectly smooth add a pinch of salt and lastly the stiffly-whisked egg whites. Beard the oysters, dip them in the batter and fry in hot fat until golden brown. Serve immediately.

6 helpings

OYSTER PATTIES

Bouchées aux Huîtres

24 oysters
2 oz. butter
1 oz. flour
$\frac{1}{4}$ pt. fish stock *or* milk (approx.)
$\frac{1}{4}$ gill cream
2 egg yolks
$\frac{1}{2}$ teasp. lemon juice
Salt and pepper
8–9 baked puff pastry cases
Parsley

Put the oysters and their liquor into a saucepan, bring to the boil. Then drain, put the liquor aside, remove the beards and cut each oyster in half. Melt the butter in a saucepan, add the flour and cook for 3–4 min. Add the oyster liquor with enough fish stock or milk to make $\frac{1}{2}$ pt., and stir until the sauce boils. Simmer for 10 min., then add the cream, egg yolks, lemon juice and seasoning to taste; re-heat gently until the egg yolks thicken. Add the oysters, and when thoroughly hot put the mixture in the patty cases, put on the covers, garnish with parsley and serve.

8–9 patties **Cooking time—$\frac{1}{2}$ hr.**

OYSTER SOUFFLÉ

Soufflé aux Huîtres

6 large sauce oysters
2 small whitings
2 oz. butter
$1\frac{1}{2}$ oz. flour
$\frac{1}{2}$ pt. milk (approx.)
$\frac{1}{2}$ gill cream
Seasoning
3 eggs
$\frac{1}{2}$ teasp. anchovy essence

Skin the whitings, remove all the meat from the bones and pound it well. Melt the butter in a saucepan, add the flour and cook a little without browning. Add the milk and oyster liquor, stir briskly until quite smooth, then add the cream. Cook a little longer, stirring all the time. Remove the beards from the oysters, cut the oysters into dice and put them into the mixture. Season to taste with salt, pepper and nutmeg, work in the egg yolks, the anchovy essence and the pounded fish. Whisk the egg whites to a stiff froth and fold carefully into the mixture. Threequarters fill a well-buttered soufflé tin or charlotte mould and steam for about 45 min. Remove from the mould and serve with a white sauce.

6 helpings

OYSTERS À LA MARGUERITE

Huîtres à la Marguerite

1 doz. large oysters
$\frac{1}{2}$ stick of celery
$1\frac{1}{2}$ oz. butter
A little stock
Seasoning
1 dessertsp. cornflour
2 tablesp. milk
Lemon juice
24 large picked shrimps
Chopped parsley

Beard the oysters, cut them in halves and blanch them in their own liquor, which should be preserved. Wash and trim the celery using only the white portions, chop up rather finely and drain well on a cloth. Melt 1 oz. of butter in a small saucepan, add the celery and fry for about 10 min. Then add a little stock, the oysters and their liquor, and season with salt and pepper. Blend the cornflour with the milk and add to the oysters. Stir until boiling, adding a little more stock to moisten. Flavour with a few drops of lemon juice and add the shrimps. Put in the remainder of the butter and cook very gently for 5 min. Sprinkle with chopped parsley and serve.

3–4 helpings **Cooking time—20 min.**

OYSTERS À LA MARINIÈRE

Huîtres à la Marinière

18 sauce oysters
$\frac{1}{2}$ glass Chablis *or* cider
1 tablesp. chopped parsley
1 tablesp. chopped shallots
1 oz. fresh breadcrumbs
Salt and pepper
1 oz. butter
Lemon juice

Beard the oysters and put the oysters with their liquor in a basin, pour the wine over and allow to stand for about 1 hr. Mix the parsley, shallots and breadcrumbs, and season to taste with salt and pepper. Arrange the oysters in a buttered fireproof dish, pour over a little of the liquor and wine and cover with the breadcrumb mixture. Place the remaining butter in small pieces on top. Bake in a fairly hot oven (**375° F., Gas 5**) for about 15 min. Squeeze a little lemon juice on top and serve in the dish.

5–6 helpings

OYSTERS AU NATUREL *Huîtres au Naturel*

Serve the oysters *as soon after opening as possible* in the deep shell in their own liquor. With "hinges" to centre, arrange 4 to 6 oysters on individual plates.

Serve with brown bread and butter and lemon wedges.

PRAWNS *Crevettes*

Prawns are available all the year. They are usually sold cooked, and can be served cold, fried, or in soups, sauces and in made-up dishes.

TO BOIL FRESHLY-CAUGHT PRAWNS

Cooked prawns should be very red and have no spawn when cooked; much depends on their freshness and the way in which they are cooked. Wash well, then put into boiling salted water and keep them boiling for about 7–8 min. They are ready when they begin to change colour, do not overboil or they will become tasteless and indigestible.

TO SHELL PRAWNS

To shell prawns, take the head between the right-hand thumb and second finger, take the tip of the tail between the left thumb and forefinger; with the nail on the right forefinger raise the shell at the knee or angle, pinch the tail and the shell will come apart, leaving the prawn attached to the head.

CURRIED PRAWNS

Crevettes à l'Indienne

2 doz. prawns
1½ oz. butter
1 small onion
1–1½ level dessertsp. curry powder (depending on strength)
1 level dessertsp. flour
½ pt. stock
1 sour apple
1 tablesp. grated coconut
Salt
1 teasp. lemon juice

Shell the prawns and put them aside. Melt the butter in a saucepan, fry the chopped onion without browning, then add the curry powder and flour and fry slowly for at least 20 min. Add the stock, coarsely chopped apple, coconut and a little salt. Simmer gently for ½ hr., then strain and return to the saucepan. Season to taste, add the lemon juice, put in the prawns and when thoroughly hot serve with well-boiled rice.

4 helpings
Cooking time—about 1 hr.

POTTED PRAWNS or SHRIMPS

Terrine de Crevettes

1 qt. fresh prawns *or* **shrimps**
¼ lb. fresh butter
Cayenne pepper
Ground mace *or* **nutmeg**
A little salt
Clarified butter

The fish should be perfectly fresh and as large as possible. Boil, then shell and divide them slightly. Pound to a paste with the butter and seasoning. Rub through a fine sieve, press into small pots, cover with clarified butter, and when cold tie down closely.

Cooking time—8 min.

SCALLOPS

See Escallops

SHRIMPS

Shrimps are available all the year. They are usually sold cooked and served cold in soups, sauces, etc.

TO BOIL FRESHLY-CAUGHT SHRIMPS

Throw the shrimps into boiling salted water, and keep them boiling for about 5 min. Care should be taken that they are not overboiled, as they then become tasteless and indigestible; they are done when they begin to change colour.

TO SHELL SHRIMPS

Take the head between the right thumb and forefinger and with the left forefinger and thumbnail raise on each side the shell of the tail, pinch the tail, and the shell will at once separate.

MEAT

MEAT, in terms of money alone, is one of the most expensive purchases made by the housewife. Yet a closer appreciation of it shows that valued as calories per penny, or body-building value per ounce consumed, or even as satisfaction per meal eaten, it still gives good value.

The cost of weekly meat purchases can be much reduced if experience accompanies the shopping basket. Experience can only be gained by trial and error; best of all it is to be found vested in a friendly butcher, one who will anxiously advise and teach his customer all she may wish to know or indeed may be able to absorb.

Acquiring such a butcher is easier than it may seem. Look for a tradesman who sells good quality merchandise, is willing and able to prepare it for you as you may require, is capable of advising on cooking methods and times, who wraps your purchases hygienically and neatly and conducts his business from a clean and well-equipped shop. Select a shop where you can buy regularly if not exclusively. It may in fact pay you to purchase regularly at two such shops.

Surprising as it may seem it would be perfectly feasible for a housewife to give her family a different meat dish on each day of the year. And although after ten months or so her ingenuity might be a little overtaxed she would find at the end of the 365 days that the average cost of her meat dishes would be less than the present average cost of the "roast, fried steak, meat pudding round" which comes to so many tables with monotonous regularity.

Particularly surprised would be the busy housewife who combines running a home with an outside job; for during the year she would have found that many of the dishes formerly considered to take much time and cooking heat, can in fact cost less in time, cost of gas or electricity, and prime cost of meat. An example of this is the oven-prepared stew compared with fried rump steak. The former can be prepared and cooked in less working time than the latter. The secret is of course to be found in the fact that once in the oven the stew can be left on a low heat completely unattended and it is almost impossible to overcook it. A fried meal requires the constant presence of the cook.

COOKING MEAT

Palatability is most important in all food and of supreme importance in meat. There is today a tendency to look at food as so many calories to be administered so many times per day. This is a viewpoint hardly consistent with civilized living. The discriminating housewife will appreciate the importance of the correct cooking of the proper cut of meat.

Two factors influence the final cooked product: the first is the temperature; the second is the time. The meat may be brought to any given temperature by a number of means: by radiant heat (grilling or broiling), by hot air (roasting or baking), by hot water (casseroling, boiling, stewing and braising) or by contact with hot metal and fat (frying). For full details of these methods *see* p. 29.

All cooking methods tend to overlap. For example roasting will usually take place with some moisture in the oven if only from the joint. "Boiling" and stewing although often differentiated are really the same process applied to large and small pieces of meat.

Joints for roasting should always enter the oven so that the cut faces of the meat are exposed to direct heat. A rib, cooked on the bone, should be prepared by the butcher so that it will stand upright. A rolled piece of beef should be slightly flattened on one side so that it will stand erect. If the outside covering of fat varies in thickness then the thickest part should go to the top of the oven.

First weigh the meat in order to calculate the cooking time. There are three well-known methods of roasting meat:

Method 1 'Sear' or brown the meat in a very hot oven (450°F., Gas 8) for 15–20 min., then reduce heat and finish cooking in a fairly hot oven (375°F., Gas 5), see time-table below.

Method 2 Cook the meat in a fairly hot oven (375°F., Gas 5) for the whole time. To produce a juicy joint cover the roasting tin with a lid or aluminium foil, although the outside will not brown so well as when the meat is cooked uncovered.

Method 3 Cook the meat in a warm–moderate oven (335° – 350°F., Gas 3–4). This method, known as slow roasting, is suitable for cuts of cheaper, poorer quality meat.

Meat	Methods 1 and 2	Method 3
Beef (without bone)	20 min. per lb., plus 10 min.	30 min per lb., plus 30 min.
(with bone)	15 ,, ,, ,, ,, 15 ,,	20 ,, ,, ,, ,, 20 ,,
Mutton	20–25 ,, ,, ,, 20–25	30–35 ,, ,, ,, 30–35
Lamb	20 ,, ,, ,, ,, 20 ,,	30 ,, ,, ,, ,, 30 ,,
Pork (thick cut)	25–30 ,, ,, ,, 25–30	40 ,, ,, ,, ,, 40 ,,
Veal	25 ,, ,, ,, ,, 25 ,,	35 ,, ,, ,, ,, 35 ,,

The above time-table is approximate and the exact time will depend on the form and thickness of the joint, and its age and condition. A square solid piece of beef will not cook as quickly as a shoulder of mutton of equal weight.

IMPORTED MEATS

Frozen: Up to and sometimes beyond the point of retail sale frozen meat is solid and needs thawing before it can be successfully cooked. The freezing naturally produces ice crystals within the muscle tissue and damages it. On thawing the meat "drips" and so loses some of its goodness. The amount of damage done by the ice formation depends to a large extent on the rate of freezing. Smaller carcases fare better than large and for this reason frozen lamb suffers much less damage than frozen beef. In cooking either lamb or beef in the oven, basting is essential to replace as far as possible the flavour lost by the tendency to "drip". A hot oven is needed as with other meat to seal the outside, but in this case it is especially necessary to prevent loss of nutritive value.

Chilled: Meat that is chilled, is kept as nearly as possible to the freezing point without freezing (and hence ice formation) taking place. Occasionally there is a slightly objectionable flavour to the fat. This can be masked by seeing that the fat is well salted prior to roasting. It also helps to ensure that the outside of the joint is well crisped.

OFFALS

THE WORD OFFAL, often connected in the mind with waste or rubbish, is perhaps an unfortunate term for those parts of an animal which properly cooked can yield the finest of taste sensations. The most commonly known offal is undoubtedly liver.

Liver: That of the lamb, calf, pig and ox, is usually the order of preference.

Liver from any animal is the only offal which tastes better in cooking than in eating. The word taste is used rather than smell, for both senses are closely associated. Indeed the delightful smell of liver and bacon cooking together is largely the reason for the popularity of the dish. As a taste sensation most other offals are superior.

Ox tail: Properly cooked this is a delicacy and, in terms of edible meat obtained on cooking, is proportionately expensive. Ox tails should be cooked until the meat just leaves the bone. To cook longer extracts glue-like material from the bones which merely makes the gravy sticky without improving its already high nutritive value. Overcooking ruins the flavour. Tails should be brightly coloured and should carry a reasonable quantity of creamy white fat.

Hearts: Those of the pig, calf and lamb may be roasted. Being a hard, tightly packed muscle with little fat to leaven the flavour they are best served (and cooked) with a herb-flavoured stuffing. If ready prepared stuffings are used it is an advantage to "lard" the mixture with a little fat before placing in the heart. Ox hearts are fit only for braising but carefully cooked yield a flavourful, nutritious and economical dish.

Sweetbreads: Butchers will often speak of two sweetbreads. In fact "they" are one gland, the thymus, which in young animals consists of two portions, one known as the throat bread and the other the heart bread. As an animal matures, both parts tend to grow smaller and only in oxen does a useable part of the heart bread persist into adult life. Sweetbreads should be used very fresh. The heart sweetbread of the calf is firm, white, broad and rather thick. It is most suitable for serving whole. The throat sweetbread is longer, less compact and dark in colour and is more suitable for cutting into pieces. The pancreas or stomach bread is often referred to as a sweetbread but is a very different organ with a very different though not unpleasant flavour. Sweetbreads should be poached, skinned and then fried in butter until the outside is crisp. They may only be described as delicious.

Kidneys: These are the only part of the offal which is purchased as part of the carcase. They have a marked flavour and are useful for flavouring steak pies and puddings. Their proper place in the cuisine may be considered to be as part of a mixed grill. For grilling, lambs' kidneys are usually used. Pig and calf kidney may be fried. Ox kidney should be used for stewed or braised dishes.

Tongues: In former days tongues were considered to be something of a delicacy and in the great days of the Argentine Pampas herds, before the export trade developed, it was common for the Gaucho to kill an ox merely to eat the tongue. Although tongues can be consumed either fresh or salted they are usually eaten after brining. Most commonly sold is salt boiled ox tongue. It is an excellent dish if not overcooked, when it becomes dry and "chaffy" to eat. Tongues from sheep, pigs and calves can be similarly treated and as they are small can be used as a kitchen " experiment " at very little cost.

Feet: Today it is uncommon for the feet of cattle to be stewed into "cow-heel". Ox, cows' or calves' feet can provide an excellent base for aspic jellies. For the connoisseur they provide fine pickings. Pigs' feet or pettitoes are a delicacy but it is perhaps now considered indelicate to eat them; the only method is with the teeth and fingers. Like other feet they are boiled, but if they have been dry salted they should first be soaked overnight and washed for an hour or so under the tap to remove excess salt.

Tripe: This again is a connoisseur's dish little eaten it would seem today. Most generally cooked are three of the four stomachs of the ox. That from the sheep is also popular in Scotland. Cooked in milk with onions and flavoured lightly with salted butter it is a dish fit for a king's table and a gourmet's palate.

Head: The use of head meats varies with the animal. From the ox the best known meat is ox cheek. This needs prolonged cooking but has an excellent flavour. (Tongues have been separately dealt with.) The equivalent from the pig is the Bath chap, which is the cheek meat salted and boiled. The most flavourful use for this is to thinly slice it and fry it as a flavour garnish for breakfast or lunch dishes. In summer it is pleasant eaten cold but it must be thinly sliced. Sheep's heads are generally cooked by boiling either fresh or salted after they have been split in half. The meat is stripped from the bones and a brawn of fine flavour produced from the meat and the rendered stock. From all heads, brains are obtainable. A little-flavoured dish, they may be boiled and fried.

Suet: This is the hard internal fat of the sheep and ox. Calves have little internal fat and that of the pig is oily and of little use in cooking. Lamb or sheep suet is hard, white and usually carries too much flavour to be useful to the cook. Beef suet however is excellent. Its slow melting makes it invaluable in pudding crusts and in Christmas puddings.

Lites: These are the lungs of the animal and although perfectly edible they are usually set aside for consumption by domestic pets. Their food value is not great and their sale today in retail shops quite small.

Melts (milts): The spleen has been sold for food and may be eaten roasted or stewed into stock. The above remarks about lites apply to these.

Skirt: Skirts are properly considered as offals since they are trimmed from the main body of the carcase. There are three kinds of skirt. (*a*) Thick or goose skirt which is found in the hind quarter. Although rather "chewy" it may be fried. More usually it is stewed. It makes excellent puddings. (*b*) Thin skirt. This is the muscular part of the diaphragm. It is usually stewed and like goose skirt has a fine flavour. (*c*) Body skirt. This, the pillars of the diaphragm is the only one of the skirts commonly found in offal shops. It may be fried but will not be overtender. Like the other two it makes excellent puddings and has the finest flavour of the three. Skirts are only sold from the ox, those from smaller animals are left attached to the relevant joint (goose skirt in the leg and thin skirt in the fore loin or best end neck. The remnant of the body skirt will be found in the loin, but often most is trimmed away during preparation.)

Udder: The mammary gland of the cow, this again is a fine flavoured food fallen into disuse. It should be salted, smoked and fried. When so cooked its flavour is difficult for any save the expert to tell from ham.

Bones: These are offals and are often overlooked. Those who need to produce soup for large families as economically as possible will know well the value of a stock-pot (*see* p. 78). Until one is kept its full value is hard to appreciate. A separate stock of veal bones properly clarified produces the finest base possible for jellies and aspics. A point often lost sight of in discussing bones and stock-pots is that they are useless on a small scale. To boil bones occasionally is a waste of time. To cook them regularly is a great economy.

Other edible offals: Two final points are worth noting. Although tripe may perhaps not be acceptable, part of the stomach of pigs and sheep are eaten by most people in the form of sausage skins. Indeed a large part of the flavour of a properly cooked sausage comes from the skin surrounding the mixture.

The wise housewife produces in her own oven and pots one of the most valuable offals from the meat animals, namely rendered fat or dripping. This is an excellent food. Where much dripping is eaten (more than can be obtained from weekly cooking) the following plan can be adopted. Purchase from the butcher some pieces of clean beef fat. Render these in a pan in the oven together with a few fat pieces of bacon until the greaves (residue) is crisp. The fat should be strained off. When set it will be found to be excellent "dripping". If intended for use in pastry making (for which it is excellent) the bacon should be omitted.

BEEF

Beef is obtained from adult bovine animals, usually designated "cows" by the uninitiated. The cow proper is the mother animal.

Female bovines which have not borne young are characterized in the trade as heifers. They provide beef which to the layman is indistinguishable from bullock or ox beef, and as in the case of all female animals has the advantage of a lighter bone structure. This is usually partially offset by a tendency to deposit slightly more fat on and in the carcase.

The father of cattle is the bull. Bull beef is rarely met on sale in retail shops. The flesh is dark, strong in taste and usually extremely lean. In the Jewish section of the meat trade there is however a leaning towards young bull meat. This is usually well fatted but still possesses a strong flavour and is unsuitable for normal Gentile methods of cooking.

The prime supplier of quality beef is the oxen or steer or bullock. These alternative terms, of which the last is the most common, apply to a male animal castrated at an early age. The effect of this operation is to produce a quiet animal whose main interest lies in feeding. Under these conditions muscles are produced which have received the minimum of exercise and the maximum opportunity to lay down fat. The flesh should ideally be bright red when freshly cut, but after exposure to the air for a short while, the lustre of colour is lost and it assumes a colour hard to describe. The term "creamy red" may perhaps convey the colour. Certainly it is not a pink or beige red, and there should be no trace of mauve in it.

The carcase of the animal, that is the animal after the removal of head, feet, skin and internal organs, is split down the backbone into two halves called sides. Each side is then divided into two halves by cutting between the tenth and eleventh rib bone. (The cuts and cutting described are London style. Wherever it is necessary reference will be made to the terms used in other areas.) The piece that contains the forelimb and first ten rib bones is called the forequarter, and the other half of the side is called the hind quarter.

THE HINDQUARTER

The cuts into which the hindquarter is divided will be better understood from the accompanying diagram than from a description. See also plate 4.

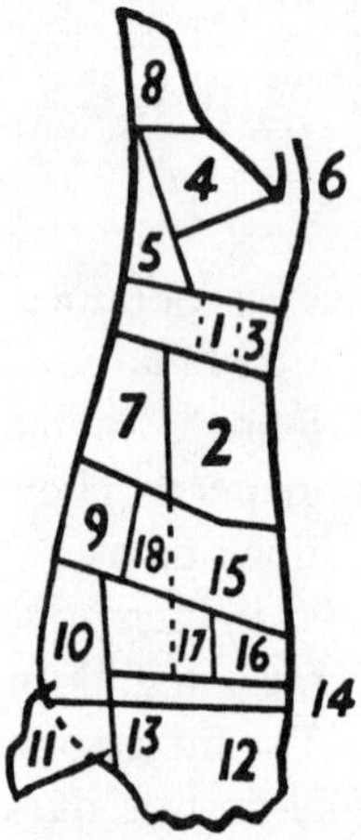

(1) The **undercut** or **fillet** is the most suitable meat for frying or grilling, having a very delicate flavour. There are, however, only 5–7 pounds of fillet in a carcase of 600–700 lb. It is therefore a very expensive cut.

(2) The **sirloin** may be considered to be the next most suitable frying cut, and on the grounds of its superior flavour, is preferred to fillet by many people. It is not often cut in England, where the most usual practice is to roast the sirloin.

(3) **Rump steak** is the most common grilling or frying cut, and the prime end of the rump is to be found in the small slices which are removed from the hip-bone.

(4) The **topside**, which is the muscle of the inside leg, (5) the **top rump**, which is the muscle of the front of the thigh, are only suitable for slow frying if they are from the highest quality of fat animal. In nearly all cases they are, together with the rump, better cooked in the oven with a small quantity of water.

The muscle of the outside of the thigh and the buttock is sold as **silverside** (6). It is suitable only for casseroling if tenderness is desired, and is eminently suitable for salting and boiling.

For those who have acquired the taste for beef fat, (7) the **hindquarter flank** (the belly of the animal) yields a cheap and delicious joint for boiling or casserole.
casserole.

(8) The **leg of beef** is well-flavoured and gives excellent gravy, but is only suitable for slow stewing or casseroling. It may be cut in two ways. In strips it shows clearly the structure of working muscle being sheathed with into thick pieces of white gristle. If cut in slices it exhibits "lines" where the various sheaths of connective tissue have been cut across. There is little to choose between the leg and the foreleg or shin except that the leg is larger and will yield bigger pieces of meat for stewing where this is required.

Several terms are now in growing use for various types of beef steaks. They are not new terms and some have already been mentioned.

Fillet: This term is used in two ways. Correctly it refers to the meat found beneath the blade part of the loin bones. It is also used for the continuation of this same muscle which is part of a whole unboned rump steak or steakpiece.

This part is properly called the undercut. Fillet or undercut may be served in several ways and under several names.

Châteaubriand: A very thick piece of fillet sufficient for two people and cut at the time of serving into two portions.

Tournedos: Thick slices of fillet for one person. Usually ¾ in. thick and a nice round shape, they are perhaps the most usual way in which the steak is cooked. They are sometimes tied to preserve their shape.

Noisettes: Neatly trimmed, round or oval shapes of fillet between half and three-quarters of an inch in thickness.

Mignons: Very fine fillet steaks which should be cooked quickly. These are often referred to as minute steaks.

Porterhouse: A steak from the wing end (wing rib) of the sirloin or forerib. In fact a slice from the part of the loin which contains no undercut or fillet.

T-bone steak: A steak cut through the sirloin so that it contains on one side at least, the "T"-shaped loin bone. It has two "eyes", that of the loin meat and that of the fillet.

Entrecote: This is a sirloin steak without the undercut and without the bone. In other words the eye meat of the loin cut into steaks.

All these steaks may be served in many different ways. For example an ordinary Châteaubriand is dipped in olive oil, salted, peppered and grilled. Garnished with hearts of artichoke, stuffed braised lettuce and Maître d'Hôtel butter it becomes *Châteaubriand Marquise*. If you sauté a sirloin steak with mushrooms and shallots in butter and then make a sauce of the vegetables with dry white wine and thick gravy it is an *Entrecôte Forestière*. With red wine instead of white and marrowbone cooked in the sauce it becomes *Entrecôte Bordelaise*. A mignon or minute steak cooked quickly in butter with a little Worcester sauce and chopped parsley is a *Bœuf Minute Diane*. The methods of cooking tournedos are legion. For example *Tournedos Andalouse* is served with grilled tomatoes on buttered toast garnished with aubergines, small onions and Madeira sauce. Cooked in butter and served with a sauce of tomatoes, mushrooms and shallots poured over the top they become *Tournedos Chasseur*. There are indeed more ways to cook steak than in the frying-pan.

THE FOREQUARTER

As in the case of the hindquarter the diagram fully explains the position of the various cuts. Commencing with:

(9) the **flank** and (10) **brisket**, which are the muscular extension of the belly

of the animal towards the chest, we find two joints suitable for salting and boiling, and for casseroling. When tender they may be finished for a short while in a very hot oven to simulate the flavour and appearance of roast beef. Whether purchased with the bone or boneless they are extremely economical joints. Properly cooked they yield a slice of meat little fatter than that obtained from the sirloin of the same animal, and have the advantage of providing at the same time an extremely fine and nutritious beef dripping.

The remarks made above about leg of beef apply equally well to (11) the **shin** or **foreleg.**

(12) The **sticking** or **neck** of the animal and (13) the **clod** or front chest muscles provide meat suitable for casseroling rather than boiling. These cuts contain less connective tissue than the shin or leg and may be distinguished from the chuck steak and blade bone by the fact that in the same animal they contain less evidence of marbling fat.

(14) The **chuck** and **blade bone** lie on the dividing line between casserole steak and roasting meat. Though sold for stewing, they need a shorter cooking time than any other cut of oven stewing meat with the possible exception of the top rump and topside.

The **foreribs** (15) are merely an extension of the sirloin and the **backribs** (16) an extension of the forerib. Since they are nearer to the harder working part of the animal than the sirloin (the forequarter is more exercised in feeding by the constant lifting and dropping of the head), they require rather more care in roasting, that is to say a lower heat, a longer time, and the addition of a little water to the pan.

The last cuts of the forequarter, the **top ribs** (17) and **flat ribs** (18) come half-way between the two types of cut and may be very slowly roasted. It is interesting here to note that the top ribs possess the peculiar quality of swelling up when placed in a hot oven. This is the reason for the colloquial term "oven busters" which is applied to this cut. In some parts of the country they are often referred to as "rising ribs".

BEEF À LA MODE

Bœuf à la mode

2 lb. rump of beef
1 glass claret
Juice of ½ lemon
1 small onion
2 cloves
Salt and pepper
Bouquet garni
1 oz. butter *or* fat
10 button onions
1 oz. flour
1½ pt. stock
2 bacon rashers
2 carrots

Trim and bone the meat. Place it in a bowl with a marinade made from the claret, lemon juice, finely-chopped onion, cloves, salt, pepper and bouquet garni. Leave for 2 hr., basting frequently. Melt the fat in a stewpan, drain the beef well and fry until brown. Fry the button onions at the same time. Remove both from the pan, add the flour and fry until nut brown. Then add the stock and the marinade in which the meat was soaked and stir until boiling. Replace the meat and the onions and season to taste. Cover the meat with the bacon rashers. Add the carrots, thinly sliced, and cook gently for 2½ hr., stirring occasionally. When tender, place on a hot dish, strain the liquid in the saucepan and pour over the meat.

8 helpings

BEEF AS MOCK HARE

1¼ lb. stewing steak
4 oz. fairly fat bacon
Seasoned flour
1 onion stuck with 3 cloves
¾ pt. stock
Bouquet garni
1 tablesp. redcurrant jelly
½ gill port (optional)
1 dessertsp. chopped pickle
Salt and pepper

GARNISH

Fried *or* baked forcemeat balls
Parsley

Wipe and trim the meat and cut into 1-in. squares. Dice the bacon, fry in a saucepan, then remove from pan. Toss the meat in seasoned flour and fry until nicely browned. Add the onion stuck with cloves, stock and bouquet garni and cook slowly until tender, 1½–2 hr. Remove the onion and bouquet garni, add the redcurrant jelly, port (if used), chopped pickle, and seasoning if required.

Serve on a hot dish. Garnish with forcemeat balls and chopped parsley.

6 helpings

BEEF BORDER

Bordure de Bœuf

1½ lb. best steak
1½ oz. butter *or* fat
1½ oz. flour
1½ gill stock
2 eggs
Salt and pepper
Mushroom ketchup *or* Worcester sauce
½ gill cream
Carrots
Green peas
1 doz. mushrooms
¾ pt. Espagnole sauce

Wipe the meat and remove any fat or skin. Mince the meat well. Melt the fat in a stewpan, add the flour, stir and cook for about 3 min. Stir in the stock and cook, stirring, until thick. Add the minced meat, the beaten eggs, seasoning, ketchup or sauce, and sieve the mixture if liked. Add the cream and place mixture in a well greased border (ring) mould. Steam gently for ¾–1 hr. Meanwhile cut pea shapes from the carrots. Cook the carrots and peas separately, toss them in butter; heat the mushrooms. Turn out the mould on to a hot dish, coat with Espagnole sauce. Fill the centre with a mixture of peas and carrots and arrange the mushrooms in heaps around the dish.

6 helpings
Cooking time—about 1½ hr.

BEEF CREAMS

Crèmes de Bœuf

¾ lb. tender lean beef
1 oz. butter *or* fat
1 oz. flour
1 gill well-flavoured brown stock
Salt and pepper
Worcester sauce
1 egg
1 teasp. finely-chopped parsley
1 tablesp. chopped mushrooms
2 tablesp. lightly whipped cream
Tomato sauce
Green peas

Wipe the meat and remove all the fat and skin. Mince the meat finely. Melt the fat in a saucepan, add the flour and cook, stirring, for a few minutes. Add the stock, bring to the boil and stir and cook for about 5 min. Add the minced meat, seasoning, Worcester sauce and egg and pound well. Put through a wire sieve, mix well with the parsley and mushrooms and mix the cream in lightly. Fill 6 large, well-greased dariole moulds and cover with greased paper. Steam very gently until firm. Turn out on to a hot dish and pour a little sauce around. Garnish with peas.

6 helpings

BEEF OLIVES

Paupiettes de Bœuf

1½ lb. good stewing steak cut in 6 slices
4 oz. veal forcemeat
¾ pt. Espagnole *or* brown sauce

Wipe and trim the slices of meat, flatten them with a wet cutlet bat or rolling pin. Spread a little forcemeat on each slice, roll up tightly and tie securely with fine string or cotton. Place the sauce in a saucepan, bring to the boil, and add the "olives". Simmer gently for about 1 hr. When cooked, untie the olives; serve on a bed of mashed potatoes.

6 helpings

Basic Recipe

BEEFSTEAK PIE

Pâté chaud de Bœuf à l'Anglaise

1½ lb. lean beefsteak
Seasoned flour
2 onions
Stock *or* water
Flaky, rough puff *or* short pastry, using 8 oz. flour, etc.
Egg *or* milk

Wipe the meat, remove the skin and superfluous fat and cut meat into small cubes. Dip the cubes in the seasoned flour and place in a pie-dish, piling them higher in the centre. Peel and finely-chop the onions; sprinkle them between the pieces of meat. Sprinkle any remaining seasoned flour between the meat. Add enough stock or water to ¼ fill the dish. Roll out the pastry ¼–½ in. thick to the shape of the pie-dish, but allow an extra 2 in. all round. Cut a strip about ¾ in. wide from around the edge of the pastry to cover the rim of the pie-dish. Dampen the rim, place the strip of pastry around with the cut side out and allow it to overlap the rim a little. Damp the join and the rest of the pastry and cover with the pastry lid. Press the edges lightly together. Trim, make a small round hole in the centre of the pie, and decorate with pastry leaves. Brush with beaten egg or milk. Place in a hot oven (**450° F., Gas 8**) until pastry is set and then reduce heat, if necessary place the pie on a lower shelf and cover with greased paper to prevent pastry becoming too brown. Heat the stock. Make a hole in the pie and pour in the hot stock before serving.

6 helpings
Cooking time—about 2 hr.

BEEFSTEAK AND KIDNEY PIE

Pâté chaud de Bœuf et Rognons à l'Anglaise

As for Beefsteak Pie, but add 2 sheep's or 6 oz. ox kidneys. Soak the kidneys, remove the skins and cores and cut into slices. Then proceed as directed in the preceding recipe, adding the sliced kidneys with the steak and onions.

BEEFSTEAK AND POTATO PIE

Pâté de Bœuf et de Pommes de Terre

As for Beefsteak Pie, adding potatoes to taste. Cut the meat in slices and dip in the seasoned flour. Cut the potatoes into slices. Place a layer of sliced potato on the bottom of the pie-dish, season, and cover with a layer of meat. Add a little onion, finely chopped. Repeat with layers of potato, meat, onion and seasoning until the dish is full. Add stock or water to ⅓ the depth of the dish. Then cover with pastry and cook as directed for Beefsteak Pie.

BEEFSTEAK PUDDING

Pouding de Bœuf à l'Anglaise

1½ lb. good stewing steak
Seasoned flour
Suet pastry using 8 oz. flour, etc.
3 tablesp. stock *or* water (approx.)

Wipe the meat; remove any superfluous skin and fat. Cut the meat into narrow strips or cubes and dip in the seasoned flour. Cut off ⅓ of the pastry for the lid. Roll the remainder out into a round about ¼ in. thick and line a greased pudding basin with it. Press well in to remove any creases. Half-fill the basin with the prepared meat and add the stock or water. Then add the remainder of the meat. Roll out the pastry reserved for the lid. Damp the edges, place the lid on top and press the edges well together. Cover with greased greaseproof paper if pudding is to be steamed, or with a pudding cloth if it is to be boiled. Place in boiling water and steam for about 3½ hr.—keep the water boiling, if necessary add more *boiling* water; *or* boil for 3 hr. Serve in the pudding basin, or turn out on to a hot dish.

6 helpings

BEEFSTEAK AND KIDNEY PUDDING

Pouding de Bœuf et de Rognon

As for Beefsteak pudding but add 2 sheep's or 6 oz. ox kidneys. Soak the kidneys, remove the skins and cores and cut into thin slices 3 in. by 2 in. Dip in seasoned flour, place a slice of kidney on each slice of meat, roll up tightly and place the rolls on end in the basin. Proceed as directed for Beefsteak Pudding.

BOILED BEEF—Unsalted

Bœuf bouilli

2½–3 lb. brisket, aitchbone *or* round of beef	**A bunch of herbs**
Salt	**Carrots**
3 cloves	**Turnips**
10 peppercorns	**Onions**
	Suet dumplings (optional)

Wipe the meat with a damp cloth and tie into a neat shape with string. Put into a pan and cover with boiling salted water. Bring to the boil again and boil for 5 min. to seal the surface. Reduce to simmering point, add the cloves, peppercorns and herbs and simmer for the remainder of the time, allowing 20 min. per lb. and 20 min. over. Skim when necessary. Add the sliced vegetables allowing enough time for them to be cooked when the meat is ready. Place the meat on a hot dish. Remove string and re-skewer meat if necessary. Arrange vegetables neatly round and serve some of the liquid separately in a sauce boat.

If suet dumplings are to be served, put them into the liquor 20 min.–½ hr. before serving.

Salt beef—silverside or topside: if very salt cover with unsalted cold water, otherwise use warm water. Bring slowly to boiling point and skim well. Continue as for fresh meat allowing a little extra boiling time.

Suet dumplings 3–4 oz. suet; ½ lb. flour; ¼ teasp. salt; 1 teasp. baking-powder; cold water. Make as for suet pastry (p. 557), form into small balls and drop into boiling stock; after 3 min. reduce heat and simmer for remainder of time.

BRAISED BEEF

Bœuf braisé

3 lb. brisket of beef	**¼ lb. fat bacon rashers**
1 large carrot	**1 oz. dripping**
1 large turnip	**Bouquet garni**
18 button onions	**6–12 peppercorns**
2 leeks	**Salt**
A few sticks of celery	**Stock**

Wipe and trim the meat and tie into a good shape. Dice a little of the carrot and turnip and put aside with the onions for garnish. Thickly slice the remainder of the carrot, turnip, leeks and celery and fry slightly in a stewpan with the bacon trimmings in the hot dripping. Place the meat on top and cover with slices of bacon. Add the bouquet garni and peppercorns tied in muslin, salt to taste and enough stock to nearly cover the vegetables. Cover with a well-fitting lid and cook as slowly as possible for about 3 hr., basting occasionally and adding more stock if necessary. When nearly ready, cook the diced vegetables and onions separately in well-flavoured stock. Make a brown gravy adding any strained stock left in the stewpan. Place the meat on a hot dish, remove string and garnish with the diced vegetables and onions. Serve the gravy separately.

BRISKET OF BEEF

Poitrine de Bœuf à la Flamande

3 lb. brisket of beef	**Allspice**
Bacon rashers	**Peppercorns**
2 onions	**Stock *or* water**
Bouquet garni	**¾ pt. brown sauce**
2 cloves	**2 carrots**
1 blade of mace	

Wipe and trim the meat. Cover the bottom of a stewpan with rashers of bacon, place the meat on them and lay more bacon on top. Add the onions, bouquet garni, cloves, mace, allspice, peppercorns and trimmings from the vegetables. Nearly cover with stock or water. Cover closely and cook very gently for 2½–3 hr., adding more boiling liquid if necessary. In the meantime make the brown sauce, using stock from the stewpan if liked. Peel and dice the carrots and cook them separately. Place the meat on a hot dish, remove any string and re-skewer if necessary. Glaze and garnish with the diced carrots. Serve with the sauce.

CARBONNADE OF BEEF

Carbonnade de Bœuf

1½ lb. good stewing steak	**½ pt. stock *or* water**
2 oz. dripping	**½ pt. ale**
2 large onions, sliced	**Salt and pepper**
1 clove of garlic	**6 thin rounds of bread**
½ oz. flour	**Mustard and vinegar *or* French mustard**

Wipe and trim the meat, removing all fat and cut into 1½-in. squares. Heat the dripping in a stewpan and brown the meat quickly on all sides. Add the sliced onions and fry until brown. Add the crushed garlic and fry lightly. Pour off the surplus fat, sprinkle in the flour and brown slightly. Add the stock or water, ale and seasoning. Place in a casserole and cook gently in a warm oven **(335° F., Gas 3)** for 1½–2 hr. When cooked, spread the rounds of bread with mustard and vinegar or French mustard, and press well down into the gravy. Return the casserole to the oven for about 15 min. without the lid and allow the bread to brown slightly. Serve in the casserole.

6 helpings

CHÂTEAUBRIAND STEAK

Château-Briand grillé

A double fillet steak not less than 1½ in. thick	**Olive oil *or* melted butter**
	Salt and pepper

Wipe the steak, remove any sinew or skin. Cover the meat with a cloth and beat carefully. Brush over with oil or melted butter and season. Place under a red-hot grill and cook both sides quickly. Reduce heat slightly and cook, turning frequently. The steak should be well browned but slightly underdone.

Serve immediately on a hot dish with Maître d'hôtel butter and potato straws or with gravy, demi-glace, tomato or Béchamel sauce.

CURRIED BEEF

Kari de Bœuf

1½ lb. lean beef	**1–2 teasp. curry paste**
2½ oz. butter *or* fat	**2 teasp. chutney**
1 large onion	**Salt and pepper**
1 sour apple	**4–6 oz. patna rice**
2 teasp. curry powder	**Juice of ½ lemon**
1¼ oz. flour	**2 teasp. jam *or* jelly**
1½ pt. strained stock *or* coconut infusion	

GARNISH

Paprika	**Gherkins**

Cut the meat into 1-in. cubes. Melt the fat in a stewpan; fry the meat lightly on both sides, then remove and keep hot. Peel and chop the onion; peel, core and slice the apple. Fry them in the fat until golden brown. Add the curry powder and flour and fry gently for 5 min. Add the strained stock or coconut infusion, curry paste, chutney and seasoning; stir until boiling. Replace the meat, cover closely, and simmer gently for 1½–2 hr. Meanwhile, boil the rice in boiling salted water for about 15–20 min. Drain on a sieve, separate the grains by pouring boiling water over; dry thoroughly. Arrange in a border on a hot dish. Add lemon juice, jelly and extra seasoning if required, to the curry. Pour the curry into the middle of the rice border. Garnish. If preferred the rice may be served separately.

6 helpings

FILLET OF BEEF DAUPHIN

Filet de Bœuf Dauphin

1½–2 lb. fillet of beef	**Dripping**
Salt and pepper	**Meat glaze**
Larding bacon	**½ pt. Madeira sauce**
Flour	**12 potato croquettes**

Wipe, trim and season the meat. Lard with the strips of bacon (p. 35), sprinkle with flour and tie into a good shape. Put into a roasting-tin with dripping. Cover with paper and put into a hot oven (**425° F., Gas 7**) for 10 min., then reduce the heat to moderate (**350° F., Gas 4**). Baste and cook until tender allowing 15 min. per lb. and 15 min. over. Baste occasionally while cooking. Remove the paper 15 min. before serving. Place fillet on a hot dish, remove string and brush over with glaze. Garnish with the potato croquettes. Pour away the fat from the roasting-tin and add any of the brown sediment to the sauce; heat and serve separately.

6 helpings

FILLETS OF BEEF—BEAUFFREMONT STYLE

Filets de Bœuf à la Beauffremont

1½–2 lb. fillet of beef
Salt and pepper
Egg and breadcrumbs
4 oz. macaroni
White stock
¾ pt. tomato sauce
¼ pt. Madeira sauce
Butter *or* fat for frying
Meat glaze
2 oz. grated cheese

GARNISH

Shredded truffle *or* chopped parsley

Cut the fillet into rounds about 1½ in. thick and 2½ in. in diameter. Season well and coat with egg and breadcrumbs. Cook the macaroni in well-flavoured stock until tender—about 20 min. Drain and add to ½ pt. of the tomato sauce. Keep hot. Add the remaining tomato sauce to the Madeira sauce and the glaze and keep hot until required. Fry the fillets in the fat in a sauté pan for 6–8 min.; arrange in a circle on a hot dish and glaze. Add the cheese to the macaroni and pile in the centre of the dish. Garnish; pour the sauce round; serve very hot.

6 helpings

FILLETS OF BEEF—GARIBALDI STYLE

Filets de Bœuf à la Garibaldi

1½–2 lb. fillet of beef
2 large truffles
Thin slices of ham *or* bacon
2 oz. beef marrow
1 egg
Salt and pepper
Pinch of nutmeg
1½ oz. butter *or* fat
Mashed potatoes
½ pt. tomato *or* piquant sauce
6–8 macaroni croquettes

Cut the meat into round fillets about ¾ in. thick and 2 in. across. Cut ½ as many slices of truffle, rounds of ham or bacon and thin rounds of marrow as there are fillets. Blanch the marrow. Pound the lean meat trimmings, marrow trimmings, egg yolk, salt, pepper and nutmeg together and pass through a wire sieve. Spread a little of this mixture (farce) on ½ the fillets, cover with a slice of marrow, add a little more farce, then a slice of truffle, more farce and lastly a round of ham or bacon. Spread a little farce on the remainder of the fillets, lay them on top of the others and press lightly together. Cover the surface with a thin layer of farce, brush over with egg white and sprinkle with chopped truffle. Melt the fat in a sauté pan and fry the fillets for about 10 min., turning carefully once only. Then cover with buttered paper and cook gently for 10 min. in the oven. Serve the fillets on a foundation of mashed or piped potato, and pour the sauce over.

Garnish with macaroni croquettes.

6 helpings

FILLETS OF BEEF MONTMORENCY

Filets de Bœuf Montmorency

1½–2 lb. fillet of beef
Salt and pepper
24 sweet cherries
¾ pt. Madeira sauce
1 tablesp. redcurrant jelly
1 tablesp. finely-grated horseradish
2 oz. butter *or* fat
Meat glaze
Peas *or* French beans

Wipe, trim and cut the meat into neat fillets and season. Stone the cherries and soak in water for about 8 min. Heat the sauce, add to it the redcurrant jelly and grated horseradish and simmer for 5 min. Add the cherries and allow to heat through. Then heat the fat and fry or grill the fillets for about 7–8 min. Arrange the fillets on a hot dish, glaze lightly, and pour a little sauce round. Garnish with peas or French beans and serve the rest of the sauce separately.

6 helpings

FILLETS OF BEEF—POMPADOUR STYLE

Filets de Bœuf à la Pompadour

1½–2 lb. fillet of beef
Salt and pepper
2 large firm tomatoes
Butter *or* fat
Meat glaze
Croûtes of fried bread
¾ oz. Maître d'hôtel butter
¾ pt. Espagnole sauce
Macedoine of vegetables

Wipe the meat and cut into rather thick round fillets of equal size, and season. Cut an equal number of slices of tomato, season and dot with a little butter and bake. Sauté the fillets in the fat, drain, glaze and serve on the fried croûtes. Place a slice of baked tomato on each fillet and place a pat of Maître d'hôtel butter on each slice of tomato. Pour a little sauce round and garnish with the macedoine of vegetables which have been tossed in butter and seasoned after cooking.

6 helpings

FILLETS OF BEEF—ROSSINI STYLE

Filets de Bœuf à la Rossini

1½ lb. fillet of beef
¼ lb. chickens' livers
2 oz. butter *or* fat
1 shallot
1½ oz. foie gras
1 tablesp. brown sauce
Salt and pepper
1 tablesp. olive oil
Meat glaze
Croûtes of fried bread
Slices of truffle
½–¾ pt. demi-glace sauce

Wipe the beef and cut into rounds 2½ in. diameter and ½ in. thick. Wash, dry and slice the liver. Melt 1 oz. of the fat in a sauté pan and fry the finely-chopped shallot slightly. Add the liver and sauté for a few minutes. Drain off the fat and pound the liver with the foie gras, brown sauce and seasoning until smooth, then pass through a wire sieve. Heat the remainder of the fat with the olive oil and fry the fillets quickly until browned on both sides. Drain and cover one side of each with the liver farce. Brush with meat glaze, place on the fried croûtes and put in the oven to become thoroughly hot. Lay a slice of truffle on the top of each fillet, arrange on a hot dish and serve the demi-glace sauce separately.

6 helpings

FILLETS OF BEEF—TRIANON STYLE

Noisettes de filets à la Trianon

1½–2 lb. fillet of beef
Salt and pepper
¼ pt. sherry (optional)
2 oz. butter *or* fat
Meat glaze
Croûtes of bread
1 gill sour cream *or* yoghourt

Wipe the meat and cut into small, plump round fillets. Put them on a dish, sprinkle with salt and pepper and pour over the sherry (if used). Cover, leave them for 2 hr., turning occasionally. Then drain the fillets and dry well in a cloth. Heat the fat in a sauté pan, skim well and fry the fillets quickly and lightly as they should be served slightly underdone. Pour off the fat and put into the sauté pan ½ gill of the liquid used in the marinade. Add 3 tablesp. meat glaze and reduce to ⅓ the original quantity. Have ready croûtes of bread the same size and number as the fillets, fry until golden brown and drain. Brush one side of the croûtes with meat glaze, place a fillet on each and arrange neatly on a hot dish. Pour a little of the reduced sauce round the dish, add the sour cream or yoghourt to the remainder, re-heat quickly and put 1 tablesp. on each fillet and serve.

6 helpings
Cooking time—about 20 min.

FILLETS OF BEEF—VIENNESE STYLE

Filets de Bœuf à la Viennoise

1¼ lb. lean tender beef
½ teasp. powdered mixed herbs
½ teasp. finely-chopped parsley
Salt and pepper
Nutmeg
Cayenne pepper
1 large egg
Flour
2 large onions
2½ oz. butter *or* fat
½–¾ pt. Espagnole sauce

Wipe and trim the meat; mince it finely. Add to it the herbs, parsley, salt, pepper, nutmeg and cayenne. Mix well and bind with beaten egg. Divide the mixture into 6–8 portions, shape into round fillets and dredge lightly with flour. Cut the onions across into slices, reserve 6–8 of the large outer rings for garnish, chop the remainder finely. Heat 1 oz. of the fat in a saucepan and fry the chopped onions lightly. Add 2 tablesp. of the Espagnole sauce, season to taste and simmer for 20 min. Heat the remainder of the fat in a sauté pan and fry the fillets. Dip the outer onion rings into the flour and fry until golden brown. Serve the fillets with a little of the chopped onion on the centre of each. Garnish with the onion rings. Pour some of the sauce around the meat and serve the remainder separately.

6 helpings **Cooking time—about 35 min.**

FILLETS OF BEEF WITH FRIED BANANAS

Filets de Bœuf aux Bananes

1½ lb. fillet beef	**Deep fat**
Salt and pepper	**Butter *or* fat**
3 bananas	**Meat glaze**
Egg and breadcrumbs	**½ pt. brown sauce**

Wipe, trim and cut the meat into neat fillets; season. Peel and cut the bananas in quarters, coat with egg and breadcrumbs and fry in deep fat. Drain and keep hot until required. Fry the fillets in hot butter or fat for about 7 min., turning frequently. Drain, glaze and arrange in a circle on a hot dish. Place the bananas in the centre and pour some of the sauce round. Serve the remainder of the sauce separately.

6 helpings **Cooking time—about 15 min.**

FILLETS OF BEEF WITH HORSERADISH SAUCE

Filets de Bœuf au Raifort

1½-2 lb. fillet of beef	**6 croûtes of bread**
Salt and pepper	**Horseradish sauce**
2 oz. butter *or* fat	**½ pt. good brown sauce**
6 large mushrooms	

Wipe and trim the meat; cut into neat fillets. Season and cook quickly in the hot fat so that they are slightly underdone. Then remove and keep hot. Fry the mushrooms and the croûtes together. Place each fillet on a croûte, arrange in a circle on a hot dish. Place a mushroom upside-down on each fillet and fill the centre with the horseradish sauce. Pour some of the brown sauce round and serve the remainder separately.

6 helpings **Cooking time—about 15 min.**

FRIED BEEFSTEAK

Bifteck frit

1½ lb. frying beef-steak, 1 in. thick	**Salt and pepper**
	Fat

Wipe the meat, remove and discard any skin, beat lightly and season to taste. Put sufficient fat to barely cover the bottom of a frying-pan. When hot, fry the steak quickly on both sides to seal the surface. Then cook more slowly until cooked to taste.

For a good gravy to serve with the steak, drain any fat from the frying-pan, keeping back the sediment. Add salt and pepper and about 1½ gills of boiling water. Boil up, skim and strain.

6 helpings **Cooking time—about 7-10 min.**

GOBBETS OF BEEF

Bouchées de Bœuf

1½ lb. lean tender beef	**6 peppercorns**
2 tablesp. rice	**2 cloves**
1 small carrot	**1 blade of mace**
½ small turnip	**Triangular slices of hot buttered toast**
1 stick of celery	**Parsley**
Salt and pepper	
Bouquet garni	

Trim, wipe and cut the meat into small dice. Put into a saucepan with just sufficient salt water to cover and simmer very gently for 40 min. Wash the rice well; shred the carrot, turnip and celery. Add them with seasoning to the meat. Put in the bouquet garni, peppercorns, cloves and mace which have been tied in muslin. If necessary add more *boiling* water or stock to barely cover. Cook for another 40 min. adding more boiling water or stock as necessary. Remove the muslin bag and serve the Gobbets on slices of hot buttered toast. Garnish with parsley. This dish may be cooked in a moderate oven **(350° F., Gas 4)** if preferred. The time for cooking will be about the same.

6 helpings

GRILLED BEEFSTEAK

Bifteck grillé

1½ lb. rump *or* fillet steak *or* sirloin	**Salt and pepper**
Oil *or* butter	**Maître d'hôtel butter**

Wipe and cut the meat across the grain into suitable slices. Beat on both sides with a cutlet bat or rolling-pin. Brush with oil or melted butter and sprinkle with salt and pepper. Place under a red-hot grill and grill quickly on both sides to seal the surfaces, thus preventing the juices from escaping. Then grill more slowly until cooked as required, a "rare" steak requires 3–4 min. for each side. Turn frequently using tongs or 2 spoons, never pierce with a fork as this would make holes through which the meat juices would escape.

Serve at once with a pat of Maître d'hôtel butter on the top.

6 helpings

HOT POT

Ragoût à l'Anglaise

1½ lb. lean beef
3 onions
3 carrots
2 lb. potatoes
Salt and pepper
Stock *or* water

Remove any fat and cut the meat into pieces. Cut the onions and carrot into thin slices and the potatoes into thicker slices. Arrange the meat, onion, carrots and potatoes in layers in a casserole and season well. The top layer should be of potatoes neatly arranged. Three-quarters fill the casserole with cold water or stock, adding more later if the dish appears to be dry. Cover and bake in a warm oven (**335° F., Gas 3**) for 2 hr. Uncover ½ hr. before serving to allow the top layer of potatoes to brown. Serve in the casserole.

6 helpings

LARDED FILLET OF BEEF

Filet de Bœuf piqué

1½–2 lb. fillet of beef (cut in 1 piece)
Salt and pepper
Larding bacon
1 large onion
1 large carrot
1 small turnip
2 sticks of celery
1 oz. butter *or* fat
Bouquet garni
Peppercorns
Brown stock
Meat glaze
½ pt. brown, Espagnole *or* tomato sauce

Wipe, trim and beat the fillet slightly. Season and tie into a good shape. Lard it in close rows with strips of bacon about 2 in. in length (p. 35). Peel and slice the vegetables. Heat the fat in a braising-tin or stewpan, add the vegetables, fry lightly then add the herbs and peppercorns. Place the fillet on top and fry for 10 min. Then add stock to nearly cover the vegetables, replenishing it as necessary. Cover the fillets with greased paper, put on the lid and cook very slowly for about 1 hr. A short time before dishing remove the lid and paper and put into a hot oven to allow the bacon to become crisp and brown. Brush with meat glaze and place on a hot dish. Strain the liquid from the saucepan and add to it the sauce, boil up and serve in a sauce-boat.

Garnish the meat with tomatoes, mushrooms, diced carrots and turnip.

6 helpings

MIGNONS OF BEEF—BOURGEOISE STYLE

Mignons de Bœuf à la Bourgeoise

1½ lb. fillet of beef
3 large carrots
24 button onions
2 medium-sized turnips
Stock
½ pt. brown sauce
2 tablesp. tomato purée
Salt and pepper
Butter *or* fat

Wipe the meat and cut into neat 2-in. pieces or small round fillets. Prepare the carrots, onions and turnips and cook them in strong stock until about half cooked. Place the brown sauce in a saucepan, add the tomato purée, boil up and season to taste. Fry the mignons of meat in hot fat for about 6 min., drain and place in one large casserole or individual casseroles. Cover the mignons with vegetables, add the sauce and cook gently on the cooker or in the oven for 20 min. If preferred the fat may be drained from the mignons when cooked and the sauce and vegetables added to the pan and cooked on the stove. In this case, serve the mignons on a hot dish, pour the sauce over and arrange the vegetables in heaps around the meat.

6 helpings

MIGNONS OF BEEF—MILANAISE STYLE

Mignons de Bœuf à la Milanaise

1½–2 lb. fillet of beef
4 oz. macaroni
Butter *or* fat
2 oz. shredded ham *or* tongue
1 finely-chopped shallot
½ bruised clove of garlic
2–4 oz. chopped mushrooms
Salt and pepper
½–¾ pt. brown sauce
1 oz. Parmesan cheese

Break the macaroni into pieces $\frac{1}{2}$ in. long and drop them into rapidly boiling salt water and cook for 20 min. or until tender. Pour off the hot water and cover with cold to prevent sticking. Wipe the meat, cut into small round fillets and trim them neatly. Fry quickly in hot butter or fat for 5–6 min. turning them once. Drain and keep hot. Add the ham or tongue, shallot, garlic, mushrooms and seasoning, and toss over heat for a few minutes. Strain off any surplus fat, add the brown sauce and stir until boiling. Next add the macaroni, simmer gently for 10 min., then add the cheese. Place the mignons in 6 individual casseroles, cover with sauce and cook gently for 15–20 min. on the stove or in a warm oven (**335° F., Gas 3**). Serve in the casseroles.

MINCED COLLOPS

1½ lb. rump steak
1 onion *or* 3 shallots
1½ oz. butter *or* fat
1¼ oz. flour
½ pt. stock *or* water
Salt and pepper
1 tablesp. mushroom ketchup *or* lemon juice *or* vinegar

GARNISH

Sippets of toast
Parsley

Mince the meat very finely. Finely chop the onion, heat the fat and fry the onion until lightly browned, then add the flour and fry lightly. Put in the minced meat and cook lightly. Add the stock or water, seasoning and the mushroom ketchup, lemon juice or vinegar. Cook very gently for 20 min., stirring occasionally. Then serve on a hot dish and garnish with sippets of toasted bread and parsley.

6 helpings

MINIATURE ROUND OF BEEF

1 large rib of beef
1 gallon water
2 lb. coarse salt
½ oz. saltpetre
6 oz. brown sugar
12 peppercorns
A bunch of mixed herbs
2–3 onions
Vegetable trimmings

GARNISH

Diced carrot and turnip

Boil the water, salt, saltpetre and sugar together for $\frac{1}{2}$ hr., skimming when necessary, then allow to become cold. Bone the meat, rub well with salt, roll up lightly and tie securely with string. Place in the cold brine and leave for 6 days, turning each day. Then drain well and wash in cold water. Place in a pan, cover with cold water, add the herbs and peppercorns and bring slowly to the boil. Boil for 5 min. Skim, add the onions and vegetable trimmings and simmer for the required time, allowing 25 min. per lb. and 25 min. over. When ready, place on a hot dish, remove the string and skewer if necessary. Serve, garnished with diced vegetables.

NOISETTES OF BEEF WITH MAÎTRE D'HÔTEL BUTTER

Noisettes de Bœuf à la Maître d'hôtel

1½–2 lb. fillet of beef
1 oz. butter
1 teasp. finely-chopped parsley
1 teasp. lemon juice
Cayenne pepper
Olive oil *or* melted butter
Salt and pepper
Fried potato ribbons

Wipe and trim the meat and cut into round fillets. Knead the butter, parsley, lemon juice and cayenne well together, form into a flat cake and chill well to become firm. Brush the fillets with the oil or melted butter, sprinkle with salt and pepper and grill for 8–10 min., turning 2 or 3 times. Place them in a nearly upright position down the centre of a hot dish, put a small pat of the prepared butter on the top of each fillet, garnish with crisply-fried potato ribbons and serve very hot.

6 helpings

NOISETTES OF BEEF WITH MUSHROOMS

Noisettes de Bœuf aux Champignons

1½–2 lb. fillet of beef
2 mushrooms
1 shallot
½ teasp. finely-chopped parsley
Salt and pepper
2 oz. butter *or* fat
Spinach *or* mashed potatoes
½ pt. brown sauce

Wipe the meat and cut into round even fillets not less than $\frac{1}{2}$ in. thick. Finely chop the mushrooms and shallot and mix well together with the parsley, salt and pepper. Place a round pat of this mixture in the centre of each fillet. Heat the fat in a sauté pan, put in the fillets with the stuffing side down, fry quickly, then turn and fry the other side a little more slowly. When cooked, arrange in a row on a foundation of spinach or mashed potatoes. Pour some sauce round the noisettes and serve the rest of the sauce separately.

6 helpings **Cooking time—about 7 min.**

PAUPIETTES OF BEEF

Paupiettes de Bœuf

6 thin slices of beef
6 oz. sausage meat
Salt and pepper
1½ oz. dripping
1 large onion
1 large carrot
½ turnip
Stock
Bouquet garni
Meat glaze
Tomato *or* brown sauce
Savoury rice

Wipe and trim the slices of meat to measure about 2 in. by 5 in. Mince the trimmings and mix with the sausage meat. Season the meat, spread with the sausage meat mixture, roll up and tie securely. Heat the fat in a saucepan, fry the rolls until well coloured, then remove. Prepare and thickly slice the vegetables, fry them lightly. Add stock to almost cover, add the bouquet garni. Place the rolls on top and cover with greased paper and a lid. Cook gently for 1½ hr., basting and replenishing the stock if necessary. 20 min. before serving, remove the lid and paper and place in a moderate oven (**350° F., Gas 4**). Remove string from the meat and place on a hot dish. Glaze, pour some of the sauce round and serve the rest separately. Serve hot with savoury rice.

6 helpings

PORTERHOUSE STEAK

Entrecôte Double

1 steak about 1½ in. thick cut from the thick end of sirloin: allow 4-6 oz. steak per person
Salt and pepper
Melted butter *or* oil

Season and brush the steak over on both sides with melted butter or oil. If possible leave oiled for 1 hr. before cooking. Grill and serve plain or with Maître d'hôtel butter, button onions fried in butter and small stuffed tomatoes or horseradish sauce.

Cooking time—about 10 min.

ROAST BEEF

Bœuf rôti

Joint of beef suitable for roasting
Salt and pepper
Beef dripping (allow 1 oz. per lb. of meat)

Weigh meat to be able to calculate cooking time. Wipe with a damp cloth. Place joint in a roasting-tin, season and add dripping.

Put roasting-tin into a very hot oven (**450° F., Gas 8**) for 10–15 min. to brown or "sear" the meat. Then reduce heat to fairly hot (**375° F., Gas 5**) and baste every 20 min. for the first ½ of the cooking time and afterwards every 30 min. Allow 20 min. per lb. and another 10 min. over for solid joints, i.e. joints without bone; and 15 min. per lb. and 15 min. over for thick joints, i.e. joints with bone.

Remove on to a hot dish when cooked, remove string and skewer with a metal skewer if necessary. Keep hot. Drain off fat from tin and make gravy from sediment in the tin.

ROAST FILLET OF BEEF

Filet de Bœuf rôti

1½–2 lb. fillet of beef
Meat glaze
½ pt. demi-glace sauce

MARINADE

2 tablesp. olive oil
1 tablesp. lemon juice *or* vinegar
1 teasp. chopped onion
1 teasp. chopped parsley
A good pinch of powdered herbs
A pinch of ground cloves
Salt and pepper

Wipe, trim and tie the meat into a good shape, place on a dish and pour over the marinade. Allow to soak in the marinade for 2–3 hr., turning and basting frequently. Drain off ½ the liquid and fold the remainder with the meat in a thick sheet of well-greased greaseproof paper or aluminium foil, fastening all ends securely. Roast for 1 hr. and remove the paper to allow the meat to brown. Place on a hot dish and brush with meat glaze. If liked a little sauce may be poured round the dish, the rest being served separately. Serve with horseradish sauce.

6 helpings

ROLLED BEEF

Roulade de Bœuf

2 lb. fillet of beef
1 gill port (optional)
1 gill vinegar
4–6 oz. savoury forcemeat
½ teasp. powdered allspice
Redcurrant jelly
Brown *or* piquant sauce *or* a good gravy

Wipe and trim the meat. Pour the wine (if used) and vinegar over the meat and let it stand for 2 days, baste frequently and turn once or twice. Then drain well, flatten slightly and cover with the forcemeat. Roll up tightly and tie securely. Place in a baking-dish, add the allspice to the liquid in which the meat was soaked and pour over the meat. Cook in a moderate oven (**350° F., Gas 4**) for about ¾ hr., basting frequently. Remove the strings and serve with a good gravy or brown or piquant sauce and redcurrant jelly.

6 helpings

ROLLED STEAK

Tranche de bœuf roulé

1½–2 lb. stewing steak about ¾ in. thick, cut in 1 piece
Salt and pepper
6–8 oz. veal forcemeat
1½ oz. fat
1 pt. stock *or* water
1 oz. flour

Wipe and trim the meat and flatten it with a rolling-pin. Season the forcemeat well, spread it on the meat, and roll up tightly and tie securely. Heat the fat in a saucepan until very hot and fry meat quickly until the whole surface is browned. Add the hot stock or water, cover closely and cook very slowly for about 2 hr. When ready, place the meat on a hot dish. Thicken the gravy with the flour which has been blended to a smooth paste with a little cold stock or water and boil for 4 min. Season to taste, strain and pour some over the meat. Serve the remainder separately. If preferred, the roll may be baked in a moderate oven (**350° F., Gas 4**) in which case it must be well basted with stock or fat.

6 helpings

RUSSIAN STEAKS

Biftecks à la Russe

¾ lb. tender steak
¾ lb. fillet of veal
1 finely-chopped shallot
2 teasp. finely-chopped parsley
Salt and pepper
2 egg yolks
Flour for dredging
Egg and breadcrumbs
Oil *or* dripping
Tomato sauce *or* 1 tablesp. yoghourt *or* sour cream (optional)

Wipe and trim the meats, removing all fat and skin. Mince the meats finely and mix well with the shallot, parsley, seasoning and egg yolks. Spread on a wet plate and leave in a cold place to become firm. Divide into 12 equal portions and form into flat cakes, using a little flour. Coat with egg and crumbs and fry in hot deep fat or oil until cooked and a good brown colour. Drain well and place in a pyramid on a hot dish. Pour a little tomato sauce over them and serve the rest separately. A tablesp. of yoghourt or sour cream may be added to the sauce.

Garnish with peas.

6 helpings

SCOTCH COLLOPS

1½ lb. good stewing steak
2 oz. butter *or* fat
2 teasp. finely-chopped onion *or* shallot
2 teasp. flour
½ pt. stock
Salt and pepper
Gravy browning
Mushroom ketchup
Sippets of fried *or* toasted bread
Parsley

Cut the meat into small neat dice. Heat the fat in a stewpan and fry the onion or shallot lightly. Add the flour and cook for about 5 min., stirring all the time. Add the stock, seasoning, a little brown colouring, and the meat. Bring slowly up to the boil, add the mushroom ketchup and simmer very slowly for 1 hr., or until tender. Season if necessary and place on a hot dish. Arrange sippets of bread around the dish and garnish with chopped parsley.

6 helpings

SMALL FILLETS OF BEEF—RICHMONT STYLE

Filets Mignons à la Richmont

1½–2 lb. fillet of beef
Salt and pepper
2 oz. butter *or* fat
24 preserved *or* stewed mushrooms
½–¾ pt. Madeira sauce
Lemon juice
2 truffles

Wipe the meat and cut the fillets into 6 slices of even size and thickness. Trim neatly and season with salt and pepper. Heat 1 oz. fat in a sauté pan and put in the fillets. Fry on one side, turn and cover the fried side with finely-chopped seasoned mushrooms, a little Madeira sauce and lemon juice. Place the remainder of the fat on top and cover with buttered paper. Place the pan in the oven and cook gently for another 10 min. Arrange the fillets on a hot dish and place a slice of truffle on each one.

Pour the remainder of the Madeira sauce around and serve hot.

6 helpings

SMOTHERED BEEFSTEAK

Etuvée de Bifteck

1½ lb. rump steak
Salt and pepper
4 Spanish onions
Seasoned flour
2 oz. dripping
½ pt. stock *or* water

Wipe the meat, beat well, then season. Cut the onions into rings and dip in seasoned flour. Melt the dripping, and when hot, fry the onion rings until crisp and lightly browned. Remove the onions, and keep hot. Fry the meat quickly on both sides to seal the surfaces, and then more slowly for about 15 min. or until tender (adding more fat if necessary). Drain and keep hot. Drain off most of the fat, add some flour and fry until brown. Add boiling stock or vegetable water, a little gravy browning, if necessary, and stir and boil for 2–3 min. Season to taste and strain. Place the meat on a hot dish, cover with the onion rings and pour the gravy over.

Serve very hot.

6 helpings

STEAK PUDDING

Pouding de Steak, cuit au Four

½ lb. good stewing steak
½ lb. ox kidney
Salt and pepper
Dripping
6 oz. flour
2 eggs
¾ pt. milk *or* water

Cut the steak into finger-shaped pieces. Cut the kidney into thin slices and season well. Fry the steak for a few minutes in the dripping to seal the surface. Mix the flour, eggs and milk or water into a smooth batter and season. Melt about ½ oz. dripping in a casserole or pie-dish and put in ½ the batter and bake until set. Place the steak and the kidney on top of the batter, fill up the dish with the remainder of the batter and bake in a hot oven (**425° F., Gas 7**) for 10 min.; then reduce to moderate (**350° F., Gas 4**) for about 1 hr. until set and well browned. Serve with a good gravy.

6 helpings

STEWED BRISKET OF BEEF

Poitrine de Bœuf à la Bourgeoise

3 lb. brisket of beef
Vinegar
Salt and pepper
2 carrots
2 onions
1 turnip
2–3 sticks of celery (optional)
1 blade of mace
10 peppercorns
Bouquet garni
1 oz. butter *or* fat
1 oz. flour

Wipe and trim the meat, rub it over with vinegar and salt and leave for 2–3 hr. Put into a stewpan, barely cover with water, add salt, bring to the boil and skim well. Cover with a well-fitting lid, simmer gently for ½ hr., then add the vegetables cut in large slices, mace, peppercorns and a bouquet garni and cook as slowly as possible for another 1½ hr. Melt the fat in a small saucepan, add the flour and cook slowly, stirring until nut brown. Take out the meat, remove the bones and place the meat on a hot dish; remove the vegetables. Strain the stock and add to the contents of the small saucepan. Season, stir until boiling and boil well for 4 min. Serve the vegetables with the meat and the sauce in a gravy boat.

STEWED STEAK

Ragoût de Steak

$1\frac{1}{2}$ lb. stewing steak	**1 large onion**
2 large carrots	**$1\frac{1}{2}$ oz. flour**
2 large turnips	**$1\frac{1}{2}$ pt. water *or* stock**
$1\frac{1}{2}$ oz. fat	**Salt and pepper**

Wipe the meat, cut off any superfluous fat, and cut the meat into neat pieces. Cut the vegetables into dice or julienne strips and keep in water until required. Put the trimmings aside for adding to the stew. Heat the fat in a saucepan and when smoking hot, fry the meat until lightly browned on both sides, then remove from the pan. Slice the onion and fry until lightly coloured. Add the flour, mix well, and cook slowly until a good brown colour. Add the water or stock, the vegetable trimmings and stir until boiling. Season, replace the meat, cover with a tightly fitting lid and simmer gently for about 2–2½ hr. or until tender. Have ready the dice or strips of vegetable which have been cooked in boiling salted water. Arrange the meat in the centre of a hot dish, pour the stock over and garnish with the vegetables.

6 helpings

TENDERLOIN OF BEEF

Filet de Bœuf

A thick piece of well-hung sirloin	**Olive oil, melted butter *or* fat**
	Salt and pepper

Wipe the meat and beat it well. Brush both sides with oil or fat and season with salt and pepper. Grill as for grilled beefsteak (*see* p. 213). Serve immediately with Maître d'hôtel butter and fried potatoes or other accompaniments if preferred.

TOAD-IN-THE-HOLE

$\frac{3}{4}$–1 lb. chuck steak	**Salt and pepper**
$\frac{3}{4}$ pt. batter	**A good gravy**
$\frac{3}{4}$ oz. dripping	

Method 1. Remove any excess fat from the meat and cut the meat into small pieces. Heat the dripping in a flat baking-tin until just smoking, pour in $\frac{1}{4}$ of the batter and bake until set. Add the chopped meat and season well. Pour in the remainder of the batter and put in a hot oven (**450° F., Gas 8**) until it has risen well. Then reduce heat and cook more slowly until ready. Serve with a good gravy.

Method 2. Prepare the meat and batter as above. Heat the dripping in a flat baking-tin and heat until just smoking. Add the chopped seasoned meat and cook in the oven for 5 min. Then pour in all the batter and bake as above for about 1 hr. Serve with a good gravy.

6 helpings

TOURNEDOS OF BEEF À LA BÉCHAMEL

$1\frac{1}{2}$–2 lb. fillet of beef	**$\frac{1}{2}$ pt. Béchamel sauce (p. 128)**
Salt and pepper	**Mashed potatoes**
Butter *or* fat	**$\frac{1}{4}$ pt. demi-glace sauce**

Trim the fillet of beef into rounds (tournedos) about 2 in. in diameter and 1 in. thick and season with salt and pepper. Grill or fry in hot fat. Cover one side of the tournedos with thick Béchamel sauce, arrange on a bed of mashed potatoes and pour a little demi-glace sauce around.

If liked, the tournedos can be served on croûtes of fried bread. Brush over with meat glaze, arrange in a circle on a hot dish. Place a heap of cooked small potatoes in the centre and sprinkle the potatoes with parsley. Pour a little Béchamel sauce round and serve the rest separately.

6 helpings

TOURNEDOS OF BEEF À LA COLBERT

Tournedos à la Colbert

$1\frac{1}{2}$–2 lb. fillet of beef	**Mashed potatoes**
2 tablesp. salad oil	**Croûtons of fried bread**

ESCHALOT SAUCE

6 shallots	**$\frac{1}{2}$ teasp. finely-chopped parsley**
1 oz. butter	**$\frac{1}{2}$ teasp. lemon juice**
$\frac{1}{2}$ pt. good gravy *or* demi-glace sauce	**Salt and pepper**
1 glass sherry (optional)	

Cut the tournedos a little smaller and thinner than directed in the preceding recipe. Chop the shallots finely, melt the fat in a sauté pan, fry them lightly, then drain well. Cool the fat slightly and strain. To the gravy or demi-glace sauce add the sherry (if used), parsley, lemon juice, well-drained shallots and seasoning. Boil well until reduced, season to taste and keep hot. Add the salad oil to the strained fat in the sauté pan, heat and fry the tournedos quickly until nicely browned. At the same time fry some small slices of potato. Arrange the tournedos in a circle on a border of mashed potatoes, and put the fried slices of potato in the centre. Garnish with the croûtons of fried bread, pour a little sauce round and serve the rest separately.

6 helpings **Cooking time—about 20 min.**

TOURNEDOS OF BEEF À LA SICILIENNE

Tournedos de Bœuf à la Sicilienne

1½–2 lb. fillet of beef
Salt and pepper
1 heaped tablesp. shredded onion
Butter *or* fat
¾ pt. brown *or* Espagnole sauce
1 glass Madeira (optional)
Cayenne pepper
Mashed potatoes

Prepare the tournedos as directed for Tournedos à la Béchamel (p. 219). Fry the shredded onion in a little butter, drain well and mix with the sauce. Add the Madeira (if used) to the sauce and the cayenne, season to taste and keep hot. Grill or fry the tournedos for 5–8 min. Arrange in a close row on a foundation of mashed potatoes. Pour a little sauce round and serve the rest separately. Garnish with vegetables in season.

6 helpings

STEWS AND OFFAL DISHES

BROWN STEW

Ragoût brun

1½ lb. neck of beef
Vinegar
2 carrots
1 turnip
2 onions
1½ oz. dripping
1½ oz. flour
1½ pt. stock *or* water
Salt and pepper

Wipe the meat and trim off any skin and superfluous fat. Cut the meat into pieces suitable for serving and place in a dish with the vinegar. Leave for about 1 hr., turning 2 or 3 times; then drain well and dry. Cut the carrots and turnip into dice or Julienne strips for garnishing and keep the trimmings. Slice the onions. Heat the fat in a saucepan and fry the meat quickly until lightly browned then remove from the pan. Fry the sliced onion until lightly browned; add the flour and cook slowly, mixing well, until a good brown colour. Add the water or stock and bring to the boil stirring all the time. Replace the meat, add the vegetable trimmings and seasoning, cover with a lid and simmer gently for about 2½ hr. or until the meat is tender. Before serving, cook the diced carrots and turnip separately. Arrange the meat in the centre of a hot dish and pour the gravy over. Garnish with the drained, diced vegetables.

6 helpings

EXETER STEW

1½ lb. lean beef
1½ oz. dripping
3 medium-sized onions
1½ oz. flour
1 teasp. vinegar
Salt and pepper

SAVOURY BALLS

4 oz. flour
¼ teasp. baking-powder
1½ oz. finely-chopped suet
1 tablesp. finely-chopped parsley
½ teasp. mixed herbs
1 teasp. salt
½ teasp. pepper
Egg *or* milk

Wipe the meat and remove all the fat. Cut the meat into pieces about 2 in. by 2½ in. Heat the fat in a stewpan until smoking hot and fry the meat until brown. Remove the meat and fry the sliced onions. Then add the flour and cook, stirring until brown. Add 1¼ pt. water and bring to the boil, stirring constantly. Simmer for a few minutes. Add the vinegar and seasoning, return the meat and simmer gently for about 2 hr. Mix the ingredients for the savoury balls together, bind with the egg or milk into a stiff mixture and make into 12 balls. Bring the stew to boiling-point about 30 min. before time for serving and drop in the balls. Simmer for the remainder of the time. Pile the meat in the centre of a hot dish, pour the gravy over and arrange the balls neatly round the base.

6 helpings

GOULASH OF BEEF

Goulash de Bœuf

1½ lb. lean beef	**2 tomatoes**
2 oz. dripping	**Salt**
2 onions	**Paprika**
1½ oz. flour	**Bouquet garni**
1 pt. stock	**6 diced potatoes**
¼ pt. red wine (optional)	**2 tablesp. sour cream (optional)**

Wipe and trim the meat, removing any skin and fat. Cut into neat pieces. Heat the fat and sauté the sliced onions with the meat, until the meat is evenly browned. Add the flour and stir until brown. Then add the stock, wine, skinned and diced tomatoes, salt, paprika, and bouquet garni. Stir, bring to the boil. If liked, transfer to a casserole and cook slowly for 1½–2 hr. in the oven, stirring occasionally, or continue cooking in saucepan for the same time. Add the diced potatoes about ½ hr. before the Goulash is ready. They should be cooked but not broken. If liked, 2 tablesp. sour cream may be stirred in before serving.

6 helpings

LEG OF BEEF STEW

Ragoût de Jarret de Bœuf

1½ lb. leg *or* shin of beef	**2 small onions**
	2 small carrots
2 tablesp. vinegar	**1 small turnip**
Bouquet garni	**Salt and pepper**

Wipe and bone the meat and cut into neat pieces. Remove any fat and skin. Put the meat into a casserole with the vinegar and leave for about 1 hr., turning 2 or 3 times. Add the bouquet garni, vegetables, seasoning, about 1 pt. water and bones. Cover closely and stew in a warm oven (**335° F., Gas 3**) for 2½–3 hr. When tender remove bones and bouquet garni and serve hot with freshly cooked vegetables.

6 helpings

SEA PIE

Pâté de Viande salée et de Légumes

1½ lb. stewing steak	**Hot stock *or* water**
Seasoned flour	**Suet pastry**
1 large onion	**using 8–12 oz. flour,**
1 carrot	**etc.**
1 small turnip	

Cut the steak into thin slices about 2 in. square. Dip the meat in the seasoned flour. Cut the prepared vegetables into thin slices or dice and place in a stewpan with the meat and cover with the hot stock or water. Simmer very gently for about 1½ hr. Roll out the suet pastry to a round a little less than the top of the stewpan and place on top of the stew. Continue cooking for 1 hr. Garnish with chopped parsley.

6 helpings

BEEF SAUSAGES

Saucisses de Bœuf

2 lb. lean beef	**Salt and pepper**
1 lb. beef suet	**Sausage skins**
¼ teasp. powdered allspice	**Fat for frying**

Mince the beef and grate the suet finely or use shredded suet. Add the allspice, salt and pepper to taste and mix well. Press the mixture lightly into the prepared skins and prick well with a fork. Fry in hot fat until well browned and cooked. If preferred the mixture may be shaped into small cakes and floured before being fried.

BULLOCK'S HEART— STUFFED AND BAKED

Cœur de Bœuf—farci et cuit au Four

1 bullock's heart	**1 oz. flour**
Veal forcemeat *or* sage and onion stuffing	**1 pt. stock *or* vegetable water**
	Redcurrant jelly *or* apple sauce
2–3 oz. dripping	

Wash the heart thoroughly under running water or in several changes of cold water. Cut off the flaps and lobes and remove all pieces of gristle. Cut away the membrane which separates the cavities inside the heart and see that it is quite free from blood. Soak for at least ½ hr. Drain and dry the heart thoroughly and stuff with the forcemeat or stuffing. Sew up the ends with fine string and place in a baking-tin with smoking hot dripping. Baste well and cook in a warm to moderate oven (**335°–350° F., Gas 3–4**) for 3 hr. Baste frequently and turn occasionally. When tender remove the string, place the heart on a hot dish and keep hot. Pour away most of the fat retaining about 1 tablesp. of the sediment. Add 1 oz. flour and stir and cook until brown. Add 1 pt. of stock or vegetable water, gradually at first, blend well and stir until boiling. Boil for 4 min. Pour a little round the heart and serve the rest separately. Serve red-currant jelly with the heart if it is stuffed with veal forcemeat and apple sauce if sage and onion stuffing is used.

6 helpings

Cow Heel

BOILED COW HEEL

Pied de Bœuf, Bouilli

2 cow heels	**1 dessertsp. finely-chopped parsley**
Stock *or* **water**	**Salt and pepper**
1 oz. butter *or* **fat**	
1 oz. flour	

Wash and blanch the heels. Put in a saucepan and cover with cold water or stock and simmer very gently for about 3 hr. Melt the fat in a saucepan, add the flour and cook without colouring. Add 1 pt. of the stock in which the cow heels were cooked, stir well until boiling, simmer for 5 min., add parsley and seasoning to taste. Remove the bones from the meat and arrange the pieces of meat on a hot dish. Pour the sauce over and serve hot.

6 helpings

FRIED COW HEEL

Pied de Bœuf frit

2 cow heels	**Finely-grated rind of ½ lemon**
1½ tablesp. seasoned flour	**Milk if necessary**
1 egg	**Breadcrumbs**
1 teasp. finely-chopped parsley	**Deep fat**
	Fried *or* **fresh parsley**

Wash and blanch the heels, and simmer gently in stock or water until the bones can easily be separated from the meat—about 3 hr. Remove the bones and press the meat between 2 plates until cold. Then cut into pieces about 1½ in. square. Dip the pieces into the seasoned flour. Beat the egg and add to it the finely-chopped parsley. and lemon rind. Add a little milk if mixture is too dry. Coat the pieces of meat thickly with the egg mixture and toss in breadcrumbs. Fry in hot, deep fat until golden brown. Serve hot, garnished with parsley.

6 helpings

Ox Kidney

KIDNEY HOT POT

Ragoût de Rognons à l'Anglaise

1 lb. ox kidney	**Salt and pepper**
¼ lb. lean bacon rashers	**Stock**
2 large onions	**1½ lb. potatoes**
3 tomatoes	**Bacon fat**
3 oz. mushrooms	**Parsley**

Soak the kidney in tepid salt water for 15 min. Wash well, skin if necessary, remove the core and any fat and cut the kidney into slices about ¼ in. thick. Cut the bacon into pieces and the onions, tomatoes and mushrooms into slices. Put alternate slices of kidney, bacon, onion, tomatoes and mushrooms in a casserole, seasoning each layer. Three-quarters fill the casserole with stock and cover the top with a thick layer of sliced potatoes. Place some bacon rinds on top. Cover and cook in a moderate oven **(350° F., Gas 4)** for 2½ hr. Remove the lid and bacon rinds ½ hr. before serving. Dot the top with small pieces of bacon fat and allow the potatoes to brown. Sprinkle with finely-chopped parsley.

6 helpings

KIDNEY WITH ITALIAN SAUCE

Rognon de Bœuf à l'Italienne

1½ lb. ox kidney	**1 pt. stock**
2 oz. seasoned flour	**12 mushrooms**
2 oz. beef dripping	**2 tablesp. sherry (optional)**
1 small onion	**Salt and pepper**
1½ oz. butter *or* **fat**	

Prepare the kidney as directed in the preceding recipe, cutting into ½-in. slices. Coat the kidney well with seasoned flour. Heat the dripping in a sauté pan and fry the kidney quickly on both sides and then more slowly for 20 min. Finely chop the onion, fry, at the same time keeping the sauté pan covered. In a stewpan, melt the fat and add the rest of the flour and cook (stirring) until a nut brown colour. Add the stock, gradually at first, stir until it boils then simmer for 5 min. Drain the kidney from the fat, place in the sauce and simmer for about $\frac{3}{4}$ hr. Add the sliced mushrooms, sherry (if used), extra seasoning if liked, and simmer for a further 15 min. Serve hot garnished with green peas.

6 helpings

STEWED KIDNEY

Ragoût de Rognons

1½ lb. ox kidney
2 oz. seasoned flour
2 oz. dripping
1 onion
1½ pt. water *or* stock
3 teasp. tomato *or* mushroom ketchup
Border of rice *or* mashed potatoes
Green peas

Prepare the kidney as directed for Kidney Hot Pot. Coat the slices of kidney with seasoned flour. Heat the dripping in a stewpan and fry the kidney until browned on both sides. Chop the onion finely and fry at the same time until lightly browned. Stir in any remaining flour and brown. Add the stock and ketchup and stir until boiling. Cover with a lid and simmer very gently for about 1½–2 hr. If cooked too quickly the kidney will become tough. When ready re-season if necessary and serve on a hot dish with a border of rice or mashed potato. Garnish with green peas.

6 helpings

Ox Liver

LIVER HOT POT

1¼ lb. ox liver
1 oz. seasoned flour
4 oz. bacon rashers
3 large onions
2 lb. potatoes
1½ teasp. powdered sage
Salt and pepper
Stock *or* water
Chopped parsley

Prepare the liver by washing thoroughly in tepid water and removing any tubes. Dry well, cut into slices $\frac{1}{4}$ in. thick and toss in the seasoned flour. Cut the bacon in pieces, slice the onions thinly, slice the potatoes. Place alternate layers of liver, bacon, onions and potatoes in a pie-dish or casserole and sprinkle with sage and seasoning. Add enough stock to barely cover the contents and place a thick layer of sliced potato on top. Cover with a lid and cook in a moderate oven **(350° F., Gas 4)** for about 2 hr. Remove the lid $\frac{1}{2}$ hr. before serving, place small pieces of dripping on top and allow the potatoes to brown. Sprinkle with chopped parsley.

6 helpings

LIVER SAVOURY

Foie de Bœuf à la Française

1½ lb. ox liver
Flour
Veal forcemeat
¼ lb. thin bacon rashers
Stock
1 oz. flour
Salt and pepper

Wash the liver thoroughly in tepid water, cut out any tubes and dry thoroughly. Cut into slices about $\frac{1}{4}$ in. thick and coat lightly with flour. Spread each slice with a thin layer of forcemeat and cover with bacon. Put into a large baking-tin, cover with a slice of bacon and pour in stock to $\frac{1}{2}$ cover the liver. Cover with a greased paper and cook in a moderate oven **(350° F., Gas 4)** for about 1½–2 hr. Add more stock as necessary. Arrange the liver on a hot dish and keep hot. Mix the 1 oz. flour to a smooth paste with a little cold stock, add $\frac{1}{4}$ pt. boiling stock or water, pour into the tin and boil up. If too thick, add more stock or water, season if necessary and strain round the liver.

6 helpings

ROAST LIVER

Foie de Bœuf rôtie

1–1½ lb. ox liver
¼ lb. fat bacon
Stock *or* water
Seasoned flour
Parsley

Wash the liver in tepid salt water, remove any skin and tubes and cut the liver in slices. Place in a deep baking-tin or dish. Lay the rashers of bacon on top and add enough stock or water to $\frac{1}{2}$ cover the liver. Bake gently for 1½–2 hr., basting well and dredging frequently with seasoned flour. Dish neatly and strain the gravy round. Garnish with parsley.

NOTE: The bacon may be cut into dice and served as a garnish, in which case it must be kept covered with 2–3 thicknesses of greaseproof paper while cooking, or it will become too crisp.

Marrow

MARROW BONES

Marrow bones (allow ½ lb. per person)
Flour
Dry toast

Scrape and wash the bones and saw in half across (your butcher will saw them for you).

Make a stiff paste of flour and water and roll it out. Cover the ends of the bones with a piece of paste to seal in the marrow and tie in a floured cloth. Stand the bones upright in a pan of boiling salt water and simmer slowly for about 2 hr. Refill the pan with boiling water if necessary. Remove the cloth and paste from each bone. Fasten a paper serviette round each one and serve with dry toast.

MARROW CROUSTADES

Beef marrow (allow 1/2 lb. per person)	**Thick brown sauce**
Baked pastry cases	**Parsley**
	Paprika

Cut the marrow into small pieces and tie in muslin. Drop into boiling water and leave for 10–15 min. Remove, drain well, remove muslin and allow to become cold. Cut marrow into small pieces, place in the pastry cases, cover with a little brown sauce, add more marrow then more brown sauce. Put in the oven for a short time to heat thoroughly and sprinkle with finely-chopped parsley and paprika pepper. Serve at once.

Ox Cheek

STEWED OX CHEEK *Tête de Bœuf en ragoût*

1 boned ox cheek	**Salt and pepper**
2 onions	**1 1/4 oz. butter *or* fat**
2 carrots	**1 1/4 oz. flour**
1 turnip	**1/2 gill sherry (optional)**
12 peppercorns	**2 teasp. lemon juice**
2 cloves	
Bouquet garni	

Wash the ox cheek well in cold water. Soak for at least 12 hr. in salted water, changing the water 2 or 3 times. Then wash well in warm water, cut into convenient sized pieces, put into a saucepan and cover with cold water. Bring to the boil and skim well. Add the thickly sliced vegetables, peppercorns, cloves, bouquet garni and salt. Simmer very gently for 1½–2 hr., or until tender, keeping the meat just covered with liquid the whole time. Have ready a brown roux made by cooking the fat and flour together until nut brown. Add to this 1¼ pt. strained liquor from the pan, stir until it boils and simmer for at least 10 min. Add the sherry (if used), lemon juice and season to taste. Put in the pieces of meat and when hot serve on a hot dish. Garnish with dice or Julienne strips of carrot and turnip, which have been cooked separately, or with spinach. The rest of the liquor makes excellent soup.

6 helpings

STUFFED OX CHEEK *Tête de Bœuf farcie*

1 cooked ox cheek	**Egg and browned breadcrumbs**
4–6 oz. veal forcemeat	**Fat for basting**

Prepare and cook the cheek as for Stewed Ox Cheek. When the bones—if left in—can be easily separated from the meat, or when the meat is tender, remove the cheek from the pan. Spread 4–6 oz. veal forcemeat over the cheek, roll up tightly and tie securely with string. Coat thickly with egg and browned breadcrumbs and bake in a moderate oven (**350° F., Gas 4**) for ¾ hr., basting frequently. Serve with a gravy made from the liquid in which the cheek was cooked.

6 helpings

Ox Tail

GRILLED OX TAIL *Queues de Bœuf grillées*

2 ox tails	**Oil *or* butter**
1 1/2 pt. well-flavoured stock	**Parsley**
Egg and breadcrumbs	**1/2 pt. piquant sauce *or* good gravy**

Wash and dry the tails and divide them at the joints. Put into a saucepan with the stock which must be well flavoured, otherwise vegetables and herbs must be added. Simmer gently for 2½ hr., and when tender drain well and put aside until cold. Coat carefully with egg and breadcrumbs, brush with melted butter or oil and grill until brown. Place on a hot dish and garnish with the parsley. Serve with piquant sauce or a good gravy.

6 helpings

STEWED OX TAIL *Queues de Bœuf en Ragoût*

2 small ox tails	**Salt and pepper**
2 oz. fat	**Bouquet garni**
2 onions	**Cloves to taste**
1 1/2 oz. flour	**Mace to taste**
1 1/2 pt. stock *or* water	**Juice of 1/2 lemon**

PLATE 9

Deep Frying

1 Melt enough fat in a deep pan over moderate heat to come half-way up pan. Check correct temp. is 360°F.

2 Quarter fill the basket with (*dried*) *chipped potatoes and lower gently into hot fat. Fry for approx. 3 min.*

3 Remove basket and re-heat fat for a few minutes to higher temp. of 375°F. Replace potatoes and cook until crisp and golden brown.

4 Drain well on crumpled kitchen paper and sprinkle them with salt.

5 Serve at once whilst very hot.

6 Cool fat; strain into clean basin, keep covered for further use. Wipe pan whilst warm with damp cloth; wash as well if preferred.

1

2

3

4

5

6

PLATE 10

Making Short Crust Pastry

1

2

1 Ensure all utensils are cold. Sift flour and salt into a bowl.

2 With a sharp knife cut, or use a grater to shred in the fat.

3 Rub in the fat with the finger tips until the mixture looks like fine breadcrumbs. Lift the hands up from the bowl so that the air is entrapped as the flour falls back into the bowl.

3

4

5

4 Using a knife, mix to a stiff dough with only the necessary amount of freshly-drawn cold water.

5 Gather the mixture together leaving the bowl clean. Dough should feel damp but not sticky.

6 On a floured surface, press the dough lightly with the fingers into rough shape required.

6

Wash the tails, dry well and remove any superfluous fat. Cut into joints and divide the thick parts in half. Melt the fat in a saucepan, fry the pieces of tail until brown, then remove from the pan. Slice the onions and fry them until light brown, add the flour, mix well and fry slowly until a good brown colour. Add the stock or water, salt, pepper, bouquet garni, cloves and mace and bring to boiling point, stirring all the time. Return the pieces of tail and simmer gently for about 2½–3 hr. Remove the meat and arrange on a hot dish. Add the lemon juice to the sauce, correct the seasoning, strain and pour over the meat. Garnish with croûtons of fried bread and diced or thin strips of cooked carrot and turnip.

6 helpings

Ox Tongue

BOILED TONGUE

Langue de Bœuf bouilli

1 ox tongue	**1 turnip**
1 onion	**A bunch of mixed herbs**
1 carrot	

Wash the tongue thoroughly and soak for about 2 hr. If the tongue is dry and rather hard soak for 12 hr. If pickled, soak for about 3–4 hr. Put the tongue into a large pan of cold water, bring slowly to the boil, skim and add the onion, carrot, turnip and bunch of herbs. Cook gently, allowing 30 min. per lb. and 30 min over. When ready, lift out tongue, remove the skin very carefully.

The tongue can then be garnished with tufts of cauliflower or Brussels sprouts and served hot with boiled poultry or ham.

To serve cold (1). After skin has been removed, shape tongue on a board by sticking a fork through the root and another through the top to straighten it. Leave until cold, trim and then glaze. Put a paper frill around the root and garnish with parsley. Decorate with a savoury butter if liked.

To serve cold (2). When skin has been removed put the tongue in a bowl or flat tin, curling it round tightly, cover with stock, put a saucer on top and press with a weight on top. Leave until cold, then turn out.

Tripe

FRICASSÉE OF TRIPE

1½ lb. dressed tripe	**1 oz. butter**
Milk	**1 oz. flour**
Salt and pepper	**Croûtons of toast**
2 Spanish onions	

Wash, blanch and scrape the tripe well. Cut into pieces about 2 in. square, put into a stewpan and cover with equal parts of milk and water. Add the seasoning and diced onions, bring to the boil and simmer gently for 1 hr. Knead the butter and flour smoothly together and add it in small pieces to the contents of the stewpan. Stir until smooth, then continue cooking for another ½ hr.

Serve on a hot dish and garnish with croûtons.

6 helpings

TRIPE À LA LYONNAISE

Gras-Double à la Lyonnaise

1½ lb. cold boiled tripe	**2 heaped teasp. finely-chopped parsley**
1 large onion	**3 teasp. vinegar**
3 oz. butter	**Salt and pepper**

Cut the tripe into pieces about 2 in. square and slice the onion. Heat the butter in a frying-pan and fry the onion until tender and golden brown. Add the tripe, parsley, vinegar, salt and pepper, and toss in the pan for a few minutes until thoroughly heated. Serve immediately.

6 helpings **Cooking time—about 15 min.**

TRIPE AND ONIONS

Tripes aux Oignons

1½ lb. tripe	**2 large onions**
½ pt. milk	**1 oz. flour**
1 teasp. salt	**Salt and pepper**

Blanch the tripe and cut into 3-in squares. Put in a saucepan with the milk, ½ pt. water and the salt; bring to the boil. Peel and slice the onions finely. Add them to the tripe and simmer very slowly for 2 hr. Mix the flour to a smooth paste with a little cold milk and add to the pan. Stir with a wooden spoon until boiling. Simmer for another 10 min., season to taste and serve.

6 helpings

LAMB

The colour of good quality lamb meat should be cherry red. There is a considerable difference in the colour of English and imported lamb due to the effect of freezing. Lamb fat should be creamy white. A brittle white fat is indicative of age, and an unduly yellow tinge is usually accompanied by an unpleasant "muttony" flavour.

The skeletal structure of the lamb is similar to that of the bullock and the cutting into sides and quarters follows the same pattern. See also plate 1.

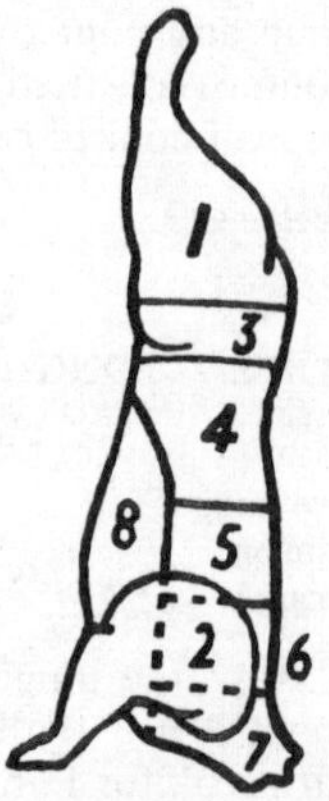

The **leg** (1), or hind limb is leaner, tougher and drier than the **shoulder** (2). It is also dearer. Both contain about the same amount of bone and both are eminently suitable for roasting.

(3) The **chump**, which is equivalent to the rump of beef, (4) the **loin** and the **best end neck** (5) are all used for chops and all equally suitable for frying and grilling. There is little to choose in tenderness, but it is generally considered that the best end provides the sweetest eating, and the loin the most tender chops.

(6) The **middle neck** and **scrag** (7) are both used for stewing, but in the case of the middle neck it is possible to cut two or three chops from the end remote from the scrag which are suitable for frying or grilling.

(8) The **breast** may be either roasted or boiled. If roasted with stuffing to which no fat has been added much of the lamb fat is absorbed, giving rise to a more palatable dish.

Three distinct types of lamb **chop** are available, chump, cut from the leg end of the loin, loin chops proper and best end neck chops. Best end chops are often served as cutlets or **noisettes.** They are prepared by removing the chine bone (back bone) and trimming away some of the meat at the rib end. Cutlets should be carefully beaten so that the meat is uniform in thickness. Best end neck may also be served as a **crown roast.** This is a double neck, i.e. the adjoining pieces from each side of the lamb cut so that it can be formed into a ring. The ends of the bones are trimmed as in the case of cutlets.

BLANQUETTE OF LAMB

Blanquette d'Agneau

2 lb. fleshy lamb-loin, neck *or* breast
Salt and pepper
1 large onion
Bouquet garni
6 peppercorns
Pinch of grated nutmeg
Stock *or* water
1½ oz. butter
1 oz. flour
1 egg yolk
2 tablesp. cream *or* milk

GARNISH

Croûtes of fried bread *or* fleurons of pastry
Button mushrooms

Cut the meat into pieces about 2 in. square and put into a stewpan with salt, sliced onion, herbs, peppercorns and nutmeg. Just cover with cold stock or water and simmer until tender—about 2 hr. When the meat is cooked, melt the butter in a saucepan and stir in the flour. Cook for a few minutes without browning. Strain ½ pt. liquor from the meat and add to the blended flour and butter. Stir until boiling then simmer for 3 min. Beat together the egg yolk and cream and add to the sauce. Stir and cook gently for a few minutes, do not allow to boil or it may curdle. Correct the seasoning. Arrange the meat on a hot dish, piling it high in the centre and strain the sauce over.

Garnish with neatly shaped croutes of fried bread or fleurons of pastry and grilled mushrooms. Serve hot.

5-6 helpings

BREAST OF LAMB—MILANAISE

Poitrine d'Agneau à la Milanaise

A breast of lamb
Salt and pepper

MIREPOIX

2 onions
2 carrots
½ turnip
½ oz. dripping
1 oz. fat bacon
Bouquet garni
Stock

MACARONI À LA MILANAISE

6 oz. macaroni
4 oz. mushrooms
2 oz. butter *or* fat
2 oz. cooked ham
2 oz. cooked tongue
1 glass white wine *or* stock
2 tablesp. tomato purée *or* sauce
1 dessertsp. flour
3 oz. grated cheese

Braise the breast of lamb as follows: bone the meat and season well with salt and pepper. Roll tightly and secure with string. Prepare the mirepoix by cutting the onions, carrots and turnip into thick pieces. Melt the dripping in a stewpan and gently fry the vegetables with the fat bacon with the lid on the pan for 10 min. Add the bouquet garni and sufficient stock to almost cover the vegetables. Bring to the boil. Place the meat on top of the mirepoix, cover with greaseproof paper and put on the lid. Cook slowly for about 2 hr. until meat is tender. Baste frequently.

While the meat is cooking prepare the macaroni à la Milanaise as follows: break the macaroni into 2-in. lengths. Cook in boiling, salted water or stock for 20 min. or until tender, then drain well. Wash and peel the mushrooms and cut into fine shreds. Put the mushrooms in a saucepan with ½ the butter and cook for a few minutes. Meanwhile cut the ham and tongue into strips and add to the mushrooms with the wine or stock and simmer for a few minutes. Now add the macaroni and tomato purée or sauce, and season carefully. Cook again until nearly dry. When ready, add the remainder of the butter mixed with the flour, this will bind the mixture together. Stir with a fork until cooked. Remove from heat and stir in the cheese. (The mixture must not boil after the cheese has been added.)

Arrange the macaroni in the centre of a hot dish and place the meat on top.

5-6 helpings
Cooking time—about 2½ hr.

CHARTREUSE À LA GASTRONOME

1 *or* 2 breasts of lamb
Ingredients for braising as for Breast of Lamb Milanaise
Lettuce stalks
Stock
Salt and pepper
½ pt. demi-glace sauce

Prepare and braise the lamb as directed for Breast of Lamb—Milanaise (above). Cook the lettuce stalks at the same time. Cut the lamb into slices and arrange alternately with layers of lettuce stalks in a cylindrical mould or basin, adding a little good stock and salt and pepper. Steam gently for 1½ hr. Unmould carefully. Serve on a hot dish with a little of the demi-glace sauce poured round. Serve the remainder in a sauce-boat.

6 helpings

DUTCH STEW

1½ lb. middle neck mutton	**½ pt. water *or* white stock**
1 oz. dripping	**Salt and pepper**
2 onions	**1 small cabbage**
	6 potatoes

Cut the meat into slices. Melt the dripping in a saucepan and fry the meat with chopped onions, stirring occasionally. Add the stock *or* water and seasoning, and simmer for 1 hr. Lift out the meat and add the shredded cabbage and the potatoes. Add more stock if needed. Place the meat on top of the vegetables and braise until the contents are tender. Serve the meat on the cabbage, with the potatoes and gravy.

6 helpings
Cooking time—about 2 hr.

EPIGRAMS OF LAMB

Épigrammes d'Agneau à la Soubise

A breast of lamb	**Salt and pepper**
2 qt. stock	**Allemande sauce (p. 133)**
1 onion	
½ turnip	**Egg and breadcrumbs**
1 carrot	**Deep fat**
Bouquet garni	**Soubise sauce**

Trim the breast of lamb, cut into 2 pieces, blanch them. Bring the stock to boiling-point, put in the meat, boil for 5 min. Add the vegetables, cut thickly, and also the bouquet garni and salt. Simmer for about 1 hr. until the meat is tender. Remove bones and press the meat between 2 dishes until cold and firm. Remove all skin and gristle and cut the meat into neat pieces for serving. Have ready the thick, nearly cold, Allemande sauce. Season the meat well with salt and pepper then completely coat with the Allemande sauce, repeat if necessary. When sauce is set and firm, dip the epigrams into beaten egg and coat with breadcrumbs. Fry quickly in deep fat until golden brown. Drain carefully. Arrange in a circle on a hot dish and serve the Soubise sauce in the centre.

6 helpings

FRICASSÉE OF LAMB

Fricassée d'Agneau

A breast of lamb	**Salt and pepper**
1 onion	**1 pt. boiling stock *or* water**
2 oz. butter *or* fat	
2 bay leaves	**1 oz. flour**
2 cloves	**1 dessertsp. roughly-chopped capers**
1 blade of mace	
6 peppercorns	

Prepare the meat and cut into 2-in. squares. Slice the onion, melt the fat, add the onion, bay leaves, cloves, mace, peppercorns, salt, pepper and meat. Cover and cook very gently for about ½ hr. stirring frequently. Add boiling stock or water and simmer for about 1½ hr. or until tender. Mix the flour smoothly with a small quantity of cold water. Gradually add to it, stirring all the time, about ½ pt. of the liquor from the saucepan. To this sauce add the meat, bring to the boil and simmer until tender. Serve on a hot dish within a border of mashed potatoes, sprinkle the capers over the meat.

4–6 helpings, depending on the quantity of meat

GRILLED LAMB CUTLETS

Côtelettes d'Agneau grillées

6–8 cutlets from the best end of neck	**Salt and pepper**
	Salad oil

Trim the cutlets to a neat uniform shape. Season with salt and pepper and brush all over with salad oil. Grill, turning 3 or 4 times for about 8 min. Cover the end of each bone with a cutlet frill. Suitable accompaniments are green peas, mashed potatoes, and a good gravy or demi-glace sauce.

6–8 helpings
Cooking time—about 10 min.

KEBABS

6 neat pieces mutton from the leg	**6 small mushrooms**
	6 small tomatoes
3 sheep's kidneys	**Oil *or* melted butter**
6 small bacon rashers	**12 bay leaves**
6 small sausages	

Trim the meat into neat even-shaped pieces. Skin the kidneys, remove the cores and cut the kidneys in halves. Soak in cold water for 5 min. Curl the bacon into rolls, prick the sausages and peel the mushrooms. Brush them all (including tomatoes) with oil or butter and thread on to 6 skewers with a bay leaf at each end. Grill for 10–15 min., turning as required. Serve on their skewers and if liked on a bed of risotto (rice cooked in stock in a casserole until stock is absorbed).

6 helpings

LAMB CHOPS WITH MUSHROOMS

Côtelettes d'Agneau aux champignons

6 lamb chops	**1 oz. flour**
1 oz. butter *or* fat	**½ pt. brown stock**
½ lb. mushrooms	**Salt and pepper**

Melt the butter *or* fat in a frying-pan. Fry the prepared chops and mushrooms, remove them as they are cooked and keep hot. This will take about 20 min. When all are removed, mix the flour with the fat and brown. Add the stock and seasoning and stir until boiling. Then replace the chops and mushrooms and heat thoroughly for about 15 min. Dish neatly. Serve with creamed potatoes and peas. Serve the gravy separately.

6 helpings
Cooking time—about 40 min.

LAMB CUTLETS AND SPINACH

Côtelettes d'Agneau aux Épinards

6–8 cutlets	**1 oz. butter *or* fat**
1 egg	**¾ pt. spinach purée**
Salt and pepper	**½ pt. gravy *or* tomato sauce**
Breadcrumbs	

Trim the cutlets. Brush them over with beaten egg, seasoned liberally with salt and pepper. Coat with breadcrumbs. Heat the fat in a frying-pan and fry the cutlets quickly until browned on both sides. Drain well and arrange in a close circle on a hot, round dish. Pile the purée in the centre and pour the sauce round.

NOTE: Peas, beans or dressed potatoes may be substituted for the spinach.

6–8 helpings **Cooking time—about 6 min.**

LAMB CUTLETS—MALMAISON STYLE

Côtelettes d'Agneau à la Malmaison

6 lamb cutlets from the best end of neck	**6 small stuffed tomatoes**
Salt and pepper	**Potatoes**
1 egg	**2 oz. butter *or* fat**
Breadcrumbs	**½ pt. demi-glace sauce**
Cooked lentils	
Cooked green peas	

Trim the cutlets to a neat uniform shape. Season with salt and pepper and coat with egg and breadcrumbs. Rub the cooked vegetables through a fine sieve, season to taste, and bind with a little egg yolk. Press into small dariole moulds and keep hot until needed. Prepare and bake the stuffed tomatoes. Cook and mash the potatoes, make into a border, brush over with egg yolk and brown in the oven. Then heat the fat in a frying-pan and fry the cutlets until lightly browned. Drain well. Arrange on the potato border. Garnish with the tomatoes and small timbales of vegetables. Serve the hot sauce separately

6 helpings

LAMB CUTLETS—RICHELIEU STYLE

Côtelettes d'Agneau à la Richelieu

6–8 lamb cutlets	**6 small stuffed tomatoes**
6 artichoke bottoms	**Mashed potatoes**
24 asparagus tips	**1 truffle**
Salt and pepper	**¼ pt. demi-glace sauce**
2½ oz. butter	

If canned artichoke bottoms are used, warm them in a little of their own liquor. Prepare and cook the asparagus tips. Then lightly season and toss them in ½ oz. of warmed butter. Prepare and bake the stuffed tomatoes. Trim the cutlets to a neat uniform shape. Heat the remaining 2 oz. butter and lightly fry the cutlets until nicely browned. Place a cutlet frill on each bone. Arrange on a border of mashed potatoes. Garnish with tomatoes. Fill the artichoke bottoms with the asparagus tips and sprinkle a little chopped truffle on each one, and place at regular intervals around the dish. Serve with the hot demi-glace sauce.

6–8 helpings

LAMB CUTLETS STEWED WITH TOMATOES

Côtelettes d'Agneau aux Tomates

6–8 lamb cutlets
4 large tomatoes
1 onion *or* shallot
1 oz. butter *or* fat
Salt and pepper
Stock *or* water (if necessary)

Trim the cutlets to a neat uniform shape. Slice the tomatoes thickly. Finely chop the onion or shallot. Heat the fat in a shallow saucepan and lightly and quickly fry the cutlets until brown on both sides. Add the onion and tomatoes and season carefully. Cover closely and cook slowly for about 1½ hr., adding a very small quantity of stock or water as needed, but if the tomatoes are juicy none will be required. When cooked, remove the cutlets and keep hot. Pass the tomatoes through a fine sieve and correct the seasoning. If more of the sauce is required, add a little stock and thicken with cornflour. Arrange the cutlets in a close circle on a hot dish and pour the sauce round.

6–8 helpings

LAMB CUTLETS WITH CUCUMBER

Côtelettes d'Agneau au Concombre

8–9 cutlets
1 large cucumber
3 oz. butter *or* margarine
Salt and pepper
Egg and breadcrumbs
Fat for frying
Mashed potatoes
¼ pt. gravy

Peel and dice the cucumber, discarding the seeds. Heat the fat in a stewpan, put in the cucumber. Season with salt and pepper, cover closely and cook very gently for nearly ½ hr. or until the pieces are tender but unbroken; drain well. Trim the cutlets into a good shape. Season both sides, dip them in beaten egg, coat with breadcrumbs and fry in hot fat in a frying-pan until lightly browned on both sides. Arrange the cutlets on a thin potato border, serve the cucumber in the centre and pour the hot gravy round.

6–7 helpings

LAMB PIE

Pâté d'Agneau

2 lb. loin, neck *or* breast of lamb
Salt and pepper
1–2 sheep's kidneys
Stock *or* water
Short crust *or* puff pastry using 6 oz. flour, etc.

Remove the fat and bones from the meat. Boil the bones for gravy. Cut the meat into neat pieces ready for serving and put in a pie-dish, sprinkling each layer with salt and pepper, and add a few thin slices of kidney. Half-fill the dish with stock or water. Cover with pastry and bake in a moderate oven (**350° F., Gas 4**) for 1½–2 hr., until the meat is tender. Strain and season the gravy made from the bones and pour into the pie just before serving.

6 helpings

LAMB SHASHLIK

1½ lb. lamb from leg *or* shoulder
1 thinly-sliced onion
¾ teasp. salt
Pinch of pepper
Juice of 1 lemon
2 tablesp. wine *or* cider
6 small tomatoes
6–9 small mushrooms
Butter *or* good dripping

Cut the meat in 1½-in. cubes, trimming off most of the fat. Place in a bowl with the sliced onion, seasoning, lemon juice and wine *or* cider. Mix well together and leave to stand overnight. When ready to cook, arrange the meat on skewers, alternating pieces of meat with a whole tomato or a mushroom. Brush with butter or dripping and grill for 15 min., turning frequently. Serve on the skewers with vegetables and potatoes or savoury rice.

6 helpings

LEG OF LAMB—FRENCH STYLE

Gigot d'Agneau à la Française

A small leg of lamb (boned)
1 carrot
1 onion
1 shallot
1 teasp. chopped parsley
1 clove of bruised garlic
Salt and pepper
2 oz. good dripping

Slice the carrot, and onion and finely chop the shallot. Mix together the parsley, shallot, garlic, salt and pepper, and then sprinkle the mixture on the inner surface of the meat. Bind into a good shape. Place in a covered baking-tin with the dripping, onion and carrot. Season well with salt and pepper. Bake for 20 min. in a fairly hot oven (**400° F., Gas 6**), then reduce heat to moderate (**350° F., Gas 4**) for the remainder of the time, allowing 20 min. per lb. and 20 min. over. For the last 10 min. remove the covering and allow the meat to brown and become crisp.

Serve on a hot dish with gravy made from the bones and the sediment in the baking tin.

6-8 helpings

NAVARIN OF LAMB

1 large breast *or* boned neck of lamb
A good pinch of sugar
1 large tablesp. flour
½ lb. skinned tomatoes
1 crushed clove of garlic
Salt and pepper
Bouquet garni
8–10 small onions
8–10 small potatoes
One A1 can peas
One A1 can small whole carrots
Chopped parsley

Cut the lamb into about 2½ oz. pieces and gently fry them in some of the fat trimmed off them. Transfer to a casserole. Pour off the fat. Sprinkle the sugar into the pan and heat until it becomes a deep gold. Work in the flour and then the chopped tomatoes (seeds discarded), then stir in enough hot water to make a sauce to cover the meat. Pour over the meat. Add the crushed garlic, a little pepper and salt and the bouquet garni. Cover, cook for 1½ hr. first in a moderate oven (**350° F., Gas 4**) reducing to **310° F., Gas 2** after ½ hr. Remove bouquet garni; add the onions and potatoes, turn up the heat to **350° F., Gas 4** and cook for a further ½–¾ hr. Add the drained peas and carrots and heat through. Sprinkle with parsley and serve.

NOISETTES OF LAMB

These are the neatly trimmed round or oval shaped pieces cut from the fleshy part of the loin of lamb. They may be cooked in the same way as cutlets but are not usually coated with egg and crumbs.

NOISETTES À LA JARDINIÈRE

Prepare the noisettes as above and place on a bed of mashed potatoes. Garnish attractively with vegetables to choice and pour a good brown gravy around the noisettes.

6 helpings

NOISETTES À L'UNION

A loin of lamb with 6 bones
1 doz. mushrooms
2½ oz. butter *or* fat
6 artichoke bottoms
¼ pt. stock
Juice of ½ lemon
1 teasp. finely-chopped parsley
¼ teasp. chopped chervil
¼ teasp. chopped chives
¼ teasp. chopped tarragon
1 teasp. meat extract
Salt and pepper
½ pt. demi-glace sauce

Remove the fillet from the loin and divide into 6 round slices—they should be entirely free from fat. Prepare and chop the mushrooms, then fry lightly in 1 oz. of the fat. Warm the artichoke bottoms in the stock. To the mushrooms add the lemon juice, parsley, herbs and meat extract, and season to taste. Fill the artichokes with this mixture and keep warm. Heat the remainder of the fat in the frying-pan and fry the noisettes quickly but carefully until light brown. Arrange neatly on a hot dish, place an artichoke bottom on each one. Pour some of the demi-glace sauce round and serve the rest separately. Serve hot.

SPANISH CUTLETS

Côtelettes à l'Espagnole

6 lamb cutlets
1 oz. dripping
Salt and pepper
2 bacon rashers
2 medium-sized onions, sliced
1 lb. tomatoes
12 chipolata sausages

Trim the cutlets to an even size and shape. Melt the dripping in a frying-pan and fry the cutlets quickly until brown. Place in a casserole and season with salt and pepper. Cut the bacon into neat dice and fry in the same pan. Remove it and fry the onions until tender and just brown. Then add the skinned and sliced tomatoes and cook together for 5 min. Add the bacon, onions and tomatoes to the casserole after correcting the seasoning. Cover the casserole and cook for ½ hr. in a moderate oven (**350° F., Gas 4**). Cook the sausages separately and serve with the meat and tomatoes.

Serve with baked or mashed potatoes.

6 helpings

LAMB

STEWED LAMB

Ragoût d'Agneau

1½–2 lb. loin, neck *or* breast	**2 sprigs of mint**
1 oz. dripping	**Stock *or* water**
A few young carrots	**Peas**
1 onion	**1 oz. flour**
Bouquet garni (parsley, thyme, bay leaf, 6 pepper-corns)	**Salt and pepper**

Trim the meat and cut into portions suitable for serving. Heat the dripping in a stewpan and put in the meat, diced vegetables, and the bouquet garni and mint tied in muslin. Cover closely and cook very gently for 10 min., stirring occasionally. Add stock or water just to cover the meat, cover closely and simmer gently until tender (about 2 hr.). About ½ hr. before cooked, add the peas a few at a time so that the temperature is not much reduced. Blend the flour to a smooth paste with a little cold water, add some of the hot liquid from the pan and stir well. Return to the stewpan and stir until boiling. When cooked, remove the herbs, season to taste and serve hot.

6 helpings

Lamb's Fry

LAMB'S FRY

1½ lb. lamb's fry	**2 tablesp. cooked macaroni**
1 small onion	**3 oz. butter *or* fat**
1 small carrot	**1 oz. flour**
Bouquet garni	**1 teasp. finely-chopped parsley**
Salt and pepper	**6 thin bacon rashers**
1 teasp. lemon juice	
Egg and breadcrumbs	

Wash the fry, put into a saucepan with the thinly-sliced onion and carrot, bouquet garni and cold water to cover. Simmer slowly for about 1 hr. Put the meat and gravy into a basin and when cold strain off the gravy and divide the meat into 2 portions. Cut half in thin slices and season with salt and pepper, sprinkle over the lemon juice, coat with egg and breadcrumbs and put aside. Dice the rest of the meat and cut the macaroni into small pieces. Melt 1 oz. fat in the saucepan, stir in the flour, cook for 3 min., then pour in about ½ pt. of the strained liquid. Stir until boiling. Season to taste and add diced meat, macaroni and parsley. Cover and keep hot without boiling. Form the bacon into rolls, fix on skewers and grill or bake until crisp. Heat the remaining 2 oz. fat in a frying-pan and cook the coated slices of fry quickly on both sides until brown. Drain well. The contents of the saucepan should be piled in the centre of a dish. Arrange the fried slices of meat round the base and garnish with bacon.

6 helpings

Lamb's Head

LAMB'S HEAD

A lamb's head	**2 oz. butter**
Salt and pepper	**2 oz. flour**
1 large onion	**¼ pt. milk**
2 carrots	**2 teasp. chopped parsley**
1 turnip	
Bouquet garni	**Croûtes of fried bread**

Split the head and remove the brains. Soak the head in cold salt water for 30 min. Scrape the bones from the nostrils and brush the teeth. Blanch the head. Place the head in a stewpan and cover with cold water and salt and pepper. When it boils skim well. Prepare and dice the vegetables, add to the stewpan with the bouquet garni and cook 3 hr. until meat is tender. Take out the head and remove ali the flesh, which should be cut into neat slices. Skin and slice the tongue neatly. Make a sauce with the butter flour, milk and ¾ pt. of the liquor from the stewpan which has been strained and well skimmed. Add the tongue and meat, season and reheat without boiling. Serve on a hot dish sprinkled with parsley and garnished with croûtes.

NOTE: The liquor may be served as broth, and the brains cooked and served as brain cakes or brains on toast.

5 helpings

Lambs' Tails

LAMBS' TAILS WITH POTATOES

4 lambs' tails	**Salt**
1 carrot	**A few bacon rashers**
1 onion	**Stock**
Bouquet garni (parsley, thyme, bay leaf, 8 peppercorns)	**Mashed potatoes**
	½ pt. tomato *or* brown sauce

Blanch and dry the tails. Slice the onion and carrot and place with the bouquet garni in a stewpan, add salt and lay the tails on the top. Cover with bacon. Add stock to nearly cover the vegetables. Cover with greaseproof paper and a close-fitting lid. Cook for about 2 hr. until meat is tender, adding a little more stock as needed. Serve on a bed of mashed potatoes with tomato sauce or brown sauce poured over.

6 helpings

Lambs' Liver

STUFFED LIVER

Foie d'Agneau farci

¾ lb. lamb's liver	**Browned breadcrumbs**
Seasoned flour	**Parsley**
4–6 oz. bacon	**1 teasp. Worcester sauce**
½ pt. stock	

STUFFING

3 oz. breadcrumbs	**2 teasp. finely-chopped onion**
3 teasp. chopped parsley	**Salt and pepper**

Wash the slices of liver, dry, and dip in the seasoned flour. Place in a greased meat-tin or fireproof dish. Mix all the ingredients for the stuffing and spread some on each slice of liver. Arrange pieces of bacon to cover the stuffing. Pour in the stock carefully, cover and cook in a moderate oven (**350° F., Gas 4**) for $\frac{1}{2}$–$\frac{3}{4}$ hr., depending on the thickness of the liver. Serve the slices sprinkled with some browned breadcrumbs and a little chopped parsley. Boil up the stock with a little thickening and add the Worcester sauce. Pour a little round the liver and serve the rest separately.

6 helpings

Lambs' Sweetbreads

CROUSTADES OF LAMBS' SWEETBREADS

Ris d'Agneau en Croustade

1½ lb. lambs' sweetbreads	**8–9 baked rough puff *or* puff pastry cases**
1 oz. butter *or* fat	**½ pt. Béchamel sauce**
Stock	
Salt and pepper	

Soak and blanch the sweetbreads. Drain and dry them. Melt the fat in a saucepan and toss the sweetbreads lightly in it, then just cover with stock. Season to taste and cook gently for about 1 hr. until tender. Drain and dry well. Fill the pastry cases with sweetbread, cover with the Béchamel sauce.

8–9 helpings

FRIED SWEETBREADS

Ris d'Agneau frit

1½ lb. lambs' sweetbreads	**Butter *or* fat**
Seasoned flour	**½ pt. good brown gravy *or* tomato sauce**
Egg and breadcrumbs	

Prepare the sweetbreads as follows: wash and soak in cold water for 1–2 hr. until free from blood. Put into a pan, cover with cold water, bring to boil and simmer for 3–5 min. then plunge into cold water. Discard fat and skin and any gristle. Press between 2 dishes until cold. Roll in seasoned flour and coat with egg and breadcrumbs. Fry in hot fat until golden brown. Serve the sauce or gravy separately.

6 helpings

Cooking time – to fry about 8 min.

SWEETBREADS—VOLTAIRE STYLE

Ris d'Agneau à la Voltaire

1 lb. lambs' sweetbreads	**Meat glaze**
1 carrot	**2 tablesp. Béchamel sauce**
1 onion	**2 egg yolks**
2 bacon rashers	**6 artichoke bottoms**
Bouquet garni	**1 oz. grated Parmesan cheese**
½ pt. good stock	
Salt and pepper	**1 oz. butter *or* fat**

Soak the sweetbreads for 2 hr., then blanch and drain them well. Put the sliced carrot, onion and bacon and bouquet garni on the bottom of a pan and $\frac{3}{4}$ cover with stock. Add salt and pepper to taste. Place the sweetbreads on top and cover with buttered paper and tightly fitting lid. Put in a moderate oven (**350° F., Gas 4**) and cook for 30–40 min., basting frequently and adding more stock if needed. When cooked, brush the sweetbreads with warm glaze and keep hot. Strain the stock into a small pan and skim well. Mix the Béchamel sauce and egg yolks together and add to the strained stock, stirring well until it thickens. Pass through a tammy cloth or nylon sieve. Drain the artichokes well after cooking, or from the liquor in which they were canned, and place in a well-greased sauté pan. In each put 1 teasp. of the prepared sauce, lay the sweetbread on top, cover with sauce and sprinkle cheese on top. Melt the remainder of the fat, pour a little on each sweetbread. Bake for 5–6 min. in a hot oven. Dish neatly and serve hot with a suitable sauce.

NOTE: For other methods of cooking lambs' sweetbreads see recipes for sweetbreads in Veal Section.

6 helpings

MUTTON

BOILED BREAST OF MUTTON

Poitrine de Mouton

A breast of mutton
2 tablesp. breadcrumbs
1 tablesp. finely-chopped suet
1 dessertsp. chopped parsley
½ teasp. mixed herbs
Salt and pepper
A little milk
Stock *or* water with vegetables, 10 peppercorns, and salt

Remove all the bones and surplus fat; flatten the meat and season well. Make the stuffing by mixing the breadcrumbs, suet, parsley, herbs, salt and pepper together. Moisten with milk. Spread the mixture on the meat, roll up lightly and bind securely with string. Put into the boiling stock or water and vegetables, and simmer for 2–3 hr., according to size.

Pour caper sauce over the meat, if liked.

NOTE: Leg and neck of mutton can be cooked in the same way.

6–8 helpings

BOILED KNUCKLE OF MUTTON

Jarret de Mouton bouilli

A knuckle of mutton
1 onion
1 carrot
¼ turnip
Good stock *or* water
Salt
Bouquet garni
8 peppercorns

Prepare the vegetables and meat. Place the meat in the stock or water with the salt, sliced vegetables, and the flavourings tied in muslin. Simmer very gently until tender–about 1¾ hr. Remove the flavourings, serve the vegetables with the meat. If liked, the stock in which the mutton is cooked may be used for making onion sauce to be served with the dish.

2–3 helpings

BONED AND STUFFED LEG OF MUTTON

Gigot de Mouton farci

A small leg of mutton, boned
2 oz. ham *or* bacon
2 shallots
4 tablesp. breadcrumbs
2 tablesp. finely-chopped suet
1 teasp. chopped parsley
½ teasp. powdered mixed herbs
½ teasp. grated lemon rind
1 saltsp. grated nutmeg
Salt and pepper
1 egg
A little milk
Brown sauce *or* gravy

Finely chop the ham or bacon and shallots, and mix well together with the breadcrumbs, suet, parsley, mixed herbs, grated lemon rind and nutmeg. Season to taste. Moisten with beaten egg and a little milk to bind the mixture lightly together. Press the mixture into the cavity left by removing the bone and secure in a neat shape with string. Roast in a moderate oven (**350° F., Gas 4**); allow 25 min. per lb. and 25 min. over. Serve with brown sauce.

BRAISED LEG OF MUTTON

Gigot de Mouton braisé

A small leg of mutton
2 onions
1 turnip
2 carrots
1 oz. dripping
Stock
Bouquet garni
10 peppercorns
2 shallots
1½ oz. butter
1½ oz. flour
Salt and pepper

Thickly slice the onions, turnip and carrots. Melt the dripping in a saucepan and sweat the sliced vegetables in it with the lid on, over a gentle heat for 5–10 min. Almost cover with stock or water, add the bouquet garni and peppercorns. Place the prepared meat on top, put a piece of greased greaseproof paper on top of the pan and cover with a good-fitting lid. Cook gently for 3–3½ hr., basting occasionally with the stock and adding more stock if necessary. About ½ hr. before serving, chop the shallots very finely, melt the butter and fry the shallots lightly. Then add the flour and cook until a good brown colour. Keep the meat hot, strain the stock and make up to 1 pt. Add the stock to the browned flour and butter and stir until boiling. Season to taste and pour a little over the meat. Serve the remainder in a sauce-boat.

Cooked tomatoes, mushrooms, diced turnips and carrots, peas, timbales of spinach or green pea purée are all suitable garnishes for this dish.

If preferred, the leg may be boned and the cavity filled with a forcemeat made as follows: equal quantities of ham and trimmings from the leg finely chopped, finely-chopped onion and a little garlic if liked. Allow an extra ½ hr. for cooking.

8–12 helpings

BRAISED MUTTON CUTLETS

Côtelettes de Mouton braisées

6 cutlets from the best end of neck
Larding bacon
1 onion
1 carrot
½ turnip
2 sticks of celery
Bouquet garni
1½ oz. dripping
½ pt. stock
Salt and pepper
Meat glaze

Trim and flatten the cutlets. Insert about 5 strips of larding bacon into the lean part of each cutlet. Thickly slice the vegetables and lightly fry them with the bouquet garni in the dripping. Then add stock to ¾ cover them; season to taste. Lay the cutlets on top, cover with greased paper and a good fitting lid. Cook gently for about 50 min. adding more stock as necessary. When cooked, brush one side of the cutlets with meat glaze and put into a hot oven to crisp the bacon.

Serve on a bed of mashed potato garnished with diced vegetables. Tomato or caper sauce are suitable for serving with this dish.

6 helpings

BRAISED MUTTON—PROVENCE STYLE

Mouton braisé à la Provençale

A small leg *or* shoulder *or* loin of mutton
Meat glaze

FARCE

2 oz. lean ham
2 oz. pork *or* veal
2 oz. breadcrumbs
6 button mushrooms
1 teasp. chopped parsley
½ teasp. mixed herbs
½ teasp. grated lemon rind
1 shallot
1 egg
Salt and pepper

MIREPOIX

2 large onions
2 carrots
1 turnip
2 sticks of celery
3 oz. good dripping *or* butter
Bouquet garni
10 peppercorns
1 qt. stock (approx.)

PROVENÇALE SAUCE

1 pt. brown sauce
1 tomato
1 onion
2 large mushrooms
½ teasp. chopped parsley
1 oz. butter
½ teasp. lemon juice

Bone the joint. Mince the ham, and pork or veal, and finely chop the shallot and parsley. Mix them with the rest of the farce ingredients. Press lightly into the cavity left by the bone and sew up the opening. Thickly slice the vegetables for the mirepoix and fry lightly in a saucepan with the dripping or butter. Add the bouquet garni and peppercorns. Place the meat on top and ¾ cover the vegetables with stock. Cover with greased paper and a tightly-fitting lid. Cook gently for 2½ hr., basting frequently and making up the stock as it reduces. Transfer the meat to a baking-tin and put in a hot oven for another ½ hr. Baste as needed. Strain the liquid and use it to make the brown sauce. Slice the tomato, onion and mushrooms, chop the parsley and add to the 1 oz. of butter melted in a saucepan. Cook for 15–20 min., then add the brown sauce and cook for another 10 min. Season carefully and strain through a sieve. Reheat, add the lemon juice and keep hot. Place the meat on a hot dish. Brush over with warm glaze. Garnish with baked tomatoes, mushrooms, or diced glazed vegetables. Serve the sauce separately.

8–12 helpings

MUTTON

BROWNED NECK OF MUTTON

Carré de Mouton rôti à brun

Best end neck of mutton (6 bones)
Stock
1 egg
1 teasp. finely-chopped parsley
¼ teasp. powdered mixed herbs
Salt and pepper
2 tablesp. breadcrumbs
2 oz. butter *or* margarine
2 oz. flour

Remove the chine bone and short bones. Fold the flap over and secure neatly. Place in a stewpan and almost cover with stock. Simmer gently for 1 hr., then drain well. Beat the egg, add the parsley, herbs and seasoning. Coat the meat thickly with this mixture. If the meat is lean add a little dripping. Cover lightly with breadcrumbs and bake in a casserole or baking-tin in a moderate oven (**350° F., Gas 4**) until well browned. Allow 25 min. per lb. and 25 min. over; baste frequently with hot fat. Heat the butter or margarine in a saucepan, add the flour and cook until brown. Then add 1 pt. stock from the stewpan, stir until boiling, correct the seasoning and serve the sauce separately.

6 helpings

CASSEROLE OF MUTTON

Casserole de Mouton

1½ lb. middle neck of mutton
1 onion
Good gravy *or* stock
Salt and pepper
Suet pastry using 4 oz. flour, etc.

Cut the meat into neat chops and remove the bones and surplus fat. Place the meat in a casserole so that it is about half full. Thinly slice the onion and place on top and barely cover with gravy or stock. Season carefully. Cover and cook gently in a moderate oven (**350° F., Gas 4**), for about 1½ hr. Roll the suet pastry to the shape of the casserole—but slightly smaller. Lay the pastry on top of the meat, replace the lid and cook gently for 1 hr. longer. Before serving, divide the pastry crust into suitable portions.

NOTE: If a casserole is not available this may be cooked in a saucepan on top of the cooker.

6 helpings

CASSEROLE OF MUTTON WITH MUSHROOMS

6 cutlets from the best end of neck
½ lb. mushrooms
Salt and pepper
½ oz. butter

Season cutlets both sides and place in a greased casserole. Cover with mushrooms and sprinkle with seasoning and a few pats of butter. Bake in a cool oven (**310° F., Gas 2**) with the lid on for 1–1½ hr.

6 helpings

EPIGRAMS OF MUTTON WITH MUSHROOMS

Epigrammes de Mouton aux Champignons

2 lb. breast of mutton
Ingredients for mirepoix see Braised Mutton (p. 235)
Stock
Egg and breadcrumbs
Deep fat
Potato purée
½ pt. mushroom sauce

Braise the mutton as directed for Braised Mutton (*see* p. 235). Simmer for about 1½–2 hr. until the meat is quite tender. Remove the meat, take out all bones, and press between 2 plates with a weight on top until cold. Cut meat into small and even, round, oval or rectangular shapes. Coat evenly with egg and breadcrumbs, fry in deep fat until golden brown. Drain well and serve on a border of potato purée with mushroom sauce poured round.

6 helpings

FRIED MUTTON CUTLETS

Côtelettes de Mouton frites

6 cutlets from the best end of neck
Egg and breadcrumbs
Deep fat
½ pt. tomato sauce

Trim and flatten the cutlets. Coat with egg and breadcrumbs—clean the bone of crumbs. Reshape the cutlets with a clean dry knife. Fry in deep fat which is faintly smoking for about 5–10 min. Fry a 1-in. cube of bread, place it in the serving dish and prop the first cutlet on it. Lean the cutlets one against the other. Pour some tomato sauce round and serve the rest in a sauce-boat. Garnish with cooked green peas.

6 helpings

GRILLED BREAST OF MUTTON

Poitrine d'Agneau grillée

A breast of mutton	**Salt and pepper**

Divide the breast into portions convenient for serving. Remove the surplus fat and skin and season the meat carefully. Grill quickly under a hot grill to seal the surfaces. Then reduce the heat and turn the meat frequently until thoroughly cooked.

Serve with tomato or piquant sauce.

6–8 helpings
Cooking time—15–20 min.

GRILLED MUTTON

6 slices about 3/4 in. thick cut from the middle of the leg	**3 tablesp. salad oil *or* oiled butter**

MARINADE

2 dessertsp. vinegar	**1 teasp. finely-chopped parsley**
1 teasp. very finely-chopped onion	**A pinch of powdered mixed herbs**
1/2 teasp. salt	**1/8 teasp. pepper**

Put the slices of meat into a dish and cover with the marinade. Leave for at least 2 hr. turning and basting occasionally. When ready, drain, dry and brush with the salad oil or melted butter. Grill, turning several times, for about 10–15 min.

Suitable accompaniments are tomato sauce and chipped potatoes or mushroom sauce, baked tomatoes and chipped potatoes or stewed mushrooms and brown sauce.

6 helpings

GRILLED MUTTON CHOPS

Côtelettes de Mouton, grillées

A loin of mutton	**Salt and pepper**
Salad oil *or* butter	**Maître d'hôtel butter**

Divide the loin into chops and trim away surplus fat. Brush well with salad oil or melted butter and season carefully. Grill for 10–15 min., turning from time to time. Serve hot with a pat of Maître d'hôtel butter on top.

Suitable accompaniments are chipped potatoes, grilled mushrooms and tomatoes and watercress.

NOTE: If liked the bone may be removed from each chop—the meat curled round and secured with a small skewer.

8–12 helpings

GRILLED MUTTON CUTLETS

Côtelettes de Mouton grillées

6 cutlets from the best end of neck	**1 1/2 oz. butter *or* fat**
Salt and pepper	**Mashed potatoes**
6 small tomatoes stuffed with mushrooms	**Breadcrumbs**
	1/2 pt. demi-glace sauce

Trim and flatten the cutlets. Season on both sides. Prepare the tomatoes and bake in a moderate oven **(350° F., Gas 4)** until tender. Melt the fat, dip in the cutlets, taking care that the sides are coated. Cover lightly with bread crumbs and press on firmly with a knife. Grill, turning them several times until cooked evenly and browned.

Arrange on a potato border and garnish with the stuffed tomatoes. Pour a little sauce round and serve the rest in a sauce-boat.

NOTE: If liked, the cutlets can be grilled without the breadcrumbs and served with tomato sauce.

6 helpings

HARICOT MUTTON

Ragoût de Mouton

6 small chops from the middle neck *or* 2 lb. scrag end	**1 large onion**
1 oz. butter *or* good dripping	**1 oz. flour**
	1 1/2 pt. stock
	Salt and pepper
	Bouquet garni

GARNISH

2 carrots	**1 turnip**

Trim off the skin and surplus fat and cut the meat into small pieces or cutlets. Put the butter or dripping into a saucepan and when smoking, fry the meat quickly and lightly. Remove the meat, chop the onion finely and fry slowly in the same fat without browning. Add the flour and fry slowly until a rich brown. Cool slightly and add the stock, seasoning and bouquet garni. Bring to the boil, put in the meat and simmer gently until tender—about

2 hr. Cut the carrots and turnip into neat dice for garnish. Add the rough trimmings to the meat. Cook the diced carrot and turnip separately in boiling salted water until just tender. Arrange the meat on a hot dish. If necessary rapidly boil the liquid in the saucepan to reduce and then strain over the meat. Garnish with the diced carrot and turnip.

6 helpings

IRISH STEW

Ragoût à l'Irlandaise

2 lb. best end of neck	**3 lb. potatoes**
1 lb. onions	**1½ pt. stock *or* water**
Salt and pepper	**Parsley**

Cut the meat into neat cutlets and trim off the surplus fat. Arrange in a saucepan layers of the meat, thinly-sliced onions, seasoning and ½ the potatoes cut in slices. Add stock or water just to cover and simmer gently for about 1½ hr. Add the rest of the potatoes—cut to a uniform size to improve the appearance on top. Cook gently in the steam for about ¾ hr. longer. Serve the meat in the centre of a hot dish and arrange the potatoes round the edge.

Pour the liquid over the meat and sprinkle with finely-chopped parsley.

Alternative method of serving: Place the meat in the centre of a hot dish. Arrange ½ the potatoes round the edge. Then sieve the liquid—onions and remaining potatoes—and pour over the meat. Sprinkle with chopped parsley.

6 helpings

LANCASHIRE HOT POT

2 lb. best end of neck	**Stock**
2 lb. potatoes	**1 oz. butter *or* margarine**
3 sheep's kidneys	
1 large onion	**½ pt. good gravy**
Salt and pepper	

Divide the meat into neat cutlets. Trim off the skin and most of the fat. Grease a fireproof baking-dish and put in a layer of sliced potatoes. Arrange the cutlets on top, slightly overlapping each other, and cover with slices of kidneys and slices of onion. Season well. Add the remainder of the potatoes. The top layer should be of small potatoes cut in halves, uniformly arranged to give a neat appearance to the dish. Pour down the side of the dish about ½ pt. hot stock seasoned with salt and pepper. Brush the top layer of potatoes with warmed fat and cover with greased greaseproof paper. Bake for about 2 hr. in a moderate oven **(350° F., Gas 4)**. Then remove the paper to allow the potatoes to become crisp and brown, cooking for a further 20 min. When ready to serve, pour some gravy down the sides of the dish and serve the rest in a gravy-boat. Serve the hot pot in the dish in which it is cooked.

6 helpings

LOIN OF MUTTON—DAUBE STYLE

Longe de Mouton à la Daube

A loin of mutton	**3 tablesp. breadcrumbs**
Stock	**A pinch of nutmeg**
1 tablesp. finely-chopped ham *or* bacon	**Salt and pepper**
	1 egg
2 tablesp. chopped suet	**A little milk**
1 teasp. finely-chopped parsley	**3 bacon rashers**
	Glaze (optional)
¼ teasp. grated lemon rind	**Tomato *or* brown sauce**

Place the bones removed from the meat at the bottom of a saucepan and cover with stock. Mix well together the ham or bacon, suet, parsley, lemon rind, breadcrumbs and nutmeg. Season well and add the egg and sufficient milk to moisten the stuffing. Spread on the inner surface of the meat, roll up and tie securely with string. Cover with the slices of bacon and fold in several thicknesses of greaseproof paper. Place in the saucepan and cover with a tightly fitting lid. Cook very slowly on the stove or in the oven for 4–5 hr., according to size. Add more stock if necessary. When ready, remove paper and bacon. If liked, brush with glaze and leave in the oven for another 10 min. Serve with tomato or brown sauce.

8–12 helpings

MUTTON CUTLETS—ITALIAN STYLE

Côtelettes de Mouton à l'Italienne

6 cutlets from the best end of neck
2–3 tablesp. salad oil
1 tablesp. lemon juice
1 teasp. finely-chopped mixed herbs
Salt and pepper
3–4 tablesp. breadcrumbs
1 tablesp. finely-chopped mushrooms
½ teasp. finely-chopped shallot
1 teasp. chopped parsley
¼ teasp. finely-grated lemon rind
A pinch of mace
1 egg
Fat for frying
⅓ pt. Italian sauce

Mix the salad oil, lemon juice, herbs and a little salt and pepper together. Pour this mixture over the cutlets and let them remain in it for 1 hr., turning 2 or 3 times. Mix together the breadcrumbs, chopped mushroom, shallot, parsley, lemon rind and mace, season with salt and pepper. Drain the cutlets, brush with beaten egg and carefully coat with the breadcrumb mixture. Fry in hot fat until brown on both sides. Serve with Italian sauce.

6 helpings
Cooking time—6–10 min.

MUTTON CUTLETS—PORTUGUESE STYLE

Côtelettes de Mouton à la Portugaise

6 cutlets from the best end of neck
1 onion *or* 2 shallots
1 oz. butter *or* fat
4 medium-sized tomatoes
1 teasp. cornflour
¼ pt. good stock
Salt and pepper
2–3 teasp. vinegar
½ teasp. castor sugar

Trim the cutlets. Slice the onion or shallots, heat the fat in a sauté pan and fry until tender and lightly browned. Add the sliced tomatoes and cook gently for ½ hr. Pass them through a fine sieve and return to sauté pan. Blend the cornflour and stock smoothly together and add to the contents of the pan. Stir until boiling and season to taste. Add the vinegar and castor sugar. Cover and keep hot. Grill the cutlets and serve in a close circle on a hot dish, with the sauce poured round.

6 helpings

MUTTON CUTLETS—VENETIAN STYLE

Côtelettes de Mouton à la Vénitienne

6 cutlets from the best end of neck
2 oz. butter *or* fat
4 oz. veal forcemeat (p. 144)
3 tablesp. finely-chopped ham
1 small truffle
1 hard-boiled egg white
Salt and pepper
½ pt. brown sauce
Mashed potatoes

GARNISH

1 tablesp. chopped hard-boiled egg white
1 tablesp. shredded cold boiled ham
1 tablesp. chopped gherkin

Prepare the cutlets and fry in the melted fat. Drain well and press lightly until cold. Cover one side of each cutlet with a layer of veal forcemeat, then cover the forcemeat with a thin layer of chopped ham. Sprinkle 3 of the cutlets with finely-chopped truffle and 3 with chopped egg white, season and place in a sauté pan. Pour some of the brown sauce round and cover with greased greaseproof paper. Cook for about ½ hr. Meanwhile heat the garnish in a bain marie, or over a saucepan of boiling water. Remove the cutlets. Add remainder of the sauce and boil up. Arrange the cutlets in a close circle on a potato border. Serve the garnish in the centre and pour the sauce round.

6 helpings

MUTTON PIE—PEMBROKESHIRE STYLE

Hot water crust pastry using 1 lb. flour, etc.
1 lb. minced mutton
¼ lb. currants
¼ lb. sugar
Salt and pepper
Stock
Egg *or* milk for glazing

When the pastry is cool enough to handle make into a large pie case or several small ones, keeping back ¼ of the pastry for the lid. Arrange the filling in layers of mutton, currants, sugar, salt and pepper and moisten with stock. Cover with the pastry lid. Bake in a fairly hot oven (**400° F., Gas 6**) for 10 min. then reduce heat to moderate (**350° F., Gas 4**) for the remainder of the time—about 1¼ hr. in all. Brush with egg or milk about 15 min before cooking is complete. Fill with stock and serve hot.

6 helpings

MUTTON PIES—CUMBERLAND STYLE

12 oz. minced mutton
Short-crust pastry using 12 oz. flour, etc.
1 onion
4 oz. mushrooms
1 dessertsp. chopped parsley
A pinch of thyme
Salt and pepper
A little good stock
Egg *or* milk

Chop and lightly fry the onion. Line 12 small round tins or small saucers with ½ the pastry. Mix together the minced mutton, chopped onion, chopped mushrooms, parsley, thyme and seasoning. Divide the mixture between the tins. Add to each a little stock to moisten. Cover with lids made from the rest of the pastry. Brush with egg or milk and bake in a moderate oven (**350° F., Gas 4**) for about 30–45 min.

6 helpings

MUTTON PUDDING

Pouding de Mouton

1 lb. lean mutton
Salt and pepper
Suet pastry using 9 oz. flour, etc.
1 *or* 2 kidneys

Follow the directions for preparation and cooking given for Beefsteak Pudding p. 208.

5–6 helpings

MUTTON ROLL

Roulade de Mouton

1½ lb. lean mutton
½ lb. ham *or* bacon
1 teasp. finely-chopped parsley
½ teasp. finely-chopped onion
3 tablesp. breadcrumbs
¼ teasp. finely-powdered herbs
A pinch of nutmeg
½ teasp. finely-grated lemon rind
Salt and pepper
1 egg
Stock *or* gravy
Flour *or* egg and breadcrumbs
Fat

Finely chop or mince the meat. Finely chop the ham or bacon and mix well with the parsley, onion, breadcrumbs, herbs, nutmeg, minced mutton and lemon rind. Season carefully. Beat the egg and add it with enough stock or gravy to moisten the mixture. Then make into a short thick roll. Enclose neatly in several thicknesses of greased greaseproof paper to keep the roll in shape and to protect the meat. Bake in a moderate oven (**350° F., Gas 4**) for about 2 hr. About ½ hr. before serving remove the paper, lightly dredge the roll with flour, or brush with egg and coat with breadcrumbs. Put into a meat-tin with hot dripping, baste well and finish cooking in a moderate oven for the remaining ½ hr. until brown. Serve with a good gravy.

NOTE: Underdone cold mutton may be used. The roll should then be cooked for about 1 hr.

6 helpings

OXFORD JOHN

1¼ lb. leg of mutton
Salt and pepper
1 tablesp. finely-chopped ham *or* bacon
1 teasp. finely-chopped parsley
1 teasp. finely-chopped onion
½ teasp. powdered mixed herbs
2 oz. butter *or* margarine
¾ oz. flour
½ pt. good stock
1 teasp. lemon juice

Cut the meat into neat thin rounds about 4 in. in diameter and season with salt and pepper. Mix together the ham or bacon, parsley, onion, herbs and a little salt and pepper; spread the mixture on one side of the meat and pile the slices one above the other. Leave for 1 hr. Then separate and fry each slice lightly and quickly in hot fat. Remove and keep hot. Sprinkle the flour into the pan, brown well and add the stock. Stir until boiling—season, add the lemon juice and replace the meat. Cook for another 10 min. just below simmering point. Serve hot.

6 helpings

SCOTCH COLLOPS

1½ lb. lean mutton chops
1 small onion
1½ oz. butter *or* fat
1 oz. flour
1½ gill stock
Salt and pepper
1½ teasp. finely-chopped parsley
Croûtes of fried *or* toasted bread

Wipe the meat and remove the bones and fat. Chop or mince the meat evenly but not too finely. Finely chop the onion. Melt the fat in a saucepan and fry the onion. Add the meat and cook quickly for a few minutes. Sprinkle in the flour, stir well, add stock and seasoning to taste and simmer very gently for ½ hr. Add the chopped parsley and serve on a hot dish. Garnish with croûtes of fried or toasted bread.

6 helpings **Cooking time—40 min.**

SCRAG OF MUTTON

Scrag end of neck of mutton
2 onions
2 carrots
½ turnip
Bacon rashers
Bouquet garni
10 peppercorns
Stock *or* water
Egg and breadcrumbs
2 oz. dripping

Wash the meat in warm salt water. Slice the onions, carrots and turnip and put in a saucepan. Lay the meat on top, cover with slices of bacon. Add the bouquet garni, peppercorns and enough stock or water to nearly cover the vegetables. Cover with a close-fitting lid and cook gently for 2½ hr. Remove the meat, brush with beaten egg and coat with breadcrumbs. Put in a tin with the hot dripping and cook in a fairly hot oven (**400° F., Gas 6**) for about ½ hr. until nicely browned. Baste occasionally. Serve with brown gravy made from the stock in which the meat was cooked.

6–8 helpings

SQUAB PIE

2 lb. neck of mutton
Salt and pepper
2 lb. apples
1 lb. onions
2 teasp. sugar
1 tablesp. mushroom ketchup (optional)
Good stock (optional)

Divide the neck into cutlets, place in a pie-dish and season well. Slice the apples and onions and add in layers sprinkled with sugar. Half-fill the dish with boiling water and cover tightly with greased greaseproof paper. Bake in a moderate oven (**350° F., Gas 4**) for 1½ hr. Before serving, see that any fat is skimmed off and also that there is sufficient gravy. If liked, add the mushroom ketchup together with some good stock.

6 helpings

STEWED MUTTON WITH RICE

Ragoût de Mouton au Riz

1 lb. neck of mutton, chined
6 carrots
3 turnips
6 onions
Salt and pepper
1–2 qt. good white stock
½ lb. rice
Parsley

Put the meat, sliced vegetables and seasonings in a casserole and cover with stock. Place in a moderate oven (**350° F., Gas 4**) for about 1¼ hr. Wash the rice well, add to the casserole and continue cooking for another 1–1¼ hr. until all the contents are tender. The rice will absorb the stock and more should be added as needed. Place the meat and vegetables on a hot dish and arrange the rice to form a neat border. Sprinkle with chopped parsley.

6 helpings

STUFFED AND ROAST LOIN OR SHOULDER OF MUTTON

Filet ou Epaule de Mouton, farci

A loin *or* shoulder of mutton
Veal forcemeat *or* sage and onion stuffing
Salt and pepper
2–3 oz. dripping

Remove all the bones from the meat. Trim off any skin and surplus fat and flatten the meat with a rolling-pin. Season the meat well with salt and pepper and spread on the forcemeat or stuffing. Roll up and tie securely with string. Melt the dripping in a covered meat-tin, put in the meat and roast in a moderate oven (**350° F., Gas 4**) until tender. Allow 25 min. per lb. and 25 min. over. Baste occasionally. A good gravy or brown sauce may be served with the meat.

Sheep's Brains

BRAIN AND TONGUE PUDDING

3 sheep's brains
3 sheep's tongues
Suet pastry using 6 oz. flour, etc.
1 teasp. finely-chopped parsley
1 shallot
1 teasp. flour
Salt and pepper
1 hard-boiled egg
¼ pt. milk

Prepare the brains as in the following recipe. Wash the tongues and simmer until the skin can be removed. Line a greased basin with suet pastry. Fill with layers of sliced tongue, cleaned and roughly chopped brains, seasoning of parsley, finely-chopped shallot, flour, and salt and pepper, and slices of hard-boiled egg. Add the milk and cover with suet pastry. Cover with greased greaseproof paper and steam for 3–3½ hr.

6 helpings

BRAINS AND EGG ON TOAST

Cervelles sur Croûtes

3 sheep's brains	**1 oz. butter**
Salt and pepper	**1 teasp. chopped parsley**
1 hard-boiled egg	
Buttered toast	

Soak the brains in salt water for ½ hr. and remove the blood and membranes with salt. Wash thoroughly and tie in muslin. Cook for 15 min. in the muslin in boiling water to which a little salt has been added. Shell and chop roughly the hard-boiled egg. Prepare and butter the toast and keep it hot. Drain the brains and chop roughly. Melt the butter in a pan and in it heat the brains and egg thoroughly. Then add the parsley and serve hot at once on the toast.

6 helpings

STEWED BRAINS

Cervelles de Mouton

3 sheep's brains	**A small bunch of parsley**
Salt and pepper	**Stock**
1 tablesp. vinegar	**Croûtons of fried bread**
3 bacon rashers	**Matelote sauce**
1 small onion	**2 teasp. lemon juice**
2 cloves	

Remove the skin from the brains with a little salt and soak in cold water for ½ hr. Have ready a saucepan of boiling water. Add the vinegar and some salt. Tie the brains lightly in muslin, and cook in the water for about 15 min., keeping just under boiling-point. Remove the muslin and place the brains in another saucepan with the bacon placed on top. Add the onion, stuck with the cloves, parsley and salt and pepper. Just cover the brains with stock and simmer gently for about 25 min. Have ready croûtons of fried bread and place the brains on them on a hot dish. Put the bacon on top of the brains and cover with matelote sauce to which the lemon juice has been added.

NOTE: Parsley sauce with lemon juice may be served instead of the matelote sauce, in which case a carrot and a bay leaf should be added to the other vegetables in the stock, and the bacon and cloves omitted.

6 helpings

Sheep's Head

SHEEP'S HEAD

Tête de Mouton

A sheep's head	**2 onions**
Bouquet garni	**1 small turnip**
10 peppercorns	**2 small carrots**
Salt and pepper	**1 oz. butter *or* fat**
2 tablesp. pearl barley *or* rice	**1 oz. flour**
	Parsley

If necessary, split the head and remove the brains. Wash the head several times, taking care to remove all splintered bones. Scrape the small bones from the nostrils and brush the teeth. Soak in salt water for 30 min. Cover with cold water and bring to the boil. Pour away the water and replace with fresh cold water and add the bouquet garni, peppercorns and salt. Boil up and skim well. Add the barley (blanched) or rice. Cook slowly for about 3 hr. Meanwhile prepare the vegetables and cut into dice; these should be added about 1 hr. before serving. Remove the skin and fibres from the brains with salt and wash in cold water. Tie the brains in muslin and cook with the head for about 15–20 min. Then chop coarsely. Heat the fat in a saucepan and add the flour. Stir over the heat and cook without browning for about 3 min., then add ¾ pt. of liquid in which the head is cooking. Stir until boiling, correct the seasoning and add the brains. Remove the head and take all the flesh from the bones. Skin and slice the tongue. Place the meat neatly on a hot dish. Pour the brain sauce over. If liked, garnish with some of the sliced tongue, vegetables and chopped parsley. Serve the broth separately.

3 helpings

Sheep's Heart

SHEEP'S HEART

Cœur de Mouton

1 sheep's heart | **½ pt. good stock**
Veal forcemeat | **¾ oz. flour**
2 oz. dripping | **Salt and pepper**

Soak the heart for about ½ hr. Wash well in clean water. Cut the pipes from the top, leave the flaps to fasten down and cut the dividing walls of the chambers. Dry thoroughly and fill the heart with forcemeat, fold over the flaps and tie or skewer to keep it in. Heat the dripping in a small meat-tin. Put in the heart, baste well and bake in a cool to moderate oven **(310°–350° F., Gas 2–4)** for 1½ hr. Gentle cooking and frequent basting are necessary to prevent the heart from becoming dry and hard. When cooked, place the heart on a hot dish and keep hot. Drain off most of the fat but keep back any sediment. Blend the flour and stock and add to the sediment to make thickened gravy. Season carefully. Pour a little round the heart and serve the rest in a gravy-boat.

NOTE: Sheep's heart may be stuffed with sage and onion stuffing and cooked in a saucepan on top of the cooker. This must be done very carefully over a very gentle heat.

6 helpings

Sheep's Kidneys

DEVILLED KIDNEYS

Rognons à la Diable

6 sheep's kidneys | **½ teasp. mixed mustard**
1½ oz. butter *or* fat | **¼ pt. stock**
1 tablesp. chopped onion | **2 egg yolks**
Salt | **Breadcrumbs**
Cayenne pepper | **Buttered toast *or* potato border**
3 teasp. chutney
2 teasp. lemon juice

Skin and well wash the kidneys. Split open and remove the cores. Cut the kidneys into neat pieces. Melt the fat in a small pan, put in the onion and cook without browning. Then add the kidney, salt, cayenne, chutney, lemon juice, mustard and stock. Cover and stew for a short time over moderate heat until the kidney is cooked. Cool slightly and stir in the egg yolks. Sprinkle in enough breadcrumbs to make a soft consistency and correct the seasoning. Serve on buttered toast or in a mashed potato border.

6 helpings | **Cooking time—about 20 min.**

FRIED KIDNEYS

Rognons frits

6 sheep's kidneys | **Salt and pepper**
¾ oz. butter *or* good dripping

Skin the kidneys and split lengthwise without quite separating the 2 parts. Remove the cores and then soak in cold water for 5 min. Dry and hold the kidneys open and flat by piercing with a skewer. Melt the butter or dripping in a frying-pan and fry the kidneys lightly and quickly on both sides. Take care not to overcook or the kidneys will be uneatable. Season with salt and pepper and pour a little of the hot gravy round. Serve as hot as possible.

6 helpings | **Cooking time—about 5 min.**

GRILLED KIDNEYS

Rognons de Mouton grillés

6 sheep's kidneys | **Salt and pepper**
Oil *or* oiled butter | **Croûtons of fried bread**

GARNISH

Maître d'hôtel butter *or* bacon rolls

Prepare the kidneys as directed in the preceding recipe and keep them open and flat with a skewer. Brush with oil or melted butter and season with salt and pepper. Grill quickly, cooking the cut side first and turning frequently. When ready, remove the skewer and serve on croûtons of fried bread on a hot dish. The hollow in the centre of the kidney may be filled with a small pat of Maître d'hôtel butter, or serve with rolls of bacon.

6 helpings
Cooking time—about 5–8 min.

KIDNEY AND BACON CROÛTES

Rognons et Bacon sur Croûtes

3 sheep's kidneys | **6 eggs**
3 bacon rashers | **6 large croûtes of bread**
4 oz. mushrooms | **2 oz. butter *or* fat**
3 skinned tomatoes | **Paprika**
Salt and pepper

Skin the kidneys, remove the cores and soak in cold water for 5 min. Chop the kidneys and bacon. Fry the bacon until crisp and keep hot. Fry the chopped mushrooms and kidney for 5 min. in the bacon fat. Halve and grill the tomatoes and season carefully with salt and pepper. Poach the eggs. Fry croûtes of bread in the fat until golden on both sides, and keep hot in the oven. Reheat the bacon in the fat and add the kidneys and mushrooms. Correct the seasoning and spread equally on the croûtes. Place an egg on each one and dredge with paprika pepper. Garnish each with ½ tomato. Serve at once.

6 helpings

KIDNEY RAMAKINS

Ramequins aux Rognons

4 sheep's kidneys
1 shallot
1½ oz. butter *or* fat
1 level dessertsp. flour
⅛ pt. sherry *or* Madeira (optional)
¼ pt. good stock *or* gravy
Salt and pepper
6 croûtons of fried bread
Parsley

Prepare the kidneys by removing the skins and cores. Soak for 5 min. in cold water. Dry and slice as thinly as possible. Finely chop the shallot. Heat the fat in a sauté pan, and fry the shallot until lightly browned. Add the sliced kidneys and toss lightly over the heat for 3–4 min. Then lift the kidneys from the pan on to a plate. Sprinkle the flour into the pan and stir and cook quickly until brown. Add the wine (if used) and the stock and stir until boiling. Season to taste. Return the kidneys to the thickened sauce and reheat, but do not boil or the kidneys will harden. Have ready the croûtons of fried bread—which should fit inside the ramakin cases and have the cases heated. Fill each case with kidney and sauce and sprinkle with chopped parsley. Serve hot.

6 helpings

KIDNEY TOAST

Rognons sur croûtes

Ingredients and directions for cooking as in preceding recipe. When cooked spread lightly on buttered toast and make thoroughly hot in the oven. Serve immediately.

6 helpings **Cooking time—10 min.**

SAUTÉD KIDNEYS

Rognons sautés

6 sheep's kidneys
2 shallots
1 oz. butter *or* fat
¼ pt. brown sauce
1 tablesp. sherry (optional)
Salt and pepper
Watercress
Croûtes of fried *or* toasted bread

Skin the kidneys and remove the cores. Soak for 5 min. in cold water. Dry and cut into ¼-in. slices. Finely chop the shallots, heat the fat in a sauté pan and fry them slightly. Then put in the sliced kidney and shake and toss over the heat for about 5 min. Drain off the surplus fat and add the brown sauce, sherry (if used) and salt and pepper. Stir over a gentle heat until thoroughly hot, but take care not to let the mixture boil. Serve as hot as possible on toast or fried bread, garnished with watercress.

6 helpings
Cooking time—about 10 min.

Sheep's Liver

LIVER À LA PROVENCALE

Foie à la Provençale

1½ lb. sheep's liver
4 oz. bacon
1½ lb. onions
Salt and pepper
1 oz. flour
½ pt. stock
Parsley

Wash the liver well. Dice the bacon and fry in a saucepan until crisp. Remove and keep hot. Chop the onions and fry in the bacon fat (covered) until tender but not brown. Season with salt and pepper. Dust in the flour, add the stock and stir until boiling. Place the slices of liver on top, cover and simmer for ¾ hr. Serve the slices of liver on a hot dish with the bacon on top and the onions heaped neatly at each end, sprinkled liberally with parsley.

6 helpings

LIVER AND BACON

Foie et Bacon

1 lb. sheep's liver
½ lb. bacon rashers
Seasoned flour
¾ pt. stock

Remove the rind and rust from the bacon. Wash the liver in cold water and remove any tubes or blood vessels. Dry the liver and, if necessary, cut in slices ½ in.–¾ in. thick. Dip each slice of liver in seasoned flour. Fry the slices of bacon and remove to a hot dish and keep hot until required. Fry the liver in the fat from the bacon lightly and quickly so that it is browned on both sides without hardening or overcooking. Remove to the hot dish, placing the bacon neatly on top. Drain off all but about 1 dessertsp. of fat, add about ¾ oz. flour and stir until browned. Add about ¾ pt. stock. Boil and season to taste. Strain round the liver.

Calves' liver may be used equally well.

6 helpings
Cooking time—about 10 min.

LIVER WITH RED PEPPERS

Foie aux Piments

1¼ lb. sheep's liver
Flour
2 oz. dripping
2 onions
4 red peppers
4 skinned tomatoes
½ pt. good stock
Salt and pepper

Wash the liver in cold water and dry well. Cut into thin slices. Dip in flour and fry quickly and lightly in the melted dripping. Remove the liver and put in a casserole. Next, fry the sliced onions and sliced peppers and when almost cooked, add the sliced tomatoes. When soft, add to the liver. Make a brown gravy from the fat in the pan, 1 oz. flour and stock. Season carefully. Pour over the liver, cover with a lid and simmer in a moderate oven (**350° F., Gas 4**) for 1 hr. When tender, correct the seasoning and pile neatly on a hot dish, pipe a potato border round or surround with cooked boiled rice.

6 helpings

LIVER WITH SAVOURY RICE

Risotto au Foie

½ lb. sheep's liver
Few shreds of saffron
½ gill hot water
1 small onion
2 oz. butter *or* fat
4 oz. Patna rice
Salt
Cayenne pepper
½ pt. strong stock
4 oz. bacon
Juice of ½ lemon
1½ gills brown sauce

Infuse the saffron in the water. Shred the onion and sauté in 1 oz. of the fat. Add the rice, mix well and cook for 2 min. Add the salt, cayenne, strained saffron and stock. Put into a casserole in a moderate oven (**350° F., Gas 4**) for 30 min. Then remove and add the remaining fat (the rice should have completely absorbed the stock by now). Well grease a border mould, carefully put in the rice and press in place with a teaspoon. Prepare and dice the bacon, fry in a saucepan until crisp and cooked, then remove. Add the prepared and neatly diced liver to the hot bacon fat and cook lightly, turning frequently. Remove the liver and add the lemon juice to the bacon fat and sediment. Stir well, add the brown sauce and boil up. Return the liver and bacon to the saucepan and reheat without boiling. Unmould the rice and warm it on a hot dish in the oven. Pile the liver and bacon in the middle.

Cooking time—about ¾–1 hr.

HAGGIS

1 sheep's paunch and pluck
1 lb. oatmeal
1 lb. beef suet
2 Spanish onions
1 teasp. pepper
2 tablesp. salt
½ nutmeg, finely-grated
Juice of 1 lemon
1½ pt. good stock *or* gravy

Soak the paunch for several hours in salt and water. Then turn it inside out and wash thoroughly several times. Wash the pluck well, just cover the liver with cold water and boil for about 1½ hr. After ½ hr. add the well-cleaned heart and lights. Chop ½ the liver coarsely and chop the other ½ with the heart and lights, very finely. Mix all together and add the oatmeal, finely-chopped suet, finely-chopped onions, salt, pepper, nutmeg, lemon juice and stock. Press this mixture lightly into the paunch and sew up the opening, allowing space for the oatmeal to swell. (If overfilled, the paunch is likely to burst.) Put the haggis into boiling water and cook gently for about 3 hr. During the first hour prick occasionally and carefully with a needle to allow the steam to escape. Usually no sauce or gravy is served with haggis. If a smaller dish is required use a lamb's paunch and pluck instead of a sheep's.

MUTTON SAUSAGES

Saucisses de Mouton

1 lb. lean, raw *or* underdone mutton	**½ teasp. powdered mixed herbs**
2 oz. ham *or* bacon	**Salt and pepper**
4 oz. suet	**2 eggs**
½ teasp. finely-chopped onion	**Stock**
	Sausage skins
4 oz. fine breadcrumbs	**Fat *or* dripping**

Chop or mince the meat very finely. Finely chop the ham or bacon and suet, and mix well with the meat, onion, breadcrumbs, herbs and ample seasoning. Stir in the beaten eggs and as much stock as necessary to moisten. Press the mixture lightly into the skins or if preferred make into neat cakes or cork-shaped pieces on a floured board. Fry in hot fat or good dripping.

6 helpings
Cooking time—8–10 min.

Sheep's Tongues

BOILED SHEEP'S TONGUES

Langues de Mouton bouillies

4–5 sheep's tongues	**½ pt. stock**
Stock	**A few capers (optional)**
Salt and pepper	
1 oz. butter	**1 tablesp. sherry (optional)**
½ oz. flour	

Soak the tongues well in salt water for 1 hr., then blanch and dry them. Put into a pan, cover with stock, season, and simmer for about 2 hr. until tender. When cooked, remove skin, trim the roots and divide each tongue lengthwise into 3. Make a sauce with the butter, flour and the ½ pt. stock. A few roughly chopped capers may be added if liked. When thickened and boiling, add the tongues and reheat with the sherry and seasonings to taste.

Serve very hot within a circle of spaghetti, spinach or potatoes.

6 helpings

BRAISED SHEEP'S TONGUES

Langues de Mouton braisées

4 sheep's tongues	**2 sticks of celery**
1 oz. butter *or* margarine	**Bouquet garni**
	6 peppercorns
1 onion	**½ pt. stock**
1 turnip	**2 bacon rashers**
1 carrot	**Meat glaze**

Prepare the tongues as in preceding recipe. Melt the fat in a stewpan and add the roughly sliced vegetables. Put on a tightly fitting lid and toss for 10 min. over a very low heat. Lay the tongues on top, add the bouquet garni, peppercorns and enough stock almost to cover the vegetables. Place the bacon on top of the tongues. Cover with greased greaseproof paper, and the lid, and cook gently for about 2 hr. or until the tongues are tender. When ready skin the tongues, cut in halves lengthwise and brush with warm glaze. Place on a greased paper in a baking-tin and put in a warm oven for a few minutes to reheat.

Serve on a bed of mashed potatoes or spinach purée. Serve with brown sauce.

6 helpings

FRIED SHEEP'S TONGUES

Langues de Mouton frites

4 sheep's tongues	**2 sticks of celery**
1 onion	**3 oz. butter *or* margarine**
1 carrot	
1 turnip	**Breadcrumbs**

Braise the tongues as directed in the preceding recipe. Warm the fat, dip the pieces of tongue in it, then coat with breadcrumbs, pressing them firmly on with a knife. Pour the remaining fat into a sauté pan and fry the tongues until the entire surface is lightly browned.

Garnish with green peas and serve with ½ pt. tomato *or* piquant sauce, if liked.

6 helpings

PORK

More and more people today realize that with the development of cold storage it is now perfectly safe to eat pork at any time of the year. In addition to its other charming features the pig is a prolific breeder, and it is safe to say that if there is a public demand for pork it will be more quickly satisfied by the producer than is the case with any other meat. Unlike beef and lamb, the whole of the pig carcase is suitable for roasting, and all except the loin suitable for boiling, especially if first salted.

The appearance of the **leg** (1) and **loin** (2) are well known. They may be either baked, the leg boiled or in the case of cutlets and chops, grilled or fried.

(7) The **belly,** comparable to the streak in bacon, is usually salted and boiled. It is perfectly suitable for roasting and if bought in the form of thin strips or rashers may be grilled.

(3) The **spare rib** of the pig is almost a parallel cut to the middle neck of lamb. It is a moist eating tender joint, equally pleasant whether roasted or grilled.

From immediately above the spare rib is lifted the **blade-bone** (4). A parallel joint to this, the blade half shoulder, may also be found in lamb. The bladebone is a roasting joint and is especially tasty if the bone is removed and the resulting space filled with stuffing. When skewered and tied with string it may be carved as easily as beef roast.

A joint which is much neglected today is (5) the **hand** and **spring** of pork. This constitutes the foreleg of the animal and in bone structure is akin to the knuckle half shoulder of lamb. Although a large joint for the smaller family to buy it is extremely cheap and may be most economically used. The knuckle portion is best removed and set aside in strong salt water for two or three days ready for boiling. The remainder may be roasted and if suitably boned and rolled it is an easy joint to carve even for beginners.

In London and the South of England the pig carcase is the only one delivered to shops with (6) the **head** attached. The effect of this is that, on the whole, the specialized offal butcher is usually the only one to stock sheeps' heads and ox cheek, together with tongues and brains. In the case of pigs' heads, however, every butcher who sells pork will have the head. They contain a considerable amount of meat in addition to the tongue and the brain. The large piece of cheek meat provides the Bath chap when salted and boiled. Cold slices of this are delicious when fried. The remainder of the head may be boiled when it is easily removed from the bones, and used for brawn, see page 274.

General quality considerations applying to beef and lamb are applicable to pork. The flesh should be a pale pink colour. Whenever there is a dark red tinge to the flesh the pork should be avoided. The fat should be white and firm to the touch. It should never be greyish in colour. Occasionally pork may be found with small black spots in the fat, particularly in the belly. This is due to a carry-over of black pigment from the skin of black or brown pigs. Although unsightly it is in no way harmful.

See also Plate 8.

BACON AND HAM

One final virtue of the pig is that it supplies us with bacon. This is obtained from a side of pork from which the head and feet have been removed. The side is then salted for a suitable time to provide green bacon. In the South of England much bacon is further treated by smoking, exposure for 24 to 48 hours to the smoke from slow-burning hardwood dust such as oak. The chine or back bone is removed prior to processing, and before slicing the other bones (rib, shoulder and thigh bones).

Bacon is usually cut into the following joints, pork equivalents are given in brackets: **gammon** (leg), boiled for ham or baked; best **back** and **long** (loin of pork), used for back rashers; **streaky** (belly of pork), cut as streaky rashers or cut with the loin as long back; **collar** (sparerib of pork), used as a boiling joint or for very lean rashers; **hock** (hand and spring of pork), used as a boiling joint.

Strictly speaking, ham should be so called only when it is obtained from the gammon. It may be cooked before or after smoking and can be specially prepared by dry salting process (York hams) or by special smoking (Bradmun hams).

BOILED PICKLED PORK

A joint of pickled ***or*** **salt pork**	**1 onion**
Broad beans	**½ turnip**
10 peppercorns	**Salt**
1 carrot	**Parsley sauce**

Soak the beans over night. Soak the meat in cold water. Cover the pork with cold water and simmer gently, allowing 25–30 min. per lb. and 25–30 min. over. When the liquid is boiling, add the peppercorns, and the carrot, onion and turnip cut in thick slices. About ½ hr. before the pork is cooked, cook the beans in boiling salted water, simmer gently until tender but whole. Drain the beans well and coat with parsley sauce. Pease pudding (p. 348) may be served in place of the beans if liked. Serve the pork in a hot dish, garnished with the vegetables.

The liquor in which the pork is cooked can be made into good pea soup.

BOSTON PORK CASSEROLE

1¼ lb. lean pork	**1 tablesp. sugar**
4 oz. haricot beans	**1 tablesp. golden syrup**
1 grated carrot	**½ teasp. dry mustard**
Salt and pepper	**½–1 pt. white stock**
2 diced celery sticks	**6 potatoes**

Soak the beans over night. Place them in a casserole with the neatly diced pork and all the other ingredients except the potatoes. The stock should just cover the mixture. Cover with a lid and cook in a cool oven (**310° F., Gas 2**) for 4 hr. Add more stock if needed. About 1 hr. before it is ready, place 6 even-sized potatoes on the top. Return to the oven and cook until tender. Serve hot.

6 helpings

BRAISED PORK, COUNTRY STYLE

4 pork chops	**Salt and pepper**
4 tablesp. cider	**2–3 large dark mushrooms**
Bouquet garni	**1 breakfastcup** ***or*** **A1 can garden peas**
3 onions	**1 breakfastcup** ***or*** **A1 can beetroots**
2 cooking apples	**6–8 oz. noodles**
Good pinch of ground cinnamon	

Trim off rind and excessive fat and quickly fry chops in them until golden brown. Place in a casserole, add cider and bouquet garni, cover and cook gently on the cooker or in a cool oven (**310°–335° F., Gas 2–3**). Meanwhile, pour off excess fat from frying-pan; peel, chop, then fry the onions and apples for a few minutes. Add the cinnamon and water to cover them, put on a lid and simmer until soft. Sieve, season to taste and turn on to the chops. Cover and cook for 1¾–2 hr. in all, adding the thickly-sliced mushrooms ½ hr. before the end. Heat the peas and beetroots separately. Trickle the noodles in salted boiling water and boil until, on testing a piece, the centre is still slightly firm. Drain the noodles, peas and beetroots. Dish the noodles with the chops on top and garnish with the mushrooms, peas and beetroots.

FRIED or GRILLED PORK CUTLETS or CHOPS

Côtelettes de Porc panées

6 bones neck ***or*** **loin of pork**	**Salt and pepper**
1 egg	**Breadcrumbs**
1 teasp. powdered sage	**1½ oz. butter** ***or*** **fat**

Trim the cutlets, removing most of the fat. Beat the egg and add to it the sage, salt and pepper. Brush each cutlet with this and then coat carefully with breadcrumbs. Heat the fat and gently fry, or grill, the cutlets for about 20 min., turning frequently until golden brown.

GRILLED TENDERLOIN

Tendrons de Porc

6 pork chops from spare rib, tenderloin ***or*** **neck**	**Marjoram**
Salt and pepper	**Castor sugar**
Sage	**Flour**
	Stock
	Apple sauce

Prepare the chops. Sprinkle both sides of the chops with a pinch of salt, pepper, sage, marjoram and castor sugar. Grill carefully until golden brown, turning several times. Keep hot and after pouring away the fat, add flour and stock to make ½ pt. fawn thick gravy. Serve the chops on a hot dish. Serve the gravy and apple sauce separately.

PORK

LOIN OF PORK—GERMAN STYLE

Longe de Porc à l'Allemande

1 loin of pork
1 large Spanish onion
½ pt. malt vinegar
6 cloves
10 fresh sage leaves
24 peppercorns
1 tablesp. salt
A pinch of thyme *or* other herbs
10 juniper berries

Remove the skin and any superfluous fat and place the meat in a deep earthenware dish. Slice the onion, and mix with the vinegar, cloves, sage, peppercorns, salt, herbs and berries. Soak the meat in this marinade for 4–5 days, turning daily. Then put the meat and marinade in a baking-dish—do *not* use a baking-tin. Add ½ pt. boiling water and cook very gently in a moderate oven (**350° F., Gas 4**), basting frequently. Allow 25 min. per lb. and 25 min. over. When cooked, strain the gravy and pour a little over the meat. Serve the rest separately.

PORK AND ONION DUMPLING

Boulette de Porc aux Oignons

1 lb. lean pork
3 onions
Suet crust pastry p. 557) **using 12 oz. flour, etc.**
Salt and pepper
Pinch of sage

Chop the pork; finely chop the onions. Roll out the suet crust pastry in a neat rectangle. On it place the pork, seasoning, sage and onion, leaving a margin all round. Roll up, securing the edges firmly. Wrap firmly in several layers of greased greaseproof paper and secure safely. Steam for 3 hr. and serve with a good brown gravy.

6 helpings

PORK AND RICE

Porc au Riz

½ lb. pork
2 oz. dripping
4 oz. chopped onion
Salt and pepper
2 teasp. chopped parsley
6 oz. rice
1 lb. skinned tomatoes
¾ pt. stock *or* water

Melt the dripping in a saucepan and fry the onion until soft but not coloured. Add the seasoning, parsley and rice, and cook carefully a little longer until rice begins to look clear. Then place a layer of rice mixture in a casserole, cover with a layer of sliced tomato, then a layer of sliced meat and finish with a layer of tomatoes. Pour the stock over, cover and cook slowly in a moderate oven (**350° F., Gas 4**) for 2–2¼ hr. Add a little more stock if required.

6 helpings

PORK CUTLETS

Côtelettes de Porc

6 pork cutlets
2 tablesp. salad oil
½ teasp. powdered sage
1 teasp. vinegar
Salt and pepper

Trim the cutlets neatly. Make a marinade with the oil, sage, vinegar, salt and pepper and pour over the cutlets. Leave to soak for 1 hr., turning frequently. Drain, then grill or fry until cooked as desired.

Serve with Robert or Soubise sauce.

6 helpings
Cooking time—about 20 min.

PORK PIE

Pâté de Porc

1 lb. lean pork
Powdered herbs
Salt and pepper
1 small onion
½ gill water *or* stock
Hot water crust pastry using 8 oz. flour etc. (p. 556)

Cut the meat into neat small dice and season to taste with herbs, salt and pepper. Place the bones, finely-chopped onion, salt and pepper in a saucepan with the water or stock and simmer for 2 hr., so that the gravy when cold will form a firm jelly. Mould the pastry with the hands or line a pie mould. Put in the filling, add some stock and cover with pastry lid. (The remainder of the stock should be reheated and added after the pie is baked and still hot.) 3 or 4 folds of greased greaseproof paper should be fastened round the pie to preserve its shape and prevent it becoming too brown. Brush the top of the pie with egg, or milk, and make a hole in the centre. Bake in a hot oven (**425° F., Gas 7**) at first and reduce heat as soon as pastry is set to moderate (**350° F., Gas 4**) for about 1½ hr. Remove the greaseproof paper or mould for the last ½ hr. and brush the sides with egg or milk.

NOTE: If preferred, small individual pies may be made. Cook for about 1 hr.

6 helpings

ROAST SUCKING PIG

Cochon de lait rôti

A sucking pig not more than 3 weeks old	**Butter *or* salad oil**
Sage and onion forcemeat	**Thick cream (optional)**

Stuff the pig with the forcemeat, then sew up the opening with fine string. Brush the entire surface of the pig with salad oil or warmed butter and wrap in several folds of well-greased greaseproof paper. Draw the legs well back and tie in a good shape. Roast in a moderate oven (**350° F., Gas 4**), according to size, allowing 25 min. per lb. and 25 min. over. Baste well and about ½ hr. before serving, remove the paper and brush with salad oil or thick cream to improve the colour and crisp the surface. Before serving, cut off the head and split the pig down centre back. Lay the 2 halves on a dish—divide the head and place ½ at each end of the dish.

Usual accompaniments are brown sauce, apple sauce, and sometimes hot currants. The currants should be washed and scalded the day before to make them plump, and then dried.

9–10 helpings

SAVOURY LOIN OF PORK

Longe de Porc farcie

3 lb. loin of pork	**½ teasp. salt**
½ teasp. powdered sage	**¼ saltsp. pepper**
1 saltsp. dry mustard	**Apple sauce**
1 tablesp. finely-chopped onion	**Brown gravy**

Score the pork with narrow lines. Mix the onion with the sage, salt, mustard and pepper and rub the mixture well into the meat. Wrap the joint in greased greaseproof paper and roast in a covered tin in a hot oven (**425° F., Gas 7**) for 10 min. and then reduce heat to moderate (**350° F., Gas 4**) for the remainder of the time. Allow 25 min. per lb. and 25 min. over. About ½ hr. before serving, remove the paper and lid and continue cooking to crisp the crackling. Serve the apple sauce and gravy separately.

6 helpings

SAVOURY TENDERLOIN OF PORK

6 pork chops from the spare rib, tenderloin *or* neck	**⅛ teasp. sage**
2 lb. Spanish onions	**1 oz. dripping**
Salt and pepper	**Mixed herbs**
	½ oz. flour

Dice the onions and mix with a small teasp. salt, ⅛ teasp. pepper, sage and ⅛ teasp. mixed herbs. Put in a casserole with ¼ pt. cold water, cover and cook gently for 1½ hr., stirring occasionally. When the onions are about half cooked, place the chops with a little hot dripping in a meat-tin. Season with salt, pepper and a pinch of herbs. Roast in a moderate oven (**350° F., Gas 4**) for 15 min., then turn them, season the other side and cook for a further 15 min. Remove the chops when cooked and pour off all the fat, leaving any sediment. Sprinkle in the flour and return to the oven to brown. Add the onions to the browned flour, mix well together and reheat. Dish the chops neatly on a hot dish, serving the onion gravy in the centre.

6 helpings

BACON AND HAM

BOILED BACON

Petit lard bouilli

Soak the bacon for at least 1 hr. in warm water—if very dry or highly salted longer is needed, and the water should be changed. Scrape the underside and the rind as clean as possible. Put into a pan with cold water, just to cover. Bring slowly to the boil and remove any scum. Simmer gently until tender, allowing about 25 min. per lb. and 25 min. over, e.g. 2 lb. will take 75 min. or 1 hr. 15 min. if a thick piece, and rather less if a thinner piece. Take joint out and remove the skin—this comes off easily when the bacon is done. If to be eaten cold, allow to cool in the water in which it was cooked. To finish—drain well then sprinkle the fat thickly with a mixture of browned breadcrumbs and brown sugar.

NOTE: Bacon can be cooked very successfully in a pressure cooker. Remove the trivet, cover joint with water, bring to boil then throw the water away. Cover again with water and pressure cook at 15 lb. pressure, allowing 12 min. per lb.

BAKED HAM

Jambon rôti

A ham
Flour
Brown sugar
Cloves

Soak the ham in water for at least 12 hr. Wipe well and trim off any rusty bits. Coat with a flour and water paste crust which must be sufficiently thick all over to keep in the gravy. Place the ham in a fairly hot oven (**400° F., Gas 6**) for about 15 min., then reduce heat to cool (**310° F., Gas 2**) and cook for the remainder of the time allowing 30 min. per lb. Remove the crust and skin, score squares in the fat and place a clove in each square, sprinkle brown sugar over the fat. Garnish the knuckle with a paper frill. Pieces of ham will need less time to cook.

BAKED HAM LOAF

8 oz. ham
4 oz. browned breadcrumbs
2 oz. sultanas
1 large cooking apple
4 oz. corned beef
1 tablesp. finely-chopped parsley
1 teasp. grated lemon rind
Pinch of allspice
Pinch of grated nutmeg
Salt and pepper
2 eggs
Milk

Well grease a bread-tin and coat with browned breadcrumbs. Wash the sultanas well; peel, core and grate the apple. Mince the ham and corned beef and mix with the parsley, lemon rind, breadcrumbs, apple, sultanas, allspice, nutmeg and seasoning. Bind with the beaten eggs and a little milk if needed. Carefully put into the prepared bread-tin and bake in a cool oven (**310° F., Gas 2**) for about 40 min. Serve hot with gravy, or cold with salad.

6 helpings

BAKED HAM SLICE

Jambon rôti

1½–2 lb. slice uncooked ham *or* gammon 1–1½ in. thick
½ teasp. dry mustard
¼ teasp. cinnamon
2 tablesp. brown sugar
Milk

Mix the mustard, cinnamon and brown sugar and spread on both sides of the ham. Place in a casserole and add sufficient milk to barely cover the ham. Cook in a cool oven (**310° F., Gas 2**) for ¾ hr.

6 helpings

BOILED HAM (1)

Jambon bouilli

Ham
Glaze *or* raspings
Brown sugar

If the ham has been hung for a long time and is very dry and salt, soak for 24 hr., changing the water as necessary. For most hams about 12 hr. soaking is sufficient. Clean and trim off the rusty parts. Put into a saucepan with sufficient cold water to cover and simmer gently until tender, allowing 30 min. per lb. When cooked, remove the ham and strip off the skin. Sprinkle the ham with a mixture of equal quantities of raspings and brown sugar. If to be eaten cold, after removing skin, put the ham back into the water until cold to keep it juicy. Before serving, sprinkle on the raspings and sugar, or glaze, if preferred.

NOTE: To ensure that the ham is sweet insert a sharp knife close to the bone—when withdrawn there should be no unpleasant smell.

BOILED HAM (2)

One 2 lb. ham
Vinegar
1 onion
1 head of celery
1 turnip
A bunch of savoury herbs
Raspings

Prepare the ham as in the preceding recipe and let it soak for a few hours in vinegar and water, mixed together in the proportion of 1 teasp. of vinegar to 1 pt of water. Then put the ham into cold water and bring to the boil. When boiling add the sliced vegetables, and herbs. Simmer gently until tender, allowing 30 min. per lb.

Then remove the skin, cover the ham with raspings and put a paper frill round the knuckle.

HAM AND EGG FLAN

Short *or* flaky pastry (p. 557), using 4–6 oz. flour	**¾ pt. milk *or* unsweetened evaporated milk**
6 oz. thinly-sliced ham	**Salt and pepper**
3 eggs	

Roll out the pastry thinly and line a flan case or sandwich-tin. Dice the ham and put into the flan. Lightly beat the eggs, add the milk, season well and pour on top of the ham. Bake on middle shelf of a moderate oven (**350° F., Gas 4**) until the pastry is cooked and the filling set.

6 helpings
Cooking time—about 45 min.

HOME BAKED HAM AND BEANS

½ lb. ham	**Salt and pepper**
½ lb. haricot beans	**2 cloves**
½ lb. tomatoes	**½ pt. water *or* stock (approx.)**
1 onion	
1 cooking apple	

Soak the beans overnight. Skin and slice the tomatoes; chop the onion and the apple finely. Put them in a casserole with the beans, seasoning, cloves and sufficient stock or water to cover. Put on lid and cook in a warm oven (**335° F., Gas 3**) for about 2 hr. until the beans are tender. Add extra water or stock as needed. Grill the ham, cut into small pieces and add to the casserole. Reheat, remove cloves and serve.

PINEAPPLE HAM SLICES

12 oz. cooked ham	**3 tablesp. sherry, cider *or* pineapple juice**
1 teasp. mixed mustard	**6 slices of pineapple**
1 tablesp. mayonnaise	**4 gherkins (optional)**

Mince the ham and mix with the mustard, mayonnaise and sherry, cider or juice. Drain the pineapple slices and cover neatly with ham mixture. Place in a greased fireproof dish or meat-tin and bake in a moderate oven. (**350° F., Gas 4**) for 10–15 min. Serve garnished with slices of gherkin if liked.

6 helpings

STUFFED HAM

Jambon farci

1½–2 lb. slices of ham—about ¼ in. thick	**1 egg**
6–8 apricots *or* 2 apples	**A little flour**
3 oz. breadcrumbs	**1 cup milk**
Salt and pepper	**½ cup water *or* syrup from canned apricots**

If dried apricots are used, soak overnight and stew until tender before using. Cut the slices of ham in two. Chop the apricots or apples and mix with the breadcrumbs and seasoning and bind lightly with beaten egg. Spread this mixture over half the slices of ham and make into sandwiches. Coat lightly with flour and place in a casserole. Pour over the milk and water, or syrup, and bake in a moderate oven (**350° F., Gas 4**) for 30–40 min. Remove lid of casserole for last 10 min.

6 helpings

Pig's Cheek

PIG'S CHEEK

A pig's cheek	**Browned breadcrumbs**

If the cheek has been cured and dried, soak it for 5–6 hr., if not, wash well in several waters. Cover the meat with warm water and simmer gently for 2½ hr. Then remove the cheek, strip off the skin and cover the cheek thickly with lightly browned crumbs. Bake for about ½ hr. in a moderate oven (**350° F., Gas 4**). Serve hot or cold. Baking the meat is not essential and can be omitted if liked.

3–4 helpings

Pig's Ears

PIG'S EARS

Oreilles de Porc

4 pig's ears	**½ pt. brown sauce (p. 119)**
Stock *or* water	
Frying fat	

STUFFING

4 tablesp. breadcrumbs
2 tablesp. finely-chopped veal
2 tablesp. finely-chopped suet
1 teasp. finely-chopped parsley
½ teasp. anchovy essence
Salt and pepper
1 egg

Wash the ears well and soak for 5–6 hr. Cover with stock or water and simmer gently 1½ hr. Mix together the breadcrumbs, veal, suet, parsley and anchovy essence. Season well with salt and pepper and moisten slightly with the beaten egg. Raise the skin of the upper side of the ears, insert the forcemeat lightly and secure the openings. Fry in shallow hot fat until lightly browned, then drain off the fat. Add stock, cover closely and either simmer on the stove or in a moderate oven (**350° F., Gas 4**) for about 1 hr. Drain well. Serve with the sauce poured over.

2 helpings

Pig's Feet

PIG'S FEET AND EARS IN JELLY

Pieds et Oreilles de Porc à la Gelée

4 pig's feet
2 pig's ears
1 dessertsp. finely-chopped parsley
½ teasp. finely-chopped sage
Salt and pepper

Wash the feet and ears well in salt water. Barely cover with cold water and simmer gently until the bones can be easily withdrawn. Cut the meat into neat dice and replace in the liquid. Add the parsley, sage, salt and pepper to taste. Simmer gently for 15 min.

Turn into a mould or basin and leave until cold and set.

3–4 helpings

STUFFED PIG'S FEET *Pieds de Porc, farcis*

4 pig's feet
Salt
1 tablesp. flour
1 egg
Breadcrumbs
Frying fat

STUFFING

2 tablesp. cooked and finely-chopped onion
1 tablesp. breadcrumbs
1 tablesp. oiled butter
½ teasp. salt
½ teasp. powdered sage
½ teasp. mixed mustard
¼ teasp. pepper

Put the feet into a saucepan with 1 teasp. salt. Cover with cold water and simmer for about 3 hr. Mix the ingredients for the stuffing. When the feet are done, split them, remove the bones and press the stuffing into the cavities. Replace the halves together and press between 2 dishes with a weight on top until cold. When ready for use, cut the feet into slices about 1 in. thick. Roll each piece in flour and brush with beaten egg and coat with breadcrumbs. Fry in hot fat until golden brown. Serve hot garnished with parsley.

6 helpings

Pig's Fry

PIG'S FRY

1½–2 lb. pig's fry which consists of the heart, lights, liver and sweetbread
Salt and pepper
Flour
Sage
Frying fat

Wash the fry well. Cover with cold water, add a little salt and boil gently for ½–¾ hr. Drain, dry well, and cut into thin slices. Coat lightly with flour seasoned with salt and pepper and a little sage. Fry in hot fat until nicely browned then remove and keep hot. Sprinkle a little flour on the bottom of the frying-pan, let it brown, then pour in some of the stock in which the fry was boiled, season to taste. Serve the fry with a little of the gravy poured round and serve the rest separately.

6 helpings

PIG'S FRY—BAKED WITH HERBS

1½–2 lb. pig's fry
Salt and pepper
Powdered sage
Flour
2–3 onions
3 lb. potatoes
Stock *or* water

Wash the fry and dry well. Cut it into thin slices. Place a layer of the fry on the bottom of a well-greased pie-dish. Season with salt, pepper and sage, and dredge liberally with flour. Cover with a layer of sliced onion, then a layer of sliced potato. Repeat the layers until all the ingredients are used up, ending with a layer of potato. Three-quarters fill the dish with boiling stock or water. Cover with greased greaseproof paper, and bake for 2½ hr. in a moderate oven (**350° F., Gas 4**). About ½ hr. before serving, remove the paper to allow the potatoes to brown.

6 helpings

Pig's Head

BOILED PIG'S HEAD

Tête de Porc bouillie

A pig's head	**Salt**

Clean the head thoroughly. Remove the hair, eyes, snout and brains if this has not been done by the butcher. Soak well in salt water for 2 hr., changing the water 3 or 4 times. Drain the head well, place in a large saucepan and just cover with cold water. Simmer for 3–3½ hr. or until tender.

FAGGOTS or "SAVOURY DUCKS"

1 lb. pig's liver *or* fry	**Salt and pepper**
2 medium-sized onions	**A pinch of grated nutmeg**
4 oz. fat pork	**1 egg**
A pinch of thyme	**Breadcrumbs**
½ teasp. powdered sage	**A pig's caul**
A pinch of basil	

Slice the liver, onions and pork thinly. Put in a saucepan with the thyme, sage, basil, salt, pepper and nutmeg and barely cover with water. Simmer for ½ hr., then strain off the liquid and save for the gravy. Mince the contents of the stewpan finely. Add the beaten egg and sufficient breadcrumbs to make into a fairly firm mixture and mix thoroughly. Form into balls and enclose each one in a piece of caul. Place in a baking-tin, and add a little gravy. Bake in a fairly hot oven (**400° F., Gas 6**) until nicely browned. Serve with a good thickened gravy. If preferred, the mixture can be pressed into a well greased baking-tin and marked into squares. Cover with caul and cut into squares after cooking.

6 helpings

SAUSAGES—to make

1 lb. pork	**Salt and pepper**
1 lb. lean veal	**6 sage leaves (optional)**
1 lb. beef suet	**⅛ teasp. marjoram (optional)**
½ lb. breadcrumbs	**¼ teasp. savoury herbs (optional)**
Grated rind of ½ lemon	**Sausage skins**
⅛ teasp. grated nutmeg	

Remove all the skin and gristle from the pork. Chop or mince the pork, veal and suet together very finely. Add the breadcrumbs, lemon rind, nutmeg, seasoning and the herbs if desired, which must all be very finely chopped. Mix together very thoroughly and then put into skins. Alternatively, the mixture may be formed into meat cakes, floured and fried.

SAUSAGES—to boil

Prick the sausages with a fork, throw them into boiling water, and cook gently for 15 min. Serve on hot buttered toast or mashed potato.

SAUSAGES—to fry

Prick the sausages well with a fork, as this prevents the skins breaking. Put into a frying-pan containing a little hot fat and fry gently, turning 2 or 3 times, to brown them equally.

Serve on hot buttered toast or with mashed potatoes.

Pig's Tongues

PIG'S TONGUES

Trim off the roots and wash the tongues thoroughly several times in salt water. See recipes for Sheep's Tongues p. 246.

VEAL

Once the preceding facts about beef, pork and lamb have been acquired there is little that needs to be added on veal. The carcase is only sparsely fatted in all except the largest calves and even in these there is not the same percentage of fat as would be found on other meat. The flesh is usually described as pink but the colour is darker than that of pork. The cuts follow the same pattern as lamb cutting and are described by the same names. Occasionally the shoulder is called an **oyster of veal** after the fore knuckle has been removed.

The meat from the hind and fore knuckles, equivalent to the shin and leg of beef together with the scrag and middle neck are used for stewing. All the other cuts are suitable for roasting or frying. Due to the absence of fat, veal is rather dry and tasteless unless cooked with a moist, fat-containing stuffing, or served with a sauce. The breast, stuffed and roasted, is probably the most tasty and the most economical cut.

BRAISED NECK OF VEAL

Carré de Veau braisée

2½ lb. best end of neck of veal
1½ oz. fat
2 oz. bacon
2 onions
2 carrots
1 small turnip
Bouquet garni
2 cloves
1 blade of mace
12 peppercorns
Salt and pepper
Stock
¾ oz. flour
Meat glaze
1 tablesp. capers
1 teasp. lemon juice

Detach the short pieces of rib bones which have been sawn across and fold the flap under. Melt ¾ oz. of the fat in a stewpan and fry the bacon and vegetables slightly. Add the bouquet garni, cloves, mace, peppercorns, and seasoning, nearly cover with stock and bring slowly to the boil. Place the meat on the bed of vegetables, cover with greased paper and a well-fitting lid and cook gently for about 2 hr., adding more stock as necessary and basting occasionally. Then place in a moderate oven (**350° F., Gas 4**) for ½ hr., removing the lid for the last 15 min. Meanwhile melt the remaining ¾ oz. fat in a small pan, add the flour and fry gently until nut brown. When the meat is tender, remove to a hot dish, brush over with glaze and keep hot. Strain the liquid, add to the brown roux and stir until smooth. Add more stock if necessary and simmer for 5 min. Add the capers and lemon juice, season to taste and serve separately. Garnish the meat with the vegetables and serve very hot.

6 helpings

CASSEROLE OF VEAL

Veau en Casserole

1½ lb. lean stewing veal
1 pt. thick Velouté sauce
2 doz. button mushrooms
Salt and pepper
2 teasp. lemon juice

GARNISH

Bacon rolls
Crimped slices of lemon

1

2

3

4

5

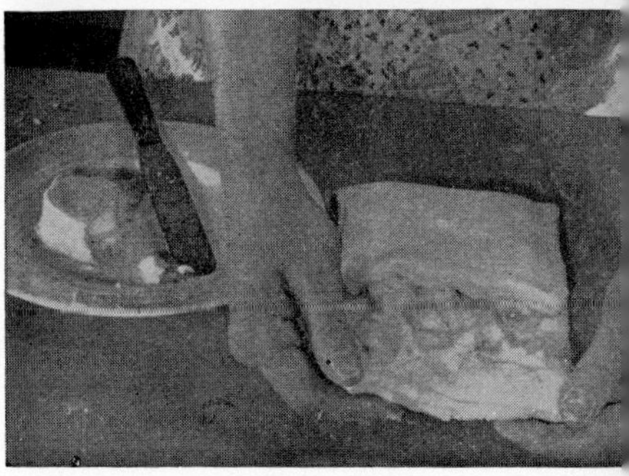
6

PLATE 11

Making Flaky Pastry

1 *If a mixture of butter and lard is being used, first blend the two together with a round-bladed knife.*

2 *Sift the flour and salt into a bowl. Divide fat into four equal portions.*

3 *Lightly rub quarter of the fat into the flour. Next mix to a soft dough with cold water and lemon juice.*

4 *Roll dough out into an oblong shape.*

5 *Place quarter of the fat in small pieces on the top ⅔ of the pastry.*

6 *Fold the bottom third of the pastry up and the top third downwards.*

7 *With the rolling pin, press edges lightly together, make a half turn, and press ridges in the pastry to distribute the air evenly. Allow dough to relax. Roll out and repeat with the other two portions of fat.*

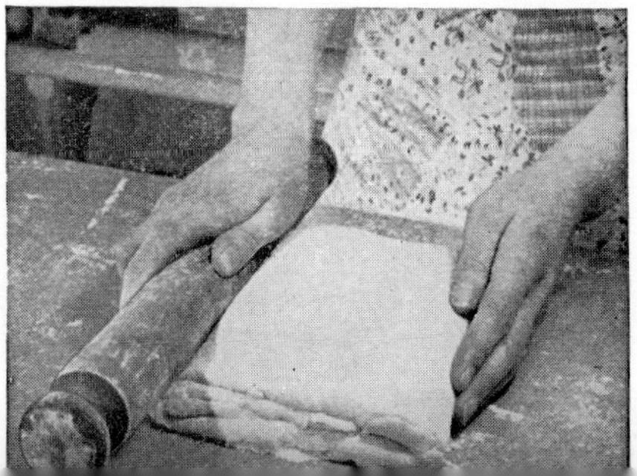
7

1

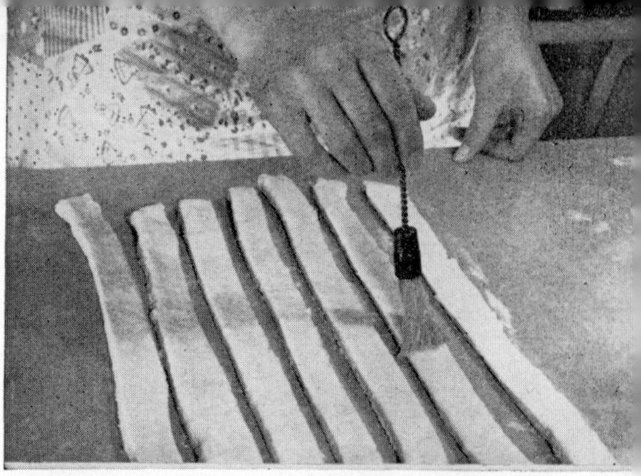

2

3

4

5

PLATE 12
Making Pastry Cones

1 Roll out the pastry to about $\frac{1}{8}$ inch thickness and cut into strips $\frac{1}{2}$ inch wide and 12–13 inches long.

2 Damp the strips lightly with water.

3 Wind round the horn cases, starting from point at the base and working upwards. The moist surface should be kept on the outside.

4 Finish with overlap on the underside of the tin and trim neatly.

5 Allow to stand for about 1 hour. Brush over the surface of the cones with milk or egg and milk.

Wipe and trim the meat, discarding any skin or fat. Cut into neat pieces and put into a casserole. Bring the sauce to boiling point and pour over the veal, adding the mushrooms and seasoning. Stand the casserole in a pan of water and simmer very gently in a warm to moderate oven (**335°–350° F., Gas 3–4**) for about 1½ hr. When tender, stir in the lemon juice, place the grilled bacon rolls on top, and garnish with lemon. Serve in the casserole.

6 helpings

CASSEROLE OF VEAL WITH DUMPLINGS

1½ lb. lean stewing veal	**¼ pt. tomato purée *or* pulp**
2 onions	**Salt and pepper**
2 tablesp. oil *or* lard	**Bouquet garni**
1–2 cloves of garlic	**Suet pastry using 3–4 oz. flour, etc.**
½ pt. white stock	**Parsley**

Wipe the meat, remove any skin and bone, and cut the meat into small pieces. Slice the onions, heat the oil and cook the onions and garlic until light brown. Add the meat and cook quickly until lightly browned. Pour off the surplus fat and add the stock, tomato purée or pulp, seasoning and the bouquet garni. Place in a casserole with a well fitting lid and cook in a moderate oven (**350° F., Gas 4**) for 1¼ hr. When ready, remove the bouquet garni and skim off any fat. Have ready 12 small dumplings made from the suet pastry. Drop them into the casserole and return to the oven for ½ hr. Serve in the casserole sprinkled with parsley.

6 helpings

COLLOPS OF VEAL

Paupiettes de Veau

1½ lb. fillet of veal	**Butter *or* fat for frying**
6 bacon rashers	**¾ oz. flour**
Salt and pepper	**½ pt. stock *or* water**
4 oz. veal forcemeat (p. 144)	**1 tablesp. lemon juice**
Egg and breadcrumbs	**Pinch of ground mace**

GARNISH

Slices of lemon	**Fried forcemeat balls**
Parsley	

Cut the meat into very thin strips about 3 in. by 2 in. After removing the rind place the bacon rashers on a board and stretch with a palette knife. Cover each piece of meat with a piece of bacon, season well, spread lightly with forcemeat and roll up. Coat with egg and breadcrumbs and fry gently in hot fat. If forcemeat balls are to be used for the garnish, fry them at the same time. Drain well and keep hot. Pour away surplus fat, leaving about ¾ oz. in the pan and any sediment. Add the flour and cook until light brown. Add boiling stock or water, lemon juice, a pinch of mace and seasoning to taste and simmer gently for 5 min., then strain. Arrange the collops on a hot dish.

Garnish with sliced lemon, sprigs of parsley and fried forcemeat balls. Serve the sauce separately.

6 helpings

CURRIED VEAL

1½ lb. lean veal	**2 heaped teasp. curry paste**
2½ oz. butter *or* margarine	**2 heaped teasp. chutney**
2 onions	**Salt**
2 apples	**6 oz. rice**
1 clove of garlic (optional)	**2 heaped teasp. red-currant jelly**
1 oz. flour	**Lemon juice**
1–2 heaped teasp. curry powder	**Cayenne pepper**
1½ pt. light stock *or* coconut infusion	

GARNISH

Chilli skins *or* paprika pepper	**Crimped slices of lemon**
Sliced gherkin	**Parsley**

Trim, wipe and cut the meat into 1-in. cubes. Heat the fat and fry the meat lightly until sealed and lightly browned. Then remove. Fry the finely-chopped onions and apples and the minced garlic for about 7 min. without browning too much. Add the flour and curry powder to the apple and cook for at least 5 min. to get rid of the raw flavour. Add the stock or coconut infusion, curry paste, chutney and salt and whilst stirring bring slowly to the boil. Return the meat to the pan and simmer very slowly for about 2 hr., stirring occasionally. Cook the rice and arrange as a border on a hot dish and keep hot. Add to the curry the redcurrant jelly, lemon juice, cayenne pepper to taste and place in the centre of the dish. Garnish with chilli skins or paprika pepper, gherkin, lemon and parsley.

NOTE: Curry can be served with any of the following accompaniments: pappadums; slices of hard-boiled egg; cubes of cucumber in coconut milk; green olives; Bombay duck; shredded coconut; cubes of salted almonds; sliced banana; variety of chutneys; fresh melon; chillies; silver onions; guava jelly; preserved ginger; diced pineapple.

6 helpings

To make coconut infusion

Add 1½ pt. boiling water to 2 heaped tablesp. coconut. Infuse for 15–20 min., strain and use as stock.

ESCALLOPS OF VEAL—VIENNESE STYLE

Escalopes de Veau à la Viennoise

1¼–1½ lb. fillet of veal cut in 6 slices
Salt and pepper
Flour
Egg and breadcrumbs
Oil *or* butter for frying
Lemon juice

BEURRE NOISETTE

2 oz. butter
Salt and pepper
Cayenne pepper

GARNISH

6 stoned olives
6 boned anchovy fillets
1 hard-boiled egg
1 tablesp. chopped parsley
Crimped slices of lemon

Wipe the meat, season, dip in flour and coat with egg and breadcrumbs. Heat the oil or butter and fry the escallops for about 5 min. until golden brown. Make the beurre noisette by heating the butter in a saucepan until golden brown, then seasoning with salt, pepper and cayenne. Place the escallops slightly overlapping on a hot dish. Sprinkle with lemon juice and pour over the beurre noisette. Garnish with olives wrapped in anchovy fillets. Place the chopped egg white, sieved egg yolk and chopped parsley at either end of the dish. Serve with crimped lemon slices.

6 helpings

FILLETS OF VEAL

Filets de Veau

1¼–1½ lb. fillet of veal
1 egg
½ teasp. finely-chopped parsley
¼ teasp. thyme
2 teasp. grated lemon rind
1 teasp. lemon juice
Breadcrumbs
2 oz. butter *or* fat
Bacon rolls
Mashed potatoes

SAUCE

½ oz. flour
½ pt. white stock
½ teasp. lemon juice
A little gravy browning
Salt and pepper
1–2 tablesp. cream (optional)

Cut the veal into slices about ½ in. thick, then cut each slice into rounds of about 2¼–2½ in. diameter. Beat with a wooden spoon or rolling-pin. Beat the egg and add to it the parsley, thyme, lemon rind and lemon juice. Soak the fillets in this mixture for about ½ hr. then coat with crumbs. Fry in the hot fat until golden brown on both sides, then reduce heat and cook more slowly for 7–10 min. in all. Drain thoroughly and keep hot together with the fried or grilled bacon rolls. To make the sauce, add the flour to the fat remaining in the pan and fry lightly. Add the stock, stir until it boils, then add the lemon juice, gravy browning and seasoning and simmer for 3 min. Add the cream, if liked. Serve the fillets in a circle on a border of mashed potatoes, pile the bacon rolls in the centre and pour the strained sauce round.

6 helpings

FILLETS OF VEAL—MILAN STYLE

Filets de Veau à la Milanaise

1½ lb. fillet of veal
2 oz. butter *or* fat
3 bacon rashers
1 shallot
2 large tomatoes
Salt and pepper
1 pt. brown sauce
2 tablesp. sherry (optional)
3 oz. spaghetti
12 stoned olives

Wipe, trim, season the meat and cut into neat pieces. Heat the fat and fry the meat quickly and lightly. Drain off the surplus fat and place the meat in a casserole with the diced bacon, finely-chopped shallot and skinned sliced tomatoes. Season to taste. Bring the sauce to the boil, add the sherry (if used) and pour on to the veal. Cook gently for 1 hr. Cook the spaghetti in boiling salted water for 5 min. Rinse with cold water and add to the casserole for 15 min. before serving. Garnish with stoned heated olives.

6 helpings

FILLETS OF VEAL—TALLEYRAND STYLE

Filets de Veau à la Tallyrand

1¼–1½ lb. fillets of veal	**¾ pt. white sauce**
Butter *or* fat	**Mashed potatoes**
1 small onion *or* 2 shallots	**1–2 egg yolks**
4 medium-sized mushrooms	**2 teasp. lemon juice**
	2 teasp. chopped parsley
	Salt and pepper

Cut the meat into neat rounds or pieces and flatten slightly with a wooden spoon. Sauté briskly in the butter without browning. Chop the onion or shallots and mushrooms finely, add to the meat and continue cooking for 3–4 min. Drain off surplus fat. Add the white sauce and cook the fillets gently for about 1 hr. Then remove fillets and place in a single row on a foundation of mashed or piped potato. Add the egg yolks, lemon juice and parsley to the sauce and cook without boiling until it thickens. Season to taste and pour over the fillets.

6 helpings

FLADGEON OF VEAL

¾ lb. lean veal	**Salt and pepper**
¼ lb. suet	**2 eggs**
3 oz. breadcrumbs	**Gravy *or* milk**
1 teasp. finely-grated lemon rind	**¼ pt. stock**
Pinch of nutmeg	**Parsley**

Finely mince the veal and suet and mix with the breadcrumbs, lemon rind, nutmeg and seasoning to taste. Stir in 1 egg and as much gravy or milk as is required to thoroughly moisten the mixture. Half-fill a greased pie-dish with the mixture and bake for 1 hr. in a fairly hot oven (**375° F., Gas 5**). Beat up the other egg, add stock, seasoning to taste, and pour over the contents of the pie-dish. Bake until set. Garnish with parsley and serve in the dish.

4 helpings

FRICANDEAU OF VEAL

Fricandeau de Veau

2 lb. piece of fillet veal	**Stock**
Larding bacon	**Bouquet garni**
2 onions	**2 cloves**
2 carrots	**6 peppercorns**
1 turnip	**Salt and pepper**
2 sticks of celery	**Meat glaze**
1 oz. butter *or* fat	**1½ lb. sorrel *or* spinach purée**
1 oz. bacon cut in pieces	**Espagnole sauce** (p. 130)

Trim and wipe the meat and beat with a rolling-pin. Lard the best side closely with strips of larding bacon. Slice the onions thickly, cut the carrots and turnip in blocks, cut up the celery roughly. Melt the fat and fry the bacon and the prepared vegetables. Then lay the meat on top and fry gently for about 15 min. Add stock to cover the vegetables, the bouquet garni, flavourings and seasoning. Cover with greased paper and a lid and cook gently for about 1 hr., adding more stock as necessary. Remove the lid and paper and put into a fairly hot oven (**400° F., Gas 6**) for 15 min. to crisp and brown the lardoons. Brush the meat with glaze, place on a hot dish larded side uppermost on a bed of purée and serve the remainder of the sorrel or spinach separately.

Pour a little Espagnole sauce round the meat, and serve the remainder in a sauce-boat. The liquid from the braising tin should be strained, reduced, skimmed to remove all fat and poured round the meat or added to the sauce.

6 helpings

FRICANDELLES OF VEAL WITH TOMATO SAUCE AND OLIVES

1¼ lb. lean veal	**6 oz. bread**
4 oz. fat	**Milk**
3 oz. finely-chopped onion	**¼ pt. water (approx.)**
	Salt and pepper
¼ teasp. finely-chopped parsley	**Paprika**
	Flour
¼ teasp. powdered lemon thyme	**Oil *or* fat**
	¾ pt. tomato sauce

GARNISH

Stoned black olives	**Slices of lemon**

Mince the veal finely. Mix the meat, fat, onion, parsley and thyme together with the bread which has been soaked in milk, then squeezed very dry. Mince the mixture. Add the water very gradually whilst working the mixture well with the hand. Season well with salt, pepper and paprika and shape into balls about the size of a large walnut. Roll lightly in flour and fry until golden brown in the fat. Place in a casserole or pan, pour over tomato sauce just to cover and cook very gently for about ½ hr. Serve in the casserole or if cooked in a pan, place on a hot dish and garnish with black olives and slices of lemon.

6 helpings

GRENADINES OF VEAL

Grenadins de Veau

1½ lb. fillet of veal	**1 clove**
Strips of larding bacon	**1 pt. stock**
	Meat glaze
1 onion	**1 oz. flour**
1 carrot	**A border of mashed *or* piped potatoes**
½ turnip	
2 sticks of celery	**Peas *or* asparagus tips *or* macedoine of vegetables**
2 oz. butter *or* fat	
Bouquet garni	
6 peppercorns	

Cut the meat into slices ½ in. thick and cut each slice into rounds about 2 in. diameter (grenadines). Lard them on one side with thin strips of bacon about 1½ in. long. Slice the onion, carrot and turnip, chop the celery. Melt 1 oz. of the fat in a stewpan, put in the bouquet garni, peppercorns, clove and vegetables and fry lightly. Lay the grenadines on top, cover and fry gently for 10 min., then add enough stock to cover the vegetables. Cover the grenadines with greased paper, replace the lid and cook gently for 1 hr., adding the rest of the stock as necessary. Remove the grenadines and place them in the oven to brown and crisp the bacon. Brush with meat glaze. Meanwhile make a brown roux with the remaining fat and the flour. Strain about ¾ pt. of liquid from the stewpan and add to the roux. Stir until boiling then simmer for 5 min. Season to taste. Have ready the mashed or piped potato border on a hot dish. Arrange the grenadines in a circle and fill the centre with peas, asparagus tips or macedoine of vegetables. Pour some of the sauce round and serve the rest separately.

6 helpings

GRENADINES OF VEAL—MARCHAND

Grenadines de Veau à la Marchand de Vin

1½ lb. fillet of veal	**1 gill tomato sauce**
Strips of larding bacon	**1 gill brown sauce**
2 shallots	**1 teasp. finely-chopped parsley**
2 oz. butter *or* fat	
1 gill claret	**Salt and pepper**

Prepare and lard the grenadines as directed in the previous recipe. Chop the shallots finely, melt the fat in a small saucepan and fry them without browning. Pour the surplus fat into a sauté pan, add the claret to the shallots and boil until well reduced. Add the tomato and brown sauce, the parsley, salt and pepper and boil well until reduced by one third. Re-heat the butter in the sauté pan and fry the grenadines until lightly browned on both sides. Pour off any remaining fat, add the reduced sauces, cover with a lid and cook very gently for about 15 min. Serve the grenadines on a potato border, garnished with strips of bacon, strain the sauce over the grenadines and serve.

6 helpings

HARICOT OF VEAL

Haricot de Veau

2½ lb. neck of veal	**1½ pt. stock**
2 onions	**Salt and pepper**
1½ oz. dripping	**6 oz. cooked haricot beans**
1½ oz. flour	

GARNISH

2 carrots	**1 turnip**

Wipe and trim the meat and cut it into pieces convenient for serving. Cut the carrots and turnip into neat dice or strips (these are cooked separately for the garnish). Reserve the trimmings for flavouring. Slice the onion, heat the dripping and fry the meat and onion lightly. Remove to a plate, sprinkle the flour on to the fat and cook slowly until well browned, add the stock, stir until boiling and season to taste. Put in the meat and onion and vegetable trimmings and simmer gently for 1½ hr. Strain the sauce and return to the pan with the cooked haricot beans and simmer for a further 15 min. Lift out the meat, place on a hot dish, pour the sauce over and garnish with the dice or strips of carrot and turnip.

6 helpings

LARDED AND ROAST VEAL

Poitrine de Veau rôtie

2½–3 lb. neck of veal	**Bouquet garni**
Larding bacon	**10 peppercorns**
2 carrots	**Stock**
1 onion	**Fat for basting**
1 small turnip	**1 oz. butter** *or* **margarine**
2 sticks of celery	
Salt and pepper	**1 oz. flour**

Fold the flap of the joint under if not already done. Lard the upper surface in close rows with thin 1½ in. strips of bacon. Slice the carrots, onion, turnip and celery and place in a saucepan with the salt, bouquet garni, peppercorns and enough stock to barely cover the vegetables. Lay the meat on top, cover with greased paper, put on the lid and cook gently for 2 hr., adding more stock when necessary. Heat some dripping in a baking-tin, put the meat in, baste well and bake in a moderate oven (**350° F., Gas 4**) for ½ hr., basting after 15 min. Have ready a brown roux made from the 1 oz. fat and flour, add ¾ pt. of stock from the saucepan and stir until boiling. Then simmer for 5 min. and season to taste. Serve the meat on a hot dish and serve the sauce separately.

6 helpings

LOIN OF VEAL—DAUBE STYLE

Longe de Veau à la Daube

2½–3 lb. chump end of loin of veal	**1 onion**
	Bouquet garni
4 oz. veal forcemeat	**1 blade of mace**
1 pt. veal stock *or* **water**	**10 peppercorns**
	Salt and pepper
A few rashers of lean bacon	

Bone the meat, fill the cavity with forcemeat and tie into a good shape. Put the stock or water into a pan, bring to the boil and put in the meat. Cover with the bacon, add the sliced onion, flavourings and seasoning and boil for 5 min., then reduce to simmering point and simmer gently for 2½ hr., basting the meat with stock. Do not add more liquid unless essential. When tender, place the meat on a hot dish, strain the remaining liquid into a small saucepan and boil rapidly until reduced to a glaze. Brush the meat thickly with the glaze.

Serve with tomato sauce.

POT PIE OF VEAL

Pâté de veau et pommes de terre

1¼ lb. lean veal	**1 lb. potatoes**
½ lb. pickled pork	**Puff** *or* **rough puff pastry using 6 oz. flour, etc.**
Salt and pepper	
Stock	

Cut the meat into pieces convenient for serving and cut the pork into thin small slices. Place the meat and pork in layers in a large pie-dish, seasoning each layer well with salt and pepper, and fill the dish ¾ full with stock. Cover with a lid and cook in a moderate oven (**350° F., Gas 4**) for 1½ hr. Meanwhile parboil the potatoes and cut in thick slices. After cooking for 1½ hr., allow the meat to cool slightly. Add more stock if necessary, place the potatoes on top, cover with pastry and make a hole in the top. Bake in a very hot oven (**450° F., Gas 8**) until the pastry is set, reduce heat and cook more slowly for the remainder of the time, making 40–50 min. altogether. Add more hot stock through the hole in the top.

Garnish with parsley and serve.

6 helpings

QUENELLES OF VEAL

Quenelles de Veau

1 lb. fillet of veal	**Salt and pepper**
1 oz. butter	**1 tablesp. cream (optional)**
2 oz. flour	
¼ pt. veal stock	**¾ pt. Béchamel *or* Velouté sauce**
2 eggs	

GARNISH

Parsley *or* dried truffle	**Green peas**

Pass the veal twice through a mincer or chop it very finely. Then make a panada: melt the butter in a pan, add the flour and cook slightly. Add the stock and stir and cook until the mixture becomes very thick and smooth, then allow to cool. Pound the panada and meat together, and the eggs 1 at a time, seasoning to taste and pound all well together. Rub the mixture through a sieve and add cream if used. Shape the mixture into oval quenelles with 2 dessertspoons previously dipped in hot water. Place them in a greased sauté pan. Gently pour in enough boiling water to cover and cover with a sheet of greased paper. Poach very gently without boiling for about 20 min. until firm. Drain, coat with sauce and decorate with chopped parsley or chopped dried truffle. Garnish with peas.

5 helpings

RAGOÛT OF VEAL

Ragoût de Veau

2½ lb. neck, breast *or* knuckle of veal	**Hot water**
	Salt and pepper
1½ oz. dripping	**1½ oz. butter *or* fat**
1 onion	**1½ oz. flour**

GARNISH

2 carrots	**Chopped parsley**
2 turnips	**Bacon rolls**

Cut the meat into pieces convenient for serving. Heat the dripping in a saucepan, fry the meat until lightly browned, then remove it. Fry the sliced onion for a few minutes, then drain off the surplus fat. Return the meat to the saucepan, cover with hot water and add seasoning. Cover with a lid and cook slowly until a pale brown colour. Meanwhile dice the vegetables for the garnish and add the trimmings to the meat. Cook the diced vegetables separately, strain then toss in a little butter. Add the chopped parsley and keep hot. When pale brown, remove the meat and keep hot. Strain the liquid in the saucepan and make up to ¾ pt. with water, if necessary. Add to it the blended fat and flour and cook and stir for 4 min. Season to taste, return the meat and simmer gently for ½ hr. Garnish with grilled bacon rolls and the diced vegetables.

6 helpings

STEAMED VEAL

1½–2 lb. cushion of veal	**1 oz. flour**
Salt and pepper	**½ pt. milk**
3 sticks of celery	**1–2 egg yolks**
1 oz. butter	**1–2 teasp. lemon juice**

Wipe, trim and season the veal and tie into a good shape. Place in a steamer with about 3 tablesp. water and the celery cut into 1-in. pieces. Steam for about 1½–2 hr. When the veal is nearly ready, melt the fat in a saucepan and add the flour. Cook for a few minutes, stirring well to avoid discolouring. Place the veal on a hot dish, remove string and keep hot. Add the strained liquid in which the veal was cooked, and the milk, to the roux in the pan and stir well until boiling. Stir whilst cooking for 5 min. Remove pan from heat, add the egg yolks and stir well. Add the lemon juice and more seasoning if required, and pour over the veal.

Garnish if liked with sprigs of cauliflower and grilled bacon rolls.

6 helpings

STEWED BREAST OF VEAL

2½ lb. breast of veal	**12 peppercorns**
2 onions	**Salt**
2 small carrots	**1 pt. parsley sauce *or* piquant sauce**
1 small turnip	

Wipe the meat and place in a pan with as much cold water as will cover it. Bring to the boil and skim. Add the vegetables, cut into dice, peppercorns and salt to taste. Cover with a well fitting lid and simmer gently for 2½–3 hr. Prepare the sauce using some of the veal stock.

Place the veal on a hot dish, pour over sufficient sauce to cover the meat and serve the remainder in a sauce-boat.

6 helpings

STEWED, ROLLED BREAST OF VEAL

$2\frac{1}{2}$–3 lb. breast of veal	**Stock; *or* water and 2 onions, 1 carrot, $\frac{1}{2}$ turnip and a little celery salt**
Salt and pepper	**Brown gravy**
Veal forcemeat	

GARNISH

Forcemeat balls	**Slices of lemon**
Bacon rolls	

Wipe and bone the meat and flatten with a rolling-pin. Season it and spread with a thin layer of forcemeat. Roll up the meat and skewer or tie securely. Form the rest of the forcemeat into balls for frying. Have ready a saucepan of sufficient boiling stock to cover the joint. Place the meat in it, bring to the boil again, skim and simmer very gently for about 3 hr. If water is used the vegetables should be added when the water boils. Prepare the gravy. Just before the veal is ready, fry the forcemeat balls and grill the bacon rolls. Place the veal on a hot dish, remove the skewers or string, and pour a little gravy over the meat if liked. Garnish with forcemeat balls, bacon rolls and cut lemon. Serve the remainder of the gravy separately.

NOTE: If liked the meat can be simmered with the bones. Use $\frac{1}{2}$ veal liquor and $\frac{1}{2}$ milk to make parsley sauce to coat the meat. Use neat pieces of carrot as additional garnish.

6 helpings

STEWED KNUCKLE OF VEAL

A large knuckle of veal	**Bouquet garni**
1 onion	**Salt and pepper**
1 carrot	**$1\frac{1}{2}$–2 oz. rice**
$\frac{1}{2}$ turnip	**1 pt. parsley sauce**
2 sticks of celery	

GARNISH

Boiled bacon, ham *or* bacon rolls grilled *or* fried	**Slices of lemon**

Wipe the meat, separate the shank bone and put it with the meat into a saucepan with enough water to cover. Bring to the boil, skim well, add the vegetables cut into dice, the bouquet garni and salt. The ham or bacon for the garnish should be boiled separately and served on a separate dish. Simmer the veal gently until tender—about 3 hr.—add the washed rice $\frac{1}{2}$ hr. before serving. Remove the meat from the broth and keep it hot. Take out the bones and bouquet garni, season the broth to taste, and serve it separately. Pour a little parsley sauce over the meat and serve the rest in a sauce-boat. If boiled bacon is not being served, garnish with bacon rolls and slices of lemon.

6 helpings

STEWED, STUFFED FILLET OF VEAL

Filet de Veau étuvé

$1\frac{1}{2}$ lb. fillet of veal	**1 pt. stock *or* water and vegetables**
4–6 oz. veal forcemeat	**1 oz. butter**
1 oz. dripping	**1 oz. flour**
A few mushrooms *or* mushroom stalks	**1–2 teasp. lemon juice**
Salt and pepper	

GARNISH

Bacon rolls	**Slices of lemon**
Parsley	

Flatten the meat well with a rolling-pin, spread on the forcemeat, roll up and tie securely. Melt the dripping in a stewpan and fry the meat until the entire surface is nicely browned. Drain off the fat. Add the mushrooms, stock or water and sliced vegetables and seasoning. Cover and simmer gently for about $1\frac{1}{2}$ hr. keeping the liquid just at simmering point. Meanwhile melt the butter in another pan, add the flour and cook gently until a light brown colour. Then add $\frac{3}{4}$ pt. of the strained liquid in which the meat was cooked and stir until boiling. Simmer for 10 min. then add lemon juice and seasoning to taste. Remove the string and serve the meat on a hot dish. Pour a little of the sauce over and serve the rest separately. Garnish with bacon rolls, parsley and slices of lemon.

6 helpings

VEAL À LA ROMAINE

Poitrine de Veau à la Romaine

The thick end of a breast of veal (about 2¼ lb.)
¾ lb. sausage meat
1 large onion
1 carrot
½ turnip
Bouquet garni
6 peppercorns
Salt and pepper
½ lb. Carolina rice
2 oz. grated cheese
Meat glaze
Slices of lemon

Remove all bones and tendons, trim meat neatly and season well. Spread the sausage meat evenly over the inner surface of the meat, roll up and tie securely with string. Slice the onion, carrot and turnip and place with the bones and trimmings in a stewpan. Add the bouquet garni, peppercorns and salt, add water to cover the vegetables. Place the meat on top and cover with greased paper and a well-fitting lid. Cook very gently for about 2½ hr. Baste occasionally and add more water or stock when necessary. Cook the rice in about 1½ pt. of boiling stock (taken from the pan) until the stock is absorbed, season to taste and stir in the cheese. Place the rice on a hot dish and put the meat on top. Brush the meat with glaze and garnish with slices of lemon.

6 helpings

VEAL CUTLETS

Côtelettes de Veau

1½ lb. fillet *or* neck of veal
2 eggs *or* 1 egg and milk
1 teasp. finely-chopped parsley
¼ teasp. powdered thyme
½ teasp. finely-grated lemon rind
Salt and pepper
½ oz. butter
Breadcrumbs
Butter *or* fat for frying

GARNISH

Parsley
Slices of lemon

Cut the meat in slices about ½ in. thick and trim into neat fillets. Beat the eggs, or egg and milk, and mix with the parsley, thyme, lemon rind, seasoning and ½ oz. melted butter. Brush the cutlets with this mixture and coat carefully with breadcrumbs. Fry in hot butter or fat for about 10–15 min. Fry both sides quickly first, then cook more slowly, turning as required, until golden brown. Drain well and place on a hot dish. Garnish with parsley and slices of lemon.

Serve with tomato, demi-glace or piquant sauce, or gravy.

6 helpings

VEAL CUTLETS—MAINTENON STYLE

Côtelettes de Veau à la Maintenon

1½ lb. fillet *or* neck of veal
Butter *or* fat
1 oz. ham
1 shallot
1 oz. flour
¾ pt. white stock
Few strips of lemon rind
Salt and pepper
Oil *or* butter

Cut the veal into neat cutlets, allowing 2 per person. Fry until slightly browned in hot fat and put aside. Finely shred the ham and finely chop the shallot. Melt 1 oz. fat in a stewpan, add the ham and shallot and sauté for a few minutes. Add the flour and cook slowly until light brown. Add the stock, lemon rind, seasoning to taste and bring to the boil, stirring constantly. Simmer for 15 min., then add the cutlets and cook very gently just below simmering point until the meat is tender. Test with a skewer. Take out the cutlets, strain the sauce and leave to become cold. Take one sheet of greaseproof paper or aluminium foil per cutlet and cut away the corners. Brush both sides with oil or butter. Place one cutlet on each, cover with sauce and fold and fasten so that the sauce cannot escape. Bake in a fairly hot oven (**375° F., Gas 5**) for 15 min. Serve in the paper cases.

6 helpings

VEAL CUTLETS WITH ITALIAN SAUCE

Côtelettes de Veau à l'Italienne

1½ lb. fillet *or* neck of veal
1 egg
Salt and pepper
Breadcrumbs
Butter *or* oil
¾ pt. Italian sauce

GARNISH

Parsley
Slices of lemon

Cut and trim the meat into neat cutlets. Beat and season the egg, brush the cutlets with egg and then coat with breadcrumbs. Press the crumbs on firmly then coat the cutlets with butter or oil. Grill under a red-hot grill, brushing occasionally with hot fat to prevent the breadcrumbs burning. Arrange neatly on a hot dish and garnish with parsley and lemon. Pour some sauce round and serve the rest separately.

6 helpings

VEAL CUTLETS WITH OYSTERS

Côtelettes de Veau aux Huîtres

1¼–1½ lb. fillet of veal	**¾ pt. white sauce**
1½ oz. butter *or* margarine	**12 sauce oysters**
3 shallots	**2 teasp. lemon juice**
	Salt and pepper
	Cayenne pepper

Cut the meat into pieces of equal size and thickness. Flatten slightly with a wooden spoon and trim into round or oval shapes. Melt the fat in a frying-pan and add the finely-chopped shallots and the cutlets. Fry for about 10 min. but do not allow to colour. Have the white sauce at simmering point and add the cutlets and shallots. Cover and simmer very gently for ½ hr. Beard the oysters, add the oysters to the sauce with the oyster liquid, lemon juice, salt, pepper and cayenne to taste. Simmer for another 5 min. Care must be taken not to overcook the oysters or they become hard and indigestible, but they must remain in the sauce until they lose their flabbiness.

Arrange the cutlets on a hot dish and pour the sauce over.

6 helpings

VEAL OLIVES

Olives de Veau

1½ lb. fillet of veal	**1½ oz. butter *or* fat**
8 thin bacon rashers	**1 pt. brown sauce**
4–6 oz. veal forcemeat	

GARNISH

Mashed potatoes	**Slices of lemon**
Green peas	**Spinach purée**

Prepare the veal and cut it into 8 thin slices about 4 in. by 3 in. and season. Place a slice of bacon on each piece of meat and spread with a thin layer of forcemeat. Then roll up tightly and fasten securely with fine string. Heat the fat in a saucepan and fry the rolls (olives) until lightly browned. Pour off the surplus fat and add the hot brown sauce to the olives. Cover and simmer gently for about 1½ hr. When tender, remove the string and place the olives on a bed of mashed potato and pour the sauce over. Garnish with green peas and slices of lemon and serve with spinach purée.

6 helpings

VEAL OLIVE PIE

Pâté aux paupiettes de Veau

1½ lb. fillet of veal	**Flaky *or* rough puff pastry using 6–8 oz. flour, etc.**
8 thin bacon rashers	**Egg *or* milk**
4–6 oz. veal forcemeat	**Parsley**
2 hard-boiled eggs	
Veal forcemeat balls	
½ pt. good stock *or* gravy	

Prepare the olives as directed for Veal Olives and tie securely. Place them in a pie-dish and mix with slices of hard-boiled egg and fried forcemeat balls. Half-fill the dish with well-seasoned stock or gravy. Cover with pastry, brush with egg or milk and decorate. Place in a very hot oven **(450° F., Gas 8)** and reduce to fairly hot **(375° F., Gas 5)** when the pastry is set and brown. When the pastry is cooked add some more stock. Garnish with parsley and serve hot or cold.

6 helpings

VEAL PARISIAN

Veau à la Parisienne

1½ lb. fillet of veal	**¾ pt. Madeira sauce**
Salt and pepper	**1 dessertsp. chopped parsley**
2 tablesp. olive oil	**Croûtons of fried bread**
1 tablesp. finely-chopped onion	**Parisian potatoes**

Wipe, trim and cut the meat into neat fillets. Season well. Heat the oil and fry the fillets lightly. Fry the chopped onion lightly. Then add the sauce and cook gently for ½–¾ hr. until the meat is tender. Add the chopped parsley and arrange on a hot dish. Serve with croûtons of fried bread and Parisian potatoes.

6 helpings

VEAL PUDDING

Pouding de Veau

1½–2 lb. veal
6 oz. ham, bacon *or* pickled pork
Suet pastry using 8 oz. flour, etc.
Salt and pepper
1 gill stock
Good gravy
Parsley

Wipe the meat, remove bones and gristle, and cut the meat into rather small neat pieces. Cut the ham, bacon or pork into narrow strips. Line a greased basin thinly with suet pastry, put in alternately, the meat, thin layers of ham and seasoning. Add the stock when the basin is ½ full. Put on a lid of pastry and cover with greased paper. Place the basin in a steamer or in a saucepan containing water to ½ the depth of the basin, replacing it with *boiling* water as it reduces. Steam for 3 hr. and serve in the basin. Garnish with sprigs of parsley and serve with a good gravy.

6 helpings

Calf's Brains

CALF'S BRAINS AU GRATIN

Cervelles de Veau au Gratin

1 set of calf's brains
½ pt. white sauce
6 button mushrooms
1 tablesp. cream
½ teasp. lemon rind
2 oz. finely-grated cheese
White breadcrumbs
Parsley

Prepare the brains as directed for Calves' Brain Cakes and cut into small pieces. Put the sauce in a small saucepan, add the brains and chopped mushrooms and heat without boiling. Remove from the heat and add the cream, seasoning if necessary and the lemon rind. Have ready 6 greased scallop shells and sprinkle them with breadcrumbs. Put some of the mixture in each shell and sprinkle with more crumbs. Cover with grated cheese and brown quickly under the grill. Serve at once garnished with parsley.

6 helpings

CALVES' BRAIN CAKES

2 calves' brains
2 small onions
Pinch of sage
Salt and pepper
1–2 teasp. lemon juice *or* vinegar
8 peppercorns
1 bay leaf
Fat
2–3 eggs
Breadcrumbs
Parsley

Wash the brains under running cold water or in several changes of water, and remove any clots of blood, loose skin and fibres. Then soak in cold water for at least 1 hr., changing the water 2 or 3 times. Put the brains in a saucepan, cover with cold water, and add the sliced onions, sage, salt, lemon juice or vinegar. Add the peppercorns and bay leaf tied in muslin. Bring to the boil and simmer for about 10 min. or until firm. Remove the muslin bag and allow the mixture to cool. Chop the brains, add seasoning to taste and sufficient beaten egg to bind the ingredients. Stir well over a low heat until the mixture thickens. Then spread on a plate in the form of a large round cake and allow to cool. When cold divide into equal small portions and form each into a cake. Coat with egg and breadcrumbs and fry in hot fat until light golden brown. Drain well and serve on a hot dish garnished with parsley.

6 helpings

CALVES' BRAINS WITH BLACK BUTTER SAUCE

Cervelles de Veau au Beurre Noir

2 calves' brains
¾ pt. good stock

SAUCE

2 oz. butter
1 teasp. vinegar *or* lemon juice
1 teasp. finely-chopped parsley
Salt and pepper

Prepare the brains as directed for Calves' Brain Cakes. Bring the stock up to just below boiling-point, add the brains and simmer gently for about 10 min. Drain well, place on a hot dish and keep hot. Heat the butter in a small pan until a nut-brown colour, taking care not to burn it. Add the vinegar or lemon juice, the finely-chopped parsley, salt and pepper as required. Pour over the brains and serve at once.

6 helpings
Cooking time—about 25 min.

CROUSTADES OF CALF'S BRAINS

Croustades aux Cervelles

Short-crust pastry (p. 557) using 6 oz. flour, etc.	**½ pt. good white sauce**
1 set of calf's brains	**1 tablesp. cream *or* milk**
1 small onion	**1 egg yolk**
1 tablesp. vinegar	**Pinch of powdered mace**
Salt	**1 teasp. lemon juice**

Line some small deep oval or round moulds with pastry. Bake them "blind" (*see* p. 558) in a fairly hot oven (**400° F., Gas 6**). Take the pastry cases out of the moulds and return them to the oven until brown and crisp. In the meantime, prepare and cook the brains as directed for Calves' Brain Cakes (*see* p. 266), excluding the herbs. Then drain well and cut into dice. Add to the white sauce, the cream or milk and egg yolk mixed together, the mace and diced brains. Stir continuously and heat very gently without boiling until the sauce thickens. Add the lemon juice, re-season if necessary and fill the pastry cases with the mixture. Garnish with parsley. Serve hot or cold.

6 helpings

FRIED CALVES' BRAINS

Cervelles de Veau frites

2 calves' brains	**Salt**
1 tablesp. vinegar *or* lemon juice	**1 tablesp. olive oil**
1 onion	**½ gill tepid water**
Pinch of sage	**1 egg white**
2 oz. flour	**Deep fat**
	Parsley

Prepare and cook the brains as directed for Calves' Brain Cakes (p. 266), excluding the peppercorns and bay leaf. Strain, dry well and cut the brains into fairly thin slices. Make a batter by sifting the flour and salt and mixing smoothly with the oil and tepid water. Whisk the egg white until stiff and then fold lightly into the batter. Have ready a pan of hot deep fat. Dip each slice of brain into the batter, drain slightly and then drop into the hot fat. Fry until golden brown, turning as necessary. Drain well, place on a hot dish and garnish with parsley.

6 helpings

Calves' Ears

CALVES' EARS

Oreilles de Veau farcies

6 ears which must be cut very deeply from the head	**2 small onions**
½ pt. milk	**3 cloves**
Salt and pepper	**6 peppercorns**
Veal forcemeat (p. 144)	**12 mushrooms**
¾ pt. white stock	**1–2 egg yolks**
	2 tablesp. cream *or* milk

GARNISH

Parsley	**Fried forcemeat balls (optional)**
Slices of lemon	**Cayenne pepper**

Wash, blanch and drain the ears thoroughly. Put them in a pan with the milk, salt and water to cover, and stew gently for 1 hr. Drain and dry well, reserve the milk. Stuff the insides with veal forcemeat, fold and tie securely and place in a pan with the stock, onions stuck with the cloves, and the peppercorns. Cook gently for 1 hr. more. Meanwhile prepare the mushrooms and stew in the milk in which the ears were cooked. Remove the ears from the stock, remove the string and keep as hot as possible. Mix the egg yolk(s) and cream or milk together, add the strained stock and milk and stir all the time until it thickens. Then add the mushrooms and season to taste. Place the ears on a hot dish and pour the sauce round.

Garnish with parsley, sliced lemon and if liked small fried forcemeat balls and cayenne,

6 helpings
Cooking time—about 2¼ hr.

Calves' Feet

FRICASSÉE OF CALVES' FEET

Pieds de Veau en fricassée

3-4 calves' feet (feet boiled down for jelly may be used)	**2 tablesp. diced and cooked ham *or* bacon**
1 onion	**1 teasp. finely-chopped parsley**
2 carrots	**1 teasp. lemon juice**
8 peppercorns	**Salt and pepper**
1 pt. white sauce	**Nutmeg**

If the feet have already been cooked for jelly, remove all the bones and cut the meat into equal sized pieces. If the feet are uncooked, they will first have to be prepared as follows. Wash and scald them and bone the upper part. Then remove the shank bone, split in two and soak in cold water for 2 hr. Wash again and put into a saucepan with some salt, water to cover, the sliced onion and carrots, and peppercorns. Cook slowly for about 1½ hr., until tender. Remove the remaining bone and cut the meat in pieces. Add to the white sauce the pieces of meat, the diced ham or bacon and heat thoroughly. Add the parsley, lemon juice, seasoning and nutmeg to taste, and serve.

6 helpings

Calf's Head

BOILED CALF'S HEAD

Tête de Veau bouillie

½ calf's head
Salt
Vinegar *or* lemon juice (optional)
1 pt. parsley *or* tomato sauce

STOCK

1 onion
1 carrot
1 turnip
1 stick of celery
Bouquet garni
6 peppercorns
Boiling water

GARNISH

Bacon
Wedges of lemon

Remove the brains and tongue, and wash the head thoroughly until free from blood. Pay special attention to the ears and nostrils. Soak in cold water for several hours, changing the water 3 or 4 times. Blanch the head by putting in a pan with cold salt water, and a little vinegar or lemon juice if liked, bringing to the boil and boiling for 10 min. Then drain, and wash well in cold water. Place in a pan of boiling water with the tongue, onion, carrot, turnip, celery, bouquet garni, peppercorns and salt. Simmer gently for 3 hr., removing any white scum. Tie the prepared brains in a muslin bag and add to the stock 20 min. before serving. Dice and fry the bacon, or form into rolls and grill. Place the head on a hot dish and cut the meat from the bone in neat pieces. Skin and slice the tongue, chop the brains. Coat the meat with parsley or tomato sauce, if tomato sauce is used sprinkle with a little parsley. Garnish with the bacon, chopped brains, sliced tongue and quarters of lemon. Serve very hot.

10 helpings
Cooking time—about 3½ hr.

CALF'S HEAD WITH TOMATO SAUCE

Tête de Veau à la Tomate

1¼ lb. cooked boned calf's head
4–5 oz. macaroni *or* spaghetti
½ pt. tomato sauce
Salt and pepper

GARNISH

Parsley
Croûtons of fried *or* toasted bread

Cut the remains of the calf's head into small neat pieces. Break the macaroni or spaghetti into pieces about ¾ in. long and boil rapidly until tender in a large saucepan of boiling salt water. Drain the macaroni, rinse with cold water and place with the meat in the tomato sauce. Heat thoroughly, season to taste and serve on a hot dish. Sprinkle with chopped parsley and garnish with croûtons of fried or toasted bread.

6 helpings

FRIED CALF'S HEAD

Fritot de Tête de Veau

The remains of a cooked calf's head
Deep fat
Parsley

MARINADE

2 tablesp. olive oil *or* melted butter
1 tablesp. lemon juice *or* vinegar
1 teasp. finely-chopped shallot *or* onion
½ teasp. mixed herbs
Salt and pepper

BATTER

4 oz. flour
½ teasp. salt
¼ pt. tepid water
2 tablesp. olive oil
1 egg white

Cut the meat into strips about 2 in. by 1 in. and place in a deep dish. Beat the oil or butter and lemon juice or vinegar well together with a fork and add the rest of the ingredients for the marinade. Pour over the meat and allow to stand for at least 1 hr. Drain well. Sift the flour and mix to a smooth batter with the salt, tepid water and oil. Fold in the stiffly-beaten egg white as lightly as possible. Dip the strips of meat into the batter and fry in hot deep fat until light golden brown. Drain thoroughly and pile on a hot dish, garnish with fresh or fried parsley.

NOTE: If a more elaborate dish is required, the fried meat may be dished in a circle on a border of piped potato, the centre filled with spinach purée, asparagus tips or macedoine of carrot and turnip and a good brown sauce poured round.

6 helpings

Calf's Heart

BAKED CALF'S HEART

Cœur de Veau rôti

A calf's heart	**Flour for dredging**
4 oz. veal forcemeat	**½ pt. brown gravy**
2 oz. fat	

GARNISH

Rashers of bacon	**Forcemeat balls**
Parsley	

Wash the heart thoroughly under running cold water or in several changes of cold water. Cut off flaps and lobes and remove any pieces of gristle. Cut away the membrane which divides the 2 cavities and see that the inside is quite free from blood. Soak in cold water for ½–1 hr. Wash again and dry well. Fill the inside with the forcemeat and sew up the ends with fine string. Heat the fat in a roasting-tin and put the heart in it. Baste well and cover with greased paper. Bake for about 1½ hr. in a fairly hot oven (**375° F., Gas 5**). Turn and baste often, and ½ hr. before serving remove the paper, dredge well with flour, re-baste and put back in the oven. When ready, place on a hot dish and use the fat and flour in the tin to enrich or form the base for the brown gravy. Garnish with rashers of bacon which have been fried or grilled, and sprigs of parsley. If liked, some of the stuffing can be made into balls and cooked for the last ½ hr. with the heart and served as garnish.

4 helpings

Calves' Kidneys

CALVES' KIDNEYS—STEWED

Rognons de Veau sautés

3 calves' kidneys	**1 tablesp. sherry (optional)**
Seasoned flour	**Salt and pepper**
1 onion	**1 dessertsp. finely-chopped parsley**
2 oz. butter *or* dripping	**Croûtons of fried bread *or* pastry**
6 mushrooms	
½ pt. stock *or* gravy	

Wash the kidneys well, remove any skin and cut out the cores with scissors. Soak in tepid salt water for 10–15 min. Wash well in clear tepid water. Cut the kidneys in halves lengthwise. Cut each half into slices about ⅛ in. thick and toss in seasoned flour. Chop the onion finely, heat the fat and cook it until lightly coloured. Then add the sliced mushrooms and prepared kidney and cook quickly until browned. Pour off any surplus fat and add the stock or gravy, the sherry (if used) and seasoning. Stir until boiling and simmer very gently for ½ hr. Add the chopped parsley, stir well and serve on a hot dish. Garnish with croûtons of fried bread or pastry.

6 helpings

CALVES' KIDNEY WITH SCRAMBLED EGGS

Rognons aux Œufs brouillées

3 calves' kidneys (small)	**½ gill sherry (optional)**
2 shallots *or* 1 small onion	**5–6 eggs**
3½–4 oz. butter	**1 gill milk**
½ pt. Espagnole sauce	**Salt and pepper**
	Parsley

Prepare the kidneys as directed in the previous recipe. Cut into very thin slices and season well. Chop the shallots or onion very finely, melt 1 oz. butter in a pan and fry them lightly. Then add the slices of kidney, frying these quickly on both sides and shaking the pan well. Pour off any surplus fat. Pour the Espagnole sauce over the kidneys, add the sherry if used and cook slowly for 15 min. Beat up the eggs and add the milk and seasoning. Arrange the kidney in a circle on a hot dish and keep hot. Keep the sauce hot. Heat the remaining butter and scramble the eggs gently until the mixture starts to thicken. Pile the scrambled egg in the centre of the circle of kidneys and pour the hot sauce round. Sprinkle with parsley and serve at once.

6 helpings

Calf's Liver

CALF'S LIVER AND SAVOURY RICE

Riz Savoureux au Foie de Veau

1¼ lb. calf's liver	**Salt and pepper**
1½ oz. butter *or* margarine	**¼–½ teasp. powdered saffron**
1 onion	**Seasoned flour**
2 cloves of garlic (optional)	**Butter *or* oil for frying**
6 oz. Patna rice	**½ pt. brown sauce**
¾ pt. well-flavoured white stock	**Juice of ½ lemon *or* 2 tablesp. wine**

GARNISH

Fried *or* grilled bacon rolls	**Paprika**
	Green peas

Wash the liver well in tepid salt water, remove any skin and tubes and dry well. Heat 1 oz. of the fat in a saucepan and sauté the finely-chopped onion and garlic without colouring it. Add the well-washed rice, mix well and cook for a few minutes. Add the stock, seasoning and saffron and cook very slowly for about ½–¾ hr. on top of the cooker, or in the oven until the rice is tender and has absorbed all the stock. Add the remaining fat, mix well and press well into a border mould or 6 individual moulds. Put aside until set. Slice the liver finely, dip in seasoned flour and fry in a little butter or oil. Drain well. Bring the brown sauce to the boil, add the lemon juice or wine and the liver and heat. Turn the rice on to a hot dish and heat in the oven. Place the liver and sauce in the centre (if a border mould) or round the rice and garnish.

6 helpings

CALF'S LIVER—HUNGARIAN STYLE

Foie de Veau à la Hongroise

1½ lb. calf's liver	**2 tablesp. finely-grateu onion**
Flour	
Salt and paprika pepper	**1½ gills fresh *or* sour cream**
2 oz. butter	

Wash the liver well in tepid salt water, remove any skin and tubes and dry well. Cut into ½-in. slices and dip into flour which has been well seasoned with salt and paprika pepper. Fry in hot butter quickly on both sides, then more slowly until tender. Fry the onion for about 5 min. Remove the liver and arrange the slices down the centre of a hot dish—keep hot. Pour away the surplus fat from the pan, add the cream to the onion in the pan, heat slightly, season to taste and pour over the liver. Sprinkle with paprika.

6 helpings

CALF'S LIVER WITH ONION PURÉE

Foie de Veau à la Clermont

1¼–1½ lb. calf's liver	**¾ pt. brown *or* Espagnole sauce**
2 large Spanish onions	
1½ oz. butter *or* margarine	**2 oz. fat for frying**
	Seasoned flour
¼ pt. stock	**Parsley**

Wash the liver well in tepid salt water, remove any skin and tubes and dry well. Peel and blanch the onions, cut into very small dice and fry in the 1½ oz. fat until golden brown. Pour off any surplus fat. Add stock and cook slowly, adding the sauce as the stock boils away, until a thick purée is obtained. Cut the liver into slices, dip in seasoned flour and fry in the hot fat. Spread the purée lightly on a hot dish, arrange slices of liver on top and sprinkle with parsley.

6 helpings

LIVER SAUSAGES

Saucissons de Foie de Veau

1 lb. calf's liver	**1 heaped teasp. salt**
¾ lb. fat bacon	**¼ teasp. pepper**
½ lb. breadcrumbs	**Good pinch of dry mustard**
1 teasp. finely-chopped parsley	**2 eggs**
¼ teasp. powdered thyme	**Milk**
	Sausage skins
¼ teasp. finely-grated lemon rind	**Frying fat**
¼ teasp. grated nutmeg	**Fried bread *or* mashed potato**

Prepare the liver, chop it very finely and mix it together with the finely-chopped bacon.

Add the breadcrumbs and rest of the dry ingredients and mix thoroughly. Stir in the eggs and add a little milk if necessary. Press the mixture into the skins, leaving room for the bread to swell. Put aside for 5–6 hr. Before cooking, prick well, then fry in hot fat until well browned, frying the bread in the same fat. Serve on fried bread, toast or mashed potatoes.

If preferred, the sausages may be shaped and floured instead of being put into skins, in which case the mixture should be a little less moist.

5-6 helpings

Calves' Sweetbreads

BRAISED SWEETBREADS

Ris de Veau braise

2 calves' heart sweetbreads	**Bouquet garni**
1 oz. fat	**6 peppercorns**
1 small onion	**Salt and pepper**
1 small carrot	**¾ pt. stock**
½ small turnip	**Croûte of fried bread**

Prepare the sweetbreads as follows: wash and soak in cold water for 1–2 hr. until free from blood. Put into a pan, cover with cold water, bring to boil and simmer for 3–5 min. then plunge into cold water. Discard fat and skin and any gristle. Press between 2 plates to retain shape.

Melt the fat in a stewpan or meat-tin, add the sliced vegetables and fry for about 10 min., then add the bouquet garni, peppercorns, salt and pepper and almost cover with stock. Place the sweetbreads on top of the vegetables and cover with greased greaseproof paper. Bring to the boil, baste the sweetbreads well and cook in a moderate oven (**350° F., Gas 4**) for about 1 hr. with the lid on. Add more stock as necessary and baste occasionally. Meanwhile cut a croûte of bread 2 in. thick and fry until golden brown. Drain well. Place the croûte on a hot dish with the sweetbreads on top.

6 helpings

VARIATIONS

1. Brush the sweetbreads with glaze or tomato sauce and serve with peas or a macedoine of vegetables.

2. Serve with Italian sauce and mushrooms.

3. Serve with Quenelles of Veal, and a sauce made from the liquid left after braising to which is added ½ pt. Madeira or demiglace sauce.

4. Serve with mushrooms cooked in sauce Suprême, peas, haricot beans or a macedoine of vegetables.

ESCALLOPS OF SWEETBREADS

Escalopes de Ris de Veau

2 calves' heart sweetbreads	**Ingredients for braising as Braised Sweetbreads**
	Meat glaze

Prepare, blanch and braise the sweetbreads as directed for Braised Sweetbreads. Braise for about 40 min. Remove the sweetbreads, cut into neat slices and place in a baking-tin. Brush with glaze and ½ cover with the liquid they were cooked in. Put in a fairly hot oven (**375° F., Gas 5**) for 10 min. The sweetbreads may be served on a border of mashed potato and sprinkled with a little chopped truffle. Serve with peas or spinach purée, and tomato sauce if liked.

6 helpings

FRIED TRIPE

Tripe frite

1½ lb. dressed tripe	**Deep fat**
Salt and pepper	**Fried sliced onions**
Coating batter	**Parsley**

Wash and blanch the tripe, and cut into 3-in. squares. Make the batter and season well. Dip the tripe into the batter and fry in the hot deep fat until crisp and brown. Drain well. Serve hot with fried sliced onions and garnished with chopped parsley.

6 helpings

COLD DISHES AND POTTED MEATS

Beef

BRAISED BEEF IN ASPIC

Filet de Bœuf Braisé en Gelée

1½ lb. fillet of beef previously braised	**1¼ pt. aspic jelly**
1 jar of meat paste	**Cooked peas**
French mustard	**Cooked carrots**

It is better to braise the beef the previous day if possible and allow it to become quite cold. Trim into an oblong shape and cut lengthwise into slices. Spread each slice alternately with meat paste and mustard, put the slices together again and press between 2 boards. Set a layer of aspic jelly at the bottom of a cake- or bread-tin and decorate with cooked peas and rings of cooked carrots. Pour on another layer of cold, liquid aspic jelly and allow it to set. Place the prepared beef on top, fill up the mould with aspic jelly and allow to set. Unmould on to an oval dish and decorate with chopped aspic. Serve with salad and mayonnaise.

6 helpings

COLLARED BEEF

Bœuf épicé

7 lb. thin end of flank of beef	**1 dessertsp. powdered sage**
2 oz. brown sugar	**A bunch of mixed herbs**
6 oz. salt	**½ teasp. powdered allspice**
1 oz. saltpetre	**Salt and pepper**
1 large handful parsley	**Stock *or* water**

Choose tender beef which is not too fat. Place it in a dish, rub in the sugar, salt and saltpetre and leave in the pickle in a cold place for 7–8 days. Turn and rub the meat every day. Bone the beef, remove all the gristle and coarse skin of the inside part and wash well. Sprinkle it thickly with chopped parsley, sage, herbs, allspice and seasoning. Roll the meat up in a cloth as tightly as possible, tie securely and boil gently for 6 hr. in stock or water to which the bones and some vegetables have been added. Remove the meat from the pan and leave under a heavy weight until cold.

20 helpings

GALANTINE OF BEEF

Galantine de Bœuf

1 lb. good stewing steak	**¼ pt. stock**
½ lb. bacon	**Raspings *or* meat glaze and a little butter *or* aspic jelly**
6 oz. breadcrumbs	
Salt and pepper	
1 egg	

Cut the steak and bacon into very small pieces. Add the breadcrumbs, season liberally and mix well together. Beat the egg, add to it the stock and stir into the dry ingredients. Shape the mixture into a short thick roll and tie tightly in a greased cloth in a good shape. Boil gently in stock, or in water with vegetables added for flavour, for about 2 hr. or if preferred, steam for 2½–3 hr. When cooked, tightly retie in a dry cloth and press until cold. Before serving, roll in raspings or brush over with dissolved meat glaze and decorate with creamed butter or chopped aspic jelly.

6 helpings

POTTED BEEF

Terrine de Bœuf

2 lb. lean beef	**A good pinch of powdered allspice**
A pinch of powdered cloves	**Salt and pepper**
A pinch of powdered mace	**½–1 teasp. anchovy essence**
	Clarified butter

Wipe, trim and cut the meat into small pieces. Put into a stone jar or casserole with

1 tablesp. water, the cloves, mace, allspice, salt and pepper. Cover with several thicknesses of greased paper and a lid and place in a pan of boiling water, or in the oven in a tin of boiling water. Cook gently for about 3 hr., replenishing the water as it reduces. Then pound the meat well, adding juice from the meat and a few drops of anchovy essence by degrees. Season to taste, rub through a fine wire sieve, press into pots and cover with melted clarified butter.

PRESSED BEEF

Bœuf pressé

Salt brisket of beef	**Bouquet garni**
1 onion	**10 peppercorns**
1 carrot	**Meat glaze**
½ turnip	

Weigh the meat. Wash it well, or if very salt soak for about 1 hr. in cold water. Put into cold water and bring slowly to boiling point. Skim well. Cut the prepared vegetables into large pieces, add to the meat with the bouquet garni and peppercorns, and simmer gently, allowing 25 min. per lb. and 25 min. over. Take the meat out, remove the bones and press between 2 boards or dishes until cold. Then brush over with meat glaze.

POTTED OX TONGUE

Terrine de Langue de Bœuf

1 cooked ox tongue	**Cloves**
3 oz. clarified butter to each 1 lb. of tongue	**Nutmeg**
	Cayenne pepper
	Salt and pepper
Powdered mace	**Extra clarified butter**

Chop the tongue finely, then pound it well. Add gradually the clarified butter in the proportion stated above and the flavourings and seasoning to taste. When the mixture is reduced to a moist smooth paste, rub through a fine sieve, press into pots and cover with melted clarified butter.

SAVOURY ROLLED OX TONGUE

Langue de Bœuf Roulée aux Fines Herbes

1 pickled ox tongue	**2 sliced carrots**
Bouquet garni	**1 sliced turnip**
2 onions stuck with 2 cloves	**Aspic jelly**

Wash the tongue, put into tepid water and bring slowly to the boil. Skim well and add the herbs, onions, carrots and turnip. Simmer gently until tender allowing 3–4 hr., according to size. Skim when necessary. When cooked, the tip of the tongue should be easily pierced with a metal skewer. Plunge the tongue into cold water and remove the skin. Trim the root, reserving the edible parts. Roll up the tongue and put into a greased cake-tin. Place the trimmings in the centre and leave with a weighted dish on top. When cold, pour on enough cold, liquid aspic to fill the tin. Turn out carefully when set and garnish with salad.

6 helpings

Lamb

COLD LAMB CUTLETS

Côtelettes d'Agneau à la Gelée

Lamb cutlets	**Mayonnaise *or* French salad dressing**
Salt and pepper	
Aspic jelly	**Lettuce**
Cooked peas and beans	

Prepare the cutlets by trimming to a neat uniform shape. Beat them with a cutlet bat or rolling-pin. Then season with salt and pepper and cook either by grilling, or by frying in smoking hot oil or fat, or by braising. Grilling or frying are more simple methods, but braising is recommended because of the fine flavour imparted by this method of cooking. Press between 2 dishes with a weight on top until quite cold. Dissolve the aspic and pour a ⅓ into a sauté pan or large dish rinsed out with cold water. Allow to set. Brush the cutlets with cold, liquid aspic and lay them about ½ in. apart on the jelly with the bones all curving the same way. Pour the remaining jelly gently over and leave to set. Then turn out on to a sheet of greaseproof paper rubbed with ice. With a sharp knife dipped in hot water, cut out the cutlets and arrange them in a circle on a round dish, with the bones pointing to the inside of the circle. Fill up the centre with the cooked vegetables mixed with mayonnaise or French dressing. Shredded lettuce may be arranged outside the circle of cutlets. Garnish with neatly cut cubes of aspic or small piles of chopped aspic.

LAMB CUTLETS À LA MAYONNAISE

Côtelettes d'Agneau à la Mayonnaise

6 lamb cutlets
Potted foie gras *or* farce
Mayonnaise sauce
Aspic jelly *or* gelatine
Radishes
Chervil *or* lettuce
Green salad

Braise or grill the lamb cutlets or sauté in butter. Then press between 2 plates with a weight on top until cold. Trim the cutlets neatly, making them all the same shape and size if possible. Coat 1 side with potted foie gras or any other farce; be careful to keep the cutlets lying one way up so that they can be dished neatly. Smooth the farce with a wet knife and place on a wire draining tray over a dish. Add to the mayonnaise a little stiff aspic jelly or dissolved gelatine which is beginning to set. Carefully coat the cutlets with this mixture. Decorate with tiny rounds of radish (like berries) and one or two leaves of chervil or lettuce. If a very glossy finish is required, pour a layer of cold, liquid aspic over the top. Keep cold and serve with green salad.

6 helpings

CHAUDFROID OF MUTTON CUTLETS

6 cutlets from the best end of neck
Mirepoix as for Braised Mutton—Provence style (p. 235)
Salt and pepper
6 oz. liver farce
½ oz. gelatine
⅓ pt. Béchamel sauce
½ pt. tomato sauce

Braise the neck as directed for Braised Mutton—Provence style. When cold, cut into neat cutlets and remove all the surplus fat. Season on both sides with salt and pepper. Cover one side of the cutlets with a thin layer of liver farce. Carefully dissolve the gelatine in 2 tablesp. cold water and divide equally between the Béchamel and tomato sauces which should be warm when the gelatine is added. Cool the sauces slightly, then coat the covered sides of the cutlets, making ½ red and the other ½ white. Leave in a cool place until set, then arrange in a circle in alternate colours and place a frill on each cutlet. Serve with dressed salad in the centre.

Noisettes of mutton may also be served in this way.

6 helpings **Time—2 hr.**

Pork

BRAWN

A pig's head weighing about 6 lb.
2 tablesp. salt
¼ teasp. powdered cloves
⅛ teasp. powdered mace
1½ lb. lean beef
1 teasp. pepper
1 onion

Clean the head well and soak in water for 2 hr. Place in a saucepan with the rest of the ingredients and almost cover with cold water. Boil for about 3 hr. or until quite tender. Take out the head and remove all the flesh. Put the bones back into the liquid and boil quickly until well reduced so that it will form a jelly when cold. Roughly chop the meat with a sharp knife, work quickly to prevent the fat settling in and put into a wet mould, basin or cake-tin. Pour some of the hot liquid over the meat through a strainer. Leave until quite cold and turn out when set.

The liquor in which the meat was cooked will make excellent soup, and the fat, if skimmed off and clarified well will answer the purposes of lard.

GALANTINE OF PORK

Galantine de Porc

1½ lb. belly pork (preferably salted)
Salt and pepper
Gherkins
Stock *or* water with 2 onions, 1 carrot and ½ turnip
Meat glaze (optional)
Parsley (optional)

Season the inside of the meat well with salt and pepper and arrange thin slices of gherkin all over it. Roll up tightly and secure with string, then secure tightly in a cloth. Just cover with stock or water and vegetables and simmer gently for about 3 hr. When cooked, press between 2 dishes until cold, then remove the cloth.

The meat may be brushed with glaze and served garnished with parsley.

6 helpings

POTTED HAM

Terrine de Jambon

2 lb. lean ham
½ lb. fat ham
¼ teasp. ground mace
¼ teasp. pepper
¼ teasp. grated nutmeg
⅛ teasp. cayenne pepper
Clarified butter

Pass the ham through a mincing machine 2 or 3 times or chop very finely. Then pound well and rub through a fine sieve. Add gradually the mace, pepper, nutmeg and cayenne and mix well together. Put into a well greased pie-dish, and cover with greased greaseproof paper. Bake in a moderate oven (**350° F., Gas 4**) for about ¾ hr. When cooked, press into small pots and cover with clarified butter.

Cooking time—about ¾ hr.

Veal

GALANTINE OF VEAL *Galantine de Veau*

A small breast of veal	**Stock *or* water**
1½ lb. sausage meat	**2 onions**
3 bacon rashers	**1 turnip**
1–2 hard-boiled eggs	**1 carrot**
Salt and pepper	**6 peppercorns**
⅛ teasp. ground mace	**Meat glaze**
Pinch of grated nutmeg	**Parsley**

Bone the veal and flatten out well. Season well and spread on ½ the sausage meat in an even layer. Place narrow strips of bacon and slices of hard-boiled egg on top and sprinkle with the seasoning, mace and nutmeg. Cover with the remainder of the sausage meat and roll up tightly. Wrap in a cloth and tie the ends tightly. Put in a pan of boiling stock or water to which the veal bones, sliced vegetables, peppercorns and seasoning have been added. Cook gently for 3 hr., then remove the cloth, roll up tightly in a clean dry cloth or greaseproof paper and press between 2 dishes until cold. When cold, remove the cloth, brush with liquid glaze and garnish with parsley.

6 helpings

POTTED VEAL *Pâte de Veau*

1 lb. veal	**1 blade of mace**
¼ lb. ham	**Butter *or* margarine**
2 tablesp. water	**Salt and pepper**
1 bay leaf	**Cayenne pepper**
6 peppercorns	**Powdered mace**

Finely chop the veal and ham. Place them in a well-greased stone jar with the water and the spices tied in a piece of muslin. Cover the jar with greased greaseproof paper and either stand in a saucepan of boiling water or place in a moderate oven (**350° F., Gas 4**) for 2½ hr. Remove the spices and pound the meat finely adding as much liquid from the jar, and butter, as is required to make a very smooth paste. Season with salt, pepper and cayenne, adding powdered mace to taste and pass through a sieve. Press into small jars, make smooth on top, and cover with melted clarified butter.

PRESSED VEAL

A breast of veal	**1 carrot**
Salt and pepper	**½ turnip**
1 large onion	**Bouquet garni**
A few sticks of celery *or* ¼ teasp. celery seeds	**10 peppercorns**

Wipe the meat and remove the skin, bones and gristle. Trim the meat neatly, season well, roll up tightly and tie with string. Slice the onion, celery, carrot and turnip and put into a saucepan with the bones and trimmings, bouquet garni, peppercorns and salt and put the meat on top. Add water to the depth of the vegetables. Cover the meat with greased paper, put on the lid and cook gently for 3 hr., basting occasionally. When the meat is tender, place it between 2 dishes or boards with weights on top, until quite cold. Strain the stock and on the following day boil rapidly until reduced to a glaze. Add colouring if liked. Trim the meat and brush it over with the glaze.

RAISED VEAL, PORK AND EGG PIE (Plate 26)

Hot water crust pastry (p. 556) **using 12 oz. flour etc.**	**1½ level teasp. salt**
	¼ level teasp. pepper
	3 hard-boiled eggs
1 lb. stewing veal	**¼ pt. (approx.) seasoned stock from veal and pork bones**
1 lb. lean stewing pork	
1 oz. flour	

Grease a 7 in. tin with lard. Make the pastry and when cool enough to handle, knead well. Cut off ¼ of the dough and keep this covered in a warm place until required. Roll out remaining dough to a round 2 in. wider than the base of the tin. Line the tin with the dough working up the sides with the fingers.

Cut the meat into small pieces, removing any gristle and fat. Mix together the flour, salt and pepper and toss the pieces of meat in this. Put half the meat into the pastry case and put in the peeled eggs. Add the remainder of the meat and 2 tablesp. water. Roll out the remaining piece of pastry to a round slightly larger than the top of the tin. Damp the edges and cover the pie. Pinch the edges. Brush with beaten egg. Bake for 15 min. in a very hot oven (**450° F., Gas 8**), then reduce heat to very cool (**290° F., Gas 1**) and continue cooking for 2½ hr. The bones from the veal and pork should meanwhile be cooked with a little water in a covered saucepan or casserole in the oven while the pie is cooking. When the pie is cooked it should be filled with the seasoned stock from the bones. Allow to cool completely before serving.

Individual pies. If preferred, the above amounts may be made into 6 individual pies. The egg should be cut into small pieces for the smaller pies.

VEAL AND HAM PIE (1)

2½ lb. neck *or* breast of veal
Salt and pepper
1½ lb. ham *or* bacon
2 hard-boiled eggs
Forcemeat balls
Puff *or* rough puff pastry
Pinch of ground mace
Grated rind of 1 lemon

Cut the meat into 1½ in. square pieces. Put into a fireproof dish or saucepan, season with salt and pepper, cover with cold water, and cook gently either in the oven or on the stove for 2 hr. Meanwhile cut the ham into narrow strips, the eggs into thin slices, make the forcemeat balls, and fry them lightly in a little hot dripping. Roll out the pastry to a suitable thickness and cut a piece to cover the top of the pie-dish. Line the edge of the dish with the trimmings. Allow the meat to cool slightly, then cover the bottom of the pie-dish with meat, add a few strips of bacon and slices of egg. Sprinkle lightly with salt, pepper, mace, lemon rind, then intersperse with forcemeat balls. Repeat until the dish is full then half-fill the dish with gravy. Put on the pastry cover, moisten and press the edges together. Make a hole in the centre of the top, decorate with pastry leaves, brush over with egg, and bake for 45–60 min. in a fairly hot oven (**375° F., Gas 5**). As soon as the pie is baked add a little more well-seasoned gravy through the hole in the top, and when served hot serve with gravy made from the liquor in which the meat was stewed.

8-10 helpings

VEAL AND HAM PIE (2)

¾ lb. sliced York ham
¾ lb. fillet of veal
2 hard-boiled eggs
½ teasp. mixed herbs
½ teasp. pepper
¼ teasp. ginger and nutmeg (mixed together)
Jelly stock
½ lb. puff pastry

Line a pie-dish with slices of ham. Fill with small slices of ham and ¼ in. thick slices of the veal fillet. With each layer place thick slices of the eggs and sprinkle with the mixed herbs and seasoning. When the dish is filled moisten with the stock, cover with puff pastry and cook in a medium oven until the pastry is just browned. Remove and cook slowly on a low heat for a further 15 min. When cold pierce the crust in 2 places and fill with stock to replace that which has evaporated. Allow to set, serve cold.

VEAL CAKE or VEAL MOULD

1 lb. lean fillet of veal
½ lb. lean bacon
2 hard-boiled eggs
2 teasp. finely-chopped parsley
2 teasp. finely-grated lemon rind
Salt and pepper
¾ pt. jellied veal stock
¼ oz. gelatine (if required)
Parsley *or* salad

Dice the veal and bacon. Cut the eggs into slices and arrange some of them in a pattern on the bottom of a greased mould. Mix the parsley, lemon rind and seasoning together. Place a thick layer of veal in the mould, cover with a thin layer of bacon, a layer of sliced egg and a layer of the parsley and lemon mixture. Repeat the layers until the mould is full. Pour in the jellied stock, cover with greased greaseproof paper and bake in a moderate oven (**350° F., Gas 4**) for 2–2½ hr. Fill up the mould with extra stock, adding ¼ oz. gelatine to ½ pt. stock if the stock is not stiff enough. When cold, turn out the mould and garnish with parsley or salad.

6 helpings

POULTRY

BIRDS AS FOOD

THERE is no bird, nor any bird's egg, that is known to be poisonous, though they may, and often do, become unwholesome because of the food that the birds eat, which at all times greatly changes the quality of the flesh, even in birds of the same breed.

Wild ducks and other aquatic birds are often rank and fishy-flavoured. Pigeons fatten and waste in the course of a few hours. The pronounced flavour of grouse is said to be due to the heather shoots on which they feed.

AGE AND FLAVOUR OF CHICKENS

The flesh of young chickens is the most delicate and easily assimilated of bird meats, which makes it especially suitable for invalids and people with weak digestion.

Few birds undergo so great a change with regard to the quality of their flesh as the domestic fowl. When quite young, cocks and hens are equally tender, but as chickens grow older the flesh of the cock is the first to toughen, and a cock over a year old is fit only for conversion into soup. A hen of the same age affords a substantial and palatable dish.

Birds of all sizes may now be obtained all the year round, so that a variety of recipes may be used, according to the bird chosen. The youngest birds may be called Baby Chicks, Spring Chickens or Squabs (French—*poussins, petits poulets*) these are usually grilled or fried, and have a delicate flavour.

The birds likely to be the most popular in the average household are cockerels, broilers or roasting chickens and fowls and capons (French—*poulets de grain*, *poulets reine*, *poulardes*, *chapons*). These may be cooked in a number of ways, two of the most popular being roasting and braising. Most frozen chickens are broilers. Older birds used for boiling may also be an economical purchase for the housewife (French-*poules*).

TO CHOOSE POULTRY

As a rule small-boned birds are an economical purchase; they should be plump and not devoid of fat.

When fresh, they should be free from any tainted smell, the eyes clear and not sunken, the feet limp and pliable. The legs should be soft and smooth, and the breast-bone and wing-tips pliable.

The signs of an old fowl are its stiff, horny-looking feet, long spurs, dark-coloured and hairy thighs, stiff beak and hard bones.

CHAPONS AND POULARDES: The male fowl, the capon (chapon), and the female bird, the poularde, are both, by treatment while young, made incapable of generating, with the result that their size is increased, and they become fatter than ordinary fowls. The flesh of these birds does not toughen with age, and even when three years old they are as tender as chicken—with a delicate flavour. The flavour of the poularde is considered more delicate than that of the capon (chapon), but the latter is the larger bird. They may be boiled, braised, roasted or otherwise prepared, according to the directions given for cooking chickens and fowls.

TURKEYS: These when young have smooth black legs and short spurs. The eyes of a fresh bird are bright and not sunken. Choose one which has a broad, plump breast and white flesh, the best being from seven to nine months old. The flesh of the hen is usually found to be more tender than the cock.

An old bird will have pale or reddish, rough legs, and the spurs will be long.

DUCKS: When young these usually have yellow feet and bills. The under-bill should be so soft that it will bend back easily, and the webbing of the feet should be soft; the breast should be meaty. (French: duck—*canard*: duckling—*caneton*.)

GEESE: The signs of freshness in a goose are the same as those in a duck, and the former should still have some down on its legs. A gosling or green goose is one up to four months old.

DRESSING POULTRY

Plucking: The removal of the feathers some time after the bird has been killed is a slow business. If a strong hook firmly fixed to a wall is available, plucking can be facilitated by tying the two feet of the bird together with strong string, and hanging the bird over the hook. Draw out one wing and pull out the under feathers, taking a few at a time. Work towards the breast and then down to the tail. Repeat on the other side. Only half the neck need be plucked, for the half remaining towards the head is cut off. The flight feathers (large quilled feathers at the ends of the wings) need hard pulling to remove and are best snapped away from the direction of growth. Small hairs may be singed away with a taper; burnt feathers, however, will impart an unpleasant flavour to the bird.

Drawing: Half way along the neck, cut a ring round the outer skin and pull or cut off the head. Slip the knife under the skin and cut back towards the body. Holding the neck in a dry cloth, pull the skin loose. At the base of the neck cut through the meat and then, still holding the neck in a dry cloth, twist firmly round until it is detached from the body. (Keep the neck for stock.) Push the index finger into the crop cavity to loosen the crop and gizzard.

Turn the bird around and with a sharp knife cut the skin on the leg, place over a board or table edge and snap the bone. Grasp the foot in one hand and the thigh of the bird in the other and pull off the foot with the tendons. There should be seven tendons.

To remove the viscera make a slit of about two to three inches, above the vent, taking care not to cut into the rectal end of the gut. Insert the first two fingers of the right hand, knuckles upwards, and gently draw out the intestines. Several attempts will have to be made in the first instance to remove all the organs, including the crop, which has to be pulled with the gizzard from the neck end, out to the back of the bird. When they are free, trim the end of the intestines and the vent away. The liver can now be separated from the gall bladder, taking care not to break the former. The meaty outside of the crop can be skinned or cut away from the gritty contents.

The lungs, which are bright red, lie close to the ribs. They are best removed by wrapping the index finger in a dry cloth and pushing in turn down from the back bone and out along each rib.

Burn the inedible waste, i.e. head, intestines, lungs, crop, feet, container of grit from the gizzard, etc., immediately. The giblets, i.e. the neck, gizzard, liver and heart, should be kept away from the bird so that its flesh will not be discoloured.

Wipe the inside of the bird with a dry cloth. Do not wet it by washing unless the bird is to be cooked immediately.

Trussing: The object of trussing a bird is to ensure that when cooked it looks attractive. Often lost sight of is the fact that poultry can be cooked as well untrussed or semi-trussed as it can be when fully trussed. The easiest way to truss is with a needle, similar in size to a packing needle, which can readily be obtained.

When the bird is clean lay it down with the breast uppermost and away from you. Thread the needle and pass it through the left leg just above the thigh bone and near to the joint between the thigh and leg bone. (When the leg is folded down against the bird these two bones form a "V" shape with the apex of the "V" pointing towards the front of the bird.) Pass the needle on through the body, out the other side, and through the other leg joint. The legs should be pushed tight against the body during this operation.

The string should now be passing through the body and the leg joints. Leaving sufficient on either side, turn the bird breast downwards and carry the string through the elbow joint of the wing on each side, then twist the end of the wing under the neck of the bird to hold the neck flap of skin. The two ends may now be drawn together not too tightly and tied off. (The expert trusser will perform the whole of this job by threading and running the string with the needle. In the way described above it is easier to discover where the strings should pass.) It now only remains to tie down the legs. This may simply be done by looping the string over the ends of the drum sticks and drawing them together, tying off round the tail end of the "parson's nose". To make this operation easier a slit may be cut in the flesh above the original vent cut and the "parson's nose" pushed through. The legs may also be tied down, using the needle on each leg end in turn. The packing needle and string can also usefully be used to repair any tears that have occurred during plucking or drawing. When trussed the skin should be as complete as possible in order to prevent the loss of fat from the bird during cooking, so resulting in over dryness and an unpalatable meat.

Boning poultry and game: Birds are invariably plucked and singed before boning, but not drawn. The crop, however, should be removed, the wings and legs cut off at the first joint, and the tendons of the legs carefully drawn at the same time. To bone the bird, use a small sharp knife, and first remove the merry-thought at the neck—a very simple matter. Cut the skin down the centre of the back and raise the flesh carefully on either side, sever the wing joints, and continue to detach the flesh, keeping the blade of the knife close to the bone. When the legs are reached, dislocate the joints, cut the connecting tendons, but leave both wings and legs intact until the breast and backbones have been removed, together with the viscera. Turn the body completely inside out; take the thigh bones of one of the legs in the left hand and strip the flesh downwards. Repeat this until all the small bones are removed. The bird may then be turned right side out again, when it will be found completely boned and should be quite whole.

Both large and small birds may be boned in this way. They are then stuffed, re-shaped and trussed, or rolled into galantines.

Jointing poultry: see plate 6.

ACCOMPANIMENTS

Whilst the choice of accompaniment to a particular dish is largely a personal one depending on individual taste, we list below the usual accompaniments to the following dishes:

ROAST CHICKEN: Thin brown gravy, bread sauce, bacon rolls, green salad, game chips, watercress to garnish, veal forcemeat stuffing.

ROAST DUCK: Thickened gravy, sage and onion stuffing, apple-, cranberry- *or* orange-sauce, watercress to garnish .

ROAST WILD DUCK: Port wine- *or* orange-sauce *or* orange salad.

ROAST TURKEY: Thickened gravy, veal- *or* chestnut-stuffing, sausage-meat stuffing, bacon rolls, grilled sausages, bread- *or* cranberry-sauce.

ROAST GOOSE: Thickened gravy, sage and onion stuffing, apple-sauce.

GENERAL HINTS

(*a*) Chicken is stuffed at the neck-end, duck and goose are stuffed from the vent-end, turkey is stuffed with veal- *or* chestnut-stuffing in the crop and with sausage-meat-stuffing in the body.

(*b*) Chickens and game birds may be roasted for a little while at the beginning of the cooking time, on the breast. This will make the breast-meat more moist. It should not be done with duck or goose. All birds should be roasted on a trivet, not resting in the tin in basting fat.

(*c*) Sufficient garnish should be served with each dish to provide some with each portion served. When dishes are to be served hot, the garnish must be ready in advance and arranged quickly. If the process takes time, the serving dish may be placed in a shallow tin of hot water to ensure that the food is served very hot.

(*d*) Frozen chickens or chicken portions can be utilized in many of the following recipes.

(*e*) The use of metal foils for cooking can be recommended (1) to ensure a tight-fitting lid when stewing or braising, (2) to wrap birds during roasting when a covered roaster is not available or proves too small. Before cooking is completed the foil should be turned back from the breast and legs of the bird to allow the skin to become crisp and brown.

(*f*) If a good stock is not available it may be produced quickly by using one of the reliable makes of consommé soup-mix now on the market.

(*g*) When the method of cooking is in a casserole or by stewing, some dry cider or dry wine may be substituted for some of the stock.

CHICKEN

BOILED CHICKEN—TURKISH STYLE

Poulet bouilli à la Turque

1 chicken *or* fowl	**½ pt. tomato sauce** (p. 127)
1 oz. butter	**1 teasp. cornflour**
1 finely-chopped shallot	**Salt and pepper**

GARNISH

½ lb. boiled rice

Truss and boil the chicken, cut into neat joints, remove skin. Melt the butter, fry shallot lightly, add tomato sauce, heat it, then add the pieces of chicken, simmer gently for 35 min. Correct the seasoning. Blend the cornflour, with a little cold water or stock, add it to the sauce and boil for 3 min.

Arrange a border of boiled rice in a hot dish, put in the chicken, strain the sauce over.

6 helpings
Cooking time—2–2½ hr.

BOMBS OF CHICKEN

Petites Bombes de Volaille

Clarified butter	**1 egg**
Chopped parsley	**Salt and pepper**
½ lb. raw chicken	**2 tablesp. cream *or* milk**
1 oz. flour	**½ pt. Béchamel sauce** (p. 128)
½ oz. butter	
½ gill water	

Have ready the bomb (small) moulds, thickly coated with clarified butter (p. 35), and sprinkle the entire surface with finely-chopped parsley.

Mince or chop chicken finely. Melt butter in a small saucepan, stir in flour, add water, boil well. Turn panada or culinary paste on to a plate to cool. Pound chicken in a bowl until smooth, add panada gradually, then add egg. Season the mixture, rub it through a fine wire sieve. Add slightly-whipped cream *or* milk. Pipe mixture into moulds. Place these in a saucepan, containing boiling water to about half their depth, cover with buttered paper, put on lid, simmer gently 20–25 min.

Arrange in 2 rows on a hot dish, pour hot sauce round and serve.

10–12 bombs

CANNELONS OF CHICKEN

Cannelons de Volaille

Chicken croquette mixture (p. 611)	**Egg and breadcrumbs**
Rough puff pastry (p. 556) **using 4 oz. flour, etc.**	**Frying fat**
	Fried parsley

Roll out pastry as thinly as possible. Cut into 1½ in. squares. Place a little chicken mixture in centre of each square, roll up rather tightly. Coat with egg and fresh breadcrumbs, fry in hot deep fat until golden brown, drain well.

Serve very hot, garnished with parsley.

6–8 helpings
Cooking time—15 min.

CHICKEN À LA MARENGO

Poulet sauté à la Marengo

1 chicken	**½ glass sherry (optional)**
¼ pt. olive oil	**1 doz. button mushrooms**
1 pt. Espagnole sauce (p. 130)	**6 stoned olives**
Salt and pepper	**1 truffle**
2 ripe tomatoes	

GARNISH

Fleurons of pastry *or* croûtes of fried bread	**Truffle**
Olives	**Mushrooms**

Joint chicken (plate 6). Remove skin and excess fat. Fry joints in oil until golden brown, drain well, pour away oil. Heat Espagnole sauce with tomato pulp, add chicken, sherry (if used), whole olives and mushrooms, truffle in large pieces, and season. Simmer gently until chicken is tender—about ¾ hr.

Pile in centre of hot dish, strain sauce over and garnish. Place fleurons *or* croûtes round the dish.

6 helpings

CHICKEN À LA MINUTE

Poussin à la Minute

3 baby chickens (poussins)	**½ pt. milk (approx.)**
2 oz. butter	**4 button onions**
1 oz. flour	**2 egg yolks**
Salt and pepper	**¼ pt. cream**

Cut the prepared chickens into quarters. Melt the butter in a saucepan, fry chicken in butter until golden brown. Sprinkle with flour, salt and pepper and stir until flour is golden brown. Just cover with boiling milk, add the blanched onions, cover tightly and cook gently until tender—about ½ hr. Remove onions, remove chicken and keep hot. Stir egg yolks and cream together; add to pan; heat gently until thick. Return chicken and continue to heat without boiling for a few more minutes. Correct seasoning and serve.

6 helpings
Cooking time—about ¾ hr.

CHICKEN—COUNTRY CAPTAIN (INDIAN)

1 roasting chicken
2 oz. fat
1 small onion
½ oz. flour
Salt and pepper
1 teasp. curry powder
1 teasp. curry paste
1 pt. stock
3 Spanish onions
2 oz. almonds

Joint the chicken, fry in a saucepan, in some of the melted fat with the small onion (sliced), until golden brown. Mix together flour, salt, pepper, curry powder and curry paste, sprinkle into pan, stir and fry until well browned. Pour off any surplus fat. Add hot stock, bring to boiling point, cover tightly and cook until chicken is tender—about 1¼ hr. Correct seasoning. Blanch and dice Spanish onions, fry until brown and crisp. Blanch and fry almonds (preferably in oil).

Serve the chicken piled on a hot dish, with onion dice and almonds on top. Serve with plain boiled rice.

6 helpings

CHICKEN CREAM

Crème de Volaille

½ lb. raw chicken
1 egg
⅛ pt. coating Béchamel sauce (p. 128)
⅛ pt. double cream
Salt and pepper
1 pt. pouring Béchamel sauce

GARNISH

Truffles *or* mushrooms

Brush 1 large mould (approx. 5 in. diameter, 3–4 in. deep) with clarified butter. (Individual moulds may be used if preferred.)

Chop and pound chicken until smooth, add egg and coating sauce gradually, sieve if desired very smooth. Whip cream stiffly, fold into mixture, season. Put mixture into prepared mould, cover with buttered paper, steam gently until firm—25 to 30 min. Meanwhile, make 1 pt. Béchamel sauce. Dish the cream, pour some sauce over.

Garnish with truffles or mushrooms.

Serve remainder of sauce in a sauce-boat.

4 helpings

CHICKEN EN CASSEROLE

Poulet en Casserole

1 chicken
1 oz. flour
Salt and pepper
2 oz. butter *or* dripping
4–6 oz. streaky bacon
1 shallot
2 oz. chopped mushrooms
1 pt. stock

Joint the chicken, dip joints in flour and seasoning. Melt the fat in a casserole; fry the bacon, cut in strips; add chicken, mushrooms and chopped shallot. Fry until golden brown, turning when necessary. Add hot stock, sufficient just to cover the chicken, simmer until tender—about 1½ hr. Correct the seasoning. Serve in the casserole.

6 helpings

CHICKEN ESCALOPES

Escalopes de Poulet

2 large raw chicken legs
½ lb. lean veal and ¼ lb. bacon *or* ¾ lb. sausage meat
6 mushrooms
1 truffle (optional)
Salt and pepper
1 egg
3 oz. butter
1 onion
1 carrot
½ small turnip
1 stick celery
Bouquet garni
1 pt. stock
1½ oz. flour
Lemon juice
1 tablesp. sherry (optional)
Spinach purée

Chop and pound veal and bacon until smooth. Add the diced mushrooms and truffle, season well, bind with egg. Bone chicken legs, stuff with farce, shape into rolls. Put 1½ oz. butter and the vegetables, sliced, into saucepan, lay chicken legs on top; cover, fry gently for 20 min., add bouquet garni. Add stock to ¾ the depth of the vegetables; place a buttered paper over; put on lid, simmer gently for 1 hr. Meanwhile, melt remaining butter, stir in flour, cook very gently (about ½ hr.) until a brown roux (paste) is formed. Remove chicken legs when cooked, keep them hot. Gradually strain stock on to roux, stirring (*or* pour on rapidly, whisking at the same time). Bring to boiling point, simmer 20 min.; add lemon juice and sherry; season to taste. Cut chicken legs into ½-in. slices, arrange slightly overlapping on bed of spinach; strain sauce over.

4–6 helpings
Cooking time—2 hr.

CHICKEN FORCEMEAT

Farce de Volaille

½ lb. raw boneless chicken	**½ gill stock**
1 oz. butter	**1 egg**
1 oz. flour	**Salt and pepper**
	Nutmeg

Melt the butter, stir in the flour, add stock (chicken stock if possible), boil 3–5 min., allow panada to cool. Chop and pound chicken, add egg and panada gradually, season well. Sieve if required very smooth.

NOTE: Before moulding or shaping the farce, test the consistency (it should not crack when handled and should retain an impression of the spoon). If necessary, soften with cream *or* milk.

Use for quenelles, cutlets, boudins, bombes, timbales.

CHICKEN FOR INVALIDS

See Chicken Ramakins; Chicken Soufflé; Chicken Panada.

CHICKEN JELLY

Gelée de Volaille

1 chicken *or* fowl	**Salt and pepper**

Joint the chicken, place the pieces in a casserole with 1 pt. cold water and a little seasoning. Cover. Cook in a warm oven **(335° F., Gas 3)** for 2 hr. Cut flesh from bones in thin slices, arrange the meat in a wetted mould or pie-dish leaving as much space as possible at the sides and between the layers for stock. Place the bones, trimmings and stock in a pan, boil rapidly for ½ hr. Strain this stock, season it, and pour over the chicken. Leave to set.

Turn out, and serve with suitable accompaniments.

6 helpings

CHICKEN LEGS AS CUTLETS

Cuisses de Volaille en Côtelettes

2 chicken legs	**8 peppercorns**
Salt and pepper	**½ pt. stock**
2 onions sliced	**2 rashers of bacon**
2 carrots sliced	**½ pt. Espagnole sauce** (p. 130)
1 small turnip sliced	
Bouquet garni	**Glaze (optional)**

Remove thigh-bones from chicken, but leave drumsticks, season the meat. Fold the skin under, and shape as much like a cutlet as possible. Wrap each leg in muslin, and fasten securely. Place vegetables, bouquet garni and peppercorns in a saucepan, add sufficient stock to barely cover the vegetables. Lay the chicken on the vegetables, covering each piece with bacon. Lay a piece of greased paper on top, and put on a tightly-fitting lid. Simmer gently until tender, about 1¼–1½ hr. Remove muslin, dish the chicken and pour the sauce over.

For an alternative method of serving: remove the pan-lid about 15 min. before the chicken is cooked, place the pan in a hot oven **(400°–425° F., Gas 6–7)** to brown the meat. Glaze the legs and pour the sauce round.

2 large helpings

CHICKEN LIVER PATTIES

Pâtés de Foie de Volaille

4 chicken livers	**Salt and pepper**
1 oz. butter	**¼ pt. brown sauce** (p. 119)
Rough-puff pastry (p. 556) **using 4 oz. flour, etc.**	**Egg *or* milk**

Remove gall, wash and trim livers, then cut into small pieces. Toss the pieces in butter over a low heat for 5 min. Line patty tins with ½ the pastry, put in the liver, season well, and add a little brown sauce to each. Cover with pastry, brush with egg *or* milk, bake in a fairly hot oven (**375° F., Gas 5**) for 20–30 min. Serve hot or cold.

4–6 helpings

CHICKEN MAYONNAISE

Mayonnaise de Volaille

1 cold boiled chicken *or* fowl	**¾ pt. mayonnaise sauce** (p. 135)
½ pt. aspic jelly	**Truffle *or* pickled walnut**
	Chervil

Joint chicken (plate 22), remove skin and excess fat, and as much bone as possible. Trim joints to a neat shape. Melt aspic jelly; when almost cool, blend ¼ pt. carefully into mayonnaise. A smooth glossy sauce will be obtained by passing it through a tammy cloth, (i.e. a piece of well-washed flannel). This is most easily done by twisting the ends of the cloth containing the sauce in opposite directions. Place the pieces of chicken on a wire cooling-tray, and mask them with the sauce when it is of a good coating consistency. Use a small ladle or tablespoon. Decorate when almost set with cut shapes of truffle (pickled walnut is cheaper, but must previously be drained on clean blotting-paper) and chervil, *or* other colourful garnish. Mask with a thin layer of the remaining aspic jelly.

Arrange on a bed of dressed salad, *or* on a dish flooded with coloured aspic. Decorate the edge of the dish with endive, cucumber and blocks of aspic jelly, if liked.

6 helpings

CHICKEN PANADA

Panade de Volaille

½ lb. raw chicken	**⅛ pt. good white sauce *or* ⅛ pt. cream**
Pepper and salt	

Remove skin and bone from chicken, put meat through a fine mincer. Place in a buttered jar, cover tightly, and stand jar in a pan of boiling water. Simmer gently for 1 hr. Pound the chicken thoroughly (sieve if desired), add liquid from jar, season to taste. Stir in the sauce *or* half-whipped cream.

Serve hot *or* cold on toast, *or* in ramakin cases.

Sufficient for 6 rounds of toast

CHICKEN PANCAKES

Crêpes de Volaille

See Game Pancakes

CHICKEN PIE

Pâté de Volaille à l'Anglaise

1 large *or* 2 small chickens	**Rough puff pastry** (p. 556) **using 8 oz. flour, etc.**
Veal forcemeat	**Salt and pepper**
½ lb. ham *or* bacon	**¾ pt. chicken stock**
2 hard-boiled eggs	**Egg for glazing**

Joint chicken, boil bones, gizzards, and trimmings for stock. Parboil the chicken liver, chop finely and mix with veal forcemeat. Cut ham into strips and eggs into sections. Make pastry. Arrange chicken and other ingredients in layers in a 1 pt. pie-dish, seasoning each layer carefully, then three-quarters fill the dish with stock. Cover pie-dish with pastry, decorate and glaze with beaten egg yolk. Bake 1½—2 hr. until meat is cooked. Until the pastry is set, have the oven hot (**425° F., Gas 7**), then lower the heat (**350°–375° F., Gas 4–5**) until cooking is complete. Before serving, add remainder of hot stock to pie.

6–8 helpings
Cooking time—about 2½ hr.

CHICKEN PILAFF

Pilau de Volaille

1 chicken *or* fowl	**6 black peppercorns**
3 pt. stock *or* 3 pt. water and 2 lb. scrag-end neck of mutton	**4 oz. butter**
	6 oz. Patna rice
	Salt and pepper
2 large Spanish onions	**1 tablesp. curry paste**
1 carrot	**2 small onions (shallots)**
1 blade mace	

Joint the chicken (plate 6), put the backbone, giblets, bones and trimmings and stock (*or* water and the mutton cut into small pieces) into a saucepan; add outside layers of Spanish onions, carrot, mace and peppercorns. Simmer gently 2–3 hr., strain. Dice remainder of Spanish onions, fry in a saucepan until lightly browned in 2 oz. of the butter, add the washed and drained rice, 1½ pt. stock and seasoning. Cook gently until rice has absorbed stock. Fry chicken slowly in remaining butter until lightly brown, put into rice with curry paste and mix well, retaining the butter. Cook gently until chicken and rice are tender, adding more stock if necessary. Cut small onions into rings, fry until golden brown in the butter in which the chicken was fried.

Pile the pilaff on a hot dish, pile rings of fried onion on top. Serve very hot.

6 helpings
Cooking time—about 1½ hr., excluding stock

CHICKEN RAMAKINS

Soufflés de Volaille en Caisses

6 oz. raw chicken
2 eggs
Salt and pepper
2 mushrooms
1 truffle *or* extra mushrooms
2 tablesp. cream
½ oz. butter

Chop or mince chicken very finely, add egg yolks gradually, making mixture as smooth as possible. (Sieve if desired.) Season well. Add chopped mushrooms and truffle to the chicken mixture, lightly stir in half-whipped cream. Fold stiffly-beaten egg-whites into mixture, add more liquid (milk) if stiff. Three-quarters fill 8 well-buttered china or paper ramakin cases with the mixture. Cook in a fairly hot oven (**375° F., Gas 5**) 15–20 min. until well-risen, firm and well-browned. Serve at once.

8 helpings

CHICKEN SAUTÉ

Poulet Sauté

See Chicken à la Marengo, p. 282, *and Fried Fowl with Peas*, p. 613.

CHICKEN SOUFFLÉ

Soufflé de Volaille

½ lb. raw chicken meat
1½ oz. butter
1 egg yolk
Salt and pepper
2 tablesp. cream
2 egg whites
½ pt. Béchamel sauce

GARNISH

Truffle *or* mushrooms

Mince chicken finely, gradually add butter and egg yolk, season well, sieve if desired. Stir in half-whipped cream, fold in stiffly-beaten egg whites. Place in a well-buttered soufflé mould or straight-sided tin; cover with greased paper and steam gently and evenly 50–60 min. (Individual moulds 25 min.)

Turn out on to a hot dish, coat quickly with sauce.

Garnish; and serve at once.

6 helpings

CHICKEN SPATCHCOCK

Poulet à la Crapaudine

1 spring chicken
1 oz. butter
Salt and pepper

GARNISH

Grilled bacon rolls

Split the prepared bird in half, cutting through the back only, cut off the legs and wings at the first joints, flatten as much as possible and keep in shape with skewers. Brush with melted butter, season lightly and grill until flesh is cooked—about 20 min. Brush with more butter if necessary and turn frequently to ensure even browning.

Remove skewers, dish up, garnish with bacon rolls; serve with Tartare *or* Piquant sauce.

1–2 helpings

CHICKEN VOL-AU-VENT

Vol-au-Vent de Volaille

6 oz. cooked chicken
Puff-pastry (p. 555) **using 8 oz. flour, etc.**
2 oz. cooked ham *or* tongue
2 truffles (optional)
2–4 oz. mushrooms
Salt, pepper, nutmeg
½ pt. Béchamel sauce
Egg *or* milk to glaze

Prepare pastry, roll out to ¾ in. thickness; cut into a round or oval shape and place on a wet baking sheet. Cut an inner ring through half the depth of the pastry and brush top of pastry (not sides) with beaten egg. Bake in a hot oven (**425°–450° F., Gas 7–8**) until well risen, firm and brown—about 25 min. Dice chicken and ham, slice mushrooms and truffles; add all these to the Béchamel sauce, season well and heat thoroughly. Lift centre from vol-au-vent case and reserve for lid, clear any soft paste which may be inside, fill with the mixture, and replace lid. See plate 18 for method of making a vol-au-vent case.

A separate piece of pastry the size of the lid may be baked with the large case, and used as a lid for the filled case; this has a better appearance.

6 helpings

CHICKEN WITH RICE AND TOMATOES

Poulet au riz à la Milanaise

1 chicken
Larding bacon
2 onions
2 carrots
1 turnip
Bouquet garni
10 peppercorns
1½ pt. stock (approx.)
½ lb. rice
¼ pt. tomato purée
3 oz. grated Parmesan cheese

Truss the chicken (p. 279). lard the breast closely (p. 35) or lay fat bacon over; wrap in greased paper. Cut vegetables into thick slices, place in pan with bouquet garni, peppercorns and sufficient stock to cover vegetables, not more. Put chicken on bed of vegetables, cover with a tightly-fitting lid, cook gently for about 1½ hr., until bird is tender, adding more stock if necessary. Wash and blanch rice; cook in good stock until tender and dry, then stir in tomato purée and cheese; season to taste. Remove paper and trussing strings from chicken; place in a hot oven (**425°–445° F., Gas 7–8**) until bacon is crisp.

Serve in a border of the rice mixture.

6 helpings

CHICKEN WITH SUPRÊME SAUCE

Poulet bouilli à la Sauce Suprême

1 chicken
1½ pt. white stock (approx.)
¾ pt. Suprême sauce

GARNISH

Truffle *or* macédoine of vegetables

Truss the chicken, poach it in the stock until tender, then divide into neat joints. Arrange the joints on a hot dish, pour the sauce over, and garnish with chopped truffle *or* macédoine of vegetable piled at either end of the dish.

4–6 helpings
Cooking time—about 1½–2 hr.

CURRIED CHICKEN

Kari de Volaille

1 chicken
2 oz. butter
1 chopped onion
1 dessertsp. flour
1 tablesp. curry powder
1 dessertsp. curry paste
¾ pt. white stock
1 chopped apple
1 dessertsp. chutney
1 tablesp. lemon juice
Salt and pepper
1 oz. sultanas
1 oz. blanched almonds
1 dessertsp. desiccated coconut
2 tablesp. cream *or* milk (optional)

GARNISH

Fans of lemon
Gherkin fans
Red pepper

Divide chicken into neat joints, remove skin, fry joints lightly in hot butter, remove from saucepan and drain. Fry onion lightly, add flour, curry powder and paste, and fry very well, stirring occasionally. Stir in stock, bring to boil. Put in all other ingredients except the cream, put in chicken joints. Have the coconut tied in muslin, and remove after 15 min. Simmer gently about 1¼ hr., adding a little more stock if necessary. Dish the chicken, add the cream to the sauce and pour the sauce over the chicken, straining if liked. Garnish.

ACCOMPANIMENTS: Dry boiled Patna rice sprinkled with paprika pepper, mangoe chutney, Bombay Duck, Poppadums, fresh grated coconut, gherkins, pickled pimentoes. These are served separately, not in the dish with the curry. Bombay Duck and Poppadums are grilled before serving.

6 helpings **Cooking time—1¾ hr.**

DEVILLED CHICKENS (POUSSINS)

Poussins à la Diable

1 poussin per portion
1 dessertsp. olive oil
Salt and pepper
Pinch of ground ginger
Pinch of mustard
1 teasp. chopped parsley
1 teasp. chopped shallot

CHICKEN

Split and skewer the baby chicken, sprinkle with the olive oil. Season with salt, pepper, ginger and mustard and sprinkle the parsley and shallot over. Allow to stand for about 1 hr., turning occasionally. Grill until tender.

Serve very hot.

FONDUE OF CHICKEN

Fondue de Volaille

See Chicken Ramakins, p. 286.

FRICASSÉE OF CHICKEN

Fricassée de Volaille

1 boiled *or* 1 lb. can of chicken	**1 egg**
1 pt. Velouté sauce	**Salt and pepper**
½ gill cream *or* milk	**Juice of 1 lemon**

GARNISH

Chopped parsley	**Sippets of fried bread, *or* potato border**

Before chicken is quite cold, cut into joints, remove skin and excess fat. Make sauce, thoroughly heat chicken in it, add cream and egg, stir over a low heat until the sauce thickens (do not boil). Season, add lemon juice.

Arrange chicken in entrée dish, strain sauce over and garnish.

NOTE: If a potato border is used, pipe or fork this into the dish, before arranging the chicken for serving.

6 helpings
Cooking time—20 min. (excluding sauce)

FRITOT OF CHICKEN

Fritot de Poulet

1 cold cooked chicken	**Frying fat**

MARINADE

2–3 tablesp. olive oil	**1 teasp. chopped parsley**
1 tablesp. lemon juice	**½ teasp. mixed herbs**
1 teasp. finely chopped onion	**Salt and pepper**

BATTER

4 oz. flour	**2 egg whites**
¼ pt. tepid water	**1 saltsp. salt**
1 tablesp. olive oil	

GARNISH

Fried parsley

Cut chicken into small joints, skin and trim the pieces neatly and place them in a deep dish. Mix together all ingredients for the marinade, pour over the chicken, and leave for 1½ hr., turning the chicken frequently. Mix flour, salt, water and olive oil to a smooth batter, allow to stand for 1 hr. Fold stiffly-beaten egg whites into the batter. Drain the chicken, dip each piece in the batter, fry in hot deep fat until golden brown. Drain.

Serve piled on a dish-paper, garnished with the parsley. Serve with tartare or tomato sauce.

6 helpings

GRILLED CHICKEN—WITH MUSHROOM SAUCE

Poulet grillé aux Champignons

1 chicken	**Croûte of fried bread**
½ pt. Espagnole sauce (p. 130)	**½ lb. lean raw ham**
1 can button mushrooms	**Salad oil *or* butter for frying and grilling**
Salt and pepper	

GARNISH

Ham	**Mushrooms**

Make Espagnole sauce, add mushrooms to it, correct seasoning and keep the sauce hot. Divide chicken into pieces convenient for serving, brush them with salad oil or oiled butter. Cut a slice of bread to fit the serving dish, fry this until lightly browned. Cut the ham into short strips and fry this. Grill prepared chicken until tender—about 15–20 min.

Pile chicken on the croûte, strain sauce round, and garnish.

4 helpings
Cooking time—about 30 min.

POTTED CHICKEN

Terrine de Volaille

Trimmings of cold roast chicken	**Nutmeg**
3 oz. cooked ham	**2 oz. butter**
Salt and pepper	**Clarified butter**

Mince chicken and ham very finely, season well, add pinch of nutmeg, and work in butter gradually, making the mixture as smooth as possible. Press paste into small pots, cover contents with clarified butter.

PURÉE OF CHICKEN—WITH RICE

Purée de Poulet au Riz

6 oz. cooked chicken
6 oz. rice
1 pt. white stock (approx.)
3 oz. boiled ham
3 tablesp. cream *or* milk
Salt and pepper

GARNISH

1 truffle *or* ¼ lb. cooked mushrooms

Blanch rice, drain well, throw into boiling stock, cook until tender, strain and put to dry, retaining the stock. Chop the chicken and ham very finely, gradually add stock to moisten. The mixture may be sieved if desired. Stir in cream *or* milk; stir in enough stock to make the mixture a thick creamy consistency, season well, and heat thoroughly.

Arrange the rice in a border in a shallow dish, put the mixture in the centre, sprinkle with chopped truffle *or* mushroom. Serve very hot.

4 helpings
Cooking time—about 1 hr.

RÉCHAUFFÉ OF CHICKEN

Réchauffé de Poulet

See Hashed Fowl, (p. 613).

ROAST CHICKEN

Poulet rôti

1 roasting chicken
Salt and pepper
2–3 rashers of bacon
½ pt. stock
Fat for basting

GARNISH

Bunches of clean watercress

Truss chicken for roasting, season lightly and cover with bacon. Roast on a trivet in the roasting tin in a fairly hot oven **(375°–400° F., Gas 5–6)** until tender 1–1½ hr. Baste frequently. The chicken may be roasted on the breast for a little while at the beginning, this will make the breast-meat more moist. (Prick the thigh to test for tenderness—if there is any trace of blood the chicken is not cooked.) The bacon may be removed 10–15 min. before serving, to allow the breast to brown. When the chicken is cooked place on a hot meat dish, remove trussing string, and keep hot. Make the gravy: pour excess fat from roasting tin but retain sediment; pour in stock, boil 2–3 min. Season to taste, strain into a hot sauce-boat.

Have ready the watercress washed, drained and lightly seasoned, garnish the chicken; serve with the gravy and bread sauce.
See also Accompaniments (p. 281).

ROAST CHICKEN—FRENCH STYLE

Poulet rôti à la française

1 roasting chicken
1 oz. butter
1 small onion
1 carrot
2 or 3 rashers of bacon
Salt and pepper
1½ gill stock

GARNISH

Watercress

Truss chicken for roasting, spread the breast thickly with butter. Slice vegetables, place in roasting tin with bacon and the washed liver and heart of the bird; fry gently. Place bird on mirepoix of vegetables (p. 290), roast in hot oven **(425° F., Gas 7)** until tender, 1–1½ hr., covering the breast with buttered paper if it browns too quickly; baste if necessary. Remove trussing string, keep chicken hot. Drain fat from roasting tin, add stock, boil 2–3 min., season and strain into gravy-boat.

Garnish; serve with gravy and bread sauce.

5–6 helpings

ROAST CHICKEN (Quick)

1 roasting chicken
Salt and pepper
2 rashers of streaky bacon
Fat for basting

Joint the chicken, season the pieces, lay them in a roasting tin with the bacon (cut into small pieces) over. Bake in a fairly hot oven **(375°–400° F., Gas 5–6)** for about 40 min., basting when necessary. Should the chicken look too dry, cover with a buttered paper. Make the gravy as for Roast Chicken.

5–6 helpings

CHICKEN

ROAST CHICKEN—STUFFED WITH HERBS

Poulet rôti aux fines herbes

1 chicken
1½ oz. butter
1 tablesp. chopped onion
2 tablesp. chopped carrot
1 oz. flour
¾ pt. stock
Salt and pepper
1 glass white wine *or* cider (optional)
1 teasp. parsley
1 teasp. chervil
1 teasp. tarragon

FORCEMEAT

2 tablesp. breadcrumbs
1 teasp. chopped shallot
1 teasp. chopped tarragon
1 teasp. chopped parsley
1 teasp. chopped chervil
Salt and pepper
Liver from chicken
1 oz. oiled butter (approx.)

Remove gall bladder, wash and chop the liver finely. Mix the chopped liver with breadcrumbs, forcemeat herbs, seasoning and sufficient oiled butter to moisten. Stuff the bird with forcemeat, truss for roasting. Roast in moderately hot oven (**350°–375° F., Gas 4–5**) until tender, 1–1½ hr.; basting frequently. Melt 1½ oz. butter in a saucepan; fry onion and carrot lightly, stir in flour, cook gently until lightly-browned. Stir in stock, boil until cooked, add seasoning and wine (if used) together with 1 teasp. each of parsley, chervil, tarragon *or* other herbs, as liked. Simmer sauce gently ¼ hr. Remove trussing strings from bird.

Serve with a little sauce poured round; and serve remainder of sauce in a sauce-boat.

4–6 helpings

SMOTHERED CHICKEN

Étuvé de Poulet

1 boiled fowl
1 pt. white sauce

Divide the hot cooked fowl into neat joints; arrange them in a hot dish. Coat with the hot sauce and serve.

The dish may be garnished with mushrooms and parsley if desired.

6 helpings

TIMBALES OF CHICKEN

½ lb. raw chicken
3 oz. macaroni
1½ oz. butter
1 egg yolk
Salt and pepper
2 tablesp. cream
2 egg whites
½ pt. Béchamel sauce

Put macaroni into rapidly-boiling salted water and cook until tender—about 15 min. Drain well. Cut macaroni into thin rings and line 6 well-buttered timbale moulds as evenly as possible with the rings (use the point of a needle to fix them in position). Prepare chicken mixture as for Chicken Soufflé (p. 286) and fill into moulds. Cover moulds with buttered paper, steam 25–35 min.

Serve hot with sauce poured round.

6 helpings

DUCK

BRAISED DUCK—WITH CHESTNUTS

Canard braisé à la française

1 duck
1 pt. stock
Larding bacon (optional)
2 oz. butter
¾ pt. Espagnole sauce (p. 130)
1 glass port wine (optional)
1 dessertsp. redcurrant jelly

MIREPOIX

2 onions
1 small turnip
2 carrots
1 stick celery
Bouquet garni
6 black peppercorns
2 cloves

STUFFING

1 lb. chestnuts
1 Spanish onion
Salt and pepper
1 egg

Boil chestnuts, remove skins and chop or mince nuts finely for stuffing. Cook Spanish onion in water until tender, chop finely, add to chestnuts, season well and bind with egg. Stuff duck with chestnut mixture, truss, lard with bacon, if liked. Slice vegetables for mirepoix (foundation), place in a large saucepan with butter, lay duck on vegetables, cover pan, fry gently for 20 min.; then add bouquet garni, spices, and enough stock to come three-quarters of the depth of mirepoix. Cover with a buttered paper, put on lid, simmer gently until duck is tender—about 2 hr. Add more stock if necessary to prevent burning. Heat Espagnole sauce, add wine (if used) and jelly, re-heat and season to taste. Remove paper and trussing string from duck, and place it in a hot oven (**425°–450° F., Gas 7–8**) to crisp the bacon.

Serve on a hot dish, with a water-cress garnish, if liked; serve sauce separately.

4–5 helpings
Cooking time—about 3 hr. in all

DUCK EN CASSEROLE

Canard en casserole

1 duck	**4 shallots**
¾ oz. flour	**¾ pt. stock (approx.)**
Salt and pepper	**½ pt. green peas**
4 oz. mushrooms	**1 teasp. chopped mint**

Cut duck into joints, remove all skin, dip the joints in seasoned flour. Place duck, chopped mushrooms and chopped shallots in a casserole. Just cover with stock, put on a tightly-fitting lid and cook in a fairly hot oven (**375°–400° F., Gas 5–6**) about ¾ hr. Add shelled peas and mint and continue cooking until duck is tender—about another ½ hr. Correct seasoning.

Serve from the casserole.

4–5 helpings

DUCK—ROUENNAISE STYLE

Canard à la Rouennaise

1 large "Rouen" duck	**½ pt. stock**
2 oz. butter	**1 glass claret (optional)**
1 tablesp. chopped shallot	**Bouquet garni**
1 dessertsp. flour	**Lemon juice**

STUFFING

Heart and liver of the duck	**1 small onion**
2 tablesp. breadcrumbs	**1 oz. butter**
1 teasp. chopped parsley	**Salt and pepper**

Prepare stuffing: remove gall bladder from liver, wash liver and heart, chop finely. Parboil onion, chop finely and add to liver and heart with breadcrumbs, parsley, melted butter and seasoning. Stuff duck with this mixture, truss, and fry with chopped shallot in the butter, until brown. Remove duck, stir in flour and brown it, stir in stock, bring to boiling-point, add claret (if used). Replace duck in pan, add bouquet garni and lemon juice, cover with a tightly-fitting lid. Cook in a moderate oven (**350° F., Gas 4**) until duck is tender—1–1½ hr. Remove trussing strings, joint the duck but keep it in shape.

Serve on a hot dish with sauce strained over.

4–5 helpings **Cooking time—1½ hr.**

FILLETS OF DUCK

Filets de Canard à la Bigarade

1 duck	**2 small oranges**
Duchess potato mixture (p. 350)	**1 teasp. salad oil**
½ pt. Bigarade sauce (p. 130)	

Truss duck, roast in a fairly hot oven (**375°–400° F., Gas 5–6**) until tender, basting when necessary. Make the potato mixture, pipe in a border round the serving dish, brown and keep hot. Grate the orange rind, add it to the Bigarade sauce, and keep hot. Remove pith and skin from the orange sections, heat them in a basin over hot water, and before serving mix with the salad oil. Remove the breast from the duck, cut it into neat strips and arrange them overlapping each other within the potato border. Pour the sauce over, and garnish with the orange.

The remainder of the duck may be made into a salmi or hash.

See Salmi of Duck (p. 292) *or Hashed Fowl* (p. 613).

4 helpings
Cooking time—1¼–1½ hr.

HASHED DUCK

Canard au Vin Rouge

1 cold roast duck	**1 pt. stock**
1 onion	**1 orange**
1 oz. butter	**1 glass claret**
1 oz. flour	**Salt and pepper**

Carve duck ready for serving. Chop onion finely, put into a saucepan, fry in butter, stir in flour and cook gently until brown. Add stock, stir until boiling, allow to simmer 10 min. Cut orange rind into very thin strips, add to the sauce with the orange juice, claret and pieces of duck. Season. Simmer very gently for ½ hr. Dish the meat and pour sauce over.

4 helpings **Cooking time—about 1 hr.**

DUCK

ROAST DUCK

Canard rôti

1 duck	**½ oz. flour**
Fat for basting	**½ pt. stock**
Sage and onion stuffing	**Salt and pepper**
	Apple sauce

Fill duck with sage and onion stuffing, truss for roasting. Baste well with hot fat, roast in a fairly hot oven (**375°–400° F., Gas 5–6**) 1–1½ hr. basting frequently. Keep duck hot, pour fat from roasting tin, sprinkle in flour and brown it. Stir in stock, simmer 3–4 min., season and strain. Remove trussing strings from duck.

Serve gravy and apple sauce separately. *See also Accompaniments* (p. 281) *and Italian Fennel and Cucumber Salad* (p. 376).

4–5 helpings **Cooking time—1½ hr.**

ROAST DUCK—WITH ORANGE

Canard rôti à l'Orange

1 duck	**1 large orange**
Fat for basting	**1 tablesp. brandy *or* red wine**

Truss and roast duck in a fairly hot oven (**375°–400° F., Gas 5–6**) for 1–1¼ hr., until tender, basting if necessary. Meanwhile, stand the orange in a pan of boiling water for about 3 min., remove skin, cut orange into sections, soak these in brandy *or* wine. Remove all white pith from the skin, cut the latter into thin strips, boil in a little water for about 5 min., drain. Heat the orange sections gently in the brandy. Remove trussing strings from duck.

Serve with strips of rind and hot orange sections as a garnish.

4–5 helpings

SALMI OF DUCK

Salmis de Canard aux Olives

1 duck (*or* trimmings from 2 cold roast ducks)	**1½ oz. butter**
	1 oz. flour
	¾ pt. stock
1 Spanish onion	**12 stoned French olives**
Fat for basting	

Slice onion into roasting tin, put prepared duck on top, baste with hot fat and roast in a fairly hot oven (**375°–400° F., Gas 5–6**) until tender. Melt butter, add flour and cook slowly until the roux browns, stir in stock and simmer until required. If a whole duck has been used, remove trussing string, cut duck into small joints and add with the olives to sauce, season and reheat thoroughly. Sieve (or finely chop) the onion, add to the duck. Drain off the fat and add the sediment from the roasting tin to the sauce.

The salmi may be dished on a croûte of fried bread placed in the centre of a hot dish with sauce and olives poured over, if liked.

4 helpings **Cooking time—about 1 hr.**

STEWED DUCK (Whole)

Canard à l'Anglaise

1 duck	**1 pt. stock**
Fat for basting	**4 sage leaves**
2 onions	**2–3 strips lemon-thyme**
2 oz. butter	**Salt and pepper**
1½ oz. flour	

Truss duck, baste with hot fat, cook in a hot oven (**425°–450° F., Gas 7–8**) until well-browned, basting frequently. Slice onions, fry until golden brown in butter, remove them, and brown the flour in the butter. Place duck in a large saucepan, barely cover it with hot stock, add fried onions, sage and lemon-thyme. Cover with a closely-fitting lid, and simmer gently until tender—about ¾ hr. When duck is cooked, strain sauce from pan, and stir ¾ pt. of it into the brown roux; stir until boiling, cook 5 min. and season.

Serve the duck with gravy and 1 pt. green peas, handed separately.

4–5 helpings **Cooking time—1¼–1½ hr.**

STEWED or BRAISED DUCK

Canard en Ragôut

1 duck	**1½ oz. butter**
2 onions, sliced	**1½ oz. flour**
2 sage leaves	**1 pt. brown stock**
Bouquet garni	**Salt and pepper**

Truss duck, roast it in a hot oven (**425°–450° F., Gas 7–8**) for 20 min. Place in a saucepan with herbs and onions, cover tightly and cook slowly for ¾ hr. Melt butter, add flour and brown well, stir in stock, simmer 20 min. and strain. When duck is tender, remove trussing strings. Add sediment from pan to the sauce; season and serve in a sauce-boat.

Some mushrooms may be added to the sauce if desired.

4–5 helpings **Cooking time—about 1¼ hr.**

STUFFED DUCKLING

Caneton à la Rouennaise

1 large "Rouen" duckling	**¾ pt. brown sauce** (p. 119).
Fat for basting	**Sections of 1 large orange**

STUFFING

1 chicken liver	**Salt and pepper**
1 duckling liver	**Nutmeg**
½ teasp. parsley	**1 oz. butter**
¼ teasp. thyme	**1 egg**
3 oz. breadcrumbs	

Blanch chicken and duckling livers, chop them finely, add herbs, breadcrumbs, melted butter, pinch of nutmeg, salt and pepper, then bind with egg. Stuff duckling with liver mixture; truss, baste well with hot fat, roast in hot oven (**425°–450° F., Gas 7–8**) for ½ hr., basting frequently. Drain off all fat, pour hot brown sauce into baking tin and continue cooking until duckling is tender—about 20 min. Baste frequently with sauce.

Serve on a hot dish. Strain a little sauce round, garnish with orange (heated in a little wine *or* stock, over a pan of hot water), and serve remainder of sauce separately.

4 helpings **Cooking time—1 hr.**

ZÉPHIRES OF DUCK

Zéphires de Canard

See Zéphires of Wild Duck, p. 309.

FOWL

BOILED FOWL

Poulet bouilli

1 fowl	**Bouquet garni**
1 onion	**1½ oz. butter**
1 carrot	**1½ oz. flour**
½ lemon	**¾ pt. stock**
Salt	

GARNISH

Truffle *or* **mushroom**	**Sprigs of parsley** *or* **sieved yolk of hard-boiled egg**

Truss the fowl, inserting some pieces of vegetable in the body. Rub breast of bird with lemon, wrap in buttered paper and put in pan with sufficient stock or water to cover. Add remainder of vegetables (sliced), salt and bouquet garni and cook gently until fowl is tender (about 2 hr.). Meanwhile melt butter in a saucepan, add flour and cook without browning; gradually stir in the stock and boil for 10 min., stirring all the time; season. Use some of the liquor from stewpan if no stock is available. Remove trussing string from fowl.

Place on a hot dish, coat with sauce; garnish.

5–6 helpings

CURRIED FOWL

Poulet à l'Indienne

Remains of 2 cold roast fowls	**¾ pt. stock**
	1 sliced apple
1 sliced onion	**1 teasp. chutney** *or* **redcurrant jelly**
2 oz. butter	
1 tablesp. flour	**1 dessertsp. lemon juice**
1 tablesp. curry powder	**Salt and pepper**

Cut fowl into neat pieces (use bones and trimmings for stock). Fry sliced onion lightly in butter in a saucepan, stir in flour and curry powder, cook 3 min. Stir in stock, bring to boil. Add sliced apple, chutney, lemon juice and seasoning; simmer gently for ½ hr. Put in fowl, keep hot but not simmering for ½ hr. Dish fowl, pour sauce over (strain if liked).

Garnish and serve accompaniments as for Curried Chicken.

GALANTINE OF FOWL

Galantine de Volaille

1 boned fowl	**2 truffles** *or* **6 mushrooms**
Salt and pepper	
1 lb. sausage meat	**½ oz. pistachio nuts** *or* **almonds**
¼ lb. boiled ham *or* **tongue**	
	1½ pt. stock (approx.)
2 hard-boiled eggs	**1 pt. chaudfroid sauce**
	½ pt. aspic jelly

FOWL

GARNISH—selection of:

Pimento	**Lemon rind**
Truffle	**Hard-boiled egg**
Mushroom	

Bone the fowl (p. 280), cut down the centre of the back (this may be done before boning, as it makes the process easier), spread it out, and distribute the flesh as evenly as possible, season well. Spread with ½ of sausage meat, arrange narrow strips of ham *or* tongue, slices of egg, chopped truffles *or* mushrooms and chopped, blanched nuts on the sausage, season well, then cover with remainder of sausage. Fold over the back skin and stitch firmly. Wrap bird in clean cloth and fasten securely. Simmer gently in stock 2½ hr.; allow to cool a little in the stock, then press between 2 large boards or plates until quite cold. Unwrap, skin, and wipe free from excess grease.

Coat with chaudfroid sauce, garnish, and mask with aspic jelly.

If preferred the galantine may be brushed with glaze, instead of using chaudfroid sauce, and garnished with aspic jelly.

8–10 helpings

GRILLED FOWL WITH MUSHROOM SAUCE

See Grilled Chicken—with Mushroom Sauce, (p. 288), *and substitute a fowl for the chicken.*

RAGOÛT OF FOWL

Ragoût de Volaille

1 fowl	**1½ oz. flour**
2½ oz. butter	**1¼ pt. stock**
1 onion	**¼ lb. ham *or* bacon**
Salt and pepper	

Joint fowl (plate 6), heat the butter in a saucepan, fry the joints in this until lightly browned; remove and keep them hot. Fry the sliced onion lightly, sprinkle in the flour, and brown this slowly; add the stock, stir until boiling, season carefully. Replace the joints in the sauce, add diced ham *or* bacon, cover with a tightly-fitting lid and cook gently until fowl is tender—2–2½ hr. Correct the seasoning, serve with the sauce strained over.

5–6 helpings

ROAST FOWL—GERMAN STYLE

Poulet rôti aux Marrons

1 fowl	**1 oz. flour**
1 lb. chestnuts	**1 pt. stock**
Veal forcemeat	**Salt and pepper**
Basting fat	
1 oz. butter	

GARNISH

Slices of lemon	**1 lb. fried sausages**

Make a slit in the chestnut skins, put them into boiling water and cook for 15 min. Remove both skins, and bake until tender. Stuff the body of the bird with chestnuts, retaining about 1 dozen. Stuff the crop with veal forcemeat. Truss the bird (p. 279), and roast in a fairly hot oven (**375°–400° F., Gas 5–6**) until tender—1½–2 hr., basting frequently. Melt butter, add flour and brown slightly; add stock, stir until boiling, season to taste; add remaining chestnuts and simmer 15 min. Remove trussing strings.

Serve bird with sausages and garnished with lemon. Serve the sauce separately.

5–6 helpings

Cooking time—about 2 hr.

STEWED FOWL—WITH RICE

Poulet au Riz

1 fowl	**Bouquet garni**
2 onions	**4 oz. rice**
3–4 sticks of celery	**Salt and pepper**
2 pt. stock	

Slice the vegetables and place a few pieces inside the body of the fowl. Truss the bird for boiling, place in a large saucepan or casserole, add the stock and bring to boiling point. Add remainder of vegetables, and bouquet garni, tied in muslin. Cover closely, and cook very gently for 1 hr., then add well-washed rice and seasoning. Continue cooking gently until fowl and rice are tender—about 2 hr. The rice should absorb nearly all the stock. Dish the fowl, removing strings. Remove vegetables and bouquet garni from the rice, correct the seasoning of this, and serve with the bird.

5–6 helpings

Cooking time—about 2–2½ hr.

GIBLETS

GIBLET PIE

Pâté aux Abatis à l'Anglaise

1 set of goose giblets	**1 lb. rump steak**
1 onion, sliced	**Puff pastry** (p.555) **using 6 oz. flour, etc.**
Bouquet garni	
Salt and pepper	**Egg *or* milk for glazing**

Wash the giblets, put in a saucepan with sliced onion, bouquet garni and seasoning, cover with cold water, simmer gently 1½–2 hr. Slice the steak thinly, and season it. Place alternate layers of steak and giblets in a pie dish (approx. 1½ pt. size) which should be filled, and strain over enough stock to come ¾ of the way up the dish. Cover the pie with puff pastry (allowing the meat to cool first, if possible) and bake in a hot oven (**425°–450° F., Gas 7–8**) until pastry is set—about 20 min.—then lower heat to moderate (**350°–375° F., Gas 4–5**) and continue cooking until meat is tender—about 60 min. more. Fill up the pie with the remainder of the hot stock.

The pie may be glazed with egg *or* milk, about 20 min. before it is ready.

6 helpings **Cooking time—1¼–1½ hr.**

STEWED GIBLETS

Abatis en Ragoût

1 set of goose giblets	**1 oz. flour**
Stock	**Salt and pepper**
1 oz. butter	

Wash the goose giblets. Cover with stock and water and stew until tender. Remove the liver, neck and tendons as soon as tender leaving the gizzard until it can be pierced with a fork. Heat butter in a saucepan, stir in flour and brown slowly. Strain ¾ pt. of stock from giblets, and stir into roux. Bringing to boiling point, season, add giblets and re-heat thoroughly. Serve very hot.

3–4 helpings **Cooking time—about 1½ hr.**

GOOSE

ROAST GOOSE

Oie rôtie

1 goose	**Fat for basting**
Sage and onion stuffing	**Flour**

Prepare the goose, make the stuffing and insert this in the body of the bird. Truss the goose (p. 279), and prick the skin of the breast. Roast bird in a fairly hot oven (**375°–400° F., Gas 5–6**) 2½ hr.—until tender. When almost cooked, dredge breast with flour, baste with some of the hot fat and finish cooking. Remove trussing string; dish the bird.

Serve with apple sauce (p. 124) and beef gravy handed separately.

Gravy made from goose giblets is very rich, but may be served instead of beef gravy, if desired.

8–10 helpings

ROAST GOOSE—WITH POTATO STUFFING

Oie farcie aux Pommes de terre

1 goose	**1 oz. butter**
1 lb. potatoes	**1 small onion**
Salt and pepper	**Milk**
2 teasp. sage	

Prepare the goose. Boil, drain and mash the potatoes well, season them thoroughly; add sage, melted butter, and the onion (finely diced); moisten with milk. Stuff the bird with the potato mixture, truss. Cook and serve as directed for Roast Goose.

NOTE: The peel of an orange may be mixed with the potato.

ROAST GREEN GOOSE OR GOSLING

Oison rôti

Geese are called green until about 4 months old—they are not stuffed usually.

1 green goose	**Salt and pepper**
2 oz. butter	

GARNISH

Watercress

Prepare the goose, mix together the butter, salt and pepper, and place this in the body. Truss the bird, and cook in a moderate oven (**350°–375° F., Gas 4–5**) for about 1 hr., basting with fat if necessary. Dish the bird. Garnish with the watercress.

Brown gravy and gooseberry jelly, or gooseberry sauce (p. 124) may be served, if desired.

5–6 helpings

GUINEA FOWL

ROAST GUINEA FOWL

Pintade rôtie

1 guinea fowl
2 oz. butter
Salt and pepper
2 slices fat bacon

GARNISH

Watercress
French dressing

Prepare the bird (p. 278), mix the butter and seasoning, place in body of bird. Truss the bird, lay slices of bacon over the breast, and roast in a moderately hot oven **(350°–375° F., Gas 4–5)** 1–1½ hr., basting frequently. When the bird is almost cooked, "froth" the breast, i.e. dredge with flour, baste and finish cooking. Wash and dry watercress, toss lightly in French dressing (p. 380). Remove trussing strings from bird and garnish.

Serve with browned crumbs, bread sauce, and Espagnole sauce (p. 130) handed separately.

4-5 helpings

TURKEY

BOILED TURKEY

Dinde bouillie

1 turkey
1 lb. sausage meat
Stock *or* water
2 onions
2 carrots
1 small turnip
Bouquet garni
Salt
1 pt. celery sauce

GARNISH

Veal forcemeat
Boiled celery
Egg and breadcrumbs

Stuff the turkey with seasoned sausage meat, truss for boiling (p. 279). Place in a large pan, cover with boiling stock *or* water; add large pieces of onion, carrot, turnip, the bouquet garni and a little salt. Cover, boil gently until tender—about 2½ hr. for 9 lb. bird (this may vary considerably—test the thigh of the bird with a thin skewer). Make forcemeat into small balls, egg and crumb, fry in deep fat, also cook celery and make sauce. Remove trussing strings from bird. Garnish with forcemeat balls; and serve celery and sauce separately.

Boiled ham *or* tongue is usually served with this dish.

DEVILLED TURKEY LEGS

Cuisses de Dinde à la Diable

2 turkey legs
Salt and pepper
Cayenne pepper
Mixed mustard *or* French mustard
Butter

Remove skin from turkey, criss-cross with deep cuts. Sprinkle well with seasoning and a little cayenne, if required very hot. Spread with mixed mustard (*or* French mustard) pressing well into the cuts and leave for several hours. Grill 8–12 min. until crisp and brown, spread with small pieces of butter mixed with cayenne, and serve immediately.

4 helpings

FRICASSÉE OF TURKEY

Fricassée de Dinde

See Fricassée of Chicken (p. 288).

ROAST TURKEY

Dinde rôtie

1 turkey
1–2 lb. sausage meat
1 lb. veal forcemeat
2–3 rashers streaky bacon
Fat for basting

Stuff crop of bird with veal forcemeat and put seasoned sausage meat inside body of bird. Truss for roasting (p. 279). Lay bacon rashers over the breast, roast in a pre-heated hot oven **(425° F., Gas 7)** for 15–20 min. then reduce heat to moderate **(350° F., Gas 4)**, basting frequently. The cooking time will vary according to the size and quality of the bird—as a general guide, allow 15 min. per lb. for a turkey under 14 lb. weight, and 12 min. per lb. if over 14 lb. About 20 min. before serving remove the bacon to allow the breast to brown. Remove trussing string; serve on a hot dish.

Serve with gravy, sausages and bread sauce (p. 122) if liked, or cranberry sauce (p. 124). *See also Accompaniments* (p. 281).

ROAST TURKEY POULT

Dindonneau rôti

1 young turkey
Fat for basting

Truss bird for roasting, (p. 279), cover breast with 2 or 3 folds of buttered paper, and roast in a hot oven **(425°–450° F., Gas 7–8)** until tender—about 1 hr.—basting if necessary. Allow skin to brown lightly, remove trussing string.

Serve with thin gravy and fried bacon *or* boiled ham handed separately.

5–6 helpings **Cooking time—about 1–1½ hr.**

ROAST TURKEY—WITH CHESTNUTS

Dinde farcie aux Marrons

1 turkey	**Cream *or* milk**
2 lb. chestnuts	**1–1½ lb. sausage meat *or* 1 lb. veal forcemeat**
½ pt. stock	**2–3 slices bacon**
2 oz. butter	**Fat for basting**
1 egg	
Salt and pepper	

Slit the skins of the chestnuts, cook in boiling water for 15 min., then remove skins. Now stew chestnuts in stock for 1 hr.—drain and chop or sieve them. Add melted butter, egg, seasoning and sufficient cream *or* milk to moisten the stuffing. Fill the crop of the bird with the chestnut stuffing, and the body of the bird with seasoned sausage meat. Truss the bird for roasting. Cover the bird with bacon, roast in a moderate oven **(350° F., Gas 4)** until tender (allow 15 min. per lb. for a turkey weighing under 14 lb., and 12 min. per lb. for a turkey over 14 lb.). Baste well. Remove bacon towards end of cooking to allow the breast to brown. Remove trussing string, dish. Serve gravy separately.

NOTE: If the turkey is large the breast meat may dry up in a small oven before the legs and thighs are cooked. Either remove legs before roasting and cook separately, or take turkey from oven when breast is ready and cook the legs according to any suitable recipe, for use at another meal.

See also General Hints, (p. 281).

ROAST TURKEY—WITH CHIPOLATA GARNISH

Dinde à la Chipolata

1 turkey	**2 or 3 slices bacon**
2 lb. sausage meat	**Fat for basting**
1 lb. veal forcemeat	**Espagnole sauce**

GARNISH

½ pt. carrot parisienne	**½ oz. butter**
½ pt. turnip parisienne	**½ pt. stock**
1 can mushrooms	

Prepare and stuff the turkey (reserving ½ lb. sausage meat) and roast (*see* previous recipes). Make Espagnole sauce. Cut the balls of carrot and turnip and sweat these in the butter; after all fat is absorbed, add the stock, cook them, add the mushrooms for a few minutes to heat them. Meanwhile, shape the remaining ½ lb. sausage meat into small rolls, flour them lightly and fry. Remove the trussing string from the bird.

Serve the bird and garnish with the well-drained vegetables. Serve the sauce separately.

STEWED or BRAISED TURKEY

Dinde braisée

1 small turkey	**Bouquet garni**
2–4 oz. butter	**Salt and pepper**
2 onions, sliced	**Stock**
2 carrots, sliced	**2 slices streaky bacon**
1 turnip, sliced	

Truss bird as for roasting (p. 279). Melt butter in a large pan or roasting tin, and brown turkey in the fat. Remove turkey, place vegetables, bouquet garni and seasoning in pan, adding sufficient stock to almost cover the vegetables. Place turkey on bed of vegetables, lay bacon slices on the breast, cover and cook gently on top of the stove or in a moderate oven **(350° F., Gas 4)** until bird is tender. Remove trussing string, dish bird.

8 helpings

GAME

GAME BIRDS, WHICH ARE wild, are protected by the law, and they may be killed or sold only during specified months of the year. The following table shows when the various birds are in season.

Game	*In season*
Grouse	August 12–December 10
Blackcock	August 20–December 10
Capercailzie	August 20–December 10
Ortolan	November–January
Partridge	September 1–February 1
Pheasant	October 1–February 1
Plover	October–February
Ptarmigan	September–April
Snipe	October–February
Wild Duck	August–March
Teal	October–February
Wigeon	October–February

NOTE: Some supplies of frozen game are now imported and may be available out of season.

TO CHOOSE GAME

Young birds are usually much better for the table than old ones, the former being more delicate in flavour and much more tender. The size of the spur, the smoothness of the legs and the tenderness of the pinion are the best guides in choosing a young bird. A bird in good condition should have a thick, firm breast. Choose those which have moist supple feet, and which have not been badly shot.

Three of the most popular game birds in this country are:

(1) **Grouse**—a young bird will have soft downy feathers on the breast and under the wings, the wings will be pointed.

(2) **Partridge**—the grey partridge is considered the best of the species. The young can be distinguished by the fact that the long wing-feather is pointed, not rounded as in older birds.

(3) **Pheasant**—the young bird will have short, not very sharp spurs, and a light plumage.

Recipes for other birds are included in this chapter.

TO KEEP GAME

All water birds should be eaten as fresh as possible, as their flesh is oily and soon becomes rank. Most game is kept until putrefaction has begun, but the length of time of keeping will vary according to the weather and individual taste. In warm, close weather, game should not be kept as long as in cool or breezy weather. The game is kept undrawn and unplucked, and should be kept hanging up in a current of air. A good sprinkling of pepper may be applied to the feathers, as it helps to keep flies away. Unless required very "high", it is ready when the tail feathers come out easily when pulled. As soon as the birds are ready, pluck them carefully, so as not to break the skin, draw them if they are to be cooked drawn, and wipe them thoroughly with a damp cloth. If the game has become too "high" it may be washed with salted water containing vinegar, and then rinsed. Fresh powdered charcoal, tied in muslin and left in the crop during cooking, will also help to remove any taint.

Portions and cooking times are given in the recipes, but birds vary in size and condition, so that this information is intended only as a guide to the cook and cannot always be quite accurate.

DRESSING GAME

The directions given on p. 278 can be applied to any bird to be plucked, drawn and trussed for cooking. With smaller birds such as grouse and pigeons great care must be taken in each operation as the work is rather more delicate. One-finger operation is needed for both of these.

Snipe, plover, quails and woodcock are cooked undrawn, merely being plucked, wiped clean, and served with the head on.

COOKING GAME

Young game birds are usually roasted. As there is little fat on game they must be either larded or barded before roasting. Grouse Pudding (p. 302) and Partridge with Cabbage (p. 303) are excellent for tough birds.

ACCOMPANIMENTS for game are usually watercress and/or green salad with French dressing, thin gravy, game chips, bread sauce and browned (fried) breadcrumbs.

GAME

FRENCH GAME PIE

Pâté de Gibier

1 blackcock, pheasant *or* partridge
¾ lb. lean veal
¾ lb. lean pork
Mixed spice *or* herbs
2–3 rashers bacon
1 truffle *or* 8 mushrooms
Salt and pepper
¼ pt. stock *or* water
Puff pastry (p. 555) using 8 oz. flour, etc.

Chop or mince the veal and pork finely; season well with spice *or* herbs, salt and pepper; add finely chopped truffle *or* mushrooms. Cut the bird into neat joints, season the pieces lightly. Put a layer of meat in the bottom of a pie-dish, then some game, bacon and more forcemeat until dish is full. Moisten with ¼ pt. water *or* stock. Cover with puff pastry, glaze and bake in a fairly hot oven **(375°–400° F., Gas 5–6)** 1½–1¾ hr., lowering the heat after 20 min. to **(350°–375° F., Gas 4–5)**.

Serve hot or cold.

6–8 helpings

GAME PANCAKES

Crêpes de Gibier

BATTER

4 oz. flour
Salt and pepper
1 egg
½ pt. milk

FILLING

4 oz. cooked game
2 oz. mushrooms
Salt and pepper
Sauce *or* cream

Mix the pancake batter; allow to stand.

Mince or chop the cold cooked game. Cook and chop the mushrooms; mix with the game, season, moisten with sauce *or* cream and heat gently. Fry the pancakes, stuff and roll each.

Serve very hot. Keep the first pancakes hot between 2 plates over a pan of boiling water, until all are ready. Chicken may be used up in the same way, when some grated cheese grilled on top of the rolled pancakes is a pleasant addition.

4 helpings **Cooking time—about 10 min.**

GAME PIE

Pâté de Gibier

See French Game Pie and Raised Pie.

HASHED GAME

Hachis de Gibier

See Salmi of Wild Duck, p. 615.

POTTED GAME

Terrine de Gibier

Cooked game
Butter *or* stock *or* gravy
Salt and pepper
Cayenne pepper
Clarified butter

Remove skin and bone from game, chop or mince meat very finely. Pound until smooth, gradually adding strong game stock *or* gravy *or* oiled butter, until mixture is moist. Season well.

Press into small pots, cover with clarified butter.

Use as a savoury spread, or in pastry cases.

RAISED PIE

Pâté de Gibier

½ lb. game
½ lb. pork
½ lb. veal
Salt and pepper
Veal forcemeat
½ pt. good stock (approx.)
Egg to glaze

HOT WATER CRUST PASTRY

½ lb. flour
Pinch of salt
¼ pt. water *or* milk and water
3 oz. lard

Remove skin and bones from the game, cut into small pieces, mix with pork and veal (also cut finely); season well.

Prepare and mould pastry: sift flour and salt into a warm basin. Put the milk and water (or water) and lard to boil, then pour into middle of flour and mix well with wooden spoon until cooler. Knead with the hands until smooth, keep warm throughout or the moulding may be extremely difficult—but avoid overheating. Cut off ¼, roll to shape for the lid. Raise remainder with the hands to a round or oval shape.

When the lower part of the pie has been raised to the required shape and thinness, line it with veal forcemeat to support the lower part of the pie. Line the sides with forcemeat, put in the prepared meat, cover with a thin layer of forcemeat, add some stock and put on the cover. Fasten 3 or 4 folds of greased, greaseproof paper round the pie to preserve its shape and prevent it becoming too brown. Brush the top of the pie with egg and make a hole in the centre. Bake in a hot oven (**425° F., Gas 7**) and reduce heat to moderate (**350° F., Gas 4**) as soon as pastry is set.

The pie may be baked in a tin (choose one with a loose base), if desired. Prepare and bake the pie, removing it from the tin and glazing top and sides with egg about 30 min. before cooking is complete. If the pie is required cold, return to the tin when cooked and leave it until cold—this prevents the pastry from becoming hard.

6 helpings
Cooking time—about 2 hr.

GROUSE

BLACKCOCK FILLETS À LA FINANCIÈRE

Filets de Petit Coq de Bruyère à la Financière

2 blackcocks	**½ pt. brown sauce** (p. 119)
1 medium-sized onion	**12 button mushrooms**
1 small carrot	**1 glass sherry** *or* **Madeira (optional)**
½ turnip	**Salt and pepper**
¼ pt. stock	
3 rashers of bacon	

Joint birds and cut into fillets. Slice vegetables and lay these in a sauté-pan with the bacon; put the fillets on top. Add the stock, cover with a buttered paper and close-fitting lid, simmer gently 30 min. Make brown sauce, add mushrooms (if fresh, fry first in butter), and wine (if used); season to taste; keep sauce hot.

When fillets are cooked, arrange on a hot dish, strain the sauce over and use mushrooms and bacon for garnishing.

5–6 helpings

GRILLED BLACKCOCK

Petit Coq de Bruyère grillé

2 blackcocks	**1 pt. brown sauce**
2 oz. melted butter	**1 teasp. lemon juice**
Salt and pepper	**Anchovy essence**

Split birds down the back, cut off legs at the first joint, skewer as flat as possible. Brush with melted butter, season lightly, grill 20–30 min., turning frequently and brushing with more butter if necessary. Make the sauce, add lemon juice, anchovy essence and seasoning to taste.

Serve the birds with potato chips *or* straws and serve sauce separately.

6 helpings

ROAST BLACKCOCK

Petit Coq de Bruyère rôti

2 blackcocks	**Rashers of bacon**
2 oz. butter	**Buttered toast**
Salt and pepper	

Let the birds hang for a few days or they will be tough and tasteless.

Pluck and draw the birds. Cut off the heads. Wipe the insides and outsides well with a damp cloth (washing spoils the flavour). Insert seasoned butter in the birds, truss them, and cover with bacon. Roast in a fairly hot oven (**375°–400° F., Gas 5–6**) for 45–60 min., basting frequently. Remove trussing string.

Serve on buttered toast (*or* croûtes of fried bread) with gravy, bread sauce and fried crumbs served separately.

6 helpings

ROAST CAPERCAILZIE

Coq de Bruyère rôti

1 capercailzie	**1 or 2 slices bacon**
¼ lb. beef steak	**Fat for basting**

GARNISH

Watercress	**French dressing**

Prepare the bird (p. 278), place the steak inside it, and truss. (The steak improves the flavour, and may afterwards be used in the preparation of a cold meat dish.) Cover the bird with bacon, roast in a fairly hot oven (**375°–425° F., Gas 5–7**) for about 1 hr., basting if necessary. Remove bacon about 15 min. before bird is cooked, baste, dredge with flour, baste and return to oven. This "frothing" will give a brown, crisp skin.

Serve (without the steak) garnished with watercress tossed in French dressing, and with gravy, bread sauce and fried breadcrumbs served separately.

6 helpings **Cooking time—1 hr.**

GROUSE PIE

Pâté de Coq de Bruyère

2 grouse
¾ lb. rump steak
2–3 slices of bacon
2 hard-boiled eggs
Salt and pepper
½ pt. good stock
Puff pastry (p. 555), **using 8 oz. flour, etc.**

Joint the birds and discard vent-end parts of the backs, as these will impart a bitter flavour to the pie. Slice the steak thinly, slice eggs and cut the bacon into strips. Line the bottom of a pie-dish with pieces of seasoned meat, cover with a layer of grouse, add some bacon, egg and seasoning. Repeat until dish is full. Add sufficient stock to ¾ fill the pie-dish, cover with puff pastry and bake 1½–1¾ hr. The first 15 min. of this time, have the oven hot (**425°–450° F., Gas 7–8**) then lower the heat to moderate (**350°–375° F., Gas 4–5**) or cover the pastry with greaseproof paper so that the filling may cook a further 1¼–1½ hr. Glaze the pie ½ hr. before cooking is complete. Simmer the necks and trimmings of the birds in the remaining stock, strain, season and pour into the pie before serving.

Finely-chopped mushrooms, parsley and shallots may be added to the pie, if liked.

6–8 helpings
Cooking time—1¾ hr.

GROUSE PUDDING

Pouding de Coq de Bruyère

This is an excellent method of using a tough bird.

1 grouse
1 lb stewing steak
1 oz. flour
Salt and pepper
Suet pastry (p. 557), **using 8 oz. flour, etc.**
½ pt. stock

Cut the steak, and the flesh from the bird, into small pieces. Dip them in seasoned flour. Make the suet pastry, line a greased basin with ⅔ of it, put in the meat and half the stock. Cover with remainder of pastry, make a hole in the lid, cover with greased paper and steam 4–6 hr., adding the remaining stock (hot) after half the cooking time. Onions *or* mushrooms may be added to the pudding, if liked.

6 helpings

ROAST GROUSE

Coq de Bruyère rôti

A brace of grouse
8 oz. rump steak *or* 2 oz. butter
Salt and pepper
2 rashers of bacon
Flour
2 croûtes fried bread or toast

Prepare the birds (p. 278), insert a piece of seasoned steak or butter into the body of each; truss for roasting. (If steak is used it can afterwards be used for a cold meat dish, it is inserted to flavour the birds and is not meant to be served with them.) Cover the breast of the birds with bacon, roast in a fairly hot oven (**375°–400° F., Gas 5–6**) until tender—about 30 min. Baste if necessary. When almost cooked, remove bacon, baste, dredge with flour, baste again and return to oven. Toast or fry the bread and place pieces in the baking-tin beneath the birds after 15 min. cooking, so that they will absorb any liquid which comes from the birds.

Dish birds on the croûtes of bread, and serve with gravy, bread sauce and fried breadcrumbs.

5–6 helpings
Cooking time—about 30 min.

ORTOLAN

ROAST ORTOLAN

Ortolan rôti

4 ortolans
Butter for basting
2 rashers of bacon
4 bay leaves
4 croûtes of fried bread *or* toast

GARNISH

Watercress

Remove head, neck and crop from each bird but let the trail remain; truss for roasting. Place a bay leaf on each, and cover with strips of bacon. Place the birds (not touching each other) on a long skewer and roast on the croûtes of bread 10–15 min. in a moderate-fairly hot oven (**350°–375° F., Gas 4–5**) basting frequently with hot butter. When cooked, remove skewer and trussing strings, but leave bacon (this may be brushed with glaze).

Serve birds on the croûtes, garnished with watercress. Serve with gravy and fried breadcrumbs.

4 helpings

PARTRIDGE

ESCALOPES OF PARTRIDGE

Escalopes de Perdreau

1 partridge	**½ turnip**
1 hard-boiled egg	**Bouquet garni**
2 slices bacon	**½ pt. stock**
1 small onion	**Potato border**
1 carrot	**¾ pt. brown sauce**

STUFFING

4 oz. cold roast partridge	**2 oz. raw ham *or* bacon**
1 teasp. chopped parsley	**Pinch of mixed herbs**
1 tablesp. chopped suet	**Salt and pepper**
1 tablesp. breadcrumbs	**1 egg**

Make the stuffing: chop partridge and ham, add suet, parsley, breadcrumbs, herbs, seasoning and egg. Split the whole partridge down the back, remove bones, flatten as much as possible, and season well. Spread half the stuffing on the bird, lay on slices of hard-boiled egg, some bacon cut in strips, then remainder of stuffing, form the bird into a roll and stitch securely with white cotton. Lay sliced vegetables and herbs in a pan with remainder of bacon, almost cover with stock and lay bird, wrapped in buttered paper, on top, cover tightly, simmer 1½–2 hr. Pipe a potato border round a dish, glaze and brown it. When bird is cooked, remove paper and cotton, cut bird in slices, arrange these in the border and pour over the brown sauce.

A variation of this dish is made by substituting veal for partridge in the stuffing, and serving garnished with spinach or mushroom.

6 helpings

GRILLED PARTRIDGE

Perdreaux grillés

A brace of partridge	**2 oz. butter**
Salt and cayenne pepper	

GARNISH

Grilled tomato	**Mushrooms**

Pluck and draw the birds (p. 278), split in half, wipe the insides thoroughly with a damp cloth. Season with salt and cayenne. Grill about 20 min., turning frequently, and brush with butter just before serving.

Garnish quickly, and serve with mushroom *or* brown sauce (p. 119) handed separately.

4 helpings

HASHED PARTRIDGE

Hachis de Perdreau

See Salmi of Wild Duck.

PARTRIDGE—WITH CABBAGE

Perdreaux au Chou

2 partridges	**1 onion**
1 small cabbage	**Bouquet garni**
4 oz. bacon	**Fat for frying**
Salt and pepper	**1 pt. stock**
Nutmeg	

GARNISH

½ lb. Chipolata sausages

Prepare the birds (p. 278).

Separate, wash and blanch cabbage leaves, drain well. Line a saucepan with the bacon and some of the leaves, well seasoned. Add a little nutmeg, the onion (sliced) and the bouquet garni. Split the partridges and fry in the fat until brown and crisp. Lay the birds in the saucepan, cover with remaining cabbage and add sufficient stock to come half-way up the pan. Cover tightly, simmer gently for about 2 hr., adding more hot stock if necessary. Correct the seasoning. Fry the sausages, dish the birds on a bed of cabbage with the sausages round.

NOTE: This is an excellent method of

preparing any game bird which is not tender enough to be roasted.

6 helpings

POTTED PARTRIDGE

Pâté de Perdreaux

See Potted Game, (p. 300).

ROAST PARTRIDGE

Perdreau rôti

1 partridge	**Butter *or* dripping**
1 rasher of bacon	**Toast *or* fried bread**

Pluck, draw and truss bird as for roasting a chicken. Cover breast with bacon, roast in a fairly hot oven **(375°–400° F., Gas 5–6)** about 30 min., basting frequently with butter *or* dripping. (A piece of seasoned butter may be put in the body of the bird if liked.) 10 min. before serving, remove bacon, baste, dredge with flour, baste and return to oven to complete cooking. Remove trussing string.

Dish bird on croûte of bread. Serve with brown gravy, bread sauce (p. 122) and fried breadcrumbs.

4 helpings

STUFFED PARTRIDGE FILLETS

Filets de Perdreau farci

1 partridge	**¼ lb. liver stuffing** (p. 143)
1 oz. butter	**Egg and breadcrumbs**
Potato border	**Frying fat**
½ pt. Espagnole sauce (p. 130)	

GARNISH

Purée of spinach *or* mushroom

Remove breast meat intact from prepared bird, bone legs and wings, and trim pieces into a good shape. Fry pieces gently in butter, press between 2 plates until cold. Pipe potato border, glaze and brown. Make sauce. Spread one side of each portion of partridge with liver farce, coat with egg and breadcrumbs; fry in deep fat. Arrange the joints in a circle within the potato border, strain the sauce over, and pile vegetable purée in the centre.

NOTE: This recipe may be employed to use up cold cooked birds of all kinds—proceed from "Pipe potato border, . . ."

4 helpings
Cooking time—25 min. (excluding sauce)

PHEASANT

BOILED PHEASANT

Faisan bouilli

1 pheasant	**½ small turnip**
Stock *or* water	**Bouquet garni**
1 onion	**1pt. Oyster sauce**
1 carrot	

FORCEMEAT

12 small oysters	**Nutmeg**
2 tablesp. breadcrumbs	**Salt, cayenne pepper**
1 tablesp. chopped suet	**1 egg**
½ tablesp. chopped parsley	

Open and beard oysters. Add them with their liquor to breadcrumbs, finely chopped suet and parsley, season with nutmeg, salt and pepper and bind with egg. Prepare, stuff, and truss the bird as for roast chicken. Wrap it in well-greased paper and immerse it in boiling stock *or* water. When the stock reboils add the sliced vegetables and bouquet garni to the pan; simmer gently about 1 hr.

Remove trussing strings and serve on a hot dish with a little oyster sauce poured round, serve the remainder of the sauce in a sauce-boat.

If preferred, chestnut stuffing may be substituted for oyster stuffing, or the bird may be cooked with some pieces of vegetable in the body instead of stuffing, and served with celery *or* oyster sauce.

Should the bird be required cold, it will be better left to cool in the pan of liquid.

4–5 helpings

GRILLED PHEASANT

Faisan grillé

1 pheasant	**Salt and cayenne pepper**
2 oz. butter	**Egg and breadcrumbs**

GARNISH

Grilled mushroom	**Watercress**
Tomato	

Joint the bird, season it, fry in butter until lightly browned, press between 2 plates until cold. Coat with egg and breadcrumbs, grill about 25 min., turning frequently, and brushing with melted butter after the coating has set.

Garnish and serve immediately, piled on a hot dish. Serve with mushroom sauce.

NOTE: If the bird is small it may be split down the back and treated like blackcock

Alternative sauces—Madeira, piquant.

4–5 helpings

PHEASANT CUTLETS

Côtelettes de Faisan

1 pheasant	**Frying fat *or* butter**
Salt and pepper	**½ pt. Espagnole sauce**
Egg and fresh breadcrumbs	

Joint pheasant, remove bones keeping joints as whole as possible. Trim pieces neatly, fold the skin under, form into a good shape. Season, coat with egg and breadcrumbs. Fry gently in hot fat *or* butter for about 10 min., until well browned; drain well. Insert a small cleaned bone into each cutlet, put on a cutlet frill.

Serve immediately with the sauce poured round.

4 helpings

ROAST PHEASANT

Faison rôti

1 pheasant	**1 slice bacon *or* strips of larding bacon**
¼ lb. beef steak	**Butter *or* dripping**

GARNISH

Watercress	**French dressing**

Pluck and draw the bird (p. 278), but leave the head on. Insert the steak in the body of the bird (this improves the flavour and keeps the bird moist, but is not intended to be eaten with it, the steak can be used for a cold meat dish later). Truss the pheasant as for a roasting chicken. Cover the breast with strips of bacon, *or* lard it with the prepared larding bacon (p. 35). Roast bird in a moderate oven **(350° F., Gas 4)** until tender, 40–50 min., basting when necessary. When bird is almost cooked, "froth" the breast (*see Roast Capercailzie*, (p. 301). Remove trussing string.

Garnish with watercress tossed in French dressing and serve with brown gravy, bread sauce and fried breadcrumbs.

If preferred, the head may be removed and the bird ornamented with the best tail feathers before serving. The feathers should be washed, baked until dry in a cool oven, and stuck fanwise into the vent-end of the cooked bird.

4–5 helpings
Cooking time—40–50 min.

ROAST PHEASANT WITH MUSHROOMS

Faisan rôti aux Champignons

1 pheasant	**2 oz. butter**
Fat bacon	**Salt and cayenne pepper**
12 large mushrooms	**Lemon juice**

Prepare bird as described in previous recipe. Roughly chop the mushrooms, mix with the butter, season well with salt and cayenne pepper; add a few drops of lemon juice. Stuff the bird with this mixture, proceed as for Roast Pheasant.

4–5 helpings
Cooking time—40–50 min.

SALMI OF PHEASANT

Salmis de Faisan à la Moderne

1 pheasant	**½ pt. brown sauce** (p. 119)
2 oz. butter	**1 glass Madeira (optional)**
¼ teasp. grated lemon rind	**6–8 slices goose liver**
2 shallots	**6–8 mushrooms (*or* sliced truffle)**
¼ teasp. thyme	**Salt and pepper**
1 bay leaf	

GARNISH

Croûtes of fried bread

Pluck, draw and truss bird for roasting. Baste it well with hot butter, roast in a hot oven **(425°–450° F., Gas, 7–8)** for 30 min., basting frequently. Pour the butter used for basting into a saucepan, add grated lemon rind, chopped shallots, thyme and bay leaf. Joint the bird, lay aside breast, wings and legs, and cut remainder into neat pieces, adding these to the saucepan and frying well. If any fat remains, pour it from the saucepan, put in the brown sauce, wine (if used), season and simmer 10 min. Add remainder of pheasant, heat thoroughly. Meanwhile, re-heat the butter, fry in it the slices of goose liver and the mushrooms. Correct seasoning of sauce.

Serve pheasant with liver and mushrooms on top, strain sauce over, garnish with croûtes.

4–5 helpings
Cooking time—about 1¼ hr. in all

PIGEONS

CURRIED PIGEONS

Kari de Pigeons

3 pigeons
1½ pt. curry sauce
2 oz. butter *or* 6 tablesp. salad oil
6 oz. boiled Patna rice

Make curry sauce. Divide pigeons into quarters, fry in butter *or* oil until well browned, drain. Put the birds into the curry sauce and simmer until tender, 30–45 min.

Serve with rice and other accompaniments (*see Curried Chicken*, p. 287).

6 helpings
Cooking time—about 1½ hr. in all

GRILLED PIGEONS

Pigeons grillés

3 pigeons
Salt and pepper
2 oz. butter *or* salad oil

Split pigeons down the back, flatten them with a cutlet-bat (or the back of a large, wet wooden spoon) and skewer them flat. Brush all over the meat with oiled butter *or* salad oil; season. Grill for 20 min., turning frequently, serve very hot.

Serve with 1 pt. tomato *or* mushroom sauce (pp. 127, 117) in a sauce-boat.

6 helpings

JUGGED PIGEONS

Civet de Pigeons

3 pigeons
3 oz. butter
1 onion
1 pt. good beef stock
Salt and pepper
1 oz. flour
1 glass port *or* claret (optional)

GARNISH
Balls of fried veal forcemeat

Truss pigeons as for roasting and fry them until well-browned in 2 oz. of the butter. Place birds in a casserole. Brown sliced onion in butter, and add to the pigeons, together with stock and seasoning. Cover and cook in a moderate oven (**350° F., Gas 4**) for 1¾ hr. Knead together the flour and remaining 1 oz. butter and drop in small pieces into the stock; continue cooking ½ hr, adding wine if used, half-way through this period.

Serve pigeons with the sauce poured over, garnished with forcemeat balls.

6 helpings

PIGEON PIE

Pâté de Pigeon

2 pigeons
½ lb. rump steak
¼ lb. ham *or* bacon
¾ pt. good stock
2 hard-boiled eggs
Salt and pepper
Puff pastry (p. 555) using 8 oz. flour, etc.
Egg *or* milk to glaze

Remove the feet from the pigeons and split each bird in two. Cut the steak in small thin slices, cut the bacon in strips and slice the eggs. Put all ingredients in layers in a pie-dish, seasoning the layers well, and seasoning each half-bird, ¾ fill the dish with stock. Cover pie with puff pastry, glaze, and cook in a hot oven (**425°–450° F., Gas 7–8**) until pastry is risen and set, then lower heat to moderate (**350°–375° F., Gas 4–5**) and bake for 1 hr. more. Cut the toes off the feet, and scald the latter. Before serving the pie, fill it with the remainder of the hot seasoned stock and fix the feet in an upright position in the hole previously made in the pastry.

6 helpings

PIGEON PUDDING

Pouding de Pigeon

3 pigeons
½ lb. steak
1 oz. flour
Salt and pepper
2 hard-boiled eggs
Suet crust pastry (p. 557) using 12 oz. flour, etc., and add ¼ teasp. mixed herbs
¼ pt. stock

Split the prepared pigeons in half, remove skin. Cut steak into small pieces. Dip the pieces of pigeon and steak into seasoned flour. Cut eggs into sections. Line a basin with suet crust pastry, put in the prepared pigeon, steak and egg, add the stock; cover with crust. Steam the pudding at least 3 hr. and serve with extra hot stock *or* thin gravy.

6 helpings

PIGEON WITH OLIVES

Pigeons aux Olives

3 pigeons	**24 (or more) stoned olives**
2 oz. butter	**¼ pt. stock**
1 pt. Espagnole sauce	

Split each pigeon into quarters, fry in butter until well browned. Put the birds into the hot Espagnole sauce, cover and simmer until birds are cooked—about ¾ hr. Thoroughly heat olives in stock.

Dish the pigeons, pour the sauce over, and garnish with the olives.

6 helpings

POTTED PIGEON

Terrine de Pigeon

See Potted Chicken, (p. 288).

ROAST PIGEON

Pigeon rôti

3 pigeons	**Lemon juice**
3 oz. butter	**1 rasher fat bacon**
Salt and pepper	**3 croûtes of fried bread**

GARNISH

Watercress	**French dressing**

Wipe the birds with a damp cloth, insert in each 1 oz. butter mixed with lemon juice and seasoning. Truss each and cover with a piece of bacon. Roast pigeons in a fairly hot oven **(375°–400° F., Gas 5–6)** until tender, 20–30 min., basting if necessary. Remove bacon 10 min. before cooking is completed to allow birds to brown. Remove trussing strings, replace bacon.

Serve each bird on a croûte of fried bread, garnish with washed watercress tossed in French dressing and serve with Espagnole, tomato *or* piquant sauce handed separately.

6 helpings

STEWED PIGEON

Compote de Pigeon à la Bourgeoise

3 pigeons	**12 shallots *or* 1 onion**
2 oz. butter	**6 new carrots**
1 pt. Espagnole sauce (p. 130)	**½ pt. garden peas**
1½ glasses claret (optional)	**Salt and pepper**
	3 croûtes of fried bread

Split each bird into quarters, fry in butter until browned. Put the pigeons into the hot Espagnole sauce, simmer until birds are cooked—about ¾ hr., add the claret (if used) and correct seasoning just before serving. Fry shallots *or* diced onion in butter, boil carrots and peas separately, drain well and keep hot.

Serve the pigeons on croûtes of fried bread, strain the sauce over, and pile vegetables at either end of the dish.

6 helpings

PLOVER

Under the provision of the Protection of Birds Act, 1954, some plovers are protected at all times by special penalties, i.e. Kentish plover, little ringed plover. Plover which may be killed or taken outside the close season (21st February to 31st August) are the golden plover and the grey plover.

ROAST PLOVER

Pluvier rôti

3 plovers	**1 glass port *or* claret (optional)**
1½ oz. butter	**Juice of 1 lemon**
3 rashers bacon	
6 croûtes of toast	
1 pt. brown sauce (p. 119)	

GARNISH

Watercress	**Sections of lemon**

Pluck and truss the birds (do not draw them). Brush with warm butter, tie a rasher of thin bacon over each breast, and roast in a moderate-fairly hot oven (**350°–375° F., Gas 4–5**) for 15–20 min. according to taste. Place slices of toast in the roasting tin to catch the trail as it drops from the birds. Baste frequently with butter, and shortly before serving remove the bacon, dredge lightly with flour, and baste well to give the breasts a light brown appearance. Make the brown sauce, add to it the wine (if used) and lemon juice.

Serve the plovers on the toast. Garnish; serve sauce separately.

NOTE: Oiled butter, with lemon juice added to it, may be served instead of brown sauce.

6 helpings

PTARMIGAN

ROAST PTARMIGAN

Perdrix blanches rôties

3 ptarmigan
1½ oz. butter
3 rashers of bacon
Croûtes of toast

Pluck, draw and truss the birds; baste with hot butter. Tie a piece of fat bacon over each bird, roast them in a fairly hot oven (**375°–400° F., Gas 5–6**) 30–35 min., basting frequently. The toast should be put under the birds when they are cooking to catch the gravy that drops from them. "Froth" the birds before serving (*see Roast Guinea Fowl*, p. 296).

Serve the birds on the toast. Serve with gravy, bread sauce and fried breadcrumbs.

6 helpings (unless birds are very small)

SNIPE

ROAST SNIPE

Bécassines rôties

3 snipe
2 oz. butter
3 pieces bacon
3 slices toast

GARNISH

Watercress

Snipe, ortolan, plover and woodcock, are dressed without being drawn. Truss for roasting, but skin the head and leave it on. Pass the bird's beak through the legs and body instead of a skewer. Brush over with warm butter, tie a thin slice of fat bacon over each breast, and place in a moderate oven (**350° F., Gas 4**). Put the toast under them to catch the drippings from the trail, baste frequently with butter, and roast for about 15 min.

Dish on the toast, garnish, and serve with gravy handed separately.

6 helpings (unless birds are very small)

WILD DUCK

Under the provision of the Protection of Birds Act, 1954, some wild duck are protected by special penalties during the close season, i.e. common scoter, garganey teal, goldeneye, long-tailed duck, scaup-duck and velvet scoter. Wild duck which may be killed or taken outside the close season (21st February to 31st August) are: the common pochard, gadwall, mallard, pintail, shoveller, teal, tufted duck and wigeon.

RAGOÛT OF WILD DUCK

Ragoût de Canard Sauvage

If using cold, cooked duck, follow the recipe and method for Salmi of Wild Duck (p. 615). Otherwise roast according to recipe for Roast Wild Duck. Then proceed as for Salmi.

ROAST TEAL

Sarcelle rôtie

Teal
Bigarade sauce
Butter for basting

GARNISH

Watercress
Sections of lemon

Pluck, draw and truss birds for roasting (p. 279). Brush them with melted butter, roast in a fairly hot oven (**375°–400° F., Gas 5–6**) 25–30 min., basting frequently.

Serve on a hot dish; garnish. Serve the Bigarade sauce separately.

1 helping is a half or a whole bird, according to size

ROAST WIGEON or WIDGEON

Canard siffleur rôti

1 wigeon
Butter for basting

SAUCE

1 pt. Espagnole sauce (p. 130)	**Juice of 1 lemon**
1 glass port *or* claret (optional)	**Juice of 1 orange**
	Salt and pepper
	Castor sugar

GARNISH

Watercress	**Sections of lemon**

Truss bird for roasting. Baste well with hot butter, roast in a fairly hot oven (**375°–400° F., Gas 5–6**) about 20–30 min. according to size and age of bird. Baste well. "Froth" the bird before serving (*see Roast Guinea Fowl*, p. 296). Meanwhile, heat the sauce, add the wine (if used), fruit juices, a pinch of sugar and seasoning to taste. Re-heat thoroughly.

Garnish and serve. Serve sauce separately.

2–3 helpings

ROAST WILD DUCK

Canard Sauvage rôti

1 wild duck	**Butter for basting**

Pluck and draw the bird, cut off the head. Cut off the toes, scald and scrape the feet, truss the bird with the feet twisted underneath the body. If the fishy taste is disliked, cover a deep roasting-tin to a depth of ½ in. with boiling water, add 1 tablesp. salt, put in the bird and bake it for 10 min., basting frequently with the salt water. Drain, sprinkle lightly with flour, baste well with hot butter and roast in a moderate oven (**350° F., Gas 4**) for 20–30 min., basting frequently. The birds should always be served rather underdone, or the flavour is lost. The breast meat has much the best flavour.

Serve with Bigarade or Port Wine sauce (pp. 130, 126) and orange salad.

ORANGE SALAD: Allow the oranges to stand in boiling water for a few minutes, peel them and remove all pith. Cut fruit into thin slices, removing pips. Sprinkle slices with a little sugar and French dressing, to which a little brandy may be added if liked.

3 helpings

ZÉPHIRES OF WILD DUCK

Zéphires de Canard Sauvage

1 wild duck	**Pepper and salt**
1 egg	**Mixed spice**
⅛ pt. salmi sauce (p. 133)	**1 oz. butter**
½ glass port (optional)	**1 pt. Espagnole sauce (p. 130)**

PANADA

½ pt. water	**1 oz. butter**
4 oz. flour	**Pinch of salt**

GARNISH

Fleurons of puff pastry	**Spinach**
Glacé cherries	

Make panada; put the water, butter and salt into a small saucepan. Heat until boiling, then stir in gradually the sifted flour, and work vigorously with a wooden spoon over the heat until the panada leaves the sides of the pan clear. Spread on a plate to cool.

Remove meat from duck, chop and pound it until very smooth, add panada and egg slowly. Mix in salmi sauce, port (if used), seasoning and spice. Sieve if required very smooth. Butter 8 moulds, fill with mixture, cover with buttered paper, and steam (or poach in a roasting tin) until firm and set. Turn the moulds out in a circle, place a fleuron of puff pastry on each and ½ a glacé cherry, pile spinach in centre and pour the hot Espagnole sauce round.

4 helpings **Cooking time—about 20–30 min.**

WOODCOCK

ROAST WOODCOCK

Bécasse rôtie

3 woodcocks	**3 rashers of bacon**
2 oz. butter	**3 slices of toast**
	Flour

Pluck and truss the birds (do not draw them). As the skin of these birds is particularly tender, they must be plucked very carefully. Brush with oiled butter, tie a slice of bacon over each and roast in a fairly hot oven (**375°–400° F., Gas 5–6**) 15–20 min., placing slices of toast beneath the birds, to catch the trail as it drops from them. Before they are cooked, remove bacon, dredge with flour, baste and return to oven to brown.

Serve on the toast garnished with watercress. Serve with good brown gravy.

6 helpings (unless birds are small)

VENISON, HARE AND RABBIT

VENISON should always be well hung before cooking, and the flavour may be further improved if the meat is marinaded before use. The choicest part of the animal is the haunch, i.e. leg and loin in one joint—and this is usually roasted. The best end of neck may be boned, rolled and roasted but the neck and shoulder are usually made into stews and pies. An abundance of clear creamy-white fat is an indication of good quality meat, that of the buck being preferred to the doe.

Venison should be hung for about 14 days in a cool dry place, but it should be inspected carefully every day. It may be rubbed with a mixture of ground ginger and black pepper to preserve it. To test the meat, run a small sharp knife into the flesh near the haunch bone; if it has an unpleasant smell when withdrawn, the meat should be washed with warm milk and water, dried thoroughly and covered with more of the preserving mixture. The latter should be washed off before the meat is cooked.

Hares may be roasted or jugged when young, and made into soup when old. The young ones have smooth sharp claws, a narrow cleft in the lip and soft ears which will tear readily; they have short stumpy necks and long joints. A leveret is a hare up to 1 year old; it will have a small bony knot near the foot, which is absent in a full-grown hare. Hares should be well hung, for 7 or 8 days, in a cool dry place. They should hang, unskinned, by the hind legs, with the head in a tin cup, to catch the blood. Hares are not paunched until required for cooking.

Skinning hares: In many respects the dressing of a hare resembles that of poultry. The main difference is that a furry skin has to be removed instead of feathers. This is achieved by first cutting off the feet above the foot joint. The feet can be jointed off with a small thin-bladed knife. Next carefully cut through the skin straight down the belly, taking care not to cut into the meat. Then gently ease back the skin away from the flesh and work round each side until the centre of the hare is completely freed from its skin. Now push forward one hind leg and work the skin free. Repeat with the other and then pull the skin away from the tail. Holding the skinned hindquarters in the left hand, gently pull the skin up the back and over the shoulder, working each foreleg through in turn. The skin must now be eased with a knife from the neck and head. Cut carefully round the base of each ear to free the fur but take care not to cut off the ears, which are left on for cooking.

When free of skin, carefully cut through the skin of the belly from the chest to the legs and draw out the viscera (this is known as paunching). Wipe dry with a clean cloth. The kidneys, found in the back embedded in a little fat, are left in position. The liver and heart is cooked and care should be taken in detaching the greenish gall bladder from the liver.

Trussing hares: A hare may be trussed with a needle and string. The desired effect is of the animal crouching prone on the dish. Sew a back leg into each side and also a foreleg (shoulder). Pass a string from front to rear, passing round the neck, and draw tight to cause a small arch in the back.

Jointing hares: see plate 3.

Rabbits have the same characteristics, when young, as hares. They are paunched before being hung and they should not be hung for longer than a day. Young ones are suitable for roasting, older ones for stewing, or boiling.

They are dressed as for hares except that the ears and eyes are removed. They may be trussed like a hare. In this case the forelegs are jointed off and sewn back in position. Either rabbit or hare may easily be jointed with a stout-bladed knife which can be tapped through the bones.

Many of the rabbits now on sale are frozen imported animals.

Animal	*Season*
Hares . . .	September–March
Rabbit . . .	September–March
Venison Buck . .	July–September
Doe . .	October–December

VENISON

CHOPS AND STEAKS OF VENISON

Côtelettes et tranches de Venaison

Venison chops are cut from the loin, and a thick slice from the leg is served as a steak. Both should be grilled and served with a sauce made from equal quantities of oiled butter, red wine and dissolved redcurrant jelly.

POTTED VENISON

Terrine de Venaison

2 lb. venison
½ glass port *or* a little stock *or* gravy
4 oz. butter
Salt and pepper
Clarified butter

Put the venison into a stewing jar with a close-fitting lid. Add wine if used, or a little stock, 4 oz. butter, salt and pepper. Cover jar with 2 or 3 thicknesses of buttered paper, press lid down tightly, cook in a cool oven

(**310°–335° F., Gas 2–3**) for 2 hr. Drain well, chop or mince very finely, moistening gradually with gravy. Sieve if required, correct the seasoning. Press into small pots, cover with clarified butter.

ROAST HAUNCH OF VENISON

Quartier de Chevreuil rôti

A haunch of venison
Clarified butter *or* dripping
Flour
Brown sauce *or* gravy
Redcurrant jelly

Saw off knuckle-bone, brush joint well with clarified butter *or* dripping and wrap in well-greased paper. Make a stiff paste of flour and water, put it over the joint, cover with another well-greased paper and tie securely with string. Roast the joint in a moderate oven (**350° F., Gas 4**) for 3–4 hr. and baste frequently. After 2½ hr., remove paste and papers, dredge lightly with flour, baste well with hot butter until the joint acquires a good brown colour.

Serve as hot as possible. Serve gravy *or* sauce and redcurrant jelly separately.

12 (or more) helpings
Cooking time—allow 25 min. per lb.

ROAST NECK OF VENISON

Carré de Venaison rôtie

Let the neck remain attached to the shoulder until required for use, so as to preserve the appearance of both joints.

Remove the chine bone and short bones. Fold the flap under and fasten in a neat shape. Cook according to instructions given in Roast Haunch of Venison.

STEWED VENISON

Ragoût de Venaison

Shoulder of venison
Thin slices of mutton fat
1 glass port (optional)
Salt and pepper
1½ pt. stock
½ teasp. peppercorns
½ teasp. allspice

If port is used soak the mutton fat in it for 2–3 hr. Bone the venison, flatten with a cutlet-bat, season well, cover with slices of mutton fat. Roll up lightly, tie securely with tape, place in boiling stock together with bones, peppercorns, allspice and the port in which the fat was soaked. Simmer gently 3–3½ hr.

Serve with redcurrant jelly, handed separately.

10–12 helpings

VENISON CUTLETS

Côtelettes de Venaison

6 cutlets of venison
3 oz. butter (approx.)
1½ pt. good gravy *or* sauce
Salt and pepper

GARNISH
Mushrooms

Cut 6 cutlets from the best end of the neck of venison, trim the bones at the end, flatten and trim cutlets. Brush with melted butter; season. Heat gravy *or* sauce, trim mushrooms (peel them if necessary), brush with melted butter. Grill the cutlets, brushing with more butter if necessary. Grill mushrooms.

Place a dab of butter on each cutlet, serve very hot. Garnish with mushrooms. Serve sauce separately. Alternatively, the mushrooms may be stewed in the sauce.

6 helpings **Cooking time—20–25 min.**

HARE

CIVET OF HARE

Civet de Lièvre

1 young hare
¼ lb. fat bacon
2 oz. butter
2 oz. flour
1 pt. good stock
Bouquet garni
Salt and pepper
2 doz. button onions
1 glass port *or* claret (optional)

GARNISH
Croûtons of fried bread

Divide hare into small joints, dice bacon and fry lightly in 1½ oz. butter in a saucepan. Remove bacon. Sprinkle flour into butter, and put in hare. Fry until brown, turning hare frequently. Replace bacon, add stock, bouquet garni, seasoning; stir until boiling, then simmer gently about 1¼ hr. Skin onions, fry until brown in remaining butter; add them with the wine, to the stew, about 20 min. before hare is cooked. Correct seasoning.

Serve hare piled on a hot dish, strain the sauce over and garnish with the croûtons.

4–5 helpings

GRILLED HARE

Lièvre grillé

Remains of roast hare | **Salt**
Butter | **Cayenne pepper**

Separate meat into neat pieces, brush with oiled butter and season highly. Grill under a hot grill until well-browned, turning frequently and brushing with more butter if necessary.

Serve very hot. Serve with sauce or gravy.

Cooking time—about 10 min.

HARE (COLD) PIE

Pâté de Lièvre

½ lb.– ¾ lb. cooked hare
½ lb. streaky bacon
4 oz. breadcrumbs
Gravy *or* stock
Salt and pepper
Worcester sauce
1 lb. creamed potatoes
1 oz. butter

Cut hare into small pieces; fry and cut up the bacon, mix with hare, breadcrumbs and enough gravy or stock to moisten well. Place a layer of mixture in the bottom of a greased pie-dish; season well; add a little sauce. Cover with a layer of seasoned creamed potato; repeat until all mixture is used, finishing with a layer of potato. Put the butter, cut in small pieces, on the top; brown and heat thoroughly in a hot oven (**425°–450° F., Gas 7–8**). Serve with a good gravy.

4–5 helpings
Cooking time—about 20 min.

HARE EN CASSEROLE

Lièvre en Casserole

1 hare
3 oz. butter
1 onion
3 cloves
Bouquet garni
Salt and pepper
1½ pt. stock *or* equal quantities stock and stout *or* cider
1 oz. flour
Veal forcemeat
Fat for frying

Prepare the hare and cut into pieces convenient for serving. Fry pieces in 2 oz. of the butter until brown then pack closely in a casserole. Slice and fry onion, add to casserole with cloves, bouquet garni, seasoning, stock (*or* equal quantities stock and stout, *or* cider). Cover closely, simmer about 2½ hr., until hare is tender. Knead remaining 1 oz. butter and flour together, divide into small pieces, drop into casserole, about ½ hr. before serving. Shape forcemeat into small balls, fry in hot fat, drain well, add to casserole 5 min. before serving. Remove bouquet garni, correct seasoning.

Serve with redcurrant jelly handed separately.

6 helpings **Cooking time—about 3 hr.**

HASHED HARE

Hachis de Lièvre

Remains of cold roast hare
¾ pt. brown sauce
1 glass port, *or* claret, *or* cider (optional)
Salt and pepper

Trim hare into neat pieces. Make stock with bones and trimmings and use this instead of wine if liked. Make brown sauce, add wine if used, put in pieces of hare and heat very thoroughly.

Serve with redcurrant jelly handed separately.

JUGGED HARE

Civet de Lièvre à l'Anglaise

1 hare
3 oz. butter
Salt and pepper
1 onion
4 cloves
1 glass port *or* claret (optional)
1 tablesp. lemon juice
12 peppercorns
Bouquet garni
1½ pt. stock
1 oz. flour
Veal forcemeat
Fat for frying

Prepare hare as in Notes on Trussing (p. 311), and cut into neat small pieces. Heat 2 oz. of the butter, fry the pieces of hare in it until brown. Put hare in a casserole with salt, onion stuck with cloves, half the wine (if used), lemon juice, peppercorns, bouquet garni and hot stock. Place a tight lid on the casserole, cook in a moderate oven (**350° F., Gas 4**) about 3 hr. Knead flour and remaining butter together, stir into the stock about ½ hr. before serving. Add remaining wine and season to taste. Make forcemeat, form into small balls and fry. Gently heat blood from hare, stir into gravy, allow to thicken.

Serve hare piled on a hot dish, strain sauce

over, arrange forcemeat balls round dish. Serve with redcurrant jelly handed separately.

5–6 helpings

POTTED HARE

Terrine de Lièvre

1 hare	**1 blade mace**
2 rashers of bacon	**2 bay leaves**
Bouquet garni	**Salt and cayenne**
3 cloves	**Stock**
10 peppercorns	**Clarified butter**

Prepare hare as in Notes on Trussing (p. 311), cut into small, neat pieces. Line the base of a saucepan or casserole with bacon, pack the pieces of hare closely on top, add the bouquet garni, cloves, peppercorns, mace, bay leaves, seasoning, and just cover with stock. Cook slowly for about 3 hr., adding more stock as necessary. Remove bones, chop and mince hare and bacon finely, moisten with more stock, season well, put in small pots and cover with clarified butter. The mixture may be sieved if desired.

NOTE: Cold cooked hare may also be potted. Moisten it with good stock or gravy.

ROAST HARE

Lièvre rôti

1 hare	**Pinch of thyme**
Veal forcemeat	**1½ oz. flour**
Fat bacon	**¾ pt. stock**
Milk	**1 glass port (optional)**
2 oz. butter	**Salt and pepper**
1 teasp. chopped shallot	**Redcurrant jelly**
½ teasp. chopped parsley	

Skin, draw and truss the hare (p. 311), reserving the liver. After inserting the forcemeat, sew up the hare, cover with bacon, bake in a fairly hot oven (**375°–400° F., Gas 5–6**) 1½–2 hr. until tender, basting frequently with milk, and a little butter, if liked. Meanwhile, remove gall-bladder from liver, wash the liver, put into cold water, bring to the boil and boil for 5 min., chop very finely. Melt the butter, add the liver, shallot, parsley and thyme. Fry for 10 min. Lift the liver mixture from the butter, put in the flour, brown the roux. Stir in the stock (*or* milk used for basting), bring to boiling point; add the liver mixture, season, simmer for 10 min.; add wine if used. Remove bacon from hare, dredge with flour, baste and allow to brown. Remove trussing strings and cotton.

Serve on a hot dish. Serve the liver sauce and redcurrant jelly separately.

5–6 helpings

LEVERET

ROAST LEVERET

Levraut rôti

2 leverets	**Flour**
Butter *or* dripping for basting	**Redcurrant jelly**

Prepare and truss as for a hare (p. 311), but do not stuff the leverets. Roast them in a fairly hot oven (**375°–400° F., Gas 5–6**) 40–50 min., basting them well with butter *or* dripping. A few minutes before serving, dredge with flour, rebaste and leave to brown. Remove trussing strings.

Serve with plain gravy in the dish; serve the redcurrant jelly separately.

5–6 helpings

RABBIT

BARBECUE OF RABBIT

Lapin grillé

1 very young rabbit	**2 tablesp. good gravy**
Salt and pepper	**1 tablesp. lemon juice**
Olive oil *or* butter	**1 teasp. French mustard**

GARNISH

Slices of lemon	**Fried parsley**

Cut off the head of the rabbit. Allow the rabbit to lie in salted water for 1 hr.; dry it thoroughly. Score the back and legs closely, season, brush with olive oil *or* melted butter. Heat the gravy, add to it lemon juice and mustard, correct the seasoning. Grill the rabbit 20–25 min., basting and turning it frequently. Divide into neat joints and place on a hot dish. Pour the sauce over; garnish.

3–4 helpings

BOILED RABBIT

Lapin bouilli

1 rabbit
1 onion
1 carrot
½ turnip
Bouquet garni
6 peppercorns
1 teasp. salt
Onion sauce
Bacon

Truss the rabbit (see notes on Trussing, p. 311), put it into boiling water. When the water re-boils, add the vegetables cut in pieces, the bouquet garni, peppercorns and salt. Cook gently for 45–60 min.—until the rabbit is tender. Remove the skewers.

Serve the rabbit, coated with onion sauce. Any extra sauce serve separately. Fried or boiled bacon may be served separately *or* the bacon may be rolled, grilled, and used as garnish. The liquor in which the rabbit is cooked may be made into broth or soup.

4 helpings

BORDER OF RABBIT

Bordure de Lapin

2 rabbits
Larding bacon
Mirepoix (see Braised Duck with Chestnuts, (p. 290)
¾ pt. stock
1 oz. butter
½ oz. flour
4 tablesp. stock *or* water
1 egg
Salt and pepper
Nutmeg
Brown sauce
Glaze

Prepare rabbits as directed for Rabbit Cutlets (p. 317), lard the pieces of back meat neatly with bacon (p. 35). Place the vegetables for the mirepoix in a saucepan, add stock from the ¾ pt. stock to nearly cover them, lay the back meat fillets on top. Cover with a greased paper, cover with a tightly-fitting lid, and cook gently for about 1 hr., adding more stock as necessary. Put the fillets into a hot oven for a few minutes to crisp the bacon.

Meanwhile melt the butter, stir in the flour, stir in 4 tablesp. stock and cook mixture until it leaves the sides of the pan—allow to cool. Chop or mince the remainder of the meat finely, add to it the cool panada, add the egg, seasoning and nutmeg; mix well. Press this mixture into a well-buttered border mould, cover and steam until firm—about 35 min.

Glaze the fillets of rabbit, and keep hot. Turn out the mould, arrange the fillets within the border, pour the sauce round and serve.

6 helpings

CREAM OF RABBIT

Crème de Lapin

½ lb. raw rabbit
1 small egg
¼ pt. thick white sauce
Salt and pepper
½ pt. brown sauce

Chop and mince the rabbit finely, pounding it until smooth. Work in the egg, add the white sauce, season well and sieve if required very smooth. Press lightly into 6 well-buttered moulds, cover with greased paper, steam gently until firm.

Serve with the brown sauce poured round the moulds.

6 moulds
Cooking time—20–30 min. to steam

CURRIED RABBIT

Lapin au Kari

1 rabbit
2 oz. butter
1 chopped onion
1 dessertsp. flour
1 tablesp. curry powder
1 dessertsp. curry paste
¾ pt. white stock
1 chopped apple
1 dessertsp. chutney
1 tablesp. lemon juice
Salt and pepper
1 oz. sultanas
1 oz. blanched almonds
1 dessertsp. desiccated coconut
2 tablesp. cream *or* milk (optional)

GARNISH

Fans of lemon
Red pepper
Gherkin fans

Wash, dry and joint the rabbit. Heat the butter in a saucepan, dry joints lightly, remove and drain. Fry onion lightly, add flour, curry powder and paste, and fry very well, stirring occasionally. Stir in stock, bring to boil. Put in all other ingredients except the cream, put in rabbit joints. Have the coconut tied in muslin, and remove after 15 min. Simmer gently about 1½ hr., adding a little more stock if necessary. Add cream or milk (if used).

Dish the rabbit, pour the sauce over, straining if liked. Garnish. For accompaniments see Curried Chicken.

3–4 helpings

FRICASSÉE OF RABBIT

Fricassée de Lapin

1 young rabbit	**1 blade mace**
White stock	**6 white peppercorns**
2 onions, sliced	**Salt and pepper**
1 carrot, sliced	**½ pt. milk (if required)**
½ turnip, sliced	**2 oz. butter**
2 sticks celery	**1½ oz. flour**
Bouquet garni	

Prepare the rabbit (p. 311), cut into neat joints, place in a saucepan and just cover with stock. Bring to boiling point, add prepared vegetables, herbs, mace, peppercorns and seasoning. Cover tightly, cook gently until rabbit is tender—about 1¼ hr.; add some milk, if necessary. Meanwhile, melt butter, add flour, stir and cook gently without browning, then keep the roux hot. Remove rabbit from pan and keep it hot. Strain ¾ pt. stock from the pan, stir this into the roux and allow to simmer for 10 min. Sieve the vegetables, add to the sauce, correct the seasoning, put rabbit in, re-heat thoroughly, then serve.

3–4 helpings

JUGGED RABBIT

Civet de Lapin

1 rabbit	**1 pt. good stock**
2½ oz. butter	**1 glass port *or* claret (optional)**
1 medium-sized onion	
2 cloves	**1 dessertsp. lemon juice**
8 peppercorns	**1 oz. flour**
Bouquet garni	**Veal forcemeat**
Salt and pepper	**Redcurrant jelly**

Wash, dry, and joint the rabbit neatly. Fry the joints in 1½ oz. of the butter until brown, then follow directions for Jugged Hare.

Serve the redcurrant jelly separately.

3–4 helpings
Cooking time—about 2 hr.

LARDED AND BRAISED RABBIT

Lapin piqué et braisé

1 rabbit	**Salt and pepper**
Larding bacon	**Bouquet garni**
2 oz. dripping	**1 oz. butter**
Stock	**1 oz. flour**

Wash, dry, and joint the rabbit, lard each piece with strips of chilled fat bacon (p. 35). Heat the dripping in a saucepan, fry rabbit until lightly browned, pour off excess fat, cover with stock, add seasoning and bouquet garni. Cover tightly. Stew gently until rabbit is tender—1¼–1½ hr. Knead butter and flour together and add in small pieces to the stew 20 min. before serving. Pile the rabbit on a hot dish; strain the sauce over.

3–4 helpings

RABBIT À LA MINUTE

Lapin à la Minute

1 young rabbit	**¾ pt. stock**
4 oz. butter	**2 teasp. chopped parsley**
Salt and pepper	
½ saltsp. mace	**2 tablesp. chopped mushrooms**
1 oz. flour	

Wash, thoroughly dry, and joint, the rabbit. Heat 2½ oz. of the butter in a saucepan, put in the rabbit, sprinkle with salt, pepper and mace. Put on a tightly-fitting lid and cook gently 45 min., turning and basting the rabbit frequently. Meanwhile melt the remaining butter in another pan, stir in the flour, cook gently for a few minutes without browning, stirring constantly. Add the stock gradually, stir it in. Bring to the boil, simmer 10 min. then pour over the rabbit. Add parsley and mushrooms. Continue to cook gently until rabbit is tender (about 20 min.). Correct seasoning and serve.

4 helpings

RABBIT—AMERICAN STYLE

Lapin à l'Americaine

1 rabbit	**¼ pt. tomato purée**
2 oz. dripping	**Salt and pepper**
Stock	**Castor sugar**
1½ oz. butter	**1 teasp. lemon juice**
1 oz. flour	

Wash and dry the rabbit thoroughly. Divide into neat joints. Heat the dripping in a saucepan, fry the pieces of rabbit until well browned, drain away any surplus fat, add sufficient stock to just cover the rabbit, cover with a closely-fitting lid and cook until tender, about 1–1¼ hr. Meanwhile, melt the butter in another saucepan, stir in the flour, and cook gently until the roux is nut-brown, then stir in the tomato purée. When ready, remove rabbit and keep it hot. Strain and stir ¾ pt. of the stock into the blended flour, butter and purée, stir until boiling, season, add a pinch of sugar and lemon juice. Put the rabbit in the sauce, make thoroughly hot, serve as quickly as possible.

3–4 helpings

RABBIT CUTLETS

Côtelettes de Lapin

2 rabbits	**Egg and breadcrumbs**
Butter *or* frying fat	**Brown sauce**
Liver farce	

GARNISH

Fried parsley

Cut off the legs and necks of the rabbits. (These may be made into a ragoût or pie.) Remove the flesh from the back of each rabbit, keeping it whole, and divide into neat, even-sized pieces. Flatten the portions, then fry gently 10–15 min. in hot butter *or* fat, press between 2 plates until cold. Cover 1 side of each piece with liver farce, coat with egg and breadcrumbs twice, fry in deep fat until golden brown, drain well.

Garnish. Serve sauce separately.

4–5 helpings

RABBIT EN CASSEROLE

Lapin en Casserole

1 large rabbit	**Salt and pepper**
Strips of fat bacon (optional)	**1 oz. flour**
	1 pt. stock
2 oz. butter	**Bouquet garni**
2 onions	
2 slices lean bacon	

Wash and joint the rabbit. If desired, lard the joints with strips of fat bacon (see p. 35). Heat the butter in a casserole and brown in it the rabbit, sliced onions and lean bacon (diced). When well-browned, add salt and pepper; sprinkle in flour, and when this has browned, stir in stock. Bring to boiling point, add bouquet garni. Cover tightly and cook slowly in a moderate oven **(350° F., Gas 4)** for 2–2½ hr. Remove bouquet garni and correct seasoning.

Serve from the casserole.

4–5 helpings

RABBIT PIE

Pâté de Lapin

1 rabbit	**½ pt. stock**
½ lb. beef steak	**Puff pastry**(p.555) **using 8 oz. flour, etc.**
½ lb. bacon *or* pickled pork	**Egg for glazing**
Salt and pepper	

Wash, dry, and joint the rabbit, dice the beef and bacon *or* pork. Place these ingredients in layers in a pie-dish, season well, ¾ fill dish with stock. Cover with pastry. Bake 1¾–2 hr. in a hot oven **(425°–450° F., Gas 7–8)** for 15 min., and in a moderate oven **(350° F., Gas 4)** for the remainder of the time. Glaze with egg 20 min. before pie is cooked. Add remainder of seasoned stock and serve hot or cold. If the pie is required cold, forcemeat balls and sliced hard-boiled egg will be an improvement.

6–8 helpings

Cooking time—1¾–2 hr.

RABBIT PIE—DARTMOOR

2 rabbits	**½ small onion**
Short crust pastry using 12 oz. flour, etc.	**Salt and pepper**
	¼ pt. milk
2 oz. cooked macaroni	**Egg *or* milk for glazing**
1 oz. grated cheese	

Wash and joint the rabbits. Stew the pieces of rabbit until tender, when tender remove flesh from bones. Line a pie-plate with half the pastry; put in the macaroni, rabbit, cheese, chopped onion and seasoning. Moisten with milk, cover with remainder of pastry, glaze with egg *or* milk, bake in a fairly hot oven **(375°–400° F., Gas 5–6)** for about 30 min.

6 helpings

RABBIT PIE—DURHAM

½ lb. cooked rabbit
Short crust pastry (p. 557) **using 8 oz. flour, etc.**
2 oz. cooked bacon
Salt and pepper
4 eggs
Egg *or* milk for glazing

Line a pie-plate with half the pastry. Chop the rabbit and bacon, mix together and place in 4 piles on the pastry. Between each pile of meat, drop a raw egg, keeping the yolks whole. Season the filling, cover with remainder of pastry, glaze and bake in a fairly hot oven (**375°–400° F., Gas 5–6**) for about ½ hr.

Serve hot.

4 helpings

RABBIT PUDDING

Pouding de Lapin

1 rabbit
1 oz. flour
Salt and pepper
½ lb. pickled pork
Suet crust pastry using 8 oz. flour, etc.

Wash, dry and joint the rabbit, putting head, neck, liver and kidneys to stew for gravy. Mix flour with 1 teasp. salt and ¼ teasp. pepper and dip joints of rabbit in this. Dice the pork. Line a greased basin with ¾ of the pastry, fill with rabbit and pork, add a little cold water, cover with remaining pastry. Cover with greased paper, steam 2½–3 hr.

Serve hot with gravy handed separately.

6 helpings

RABBIT SOUFFLÉ

Soufflé de Lapin

6 oz. raw rabbit
2 oz. butter
2 oz. flour
½ pt. milk
2 eggs
Salt and pepper
Brown sauce

Melt butter in a saucepan, add the flour and cook for 3 min. Stir in the milk, simmer gently 10 min., then cool. Chop and pound rabbit until smooth, work in egg yolks, cooled sauce and seasoning. Fold in the stiffly-beaten egg whites and half fill a well-buttered soufflé (straight-sided) tin with the mixture. Cover with greased paper. Steam gently 40–50 min.

Turn on to a hot dish and serve immediately. Serve the sauce separately.

NOTE: Alternatively, the soufflé may be baked (uncovered) in a fairly hot oven (**375°–400° F., Gas 5–6**) for about 25 min.—until well risen and set. Make a deep channel with the handle of a teaspoon all round the soufflé, about ½ in. from the edge, the mixture will split along this line and the centre rise evenly.

6 helpings

RABBIT STEWED IN MILK

Lapin au lait

1 rabbit
1 small onion
Salt and pepper
1 small blade mace
1 pt. milk
1 teasp. cornflour

Wash and joint the rabbit. Blanch head and neck in strongly salted water. Pack the joints in a pie-dish or casserole; sprinkle with finely chopped onion; add seasoning and mace. Three quarters fill the dish with milk, cover and cook in a fairly hot oven (**375°–400° F., Gas 5–6**), 1¼–1½ hr. Blend the cornflour with a little cold milk, boil and add to the liquid in the pie-dish. Allow to cook another 10 min. Remove the head.

Serve remainder of rabbit piled on a hot dish, with the sauce strained over.

3–4 helpings
Cooking time—about 2 hr.

RABBIT STEW—RICH

Gibelotte de Lapin

1 rabbit
4 oz. streaky bacon
18 button onions
2 oz. butter
1½ oz. flour
1 pt. good stock
Bouquet garni
2 cloves
Salt and pepper
1 glass claret (optional)

Wash, dry and joint the rabbit, put the liver aside. Dice the bacon, peel the onions. Melt the butter in a large saucepan, fry onions and bacon until brown, then lift out. Fry rabbit lightly, sprinkle in flour and continue frying until well browned. Replace onions and bacon, add hot stock, bouquet garni, cloves and seasoning, cover tightly and stew gently until rabbit is tender—about 1¼ hr. About 15 min. before serving, add claret if used, put in liver (washed and cut into small pieces) and finish cooking.

Pile the rabbit on a hot dish, strain the sauce over and garnish with bacon dice and onions.

3–4 helpings
Cooking time—about 2 hr.

RABBIT VENISON

Lapin venaison

1 rabbit	**1 teasp. sage**
¾ oz. flour	**1 onion**
Salt and pepper	**¼ pt. stock**
3 rashers streaky bacon	**1 oz. butter**
4 oz. breadcrumbs	

Wash and joint the rabbit, dip joints in seasoned flour, place half of them in a greased casserole. Cut the bacon into small strips, lay these in casserole. Add remainder of rabbit, breadcrumbs mixed with sage, the chopped onion and stock. Cover casserole, cook in a warm oven (**335° F., Gas 3**) for 2½ hr. Remove the lid, put the butter on top (in small pieces) and return to oven for another ½ hr. Correct seasoning.

Serve from casserole with potatoes baked in their jackets.

4–5 helpings

RAGOÛT OF RABBIT

Ragoût de Lapin

1 rabbit	**1 pt. stock**
4 oz. streaky bacon	**Salt and pepper**
2 oz. butter	**1 carrot**
1 onion	**½ small turnip**
1½ oz. flour	**6 peppercorns**

GARNISH
Macédoine of vegetables

Wash, dry and joint the rabbit; dice the bacon. Heat the butter in a saucepan, fry rabbit in it until well browned; remove rabbit and keep hot. Fry diced onion, put in flour, stir and fry until well browned. Add boiling stock; boil for 10 min. Return rabbit to pan, add seasoning, diced carrot and turnip, bacon and peppercorns. Cover tightly. Stew gently until rabbit is tender—about 2 hr. Correct seasoning.

Serve rabbit on a hot dish with sauce strained over. Garnish at either end with macédoine of vegetable.

3–4 helpings

SANDRINGHAM RABBIT

Lapin, Sandringham

1 rabbit	**1 small shallot**
Salt and pepper	**2 oz. suet**
2 large tomatoes	**1 egg**
1 teasp. grated lemon rind	**1 rasher of bacon**
2 oz. breadcrumbs	**Fat for basting**
1 teasp. chopped parsley	**Tomato *or* brown sauce**
½ teasp. thyme	

GARNISH
Bacon rolls

Wash rabbit, season it well. Skin and finely chop tomatoes, mix with lemon rind, breadcrumbs, parsley, thyme, chopped shallot and suet. Mix with a small egg. Stuff the rabbit with this mixture, truss it and lay the bacon over the back. Roast the rabbit 50–60 min. in a fairly hot oven (**375°–400° F., Gas 5–6**) basting if required. Remove bacon about 10 min. before serving. Remove trussing strings.

Serve rabbit garnished with grilled bacon rolls. Serve sauce separately.

3–4 helpings

SCOTCH RABBIT

Lapin Écossais

1 rabbit	**2 tomatoes**
¼ lb. pork *or* bacon	**1 small onion**
1 cabbage	**Bouquet garni**
Salt and pepper	**½ pt. stock (approx.)**

Wash the rabbit, cut the flesh from the bones (the bones can be used to make stock). Mix flesh with chopped pork *or* bacon. Separate and wash cabbage leaves; blanch and season them. Line a saucepan with some of the cabbage, put in the meat, chopped tomato and onion, seasoning and bouquet garni. Cover closely with more cabbage leaves (an extra piece of bacon may be put on top if liked); add the hot stock, cover tightly, and simmer for about 2½ hr. Correct seasoning, remove bouquet garni and serve.

Kale may be used instead of cabbage.

4 helpings

VEGETABLES

COOKING OF VEGETABLES

VEGETABLES CAN form one of the most interesting parts of the meal yet they are often served without variety or originality, lacking both flavour and nutritive value. They are all too often considered by the cook to be the least important part of the meal.

The general level of vegetable culture is high but there is a tendency for most growers to keep back vegetables until they are of large size and have really passed the stage at which they should be eaten. There is no excuse for this in the case of the private gardener, who should supply the housewife with really young, tender vegetables. Small young peas, carrots, new potatoes and Brussels sprouts have a flavour entirely different from that of the large, fully grown vegetable. This excellent flavour is also partly the result of being able to reduce cooking time to a minimum.

The private gardener all too often grows, not only the same limited variety of vegetables year after year, but also too large a quantity of each vegetable. Encouraged by a housewife eager to introduce more variety into her vegetable cookery, he would no doubt find it interesting to experiment with some of the less well-known vegetables, growing these at the same time as the well-tried favourites.

More time, thought and care could with advantage in many cases be given to the cooking of vegetables. This does not mean the elaborate preparation of vegetable dishes. Simple methods which retain and enhance the natural flavour of the vegetables are best. The traditional British habit of cooking vegetables for too long a time in too much water is now almost a thing of the past. Much excellent propaganda, stressing the undesirability of this method from the nutritive point of view, has resulted in a widespread acceptance of more conservative methods of cooking vegetables. The use of butter or margarine in the cooking or serving of vegetables is not sufficiently practised in Great Britain, nor is the use of such herbs as parsley, chives, mint and savory in salads or cooked vegetable dishes.

Vegetables may be insipid in flavour through lack of seasoning. Sufficient salt should be used during the cooking and the vegetable tasted and reseasoned, if necessary, before serving. Potatoes, particularly when served as mashed potatoes, often lack flavour and are much improved by the addition of grated nutmeg. Vegetables which have little flavour in themselves are improved by being served with a well-flavoured sauce, which should be made with part, at any rate, of the cooking liquid from the vegetable.

The flavour of vegetables can be fully appreciated only if they are served immediately cooking is completed. If the vegetable is kept hot, even for a short period, the flavour is spoilt, and in the case of cauliflowers and most green vegetables, becomes strong and unpleasant.

VALUE OF VEGETABLES IN THE DIET

Vegetables are essential to the diet because they are a most valuable source of Vitamin C. They also contain Vitamins A and B1 (thiamine); certain mineral elements, chiefly calcium, phosphorus and iron; carbohydrate in the form of starch, sugar and roughage and a small quantity of useful second-class protein.

GREEN VEGETABLES

Green vegetables are of nutritional importance chiefly because of the Vitamin C and A which they contain.

Vitamin C is present in all green vegetables—turnip-tops, Brussels sprouts, cabbage and watercress being very good sources of the vitamin. The amount to be found in the vegetable is highest when the plants are making most rapid growth, in spring and early summer. Unfortunately, however, Vitamin C is rapidly lost after the vegetable is cut or pulled from the ground. Storage of green vegetables for even a short time, particularly in a warm atmosphere, causes considerable loss of the Vitamin, spinach losing as much as 40% of its Vitamin C in 1 day. Where possible, therefore, it is desirable to grow vegetables in the garden and to cook them within an hour of cutting.

Vitamin C is always lost to a certain extent when a vegetable is cooked. Where the cooking method is poor, the loss is considerable. Vitamin C is very easily soluble in water, therefore green vegetables should be soaked for the minimum of time and cooked in only a small quantity of water until just tender. The cooking liquid should be used for gravies or soups. The destruction of Vitamin C by heat, particularly in the presence of air, is also considerable. The vegetables should be cooked in a pan with a tight-fitting lid and should be served immediately they are cooked. If they are kept hot the loss of Vitamin C is greatly accelerated when bicarbonate of soda is used in the cooking water. Use of bicarbonate of soda is to be deplored in any case, as it spoils flavour and texture as well as being destructive not only of Vitamin C but also of Vitamin B1 (thiamine). Finally, Vitamin C is destroyed by plant enzymes present in the green vegetable which come into contact with the Vitamin C when vegetables are grated, and to a lesser extent when they are cut or shredded. If, however, the green vegetable is placed, immediately after shredding, into rapidly boiling water the enzymes themselves are destroyed. By putting a little of the green vegetable into the pan at a time, the water scarcely goes off the boil and very little Vitamin C is lost by enzyme action. This also explains the dietetic reason for plunging parsley into boiling water prior to chopping it (*see To chop parsley*, p. 40).

Vitamin A is present in the form of carotene in green vegetables. The amount present is proportional to the greenness of the vegetable. The darker green outer leaves of cabbage, lettuce, endive, etc. should always be used. Vitamin A is not water-soluble and is not destroyed in the cooking of green vegetables provided that the cooking is rapid and the vegetable served as soon as possible after cooking.

Green vegetables are quite good sources of Vitamin B1 (thiamine). Like Vitamin C it is very easily soluble and is rapidly destroyed in the presence of bicarbonate of soda.

Green vegetables also contain mineral elements. Watercress and sprouting broccoli are excellent sources of calcium; parsley, mustard and cress, turnip tops and endive all contain iron, but there is some doubt as to whether iron from vegetable sources is available or not.

A small amount of second class protein is present in green vegetables.

Lastly green vegetables have their value in the diet as suppliers of indigestible cellulose or roughage which stimulates the muscles of the digestive tract and has a laxative effect.

ROOTS AND TUBERS

Potatoes are the most important of these vegetables. The high proportion of starch which they contain makes them a valuable source of calories in the diet. The starch cells must be ruptured by cooking before the starch can be eaten and digested.

The potato contains Vitamin C, not in large quantity, but owing to the amount of potato eaten in the diet, it forms a useful contribution. This is particularly true in households where other sources of Vitamin C are too expensive. New potatoes are rich in the Vitamin, particularly when freshly dug, but Vitamin C being so rapidly lost in storage of vegetables, is scarcely to be found at all in old potatoes used in March or April. The potato is also a source of second class protein.

Where possible potatoes should be cooked in their skins to retain maximum food value and flavour.

Beetroots, carrots, swedes, parsnips and onions all provide sugar in the diet. The sugar is very soluble, hence the undesirability of boiling these vegetables in a large quantity of water for a long time. This method of cooking is still the one used for cooking root vegetables in most households. Not only is sugar lost but much of the flavour of the vegetable. The flavour is delicious if they are cooked "conservatively" (*see Carrots conservatively cooked*, p. 334). Beetroots retain their sweet flavour if baked or cooked in a pressure cooker rather than boiled in the usual way.

Carrots are exceptional among root vegetables in containing a large amount of Vitamin A in the form of carotene.

Like green vegetables, root vegetables also supply roughage in the diet which has a useful laxative effect.

PEAS AND BEANS

Fresh peas and beans contain the vitamins and mineral salts to be found in green leafy vegetables. Their vitamin B1 content is higher, however, and peas contain the same percentage of iron as watercress.

Peas and broad beans contain sugar and rather a higher percentage of second class protein than most other vegetables, usually about 6% as compared with 3% or much less in some other vegetables.

Dried peas and beans (usually called "pulses") must not be confused with the fresh vegetables, particularly from a dietetic point of view. They contain no Vitamin C and very little Vitamin A. Figures given for their protein value are apt to be misleading. When soaked and cooked they contain 7% to 8% protein, about $\frac{1}{3}$ of that of cooked lean meat. Before soaking and cooking the percentage is 20%, and it is this figure which gives the impression that they contain as much protein as meat.

Pulses are palatable only when really well cooked and though sometimes served as a separate vegetable, they are probably enjoyed and digested best if sieved and served in the form of soup.

DEHYDRATED VEGETABLES

Dried peas and beans have been used by the British cook for centuries. The new dehydrated vegetables are in quite a different category. They were used extensively by the armies of the Second World War and dried potato in powder form was used in most homes. Dehydrated carrot and other root vegetables including potato, dehydrated cabbage and mixtures of these vegetables, cut in strips are now available in the shops. They are dried in such a way that the Vitamin C is unharmed and carotene and other nutritive factors are not affected. Their flavour and appearance when cooked is excellent. Clear instructions as to amount of liquid and time for cooking are supplied with the vegetables.

FROZEN VEGETABLES

Frozen vegetables are now used extensively. Their popularity is no doubt due to the fact that no preparation is needed before cooking them, and to the excellent quality of the vegetables. The latter is particularly appreciated by housewives in large towns who have no opportunity of gathering fresh vegetables from the garden. Frozen peas cooked with a little sugar and sprig of mint and tossed in butter or margarine before serving are almost indistinguishable from peas gathered from the garden at the height of the season, and are far superior to field peas bought from a greengrocer, particularly in a dry growing season when skins are often tough. Their value in the diet is equal to that of fresh vegetables, provided that they are cooked before they have thawed out.

CANNED AND BOTTLED VEGETABLES

Present-day canned and bottled vegetables contain the same amount of Vitamin C as well-cooked vegetables. The vegetables are always blanched before being put into cans; this destroys the plant enzymes, but some of the Vitamin C is lost in the water. During processing, both Vitamin B1 and C diffuse out of the vegetable into the surrounding liquid, so this should be utilized. After the can is opened the vegetable should be used as soon as possible. If kept hot in the presence of air the vegetables will lose Vitamin C just as freshly cooked vegetables do.

ARTICHOKES

Globe artichokes are in season from July to October.

BOILED GLOBE ARTICHOKES

Artichauts au naturel

6 globe artichokes
Salt
1 tablesp. lemon juice
½ pt. Hollandaise sauce
or **½ pt. mushroom sauce**
or **2 oz. melted butter**

Soak the artichokes in cold, salt water for at least 1 hr. to ensure the removal of all dust and insects. Wash them well. Cut off the tails and trim the bottoms with a sharp knife. Cut off the outer leaves and trim the tops of the remaining ones with scissors. Put into a pan with just sufficient boiling water to cover them, adding salt and the lemon juice. Cook until tender, 15–45 min., according to size and freshness (when cooked the leaves pull out easily). Test frequently after 15 min. as they are apt to break and become discoloured if over-cooked. Remove from water and drain them well by turning them upside down.

Serve with Hollandaise sauce *or* melted butter *or* mushroom sauce.

6 helpings
Cooking time—15–45 min.

GLOBE ARTICHOKES—FRENCH METHOD OF COOKING

Artichauts aux fines herbes

6 globe artichokes
Salt
1 tablesp. lemon juice
A small bunch of savoury herbs
Melted butter

Prepare and cook artichokes as in preceding recipe, but add the bunch of herbs to the cooking water.

Drain the artichokes well and serve with melted butter.

6 helpings
Cooking time—15–45 min.

STUFFED GLOBE ARTICHOKES

Artichauts farcis

6 globe artichokes (cooked)
1 teasp. finely-chopped onion
2 tablesp. finely-chopped mushrooms
½ oz. butter *or* **margarine**
3 tablesp. chopped ham
1 tablesp. breadcrumbs
Brown sauce *or* **egg to bind**
Salt and pepper

Remove the inner leaves and the "chokes" from the artichokes. Fry the onion and mushrooms in the butter, add the other ingredients and sufficient brown sauce or egg to bind. Season the mixture carefully and fill the artichokes with it. Put them into a greased, fireproof dish, cover with greased paper and bake for 10–15 min. in a fairly hot oven (**375° F., Gas 5**) to ensure they are served hot.

6 helpings **Cooking time—1–1¼ hr.**

OTHER STUFFINGS:

(1) Cooked, chopped chicken liver, mushrooms, onion, chicken stock.

(2) Hard-boiled egg, lemon juice, spinach purée.

ARTICHOKE BOTTOMS

Fonds d'Artichauts

Where economy does not have to be considered, globe artichokes may be cooked as in the preceding recipes and only the bottoms or "fonds" used. After cooking, the leaves are carefully pulled out of the artichokes so that the bottoms are retained, unbroken.

The bottoms may be served quite simply, tossed in hot butter or coated with a good sauce; they may be fried; or they may be stuffed with vegetable, meat or cheese fillings piled into the natural cavity in the centre of each.

FRIED ARTICHOKE BOTTOMS

Fonds d'Artichauts frits

6 artichoke bottoms
Fried parsley
Deep fat for frying

BATTER

2 oz. flour
Pinch of salt
1 dessertsp. salad oil
4 tablesp. tepid water (approx.)
1 egg white

Cut the cooked artichoke bottoms into 3 or 4 pieces according to size.

Sift the flour and salt and mix to a smooth batter with the oil and sufficient tepid water to give a coating consistency. Leave to stand for ½ hr. Fold in the stiffly whipped egg white just before frying. Dip the pieces of artichoke into the batter on a skewer and lower each piece carefully into hot deep fat at 340° F. Turn them during frying as they will float, and when golden brown (5–7 min.) remove from the fat. Drain well and serve garnished with fried parsley.

NOTE: The bottoms will have more flavour if soaked for ½ hr. before coating and frying, in a marinade of olive oil, lemon juice, pepper, salt and herbs.

4–6 helpings
Cooking time—5–7 min. to fry the bottoms

STUFFED ARTICHOKE BOTTOMS

Fonds d'Artichauts farcis

Artichoke bottoms
1 tablesp. of stuffing for each (approx.)
Butter *or* margarine

STUFFINGS

(1) **Cooked rice well seasoned and flavoured with cheese, preferably Parmesan** *or*

(2) **Fried, finely chopped shallot, young cooked peas, mint, seasoning** *or*

(3) **Cooked sausage meat, chopped chives, French mustard** *or*

(4) **Finely chopped fried onion, mushroom, and a little tomato purée.**

Toss the cooked artichoke bottoms in hot butter or margarine. Pile the hot, well-flavoured stuffing on each bottom. Serve immediately.

Allow 1 artichoke bottom for each person
Cooking time—5–7 min. to fry the bottoms

JERUSALEM ARTICHOKES

Jerusalem artichokes are seasonable from October to April.

BOILED JERUSALEM ARTICHOKES

Topinambours au naturel

1½–2 lb. Jerusalem artichokes
White vinegar *or* lemon juice
Salt
¾ pt. white sauce

Scrub, scrape and rinse the artichokes, using 1 teasp. of white vinegar or lemon juice in each water to keep the vegetable white. Put into sufficient boiling, salted water to cover the vegetable, adding 1 teasp. white vinegar or lemon juice to each quart of water. Simmer gently till just tender, about 20 min. Drain well and serve in a hot vegetable dish with the white sauce poured over.

5–6 helpings **Cooking time—about 20 min.**

BAKED JERUSALEM ARTICHOKES

Topinambours rôties

2 lb. Jerusalem artichokes
Lemon juice *or* white vinegar
Salt and pepper
Dripping

Prepare and parboil the artichokes 5 min. Drain them and shake the pan over heat to dry them. Put into hot dripping in a roasting tin or in the tin containing the roast joint. Roll the artichokes in the fat and cook in a fairly hot oven (**375° F., Gas 5**) till brown and tender (about 1 hr.) turning them during cooking. They will not be a good colour but are of excellent flavour.

4–6 helpings
Cooking time—to parboil, 5 min.; to bake about 1 hr.

FRIED JERUSALEM ARTICHOKES (1)

Topinambours frits

1½ lb. Jerusalem artichokes
Coating batter (double quantity) (p. 399)
Fried parsley

Prepare and parboil the artichokes (about 15 min.). Cut them into slices ½ in. thick and season them well. Make the batter, dip in the slices of artichokes and fry in hot fat, at 340° F. until golden brown (5–7 min.), turning them during cooking. Drain well and serve very hot with fried parsley.

6 helpings
Cooking time—15 min. to parboil artichokes
5–7 min. to fry them

FRIED JERUSALEM ARTICHOKES (2)

1½ lb. Jerusalem artichokes	**Deep frying fat**
Lemon juice *or* white vinegar	**Salt and pepper**

Prepare the artichokes. Slice them very thinly and soak them for 10 min. in water to which lemon juice or vinegar has been added. Drain them thoroughly and then dry them in a cloth. Sprinkle gradually into hot, deep fat at 320° F. Remove when golden brown, drain well, sprinkle with salt and pepper and serve at once.

6 helpings
Cooking time—to fry, 3–5 min.

MASHED JERUSALEM ARTICHOKES

Purée de Topinambours

2 lb. Jerusalem artichokes	**1 oz. butter *or* margarine**
Lemon juice *or* white vinegar	**2 tablesp. milk**
	Salt and pepper
	Chopped parsley

Prepare and cook as in Boiled Jerusalem Artichokes (p. 326). Drain well and shake the pan over a low heat to dry the artichokes slightly. Mash with a fork or potato-masher or rub through a nylon sieve. Heat the butter or margarine in the pan and beat in the purée. Stir over heat until thoroughly hot. Season well. Serve in a hot vegetable dish and sprinkle with chopped parsley.

NOTE: To ⅔ artichoke purée may be added ⅓ potato *or* carrot purée.

5–6 helpings
Cooking time—30–35 min.

ASPARAGUS

Asparagus is in season from March to July.

ASPARAGUS—BOILED

Asperges au naturel

1 bundle of asparagus	**2 oz. butter**
Salt	**Lemon juice**

Trim the hard white ends of the asparagus to suitable lengths for serving. Scrape the stalks with a sharp knife, working downwards from the head. Wash them well in cold water. Tie them into small bundles with the heads in one direction. Re-trim the stalks evenly. Keep them in cold water until ready to cook. Cook very gently, with the heads off the source of heat, in just enough salted boiling water to cover. When tender (in about 15–20 min.), drain and serve on a folded table napkin. Serve with melted butter, seasoned and lightly flavoured with lemon.

NOTE: To ensure that the tender point of the asparagus is not overcooked by the time that the stem is ready, the asparagus should be cooked "standing". This can be achieved in an "asparagus boiler", a narrow very deep pan. A bottling jar half-filled with boiling water, stood in a deep saucepan of boiling water, serves as a very good substitute. The asparagus is placed stems down in the jar and the points cook more slowly in steam only. Allow 30 min. for this method of cooking.

Allow 6 or 8 medium-sized heads per person

ASPARAGUS—FRENCH STYLE

Asperges à la Bonne Femme

50 heads of asparagus	**1 sprig of thyme**
½ pt. milk	**1 oz. flour**
1 small lettuce—finely shredded and in short lengths	**1 oz. butter**
	1 egg
	Salt and pepper
1 small onion—par-boiled and finely chopped	**1 teasp. lemon juice**
	Croûtes of buttered toast *or* fried bread
1 bay leaf	

GARNISH

Chopped parsley	**Cucumber strips**

Prepare the asparagus (*see Asparagus—Boiled*) and tie into bundles. Bring the milk to boiling-point, put in the asparagus, lettuce, onion, bay leaf, thyme and a little salt. Simmer gently about 20 min. Drain the asparagus well, cut off the points and edible parts of the stalks and keep them hot. Strain the milk and make a white sauce with it and the flour and butter. Cool it slightly, add the beaten egg and cook until it thickens, without boiling. Season and add lemon juice. Pile the asparagus on the croûtes, coat with sauce and garnish with chopped parsley and cucumber strips. **Serve** as a vegetable entremet *or* as an entrée for a vegetarian dinner.

Allow 1 croûte for each person and 1 or 2 over
Cooking time—30–40 min.

ASPARAGUS ROLLS

Petits Pains aux Asperges

50 heads of asparagus	**1 egg**
6 small French rolls	**Salt and pepper**
½ pt. white sauce (p. 115)	**Lemon juice**

Cut off the tops of the rolls and scoop out the inside. Heat the shells of crust in the oven till they are very crisp. Cook the asparagus in the usual way, cut off the points and keep them hot and rub the stalks through a fine sieve (stainless metal *or* nylon). Stir the asparagus purée and the beaten egg into the white sauce. Cook until the mixture thickens (without boiling or the egg will curdle). Season well and use a little lemon juice or additional flavour. Fill the crisp rolls, piling the mixture high, garnish the top of each with asparagus points. Put the tops of the rolls on again like lids, and serve very quickly.

NOTE: This dish may be served as a vegetable entremet, luncheon dish or as a vegetarian entrée.

6 helpings
Cooking time—about 40 min.

ASPARAGUS WITH EGGS

Asperges aux œufs

50 heads of asparagus	**3 sprigs of thyme**
1 pt. milk	**2 oz. butter**
1 large lettuce, finely shredded	**2 oz. flour**
	1 egg
1 medium-sized onion, parboiled	**Salt and pepper**
	1 teasp. lemon juice
1 bay leaf	**6 poached eggs**

Prepare the asparagus, then cut off the points and keep them covered until required. Bring the milk to boiling-point, put in the asparagus stalks, lettuce, onion cut in small pieces, bay leaf, thyme, and salt and simmer gently for about 20 min. Rub through a fine sieve (stainless metal or nylon). Make a sauce with the fat, flour, milk and asparagus purée. Cool slightly and add the beaten egg. Cook until the mixture thickens, without boiling. Boil the asparagus tops 10–15 min. Poach the eggs and trim neatly to a nice round shape, chop the trimmings finely and add to the sauce. Season the sauce well and add lemon juice, then pour it down the centre of a hot dish. Arrange the eggs on either side, and garnish the top of the thick sauce, between the 2 rows of eggs, with the asparagus points.

6 helpings
Cooking time—about 40 min.

AUBERGINE (EGG PLANT)

Aubergines are used extensively in the East where they are considered a great delicacy. It is essential that they should be fresh and they are at their best in July and August before the seeds form in them. Fresh aubergines have a smooth, very glossy skin and are firm to the touch.

AUBERGINES WITH POACHED EGGS

Aubergines aux œufs pochés

3 aubergines	**1 tablesp. breadcrumbs**
½ oz. butter	**Salt and pepper**
¼ pt. tomato pulp	**6 small poached eggs**
2 tablesp. chopped ham	**Chopped parsley**

Boil the aubergines in slightly salted water until tender, or steam them. Halve them lengthwise, and remove seeds if necessary. Heat the butter, add the tomato pulp, ham, breadcrumbs and stir over heat. Season well, then fill the cavities of the aubergines with the mixture. Put into a greased dish in a moderate oven (**350° F., Gas 4**) and heat thoroughly. Place a neatly trimmed poached egg on each half; garnish with parsley and serve.

6 helpings
Cooking time—about 1 hr. altogether

BAKED AUBERGINE WITH CHEESE

Aubergine au Parmesan

4 aubergines
1 heaped tablesp. grated Parmesan cheese
½ pt. Béchamel sauce (p. 128)
Salt and pepper
1 tablesp. breadcrumbs
½ oz. butter

Parboil the aubergines for 10 min., then slice rather thickly, remove the seeds, if any, and arrange slices neatly in a fireproof dish. Mix the cheese into the Béchamel sauce, season to taste, and coat the aubergines with it. Cover lightly with the breadcrumbs, sprinkle the surface with the melted butter. Bake in a fairly hot oven, (**375° F., Gas 5**) for ½ hr.

6 helpings

FRIED AUBERGINE

Aubergines frites

4 aubergines
Flour
Cayenne pepper
Salt
1 finely-chopped onion
Salad oil *or* butter

Slice the aubergines about ½ in. thick, lay them out on a flat dish, sprinkle with salt and put on a weight (this hastens the process of removing the moisture). After ½ hr. wipe them with a cloth, then coat them lightly with flour seasoned with cayenne and salt. Fry the onion in the oil or butter until lightly browned, drain and keep the onion hot. Replace the butter in the pan and fry the aubergine until both sides are lightly browned. Drain and dish. Sprinkle the onion on the aubergine; serve with tomato sauce, if liked.

6 helpings
Cooking time—to fry the aubergine, about 15 min.

BEANS

French beans are in season from May to November. Runner beans are in season from August to October. Broad beans are in season from June to August.

BOILED FRENCH or RUNNER BEANS

Haricots Verts au Naturel

1½ lb. French *or* runner beans
1 oz. butter *or* margarine
Salt

Wash, top and tail and string the beans. Do not cut up French beans *or* young runner beans as they lose their flavour in cooking. For older scarlet runners, slice thinly, or, for better flavour, cut into diamonds, i.e. slice them in a slanting direction. Have ready just enough boiling salted water to cover them and cook them with the lid on the pan. When tender (15–20 min.), drain and reheat in butter or margarine. Serve immediately.

4–6 helpings

BEANS—FRENCH METHOD OF COOKING

Haricots Verts à la Maître d'Hôtel

1½ lb. French beans
2 oz. butter *or* margarine
Juice of ½ lemon
1 tablesp. chopped parsley
Salt and pepper

Cook as in preceding recipe, drain well and shake in the pan until most of the water has evaporated. Add butter, parsley, lemon juice and seasoning and shake over heat for a few minutes. Serve immediately.

4–6 helpings **Cooking time—15–20 min.**

BROAD BEANS WITH CREAM SAUCE

Fèves à la Poulette

2 lb. broad beans
½ pt. veal *or* chicken stock
A bunch of herbs (thyme, sage, savory, marjoram, parsley stalks)
1 lump of sugar
1 egg yolk
¼ pt. single cream *or* evaporated milk
Salt and pepper

Shell the beans and cook them in the stock with the lump of sugar and the bunch of herbs. When the beans are tender, lift out the herbs. Beat the egg yolk with the cream and stir it carefully into the saucepan. Reheat, stirring all the time until almost simmering. Season and serve at once. If preferred, the herbs may be finely chopped and left in the sauce.

If the beans are really large strain them from the liquid when they are tender and skin them before returning them to the thickened sauce.

4–6 helpings **Cooking time—20–40 min.**

BROAD BEANS WITH PARSLEY SAUCE

Fèves à la Maître d'Hôtel

2–3 lb. broad beans
Salt
2–3 savory leaves (if available)
Parsley sauce

Wash the beans and shell them. If not to be cooked immediately, cover down with some of the washed pods as this prevents the skins of the beans from drying out and becoming slightly toughened. Cook gently in just enough boiling salted water to cover, with the savory leaves in the water. When tender, 15–35 min. according to size and age, drain well. Make a good parsley sauce with ½ milk and ½ bean water and well flavoured with lemon juice. Reheat the beans in the sauce and serve immediately.

NOTE: When really young, broad beans should have heads, tails and strings removed as for runner beans, and be cooked whole in the pods. The pods are eaten after tossing them in melted butter. The pod is quite tender, with an excellent flavour, and a very economical dish can be produced by this method.

When really mature, it is often necessary to skin the beans after cooking and before tossing them in the parsley sauce.

4–6 helpings (according to yield)

BROAD BEANS WITH SPANISH SAUCE

Fèves à l'Espagnole

2 lb. broad beans
¾ pt. good brown stock
1 small onion (finely-chopped)
2 *or* 3 sprigs of thyme
1 bay leaf
Salt and pepper
6 *or* 8 button mushrooms
1 oz. butter *or* margarine
1 oz. flour
1 teasp. parsley (finely-chopped)
Lemon juice

Shell the beans and cook them in the boiling stock with the onion, thyme, bay leaf and a little salt. Meanwhile, fry the mushrooms in the butter, without browning. Add them to the pan containing the cooked beans, leaving the butter behind. Add the flour to the butter and cook until it is golden brown. Stir into it the beans, mushrooms and stock, having lifted out the sprig of thyme and the bay leaf. Stir over heat until just boiling. Add parsley and lemon juice and season carefully. Serve very hot.

If liked, garnish the dish with bacon rolls and crescents of fried bread. Vegetarians could substitute vegetable stock for the meat stock and garnish with small dice of nut meat fried in oil.

4–6 helpings
Cooking time—35–40 min.

HARICOT BEANS

All the following recipes given for Haricot Beans may be used for similar beans such as Butter Beans, American Lima Beans, Flageolets (green haricots), etc.

BOILED HARICOT BEANS

Haricots de Soisson au beurre

½ lb. haricot beans
1 oz. butter *or* margarine
Salt and pepper
Chopped parsley

Soak the beans overnight in boiling water. Drain them and well cover with cold, salted water. Bring slowly to boiling point and simmer very slowly until tender, 2–2½ hr. Drain off the water and shake them gently over the low heat to dry them. Toss them in butter and season with pepper and salt. Serve hot, sprinkled with freshly chopped parsley.

6 helpings

HARICOT BEANS AND MINCED ONIONS

Haricots à la Lyonnaise

½ lb. haricot beans
2 medium-sized onions (minced *or* chopped very finely)
1 oz. butter *or* margarine
Seasoning
Chopped parsley

Cook the beans. Fry the onions slowly in the butter until tender and golden brown. Mix together the onions and beans, season and serve hot sprinkled with parsley.

6 helpings
Cooking time—2–2¼ hr.

HARICOT BEANS WITH CHEESE

Haricots au gratin

½ lb. haricot beans
1 oz. butter *or* margarine
1 egg yolk
2 oz. grated cheese (preferably Parmesan)
Cayenne pepper and salt
1 tablesp. cream *or* evaporated milk
1 tablesp. chopped parsley
Sippets of fried bread

Cook the beans. Melt the fat, add all the other ingredients except 1 dessertsp. of the cheese. Shake over the heat till thoroughly hot. Put into a hot, greased fireproof dish, sprinkle with the rest of the cheese and brown quickly under a hot grill.

4 helpings
Cooking time—2½ hr.

BEETROOT

When small, young and juicy, this vegetable makes a very excellent addition to winter salads, and may easily be converted into an economical and quickly-made pickle (*see* p. 653). Beetroot is more often served cold than hot; when served hot it should be served with sour-sweet sauce (p. 127) or melted butter.

Beetroot is obtainable throughout the year.

BAKED BEETROOT

Small young beetroots

Wash the beetroots carefully. If the skin has been damaged in any way, cover the damaged part with a little flour and water paste. Put them into a baking-dish and bake in a moderate oven **(350° F., Gas 4)**, until tender, about 1 hr. This method is excellent for young beetroots, all the flavour and sweetness of the beetroot being retained.

NOTE: The beetroots may be wrapped in greased papers or covered with aluminium foil before baking.

BOILED BEETROOT

Beetroots

Wash the beetroots very carefully, but do not break the skins, or they will lose colour and flavour during cooking. Put them into sufficient boiling water to cover them and boil them gently until tender, 1½–2½ hr. according to size and age. Unless to be served as a hot vegetable, leave them to cool in the cooking water before rubbing off the peel. If to be served hot, serve them with melted butter.

Beetroots are cooked most successfully and quickly in a pressure cooker, taking 15–40 min. according to size and age, with the cooker set at 15 lb. pressure.

Cooking time (in a pressure cooker)—*small* beetroots 15 min., *medium* beetroots 20 min., *large* beetroots 35–40 min.

POLISH BEETROOT

Betterave à la Polonaise

2 lb. cooked, peeled beetroots
1 small onion—finely chopped
½ oz. margarine
½ oz. flour
½ bottle of yoghourt
1 dessertsp. finely-grated horseradish *or* 1 dessertsp. bottled horse-radish sauce
Salt and pepper
A little sugar, if necessary
Chopped parsley

Grate the beetroot. Melt the fat and fry the onion in it, carefully and thoroughly. Stir in the flour, add the yoghourt and bring to the boil. Add the beetroot and horseradish and heat thoroughly. Season carefully, adding a little more yoghourt if the flavour is too sweet, or a little sugar if too sharp. Serve very hot and decorate with lines of parsley.

This is a very pleasant way of serving beetroot as a hot vegetable and is a very quick dish if cooked beetroots are purchased or available.

6 helpings **Cooking time—15 min.**

BROCCOLI

This vegetable is known to the cook in three different forms:

(1) Most of the cauliflowers which are sold between October and June come from the broccoli plant, which is very hardy. (The cauliflower plant proper, is less hardy and supplies the typical white heads during the summer and early autumn, before the frosts appear). This form of broccoli is cooked by all the methods suggested for CAULIFLOWER.

(2) The Calabresse, green or Italian sprouting broccoli, produces a medium-sized green central head which is usually available in March. It is cooked like cauliflower and served with melted butter.

After the central head is cut, shoots appear from every leaf joint, each shoot having a tiny head. The shoots are cut with about 6 in. of stem and provide an excellent vegetable for two or three months. The stems should be cut into short lengths and cooked, with the tiny heads, in boiling salted water as for any green vegetable; or they can be tied in bundles and cooked and served like asparagus.

(3) Early purple sprouting and white sprouting broccoli come into season at the beginning of April. The tiny heads should be cut off with about 2 in. of stem and adjoining leaves and cooked whole in boiling salt water like any other green vegetable. The more the heads are cut off the more prolific is the growth.

As purchased from the greengrocer, there is often a great deal of stem and leaf with the heads. The really coarse stems should be discarded and the rest shredded with the leaves and added to the pan before the small heads.

BRUSSELS SPROUTS

Sprouts are in season from September to March.

BOILED BRUSSELS SPROUTS

Choux de Bruxelles au naturel

1½ lb. Brussels sprouts
Salt
1 oz. butter *or* **margarine (optional)**

Choose small, close, sprouts. Remove shabby outer leaves by cutting the end, then make a cross cut on the bottom of each stalk. Soak in cold water, containing 1 teasp. of salt per quart, for 10 min. only. Wash thoroughly under running water if possible. Choose a suitably sized pan and put in enough water to ¼ fill it only, with ½ teasp. salt to 1 pt. of water. When boiling, put in half the sprouts, the largest ones if variable in size, put on lid and bring quickly to boil again. Add rest of sprouts and cook until all are just tender, with the lid on the pan all the time. Drain in a colander and serve immediately in a hot vegetable dish or toss in melted butter before serving. Sprouts should be served quickly as they soon cool.

NOTE: By this method the sprouts retain their maximum colour, flavour and nutritive value.

On no account should soda be used in the cooking of green vegetables.

6 helpings
Cooking time—15 min.

BRUSSELS SPROUTS AU JUS

Choux de Bruxelles au Jus

1½ lb. Brussels sprouts
1 pt. stock

Prepare and cook sprouts as in preceding recipe but use stock instead of water and ½ the quantity of salt. Drain and dish the sprouts. Reduce the stock to a thin glaze by quick boiling and pour it over the sprouts.

6 helpings
Cooking time—15–20 min.

BRUSSELS SPROUTS WITH CHESTNUTS

Choux de Bruxelles aux Marrons

1½ lb. Brussels sprouts
1 dozen cooked chestnuts
3 oz. ham
4 tablesp. cream
Salt and pepper

Boil the sprouts and drain them, *see above*. Cook the chestnuts separately and chop them. Put the sprouts, chestnuts, finely chopped ham and cream into a warm casserole. Put on the lid and reheat gently in a moderate oven (350° F., Gas 4).

6 helpings
Cooking time—in the oven, 15 min.

FRIED BRUSSELS SPROUTS

Choux de Bruxelles frits

1 lb. small, tight Brussels sprouts, cooked
Coating batter (double quantity) *see Fried Artichoke bottoms* (p. 325) *or*
Yeast batter:

½ oz. margarine
¼ pt. milk
¼ lb. flour
¼ oz. yeast
¼ teasp. salt

Prepare the batter, if using yeast batter: warm the milk to blood heat with the margarine, and cream the yeast with a little of it Add the rest of the milk to the yeast, then add all to the warmed flour and salt. Beat till smooth. Put to rise in a warm place till doubled in size. Cook the sprouts so that they are just tender. Drain well. Dip them in the batter on a skewer and lower each piece carefully into hot, deep fat at 340° F. Turn them during frying as they will float, and when golden brown, 5–7 min., remove from the fat. Drain well and serve garnished with fried parsley.

NOTE: The yeast batter gives a pleasant, very crisp result. Tomato sauce is an excellent accompaniment if the sprout fritters are to be served as a separate course.

4 helpings

CABBAGE

Cabbage is obtainable throughout the year.

BOILED CABBAGE

Choux au naturel

1 large, fresh cabbage (about 2 lb.)
Salt

Cut across the end and remove only the very thick, coarse piece of stalk and shrivelled or discoloured outer leaves. Pull off the green leaves and put to soak, with the heart cut into 4 pieces, in cold water with 1 teasp. of salt per quart of water. Soak for 10 min. only. Wash thoroughly under running water if possible. Choose a suitably-sized pan and put in enough water to $\frac{1}{4}$ fill it only, with $\frac{1}{2}$ teasp. of salt to 1 pt. of water. Cut out the stalk from the green leaves and heart of the cabbage, shred it and put on to cook with the lid on the pan. Shred the green outer leaves and add these to the pan. Replace lid and bring to boil again quickly, while shredding the cabbage heart. Add the heart to the pan a handful at a time so that the water barely goes off the boil. Cook with lid on pan until the cabbage is just tender. Drain well in a colander but do not press out liquid. Serve in a hot dish and send to table immediately.

NOTE: *See Boiled Brussels Sprouts.*

6 helpings **Cooking time—10–15 min.**

POLISH CABBAGE

Choux à la Polonaise

1 lb. cabbage heart
1 oz. bacon
½ oz. bacon fat
1 small onion, finely-chopped
Salt and pepper
¼ pt. boiling water
1 cooking apple *or* 2 tomatoes
1 dessertsp. flour

Cut the bacon into small pieces and fry lightly in a saucepan, with the bacon fat. Add the onion and fry it. Shred the cabbage finely and add to the bacon and onion, stirring it well. Add boiling water and a little salt and simmer gently until the cabbage is almost soft. Add the apple, chopped, or the skinned and cut up tomatoes and cook until the cabbage is quite soft. Stir in the flour and boil for 2–3 min. until the flour is cooked. Dish very hot.

4–6 helpings
Cooking time—45 min. (approx.)

STUFFED CABBAGE

Choux farcis

6 large leaves of cabbage
4 oz. cooked rice
2 teasp. very finely-chopped onion
4 oz. fresh minced meat
Powdered mace
Pepper and salt
Worcester sauce
Stock
Arrowroot

Wash and boil the cabbage leaves for 5 min. in salt water. Drain. Mix the filling, moistening it with stock and flavouring it carefully. Form into rolls. Remove a little of the coarse vein of the cabbage leaves. Wrap each roll of filling in a cabbage leaf and tie with cotton or secure with a cocktail stick. Place in a saucepan, barely cover with stock, put on lid and simmer very gently 45 min. Lift on to a hot dish and thicken stock by boiling it with blended arrowroot (1 teasp. to $\frac{1}{4}$ pt. of stock). Season carefully. Pour sauce over cabbage rolls and serve immediately.

6 helpings
Cooking time—about 1 hr. (approx.)

RED CABBAGE

RED CABBAGE WITH APPLES

Choux aux Pommes

1 small red cabbage	**1 tablesp. golden syrup**
1 oz. margarine	**Juice of ½ lemon**
1 onion chopped very fine	**2 tablesp. vinegar**
2 cooking apples	**Salt**

Melt the fat. Add the onion and fry gently until light brown. Add cabbage finely shredded, peeled and sliced apples, and syrup. Cook over very gentle heat for 10 min., shaking pan frequently. Add lemon juice, vinegar and salt and simmer covered, 1–1½ hr. Stir occasionally. Season and serve.

6 helpings **Cooking time—1½–2 hr.**

RED CABBAGE WITH CHEESE

Choux au fromage

1 small red cabbage	**4 oz. grated cheese**
¼ pt. boiling water	**2 teasp. vinegar**
1 teasp. quince jelly	**Salt and pepper**

Soak, wash and slice the cabbage thinly. Boil gently in the water with the jelly and a little salt added. Add the cheese and vinegar and mix well. Season and serve hot.

6 helpings
Cooking time—¾–1 hr.

STEWED RED CABBAGE

Choux au Jambon

1 small red cabbage	**¼ pt. vinegar**
1 slice of ham	**Salt and pepper**
½ oz. butter *or* **margarine**	**1 tablesp. granulated sugar**
1 pt. stock	

Soak, wash and slice the cabbage thinly. Put into a stewpan with the ham (diced), the butter, ½ pt. of stock, and the vinegar. Put on the lid and stew gently 1 hr. When very tender add the rest of the stock, sugar and seasoning. Mix and stir over heat until nearly all the liquor has dried away. Serve at once.

This is an excellent dish to serve with sausages.

6 helpings
Cooking time—1¼ hr.

CARDOONS

This is a very good vegetable, not used sufficiently by most cooks. In the South of France where the very prickly variety, *Cardon de Tours*, is grown, it is a very highly favoured vegetable, and both roots and stalks are used.

Cardoons are in season from October throughout the winter.

BOILED CARDOONS

Cardons au naturel

2 lb. cardoons	**Salt**
¾ pt. white sauce (p. 115)	**1 tablesp. lemon juice**

Discard the outer stems, which are very tough. Cut the inner stalks into 3-in. lengths, remove the prickles, cover with boiling salted water and lemon juice and cook very gently for 15 min. Drain and rub off the skins with a cloth. Put into fresh, boiling salted water and continue to cook very gently for another 1–1¼ hr. Drain well and coat with white sauce. Serve immediately.

6 helpings
Cooking time—1¼–1½ hr.

CARROTS

Carrots are obtainable throughout the year.

CARROTS—CONSERVATIVELY COOKED

1½ lb. carrots	**½ teasp. salt**
1 oz. butter *or* **margarine**	**½–1 gill boiling water**
	Chopped parsley

Cut off the green tops, scrub and scrape the carrots. Slice them thinly if old carrots (or leave whole if really young). Fat steam the carrots for 10 min., i.e. shake them in the melted fat, well below frying temperature, with the lid on the pan until the fat is absorbed. Add the liquid (less for young carrots) and the salt, and simmer gently until the carrots are tender—15–30 min. according to age of carrots. Serve hot, with the small amount of liquid remaining, and garnished with parsley.

NOTE: This method should be employed for

cooking most root vegetables, e.g. parsnips, turnips, swedes, onions, etc., and should replace "boiling". Both flavour and food value are conserved.

6 helpings

CARROTS—GERMAN STYLE

Carottes à l'Allemande

1½ lb. carrots	**1 oz. flour**
2 oz. butter *or* **margarine**	**Nutmeg**
1 dessertsp. finely-chopped onion	**1 tablesp. chopped parsley**
1 pt. stock	**Salt and pepper**

Prepare and cook the carrots as in preceding recipe, using 1 oz. butter, but add the onion and use the stock for cooking. Pour the carrots into a colander, retaining the liquid and making it up to ¾ pt. Melt the other ounce of butter, stir in the flour and cook until browned. Add the ¾ pt. stock and stir till boiling. Add the carrots to the boiling stock, stir in the grated nutmeg and parsley, season. and serve.

6 helpings **Cooking time—¾–1 hr.**

CARROTS WITH CIDER

Carottes à la Normande

1½ lb. young carrots	**Salt and pepper**
3 oz. butter	**A wineglassful of cider**
4 tablesp. cream	**Lemon juice**

Cook the carrots (*see Carrots—Conservatively Cooked*). Drain off any liquid left. Melt the remaining 2 oz. of butter and, when hot, stir in the cream gradually. Season with salt and pepper. Add the cider gradually and a few drops of lemon juice. Put the carrots back into this sauce and gently cook them in it for 10 min. Serve immediately.

6 helpings **Cooking time—about 45 min.**

GLAZED CARROTS

Carottes glacées

1½ lb. young carrots	**¼ teasp. salt**
2 oz. butter	**Good stock**
3 lumps sugar	**Chopped parsley**

Melt the butter in a saucepan, Add the scraped, whole carrots, sugar, salt and enough stock to come half-way up the carrots. Cook gently, without a lid, shaking the pan occasionally until tender. Remove the carrots and keep them hot. Boil the stock rapidly until reduced to rich glaze. Replace the carrots 2 or 3 at a time, turn them until both sides are well coated with glaze. Dish, sprinkle with chopped parsley and serve.

6 helpings **Cooking time—about ¾ hr.**

CAULIFLOWER

Cauliflowers are in season from June to October. *See Broccoli*

BOILED CAULIFLOWER WITH WHITE SAUCE

Choufleur à la Sauce blanche

1 large cauliflower	**Salt**
½ pt. white sauce made with ½ milk and ½ cauliflower water	

Trim off the stem and all the leaves, except the very young ones. Soak in cold water, head down, with 1 teasp. salt per qt. of water, for not more than 10 min. Wash well. Choose a suitably sized pan and put in enough water to ¼ fill it, with ½ teasp. salt to 1 pt. water. Put in cauliflower, stalk down, and cook with lid on pan until stalk and flower are tender. Lift out carefully and drain. Keep hot.

Coat the cauliflower with the sauce and serve immediately.

NOTE: To reduce cooking time, the cauliflower may be quartered before cooking or broken into large sprigs.

6 helpings **Cooking time—20–25 min.**

CAULIFLOWER WITH CHEESE

Choufleur au gratin

1 large cauliflower
¾ pt. cheese sauce
Salt
1 heaped tablesp. grated cheese (dry Cheddar) *or* **1 dessertsp. grated Cheddar cheese and 1 dessertsp. grated Parmesan cheese**

Cook the cauliflower as in preceding recipe, drain well and dish up in a fireproof dish. Coat with thick cheese sauce. Sprinkle with grated cheese and immediately brown under a hot grill or in the top of a hot oven (**425° F., Gas 7**). Serve immediately.

4 helpings
Cooking time—25–30 min.

FRIED CAULIFLOWER

Choufleur en fritot

1 medium-sized cauliflower
Coating batter (double quantity) (*see Fried Artichoke Bottoms*, p. 325) *or* **yeast batter** (*see Fried Brussels Sprouts*)

Cook the cauliflower whole till only just tender. Divide into sprigs the size of a large walnut. Fry as in Fried Brussels Sprouts, p. 332.

4 helpings
Cooking time—5–7 min. to fry

POLISH CAULIFLOWER

Choufleur à la Polonaise

1 large cauliflower
Salt
1½ oz. butter
2 hard-boiled eggs
2 oz. fine stale bread-crumbs

Cook and drain the cauliflower. Heat the butter in a pan until just browning. Stir in the finely chopped hard-boiled eggs, then the crumbs. Mix well. Dish the cauliflower and pour the crumb mixture over it. Serve immediately.

6 helpings
Cooking time—35-40 min.

CELERIAC or TURNIP ROOTED CELERY

This vegetable with its flavour of celery has many uses. It can be grated raw in salads, used for flavouring soups and is excellent cooked in various ways. The thick root only is used. It stores well.

Celeriac is in season from October to April.

CELERIAC WITH WHITE SAUCE

Céléri-rave à la Sauce blanche

3 roots of celeriac
¾ pt. good white sauce
Salt
Lemon juice

Scrub the root well, then peel thickly. (If the roots are spongy discard them as useless.) Cut into ½-in. slices and stew them slowly in boiling, salted vegetable stock or water till tender—about 45 min. Drain. Make a good white sauce with ½ pt. milk and cooking liquid. Season and add a little lemon juice. Coat the celeriac and serve immediately.

NOTE: The vegetable stock can be water in which onions, Jerusalem artichokes, etc., have been cooked.

6 helpings **Cooking time—45 min. approx.**

FRIED CELERIAC *Céléri-rave frit*

3 roots of celeriac
Butter *or* margarine
Finely-chopped parsley

Cook the celeriac as in preceding recipe. Drain well and dry in a cloth. Fry in butter *or* margarine until golden brown. Drain and dish hot, sprinkled with finely-chopped parsley.

6 helpings
Cooking time—45 min. to boil, 6–8 min. to fry

CELERY

This vegetable is most commonly eaten raw. It may be cooked in a variety of ways and the outer stems, unsuitable for eating raw, should always be used in soups, stews and for flavouring in some sauces and fish dishes.

Celery is in season from September to February.

BRAISED CELERY

Céléri braisé

4 heads of celery
Stock
Glaze (if available)

MIREPOIX

½ oz. dripping
½ oz. bacon
2 large carrots
1 small turnip
2 onions
Bouquet garni (thyme, marjoram, sage, parsley)
1 blade of mace
6 white peppercorns
1 bay leaf
Salt

Trim the celery but leave the heads whole. Wash them well and tie each securely. Prepare the mirepoix. Fry the bacon in the dripping in a large saucepan, then fry all the vegetables cut in pieces ¾ in. thick, until lightly browned. Add herbs, spices and ½ teasp. of salt and enough stock to come ¾ of the way up the vegetables. Bring to boiling-point. Lay the celery on top. Baste well with the stock in the pan and cover closely with greased paper or metal foil. Put on lid and cook until the celery is soft (about 1½ hr.). Baste several times during cooking. Dish the celery and keep hot. Strain the liquor, put it back in the pan and add 1 teasp. of glaze if available. Reduce by boiling quickly until of glazing consistency. Pour over the celery.

NOTE: Use the coarse outer stems of the celery for soups. A few pieces may be cut up and fried for the mirepoix. The cooked mirepoix can be served sprinkled with parsley as a separate vegetable dish or if sieved and thinned down with stock it makes an excellent soup.

4–8 helpings, according to the size of the celery heads

CELERY WITH WHITE SAUCE

Céléri à la Sauce blanche

2 large heads of celery	**Salt**
½ pt. good white sauce	**Lemon juice**

Trim off the green tops of the celery, reserving a few pale green ones. Remove the very tough outer stalks. Separate the other stalks and wash or, if necessary, scrub in cold water. Rinse and reserve the tender hearts for eating raw. Scrape the stalks to be cooked, cut into suitable lengths for cooking and tie in bundles. Stew in barely sufficient boiling water, slightly salted, to cover the celery. If possible, cook in vegetable water from cooked artichokes, onions etc. When tender (in about 1 hr.), drain. Make a good white sauce with ½ milk and ½ cooking liquid. Season and add a little lemon juice. Coat the celery with the sauce, garnish with some of the pale green leaves and serve immediately.

NOTE: The celery may be cooked in milk, with the addition of 1 finely chopped onion. When cooked, the celery may be served as above, with the addition of 2 tablesp. of cream to the sauce just as the pan is removed from the heat.

4–6 helpings
Cooking time—1 hr.

FRIED CELERY

Céléri en fritot

1 large head of celery *or* **2 small heads**
Coating batter, double quantity (*see Artichoke Bottoms*, p. 325) *or* **yeast batter** (*see Fried Brussels Sprouts)*

Cook the celery as for Celery with White Sauce until just tender. Cut into 2-in. lengths. Fry as for Fried Brussels Sprouts p. 332.

4 helpings
Cooking time—5–7 min. to fry

CHESTNUTS

CHESTNUTS AU JUS

Marrons au jus

2 lb. chestnuts	**Cayenne pepper**
2 cloves	**Salt**
1 small onion	**1 dessertsp. glaze (if available)**
1 outside stick of celery	**Fleurons of pastry**
1 bay leaf	
1 blade of mace	
1 pt. good brown stock	

Take a sharp knife and make an incision in each chestnut, in the shell only. Put into a saucepan and cover with cold water. Bring to the boil and cook for 2 min. Drain and peel and skin them while very hot. Stick the cloves into the onion and put chestnuts, onion, celery, bay leaf and mace into the boiling stock. Season. Simmer about 1 hr. until the chestnuts are tender. Strain and keep the chestnuts hot. Return stock to pan, add the glaze if available and reduce to a glazing consistency. Pile the chestnuts in a hot vegetable dish, pour the glaze over and decorate with fleurons of pastry.

6 helpings
Cooking time—1¼ hr.

CHESTNUT PURÉE

Purée de Marrons

2 lb. chestnuts	**1 tablesp. cream**
Veal *or* chicken stock	**Seasoning**
½ oz. butter	

Peel and skin chestnuts as in preceding recipe. Put them into the boiling stock with a little salt and stew gently until tender (use barely enough stock to cover). Strain. Put the chestnuts through a wire sieve. Put them back into the pan, add the butter and enough of the cooking liquor to give a thick purée. Add the cream and season carefully. Serve in a hot vegetable dish. Put tiny pieces of butter on the surface to prevent a crust forming, if the purée must be kept waiting.

4–6 helpings
Cooking time—1¼ hr. (approx.)

CHICORY

This vegetable is used extensively in France, particularly in its raw state, with a French dressing. It is an excellent vegetable either raw or cooked. The bitter flavour, disliked by some, is disguised by the French dressing and can be removed from cooked chicory by blanching for five minutes prior to the cooking process itself.

Chicory is in season from September to April.

CHICORY AND WHITE SAUCE

Barbe-de-Capucin à la Sauce blanche

6 large heads of chicory	**Salt**
¾ pt. good white sauce	**Lemon juice**

Cut off the end of the chicory and the outer leaves. Split each head to within ½ in. of the end and wash well between the leaves. Blanch, by bringing to the boil in just enough water to cover and boiling 5 min. Drain, then tie the heads together in bundles of 2 and cook in boiling salted water until just tender. Finish and serve as for Celery with White Sauce.

6 helpings **Cooking time—30–40 min.**

BRAISED CHICORY

Barbe-de-Capucin braisé

6 large heads of chicory	**Glaze, if available**
Stock	**Mirepoix** (*see Braised Celery*, p. 336)

Prepare and blanch chicory as in preceding recipe. Braise and serve as for Braised Celery.

4–6 helpings **Cooking time—1–1¼ hr.**

CHICORY AND HAM

12 small heads of chicory	**2 oz. dry, grated Cheddar cheese *or* 2 oz. grated Parmesan cheese**
12 thin slices of ham	**1 oz. dry white breadcrumbs**
¾ pt. cheese sauce	**1 oz. butter *or* margarine**

Prepare and cook chicory as for Chicory and White Sauce. Drain and dry each head in a cloth. Wrap each head in a slice of ham and put into a warm, fireproof dish. Coat with thick cheese sauce. Sprinkle with the mixture of cheese and crumbs, then with the melted butter or margarine. Bake in a fairly hot oven (**375° F., Gas 5**) for 20–30 min. until hot and browned on top.

6 helpings **Cooking time—1 hr.**

CORN, INDIAN CORN, SWEET CORN, or MAIZE

In cookery corn always means Maize or Indian Corn. It is grown extensively in America, where it is considered a great delicacy. Early ripening varieties from America have made it a fairly well-known vegetable with British cooks. It is not, however, eaten at its best in Britain, as it is often allowed to ripen too long, and it should be freshly cut when cooked. When ripe enough to cut, the milk of the grain should exude when the grain is pierced with the finger-nail. After this stage it is useful only as food for poultry.

Corn is seasonable from May to August.

BAKED CORN ON THE COB

Maïs rôti

6 ears *or* cobs of corn, freshly picked
2 oz. butter
Seasoning

Method 1. Remove outer and inner husks and the silk. Melt the butter in a roasting dish. Roll the cobs in it, so that they are lightly coated with butter. Season. Roast in a fairly hot oven (**375° F., Gas 5**) turning them frequently.

6 helpings
Cooking time—35 min. (approx.)

Method 2. Prepare as above but place the cobs in the roasting dish (without butter) and just cover them with milk. Bake for about 45 min. Drain; season with salt and pepper. Toss in melted butter and place under a hot grill for a few minutes before serving.

6 helpings
Cooking time—1 hr. (approx.)

BOILED CORN ON THE COB

Maïs bouilli

6 ears *or* cobs of corn freshly picked
Seasoning
Butter

Remove the outer husks of the corn. Open the tender, pale green inner husks and take away all the silk surrounding the corn. Replace the inner husk and tie securely; place the ears in a saucepan with sufficient boiling water to cover them. Simmer gently 15–20 min. Drain and remove strings and husks. Serve with melted, seasoned butter. The flavour is always best if the corn is torn from the cob with the teeth, each guest being supplied with melted butter in which to dip the corn. Eating it this way is most pleasant but very messy.

6 helpings
Cooking time—about 20 min.

CORN PUDDING

Pouding de Maïs

6 large ears *or* cobs of corn
2 eggs
4 oz. flour
1 teasp. salt
½ teasp. pepper
1 pt. milk

Remove the husks and the silk from the corn, cut downwards through the centre of each row of grains, then remove them with the back of a knife. Beat the eggs and add them, stirring carefully, to the sifted flour, salt and pepper. Stir in the milk, then the corn. Pour into a greased pie-dish and bake in a moderate oven (**350° F., Gas 4**) about 1 hr. Serve hot.

6 helpings

STEWED CORN

Maïs bouilli

6 ears *or* cobs of corn, freshly picked
1 oz. butter
1 oz. flour
¾ pt. milk
Salt and pepper

Prepare the corn as in preceding recipe. Place the grains in a saucepan, with sufficient boiling water to cover, and cook gently 15–20 min. Drain well. Make a sauce with the flour, fat and milk. Season well. Stir in the corn and when thoroughly hot, serve.

6 helpings

CUCUMBER

Cucumbers are usually eaten uncooked or pickled. Cucumber is most digestible if the skin is left on and the cucumber sliced thickly to ensure that it is well chewed. The rind is rich in salts and flavour, and contains minute amounts of substances which help in digestion of the pulp of the cucumber.

There are a number of pleasant ways of using cucumber as a cooked vegetable. As with marrow, which, like the cucumber, contains a high percentage of water, it should be steamed rather than stewed or boiled.

Cucumbers are obtainable all the year round but are cheapest in July and August.

CUCUMBER WITH SAUCE

Concombre à la Poulette

2 large cucumbers
1 oz. butter *or* margarine
1 teasp. finely-chopped shallot
¾ pt. white sauce (p. 115)
1 egg
1 teasp. finely-chopped parsley
Salt and pepper

Peel the cucumber and steam it until tender (about 20 min.). Drain well and cut into 1-in. slices. Melt the butter in a saucepan, put in the shallot and cook it without browning. Add the sliced cucumber, toss over heat for a few minutes, then stir in the white sauce. Just before boiling-point is reached, add the well-beaten egg and parsley, stir and cook gently until the egg thickens. Season and serve hot.

6 helpings **Cooking time—30 min. approx.**

FRIED CUCUMBERS

Concombres frits

2 cucumbers	**Butter *or* margarine**
Flour	**Seasoning**

Wash the cucumbers and cut into 1-in. slices. Steam for 15 min.; then dry them on a cloth. Dredge them lightly with flour. Fry in butter *or* margarine till golden brown, turning them frequently. Drain well. Season with pepper and salt and serve immediately.

6 helpings
Cooking time—15 min. to steam; 7–10 min. to fry

STEAMED CUCUMBERS

2 cucumbers	**Salt**
¾ pt. white *or* Hollandaise sauce	**Lemon juice**
	Fresh tarragon leaves

Wash the cucumbers. Steam them whole until tender. Drain and cut into 2-in. lengths. Stand the pieces upright in a hot dish and coat with a well flavoured sauce containing a little lemon juice. Garnish with a little finely-chopped, fresh tarragon.

6 helpings **Cooking time—25–30 min.**

STUFFED CUCUMBERS

Concombres farcis

2 large cucumbers	**¼ teasp. mixed herbs**
1 oz. margarine	**1 egg**
½ lb. minced cold meat e.g. ham, veal, beef, chicken	**A little stock**
	Seasoning
	Worcester sauce
2 heaped tablesp. fresh breadcrumbs	**Croûtes of fried bread**
1 tablesp. finely-chopped parsley	

Wash and peel the cucumbers and cut into 2-in. lengths. Scoop out the centres with a teaspoon. Steam until soft—about 15 min. While the cucumber is cooking, heat the margarine in a saucepan. Stir in the meat, breadcrumbs, parsley and herbs, heat thoroughly, add the beaten egg and enough stock to give a soft stuffing. Season well, adding Worcester sauce for extra flavour, if necessary. Drain the cucumber and put each piece on a croûte of bread. Fill with the hot stuffing, which should be piled up high. Garnish with chopped parsley.

Serve tomato sauce (p. 127) or brown sauce (p. 119) with the stuffed cucumber.

6 helpings
Cooking time—35 min. approx.

NOTE: Other fillings for stuffed cucumber are as follows:

(1) Hard-boiled eggs finely-chopped and mixed with thick cheese sauce.

(2) Macedoine of vegetables in a thick cheese sauce.

(3) Finely-chopped cooked mushrooms mixed with chopped onion and bacon and thickened with breadcrumbs or white sauce.

DANDELION LEAVES

STEWED DANDELION LEAVES

Feuilles de Dents de Lion

2 lb. young, tender dandelion leaves	**Salt and pepper**
1 oz. butter *or* margarine	**1 tablesp. cream**

Wash the leaves thoroughly and soak in cold water for 1 hr. Cook in boiling salted water, the water should come ¼ of the way up the pan before the leaves are put into it. When tender (in 20–30 min.) drain them well, like spinach. Chop them and reheat with butter and cream. Season and serve hot.

NOTE: Dandelion leaves are suitable for cooking in the Spring.

6 helpings

EGG PLANT (*see Aubergine*)

ENDIVE (*Chicorée*)

This vegetable is generally served as a salad but may also be served as a hot vegetable.

Endive is in season from November to March.

BRAISED ENDIVE

Chicorée braisé

6 heads of endive
Stock
Glaze, if available
Mirepoix (*see Braised Celery*, p. 336)

Cut off the stumps of the endive and discard any outer leaves that are discoloured or tough. Wash in several waters, then parboil in salted water 10 min. to remove bitter flavour. Drain well; pressing out water with the fingers. Braise and serve as for Braised Celery.

6 helpings
Cooking time—approx. 1½ hr. altogether

STEWED ENDIVE

Purée de Chicorée

6 heads of endive
1 oz. butter *or* margarine
1 oz. flour
¾ pt. stock
1 tablesp. of lemon juice
Salt and pepper

Prepare and blanch endive as in preceding recipe. (The whitest and best parts of the endives can be put aside to use raw as a salad.) Drain well and chop finely. Melt the butter in a saucepan, stir in flour, cook slightly without browning, add stock and stir until boiling. Add the endive and lemon juice, season and simmer until the endive is quite hot. Serve.

6 helpings
Cooking time—approx. 45 min. altogether

KOHL-RABI

This is a vegetable which resembles turnip in flavour, but is grown much more easily and should be eaten soon after it is taken from the ground as its flavour is spoilt by storing.

It may be served in any way suitable for Turnips, but as its characteristic flavour is in and near the skin, it should, where possible, be cooked in the skin.

LEEKS

Leeks are in season from August to May.

BOILED LEEKS

Poireaux au naturel

12 leeks
Salt
¾ pt. white sauce

Trim off the roots and outer leaves and as much of the tops as necessary. Split from the top to within 1 in. of the bottom. Wash very thoroughly under running water, separating each leaf with the fingers to ensure that no grit is left between the leaves. Drain and tie in bundles. Boil in as little water as possible (barely enough to cover), with 1 teasp. salt to 1 pt. water. Cook until tender—30–40 min. Drain well and coat with white sauce made with ½ milk and ½ leek water.

6 helpings

BRAISED LEEKS

Poireaux braisés

12 leeks
Stock
Glaze, if available
Mirepoix (*see Braised Celery*, p. 336)

Prepare leeks as in preceding recipe. Braise and serve as for Braised Celery.

4–6 helpings
Cooking time—1½ hr.

LENTILS

BOILED LENTILS

Lentilles bouillies

¾ lb. lentils
Bouquet garni
1 ham bone (if available) *or* bacon rinds
1 onion
1 clove
Salt and pepper
½ oz. butter *or* margarine

Put the lentils into cold water with the herbs, ham bone, onion stuck with the clove, and a little salt. Bring to boiling point and cook until the lentils are soft—about 1 hr. Strain the lentils, toss in a little melted butter *or* margarine; season and serve. If preferred, sieve the lentils before tossing in butter.

6 helpings

LETTUCES

Though generally served as the principal ingredient in a salad, lettuces may also be served as a cooked vegetable.

BRAISED LETTUCES

Laitue braisé

6 heads of lettuce
Stock
Glaze, if available
Mirepoix (*see Braised Celery*, p. 336)

Braise as for Braised Endive.

STEWED LETTUCE

Laitue au Jus

6 small lettuces
1 oz. butter *or* margarine
1 oz. flour
½ pt. stock
1 dessertsp. chopped chives
1 bay leaf
1 dessertsp. chopped parsley
Salt and pepper

Wash the lettuces well. Plunge into boiling salt water and simmer 2 min. Plunge into cold water, drain. Melt the butter in a saucepan, add the flour, mix well, then add stock and stir until smooth and thick. Add chives, bay leaf, parsley, and a little salt and put in the lettuces. Cook gently for ½ hr., stirring from time to time. Re-season and serve.

6 helpings
Cooking time— ½ hr. (approx.)

LIMA BEANS *see Haricot Beans*

MUSHROOMS

Mushrooms are obtainable all the year.

BAKED MUSHROOMS

Champignons au beurre

18–24 flap mushrooms
Salt and pepper
Powdered mace
Butter *or* margarine

Wash the mushrooms under running water, peel the caps and trim the ragged ends of the stalks. Put into a baking-dish, gills of the mushrooms uppermost, sprinkle with salt and pepper and a very little mace and put a tiny piece of butter on each. Cover and cook 25–30 min. in a fairly hot oven (**375° F., Gas 5**).

If possible, cook in a fireproof glass dish with a lid and serve in the same dish, thus retaining all the flavour of the mushrooms.

6 helpings

FRIED MUSHROOMS

Champignons frits

1 lb. flap mushrooms
Butter *or* margarine *or* bacon fat
Salt and pepper

Wash and peel the mushrooms, trim the stalks. Melt the fat and fry the mushrooms in it for 15 min. Drain and serve hot, seasoned with salt and pepper.

Small rounds *or* squares of bread may be fried in the fat, after removing the mushrooms, and the mushrooms served on the bread.

6 helpings
Cooking time—about 15 min.

GRILLED MUSHROOMS

Champignons grillés

12 flap mushrooms
Salt and pepper
Butter *or* bacon fat
Buttered toast
Chopped parsley
Lemon juice

Wash, peel and trim the stalks. Season and brush with melted butter *or* bacon fat. Cook under a hot grill, turning them once. Serve in a hot dish or on rounds of buttered toast, with a sprinkling of chopped parsley and a squeeze of lemon juice.

NOTE: A pinch of very finely-chopped marjoram, sprinkled on each mushroom prior to grilling, imparts an excellent flavour.

6 helpings
Cooking time—10 min. (approx.)

MUSHROOMS STEWED WITH WINE

1 lb. button mushrooms
6 rashers of streaky bacon
1 teasp. finely-chopped chives
1 teasp. finely-chopped parsley
Salt and pepper
White wine *or* cider
Flour

Wash and peel the mushrooms, trim the stalks. Cut up the bacon into small pieces and cook in a saucepan 15 min. Add the mushrooms, chives and parsley and a little salt. Moisten with white wine or cider, dredge lightly with flour and stew very gently until the sauce is quite thick. Re-season.

6 helpings
Cooking time—40 min. (approx.)

MUSHROOMS WITH CHEESE

Champignons au gratin

18–24 flap mushrooms
Salt and pepper
1 tablesp. finely-chopped chives
1 tablesp. finely-chopped parsley
1 tablesp. fresh breadcrumbs
2 tablesp. grated Parmesan cheese
½ oz. butter

Wash, peel, stem the mushrooms. Grease a baking-dish and put in the mushrooms, gills uppermost. Season. Sprinkle with the parsley and chives, then with the breadcrumbs and cheese mixed. Lastly sprinkle with the melted butter. Bake for 25 min. in a fairly hot oven (**375° F., Gas 5**).

6 helpings
Cooking time—25 min.

STEWED MUSHROOMS

Champignons à la crème

1 lb. flap *or* button mushrooms
2 oz. butter *or* margarine
1 dessertsp. arrowroot
¼ pt. stock
Lemon juice
2 tablesp. cream
Salt and pepper
Chopped parsley
Fleurons of pastry

Wash and peel the mushrooms, trim the stalks. Melt the butter in a saucepan and fry the mushrooms in it slowly, about 10 min. Blend the arrowroot with the stock. Add to the pan and stir till boiling. Simmer 20–30 min. Add lemon juice and cream and season carefully. Dish and garnish with parsley and fleurons of pastry.

NOTE: This mixture may be used to fill small French rolls (*see Asparagus Rolls*, p. 328).

6 helpings
Cooking time—30–40 min.

STUFFED MUSHROOMS

Champignons farcis

6 medium-sized mushrooms
½ oz. butter *or* margarine
1 small onion finely-chopped
1 tablesp. finely-chopped ham
1 dessertsp. fresh breadcrumbs
1 teasp. grated Parmesan cheese
1 teasp. chopped parsley
Brown sauce
Salt and pepper
6 round croûtes fried *or* toasted bread

Wash, peel and remove stalks from mushrooms. Trim the mushrooms to neat, round shapes with scissors and use the trimmings in the stuffing. Melt the butter in a saucepan, add the onion and mushroom trimmings (finely-chopped) and cook 10 min. Add the other ingredients, with sufficient sauce to bind. Stir till well mixed and hot. Season carefully. Pile on the underside of the prepared mushrooms. Put on to a greased tin, cover with greased paper or metal foil and bake in a fairly hot oven (**375° F., Gas 5**) about 20 min. Serve on the fried or toasted croûtes.

6 helpings
Cooking time—about 30 min.

NETTLES

Young nettles are very pleasant to eat, resembling spinach. The young tops should be gathered, washed and cooked like spinach, cooking them over a low heat at first until the water has run off the leaves and there is no fear that they will burn on the bottom of the pan.

Gloves must be worn when gathering and preparing the nettles.

OKRA (*Gumbo*)

This is an aromatic bean native to the West Indies, where it is known as Gumbo. It is now grown extensively in India, West Africa and the Southern States of America, and to a lesser extent in the South of France. The young green pods are sometimes pickled and the older pods preserved in cans for export. Okra has a peculiar flavour, often thought disagreeable to an unaccustomed palate. It is exceedingly mucilaginous, the pods in the tin being surrounded by a substance of greater viscidity than gum.

BOILED OKRA

Gumbo bouilli

24 fresh okras
2 oz. butter
2 tablesp. cream *or* milk
Salt and pepper

Wash the okras in cold water, drain them well and trim both ends. Place in barely enough salted water to cover, cook gently for 15 min., or until tender, and drain well. Heat the butter and cream in the saucepan, put in the okras, sprinkle with salt and pepper, shake over heat for a few minutes, then serve.

6 helpings
Cooking time—20–30 min.

CANNED OKRAS (to serve as a vegetable)

1 can okras
½ oz. butter *or* margarine
Salt and pepper

Turn the contents of the can into a saucepan and heat. Drain. Toss in melted butter *or* margarine. Season and serve.

OKRA AND AUBERGINE

24 fresh okras
1 aubergine
2 tomatoes
1 oz. butter *or* margarine
1 finely-chopped onion
Salt and pepper
1 tablesp. finely-chopped parsley

Wash and slice the okras. Peel the aubergine, remove seeds, if necessary, and slice in pieces similar in size to the pieces of okra. Peel and slice the tomatoes. Melt the butter in a saucepan. Add okras, aubergine, tomatoes, onion and a little salt. Stew till tender—about 35 min.—stirring frequently. Stir in the parsley, season carefully and serve.

6 helpings
Cooking time—about 35 min.

SCALLOPED OKRAS AND TOMATOES

½ can okras *or* 1 small can
A little milk
1 oz. butter *or* margarine
1 oz. flour
4 sliced tomatoes
2 tablesp. fresh breadcrumbs
Salt and pepper
Butter *or* margarine
6 scallop shells

Drain the okras and make up the juice to ½ pt. with milk. Make a sauce with the butter, flour and liquor. Cut the okras into small pieces and the slices of tomato into halves or quarters. Mix them together with 1½ tablesp. breadcrumbs and season. Place the mixture in greased scallop shells. Cover with the sauce. Cover lightly with the rest of the breadcrumbs and sprinkle with melted butter. Bake in a fairly hot oven (**375° F., Gas 5**) 15–20 min. Serve hot in the scallop shells.

6 helpings

ONIONS

The name Spanish onion is often given to any large onion of mild flavour.

If strong onion flavour is disliked, onions should be blanched prior to the actual cooking.

BAKED ONIONS

Oignons rôtis

6 large onions
Salt and pepper
A little margarine *or* butter
A little milk

Method 1. Peel the onions and cook in boiling, salted water 20 min. Drain and place in a fireproof dish. Sprinkle with salt and pepper. Put a small pat of margarine *or* butter on the top of each and pour enough milk in the dish to come ⅓ of the way up the onions. Cover with a greased paper. Bake in a moderate oven (**350° F., Gas 4**) until tender, basting frequently with the milk. Serve with any milk and onion liquor in the dish.

6 helpings
Cooking time—to bake the onions about 1½ hr.

Method 2. Boil the onions till tender, in their skins. Drain and dry in a cloth and wrap each onion in well-greased paper or in "cropar" paper. Bake in a moderate oven

(**350° F., Gas 4**) for an hour. Unwrap and serve in their skins with butter or margarine.

6 helpings

Cooking time—to boil 1½ hr.; to bake 1 hr.

Method 3. Trim off the roots of the onions, wipe, but do not skin. Put a little margarine, butter *or* dripping in a fireproof dish, or roasting-tin. Place the onions in it and bake until tender in a fairly hot oven (**375° F., Gas 5**). Take out the onions and peel them. Put them back in the dish, season with salt and pepper, and baste well, using a little extra fat if necessary. Reheat for 10 min.

6 helpings

Cooking time—to bake 1½–2 hr.

BOILED ONIONS

Oignons bouillis

6 large onions	**¾ pt. white sauce** (p. 115)
Salt and pepper	**Lemon juice**

Cut off the root and top of the onion, the brown skin and inner layer of skin. Put into cold water, bring to the boil and strain if a mild flavour is required. Put into boiling water (just enough to cover) with 1 teasp. salt to 1 pt. of water. Boil gently 1½–2 hr. according to size. Make a white sauce with ½ milk and ½ onion water. Season and flavour with a little lemon juice. Coat the onions and serve very hot.

6 helpings

Cooking time—1½–2 hr.

BRAISED ONIONS

Oignons braisés

6 large onions	**Mirepoix** (*see Braised Celery*, p. 336)
Stock	
Glaze, if available	

Prepare and blanch the onions. Braise and serve as for Braised Celery.

NOTE: If small onions, shallots, or button onions are to be braised, tie them loosely in a muslin bag before placing on the mirepoix, so that they are easy to remove after cooking.

6 helpings

Cooking time—1¾–2 hr.

FRIED ONIONS (1)

Oignons frits

6 large onions	**Frying fat**
	Salt and pepper

Peel and slice the onions. Heat enough frying fat in a frying-pan to cover the bottom of the pan. Fry the onions slowly until golden brown and quite soft, stirring them occasionally during frying. Drain well, season and serve hot.

6 helpings **Cooking time—20 min.**

FRIED ONIONS (2)

6 large onions	**A little flour**
A little milk	**Salt and pepper**

Peel the onions and cut into slices ¼ in. thick. Separate into rings. Dip in milk, then toss in seasoned flour. Fry them in deep fat, adding the rings gradually to the fat, at 340° F., until golden brown. Drain well, season and serve at once.

6 helpings **Cooking time—5–7 min.**

GLAZED ONIONS

Oignons glacés

1½ lb. button onions	**2 teasp. castor sugar**
2 oz. butter *or* **margarine**	**A little stock**

Peel the onions. Heat the butter *or* margarine in a wide saucepan. Add the onions and toss them in the fat for a few minutes. Sprinkle them with the sugar and continue to shake them in the pan over a gentle heat until they are soft. Unless they are really small onions, toss them for 5 min., then add stock barely to cover and let them simmer very gently without a lid on the pan until they are soft and the liquid is reduced to a glaze. Season and use as a garnish.

6 helpings **Cooking time—15–35 min.**

ONIONS—ITALIAN STYLE

Oignons à l'Italienne

1½ lb. button onions	**2 cloves**
Salt	**4 white peppercorns**
2 tablesp. olive oil	**2 tablesp. wine vinegar**
2 bay leaves	**1 tablesp. sugar**

Choose small onions equal in size. Cook gently in boiling, salted water, in their skins. When tender, drain and peel them. Heat the oil, add bay leaves, cloves, peppercorns. Shake these in the oil for a few minutes. Add the onions and simmer very gently for about 5 min. Stir in the vinegar and sugar and continue cooking until the liquid is reduced to a syrup. Serve hot.

6 helpings **Cooking time—altogether 45 min.**

ONIONS WITH APPLES

Oignons aux pommes

¾ lb. onions
1 lb. cooking apples
1½ oz. butter *or* margarine
2 teasp. sugar

Peel and blanch the onions. Drain and cut into slices. Wash, peel and core the apples. Slice them. Heat the fat in a pan; add the onions, apples and sugar. Put on the lid and simmer gently until tender, about ½ hr. Season and serve.

6 helpings

ONIONS WITH CHEESE

Oignons au gratin

6 large onions
Salt and pepper
¾ pt. cheese sauce
1 heaped tablesp. dry, grated Cheddar cheese *or* 1 dessertsp. dry, grated Cheddar cheese *and* 1 dessertsp. grated Parmesan cheese

Cook the onions as for Boiled Onions. Slice thickly and coat with thick cheese sauce. Sprinkle with the grated cheese and brown under a hot grill or in the top of a hot oven. Serve immediately.

6 helpings
Cooking time—1½–2 hr.

ONIONS WITH TOMATOES

Oignons aux tomates

6 large onions
2 oz. butter *or* margarine
½ lb. tomatoes
2 bay leaves
2 cloves
2 tablesp. cider
½ pt. stock

Peel and blanch the onions. Cut them into slices. Heat the fat in a pan. Add the onion slices and fry gently until golden brown. Add the tomatoes (skinned and sliced), bay leaves, cloves, cider and stock. Simmer until tender, ¾–1 hr. Season and serve with any liquor remaining.

6 helpings **Cooking time—1–1¼ hr.**

STEWED ONIONS

Oignons au jus

6 large onions
1 pt. brown stock
Salt and pepper
Small bunch of herbs

Peel the onions and blanch them. Put them into a pan which will just hold them standing side by side. Add the stock, bunch of herbs, and a little salt and put on the lid of the pan. Simmer gently 1½ hr. Season and serve in a hot dish with the cooking liquid poured round.

6 helpings **Cooking time—about 1½ hr.**

STUFFED ONIONS

Oignons farcis

6 large onions
4 tablesp. finely-chopped liver *or* cooked ham *or* any cooked meat
1 tablesp. finely-chopped cooked onion
1 tablesp. breadcrumbs
½ teasp. finely-chopped fresh sage *or* ½ teasp. dried sage
Salt and pepper
1 egg
Butter *or* margarine
¾ pt. brown sauce (p. 119)

Peel and steam the onions gently until almost soft, about 1 hr. Lift out the centre of each onion with a teaspoon handle. Chop the onion centres and add to the stuffing. Mix the stuffing ingredients with the beaten egg. Season well. Press it firmly into each onion and pile neatly on top. Sprinkle the top of each onion with a little melted butter *or* margarine. Pin a band of stiff, greased paper round each onion to prevent splitting. Put into a greased, fireproof dish and bake 30–40 min. in a moderate oven (**350° F., Gas 4**). Serve with the sauce poured round.

6 helpings
Cooking time—about 1¾ hr.

PARSLEY

Parsley is used extensively by the cook as a garnish for all types of savoury dishes and adds considerably to their Vitamin C value. If chopped by the method on p. 40, it is bright green in colour, retains most of its Vitamin C and is chopped quickly, without leaving a stain on the chopping board.

FRIED PARSLEY

Persil frit

Remove stalks from the parsley, leaving it in sprigs. Wash it, shake well and dry in a cloth for at least 1 hr. before frying. Put into the basket of a deep fat pan. Dip the basket just into the hot fat at 340° F., remove quickly, dip again and remove, then plunge into the fat and leave it in until most of the bubbling has ceased and the parsley is bright green and crisp. Drain very well on absorbent paper. Serve hot with many savoury dishes, particucularly with fish.

NOTE: The high water content of parsley causes hot fat to bubble fiercely and if the parsley is plunged straight into the fat and left there, the fat may come over the top of the pan and cause a fire.

PARSNIPS

Parsnips are in season from October to March.

PARSNIPS—CONSERVATIVELY COOKED

2 lb. parsnips	**½ teasp. salt**
1 oz. butter *or* margarine	**1 gill boiling water**
	Chopped parsley

Scrub and scrape the parsnips and slice them thinly. Fat steam the parsnips for 10 min., i.e. shake them in the melted fat, well below frying temperature with the lid on the pan until the fat is absorbed. Add the boiling water and the salt, and simmer gently until the parsnips are tender.

Serve hot with the small amount of liquid remaining, and garnish with chopped parsley.

6 helpings
Cooking time—30–45 min.

BAKED PARSNIPS

Panais rôtis

2 lb. parsnips	**Dripping**
Salt	

Prepare the parsnips, cut off the thin end and leave whole, cut the thick end lengthwise, then across, i.e. into quarters. Boil the parsnips in just enough salt water to cover, for 10 min. Strain off the water and dry the parsnips over a low heat. Put into hot dripping in a roasting-tin, or in the tin containing the roast joint. Roll the parsnips in the fat and cook till brown and tender—¾–1 hr., turning them during cooking. The high sugar content of the parsnips gives them an excellent flavour and a very pleasant brown colour when baked.

PEAS

Peas are in season from May to September.

GREEN PEAS

Petits Pois Verts à l'Anglaise

2 lb. peas	**A little sugar**
Salt	**½ oz. butter *or* margarine**
Sprig of mint	

Shell the peas. Have sufficient boiling, salted water to cover the peas. Add the peas, mint and sugar. Simmer gently until soft, from 10–20 min. Drain well. Reheat with butter *or* margarine and serve in a hot vegetable dish.

NOTE: If the peas must be shelled some time before cooking, put them in a basin and cover them closely with washed pea-pods.

4–6 helpings (according to yield)
Cooking time—10–20 min.

GREEN PEAS—FRENCH STYLE

Petits Pois à la Française

2–3 lb. green peas (1½ pt. shelled peas)	**2 oz. butter *or* margarine**
4 very small onions *or* spring onions	**2 teasp. sugar**
	Salt and pepper
1 lettuce	**Egg yolk (optional)**

Shell the peas. Peel the onions. Remove the outer leaves of the lettuce, wash the heart, leaving it whole. Put the peas into a thick saucepan, add the lettuce heart, onions and the butter cut into small pieces. Stir in the sugar and a little salt. Cover with the lid and cook over a very low heat, about 1 hr., shaking the pan occasionally. Re-season and serve. The liquid in the pan may be thickened with an egg yolk before serving.

6 helpings
Cooking time—about 1 hr.

PEA PURÉE

Purée de pois

¾ lb. green *or* yellow split peas	**2 carrots**
4 oz. fat bacon	**2 cloves**
2 small onions	**Bunch of herbs**
	Salt and pepper

Soak the peas overnight. Cut up the bacon and put it into a saucepan with the peas, sliced onions and carrots, bunch of herbs, and enough cold, salted water to cover. Simmer gently until the peas are tender, 2–2½ hr. Drain off liquid, but reserve it. Rub ingredients through a sieve. Reheat with a little of the cooking liquid added, if necessary, to give a fairly thick purée. Season and serve.

NOTE: Pea purée is excellent with grilled or fried sausages, *or* bacon *or* bacon and eggs.

6 helpings
Cooking time—about 3 hr.

PEAS WITH HAM

Petits pois au lard

2–3 lb. green peas (1½ pt. shelled peas)	**2 oz. lean, cooked ham, diced**
½ small onion, finely-chopped	**½ pt. stock**
1 oz. butter *or* margarine	**Pinch of castor sugar**
1 teasp. flour	**Pinch of grated nutmeg**
	Salt and pepper

Cook the peas and drain them well. Fry the onion until lightly browned in the fat. Add the flour and ham, stir over heat for a minute or two, then add the peas, stock, sugar and nutmeg. Simmer until the peas are thoroughly reheated, about 10 min. Season and serve.

6 helpings
Cooking time—about ¾ hr.

CANNED or BOTTLED PEAS (to dress)

1 can *or* bottle of peas	**Sprig of mint**
Butter *or* margarine	**Sugar**
	Salt and pepper

Strain the peas and rinse them well. Melt ½–1 oz. butter *or* margarine in a saucepan (the amount depends upon the size of the can of peas). Add a sprig of mint, the peas, salt and little sugar. Cover down closely with a butter or margarine paper, then the tightly-fitting lid of the pan. Leave over a very low heat, shaking the pan occasionally until the peas are hot, about 15–20 min. Re-season and serve.

NOTE: If available 1 or 2 outside lettuce leaves may be put into the pan (whole) and removed before serving the peas. The peas may also be served as in preceding recipe, with ham.

DRIED PEAS

Dried peas	**½ level teasp. bicarbonate of soda *or* a piece of washing soda the size of a cherry**
2 qt. boiling water to each 1 lb. peas	

Pour the boiling water on to the required weight of peas, add the soda, and leave to soak overnight.

Rinse the peas thoroughly after soaking, cook in plenty of boiling, salted water until the peas are soft—1–1½ hr. approximately.

To improve the flavour, add a sprig of mint, bunch of herbs (a small sprig of marjoram, sage, thyme and a few parsley stalks) or an onion stuck with 2 or 3 cloves.

PEASE PUDDING

Pouding aux pois à l'Anglaise

1½ pt. split peas	**2 oz. butter *or* margarine**
1 small onion	**2 eggs**
Small bunch of herbs	**Salt and pepper**

Soak the peas overnight, remove any discoloured ones. Rinse and cover with cold, salted water. Bring slowly to boiling point in the water, to which has been added the onion (whole) and the bunch of herbs. Simmer very slowly until tender—2–2½ hr. Drain well and rub through a sieve. Add the butter, cut in small pieces, the beaten eggs, pepper and salt. Beat well until the ingredients are well incorporated. Tie tightly in a floured cloth and simmer in water for an hour. Turn out and serve very hot.

NOTE: Pease pudding is served with hot pickled pork.

6 helpings
Cooking time—about 3½ hr.

PEPPERS or CAPSICUMS

The large peppers used as a vegetable are variously known as Spanish peppers, Long peppers, Green or sweet peppers, Bell peppers or Red peppers according to their shape and colour. They are a very popular vegetable in America and Spain and are being used more extensively than formerly in Britain.

Peppers are in season from August to November.

FRIED PEPPERS

Piment frit

4 green peppers
Butter *or* margarine *or* deep fat
Egg and breadcrumbs (if to be fried in deep fat)

Wash the peppers. Parboil in salted water for 5 min. Drain and cut into strips or rings. Remove seeds and inner partitions. Toss in hot butter or margarine in a frying-pan for 5–10 min. *or* dip in egg and breadcrumbs and fry in deep fat (**360° F.**) 5–7 min. Drain well and serve hot.

4–6 helpings

STUFFED PEPPERS

Piment farci

6 Small *or* 3 large peppers
Stuffing, *see Stuffed cabbage, Stuffed onions, Stuffed tomatoes, or Stuffed vegetable marrow*
1 tablesp. breadcrumbs
A little melted butter *or* margarine

Wash and parboil the peppers as in preceding recipe. Drain, cut in ½ lengthwise and remove seeds. Fill the halved peppers with the stuffing, sprinkle with a few breadcrumbs and a little melted fat. Pack tightly into a greased, fireproof dish and bake for 35 min. in a fairly hot oven (**375° F., Gas 5**).

6 helpings
Cooking time—about 40 min.

POTATOES

ANNA POTATOES

Pommes de terre Anna

2 lb. even-sized waxy potatoes
Salt and pepper
Melted clarified butter *or* margarine

Grease a thick cake-tin and line the bottom with greased paper. Peel and trim the potatoes so that they will give equal sized slices. Slice them very finely and arrange a layer of slightly overlapping slices. Sprinkle with clarified fat and seasoning. Make a second layer of potato and repeat. Continue until the tin is full, pressing each layer well into the tin. Cover with greased paper and a lid and bake in a a fairly hot oven (**375° F., Gas 5**) for about 1 hr. Look at the potatoes from time to time and add more clarified butter if they become dry. Turn out on to a hot dish and serve at once.

6 helpings
Cooking time—about 1 hr.

BAKED POTATOES—IN THEIR JACKETS

Pommes de terre en robe de chambre

6 large potatoes
Butter *or* margarine *or* bacon fat

Scrub the potatoes, rinse and dry them. Brush with melted butter, or margarine or bacon fat or rub with a greasy butter paper. Prick with a fork. Bake on the shelves of a fairly hot oven (**375° F., Gas 5**) until soft—about 1½ hr., turning them whilst they are cooking. Cut a cross in the top of each, insert a pat of butter or margarine. Serve in a hot vegetable dish.

6 helpings **Cooking time—about 1½ hr.**

BAKED AND STUFFED POTATOES

Pommes de terre farcies

6 large potatoes

STUFFING, choice of:

(1) **3 oz. grated cheese; 1 oz. butter *or* margarine; a little milk; seasoning; nutmeg**
(2) **3 oz. chopped, fried bacon; a little milk; seasoning**
(3) **3 oz. mashed, cooked smoked haddock; chopped parsley; lemon juice; a little milk; nutmeg**
(4) **2 boned kippers, cooked and mashed; a little milk**
(5) **2 oz. grated cheese; 1 oz. butter; chopped parsley; a little milk; seasoning; 2 egg yolks stirred into the filling; 2 egg whites folded in at the end**

Scrub, rinse and dry the potatoes and grease as in preceding recipe. With a small sharp knife, cut through the skin of the potatoes to give the appearance of a lid. Bake as for Potatoes in Jackets. Lift off lids carefully, scoop out cooked potato from skins, including lids, taking care not to split the skins. Mash the potato in a basin and add the ingredients of any one of the stuffings listed above. Mix well and season thoroughly. Fill the potato skins with the mixture, piling it high. Fork the tops and brush with a little egg, or sprinkle with a little grated cheese (if an ingredient of the stuffing). Put back in the oven and bake till thoroughly hot and golden brown. Serve in a hot dish garnished with parsley and with the skin "lids" replaced, if liked.

NOTE: A stuffing consisting of cooked minced meat in a sauce or gravy, *or* of cooked mixed vegetables *or* flaked fish in a sauce may replace the floury meal of the potato entirely. The latter should then be mashed and served separately *or* mashed and piped round the opening of the potato after it has been stuffed and before returning it to the oven.

6 helpings
Cooking time—about 2 hr.

BOILED POTATOES

Pommes de terre au naturel

2 lb. even-sized potatoes	**Salt**
	Chopped parsley

Scrub the potatoes. Peel thinly. Rinse and put into a saucepan with sufficient *boiling* water just to cover them and 1 teasp. salt to each quart of water. Boil gently 25–40 min. according to age and size. Test with a fine skewer and if tender, drain off the water and put the saucepan back on a very low heat, with the lid tilted to allow steam to escape. Serve hot, sprinkled with chopped parsley.

NOTE: The potatoes have a better flavour if boiled in their skins. In this case peel off a thin strip of skin, round the middle of each potato. This facilitates skinning after cooking.

6 helpings
Cooking time—25–40 min.

BOILED POTATOES—IRISH WAY

Pommes de terre à l'Irlandaise

2 lb. potatoes	**Salt and pepper**

Boil the potatoes in the usual way but without peeling them. When cooked, add sufficient cold water to the pan to reduce the temperature of the cooking water several degrees below boiling-point. Leave 2–3 min. Pour off the water. Cover the potatoes with a folded cloth, and stand the pan near the heat until the steam has evaporated. Peel them quickly and serve in an uncovered dish, so that the steam can escape, otherwise the potatoes may be watery.

6 helpings **Cooking time—about 40 min.**

DUCHESS POTATOES

Pommes de terre Duchesse

1 lb. old potatoes	**2 yolks *or* 1 whole egg**
1 oz. butter *or* margarine	**Salt and pepper**
Cream *or* top of milk	**Grated nutmeg**

Prepare and cook the potatoes as for Boiled Potatoes. Put through a sieve. Mash with the fat, beaten egg and sufficient cream to give a smooth mixture, which stands up in soft peaks when drawn up with the wooden spoon. Season well and add grated nutmeg. Pipe through a star vegetable pipe, on to a greased baking-sheet. Sprinkle with a little beaten egg and bake in a hot oven (**400° F., Gas 6**), until crisp and brown. Serve in a hot uncovered dish.

NOTE: If a "pipe" is not available, keep the mixture a little stiffer and shape on a floured board into small cork shapes, diamonds, rounds or triangles. Decorate the tops with criss-crosses made with the back of a knife.

If more convenient, the mixture may be shaped or piped on to the tin and left in a cool place for baking at a later time.

6 helpings Cooking time—to bake, 15 min.

MASHED POTATOES

Purée de Pommes de terre

2 lb. potatoes	**A little milk**
1 oz. butter *or* margarine	**Salt and pepper**
Chopped parsley	**Grated nutmeg**

Prepare and cook potatoes as for Boiled Potatoes. Pass them through a wire sieve, *or* through a potato masher, *or* mash with a fork or the end of a rolling-pin. Melt the fat (in one corner of the pan if the potatoes have been mashed in the pan itself) and beat in the potatoes. Add milk gradually and beat well until the mixture is thoroughly hot, and smooth. Season well and add a little grated nutmeg. Serve in a hot dish. Sprinkle with chopped parsley.

NOTE: If mashed potatoes are to be served with sausages, use a little of the sausage fat instead of butter *or* margarine.

Successful mashed potato depends upon the use of a floury type of potato, thorough drying of potatoes after the water has been strained off them, and the thorough mashing of the potatoes before fat and milk are added.

6 helpings
Cooking time—30–45 min.

MASHED POTATOES—FRENCH STYLE

Purée de Pommes de terre à la Pernollet

2 lb. potatoes	**Milk**
1 oz. butter *or* margarine	**Salt and pepper**
	Chopped parsley

Peel potatoes and slice them. Put into a pan, add fat and cover with cold milk. Cook very gently. As soon as they are tender, mash them in the pan. Season and beat well. Serve in a hot dish. Sprinkle with chopped parsley.

NOTE: This is an excellent method for cooking potatoes.

6 helpings
Cooking time—25–30 min.

NEW POTATOES—BOILED

Pommes de terre nouvelles bouillies

2 lb. new potatoes, even-sized	**1 oz. butter *or* margarine**
Salt and pepper	**Parsley**
Mint	

Where possible dig the potatoes just before cooking. Scrub with a stiff brush. (This should be sufficient to remove the skin. If the potatoes are not freshly dug, scrape them to remove skins.) Rinse. Cook as for old potatoes but with mint in the water. When dried, add fat, chopped parsley and chopped mint to the saucepan. Toss the potatoes gently in the fat. Serve hot.

New potatoes are in season from May to July.

4–6 helpings
Cooking time—15–30 min. according to size and freshness

POTATO BALLS or CROQUETTES

Croquettes de Pommes de terre

1 lb. cooked potatoes	**Optional: 1 teasp. chopped parsley *or* 2 tablesp. dry grated cheddar cheese *or* 2 tablesp. grated Parmesan cheese**
1 oz. butter *or* margarine	**Egg and breadcrumbs**
2 egg yolks *or* 1 whole egg	**Deep fat**
Salt and pepper	

Put the potatoes through a sieve and mash in a saucepan with the fat, beaten egg, and parsley or cheese if used. Season well. Form into small balls or into rolls. Coat twice with egg and crumbs. Fry in hot deep fat at 380° F., for 4–5 min. Drain well and serve immediately.

6 helpings

POTATOES—BAKED IN FAT

Pommes de terre rôties

2 lb. even-sized potatoes	**Salt and pepper**
	Dripping

Peel the potatoes and cut in halves or even

in quarters if very large. Parboil and strain off the water and dry the potatoes over a low heat. Put into hot dripping in a roasting-tin, or in the tin containing the roast joint. Roll the potatoes in the fat and cook till tender and brown.

Cooking time—to parboil, 10 min.; to bake, 1 hr. (approx.)

POTATOES—GERMAN METHOD OF COOKING

Pommes de terre à l'Allemande

2 lb. medium-sized potatoes
2 oz. butter *or* margarine
2 oz. flour
2 tablesp. vinegar
¾ pt. stock
Salt and pepper

Peel and slice the potatoes thinly. Brown the flour lightly in the fat and make a sauce with the stock and vinegar. Bring to the boil, season. Add the sliced potatoes and simmer very gently until tender. Serve hot.

6 helpings
Cooking time—about 25 min.

POTATOES WITH CHEESE

Pommes de terre au gratin

2 lb. potatoes
1 oz. butter *or* margarine
¼ pt. milk
2–3 oz. dry grated Cheddar *or* Parmesan cheese
Salt
Cayenne pepper

Cook, then mash the potatoes smoothly with the fat and milk. Stir in the cheese. Season well. Put into a greased pie-dish. Sprinkle the top with grated cheese. Reheat and brown under the grill or in the top of a hot oven.

5–6 helpings
Cooking time—45 min.

FRIED POTATOES

Potatoes may be fried in any of the following ways.

LYONNAISE POTATOES

Pommes de terre Lyonnaise

2 lb. potatoes
½ lb. onions
3 oz. butter *or* margarine
Chopped parsley
Salt and pepper

Cook the potatoes in their skins until nearly soft. Peel and slice thinly. Slice the onions thinly across and cook them slowly in the butter in a frying-pan until just golden coloured. Remove the onions and keep them hot. Toss the potatoes in the fat as for Sauté Potatoes. Add the onions to them and mix. Season well with salt and pepper. Serve in a hot dish and sprinkle with chopped parsley.

6 helpings
Cooking time—to fry, 15 min.

PARISIAN POTATOES

Pommes de terre Parisienne

2 lb. potatoes
2–3 oz. butter *or* margarine
Salt

Scrub, rinse and peel the potatoes. Using a round vegetable scoop, scoop small balls from the potatoes. Boil them until nearly tender and drain them well. Heat the butter in a frying-pan or sauté pan and fry the potatoes in it, tossing them all the time until they are brown. Season and serve.

6 helpings
Cooking time—to fry, about 10 min.

POTATO CHIPS and POTATO STRAWS

Pommes de terre frites à l'Anglaise and *Pommes de terre en Allumettes*

6 medium-sized potatoes
Deep fat
Salt

Scrub and rinse the potatoes. Peel them thinly. For chips—cut into sticks about 2 in. long and ½ in. wide and thick. For straws—cut into strips the size of a wooden match. Drop them into cold water as they are cut. Rinse and drain and dry in a clean cloth. Put them into the frying-basket and lower them gently into hot deep fat at 360° F. (Keep the heat fairly high as the potatoes will have cooled the fat.) When the potatoes are soft but *not*

PLATE 13
Egg Dishes

Cheese soufflé (see page 578) a most appetising hot savoury.

Left, a jam omelet (see page 407) and an example of an English-type omelet. Centre, an omelette fines herbes (see page 687), and an excellent example of a French omelette. Right, a plate of meringues (see page 539) for afternoon tea.

PLATE 14

Dressing a Crab

1 Wipe the crab with a damp cloth and remove the claws and legs by twisting inwards and towards you. 2 Place the thumbs under the tail flap and push upwards until the body breaks away from the shell. 3 and 4 Remove the mouth and stomach bag with the thumbs as shown. 5 Ease round the inside of the shell to loosen the meat, and turn it into a basin.

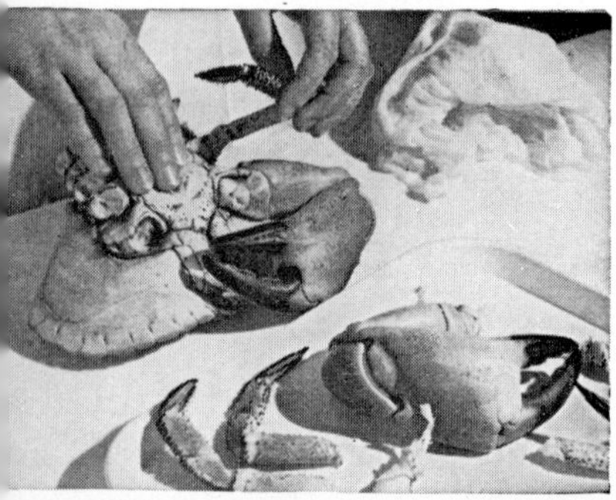
1

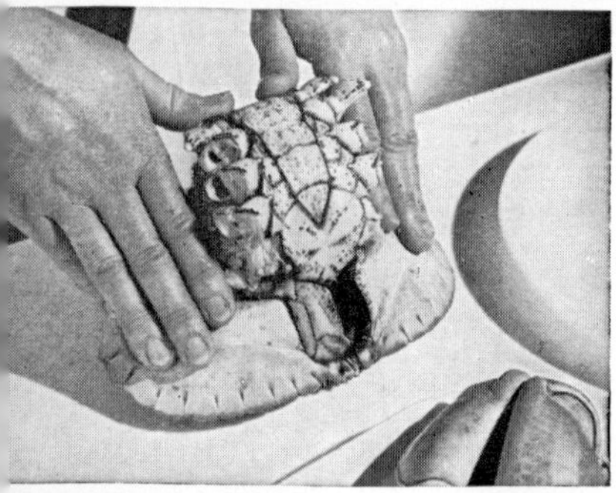
2

3

4

5

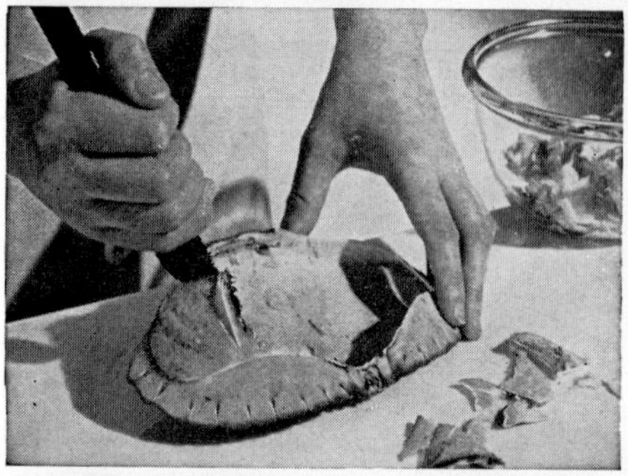
6

7

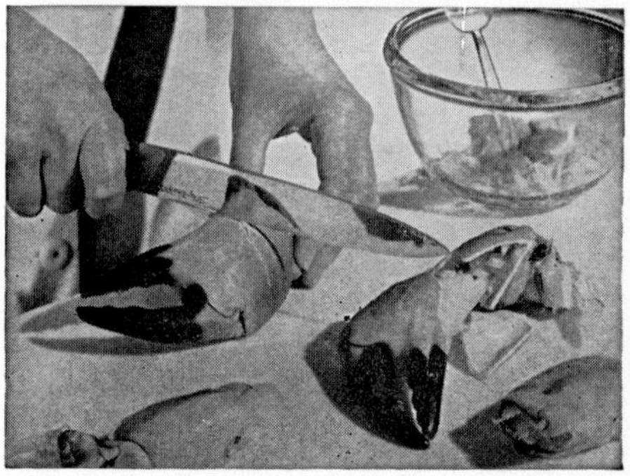
8

6 Trim shell by tapping 'false' line round shell cavity with a knife handle and press with the thumbs till edges of shell wall break away. 7 Remove 'dead men's fingers'. Remove meat. Scoop white meat from leg sockets, keeping free of bone. 8 Twist off joint from both claws and empty meat into a basin. With the back of a heavy knife tap sharply round the centre of the broadest part of the claws till the shell cracks apart.

brown—about 3 min. for chips and 1 min. for straws—lift out the basket and heat the fat to 375° F. Put back the basket and leave in the fat until the potatoes are crisp and golden brown—about 3 min. for chips and 2 min. for straws.

Drain on absorbent paper, sprinkle with salt and serve immediately.

NOTE: If potato chips or straws are to be served with fried fish or any other fried dish, the second frying of the potatoes to brown and crisp them should be done after the fish, etc., is fried. In this way the potatoes will be sent to table in their best condition.

6 helpings
Cooking time—for chips, about 6 min.
for straws, about 3 min.

POTATO CRISPS

6 egg-sized, waxy potatoes	**Deep fat**
	Salt

Scrub and rinse the potatoes but do not peel unless the skins are very tough and blemished. Slice very thinly with a sharp knife or on a potato slicer bought for the purpose. Drop them into cold water as they are cut. Drain and rinse and dry well between the folds of a clean cloth. Sprinkle gradually into hot deep fat, at 320° F., and fry till golden and crisp. Remove from the fat as they brown and drain on absorbent paper. Keep them hot while frying the rest. Sprinkle with salt.

They can be kept in an air-tight tin for some time and be reheated when necessary.

NOTE: To the professional cook or chef these are known as "chips". They are served with grills and with poultry and game but may also be served with many meat and fish dishes.

6 helpings
Cooking time—3–4 min.

SAUTÉ or TOSSED POTATOES

Pommes de terre sautées

6 medium-sized potatoes (waxy ones)	**1–2 oz. butter or margarine**
	Seasoning

Cook the potatoes, preferably in their skins, until only just soft. Let them dry thoroughly then peel and slice them ¼-in. thick. Heat the fat in a frying-pan and put in the potatoes. Season them with salt and pepper. Toss in the fat until they are light brown and have absorbed all the fat.

Serve at once.

4–6 helpings

PUMPKIN

Pumpkin may be served as a vegetable *or* as the main ingredient of the filling for Pumpkin Pie *or* with equal quantities of apple as a Pumpkin and Apple Pie.

Pumpkin is in season from July to October.

FRIED PUMPKIN

Potiron frit

2 very small pumpkins
Coating batter (double quantity), *see Fried Artichoke Bottoms* (p. 325) *or* **yeast batter,** *see Fried Brussels Sprouts* (p. 332) *or* **egg and breadcrumbs**

Peel and boil the pumpkins in salt and water until tender. Drain well. Cut into 1½-in. squares or into strips, remove the seeds. Coat with egg and crumbs *or* dip in batter and fry in deep hot fat at 340° F. Turn them during frying as they will float, and when golden brown remove from the fat. Drain well, serve hot.

6 helpings
Cooking time—to fry, 7 min.

MASHED PUMPKIN

Purée de potirons

2 young pumpkins	**2 tablesp. milk** *or* **cream**
1 oz. butter *or* **margarine**	**Salt and pepper**
	Chopped parsley

Prepare the pumpkins and cook them as in Vegetable Marrow—Conservatively Cooked (p. 360). Drain off any liquid left in the pan and reserve it for a soup or gravy. Mash pumpkins with a fork or masher or rub through a nylon sieve. Heat the fat in the pan and beat in the pumpkin purée. Add the milk *or* cream. Stir over heat until thoroughly hot, season well. Serve in a hot dish and sprinkle with chopped parsley.

6 helpings
Cooking time—about 30 min.

PUMPKIN PIE

½ pt. pumpkin (cooked and sieved)
¼ teasp. ground ginger
¼ teasp. nutmeg
Good pinch of cinnamon
3 eggs
2 tablesp. brandy
¼ pt. milk (approx.)
4 oz. castor sugar (approx.)
Short crust pastry (p. 557), **using 8 oz. flour, etc.**

Put the pumpkin in a mixing-bowl. Stir in the spices, the well beaten eggs, the brandy and sufficient milk to give a consistency of thick batter. Sweeten to taste. Turn into a deep 9-in. pie-plate lined with pastry. Cover with pastry. Bake in a fairly hot oven (**375° F., Gas 5**) about 45 min. Serve hot.

Note: Pumpkins should be peeled, sliced and the seeds removed before boiling in slightly salted water until tender.

5–6 helpings

RADISHES (*Radis*)

Although generally eaten raw, radishes can be used very successfully as a flavouring and as a garnish in place of turnip, particularly when turnips are poor in quality or when new turnips are very expensive.

Radish tops are a valuable source of Vitamin C and may be cooked as a green vegetable.

SALSIFY, SALSAFY or VEGETABLE OYSTER

This vegetable is very popular on the European continent. It is an excellent root vegetable. The name Vegetable Oyster or Oyster Plant was given to it many years ago when it must have had a flavour somewhat resembling oysters. It does not possess that flavour today.

The young leaves of salsify may be used in salads.

Salsify is seasonable from December to March.

BOILED SALSIFY

Salsifis bouillis

2 lb. salsify
White vinegar *or* lemon juice
Salt
¾ pt. white *or* Béchamel Sauce

Wash and scrape the roots, using vinegar or lemon juice in the water (see Boiled Jerusalem Artichokes). Scrape gently so that only the outside peel is removed. Cut into 4-in. lengths, cook and serve as for Jerusalem Artichokes.

6 helpings **Cooking time—30–40 min.**

FRIED SALSIFY (1)

Salsifis frits

1½ lb. salsify
Coating batter (double quantity), *see Fried Artichoke bottoms,* *or* **yeast batter**
Fried parsley

Prepare and parboil the salsify (about 15 min.). Cut them into slices ½ in. thick and season them well. Make the batter, dip in the slices of salsify and fry in hot fat, at 340° F., until golden brown (5–7 min.), turning them during cooking. Drain well and serve very hot with fried parsley.

6 helpings
Cooking time—15 min. to parboil salsify, 5–7 min. to fry them

FRIED SALSIFY (2)

6 salsify
1–2 oz. butter *or* margarine
Seasoning

Cook the salsify, preferably in their skins, until only just soft. Let them dry thoroughly then peel and slice them ¼ in. thick. Heat the fat in a frying-pan and put in the salsify. Season them with salt and pepper. Toss in the fat until they are light brown and have absorbed all the fat. Serve at once.

4–6 helpings

SAVOY

See recipes for cooking Cabbage.

SEAKALE

This is an excellent vegetable and can be used raw in salads, or cooked and served with a good sauce. It grows in the wild state on the beaches of certain parts of Hampshire and on the sea-coasts of Western Europe. Its high price when bought probably prevents cultivated seakale from being a more popular vegetable.

Seakale is in season from December to May.

BOILED SEAKALE

Chou-marin bouilli

2 lb. seakale
Salt

¾ pt. white sauce (p. 115) *or* **¾ pt. Béchamel sauce** (p. 128) *or* **½ pt. Hollandaise sauce** (p. 126) *or* **melted, seasoned butter**

Cut off the stump and any broken or discoloured leaves. Wash. Tie into bundles. Cook very gently in just enough boiling, salted water to cover, until tender, 25–30 min. Seakale hardens if cooked longer. Drain and serve with melted butter, or coat with one of the sauces suggested.

6 helpings
Cooking time—25–30 min.

SORREL

Sorrel is in season from May to October.

SORREL PURÉE

Purée d'oseille

3 lb. sorrel
1 oz. butter *or* **margarine**
1–2 tablesp. cream
A little flour
Salt and pepper

Pick over the sorrel, remove the stalks and wash it in several waters. Put into a large saucepan enough water to cover the bottom. Bring to the boil. Add the sorrel and cook it gently about 20 min., turning it over and pressing it down repeatedly with a spoon, to equalize the cooking. Drain well and rub through a fine sieve. Return it to the pan with the butter, cream and salt and pepper. Stir over heat for about 8 min., dredging in gradually enough flour to give a thick consistency.

NOTE: A little sugar may be added during cooking to counteract the acidity of the vegetable. Sorrel is excellent served with eggs, veal or white fish.

6 helpings **Cooking time—about 30 min.**

SPINACH

Spinach is in season all the year as there is a winter and summer variety.

BOILED SPINACH (1)

Épinards en Branches

3 lb. spinach
1 oz. butter *or* **margarine**
2 tablesp. cream (optional)
Salt and pepper

Pick over the spinach carefully and wash it in at least 3 waters. Break off the stalks and at the same time pull off the central ribs if coarse. (Young, summer spinach need not be stripped of the central ribs.) Put the wet leaves into a saucepan, without additional water. Cook slowly until tender, about 15 min., stirring the spinach in the pan occasionally. The pan should have a tightly-fitting lid. Drain well, pressing out the water. Reheat in the butter. Add the cream, if used, and mix it well with the spinach. Season and serve hot.

5–6 helpings
Cooking time—about 25 min.

BOILED SPINACH (2)

Purée d'Épinards

3 lb. spinach **Salt and pepper**
(*a*) **1 oz. butter** *or* **margarine and a little cream** *or*
(*b*) **a roux: 1 oz. butter** *or* **margarine and 1 oz. flour** *or*
(*c*) **a panada: 2 rounded teasp. cornflour and 1 gill spinach liquor**

GARNISH

Fleurons of pastry, ***or*** **sieved egg yolk,** ***or*** **crescents of fried bread**

Cook as for Boiled Spinach (1) and drain well. Chop finely with a stainless knife or rub through a hair, nylon or stainless metal sieve. Reheat with either (*a*) the butter and a little cream if liked, *or* (*b*) with the roux, *or* (*c*) with the panada. Season well. Serve hot. Garnish if liked, with fleurons of pastry, sieved egg yolk *or* crescents of fried bread.

NOTE: If the spinach is to be sieved, the central rib need not be stripped from the spinach. A little grated nutmeg may be added for additional flavour.

5–6 helpings **Cooking time—25 min.**

SPINACH—ITALIAN STYLE

Épinards à l'Italienne

2 lb. spinach	**Salt and pepper**
2 tablesp. olive oil	**1 oz. sultanas**
1 clove of garlic	**1 oz. pine kernel nuts**

Cook the spinach, press out the water well, and chop the spinach coarsely. Warm the oil in a wide pan. Add the spinach, finely-chopped garlic, salt and pepper. Turn the spinach over and over in the pan to heat it thoroughly without frying it. Add the sultanas, washed in boiling water to make them plump, and the nuts.

Reheat and serve hot.

4–6 helpings **Cooking time—about 30 min.**

SPINACH SOUFFLÉ

Soufflé aux Épinards

½ pt. spinach purée	**3 eggs**
Good 1 oz. butter *or* **margarine**	**Salt and pepper**
Good 1 oz. flour	**1 egg white**

Melt the butter and stir in the flour. Cook for a few seconds without browning. Add the spinach purée and boil till thick. Cool slightly. Add the 3 beaten egg yolks and season. Fold in the 4 stiffly whipped egg whites. Turn into a greased pie-dish *or* china *or* fireproof soufflé case. Bake in a moderate oven (**350° F., Gas 4**) about 45 min.

4–5 helpings

SPINACH WITH POACHED EGGS

Épinards au œufs pochés

Spinach purée (as in Boiled Spinach (2))	**Fleurons of pastry** *or* **crescents of fried bread**
6 poached eggs	

Poach the eggs in as plump a form as possible. Trim the edges and put the trimmings on the bottom of a hot dish. Serve the spinach on top, flattening the surface. Arrange the poached eggs on it, garnish the base with fleurons of pastry *or* crescents of fried bread.

SPRING GREENS

(*See Cabbage*, p. 333)

SWEET POTATOES

Sweet potatoes may be served as a vegetable or in the sweet course and are in season from September through the winter.

BAKED SWEET POTATOES

6 even-sized sweet potatoes	**Butter** *or* **margarine**
	Salt and pepper

Scrub the potatoes well and rub them all over with a greasy butter or margarine paper. Bake in a fairly hot oven (**375° F., Gas 5**), until soft. Serve with butter, salt and pepper or scrape out the soft inside, mash with butter, season and serve hot.

6 helpings
Cooking time—about 1 hr.

SWEET POTATO FRITTERS

¾ lb. sweet potatoes	**Salt**
2 oz. butter *or* **margarine**	**Egg and breadcrumbs**
	Deep fat
1½ oz. flour	**Sugar**
2 large eggs	**Ground cinnamon**

Bake the potatoes as in preceding recipe. Mash the floury potato meal very thoroughly and add to it the melted butter, flour, beaten eggs and a little salt. Beat well over a low heat. Cool the mixture, then shape into small flat cakes. Coat twice with egg and breadcrumbs. Fry in deep fat at 380° F. for 3–4 min. until golden brown. Drain well and serve as a sweet with sugar and cinnamon.

6 helpings
Cooking time—to fry, about 4 min.

TOMATOES

BAKED TOMATOES

Tomates rôties

6 large tomatoes
A little butter *or* margarine
Salt and pepper
Castor sugar
Finely-chopped tarragon (optional)

Wash the tomatoes and cut them in halves. Put them in a greased, deep fireproof dish. Season and sprinkle each with a pinch of sugar and a pinch of chopped tarragon, if used. Put a tiny piece of butter on each or cover with a well greased paper. Bake in a moderate oven (**350° F., Gas 4**) until soft—about 20 min.

6 helpings

DEVILLED TOMATOES

Tomates à la Diable

6 tomatoes
2 oz. butter *or* margarine
Yolks of 2 hard-boiled eggs
Salt
Cayenne pepper
½ teasp. mixed mustard
A little sugar
2 tablesp. vinegar
2 eggs

Peel and slice the tomatoes and cook them slowly in a saucepan with ½ oz. of the butter. Mix the rest of the butter with the hard-boiled egg yolks, stir in the salt, pepper, mustard, about 1 saltsp. of sugar and the vinegar. Lastly add the beaten eggs. Put the mixture into another small pan and stir over a gentle heat until it thickens. Re-season. Place the tomatoes in a hot dish and pour the sauce over them.

5–6 helpings
Cooking time—about 30 min.

FRIED TOMATOES

Tomates frites

6 large tomatoes
Butter *or* margarine *or* bacon fat for frying
Salt and pepper

Wash the tomatoes and cut in halves. Fry in hot fat, turning them once during frying. Season. Serve hot.

6 helpings
Cooking time—about 6 min.

SCALLOPED TOMATOES

Tomates en Coquille

1 lb. ripe tomatoes
1 oz. butter *or* margarine
1 teasp. finely-chopped onion
3 tablesp. fine breadcrumbs
Sugar
Nutmeg
Salt and pepper

Scald the tomatoes for 1 min. in boiling water. Cut them in slices, roughly, and rub through a fine hair, nylon or stainless metal sieve. Heat ½ oz. of the butter in a pan and fry the onion in it until lightly browned. Add the tomato pulp and cook for a few minutes. Stir in 2 tablesp. of the crumbs, a good pinch each of sugar and freshly grated nutmeg. Heat and stir the mixture well. Season. Pour into greased, deep scallop shells. Sprinkle with the rest of the crumbs and finally with the remaining ½ oz. butter, melted. Bake near the top of a fairly hot oven (**375° F., Gas 5**) or under the grill until golden brown.

6 shells
Cooking time—in the oven, 15 min.; under the grill, 5 min.

STUFFED TOMATOES

Tomates farcies

6 large firm tomatoes
1 teasp. finely-chopped onion
1 teasp. finely-chopped mushroom
½ oz. butter *or* margarine
1 heaped tablesp. finely-chopped cooked ham
1 tablesp. fresh breadcrumbs
½ teasp. chopped parsley
Salt and pepper
1 teasp. dry grated cheese
6 rounds of fried *or* toasted bread

Wash and dry the tomatoes. Cut a small round from each tomato at the end opposite the stalk. Scoop out the centre with the handle of a teaspoon. Fry the onion and the mushroom in the butter or margarine until cooked. Add the ham, crumbs, parsley and sufficient tomato pulp to bind the mixture. Season well. Fill the tomatoes with the mixture, piling some on top. Bake in a moderate oven (**350° F., Gas 4**) until the tomatoes are soft—about 20 min. Sprinkle the tops with cheese, replace the lids and serve on the fried or toasted bread. Garnish with parsley.

NOTE: For alternative fillings see Stuffed Cabbage, p. 333, Stuffed Vegetable Marrow, p. 359.

For a vegetarian filling replace the ham and cheese in the above recipe with chopped mushrooms *or* chopped nut meat.

6 helpings
Cooking time—to bake, about 20 min.

TURNIPS AND SWEDE-TURNIPS

Swedes differ from turnips in that the flesh is orange in colour, and not the pure white of that of the turnip. Swedes have a sweeter, milder flavour than the turnip. There are two varieties of turnip—the summer ones, which do not store well and are pulled when about the size of a tennis ball, and main crop turnips, which are much larger in size and are left in the ground or pulled about November for storage. Swedes are left in the ground to mature fully and are always large in size.

In certain parts of England, e.g. Cornwall, the term "turnip" is applied to the orange-fleshed swede, the white turnip finding no favour there.

Swedes may be cooked and served in all the ways described later for turnips except where the recipe requires small young turnips.

They are in season in late autumn and winter.

TURNIPS—CONSERVATIVELY COOKED

2 lb. turnips
1 oz. butter *or* margarine
½ teasp. salt
½-1 gill boiling water
Chopped parsley

Scrub and peel the turnips thickly. If large, cut into quarters, then slice thinly (if young turnips, slice the whole turnip). Fat steam the turnips for 10 min., i.e. shake them in the melted fat, well below frying temperature with the lid on the pan until the fat is absorbed. Add the liquid and the salt, and simmer gently until the turnips are tender, 15–30 min. according to age of turnips. Serve hot with the small amount of liquid remaining, and garnished with chopped parsley.

6 helpings

GLAZED TURNIPS

Navets glacés

1½ lb. young turnips
2 oz. butter
3 lumps sugar
¼ teasp. salt
Good stock
Parsley

Melt the butter in a saucepan. Add the scraped, whole turnips, sugar, salt and enough stock to come halfway up the turnips. Cook gently, without a lid, shaking the pan occasionally, until tender. Remove the turnips and keep them hot. Boil the stock rapidly until reduced to a rich glaze. Replace the turnips 2–3 at a time, turn them until both sides are well coated with glaze. Dish, sprinkle with chopped parsley and serve.

6 helpings
Cooking time—about ¾ hr.

MASHED TURNIPS

Purée de Navets

2 lb. turnips
1 oz. butter *or* margarine
2 tablesp. milk
Salt and pepper
Chopped parsley

Prepare the turnips and cook them as in Turnips—Conservatively Cooked. Drain off any liquid left in the pan and reserve it for a soup or gravy. Mash turnips with a fork or rub through a nylon sieve. Heat the butter or margarine in a pan and beat in the purée, add the milk. Stir over heat until thoroughly hot. Season well. Serve in a hot vegetable dish and sprinkle with chopped parsley.

6 helpings
Cooking time—35–50 min.

STUFFED TURNIPS

Navets farcis

6 even-sized, young turnips	**1 tablesp. breadcrumbs**
4 tablesp. finely-chopped liver *or* cooked ham *or* any cooked meat	**½ teasp. finely-chopped fresh sage *or* ½ teasp. dried sage**
1 tablesp. finely-chopped cooked onion	**Salt and pepper**
	1 egg
	Butter *or* margarine
	¾ pt. brown sauce (p. 119)

Peel and steam the turnips gently until almost soft—about 1 hr. Lift out the centre of each turnip with a teaspoon handle. Chop the turnip centres and add to the stuffing. Mix the stuffing ingredients with the beaten egg. Season well. Press the stuffing firmly into each turnip and pile neatly on top. Sprinkle the top of each turnip with a little melted butter *or* margarine. Pin a band of stiff, greased paper round each turnip to prevent splitting. Put into a greased, fireproof dish and bake 30–40 min. in a moderate oven (**350° F., Gas 4**).

Serve with the sauce poured round.

6 helpings
Cooking time—about 1¾ hr.

TURNIPS WITH CREAM

Navets à la crème

As for Turnips—Conservatively Cooked. Stir in 1 tablesp. cream just before serving.

6 helpings
Cooking time—20–35 min.

TURNIP GREENS

These, when young, provide a most pleasant green vegetable, very rich in Vitamin C.

The stalks should be removed and the leaves shredded and cooked like cabbage.

VEGETABLE MARROW

Vegetable marrows should be cut and used as a vegetable when small and young. The tiny French marrows known as "Courgettes" and the Italian "Zucchini" are better flavoured, and much more interesting as a vegetable than the large English marrow. Vegetable marrow is in season from July to October.

FRIED VEGETABLE MARROW

Courge frite

2 very small marrows
Coating batter (double quantity), *see Fried Artichoke Bottoms* (p. 325) *or* **yeast batter,** *see Fried Brussels Sprouts* (p. 332) *or* **egg and breadcrumbs**

Peel and boil the marrows in salt and water until tender. Drain well. Cut into 1½ in. squares or into strips, remove the seeds. Coat with egg and breadcrumbs *or* dip in batter and fry in deep hot fat at 340° F. Turn them during frying as they will float, and when golden brown remove from the fat. Drain well, serve hot.

6 helpings
Cooking time—to fry, 7 min.

MASHED VEGETABLE MARROW

Purée de Courge

2 young marrows	**2 tablesp. milk *or* cream**
1 oz. butter *or* margarine	**Salt and pepper**
	Chopped parsley

Prepare the marrows and cook them as in Vegetable Marrow—Conservatively Cooked. Drain off any liquid left in the pan and reserve it for a soup or gravy. Mash marrows with a fork or masher, or rub through a nylon sieve. Heat the fat in the pan and beat in the purée. Add the milk *or* cream. Stir over heat until thoroughly hot. Season well. Serve in a hot dish and sprinkle with chopped parsley.

6 helpings
Cooking time—about 30 min.

STUFFED VEGETABLE MARROW

Courge farcie

2 small vegetable marrows	**¾ pt. brown sauce *or* tomato sauce**

STUFFING

1 small finely-chopped onion	**1 tablesp. chopped parsley**
½ lb. cooked ham *or* nut meat for vegetarians	**2 oz. breadcrumbs**
	1 egg
	Seasoning
6 mushrooms, chopped	**1 gill stock (approx.)**
2 oz. butter *or* margarine	

COATING

Browned crumbs	**Melted butter *or* margarine**

Peel the marrows and cut into halves lengthwise *or* cut into rings, about 2 in. thick. Remove the seeds with a tablespoon and steam the marrow until almost soft. Drain carefully. Fry the chopped mushrooms and onion in the butter until cooked—about 10 min. Add all the other ingredients and bind with the egg and enough stock to make a soft stuffing. Season well. Stuff the marrow halves or rings of marrow with filling. Sprinkle browned crumbs on top, then a little melted butter. Bake in a fairly hot oven (**375° F., Gas 5**). Serve with brown *or* tomato sauce.

6 helpings
Cooking time—about 1 hr.

VEGETABLE MARROW—CONSERVATIVELY COOKED

2 small marrows	**½ teasp. salt**
1 oz. butter *or* margarine	**¾ pt. white sauce**
½–1 gill boiling water	

Peel the marrows. Cut into halves lengthwise and scrape out the seeds and pith with a tablespoon. Cut into pieces, about 2 in. square. Fat steam the pieces for 10 min., i.e. shake them in the melted fat, well below frying temperature with the lid on the pan until the fat is absorbed. Add the liquid and the salt, and simmer gently until the marrow is tender, about 15 min. Drain well, retaining the cooking liquor for use in making the white sauce. Dish the marrow in a hot dish and coat with the sauce. Serve immediately.

6 helpings
Cooking time—about 25 min.

YAMS

The yam resembles the potato but has a thicker skin and often weighs as much as 2 lb. The flesh is very white and floury when cooked and is sweeter in flavour than potato.

BAKED YAMS

Ignames rôties

Yams	**Salt and pepper**
Butter *or* margarine	

Scrub and rinse the yams. Bake in a fairly hot oven (**375° F., Gas 5**) until soft. Serve with butter, salt and pepper.

1 yam for 2 to 3 helpings
Cooking time—about 2 hr.

BOILED YAMS

Ignames au naturel

Yams	**Salt**

Scrub, peel and rinse the yams. Boil as for potatoes (p. 350). Drain dry and serve *or* mash as potatoes.

NOTE: Yams may also be cooked in most of the ways suitable for potatoes.

1 yam for 2 to 3 helpings
Cooking time—about 35 min.

MIXED VEGETABLES

MIXED VEGETABLES—CONSERVATIVELY COOKED

1½ lb. mixed vegetables:
In winter: **parsnip, turnip, carrot, leek, cauliflower**
In summer: **new carrots, new turnips, broad beans, peas, spring onions, tomato**

1 oz. butter *or* margarine	**Salt and pepper**
	Chopped parsley
½–1 gill boiling water	

Prepare all the vegetables. Cut the winter vegetables into thin slices, cutting the slices in halves or quarters when large. Break the cauliflower into sprigs. Leave most of the summer vegetables whole, cutting the carrots in thick slices, if not really small, trimming the spring onions rather short and cutting the tomatoes into wedges. Melt the fat in a saucepan. Add the vegetables to it at intervals, starting with the ones which take the longest time to cook. Put the lid on the pan after each addition and toss the vegetables in the fat. (Do not add the tomatoes to the summer vegetables until 5 min. before serving.) Add the liquid and the salt (use very little water with the summer vegetables), and simmer gently until the vegetables are tender. Serve hot, sprinkled with chopped parsley.

NOTE: Although vegetables are mixed in a salad, a dish of mixed cooked vegetables is infrequently served. The combination of flavours is most pleasing particularly where very little water is used as in this method of cooking.

6 helpings
Cooking time—winter vegetables, about ¾ hr.
summer vegetables, about ½ hr.

MIXED VEGETABLES FOR GARNISH

Macédoine de Légumes

Carrots	**Cauliflower**
Turnips	**French *or* runner beans**
Peas	**Salt**

Wash and scrape or peel the carrots and turnips. Dice them very neatly or cut out small balls with a vegetable scoop. Wash and divide cauliflower into neat sprigs. Cut beans into diamond shapes. Cook each vegetable separately in the minimum of boiling salted water until just tender. Drain well. Use one vegetable only as a garnish *or* mixtures of any *or* all of the above.

MIXED VEGETABLES WITH CHEESE

Légumes au gratin

Conservatively cooked mixed vegetables (p. 360)	**1 heaped tablesp. dry grated Cheddar cheese *or* 1 dessertsp. dry grated Cheddar cheese *and* 1 dessertsp. grated Parmesan cheese**
¾ pt. cheese sauce	

After cooking the vegetables drain off any cooking liquor. Make the cheese sauce, using up the cooking liquor. Coat the vegetables with the sauce, sprinkle with grated cheese and immediately brown under a hot grill or in the top of a hot oven.

NOTE: If the mixture of vegetables is stirred into enough thick cheese sauce to bind it, it can be used as a very pleasant vegetarian stuffing for peppers, marrow and potatoes.

6 helpings
Cooking time—about 1 hr.

MIXED VEGETABLES—CURRIED

Légumes en Kari

Conservatively cooked vegetables,	**¾ pt. curry sauce** (p. 123)
	6 oz. boiled, dry, Patna rice

After cooking the vegetables, drain off any cooking liquor. Make the curry sauce, using up the vegetable liquor, and let it simmer for at least 2 hr. Reheat the cooked vegetables carefully in it. Flavour carefully. Serve with a separate dish of hot, dry rice and any of the usual accompaniments for curry.

6 helpings **Cooking time—about 3 hr.**

VEGETABLE PIE

Pâté aux Légumes

Conservatively cooked vegetables	**8 oz. well-cooked haricot beans *or* a small can of nut meat**
Meat extract	
1 teasp. mixed herbs	**Short pastry using 8 oz. flour, etc. *or* 8 oz. cheese pastry *or* 1½ lb. mashed potatoes**

After cooking the vegetables, stir in the herbs, meat extract, beans, or nut meat cut in small cubes. Put into a pie-dish and cover with pastry *or* mashed potato. (If mashed potato is used, decorate the surface and dot with small pieces of fat). Bake in a fairly hot oven (**400° F., Gas 6**) until the pastry is cooked or the potato browned.

6 helpings
Cooking time—about 40 min. in the oven if pastry is used.
about 25 min. in the oven if potato is used.

SALADS

ALTHOUGH LETTUCE frequently forms the foundation of salads, there are few vegetables and edible plants that may not be used in salad-making. Originally a salad consisted of uncooked, edible leaves of various plants but today the name is applied to mixtures which may include cooked and uncooked vegetables, herbs, fruits, meat and fish.

On the Continent mixtures of cold, cooked vegetables are made into tempting salads, a practice which, apart from the use of cold cooked beetroots and potatoes, is rarely to be found in England. Cooked peas, beans, carrots, cauliflower sprigs and parsnips can be made into very pleasing salads, with the addition of watercress or fine cress and chopped parsley to add Vitamin C and green colour.

In France a salad is composed of one vegetable only, for the French cook will on no account mix two or more vegetables or salad plants. Dressed with oil, wine vinegar and seasoning the delicate flavour of the individual plant is fully appreciated.

In America fruits of all kinds are mixed with vegetables in a salad so that it is sometimes a little difficult to decide whether the salad forms part of a savoury or sweet course. Fruits such as grapefruit, orange, pineapple, grapes, used in moderation, provide a most refreshing addition to a vegetable salad. Dried fruits such as raisins, chopped dates or figs are also most pleasing in a salad.

To ensure success in salad making it is essential that all vegetables and fruits used are in perfect condition. Leafy salad plants should be young, crisp and freshly gathered. They must be properly washed in several waters or under running water. As much water should be removed as possible, after washing, by shaking the plants in a salad shaker or colander, allowing them to drain well and then drying in a clean cloth held by the corners. If possible they should be put into a covered container in the refrigerator to crisp them before use. Lettuce leaves, which need to be mixed into a salad should always be cut with a stainless knife or torn with the fingers.

Vegetables which are usually eaten cooked, should be very finely divided when to be eaten raw in a salad, or they will be indigestible. Carrots and young turnips should be grated; cabbage should be finely chopped; and cauliflower grated or broken into tiny sprigs.

All salads should be mixed with a dressing just before serving. The dressing adds considerably to their flavour, digestibility and food value.

Salads offer considerable scope for the cook to show her skill and initiative in producing a cool, inviting and dainty dish.

A. FRUIT AND VEGETABLE SALADS

APPLE AND CUCUMBER SALAD

Salade de pommes et Concombres

1 cucumber
3 dessert apples
Salt and pepper
Lemon juice
Cream *or* evaporated milk
Finely-chopped mint (optional)

Slice the cucumber thinly; quarter, core and slice the apples. Season lightly and sprinkle with lemon juice. Stir in a little cream *or* evaporated milk. Pile in a salad bowl. Sprinkle with a little mint, if liked.

6 helpings

APPLE AND POTATO SALAD

Salade de pommes aux pommes de terre

3 dessert apples
3 cooked potatoes
French dressing (flavoured with mustard)
Chopped chives
Chopped parsley

Cut the apples and potatoes into small dice. Mix and dress with French dressing. Pile in a salad bowl and garnish with chives and parsley.

4–6 helpings

APPLE, CELERY AND NUT SALAD

Salade de pommes, céleri et de noix

2 cooking apples
4 oz. black *or* white grapes
1 large *or* 2 small celery hearts
Mayonnaise sauce *or* salad dressing
6 crisp lettuce leaves (preferably Cos)
6 walnuts

Quarter, core and slice the apples thinly; halve the grapes and remove the pips; cut the celery into shreds. Mix together lightly with mayonnaise or salad dressing. Pile the mixture into the lettuce leaves and garnish with halved walnuts.

NOTE: Oranges may be substituted for apples.

6 helpings

APPLES FILLED WITH BANANA AND NUT SALAD

Salade de Bananès aux Pommes

6 small rosy apples
4 lettuce leaves
1 tablesp. coarsely-chopped nuts
2 bananas
Salad dressing
Watercress *or* fine cress

Wash and dry the apples; cut a small piece off the top of each, and carefully scoop out most of the inside with a teaspoon. Shred the lettuce leaves and mix very lightly with nuts, sliced banana, a little of the apple pulp (chopped), and salad dressing. Fill the polished apple cases with the mixture. Serve on individual plates, decorating each with watercress or tiny bunches of fine cress.

6 helpings

BANANA SALAD

Salade de Bananes

6 bananas
Lemon juice
Mayonnaise sauce *or* salad dressing
Chopped parsley
Watercress
French dressing

Cut the bananas into rounds $\frac{1}{8}$ in. thick and put them into a salad bowl containing about 1 tablesp. lemon juice. Mix lightly, and pile in the dish. Coat with salad dressing or mayonnaise, sprinkle with parsley. Arrange watercress around the dish and sprinkle it with French dressing.

NOTE: Coarsely chópped walnuts may be added to this salad.

6 helpings

BANANA AND CELERY SALAD

Salade de Bananes et Céleri

6 bananas	**⅛ pt. mayonnaise sauce** *or*
1 celery heart	**⅛ pt. salad dressing**
6 walnuts	**1 orange**
Seasoning	**Watercress**

Slice the bananas thinly, cut the celery into fine shreds and shred the walnuts. Mix lightly with a little seasoning and the mayonnaise sauce or salad dressing. Pile neatly in a salad bowl and garnish with a neat border of orange sections and watercress.

6 helpings

BANANA, RAISIN AND CARROT SALAD

Salade de Bananes aux Raisins et Carrottes

6 bananas	**French dressing made with lemon juice**
2 oz. seedless raisins	**Chopped parsley**
1 oz. almonds	
2 large carrots	

Slice the bananas thinly and mix lightly with the raisins, coarsely-chopped almonds, finely-grated carrot and French dressing. Pile in a salad bowl and sprinkle lavishly with chopped parsley.

6 helpings

CHERRY SALAD

Salade de Cerises

1 lb. Morello cherries	**1 dessertsp. brandy** *or* **Kirsch**
1 tablesp. olive oil	**Finely-chopped tarragon**
1 teasp. lemon juice	**Finely-chopped chervil**
3 or 4 drops of tarragon vinegar	**1 teasp. castor sugar**

Stone the cherries. Crack some of the stones and mix the kernels with the cherries. Mix the oil, lemon juice, vinegar, brandy or kirsch, a very small quantity of tarragon and chervil and the sugar. Pour over the cherries.

Serve with roast game or duck.

4–6 helpings

GRAPE SALAD

Salade de Raisins

1 lb. green grapes	**French dressing**

Skin, halve and remove pips from the grapes. Place the grapes in a salad bowl and mix lightly with the dressing.

4–6 helpings

GRAPEFRUIT AND CHICORY SALAD

Salade de Barbe-de-Capucin

3 grapefruits	**French dressing made with grapefruit juice**
3 small heads chicory	**Fine cress**
2 oz. seedless raisins	

Halve the grapefruits and remove the pulp in sections. Remove the partitions from the halved shells. Shred the chicory, reserving some neat rounds for garnish. Mix the grapefruit pulp, raisins and chicory lightly with the dressing. Fill the grapefruit shells with the mixture. Decorate with tiny bunches of cress and rounds of chicory.

6 helpings

MELON SALAD

Salade de Mélon

¼ of a medium-sized melon	**1 bunch watercress**
Salt and pepper	**French dressing**
Paprika pepper	**Mayonnaise sauce**
1 teasp. castor sugar	**Lemon**
Lemon juice	**Cucumber**

Cut the peeled melon into fine shreds. Mix lightly with seasoning, a pinch of paprika pepper, sugar, and a little lemon juice. Cover. If possible, leave on ice. Toss the watercress in French dressing. Pile the melon in a salad bowl, cover with mayonnaise. Decorate with thin slices of lemon and cucumber. Surround with a border of the watercress.

6 helpings

ORANGE SALAD

Salade d'oranges

4 sweet oranges	**Chopped tarragon and chervil** *or* **chopped mint**
½ teasp. castor sugar	
1 tablesp. French dressing	

Peel the oranges thickly with a saw-edged knife, so that all pith is removed. Cut out the natural orange sections. Place in a salad bowl, sprinkle with sugar. Pour the dressing over and sprinkle with tarragon and chervil, if obtainable, or with chopped mint.

4–6 helpings

PEARS FILLED WITH NUT AND DATE SALAD

3 ripe dessert *or* canned pears
1 small crisp lettuce
4 oz. chopped dates
2 oz. chopped walnuts
Chopped parsley
French dressing *or* salad dressing

Peel and halve the pears. Remove the cores with a sharp teaspoon, then scoop out a little of the pulp of the pears to leave a hollow for the filling. Shred a few lettuce leaves very finely and mix with dates, walnuts, chopped parsley and finely diced pear pulp and French dressing *or* salad dressing. Place the halved pears on small crisp lettuce leaves on individual plates. Pile the mixture on each piece of pear.

NOTE: If fresh pears are used, squeeze lemon juice over them to prevent discoloration.

6 helpings

PINEAPPLE SALAD

Salade d'Ananas

1 small pineapple
1 celery heart
Mayonnaise sauce *or* salad dressing
Thin slices of lemon

Peel and core the pineapple and cut into fine shreds. Cut the celery into small shreds and mix it with the pineapple. Toss in sufficient salad dressing or mayonnaise to moisten and season it. Serve ice cold, garnished with lemon.

4–6 helpings

STRAWBERRY AND TOMATO SALAD

Salade de fraises et tomates

¾ lb. firm strawberries
6 tomatoes
Salt
Paprika pepper
Lemon juice
Mayonnaise sauce
Lettuce heart
Thinly-sliced cucumber

Cut the strawberries into quarters. Skin the tomatoes, cut in halves, remove the seeds and the pulp, then cut them into thin slices. (The tomato pulp may be sieved and used for cocktails, etc.) Season the slices with a little salt and the paprika pepper and sprinkle with lemon juice. Just before serving, mix the strawberries and tomatoes and put into a salad bowl. Add a little mayonnaise, barely to cover the fruit. Place the lettuce heart in the centre of the dish and garnish the base with thinly-sliced cucumber.

6 helpings

B. VEGETABLE SALADS

ARTICHOKE SALAD

Salade d'Artichauts

6 cooked globe artichokes (small ones)
French dressing *or* Vinaigrette sauce

When quite cold, serve the artichokes on a suitable dish. Hand the sauce separately.

6 helpings

ARTICHOKE AND ASPARAGUS SALAD

Salade d'Artichauts et Asperges

6 cooked globe artichokes (small ones)
1 bundle of small asparagus (sprue)
French dressing

Cook the artichokes and when drained and cold remove the chokes and centre leaves. Fill the cavity with the asparagus, cooked and cut into ½-in. lengths, using the tips and green part only. Baste dressing over the asparagus. Serve the rest of the dressing in a sauceboat.

6 helpings

ASPARAGUS SALAD

Salade d'Asperges

50 heads of asparagus, cooked
Mayonnaise sauce *or* Vinaigrette sauce *or* salad dressing

Chill the asparagus thoroughly then coat

the tips with sauce, dish neatly and serve immediately.

NOTE: This is a simple but excellent salad.

6 helpings

ASPARAGUS AND CAULIFLOWER SALAD

Salade d'Asperges et choufleur

30 heads of asparagus, cooked
1 cauliflower, cooked
Mayonnaise sauce *or* salad dressing
Finely-chopped parsley
Finely-chopped tarragon
Finely-chopped chervil

Cut off the points of the asparagus. (The rest of the tender part of the asparagus should be eaten as a hot vegetable.) When cold, mix lightly with most of the cauliflower, cut into neat sprigs. Toss carefully in the mayonnaise or salad dressing. Dish and sprinkle with the chopped herbs. Garnish with a border of cauliflower sprigs.

6 helpings

BEETROOT SALAD

Salade de Betterave

2 cooked beetroots
French dressing
Grated horseradish

Slice or dice the beetroot and arrange neatly. Baste with French dressing, after sprinkling with freshly grated horseradish.

NOTE: If preferred, dry mustard may be added to the French dressing and the horseradish omitted.

6 helpings

BEETROOT AND CELERY SALAD

Salade de Betterave et Céleri

2 cooked beetroots
2 dessert apples
2 oz. shelled walnuts
1 large celery heart *or* 2 heads chicory
Chopped parsley
French dressing
1 bunch watercress

Cut neat rounds of beetroot for garnish, then dice the rest. Mix the diced apples, chopped walnuts, diced celery or chicory and beetroot; chopped parsley. Toss lightly in the French dressing. Pile in a salad bowl. Make a border of the rounds of beetroot and tiny bunches of watercress. Decorate the top with curled celery.

NOTE: This is an excellent salad for winter.

6 helpings

BROAD BEAN SALAD

Salade de fères

1 pt. very small, young broad beans, cooked
French dressing *or* Vinaigrette sauce
Rounds of young carrots (cooked)
Finely-chopped savory *or* chives

Dress the cold broad beans with French dressing or vinaigrette sauce. Garnish with rounds of cooked young carrots and sprinkle with a little chopped savory or chopped chives.

4–6 helpings

BRUSSELS SPROUTS SALAD—COOKED

Salade de Choux de Bruxelles

2 lb. small, compact Brussels sprouts, cooked
French dressing *or* salad dressing
Beetroot

Toss the sprouts lightly in the dressing and pile them in a salad bowl. Garnish with a border of diced or neatly sliced beetroot.

6 helpings

BRUSSELS SPROUTS SALAD—UNCOOKED

Salade de Choux de Bruxelles

1 lb. very young Brussels sprouts
Salt
French dressing

Prepare the brussels sprouts in the usual way, taking care to discard any coarse leaves. Shred very finely. Sprinkle with a little salt and dress with French dressing.

6 helpings

CABBAGE SALAD

Salade de chou

1 lb. of the heart of a white cabbage
Salt
French dressing

Prepare the cabbage in the usual way. Shred very finely. Sprinkle with a little salt and dress with French dressing.

6 helpings

CABBAGE, BEETROOT AND CARROT SALAD

Salade de chou, de betterave et de carrottes

¼ of the heart of a white cabbage
1 celery heart
1 tablesp. raisins *or* sultanas
1 small cooked beetroot
2 carrots
Fine cress
Salad dressing
1 teasp. lemon juice
Chopped parsley

Chop the cabbage very finely. Shred the celery; chop the raisins. Cut the beetroot into tiny dice. Grate the carrot finely. Mix the cabbage lightly with most of the beetroot and carrot and with all the celery and raisins and some salad dressing. Pile on a flat salad dish. Garnish with small heaps of beetroot and carrot, separated by little bunches of cress. Sprinkle the carrot and beetroot with a little lemon juice and finely-chopped parsley before serving.

6 helpings

CARROT SALAD

Salàde de Carottes

3 large carrots
1 lettuce
French dressing
Finely-chopped parsley

Grate the carrots finely and serve on a bed of lettuce leaves. Sprinkle with the French dressing. Garnish with chopped parsley.

NOTE: Grated, raw carrot can be used with success in many salads. It should be grated very finely to be digestible and sprinkled with lemon juice or French dressing as soon as grated to retain its bright colour.

6 helpings

CAULIFLOWER SALAD—COOKED

Salade de Choufleur

1 large cauliflower
Vinaigrette sauce

Steam the cauliflower then divide carefully into small sprigs. Arrange the sprigs neatly in a salad bowl and pour the sauce over while the cauliflower is still warm. Serve when quite cold.

6 helpings

CAULIFLOWER SALAD—UNCOOKED

Salade de Choufleur

1 medium-sized cauliflower
1 small bunch of radishes
Mayonnaise sauce *or* salad dressing
Lettuce leaves

Grate the raw cauliflower and the radishes, leaving a few radishes for decoration. Mix with mayonnaise or salad dressing and pile on a bed of crisp, young lettuce leaves. Garnish with finely-cut, overlapping rounds of radishes.

NOTE: Tomato mayonnaise is excellent with this salad.

6 helpings

CELERY SALAD

Salade de Céleri

2–3 celery hearts
Mayonnaise sauce (p. 135) ***or* tomato mayonnaise**
Crisp lettuce leaves
Chervil
Tarragon

Shred the tender sticks of celery and mix with the mayonnaise. Pile on the crisp lettuce leaves. Sprinkle with chopped chervil and tarragon and decorate with curls of celery.

For directions for making celery curls, *see* p. 38.

6 helpings

CELERY AND CHESTNUT SALAD

Salade de Céleri et de Marrons

½ lb. stewed chestnuts
1 dessert apple
2 celery hearts
Salad dressing (p. 380)
Crisp lettuce leaves

Cut the chestnuts into fairly large pieces. Dice the apple, shred the celery. Mix lightly with the dressing. Pile on a dish decorated with small, crisp lettuce leaves. Garnish with curled celery, *see* p. 38.

4–6 helpings

For other uses of celery in Salads *see Beetroot and Celery Salad*; *Apple, Celery and Nut Salad*; *Banana and Celery Salad*; *Pineapple Salad*

CHICORY SALAD

Salade de Barbe-de-Capucin

6 heads of chicory
French dressing *or* Vinaigrette Sauce

Prepare, wash and drain the chicory well, having split each head in ½ lengthwise. Toss in the French dressing.

NOTE: Chicory cut in shreds may be added to many salads, its crisp texture making it a very pleasant addition. It is most useful as a substitute for celery when the latter is of poor quality or out of season.

6 helpings

CUCUMBER SALAD

Salade de Concombre

1 large cucumber
Salt
French dressing
Chopped parsley
Chopped tarragon

Slice the cucumber ("Ridge" cucumbers must be peeled prior to slicing. For other cucumbers see note in Vegetable Section under Cucumber, p. 339). Put on a china plate and sprinkle with salt. Tilt the plate slightly so that the water may drain off easily and leave for ½ hr. Rinse quickly in a colander and drain. Dish and pour over the French dressing. Sprinkle with parsley and tarragon.

6 helpings

CUCUMBER AND MINT SALAD

Salade de Concombre et Menthe

1 large cucumber *or* 2 ridge cucumbers *or* 2 pickled cucumbers
1 bottle of yoghourt
1 tablesp. vinegar
2 tablesp. chopped mint
Sugar

Mix the yoghourt with the vinegar; add the mint and a little sugar. Stir in the peeled, sliced cucumber. Pile in a salad bowl.

6 helpings

STUFFED CUCUMBER SALADS

Salade de concombres

1 large cucumber
Tomatoes
Macedoine of vegetables, cooked and cold
Salad dressing *or* mayonnaise sauce
Parsley
Fine cress

Cut the cucumber into 1-in. rings and scoop out the centres with a teaspoon. Peel the tomatoes and cut into slices, one for each ring of cucumber. (Any tomato left over should have pips and pulp removed and be neatly diced and added to the macedoine.) Mix the macedoine of vegetables with mayonnaise or salad dressing and chopped parsley. Place the tomato slices on a flat dish; put a cucumber ring on each; fill with the vegetable mixture. Decorate with tiny bunches of cress.

6 helpings

ENDIVE SALAD

Salade de Chicorée

2 heads of endive
French dressing *or* Vinaigrette sauce (p. 380)

Prepare endive as *Lettuce*, (p. 369). Dress with French dressing and serve at once.

6 helpings

ENDIVE, CELERY AND BEETROOT SALAD

Salade de Chicorée, céleri et Betterave

2 heads of endive
Salad dressing (pp. 378–380)
Celery curls
Cooked beetroot
Fine cress

Toss the tufts of endive in salad dressing and pile them in a salad bowl. Sprinkle with celery curls. Surround with a border of neatly sliced beetroot and tiny bunches of cress.

6 helpings

ENDIVE SALAD WITH BACON

Salade de chicorée au petit lard

2 heads of endive
4 streaky rashers of bacon
Salt and pepper
2 tablesp. vinegar (preferably wine vinegar)

Use only the white hearts of the endive and divide the tufts into short pieces. Cut the bacon, with scissors, into fine shreds and fry it until golden brown. Drain on absorbent paper. Mix bacon with endive, add a little salt, freshly ground pepper, and the vinegar; mix thoroughly.

4–6 helpings

LETTUCE SALAD

Salade de laitue

Lettuce, of the cabbage or cos variety, prepared correctly and dressed with a French dressing *or* Vinaigrette Sauce, provides the finest of all salads.

To prepare lettuce 1. Cut off the stump of the lettuce and discard the coarse outer leaves only. 2. Separate all the leaves and wash them leaf by leaf under running water if possible, otherwise in several waters in a basin. 3. Put into a salad shaker or a clean tea-towel and swing them to shake out the water. 4. Leave to drain. 5. If possible put into a covered box *or* into a casserole with a lid in the refrigerator for at least ½ hr. before dressing them for table.

The salads in which lettuce is used as a foundation, are so numerous that it is unnecessary to name them all here.

See also note under Bacon and Potato Salad (p. 321).

MIXED VEGETABLE SALAD
(using cooked summer vegetables)

3 large new potatoes
3 new turnips
½ pt. shelled peas
½ bunch new carrots
1 tablesp. chopped parsley
1 teasp. chopped mint
Salad dressing

Cook the vegetables and slice the carrots, potatoes and young turnips. Save some of each vegetable for garnish and toss the rest in the salad dressing with the herbs. Put the mixture in a suitable dish and garnish with the remainder. Baste with a little French dressing.

4–6 helpings

MIXED VEGETABLE SALAD
(using cooked winter vegetables)

Salade de Légumes à la Jardinère

1 cauliflower
2 large carrots
1 parsnip *or* 2 turnips
1 cooked beetroot
1 small can of peas
Salad dressing (pp. 378–380)
Watercress *or* fine cress
A little French dressing

Steam the cauliflower, carrots, parsnip or turnips. Divide the cauliflower into sprigs. Dice the carrots, parsnip or turnip, and beetroot, or cut into neat rounds with a cutter. Rinse and drain the peas. Mix all trimmings and uneven pieces of vegetable lightly with salad dressing—include some of the peas. Put this mixture into a dish, preferably oblong in shape. Cover with lines of each vegetable, very neatly arranged and with suitable colours adjoining. Garnish the edges with watercress or fine cress. Baste the surface with French dressing.

6 helpings

MUSHROOM SALAD

Salade de Champignons

1 lb. mushrooms
1 onion, finely chopped
Salad oil
Vinegar *or* lemon juice
Salt and pepper

Prepare the mushrooms and leave whole, if small; if large, cut in quarters. Fry the onion gently in the oil until cooked. Drain it. Fry the mushrooms in the same oil. Pour the contents of the pan into a salad dish. Add the onion, seasoning, and about 1 tablesp. vinegar or lemon juice. Serve when cold.

6 helpings

ONION SALAD

Salade d'Oignons

3 large mild onions
3 firm tomatoes
French dressing *or* Vinaigrette sauce

Parboil the onions and leave to cool. Slice them as finely as possible. Arrange in a dish with slices of peeled tomatoes. Pour over the French dressing or vinaigrette sauce.

6 helpings

POTATO SALAD (1)

Salade de Pommes de Terre

6 large new potatoes *or* waxy old potatoes
French dressing *or* Vinaigrette sauce
2 heaped tablesp. chopped parsley
1 teasp. chopped mint
1 teasp. chopped chives *or* spring onion
Salt and pepper

Cook the potatoes until just soft, in their skins. Peel and cut into dice whilst still hot. Mix while hot with the dressing and the herbs and a little seasoning. Serve cold.

6 helpings

POTATO SALAD (2)

6 large, new potatoes *or* waxy old potatoes
½ pt. salad dressing (pp. 378–380)
2 finely-chopped spring onions *or* 1 heaped teasp. finely-chopped chives
1 tablesp. chopped parsley
Salt and pepper
Radishes *or* tomatoes
Fine cress

Prepare potato salad as in preceding recipe. Garnish with overlapping rounds of radish or wedges of tomato from which the pips have been removed, and tiny bunches of fine cress.

6 helpings

POTATO SALAD—HOT

6 large new potatoes *or* waxy old potatoes
Salt and pepper
1 heaped tablesp. chopped parsley
1 tablesp. chopped chives *or* spring onion
4 tablesp. French dressing
1 tablesp. lemon juice

Cook the potatoes as in preceding recipe. Peel and slice and put a layer of slices in a hot fireproof dish. Sprinkle with mixed parsley and chives and lemon juice. Continue until all the potato is used. Bring the French dressing to the boil and baste over the potatoes. Cover and put into a moderate oven (**350° F., Gas 4**) until the contents are very hot.

6 helpings

RED CABBAGE AND APPLE SALAD

Salade de chou rouge

½ small red cabbage
3 dessert apples
French dressing (with mustard)
Fine cress

Shred the red cabbage very finely. Shred the peeled, cored apples in equally fine shreds. Mix lightly with the dressing and serve in a salad bowl with tiny bunches of fine cress.

6 helpings

SALSIFY SALAD

Salade de Salsifis

1½ lb. cooked salsify
Mayonnaise sauce *or* salad dressing

Cut the salsify into 2-in. lengths. Pile in a salad bowl and coat with mayonnaise sauce or salad dressing.

6 helpings

TOMATO IN SALADS

For all salads containing sliced tomatoes, the tomatoes should be skinned first. The removal of the pips from the tomatoes is a matter for personal choice.

To skin tomatoes

There are 3 methods of skinning tomatoes. The 1st and 2nd methods listed below are excellent where only a few tomatoes have to be skinned. The 3rd method is preferable where a large number of tomatoes have to be skinned.

1. Rub the surface of the tomatoes firmly with the back of a knife. Slit and remove the skin.
2. Impale the tomato on a fork and hold over a low gas flame, turning it in the flame until the skin wrinkles and splits. (A gas taper may be used instead of the gas burner.) Remove the skin and cool the tomato.
3. Cover the tomatoes with boiling water and leave for 1 min. Drain and plunge the tomatoes immediately into cold water. Slit and remove the skins.

   Care must be taken to avoid leaving the tomatoes too long in the boiling water and thus partially cooking them.

TOMATO SALAD

Salade de Tomates

6 large firm tomatoes
Salt and pepper
French dressing
Finely-chopped parsley

Skin and slice the tomatoes. Season lightly. Pour the dressing over the tomatoes. Sprinkle with chopped parsley.

6 helpings

TOMATO AND ARTICHOKE SALAD

Salade d'Artichauts et Tomates

6 tomatoes
6 cooked *or* canned artichoke bottoms
Mayonnaise sauce *or* salad dressing

Skin and slice the tomatoes. Split the artichoke bottoms in halves. Arrange neatly in a dish. Pour over a little mayonnaise sauce or salad dressing.

6 helpings

TOMATO AND ONION SALAD

Salade d'Oignons et Tomates

6 tomatoes
1 large onion
Salad dressing *or* **French dressing** (pp. 378–380)

Boil *or* bake the onion until almost tender. When cold chop it finely. Skin and slice the tomatoes, sprinkle the onion over them and add a little salad dressing or French dressing.

NOTE: 1 dessertsp. finely-chopped chives, *or* 3 spring onions, finely chopped may be substituted for the cooked onion.

6 helpings

STUFFED TOMATO SALADS

Salade de Tomates Farcies

6 large firm tomatoes
Crisp lettuce leaves

STUFFING, choice of:

1. **Finely-shredded lettuce leaves; cold cooked asparagus tips; salad dressing** *or*
2. **Chopped celery; finely-diced cooked carrot; canned peas; salad dressing** *or*
3. **Chopped hard-boiled egg; chopped gherkins; salad dressing** *or*
4. **Chopped shrimps** *or* **prawns; finely-shredded lettuce leaves; salad dressing**

Cut off the tops of the tomatoes, take out the centres and the pulp. Use a little of the pulp with the stuffing. Mix the chosen stuffing and fill the tomatoes. Put back the tops. Garnish with tiny sprigs of parsley or with a suitable ingredient of the filling. Dish on crisp lettuce leaves on individual dishes or plates.

6 helpings

TURNIP SALAD—COOKED

Salade de Navets

6 young turnips
Sliced beetroot
Salad dressing *or* **French dressing**

Cook the turnips by steaming them. Slice and cut into strips or dice them. Mix with salad dressing and pile in a salad bowl. Decorate the dish with diced or neatly sliced beetroot.

6 helpings

TURNIP SALAD—UNCOOKED

Salade de Navets

1 bunch young turnips
Salt
French dressing
Chopped parsley

Peel the turnips and grate them finely. Put them on a china dish and sprinkle with salt. Leave for an hour. Drain off the liquid. Mix with French dressing and sprinkle with chopped parsley.

6 helpings

C. MEAT, FISH AND EGG SALADS

BACON AND POTATO SALAD

6 large new potatoes
2 spring onions
Salt and pepper
2 tablesp. vinegar
6 oz. lean bacon
Mayonnaise sauce (p.380)
1 tablesp. finely-chopped parsley

Steam the potatoes and peel after cooking. Dice them while hot and put into a basin with the finely-chopped onions. Season them and baste with the vinegar. Cut the bacon into dice and fry it slowly until browned. Drain from the fat and add to the potatoes; mix lightly with mayonnaise sauce taking care not to break the potato. Dish, sprinkle with parsley.

NOTE: Endive and lettuce may be made into a salad with bacon in the same way but mix with vinegar, salt and pepper only and omit the mayonnaise.

6 helpings

HAM SALAD WITH PINEAPPLE

½ lb. cooked ham
1 small fresh pineapple *or* **1 small can of pineapple**
Mayonnaise sauce *or* **salad dressing**
Sliced gherkins

Cut the ham into short strips. Cut the pineapple into small dice. Toss lightly with mayonnaise sauce or salad dressing. Garnish with slices of gherkin.

4–6 helpings

CHICKEN SALAD

Salade de Volaille

1 small cooked boiling fowl *or* remains of a cooked chicken *or* turkey
1 celery heart (if in season)
1 large lettuce
1 dessertsp. caper vinegar
Salt and pepper
¼ pt. mayonnaise sauce
2 hard-boiled eggs
Olives *or* gherkins
1 tablesp. capers

Cut the chicken into neat, small pieces. Shred the celery and the outer leaves of lettuce. Mix lightly with the vinegar and a little salt and pepper. Pile in a salad bowl and coat with the mayonnaise sauce. Garnish with lettuce leaves, slices of hard-boiled egg, stoned olives or strips of gherkins, and capers.

6 helpings

DUCK SALAD

Salade de Canard

½ a cold duck
1 small heart of celery
Salt and pepper
3 tablesp. French dressing
2 slices unpeeled orange
1 cabbage lettuce
½ bunch watercress
Mayonnaise sauce (p. 135)
1 teasp. chopped parsley
1 teasp. chopped olives (optional)

Cut the duck into 1-in. dice, and the celery into fine strips. Mix in a basin with seasoning and 2 tablesp. French dressing and leave to stand. Cut the orange slices into quarters or eighths. Line the salad bowl with lettuce leaves and sprigs of cress. Decorate with the orange sections and baste with 1 tablesp. French dressing. Place the duck mixture in the centre and cover with a thin layer of mayonnaise. Sprinkle with parsley and olives.

6 helpings

GAME SALAD

Salade de Gibier

1 lb. of remains of cold game
2 lettuces
1 hard-boiled egg
Mayonnaise sauce (p. 135)
Cayenne pepper and salt
Beetroot

Dice the meat. Shred the lettuce finely. Stamp out star-shaped pieces of egg white and beetroot. Mix the meat and chopped egg yolks and remains of whites. Arrange meat, lettuce and mayonnaise in alternate layers in a salad bowl, seasoning each layer, and pile in pyramid shape. Cover the surface with a thin layer of mayonnaise sauce. Garnish with the stars of beetroot and egg white.

6 helpings

ANCHOVY CHEQUER BOARD SALAD

1 lb. cod fillet *or* other white fish
2 tablesp. water
2 tablesp. lemon juice
1 level tablesp. chopped parsley
1 level tablesp. chopped chives
Salt and pepper
Lettuce leaves
1 small can (2 oz.) anchovy fillets
Hard-boiled egg *or* olives

GARNISH

Radish roses
Parsley

Place the fish in a fireproof dish with the water. Cover and cook in a fairly hot oven (**375° F., Gas 5**) for 20 min.; allow to cool. Remove any skin and bones, flake the fish, then moisten it with the lemon juice and stir in the parsley and chives with seasoning to taste. Arrange neatly on a bed of shredded lettuce, flattening and smoothing the top. Place the anchovy fillets diagonally on top in a squared pattern, filling the spaces with rings of hard-boiled egg or slices of stoned olives. Garnish with radish roses and parsley.

4 helpings

CRAB SALAD (1)

Salade de Crabes

1 large cooked crab *or* 2 small cooked crabs
2 celery hearts *or* the heart of 1 endive
2 tablesp. olive oil
2 tablesp. tarragon vinegar
1 tablesp. chilli *or* caper vinegar
1 dessertsp. chopped parsley
Salt and pepper
Crisp lettuce leaves
2 hard-boiled eggs
1 tablesp. capers
12 stoned olives
Anchovy butter

Cut the meat of the crabs into convenient-sized pieces. Shred the celery or endive, add to the crab meat and mix lightly with the oil, vinegar, parsley and seasoning. Serve on a bed of lettuce leaves; garnish with slices of hard-boiled egg, capers and olives stuffed with anchovy butter.

6 helpings

CRAB SALAD (2)

1 large cooked crab	**Salt and pepper**
2 lettuces	**2 oz. smoked salmon (optional)**
½ pt. cooked asparagus tips	**Finely-chopped parsley**
1 hard-boiled egg	**Chopped chives**
Vinaigrette sauce (p. 380)	

Mix the shredded crab meat with the shredded outer leaves of the lettuce and the asparagus tips. Slice the egg, retain the rings of white and sieve the yolk. Mix the yolk with the vinaigrette sauce. Mix the crab, lettuce and asparagus lightly with the vinaigrette sauce and season carefully. Put into a salad bowl and garnish with the inner lettuce leaves, rings of egg white and strips of smoked salmon. Sprinkle with parsley and chives.

6 helpings

FISH SALAD

Cold cooked fish	**1 lettuce**
Salt and pepper	**1 lemon**
⅛ pt. tartare sauce *or* ⅛ pt. mayonnaise sauce	

Use any cold cooked fish divided into large flakes. Season it and mix with the tartare sauce and a little shredded lettuce. Decorate a dish with the crisp, inner lettuce leaves and slices of lemon and arrange the fish on the dish.

4 helpings

LOBSTER SALAD (1)

Salade de Homard

1 large cooked lobster	**2 hard-boiled eggs**
1 endive	**12 stoned olives**
1 lettuce	**3–4 gherkins**
½ pt. mayonnaise sauce	**1 teasp. capers**
	12 anchovy fillets
Salt and pepper	**½ bunch watercress**

Remove all the meat from the lobster and cut into neat pieces. Break the endive into tufts, shred the lettuce coarsely. Arrange the lobster and salad in layers with a little mayonnaise and seasoning. Coat with mayonnaise. Decorate with slices of hard-boiled egg, olives, gherkins, capers, anchovy fillets, the small inner lettuce leaves and watercress.

6 helpings

LOBSTER SALAD (2) (served in the shell)

Salade de Homard en Coquille

1 cooked lobster	**1 lettuce**
Salt and pepper	**1 lemon**
⅛ pt. tartare sauce *or* ⅛ pt. mayonnaise sauce	

Split the lobster, remove all the meat. Cut the meat into small dice, season it and mix with the tartare sauce and a little shredded lettuce. Fill the cleaned, trimmed lobster shells with the mixture. Decorate a dish with the crisp, inner lettuce leaves and slices of lemon and arrange the shells on the dish.

4 helpings

MINT AND PARSLEY FISH SALAD

Salade de Poisson à la Menthe et au Persil

¾ lb. cooked, flaked white fish (approx.)	**1 lettuce**
Salt and pepper	**Mayonnaise *or* salad cream**
1 tablesp. lemon juice	**Tomatoes, carrots *or* other salad vegetables**
1 level tablesp. chopped mint	**Lemon wedges**
1 level tablesp. chopped parsley	

Season the fish to taste, mix with the lemon juice and chopped herbs, reserving 1 teasp. mixed parsley and mint for garnish. Shred the outside leaves of the lettuce and arrange in the serving dish. Pile the fish mixture on the lettuce and cover completely with mayonnaise. Sprinkle with the teaspoonful of chopped herbs and arrange the rest of the lettuce and the other salad vegetables around.

Garnish with sprigs of parsley, mint and lemon wedges.

4 helpings

PICNIC SALAD

1 lb. cooked haddock
1 medium sized carrot
1 level tablesp. chopped parsley
1 level tablesp. chopped chives
3 tablesp. French dressing
Lettuce leaves

Remove all skin and bone and flake the fish. Grate the carrot and add with the parsley and chives to the fish. Toss all together with the French dressing and serve on crisp lettuce leaves, as one salad or as individual portions.

4 helpings

RADISH, CUCUMBER AND FISH SALAD

Salade de Poisson au Radis et au Concombre

1 lb. cooked cod *or* haddock fillet
8 oz. cucumber
2 oz. radishes (about 15)
French dressing *or* salad cream
Salt and pepper
Lettuce

Remove any skin and bone and flake the fish finely. Cut the cucumber into ¼-in. dice, slice the radishes. Mix the cucumber and radishes with the fish and moisten with dressing or salad cream, adding salt and pepper to taste. Pile on a bed of lettuce and serve at once. Garnish with radish roses.

4 helpings

SHRIMP or PRAWN SALAD

Salade de Crevettes

1 pt. picked shrimps
2–3 tablesp. mayonnaise sauce
Slices of cucumber
Crisp, inner lettuce leaves

Mix shrimps lightly with the mayonnaise sauce and pile in a salad bowl. Garnish with shreds of lettuce and cucumber.

5–6 helpings

SHRIMP AND ASPARAGUS SALAD

Salade d'Asperges aux Crevettes

25 cooked heads of asparagus
1 pt. picked shrimps
3 tablesp. mayonnaise sauce
2 hard-boiled eggs

Cut the green part of the asparagus into ½-in. pieces. Mix very lightly with the shrimps and mayonnaise sauce. Pile on a salad dish with a border of slices of hard-boiled egg and asparagus tips.

6 helpings

EGG SALAD

Salade aux œufs

6 hard-boiled eggs
2 tablesp. cream (optional)
Mayonnaise sauce
1 tablesp. chopped parsley
1 crisp lettuce
Salt and pepper
1 tablesp. capers
Beetroot

Slice the eggs thickly. Whip the cream (if used) till stiff and add to the mayonnaise sauce with 1 teasp. of the parsley. Arrange a layer of lettuce leaves in the salad bowl, add a layer of mayonnaise, then a layer of slices of egg and so on until all the egg and lettuce is used, piling the centre high. Season each layer. Garnish with capers and neat slices of beetroot, sprinkle with rest of the parsley.

6 helpings

EGG AND CARROT SALAD

Salade aux œufs et carrotes

4 hard-boiled eggs
12 young carrots
French dressing *or* Vinaigrette sauce
Salt and pepper
Mustard and cress

Slice the carrots thinly. Slice the eggs. Arrange alternately in overlapping slices. Pour over the dressing. Season. Garnish with tiny bunches of mustard and cress.

4–6 helpings

D. NATIONAL SALADS

AMERICAN SALADS

Many of the Fruit and Vegetable Salads (pp. 363–5) are typical American Salads. So popular is the salad in America that it would be impossible to list the wide variety of vegetable mixtures employed. American salads are served very cold.

AMERICAN ASPARAGUS SALAD

Salade d'Asperges Americaine

2 grapefruits
½ pt. cooked asparagus tips
2 tablesp. lemon juice
1 tablesp. Worcester sauce
2 tablesp. tomato ketchup
Salt and pepper

Halve the grapefruits and remove the pulp in sections. Mix it with the asparagus tips. Mix the lemon juice, Worcester sauce, tomato ketchup and a little seasoning and pour on to the grapefruit and asparagus. Toss together lightly. Dish and serve very cold.

4–6 helpings

AMERICAN CABBAGE SALAD

Cole Slaw

½ small white cabbage	**Good pinch of salt**
1 tablesp. vinegar	**1 teasp. melted butter**
6 peppercorns	**2 tablesp. cream**
	1 egg

Chop the cabbage very finely and put into a china bowl. Boil 1 tablesp. of vinegar for 2 min. with the peppercorns and salt, then strain it and put into a basin. Melt the butter, add the cream and the egg yolk and well-beaten egg white; stir into the cooled vinegar. Put the basin over hot water and stir the sauce continually until it thickens, but do not let it boil. When cold, pour over the cabbage. Serve very cold.

4–6 helpings

DANISH SALAD

Salade Danoise

4 tomatoes	**¼ pt. pickled button onions**
1 lb. cooked French beans	**Mayonnaise sauce (p. 135)**
½ pt. cooked green peas	**Sprigs of dill**

Skin and slice the tomatoes; cut the beans into thick slices. Mix the beans, peas and onions with mayonnaise sauce. Pile on a dish and garnish with sliced tomato and sprigs of dill.

4–6 helpings

DUTCH SALAD or FLEMISH SALAD (1)

Salade à l'Hollandaise

1 cooked beetroot	**French dressing with mustard**
2 cooked potatoes	**6 anchovy fillets**
1 heart of celery	**Watercress**

Cut the beetroot, potatoes and celery into strips. Mix lightly with the dressing and pile in a salad bowl. Decorate with strips of anchovy fillets and small bunches of watercress.

4–6 helpings

DUTCH SALAD or FLEMISH SALAD (2)

2 salted and/or pickled herrings	**Finely-chopped dill pickles**
6 oz. cooked potato	**Finely-chopped raw onion**
6 oz. cooked beetroot	**Mayonnaise sauce *or* salad dressing**
6 oz. cooking apple	**Hard-boiled egg**
Salt and pepper	

GARNISH
Fans of dill pickle

Separate the herrings into flakes. Dice the potato, beetroot and apple. Mix the ingredients slightly with mayonnaise sauce or salad dressing; or mash all together. Pile in a lettuce-lined salad bowl. Garnish with fans of dill pickle and slices of egg.

6 helpings

ENGLISH SALAD or SUMMER SALAD

1 large lettuce	**Bunch of watercress *or* box of mustard and cress**
½ small cucumber	**2 hard-boiled eggs (optional)**
3 tomatoes	
½ bunch radishes	
A few spring onions	
Salad dressing	

Reserve the best lettuce leaves and shred the rest. Slice the cucumber thinly, skin and slice the tomatoes, slice the radishes. Leave the onions whole. Mix the shredded lettuce leaves lightly with some of the cucumber, radishes and salad dressing. Line a salad bowl with the lettuce leaves. Pile the mixture in the middle and garnish with small bunches of watercress, sliced tomatoes, radishes, cucumber and hard-boiled egg. Hand the onions separately or arrange on the salad so that they may be avoided if not liked.

6 helpings

FRENCH SALADS

A typical French salad consists of one vegetable only, dressed with a simple French dressing comprising oil, vinegar, seasonings and a little mustard if liked, or with a vinaigrette sauce.

For examples of this type of salad, *see Vegetable Salads*.

FRENCH CARROT SALAD

Carottes Marinées

1½ lb. young carrots
1 dessertsp. French mustard

MARINADE

¼ pt. water
¼ pt. wine vinegar
¼ pt. white wine
1 level teasp. salt
1 level teasp. sugar
Sprig of parsley
Sprig of thyme
1 bay leaf
1 crushed clove of garlic
Good pinch cayenne pepper
¼ pt. olive oil

Mix all the ingredients of the marinade and bring to the boil. Slice thickly or quarter the carrots and cook them in the marinade until just soft. Drain them and strain the liquor. Mix the mustard into the liquor and pour over the carrots. Leave till quite cold. Serve.

NOTE: This salad is improved if prepared the day before it is to be served.

6 helpings

FRENCH COLD MEAT SALAD (1)

Salade de Viande à la Francaise

1½ lb. cold roast *or* boiled meat
2 shallots
4 anchovy fillets
Vinaigrette sauce (p. 380)
Gherkins
Capers

Cut the meat into strips, about 2½ in. by 1 in. Chop the shallots and anchovy fillets finely and mix with the meat and Vinaigrette sauce. Cover and leave 2 hr., stirring the mixture occasionally. Pile in a pyramid in a salad bowl and garnish with strips of gherkin and chopped capers.

6 helpings

FRENCH COLD MEAT SALAD (2)

Salade de pois verts Toulousienne

1 lb. cold meat (beef, mutton *or* veal)
1 pt. cooked green peas
Celery salt
Pepper
Crisp lettuce leaves
Mayonnaise sauce *or* salad dressing
Mustard
Finely-chopped mint

Dice the meat, mix with the peas and season with pepper and celery salt. Arrange in individual lettuce cups and baste with mayonnaise sauce or salad dressing flavoured with a little mustard and chopped mint.

6 helpings

FRENCH COLD MEAT SALAD (3)

Bœuf en Salade

1 lb. cold cooked beef (fresh *or* salt)
½ lb. tomatoes
½ lb. cooked potatoes
Salt and pepper
Vinaigrette sauce (p. 380)
2 hard-boiled eggs

Put a layer of sliced, skinned tomatoes in a salad bowl. Season lightly then add a layer of thin slices of beef, then a layer of cooked potatoes, also seasoned. Pour over the Vinaigrette sauce, and garnish with quarters of hard-boiled egg.

NOTE: The beef from brown stock may be used to form an economical base for this salad.

6 helpings

ITALIAN SALAD

Salade Italienne

½ lb. cold roast veal
½ lb. cooked potatoes
¼ lb. beetroot
¼ lb. gherkins
1 tablesp. capers
Salt and pepper
Mayonnaise sauce *or* salad dressing
12 stoned olives
Crisp lettuce leaves
12 slices salami sausage
1 lemon

Dice the veal, potatoes and beetroot. Slice the gherkins. Mix them with the capers and seasoning and pile in a salad bowl. Pour over the mayonnaise and garnish with the olives, lettuce leaves, salami sausage and slices of lemon.

6 helpings

ITALIAN FENNEL AND CUCUMBER SALAD

Salade de concombre et de fenouil

½ large cucumber
6 radishes
1 root of fennel
1 teasp. chopped mint
Salt and pepper
1 clove garlic finely chopped
2 tablesp. olive oil
1 tablesp. lemon juice
2 hard-boiled eggs

Dice the unpeeled cucumber; slice the radishes and the root of fennel; mix together. Add the mint, season with salt and pepper, garlic, olive oil and lemon juice. Serve garnished with quartered hard-boiled eggs.

NOTE: If orange sections are added this is an excellent salad to serve with roast duck.

4–6 helpings

ITALIAN SALAD OF YELLOW PEPPERS

Salade de Poivres

4 large yellow peppers
1 bunch radishes
1 celery heart
3 tomatoes
Olive oil

Cut the peppers into strips and the radishes into thin rounds. Slice the celery and the skinned tomatoes. Mix lightly and sprinkle lavishly with oil.

6 helpings

POLISH SALAD (1)

Salade à la Polonaise

½ lb. small cooked potatoes
¾ lb. cold roast meat *or* poultry
6 gherkins
3 pickled mushrooms
1 small raw onion
3 sprigs pickled cauliflower
1 hard-boiled egg
Salad dressing *or* sour cream *or* yoghourt
Salt and pepper
1 lettuce
1 dessertsp. chopped parsley

Cook the potatoes in their skins and leave till cold before peeling them. Cut meat into small pieces. Slice the gherkins and mushrooms, chop the onion, cauliflower and hard-boiled egg. Mix all together with salad dressing and seasoning. Arrange in a salad bowl with a border of crisp lettuce leaves. Sprinkle with chopped parsley.

4–6 helpings

POLISH SALAD (2)

2 large cooked carrots
2 cooked potatoes
1 medium cooked beetroot
1 small raw leek
Salt and pepper
Mayonnaise sauce *or* salad dressing

Dice the carrots, potatoes and beetroot. Add the finely-chopped leek. Season and mix lightly with mayonnaise sauce or salad dressing.

4–6 helpings

ROMAN SALAD

Salade Romaine

2 cos lettuces
Vinegar
Honey
1 finely-chopped onion

Separate the lettuces into leaves, discarding the coarse outer leaves. Baste with vinegar sweetened to taste with honey. Sprinkle with onion.

6 helpings

RUSSIAN SALAD

1 small cauliflower
¼ pt. peas
¼ pt. vegetables (carrot, turnip, French beans)
3 potatoes
1 small cooked beetroot
2 tomatoes
Aspic jelly
2 oz. diced ham *or* tongue
2 oz. cooked fish (shrimps, prawns, lobster)
2 oz. smoked salmon (optional)
3 gherkins
1 dessertsp. capers
A few lettuce leaves
Mayonnaise sauce *or* salad dressing
1 hard-boiled egg (white only)
6 stoned olives
6 anchovy fillets

Method 1. Prepare and cook all the vegetables (or use canned or bottled vegetables). Drain them well. Divide the cauliflower into small sprigs, dice all the other vegetables except the peas. Skin and slice the tomatoes. Line a border mould with aspic jelly and decorate it with a little of the diced vegetables. Set layers of vegetables, meat, fish and pickles alternately with jelly in the mould; do not use all the vegetables. When set, turn out. Toss shredded lettuce and remaining vegetables in mayonnaise or salad dressing and pile in the centre of the mould. Decorate with egg white, olives and anchovy fillets.

Method 2 (without aspic jelly). Put layers of vegetables, meat and fish in a salad bowl, season with salt and pepper and a pinch of castor sugar and cover each layer with mayonnaise sauce. Arrange in pyramid form. Cover lightly with mayonnaise. Decorate with beetroot, diced egg white, olives, capers, anchovies and shredded salmon.

Method 3. Mix the vegetables lightly and stir into them aspic mayonnaise (p. 135). Pour into a cylindrical mould. Turn out when set and decorate as in preceding method.

NOTE: Meat may be omitted from a Russian Salad.

6 helpings

SPANISH SALAD (1)

Salade à l'Espagnole

6 tomatoes
3 cooked potatoes
2 cooked red peppers
½ lb. French beans
Salt and pepper
French dressing *or* salad dressing

Slice all the vegetables, cutting the beans into short pieces. Arrange in neat rows, season and baste with French or salad dressing.

4-6 helpings

SPANISH SALAD (2)

1 large Spanish onion
1 cucumber
6 firm tomatoes
Salt and pepper
French dressing
2 tablesp. grated Parmesan cheese
6 stoned Spanish olives

Cut the onion into very thin slices. Slice the cucumber finely and the tomato into thicker slices. Arrange in layers, seasoning each layer, and sprinkling it with French dressing and grated cheese. Garnish with stoned olives.

6 helpings

SWEDISH SALAD

Salade à la Suédoise

4 oz. cold roast beef
1 pickled herring
4 oz. cooked potatoes
4 oz. cooking apples
4 oz. cooked *or* pickled beetroot
1 tablesp. chopped gherkin
1 tablesp. chopped capers
Chopped chervil
Chopped tarragon
Oil
Vinegar
1 hard-boiled egg
3 anchovy fillets
6 bearded oysters (optional)

Dice the beef, herring, potatoes, apples and beetroot. Mix with the gherkin, capers, herbs and moisten with a little oil and vinegar. Pile in a dish and garnish with hard-boiled egg, anchovy fillets and if liked 6 bearded oysters.

NOTE: This salad is often served with stiffly-beaten sour cream coloured with pickled beetroot juice.

4-6 helpings

SWISS SALAD

Salade Suisse

3 small cooked potatoes
1 cooked carrot
½ small cooked beetroot
1 small cooking apple
2 oz. tongue
1 cooked herring
Chopped parsley
Salad dressing

Dice the potatoes, carrot, beetroot, apple and tongue. Divide the herring into flakes. Mix all together lightly with chopped parsley and salad dressing. Pile in a salad bowl.

4-6 helpings

SALAD DRESSINGS

LEMON JUICE may be used in all the following recipes, in place of vinegar, if preferred.

The salad dressings have been divided into, first, uncooked dressings, then cooked dressings.

Recipes for Mayonnaise Sauce, Rémoulade Sauce and Tartare Sauce will be found in the section on Sauces.

CHIFFONADE DRESSING

2 hard-boiled eggs
2 tablesp. very finely-chopped parsley
2 tablesp. very finely-chopped red pepper
1 teasp. very finely-chopped shallot
French dressing

Chop the eggs very finely. Add the parsley, red pepper and chopped shallot and enough French dressing to give the desired consistency. Use very cold.

CLARET DRESSING

¼ pt. claret
1 teasp. lemon juice
1 clove of garlic
1 teasp. finely-chopped shallot
Salt and pepper

Mix all the ingredients together and leave to stand overnight. Strain and pour over a salad previously tossed in a little salad oil.

CREAM AND EGG SALAD DRESSING (1)

2 raw egg yolks
Salt and pepper
1 level saltsp. mixed mustard
2 tablesp. salad oil
2 tablesp. double cream
1 tablesp. wine *or* malt vinegar
1 teasp. tarragon vinegar
½ teasp. finely-chopped onion *or* spring onion *or* chives

Add salt, pepper and mustard to the raw egg yolks and stir with a wooden spoon in a small basin until the yolks are thick. Add the oil drop by drop, beating the mixture vigorously; stir in the cream, then beat in the vinegar slowly. Stir in the onion.

CREAM AND EGG SALAD DRESSING (2)

2 hard-boiled eggs
1 level teasp. mixed mustard
1 level saltsp. salt
Good pinch pepper
2 tablesp. double cream
1 tablesp. vinegar (wine *or* malt and a little tarragon)

Mash or sieve the egg yolks and add to them the mustard, salt, pepper and the cream gradually. When quite smooth, add the vinegar drop by drop, beating the mixture vigorously.

NOTE: The whites of egg should be used in, or for garnishing, a salad. Oil may be substituted for the cream.

CREAM AND POTATO SALAD DRESSING

2 level tablesp. floury cooked potato
1 level saltsp. salt
Pepper
Good pinch castor sugar
1 level saltsp. mixed mustard
2 tablesp. double cream
1 tablesp. wine *or* malt vinegar

Sieve the potato and when cold mix with salt, pepper, sugar and mustard. Add the cream. Stir in the vinegar drop by drop.

NOTE: Oil may be used instead of cream.

CREAM DRESSING USING SOUR CREAM

Sour, thick cream
Salt and pepper
Mixed mustard *or* French mustard
Castor sugar

Stir the cream until smooth. Flavour with salt, pepper, mustard and castor sugar. Add a little milk or top of the milk if too thick.

CREAM SALAD DRESSING (1)

½ level teasp. mixed mustard *or* French mustard
1 level saltsp. salt
1 saltsp. castor sugar
4 tablesp. double cream
1 tablesp. vinegar (wine *or* malt with a little tarragon)

Mix the mustard, salt and sugar smoothly together. Stir in the cream. Add the vinegar drop by drop, beating mixture all the time.

CREAM SALAD DRESSING (2)

1 level saltsp. mixed *or* French mustard
1 level saltsp. salt
Pepper to taste
Good pinch castor sugar
2 tablesp. double cream
1 tablesp. oil
1 dessertsp. vinegar (wine *or* malt with a little tarragon)

As in preceding recipe but add oil drop by drop to cream mixture before adding vinegar.

EVAPORATED MILK DRESSING

4 tablesp. evaporated milk
1 tablesp. vinegar (wine *or* malt)
1 level saltsp. mixed mustard
Good pinch castor sugar
1 level saltsp. salt

Whisk the milk until thick. Add the vinegar drop by drop, stirring vigorously. Add the flavourings.

FRENCH DRESSING
(see Vinaigrette Sauce, below)

2–3 tablesp. olive oil
1 tablesp. wine vinegar
Pepper and salt

Mix the oil and seasoning. Add the vinegar gradually, stirring constantly with a wooden spoon so that an emulsion is formed.

NOTE: A pinch of sugar, a little mustard and one or two drops of Worcester sauce may be added.

Lemon juice may be used in place of vinegar. Where suitable, orange or grapefruit juice may also be used.

A graduated medicine bottle is most useful for making French dressing. The oil and vinegar can be measured accurately without waste, and the dressing vigorously shaken to mix it. It can be stored in the larder or refrigerator, the bottle being well shaken before the dressing is used.

MAYONNAISE—COOKED

1 teasp. castor sugar
1 teasp. salt
1 level teasp. dry mustard
Good pinch pepper
1 tablesp. salad oil
3 egg yolks
⅛ pt. vinegar (1 teasp. to be tarragon)
½ pt. milk *or* single cream

Mix the sugar, salt, mustard and pepper. Stir in the oil then the well-beaten egg yolks. Add the vinegar gradually and lastly the milk or cream. Cook in the top of a double saucepan, or in a basin placed in a saucepan containing sufficient boiling water to come halfway up the basin, stirring it all the time until the mixture thickens like custard. Re-season when cold.

NOTE: This salad dressing will keep well if put in a cool larder or in the refrigerator.

MAYONNAISE (economical recipe)

3 rounded teasp. flour
1 teasp. castor sugar
1 teasp. salt
1 level teasp. dry mustard
Good pinch pepper
1 tablesp. melted butter *or* margarine
1 egg yolk
⅛ pt. vinegar
½ pt. milk

Proceed as in preceding recipe, mixing the flour with the sugar, salt, mustard and pepper, and adding the melted butter *or* margarine before the egg yolk, etc. Bring just to the boil to cook the flour.

SALAD DRESSING
(with foundation of Béchamel Sauce)

This is an excellent salad dressing, very smooth in texture, of excellent flavour and and good keeping qualities. It is the best dressing to use for a potato salad.

1 egg *or* 2 yolks
½ pt. Béchamel sauce (made with all milk) (p. 128)
2 tablesp. wine *or* malt vinegar
1 tablesp. tarragon vinegar
Salt and pepper
A little castor sugar

Beat the egg or egg yolks. Cool the Béchamel sauce until the hand can be placed in comfort on the bottom of the pan. Stir in the egg and cook without boiling. Wring through muslin and when cooled a little, stir in the vinegars gradually and the seasoning and sugar. Leave until quite cold, then taste and reseason if necessary.

SALAD DRESSING
(with foundation of custard)

½ pt. milk
½ oz. custard powder (an unflavoured one if possible)
½ oz. margarine
3 tablesp. vinegar
A little castor sugar
Salt and pepper
1 level teasp. mixed mustard

Make the custard, putting the margarine in the pan with the milk at the beginning. Cool the custard, stirring it from time to time to prevent the formation of a skin. When cool stir in the vinegar, sugar, mustard and seasoning. When cold, correct the seasoning.

NOTE: This salad dressing will keep for several days in a cool place.

VINAIGRETTE SAUCE

This consists of a simple French dressing to which the following are added:

1 teasp. finely-chopped gherkin
½ teasp. finely-chopped shallot *or* chives
½ teasp. finely-chopped parsley
1 teasp. finely-chopped capers
½ teasp. finely-chopped tarragon and chervil (if available)

HOT SWEETS

MILK PUDDINGS

MILK puddings are basically made with a farinaceous ingredient, sugar and milk. Eggs may be added, if liked, or any other suitable flavouring such as grated lemon or orange rind, grated nutmeg, ground cinnamon or flavouring essences. Bay leaf, orange or lemon rind can be infused in the milk, provided they are removed before serving unless the rind is finely grated. If a vanilla pod is available it can be stored in a jar of sugar and the flavoured sugar used for sweetening puddings.

Skimmed and dried milk can be used for making milk puddings, and ½–1 oz. butter or suet added to each pint of milk will make up the deficiency of fat. If *sweetened condensed milk* is used the amount of sugar in the recipe should be decreased accordingly. *Evaporated and condensed milks* should be made up to the equivalent of fresh milk by following the directions on the tin.

The addition of egg to a milk pudding increases the nutritive value and the pudding is made much lighter if the whites are whisked before being added. The egg must not be added until the grain is fully cooked otherwise the prolonged cooking necessary to cook the grain would overcook the eggs and cause them to curdle. Baking for about 30 min. in a warm oven **(335° F., Gas 3)** is usually long enough to cook the eggs and brown the top of a one pint pudding.

The correct consistency of a boiled or baked milk pudding is such that it will just flow over the plate when served. This result is achieved by using the correct quantities of ingredients and slow cooking to prevent excessive evaporation. Extra milk can sometimes be added if the pudding becomes too thick.

STEAMED MILK PUDDINGS

Boiling and baking are the more common methods by which milk puddings are made, but they can also be steamed and unmoulded provided that they contain at least 2 eggs to each pint of liquid in addition to the farinaceous ingredient. The basin or mould must be well greased, the pudding covered with greased paper and allowed to steam very gently until set.

GENERAL HINTS FOR MAKING MILK PUDDINGS

1. Avoid using thin saucepans; rinse out the saucepan with cold water before using, *or* lightly grease with butter to lessen the risk of burning.
2. Puddings cooked in a saucepan must be stirred well from the bottom of the pan and only just allowed to simmer.
3. If a double saucepan is used, little attention is required, but the pudding will take longer to cook.
4. A pinch of salt added to all puddings improves the flavour.
5. Finely-shredded suet, *or* flakes of butter *or* margarine, put on to the top of all baked puddings improves the flavour and also increases the fat content.
6. Grease the pie-dish to facilitate cleaning afterwards.
7. In puddings where eggs are included, the mixture must be cooled slightly before the egg yolks are added.
8. For instructions for making meringue see page 38.

FLAVOURINGS

Ground cinnamon: Sprinkle on top of large grain puddings *or* mix with any type of milk pudding.

Nutmeg: Grate on top of large grain milk puddings and baked puddings.

Lemon *or* orange rind: Cut thin strips of lemon *or* orange rind avoiding white pith. Add at commencement of cooking and remove before serving.

Lemon *or* orange rind (grated): Add to milk pudding just before serving.

Dried fruit: Sultanas, seedless and stoned raisins, chopped dates and finely-chopped candied peel can be added to all puddings at commencement of cooking.

Essences: Add to small- and powdered-grain puddings at the end of boiling.

Cocoa: Blend first with a little of the milk; then add to the rest of the milk. Extra sugar may be required.

Chocolate: Grate plain chocolate and dissolve in a little warm milk, add to rest of milk.

LARGE GRAIN PUDDINGS

(Large sago, whole rice (Carolina-type or short grain), flaked tapioca, flaked rice)

Basic Recipe

4 oz. grain
2 pt. milk
2–3 oz. sugar
½ oz. finely-shredded suet *or* butter (optional)
Grated nutmeg *or* other flavouring

Grease a pie-dish with butter. Wash the grain in cold water if necessary, and put it into the pie-dish with the milk. Leave to stand for about ½ hr. Add the sugar, flake the fat on to the top and add any flavouring required. Bake slowly (**310° F., Gas 2**) until the pudding is brown on top and of a thick creamy consistency.

6 helpings
Cooking time—about 2½ hr.

LARGE GRAIN PUDDINGS—WITH EGGS

(Large sago, whole rice, flaked tapioca, flaked rice)

Basic Recipe

4 oz. grain
2 pt. milk
2–4 eggs
2–3 oz. sugar
Flavouring

Wash the grain in cold water, if necessary. Put the grain and milk into a strong *or* double saucepan and cook slowly until the grain is tender. Remove from the heat and allow to cool slightly. Separate the eggs and whisk the whites stiffly. Stir into the pudding the egg yolks, sugar and flavouring, and lastly stir in lightly the stiffly-whisked whites. Pour into a well buttered pie-dish and bake in a warm oven (**335° F., Gas 3**) about 30–40 min. until the top is brown.

6 helpings

Variations

APPLES AND RICE

Pommes au Riz

3 oz. rice
Pinch of salt
1½ pt. milk
Rind of 1 lemon
1 oz. butter
3 oz. granulated sugar
6 cooking apples
2 tablesp. raspberry jam *or* butter and sugar

Wash the rice and simmer it in the milk (with the salt and strips of lemon rind) until tender and most of the milk has been absorbed. Stir in the butter and granulated sugar and remove the lemon rind. Peel and core the apples and place them in a large pie-dish. Fill the cavities with raspberry jam *or* butter and sugar. Carefully fill the spaces between the apples with rice. Bake in a cool oven (**310° F., Gas 2**) for about ¾–1 hr. until the apples are tender but not broken.

6 helpings

APPLE SNOWBALLS

Ballons de Pommes à la Neige

To each apple allow:

1½ oz. rice
½ pt. milk *or* milk and water
Pinch of salt
1½ oz. sugar
1 clove (optional)

Simmer the rice in the milk with the salt until the rice is tender and all the milk is absorbed. (1 tablesp. of sugar to every pt. of milk may be added if liked.)

Peel and core the apples, keeping them whole. Put a clove (if used) into the centre and stand each apple on a base of cooled rice on a pudding cloth. Fill the centre of the apple with sugar and then cover the apple with rice. Tie the apples in the pudding cloth and drop into boiling water. Boil very gently for about 45 min.

Serve with castor sugar.

1 apple per helping

BARLEY PUDDING

Orge au lait

4 oz. pearl barley
2 pt. milk
Pinch of salt
2 oz. butter *or* margarine
2 eggs
2 oz. sugar
Grated rind of 1 lemon

Wash and blanch the barley by putting it into a saucepan with enough cold water to cover well. Bring quickly to the boil, strain, and rinse in cold water. Leave the barley to soak overnight in just enough cold water to cover. Put it into a saucepan with the milk, salt and butter and simmer slowly until the barley is tender, about 1 hr. Leave to cool slightly. Separate the eggs. Stir into the barley the sugar, egg yolks and grated lemon rind. Stir in lightly the stiffly-whisked egg whites. Pour into a buttered pie-dish and bake in a moderate oven (**350° F., Gas 4**) for 20–30 min., until nicely browned.

6 helpings

CARAMEL RICE PUDDING

Pouding Caramel au Riz

4½ oz. rice	**2 eggs**
1½ pt. milk	**1½ oz. castor sugar**
Pinch of salt	

CARAMEL

3 oz. loaf sugar	**½ gill water**

Heat a charlotte mould and have ready a thickly folded band of newspaper so that the hot mould may be encircled with it and held firmly in one hand. Prepare the caramel by heating the loaf sugar and water together; stir until it boils; then remove the spoon and allow to boil without stirring until golden brown. Pour the caramel into the warm charlotte mould and twist round, until the sides and base are well coated with the caramel. Wash the rice and simmer in the milk, with the salt, until the rice is soft and all the milk has been absorbed. Cool slightly and add the beaten eggs and sugar. Turn into the caramel-lined mould, cover with greased paper and steam for 1 hr. until firm.

Serve either hot or cold.

6 helpings

EMPRESS PUDDING

Pouding à l'Impératrice

4 oz. rice	**2 oz. castor sugar**
Pinch of salt	**Trimmings of pastry**
2 pt. milk	**Jam *or* stewed fruit**
2 oz. butter *or* margarine	

Simmer the rice in the milk with a pinch of salt until it is tender. Add the fat and sugar. Line the sides of a pie-dish with the trimmings of pastry. Spread a layer of rice on the bottom of the dish. Cover with jam *or* stewed fruit. Repeat until the dish is full, finishing with a layer of rice. Bake in a moderate oven (**350° F., Gas 4**) until browned.

Serve with custard.

6–7 helpings
Cooking time—½ hr.

GENEVA PUDDING

Pouding à la Genevoise

3 oz. rice	**1 oz. butter**
1½ pt. milk	**¼ teasp. ground cinnamon**
Pinch of salt	
3 oz. sugar	**3 tablesp. water**
2 lb. cooking apples	

Wash the rice and let it simmer in the milk with the salt until cooked. Add ½ oz. sugar. While the rice is cooking wipe the apples and chop them roughly; put them in a saucepan with the butter, cinnamon and 3 tablesp. of water. Simmer very gently until tender; then put the mixture through a fine sieve. Add the rest of the sugar (2½ oz.). Well grease a pie-dish with butter and arrange the rice and apple purée in alternate layers, with rice forming the bottom and top layers. Bake in a moderate oven (**350° F., Gas 4**) until brown.

6 helpings
Time—1¼ hr.

LEMON RICE

Riz au Citron

3 oz. rice	**1½ oz. granulated sugar**
1½ pt. milk	**2 eggs**
Juice and rind of 1 lemon	**3 tablesp. jam**
Pinch of salt	**2 oz. castor sugar**

Simmer the rice in the milk, with the lemon rind and salt until the grain is tender. Remove the rind and stir in the granulated sugar. Cool slightly. Separate the eggs and stir into the rice the egg yolks and lemon juice. Pour into a buttered pie-dish and bake in a warm oven (**335° F., Gas 3**) until set, about 20–30 min. Spread a layer of jam on top. Whisk the egg

PLATE 15

Decorating Tarts

A few simple finishing touches like the ones outlined below will soon transform even the plainest tarts and pies into fancy party dishes.

1 *With a sharp knife make even cuts about 1 inch apart and 1 inch in depth round the edge of the tart. Damp with a pastry brush and fold alternate pieces down, pressing them only very lightly.*

2 *Roll out pastry trimmings to a thickness of $\frac{1}{8}$ inch and cut out small circles. Damp the edge of the tart and press cut outs on edge so that they overlap.*

3 *Make cuts as in 1. Moisten and fold pieces so that they overlap to give a sunray effect.*

4 *Decorate the edge with a fork then arrange fleurons (cut with a fluted pastry cutter from pastry scraps) on the filling.*

5 *Shows three ways of folding an edge after cutting (see 1 above).*

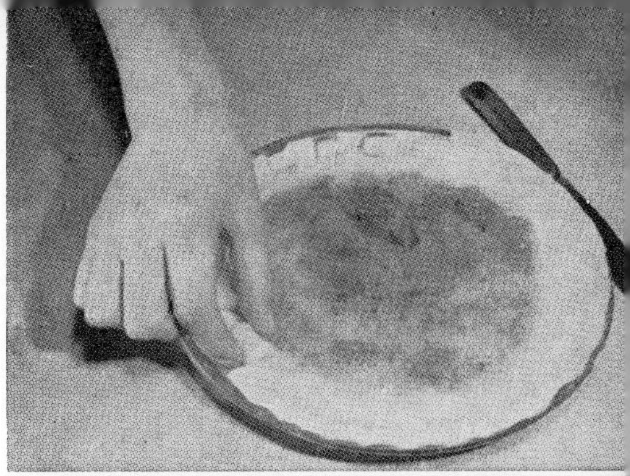
1

2

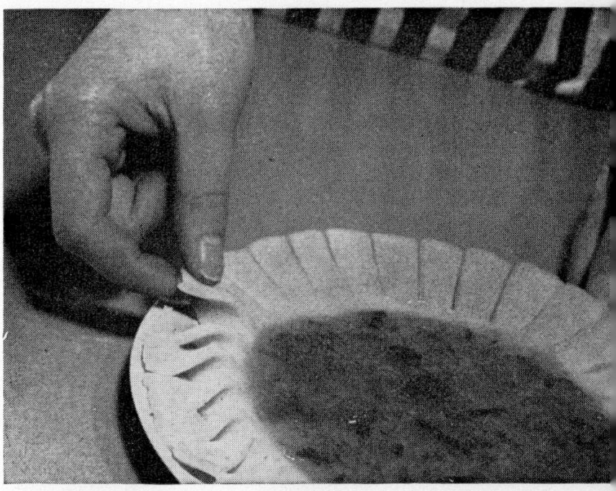
3

4

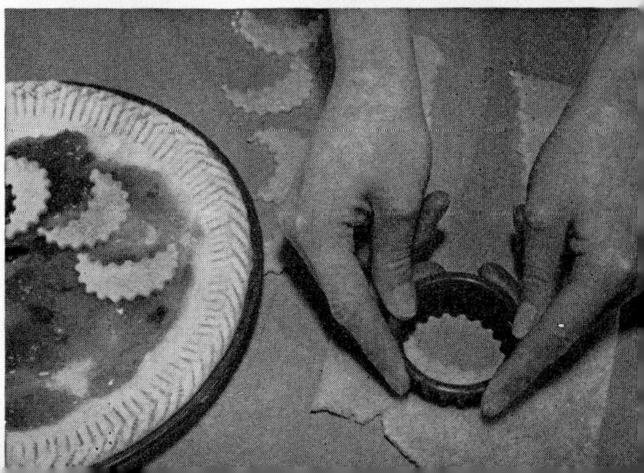

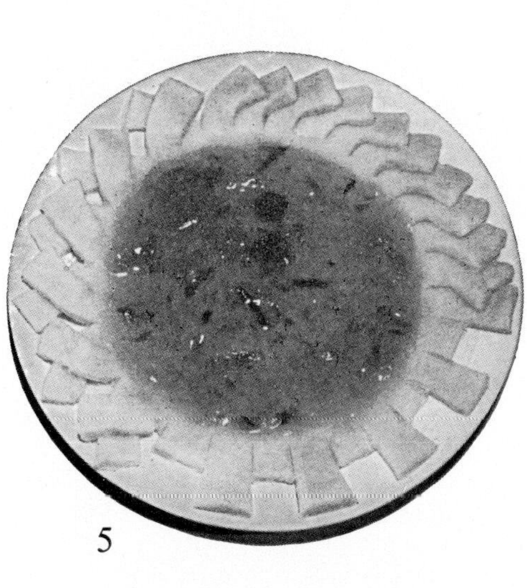
5

whites stiffly and stir the castor sugar in lightly. Pile on top of the pudding and dredge with castor sugar. Cook in a very cool oven (**290° F., Gas 1**) until the meringue is coloured, about 20–30 min.

6 helpings

MACARONI PUDDING

Macaroni au lait

4 oz. macaroni	**Grated rind of 1 lemon**
Salt	**1½ oz. butter *or* margarine**
1½ pt. milk	
2 oz. sugar	**1–3 eggs**

Break the macaroni into ½-in. lengths and throw into boiling salted water. Cook for 10 min. until just tender. Strain the macaroni and put it into the saucepan with the milk and simmer until quite soft. Cool slightly. Add the sugar, lemon rind and butter. Separate the eggs and stir in the beaten yolks, stir for a few minutes but do not let it boil. Whip the egg whites stiffly and fold lightly into the mixture. Remove the lemon rind. Pour into a buttered pie-dish and cook until brown in a moderate oven (**350° F., Gas 4**)—about 20–30 min.

6 helpings

PEARS AND RICE

Poires au Riz à la Marquise

4 oz. rice	**2 eggs**
1½ pt. milk	**1 can *or* bottle of pears**
Pinch of salt	**1 tablesp. maraschino**
4 oz. castor sugar	***or* curacao *or* vanilla**
Grated rind of ½ lemon	**essence**
¼ oz. butter	

Wash the rice and put it in a saucepan with the milk and salt. Cook until tender. Add 2 oz. of the sugar, lemon rind and the butter. Separate the eggs and stir the beaten yolks into the mixture. Return to the heat and cook until thick. Press the mixture into a flat round mould, such as a sponge-cake tin. Leave for a little while and then turn out on to a hot fireproof dish.

Meanwhile, strain the syrup from the pears into a saucepan and boil rapidly until considerably reduced. Add the maraschino *or* curacao *or* a few drops of vanilla essence; put in the pears to heat them through. Arrange the pears in a pyramid form on top of the rice. Add a little syrup. Dredge with castor sugar. Stiffly whip the egg whites and lightly fold in the remaining 2 oz. sugar, and pile on top of the pears. Bake in a very cool oven (**290° F., Gas 1**) until the meringue is set and golden brown.

Serve with the rest of the syrup.

NOTE: This can also be made in an oven-glass pie-dish by pressing the rice into the dish and arranging the pears and meringue on top.

6–7 helpings
Time—1¼ hr.

RICE CROQUETTES

Croquettes de Riz

4 oz. rice	**2 oz. castor sugar**
1½ pt. milk	**1 egg**
Pinch of salt	**Egg and white bread-crumbs**
½ oz. butter	
Lemon rind	**Frying-fat**

Wash and drain the rice; put it into a pan with the milk, salt, butter and thinly-cut lemon rind. Cook until the rice is tender, all the milk absorbed and the mixture is thick. Remove the lemon rind. Add the sugar and beaten egg, and reheat to cook the egg. Spread the mixture on a plate and leave to cool. When almost cold, form into pear or cork-shapes and coat with egg and crumbs. Fry in deep fat which is just beginning to haze. Cook until golden brown. Drain well.

Dredge well with castor sugar and serve.

NOTE: If shallow fat is used it should come half-way up the croquette and then the croquette must be turned over.

6 helpings

RICE MERINGUE PUDDING

Pouding de Riz méringue

3 oz. rice	**1½ oz. granulated sugar**
1½ pt. milk	**1 oz. butter**
Pinch of salt	**2 eggs**
1 bay leaf	**2 oz. castor sugar**

Put the rice, salt, milk and bay leaf into a saucepan and simmer gently until the rice is

A Selection of Interesting Dishes (opposite)

tender. Remove the bay leaf. Cool slightly and stir in the granulated sugar, butter and beaten egg yolks. Pour into a buttered pie-dish. Whisk the egg whites stiffly and stir in lightly the castor sugar. Pile on top of the rice, dredge with castor sugar and bake in a very cool oven (**290° F., Gas 1**) until the meringue is crisp and golden; about ¼–½ hr.

6 helpings

SPAGHETTI PUDDING

Spaghetti au lait

As for Macaroni Pudding (p. 385) substituting spaghetti for macaroni.

SWEDISH RICE

Riz à la Suèdoise

¾ lb. rice
Salt
1½ lb. cooking apples
¾ pt. milk
Rind of 1 lemon
3 oz. sugar
Pinch of ground cinnamon
Wineglass of sherry
¼ lb. raisins, stoned and roughly chopped

Wash the rice and throw it into slightly salted boiling water. Boil for 3 min. then strain off the water. Peel, core and thinly slice the apples. Add the milk, lemon rind and the apples to the rice; cook until tender. Remove the lemon rind. Add the sugar, ground cinnamon, wine and prepared raisins. Cook for 3–4 min. longer.

Serve with cream.

6 helpings

TAPIOCA CREAM PUDDING

Tapioca au lait à la Crème

2½ oz. tapioca
1½ pt. milk
Pinch of salt
½ oz. butter *or* margarine
1½ oz. sugar
¼ teasp. almond essence
3 eggs
3 oz. crushed ratafias

Wash and soak the tapioca in the milk with the salt for 1–2 hr. Simmer the tapioca in the milk until cooked. Add the butter, sugar and almond essence. Separate the eggs and add the egg yolks. Pour into a well-buttered pie-dish and bake in a moderate oven (**350° F., Gas 4**) until just set. Stiffly whisk the egg whites and fold in lightly, the crushed ratafias. Pile on top of the tapioca. Reduce the heat of the oven to cool (**290°–310° F., Gas 1–2**) and bake until a pale golden brown on top; about 30 min.

6 helpings

VERMICELLI PUDDING

Vermicelle au lait

1½ pt. milk
1 bay leaf *or* pinch of ground cinnamon *or* orange *or* lemon rind
3 oz. vermicelli
Pinch of salt
1½ oz. sugar
2–3 eggs

Bring the milk slowly to the boil, with the flavouring ingredient (not ground cinnamon); then remove the flavouring. Add the vermicelli, broken into short pieces, and the salt. Simmer until tender, then cool slightly. Separate the eggs. Add the sugar, ground cinnamon (if used) and egg yolks and stir well. Lightly stir in the stiffly-whipped egg whites. Pour into a well-buttered pie-dish and bake in a moderate oven (**350° F., Gas 4**) until golden brown—about 20–30 min.

6 helpings
Cooking time—about 1 hr. altogether

WINDSOR PUDDING

1½ oz. rice
¾ pt. milk
2 lb. cooking apples
2 oz. castor sugar
Grated rind and juice of ½ lemon
3–4 egg whites

Wash the rice and stew it in the milk until the rice is tender and all the milk has been absorbed. Wipe the apples, cut them roughly and stew them in as little water as possible. When soft, pass them through a fine sieve into a mixing bowl. Stir in the sugar, rice, lemon rind and juice. Whisk the egg whites stiffly and fold them lightly into the mixture. Put into a greased basin; cover. Steam very gently for about 40 min.

Serve with custard sauce made from the egg yolks.

6 helpings

MEDIUM OR SMALL GRAIN PUDDINGS

(Semolina, ground rice, small sago, crushed tapioca)

Basic Recipe

2 pt. milk — **3 oz. grain**
Flavouring (*see* p. 382) — **2–3 oz. sugar**

Heat the milk and infuse the flavouring for about 10 min. then remove the flavouring. Sprinkle the grain into the milk, stirring quickly to prevent lumps forming. Continue stirring until the mixture has simmered long enough for the grains to become transparent and cooked through—usually about 15 min. Add the sugar and essence (if used for flavouring). The pudding can then be (*a*) served as it is, *or* (*b*) poured into a well-buttered pie-dish, and put into a moderate oven (**350° F., Gas 4**) for 20–30 min. until the top is browned.

6 helpings

SMALL GRAIN PUDDINGS—WITH EGGS

(Semolina, ground rice, small sago, crushed tapioca)

Basic Recipe

2 pt. milk — **2–4 eggs**
Flavouring (*see* p. 382) — **2–3 oz. sugar**
3 oz. grain

Heat the milk, and infuse the flavouring for about 10 min. then remove it. Sprinkle the grain into the flavoured milk, stirring quickly to prevent lumps forming. Continue stirring until the mixture has simmered long enough for the grain to become transparent and cooked through—about 15 min. Leave to cool slightly. Separate the eggs and stir in the egg yolks. Add the sugar and flavouring essence (if used), and lastly stir the stiffly-beaten egg whites into the pudding. Pour into a well-buttered pie-dish and bake in a warm oven (**335° F., Gas 3**) until the top is nicely brown—about 30–40 min.

6 helpings

Variations

CHOCOLATE SEMOLINA

Semoule au Chocolat

3 oz. plain chocolate — **2 oz. sugar**
½ gill milk — **A few drops of vanilla essence**
1½ pt. milk
2½ oz. semolina

Grate the chocolate and leave to dissolve in ½ gill milk. Heat 1½ pt. milk, sprinkle in the semolina, stirring well, and simmer until the semolina is cooked through. Slightly warm the chocolate if it is not completely dissolved and add to the semolina with the sugar and vanilla essence. Reheat and serve.

NOTE: ¾–1 oz. of cocoa may be used instead of the chocolate. Blend the cocoa with a little of the milk and add it before sprinkling in the semolina.

4–5 helpings — **Cooking time—30 min.**

HASTY PUDDING

1½ pt. milk — **1 oz. sugar**
2½ oz. sago *or* semolina *or* ground rice

Heat the milk to almost boiling, then sprinkle in the sago, semolina *or* ground rice stirring briskly. Simmer until the grain is cooked and the mixture begins to thicken—about 10–15 min. Add the sugar.

Serve with cream, sugar, jam or treacle.

6 helpings

HONEY PUDDING (1)

1 gill milk — **Grated rind of ½ lemon**
1 oz. semolina — **½ teasp. ground ginger**
1 oz. butter — **2 eggs**
4 oz. honey — **6 oz. breadcrumbs**

Grease a 1–1½ pt. mould *or* basin.

Heat the milk in a saucepan; sprinkle in the semolina, and, stirring well, cook for 10 min. Add the butter, honey, lemon rind, ginger, the egg yolks and the breadcrumbs. Beat well. Whisk the egg whites stiffly and stir them lightly into the rest of the ingredients. Turn the mixture into the mould *or* basin; cover. Steam gently for 1¾–2 hr. Serve with almond sauce.

5–6 helpings

NOTE: See p. 418 for Honey Pudding (2).

TIMBALES OF SEMOLINA

Timbales de Semoule

1 pt. milk	**2 tablesp. cream *or* top of milk**
3 oz. semolina	**6–7 apricot halves**
2 oz. sugar	**½ pt. apricot syrup (approx.)**
A few drops of vanilla essence	**Maraschino (optional)**
2 eggs	

DECORATION

Glacé cherries	**Angelica**
Almonds	

Heat the milk, sprinkle in the semolina, stirring briskly, and simmer until the semolina is cooked through. Cool slightly; then add the sugar, and vanilla essence. Separate the eggs and stir in the beaten yolks. Beat the mixture until it is nearly cold; then add the cream and stir in lightly the stiffly-whipped egg whites. Three-quarters fill well-greased timbale or dariole moulds with the mixture. Cover with greased paper and steam very gently for about ½ hr. until set.

Meanwhile, heat the apricots between 2 plates. Boil the apricot syrup until well reduced and flavour with a little maraschino, if liked. When the moulds are cooked and set, unmould them on to a hot dish.

Place half an apricot on top of each, decorate with glacé cherry, chopped almonds and angelica. Pour the syrup round and serve.

6–7 helpings

POWDERED GRAIN PUDDINGS

(Arrowroot, cornflour, custard powder, finely ground rice, powdered barley, fine oatmeal)

Basic Recipe

2½ oz. powdered grain	**2–3 oz. sugar**
2 pt. milk	**Flavouring (*see* p. 382)**

Mix the grain to a smooth paste with a little of the milk and put the rest of the milk on to boil. Pour the boiling milk quickly on to the blended paste, stirring vigorously to prevent lumps forming. Return the mixture to the saucepan, heat until it thickens, then simmer for 2–3 min. to completely cook the grain, stirring continuously. Add the sugar. The pudding can then be served as it is, *or* poured into a well-buttered pie-dish and baked in a moderate oven (**350° F., Gas 4**) until the top is browned, about 20–30 min.

6 helpings

POWDERED GRAIN PUDDINGS—WITH EGGS

(Arrowroot, cornflour, custard powder, finely ground rice, powdered barley, fine oatmeal)

Basic Recipe

2½ oz. powdered grain	**2–3 oz. sugar**
2 pt. milk	**Flavouring (*see* p. 382)**
2–4 eggs	

Mix the grain to a smooth paste with a little of the milk and put the rest of the milk on to boil. Pour the boiling milk quickly on to the blended paste, stirring vigorously to prevent lumps forming. Return the mixture to the saucepan, heat until it thickens, then simmer for 2–3 min. to completely cook the grain, stirring continuously. Allow the mixture to cool. Separate the eggs and whisk the whites stiffly. Stir into the pudding the egg yolks, sugar, any flavouring essence and lastly stir in lightly the stiffly-whisked egg whites. Pour into a well-buttered pie-dish and bake in a warm oven (**335° F., Gas 3**) until the top of the pudding is nicely browned, about 30–40 min.

6 helpings

Variations

ARROWROOT PUDDING—STEAMED

Pouding à l'Arrowroot

1½ oz. arrowroot	**½ teasp. vanilla essence *or* grated lemon rind**
1½ pt. milk	**3 eggs**
2 oz. castor sugar	

Mix the arrowroot to a smooth paste with a little of the milk. Boil the remainder of the milk and pour over the arrowroot paste, stirring well. Return to the saucepan, stir, and simmer gently until the mixture thickens.

Leave to cool slightly and stir in the flavouring, sugar and well-beaten eggs. Pour into a 2 pt. greased basin, cover with greased paper and steam for 1½ hr.

Turn out and serve with custard or wine sauce.

6 helpings

DEVONSHIRE RUM

Cold Christmas pudding	**½ oz. castor sugar**
1 oz. cornflour	**1 egg**
1 pt. milk	**Wineglass of rum**

Grease a pie-dish and fill it with strips of pudding crossed lattice fashion. Mix the cornflour smoothly with a little of the milk. Put the rest of the milk on to boil. When boiling remove from the heat and add the blended cornflour, slowly, but stirring thoroughly to prevent lumps forming. Return to heat and cook for 3 min. Add the sugar, beaten egg and the rum. Pour the sauce over the pudding. Bake gently in a moderate oven **(350° F., Gas 4)** until the mixture is set.

If preferred, the pudding may be steamed for 2 hr. in a basin.

6 helpings
Cooking time (baked)—½ hr.
(steamed)—2 hr.

CUSTARDS AND CUSTARD MIXTURES

BASICALLY THESE are made from a mixture of eggs, milk and sugar, cooked very slowly to just set the mixture. Custards can be cooked by "boiling", baking or steaming but they must be cooked very carefully and slowly since over-cooking will cause the mixture to curdle. A custard which is to be turned out requires at least the equivalent of four eggs to one pint of liquid, otherwise it is liable to break.

POURING CUSTARDS

These are made by heating and maintaining the mixture at a temperature below boiling point until the eggs cook evenly through the mixture. The use of a double saucepan for this purpose lessens the risk of curdling.

BAKED CUSTARDS

The pie-dish should be well greased and then placed in a tray of warm water and baked slowly at about **335°–350° F., Gas 3–4**, until the custard is set. Take out of the water immediately to prevent further cooking.

STEAMED CUSTARDS

The basin must be well greased and the custard covered with greased paper to prevent the condensing steam from dripping into it. Only a very gentle flow of steam should be maintained to prevent overcooking. For detailed notes on steaming, *see* p. 410.

CUSTARDS

FLAVOURINGS

Custards can be flavoured with grated nutmeg; cinnamon; vanilla, lemon *or* almond essence; or by infusing a bay leaf *or* thinly-cut strips of lemon rind (avoid the white pith) in the milk for a few minutes then removing them.

BAKED CUSTARD

Crème cuite au four

1½ pt. milk	**3 eggs**
Flavouring (*see above*)	**1½ oz. castor sugar**

Beat the eggs with the sugar. Add the warmed milk and flavouring. Strain into a greased pie-dish. Stand the pie-dish in a tray of warm water and bake slowly in a warm–moderate oven (**335°–350° F., Gas 3–4**) until the custard is set in the centre, about 50 min.

6 helpings

CUP CUSTARD

To make ¾ pt.

½ pt. milk	**1 oz. castor sugar**
Flavouring: lemon rind *or* vanilla essence	**2 tablesp. double cream (optional)**
1 egg and 1 yolk *or* 3 egg yolks	

Warm the milk, infusing the lemon rind if used. Mix eggs and sugar to a liquid. Pour the warmed milk over the eggs and strain the custard into a pan previously rinsed with cold water. Cook the custard gently until the eggs have coagulated and thickened the milk. To ensure that this occurs evenly and forms a smooth creamy texture, stirring should be brisk and thorough. If the custard is cooked in a saucepan, a wooden spoon will be found most suitable for this as the thick edge of the spoon works smoothly over the base of the pan, keeping it clear. If the custard is cooked in a double saucepan over hot water, a whisk is better as thickening takes place from the sides as well as from the base. Do not let the custard boil. When the custard coats the spoon, pour into a cool bowl, and add the vanilla if used. Add the cream (if used) and stir in lightly. Stir frequently during cooling so that a skin does not form on the surface.

NOTE: A thinner pouring custard can be made by using 1 pt. milk and 2 eggs.

Time—15 min.

STEAMED CUSTARD

1 pt. milk	**4 eggs**
Flavouring (*see* above)	**1 oz. castor sugar**

Warm the milk and flavouring. Beat the eggs and sugar together. If bay leaf or lemon rind has been used to flavour, remove from the milk before pouring it on to the eggs and sugar; stir well. Pour the mixture into a buttered mould, cover with greased paper and steam very gently for about 40 min. Turn out and serve with wine sauce (p. 140).

5–6 helpings
Time—50 min.

Variations

BANANA CUSTARD

Crème aux Bananes

1 pt. cup custard	**1 lb. bananas**

Make the custard and when cooked add the sliced bananas. Leave to stand for 3–4 min. Pour into a dish or into individual glasses and serve.

Time—25 min.

BORDER OF PEARS

Bordure de Poires à la Reine

½ lb. loaf sugar	**1 gill milk**
1 pt. water	**2 oz. castor sugar**
A few drops of cochineal	**Grated rind of ½ lemon**
2 lb. small stewing pears	**1 oz. butter**
2 eggs	**3 individual sponge cakes**
1 egg yolk	

Make a syrup by slowly heating together the loaf sugar and water and then boiling rapidly for a few minutes; add a few drops of cochineal to just colour the syrup pink. Peel, halve and core the pears and put immediately into the syrup and stew until tender; about ½ hr. Take out the pears and reduce the syrup by rapid boiling to just over ½ pt., reheat the pears in the syrup before serving. Meanwhile beat together the eggs, warmed milk, castor sugar, lemon rind and melted butter. Slice the sponge cakes and arrange them in a buttered border mould. Pour the custard on to the sponge cakes. Stand the mould in a tray containing sufficient cold water to come about halfway up the sides of the mould. Bake 40 min. in a warm oven **(335° F., Gas 3)** until set.

Turn out on to a hot dish, arrange the pears on the border or in the centre and pour the syrup round.

Serve either hot or cold.

6 helpings
Cooking time—altogether 1¼ hr.

BREAD AND BUTTER PUDDING

Pouding au Pain beurré

6 thin slices of bread and butter	**3 eggs**
2 oz. sultanas *or* **currants** *or* **stoned raisins** *or* **chopped candied peel**	**1½ oz. sugar**
	1½ pt. milk

Grease a 2 pt. pie-dish. Cut the bread into squares or triangles and put them neatly in the dish. Remove the crust, if preferred. Sprinkle the fruit over. Beat the eggs with the sugar, add the milk and pour over the bread; it should only half-fill the dish. Leave to soak at least 30 min. Bake in a moderate oven **(350° F., Gas 4)** until the custard is set; about 1 hr.

5–6 helpings

CABINET PUDDING

Pouding de Cabinet

6 individual sponge cakes *or* **12 savoy biscuits**	**1 pt. milk**
8 ratafias	**4 eggs**
1 oz. castor sugar	**A few drops of vanilla essence**

DECORATION

Angelica	**Glacé cherries**

Grease a 1 pt. soufflé (straight-sided) mould and put a round of greased paper in the bottom, to fit exactly. Decorate the bottom of the mould with a bold design of cherries and angelica. Line the sides with slices of cut sponge cakes. Crumble the trimmings of cake and ratafias and put them into the mould.

Add the sugar to the milk and warm slightly. Add the well-beaten eggs and vanilla essence. Pour the mixture into the mould and leave to stand for about 1 hr., if time allows. Cover with greased paper and steam gently 1–1½ hr. Remove paper, turn out, and peel off top paper.

Serve with jam sauce.

6 helpings
Cooking time—1–1¼ hr.

CABINET PUDDING—PLAIN

4 oz. stoned raisins	**1 oz. sugar**
½ lb. bread	**1 pt. milk**
4 eggs	**Vanilla essence**

Grease a 2 pt. pudding basin and decorate the base and sides by pressing on some halved raisins.

Cut the bread into ¼-in. dice. Beat the eggs. Heat the sugar and milk slightly and stir into the beaten egg. Add vanilla essence to taste. Add the bread and rest of the raisins and leave to soak for ½ hr. Pour into the basin, cover with greased paper and steam gently 1¼–1½ hr. until the pudding is firm in the centre.

Serve with jam sauce.

6 helpings **Cooking time—1¼–1½ hr.**

CANADIAN PUDDING

Pouding Canadien

1 oz. stoned raisins	**Rind of 1 small lemon**
6 oz. corn meal	**2 oz. sugar**
2 pt. milk	**3 eggs**

Grease, then decorate a basin with the raisins. Mix the meal with a little of the cold milk; infuse the lemon rind in the remainder of the milk for 15 min. Remove the lemon rind; pour the boiling milk over the blended corn meal, stirring well. Return to the pan, add the sugar, and simmer gently for 10 min. When cool, add the well-beaten eggs. Pour the mixture carefully into the decorated mould.

Cover. Steam slowly for 1½–2 hr. until firm to the touch.

6–7 helpings

CARAMEL CUSTARD

Crème au Caramel

4 eggs
1 oz. castor sugar
¾ pt. milk
A few drops of vanilla essence

CARAMEL

3 oz. loaf sugar
½ gill cold water

Have ready a warm charlotte *or* plain mould and a thickly-folded band of newspaper to encircle it so that the mould can be firmly held in one hand. Prepare the caramel by heating the loaf sugar and water together, stir until it boils, then remove the spoon and allow to boil without stirring until it is golden brown. Pour the caramel into the warm mould and twist round until the sides and base are well coated with caramel.

Work together the eggs and sugar without beating them and pour on to them the warmed milk. Add the vanilla essence. Strain the custard into the mould and cover with greased paper. Steam very slowly for about ¾ hr. until the custard is firm in the middle; *or* the caramel custard may be baked by leaving it uncovered, standing it in a tray of warm water, and baking in a warm oven (**335° F., Gas 3**) until the custard is set in the centre: about 40 min. Turn out carefully, so that the caramel runs off and serves as a sauce.

NOTE: Small caramel custards can be made in dariole moulds; cook for about 20 min.

6 helpings

CORN PUDDING

Pouding à l'Indienne

3 oz. corn meal
1 pt. milk
1½ oz. castor sugar
¼ teasp. grated lemon rind
2 eggs

Mix the meal with a little cold milk. Boil up the remainder of the milk. Add the blended meal, sugar and lemon rind. Stir well and cook gently for a few minutes until the mixture thickens. Cool; and add the well-beaten eggs. Half-fill well-buttered moulds *or* a pie-dish with the mixture. Bake in a fairly hot oven (**375° F., Gas 5**) 30 min. for small puddings and 40–45 min. for a large pudding.

CRÈME BRÛLÉE

½ pt. milk
½ oz. cornflour
½ pt. cream
A few drops of vanilla essence
3 eggs
2 oz. castor sugar
Ground cinnamon

Mix the cornflour with a little of the milk and put the rest of the milk and cream on to boil. When boiling, pour on to the cornflour paste, stirring well. Return to the pan and simmer for 2–3 min. Add the vanilla essence and stir in the well-beaten eggs. Whisk over a low heat until the mixture thickens, but do not allow to boil. Add 1 oz. sugar to sweeten. Pour into a well-greased soufflé dish, sprinkle well with cinnamon and the rest of the sugar and bake in a fairly hot oven (**400° F., Gas 6**) until the mixture is set and well browned, about ¼ hr., or brown under the grill.

NOTE: *See also* another recipe for Crème Brûlée in Cold Sweets.

6 helpings

CUSTARD PIE

Tourte à la Crème

3 level tablesp. cornflour
1½ pt. milk
3 eggs
1½ oz. castor sugar
A little grated nutmeg
Short crust pastry (p. 557) using 6 oz. flour, etc.

Blend the cornflour with a little of the cold milk and put the rest of the milk to boil. Pour the boiling milk on to the blended cornflour, stirring well. Return to pan, re-boil 2–3 min.; remove from heat. Work together the eggs and sugar, and when the cornflour mixture is cooler add this to the worked eggs.

Line a 9-in. flan ring or a shallow heat-proof glass dish with short crust pastry and prick the base finely. Pour in the custard mixture, dust with a little grated nutmeg, if liked, and bake in a fairly hot oven (**375° F., Gas 5**) until the pastry is browned, then reduce the heat to **335° F., Gas 3,** until the custard is set —45 min.

NOTE: To ensure that the base of the pastry case is cooked through, place the flan ring or dish on a solid baking sheet in the oven.

6 helpings

FOREST PUDDING

4 stale individual sponge cakes	**1 oz. sugar**
Jam	**3 eggs**
Grated rind of ½ lemon	**1½ pt. milk**

Slice the sponge cakes thinly, spread half of them with jam, cover with the remaining halves and put into a well-buttered pie-dish, which they should half-fill. Sprinkle with lemon rind. Beat together the sugar and eggs and pour on the milk. Pour the custard over the sponge cakes and leave to stand for 1 hr. Bake very slowly for 40–50 min. in a warm–moderate oven (**335°–350° F., Gas 3–4**) until the custard is set and the pudding browned on top.

6 helpings

ITALIAN PUDDING (1)

Pouding à l'Italienne

2 eggs	**½ lb. stoned raisins**
½ oz. castor sugar	**2 oz. finely-chopped mixed peel**
¾ pt. milk	**¼ teasp. ground nutmeg**
2 oz. cake-crumbs	**1 lb. cooking apples**
½ lb. stoned dates	

Make a custard by beating together the eggs and sugar and pouring on the warmed milk. Stir in the cake-crumbs. Mix together the dates, raisins, peel and nutmeg. Peel, core and slice the apples thinly. Put the apple slices at the bottom of a well-buttered pie-dish, add the mixed fruit and then cover with the custard mixture. Bake in a warm oven (**335° F., Gas 3**) for ¾–1 hr., until firm and set.

Serve hot or cold.

5–6 helpings

NOTE: See p. 418 for Italian Pudding (2).

JENNY LIND PUDDING

4 stale individual sponge cakes	**1 oz. desiccated coconut**
4 coconut cakes	**1 pt. milk**
12 ratafias	**2 eggs**
	¾–1 oz. castor sugar

Slice the sponge cakes and put them in a buttered pie-dish interspersed with the coconut cakes and ratafias. Simmer the coconut in the milk until tender—about 15 min., cool slightly. Beat the eggs and sugar together and add to the milk and coconut. Pour the custard over the other ingredients and bake gently (about **335° F., Gas 3**) until the mixture is set.

5–6 helpings
Time—50–60 min.

MADEIRA PUDDING

Pouding au Madère

6 oz. bread, cut into ¼-in. dice	**¾ pt. milk**
3 oz. castor sugar	**3 eggs**
1 teasp. grated lemon rind	**1 wineglass sherry *or* Madeira (optional)**

Mix together in a basin the bread, sugar and lemon rind. Heat the milk to about blood heat and pour it on to the well-beaten eggs. Add the sherry *or* Madeira, if used, and pour this over the bread, sugar and lemon rind mixture. Leave to soak for 15–20 min. Pour into a well-buttered mould or basin, cover and steam very gently for 2 hr.

Serve with custard, wine or jam sauce (pp. 138, 139, 140).

5–6 helpings

MARMALADE PUDDING (1)

Pouding à la Confiture d'Oranges

4 tablesp. marmalade	**1 oz. sugar**
1 oz. butter *or* margarine	**½ pt. breadcrumbs**
1 pt. milk	**3 eggs**
	2–4 oz. castor sugar

Butter a 2 pt. pie-dish and cover the bottom of the dish with a layer of marmalade. Heat together the butter, milk and 1 oz. sugar. Add the breadcrumbs and leave to stand for about 10 min. Beat together 1 whole egg and 2 egg yolks and stir well into the breadcrumb mixture. Pour half the breadcrumb mixture into the dish; add another layer of marmalade, and put the remainder of the breadcrumb mixture on top. Bake in a moderate oven (**350° F., Gas 4**) until the mixture is set. Whip the egg whites stiffly, fold in the 2–4 oz. castor sugar and pile on top of the pudding. Dredge well with castor sugar. Bake in a very cool oven (**290° F., Gas 1**) for about 20–30 min. until the meringue is fawn and crisp.

Cooking time—1 hr. **5-6 helpings**

NOTE: See p. 418 for Marmalade Pudding (2).

NEWMARKET PUDDING

2 eggs
3 oz. sugar
½ pt. milk
5 individual sponge cakes
2 oz. finely-chopped peel
2 oz. muscatel raisins (halved)
1 oz. currants
3 tablesp. redcurrant jelly

Beat together the eggs and sugar and stir in the milk. Slice the sponge cakes and place them in layers alternately with a mixture of peel, raisins and currants. Pour in the custard, cover with greased paper and steam gently for 1–1¼ hr., until set. Warm the redcurrant jelly, turn out the pudding and coat with the jelly just before serving.

5–6 helpings
Cooking time—1–1¼ hr.

OATMEAL PUDDING

Pouding d'Avoine

1½ oz. fine oatmeal
½ oz. plain flour
1½ pt. milk
1–2 eggs
¼–½ teasp. salt

Blend the oatmeal and flour to a smooth paste with some of the milk. Put the rest of the milk on to boil. Add the blended mixture carefully, stirring well. Cook gently for 5 min. Cool slightly. Stir in the well-beaten egg(s). Add salt to taste. Pour into a buttered pie-dish. Bake gently in a moderate oven (**350° F., Gas 4**) for about 20 min.

Serve with cream and sugar, or golden syrup.

4 helpings **Time—40 min.**

QUEEN OF PUDDINGS

Reine des Poudings

1 pt. milk
½ pt. breadcrumbs
2 oz. butter *or* margarine
Grated rind of 2 lemons
2 oz. granulated sugar
2 eggs
3 tablesp. jam
2–4 oz. castor sugar

Heat the milk and add to it the breadcrumbs, fat, lemon rind and granulated sugar. Leave to soak for 30 min. Separate the eggs and stir in the yolks. Pour the mixture into a buttered pie-dish and bake in a moderate oven (**350° F., Gas 4**) until set—about ¾ hr. When the pudding is set, spread the jam on top. Whip the egg whites very stiffly, add 1 oz. of castor sugar and whip again until stiff; then stir in lightly the rest of the sugar. Spread over the pudding, put into a very cool oven (**265° F., Gas ½**) until the meringue is set and golden brown.

5-6 helpings

QUEEN'S PUDDING

Pouding à la Reine

¼ lb. biscuit- *or* cake-crumbs
1 pt. milk
2 oz. sugar
2 eggs
Vanilla essence
6–9 apricot halves (preserved, i.e canned *or* bottled)
Glacé cherries for decoration

APRICOT SAUCE

½ pt. apricot syrup
Sugar to taste
1 tablesp. kirsch *or* rum

Rub the biscuit- or cake-crumbs through a fine sieve. Heat the milk, add the crumbs, leave to stand for 10–15 min. until soft; then beat until smooth. Beat in the sugar and eggs. Flavour with vanilla essence. Grease a plain mould or basin with butter, line the base with a round of greased paper and sprinkle with castor sugar. Pour in the mixture and cover with paper. Stand the mould in a tin of hot water, and bake in a warm oven (**335° F., Gas 3**) until the mixture is firm to the touch; about ¾ hr.

Meanwhile make the apricot sauce by boiling the apricot syrup with sugar added to taste until it is slightly reduced, then add the rum *or* kirsch.

When the pudding is set in the middle, leave it to stand a few minutes and then carefully unmould on to a dish. Tear off the paper, arrange apricot halves round the dish, decorate pudding with cherries, and pour round it the apricot sauce.

6 helpings

SAVOY PUDDING

Pouding de Savoie

8 oz. stale savoy *or* sponge cake
2 oz. finely chopped mixed peel
1½ gill milk
2 oz. warmed butter
1 wineglass sherry *or* Marsala (optional)
4½ oz. castor sugar
3 eggs

Pass the cake through a fine wire sieve. Add the peel, milk, warmed butter, wine and 1½ oz. of the sugar. Separate the eggs and add the yolks to the mixture. Beat well and pour the mixture into a buttered pie-dish. Bake in a moderate oven **(350° F., Gas 4)** until the pudding is set—about ¾ hr. Stiffly whisk the egg whites, stir in the remaining 3 oz. of sugar lightly, and pile on top of the pudding. Bake in a very cool oven **(265°–290° F., Gas ½–1)** to set and colour the meringue, about ½ hr.

5–6 helpings

SAXON PUDDING

Pouding à la Saxonaise

4 individual sponge cakes
6 macaroons
18 ratafias
2 eggs
½ pt. milk
¼ pt. cream
1 glass sherry (optional)
1 oz. sugar
A few drops of vanilla essence

DECORATION

2 oz. almonds
A few glacé cherries
Angelica

Blanch, peel, shred and bake the almonds until golden brown, in a cool oven (p. 512). Well-butter a plain charlotte mould and decorate the sides with the almonds and the bottom with halves of cherries and strips of angelica. Fill the mould with alternate layers of sliced sponge cake and pieces of macaroon and ratafias. Beat together the eggs, milk, cream, wine (if used), sugar and vanilla essence and pour this into the mould. Cover with greased paper and leave to stand for 1 hr. Steam for 1½–1¾ hr.

Turn out and serve with fruit syrup or sauce. If liked, the pudding can be served cold with whipped cream.

5–6 helpings

VIENNESE PUDDING

Pouding à la Viennoise

1 oz. almonds
½ pt. milk
2 eggs
3 tablesp. sherry (optional)
5 oz. white bread cut into ¼-in. dice
2 oz. castor sugar
3 oz. sultanas
2 oz. finely-chopped candied peel
Grated rind of 1 lemon

CARAMEL

1 oz. loaf sugar
4 tablesp. water

Blanch, shred and, if liked, the almonds can be browned in a very cool oven (p. 512). Put the loaf sugar into a small saucepan with 4 tablesp. of water and heat gently, stirring well until all the sugar is dissolved, without boiling. Remove the spoon, bring to the boil without stirring until light brown. Remove from the heat and add the milk quickly. Reheat gently until the caramel has dissolved in the milk. Allow to cool, then add the well-beaten eggs and sherry (if used). Meanwhile mix together the bread dice, castor sugar, cleaned sultanas, peel, almonds and lemon rind and pour the custard mixture on to this. Leave to stand for 1 hr. Pour into a well-buttered mould, cover with greased paper and steam for 2 hr. until set.

Turn out and serve with custard or arrowroot sauce.

6–7 helpings

BATTERS

BATTERS ARE MADE from a basic mixture of flour, milk and egg. The flour (with salt added for flavouring) is worked to a slack consistency with the eggs and some of the liquid, so that it can be beaten more easily until smooth and viscous. The rest of the liquid is then stirred in. The mixture is left to stand for half an hour before use.

The lightness of a batter depends on the quick formation of steam within the mixture and the quick cooking of the flour. A baked batter therefore requires a hot oven (**425° F., Gas 7**); the temperature can be reduced when the flour is almost cooked. It is best to put the batter at the top of the oven to begin with; then to move it to a lower shelf at reduced heat (**375° F., Gas 5**) to finish cooking.

Batter mixtures may also be steamed. See notes on steaming (p. 410).

Coating batters are dealt with in the section on fritters (p. 398).

Basic Recipe

BATTER PUDDING

½ lb. plain flour
¼ teasp. salt
2 eggs
1 pt. milk
1 tablesp. cooking fat *or* lard

Sift the flour and salt into a basin. Make a well in the centre of the flour and break the eggs into this. Add about a gill of the milk. Stir gradually working the flour down from the sides and adding more milk, as required, to make a stiff batter consistency. Beat well for about 5 min. Add the rest of the milk. Cover and leave to stand for 30 min. Put the fat into a Yorkshire pudding tin and heat in the oven until hot. The fat should just be beginning to smoke. Quickly pour in the batter and leave to cook in a hot oven (**425° F., Gas 7**) at the top of the oven until nicely browned. Reduce the heat to **375° F., Gas 5**, and finish cooking through for 10–15 min.

Serve with wine-, syrup-, or jam-sauce (*see* Sauce Section, pp. 136–140).

6 helpings
Time (Large pudding)—35–40 min.
(Individual puddings)—20–25 min.

STEAMED BATTER PUDDING

1 pt. milk
¼ teasp. salt
2 eggs
½ lb. plain flour

Prepare the mixture as in previous recipe. Pour it into a well-greased pudding basin. Cover with a greased paper and steam for 2 hr.

Serve with a fruit- or sweet-sauce.

6 helpings **Cooking time—2 hr.**

Variations

BATTER PUDDING WITH APPLES

½ lb. plain flour
¼ teasp. salt
2 eggs
1 pt. milk
1 lb. apples
2 oz. granulated sugar
¼ teasp. ground cinnamon *or* grated lemon rind
½ oz. butter

Prepare the batter as for Batter Pudding. Cover and leave to stand for 30 min.

Core, peel and slice the apples thinly. Sprinkle them with the sugar and cinnamon *or* lemon rind. Spread them over a well-greased Yorkshire pudding tin. Pour the batter over, flake the butter on top, and bake in a hot oven (**425° F., Gas 7**) until brown, 20–25 min. Reduce the heat to **375° F., Gas 5**, and finish cooking. Dredge with sugar before serving.

6 helpings **Cooking time—30–40 min.**

BATTER PUDDING WITH DRIED FRUIT

½ lb. plain flour
¼ teasp. salt
2 eggs
1 pt. milk
1–2 tablesp. cooking fat
4 oz. mixed dried fruit
¼ teasp. mixed spice *or* ground cinnamon *or* grated lemon rind
Castor sugar

Prepare the batter as given for Batter Pudding. Heat the fat in a Yorkshire pudding tin until very hot. Pour in the batter and sprinkle in the mixed dried fruit and spice. Bake in a hot oven (**425° F., Gas 7**) for about 20–25 min. until brown. Reduce the heat of the oven to **375° F., Gas 5**. Lower the pudding in the oven and finish cooking through for 10–15 min.

Dredge well with castor sugar before serving.

6 helpings

BLACK CAP PUDDING

2 oz. currants
½ lb. plain flour
2 oz. castor sugar
Pinch of salt
2 eggs
1 pt. milk

Well grease 8–9 dariole moulds and sprinkle the cleaned currants at the base of each. Put the flour, sugar and salt into a basin and make a well in the centre. Break the eggs into the well, add a little of the milk, stir, and gradually work down the flour from the sides, adding more milk as required until a stiff batter consistency is obtained. Beat well for 5 min., add the rest of the milk. (If time allows, let it stand for ½ hr.) Two-thirds fill the moulds with the mixture, cover with greased paper and steam 30 min. until set.

NOTE: This may be cooked as one large pudding in a basin—steam for 1 hr.

6 helpings

CRÊPES SUZETTE

½ pt. batter
Icing sugar
Brandy *or* rum

FILLING

2 oz. butter
3 oz. castor sugar
Rind of ½ orange, grated
2 teasp. orange juice
1 teasp. lemon juice
1 tablesp. Kirsch *or* Curacao

Make the batter and leave it to stand. Cream together the butter and sugar for the filling until very soft, then work in the orange juice, orange rind, lemon juice and liqueur. Make a very thin pancake, spread with some of the filling, roll up and dredge with icing sugar. Put into a warm place while the rest of the pancakes are being made. Just before serving pour over the rum or brandy and light up. Serve immediately.

FRENCH PANCAKES

Crêpes à la Française

½ pt. milk
2 oz. butter *or* margarine
2 oz. castor sugar
2 eggs
2 oz. plain flour
A little grated lemon rind
4 tablesp. jam (approx.)

Warm the milk. Cream the fat and sugar until soft. Well whisk the eggs and beat them gradually into the creamed fat and sugar. Stir in the flour. Add the warmed milk and lemon rind. Beat well. Leave to stand for ½ hr.

Grease 6 small deep plates *or* large saucers and pour an equal quantity of batter into each. Bake in a fairly hot oven (**400° F., Gas 6**) for about 5–10 min., until the batter rises; then more slowly (**350° F., Gas 4**) for about another 10 min., until firm and brown on top.

Turn a pancake out on to a hot dish, spread quickly with melted jam; lay another pancake on top, and so on until the last pancake is put on top.

Dredge well with castor sugar and serve quickly.

NOTE: This is sometimes known as **Angel Pudding**—*Pouding des Anges*.

5–6 helpings

FRUIT BATTER—STEAMED

Pâte de fruits à l'étuvée

6 oz. plain flour
¼ teasp. salt
3 eggs
¾ pt. milk
1 lb. fresh fruit
¼ teasp. ground cinnamon *or* grated lemon rind
2 oz. sugar

Prepare the batter as for Batter Pudding (p. 396). Leave to stand for about 30 min. Put the prepared fruit, spice and sugar into a well-greased basin and pour over the batter. Cover with well-greased paper and steam for about 2 hr.

5–6 helpings

PANCAKES

Crêpes

Batter as for Batter Pudding (p. 396)
A little cooking fat
Lemon
Castor sugar

Prepare the batter. Leave to stand for ½ hr. then pour into a jug. Use a small clean frying pan or omelette pan.

If the pan is new or has been washed frequently, melt in it about ½ oz. cooking fat; heat until it is smoking hot, twisting the pan so that the sides are coated with fat. Pour away all the fat and wipe the pan clean with a soft cloth or pieces of kitchen paper, otherwise the pancakes may stick.

Put about ¼ oz. of cooking fat into the cleaned frying pan and heat until it is just beginning to smoke. Quickly pour in enough batter to coat thinly the bottom of the pan, tilting the pan to make sure that the batter runs over evenly. Move the frying pan over a quick heat until the pancake is set and browned underneath. Make sure that the pancake is loose at the sides and either toss or turn with a broad bladed knife or fish slice. Brown on the other side and turn on to a sugared paper. Sprinkle with sugar and lemon juice, roll up and keep hot while cooking the rest.

Serve dredged with castor sugar and pieces of cut lemon.

6 helpings

NOTE: Other flavourings such as jam, orange, tangerine or brandy may be used, as follows:

Jam pancakes—*Crêpes de Confiture:* Spread with jam before rolling up.

Orange pancakes—*Crêpes d'Orange:* Make the pancakes but sprinkle with orange juice and serve with pieces of cut orange.

Tangerine pancakes—*Crêpes d'Orange de Tanger:* Add grated tangerine rind to the batter. Sprinkle with tangerine juice before rolling up.

With **brandy filling**: Cream together 2 oz. butter and 1 oz. castor sugar until soft. Work in 1 tablesp. brandy and 1 teasp. lemon juice. Spread the pancakes with this mixture. Roll up and put immediately into the serving dish.

YORKSHIRE PUDDING

Pouding à la Yorkshire

1 pt. batter as for Batter Pudding
2 tablesp. dripping

Prepare and cook as for Batter Pudding but cook the pudding in meat dripping. Start cooking on the top shelf above the meat and finish off below the meat on a lower shelf.

Serve with roast beef.

NOTE: In Yorkshire this pudding is served with gravy, as a separate course, before the meat.

6 helpings
Cooking time—about 35 min.

FRITTERS

FRITTERS ARE USUALLY made from a batter mixture, used as a coating or as a means of cohering a mixture. They are fried in fat.

Fritters can be varied by using: dessert **gooseberries; prunes** soaked, the stones removed and the cavity filled with an almond *or* marzipan; ripe **pears** cut into quarters soaked in a little liqueur *or* lemon juice before coating; **strawberries; figs; stale cake** *or* **pudding,** cut into suitable pieces, soaked lightly in fruit syrup *or* liqueur; **small fresh fruit** coated and dropped into the fat in spoonfuls.

GENERAL HINTS

1. The batter should be thick enough to coat the food to be fried.
2. The frying fat should be at least one inch in depth. Coated food can be fried in deeper fat.
3. The fat must be hot enough to seal the batter immediately so that the food

inside does not become greasy, but not so hot as to burn the coating before the filling is cooked or heated through.

4. When hot enough the fat should just show signs of hazing. It can be tested by dropping a small spot of batter into the fat. If the fat is at the correct temperature the batter will sink, rise to the surface immediately and then begin to colour.
5. Cook only small amounts at a time and finish cooking on one side before turning the food over.
6. Allow the fat time to reheat before putting in another batch.
7. Drain the fried food well on kitchen paper, which will absorb the surplus fat before serving.
8. Strain the fat after use.

The following batters can be used for coating. A yeast batter is given in the recipe for Apricot Fritters (p. 400).

COATING BATTER (1)

2 oz. plain flour
Pinch of salt
1 dessertsp. salad oil *or* oiled butter
½ gill warm water
1 egg white

Sift together the flour and salt. Mix to a smooth consistency with the oil and water. Beat well and leave to stand for at least 30 min. Just before using, stiffly whisk the egg white and then stir it lightly into the batter.

COATING BATTER (2)

4 oz. plain flour
Pinch of salt
1 tablesp. salad oil *or* melted butter
1 gill warm water (approx.)
1 teasp. baking powder

Sift together the flour and salt. Mix to a smooth consistency with the oil and water until the mixture is thick enough to beat. Beat well; then add water until the mixture is of a consistency to coat the back of a wooden spoon. Leave to stand for at least 30 min. Just before using, stir in the baking powder.

COATING BATTER (3)

4 oz. plain flour
Pinch of salt
1 egg
1 gill milk

Sift together the flour and salt. Make a well in the centre of the flour and add the egg and some of the milk. Mix gradually to a stiff consistency, using more milk as required. Beat well. Add the rest of the milk. Leave to stand for about 30 min. before using.

ALMOND FRITTERS

Beignets d'Amandes

2 eggs
1 oz. castor sugar
½ oz. cornflour
2 oz. ground almonds
A few drops of vanilla
Frying-fat

Beat the egg yolks and the sugar together until thick and creamy. Stiffly whisk the egg whites. Stir the cornflour, almonds and vanilla essence into the creamed yolks and sugar. Lightly stir in the egg whites. Drop the mixture in teaspoonfuls into frying fat (which is just beginning to haze and which is at least 1 in. in depth). Fry until golden brown underneath. Turn, and when cooked on the other side drain well.

Dredge with castor sugar and serve at once.

5–6 helpings
Time—30 min.

APPLE FRITTERS

Beignets de Pommes

1 lb. cooking apples
Castor sugar
Deep fat
Coating batter
Lemon juice

Peel the apples, core them with an apple corer and cut into rings about ¼ in. thick. Put the apple rings on to a plate and sprinkle with lemon juice and sugar. Let them stand for a few minutes. Using a skewer dip them into the batter, then drop them into deep fat which should just be beginning to haze. Cook until golden brown—about 4 min. and then lift out with a skewer.

Dredge well with castor sugar before serving.

4 helpings
Time—20 min.

APRICOT FRITTERS

Beignets d'Abricots

12 apricot halves (fresh *or* preserved)
Fat for frying
Castor sugar
Ground cinnamon

YEAST BATTER

¼ oz. yeast
¼ teasp. castor sugar
1½ gill warm milk (approx.)
6 oz. plain flour
Pinch of salt
1 oz. melted butter

Make the batter by creaming the yeast and sugar and adding a little milk. Sift together 2 oz. of the flour and the salt into a warm bowl. Mix to a batter consistency with the yeast mixture, adding more milk if required. Leave to rise until double its size. Meanwhile, drain the apricots from the syrup. When the dough is risen add the rest of the flour and warm milk to make a batter consistency, and work in the melted butter. Leave to rise again in a warm place. Coat the apricots thinly with the batter and place them on a well-buttered paper. Leave in a warm place for 30 min. Fry in hot fat until nicely brown.

Drain well and dredge with plenty of castor sugar and cinnamon, before serving.

12 fritters

BANANA FRITTERS

Beignets de Bananes

4 firm bananas
Coating batter
Frying-fat
Castor sugar

Prepare the batter. Cut each banana lengthwise and across the middle, making four portions. Coat with batter. Fry in hot fat, which is just beginning to haze.

Sprinkle well with castor sugar and serve immediately.

6 helpings

BREAD AND BUTTER FRITTERS

Beignets de Pain beurré

Coating batter
6 thin slices of bread and butter
Jam
Fat for frying
Castor sugar
Ground cinnamon

Make the batter. Spread the slices of bread and butter well with jam. Make into sandwiches and cut into four. Dip into the batter and fry in fat which is at least 1 in. deep and which is just showing signs of smoking or hazing. Turn and fry to a golden brown. Drain well.

Dredge with plenty of castor sugar and cinnamon.

Serve immediately.

4–5 helpings
Cooking time—5 min.

BREAD FRITTERS

Beignets de Pain

6 slices of bread, about ¼ in. thick, cut into halves *or* 3 French dinner rolls cut into slices
1 egg
1 egg yolk
¾ pt. milk
¼ teasp. ground cinnamon
½ oz. castor sugar
½ small glass of maraschino (optional)
Clarified butter *or* frying-fat

Cut the crusts off the bread and place the bread in a deep dish. Beat the egg and egg yolk, add the milk, cinnamon, sugar and maraschino, if used. Stir well, and pour over the bread. Leave to soak for 10 min. Carefully lift out the slices of bread and let them drain. Fry in hot fat or clarified butter until golden brown on both sides.

Drain, sprinkle with castor sugar and cinnamon.

Serve immediately.

6 helpings **Cooking time—10 min.**

CURRANT FRITTERS

Beignets de Groseilles rouges

2 eggs
1 oz. castor sugar
¼ pt. milk
2 oz. plain flour
Pinch of salt
3 oz. currants
4 oz. boiled rice
Pinch of nutmeg
Fat for frying

Beat together the egg yolks, sugar and milk. Gradually stir some of the mixture into the sifted flour and salt until a thick batter is formed; beat well. Add the rest of the milk and egg. Whisk the egg whites stiffly, and stir them in lightly. Add the currants, rice and nutmeg. Drop the mixture in spoonfuls into hot shallow fat and fry on both sides until crisp and golden brown.

Drain well, sprinkle with castor sugar and serve.

4-5 helpings
Cooking time—10-15 min.

CUSTARD FRITTERS

Beignets à la crème cuite

2 oz. plain flour
2 oz. cornflour
1 pt. milk
2 oz. castor sugar
Pinch of salt
4 egg yolks
A few drops of vanilla essence
Egg and fresh bread-crumbs
Fat for frying

Mix the flour and cornflour smoothly with a little of the milk. Boil the rest of the milk. Pour the boiling milk over the paste, stirring well. Return the mixture to the saucepan, and cook gently for about 4 min. Stir in the sugar, salt and egg yolks. Continue cooking for a few minutes. Add the vanilla essence. Spread the mixture to a depth of 1 in. on a dish and leave to set. When cold, cut into rounds and coat with egg and breadcrumbs. Fry in fat (which is just beginning to haze) until golden brown.

Serve quickly with a wine- or jam-sauce.

4 helpings
Time—to make the mixture 15 min.
—to fry 4-5 min. per batch

GOOSEBERRY FRITTERS

1 lb. large gooseberries
Fat for frying

BATTER

2 oz. plain flour
Pinch of salt
2 tablesp. cream *or* milk
2 tablesp. water
2 eggs

Sift together the flour and salt. Mix to a stiff batter with the milk, water and egg yolks (*see* p. 399). Beat well and leave to stand for at least ½ hr.

Top, tail, wash and dry the gooseberries. Stiffly whisk the egg whites and stir into the batter then add the gooseberries. Take up 2–3 gooseberries at a time, using a greased tablespoon, and lower them into the deep fat which should just be beginning to haze, without separating them. Fry a golden brown, drain well.

Sprinkle with plenty of sugar and serve.

6–7 helpings
Cooking time—6-8 min.

INDIAN FRITTERS

Beignets à l'Indienne

3 oz. plain flour
Pinch of salt
Boiling water
2 eggs
2 egg yolks
Frying-fat
Jam *or* jelly

Sift the flour into a basin with a pinch of salt. Stir in a good ½ gill of boiling water and beat to form a very stiff smooth paste. Leave to cool slightly. Beat in the eggs and egg yolks gradually and thoroughly. Have ready the deep fat, just beginning to haze. Half fill a tablespoon with the mixture, put a teaspoonful of jam *or* jelly in the centre and cover with some more of the batter mixture and drop this into the hot fat. Cook until golden brown, about 3 min.; drain well.

Dredge with castor sugar or serve with a sauce made from jam *or* jelly similar to the filling.

5–6 helpings
Cooking time—15-20 min.

ORANGE FRITTERS

Beignets d'Oranges

Coating batter
4 oranges
Fat for frying
Castor sugar

Prepare the batter. Remove the peel and

pith from the oranges; divide them into pieces of 3–4 segments. Carefully cut into the centre to remove pips. Dip into the batter and fry in hot fat until golden brown about 3–4 min. Drain well.

Dredge with castor sugar and serve at once.

6 helpings

PINEAPPLE FRITTERS

Beignets d'Ananas

Coating batter
2 cans small pineapple rings
Fat for frying
Castor sugar

Make the batter. Drain the pineapple well. Dip each ring into batter and then using a skewer, lower the ring into the deep fat which should be just hazing. Cook until crisp and nicely browned. Drain; dredge with castor sugar and serve at once.

If liked, serve with pineapple sauce made from the syrup.

Allow 2 fritters for each helping

POLISH FRITTERS

Beignets à la Polonaise

6 pancakes
Apricot marmalade
2 oz. breadcrumbs
4 oz. finely-crushed macaroons
1 egg
Fat for frying
Castor sugar
Ground cinnamon

Make the pancakes. Spread each one with apricot marmalade and roll up firmly. Trim off the ends and cut each pancake across in half. Mix together the breadcrumbs and macaroons. Coat each piece of pancake with egg; roll in the crumb mixture and fry in hot fat until nicely brown. Drain well.

Sprinkle with castor sugar and cinnamon and serve.

6 helpings

RICE FRITTERS

3 oz. rice
1½ pt. milk
½ oz. butter
1½ oz. granulated sugar
2 tablesp. orange marmalade
2 eggs
Coating batter
Fat for frying
Castor sugar
Quarters of orange *or* lemon (optional)

Simmer the rice in the milk until all the milk is absorbed. Add the butter, granulated sugar, marmalade and beaten eggs; cook gently until the mixture thickens. Spread the mixture on to a dish, to the thickness of ½ in. When cold, cut into strips *or* squares. Dip these into the batter and fry in hot fat until crisp and brown. Drain well.

Dredge with castor sugar and serve with quarters of orange *or* lemon if liked.

5–6 helpings
Time to fry—4–5 min. per batch

SOUFFLÉ FRITTERS

Beignets soufflés

4 oz. flour
Pinch of salt
½ pt. water
4 oz. butter *or* margarine
3 large eggs
Vanilla essence
Fat for frying
Castor sugar

Make choux pastry: sift the flour and salt. Put the water and fat in a saucepan and when the fat has melted bring to boiling point. Add the sifted flour all at once and beat well over the heat until the mixture leaves the sides of the pan—about 1 min. Allow to cool slightly and add the beaten eggs gradually and then vanilla essence to taste, beating well.

Heat the deep fat until it is just beginning to haze. Grease a dessertspoon and, with it, drop small spoonfuls of the pastry into the fat. Cook gently until crisp and lightly browned. Drain well.

Dredge with castor sugar and serve hot.

NOTE: It is advisable to test a fritter from each batch to ensure that the centre is cooked, since the time of cooking depends on the temperature of the fat.

5–6 helpings
Cooking time—7–10 min.

STRAWBERRY FRITTERS

Beignets de Fraises

Proceed as for Gooseberry Fritters (p. 401), substituting strawberries for gooseberries.

Cooking time—6–8 min.

HOT SOUFFLÉS

SOUFFLÉS CAN BE either steamed or baked. The mixture depends for its lightness on the introduction of air incorporated into the egg whites by whisking.

PREPARATION OF THE SOUFFLÉ TIN OR MOULD

Grease with clarified butter or a tasteless cooking fat. Tie a double band of greased paper to come 3 in. above the top and half-way down the side of the tin, to support the mixture as it rises, although this is not always so necessary with baked soufflés, as the outside becomes firm as it rises. The cut edges of the paper should be at the top. If the soufflé is to be steamed, cut a circle of greased paper for the top of the tin to prevent condensing water dripping on to the soufflé during steaming.

STEAMED SOUFFLÉS

These are cooked in a steamer *or* a saucepan containing sufficient boiling water to come half-way up the sides of the pan. To prevent the soufflé tin from being in direct contact with the bottom of the saucepan, stand it on an upturned saucer or plate.

Steam gently but steadily and avoid moving or jolting the steamer in any way. When cooked, the soufflé should be well risen and just firm to touch. Turn out immediately on to a hot dish and serve at once with a suitable sauce.

BAKED SOUFFLÉS

These are served in the dish in which they are baked—either in a large dish, in individual fireproof china dishes, or in paper cases. The dish should be greased and the mixture should only three-quarters fill it before cooking. Soufflés tend to sink very easily, so during cooking avoid unnecessary opening of the oven door; close it gently as a sudden cold draught or jolting of the oven could cause the mixture to fall. When cooked, the soufflé should be well risen and firm.

Serve at once with a suitable sauce.

GENERAL HINTS

1. Before beginning to make the soufflé, prepare the tin or mould, and see that the steamer or oven is on.

2. Whisk the egg whites as stiffly as possible, until they stand up in points. Fold them very carefully into the mixture taking care not to push out the entrapped air. Only half-fill the mould. Cook straight away.
3. Time the preparation and cooking so that the soufflé can be served as soon as it is cooked. The mixture falls very quickly after removal from the heat.

APRICOT SOUFFLÉ

Soufflé aux Abricots

3/8 pt. apricot purée
1½ oz. butter
1½ oz. plain flour
4 egg yolks
2 oz. castor sugar
Cochineal
6 egg whites

Prepare the soufflé tin (*see* p. 403). Make the apricot purée by rubbing either stewed or tinned apricots through a fine sieve and thinning down the purée with some of the syrup.

Melt the butter in the saucepan, add the flour and cook slowly for a few minutes. Stir in gradually the apricot purée; continue cooking until the mixture thickens. Leave to cool. Beat in the egg yolks singly and the sugar. Add a few drops of cochineal to bring up the apricot colouring. Stiffly whisk the egg whites; fold them into the mixture. Pour into the soufflé mould, cover and steam gently, about 50–60 min.

Turn out and serve at once with apricot- (p. 136) or custard- (p. 138) sauce.

6 helpings

CHOCOLATE OMELET SOUFFLÉ

Omelette Soufflée au Chocolat

As for Omelet Soufflé (p. 405) but omit the flour and jam. Add 2 oz. finely-grated plain chocolate to the egg yolks and sugar.

4 helpings
Cooking time—15–20 min.

CHOCOLATE SOUFFLÉ

Soufflé au Chocolat

2 oz. finely-grated plain chocolate
3/8 pt. milk
1½ oz. butter
1½ oz. plain flour
4 egg yolks
3 oz. castor sugar
½ teasp. vanilla essence
5 egg whites

Prepare the soufflé tin (p. 403). Dissolve the chocolate in the milk. Melt the butter, add the flour and let it cook for a few minutes without colouring. Add the milk and beat well until smooth. Reheat until the mixture thickens and comes away from the sides of the pan. Allow to cool slightly. Beat in the egg yolks well, one at a time, add the sugar and vanilla essence. Stiffly whisk the egg whites and fold them lightly into the mixture. Turn into the mould; cover, and steam very gently for about 1 hr.

6 helpings

CUSTARD SOUFFLÉ

Soufflé à la Crème

Butter
3 oz. plain flour
¾ pt. milk
4 eggs
2 oz. castor sugar

Well butter a pie-dish. Melt 3 oz. butter in a saucepan, add the flour and stir over the heat until well cooked but not coloured. Add the milk; beat well until smooth. Reheat stirring continuously until the mixture thickens and comes away from the sides of the pan. Let it cool slightly. Beat in the egg yolks singly and add the sugar. Stiffly whisk the egg whites and fold them lightly into the mixture. Turn into the pie-dish and bake in a fairly hot oven (**375° F., Gas 5**) for 25–30 min.

Serve with a wine- or fruit-sauce.

6 helpings

GINGER SOUFFLÉ

Soufflé au Gingembre

1 oz. cornflour
¼ pt. milk
2 oz. butter
2 oz. castor sugar
¼ pt. syrup from the preserved ginger
4 egg yolks
2 oz. preserved ginger
5 egg whites

Blend the cornflour with a little milk. Heat the rest of the milk in a saucepan; add the butter and cornflour paste. Stir well and heat gently until the mixture thickens. Work in the sugar and ginger syrup. Separate the eggs and beat the yolks into the mixture one at a time. Add the preserved ginger (cut into small pieces). Stiffly whisk the egg whites and fold them into the mixture. Three-quarters fill individual paper soufflé cases. Bake in a fairly hot oven (**375° F., Gas 5**) about 15 min. until firm and well risen.

Dredge with castor sugar and serve.

6 helpings

LEMON SOUFFLÉ

Soufflé au Citron

Butter	**Finely-grated rind of 1½ lemons**
1½ oz. plain flour	**1½ oz. castor sugar**
⅜ pt. milk	**2 teasp. lemon juice**
5 egg yolks	**6 egg whites**

Butter and prepare a soufflé mould (see p. 403). Melt 1½ oz. butter, stir in the flour and cook for a few minutes. Add the milk gradually, beating well, and continue cooking until the mixture thickens. Leave it to cool. Beat in the yolks one at a time. Stir in the lemon rind, sugar and lemon juice. Stiffly whisk the egg whites and fold them into the mixture. Pour into the mould, cover with a buttered paper. Steam for 50–60 min. until firm on top.

6 helpings

OMELET SOUFFLÉ

Omelette Soufflée

4 egg yolks	**6 egg whites**
3 oz. castor sugar	**2 tablesp. warmed jam**
½ teasp. vanilla essence	**Vanilla sugar**
½ oz. plain flour	

Well butter a soufflé dish. Cream together the egg yolks and sugar, add the vanilla essence and stir in the flour. Stiffly whisk the egg whites and fold them lightly into the yolk mixture. Pour half the mixture into the soufflé dish; add a layer of jam and pour the rest of the mixture on top.

Dredge well with vanilla sugar. Bake in a fairly hot oven (**375° F., Gas 5**) for 15–20 min., until well risen and set. Serve at once.

5–6 helpings

ORANGE SOUFFLÉ

Soufflé à l'Orange

Butter	**Finely-grated rind of 1½ oranges**
1½ oz. plain flour	**Juice of ½ orange**
⅜ pt. milk	**1½ oz. castor sugar**
5 egg yolks	**6 egg whites**

Butter and prepare a soufflé tin (*see* p. 403). Melt 1½ oz. butter, stir in the flour and cook for a few minutes. Add the milk gradually, beating well. Continue cooking until the mixture thickens. Leave it to cool, then beat in the yolks one at a time. Stir in the orange rind, juice and sugar. Stiffly whisk the egg whites and fold these into the mixture. Pour the mixture into the mould; cover with a buttered paper. Steam for 50–60 min. until firm on top.

Serve immediately.

5–6 helpings

PINEAPPLE SOUFFLÉ

Soufflé à l'Ananas

1½ oz. butter	**A few drops of vanilla essence**
1½ oz. plain flour	**3 oz. preserved pineapple**
⅜ pt. milk	**6 egg whites**
4½ egg yolks	**Angelica (optional)**
1½ oz. castor sugar	

Well butter and prepare a soufflé tin (see p. 403). If liked, the bottom can be decorated with angelica and pineapple. Melt 1½ oz. butter, stir in the flour and cook very slowly for a few minutes. Add the milk gradually, beating all the time, continue cooking for a minute longer. Let the mixture cool slightly. Beat in the egg yolks one at a time then add the sugar, vanilla essence and diced pineapple. Stiffly whisk the egg whites and fold them lightly into the mixture. Pour the mixture into the prepared soufflé tin; cover with a buttered paper. Steam gently for 45–60 min. until firm on the top.

Unmould and serve immediately, with pineapple sauce.

NOTE: If canned pineapple is used, drain the fruit well and substitute half the milk with pineapple juice.

5–6 helpings

HOT SOUFFLÉS

RASPBERRY SOUFFLÉ

Soufflé aux Framboises

½ lb. ripe raspberries
2 oz. cornflour
2 oz. castor sugar
⅛ pt. cream
3 eggs
2 oz. cake- *or* bread-crumbs

Butter a soufflé dish. Pass the raspberries through a fine nylon sieve. Mix together the cornflour, sugar and raspberry pulp to a smooth consistency. Add the cream. Separate the eggs, beat the egg yolks into the mixture and add the cake-crumbs. Stiffly whisk the egg whites and fold them into the mixture. Turn the mixture into the soufflé dish and bake in a fairly hot oven (**400° F., Gas 6**) for 25–30 min.

4 helpings

RICE AND APPLE SOUFFLÉ

Soufflé de Riz aux Pommes

1 lb. cooking apples
2 tablesp. water
1 oz. butter
1 clove
Pinch of ground cinnamon
Rind of ½ lemon
2–3 oz. moist sugar
2 oz. ground rice
¾ pt. milk
2 oz. castor sugar
2 eggs

Butter a soufflé dish. Wipe the apples, chop them roughly and cook with 2 tablesp. of water, the butter, clove, cinnamon, lemon rind and moist sugar, until tender. Rub through a fine sieve. Mix the ground rice with a little of the cold milk. Boil the rest of the milk, pour in the blended rice, stir well and cook gently for 10 min. Add the castor sugar and leave the mixture to cool. Separate the eggs and beat the yolks into the mixture one at a time. Stiffly whisk the egg whites and fold into the mixture. Fill the soufflé dish with alternate layers of the rice and the apple purée, piling the last layer of rice into a pyramidal form. Dredge with castor sugar and bake in a fairly hot oven (**375° F., Gas 5**) about 30 min.

5-6 helpings

STRAWBERRY SOUFFLÉ

Soufflé de Fraises

Strawberries to make ¼ pt. pulp
1½ oz. butter
2 oz. plain flour
¼ pt. cream *or* top of milk
3 eggs
2 oz. castor sugar
A few drops of cochineal
½ lb. strawberries, cut into dice

Butter a soufflé dish. Reduce strawberries to a ¼ pt. pulp by crushing them with a fork, sweeten to taste. Melt the butter, add the flour and cook for a few minutes. Stir in the milk *or* cream and continue cooking until the mixture thickens. Leave to cool. Beat in the egg yolks. Work in the strawberry pulp and sugar. Add a few drops of colouring if necessary and the ½ lb. diced strawberries. Stiffly whisk the egg whites and fold these into the mixture. Turn into the mould and bake in a fairly hot oven (**400° F., Gas 6**) 35–40 min.

Serve with a fruit syrup or sweet sauce.

6–7 helpings

VANILLA SOUFFLÉ

Soufflé à la Vanille

1½ oz. butter
1½ oz. plain flour
⅜ pt. milk
4 egg yolks
1½ oz. castor sugar
½ teasp. vanilla essence
5 egg whites

Prepare the soufflé tin according to the method of cooking. If the soufflé is to be baked, butter the mould well, if steamed *see* p. 403.

Melt the butter, stir in the flour and cook gently for a few minutes without colouring. Add the milk, stir well until smooth. Reheat stirring continuously until the mixture thickens and leaves the sides of the pan. Leave to cool. Beat in the egg yolks, sugar and vanilla essence. Whisk the egg whites stiffly and fold them in lightly. Pour the mixture into the mould or tin and cover. Steam for ¾–1 hr. or bake in a fairly hot oven (**375° F., Gas 5**) for 30—35 min.

6 helpings

SWEET OMELETS

GENERAL HINTS

1. The pan should be the correct size for the number of eggs used. A two-egg omelet requires a pan of about 6 in. diameter.
2. The pan should be absolutely clean and should be kept only for omelet making. Do not wash it after use but wipe it out with a clean dry cloth, rubbing off any burnt egg with a little salt.
3. An old pan is better for omelets; a new pan needs to be proved. Heat a little fat (about ½–1 oz.) in a new pan until a haze appears; pour off the fat and wipe the pan with a clean dry cloth.
4. A palette knife or fish slice is useful for folding the omelets.
5. Overcooking will make the omelet tough. It is cooked when the egg on top is just set. When making an omelet in which the yolks and whites of egg have been separated it is often necessary to finish cooking it under the grill for a minute.
6. Serve an omelet as soon as it is cooked.

NOTE: For directions for making Savoury Omelets, *see* p. 686.

JAM OMELET

2 eggs
1 oz. castor sugar
A few drops of flavouring, if liked
½ oz. unsalted butter
1 tablesp. warmed jam

Cream together the egg yolks, sugar and flavouring. Whisk the whites stiffly and mix them lightly with the yolks and sugar. Heat the butter in the omelet pan and take off any scum. Pour in the omelet mixture and cook without stirring over a moderate heat until it just sets. Brown off the top by putting it into a hot oven (**425° F., Gas 7**) or by putting it under a hot grill for a minute. Spread the jam in the centre and fold the omelet over, away from the handle of the pan, and then tip it out on to a hot dish.

Dredge with sugar and serve at once.

2 helpings **Time—15 min.**

RUM OMELET

Omelette au Rhum

3 eggs
½ oz. castor sugar
1 tablesp. cream
2 tablesp. rum
½ oz. unsalted butter

Beat the eggs well and stir in thoroughly the sugar, cream and one tablesp. of rum. Heat the butter and take off any scum. Pour in the egg mixture and cook over a fairly quick heat. Stir until the mixture begins to set; then fold it over away from the handle of the pan. Cook for another minute and then tip it out on to a hot dish.

Pour round a tablesp. of rum and light, if liked. Serve at once.

NOTE: This omelet can be varied by using a liqueur instead of rum for flavouring.

2 helpings

SWEET OMELET

Omelette Sucrée

2 eggs | **½ oz. castor sugar**
Pinch of salt | **½ oz. unsalted butter**
1 tablesp. cream *or* top of the milk

Beat the eggs thoroughly with the salt, cream and castor sugar. Heat the butter in an omelet pan and remove any scum. When the butter is really hot pour in the omelet mixture and stir until it begins to set. Fold away from the handle of the pan. Cook for another minute and then tip out on to a hot dish.

Dredge with castor sugar and serve at once.

NOTE: Any sweet filling can be added, such as warmed jam, fruit purée *or* diced soft fruit. It should be spread evenly in the centre just before the omelet is folded over.

2 helpings

PUDDINGS

PUDDINGS ARE MADE basically from flour, breadcrumbs or cake-crumbs, fat, sugar, eggs and a raising agent. By using breadcrumbs or cake-crumbs and flour instead of all flour in suet mixtures, a lighter pudding is obtained. A good pinch of salt is added for each ½ lb. of flour used.

When the proportion of baking-powder to flour is 1 teasp. to ½ lb., self-raising flour is a satisfactory alternative.

The fat is worked into the mixture in various ways, as follows:

(*a*) CHOPPED-IN METHOD (SUET)

Either beef or mutton suet can be used, although beef suet is generally preferred as mutton suet sometimes gives a predominating flavour to the pudding. Shredded packet suet is, of course, ready for use and requires no further chopping.

To prepare suet remove the skin and fibrous tissue from the suet. Sprinkle the suet liberally with some of the measured flour or bread-crumbs. Shred or cut it down in flakes; then chop it finely. (A quick and easy method of chopping is to use a cook's knife. The handle, held in the right hand, is raised and lowered quickly, while the point of the knife is held down on the board by the thumb and first finger of the left hand.) Add more measured flour if

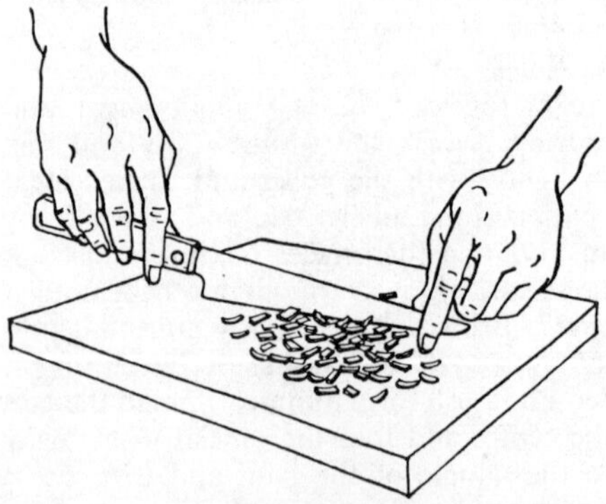

Chopping suet

the suet becomes sticky. Mix all the other dry ingredients with the suet. Stir in the eggs and sufficient milk to obtain the consistency required by the recipe.

(*b*) RUBBED-IN METHOD

Sift the flour, salt and raising agent into a mixing bowl. Cut the fat (generally butter or margarine) into small pieces. With the tips of the fingers, rub the fat into the flour, lifting it above the bowl so that, in falling back between the fingers, the mixture becomes aerated. Continue this until all the lumps of fat have been worked down and the mixture resembles breadcrumbs. Add the rest of the dry ingredients. Stir in the beaten eggs and liquid, according to the recipe.

(*c*) CREAMING METHOD

This method is used for richer puddings, where the amount of fat is often too great to be rubbed in, or where flour is not used in the recipe. Castor sugar should be used, as the small crystals are more easily dissolved.

Work the fat and sugar well together—using either a wooden spoon or the hand—until the mixture is lighter in colour and of the consistency of thick cream. Add any essences at this stage. (In cold weather, a warm bowl or hot dish-cloth round the bowl will facilitate the creaming, but on no account should the mixture be allowed to oil as a result of too much heat.) Beat the eggs. Add the beaten egg a little at a time, beating well between each addition so that the mixture remains smooth. Curdling of the mixture may occur if the egg is added too quickly or if the egg used has come direct from the refrigerator. Sift in the flour, salt and baking-powder. Stir in lightly, adding the rest of the ingredients.

(*d*) CREAMING OF YOLKS AND SUGAR METHOD

Each egg should be broken separately in a saucer or cup so that if there should be one bad egg it will not spoil the others. Put the yolks into a basin with the sugar. Whisk until lighter in colour and frothy. Stir in lightly the other ingredients, proceeding according to the recipe.

CONSISTENCIES OF MIXTURES

A *dropping consistency* is reached when the mixture will just drop off a spoon when it is shaken lightly. For a *soft dropping consistency* the mixture should drop easily from the spoon. For a *slack consistency* the mixture should fall easily from the spoon.

DRIED FRUITS

Currants, raisins, sultanas, etc., are best cleaned when they are bought. Remove the stalks and rubbish. Wash thoroughly in cold water, dry in a clean cloth, and then lay them out on a tray in a warm place to finish drying. Store them in dust-proof tins or jars, so that they are ready for use. Raisins can be stoned before storing.

STEAMED AND BOILED PUDDINGS

The mould or basin in which a pudding is cooked should be well-greased with fresh butter, clarified butter *or* margarine (p. 35), *or* cooking fat. Always prepare the mould or basin and the covering before the pudding is mixed.

STEAMED PUDDINGS—GENERAL HINTS

1. Have the steamer ready before the pudding is mixed. There should be plenty of boiling water in the steamer. If a steamer is not available, the pudding can be *partly steamed*, by standing it on an old plate, saucer or pastry cutter (to prevent direct contact with the source of heat) in a saucepan, with just enough water to reach half-way up the mould or basin. Put a tightly-fitting lid on the saucepan and simmer gently. If the water boils away, add more *boiling* water to replace it.
2. Where gentle steaming is indicated in the recipe, the water below the steamer should only simmer.
3. The basin or mould should not be more than three-quarters full.
4. Always cover the pudding with greased paper before steaming; this acts as a waterproof cover against condensing steam. Use a piece of strong paper, such as greaseproof, grease it well and place it greased side down on the basin. Turn the edges under and twist them securely below the rim of the basin.
5. After taking the pudding out of the steamer, leave it for a minute or two, to allow it time to shrink slightly from the sides of the mould or basin, before turning it out.
6. If puddings are steamed in a pressure cooker, follow the manufacturer's instructions regarding time and pressure.

BOILED PUDDINGS—GENERAL HINTS

1. The pudding can be boiled in a basin covered with a cloth *or* in a cloth only.

2. The cloth should be clean and well floured before use. Lay the cloth over the top of the basin and tie it with string under the rim, using a loop knot which can be easily untied. Gather the four corners of the cloth up on top and either tie them together or pin them with a safety pin. Roly-poly types of puddings are rolled in the floured cloth forming a sausage-shape, and tied loosely at either end, to allow room for the pudding to swell.
3. If a basin is used, fill it completely.
4. The water must be boiling rapidly when the pudding is put in and then should simmer gently.
5. The water must completely cover the pudding and be deep enough to float those boiled in cloths; otherwise a plate or saucer must be placed at the bottom of the pan.
6. As the water boils away, *boiling water* must be added.
7. The pudding should be allowed to stand a minute or two before being turned out in order that some of the steam may escape, causing the pudding to shrink and thus be less liable to break.

CHRISTMAS PUDDINGS

After the first boiling, the cloth should be taken off and a clean, dry, well-floured cloth tied on to the pudding. Cover or wrap in greaseproof paper and store in a cool larder. Give at least another 1½ hours' boiling before serving.

ALMA PUDDING

2 oz. currants
2 oz. sultanas
4 oz. butter *or* margarine
6 oz. castor sugar
2 eggs
8 oz. plain flour
1 rounded teasp. baking-powder
Grated rind of 1 lemon

Clean and pick over the currants and sultanas. Grease a pudding basin.

Cream together the fat and sugar. Beat in the eggs gradually. Add the sifted flour, baking-powder, currants, sultanas, and lemon rind. Mix to a soft consistency. Put the mixture into the basin: cover with a greased paper and steam for 2 hr.

5–6 helpings

ALMOND PUDDINGS

3 oz. butter
3 oz. castor sugar
3 eggs
6 oz. ground almonds
3 tablesp. cream *or* top of the milk

Grease seven or eight dariole moulds.

Cream together the butter and sugar, until soft. Separate the eggs, and work in the egg yolks. Stir in the ground almonds and cream *or* milk. Whisk the egg whites until stiff, and fold them in lightly. Three-quarters fill the moulds with the mixture. Cover with greased paper and steam for ¾–1 hr., until firm.

Turn out and serve with apricot sauce.

7–8 helpings

APPLE DUMPLINGS—BOILED

Pommes enrobées

6 apples	**3 oz. moist *or* brown sugar**
Suet crust pastry (p. 557) using 12 oz. flour, etc.	**6 cloves**

Core and peel the apples. Divide the pastry into 6 portions and roll each into a round. Put an apple into the centre of the round of pastry and work the pastry round the apple until it nearly meets. Fill the centre of the apple with sugar and a clove. Damp the edges of pastry and join them firmly together. Tie each apple dumpling in the corner of a well-floured pudding cloth. Put the dumplings into boiling water and boil gently, from 40–50 min.

6 helpings

APPLE PUDDING—STEAMED

Pouding de Pommes

4 oz. apples (after peeling and coring)	**4 oz. moist sugar**
4 oz. breadcrumbs	**Pinch of nutmeg**
4 oz. finely-chopped suet	**Pinch of salt**
	2 eggs
	¼ pt. milk

Chop the apples coarsely. Mix together the breadcrumbs, suet, sugar, nutmeg and salt. Add the apples. Beat the eggs. Stir in the eggs and milk, and mix well. Leave to stand for 1 hr. to allow the bread to soak. The mixture should then drop easily from the spoon. If it is too stiff, add a little more milk. Pour into a well-greased basin, cover, and steam for 2 hr.

Serve with custard sauce.

NOTE: *See also Fruit Pudding with Suet Crust* (p. 417).

5–6 helpings

APRICOT PUDDING

Pouding d'Abricots

6 pieces canned apricots	**2 eggs**
3 oz. butter *or* margarine	**Rind of ½ lemon**
3 oz. castor sugar	**3 oz. plain flour**
	¼ teasp. baking-powder

Grease a 1½ pt. basin. Drain the apricots well and cut them into small pieces.

Cream together the fat and sugar and when really soft beat in the eggs gradually. Stir in the grated lemon rind, apricots and the sifted flour and baking-powder. Turn the mixture into the basin, cover and steam steadily 1¼–1½ hr.

Serve with apricot sauce.

4 helpings

BACHELOR'S PUDDING (1)

4 oz. chopped apple (after peeling and coring)	**Pinch of salt**
4 oz. breadcrumbs	**Grated rind of ½ lemon**
4 oz. currants	**2 eggs**
3 oz. castor sugar	**Milk if required**
¼ teasp. ground nutmeg	**1 small teasp. of baking-powder**

Grease a pudding basin.

Mix the coarsely-chopped apple, breadcrumbs, currants, sugar, nutmeg, salt and grated lemon rind. Stir in the well-beaten eggs. Leave to stand for 30 min. Add milk, if necessary, to reduce the mixture to an easy dropping consistency. Finally, stir in the baking-powder. Turn the mixture into the basin; cover with greased paper. Steam for 2½–3 hr. Serve with custard or vanilla sauce.

5–6 helpings

BARONESS PUDDING

Pouding à la Baronne

4 oz. finely-chopped suet	**1 rounded teasp. baking-powder**
6 oz. stoned raisins	**Pinch of salt**
8 oz. plain flour	**1 gill milk (approx.)**
2 oz. castor sugar	

Grease a 1½ pt. pudding basin. Prepare the suet and raisins.

Mix together the sifted flour, baking-powder and salt with the raisins, suet and sugar. Add enough milk to mix to a soft dropping consistency. Put the mixture into the basin; cover with a greased paper. Steam 1½–2 hr.

Serve with custard, brandy- *or* lemon-sauce *or* well-dredged with sugar.

6 helpings
Cooking time—1½–2 hr.

BRANDY PUDDING

Pouding au Cognac

1 oz. glacé cherries
1 stale French roll
2 oz. macaroons *or* ratafias
4 oz. castor sugar
1 wineglass brandy
4 eggs
½ pt. cream
½ pt. milk
½ teasp. grated lemon rind
Grated nutmeg

Grease and decorate a mould or basin with the halved cherries. Line the mould with thin slices of roll. About ½ fill the mould with alternate layers of macaroons and thinly sliced roll; adding a few cherries, 1 oz. sugar and the brandy. Mix the eggs, cream and milk together; add the rest of the sugar, the lemon rind and a little nutmeg and pour the whole into the mould. Let it stand for 1 hr. Then cover and steam gently for 1½ hr. Serve with lemon sauce.

6-7 helpings

BREAD PUDDING (1)

6 oz. raisins *or* currants
3 oz. finely-chopped suet
1 lb. stale bread
2 oz. chopped candied peel
Good pinch of ground nutmeg
3 oz. castor sugar
1 egg
¼ pt. milk (approx.)

Any scraps of stale bread can be used for this. Grease a basin, clean the fruit and prepare the suet. Break the bread into small pieces, cover with cold water and leave to soak for at least ½ hr. Strain and squeeze the bread dry; beat out all the lumps with a fork. Add the suet, fruit, nutmeg and sugar. Mix to a stiff consistency with the egg and milk. Put into the basin; cover. Steam *or* boil for 2 hr.

5-6 helpings

NOTE: See p. 425 for Bread Pudding (2).

BROWN BREAD PUDDING

Pouding au Pain bis

3 oz. raisins
3 oz. sultanas
4 oz. finely-chopped suet
8 oz. brown bread-crumbs
3 oz. castor sugar
2 eggs
A little milk

Grease a basin; clean the fruit; prepare the suet if shredded suet is not used.

Mix together the breadcrumbs, sugar, fruit and suet. Add the beaten eggs and some of the milk, and mix to a dropping consistency. Leave to stand for ½ hr. Add more milk if the mixture is too stiff, to make a soft dropping consistency. Put into the basin; cover. Steam or boil for 2½–3 hr.

Serve with custard or wine sauce, pp. 138, 140.

6-7 helpings

CANARY PUDDING

Pouding Échaudé

6 oz. butter *or* margarine
6 oz. castor sugar
3 eggs
Grated rind of ½ lemon
6 oz. plain flour
1 level teasp. baking-powder

Grease a 1½ pt. pudding basin *or* mould.

Cream together the fat and sugar until soft and lighter in colour. Beat in the eggs gradually. Add the lemon rind. Stir in lightly the sifted flour and baking-powder. Pour into the basin *or* mould. Cover with a greased paper. Steam 1½ hr.

Turn out and serve with jam sauce.

6 helpings

CHOCOLATE PUDDING (1)

Pouding au Chocolat

8 oz. plain flour
1 teasp. baking-powder
Pinch of salt
4 oz. butter *or* margarine
4 oz. castor sugar
1 oz. cocoa
2 eggs
Milk to mix
A few drops of vanilla essence

Grease a 2 pt. basin.

Sift together the flour, salt and baking-powder. Rub in the fat. Add the sugar and cocoa. Mix to a soft dropping consistency with the beaten eggs and milk. Add vanilla essence to taste. Put the mixture in the basin; cover. Steam for 2 hr. Serve with chocolate sauce.

6 helpings

CHOCOLATE PUDDING (2)

3 oz. plain chocolate
2 tablesp. milk
6 oz. butter
6 oz. castor sugar
A few drops of vanilla essence
3 eggs
6 oz. plain flour
¾ teasp. baking-powder

Grease a mould or basin.

Grate the chocolate and heat with the milk in a small saucepan until dissolved. Cream the butter, sugar and melted chocolate together. Add a few drops of vanilla essence. Beat in the eggs. Sift in the flour and baking-powder and mix to a soft dropping consistency. Pour the mixture into the mould *or* basin. Steam for 2 hr. Serve with custard, chocolate, *or* sherry sauce.

6 helpings

CHRISTMAS PUDDING (1)

Pouding de Noël

6 oz. finely-chopped suet
6 oz. raisins, stoned and halved
6 oz. sultanas
6 oz. currants
1½ oz. whole almonds
3 oz. plain flour
Pinch of salt
¼ teasp. grated nutmeg
3 oz. breadcrumbs
6 oz. moist brown sugar
3 oz. chopped candied peel
Grated rind of 1 lemon
2 eggs
1 small wineglass brandy, sherry, stout *or* fruit juice (optional)
A little milk

Grease two 1½ pt. basins; finely chop or shred the suet, clean the fruit, blanch, skin and chop the almonds.

Sift the flour, salt and nutmeg into a mixing bowl. Add the breadcrumbs, suet, sugar, dried fruit, peel, grated lemon rind and almonds. Beat the eggs well, and stir them and the flavouring (if used) into the mixture. Add milk and mix to a soft dropping consistency. Put the mixture into the basins; cover; steam for 5–6 hr.

For storing Christmas Puddings, *see* p. 411.

CHRISTMAS PUDDING (2)—FRUITARIAN PLUM PUDDING (Without suet)

½ lb. figs
8 oz. peeled sweet almonds
4 oz. shelled Brazil nuts
4 oz. pine kernels
4 oz. currants
8 oz. raisins, stoned and halved
4 oz. sultanas
2 small cooking apples
1 teasp. mixed spice
4 oz. moist brown sugar
½ lb. breadcrumbs
4 oz. chopped candied peel
Pinch of salt
Rind and juice of 1 large lemon
4 oz. butter *or* margarine
4 oz. honey
3 eggs

Grease two 1½ pt. basins. Wash, chop (or mince) the figs; chop the nuts; prepare the dried fruit; core, peel and chop the apples.

Mix together the fruit, nuts, spice, sugar, breadcrumbs, candied peel, salt and grated lemon rind. Warm the butter and honey together. Beat the eggs and add them to the butter and honey. Stir into the dry ingredients. Add the lemon juice and stir well to thoroughly mix the ingredients. Put the mixture into the basins; cover. Boil for 3 hr.

12 helpings

CHRISTMAS PUDDING (3)—RICH

10 oz. sultanas
10 oz. currants
½ lb. raisins
2 oz. sweet almonds (skinned and chopped)
1 level teasp. ground ginger
½ lb. plain flour
Pinch of salt
1 lb. soft brown sugar
½ lb. mixed finely-chopped candied peel
1 level teasp. mixed spice
1 level teasp. grated nutmeg
½ lb. breadcrumbs
10 oz. finely-chopped *or* shredded suet
6 eggs
½ gill stout
Juice of 1 orange
1 wineglass brandy
½ pt. milk (approx.)

Grease three 1 pt. pudding basins. Prepare the dried fruit; stone and chop the raisins; chop the nuts.

Sift the flour, salt, spice, ginger and nutmeg into a mixing bowl. Add the sugar, breadcrumbs, suet, fruit, nuts and candied peel. Beat the eggs well and add to them the stout, orange juice and brandy, and stir this into the dry ingredients adding enough milk to make the mixture of a soft dropping consistency. Cover and boil steadily for 6–7 hr. Take the puddings out of the water and cover them with a clean dry cloth and, when cold, store in a cool place until required.

When required, boil the puddings for 1½ hr. before serving.

3 puddings (each to give 6 medium helpings)

CHRISTMAS PUDDING (4)—INEXPENSIVE

1 apple
1 lb. mixed dried fruit (sultanas, currants, raisins)
4 oz. plain flour
1 oz. self-raising flour
Pinch of salt
4 oz. breadcrumbs
4 oz. moist brown sugar
½ lb. shredded suet *or* finely-chopped suet
6 oz. mixed chopped candied peel
Juice and rind of 1 lemon
2 eggs
Milk to mix
A little caramel *or* gravy browning
A few drops of almond essence

Grease two small basins or one large basin; peel, core and chop the apple; prepare the dried fruit.

Sift together the plain flour, self-raising flour and salt into a mixing bowl. Add the breadcrumbs, dried fruit, sugar, suet, candied peel and grated lemon rind. Beat the eggs and milk together and stir them into the dry ingredients with the lemon juice, adding more milk to make the mixture of a soft dropping consistency. Add a little caramel *or* gravy browning to slightly darken the mixture (about a level teasp.), and the almond essence. Mix well in. Turn into the basin, cover and boil for 4 hr.

12 helpings

CHRISTMAS PUDDING (5)

3 oz. currants
3 oz. raisins, stoned and halved
1½ oz. grated raw carrot *or* finely-chopped apple
2 oz. plain flour
3 oz. breadcrumbs
3 oz. finely-shredded suet
1½ oz. finely-chopped candied peel
1 teasp. grated lemon rind
3 oz. moist brown sugar
¼ teasp. grated nutmeg
Pinch of salt
2 eggs
1 gill milk (approx.)
1 level teasp. baking-powder

Grease a basin; prepare the fruit; wash, peel and grate the carrot, *or* peel, core and chop the apple.

Mix well together the sifted flour, salt, nutmeg, breadcrumbs, suet, dried fruit, candied peel, lemon rind, sugar and carrot *or* apple. Beat the eggs and stir into the dry ingredients with sufficient milk to moisten. Cover and let the mixture stand for 1 hr. When ready stir in the baking-powder, turn into a well greased basin, cover, boil for 6 hr. *or* steam for 7 hr.

6 helpings

COCONUT PUDDING

Pouding de Noix de Coco

6 oz. flour
Pinch of salt
1 rounded teasp. baking-powder
2 oz. butter *or* margarine
2 oz. sugar
2 oz. desiccated coconut
1 egg
Milk to mix

Grease a 1½ pt. pudding basin. Sift together the flour, salt and baking-powder. Rub in the fat and add the sugar and coconut. Mix to a soft dropping consistency with the beaten egg and milk. Put the pudding mixture into the basin and cover with a piece of greased paper. Steam for 1½–2 hr.

4–6 helpings

CUMBERLAND PUDDING

8 oz. peeled, cored and coarsely-chopped apple
8 oz. plain flour
Pinch of salt
1 rounded teasp. baking-powder
4 oz. finely-chopped *or* shredded suet
6 oz. currants
3 oz. soft brown sugar
A little grated nutmeg
2 eggs
½ gill milk (approx.)

Grease a 1½ pt. pudding basin. Mix the apples with the sifted flour, salt and baking-powder. Add the suet, currants, sugar and nutmeg. Beat the eggs well and stir them into the mixture adding milk to make a soft dropping consistency. Turn into the basin. Cover securely with greased paper and steam 2½ hr.

6 helpings

CURRANT PUDDING

Pouding aux Groseilles

12 oz. plain flour
2 rounded teasp. baking-powder
Pinch of salt
6 oz. currants
6 oz. finely-chopped suet
1½ gill water (approx.)
Lemon
Castor sugar

Sift together the flour, salt and baking-powder. Add the suet and currants and mix with the water to make a soft pliable dough. Form into a roll and put into a floured pudding cloth. Roll up loosely and tie at each end to form a sausage-shape. Put the pudding into boiling water and let it boil gently for 2–2½ hr. Turn out and serve with cut lemon and plenty of castor sugar.

6 helpings

DATE PUDDING

8 oz. plain flour
Pinch of salt
1 rounded teasp. baking-powder
3–4 oz. butter *or* **margarine**
3 oz. castor sugar
6 oz. chopped stoned dates
1 egg
Milk

Grease a basin. Sift together the flour, salt and baking-powder. Rub the fat into the flour. Add the sugar and dates and mix well together. Mix to a soft dropping consistency with the egg and milk. Put into the basin. Cover with a greased paper and steam for 1½ hr. ,until firm in the centre.

6 helpings

DATE ROLY POLY

Roulade aux Dattes

6 oz. dates
12 oz. plain flour
2 rounded teasp. baking-powder
¼ teasp. salt
4–6 oz. finely-chopped suet
Water to mix

Chop the dates. Sift together the flour, baking-powder and salt. Add the suet and dates. Add sufficient water to mix to a soft, but firm, dough. Form into a roll and place at the end of a well-floured pudding cloth. Roll up loosely and tie firmly at either end, into a sausage-shape. Drop into boiling water and simmer 2–2½ hr.

Serve with custard.

NOTE: For dates the same weight of the following may be substituted—**currants, sultanas,** stoned **raisins** or **figs,** and the pudding named accordingly.

DELHI PUDDING

1 lb. cooking apples
6 oz. raisins
3 oz. brown sugar
¼ teasp. ground nutmeg
Grated rind of 1 lemon

SUET CRUST PASTRY

6 oz. finely-chopped suet
12 oz. plain flour
¼ teasp. salt
2 rounded teasp. baking-powder
Water to mix

Grease a basin. Peel, core and thinly slice the apples. Stone and halve the raisins. Mix together the apples, raisins, sugar, nutmeg and lemon rind.

In another bowl mix the flour, baking-powder, salt and suet with sufficient water to make a soft, but firm, dough. Divide the dough into two equal portions. Use one portion to line the pudding basin from the other portion reserve one piece to make the lid and roll the rest out thinly.

Put a layer of the apple mixture into the lined basin. Cover with a round of thinly rolled pastry, moistening the edges with water to join it securely to the pastry lining the basin. Add alternate layers of apple mixture and pastry until the basin is full. Place on top the pastry reserved for the lid. Cover with greased paper. Steam gently for 3 hr.

DUCHESS PUDDING

Pouding à la Duchesse

½ oz. pistachio nuts
3 oz. macaroons
3 oz. butter *or* **margarine**
3 oz. castor sugar
3 eggs
4 tablesp. orange marmalade
1 level dessertsp. ground rice

Grease a mould (or 1½ pt. pudding basin) with butter. Blanch, peel and chop the pistachios roughly; sprinkle half of them round the sides and bottom of the mould. Crush the macaroons.

Cream together the fat and sugar. Separate the eggs. Work in the egg yolks and marmalade. Stir in the macaroons. Stiffly whisk the egg whites and fold them in lightly. Sprinkle

PLATE 17

Chocolate Soufflé and Apricot Trifle

Above: a cold sweet for a hot day—chocolate soufflé, decorated with piped cream (see page 454). On right: apricot trifle—a quickly-made cold sweet (see page 456).

PLATE 18

Making a Vol-au-vent

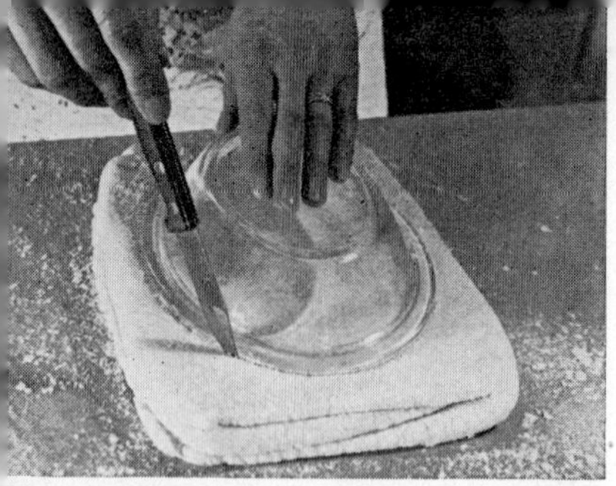

1

1 Roll out the puff pastry to a thickness of about $\frac{3}{4}$ inch. Place a dish on the top of the rolled pastry and mark out the shape.

2

2 Cut out the shape with a knife. During this operation make sure that the knife cuts cleanly and does not drag or twist the pastry.

3

3 Place on a wet baking sheet. Mark the inner ring and cut down to about $\frac{1}{2}$ the depth of the pastry.

4

4 Brush over the marked top of the pastry with the beaten egg mixture.

5

5 Mark slanting cuts outwards from the inner ring—again taking care not to drag or twist the pastry.

6 When baked remove the inner ring (the lid) and scoop out the soft inside ready to take the filling.

6

in the ground rice and the rest of the pistachios at the same time. Put the mixture into the mould; cover. Steam slowly for 1¼–1½ hr.

Serve with marmalade sauce.

5–6 helpings

FIG PUDDING

Pouding aux Figues

8 oz. dried figs	**4 oz. castor sugar**
4 oz. plain flour	**Pinch of salt**
4 oz. finely-chopped suet	**Pinch of ground nutmeg**
4 oz. breadcrumbs	**1–2 eggs**
1 level teasp. baking-powder	**1½ gills milk (approx.)**

Grease a 2 pt. basin. Wash, dry and chop the figs.

Mix the flour, suet, breadcrumbs, baking-powder, sugar, salt, nutmeg and figs. Beat the egg with some of the milk and stir into the mixture. Add milk as necessary to make the mixture of a dropping consistency. Put it in the basin; cover. Steam for 2½ hr.

Serve with a custard or sweet sauce.

6 helpings

FINGER PUDDING

Pouding aux Biscuits à la cuillère

3 eggs	**Pinch of ground cloves**
4½ oz. castor sugar	**2 oz. melted butter *or* margarine**
4½ oz. ground almonds	**1½ oz. crushed savoy *or* finger biscuits**
½ teasp. grated lemon rind	
¼ teasp. ground cinnamon	

Grease a mould.

Separate the eggs. Beat the yolks and sugar together until light and creamy. Add the ground almonds, lemon rind, cinnamon, cloves, the melted fat and the crushed biscuits. Mix well. Stiffly whisk the egg whites and fold them in lightly. Pour the mixture into a well-greased mould. Steam gently for 1–1¼ hr.

5–6 helpings

FRUIT PUDDING WITH SUET CRUST

Pouding aux Fruits

1–1½ lb. fresh fruit (*see below*)	**2–3 oz. granulated sugar**

SUET CRUST PASTRY

½ lb. plain flour	**Pinch of salt**
1 teasp. baking-powder	**3 oz. finely-chopped suet**

Prepare the fruit and mix it with the sugar.

Sift the flour and baking-powder, add the suet and salt. Mix with sufficient water to make a soft, but firm, dough. Grease and line a basin (*see below*). Fill to the top with the fruit and sugar and add ¼ gill of cold water. Put on the top crust.

To boil: Cover with a well-floured cloth and boil for 2½–3 hr.

To steam: Cover with greased paper and steam for 2½–3 hr.

6 helpings

NOTE: *To line a basin*—cut off one quarter of the pastry for the top. Roll the remaining pastry ½ in. larger than the top of the basin, drop the pastry into the greased basin, and with the fingers work the pastry evenly up the sides to the top. Roll out the lid to the size of the top of the basin, wet the edges and secure it firmly round the inside of the pastry lining the basin.

SUGGESTED FILLINGS

Apples	**Damsons**
Blackberries and apples	**Gooseberries**
Blackcurrants	**Plums**
Cranberries	**Rhubarb**

GINGERBREAD PUDDING

Pouding au Pain d'Épice

½ lb. plain flour	**¼ lb. finely-chopped suet**
Pinch of salt	**½ lb. golden syrup**
1 teasp. baking-powder	**1 egg**
1 teasp. ground ginger	**Milk to mix**

Grease a 2 pt. mould or basin.

Sift together the flour, salt, baking-powder and ginger, and mix with the suet. Slightly warm the syrup, if it is very thick. Beat together the syrup, egg and a little milk. Stir this into the dry ingredients, mixing well. Add more milk, if necessary, to make the mixture of a dropping consistency. Put into a well-greased mould *or* basin; cover. Steam for 2½ hr.

5–6 helpings

BOILED PUDDINGS

GINGER PUDDING

Pouding au Gingembre

½ lb. plain flour
1 level teasp. ground ginger
Pinch of salt
1 level teasp. bicarbonate of soda
4 oz. finely-chopped suet
3 oz. sugar
1 tablesp. treacle
1 egg
Milk to mix

Grease a 2 pt. basin. Prepare the suet.

Sift the flour, ginger, salt and bicarbonate of soda into a bowl. Add the finely-chopped suet and sugar. Stir in the treacle, beaten egg and sufficient milk to make a soft dropping consistency. Put the mixture into the basin; cover. Steam for 2 hr.

Turn out and serve with syrup sauce.

6 helpings

GOLDEN PUDDING

Pouding Doré

4 oz. marmalade
4 oz. plain flour
4 oz. breadcrumbs
3 oz. finely-chopped suet
2 oz. castor sugar
1 rounded teasp. baking-powder
Pinch of salt
2 eggs
1 gill milk (approx.)

Grease a 2 pt. pudding basin. Put 2 oz. marmalade at the base.

Mix together the flour, breadcrumbs, suet, sugar, baking-powder and salt. Beat together the eggs, remaining 2 oz. marmalade and a little of the milk. Stir this into the dry ingredients and, using milk as required, mix to a very soft dropping consistency. Put the mixture into the basin, cover with greased paper. Steam for 1½–2 hr.

Serve with marmalade sauce.

6 helpings

HONEY PUDDING (2)

2 dessertsp. honey
6 oz. flour
Pinch of salt
1 rounded teasp. baking-powder
3 oz. butter *or* margarine
2 oz. sugar
1 egg
Milk to mix

Grease a 1½ pt. pudding basin, and put 1 dessertsp. of honey in the bottom. Sift together the flour, salt and baking-powder. Rub in the fat and add the sugar. Beat together the egg and 1 dessertsp. of the honey and stir into the dry ingredients with enough milk to make a dropping consistency. Put the pudding mixture into the basin, cover with a piece of greased paper. Steam for 1½–2 hr.

4–6 helpings

NOTE: See p. 387 for Honey Pudding (1).

ITALIAN PUDDING (2)

1 oz. cake crumbs
1 oz. breadcrumbs
6 macaroons, pounded
1 oz. finely-chopped candied peel
½ oz. sultanas
½ oz. pistachio nuts, shredded
1 tablesp. rum *or* brandy
2 eggs

Put the cake crumbs, breadcrumbs, macaroons, peel, sultanas and pistachios into a bowl. Beat together the brandy and eggs, and stir into the mixture. Turn into a well-greased mould. Steam gently 1–1¼ hr. Serve with custard sauce.

3 helpings

NOTE: See p. 393 for Italian Pudding (1).

LEMON PUDDING (1)

6 oz. flour
Pinch of salt
1 rounded teasp. baking-powder
2 oz. butter *or* margarine
2 oz. sugar
Juice and rind of 1 lemon
1 egg
Milk to mix

Grease a 1½ pt. pudding basin. Sift together the flour, salt and baking-powder. Rub in the fat and add the sugar and grated lemon rind. Mix to a soft dropping consistency with the beaten egg, lemon juice and milk. Put the pudding into the greased basin and cover with a piece of greased paper. Steam for 1½–2 hr.

4–6 helpings

MARMALADE PUDDING (2)

Rind of 1 lemon
4 oz. plain flour
Pinch of salt
1 level teasp. baking-powder
4 oz. breadcrumbs
4 oz. finely-chopped suet
4 oz. sultanas
2 oz. castor sugar
4 tablesp. marmalade
2 eggs
1 gill milk (approx.)

Grease a basin. Grate the lemon rind.

Sift together the flour, salt and baking-powder. Mix with the breadcrumbs, suet, lemon rind, sultanas and sugar. Stir in the marmalade, beaten eggs and milk. Use enough milk to make the mixture of a dropping consistency. Put into the basin; cover; steam for 1½–2 hr. Serve with marmalade sauce.

6 helpings

NOTE: See p. 393 for Marmalade Pudding (1).

NEWCASTLE PUDDING

1 oz. glacé cherries
4 oz. butter *or* margarine
4 oz. castor sugar
2 eggs
6 oz. plain flour
Pinch of salt
1 teasp. baking-powder
A little milk

Grease a mould *or* 1½ pt. basin and decorate with the cherries.

Cream the butter and sugar. Gradually beat in the eggs. Sift in the flour, salt and baking-powder and mix to a soft dropping consistency with a little milk. Put the mixture into the basin *or* mould; cover. Steam for 1½–2 hr. Turn out and serve with jam sauce.

6 helpings

PATRIOTIC PUDDING

3 tablesp. red jam
4 oz. butter *or* margarine
½ lb. plain flour
Pinch of salt
1 heaped teasp. baking-powder
4 oz. castor sugar
1 egg
½ gill milk (approx.)

Grease a 2 pt. basin and cover the bottom with the jam.

Rub the fat into the sifted flour, salt and baking-powder and mix in the sugar. Beat the egg and add it to about ½ gill milk. Stir this into the dry ingredients to make the mixture of a soft dropping consistency, adding more milk if required. Put into the basin; cover with a greased paper. Steam for 1½–2 hr.

Turn out and serve with jam sauce.

6 helpings

PLUM PUDDING

4 oz. finely-chopped suet
4 oz. raisins
4 oz. currants
4 oz. plain flour
Pinch of salt
1 rounded teasp. baking-powder
4 oz. breadcrumbs
4 oz. moist sugar
¼ teasp. ground mace
¼ teasp. grated nutmeg
1 egg
1 gill milk (approx.)

Grease a 2 pt. basin. Prepare the suet, raisins and currants.

Sift the flour, salt and baking-powder and mix with the breadcrumbs, suet, sugar, raisins, currants, ground mace and grated nutmeg. Stir in the beaten egg and milk and mix to a dropping consistency. Turn into a well-greased basin; cover. Boil for 4–5 hr. *or* steam for at least 5 hr.

Serve with melted butter sauce.

6 helpings

POUND PUDDING

½ lb. finely-shredded suet
½ lb. raisins, stoned and halved
½ lb. currants
1 oz. finely-chopped candied peel
Pinch of salt
¼ lb. plain flour
1 level teasp. ground ginger
¼ lb. sugar
¼ lb. breadcrumbs
¼ of a nutmeg, grated
1 egg
¼ pt. milk

Grease a 2 pt. mould or basin. Prepare the suet, raisins, currants and peel.

Sift together the salt, flour and ginger and mix with the sugar, breadcrumbs, raisins, currants, candied peel and nutmeg. Stir in the beaten egg and milk; mix to a dropping consistency, adding more milk as necessary. Turn into a well-buttered mould *or* basin; cover. Boil for 3–3½ hr.

5–6 helpings

PRIMROSE PUDDING

4 oz. butter *or* margarine
4 oz. castor sugar
2 eggs
Grated rind of ½ lemon
Vanilla essence to taste
6 oz. plain flour
1 level teasp. baking-powder
A few drops of yellow colouring
3 tablesp. milk (approx.)

Grease a 1½ pt. mould.

Cream together the fat and sugar. Beat in the eggs one at a time. Add the lemon rind and vanilla essence. Sift in the flour and baking-powder; stir in lightly. Add yellow colouring. Mix with enough milk to make a soft dropping consistency. Pour into a well-buttered mould; cover. Steam for 1½ hr.

Turn out and serve with custard-, wine-, or vanilla-sauce.

6 helpings

BOILED PUDDINGS

PRINCE ALBERT PUDDING

1 lb. prunes
1 pt. water
A few strips of lemon rind
1 oz. brown sugar
4 oz. butter *or* margarine
4 oz. castor sugar
2 eggs
Rind of ½ lemon
1½ oz. rice flour
4 oz. brown bread-crumbs

SAUCE

1 teasp. arrowroot
½ pt. prune syrup
½ oz. granulated sugar
Juice of ½ lemon
Cochineal

Wash and soak the prunes in the water overnight. Stew them with the strips of lemon rind and brown sugar until soft. Strain them (reserving the liquid for the sauce) and remove the stones.

Line a dry mould or basin completely with the prunes, as follows: halve each prune; dip in clarified butter *or* margarine, and press skin-side against the mould. Chop any prunes left over.

Cream the butter and castor sugar together. Separate the eggs; beat in the yolks. Add the grated lemon rind, chopped prunes, rice flour and brown breadcrumbs. Fold in the stiffly-whisked egg whites. Turn mixture into the mould; cover. Steam gently for 1¾ hr.

Meanwhile make the sauce; blend the arrowroot with some of the prune syrup. Boil the remainder of the syrup and pour over the blended arrowroot; return to pan and simmer for 3 min. Add the sugar and juice of ½ lemon and colour pink with a few drops of cochineal.

Turn out the pudding and coat with the sauce.

6 helpings

ROLY POLY

Roulade

12 oz. plain flour
2 rounded teasp. baking-powder
6 oz. finely-chopped suet
Pinch of salt
Water to mix
Jam

Sift the flour and baking-powder, add the suet and salt. Mix with sufficient water to make a soft, but firm, dough. Roll it into a rectangle about ¼ in. thick. Spread with jam almost to the edge. Damp the edges and roll up lightly. Seal the edges. Wrap the pudding in a scalded well-floured cloth; tie up the ends. Put into fast boiling water. Simmer for 2–2½ hr.

6 helpings

SNOWDON PUDDING

4 oz. raisins
1 oz. glacé cherries
4 oz. finely-chopped beef suet
4 oz. breadcrumbs
1 oz. ground rice
4 oz. castor sugar
Rind of 1 lemon
Pinch of salt
2 eggs
2 tablesp. marmalade
½ gill milk (approx.)

Grease a 2 pt. mould (or basin) with butter. Prepare the raisins and halve the cherries. Decorate the bottom and sides of the mould with some of the raisins and cherry halves.

Put the remainder of the fruit into a mixing bowl. Add the suet, breadcrumbs, ground rice, sugar, grated lemon rind and salt. Beat together the eggs, marmalade and a little of the milk. Add to the other ingredients; use sufficient milk to moisten, and mix well. Pour the mixture into the prepared mould. Cover with a greased paper. Steam for 2–2½ hr.

Serve with marmalade sauce.

6 helpings

SPICED RHUBARB PUDDING

Pouding à la Rhubarbe épicé

1 lb. rhubarb
2 oz. sultanas
2 oz. currants
2 oz. raisins
2 oz. brown sugar
1 level teasp. mixed spices
1 teasp. ground cinnamon
Suet crust pastry using 8 oz. flour, etc. (p. 557)

Grease a 2 pt. basin. Clean the dried fruit.

Wipe and cut the rhubarb into pieces about ½ in. in length and mix with the dried fruit, sugar and spices.

Make the suet crust pastry. Divide the crust into 3 portions varying in size. Put the smallest portion at the bottom of the basin; cover it with ½ of the rhubarb mixture. Roll out the second piece of crust and put it on top. Add the rest of the rhubarb mixture; cover with the third piece of rolled-out crust.

Cover with grease-proof paper. Steam for 2–2½ hr.

6 helpings

SPOTTED DICK

Pouding aux raisins de Corinthe

12 oz. plain flour	**6 oz. finely-chopped suet**
2 rounded teasp. baking-powder	**4 oz. castor sugar**
	6 oz. currants
Pinch of salt	**Milk to mix**

Sift together the flour, baking-powder and salt. Add the suet, sugar and fruit and mix with the milk to a soft dough. Form into a roll and turn on to a well-floured cloth. Roll up the cloth loosely, and tie at both ends, leaving enough room for the pudding to swell. Drop into boiling water and simmer for 2 hr; *or* steam for 2½ hr.

Serve with custard *or* lemon sauce.

6 helpings

SUET PUDDING

Pouding Roulé à l'Anglaise

12 oz. plain flour	**4–6 oz. finely-chopped suet**
¼ teasp. salt	**Water to mix**
2 rounded teasp. baking-powder	

Sift the flour, salt and baking-powder. Mix in the suet. Add cold water, stirring gradually until a stiff dough is formed. Shape the dough into a roll. Put the dough into a scalded, well-floured pudding cloth and roll up loosely. Tie the ends securely with string. Put into a saucepan of boiling water and boil gently for 1½–2 hr., adding more boiling water, if necessary, to keep the pudding covered. Serve with jam-, treacle-, fruit- or marmalade-sauce.

6–7 helpings

SULTANA PUDDING

Pouding aux Raisins de Smyrne

4 oz. butter *or* **margarine**	**4 oz. castor sugar**
	4 oz. sultanas
½ lb. plain flour	**2 eggs**
Pinch of salt	**Milk to mix**
1 heaped teasp. baking-powder	**A few drops vanilla essence**

Grease a 2 pt. basin. Clean the sultanas. Rub the fat into the sifted flour, salt and baking-powder. Add the sugar and fruit. Mix with beaten egg, milk and vanilla essence to a soft dropping consistency. Put the mixture into the basin; cover. Steam for 1½–2 hr.

Turn out, dredge with sugar, and serve with custard or lemon sauce.

6 helpings

SYRUP SPONGE PUDDING

Pouding de Savoie au Sirop

6 oz. plain flour	**Pinch of salt**
6 oz. breadcrumbs	**1 egg**
4 oz. finely-chopped suet	**2 tablesp. golden syrup**
2 oz. castor sugar	**1 tablesp. treacle**
1 teasp. ground ginger	**Milk to mix**
1 level teasp. bicarbonate of soda	

Grease a basin and, if liked, put an extra tablesp. of golden syrup in the bottom. Mix together the flour, breadcrumbs, suet, sugar, ginger, bicarbonate of soda and salt. Beat the egg with the golden syrup, treacle and a little of the milk. Stir this into the other ingredients, using more milk if required, to mix to a very soft dropping consistency. Put the mixture into the basin; cover with greased paper. Steam for 1½–2 hr.

6–7 helpings

TRANSPARENT PUDDING

Pouding transparent

3 oz. butter *or* **margarine**	**3 eggs**
	2 tablesp. apricot jam
3 oz. sugar	

Well butter 6 dariole moulds.

Cream together the fat and sugar until lighter in colour and quite soft. Add each egg separately and beat well. One-third fill each mould with this mixture and put a dessertsp. of apricot jam on top; then cover with the remaining mixture, so that the moulds are about ¾ full. Cover with greased paper. Steam slowly for about 25 min. Let the puddings cool slightly before turning them out, to lessen the risk of their breaking.

Serve at once with custard.

6 helpings

TREACLE LAYER PUDDING

Pouding à la Mélasse

2 oz. breadcrumbs
Rind of 1 lemon
½ lb. treacle *or* golden syrup (approx.)

SUET CRUST PASTRY

4–6 oz. finely-chopped *or* shredded suet
12 oz. plain flour
Pinch of salt
2 rounded teasp. baking powder
Water to mix

Sift flour, salt and baking-powder and mix with suet and sufficient water to make a soft, but firm, dough. Divide the dough into two equal portions, using one portion to line a 2 pt. basin. From the other portion cut off enough to make the lid; roll out the remainder thinly.

Mix the breadcrumbs and grated lemon rind. Put a layer of treacle in the basin; sprinkle well with the breadcrumbs. Cover with a round of the thinly-rolled pastry. Moisten the edge of it with water and join securely to the pastry at the side of the basin. Add another layer of treacle, crumbs and pastry; then more treacle and crumbs. Finally cover with the rolled-out top as the last layer of pastry Cover with greased paper. Steam for 2½ hr.

6–7 helpings

WELSH PUDDING

Pouding à la Galloise

8 oz. castor sugar
8 oz. breadcrumbs
Pinch of salt
8 oz. finely-chopped suet
Finely grated rind of 1 lemon
2 eggs
Juice of 2 large lemons
Milk to mix

Grease a 2 pt. basin.

Mix together the sugar, breadcrumbs, salt, suet, and lemon rind. Add the eggs, lemon juice and enough milk to make a mixture which just drops from the spoon. Turn into the basin; cover. Steam *or* boil for 3–4 hr.

5–6 helpings

BAKED PUDDINGS

GENERAL HINTS

1. Well-butter the dish, tin or mould, so that the pudding is easily turned out or served.
2. Wipe round the edges of the pie-dish before baking.
3. The pudding is easier to handle if it is placed on a baking sheet while cooking.
4. Oven settings may vary with different cookers, so that the average settings in the recipes are given for general guidance. The numbers used for gas markings are those approved by the British Standards Institute and now adopted by most of the manufacturers of gas cookers.

ALMOND CASTLES

Châteaux d'Amandes

3 oz. butter
3 oz. castor sugar
3 eggs
3 tablesp. cream *or* milk
1 tablesp. brandy (optional)
6 oz. ground almonds

Grease 8 dariole moulds.

Cream together the butter and sugar. Stir in the egg yolks, cream or milk, brandy (if used) and almonds. Whisk the egg whites to a stiff froth and add lightly to the rest of the ingredients. Three-quarters fill the moulds. Bake in a warm oven (**335° F., Gas 3**) 20–25 min., until the puddings are firm in the centre and golden brown.

Turn out and serve with custard.

If liked the puddings may be steamed—cover with greased paper and steam 40–50 min. until firm.

6–7 helpings

APPLE CHARLOTTE (1)

Charlotte de Pommes

2 tablesp. browned crumbs (cake *or* bread)
6 oz. finely-chopped suet
6 oz. white bread-crumbs
Grated rind of 1 lemon
2 lb. cooking apples
4 oz. brown sugar

Grease a 2 pt. pie-dish with butter and coat with the 2 tablesp. browned crumbs. Mix together the suet, 6 oz. breadcrumbs and lemon rind. Peel, core and slice the apples. Fill the pie-dish with alternate layers of the crumb mixture and apples, sprinkled with sugar, finishing with a layer of crumb mixture. Press down lightly. Cover with greased paper. Bake in a moderate oven (**350° F., Gas 4**) about 1¼–1½ hr., until the apples are soft.

Loosen the edges of the charlotte with a knife and turn out on to a hot dish.

6–7 helpings

APPLE CHARLOTTE (2)

2 lb. cooking apples
4 oz. brown sugar
1 lemon
8 thinly cut slices of bread and butter
Castor sugar

Grease a 2 pt. pie-dish with butter. Peel, core and slice the apples. Place a layer in the bottom of the pie-dish and sprinkle with sugar, grated lemon rind and lemon juice. Cover with thin slices of bread and butter. Repeat until the dish is full, finishing with a layer of bread and butter. Cover with greased paper. Bake in a moderate oven (**350° F., Gas 4**) for ¾–1 hr.

Turn out of the dish and dredge well with castor sugar before serving.

5–6 helpings

APPLE CRUMBLE

Pommes au gratin

1½ lb. apples
4 oz. brown sugar
A little grated lemon rind
½ gill water (approx.)
3 oz. butter *or* margarine
6 oz. plain flour
3 oz. castor sugar
¼ teasp. ground ginger

Peel, core and slice the apples into a pan. Add ½ gill water, 4 oz. brown sugar and lemon rind. Cook gently with lid on the pan until soft. Place in a greased 2 pt. pie-dish. Rub the fat into the flour until of the consistency of fine breadcrumbs. Add the castor sugar, ground ginger and mix well. Sprinkle the crumble over the apple; press down lightly. Bake in a moderate oven (**350° F., Gas 4**) until golden brown, and the apples are cooked—about 30–40 min., depending on the cooking quality of the apples.

Dredge with castor sugar and serve with custard *or* cream.

NOTE: For apples the same weight of the following may be substituted: **damsons, gooseberries, plums, raspberries *or* rhubarb,** and the crumble named accordingly.

6 helpings

APPLE DUMPLINGS

Pommes enrobées

Short crust pastry (p. 557), 12 oz. for large apples *or* 8 oz. for small apples
2 oz. brown sugar
A little grated lemon rind *or* ground cinnamon
6 cooking apples
12 cloves (optional)

Make the short crust pastry; divide into six portions, shaping each into a round.

Mix the sugar and grated lemon rind or cinnamon. Peel and core each apple and put it on a round of pastry. Work the pastry round the apple until it is almost covered. Press the cloves, if used, into the centre of the apple; then fill the cavity with the sugar mixture. Seal the pastry edges by moistening slightly with water. Place the dumplings join downwards on a greased baking sheet. Brush them with milk and dredge with castor sugar. Bake for about 30 min. in a fairly hot oven (**400° F., Gas 6**).

6 helpings

APPLE PUDDING (1)

Pouding de Pommes

2 lb. cooking apples
½ gill water
6 oz. castor sugar
2 oz. butter *or* margarine
1–2 eggs
4 oz. breadcrumbs

Peel, core and cut the apples into slices, stew with ½ gill water until tender. Stir in the sugar, fat, and well-beaten egg. Butter a 2 pt. pie-dish. Coat the bottom and sides thickly with the crumbs. Add the apple pulp and finish with a layer of crumbs. Put a few flakes of butter on the top and bake in a moderate oven (**350° F., Gas 4**) for ¾ hr.

4-5 helpings

APPLE PUDDING (2)

5 oz. butter	**1 egg**
3 oz. demerara sugar	**Vanilla essence**
1 level teasp. cinnamon	**8 oz. self-raising flour**
1 lb. cooking apples	**Pinch of salt**
4 oz. sugar	**Milk to mix**

Grease a 2 pt. pie-dish. Melt 1 oz. of the butter, demerara sugar and the cinnamon in a saucepan and add the peeled, cored and sliced apples. Cook for about 5 min. Cream together the remainder of the butter and 4 oz. sugar and beat in the egg. Add a few drops of vanilla essence. Stir in the sifted flour and salt and mix to a dropping consistency with the milk. Put the apple mixture into the bottom of the pie-dish and spread the pudding mixture on top. Bake until firm and set—about 45–50 min., first in a moderate oven (**350° F., Gas 4**) then reduce heat after ½ hr. to warm (**335° F., Gas 3**).

APPLE SNOW

2 lb. cooking apples	**2 eggs**
Lemon rind	**½ pt. milk**
4 oz. sugar	**½ oz. castor sugar**
1 tablesp. cream (optional)	**2 oz. castor sugar**

Peel, core and slice the apples. Stew with the lemon rind in ½ gill water until tender. Put through a fine nylon sieve. Add the 4 oz. sugar and cream, if used. In another bowl separate the eggs. Heat the milk and pour on to the well-beaten yolks; return to the pan and heat gently until the mixture thickens. Add ½ oz. sugar. Put the apple purée into a buttered pie-dish; pour the custard on top. Put into a warm oven (**335° F., Gas 3**) until set—about 40 min. Stiffly-whisk the egg whites; stir in lightly the 2 oz. castor sugar. Pile on top of the mixture. Bake in a very cool oven (**290° F., Gas 1**) until meringue is slightly coloured.

6 helpings

NOTE: See also p. 457.

BACHELOR'S PUDDING (2)

8 oz. plain flour	**2 oz. sultanas**
Pinch of salt	**2 oz. raisins, stoned and halved**
4 oz. castor sugar	**1 egg**
1 teasp. baking-powder	**1 gill milk (approx.)**
3–4 oz. chopped suet	

Butter a pie-dish. Mix sifted flour, salt and baking-powder with the sugar, suet, sultanas and raisins. Beat the egg with some of the milk and add to the mixture. Mix to a soft dropping consistency, adding more milk if necessary. Put into the pie-dish. Bake in a moderate oven (**350° F., Gas 4**) for 1–1¼ hr.

When ready, turn out of the dish, dredge with castor sugar, serve with a fruit sauce.

5–6 helpings

NOTE: See p. 412 for Bachelor's Pudding (1).

BAKED APPLES

Pommes cuites au four

6 cooking apples	**½ gill water**
2 oz. demerara sugar	

FILLING, choice of:—

1. **2 oz. moist sugar and 2 oz. butter**
2. **Blackcurrant *or* raspberry *or* strawberry *or* apricot jam**
3. **3 oz. stoned dates *or* sultanas *or* currants *or* raisins, 2 oz. moist sugar and 1 teasp. ground cinnamon**

Prepare the filling. Wash and core the apples. Cut round the skin of the apple with the tip of a sharp knife, ⅔ of the way up from the base. Put the apples into a fireproof dish and fill the centres with the chosen filling. Sprinkle with the demerara sugar. Add the water. Bake in a moderate oven (**350° F., Gas 4**) until the apples are soft in the centre—about ¾–1 hr. depending on the cooking quality of the apples.

6 helpings

BAKED JAM ROLL

12 oz. plain flour	**6 oz. finely-chopped suet**
1 teasp. baking-powder	**Jam**
Pinch of salt	

Mix the flour, baking-powder, salt and suet with sufficient water to make a soft, but firm, dough. Roll the dough into a rectangle about ¼ in. thick. Spread with jam almost to the edges, damp the edges and roll up lightly. Seal the edges. Put on to a well-greased baking sheet. Cook in a fairly hot oven **(400° F., Gas 6)** until cooked through; about 1 hr.

6 helpings

BANANA PUDDING

Pouding de Bananes

1½ oz. butter *or* margarine
6 oz. castor sugar
3 eggs
6 oz. plain flour
¾ gill of top of the milk *or* cream
3 bananas

Cream the fat and sugar together until soft. Beat in the egg yolks. Stir in the sifted flour and milk (or cream) alternately. Add the thinly sliced bananas. Whisk the egg whites to a stiff froth, and add them lightly to the rest of the ingredients. Pour the mixture into a well-buttered dish. Bake in a warm oven **(335° F., Gas 3)** for ¾–1 hr. until the pudding is firm and golden brown.

6–7 helpings

BETSY PUDDING

1 small stale white loaf
1½ pt. milk
2 oz. finely-chopped suet
2 oz. castor sugar
2 eggs
8 tablesp. jam *or* sweetened stewed fruit

Cut the crust off the bread and break the bread into small pieces. Cover with the boiling milk and leave to stand for ½ hr. Beat the mixture well to make it smooth and add the suet, sugar and well beaten eggs. Stir well. Put a layer of this into the bottom of a well greased pie-dish, cover with jam *or* stewed fruit. Add another layer of bread mixture, repeat until the dish is full, ending with a good layer of the bread mixture. Bake in a moderate oven **(350° F., Gas 4)** for about 1 hr. until set.

6 helpings

BREAD PUDDING (2)

8 oz. stale bread
4 oz. currants *or* raisins *or* sultanas
2 oz. brown sugar
2 oz. finely-chopped suet
1 oz. chopped peel
½ teasp. mixed spice
1 egg
A little milk

Break the bread into small pieces and soak in cold water for at least ½ hr.; then strain and squeeze as dry as possible. Put into a basin and beat out the lumps with a fork. Add the dried fruit, sugar, suet, peel and mixed spice and mix well. Add the egg and enough milk to enable the mixture to drop easily from the spoon. Put into a greased tin. Bake in a warm oven **(335° F., Gas 3)** for about 1 hr.

When done, turn out on to a hot dish. Dredge with sugar and serve with custard or vanilla sauce.

5–6 helpings

NOTE: See p. 413 for Bread Pudding (1).

BROWN BETTY PUDDING

6 oz. breadcrumbs
2 lb. cooking apples
1 lemon
4 tablesp. golden syrup
4 oz. demerara sugar
2 tablesp. water

Grease a 2 pt. pie-dish. Coat it with a layer of breadcrumbs. Peel, core and thinly slice the apples. Fill the pie-dish with alternate layers of apples, grated lemon rind and breadcrumbs. Heat the syrup, sugar and water in a pan, add the lemon juice and pour this over the mixture. Bake in a warm oven **(335° F., Gas 3)** 1¼–1½ hr. until the pudding is brown and the apple cooked.

6 helpings

CASSELL PUDDINGS

Jam
2 eggs
4 oz. castor sugar
4 oz. plain flour
Grated rind of 1 lemon
4 oz. butter *or* margarine

Grease 6–7 dariole moulds, and put about a teaspoonful of jam in the bottom of each. Separate the eggs. Whisk the egg whites until stiff. Add the yolks and sugar and whisk for about 5 min. Stir in lightly the flour, lemon rind and the slightly melted fat. Three-quarters fill each mould with the mixture. Bake in a moderate oven (**350° F., Gas 4**) until firm and golden brown—about 25 min.

Turn out and serve with custard sauce.

6–7 helpings

CASTLE PUDDINGS

Poudings à la Château

4 oz. butter *or* margarine	**1 level teasp. baking-powder**
4 oz. castor sugar	**Grated rind of ½ lemon *or* a few drops of vanilla essence**
2 eggs	
4 oz. plain flour	

Grease 6–7 dariole moulds. Cream together the fat and sugar until soft and lighter in colour. Beat in the eggs gradually. Stir in the sifted flour, baking-powder, lemon rind *or* vanilla essence. Three-quarters fill the moulds. Bake in a moderate oven (**350° F., Gas 4**) until set and golden brown—about 25 min.

Turn out and serve with jam sauce.

NOTE: These may be steamed: cover with greased paper; steam for about 50 min.

CHERRY PUDDING

Pouding aux Cerises

1 lb. cooking cherries	**2 oz. castor sugar**
½ gill water	**Pinch of salt**
3 oz. moist sugar	**3 eggs**
3 oz. plain flour	**Grated rind of ½ lemon**
2–3 tablesp. milk (approx.)	**Pinch of ground cinnamon**
1 gill cream *or* milk	

Stone the cherries and stew them very gently (to keep them whole) in a small saucepan with the water and moist sugar. Allow to cool. Blend the flour with the 2–3 tablesp. of milk, so that it is smooth and "runny". Boil the cream *or* milk and add to it the blended flour, beating well to keep the mixture smooth. Bring to the boil again and add the castor sugar and salt. Cool the mixture. Separate the eggs. Beat the egg yolks into the mixture. Add the lemon rind and cinnamon, and lastly the stiffly-whisked egg whites. Put into a well-greased mould or pie-dish a layer of cherries and a layer of mixture alternately until the mould is full. Cover with greased paper. Bake in a fairly hot oven (**400° F., Gas 6**) for about 40 min.

Serve with a sweet sauce or fruit syrup.

5–6 helpings

CHESTNUT PUDDING

Pouding aux Marrons

6 oz. chestnuts, weighed after the skins have been removed	**2 oz. flour**
Pinch of salt	**2 oz. cake crumbs**
1 oz. plain chocolate	**3 eggs**
½ pt. milk	**½ teasp. vanilla essence**
2 oz. butter *or* margarine	**1 oz. castor sugar**

Wash the chestnuts, make a slit in each and boil in water for about 10 min. Remove both skins and put the chestnuts into a saucepan with a very little water and the salt. Cook until tender, strain, dry and rub through a fine sieve.

Grate the chocolate and put it in the milk and simmer until dissolved. Allow to cool slightly.

In another pan melt the fat, stir in the flour, cook for 2–3 min. Work in the milk and chocolate gradually, keeping the mixture smooth: stir until it boils. Add the cake crumbs and continue cooking until the mixture leaves the sides of the pan. Allow to cool. Separate the eggs. Beat into the mixture the egg yolks, chestnut purée, vanilla essence and sugar. Whisk the egg whites to a stiff froth and fold them lightly into the mixture. Pour into a well-buttered mould. Cover with buttered paper. Bake in a fairly hot oven (**375° F., Gas 5**) for 1 hr. *or* steam for 1½ hr.

Serve with vanilla *or* custard sauce.

6–7 helpings

CHOCOLATE PUDDING (3)

6 oz. plain flour	**4 oz castor sugar**
Pinch of salt	**1 oz. cocoa**
1 rounded teasp. baking-powder	**1 egg**
3 oz. butter *or* margarine	**Milk to mix**
	A few drops of vanilla essence

Sift together the flour, salt and baking-powder. Rub in the fat. Add the sugar and cocoa; mix well. Add the beaten egg and milk and mix to a dropping consistency. Add the vanilla essence. Put into a greased tin or pie-dish. Bake in a fairly hot oven (**375° F., Gas 5**) for 30–40 min.

Dredge well with castor sugar and serve with chocolate *or* custard sauce.

6 helpings

NOTE: See p. 413 for Chocolate Puddings (1)–(2)

COBURG PUDDINGS

3 oz. butter
3 oz. castor sugar
2 eggs
3 oz. plain flour
¼ teasp. ground nutmeg
1 level teasp. baking-powder
3 oz. currants
½ pt. milk (slightly warm)
1 tablesp. brandy

Cream the butter and sugar until soft. Beat the eggs in gradually. Sift in the flour, nutmeg and baking-powder. Mix in all the other ingredients. Pour into well-greased moulds (use 6 large moulds *or* 12 small dariole moulds) to ¾ fill and bake in a fairly hot oven (**375° F., Gas 5**) for ½ hr. Serve with wine sauce.

COLLEGE PUDDING

4 oz. flour
½ teasp. baking-powder
Pinch of salt
½ teasp. mixed spice
4 oz. breadcrumbs
3 oz. finely-chopped suet
3 oz. castor sugar
2 oz. currants
2 oz. sultanas
1–2 eggs
1 gill milk (approx.)

Grease 6–7 dariole moulds. Sift together the flour, baking-powder, salt and spice. Add the breadcrumbs, suet, sugar, currants and sultanas, and mix well together. Well beat the eggs. Add to the dry ingredients and mix to a soft dropping consistency, adding milk as required. Half-fill the moulds with the mixture. Bake in fairly hot oven (**375° F., Gas 5**) for about 25 min.; *or* cover with greased paper and steam for 35–40 min.

Serve with wine-, orange-, brandy- or custard-sauce.

COTTAGE PUDDING

½ lb. plain flour
Pinch of salt
1 rounded teasp. baking-powder
4 oz. butter *or* **margarine**
3 oz. sugar
4 oz. raisins
1 egg
½ gill milk (approx.)

Grease a Yorkshire pudding tin (10 in. by 8 in.). Sift together the flour, salt and baking-powder. Rub the fat into the flour. Add the rest of the dry ingredients. Mix to a stiff consistency with the egg and milk, so that the mixture will just drop from the spoon. Spread in the tin. Bake in a fairly hot oven (**375° F., Gas 5**) until firm in the centre and golden brown; about 35–40 min.

5–6 helpings

EVE'S PUDDING

Pouding d'Eve

1 lb. apples
2 tablesp. water
2–4 oz. granulated *or* **demerara sugar**
4 cloves (optional)
4 oz. butter *or* **margarine**
4 oz. castor sugar
2 eggs
Grated rind of ½ lemon
4 oz. plain flour
1 level teasp. baking-powder

Peel, core and thinly slice the apples. Put them into a small saucepan with the water. granulated *or* demerara sugar, and cloves if used. Cook very slowly (with the lid on the pan) until the apples are soft, stirring occasionally to prevent them from burning. Remove the cloves. Put the apples into the bottom of a well-greased pie-dish.

Cream together the fat and castor sugar. Beat in the eggs gradually. Add the grated lemon rind. Sift in the flour and baking-powder. Mix to a soft dropping consistency. Spread this mixture over the apples. Bake in a moderate oven (**350° F., Gas 4**) for 40–45 min.

4 helpings

EXETER PUDDING

5 oz. breadcrumbs
1 oz. ratafias
3½ oz. finely-shredded suet
2 oz. sago
3 oz. castor sugar
½ teasp. grated lemon rind
3 eggs
2–3 tablesp. milk *or* **cream**
1 wineglass rum (optional)
2 individual sponge cakes
Jam

SAUCE

3 tablesp. blackcurrant jelly
3 tablesp. water
1 wineglass sherry (optional)

Coat a well-buttered mould *or* pie-dish with some of the breadcrumbs. Cover the bottom with some of the ratafias.

Mix together the rest of the breadcrumbs, suet, sago, sugar and grated lemon rind. Stir in the well-beaten eggs, milk and rum (if used). Put some of the mixture into the lined dish. Cover with slices of sponge cake. Spread thickly with jam and place a few ratafias on top. Repeat this until all the ingredients are used up, finishing with the breadcrumb mixture. Bake gently in a moderate oven (**350° F., Gas 4**) for about 1 hr.

Make the sauce by boiling together the blackcurrant jelly, water and sherry (if used).

5–6 helpings

FRUIT PUDDING—Quick Method

Pouding aux Fruits

1 pt. sweetened, stewed fresh fruit	**3 oz. butter** *or* **margarine**
8 oz. plain flour	**3 oz. castor sugar**
1 heaped teasp. baking-powder	**2 eggs**
Pinch of salt	**Milk to mix**

Grease a pie-dish. Strain the syrup from the fruit and lay the fruit at the bottom of the pie-dish. The syrup can be used for making a sauce to serve with the pudding. (Left-over stewed fruit can be used for this purpose; it is not essential to have the exact amount but there should be enough fruit to cover the pie-dish to a depth of at least ½ in.)

Sift together the flour, baking-powder and salt, and rub in the fat. Add the sugar. Mix to a dropping consistency with the beaten eggs and milk. Spread this mixture over the fruit. Bake in a fairly hot oven (**375° F., Gas 5**) for 40–45 min., until the pudding mixture is cooked through and brown on top.

Dredge well with castor sugar. Serve with fruit- *or* custard-sauce *or* thin cream.

NOTE: If raw fruit is used, prepare it in the usual way. Stew it in as little water as possible, sweeten to taste and let it cool before putting the pudding mixture on top.

6 helpings

FRUIT SPONGE

1 lb. fresh fruit (e.g. apricots, peaches, gooseberries)	**3 oz. butter** *or* **margarine**
Sugar to taste	**3 oz. castor sugar**
	2 eggs
	4 oz. self-raising flour

Prepare the fruit according to kind. Grease a 1½ pt. pie-dish and arrange the fruit in the bottom. Sprinkle with sugar to taste and add a little water if required. Cream together the fat and 3 oz. sugar. Add the well-whisked eggs gradually, beating well between each addition—if sign of curdling, add some flour. Sift flour and stir lightly into the creamed fat and egg. Spread the sponge mixture over the fruit, and bake in the middle of a moderate oven (**350° F., Gas 4**) for 35–40 min. Serve hot or cold.

NOTE: This can be made with canned fruit if liked, drain the fruit from the juice before arranging in the pie-dish.

LEMON PUDDING (2)

Pouding au Citron

2 oz. butter *or* **margarine**	**Rind and juice of 1½ lemons**
4 oz. castor sugar	**6 oz. plain flour**
3 eggs	**½ pt. milk**

Grease a 2 pt. pie-dish.

Cream together the butter and sugar until soft. Beat in the egg yolks. Add the grated lemon rind and the sifted flour. Stir in the milk and lemon juice. Fold in the stiffly-whisked egg whites. Pour the mixture into the buttered pie-dish. Bake in a moderate oven (**350° F., Gas 4**) for 45 min., until firm and brown.

4 helpings

NOTE: See p. 418 for Lemon Pudding (1)

RAISIN PUDDING

Pouding de Raisins

See Cottage Pudding (p. 427).

RASPBERRY PUDDING

Pouding de Framboises

1 lb. raspberries
3 oz. granulated sugar
4 oz. butter *or* margarine
4 oz. castor sugar
2 eggs
6 oz. plain flour
1 rounded teasp. baking-powder
2–4 tablesp. milk (approx.)

Grease a pie-dish. Put the cleaned and washed raspberries, with the granulated sugar, in the bottom of the dish.

Cream together in a mixing bowl the butter and castor sugar. Beat in the eggs gradually. Stir in the sifted flour and baking-powder, adding milk to make an easy dropping consistency. Spread this mixture over the fruit. Bake in a moderate oven **(350° F., Gas 4)** until the pudding is cooked and nicely browned—about 1–1¼ hr.

Well dredge with castor sugar before serving. Serve with cream *or* custard sauce.

6 helpings

SOMERSETSHIRE PUDDING

3 oz. butter *or* margarine
3 oz. sugar
2 eggs
¼ teasp. vanilla essence
4 oz. plain flour
1 level teasp. baking-powder

Grease 6–7 dariole moulds.

Cream the fat and sugar together. Beat in the eggs and flavouring. Sift in the flour and baking-powder and mix to a soft dropping consistency. Put the mixture into the moulds and bake in a fairly hot oven **(375° F., Gas 5)** until brown and cooked through—about 20 min. Serve with jam- *or* custard-sauce.

NOTE: These puddings can also be served cold, with the inside scooped out and the cavity filled with jam *or* stewed fruit and whipped cream.

4 helpings

YEAST MIXTURES

BABAS WITH RUM SYRUP

Babas au Rhum

½ lb. plain flour
Pinch of salt
½ oz. yeast
1 oz. castor sugar
1 gill milk
4 eggs
4 oz. butter
2 oz. currants

RUM SYRUP

3 oz. granulated sugar
1 gill water
Rind of ½ lemon
1 wineglass rum
1 wineglass sherry

Grease 9 dariole or baba moulds.

Sift the flour and salt into a warm basin. Cream the yeast with a pinch of castor sugar, and add to it the gill of warm milk. Mix this into the flour to form a soft dough. Beat well until the dough leaves the sides of the basin clean. Cover the basin with a damp cloth and leave the dough to rise in a warm (but not hot) place until about twice its size. When the dough has risen sufficiently add 2 eggs, the melted butter and castor sugar, beat well in. Then add the rest of the eggs and the currants and beat again for 5–10 min., until the dough is smooth and glossy. Half-fill the moulds with the mixture. Put them in a warm place until the mixture has risen to the top of the moulds. Bake in a fairly hot oven **(425° F., Gas 7)** for about 20–25 min. until brown and firm.

Put the granulated sugar and water into a pan with the thinly peeled lemon rind. Boil for 10 min., add the rum and sherry; strain.

Reheat the syrup. Soak the babas in it for a minute; lift them out and serve immediately, with the syrup poured round.

9 babas

BABAS WITH KIRSCH

Babas au Kirsch

Babas—*see Babas with Rum Syrup*.

SYRUP

6 oz. granulated sugar
1½ gills water
Rind of ½ lemon
Kirsch to flavour

Boil the sugar and water together with the thinly peeled lemon rind for 10 min. Strain; reboil and add the kirsch. Soak the babas in the syrup for 1 min. and serve immediately.

9 babas

NORFOLK DUMPLINGS

Boulettes Norfolk, bouillies

Boiling water
Salt

BREAD DOUGH

8 oz. plain flour	**½ oz. lard**
½ teasp. salt	**¼ pt. warm water (approx.)**
½ oz. yeast	
Small pinch of sugar	

Make the dough: sift the flour and salt into a basin. Cream the yeast with the sugar and add the warm water and the melted fat. Mix to an elastic dough. Knead well until smooth, cover with a cloth, and set in a warm place to rise to double its size. Knead again until there are no large holes in the dough when cut.

Roll into small balls. Leave in a warm place to rise slightly. Drop into gently boiling salted water. Simmer for 6–7 min. Strain.

Serve with one of the following: jam, treacle, golden syrup, *or* butter and sugar.

8 helpings

PUDDING À L'AMBASSADRICE

Savarin mixture cooked in a plain mould.

CUSTARD FILLING

1 oz. butter	**½ gill cream**
1 oz. plain flour	**1 dessertsp. castor sugar**
1 gill milk	
1 egg yolk	

CARAMEL

2 oz. loaf sugar	**½ gill water**

CUSTARD

1½ gills milk	**1 egg yolk**
½ gill cream	**1 dessertsp. castor sugar**
2 eggs	

Cook the savarin and leave to cool.

Make the custard filling: melt the butter, add the flour, work in the milk and then bring to the boil, stirring well. Add the beaten egg yolk, cream and sugar; and cook gently until the mixture thickens. Leave to cool.

Heat a soufflé tin and have ready a thickly folded band of newspaper to encircle the tin so that it can be held firmly in one hand. Prepare the caramel by heating together the loaf sugar and water, stir until it boils, then remove the spoon and allow to boil without stirring until it is golden brown. Pour the caramel into the warm soufflé tin and twist round until the sides and bowl are well coated with caramel.

Slice the savarin, spread it with the custard filling and pile it into the soufflé tin.

Make the custard: warm the milk and cream and pour it on the 2 beaten eggs and egg yolk, add the sugar. Strain over the savarin mixture; cover. Steam very gently for about 45 min. until firm.

SAVARIN

4 oz. plain flour	**1 egg**
Pinch of salt	**¼ oz. sugar**
¼ oz. yeast	**1½ oz. butter**
¼ gill warm water	

RUM SAUCE

3 oz. loaf sugar	**1–2 tablesp. rum**
¼ pt. water	**Juice of ½ lemon**

DECORATION

Apricot jam	**Blanched almonds, browned**

Sift the flour and salt into a basin and put it to warm. Cream the yeast with the tepid water. Make a well in the centre of the flour and pour in the yeast mixture. Sprinkle over the top with a little of the flour from the side of the bowl. Leave to prove for 10–15 min. in a warm place. Add the egg gradually, beating well to a smooth elastic dough, using a little more tepid water if necessary. Knead well. Put the dough back into the basin and press down, sprinkle the sugar on the top and put on the butter in small pieces. Cover with a damp cloth and leave in a warm place to double its size. Beat well again until all the sugar and butter is absorbed. Grease a border mould and fill it ⅓ of the way up with the mixture.

Leave to prove in a warm place until the mixture just reaches the top of the mould. Then bake in a fairly hot oven **(400° F., Gas 6)** for about 20 min.

Make the sauce: boil the water and sugar steadily for about 10 min. Add the rum and the lemon juice.

Turn the savarin out on to a hot dish, prick with a needle or hat pin and soak well in the sauce. Coat with hot sieved apricot jam and decorate with spikes of almonds etc. Serve with the rest of the sauce poured round.

4 helpings

COLD SWEETS

CEREAL MOULDS

CEREAL MOULDS ARE composed of whole or ground cereals, milk and sugar, flavouring and sometimes a little gelatine to ensure a firm set. They are easily digested and are eminently suitable for young children and invalids. Great care must be taken during the cooking of the starch to avoid too much evaporation of liquid otherwise the consistency may be too stiff. A small nut of butter added during the cooking improves both flavour and texture.

Whole grain, such as rice (Carolina or Carolina-type), large sago, large tapioca, and barley, should be simmered gently in the milk until every grain is soft and the milk is almost absorbed. To accomplish this without burning, and without excessive evaporation, use (*a*) a double saucepan, *or* (*b*) a thick-bottomed pan, standing over low heat or in a cool oven.

Keep covered and stir occasionally to ensure even cooking of the grain. Cooking time 1½–2 hr.

Small grain, such as semolina, ground rice, small sago and tapioca should be sprinkled dry into near boiling milk and cooked gently until the grain is soft and clear. Continuous stirring is necessary to ensure smoothness, and excessive evaporation must be avoided by keeping the heat low. Cooking time 10–15 min.

Powdered grain, such as cornflour, arrowroot, custard powder and flour, should be blended with sufficient cold milk to make a thin cream. The rest of the milk is heated almost to boiling-point and poured on to the blended grain, stirring continuously. Pour back into the pan and boil gently, still stirring, until all the starch grains are quite cooked. Cooking time 4–5 min.

The consistency of cereal mixtures ready for moulding should be such that if a spoonful is dropped back on to the surface of the hot mixture, it will merge into it only when gently shaken; and this should be achieved either by further evaporation if the consistency is too slack or by adding a little milk if too stiff. A cereal mould of too stiff a texture is very unpalatable, but if too thin it may be poured into a bowl and served semi-set.

Choose china or glass moulds for preference, as the cold wetted surface causes instant gelatinization of the surface starch and imparts a clean, glossy surface to the mould when turned out. Pour in quickly, and from a slight height so that, by its own weight, the mixture can drive all the air out of the mould and force itself into the hollows of the shape. This will ensure a well-formed mould free from holes. If cereal mixtures are to be set in border moulds, which are metal, a little margarine *or* butter *or*, best of all, pure olive oil, should be used to grease the inside. A sharp tap on the side of this type of mould should be all that is necessary to dislodge the mixture.

A china or glass mould may be turned out quite cleanly if the cereal mixture is first gently loosened from the lip of the mould with the tips of the fingers, then inverted on to the hand or dish and dislodged by a sharp jerk of the wrist. If the surface of the dish is moistened the mould can be moved to an exact position.

WHOLE GRAIN MOULDS

(Rice, large sago, large tapioca)

Basic Recipe

WHOLE RICE MOULD

Gâteau de Riz

6 oz. rice
1 qt. milk
3 oz. castor sugar
Flavouring (*see above*)
½–1 oz. fresh butter (optional)

Wash the rice and put it with the milk into a double saucepan, or a thick pan standing over a very low heat. Simmer very gently, with the lid on the pan to prevent undue evaporation. Stir occasionally to prevent the rice from settling on the bottom of the pan, and cook until the rice is quite tender and the milk almost absorbed. Sweeten to taste, add flavouring if required, stir in the butter if used. Pour quickly into a cold, wet basin or mould. Turn out when set and serve with stewed, canned, or fresh fruit, jam, jelly, etc.

6 helpings
Cooking time—2–3 hr. **Setting time—2 hr.**

FLAVOURINGS

Lemon *or* **Orange**: Wash fruit, dry well and grate rind finely; stir into the cooked mixture just before moulding. Alternatively, peel rind in thin strips, avoiding white pith and infuse in mixture during cooking; remove before adding sugar and butter.

Coffee: Add coffee essence to taste, with the sugar.

Variations

CHOCOLATE RICE MOULD

Gâteau de Riz au Chocolat

6 oz. rice
2 oz. cocoa *or*
3 oz. chocolate
1 qt. milk
4 oz. castor sugar
Vanilla *or* **coffee essence** *or* **1 teasp. brandy** *or* **rum**
1 oz. fresh butter

Make as the basic recipe for Whole Rice Mould, blending the cocoa with a little of the warm milk. If chocolate is used, chop roughly and add to the mixture ½ hr. before moulding. Flavour with essences *or* spirits just before moulding.

6 helpings
Cooking time—2–3 hr. **Setting time—2 hr.**

CREAMED RICE

Riz à la Crème

To 1 pint of cold rice mould, add whipped cream *or* cream and custard, to produce a soft, creamy consistency. Pour into serving dishes and flavour and decorate in any of the following ways:

1. **Chocolate**: Grate chocolate coarsely over the top.
2. **Coffee**: Stir in coffee essence to taste.
3. **Orange**: Stir in finely-grated orange rind just before serving.
4. **Fruit**: (fresh, canned, preserved *or* stewed e.g. peaches, pineapple, dessert apples, dates.)
   (*a*) Drain the fruit from the juice, chop or shred, and stir into the rice.
   (*b*) Arrange fruit attractively on top of the rice, either in slices, quarters, halves *or* even a purée. The dish may be finished by piling up on top a meringue (p. 461) and drying it to a golden brown in a cool oven **(310° F., Gas 2)** *or* finished as for Peach Condé (see below).

4 helpings

CREAMED RICE WITH SHERRY

Crème de Riz au Sherry

3 oz. rice	**1 tablesp. castor sugar**
1 pt. milk	**2 tablesp. sherry**
½ pt. double cream	

Cook the rice in the milk until quite tender. Drain well in a sieve until cold. Whip the cream until thick, stir in the rice, sugar and the sherry. Serve in individual dishes and decorate with strips of glacé cherry or chopped preserved ginger.

6 helpings

PEACH CONDÉ

Pêche Condé

1 pt. cold rice mould (p. 432)	**1 small can peaches**
⅛ pt. double cream *or* **cream and custard**	**1 level teasp. arrowroot**

Stir the cream into the cold rice mould to produce a soft, creamy consistency. Pour into serving dishes. Drain the fruit from the juice and arrange attractively on top of the rice. Make up the fruit juice to ¼ pt. with water. Blend the arrowroot with the fruit juice and boil until clear. Pour carefully over the fruit. Finish by decorating with whipped cream.

NOTE: Apricots or pineapple may be substituted for peaches.

4 helpings

SMALL GRAIN MOULDS

(Semolina, ground rice, tapioca, small sago)

Basic Recipe

SEMOLINA MOULD

Gâteau de Semoule

1 qt. milk	**3 oz. castor sugar**
4 oz. semolina	**Flavouring** (*see below*)

Rinse a thick saucepan, put in the milk and heat to boiling point. Sprinkle in the semolina, stirring continually. Boil gently, stirring all the time, until the grain is quite cooked, and appears transparent when lifted on the back of a spoon (7–8 min.). Add sugar and stir well. Pour quickly into a cold, wet mould.

6 helpings
Cooking time—10 min.
Setting time—2 hr.

FLAVOURINGS

Lemon *or* **Orange**: Infuse thin strips of rind with the milk during heating. Remove before adding the grain.

Coffee: Add 1 tablesp. coffee essence, with the sugar.

Chocolate: Melt 3 oz. chocolate in the milk, *or* blend 1½ oz. cocoa with some of the milk. Add rum, brandy, sherry *or* vanilla essence.

Variations

APPLE SEMOLINA

Semoule aux Pommes

2 lb. cooking apples	**1½ pt. milk**
3–4 oz. sugar	**2 oz. castor sugar**
3 oz. semolina	**¼ pt. double cream** *or* **custard**

CEREAL MOULDS

DECORATION

Glacé cherries	**Angelica**

(*a*) Wash, core apples and bake in a moderate oven (**350° F., Gas 4**) until fallen; remove skins *or* (*b*) peel, core and cook gently to a purée in a thick pan with 1 tablesp. water. Sweeten while hot with 3-4 oz. sugar and spread in the bottom of a glass dish. Cook the semolina in the milk until quite tender and the grain is clear. Stir in the castor sugar. Cool, stirring occasionally to prevent a skin forming, and when lukewarm stir in the cream *or* custard. Pour smoothly over the apple purée, and leave to go cold. Decorate the top with slices of glacé cherry and tiny leaves of angelica.

6 helpings
Cooking time—15 min.

APRICOT MOULD

Gâteau d'Abricots

1½ pt. milk	**4 tablesp. apricot jam**
2½ oz. ground rice	**1 oz. castor sugar**
1 tablesp. hot water	**½ gill double cream**

Heat the milk and when boiling, sprinkle in the ground rice. Cook the rice gently until quite soft—about 7 min., stirring all the time. Stir 1 tablesp. hot water into the apricot jam and sieve. Add to the ground rice and milk. Add sugar to sweeten to taste. Pour quickly into a wet 1½ pt. border-mould. When quite cold and set, turn out and pile sweetened whipped cream into the hollow.

6 helpings
Cooking time—10 min.
Setting time—2 hr.

BANANA AND TAPIOCA SPONGE

Gâteau de Tapioca aux Bananes

6 bananas (not over-ripe)	**1 pt. milk**
	2 oz. tapioca
2 oz. granulated sugar	**Sugar to taste**
¼ pt. water	**2–3 egg whites**
Juice of ½ lemon	

Slice bananas and cook to a purée with the granulated sugar and water (5–10 min.). Add strained lemon juice and beat to a smooth cream. Boil the milk, sprinkle in the tapioca and cook gently for about 15 min., stirring all the time. Add banana purée, taste and re-sweeten if necessary. Whisk egg whites stiffly and fold lightly into the banana tapioca mixture. Stir lightly until cool and serve piled up in a glass dish. Chill if liked.

6 helpings
Cooking time—35 min.

CARAMEL MOULD

Gâteau de Caramel

1 lemon	**3 oz. ground rice**
1½ pt. milk	**1 oz. castor sugar**

CARAMEL

2 oz. loaf *or* **granulated sugar**	**1 tablesp. cold water**

Heat a tin charlotte or soufflé mould and have ready a thickly folded band of newspaper so that the hot tin may be encircled with it and held firmly in one hand. Melt loaf sugar in the water in a thick, very small pan, and when dissolved, boil quickly until it becomes dark golden brown. Do not stir. Pour at once into the hot tin mould, and rotate quickly to coat the sides and base of the mould. Finally, place mould on a firm flat board so that excess caramel may flow to the base and set level. Keep in a warm place, as draughts may cause the caramel coating to crack.

Cut thin strips of lemon rind and infuse in the milk, slowly. Remove the rind when the milk boils, sprinkle in the rice, stirring all the time and cook until grain is soft and smooth, about 8–10 min. Sweeten to taste. Pour into the coated mould and leave in a cool place to set. Turn out and serve with cream.

6 helpings

CRÈME DE RIZ

1 pt. milk	**2 tablesp. cold water**
2 oz. ground rice	**2 oz. castor sugar**
½ oz. powdered gelatine	**Flavouring** (*see* p. 433)
	¼–½ pt. double cream

Heat the milk and when boiling, sprinkle in the rice. Cook gently, stirring continuously, until quite soft and smooth—15–20 min. Avoid too much evaporation. Soak gelatine in the 2 tablesp. cold water, for 5–10 min., then warm until dissolved. Sweeten and flavour the rice, stir in the gelatine and allow to cool, stirring lightly from time to time. When quite cool, but not set, fold in the whipped cream. Pour into a cold wet mould and leave to set.

NOTE: This recipe may be used for whole rice, or for semolina.

4 helpings
Cooking time—½ hr.
Setting time—2 hr.

RICE À L'IMPÉRATRICE

Riz à l'Impératrice

Proceed as for Crème de Riz (p. 434), but set in an oiled border mould, and decorate with fruit when turned out. Either: (*a*) Fill the central hollow with fruit salad and piped whipped cream *or* (*b*) Place selected fruit, e.g., apricot halves on the top of the border, glaze with apricot juice thickened with arrowroot (1 level teasp. to ½ pt. juice), and decorate with piped whipped cream, and angelica.

TAPIOCA CREAM

Crème au Tapioca

½ pt. packet red jelly	**1 bay leaf**
1 tablesp. sherry (optional)	**2 pt. milk**
	1½ oz. tapioca
1 tablesp. redcurrant *or* crab-apple *or* bramble jelly	**2 oz. castor sugar**
	2 egg yolks
	2 tablesp. double cream
Rind of ½ lemon	

Make the jelly to just less than ½ pt., inclusive of sherry (if used) and preserves, and add these when jelly is cool. Pour into a wet border mould and leave to set. Cut thin strips of lemon rind without white pith; infuse in the milk with the bay leaf. When milk boils, remove flavourings and sprinkle in tapioca, stirring continuously. Cook gently 15–20 min. until smooth and soft. Add sugar, cool slightly, and add beaten egg yolks. Re-heat to cook the yolks, but do not boil. Allow to cool, then lightly stir in whipped cream. Pour into the border mould and leave to set.

6 helpings
Cooking time—1 hr.
Setting time—2 hr.

POWDERED GRAIN MOULDS

(Cornflour, arrowroot)

Basic Recipe

CORNFLOUR MOULD

Gâteau à la crème de maïs

3 oz. cornflour	**2 oz. castor sugar**
2 pt. milk	**Flavouring (*see below*)**

Blend cornflour with a little cold milk to a thin cream. Boil remainder of milk and pour on to the blended cornflour, stirring continuously. Return mixture to the pan and heat until boiling. Cook gently for 4 min., stirring all the time. Add sugar to taste, and flavouring essences, if used. Pour quickly into a wetted mould. Turn out when set.

6 helpings
Cooking time—15 min.
Setting time—2 hr.

FLAVOURINGS

Lemon *or* orange: Infuse thinly-cut strips of lemon *or* orange rind with the milk. Remove rind before pouring milk on to cornflour.

Chocolate: Blend 1½ oz. cocoa with the cornflour. Extra sugar may be desired, and also a flavouring of vanilla, rum *or* coffee essence.

Coffee: Add 1 tablesp. coffee essence with the sugar, and taste before adding more, as essences vary in strength.

Custard: Add beaten egg yolk to cooled mixture and re-heat until cooked ; *or* replace 1 oz. cornflour with 1 oz. custard powder.

Variations

AMBROSIA MOULD

Gâteau Ambroisie

3 oz. cornflour	**4 oz. sugar**
2 pt. milk	**¼ pt. sherry**
2 oz. butter	

Blend cornflour with a little of the milk to a thin cream. Boil remainder of the milk with the butter. Pour over blended cornflour, return to pan and cook thoroughly. Add sugar and sherry; pour into a wetted mould. Turn out when cold and serve with wine sauce.

6 helpings
Cooking time—10 min.
Setting time—2 hr.

BANANA MOULD

Gâteau de Bananes

2 oz. cornflour	**2 egg yolks**
2 pt. milk	**½ teasp. vanilla essence**
2 oz. castor sugar	**2 bananas**

Blend the cornflour with a little milk and heat the remainder of the milk. Proceed as for cornflour mould, cooking well. Stir in the sugar, cool, and add the beaten yolks. Re-cook until the mixture thickens, stir well. Stir in the vanilla essence, add the thinly-sliced bananas and pour into a wetted mould.

6 helpings
Cooking time—10–12 min.
Setting time—2 hr.

BUTTERSCOTCH MOULD

Gâteau de Caramel au Beurre

1 oz. cornflour	**1 oz. butter**
1 pt. milk	**2 egg whites**
5 oz. soft brown sugar	**1 teasp. vanilla essence**

Blend cornflour and make as for cornflour mould (p. 435). Melt the sugar in a thick pan, stir in the butter and pour into the cornflour mixture. Beat well. Stiffly whisk egg whites and beat 2 tablesp. into the cornflour mixture to soften it a little. Fold in the remaining foam very lightly. Flavour with vanilla and pile into a glass dish *or* mould, and chill.

6 helpings
Cooking time—20 min.

COCONUT MOULD

Gâteau de Coco

2½ oz. cornflour	**2–3 oz. castor sugar**
2 pt. milk	**Carmine colouring**
2 oz. butter	**Pink desiccated coconut**
2 oz. desiccated coconut	

Blend cornflour with sufficient of the milk to mix to a smooth cream. Heat remaining milk with butter and proceed as for cornflour mould. Add coconut and sugar and colour a very pale pink. Pour quickly into a wet mould. Turn out when set and sprinkle pale pink coconut lightly all over.

6 helpings
Cooking time—15 min.
Setting time—2 hr.

To colour coconut: Tint 1 teasp. cold water with 2–3 drops only of colouring. Stir into white desiccated coconut until evenly coloured. Spread thinly over a sheet of greaseproof paper to dry thoroughly. Store in a stoppered jar.

FRUIT MOULD

Fruits moulés

1 pt. mixture as for cornflour mould (p. 435)	**½ lb. stewed fruit**

Put a thick layer of cornflour mixture at the bottom of a mould. When set, place a tumbler in the centre, and fill the space between the two with cornflour mixture. When the mixture is firm, remove the tumbler, fill the cavity with stewed fruit, and cover with a layer of cornflour mixture. When set, turn out, and serve with custard or whipped cream.

NOTE: If liked, Ground Rice Mould can be substituted for cornflour mould.

5–6 helpings
Time—about 2 hr.

GOLDEN MOUSSE PRALINE

4 oz. almond brittle *or* **almond rock**	**½ pt. water**
1 egg	**1 dessertsp. cornflour**
1½ oz. loaf sugar	**Pinch of salt**
1 orange	**½ pt. evaporated milk**
1 dessertsp. powdered gelatine	**One No. 1 tall can strawberries**

Pass the almond brittle through a mincing machine or crush it with a rolling pin between 2 sheets of greaseproof paper. Beat the egg into it. Rub the lumps of sugar hard on the orange rind to absorb its zest. Wet the gelatine with ½ the water and heat only enough to dissolve it. Add the orange-flavoured sugar and break it down. Add to the almond brittle-egg mixture. Blend the remaining water with the cornflour and stir over a low heat until cooked. Add the salt and stir into the other mixture. Leave until lukewarm, then stir in the evaporated milk. When cold and beginning to thicken, whip until very frothy. Turn into a greased mould and leave to set.

Turn out and garnish with the strawberries in their syrup.

5–6 helpings

NEAPOLITAN MOULD

Gâteau napolitain

3 oz. cornflour
2 pt. milk
½–1 oz. butter
2 oz. sugar
Colourings: sap green, carmine
Flavourings: almond, raspberry and coffee essences

Blend cornflour and make as for cornflour mould. Whilst cornflour is cooking warm 2 basins. Sweeten cornflour mixture to taste. Pour ⅓ quickly into a heated basin, colour pale pink and flavour with raspberry essence. Stir quickly and pour into a wetted mould. Pour ½ the remaining cornflour mixture into a heated basin, colour pale green and flavour with almond essence. Stir quickly and pour on the top of the set pink mixture. (This should be done lightly and slowly, pouring around the sides of the mould so that the second layer puts no great weight on the surface of the first). Flavour the remaining ⅓ of the mixture with coffee essence and pour on to the set green mixture, taking care, as before, not to pour too heavily. Leave to set and turn out when cold.

6 helpings
Cooking time—20 min. **Setting time—2 hr.**

SEA-FOAM PUDDING

Pouding à l'Ecume de la Mer

2 large lemons
2½ oz. cornflour
1½ pt. water
4–5 oz. sugar
3 egg whites

Wash lemons. Remove rind in thin strips, avoiding white pith as this is bitter. Blend cornflour with sufficient of the water to form a thin cream. Infuse lemon rind in remaining water; when boiling, remove rind and pour on to blended cornflour, stirring all the time. Return to pan and cook gently but thoroughly, 4–5 min. Add sugar, and juice of lemons. Whisk egg whites to a stiff foam, and pour cornflour mixture gently and smoothly into them, whisking continuously. When frothy, and still liquid, pour into a wet mould.

Turn out when set, and serve with custard sauce.

6 helpings
Cooking time—½ hr.
Setting time—2 hr.

SWISS CREAM

Crème à la Suisse

¼ lb. ratafia biscuits *or* sponge cake
3–4 tablesp. sherry
1¼ oz. cornflour
1 pt. milk
1 lemon
2 oz. castor sugar
¼–½ pt. double cream
2 teasp. chopped *or* grated nuts *or* glacé fruits

Put the ratafia biscuits or cake in the bottom of a glass dish, or individual dishes, and soak with sherry. Blend the cornflour with sufficient of the milk to make a smooth cream. Heat the remainder of the milk slowly with thin strips of lemon rind. Strain on to the blended cornflour, return to the pan and cook thoroughly but gently for 3–4 min. Stir in the sugar. Allow to cool. Whip the cream slightly and add it and the juice of the lemon gently and gradually to the cool cornflour cream. Re-sweeten if necessary. Pour over the soaked biscuits or cake and leave to go cold.

Decorate with chopped nuts, or tastefully arranged glacé cherries and thinly cut strips of angelica.

4–6 helpings
Cooking time—25 min.

JELLIES

JELLIES MAY BE MADE from fruit juices, fruit purées, milk flavoured with essences, or water and wine, set into a jellied form by the addition of gelatine. To be palatable, a jelly should be only just sufficiently set to stand upright when turned from the mould, and to achieve this consistency the measuring and weighing of ingredients must be exact. Manufacturers of gelatine recognize this expediency and always state the amount of gelatine required to set a given quantity of liquid. The gelatine used in compiling these recipes was a popular high-grade powdered product, but whatever the quality and the form, the manufacturer's instructions must always be followed.

For general purposes 1 pint of thin liquid will be set by ¾ oz. gelatine, but when a slightly firmer "set" is required 1 oz. to 1 pint is advisable. The larger amount of gelatine will be required for example:

(*a*) In hot weather.

(*b*) When pieces of fruit are to be set in the jelly and the mould turned out, the reason being that fruit is moist and dilutes the jelly slightly, fruit is also heavy, and when turned out may be too heavy to remain suspended in a delicate and fragile jelly.

(*c*) If the jelly is to be used for lining a mould, or chopped for decoration (*see also* p. 443).

(*d*) If it is to be whipped and set in a foam.

JELLY MOULDS

Jelly moulds may be made of glass, highly-glazed china or metal. Smooth cereal and milk mixtures such as cornflour mould are most easily turned out from glass or china moulds, as the cold, wet surface of the china cools the surface of the mixture very quickly and causes a slight shrinkage from the sides. If gelatine is included in the ingredients, however, a metal mould, being a better conductor of heat, will give a cleaner and sharper outline to the turned-out shape. Tin-lined copper moulds are costly but ensure perfect form and finish and are so durable that they are handed down from one generation to the next. The expense of occasional re-lining with tin (which is essential as copper is dissolved by acids) is no more than the price of a tin-plate mould.

All moulds must be scrupulously clean. They must be quite cold when used and should be rinsed out with cold water immediately before use.

UNMOULDING JELLIES

The unmoulding of jellies can only be successfully achieved by one single, quick, and total immersion in very hot water. Repeated dipping in water that is not hot enough to loosen the mould instantly will spoil the shape. As the whole is immersed, the top of the jelly must be dried afterwards with a clean cloth.

AMBER JELLY

Gelée ambrée

¾ pt. water
1 wineglass sherry (optional)
¼ pt. lemon juice (2 lemons)
6 oz. loaf sugar
1 oz. gelatine
3 egg yolks
Thin rind of 1 lemon

Put all ingredients into a pan and allow to soak 5 min. Whisk over gentle heat until near boiling point. Do not boil or the eggs will curdle. Strain through muslin and pour into a prepared mould.

This is a delicious and nutritious sweet for an invalid.

4–6 helpings **Cooking time—½ hr.**

APPLE JELLY

Gelée de Pommes

2 lb. apples
1 pt. water
5–6 oz. sugar
2 cloves
2 small lemons
1½ oz. gelatine
4 tablesp. cold water

Wash apples, cut into quarters and core. Cook with 1 pt. of water, sugar, cloves and grated lemon rind until soft. Soak gelatine in 4 tablesp. cold water for 5 min., then heat until dissolved. Rub apples through a fine sieve, add juice of lemons and taste for further sweetening. Strain gelatine into the purée and stir well. Pour into a wet mould.

6 helpings
Cooking time—15–20 min. **Setting time—2–3 hr.**

BANANA JELLY WITH CREAM

Gelée de Bananes à la Crème

1 pt. lemon *or* orange jelly
½ oz. peeled pistachio nuts
6 bananas
¼ pt. double cream

Make the jelly and allow to cool. Chop green pistachio nuts finely and stir into 2 tablesp. jelly. Set the nut jelly in the bottom of a mould. Beat the bananas to a purée and half-whip the cream. Stir the banana purée into the remaining jelly ; add cream and fold together lightly. Fill up the mould and turn out when set.

6 helpings
Cooking time—5 min.
Setting time—2 hr.

DUTCH FLUMMERY

Crèmes aux Œufs à l'Hollandaise

1 lemon
1 pt. water
1 oz. gelatine
2 eggs
1 small wineglass of sherry *or* madeira wine
Castor sugar to taste

Wash lemon and cut thin strips of rind; infuse the rind in water. Add gelatine and simmer gently until dissolved. Beat the eggs, add wine, juice of the lemon and water with the gelatine. Strain all into a pan and stir over gentle heat until thick. Sweeten to taste and pour into a 2 pt. wetted mould. Turn out when set.

6 helpings
Cooking time—about 40 min.
Setting time—2–3 hr.

GOOSEBERRY JELLY

Gelée de Groseilles vertes

2 lb. gooseberries
1 pt. water
5–6 oz. sugar
1½ oz. gelatine
4 tablesp. cold water

Top and tail gooseberries; wash them. Cook with 1 pt. of water and the sugar until soft. Soak gelatine in 4 tablesp. cold water for 5 min., then heat until dissolved. Rub gooseberries through a fine sieve, and taste for further sweetening. Strain gelatine into the purée and stir well. Pour into a wet mould.

6 helpings
Cooking time—20 min.
Setting time—2–3 hr.

HONEYCOMB MOULD

Crème Anglaise

1 pt. milk	**2 large eggs**
Flavouring: vanilla essence *or* lemon *or* orange rind	**1 oz. castor sugar**
	½ oz. gelatine
	4 tablesp. water

If orange or lemon rind is being used for flavouring, slowly infuse thinly-cut strips of rind in the milk. Remove the rind and make a custard with the egg yolks, sugar and flavoured milk. If using essence add to the custard after the sugar. Dissolve gelatine in measured water and while still warm stir into the custard. Allow to cool. When just beginning to set, fold in the stiffly-whisked egg whites. Pour into a quart border mould and leave to set.

Turn out and serve with fruit salad piled up in the hollow. Decorate with whipped cream.

4–6 helpings

LEMON CURD JELLY

Gelée au Citron

3 large lemons	**1 oz. gelatine (light-weight)**
1½ pt. milk	
7–8 oz. sugar	**4 tablesp. water**

Wash lemons and remove rind in thin strips from two of them. Infuse rind in the milk with the sugar until the latter is dissolved. Soak the gelatine in the water and, when soft, stir into the warm milk. Do not allow the milk with gelatine to boil or curdling may occur. Strain into a bowl and allow to cool to blood-heat. Stir in the strained juice of three lemons and mould. Turn out when set.

NOTE: If curdling should occur, whisk vigorously before moulding and a fine, spongy texture will be formed.

6 helpings
Cooking time—½ hr.
Setting time—2 hr.

MILK JELLY (INVALID)

Gelée au Lait

½ oz. gelatine	**½ pt. milk**
4 tablesp. water	**1 teasp. castor sugar**
Lemon rind	

Heat the gelatine gently in the water until dissolved. Add the milk, sugar and thinly-cut strips of lemon rind. Stir over a gentle heat until sugar is dissolved—do not let it boil or it will curdle. Strain into a basin and stir from time to time until it attains the consistency of thick cream. Pour into a wet mould.

NOTE: The jelly may be flavoured with vanilla *or* coffee essences, if liked.

2 helpings
Cooking time—5 min.
Setting time—1 hr.

ORANGE CUSTARD JELLY

Gelée d'Orange à la Crème

5 oranges	**¾ oz. gelatine**
4 oz. sugar	**2 eggs**

Wash oranges and cut rind from 2 in thin strips. Strain orange juice and make up to 1½ pt. with water. Add rind, sugar and gelatine and heat gently until dissolved. Allow to cool and add well-beaten eggs. Cook again to thicken but do not boil. Strain into a wet 2-pt. mould. Turn out when set.

6 helpings
Cooking time—about 45 min.
Setting time—2 hr.

ORANGE JELLY

Gelée d'Oranges

1 pt. water	**6 oranges (1 pt. juice)**
3–4 oz. sugar	**2 lemons**
1½ oz. gelatine	**Angelica (optional)**

Put water, sugar and gelatine into a pan. Wash fruit and cut thin strips of outer rind from 3 oranges, avoiding white pith. Add strips to the pan and bring slowly to the boil. Leave to infuse, with the lid on, for 10 min. Squeeze juice from oranges and lemons and strain on to juice. Then either:

(*a*) pour into a wet metal mould; *or*

(*b*) prepare orange-skin "cups" made from half-sections of peel freed from pulp. Fill with liquid jelly, stand in patty-tins to hold upright until set, and decorate with piped cream and angelica-strip "handles" to form baskets; *or* form baskets as shown on p. 39; *or*

(*c*) allow to set in orange-skin cups then cut the halves into quarters and arrange as boats.

6 helpings
Cooking time—10 min.
Setting time—2 hr.

PORT WINE JELLY

1 pt. water
2 oz. sugar
2 tablesp. redcurrant jelly
1 oz. gelatine
½ pt. port wine
Cochineal

Put water, sugar, redcurrant jelly and gelatine into a pan and leave to soak for 5 min. Heat slowly until dissolved. Add half the port wine and colour dark red with a few drops of cochineal. Strain through double muslin; add the rest of the wine. Pour into a wet mould.

6 helpings
Cooking time—10 min. **Setting time—2 hr.**

CLEARED JELLIES

"CLEARED" JELLY is filtered through a foam of coagulated egg whites and crushed egg-shells. The pan, whisk and metal jelly-mould to be used must first be scalded. The egg whites are lightly whisked until liquid, then added with the washed and crushed egg-shells to the cooled jelly. The mixture is heated steadily and whisked constantly until a good head of foam is produced, and the contents of the pan are hot, but not quite boiling. The albumen in the egg-whites and egg-shells coagulates at 160° F., and as the hardened particles rise to the surface they carry with them all the insoluble substances with which they come in contact, forming a thick "crust" of foam. The correct temperature is reached when the foam begins to set, and care must be taken not to break up, by whisking too long, a completely coagulated foam. The whisk is removed, and heating continued to allow the foam "crust" to rise to the top of the pan. The heat is then lowered and the contents of the pan left to settle in a warm place, covered with a lid, for 5–10 minutes. The jelly is then poured through a scalded jelly cloth while the cloth is still hot, into a scalded bowl below. The bowl of strained jelly is replaced with another scalded bowl, and the jelly re-strained very carefully by pouring through the foam "crust" which covers the bottom of the cloth and acts as a filter. If the jelly is not clear and brilliant when a little is taken up in a highly-polished spoon, the filtering must be repeated immediately.

The filtering is most easily carried out using a jelly bag and stand made for the purpose, but if these are not available the 4 corners of a clean cloth can be tied to the legs of an upturned stool, and a bowl placed below the cloth.

CLEARED JELLIES

It must be remembered that repeated filtering will cool the jelly considerably and, if done too often, will result in a very poor yield of clear jelly as it will tend to solidify in the cloth. The jelly stand should be placed in a warm position during filtering and draughts should be excluded from the filter by covering the stand with a blanket. A metal container filled with hot water "planted" in the filter will assist in keeping the jelly liquid, but if the filter is at all disturbed by doing this, the resulting jelly will be cloudy, caused by the filter being broken up.

Careful filtering produces a jelly of clear brilliance, a necessary quality for lining moulds and setting decorations and fruit, otherwise the colour of these would be obscured.

MOULDS FOR CLEARED JELLIES

All moulds must be scrupulously clean, and should be scalded, as the merest trace of grease may cause cloudiness.

LINING A MOULD

To line a mould thinly and evenly with jelly, it is essential that it should be rotated quickly; therefore it is better to choose a round mould and to prepare a bed of crushed ice, into which the mould is set on its side in such a position that it can be "spun" by the thumbs. Care must be taken to prevent ice from entering the mould during spinning.

The jelly should be cold but liquid, and enough should be used to coat the side from the base to the lip—two to three tablespoonfuls. Surplus jelly should be drained from the mould while still liquid, otherwise a ridge will form in the lining. Two thin coats are preferable to one thick one, and, as speed is essential in acquiring a thin coat, spinning should be practised with an empty mould to achieve proficiency.

DECORATING A MOULD

Decorations may be placed in the base or on the lined sides of a mould, and must be covered by another thin coating of jelly before the "filling" is put in, otherwise, when the mould is turned out, they will appear to have sunk into the filling.

When the sides of the mould are set, use a teaspoon to place jelly in the base. On no account should jelly be poured into the mould, as bubbles of air can very easily be entrapped and appear as holes when the jelly is turned out. Any bubbles which do form should be gently lifted out with a teaspoon.

Decorations should be chosen for their colour-contrast, or if decorating a cream they could indicate the flavour of the cream filling; but in all cases they must be very neatly cut. Pistachio nut, blanched, skinned and cut into thin slices, gives a clear bright green trefoil shape ideal for leaves. Angelica, on the other hand, is almost invisible because it is translucent. If this is used, it must be cut rather thickly to be effective. Candied and glacé fruits, too, are not always colourful enough, but the black skin of prunes and the red and yellow of plums and apricots are very effective if cut into tiny petals, rounds and diamonds. Each piece of decoration is dipped into cold liquid jelly before being set in place. Two hat-pins will be found most suitable for this meticulous work.

FILLING THE MOULD

Moulds should always be filled to the brim, and if when moulding a cream there is insufficient cream to do this, the space should be filled with jelly. The reason for this is that when the mould is jerked to release its filling a "drop" of a mere half-inch may be enough to break the delicate texture.

UNMOULDING JELLIES AND CREAMS

The unmoulding of jellies and creams can only be successfully achieved by one single, quick, and total immersion in very hot water. Repeated dipping in water that is not hot enough to loosen the mould instantly will spoil the shape and dislodge any decoration. Charlottes lined with sponge fingers are dipped only to the rim, as any dampening of the sponge would cause the charlotte to collapse. After total immersion, quickly absorb any surface moisture with a clean cloth, and with one sharp jerk, turn out the mould on to the serving dish by gently sliding the fingers of the supporting hand from underneath the loosened jelly.

Mask the dish surrounding the jelly with piped cream or chopped jelly and, if a silver dish, rub lightly to remove any spot or mark before serving.

TO CHOP JELLY

Chopped jelly used as a decoration must be very clear and be chopped cleanly with a wet knife on wet greaseproof paper so that the light is refracted from the cut surfaces as from the facets of a jewel. The more coarsely the jelly is chopped, the better is the effect, for whilst large pieces refract the light, finely-chopped jelly has a slightly opaque appearance.

CLEARED JELLIES

CLARET JELLY

Gelée au Bordeaux

4 lemons (¼ pt. juice)
1¼ pt. water
6 oz. loaf sugar
1½ oz. gelatine
Whites and shells of 2 eggs
¼ pt. claret
Carmine

Use thinly cut rind of 2 lemons and infuse with water, sugar and gelatine. Add crushed shells and whites of eggs and lemon juice (*see* p. 441), Whisk steadily until boiling point is almost reached. Remove whisk and boil to the top of the pan. Pour in the claret without disturbing the foam "crust". Boil again to the top of the pan. Remove from the heat, cover, and leave to settle for 1 min. Filter, add the colour, drop by drop, after filtering; cool, remove froth, and mould in scalded individual moulds.

4–6 helpings
Time—45 min.

LEMON JELLY

Gelée au Citron

4 lemons
Sherry (optional)
1½ pt. water
6 oz. sugar
4 cloves
1 in. cinnamon stick
1¾–2 oz. gelatine
Shells and whites of 2 eggs

Scald a large pan, whisk and metal jelly-mould. Wash lemons and cut thin strips of rind, avoiding white pith. Extract juice and measure. Make up to ½ pt. with water *or* sherry, but if the latter is to be used, do not add until just before clearing the jelly. Put the 1½ pt. water, ½ pt. juice, rinds, sugar, flavourings and gelatine into the scalded pan and infuse, with a lid on, over gentle heat until sugar and gelatine are dissolved. Do not let the infusion become hot. Wash egg-shells and crush. Lightly whisk the whites until liquid and add, with shells, to the infusion. Heat steadily, whisking constantly, until a good head of foam is produced, and the contents of the pan become hot, but not quite boiling. Strain through the crust (*see* p. 441), and add sherry if used, to the jelly as it goes through the filter.

6 helpings
Time—1–1½ hr.

RED WINE JELLY

Gelée au Vin d'Oporto

4 lemons (¼ pt. juice)
½ lb. sugar
1½–2 oz. gelatine
1 pt. water
Whites and shells of 2 eggs
¾ pt. port wine

Infuse the thinly cut lemon rinds, sugar and gelatine in the measured water until dissolved. Add lemon juice, whites and crushed shells of the eggs and whisk steadily until boiling point is almost reached. Remove whisk and boil to the top of the pan. Pour in the port wine without disturbing the foam "crust". Boil again to the top of the pan. Remove from the heat, cover, and leave to settle for 1 min. Strain carefully (*see* p. 441). Cool, remove froth, and mould in scalded individual moulds.

4–6 helpings
Time—1–1½ hr.

WINE JELLY

Gelée au Vin

4 lemons (¼ pt. juice)
½ lb. sugar
1½–2 oz. gelatine
1 pt. water
Whites and shells of 2 eggs
¼ pt. brandy
½ pt. sherry

Infuse the thinly cut lemon rinds, sugar and gelatine in the measured water until dissolved. Add lemon juice, whites and crushed shells of the eggs and whisk steadily until boiling-point is almost reached. Remove whisk and boil to the top of the pan. Pour in the brandy and sherry without disturbing the foam "crust". Boil again to the top of the pan. Remove from the heat, cover, and leave to settle for 1 min. Strain carefully (*see* p. 441). Cool, remove froth. and mould in scalded individual moulds.

4–6 helpings
Time—1–1½ hr.

FRUIT IN JELLY

Macédoine de Fruit à la Gelée

1½ pt. very clear lemon jelly *or* wine jelly using white wine instead of sherry and brandy
Selected pieces of fruit, e.g. bananas, black and green grapes, tangerines, cherries, apricot, pineapple, etc.

Scald a metal mould, then rinse it with cold water. Cover the bottom with a thin layer of cool jelly (about $\frac{1}{8}$ in. thick). Avoid the formation of bubbles in the jelly by tilting the mould and placing the jelly in spoonfuls in the bottom. Bubbles will spoil the clear transparency of the jelly when turned out. If they do form, remove with a teaspoon. Leave to set. Cut pieces of fruit to suit the hollows and spaces of the mould, dip each piece into cold liquid jelly and set in place around and on the jelly layer. Leave to set and cover carefully with a layer of clear jelly. Allow to set. Repeat, taking care that each layer of fruit is quite firm before adding a layer of jelly—otherwise the fruit may be "floated" from its position. Fill the mould to the top.

When quite set, turn out and decorate with piped cream *or* chopped clear jelly.

6 helpings
Time (without ice)—3–4 hr.
(with ice packed around the mould)—1 hr.

INVALID CHAMPAGNE JELLY

Gelée au Vin de Champagne

1 pt. water
¼ pt. champagne
¼ pt. sherry
6 oz. loaf sugar
1½ oz. gelatine
Juice and finely-cut rind of 1 lemon
Juice and finely-cut rind of 1 orange
2 cloves
1 in. cinnamon stick
White and shell of 1 egg

Put all the ingredients into a deep saucepan and bring to the boil, whisking meanwhile. Remove whisk and allow to simmer for about 10 min. Strain through the crust (*see* p. 441). Pour the cleared jelly into a wetted mould and allow to set.

4–6 helpings
Time—about 40 min.

JELLY WITH CREAM

Gelée à la Crème

1 pt. red wine jelly (clear)
½ oz. gelatine
½ pt. double cream
¼ oz. angelica
¼ oz. glacé cherries
¼ oz. preserved ginger
¼ oz. apricots

Set a 1 in. layer of jelly in the bottom of a quart mould. Stand a tumbler in the middle and pour the remaining jelly around it. Weight the tumbler with cold water if necessary. Leave to set firmly. Dissolve gelatine by heating it gently in 2–3 tablesp. water, cool and add gradually to the whipped cream. Shred the fruits and stir into the cream. Remove the tumbler from the jelly by filling it for a minute with warm water. Fill the cavity with the cream and leave to set.

Turn out on to a silver dish, if possible, and decorate with chopped jelly.

4 helpings

MARBLED JELLY

Gelée marbrée

1½ pt. lemon *or* wine jelly (clear)
Carmine colouring
Sap-green colouring
¼ pt. double cream

Coat a quart mould with a thin layer of clear jelly (*see* p. 442). Put 3 tablesp. cool jelly into each of 3 basins and colour one red and one green. Whisk each until frothy and set. With a small teaspoon, place little balls of whisked jelly round the mould, alternating the colours. Cover carefully with cold, liquid clear jelly. Repeat until the mould is filled, the last layer being of clear jelly. Turn out and decorate with whipped cream.

6 helpings
Time (without ice)—2 hr.

NEAPOLITAN JELLY

Gelée napolitaine

1½ pt. wine jelly
Carmine colouring
Sap-green colouring
¼ pt. double cream

Divide jelly into 3, colouring $\frac{1}{3}$ red and $\frac{1}{3}$ green and leaving $\frac{1}{3}$ plain. Mould in layers of equal thickness, alternating the colours, allowing each layer to set before adding another. Turn out and decorate with piped, whipped cream.

6 helpings
Time (without ice)—2–3 hr. according to weather
(with ice packed round mould)—¾ hr.

WHIPPED JELLIES

IF JELLY is whipped or whisked just prior to setting, tiny bubbles of air are enclosed. These impart a lightness of texture both stimulating and refreshing to the palate—qualities of great appeal in hot weather. The addition of egg white, slightly whisked and then whipped with the cold liquid jelly increases the volume of the jellied foam and also adds to its nutritive value without unduly diluting the flavour, although a strongly-flavoured jelly is necessary if more than 1 egg white is used. This is a sweet very suitable for, and popular with, children and invalids.

BLACKCURRANT WHIP

Gelée de Cassis fouettée

¼ pt. blackcurrant purée and ½ pt. water *or* ¾ pt. blackcurrant juice
½ oz. gelatine
Sugar to taste

Heat the gelatine slowly in the juice *or* purée and water until dissolved. Add sugar if necessary. Cool, then whisk briskly until a thick foam is produced. When the whisk leaves a trail in the foam, pile quickly into a glass dish.

6 helpings
Time—½ hr.

COFFEE WHIP

Gelée de Café fouettée

1 pt. milk
1 tablesp. coffee essence
Sugar to taste
¾ oz. gelatine soaked and dissolved in 4 tablesp. water
1–2 egg whites (optional)

DECORATION
Chopped nuts

Heat together the milk, coffee essence and sugar. Heat the gelatine in the water until dissolved then cool slightly. Add to the cooled coffee-flavoured milk. Whisk strongly. If egg whites are used, whisk them until liquid and slightly frothy, and stir into the cool jelly just before whisking. When thick, pile into a dish and scatter chopped nuts over the top.

6 helpings
Cooking time—10 min.
Setting time—½ hr.

DAMSON WHIP

Gelée de Prune de Damas fouettée

¾ pt. damson juice
½ oz. gelatine
Sugar to taste

Proceed as for Black Currant Whip.

LEMON WHIP

Gelée au Citron fouettée

One 1 pt. lemon jelly tablet
Sugar if necessary
¾ pt. water
1 tablesp. lemon juice

Melt the jelly tablet in ¼ pt. water. Stir in ½ pt. cold water and strained lemon juice. Sweeten if necessary. When cool, whisk briskly until a thick foam is produced. When the whisk leaves a trail in the foam, pile quickly into a glass dish.

6 helpings **Time—½ hr.**

ORANGE WHIP (1)

Gelée d'Oranges fouettée

One 1 pt. orange jelly tablet
Water and orange juice to make ¾ pt.

Proceed as for Lemon Whip.

ORANGE WHIP (2)

¾ pt. strained orange juice
½ oz. gelatine
Castor sugar to taste

Proceed as for Blackcurrant Whip.

PINEAPPLE WHIP (1)

Gelée d'Ananas fouettée

One 1 pt. pineapple jelly tablet
½ pt. canned pineapple juice
¼ pt. water
Sugar if necessary

Proceed as for Lemon Whip.

PINEAPPLE WHIP (2)

¾ pt. pineapple juice **½ oz. gelatine**

Proceed as for Blackcurrant Whip (p. 446).

RASPBERRY WHIP (1)

Gelée de Framboise fouettée

One 1 pt. raspberry jelly tablet
½ pt. raspberry juice
¼ pt. water
Sugar if necessary

Proceed as for Lemon Whip (p. 446).

RASPBERRY WHIP (2)

¾ pt. strained raspberry juice
½ oz. gelatine
Sugar to taste

Proceed as for Blackcurrant Whip (p. 446).

STRAWBERRY WHIP

Gelée de Fraise fouettée

1 pt. strawberry jelly tablet
½ pt. strawberry juice
¼ pt. water
Sugar if necessary

Proceed as for Lemon Whip (p. 446).

CREAMS

CREAMS CAN BE DIVIDED into two types:— full creams and half-creams.

FULL CREAMS

These consist wholly of cream flavoured with essence or liqueurs, set with gelatine.

HALF-CREAMS

Half-creams (also known as **Bavaroise** or **Bavarian Creams**) are compounds of custard, cream and flavouring, the last being in the form of fruit purées, juices, essences, etc.

Fresh cream cannot be equalled in texture and flavour by any synthetic cream, but substitutes can be used without any modification of the recipe provided certain precautions are taken in using them:

1. EVAPORATED UNSWEETENED MILK: Boil the can of milk, unopened, for 20 min., then cool quickly. If possible chill for 24 hr., in a refrigerator. The milk will then keep for several weeks in a refrigerator providing the can is not opened; several cans can thus be boiled at one time and kept until required.

2. SYNTHETIC CREAM: Whip the cream as it is. Any sugar required for sweetening should be stirred in after whipping.

The inclusion of milk, custard, cream or ice cream in a jellied liquid increases its density and therefore less gelatine is required to set one pint of this thicker consistency; as little as a quarter of an ounce being sufficient to set one pint of a really thick liquid such as a mixture of cream and rich custard. The gelatine, dissolved in a little water, must be added at a certain temperature, if it is too hot it causes the cream to lose some of its lightness, and if too cold, it sets in small hard lumps before it is evenly distributed (should this happen whip the mixture over a bowl of hot water). Egg also has a thickening capacity as it coagulates when heated and in this state is able to hold liquid. One egg will "set" a quarter of a pint of liquid and if eggs are being added to jellies for nutritional purposes the proportion of gelatine should be adjusted accordingly.

The smoothness of cream mixtures depends largely on the ease with which their various ingredients are blended, and, to achieve this, care should be taken to combine them at a similar consistency. Custard should be cooled until its consistency is comparable with that of the jelly or fruit purée, and cream, if used, should be whipped to a similar stage. If the cream is over-whipped it may turn to butter, particularly in warm weather. If ice cream is used it will be found necessary to warm the mixture during blending as the low temperature will cause setting before the milk or cream can be added. Fresh whipped cream should be stirred in very lightly just before setting—this imparts a slight sponginess to the texture of the mixture as a small amount of air is incorporated during whipping, and this would be lost with continued stirring.

Moulds for these mixtures should be of metal and if to be decorated must be lined with jelly. For instructions on lining a mould with jelly, decorating, filling and turning out a mould *see* pp. 442–3.

FULL CREAMS

PISTACHIO CREAM

Crème aux Pistaches

4 oz. pistachio nuts
$1/4$ oz. gelatine
4 tablesp. water
2 oz. castor sugar
1 pt. double cream
Sap-green colouring

Blanch, skin and finely chop the pistachio nuts. Soak gelatine in the water, heat to dissolve. Add sugar and stir until dissolved. Whip the cream, fold in the liquid gelatine and chopped nuts, and colour pale green, adding the colouring a drop at a time. Pour into a prepared mould and leave to set.

6 helpings
Setting time—1–2 hr.

VELVET CREAM

Crème Veloutée

$1/4$ oz. gelatine
4 tablesp. water
$1\frac{1}{2}$–2 oz. castor sugar
Sherry, *or* vanilla essence
1 pt. double cream

Soak the gelatine in the cold water for 5 min. Heat gently until quite dissolved and clear. Stir in the sugar until dissolved. Add the sherry or vanilla. Whip the cream until thick and fold into it the flavoured liquid gelatine.

Pour into a prepared mould and leave to set.

6 helpings
Setting time—1 hr.

PLATE 19

Making a Flan Case

(*'Blind' Baking*)

1

1 Roll out the pastry and line a greased flan ring with it. Press to fit bottom and side so that no air bubbles form underneath.

2

2 Trim off surplus pastry by rolling across with the rolling-pin or cut it off with a sharp knife.

3

3 Decorate the top edge by pinching and twisting the pastry between the first finger and the thumb.

4

4 Cover bottom of flan with a piece of greaseproof paper and weight it to keep shape during baking.

5

5 Remove paper, rice, beans, etc., and flan ring when pastry is cooked.

Reading from top and left to right: Sultana cake (page 518); cream buns (page 569); rock buns (page 516); madeleines (page 533); orange sandwich cake (page 531); éclairs (page 571); chocolate Swiss roll (page 536); sponge cake (page 536); fruit scones (page 506); rich cakes (page 533).

Apricot baskets (see page 533) are just one simple variation of the basic recipe for small rich cakes.

PLATE 20
Cakes and Buns

HALF CREAMS

CHOCOLATE CREAM

Crème au Chocolat

4 oz. plain chocolate
½ pt. milk
3 egg yolks *or* 1 whole egg and 1 yolk
2–3 oz. castor sugar
½ oz. gelatine
4 tablesp. water
1 teasp. vanilla *or* coffee essence
½ pt. double cream

Grate the chocolate and dissolve in the milk. Beat eggs and sugar until liquid and make a thick pouring custard with the flavoured milk, straining back into the pan to cook and thicken. Do not allow to boil or the eggs may curdle. Allow to cool. Soak gelatine in the water for 5 min., then heat to dissolve. Stir the vanilla *or* coffee essence gently into the cooled custard, and add the dissolved gelatine, stirring again as it cools. Whip the cream and fold lightly into the custard mixture just before setting. Pour into a prepared mould or into glass dishes.

6 helpings
Setting time—1–2 hr.

COFFEE CREAM

Crème au Café

3 egg yolks *or* 1 whole egg and 1 yolk
2–3 oz. castor sugar
½ pt. milk
½ oz. gelatine
4 tablesp. water
2–3 teasp. coffee essence
½ pt. double cream

Beat the eggs and sugar until liquid. Heat the milk almost to boiling point and pour over the egg mixture. Strain the egg and milk back into the pan, and cook gently until thick, stirring all the time. Allow to cool. Soak the gelatine in the water for 5 min., then heat to dissolve. Stir the coffee essence into the cooled custard, and add the dissolved gelatine, stirring again as it cools. Whip the cream and fold lightly into the custard mixture just before setting. Pour into a prepared mould or into glass dishes.

6 helpings
Setting time—1–2 hr.

GINGER CREAM

Crème au Gingembre

2–3 oz. chopped preserved ginger
½ pt. milk
3 egg yolks *or* 1 whole egg and 1 yolk
Castor sugar to taste
½ oz. gelatine
4 tablesp. water
2–3 tablesp. ginger syrup
½ pt. double cream

Infuse the preserved ginger in the milk. Beat the eggs and sugar until liquid and make a thick pouring custard with the flavoured milk, straining back into the pan to cook and thicken. Allow to cool. Soak gelatine in the water for 5 min., then heat to dissolve. Stir the ginger syrup gently into the cooled custard, and add the dissolved gelatine, stirring again as it cools. Whip the cream and fold lightly into the custard mixture just before setting. Pour into a prepared mould or into glass dishes.

6 helpings
Setting time—1–2 hr.

ITALIAN CREAM

Crème à l'Italienne

1 lemon
½ pt. milk
3 egg yolks *or* 1 whole egg and 1 yolk
2–3 oz. castor sugar
½ oz. gelatine
½ gill water
½ pt. double cream

Infuse thin strips of lemon rind in the milk. Beat eggs and sugar until liquid and make a thick pouring custard with the flavoured milk, straining back into the pan to cook and thicken. Allow to cool. Soak gelatine in the water for 5 min., then heat to dissolve. Stir juice of lemon gently into the cooled custard, and add the dissolved gelatine, stirring again as it cools. Whip the cream and fold lightly into the custard mixture just before setting.

Pour into a prepared mould and leave to set. If liked the cream may be poured into individual glass dishes, which may be decorated according to personal taste with glacé fruits or chopped nuts.

6 helpings
Setting time—1–2 hr.

QUEEN MAB'S PUDDING

Pouding de la Reine Mab

1 pt. milk
3 eggs
3 oz. castor sugar
Vanilla essence
½ oz. gelatine
4 tablesp. water
2 oz. glacé cherries
1 oz. citron peel
¼ pt double cream

Make a custard with the milk, eggs and sugar, and flavour with vanilla. Soak gelatine in the water for 5 min., then heat until dissolved. Stir into the custard. Cut cherries in halves and shred the peel. Stir into the custard and lastly fold in the cream, whipped to a consistency similar to that of the cool custard. Just before setting, pour into a prepared mould. Turn out when set.

6 helpings
Setting time—1–2 hr.

RUM CREAM

Crème au Rhum

1 bay leaf
½ pt. milk
3 egg yolks *or* 1 whole egg and 1 yolk
2–3 oz. castor sugar
½ oz. gelatine
4 tablesp. water
1 wineglass of rum
½ pt. double cream

Infuse the bay leaf in the milk for 20 min. Beat eggs and sugar until liquid and make a thick pouring custard with the flavoured milk, straining back into the pan to cook and thicken. Allow to cool. Soak gelatine in the water for 5 min., then heat to dissolve. Stir the dissolved gelatine into the cooled custard. Stir in the rum. Whip the cream and fold lightly into the custard mixture just before setting. Pour into a prepared mould, or into glass dishes.

6 helpings
Setting time—1–2 hr.

VANILLA CREAM

Crème à la Vanille

3 egg yolks *or* 1 whole egg and 1 yolk
2–3 oz. castor sugar
½ pt. milk
½ oz. gelatine
4 tablesp. water
2 teasp. vanilla essence
½ pt. double cream

Beat the eggs and sugar until liquid. Heat the milk to almost boiling point and pour over the egg mixture. Strain the egg and milk back into the saucepan, and cook very gently until thick, stirring all the time. Allow to cool. Soak the gelatine in the water for 5 min., then heat to dissolve. Stir the vanilla essence into the cooled custard, and add the dissolved gelatine, stirring again as it cools. Whip the cream and fold lightly into the custard mixture just before setting. Pour into a prepared mould or into glass dishes.

6 helpings
Setting time—1–2 hr.

FRUIT CREAMS

CRÈME AUX FRUITS

Basic Recipe

½ pt. fruit purée (*see below*)
½ pt. thick, rich custard
Castor sugar to sweeten
Lemon juice (optional)
½ oz. gelatine
4 tablesp. water *or* thin fruit juice
Colouring (optional)
½ pt. double cream

Purée the fruit through a very fine sieve—nylon mesh if possible, as fresh fruit is acid. Blend with the cool custard, sweeten, and flavour with lemon juice if required. Soak the gelatine in the water *or* juice for a few minutes and heat to dissolve. Pour, while steaming hot, into the custard and fruit mixture, and stir to keep well blended until the mixture begins to feel heavy and drags on the spoon. Colour if necessary. Stir in, lightly, the whipped cream and pour into a prepared mould.

NOTE: **apricots, blackcurrants, damsons, gooseberries, greengages, peaches, raspberries** *or* **strawberries** may be used for the purée, and the cream named accordingly.

6 helpings
Setting time—1–2 hr.

Variations

GARIBALDI CREAM

Crème à la Garibaldi

½ pt. strawberry cream
½ pt. vanilla cream
½ pt. pistachio cream

Place the strawberry cream at the bottom of a prepared mould. Allow to set. Add the vanilla cream and set. Put the pistachio cream on the top. Turn out and surround with chopped jelly.

6 helpings
Setting time (with ice)—45 min.
(without ice)—2–3 hr.

ORANGE CREAM (1)

Crème à l'Orange

3 large oranges	**2 oz. castor sugar**
½ pt. milk	**¾ oz. gelatine**
3 egg yolks *or* 1 egg and 1 yolk	**¼ pt. double cream**

Infuse thin strips of rind from 2 oranges in the milk. Remove the rind, and make into a thick pouring custard with the egg yolks and sugar. Soak the gelatine in the orange juice and add sufficient water to make ½ pt. Heat to dissolve, and strain into the orange-flavoured custard. Whip the cream and fold in when the gelatine-custard mixture is thick but not set. Pour into a prepared mould and turn out when quite cold.

6 helpings
Setting time—1–2 hr.

ORANGE CREAM (2)

Two 1 pt. orange jelly tablets	**1 pt. thick pouring custard**
¼ pt. water	**½ pt. double cream**
¼ pt. orange juice *or* squash	

Melt the jellies in the water and juice. Make the custard and stir into the jelly when both are slightly cooled. Whip the cream and fold in.

8 helpings
Setting time—1–2 hr.

ORANGE CREAM (3)

Two 1 pt. orange jelly tablets	**12 oz. family block of ice cream**
¼ pt. water	**Juice of ½–1 lemon to taste**
¼ pt. orange juice *or* squash	**½ pt. milk**

Melt the jellies in the water and juice. Stir in the ice cream quickly and if the mixture sets at this stage, place the bowl over a pan of hot water and stir until liquid again. Add lemon juice as required as this mixture will be very sweet. Stir in the milk, and pour into a prepared mould. Turn out when set.

8 helpings

PINEAPPLE CREAM (1)

Crème à l'Ananas

Two 1 pt. pineapple jelly tablets	**1 pt. thick custard**
¼ pt. water	**4 oz. chopped pineapple**
¼ pt. pineapple juice	**½ pt. double cream**

Melt the jellies in the water and juice. Make the custard and stir into the jelly when both are slightly cooled. Stir in the chopped pineapple. Whip the cream and fold in.

8 helpings **Setting time—1–2 hr.**

PINEAPPLE CREAM (2)

Two 1 pt. pineapple jelly tablets	**1 family size 12 oz. block ice cream**
¼ pt. water	**½ pt. milk**
¼ pt. pineapple juice	**Lemon juice to taste**

Melt the jellies in the water and juice. Stir in the ice cream quickly and if the mixture sets at this stage, place the bowl over a pan of hot water and stir until liquid again. Add lemon juice as required as this mixture will be very sweet. Stir in the milk, and pour into a prepared mould. Turn out when set.

8 helpings

TANGERINE CREAM

Crème à l'Orange de Tanger

Two 1 pt. orange jelly tablets	**1 pt. thick custard**
¼ pt. water	**½ pt. double cream**
¼ pt. tangerine purée (sieve contents of 1 small can)	

Proceed as for Orange Cream (2).

NOTE: 1 family size 12 oz. block of ice cream, ½ pt. milk and lemon juice to counteract sweetness of ice cream, may be used instead of the custard and cream in the above recipe. Proceed as for Orange Cream (3).

8 helpings

CHARLOTTES

Charlottes are moulds lined with sponge fingers, savoy fingers, *or* wafers, and filled with various creams. Choose a mould with straight sides.

CHARLOTTE À LA ST. JOSÉ

20 savoy fingers	**1½ pt. pineapple cream** (p. 451)

DECORATION

Preserved pineapple	**½ pt. clear lemon jelly**

Line the bottom of the mould with jelly, and when set, decorate with fancily-cut pieces of preserved pineapple dipped in jelly. Allow to set, then cover with another thin layer of cold liquid jelly. When the jelly has set, line the sides of the mould with savoy fingers, having trimmed the ends so that they fit closely on to the jelly. Remove any crumbs from the surface of the jelly with the tip of a dry pastry brush. Pour the pineapple cream into the lined mould and leave to set. Trim the fingers level with the rim. Turn out and decorate with piped cream.

CHARLOTTE RUSSE

As for Gooseberry Charlotte, but fill the prepared mould with Italian cream (p. 449) using a flavouring of vanilla *or* sherry.

GOOSEBERRY CHARLOTTE

Charlotte de Groseilles vertes

20 savoy fingers	**1½ pt. gooseberry cream** (p. 450)

DECORATION

½ pt. clear lemon jelly	**Angelica**
3 glacé cherries	

Thinly coat the bottom of a mould with jelly, and, when set, decorate with neatly-cut slices of cherry and leaves of angelica. Both these fruits should be cut thickly as they are translucent and will not show clearly if too thin. Re-coat with a second layer of cold liquid jelly, sufficient only to cover the decoration. When the jelly has set, line the sides of the mould with savoy fingers, having trimmed the ends so that they fit closely on to the jelly. Remove any crumbs from the surface of the jelly with the tip of a dry pastry brush. Pour the gooseberry cream into the lined mould and leave to set. Trim the fingers level with the rim. Turn out and decorate with piped cream.

If preferred, the base of the mould may be lined with sponge fingers.

NOTE: A quicker but less satisfactory method is to pour the gooseberry cream into the mould unlined, and after turning out press trimmed savoy fingers, sugar side outwards, around the sides. Tie a ribbon round to ensure a neat finish.

6 helpings

CHARTREUSE

CHARTREUSE OF BANANAS

Chartreuse de Bananes

2 pt. clear lemon *or* **wine jelly**	**½ pt. double cream**
1 oz. pistachio nuts	**Vanilla essence**
4 bananas	**Castor sugar to taste**

Line a 1 qt. border mould with jelly. Blanch, skin, chop and dry the pistachio nuts, mix with 2 tablesp. jelly and run smoothly over the base of the mould. When set, cover with a ½-in. layer of clear jelly. Slice a banana evenly, dip each slice in jelly and arrange them, slightly overlapping, in an even layer on the jelly when set. Cover with another ½-in. layer of clear jelly and allow to set. Repeat with fruit and jelly until the mould is full, the last layer being jelly. When set, turn out and pipe the whipped cream, sweetened, and flavoured with vanilla, into the centre. Surround with chopped jelly.

NOTE: **Strawberries** or **tangerines** may be substituted for bananas and the chartreuse named accordingly.

6 helpings

Setting time (without ice)—2–3 hr. (with ice)—¾ hr.

CHARTREUSE OF MIXED FRUITS

Chartreuse de Macédoine de Fruits

As for Chartreuse of Bananas using neatly-cut and whole fruits to give a colourful border.

COLD SOUFFLÉS

SOUFFLÉS are extremely light in texture because of the air which is entrapped by whisking the ingredients and retained either by the use of gelatine, or by freezing. The eggs are separated, the yolks being whisked with the sugar and flavouring over hot water until very thick and "ropey". Warmth from the water helps to melt the sugar and lowers the surface tension so that air enters more easily. On no account should the bowl containing the egg and sugar be allowed to become hot, as this would cook the egg and make the inclusion of air impossible. The container holding the hot water should be deep enough for the bowl holding the mixture to rest firmly in the rim without touching the water. Whisking should continue until the mixture is cool, so that the dissolved gelatine, which must be added steaming hot in order to ensure even distribution throughout the mixture, does not raise the temperature of the whole too much. This is very important as a too warm mixture necessitates prolonged stirring in order to keep the various ingredients blended, and during this operation most of the air so carefully whipped in will be lost.

The cream is half-whipped—to blend easily with the thickly-whisked mixture, and the egg whites stiffly whipped. These are folded in just before setting as they hold most of the air. Pour immediately into a prepared soufflé dish.

Tie a double band of greaseproof paper around a 1 pt. china soufflé dish, so that 3 in. of the paper extends above the rim. This is so that the soufflé mixture will set when it is at least 1 in. above the rim, and on removal of the paper, will appear to have "risen" above the dish.

Basic Recipe

MILANAISE SOUFFLÉ

Soufflé à la Milanaise

2 lemons
3–4 eggs, according to size
5 oz. castor sugar
½ oz. gelatine
¼ pt. water
½ pt. double cream

DECORATION

Chopped pistachio nuts

Wash lemons, dry, and grate rind finely. Whisk the egg yolks, sugar, rind and lemon juice over hot water until thick and creamy, then remove bowl from the hot water and continue whisking until cool. Soften the gelatine in the ¼ pt. water, and heat to dissolve. Half-whip the cream. Whisk the egg whites very stiffly. Add the gelatine, steaming hot, in a thin stream, to the egg mixture, and stir in. Fold in the cream and the stiffly-whipped whites. Fold the mixture very lightly until setting is imminent—the mixture pulls against the spoon. Pour into the soufflé dish and leave to set. Remove the paper band by coaxing it away from the mixture with a knife dipped in hot water. Decorate the sides with chopped, blanched pistachio nuts, and the top with piped cream, if liked.

6 helpings
Setting time—2 hr.

COLD SOUFFLÉS

Variations

APRICOT SOUFFLÉ

Soufflé aux Abricots

½ pt. apricot purée	**Lemon juice**
4 eggs	**Carmine**
2–3 oz. castor sugar (according to sweetness of apricots)	**½ oz. gelatine**
	4 tablesp. water
	¼ pt. double cream

DECORATION

Pistachio nuts

Use the purée in place of rind and juice of lemons in Milanaise soufflé. Taste and sweeten as liked. Add lemon juice to sharpen. When thick and creamy, colour carefully with one or two drops of carmine. Finish as for Milanaise soufflé.

Decorate with chopped, blanched pistachio nuts.

6 helpings **Setting time—2 hr.**

ORANGE SOUFFLÉ

Soufflé à l'Orange

3–4 eggs according to size	**Orange colouring**
	½ oz. gelatine
4 oz. castor sugar	**4 tablesp. water**
3 oranges	**½ pt. double cream**
Rind of ½ lemon	

DECORATION

Pistachio nuts

Proceed as for Milanaise Soufflé using oranges in place of lemons. A little orange colouring may be necessary.

Decorate with chopped, blanched pistachio nuts.

6 helpings **Setting time—2 hr.**

RASPBERRY SOUFFLÉ

Soufflé aux Framboises

As for Milanaise Soufflé using raspberry purée (made from fresh raspberries) instead of rind and juice of lemons; colour suitably.

STRAWBERRY SOUFFLÉ

Soufflé aux Fraises

As for Milanaise Soufflé, using strawberry purée (made from fresh strawberries) instead of rind and juice of lemons; colour suitably.

CHOCOLATE SOUFFLÉ (Plate 17)

Soufflé au Chocolat

2 eggs	**2 oz. milk chocolate**
2 oz. sugar	**½ oz. gelatine**
12 tablesp. evaporated milk	**4 tablesp. warm water**

DECORATION

Whipped cream

Put the yolks of the eggs and sugar in a double saucepan, and whisk until thick and creamy. Whip the evaporated milk until thick, and add to the eggs and sugar. Melt the chocolate over very gentle heat, add to the egg and sugar mixture. Put the gelatine in the warm water and heat to dissolve; then stir it into the chocolate mixture. Whip up the egg-whites stiffly and stir into the chocolate mixture. Put into the prepared soufflé case. When set, remove the paper carefully, and decorate the top with cream.

6 helpings
Setting time—2 hr.

CUSTARDS

(*see also Hot Sweets—Custards*, pp. 389–90)

ECONOMICAL CUSTARD

Crème Anglaise

(*To make* 1 *pt.*)

1 teasp. cornflour	**1 egg**
1 pt. milk	**Flavouring: lemon rind** *or* **vanilla essence**
1 oz. sugar	

Blend cornflour with 1 tablesp. of the milk and heat the remainder, infusing the lemon rind if used. Remove the rind, pour the hot milk over the blended cornflour, stirring to keep smooth. Replace in saucepan and cook thoroughly by boiling gently for 2 min. stirring continuously. Add the sugar and allow to cool slightly. Beat the egg, mix with a little of the hot mixture, then add to the contents of the saucepan and cook for a few minutes until thickened. Stir in the vanilla if used. Serve hot *or* cold.

4 helpings **Time—20 min.**

APPLE CUSTARD

Crème aux Pommes

2 lb. apples | **2 oz. castor sugar**
1 tablesp. water | **1 pt. milk**
4 oz. sugar | **Vanilla essence (optional)**
3 eggs

Peel, core, slice and cook the apples in the water and sugar until pulped. Beat well, *or* sieve, and put in the bottom of an oven-glass dish. Separate the yolks and whites of the eggs and beat the yolks slightly with 1 oz. castor sugar. Stir in the milk and strain mixture into a saucepan which has been rinsed with cold water. Whisk over moderate heat to ensure even thickening but do not let the custard boil or it will curdle. Cool quickly in a bowl, stirring occasionally to prevent a skin forming and flavour with a little vanilla essence if liked. Whisk the egg whites to a stiff, dry foam and beat in 1 teasp. castor sugar to sweeten. Pour cooled custard over apple pulp and pile meringue lightly on the top. Dust surface with castor sugar and bake in a very cool oven **(290° F., Gas 1)** until the meringue is dry and crisp and is a pale, glossy, golden brown on top (20 min.).

6 helpings
Time—1½ hr.

ORANGE CUSTARD

Crème à l'Orange

4 oranges | **4 oz. granulated sugar**
1½ pt. boiling water | **3 eggs**

DECORATION

¼ pt. cream | **Candied orange peel**

Wash oranges and cut off thin strips of outer rind avoiding white pith. Put rind, water and sugar into a bowl and leave to stand, covered, for 2 hr. After 2 hr. strain into a saucepan, heat through and pour gradually over the well-beaten eggs, stirring all the time. Strain the mixture back into the rinsed pan and heat again to thicken and cook the eggs. Do not allow the custard to boil or curdling will occur. Whisk *or* stir during cooking. Allow to cool, stir in the strained juice of the oranges and pour into custard glasses. When quite cold (*or* chilled in refrigerator) pile whipped cream on top. Decorate with fine strips of candied orange peel.

6 helpings
Time—3 hr.

PINEAPPLE CUSTARD

Crème à l'Ananas

1 large can pineapple | **2 eggs**
1½ oz. cornflour | **1 oz. castor sugar**
1 pt. milk

DECORATION

Glacé cherries | **Angelica**

Drain the juice from the fruit, chop the latter and put it in the bottom of an oven-glass dish. Blend the cornflour with 3 tablesp. of the milk, heat the remainder of the milk and pour over the blended cornflour, stirring all the time. Return to the pan and cook until thick, continuing after that for 3–4 min. to cook all the cornflour. Avoid excessive evaporation. Add ½ pt. of pineapple juice and stir in the egg yolks. Re-heat almost to boiling to cook the eggs. Sweeten if necessary and pour over the pineapple. Make a meringue with the egg whites and 1 oz. castor sugar (p. 461). Pile on the top and cook until crisp and dry in a very cool oven **(290° F., Gas 1).**

Decorate with small pieces of cherry and angelica. Serve hot *or* cold.

6 helpings
Time—1 hr.

FRUIT MOULDS

APRICOT MOULD

Abricots moulés

1 lb. apricots | **3 oz. sugar**
1½ pt. water | **¾ oz. gelatine**
1 lemon

Wash apricots, and soak overnight in the measured water. Cook with thinly cut strips of lemon rind and sugar until quite soft. Remove lemon rind. Remove stones and chop apricots to a pulp. Soak the gelatine in 2 tablesp. cold water for a few minutes, then heat until dissolved. Add to the apricot mixture and flavour with lemon juice. If liked the kernels may be removed from the apricot-stones, shredded and added. Stir thoroughly and pour into a wet mould. Turn out when set and serve with thin custard.

6 helpings
Setting time—2 hr.

PRUNE MOULD

Pruneaux moulés

1 lb. prunes
1½ pt. water
1 lemon
3 oz. sugar
1 in. cinnamon stick
¾ oz. gelatine
Carmine colouring

Wash prunes, and soak overnight in the measured water. Cook with thinly cut strips of lemon rind, sugar and cinnamon until quite soft. Remove lemon rind, remove stones and chop prunes to a pulp. Soak the gelatine in 2 tablesp. cold water for a few minutes, then heat until dissolved. Add to the prune mixture and flavour with lemon juice. Colour if necessary. If liked, the kernels may be removed from the prune stones, shredded and added. Stir thoroughly and pour into a wet mould. When set, unmould and serve with thin custard.

6 helpings
Setting time—2 hr.

TRIFLES

APPLE TRIFLE

Trifle de Pommes

2 lb. cooking apples
6 oz. sugar
Grated rind of ½ lemon
6 individual sponge cakes
¾ pt. custard

DECORATION

⅓ pt. double cream
Almonds—blanched, shredded and lightly browned

Peel, quarter and core the apples and cook gently with the sugar, lemon rind and about 2 tablesp. water until soft. Beat to a smooth pulp, *or* sieve. Slice the sponge cakes and place in individual dishes *or* in a large flat glass dish. Spread the apple purée over the cake. Pour sufficient custard over the top to run smooth and leave to go cold.

Decorate with whirls of whipped cream and golden shredded almonds.

6 helpings

APRICOT TRIFLE (1)

Trifle d'Abricots

2 apricot halves per person
1 round of sponge cake ½ in. thick and slightly larger than the fruit, for each person
1 tablesp. sherry (optional)
Fruit juice
1 oz. sugar to ¼ pt. juice
⅓ pt. cream
6 pistachio nuts, blanched and chopped

If fresh fruit is used, prepare as required, dust with castor sugar and allow to stand 1 hr. to sweeten and become juicy. If canned fruit is used, drain from juice on a sieve. Soak the rounds of sponge cake in the sherry (if used) and a little fruit juice. Place in individual dishes and chill. Arrange the fruit on the top and glaze with a thick syrup made by boiling together ¼ pt. fruit juice and 1 oz. sugar. Pipe whipped cream round the edge of the sponge and decorate with chopped pistachio nuts.

APRICOT TRIFLE (2) (Plate 17)

5–6 slices Swiss jam roll
1–2 macaroons
2–3 tablesp. sherry
1 can apricots
1 pt. custard
6 oz. can cream
1 teasp. gelatine
2 teasp. boiling water
1 oz. blanched almonds

Cut the jam roll into small cubes and place with broken macaroons in the bottom of a shallow glass dish; pour the sherry and a little apricot juice over. Cut up some of the apricots and add to the dish; pour over the custard. Allow to set. Whip the cream, adding the gelatine melted in the water. Pile the cream roughly so that it is fairly high in the centre. Decorate with apricots spiked with strips of almonds.

GOOSEBERRY TRIFLE

Trifle de Groseilles vertes

As for Apple Trifle substituting gooseberries for apples. Increase sugar if necessary. Omit lemon rind.

PEACH or PINEAPPLE TRIFLE

As for Apricot Trifle substituting one peach half *or* slice of pineapple per person for apricots.

PEAR AND CHOCOLATE TRIFLE

Trifle de Poires au Chocolat

6 individual sponge cakes
6 halves of dessert *or* canned pears

SAUCE

1 oz. butter *or* margarine
¾ oz. cocoa
1 oz. flour
1 pt. milk
¼ oz. gelatine
1 tablesp. water
1 oz. sugar

DECORATION

Whipped cream
Angelica

Place sponge cakes neatly in a glass dish *or* individual dishes. Drain pears and place, rounded side uppermost, on top of the sponge cakes. Make the sauce: melt the fat in a saucepan; add cocoa, and stir well in. Add flour, mix well, and gradually mix in the milk. Soak the gelatine in the water and heat to dissolve. Bring the milk mixture to the boil, stirring all the time to keep it smooth. Sweeten. Add the dissolved gelatine and remove from heat. Stand pan in a bowl of cold water to cool slightly to a coating consistency. Pour carefully over the pears and allow to run smoothly around the dish.

Decorate when cold with piped whipped cream and angelica.

6 helpings

ST. HONORÉ TRIFLE

Trifle St. Honoré

1 round sponge cake (1 in. thick by 6 in. across)
2–3 egg whites
4 oz. castor sugar
¼ lb. macaroons *or* ratafia biscuits
¼ pt. sherry
½ pt. double cream

DECORATION

Glacé cherries
Angelica

Place sponge cake on a baking sheet. Make meringue with egg whites and sugar (p. 461). Pipe a border of meringue around the top edge of the sponge cake, and dry off in a very cool oven (**265° F., Gas ½**). Do not allow meringue to colour. Place a thick layer of macaroons *or* ratafias on top of the cake and soak well with the sherry for at least 1 hr. Avoid touching the meringue with sherry, otherwise it may crumble. Pile whipped cream on top and decorate with cherries and angelica.

6 helpings

TRIFLE—TRADITIONAL RECIPE

Trifle Anglaise

4 individual sponge cakes
Raspberry *or* strawberry jam
6 macaroons
12 ratafia biscuits
¼ pt. sherry
Grated rind of ½ lemon
1 oz. almonds (blanched and shredded)
½ pt. custard using ½ pt. milk, 1 egg and 1 egg yolk
¼ pt. double cream
1 egg white
1–2 oz. castor sugar

DECORATION

Glacé cherries
Angelica

Split the sponge cakes into two and spread the lower halves with jam. Replace tops. Arrange in a glass dish and cover with macaroons and ratafias. Soak with sherry, and sprinkle with lemon rind and almonds. Cover with the custard and leave to cool. Whisk the cream, egg white and sugar together until stiff and pile on top of the trifle. Decorate with glacé cherries and angelica.

6 helpings

MISCELLANEOUS

APPLE SNOW (Plate 21)

Pommes à la Neige

4 large baking apples (1½ lb.)
Rind and juice of 1 lemon
½ pt. milk
2–3 eggs
3 oz. granulated sugar (approx.)
4 individual sponge cakes

DECORATION

Glacé cherries

Reduce the apples to a purée. The finest flavour is obtained by washing the apples and baking them, dry, in a moderate oven (**350° F., Gas 4**) until quite soft, when the skins and cores may easily be separated from the pulp. Otherwise, peel, core, slice and cook in the minimum amount of water.

Wash the lemon, remove the rind in thin strips, avoiding any white pith, and infuse slowly in the milk. Make a cup custard with this and the egg yolks (p. 390). Sweeten to taste. Place the sponge cakes, split if liked, in the bottom of a large glass dish and pour the custard over them. Rub the apple-pulp through a fine nylon sieve and sweeten to taste. Add lemon juice to flavour and leave to cool. Whisk the egg whites until quite stiff. Whisk in the apple purée, 1 tablesp. at a time, keeping the foam firm and light. Pile the apple foam on top of the soaked sponge cakes and decorate with glacé cherries.

6 helpings

BANANA WHIP or SNOW

Banane fouettée

6 bananas
2 tablesp. soft sugar
2 teasp. lemon juice
½ pt. yoghourt
¼ pt. double cream
3 egg whites

DECORATION

Almonds

Mash bananas with sugar and lemon juice. Mix in the yoghourt and cream. Whisk egg whites to a stiff foam and fold lightly into the banana cream. Pile into dishes and sprinkle with chopped roasted almonds.

6 helpings

BLANCMANGE *See Powdered Grain Moulds* (pp. 435–437).

CABINET PUDDING—COLD

Pouding de Cabinet, froid

10–12 savoy sponge fingers
1 oz. ratafia biscuits
Custard (p. 390) **using ¾ pt. milk, 2 eggs, 1 oz. sugar)**
½ oz. gelatine
Vanilla essence
¼ pt. cream

DECORATION

Clear jelly
Glacé cherries
Angelica

Set a thin layer of clear jelly in the bottom of a 1½ pt. soufflé tin. Decorate with pieces of cherry and angelica, dipping each piece in jelly before setting in position (*see* p. 442). Cover the decoration, when set, with another thin layer of cold liquid jelly. When the jelly has set, line the sides of the tin with savoy fingers, trimming the tips so that they stand cleanly on the jelly base. Trim the fingers level with the top of the tin, and soak trimmings and ratafias in the custard.

Soften the gelatine in 2 tablesp. cold water, and heat until dissolved. Add to the custard, and sweeten if necessary; flavour carefully with vanilla. Add the cream to the cool custard mixture just before setting and pour into the mould. When set, turn out by dipping the mould in and out of water just bearably hot, taking care not to dampen the tips of the sponge fingers; invert on to a serving dish and dislodge with one sharp jerk of the hand.

6 helpings

COMPOTE OF FRUIT *See Stewed Fruit* (p. 462).

CREAM SNOW

Crème à la Neige

1 pt. cream
2 egg whites
1 tablesp. castor sugar
Vanilla essence

DECORATION

Glacé cherries
Angelica

Whip the cream. Whisk the egg whites to a stiff foam, and fold lightly into the cream with the sugar, and flavour to taste with vanilla. Pile in a glass dish, and decorate with cherries and strips of angelica.

6–7 helpings

CRÈME BRÛLÉE

½ pt. fresh milk
½ pt. cream
5 eggs
2 oz. sugar
Vanilla essence *or* **brandy**
Icing sugar
Chopped, blanched almonds (optional)

Heat milk and cream until almost boiling. Beat eggs and sugar together to blend well. Pour on the hot milk and cream, stirring well. Add vanilla *or* brandy to taste. Strain into a 1½ pt. fireproof china soufflé case. Bake very gently for approximately 1 hr. in a very cool oven. Use a water bath if oven is hotter than **265° F., Gas ½.** When set, allow to cool and dredge the surface to a depth of ⅛ in. with icing sugar. Sprinkle chopped almonds over lightly if liked. Grill until sugar has been changed to caramel.

Serve cold, with whipped cream.

NOTE: This recipe may be varied by substituting 1 pt. cream for ½ pt. fresh milk and ½ pt. cream, and using 8 egg yolks instead of 5 whole eggs. Proceed as above.

See also another recipe for *Crème Brûlée—Hot Sweets* (p. 392).

6 helpings

FLOATING ISLANDS

Iles flottantes

2 egg whites
2–3 tablesp. raspberry jam *or* redcurrant jelly
1 pt. sweetened cream

Beat the egg whites until stiff, then lightly fold in the jam or jelly a teaspoonful at a time. Whip the cream until stiff and spread lightly in the bottom of a glass dish. Drop tablespoonfuls of the egg mixture on to the cream, making each small pile as rocky as possible.

FRENCH PEARS

Poires à la française

6 large cooking pears
½ pt. water
2 oz. sugar
4 tablesp. red jam
1 teasp. carmine
1 lemon
2–3 teasp. arrowroot
1 oz. almonds, blanched and shredded
2 tablesp. claret *or* port
1 tablesp. liqueur (optional)

Wash pears and peel. Keep parings. Cut out the crown and core as far as possible, without breaking the fruit and leave on the stalks. Put into a casserole with the water, sugar, jam and carmine, and cover with parings of pears and lemon peel. Stew very gently until quite tender but whole, then lift out fruit to cool. Strain the syrup, thicken with arrowroot (blended with sufficient cold water to make a thin cream) and cook until clear—1–2 min. Stir in the shredded, blanched almonds, lemon juice, wine and liqueur. Arrange the pears in a dish and pour the sauce over them.

6 helpings
Time—45 min.

FRESH FRUIT SALAD

Macédoine de fruits frais

1 pt. water *or* fruit juice
3 oz. sugar
Selection of fruit as liked (*see below*)
Juice of 1 lemon
1 tablesp. brandy *or* kirsch (optional)
2 tablesp. sherry (optional)

Boil the water and sugar together until reduced to half quantity, but sufficient syrup should be made to cover fruit completely. Prepare the fruit according to kind:

Apples: Peel, core, quarter and slice thinly.

Oranges: Peel in a similar way to an apple, with a very sharp knife, cutting deeply enough to expose the flesh. Cupping the peeled fruit in the hand, cut the pulp cleanly from each section by loosening the thin skin from both sides. Work over a plate as juice is likely to escape.

Grapes: Remove seeds, and skins from black grapes. If black colour is required for contrast, leave a few half-grapes unskinned.

Apricots, Peaches: Slit around the natural groove, "unscrew" the two halves, skin, stone and cut each half in two or four.

Pineapple: Slice off the top cleanly, just below the leaves, using a sharp, thin knife, cut around the rim of the fruit, cutting down to the base, all round. Withdraw the inner "barrel" of fruit by means of a corkscrew. Cut fruit in slices.

Cherries: Remove stones neatly—a fine, sterilized hairpin may be kept for this purpose.

Strawberries, Raspberries: Hull carefully.

Plums: Halve and stone.

Bananas: Slice thinly. This fruit must never be chilled, unless covered, as such treatment causes discoloration.

Melon: Cut into slices and, if flesh alone is required, remove with a silver spoon. The melon may be used as a receptacle for fruit salad by cutting off the top, removing the seeds, and the flesh, with a spoon. The melon "cup" is then flavoured with kirsch and set on ice to become chilled, while the flesh is used as an ingredient of the mixed salad to be served in the melon case.

Pour the syrup over the prepared fruit and flavour with lemon juice. Cover the bowl and allow the salad to become quite cold. Stir in the liqueur and wine if used, a few minutes before serving. Serve with cream, custard, ice cream, *or* chopped nuts.

FROSTED APPLES

Pommes glacées

6 cooking apples	**1 in. cinnamon stick**
½ pt. water	**2 cloves**
4 oz. granulated sugar	**¼ pt. double cream**
1 tablesp. marmalade	

MERINGUE

2–3 egg-whites	**4 oz. castor sugar**

DECORATION

Glacé cherries	**Angelica**

Wash, core and peel apples without breaking them. Put water, peelings, granulated sugar, marmalade, cinnamon and cloves into a pan and boil to a syrup. Place apples in a buttered dish, strain the syrup over, cover with a lid *or* buttered paper and bake very gently. Drain when cooked and transfer to a baking sheet lined with kitchen paper. Whisk egg whites into a firm, sweet meringue with the castor sugar (p. 461) and coat the entire surface of each apple. Dust well with castor sugar and bake very lightly in a cool oven until the meringue is firm and faintly coloured. Leave to become quite cold.

Whip cream stiffly, sweeten with 1 teasp. castor sugar and pile a little on top of each apple, decorating it with small pieces of glacé cherry and tiny leaves of angelica.

Serve in individual glasses—on a bed of whipped cream *or* with the apple syrup poured round.

6 helpings

FRUIT FOOL

Foule de Fruit

1½ lb. fruit (approx.), *see below*	**1 pt. thick, pouring custard** (p. 390) *or* **1 pt. double cream** *or* **½ pt. custard and ½ pt. cream mixed**
Sugar according to taste and sweetness of fruit	**Ratafia biscuits** *or* **tiny macaroons for decoration**

Prepare the fruit and cook if necessary:

Gooseberries and **Damsons** will require about 1 pt. water.

Pink, forced **Rhubarb,** if cooked gently in a wet earthenware *or* oven-glass casserole requires *no* water. Sweeten with brown sugar to produce a rich pink juice.

Red- and **Black Currants** require about ¼ pt. water.

Strawberries, Loganberries and **Raspberries** should be crushed, sprinkled with castor sugar and left overnight.

Rub the softened fruit through a fine nylon sieve. Allow to cool then blend with the cream *or* cold custard; taste and sharpen with a little lemon juice if necessary. Sweeten to taste with castor sugar. Chill and serve with ratafia biscuits arranged carefully on top.

6 helpings

JUNKET

Lait caille

2 pt. fresh milk	**2 teasp. rennet**
2 teasp. castor sugar	**Flavouring** (*see below*)

Warm the milk to blood heat and stir in the sugar until dissolved. Add the rennet, stir and pour at once into serving dishes. Put in a warm place to set.

Serve with cream, if liked.

6 helpings

FLAVOURINGS

Coffee: Add to milk, coffee essence to flavour, and decorate finished junket with chopped nuts.

Chocolate: Add 2–3 oz. plain chocolate, grated and dissolved in a little of the measured milk.

Rum: Add rum to taste.

Vanilla, almond, raspberry, etc.: Add a few drops of essence.

NOTE: When using rennet in liquid or powder form, the manufacturer's instructions should be followed carefully to ensure the desired result.

LEMON CREAM

Crème au Citron

1 pt. double cream
2 tablesp. lemon juice
1 teasp. finely grated lemon rind
1 oz. ground almonds
1 oz. castor sugar

Whip the cream stiffly, adding the rest of the ingredients gradually. Sweeten to taste. Serve in individual glasses.

10 small glasses
Time—10–15 min.

MERINGUE

4 egg whites
½ lb. castor sugar *or* 4 oz. granulated sugar and 4 oz. castor sugar

Make sure that the egg whites are fresh and contain no trace of yolk, or grease. Break down with a whisk to an even-textured liquid by tapping lightly for a few moments. Whisk evenly and continuously until a firm, stiff, close-textured foam is obtained. Add the granulated sugar, *or* half the castor sugar if all castor is being used, one tablespoonful at a time, whisking the foam stiffly between each tablespoonful. Add the rest of the sugar, folding it in lightly with a metal spoon. Force through a ⅜ in. pipe into small rounds, *or* form into egg-shapes with two spoons, dipped in cold water, and place on strips of oiled kitchen paper on baking sheets. Dredge well with castor sugar and dry in a very cool oven (**290° F., Gas 1**), placed low to avoid discolouring and reduce to **265° F., Gas ½** after 1 hr. If a pure white meringue is required, *very* slow drying is essential, and this may be achieved (if cooking by gas) by leaving the oven door slightly ajar and regulating the oven temperature by turning the gas tap very low, as the regulator will not be operating while the door is open. Drying will take very much longer, even overnight, but the meringue cases will be quite crisp throughout, and will store most successfully for weeks in an airtight tin.

About 12 meringue shells
Cooking time—4–12 hr.

NOTE: Meringue for decorating fruit dishes may be required less sweet than this recipe, in which case half the sugar is whisked into the stiff foam. The mixture is then piled on the pudding *or* flan, dusted lightly with castor sugar and baked in a cool oven (**290° F., Gas 1**) for about 30–40 min.

RHUBARB AND BANANA FOOL

Foule de Rhubarbe et de Banane

6 bananas
1 lb. forced rhubarb cooked and sieved (¾ pt.)
½ pt. thick pouring custard *or* cream
Sugar to taste

DECORATION

Ratafia biscuits, macaroons *or* whipped cream

Mash the bananas and stir into the rhubarb purée until well blended. Add cream *or* custard, and sweeten to taste. Serve in a dish and decorate with ratafia biscuits, macaroons *or* whipped cream.

6 helpings

ST. CLOUD PUDDING

Pouding Froid à la St. Cloud

½ oz. butter
2 oz. almonds
Stale sponge cake
2–3 eggs according to size
2 oz. castor sugar
1 pt. strong, clear coffee *or* coffee essence in water
2 tablesp. double cream
3 tablesp. apricot jam

DECORATION

Glacé cherries
Angelica

Thickly butter a 1½ pt. soufflé tin. Blanch, shred and bake the almonds golden brown (p. 512). Sprinkle liberally over the buttered surface of the tin. Three quarters fill the tin with crumbled cake and the remainder of the almonds. Beat the eggs and sugar to a liquid, warm the coffee and pour over the egg liquid. Stir, add the cream and strain into the prepared tin. Cover with a buttered paper and steam very gently for about 1½–2 hr. Cool slightly, then turn out and leave to go cold. Heat the apricot jam with a little water (2 tablesp.) and when cool strain over the pudding.

Decorate with rings of cherry and angelica.

6-7 helpings

STEWED FRUIT

Compote de Fruit

Fresh fruit *or* dried fruit (*see below*)
Sugar (*see below*)

FLAVOURING

Lemon *or* orange rind
Cloves
½ in. cinnamon stick
Sherry
Claret

NOTE: The amount of sugar required will depend on the sweetness of the fruit, e.g. dried fruits 1–2 oz. sugar per lb. of fruit; gooseberries 2–4 oz. sugar per lb. The amount of water will vary from ¼ pt. to ½ pt. per lb. of fruit, e.g. forced rhubarb requires very little water, whereas apples and pears should be covered in order to retain their white colour. Flavourings should be added to the water at the beginning and if rind is used it should be strained from the juice before reducing it after the fruit is cooked.

Dried Fruit should be washed and soaked overnight in cold water, allowing 1 pt. water per lb. fruit. If liked, freshly made cool tea may be used instead of water.

Fresh Fruit is prepared according to kind:

Apples, Pears: May be peeled, cored and left whole if small, or quartered if large. They should be placed immediately into the sugar and water syrup as each is prepared, otherwise the air causes a brown discoloration on the peeled surface. Apples may be stewed in oven-glass or earthenware dish in the oven, 2–3 cloves added to the syrup improve the flavour.

Rhubarb: Forced rhubarb is wiped with a damp cloth, cut into suitable lengths and covered with brown sugar. If cooked very gently in oven-glass or earthenware dish, no water is required and a rich red juice is obtained. If unforced rhubarb is old, the stringy outer skin should be stripped off.

Gooseberries, Plums, any sour Stone Fruit: Should be washed, the stalks removed, the stones may be left or removed as liked; gooseberries should be topped and tailed. Cook very slowly in the sugar and water until the skins crack, so that the sweet syrup can be absorbed by the flesh. If a little skin is removed from gooseberries during the topping and tailing their flavour will be much improved.

When the fruit is cooked, drain from the syrup and place in serving dish.

Boil the syrup to reduce it to a thicker consistency, cool, and pour it over the fruit.

Time (Dried fruit)—1–2 hr.
(Fresh fruit)—½ hr. approx.

SUMMER PUDDING

12 individual sponge cakes (approx.)
2–4 oz. sugar according to sweetness of fruit
1½–2 lb. soft fruit: apples, *or* rhubarb, gooseberries, strawberries, raspberries, redcurrants, *or* black currants, *or* a mixture, as liked

Choose a 1½ pt. pudding basin *or* charlotte *or* soufflé mould. Cut sponge cakes into inch-wide fingers for lining the sides, and triangles for lining the base. Cook the selected fruit with the least possible amount of water, until pulped; and sweeten to taste. Pour into the lined mould. Cover the top with slices of sponge cake, press down with a small weighted saucer, and leave pudding to become cold. Turn out on to a dish.

Coat with either custard (p. 390), or fruit juice thickened to coating consistency with 1 level teasp. arrowroot to ½ pt. juice. Decorate with choice pieces of fruit *or* shredded almonds.

6 helpings

SYLLABUB

4 oz. castor sugar
Juice of 1 lemon
Finely-grated rind of ½ lemon
Pinch of ground cinnamon
1 small wineglass sherry *or* Madeira
Ratafia essence
1 pt. cream
10 macaroons

Mix together the sugar, lemon juice and rind, cinnamon and wine. Add a few drops of essence and stir until the sugar is dissolved. Add the cream and whip to a froth. Arrange the macaroons in the bottom of a deep dish, and as the froth is formed on the syllabub, skim it off and place it on the biscuits, until the whole of the mixture has been reduced to a froth and piled on the biscuits. Chill before serving.

7–8 helpings

TIPSY CAKE

Gâteau au Madère

1 sponge cake *or* 8 individual cakes
Raspberry jam
1 glass Madeira *or* sherry
1 pt. cup custard

DECORATION

Almonds
Angelica
Glacé cherries

Split the cake or cakes and spread half thickly with jam. Sandwich together again and place in a dish. Pour over the wine and allow to soak for 1 hr. Pour over the custard, stick the blanched almonds in like a porcupine, and decorate with cherries and angelica.

6–7 helpings

WHIPPED CREAM

Crème fouettée

1 dessertsp. sherry
1 dessertsp. brandy (optional)
Rind and juice of ½ lemon
1½ oz. castor sugar
½ pt. double cream

Put the sherry, brandy if used, lemon juice, finely grated rind and sugar into a bowl; stir until the sugar has dissolved. Add cream and stir well in, gradually increasing to a steady whipping until quite firm. Serve with fruit.

NOTE: If preferred, 1 oz. ground almonds *or* 1 oz. fine, dry brown breadcrumbs can be stirred into the cream. Serve as a rich sweet.

ZABAGLIONE

Sabayon

6 egg yolks
6 tablesp. Madeira, *or* Marsala *or* sherry
6 tablesp. castor sugar

Place an oven-glass *or* earthenware bowl over a pan of hot water. Add the ingredients and whisk continuously until the mixture is creamy and retains the impression of the whisk. Pile into glasses and serve immediately with savoy fingers.

6 glasses **Time—10–20 min.**

GÂTEAUX

APRICOT GÂTEAU

Gâteau d'Abricot

1 round of genoese pastry (p. 534) ***or* rich, light cake 6 in. diameter and 1 in. thick**
2 tablesp. sherry *or* fruit juice
2 doz. savoy fingers soft textured
2 tablesp. sieved apricot jam
A length of 1 in. wide pale coloured ribbon to tie round the sponge fingers (about 12 in.)

FILLING

1 large can apricots
½ pt. lemon jelly tablet
¾ pt. double cream
Castor sugar to taste

DECORATION

Angelica

Place the round of cake on a serving plate and sprinkle with the sherry or juice. Trim the sponge fingers so that the sides are quite straight and all are equal in length, with one end trimmed straight across. Melt the ½ pt. jelly tablet in ¼ pt. of apricot juice and allow to cool, but not set. Brush inside of trimmed end of each sponge finger to 1 in. in depth with sieved apricot jam; dip one edge only in cool jelly, and press firmly against the side of the round of cake. As each finger is so treated, the jellied edge will be in contact with the dry edge of the adjacent finger, and a firm case may be made without danger of the fingers becoming sodden and crumbling. The rounded, sugary surface of the finger faces outwards. Tie the ribbon round the finished case so that the sponge fingers are held firmly upright, and leave to set.

FILLING: Drain apricots well, and reserve 6 halves for decoration. Cut the remainder into quarters. Whip the cream until the fork leaves a trail; sweeten to taste with castor sugar. Put ¼ of the cream into a forcing bag with rose pipe, for decorating (optional). Stir the quartered apricots into the remainder of the cream. Lastly stir in ⅛ pt. of the liquid jelly, steaming hot. Pour immediately into the sponge-finger case. Arrange the 6 apricot halves (either whole *or* cut as liked) on the top, and pipe cream roses between and around to cover the surface of the cream. Decorate with leaves of angelica.

VARIATIONS: Use fresh *or* canned strawberries, *or* chopped pineapple, *or* fruit-flavoured ice cream, *or* custard cream fillings.

MERINGUE GÂTEAU

6 egg whites
12 oz. castor sugar
1½ lb. strawberries
Juice of 1 lemon
Castor sugar
¼–½ pt. double cream

Make the meringue (p. 461). Put into a plain forcing pipe (½ in.) and pipe a round base, working from the centre outwards, 6 in. in diameter. Build up the sides to a height of 1½ in. Pipe the remaining meringue into small shell shapes. Bake in a very cool oven (**265° F., Gas ½**); then cool.

Prepare strawberries, sprinkle with lemon juice and castor sugar and allow to stand until meringue case is ready. Reserve a few choice fruits for decoration; place the rest in the meringue case. Cover with the whipped cream. Decorate with meringue shells and strawberries.

NOTE: The meringue case, if completely dried by gentle cooking, will remain firm if kept in an airtight tin. It cannot retain its crispness for long after the inclusion of fruit and cream. Do not put in a refrigerator.

6 helpings

VARIATIONS: Use ice cream *or* fresh fruits *or* custard creams (pp. 449–50) for the filling.

MILLE-FEUILLE GÂTEAU

Puff pastry (p. 555) **using ½–¾ lb. flour, etc.**
2–3 tablesp. jam—strawberry *or* raspberry *or* apricot
½ pt. double cream *or* custard cream as used for vanilla cream (p. 450)
4 oz. icing sugar for glacé icing

DECORATION, selection of:

Glacé cherries
Shredded almonds
Grated chocolate
Pistachio nuts
Walnuts
Candied fruits

Roll out pastry ⅛ in. thick and cut into 7–8 rounds with a cake tin *or* plate. Rinse baking sheets with cold water, place pastry on damp surface, prick well. Bake in a very hot oven (**450° F., Gas 8**)—about 6 in. from the top—for 10 min. approximately, until golden brown and crisp. Lift off carefully and cool on a rack. Spread thinly with jam and whipped cream; place layer upon layer, without pressure. Ice the top with thick glacé icing. Decorate with chosen fruits *or* nuts.

6 helpings

VARIATIONS: Fresh *or* canned fruits, such as pineapple, apricots, mandarin oranges, guavas, may be used. Chop and mix with the cream filling, reserving choice pieces for top decoration.

SPONGE GÂTEAU

Gâteau de Savoie

2 sponge cakes 7 in. in diameter
3 tablesp. sherry *or* fruit juice
1 family block ice cream, flavoured as required (*see below*)
¼ pt. double cream, whipped and sweetened
Approx. 1 lb. fruit for garnish (*see below*)

Place one round of sponge on the serving dish and sprinkle with sherry *or* juice. Cut out the centre of the other round, leaving a 1 in. border all round. Place the border on the prepared base. Cut the ice cream quickly into chunks and pile into the hollow. Decorate the border and sides of the sponge with stars of whipped cream and suitable pieces of fruit.

Serve immediately.

NOTE: All canned and fresh fruits such as strawberries, raspberries, loganberries, apricots, peaches, are suitable, with vanilla *or* strawberry ice cream. Coffee ice cream can be sprinkled with chopped roasted almonds *or* grated chocolate.

6 helpings

ICES

ICES MAY BE broadly divided into two classes: water ices and ice creams.

WATER ICES AND SHERBETS (SORBETS)

Water ices are made from the juice of fresh fruit or fruit purée mixed with syrup or fruit syrup. Sherbets (Sorbets) are half-frozen water ices containing egg white or gelatine. They are served at formal banquets in sorbet cups or glasses immediately before the roast to clear the palate, but at more informal meals they are often served as a sweet course.

ICE CREAMS

These are sometimes composed almost entirely of cream—sweetened, flavoured, and decorated in many ways; but more frequently the so-called "ice cream" consists principally of custard, of varying degrees of richness, with the addition of fruit pulp, almonds, chocolate, coffee, liqueurs and other flavourings. The cream, when used, should be double cream; evaporated milk can be substituted for part or all of the cream but the can should first be boiled, unopened, for 20 minutes, then cooled quickly and if possible chilled for 24 hours in a refrigerator.

MAKING ICE CREAM IN A REFRIGERATOR

To obtain a smooth, evenly-textured ice cream in a refrigerator, the mixture must be frozen quickly and whisked well. The quicker the freezing the less likelihood there is of ice crystals forming, so set the refrigerator to the coldest point ½ hr. before putting the mixture to freeze, unless instructed otherwise in the recipe. Chill all ingredients and utensils before use.

Prepare the mixture, place it in the ice tray or drawer, and replace the tray in the freezing compartment.

Air acts as a deterrent to crystal formation, so remove the mixture after ½ hr. and whisk well in a chilled bowl. Replace in the tray and put back into the freezing compartment.

MAKING ICE CREAM IN A FREEZER

An ice cream freezer consists of a metal container, in which the ice cream mixture is placed—and an outer container, usually a wooden bucket; the space between the two being packed with alternate layers of crushed ice and salt. Air is incorporated into the mixture by churning.

The recipes are based on a one quart bucket type mixture; this bucket needs 7 lb. of ice and 2 lb. freezing salt (common salt may be substituted). Broken ice alone is insufficient to freeze or mould the ices.

GENERAL HINTS

1. Add sugar carefully, too much sugar will prevent the ice mixture from freezing successfully, and insufficient sugar will cause the mixture to freeze hard and rocky.
2. Do not put warm mixtures into the container, and do not fill the container as freezing increases the bulk of the mixture.
3. Raise the lid from time to time and scrape down with a wooden spatula or spoon, the thin coating of ice which will have formed on the side, and mix well with the more liquid contents.
4. Wipe the lid of the container carefully before raising it, so that no salt or salt water is allowed to get into the mixture.
5. Churn slowly at first, and more rapidly as the mixture stiffens.
6. If the ice cream is to be served unmoulded it must be frozen quite stiffly.

MOULDING ICES

If the mixture is to be moulded it should be removed from the freezer or refrigerator in a semi-solid condition, and then packed into a dry mould or bomb, well shaken, and pressed down into the shape of the mould. The mould should have a tightly-fitting lid, which must be sealed with a thick layer of lard. The mould or bomb is then wrapped in greaseproof paper and buried in broken ice and freezing salt for $1\frac{1}{2}$–2 hr.

To unmould, remove the paper and lard, wipe the mould carefully, dip it into cold water, and turn the ice on to a dish in the same way as a jelly or cream.

SYRUPS FOR WATER ICES

SYRUP (1)

2 lb. loaf sugar **1 pt. water**

Place the sugar and water in a strong saucepan. Allow the sugar to dissolve over gentle heat. Do not stir. When the sugar has dissolved, gently boil the mixture for 10 min., or, if a saccharometer is available, it should register 220° F. Remove scum as it rises. Strain, cool and store.

1 pt. syrup
Time—½ hr.

SYRUP (2)

8 oz. loaf sugar **1 pt. water**

Proceed as for Syrup (1).

WATER ICES

APPLE WATER ICE

Glace à l'eau de Pommes

1 pt. apple pulp **2 tablesp. lemon juice**
1 pt. syrup **Carmine**

Stew the apples with a minimum amount of water. Pass through a nylon sieve and stir the pulp into the hot syrup. When cold, add the lemon juice and carmine. Chill and freeze.

10–12 helpings
Time—2–2½ hr.

CIDER ICE

Glace au Cidre

1 large Bramley apple **½ pt. syrup (1)**
½ pt. cider **Juice of 1 large lemon**

Peel, core and slice the apple. Cook in a covered saucepan with 1 tablesp. of water. Pass the cooked apple through a fine hair *or* nylon sieve and add all other ingredients. Chill and freeze.

6 helpings
Time—2–2½ hr.

LEMON WATER ICE

Glace aux Citrons

6 lemons **1½ pt. syrup**
2 oranges

Thinly peel the fruit and place the rind in a basin. Add the hot syrup, cover and cool. Add the juice of the lemons and oranges. Strain, chill and freeze.

6 helpings **Time—1½ hr.**

PINEAPPLE WATER ICE

Glace à l'eau d'Ananas

½ pt. canned pineapple juice **1 pt. syrup (1)**
2 tablesp. lemon juice

Thoroughly mix all ingredients. Chill and freeze.

6 helpings
Time—1½–2 hr.

RASPBERRY or STRAWBERRY WATER ICE

Glace à l'eau de Fraises ou Framboises

1 lb. ripe strawberries *or* raspberries **Juice of 2 lemons**
1 pt. syrup

Rub the fruit through a nylon sieve and add the lemon juice. Add the syrup and a little colouring if necessary. Chill and freeze.

6 helpings
Time—1 hr.

REDCURRANT WATER ICE

Glace à l'eau de Groseilles rouges

1 lb. redcurrants **2 pt. syrup (1) *or* (2)**
½ lb. raspberries **Juice of 1 lemon**

Pick over the fruit and rub it through a fine nylon sieve. Add the syrup and lemon juice. Chill and freeze.

6–8 helpings **Time—1 hr.**

TANGERINE WATER ICE

Glace aux Tangerines

2 oz. loaf sugar **¼ pt. water**
6 tangerines **1 pt. syrup (1) *or* (2)**
2 oranges
2 lemons

Rub the sugar on the rind of the tangerines to extract some of the flavour. Place the sugar in a saucepan, add the thinly peeled rind of 1 orange, 1 lemon and the ¼ pt. water. Boil the mixture for 10 min., then add the juice of all the fruit and the syrup. Boil up, strain and cool. Freeze.

6–8 helpings
Time—1½ hr.

SHERBETS (SORBETS)

LEMON SHERBET (SORBET)

Sorbet au Citron

1 pt. water
8 oz. loaf sugar
½ pt. lemon juice
2 egg whites

Dissolve the sugar in the water. Boil it for 10 min., strain and cool. Add the lemon juice and the stiffly beaten egg whites. Freeze and serve at once.

6 helpings
Time—1½ hr.

PINEAPPLE SHERBET (SORBET)

Sorbet d'Ananas

1 pt. water
8 oz. loaf sugar
½ pt. canned pineapple juice
2 egg whites

Dissolve the sugar in the water. Boil it for 10 min.; strain and cool. Add the pineapple juice and the stiffly beaten egg whites. Freeze and serve at once.

6 helpings
Time—1½ hr.

ICE CREAM CUSTARD

Basic Recipes

CUSTARD (1)—Economical

1 oz. custard powder
1 pt. milk
4 oz. castor sugar

Blend the custard powder with a little of the milk. Boil remaining milk and pour on to the blended mixture. Return to pan and simmer—stirring continuously. Add sugar; cover, and allow to cool.

CUSTARD (2)

1 pt. milk
3 eggs
4 oz. castor sugar

Heat the milk. Beat together eggs and sugar. Add the hot milk stirring continuously. Return to pan and cook without boiling until custard coats the back of a wooden spoon. Strain, cover and cool.

ICE CREAMS

ALMOND ICE CREAM

Glace à la Crème d'Amandes

3 oz. sweet almonds
3 bitter almonds
1 teasp. orange flower water
¼ pt. milk
½ pt. cold custard
¼ pt. cream
Almond essence
1 oz. castor sugar

Blanch, chop and pound the almonds smoothly, adding the orange flower water to prevent them oiling. Warm the milk and pour over the almonds. When cool, add the custard. Partially freeze the mixture. Whip the cream and add to the mixture with almond essence to taste and the castor sugar. Complete the freezing.

6 helpings **Time—2½–3 hr.**

BANANA ICE CREAM

Glace à la Crème de Bananes

3 bananas
2 tablesp. lemon juice
½ pt. cream *or* ¼ pt. cream and ¼ pt. custard (1) *or* (2)
3–4 oz. castor sugar

Peel and slice the bananas, cover with lemon juice. Pass fruit through a nylon sieve. Add the half whipped cream, cold custard if used, and sugar. Chill and freeze.

6 helpings

BLACKCURRANT ICE CREAM

Glace à la Crème de Cassis

½ lb. ripe blackcurrants
3 oz. castor sugar
¼ pt. water
Rind and juice of 1 lemon
Few drops of carmine
½ pt. custard (1) *or* (2)
¼ pt. cream

Place blackcurrants, sugar and water, peel and strained juice of lemon and a few drops of carmine in a pan and allow to just boil. Pass through a nylon sieve. Add the custard and partly freeze. Add the whipped and sweetened cream and finish freezing.

6 helpings **Time—2½ hr.**

BURNT ALMOND ICE CREAM

Glace aux Amandes brulées

2 oz. almonds
2 oz. loaf sugar
¾ gill cream
1½ pt. custard
1 tablesp. kirsch (optional)

Blanch, shred and bake the almonds until brown. Put the sugar and a few drops of water in a saucepan and boil until it acquires a deep golden colour. Add the cream, boil up and stir into the custard. Chill, add almonds and kirsch, if used, and then freeze the mixture.

6–7 helpings **Time—2½–3 hr.**

CARAMEL ICE CREAM

Glace à la Crème de Caramel

2 oz. loaf sugar
¾ gill cream
1½ pt. custard (2)

Put the sugar into a small saucepan with a few drops of water and boil until it acquires a deep golden colour. Add the cream and when boiling stir into the custard. Chill and freeze.

6–7 helpings
Time—1½–2 hr.

CHOCOLATE ICE CREAM

Glace au Chocolat

4 oz. plain chocolate
½ gill water
½ pt. custard
1 gill cream
1–2 teasp. vanilla essence

Break chocolate roughly, place in pan, add water. Dissolve over low heat. Add melted chocolate to the custard. Cool. Add the half-whipped cream and vanilla to taste. Chill and freeze.

6–8 helpings

COFFEE ICE CREAM (1)

Glace Crème au Café

½ pt. cream
½ pt. custard (1) *or* (2)
2 tablesp. liquid coffee
2 oz. castor sugar

Half whip the cream. Add the custard, coffee and sugar. Mix well. Chill and freeze.

6 helpings

COFFEE ICE CREAM (2)

3 teasp. instant coffee
½ gill hot water
½ pt. cream
3 oz. castor sugar

Dissolve the coffee in the hot water. Cool. Half whip the cream and add castor sugar. Fold in the dissolved coffee. Chill and freeze.

6 helpings
Time—2½ hr.

GINGER ICE CREAM

Glace à la Crème de Gingembre

1 level teasp. ground ginger
½ gill ginger syrup
3 oz. chopped preserved ginger (in syrup)
½ pt. cream
¼ pt. custard (2)
2 oz. castor sugar

Dissolve the ground ginger in the syrup. Cut the preserved ginger into small dice. Half-whip the cream and add to it the custard, ginger, syrup and sugar. Chill and freeze.

6 helpings
Time—2 hr.

ORANGE ICE CREAM

Glace à la Crème d'Orange

3 oranges
2 oz. loaf sugar
1½ pt. custard (1) *or* (2)
Saffron yellow colouring
Carmine colouring

Remove the outer, yellow skin of the oranges by rubbing them with lumps of sugar. Dissolve the sugar in 1 tablesp. of hot water. Mix with the strained juice of oranges. Stir into the custard and add the colourings until the desired shade is obtained. Chill and freeze.

6–8 helpings
Time—45 min.

PINEAPPLE ICE CREAM

Glace à la Crème d'Ananas

¼ lb. canned pineapple
¼ pt. cream
¼ pt. custard (2)
¼ pt. pineapple juice
1 tablesp. lemon juice
1 oz. castor sugar

Cut the pineapple into small dice. Half whip the cream. Add the cold custard, cut pineapple, pineapple juice, lemon juice and sugar. Chill and freeze.

6 helpings **Time—2–2½ hr.**

PISTACHIO ICE CREAM

Glace Crème aux Pistaches

1½ pt. custard (2) (p. 468)
4 oz. pistachio nuts
Orange flower water
1 tablesp. noyeau
Green colouring

Blanch the nuts and remove the skins. Pound the nuts, gradually adding a little orange flower water. Add the noyeau and the colouring to the cold custard. Chill and freeze, when partially frozen add the pistachio nuts.

6–8 helpings **Time—1–1¼ hr.**

RASPBERRY ICE CREAM

Glace à la Crème de Framboises

1 small can raspberries
¼ pt. cream
¼ pt. custard (2) (p. 468)
2 oz. castor sugar

Drain the raspberries and pass through a nylon sieve. (Purée and juice together should measure ½ pt.) Mix with custard and then add the half-whipped cream. Add the sugar, and a little colouring if necessary. Chill and freeze.

6 helpings

STRAWBERRY ICE CREAM

Glace à la Crème de Fraises

¼ pt. milk
½ pt. cream
1–2 egg yolks
6 oz. castor sugar
1 lb. strawberries
1 dessertsp. granulated sugar
1 teasp. lemon juice
Carmine

Put milk and cream in a saucepan and bring nearly to boiling-point. Beat together the egg yolks and castor sugar, add to the milk and cream and stir over a low heat until they thicken. Pass the strawberries through a sieve, together with the granulated sugar. Mix with the custard, add the lemon juice and carmine to colour. Chill and freeze.

6–8 helpings **Time—About 1–1½ hr.**

TEA ICE CREAM

1 pt. custard (1) *or* **(2)** (p. 468)
½ pt. strong tea
½ gill cream
2 oz. castor sugar

Strain the tea, add the sugar and let it cool. Mix all ingredients together. Chill and freeze.

6–8 helpings **Time—35–40 min.**

VANILLA ICE CREAM (1)—Economical

Glace à la Crème de Vanille

¼ pt. cream *or* **prepared evaporated milk**
1 pt. cold custard (1)
1 teasp. vanilla essence

Half whip the cream *or* evaporated milk. Add the custard and vanilla. Chill and freeze.

6 helpings **Time—2½ hr.**

VANILLA ICE CREAM (2)

¼ pt. cream
½ pt. cold custard (2)
½ oz. castor sugar
1 teasp. vanilla essence

Half whip the cream. Add the custard, sugar and vanilla. Chill and freeze.

WALNUT ICE CREAM

Glace Crème aux Noix

4 oz. walnuts
Orange flower water
Vanilla essence
1½ pt. custard (2)

Pound the nuts, gradually adding a little orange flower water. Add the vanilla essence to the custard. Chill and freeze; when partially frozen add the walnuts.

6–8 helpings
Time—1–1¼ hr.

WHITE COFFEE ICE CREAM (Very delicate)

Crème de Café Blanc

4 oz. freshly roasted coffee berries
1 pt. cream *or* **milk**

Place the berries and the cream *or* milk in a saucepan and heat for an hour but do not let them boil. Strain. Use this mixture to make one of the basic custards (1)–(2) (p. 468) and finish as for Vanilla ice cream.

ICE PUDDINGS

NEAPOLITAN ICE PUDDING

Pouding Glace Napolitaine

½ pt. rich custard	**3 oz. castor sugar**
½ pt. cream	**½ oz. grated chocolate**
¼ pt. strawberry *or* raspberry pulp	**½ teasp. vanilla essence**

Half whip the cream and add it to the cooled custard. Divide this mixture into three. Mix the fruit pulp with ⅓ of the mixture and add 1 oz. of sugar and a little colouring, if necessary. Dissolve the chocolate in 1 tablesp. of water and add it to another ⅓ of the mixture with 1 oz. of sugar. To the remaining ⅓ of mixture add vanilla and 1 oz. of sugar. Freeze separately and then pack in layers in a suitable mould. Seal with lard, wrap in paper, and bury in ice and salt until required.

6 helpings **Time—3 hr.**

NESSELRODE PUDDING

Pouding Glace à la Nesselrode

2 dozen chestnuts	**6 oz. castor sugar**
½ pt. milk	**Vanilla essence**
4 egg yolks	**2 oz. glacé cherries**
½ pt. cream	

Parboil, shell, and skin the chestnuts. Simmer them in ¼ pt. milk until tender. Rub through a fine sieve. Heat remaining ¼ pt. milk until almost boiling, add the beaten egg yolks and cook, stirring continuously until it thickens without boiling. Add the chestnut purée and sugar. Cool. Add ½ of the half-whipped cream and vanilla. Freeze until nearly set, then stir in the chopped cherries and the remainder of the cream stiffly-whipped. Freeze until set, stirring frequently. Press into a mould, seal with lard, wrap in paper and bury in ice and salt until required.

6 helpings **Time—3 hr.**

MAPLE PARFAIT

Parfait au Sirop

1 gill syrup (1)	**2 egg yolks**
½ teasp. vanilla essence	**1½ pt. cream**
	3 oz. maple sugar

Boil the syrup until it registers 240°F. on a saccharometer. Pour the syrup over the egg yolks previously well beaten, with the vanilla. Whisk over boiling water until it has the consistency of thick cream and continue whisking without the boiling water until cold. Add the stiffly whisked cream and maple sugar. Stir over ice for some minutes. Turn into a parfait or bombe mould. Secure and seal the lid and bury in ice for 2½–3 hr.

6–7 helpings

MARASCHINO ALMOND PARFAIT

Parfait au Marasquin

3 oz. almonds (skinned and halved)	**¼ pt. syrup from the cherries**
Olive oil for frying	**1 pt. vanilla ice cream**
3 oz. Maraschino cherries	

Fry the almonds in olive oil until golden brown. Drain well. Add the cherries cut in halves, and the syrup. Beat thoroughly. Arrange alternate layers of almond and cherry mixture with ice cream in tall glasses, finishing with almonds and cherries on top.

6–8 helpings

PLOMBIÈRES

JAPANESE PLOMBIÈRE

Glace Plombière à la Japonaise

2 oz. apricot jam	**1 pt. custard** (p. 468)
Lemon juice	**4 oz. macaroons**
4 oz. ground almonds	**½ pt. cream**

Make apricot marmalade by boiling the apricot jam with a flavouring of lemon juice. Pass the flavoured jam through a sieve and add with the almonds to the hot custard. Crush the macaroons and whip the cream. Add these to the mixture when cool. Chill and freeze. Decorate with apricot marmalade and ratafia biscuits.

6 helpings

STRAWBERRY PLOMBIÈRE

Plombière de Fraises

½ pt. fresh strawberry pulp	**Few drops vanilla essence**
½ pt. rich custard	**Small pinch of mixed spice**
½ pt. cream	**1 wineglass brandy**
4 oz. castor sugar	**2 whipped egg whites**

Mix together the strawberry pulp, custard and whipped cream. Add the sugar, vanilla, spice, brandy and a little carmine if necessary. Lastly, carefully add the whipped egg whites. Freeze and mould.

6–8 helpings

VANILLA PLOMBIÈRE

Glace Plombière à la Vanille

1 pt. vanilla ice cream mixture	**¼ pt. cream**
	2 tablesp. almonds

Partially freeze the ice cream. Chop the almonds and whip the cream and add them to the ice cream. Complete the freezing.

6–8 helpings

REFRIGERATOR ICE CREAMS

LEMON ICE CREAM

Glace à la Crème aux Citrons

8 egg yolks	**Juice of 2 lemons**
½ lb. castor sugar	**½ pt. cream**

Set the refrigerator at coldest temperature. Beat the egg yolks until very thick. Add the sugar and beat again. Stir in the lemon juice. Add the half-whipped cream carefully. Pour into the tray and freeze ½ hr. Remove, stir and continue freezing for another 1½ hr.

6–8 helpings

MAPLE ICE CREAM

Glace à la Crème de Sirop

1 gill syrup (2)	**1 pt. whipped cream**
2 egg yolks	**1 teasp. vanilla essence**
2 oz. maple syrup	

Boil the syrup. Beat the egg yolks. Add syrup to egg yolks and whisk over boiling water until the mixture has the consistency of thick cream, and then whisk until cold. Add it to the whipped cream. Flavour with vanilla. Place in trays and freeze at coldest temperature for 2 hr.

MARSHMALLOW ICE CREAM

Glace Guimauvée

14 marshmallows	**3 oz. castor sugar**
¼ pt. evaporated milk	**¼ pt. cream**
¼ pt. fruit purée	

Melt the marshmallows in the evaporated milk over hot water. Cool. Add the fruit purée and sugar. Lastly fold in the half-whipped cream. Pour into the tray and freeze at medium. Stir once after the first ½ hr. and continue to freeze for a further 1½ hr.

6 helpings

VANILLA ICE CREAM

Glace à la Crème de Vanille

2 level tablesp. icing sugar	**2 egg whites**
	1 oz. glacé cherries
1 gill cream	**Vanilla essence**

Sieve the icing sugar. Whip the cream and add 1 tablesp. of the sugar. Stiffly whip the egg whites and fold in the other tablesp. of sugar. Carefully mix together the cream, egg whites, quartered cherries and vanilla. Turn into a tray of the ice chamber and freeze.

SUNDAES, ETC.

BANANA SPLIT

6 bananas	**¼ pt. whipped sweetened cream**
1 pt. vanilla ice cream (p. 470) *or* **1 family brick**	**2 oz. chopped walnuts**
½ pt. melba sauce	**8 maraschino cherries**

Peel bananas, split in half lengthways and place in small oval dishes. Place two small scoops or slices of ice cream between the halves of bananas. Coat the ice cream with melba sauce; sprinkle with chopped nuts. Decorate with piped cream and cherries.

CHOCOLATE SUNDAE

½ pt. chocolate ice cream (p. 469) *or* **1 small brick**
½ pt. chocolate sauce
½ pt. vanilla ice cream
2 oz. chopped walnuts
¼ pt. sweetened whipped cream
8 maraschino cherries

Place a scoop of chocolate ice cream in 6–8 sundae glasses; coat with chocolate sauce. Place a scoop of vanilla ice cream on top; coat with chocolate sauce. Sprinkle with chopped nuts. Pipe with cream. Decorate with cherries.

COUPE JACQUES

½ pt. vanilla ice cream (p. 470)
½ pt. strawberry ice cream
2 oz. peeled grapes
1 banana
1 peach
2 oz. raspberries
¼ pt. sweetened whipped cream

Place one portion of vanilla ice cream and one portion of strawberry ice cream in a deep dish. Chop and mix the fruit and place over the ice cream. Garnish with piped whipped cream.

6–8 helpings

CRUSHED PINEAPPLE SUNDAE

1 pt. vanilla ice cream (p. 470)
1 can crushed pineapple
¼ pt. sweetened whipped cream
8 maraschino cherries

Place a portion of ice cream in 6–8 sundae glasses. Cover with crushed pineapple. Pipe with sweetened whipped cream. Decorate with cherry.

6–8 sundaes

HAWAIIAN DREAMS

1 large can crushed pineapple
½ oz. gelatine
2 teasp. lemon juice
1 pt. vanilla *or* **chocolate ice cream**
2 oz. chopped browned almonds
¼ pt. sweetened whipped cream
6–8 maraschino cherries

Measure the crushed pineapple and make it up to 1 pt. with water. Dissolve the gelatine in a little of the liquid but do not allow to boil. Add it to the crushed pineapple with the lemon juice. Pour into individual glasses to set. Just before serving, place a scoop of ice cream on top of the set mixture. Sprinkle with nuts. Decorate with a rose of cream and place a cherry on top.

6 individual glasses

KNICKERBOCKER GLORY

1 pt. red jelly
1 pt. yellow jelly
1 small can chopped peaches
1 small can pineapple
2 pt. vanilla ice cream (p. 470) *or* **2 family bricks**
1 pt. melba sauce (p. 475)
2 oz. chopped walnuts
¼ pt. sweetened whipped cream
8 maraschino cherries

Make the jellies, allow to set, then whip with a fork. Place small portions of chopped fruit in the bottom of tall sundae glasses. Cover these with 1 tablesp. of whipped jelly. Place a scoop or slice of ice cream on top of the jelly. Coat the ice cream with melba sauce. Repeat again with fruit, jelly, ice cream and sauce. Sprinkle with chopped nuts. Pipe with sweetened whipped cream. Place a cherry on top of each.

6 individual glasses

MERINGUE GLACE CHANTILLY

1 pt. vanilla ice cream (p. 470) *or* **1 family brick**
16 meringue cases
¼ pt. sweetened whipped cream
8 maraschino cherries

Place a scoop or slice of ice cream in 8 small oval dishes. Set a meringue case on either side of the ice cream. Pipe a large rose of cream on top of the ice cream. Place a cherry on top.

8 individual dishes

OMELETTE SOUFFLÉE EN SURPRISE

1 round Genoese pastry *or* sponge cake
1 tablesp. liqueur
1 egg yolk
2 oz. castor sugar
3 egg whites
A few drops of vanilla essence
1 Nesselrode pudding (p. 471) *or* **1 pt. vanilla ice cream**

DECORATION

Glacé cherries
Angelica

Place the cake on a silver or fireproof dish and soak with liqueur. Whip the egg yolk and sugar until thick and fold in the stiffly-beaten egg whites. Add vanilla essence and place the soufflé mixture in a piping bag with a large rose pipe. Place the ice cream on top of the cake. Completely cover with piped soufflé mixture. Dredge with icing sugar and place in a very hot oven for 3 min. Decorate and serve immediately.

6–8 helpings

PEACH MELBA

Pêche Melba

4–5 firm, ripe peaches
½ gill raspberry syrup
Vanilla essence
4 oz. sugar
½ pt. vanilla ice cream

Halve and peel the peaches. Add the vanilla to the syrup and dissolve in it the sugar. Poach the peaches in the syrup until tender but not broken. Lift out the peaches, drain them on a sieve, and allow to get thoroughly cold. Serve them piled around a mound of vanilla ice cream in a silver dish. Set this dish in another dish containing shaved ice. Pour over a rich raspberry syrup, which must be previously iced. Serve at once.

NOTE: This is the original recipe created in honour of Madame Melba, it is now often made as follows:

1 pt. vanilla ice cream (p. 470)
6 canned peach halves
½ pt. melba sauce (p. 475)
¼ pt. whipped sweetened cream

Place a scoop or slice of ice cream in 6 sundae glasses. Cover with a peach half. Coat with melba sauce. Pipe a large rose of cream on top of each.

6 individual glasses

PEAR DELICE

8 pear halves
1 pt. strawberry ice cream
½ pt. chocolate sauce (p. 475)
2 oz. grated chocolate

Arrange a half of pear in 8 small flat glass dishes hollow side up. Place a scoop of ice cream in the hollow of the pears. Coat with hot chocolate sauce. Sprinkle with grated chocolate.

8 individual dishes

STRAWBERRY SUNDAE

1 pt. strawberry ice cream
1 lb. strawberries
Sugar to taste
2 oz. chopped walnuts
¼ pt. sweetened whipped cream

Place a scoop of ice cream in 8 sundae glasses. Slice and sugar the strawberries, reserving 8 small berries for decoration. Cover the ice cream with the sliced strawberries. Sprinkle with chopped nuts. Pipe with sweetened whipped cream.

Place a small whole strawberry on the top of each.

8 sundaes

TROPICAL SPLENDOUR

3 small pineapples
2 oz. castor sugar
2 tablesp. kirsch
½ pt. vanilla ice cream

Cut the pineapples in half lengthwise. Scoop out the pulp and cut into chunks. Mix it with sugar and kirsch. Pile it back into the pineapple halves and chill. Just before serving place a spoonful of vanilla ice cream on top.

6 helpings

TUTTI FRUTTI ICE CREAM

Glace Tutti Frutti

1 pt. ice cream mixture, any flavour
4 oz. mixed candied fruits
Pistachio nuts

Chop the fruits and nuts into small pieces. Half freeze the ice cream mixture, mix in the chopped fruits and nuts. Complete the freezing. Serve with Melba sauce.

RECIPES USING FAMILY BRICK ICE CREAM

DECORATED NEAPOLITAN

Wafers *or* sponge fingers
1 family brick ice cream (Neapolitan)
¼ pt. sweetened whipped cream
8 maraschino cherries
8 walnut halves
Few strips of angelica

Cut the wafers *or* sponge fingers to the same height as the brick. Place the brick on a large flat dish. Arrange the wafers *or* sponge fingers side by side round the brick putting a dab of cream on each to keep it in place. Pipe cream on top and decorate with rows of cherries and walnuts, and with leaves of angelica.

4–6 helpings

STRAWBERRY BASKET

1 sponge cake cut to size of ice cream brick
1 wineglass of sherry, liqueur *or* fruit juice
1 family brick ice cream
½ pt. sweetened whipped cream
12 ice cream wafer biscuits
½ lb. strawberries
1 strip angelica

Place the sponge cake on a silver dish and soak with sherry, liqueur *or* juice. Place the family brick ice cream on top of the sponge. Pipe a band of cream round the sides of the ice cream. Stand the wafers overlapping round the four sides and press them to the block. Pipe cream on top. Arrange the strawberries on top of the cream. Make a handle with the strip of angelica. Serve at once.

6–8 helpings

STRAWBERRY LAYER GÂTEAU

1 family brick ice cream
½ lb. strawberries
¼ pt. sweetened whipped cream
Castor sugar

Cut the family brick, which must be firm, in half horizontally. Cover the lower half with halves of strawberries. Sprinkle with castor sugar and replace the top half. Pipe with rosettes of cream and place small strawberries all over the top. Dredge with castor sugar and serve immediately.

6 helpings

SWISS CHOCOLATE LOG

1 chocolate Swiss roll
1 family brick ice cream
¼ pt. sweetened whipped cream

Cut the Swiss roll into seven slices and the family brick into six. Arrange on a long dish by sandwiching alternate slices of Swiss roll and ice cream pressed together. Pipe the whipped cream on top of the ice cream and dredge the Swiss roll with icing sugar.

6 helpings

SAUCES FOR SERVING WITH ICE CREAM

CHOCOLATE SAUCE

Sauce de Chocolat

1 rounded dessertsp. cornflour
2 rounded dessertsp. cocoa
3 rounded dessertsp. sugar
½ pt. water
3 drops vanilla essence
½ oz. butter

Blend together the cornflour, cocoa and sugar with a little of the water. Boil remaining water and pour on to blended mixture. Return to pan and boil for 2 min., stirring all the time. Add vanilla and butter.

Serve hot or cold.

COFFEE SAUCE

Sauce de Café

6 tablesp. freshly ground coffee
¾ pt. water
¼ oz. gelatine
3 egg yolks
3 oz. castor sugar

Boil the water and pour over the coffee. Strain when cool. Dissolve the gelatine in 1 tablesp. water. Beat together the egg yolks and sugar. Place all the ingredients in a saucepan. Cook slowly, without boiling, until the mixture thickens. Strain and chill. Use as required.

MELBA SAUCE

To make Melba sauce pass the required quantity of fresh raspberries through a nylon sieve and sweeten with icing sugar. The sauce is not cooked.

Use as required.

MOCK MELBA SAUCE

½ oz. arrowroot
½ pt. water
½ gill raspberry jam
Juice of ½ lemon

Blend the arrowroot with a little of the water. Boil remaining water with the jam and lemon juice. Strain it on to the blended mixture, return to the pan and boil up stirring all the time.

Cool before using.

ICED DRINKS

ICE CREAM BRANDY PUNCH

1 pt. milk
1 egg
1 wineglass brandy
1 pt. vanilla ice cream

Place in a bowl the milk, brandy and egg. Whisk well. Add the ice cream cut in small pieces. Whisk until frothy. Pour into a punch bowl and serve immediately.

6–8 glasses

ICED COFFEE

Café Frappé à la Vanille

½ pt. milk
6 oz. castor sugar
2 pt. strong, clear, hot coffee
A few drops of vanilla essence
½ pt. cream

Place the milk and sugar in a saucepan. Bring almost to the boil, add the coffee and vanilla essence, allow to cool. Strain, stir in the cream, and chill until it has the consistency of thick cream. Serve very cold, in tall glasses, and hand castor sugar separately.

MILK PUNCH

Punch au Lait

2 pt. milk
4 oz. loaf sugar
2 tablesp. brandy *or* rum
¼ pt. cream

Boil the milk, dissolve the sugar in it, strain and chill. Add the brandy *or* rum and the whipped cream. Mix well and half freeze. Serve in a half-frozen condition in small china sorbet cups and, if liked, grate a little nutmeg or cinnamon on top before serving.

6–8 helpings

DESSERT

AT FORMAL DINNERS the last course to be served is the dessert, which is composed principally of fruits in season, nuts (with or without raisins) and often ices, petits fours or dessert biscuits, dainty sweets and bonbons. Salted almonds are much appreciated after a sweet course.

The chief fruits served are grapes, peaches, nectarines, plums, cherries, apples, pears, oranges, dates and figs. The fruit looks most attractive served on a dish lined with green leaves (preferably vine leaves if available), which can form part of the table décor. If to be handed round separately, the fruit is served after the table has been cleared and dessert plates, knives and forks have been placed before each person. The fruit should of course be first washed or wiped with a damp cloth, and afterwards polished with a soft, dry cloth.

On the Continent fruit is often served instead of a sweet course, whilst in America the pudding course is referred to as the dessert.

SWEET MAKING

UNTIL RECENTLY SWEETS were not made by many housewives. Even now there exists a mistaken idea that sweet making is difficult, and that elaborate equipment is essential. Naturally success is more certain if you have a saccharometer, marble slab, crystallizing tray, sweet fork and ring, etc., but these are not indispensable. By measuring accurately, testing repeatedly, and by taking care to apply the right amount of heat, an amateur should find no difficulty in preparing many of the sweets for which recipes are given below.

Of the equipment mentioned in the following recipes, that absolutely necessary, is simple and inexpensive, and comprises a nylon or hair sieve, a palette knife and a candy hook. (A strong iron kitchen hook, which should be fixed firmly on a wall about 5 feet from the floor, according to the height of the worker, may be substituted for a candy hook.) When a sugar skimmer is not available for testing the sugar as it approaches the "small ball" degree, a piece of wire twisted to form small rings will be found a good substitute.

When cooking over gas it is advisable to have a piece of sheet-iron to place over the gas burners when a very slow continuous application of heat is required, as in making caramels, etc.

Cream of tartar is added to the syrup to prevent the sugar granulating, and bicarbonate of soda serves to whiten toffee, etc.

POINTS TO NOTE WHEN MAKING SWEETS

1. Choose a strong thick saucepan as the sugar mixture is liable to burn in a thin saucepan at high temperatures. The pan should be scrupulously clean and burnished to prevent the sugar sticking.

2. Always allow the sugar to dissolve thoroughly before the mixture reaches boiling-point. Tapping the bottom of the saucepan with the wooden spoon speeds up this process. When no further grittiness is felt the sugar will have dissolved completely.

3. While boiling to the required temperature do not stir unless the recipe specially requires it, as stirring lowers the temperature and may make the finished sweets cloudy.

4. For fudge and some caramel mixtures however, stirring is often required when nearing the end of the cooking to prevent burning and to obtain the desired "grained" consistency.

5. During boiling the sugar will splash on to the sides of the saucepan, and this may be brushed down with a clean pastry brush dipped in cold water. If this is not done, sweets which should be clear and smooth may be "sugary" and rough when finished.

6. Use waxed paper or Cellophane to wrap the sweets.

7. Most sweets need airtight storage if they are not to become sticky. When packing presentation boxes, waxed paper should be put between the rows and the layers to prevent sticking.

TO TEST THE HEAT OF BOILING SUGAR

Although sugar may be boiled, and the degree approximately gauged by applying the following tests, the process is greatly simplified by the use of a saccharometer, and more accurate results will be obtained. If using a saccharometer put it into a pan of cold water and bring to the boil before putting it into the sugar.

The different degrees to which sugar is boiled are classed as follows:

1. Small Thread	215° F.	7. Small Ball	237° F.
2. Large Thread	217° F.	8. Large Ball	247° F.
3. Small Pearl	220° F.	9. Small Crack	290° F.
4. Large Pearl	222° F.	10. Large Crack	312° F.
5. Small Blow	230° F.	11. Caramel	350° F.
6. Large Blow or Feather	233° F.		

The small thread: Dissolve 2 lb. loaf sugar in 1 pt. water, bring to boiling-point, and remove the scum. Boil for a few minutes, then dip the tip of the forefinger into the syrup and apply it to the thumb. If, on immediately separating the finger and thumb, the syrup is drawn out into a fine thread which breaks at a short distance, the sugar is boiled to the small thread (215° F.).

The large thread: Boil the syrup a little longer, and apply the same test; if the thread can be drawn longer without breaking, the syrup is boiled to the large thread (217° F.).

The small pearl: Continue the boiling for a few moments and proceed as before. When the thumb and forefinger may be separated to a little distance without breaking the thread, the sugar is boiled to the small pearl (220° F.).

The large pearl: After a little further boiling dip the forefinger in again, stretch the thumb and forefinger as far as possible, and if the thread remains unbroken the sugar has been boiled to the large pearl (222° F.).

The small blow: Boil a little longer, then take a skimmer, dip it into the syrup, drain it well over the pan, and blow through the holes. If small bubbles appear on the other side of the skimmer, the sugar is boiled to the small blow (230° F.).

The large blow or feather: After a moment's further boiling repeat the test, and when the bubbles appear in much larger quantities and fly off the skimmer when shaken, like small feathers or down, the sugar is boiled to the large blow (233° F.).

The small ball: Now dip the forefinger into a basin of cold water, then dip it into the sugar, and again quickly into the water. When the sugar can be rolled between the thumb and forefinger into a small ball it has reached the stage known by that name (237° F.).

The large ball: Continue the boiling and proceed as before; as soon as the sugar can be formed into a larger and harder ball, it is boiled to the large ball (247° F.).

The small or soft crack: Boil for a little longer, then dip in the forefinger, and if the sugar adhering to it breaks with a slight noise, and sticks to the teeth when bitten, it is boiled to the small crack (290° F.).

The large or hard crack: Boil a little longer, dip the forefinger into cold water, then into the sugar, and again quickly into the water. If the sugar breaks short and brittle, and does not stick to the teeth when bitten, it is boiled to the large crack (312° F.).

The caramel: If the boiling is prolonged beyond this stage, the sugar soon begins to acquire a golden colour, which gradually deepens until brown, and finally black, burnt sugar is obtained.

DESSERT SWEETMEATS

ALMOND STICKS

½ lb. ground *or* pounded almonds
¾ lb. icing sugar
¼ lb. granulated *or* vanilla sugar
5 egg whites
Royal icing
Vanilla essence

If the almonds are whole, blanch them and dry thoroughly in a cool oven, then pound them finely. Add the sugars by degrees to the almonds. When perfectly smooth, add the egg whites, and when well mixed, turn on to a marble slab. Knead well, roll out to about a ¼ in. thick, then cut into strips about 2 in. long and ½ in. wide. Place them on a greased and floured baking-sheet, cover with royal icing flavoured with vanilla, and bake in a very cool oven (**290° F., Gas 2**) for about ½ hr. These sticks may be served as dessert or handed round with ices instead of wafers.

BUTTERED ALMONDS, WALNUTS, or BRAZILS

½ lb. demerara sugar
6 tablesp. water
2 level teasp. glucose
Pinch of cream of tartar
2 oz. butter
2 oz. blanched browned almonds *or* dried halved walnuts or whole brazils

Dissolve the sugar in the water very slowly. Add the glucose, cream of tartar and butter. Boil to 290° F. Have sweet rings oiled and place them on an oiled slab. Place a nut in each and pour over ⅛–¼ in. of toffee. Remove from the rings when cool and wrap separately in waxed paper and store in an airtight jar or tin.

The sweets may be made without the sweet rings, if these are not available, using the toffee a little cooler and putting a teaspoonful over each nut on an oiled slab, although the finished sweets will be irregular in shape.

CANDIED CHESTNUTS

Chestnuts
Loaf sugar

Remove the shells, place the chestnuts in a pan of boiling water, boil for about 10 min., then drain and skin them. Replace in the pan, cover with boiling water, boil until tender, but not broken, and let them cool. Allow ½ pt. water to each lb. of sugar, boil to the "small crack" degree (**290° F.**), then dip in the chestnuts one at a time and place on an oiled slab.

CHOCOLATE ALMONDS

Chocolate
Vanilla essence
Almonds, blanched and dried

Dissolve the chocolate in the smallest possible quantity of hot water and flavour it to taste with vanilla essence. Dip each almond in separately and place them on an oiled slab or plates to set.

CHOCOLATE PRALINES

¼ lb. almonds
½ lb. icing sugar
Chocolate
Chocolate coating

Blanch the almonds and bake until brown. Chop them coarsely then pound them finely. Place the sugar in a sugar boiler or pan, *without water*, cook until lightly browned, stir in the almonds, and then pour on to an oiled slab. When cold, pound to a powder, mix with it sufficient chocolate dissolved in warm water to form a paste, and turn it into a tin. When cold cut into squares, and coat with dissolved chocolate.

CHOCOLATE STICKS

10 oz. castor sugar
½ lb. ground *or* pounded almonds
2 oz. finely-grated chocolate
Whites of 2 small eggs
Royal icing

Pass the sugar through a fine sieve and roll out finely any lumps. Add the sugar gradually to the almonds, then add the chocolate and egg whites. When well mixed, turn on to a board or slab, knead well, roll out about ¼ in. thick, and cut into strips about 2 in. long and ½ in. wide. Place them on a buttered and floured baking-sheet, cover with icing, and bake in a very cool oven for about ½ hr.

COCONUT CANDY

1 medium-sized coconut
1½ lb. demerara sugar
¾ pt. water

Remove the shell and rind from the coconut, and slice it thinly. Dissolve the sugar in the water, boil to the "large ball" degree (**247° F.**), then remove the pan from the heat, and grain the syrup by rubbing it with the back of the spoon against the sides of the pan. As soon as the mixture begins to grow cloudy add the sliced coconut, stir until quite thick, then pour on to an oiled tin. When sufficiently firm, mark into squares or oblongs, and when perfectly cold and firm divide into sections. White candy may be made by substituting white sugar for the demerara.

COCONUT ICE (1)

¾ lb. loaf sugar
1½ pt. water
¾ lb. glucose
Raspberry essence
Red *or* carmine colouring
1 lb. desiccated coconut
Vanilla essence

Cut greaseproof paper to fit the sides and bottom of a shallow box, or tin with straight

PLATE 21

Apple Snow and Lemon Meringue Pie

Apple snow (see page 457) makes an inviting cold sweet for a hot day.

Lemon meringue pie decorated with glacé cherries and angelica.

PLATE 22

Making a Fruit Pie

1 Fill the dish with fruit. Roll out the pastry a little larger than the pie-dish; cut off a strip from the edge to fit the dish rim.

2 Moisten edge of the pie-dish. Place strip on rim with cut edge inwards and dampen the strip.

3 Lift pastry lid with the rolling-pin to prevent stretching it and place on dish. Press strip and cover well together, trim off surplus pastry with sharp knife.

4 Knock up edge of pastry with the back of a knife held horizontally.

5 Scallop edge with the back of a knife, pressing lightly with thumb.

6 Raise the pie edge to make a few gaps to allow the steam to escape.

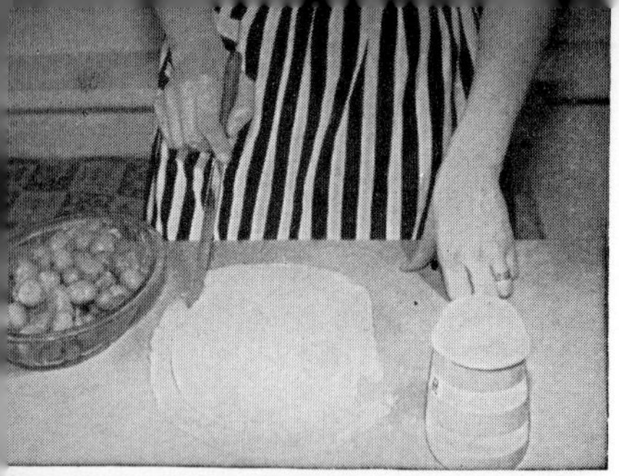

1

2

3

4

5

6

sides, and arrange it carefully. Dissolve the sugar in the water, add the glucose, and boil to the "small ball" degree (**237° F.**). Pour ½ the syrup into another pan, and keep it warm. Flavour the remainder to taste with raspberry essence, and add colouring drop by drop until a pale pink colour is obtained. Grain this pink syrup by working it against the sides of the pan; when cloudy, stir in ½ the coconut and pour the mixture into the prepared box or tin. Flavour the other portion with vanilla essence, grain it in the same way as the pink syrup, and when cloudy add the remainder of the coconut and pour it on the top of the pink ice. When quite cold and set, turn out of the box and cut into slices.

COCONUT ICE (2)

3 lb. loaf sugar	**Vanilla essence**
½ pt. water	**Carmine colouring**
½ lb. desiccated coconut	

Line a shallow tin with greaseproof paper. Boil the sugar and water to the "small ball" degree (**237° F.**), remove the pan from the heat, add the coconut, and flavour to taste. Let it cool a little, then pour ½ into the prepared tin, and stand the pan containing the remainder in hot water, to prevent it setting. As soon as the portion in the tin is set, add a few drops of carmine or cochineal to the remainder in the pan, and pour it over the ice in the tin. When cold, turn out and cut into bars.

COCONUT MERINGUE ROCKS

½ lb. castor sugar	**Vanilla essence**
4 egg whites	**Pistachio nuts**
Pinch of salt	**Granulated sugar**
2 oz. desiccated coconut	

Pass the sugar through a fine sieve. Put the egg whites with a good pinch of salt into a bowl or large basin, and whisk them to a very stiff froth. Stir in as lightly as possible the sugar and coconut, and add a few drops of vanilla essence. Have ready a baking-tin, buttered and dredged lightly with flour, and on it pile the mixture in dessertspoonfuls, about 1 in. apart. Sprinkle ½ with finely-chopped pistachios, and the rest with granulated sugar. Bake in a cool oven for 30–40 min.

DATES

Dates may be served plain or stuffed. To stuff: slit the date and remove the stone. Fill the cavity with a whole blanched almond or roll of marzipan. Roll in castor sugar.

FONDANT

2 lb. loaf *or* granulated sugar	**1 dessertsp. glucose**
1½ gills water	**Colourings**
	Flavourings

Dissolve the sugar in the water, add the glucose, bring to the boil quickly, and boil until the syrup registers **237° F.** ("small ball"). Pour on to an oiled or wetted slab, let it cool slightly (for if worked when hot it will grain), and work it with a palette knife, keeping the mass as much as possible together. When the paste is sufficiently cool, knead it well with the hands. When perfectly smooth, divide into 2–3 portions, colour, flavour and knead again separately, and use as required.

FONDANT FRUITS or NUTS

2 lb. loaf sugar	**Colouring**
1½ gills water	**Flavouring to taste**
1 dessertsp. glucose	**Fruit *or* nuts**

Dissolve the sugar in the water, bring to boiling point, add the glucose, and boil to the "small ball" degree (**237° F.**). Turn on to a marble slab, work well with a palette knife until white, then knead with the hands until perfectly smooth. Colour and flavour to taste, put a small portion into a cup, stand the cup in a tin of boiling water, and stir until the fondant has the appearance of thick cream. Any kind of fruit or nuts may be dipped one by one into the liquid fondant. Care should be taken to coat them thoroughly; cherries, grapes, etc., may be held by the stem, but nuts must be immersed and lifted out with a ring fork. During the process the fondant must be kept warm to prevent hardening.

WALNUT FONDANTS

½ lb. fondant	**Pineapple essence**
Green colouring	**18 dried walnuts**

Colour the fondant pale green and flavour it to taste with pineapple essence. Divide into 18 equal portions, form first into balls, then press them into oval cakes, the same shape and size as the walnuts. Place the cakes between two halves of walnuts, press firmly together, and let them harden in a dry and warm place.

FUDGE

1 lb. granulated sugar	**2 oz. butter**
¼ pt. milk	**½ teasp. vanilla essence**

Put sugar and milk in a saucepan and leave to soak for 1 hr. Add the butter, place over gentle heat and stir until sugar is dissolved. Then bring to boil and boil to the "small ball" degree (**237° F.**). Remove from heat, stir in vanilla, cool slightly, then beat until thick. Pour into an oiled tin; cut in squares when cold.

NOTE: Coconut, nuts or ginger may be stirred in while fudge is cooling. **Chocolate fudge**: Add 2 tablesp. cocoa or 2 oz. plain chocolate with the butter.

GINGER

Stem ginger is popular as a dessert. It may be served plain or chocolate covered.

To cover with chocolate, drain the pieces of ginger on a piece of clean muslin, then dip on a skewer into melted chocolate. Allow to harden on a cooling-tray.

HARD GLAZED FRUITS

Fresh *or* candied fruit	**A few drops of lemon juice**
½ lb. loaf sugar	
½ gill water	

Fresh fruit must be dried thoroughly; candied fruit must be washed free from sugar and afterwards dried. Dissolve the sugar in the water, add a few drops of lemon juice, and boil to the "small crack" degree (**290° F.**). Plunge the saucepan into cold water to prevent the syrup becoming over-cooked, and immediately dip in the prepared fruit one by one. Place them on an oiled tin until cold, then transfer to sheets of white paper.

MARASCHINO CREAM BONBONS

FOR THE CENTRES

Icing sugar	**1 gill hot water**
2 oz. gum arabic	**2 tablesp. maraschino**

FOR COATING

1 teasp. lemon juice	**Coffee essence**
2 egg whites	**Caramel**
¾ lb. icing sugar	

Pass the sugar through a fine nylon sieve. Soak the gum arabic in the hot water, strain, add the maraschino and as much icing sugar as will form a paste firm enough to be cut, yet moist enough to be piped, and work until elastic. Put it into a paper forcing bag, and as it is pressed out, cut it into small pieces, and let them drop on to paper thickly dredged with icing sugar. Allow these centres to remain in a warm place until they harden slightly.

Add the lemon juice and egg whites gradually to about ¾ lb. icing sugar, work until perfectly smooth, then flavour to taste with coffee essence, and colour with caramel. Dip in the centres one by one, and let them remain on a wire tray until dry.

NOTE: Curaçao or any other liqueur, orange flower water, and many flavouring essences, may be substituted for maraschino, the bonbons taking their name from the flavouring.

MARSHMALLOWS

¼ lb. gum arabic	**3 egg whites**
½ pt. water	**Caramel essence**
½ lb. icing sugar	

Soak the gum arabic in the water until soft, then heat gently until dissolved, and strain it through fine muslin. Return to the pan, add the sugar, and when dissolved, stir in the egg whites, and whisk until the mixture is quite stiff. Flavour to taste, and let it remain for about 10 hr. When ready, cut into small squares, and dredge them thickly with icing sugar.

MARZIPAN

1 lb. loaf sugar	**2 egg whites**
1½ gills water	**3 oz. sifted icing sugar**
12 oz. ground almonds	**Flavouring**

Boil the loaf sugar and water to **240° F.**, then draw the sugar boiler or pan aside, and when the syrup has cooled slightly add the almonds and egg whites. Stir over a low heat for a few minutes, then turn on to a slab, stir in the icing sugar, and work with a palette knife until cool enough to handle. Knead with the hands until perfectly smooth, add flavouring and mould into shapes.

MARZIPAN—GERMAN

1 lb. almonds	**¾ lb. castor sugar**
¼ gill orange flower water	**½ lb. sifted icing sugar**

Blanch and shred the almonds finely and pound them to a paste with the orange flower water. Put the castor sugar and pounded almonds into a pan placed in a tin of boiling water, and stir until the mixture, when touched, does not stick to the fingers. Turn on to a slab, add the icing sugar, work with a palette knife until cool enough to handle, then knead until perfectly smooth. Colour and flavour to taste and use as required.

NOUGAT

8 oz. almonds	**4 oz. honey**
4 oz. icing sugar	**2 egg whites**

Blanch and dry the almonds thoroughly. Line a box of suitable size first with white paper and then with wafer paper, both of which must be cut to fit exactly. Put the sugar, honey and egg whites into a sugar boiler or pan, and stir over a low heat until the mixture becomes thick and white. Drop a little into cold water; if it hardens immediately, remove the pan from the heat, and stir in the almonds. Dredge the slab with icing sugar, turn on to it the nougat, and form into a ball. Press into the prepared box, cover with paper, let it remain under pressure until cold, then cut up into squares.

PEPPERMINT CREAMS

1 lb. icing sugar	**1–2 drops oil of peppermint *or* 2 teasp. peppermint essence**
Whites of 2 large eggs	

Sieve the icing sugar and add the stiffly beaten egg whites and the peppermint flavouring. A very little green colour may be added if liked. Mix all well together to a firm dough-like ball and roll out, well sifted with icing sugar, to about $\frac{1}{4}$–$\frac{1}{8}$ in. thick. Cut out with a small round sweet cutter and leave on a wire tray to dry out for 12 hr. Pack into an air-tight container.

The creams may be coated with melted chocolate if desired. For this, dissolve some broken chocolate in a bowl over hot water and dip the creams into the chocolate, holding them on a fine skewer or a sweet-dipping fork. Allow to set on clean greaseproof paper.

RASPBERRY CREAM BONBONS

FOR THE CENTRES

Icing sugar	**Carmine**
2 oz. gum arabic	**Raspberry essence**

FOR COATING

¾ lb. icing sugar (approx.)	**4 oz. unsweetened finely-grated chocolate**
1 teasp. lemon juice	
2 egg whites	

Pass the sugar through a fine sieve. Soak the gum arabic in 1 gill of hot water, strain, colour and flavour to taste, stir in gradually as much icing sugar as will form a paste firm enough to be cut, yet moist enough to pass easily through a piping tube, and work it well. Have ready a paper bag with a tube attached, fill with the mixture, force out, cut off into small pieces, and let them fall on to paper covered thickly with icing sugar. Let the bonbons remain in a warm place to harden slightly while the coating is being prepared. Put about $\frac{3}{4}$ lb. icing sugar into a basin, add the lemon juice and egg whites gradually, and work until perfectly smooth. Put the chocolate with 1 tablesp. warm water into a basin, place it over a small saucepan of boiling water, stir until dissolved, and when cool, add it to the egg white and sugar. Mix thoroughly, dip in the bonbons one by one, dry on a wire tray.

ROUT CAKES or PETITS FOURS

1 lb. whole *or* ground almonds
Orange flower water
1 lb. castor sugar

If whole, blanch, dry and pound the almonds finely. Add gradually a little orange flower water to the almonds. When reduced to a fine paste, put it into the pan with the sugar, and stir over heat until dry and when touched does not stick to the finger. Form into small fancifully-shaped sweetmeats and bake in a moderately cool oven.

TURKISH DELIGHT

1 oz. gelatine
2 oz. almonds *or* pistachios
1 orange
1 lemon
1 lb. loaf sugar
1 gill water
1 tablesp. rum
½ lb. icing sugar
1–2 teasp. cornflour

Put the gelatine to soak in cold water. Blanch the almonds or pistachios and chop them coarsely. Remove the rinds of the orange and lemon in thin fine strips, place the rinds in a sugar boiler or saucepan with the loaf sugar, 1 gill water and the strained juice of the orange and lemon. When boiling add the gelatine, simmer until dissolved, then strain into a basin and add the rum. Let the mixture remain until on the point of setting, then stir in the almonds or pistachios and pour at once into a wetted tin. When perfectly set turn the jelly out, cut it into 1 in. square pieces and dust them lightly in a mixture of icing sugar and cornflour.

SWEETS, CANDIES AND TOFFEES

ALMOND ROCK (I)

¼ lb. almonds
1 lb. loaf sugar
½ pt. water
¼ lb. glucose
Almond essence

Blanch and dry the almonds thoroughly. Dissolve the sugar in the water, add the glucose, and boil to the "small crack" degree (**290° F.**). Remove the pan from the heat, add the almonds, a few drops of almond essence, return to heat, boil until golden brown, then pour on to oiled or buttered tins.

BARLEY SUGAR

2 lb. loaf sugar
1 pt. water
½ teasp. lemon juice
Pinch of cream of tartar
Yellow colouring
Lemon essence

Dissolve the sugar in the water, boil to the "small ball" degree (**237° F.**), and add the lemon juice. Continue boiling to the "large crack" (**312° F.**), add a pinch of cream of tartar, a few drops of yellow colouring, flavour to taste, and turn on to an oiled slab. When cool, cut into narrow strips, twist them into a spiral form, and when perfectly cold, store them in airtight tins or boxes.

BURNT ALMONDS

1 lb. almonds
1¾ lb. granulated sugar
Cold water

Blanch the almonds and dry them thoroughly in a cool oven. Put 1 lb. sugar and 1½ gills water into a pan, bring to the boil, then add the almonds and boil gently over a low heat. When the almonds make a slight crack-noise, lower the heat, stir until the sugar granulates, then turn on to a coarse sieve. Shake well, put the sugar that passes through the sieve into a pan, add to it 1½ gills water and the remaining ¾ lb. sugar, and let it boil to the "small or soft ball" degree (**237° F.**). Now add the almonds, which should in the meantime have been kept warm, stir until well coated, but at the first inclination they show of sticking together, remove them from the heat, and place them on the sieve as before. The second coating of sugar is frequently coloured and flavoured according to taste.

BUTTERSCOTCH

1 lb. loaf sugar
½ pt. milk
Pinch of cream of tartar
½ lb. butter

Place the sugar and milk in a pan and stir occasionally over a low heat until the sugar is dissolved. Add the cream of tartar, and the butter a small piece at a time, and boil the mixture until a little, dropped into cold water, forms a moderately hard ball. Pour on to an oiled or buttered tin, and as soon as it is sufficiently firm, mark off into small oblongs or squares, and when cold, divide the sections. Wrap each piece first in waxed paper, then in tinfoil.

CANDIED POPCORN

1 qt. popped corn	**1 oz. butter**
½ lb. castor sugar	**3 tablesp. water**

To prepare the popped corn, put the Indian maize into a wire sieve and shake it gently over a low heat until it pops. Place the sugar, butter and water in a pan, boil to the "small ball" degree (**237° F.**), add the prepared corn, and stir briskly until the corn is completely coated. Remove the pan from the heat, and continue stirring until cool, to prevent the corn sticking together.

CANDIES

TO "PULL" SUGAR

In the following recipes the sugar mixture when boiled to the required stage is then turned on to a wetted slab and left until it is cool enough to handle. At this point and working quickly the sugar is pulled, either between the hands or, where a large quantity is being handled, over an oiled hook. It will then acquire a light colour and a satin finish. As the mixture begins to set it is pulled into a long even piece as thick as required and this is quickly cut into small convenient pieces using a pair of scissors or a sharp knife.

Several colours may be introduced by dividing the hot sugar mixture into different parts to cool, adding a few drops of a different colour to each portion. These are pulled separately and then laid together for the final pulling and shaping, or one portion may be left unpulled and clear and added at the final stage of shaping. The finished appearance may thus be varied as desired.

AMERICAN CANDY

2 lb. moist sugar	**Flavouring essence**
½ pt. water	**Tartaric acid**
Cream of tartar	**1 dessertsp. golden syrup**
Colouring	

Dissolve the sugar in the water, add a good ½ teasp. cream of tartar, and boil to the "large crack" degree (**312° F.**). Pour on to an oiled slab, add a little colouring, and flavour to taste. Any flavouring substance may be used, but it should agree with the colour of the candy; thus red should be flavoured with raspberry essence, yellow with pineapple, etc. Add also a pinch of tartaric acid and the golden syrup. Work well in, fold up, then pull over an oiled hook, and cut into squares.

AMERICAN MOLASSES CANDY

3 cups demerara sugar	**1 cup molasses**
1 cup water	**½ teasp. cream of tartar**
1 oz. butter	

Dissolve the sugar in the water, add the butter and molasses, and when boiling stir in the cream of tartar. Continue the cooking until the syrup reaches the "small crack" degree (**290° F.**), then turn on to an oiled slab. When cool enough to handle, pull it over an oiled hook and when firm cut into squares.

BROWN ALMOND CANDY KISSES

2 oz. almonds	**1 oz. butter**
1 lb. demerara sugar	**4 oz. glucose**
¼ pt. water	**Caramel essence**

Blanch and chop the almonds coarsely, then bake them in the oven until golden-brown. Dissolve the sugar in the water, add the butter and glucose, and boil to the "large ball" degree (**247° F.**). Remove the pan from the heat, stir in caramel essence to taste, press the syrup against the sides of the pan with a spatula or wooden spoon to give the candy a grained appearance, and when it becomes cloudy, stir in the prepared almonds. When sufficiently firm, pile small portions on an oiled slab, using a teaspoon for the purpose. Chopped hazel nuts or coconut may be substituted for the almonds.

CANDY TWIST

1½ lb. demerara sugar	**Caramel colouring**
½ pt. water	**Almond essence**

Dissolve the sugar in the water, boil to the "small crack" degree (**290° F.**), then colour and flavour to taste. Pour the syrup on to an oiled slab, and as the edges cool fold them over. When cool enough to handle pull it over the candy-hook, cut it into 6-in. lengths, and twist them into a spiral form.

If preferred, white granulated sugar may be substituted, and the candy flavoured with vanilla, or it may be coloured red with a few drops of cochineal and flavoured with raspberry.

WHITE ALMOND CANDY KISSES

2 oz. almonds	**1 oz. butter**
1 lb. loaf sugar	**4 oz. glucose**
¼ pt. water	**Vanilla essence**

Blanch and chop the almonds and dry them thoroughly. Prepare the syrup as directed in the preceding recipe, substituting vanilla essence for the caramel flavouring.

PINEAPPLE SNOW CANDY

1 pt. clarified syrup (p. 467)	**1 egg white**
	1 tablesp. castor sugar
Yellow colouring	**Pineapple essence**

Boil the prepared syrup to the "small crack" degree (**290° F.**), and add a few drops of yellow colouring. Meanwhile whisk the egg white stiffly, and add to it the castor sugar and a few drops of pineapple essence. Line some moulds or small tins with oiled paper, and sprinkle the bottom and sides liberally with icing or castor sugar. As soon as the syrup is sufficiently boiled, plunge the pan into cold water to arrest further cooking, and let it cool slightly, then pour it on the egg white and sugar mixture, and stir briskly to a froth. When ready, pour into the prepared moulds, and turn out when perfectly set. The flavour and colour may be varied as desired, the candy of course taking its name from the flavouring ingredient.

TREACLE CANDY

1 pt. treacle	**1 tablesp. vinegar**
¾ lb. brown sugar	**1 teasp. bicarbonate of soda**
2 oz. butter	

Place the treacle, sugar, butter and vinegar in a large pan, boil until a few drops will harden immediately when dropped into cold water, then stir in the bicarbonate of soda previously dissolved in a little hot water. Pour at once into an oiled or buttered tin, turn the edges in as they cool, and as soon as the whole can be handled pull it until white, draw it into sticks and cut into short lengths.

CARAMELS

CHOCOLATE CARAMELS (1)

1 lb. loaf sugar	**3 oz. finely-grated chocolate**
½ pt. milk	
½ pt. cream	

Dissolve the sugar in the milk, add the cream and bring slowly to boiling-point. Dissolve the chocolate in a bowl standing in hot water, stir it into the syrup, and boil very gently until a little, dropped into cold water, at once hardens and snaps easily. Pour it on to an oiled slab into a square formed by bars, or, failing these, into an oiled tin. When cold, cut into squares with a caramel cutter, or buttered knife, and wrap each piece in waxed paper.

CHOCOLATE CARAMELS (2)

½ lb. loaf sugar	**1 oz. butter**
1 gill water	**2 oz. grated chocolate**
2 oz. glucose	**Acetic acid**
¼ gill cream	

Dissolve the sugar in the water, add the glucose, and boil to **280° F.** Stir in the cream, butter and chocolate, replace on the heat, and re-boil to the same temperature. Remove from the heat, stir in 2 drops of acetic acid, and pour into a well-oiled tin. When cold, mark with a caramel cutter or knife and cut into squares.

STRAWBERRY CARAMELS

2 lb. loaf sugar	**¼ oz. butter**
¼ pt. water	**Strawberry essence**
2 oz. honey	**Red *or* carmine colouring**
⅓ pt. cream	

Place the sugar in a sugar boiler or pan, add the water, and when dissolved stir in the honey, cream and butter. Boil to the "small crack" (**290° F.**), then stir in the flavouring essence and colouring ingredient, and pour on to an oiled slab. When set, cut into small squares with a caramel cutter or buttered knife.

WRAPPED CARAMELS

1 lb. loaf sugar — **1 oz. butter**
¼ pt. water — **Acetic acid**
4 oz. glucose — **Vanilla essence**
½ gill cream

Dissolve the sugar in the water, add the glucose, and boil to **280° F.** Stir in the cream and butter, reheat to the same temperature, then remove the pan from the heat and add 2 drops of acetic acid and vanilla essence to taste. Turn into an oiled tin; when sufficiently firm, mark with a caramel cutter or knife and when cold cut into squares. Wrap them in waxed paper.

FRUIT DROPS

1 lb. loaf sugar — **A few drops of acetic acid**
½ pt. water — **Fruit essence**

Boil the sugar and water to the "small ball" degree (**237° F.**), add a few drops of acetic acid, and fruit essence to taste. Grain the syrup by pressing it against the sides of the pan with the back of the spoon, let it cool slightly, then turn it on to an oiled sheet. Mark it in small squares with the back of a knife and separate them when cold.

LEMON ACID DROPS

1½ lb. loaf sugar — **Lemon essence**
½ pt. water — **1 dessertsp. tartaric acid**
½ teasp. cream of tartar

Boil the sugar, water and cream of tartar together until the mixture is pale yellow, add lemon essence to taste, and turn on to an oiled slab. Sprinkle on the tartaric acid, work it well in, and as soon as it is cool enough to handle, form into thin rolls. Cut off short pieces with scissors and roll into shape under the hand. Coat with sifted sugar, dry well and afterwards store.

ORANGE DROPS

2 lb. loaf sugar — **1 pt. water**
3–4 oranges — **Yellow colouring**

Rub some of the sugar on the oranges to obtain the zest. Boil all the sugar and the water to the "small crack" degree (**290° F.**), and add a little colouring. Cool slightly, then pour on to an oiled slab, mark off into small squares, and break them up when cold. Dry thoroughly then store.

MINT HUMBUGS

1 lb. sugar — **¼ teasp. oil of peppermint (approx.)**
4 oz. glucose — **Colouring**
½ pt. water
½ level teasp. cream of tartar

Dissolve the sugar and glucose in the water over a low heat. Add the cream of tartar and boil to the "small crack" degree (**290° F.**), then add peppermint oil to taste. Pour on to a wetted slab in 2 equal portions and colour one half—say, green. Allow to cool slightly then pull each portion separately. When setting lay the two portions together and pull into a long thick "rod". Cut into ½-in. lengths with scissors, turning the sugar ½ a turn at each cut. Wrap separately and store in an airtight tin.

TO CLARIFY SUGAR FOR SYRUP

6 lb. loaf sugar — **1 egg white**
1 qt. water

Dissolve the sugar in the water in a large pan, but do not let it become very hot. Beat the egg white, pour the warm syrup on to it and return to the pan. When the syrup boils, add ½ gill of cold water, repeat 3 times, i.e. in all ½ pt. Reduce heat for about 10 min., then strain through a jelly bag or fine muslin and use as required.

TOFFEE

¼ pt. water — **Lemon essence *or* other flavouring**
1 lb. loaf sugar
Pinch of cream of tartar

Put the water and sugar into a sugar boiler or pan, stir occasionally until dissolved, bring to boiling-point and add the cream of tartar. Boil to the "small crack" degree (**290° F.**), add flavouring and pour into an oiled tin, allow it to cool, then mark off into squares with a knife and when cold break into pieces.

ALMOND TOFFEE

5 oz. almonds
1 lb. loaf sugar
½ pt. water
Pinch of cream of tartar
Almond essence

Blanch and skin the almonds, cut them across in halves, and dry them in the oven without browning. Dissolve the sugar in the water, add the cream of tartar, and boil until a deep amber-coloured syrup is obtained. Remove the pan from the heat, add the almonds, and a few drops of almond essence, boil up again and pour on to a buttered or oiled tin.

COCONUT TOFFEE

¾ lb. granulated sugar
½ lb. demerara sugar
1½ gills water
¼ lb. glucose
¼ lb. desiccated coconut
Flavouring essence

Dissolve the sugars in the water, add the glucose and boil to the "small crack" degree (**290° F.**). Remove the pan from the heat, stir in the coconut, and boil to the "large crack" (**312° F.**). Add a few drops of flavouring essence, and pour on to oiled or buttered tins.

EVERTON TOFFEE

1 lb. demerara sugar
¼ pt. water
Good pinch of cream of tartar
4 oz. butter

Dissolve the sugar in the water, add the cream of tartar, and boil to the "large ball" degree (**247° F.**). Remove the pan from the heat, add the butter in small pieces, then boil to the "small crack" degree (**290° F.**). Pour on to buttered or oiled tins; when sufficiently set mark into squares or oblongs, and when quite cold divide and wrap each piece first in waxed paper and afterwards in tinfoil.

FRENCH TOFFEE

1 pt. golden syrup
¾ lb. granulated sugar
2 tablesp. almonds
2 tablesp. coconut
2 tablesp. vinegar
1 teasp. lemon juice
1 egg

Put the golden syrup and sugar into a sugar boiler or pan and boil to the "large crack" degree (**312° F.**). Add the almonds previously blanched and chopped coarsely, the coconut, vinegar, lemon juice and the well-beaten egg. Replace over the heat, bring to boiling-point and pour on to wetted tins. Mark with a knife as it cools.

GINGER TOFFEE

2 lb. demerara sugar
½ pt. water
1 oz. ground ginger

Dissolve the sugar in the water, bring gently to boiling-point, stirring occasionally at first, and continuously when nearing boiling-point. When the syrup has reached the "small ball" degree (**237° F.**), add the ginger, replace on the heat, stir until it begins to thicken, then pour into a tin lined with well-buttered paper. When cold, cut into diamonds, squares or any other shape required.

LEMON TOFFEE

4 oz. butter
1 lb. granulated sugar
Juice of 1 lemon
Lemon essence

Melt the butter in a pan, add the sugar, boil up slowly, stir and boil for a few minutes, then add 1 teasp. lemon juice. Continue boiling to the "small crack" degree (**290° F.**), add the rest of the lemon juice and a few drops of lemon essence, and pour on to a buttered or oiled tin. Mark into squares while cooling.

RASPBERRY TOFFEE

1 lb. sugar
1 gill cold water
Pinch of cream of tartar
Few drops of cochineal
Few drops raspberry essence

Dissolve the sugar in the water, then add the cream of tartar, bring to boiling-point, skim carefully and boil to the "large crack" degree (**312° F.**). Remove the pan from the heat, stir in the cochineal and raspberry essence, and pour into an oiled or buttered tin. Let it harden stiffly, then mark off into sections and divide when cold.

RUSSIAN TOFFEE

½ lb. loaf sugar	**1 tablesp. redcurrant jelly**
¼ lb. butter	**Vanilla *or* other flavouring**
¼ pt. cream	

Place the sugar, butter and cream in a pan, and stir over a low heat until the mixture thickens and leaves the sides of the pan clean. Add the jelly. Flavour to taste, pour on to an oiled or buttered tin and when cold cut into squares.

TOFFEE APPLES

These are best made in the autumn with the small slightly sour apples available at that time of year.

1 lb. sugar	**2 tablesp. water**
4 oz. butter	**12 apples (approx.)**

Wash the apples and put a clean stick into each so that it feels firm. Put all the ingredients for the toffee into a strong saucepan and allow the sugar to dissolve very slowly over a low heat. Boil to the "small crack" degree (**290° F.**). Dip each apple into cold water, then into the toffee and then into the cold water. Put on to an oiled slab or buttered paper to set. Use immediately as they go sticky on keeping.

TREACLE TOFFEE

1 lb. brown sugar	**2 tablesp. water**
½ lb. treacle	**1 tablesp. orange juice**
2 oz. butter	

Put all the ingredients into a saucepan and allow the sugar to dissolve over a low heat. Boil to the "small crack" degree (**290° F.**) and pour on to a buttered tin. Mark into squares when partially set and break when firm. Wrap in waxed paper and store in an airtight tin.

WALNUT TOFFEE

1 lb. walnuts	**2 lb. golden syrup**
Good pinch of bicarbonate of soda	**1 tablesp. glucose**

Blanch the walnuts, break them into small pieces or chop them coarsely. Dissolve the bicarbonate of soda in a small quantity of hot water. Bring the syrup slowly to boiling-point, add the glucose and boil to the "small crack" degree (**290° F.**). Remove the pan from the heat, stir in the prepared walnuts and bicarbonate of soda, and at once pour on to an oiled or buttered tin. When sufficiently set, mark into sections, and when perfectly cold, divide and wrap each piece in waxed paper.

BAKING

WHEN a housewife describes her domestic activity as "doing a baking", it is generally understood that she is concerned with replenishing her supply of bread, scones, buns, cakes and biscuits, and perhaps including dishes made with pastry to store in her larder.

This is a most interesting and fascinating branch of cookery, giving satisfaction to the producer no less than the consumer. As in the cultivation of flowers there is the person who has the proverbial "green fingers", so in the craft or art of baking there are fortunate people who, without any apparent effort, possess the "light hand" and whose products are of a standard immediately acceptable to all. They start with a great advantage. However, the less fortunate may acquire this skill, particularly if they approach the matter with a good background knowledge of the general requirements for success, together with the determination to "try again" if necessary.

BREAD-MAKING

BREAD has been described as the staff (not the stuff) of life and there is no doubt that the housewife is very dependent upon it for the feeding of her family. It is generally eaten in some form at every meal and helps to give a feeling of sufficiency to the eater. It is important to stress, however, that its consumption with other starchy foods is often out of proportion to what is required by the body and is one of the main causes of obesity. Fat should be eaten with bread as it assists in digesting the fat and producing energy.

Bread is obtained by baking a mixture of flour, water and salt, which is made light and porous by the use of yeast or some other means of aeration. Bread which has not been aerated is known as unleavened bread and is eaten by the Jews in commemoration at their special religious feasts.

Flour used for bread-making is primarily that obtained from the wheat grain, a white flour being obtained when all the outer husk has been removed before grinding. *Wholemeal* is the entire grain ground down. In the case of the latter, the keeping quality may be less good because of the fat content of the flour, but on the other hand a more nutritionally valuable food is obtained. For bread-making a "strong" flour is considered desirable, i.e. a flour with a high protein (gluten) content, a gluten which has cohesiveness and elasticity.

An 80% extraction of the wheat grain is recognized as desirable today and generally satisfies the producer, dietician, baker and housewife. There are other flours used in bread-making, usually in conjunction with wheat because wheat contains much more gluten than any other cereal. Rye can be made into a rather close, heavy bread, dark in colour but it is best combined with wheat. Oat flour, barley flour, maize (corn starch), potato and banana flour can all be used together with wheat. A good quality of wheat flour is creamy in colour, has a pleasant nutty smell, and when pressed with the finger, retains the impression. Buying and storage depend on the rate of consumption.

Yeast: The fermentation method of raising dough involves the use of yeast. The earliest method of aeration was to leave a small portion of dough from one baking to the next so that it could be infected by wild yeasts from the air, this was added to the new dough and so the yeasts grew in the dough forming carbonic acid gas and giving off alcohol.

The yeast which is probably used most in the home is compressed yeast. When in good condition it should have a beery smell and be a fresh putty colour.

In order to produce carbonic acid gas yeast requires warmth, moisture and food—its action is often started by mixing with a small amount of sugar. The action of yeast can be retarded by cold, by coming into direct contact with salt and a high concentration of sugar, and it can be killed entirely by great heat, e.g. too hot water for mixing. One ounce of yeast will raise three and a half pounds of flour in one hour. Milk and fat added to bread make a better keeping product, they also change the appearance and the texture of the bread. Compressed yeast may be stored in a refrigerator for a week or two because, as stated above, its action is only arrested by cold.

Particularly in America another form of yeast is commonly used and is described as "Dry granular". This yeast keeps without refrigeration. It can be bought in tins or packets and instructions for use are stated on the package. The required amount of yeast is mixed with warm water, not *hot* water (optimum temperature is 30° C. just as for compressed yeast) and it is allowed to stand without stirring for five minutes but is stirred before adding to the flour.

It is important to remember that whatever further liquid is being added to mix to the required dough, *all* the prepared yeast must be put in first.

The term "Quick Breads" is used to describe breads which are made with a raising agent which is quick in action, e.g. baking-powder bread raised with baking-powder, soda bread raised with bicarbonate of soda and cream of tartar or other acid, e.g. sour milk, and bread leavened with the latter and cooked by steam. Recipes for "Quick Breads" will be found (p. 503), while many attractive and interesting products raised with yeast are also included.

OTHER RAISING AGENTS USED IN BAKING

Baking-powder is a leavening or raising agent produced by the mixing of an acid reacting material, e.g. tartaric acid and sodium bicarbonate—this is generally blended with some starchy material. The ideal baking-powder gives the most gas (CO_2) for the least volume and weight of powder. It gives the gas slowly when cold and increasingly in the cooking dough—this means that some doughs may be left standing before baking. The baking-powder should leave a tasteless and harmless residue in the bread, etc., and it should not deteriorate in the tin with keeping. Baking-powder is used in the proportion of one to three teaspoonfuls to each pound of flour, depending on the richness of the mixture—usually the plainer the mixture (fewer eggs, less fat) the more baking-powder is required.

Egg powders are just coloured baking powders and must not be confused with dried egg.

Eggs (fresh) act as raising agents because when beaten they possess the property of holding air (a mixture of gases) which expands on heating.

Bicarbonate of Soda and Cream of Tartar (without starchy material as in baking-powders) are used in the making of scones, etc. The proportion used in scones is one teaspoonful bicarbonate of soda and two and a quarter teaspoonfuls cream of tartar to one pound of flour, or equal quantities if sour milk (acid) is used. It is most important to combine the soda with the correct amount of cream of tartar, otherwise the excess soda will affect the colour and taste of the food. The cream of tartar and the bicarbonate of soda can only act upon one another in the presence of moisture, so that they must be kept dry if they are to retain their strength.

Bicarbonate of soda is used sometimes without the cream of tartar, e.g. in the making of gingerbread or treacle pudding, where the resulting dish is required to be brown.

Self-Raising Flour may be used for some things; in this case the raising agent has been added to the flour and *generally* no more is required (p. 510). Self-raising flour is more expensive than plain flour but it has an appeal for the amateur, who in using it feels more assured of success.

YEAST MIXTURES

"*If the baker is kind to the yeast, the yeast will be kind to the baker.*"

IMPORTANT POINTS TO REMEMBER WHEN USING YEAST

1. Yeast being a plant organism (fungus) it requires warmth, moisture and food for growth. Its growth can be completely stopped by great heat, while shrinkage of the yeast buds will be caused by bringing it into contact with too much sugar or salt; and of course it will not grow if too cold. This shows quite clearly that in using yeast the flour, liquid and atmosphere should be just warm.
2. Sufficient moisture is absolutely necessary. A stiff dough will never give a successful result.
3. In most cases the growth of the yeast is started off by creaming it with a small amount of sugar.
4. There are two ways of using yeast in mixtures: (i) by direct mixing with flour and liquid to required dough and (ii) by "setting the sponge"—*see White Bread* (p. 495). The latter is considered to give a better textured bread.
5. The larger the amount of flour used, the smaller proportion of yeast is needed, e.g. where 1 oz. will raise 3½ lb. flour in 1 hour, it will take ½ oz. to raise 1 lb. flour in the same time. Again, the longer the time which can be given for raising the dough, the less yeast proportionately will be required.
6. Where fruit is being added to the dough it may be put in with advantage after the dough has risen for the first time; this prevents it from being squashed by much handling.
7. When dough is rising cover with a clean towel, to prevent surface evaporation.

8. A dough which has been raised too long will become overstretched with gas (CO_2) and will collapse, giving heavy bread.
9. After kneading the dough for a second time, it *must* be allowed to "prove" or recover from the kneading, because some of the gas will have been knocked out of it. If baked immediately after kneading, the dough will be heavy and probably uneatable.
10. When the yeast has done its work and filled the dough with gas to capacity, it must be killed off by great heat, hence the instruction in most cases to bake in a hot oven.

Tests for a good loaf: It should be of good shape, well risen, with a crisp and nicely browned crust, smooth on the bottom and should sound hollow when knocked; when cut the texture should be even with no large holes.

YEAST BREADS

WHOLEMEAL BREAD

3½ lb. wholemeal flour
3½ teasp. salt
1 teasp. sugar
1 oz. yeast
2 oz. lard
1¾ pt. warm water

Mix salt well with flour and make warm in a large basin. Cream the yeast with the sugar, add the warm water, together with the melted fat, and mix with the flour to an elastic dough. Knead well until smooth, cover with a cloth, to prevent surface evaporation, and set in a warm place to rise to double its size—about 1 hr. When the dough is sufficiently risen it has a honeycombed appearance. The first kneading distributes the yeast and softens the gluten of the flour. Knead the dough a second time to distribute the carbonic acid gas which has formed. Continue kneading until, when the dough is cut, there are no large holes in it, but do not knead too heavily. Divide into the number of loaves required. Place in warmed greased tins, making the top round. Prick and allow to prove or recover for 20 min. or until the dough is well up to the top of the tin. If the dough is over-proved it will collapse and give heavy bread. Bake in top middle of a very hot oven (**450° F., Gas 8**), (to kill the yeast), for 10–15 min. then reduce heat to fairly hot (**375° F., Gas 5**), baking in all about 1 hr. When ready the loaf should have a hollow sound when knocked on the bottom, and should be well risen and nicely browned with a crisp crust.

4 loaves
Cooking time—1 hr.

WHOLEMEAL PRUNE BREAD

Ingredients as for wholemeal bread
4–6 oz. chopped prunes
1 small tablesp. grated orange rind *or* grated candied peel
1 oz. sugar

Make as for wholemeal bread. When risen, knead dough and work in the fruit and sugar. Form into loaves and put in greased tins. Prove and bake as for wholemeal bread.

4 loaves
Cooking time—1 hr.

MALTED BROWN BREAD

3½ lb. wholemeal flour
¾ oz. yeast
1 oz. malt extract
3 teasp. salt
1¾ pt. warm water (approx.)

Put the flour into a large bowl and make a well in the centre. Mix the yeast and malt extract in the warm water and pour into the well. Stir in about ¼ of the flour to make a pool of batter (setting the sponge), cover with a clean cloth and leave in a warm place (probably the warmth of the kitchen will do) for

30 min. to 1 hr. At the end of the time sprinkle the salt well round the dry flour and mix all to an elastic dough, knead well, and form into loaves. Put into warmed greased tins and prove till risen well up the tins. Bake in a hot oven (**450°–425° F., Gas 8–7**).

3–4 loaves
Cooking time—45–60 min.

SCOTTISH BROWN BREAD

3¼ lb. wholemeal flour	**2 level teasp. bicarbonate of soda**
¼ lb. oatmeal	**1½–1¾ pt. warm water (approx.)**
3½ teasp. salt	
1 teasp. sugar	
1 oz. yeast	

Mix the wholemeal flour and oatmeal and proceed as for wholemeal bread (p. 494), adding soda dissolved in a little water. Prepare tins by greasing and dusting very thickly with flour. Oval-shaped tins give an attractive-looking loaf. Divide the dough into pieces and put in tins. Press well into shape and smooth on top. Prove for 15 min. or until well risen, with a baking sheet on top. Bake in a very hot oven (**450° F., Gas 8**) with a baking sheet and weight on top, reducing the heat after 20 min. to fairly hot (**375° F., Gas 5**). The finished bread should be floury on the outside.

3–4 loaves
Cooking time—45–60 min.

WHITE BREAD

Basic Recipe

3½ lb. white flour	**1 teasp. sugar**
3½ teasp. salt	**1¾ pt. warm water**
1 oz. yeast	

Grease 3–4 loaf tins and put them to warm. Mix salt and flour well together, cream yeast with the sugar and add to warm water. Make a well in the centre of the flour, pour the liquid into the well and sprinkle on or mix in a little of the flour to form a pool of batter and allow to stand in a warm place for 20 min. Mix to an elastic dough, using more water if required; knead well till the dough leaves the basin clean, and put to rise in a warm place until the dough has doubled its size. Then turn on to a floured board, knead again not too heavily but until there are only small holes in the dough, and put into the prepared tins. Put to prove until the dough is well up the sides of the tin then bake in a hot oven (**425° F., Gas 7**).

3–4 loaves
Cooking time—1 hr.

Variations

Nut Bread

As for white bread. Add 8 oz. chopped nuts—walnuts, peanuts, etc.

Raisin Bread

As for white bread. Add 8 oz. chopped raisins when kneading the dough for the second time.

Sultana Bread

As for white bread. Add 8 oz. sultanas when kneading the dough for the second time.

PULLED BREAD

1 lb. plain flour	**½ teasp. sugar**
1 teasp. salt	**½ oz. yeast**
½ pt. warm water	

Mix salt and flour well together, cream yeast with the sugar and add to warm water. Make a well in the centre of the flour, pour the liquid into the well and sprinkle on or mix in a little of the flour to form a pool of batter and allow to stand in a warm place for 20 min. Mix to an elastic dough, using more water if required; knead well till the dough leaves the basin clean, and put to rise in a warm place until the dough has doubled its size. After dough has risen place in greased bread tin and prove. Bake in a hot oven (**425° F., Gas 7**) for about 20 min. or just long enough to set the dough. Turn it out of the tin and with two forks separate it into irregularly shaped pieces suitable for serving. Place them on a baking-sheet and bake them in a moderate oven (**350° F., Gas 4**) for about 20 min. until crisp and lightly browned.

Cooking time—about 40 min.

SCOTTISH BREAKFAST ROLLS

1 lb. plain flour	**½ teasp. sugar**
1 teasp. salt	**½ oz. yeast**
½ pt. warm water	

Mix salt and flour well together, cream yeast with the sugar and add to warm water. Make a well in the centre of the flour, pour the liquid into the well and sprinkle on or mix in a little of the flour to form a pool of batter and allow to stand in a warm place for 20 min. Mix to an elastic dough, using more water if required; knead well till the dough leaves the basin clean, and put to rise in a warm place until the dough has doubled its size. Divide risen dough into 12 pieces, knead lightly and shape into rounds or ovals. Pat down a little and put to prove on a greased or floured baking sheet. Brush with milk *or* water and dredge with flour. Place in a hot oven **450°–425° F., Gas 8–7).**

12 rolls
Cooking time—15–20 min.

MILK BREAD

Basic Recipe

1 lb. plain flour	**2 oz. lard *or* margarine**
1 teasp. salt	**½ pt. warm milk (approx.)**
½ oz. yeast	**1 egg (optional)**
½ teasp. sugar	

Mix the salt with the warmed flour, cream the yeast with the sugar. Rub fat into flour and mix with the yeast, milk and egg if used, to a fairly soft, light dough. Beat until mixture is smooth and leaves the sides of the basin clean. Allow to stand in a warm place till twice its original size. Proceed as for White Bread (p. 495), or see following recipes.

Variations

Bread Plait

1 lb. plain flour, etc., as for Milk Bread

Roll risen dough into two strips, each 10 in. long by 5 in. or 6 in. wide. Cut each strip almost to the top in three even-sized pieces and plait them as if plaiting hair. Damp and seal the ends neatly but firmly and place on a greased baking-sheet. Allow to prove 10–15 min. Brush with egg wash and place in a hot oven (**450° F., Gas 8**). Bake 20–30 min., reducing heat after first 10 min. to **400° F., Gas 6** or **375° F., Gas 5.**

2 loaves
Cooking time—20–30 min.

Bridge Rolls or Sandwich Buns

1 lb. flour, etc., as for Milk Bread, using 1–2 eggs in mixing the dough

Make the dough as for Milk Bread and divide raised dough into required number of pieces; roll each piece into long finger-shaped buns about 3–3½ in. long. Place on warmed greased baking-sheets and pat down a little to make a good shape. Put the rolls touching one another so that they bake with soft edges. Prove for 10 min., brush with egg and milk and bake in a hot oven (**425° F., Gas 7**).

45–50 rolls
Cooking time—8–10 min.

Cheese Bread Plait

As for Milk Bread, adding 3–4 oz. finely grated cheese with the dry ingredients. Bake as for Bread Plait.

Dinner Buns

1 lb. plain flour, etc., as for Milk Bread

Make the dough as for Milk Bread then divide risen dough into required number of pieces. Shape each into a round, making sure that the underside is smooth. Place on a greased baking-sheet and flatten slightly—keep good shape. Prove for 10–15 min. then brush over with beaten egg and milk. Bake in a hot oven (**425° F., Gas 7**).

20–24 buns
Cooking time—10–15 min.

French Shapes

1 lb. plain flour, etc., as for Milk Bread

Make the dough as for Milk Bread then divide risen dough into required number of pieces, knead lightly and form into shapes, e.g.:

Small plait: Divide the dough into 3 and

shape each into a long roll, plait together sealing ends securely.

Small Twists: Divide dough into 2, shape into long rolls, twist together and secure ends.

Cottage Loaf: Cut off ⅔ of dough and make into bun shape, treat ⅓ in same way. Place smaller one on top of larger one and secure by putting little finger through centre or pierce with a wooden skewer.

"*S*" *Shape:* Make a long roll with the dough and twist into an "S" shape.

Horseshoe Shape: Roll out dough thinly and cut into triangular shapes. Roll up from the base and twist into a horseshoe shape. Pierce with skewer to represent nails.

Allow buns to prove 10–15 min., brush with egg and milk and bake in a hot oven (**425° F., Gas 7**) until cooked through and a rich golden brown.

24–28 shapes
Cooking time—10–15 min.

BRUSSELS BUN

½ lb. plain flour	**1 egg**
¼ teasp. salt	**1 gill warm milk**
1½ oz. lard *or* margarine	**3 oz. almond paste**
1 oz. sugar	**Glacé icing, using 3 oz. icing sugar**
½ oz. yeast	

Make as for Milk Bread (p. 496). Knead risen dough lightly and form into a large cake. Lay the almond paste on half, damp edge and fold in half; prove for 15 min. Bake for 30–40 min. in a hot oven (**425° F., Gas 7**), reducing heat to fairly hot (**375° F., Gas 5**) after 10 min. When cold, coat the top with glacé icing.

Cooking time—30–40 min.

CHERRY BREAD

1 lb. plain flour	**1–2 eggs**
1 teasp. salt	**2 teasp. sugar**
2 oz. lard *or* margarine	**6 oz. roughly chopped glacé cherries**
½ oz. yeast	
½ pt. warm milk (approx.)	

Grease two 6-in. cake-tins and put them to warm. Make the dough as for Milk Bread (p. 496) and mix in the cherries. When the dough has risen to double its size, knead very lightly, shape into 2 loaves and place in the prepared tins. Allow to prove 15 min. or till well up the tin; bake in a hot oven (**425° F., Gas 7**). Reduce heat after 10 min. to fairly hot (**375° F., Gas 5**).

NOTE: If liked the cherries may be worked in after dough has risen the first time.

2 loaves
Cooking time—30 min.

CROISSANTS

1 lb. plain flour	**½ pt. warm milk and water**
½ teasp. salt	**3 oz. margarine**
½ oz. yeast	
1 teasp. sugar	

Make as for Milk Bread (p. 496), omitting margarine. When the dough has risen to double its size, roll out on a floured board three times its width and spread with ⅓ of the margarine, in small pieces. Dredge lightly with flour, fold up ⅓ and down ⅓ (as for flaky pastry) and seal the edges. Repeat with the other ⅔ of margarine. Put the dough in a warm place again to rise for 30 min. Roll the dough out like pastry ⅛ in. thick, and cut into 12 pieces 5 in. square. Turn the squares over so that the smooth side comes outside and damp the surface very lightly with warm water. Beginning at one corner, roll up the square, pressing the opposite corner over to make it stick to the roll. Bend the two ends towards each other to form a crescent. Place on greased trays and allow to prove 15 min. Bake in a fairly hot oven (**425° F., Gas 7**). Brush with egg yolk and milk when almost ready, then dry them off.

12 croissants
Cooking time—15–20 min.

DISTINGUISHED BREAD

1 lb. plain flour	**1 egg**
1 teasp. salt	**1 oz. sugar**
2 oz. lard *or* margarine	**1 teasp. dried sage**
½ oz. yeast	**½ teasp. grated nutmeg**
½ pt. warm milk (approx.)	**1–2 teasp. caraway seeds**

Make the dough as for Milk Bread adding the sage, nutmeg and caraway seeds. When the dough has risen divide into two pieces;

knead lightly, make each into a round, and place in 6 in. cake tins. Prove till well up tin, and bake in a hot oven (**425° F., Gas 7**).

2 loaves
Cooking time—30 min.

GRISSINI BREAD or SALT STICKS

1 lb. plain flour	**½ oz. yeast**
1 teasp. salt	**½ teasp. sugar**
1 oz. margarine *or* lard	**3–4 tablesp. warm milk**
Enough warm water to make a fairly stiff dough	

Make as for Milk Bread (p. 496); allow to rise for 1–1½ hr. Form into long sticks 6–8 in. in length and when proved brush with egg white, bake in a hot oven (**425° F., Gas 7**) until crisp.

If liked, they may be brushed with milk and sprinkled with a little coarse salt before baking.

12 sticks
Cooking time—20–30 min.

YEAST BUNS

BATH BUNS

1 lb. plain flour	**Good ½ oz. yeast**
½ teasp. salt	**3 oz. sugar**
3 oz. fat—margarine and lard	**2 eggs**
	1½–2 gills warm milk

GLAZE

1 tablesp. water	**1 dessertsp. sugar**

Mix salt with warmed flour and rub in fat. Mix in most of the sugar. Mix to a light dough with yeast creamed with remainder of sugar, egg and milk. Put to rise till double its size, then knead lightly. Divide into 24 pieces and shape each 3½–4 in. long and 1 in. wide. Place fairly close together (so that they join up in baking) on greased baking-sheets and prove 15 min. Bake in a hot oven (**425° F., Gas 7**) 10–15 min.

To make the glaze—boil together the water and sugar until *slightly syrupy*. Brush the buns immediately they come from the oven so that the syrup dries on.

Dredge thickly with castor sugar. Break buns apart before serving.

NOTE: 2 oz. sultanas and 1 oz. chopped peel may be worked into the dough after it has risen.

24 buns
Cooking time—10–15 min.

BRIOCHE ROLLS

1 lb. plain flour	**4 eggs**
½ teasp. salt	**1 oz. castor sugar**
½ oz. yeast	**6 oz. margarine**
2–3 tablesp. tepid water	

Sift the warmed flour and salt into a basin, make a well in the middle and pour in the creamed yeast and tepid water. Allow to sponge in a warm place for about 30 min. Add the eggs, sugar and slightly warmed margarine and mix all together with additional tepid water to make a soft pliable dough. Allow dough to rise 1–2 hr., until it has doubled its size. Take ⅔ and divide it into 20–24 large balls. Divide the remaining ⅓ into 20–24 small balls. Grease patty tins, place a large ball on each tin and flatten slightly, make a small depression, damp it and fix a small ball on top. Put the little finger through the centre. Leave the rolls in a warm place to prove for 20 min. Brush with egg and sprinkle with salt, or if wanted sweet, with sugar. Bake in a hot oven (**425° F., Gas 7**).

20–24 rolls
Cooking time—15–20 min.

CHELSEA BUNS (I)

½ lb. plain flour	**½ oz. currants *or* sultanas**
¼ teasp. salt	
1 oz. lard *or* margarine	**½ oz. chopped candied peel**
½ oz. yeast	
1 gill warm milk	**1 oz. sugar**

Mix flour and salt; rub in fat, cream yeast and add to flour, with warm milk. Beat well and put to rise to double its size. Knead risen dough lightly and roll out in a square of about 10 in. Sprinkle with the fruit and sugar and roll up like a Swiss roll. Cut roll into 7 pieces and put cut side uppermost. Place buns in a greased 8 in. sandwich cake tin so that they will join together when cooked and allow to prove till up to the top of the tin. Brush with milk or egg, bake in a hot oven (**425° F., Gas 7**)

20–25 min. Make sure they are cooked well in the bottom. When buns are ready, brush over with glaze as for Bath Buns (p. 498), and dust with castor sugar. Break buns apart when cool.

7 buns
Cooking time—20–25 min.

CHELSEA BUNS (2)

1 lb. plain flour	**2 oz. sugar**
½ teasp. salt	**2 oz. margarine *or* lard**
½ oz. yeast	**1 oz. currants**
½ pt. tepid milk	**½ oz. chopped peel**
1 egg	

Mix sifted flour and salt, making a well in the centre of the flour. Crumble the yeast and mix it with ½ teasp. of sugar and about ½ gill of the warm milk; pour this into the well and add a very little flour to make a thin batter. Cover, and allow to stand in a warm place for 30 min. Add the rest of the milk, egg, sugar and melted fat and beat up to a light dough. Cover, and put to rise for 30 min. Work in the currants and chopped or shredded peel and make into buns of even size and shape. Place on a greased baking-sheet and prove for a further 10 min. Brush over with sweetened milk *or* egg and milk and bake in a hot oven **(425° F., Gas 7).**

16–20 buns
Cooking time—20–25 min.

DOUGHNUTS

½ lb. plain flour	**½ oz. yeast**
¼ teasp. salt	**½–¾ gill warm milk**
2 oz. margarine (*or* ¾ oz. lard and 1 oz. margarine)	**1 egg**
	Cinnamon sugar for coating
1 oz. castor sugar	**Fat for deep frying**

Rub the fat into the warmed flour and salt; add sugar, having taken out ½ teasp. to cream the yeast. Add the warm milk and egg to the creamed yeast and pour into the flour. Mix well (do not make too soft as the dough is to be cut out), and put to rise to double its size. Knead lightly and roll out ½ in. thick. Cut into rings, using 2½–2¾ in. cutter for outside and 1½–1¾ in. for inner ring, and prove on warm tray for 5 min. Drop into very faintly smoking fat and cook 5 min.; drain well and toss in castor sugar *or* sugar mixed with ground cinnamon to taste.

NOTE: Proving may be unnecessary, the first doughnuts may be ready to fry by the time the last are cut out.

14–16 doughnuts

Alternative Method: Divide dough into 12. Roll each piece into a ball and place a glacé cherry or a little jam in the middle. Prove 10 min. and proceed as above.

"ESS" BUNS

1 lb. plain flour	**1 oz. yeast**
½ teasp. salt	**Small ½ pt. warm milk**
Good 1 oz. sugar	**Crushed lump sugar for top**
4–6 oz. margarine	
2 eggs	

Mix sifted flour, sugar and salt together. Cream the margarine and add the egg and flour. Add creamed yeast and enough warm milk to make of the consistency of very thick batter. Allow to rise about 30 min. Divide into 24 pieces, roll each under the hand to about 6 in. long, then roll up into the shape of the letter "S". Put to prove on greased trays. When proved brush with egg wash and sprinkle with crushed sugar. Bake in a hot oven **(450°–425° F., Gas 8–7).**

24 buns
Cooking time—15–20 min.

HOT CROSS BUNS

1 lb. plain flour	**½ oz. yeast**
½ teasp. salt	**1–2 eggs**
2 oz. margarine *or* margarine and lard	**1½–2 gills milk**
	2 oz. currants *or* 2 oz. raisins and peel
4 oz. sugar	
1 teasp. mixed spice *or* cinnamon	**Short crust pastry**

Mix salt with warmed flour. Rub in fat. Add sugar, spice, creamed yeast, and eggs with the warm milk. Mix to a soft, light dough, beat well and put to rise. When well risen, knead the dough lightly, working in the fruit, and divide into 20–24 pieces. Form into round shapes, flatten slightly and put to prove for 15 min. Cut narrow strips of pastry 1½–2 in. long, brush tops of buns with egg wash *or* milk, place pastry crosses on top and bake in a hot oven (**425° F., Gas 7**).

NOTE: If there is no pastry available cut a deep cross on each bun.

20–24 buns
Cooking time—15–20 min.

LUXEMBURG BUNS

Make as for Bath Buns (p. 498). Do not glaze, but when cold, spread tops with glacé icing (p. 547). The buns look attractive if made round in shape.

PACE ROLLS

1 lb. plain flour	**½ oz. yeast**
½ teasp. salt	**2–2½ gills milk**
3 oz. moist sugar	**3–4 oz. margarine**

Mix the flour, salt and sugar together. Make a well in the centre of the flour and add the crumbled yeast and 1 gill milk; mix this with a small amount of the flour to form a pool of batter. Allow to stand in a warm place till well sponged, 20–30 min. Warm the margarine to softness (not to oil) and add to dough with enough milk to make a spongy mixture. Form into buns the size of an egg, lay them in rows 2 in. apart and allow to prove till double their size. Bake in a hot oven (**450° F., Gas 8**).

When ready they may be rubbed over with margarine.

20–24 rolls
Cooking time—15–20 min.

PIKELETS (SOMETIMES CALLED CRUMPETS)

½ lb. plain flour	**½ pt. milk and water**
½ teasp. salt	**Pinch of bicarbonate of soda**
½ oz. yeast	
½ teasp. sugar	

Warm the flour and mix with the salt. Cream yeast with sugar, add to the warmed milk and water and mix with flour to consistency of a soft batter. Cover and leave to rise 30–45 min. Dissolve the soda in 1 tablesp. warm water, add to the mixture, beating well, and put to rise again for 30 min. Grease a girdle, thick frying-pan or electric hot plate and heat until fairly hot. Grease pikelet rings or large plain cutters (3½–4 in.), place on the girdle and pour in enough batter to cover the bottom of ring to a depth of ¼ in. When top is set and bubbles burst, turn and cook on underside.

Serve hot with butter.

8–10 pikelets

PRINCESS ROLLS

¾ lb. warm plain flour	**1 teasp. castor sugar**
¾ pt. milk	**10 oz. extra flour (approx.)**
4 oz. margarine	
2 tablesp. castor sugar	**Extra butter *or* margarine**
½ teasp. salt	
Good ½ oz. yeast	

Heat the milk, 4 oz. margarine, 2 tablesp. sugar and salt, till lukewarm. Cream the yeast with the teasp. sugar and add to the milk. Mix the milk mixture with the ¾ lb. warm flour and beat well. Cover and leave in a warm place till well risen. Add enough extra flour to enable the dough to be kneaded and put to rise again. Knead lightly on a floured board and roll out to ⅓ in. in thickness. Allow the dough to shrink for a few minutes, then cut into rounds 2½–3 in. in diameter. Put a very small piece of butter on one half of the round, fold over the other half and press the edges together very tightly. Put the rolls on a greased oven tray and allow to prove 15 min. Bake in a hot oven (**425° F., Gas 7**).

30–36 rolls
Cooking time—15–20 min.

RAILWAY BUNS

1 lb. plain flour	**2 oz. lard *or* margarine**
1 teasp. salt	**½ pt. warm milk (approx.)**
½ oz. yeast	
1 oz. sugar	**1 egg (optional)**

Mix the salt with the warmed flour, cream the yeast with the sugar. Rub fat into flour and mix with the yeast, milk and egg if used, to a fairly soft, light dough. Beat until mixture is smooth and leaves the sides of the basin clean. Allow to stand in a warm place till twice its original size.

When dough is risen, roll out $\frac{1}{2}$ in. thick and cut into squares or fingers or stamp out with 2–2$\frac{1}{2}$ in. cutter. Put on to greased tins and allow to prove 10 min. Bake in a hot oven **(425° F., Gas 7)** 8–10 min. and when cooked rub over with margarine.

These make good sandwiches for a journey.

24 buns
Cooking time—8–10 min.

TEA CAKES

Brioches plates

1 lb. plain flour	**1 oz. sugar**
½ teasp. salt	**½ pt. warm milk**
2 oz. lard and margarine	**2–3 oz. currants (if liked)**
½ oz. yeast	

Sift warm flour and salt and rub in the fat. Cream the yeast with the sugar, add the warm milk to it and mix with the flour and fruit to a light elastic dough. Put to rise to double its size. Divide risen dough into 4–6 pieces, knead each into a round and roll out to the size of a tea plate. Place on greased baking sheets, prick the top neatly, and allow to prove for 15 min. Bake in a hot oven **(425° F., Gas 7)** for 20–25 min.

If liked the cakes may be brushed with egg and water before baking or rubbed over with margarine after baking.

4–6 cakes

WAFFLES

Gaufres

8 oz. plain flour	**1 pt. milk**
¼ teasp. salt	**2 oz. margarine**
¾ oz. yeast	**2–3 eggs**
½ teasp. sugar	

Sift flour and salt into a bowl. Cream the yeast with the sugar and add to it the warm milk and margarine; beat the eggs. Add the yeast, milk and egg to the flour, using more milk if required to make a pouring batter. Set aside to rise for 30–45 min. Heat and grease the waffle iron and pour in enough batter to fill the iron sections—the lid must press on the batter. The waffles are ready when nicely browned.

Serve hot with maple or ordinary syrup.

30–40 waffles

YEAST CAKES, ETC.

BUN LOAF

½ lb. plain flour	**1 oz. peel**
½ teasp. salt	**½ oz. yeast**
1 oz. margarine *or* lard	**½ teasp. sugar**
¼ teasp. mixed spice	**1¼ gills warm milk *or* enough to make a very soft mixture**
1 oz. sugar	**1 egg**
1–2 oz. currants *or* sultanas	

Mix salt with warmed flour, and rub in the fat. Add the spice, 1 oz. sugar, currants and peel. Cream the yeast with the $\frac{1}{2}$ teasp. sugar, add the dry ingredients and mix with the milk and egg to a very soft consistency. Pour into a well-greased 6-in. cake-tin and allow to rise almost to the top of the tin. Place in the top middle of a hot oven **(425° F., Gas 7)** for 10 min., then reduce heat to fairly hot **(375° F., Gas 5)** and bake an extra 20 min. until golden brown and cooked through. Brush the top with sugar and water glaze (1 dessertsp. sugar to 1 tablesp. water boiled to slight syrup), and dust with castor sugar. Avoid over-raising.

Cooking time—30 min.

CHRISTMAS BREAD

Pains de Noël

1 lb. plain flour	**¾ oz. yeast**
¼ teasp. salt	**3 eggs**
4 oz. margarine	**1½–2 gills warm milk**
½ teasp. cinnamon	**4 oz. sultanas**
¼ teasp. mixed spice	**4 oz. raisins**
3 oz. sugar	**2 oz. currants**

Sift together the warmed flour and salt; rub in the margarine. Add other dry ingredients (not fruit) to flour and mix to a light dough with the yeast creamed with a little of the sugar, eggs and milk. Beat well. Put to rise to double its size then work in the fruit. Put into greased tins (two 6 in. *or* one 8 in. *or* 10 in.) and allow to prove till well up in the tin. Bake in a fairly hot oven (**400°–380° F., Gas 6–5**) for ¾–1¼ hr. depending on size of loaf. When loaf is almost ready, brush over with sugar and water glaze. Return to oven for 5 min.

1 large or 2 small loaves
Cooking time—50–80 min.

DOUGH CAKE

¾ lb. plain flour	**2 teasp. allspice and mixed spice**
¼ teasp. salt	**8 oz. moist sugar**
6 oz. margarine	**1 oz. yeast**
8 oz. currants and raisins	**¾ pt. milk**

Mix the warmed flour with salt and rub the margarine into the flour. Add the fruit, all-spice and sugar, leaving a little sugar to cream with the yeast. Cream the yeast and mix with most of the warm milk; add to the dry ingredients and mix to a spongy light dough; adding more milk if necessary. Knead it well and put into two 6 in. greased tins. Allow to prove for 1 hr. *or* until well risen. Bake in a fairly hot oven (**400° F., Gas 6**).

2 cakes
Cooking time—1 hr.

SAFFRON CAKE

Small ½ oz. yeast	**A good pinch of saffron (infuse the saffron with ⅛ pt. of the warm water)**
½ pt. warm water	**4–6 oz. currants and raisins**
1 lb. plain flour	
½ teasp. salt	
6–8 oz. margarine	
4 oz. sugar	
2 eggs	

Cream the yeast and add the warm water to it. Stir into it enough sifted flour to make a nice soft dough. Knead it well and leave to rise in a warm place. When well risen, take the remaining flour and salt, and rub the fat into it; add the sugar, eggs and fermented dough, together with the strained saffron liquor. Knead this well and work in the currants, and stoned raisins. Put the dough into two greased ½ lb. cake-tins and leave to rise well. Bake in a fairly hot to moderate oven (**400°–350° F., Gas 6–4**) for 1–1½ hr.

2 cakes

SALLY LUNN

½ lb. plain flour	**½ oz. yeast**
¼ teasp. salt	**1 egg**
1½ oz. margarine	**1 gill warm milk (approx.)**
½ teasp. sugar	

Mix flour and salt, rub in the fat. Cream yeast with sugar, add to it the egg and milk and make a very soft dough with the flour, beat well. Put mixture in greased Sally Lunn rings on tins—2 small *or* 1 large—and allow to rise till well up the tin. Bake in a fairly hot oven (**425°–400° F., Gas 7–6**) for 20–30 min.

2 small *or* 1 large Sally Lunn

SCANDINAVIAN TEA RING

6 oz. plain flour	**Small ½ oz. yeast**
¼ teasp. salt	**½–¾ gill warm milk**
½ oz. sugar	**½–1 egg**

FILLING

1 oz. ground almonds	**Hot water to mix to a spreading consistency**
1 oz. castor sugar	

ICING

3 oz. sifted icing sugar	**Warm water to mix**

DECORATION

½ oz. blanched and chopped almonds

Mix flour and salt; add most of the sugar. Cream yeast with remainder of sugar, add warm milk and egg and mix with flour to a light but workable dough. Put dough to rise and when well risen roll out in an oblong shape. Spread with almond mixture; damp edges with water and roll up. Form into a ring or horseshoe shape; prove 10–15 min. Bake in a hot oven (**425° F., Gas 7**), reducing the heat after 10 min. to fairly hot (**375° F., Gas 5**). When cold, spread with icing and sprinkle with chopped almonds.

Cooking time—20–30 min.

SWEET BREAD TWIST

½ lb. plain flour	**Small ½ oz. yeast**
¼ teasp. salt	**½ teasp. sugar**
1 oz. lard *or* margarine	**1 gill warm milk**
1½ oz. sugar	**1 egg**

GLAZE

¼ oz. margarine	½ dessertsp. honey
½ oz. icing sugar	

Rub fat into flour and salt; add 1½ oz. sugar. Cream yeast with ½ teasp. sugar, add to warm milk with egg. Mix to a light dough and put to rise till double its size. Knead risen dough and form into a roll 2–2½ ft. long. Wind roll into a large sandwich cake tin, beginning at outside; then prove 10–15 min.

Melt together the ingredients for the glaze and brush over the roll. Bake in a fairly hot oven (**400° F., Gas 6**) reducing the heat to **375° F., Gas 5** after the first 10 min.

NOTE: Too hot an oven may cause glaze to burn.

Cooking time—20–30 min.

YEAST FRUIT CAKE (1)

¾ lb. plain flour	1 gill milk
¼ teasp. salt	2 oz. margarine
1 oz. yeast	6 oz. currants
4 oz. moist sugar	1 oz. shredded peel
1½ eggs	

Warm flour and salt. Cream yeast with a little sugar. Beat the eggs. Warm the milk and melt the margarine in it. Add the remainder of the sugar to the flour and mix to a smooth dough with milk, eggs and yeast. Put to rise to double its size, then work in the currants and shredded peel. Put dough into two greased cake-tins 6 in. in diameter (*or* 1 large tin if wished) and leave to rise till well up in the tins. Bake in a fairly hot oven (**400° F., Gas 6**) at first, then reduce heat to moderate (**350° F., Gas** 4).

1 large *or* 2 small cakes
Cooking time—45–60 min.

YEAST FRUIT CAKE (2)

½ oz. yeast	1 oz. chopped peel
4 oz. sugar	¼ teasp. ground cinnamon
3 oz. margarine	
1 egg	¼ teasp. ground nutmeg
6 oz. plain flour	¼ teasp. bicarbonate of soda
4 oz. semolina *or* ground rice	¾–1 gill milk
½ lb. dried fruit	

Cream the yeast with ½ teasp. of the sugar. Cream the fat and remainder of sugar, add the beaten egg and yeast. Mix flour, semolina, fruit and spices, and add to the mixture. Lastly, stir in the soda, dissolved in the milk. Place mixture in a greased cake-tin and bake in a fairly hot to moderate oven (**400°–350° F., Gas 6–4**) for 1¼–1½ hr.

YULE CAKE

Gâteau de Noël

1 lb. plain flour	½ pt. lukewarm milk
¼ teasp. salt	1 egg
4 oz. margarine *or* margarine and lard	¾ oz. yeast
	¾ lb. sultanas
½ level teasp. grated nutmeg	2 oz. chopped candied peel
4 oz. sugar	

Warm flour and salt and rub in the fat; add nutmeg and sugar, leaving 1 teasp. of sugar to cream with the yeast. Pour the warm milk on to the beaten egg and add to the flour with the creamed yeast. Mix to a light elastic dough and knead well. Allow to rise to double its size, then work in the fruit. Place in a greased 8 in. cake-tin and put to prove. When well risen bake in a fairly hot oven (**400° F., Gas 6**) at first, then reduce heat to moderate (**350° F., Gas 4**). Protect with paper if browning too much.

1 cake
Cooking time—1¼–1½ hr.

QUICK BREADS

BAKING-POWDER BREAD

1 lb. plain flour	Milk to mix to light spongy dough—average ½ pt.
1 teasp. salt	
2 oz. lard *or* margarine	
2 round *or* 4 level teasp. baking-powder	

Sift the flour and salt and rub in the fat until quite fine. Add the baking-powder and mix very lightly with the milk. Shape into small loaves or bake in two greased 6-in. cake-tins. Put into a hot oven **450°–425° F., Gas 8–7**).

Cooking time (Small loaves)—10–15 min.
(Large loaves)—25–30 min.

CANADIAN DATE LOAF

½ lb. plain flour
⅛ teasp. salt
2 level teasp. bicarbonate of soda
2½ oz. moist sugar
2½ oz. sultanas *or* raisins
2 oz. chopped walnuts
¼ pt. boiling water
1 lb. stoned dates
½ oz. margarine
1 egg
½ teasp. vanilla essence

Sift flour with salt and mix with other dry ingredients (not the dates). Pour the boiling water over the chopped dates and margarine and allow to cool for a few minutes. Add all the ingredients to the dates and mix thoroughly with the egg and essence. Bake in a greased loaf-tin in a fairly hot oven (**400°–350° F., Gas 6–4**).

1 loaf **Cooking time—40–60 min.**

DATE AND WALNUT LOAF

14 oz. plain flour
¼ teasp. salt
½ lb. chopped dates
4 oz. sugar
2 oz. margarine
2 level teasp. bicarbonate of soda
1½ gills boiling water
1 egg
2 oz. chopped walnuts
1 teasp. vanilla essence

Sift together the flour and salt. Put chopped dates (weigh after stoning), sugar, margarine and soda in a mixing bowl and pour the boiling water over; stir thoroughly. Add the egg, flour, walnuts and essence and beat well. Bake in a greased cake tin or large loaf tin in a fairly hot oven (**400°–350° F., Gas 6–4**).

1 loaf **Cooking time—1–1½ hr.**

MALT BREAD

1 lb. self-raising flour
2 level teasp. bicarbonate of soda
4 tablesp. golden syrup
4 tablesp. malt extract
½ pt. milk
2 eggs
2 teacups sultanas *or* raisins

Sift the flour and soda into a bowl. Melt syrup and malt in a pan with the milk and add with beaten eggs to the flour; lastly add the fruit. Pour into greased tins (cake- or bread-tins) and bake in a fairly hot oven (**400°–375° F., Gas 6–5**).

2 medium loaves **Cooking time—40–50 min.**

NORTH RIDING BREAD

1 lb. plain flour
¼ teasp. salt
4 teasp. baking-powder
¼ nutmeg (grated)
3–4 oz. lard
6 oz. demerara sugar
6 oz. currants
6 oz. raisins
3 oz. chopped mixed peel
1 tablesp. treacle
½ teasp. almond essence
½ pt. milk

Sift the flour and salt, baking-powder and nutmeg; rub in the lard and add the sugar and fruit. Stir the treacle and essence into the milk and mix all to a soft dough. Divide into two small bread- or cake-tins (½ lb. size) and bake in a fairly hot oven (**400°–375° F., Gas 6–5**).

NOTE: This bread is better if kept in a tin for a week before use.

2 loaves **Cooking time—45–60 min.**

NUT AND RAISIN BREAD

¾ lb. wholemeal flour
¼ teasp. salt
2 oz. lard *or* dripping *or* margarine
2 round teasp. baking powder
2 oz. sugar
2 oz. sultanas
4 oz. chopped nuts
1 egg
½ pt. milk

Rub the fat into the sifted flour and salt. Add remaining dry ingredients and mix to a fairly soft dough with egg and milk. Put into a well-greased tin (bread- or cake-tin) and bake in a fairly hot oven (**400°–375° F., Gas 6–5**).

1 loaf **Cooking time—1 hr.**

SOUR MILK BREAD

1 lb. plain flour
1 teasp. salt
1 round *or* 2 level teasp. bicarbonate of soda
1 round *or* 2 level teasp. cream of tartar
½ pt. sour milk *or* buttermilk (approx.)
2 oz. lard may be rubbed in; this makes a better keeping bread

Sift the flour and salt, and, if required, rub in the fat. Add the soda and tartar, making quite sure that all the lumps are sifted out of the soda. Mix to a light spongy dough with the milk. Divide the dough and form into two round cakes. Place on a greased baking sheet and bake in a hot oven (**450°–425° F., Gas 8–7**).

2 loaves **Cooking time—30 min.**

SCONES

THE otherwise good cook sometimes finds considerable difficulty in producing really light, well-shaped, nicely-browned scones, and there is no doubt that, as in pastry-making, the "light hand" is particularly essential to good results. However that may be, much success can be achieved by following the simple rules given below. Basic proportions are stated there, together with many ways in which the foundation may be varied.

It is not economically sound to heat an oven solely for making a few scones for tea, and this is where the girdle will be found a good cooking substitute. Even a strong frying-pan will do, and, of course, many people use the electric hot-plate, which is very satisfactory if carefully controlled. There is a non-grease girdle on the market, which is pleasant to use and makes for successful results if the makers' instructions are obeyed.

The plain oven scone recipe can be used for girdle cookery but it is important to remember that there is only contact heat in this case, in comparison with radiated heat and convection currents in the oven—consequently the dough must be rolled out more thinly than for oven scones.

A good method of greasing a girdle is to tie a piece of suet (hard fat) in muslin and rub the heated surface with this; it lasts for a considerable time, as suet has a high melting-point. When a girdle is hot the greased surface should show a *faint* haze rising from it. Another method of testing a hot girdle is to sprinkle on a little flour—if the flour browns within a few seconds the girdle is ready for use.

IMPORTANT POINTS TO REMEMBER WHEN MAKING SCONES

1. If the basic proportions are correct they can be varied in many different ways—see suggestions.
2. It is most essential to be accurate with proportions, e.g. too much soda will ruin the scones.
3. Whereas yeast mixtures are kept warm, scones etc. made with other raising agents should be kept as *cool* as possible. The cold air expands with the heat and so helps to make the scones lighter.
4. The best utensil for mixing scones is a round-bladed knife; it gets well down to the bottom of the bowl and can be used for mixing without *pressing* on the mixture.
5. The most important rule is to add *all* the liquid *at once* and mix lightly to a spongy dough.

6. The scones should be handled as little and as lightly as possible.
7. Scones should be cooked quickly—10 minutes in a hot oven for small scones and 15 minutes for a round of 4 or 6.
8. Cool oven scones on a cooling tray to keep the outside crisp. Girdle scones are best cooled in a tea towel to keep the skin soft.

NOTE: From experiment it has been found that better results are obtained if the scones are allowed to stand (after cutting out) for 10 minutes before cooking. This applies to scones raised with bicarbonate of soda and cream of tartar.

PLAIN SCONES

Basic Recipe

1 lb. plain flour | **2–3 oz. lard *or* margarine**
½ teasp. salt

and

2 level teasp. bicarbonate of soda and 4½ level teasp. cream of tartar with ½ pt. fresh milk

or

2 level teasp. bicarbonate of soda and 2 level teasp. cream of tartar with ½ pt. sour *or* butter milk

or

4–6 level teasp. baking-powder with ½ pt. fresh milk

Sift flour and salt and lightly rub in the fat; sift in the raising agents and mix well. Add *all the milk at once* and mix *lightly* to a *spongy* dough. Knead very lightly to make the dough smooth and roll out ½–¾ in. thick. Cut out with a 2-in. cutter, brush with egg *or* milk, if desired, and bake in a hot oven (**425°–450° F., Gas 7–8**). The dough may be divided into 4 and each piece formed into a round cake and marked into 6 with a knife.

24–30 scones
Cooking time—about 10 min.

Variations of Basic Recipe

Cheese Scones

Add 4–6 oz. grated cheese to above proportions. Cut out in finger-shapes or squares.

Cheese Whirls

Add 4–6 oz. grated cheese to the basic recipe.

Roll out dough into oblong shape. Spread with cheese and roll up like a Swiss Roll. Cut into slices and lay on greased baking-sheets with the cut side uppermost. Brush with milk or egg. If any cheese is left over, sprinkle it on and bake the whirls in a hot oven (**425°–450° F., Gas 7–8**).

20–24 scones
Cooking time—10–15 min.

Fruit Scones (Plate 20)

Add 2 oz. sugar and 2-4 oz. fruit (currants, sultanas, etc.) to the basic recipe.

Girdle Scones

Galettes

Add 2–3 oz. currants; roll out ¼ in. thick, cut into 2½ in. rounds or triangles; cook on both sides on a moderately hot girdle about 5 min. till nicely brown and edges dry. Cool in a towel.

Nut Scones

Add 2–4 oz. chopped nuts to the basic or to the wholemeal recipe.

Sweet Scones

Add 2 oz. sugar and, if liked, 1 egg.

Treacle Scones

Add 1 oz. sugar, 1 teasp. ground cinnamon, 1 teasp. mixed spice, 2 tablesp. black treacle. Put the treacle in with ⅔ of the milk, then add the rest as required.

Wholemeal Nut Scones

Use half wholemeal flour and half plain flour, add 2–4 oz. chopped nuts.

Wholemeal Scones

Use half wholemeal flour and half plain flour.

CREAM SCONES

8 oz. plain flour
¼ teasp. salt
3 oz. butter *or* margarine
1 level teasp. bicarbonate of soda
2 level teasp. cream of tartar plus ⅛ teasp.
½ gill milk
½ gill cream

Sift flour and salt and rub in the fat, add the raising agents. Mix to a light dough with milk and cream. Roll out ½–¾ in. thick, cut in rounds with cutter 2–2½ in. in diameter, place on greased baking-sheet and brush with milk or egg wash. Bake in a very hot oven **(450° F., Gas 8).**

12 scones **Cooking time—10–15 min.**

DROPPED SCONES

6 oz. plain flour
⅛ teasp. salt
1½ oz. sugar
2 eggs
1 gill milk (approx.)
1 level teasp. bicarbonate of soda
2 level teasp. cream of tartar

Mix flour, salt and sugar together, add eggs and enough milk to make a thick batter. Beat well. Stir in the dry bicarbonate of soda and cream of tartar. Drop in spoonfuls on a hot greased girdle—allow 1 dessertsp. for a small scone and 1 tablesp. for a large one. Drop from the point of the spoon to keep the scone a good shape. When there are bubbles appearing and the scone is brown on the underside, turn with a broad knife, straighten the edges and brown on the second side. Cook for 2 min. and cool in a tea-towel.

12–20 scones

FARM HOUSE SCONES

1 lb. self-raising flour
½ teasp. salt
2 level teasp. bicarbonate of soda
2 level teasp. cream of tartar
1–2 eggs
¾–1 pt. milk

Sift flour, salt and raising agents into a bowl. Mix to a very thick batter with the milk and egg—do not make the scones so soft that they cannot be lifted. Place a tablespoon of the batter on a thickly floured board and dust the top with more flour. Lift the scone in the hands and drop on to a well-floured girdle or electric hot-plate. Pat into a round shape. The girdle should be moderately hot. Cook on one side till well risen; turn over and cook the other side. When ready they should be slightly coloured, very floury and the edges should be cooked. Cool on a towel.

NOTE: When the flour on the girdle becomes brown, remove and reflour.

16–20 scones

GEORDIE'S SCONES

8 oz. plain flour
¼ teasp. salt
4 oz. fat—usually lard
½ teasp. baking-powder
3 oz. currants
¾ gills milk (approx.)

Rub fat into flour and salt; add baking-powder and currants. Mix to a stiff consistency with milk. Roll into two large cakes ½ in. thick, place on girdle and cook rather slowly until first side is browned; turn over and cook the other side. Test for readiness—there should be no soft mixture at edges. When cooked cut into wedges, butter and serve hot. Alternatively the dough may be cut into 2½ in. rounds.

2 large rounds *or* 15–20 small

INVERARY MUFFINS

1 lb. plain flour
¼ teasp. salt
1½ level teasp. bicarbonate of soda
3 level teasp. cream of tartar
2 oz. sugar
3 oz. margarine
1 egg
1½–2 gills buttermilk *or* sour milk

Sift flour, salt, bicarbonate of soda and cream of tartar into a bowl. Add sugar, melted margarine and egg and make into a soft dough with buttermilk. Roll out ½ in. thick, and cut into rounds 3–3½ in. across and cook both sides on a greased girdle.

Serve hot or cold.

12–16 muffins

ITALIAN SCONES

1 lb. plain flour	**3 level teasp. cream of tartar**
¼ teasp. salt	**1–1½ gills milk**
4 oz. margarine	**Jam**
4 oz. castor sugar	
1½ level teasp. bicarbonate of soda	

Sift the flour and salt, rub in the fat and add the sugar. Sift and add raising agents and mix to a fairly stiff consistency with the milk. Divide the mixture into two pieces and roll each into a square. Spread one square with jam and place the other square on top, brush with egg wash and mark with a knife. Bake in a hot oven (**450°–425° F., Gas 8–7**). Cut when cold.

12–15 scones
Cooking time—10 min.

LARDY JOHNS

8 oz. plain flour	**3 level teasp. baking-powder**
Pinch of salt	**Cold water *or* milk to mix**
4 oz. lard	
4 teasp. sugar	
1 oz. currants	

Sift flour and salt and rub in the lard. Add the other dry ingredients and mix to a fairly soft dough with the milk or water. Roll out ¾ in. thick, score on top and cut into 2-in. squares, brush with egg wash. Place on a greased baking-sheet and bake in a hot oven (**450°–425° F., Gas 8–7**).

10–12 scones
Cooking time—10 min.

POTATO SCONES

½ lb. cold cooked potatoes	**Salt**
½ oz. margarine	**3 oz. plain flour (approx.)**

Sift or mash potatoes very smoothly and mix with the melted margarine and salt—the amount of the latter depends on how much salt has been used in cooking the potatoes. The scones are very tasteless unless there is some salt in the mixture. Work in as much flour as the paste will take up and roll out very thinly. Cut into rounds with a 3½-in. cutter, or triangles, and prick well. Place on a moderately hot girdle and cook for 3 min. on each side. Cool in a towel.

If desired, scones may be buttered and served hot.

8–10 scones

TEA SCONES

8 oz. plain flour	**1 level teasp. bicarbonate of soda**
¼ teasp. salt	**2 eggs**
2 oz. margarine	**Water or milk to make a light spongy mixture (average ½–¾ gill)**
2 oz. castor sugar	
2 level teasp. cream of tartar	

Sift the flour and salt and lightly rub in the fat. Add the other dry ingredients and mix with the beaten eggs and water to make a light spongy dough. Roll out ¼ in. thick and cut into rounds. Bake on a greased, fairly hot girdle or in a hot oven (**450°–425° F., Gas 8–7**). If the scones are to be baked in the oven, roll the dough ½ in. thick.

12–15 scones
Cooking time—10 min.

CAKE-MAKING

ONE way of classifying cakes is as follows:

(*a*) Plain cakes and buns—where the fat is rubbed in and the proportion of fat to flour is small, e.g. rock buns.

(*b*) Plain cakes—where the fat is melted, e.g. gingerbread.

(*c*) Rich cakes—where the fat and sugar are creamed because there is a larger proportion of fat to flour, e.g. queen cakes, sandwich cakes, Dundee cake, etc.—the proportion of sugar, fruit and eggs to the pound of flour is also increased.

(*d*) Sponge cakes—where there is a large proportion of egg, with or without fat, e.g. Swiss roll.

(*e*) Miscellaneous—belonging to no definite class, e.g. jap cakes, brandy snaps.

PREPARATION OF TINS FOR BAKING CAKES

(*a*) For small cakes, e.g. queen cakes—grease with clarified fat.

(*b*) For sponge cakes (not Swiss roll)—grease with clarified fat and dust greased tins with equal quantities of castor sugar and flour mixed together —this gives a crisp outside to the cake.

(*c*) Large cake-tins—line as described below. Even for plain cakes line the bottom with paper. Treat sandwich tins in the same way. The richer the cake and the longer the baking, the thicker the paper lining should be to protect the cake during cooking.

ROUND AND SQUARE TINS

A square tin takes approximately the same amount of mixture as a round tin which measures 1 in. more in diameter than the length of one side of the square tin. If there is a difference in the depth of the tins this should, of course, be taken into account.

To line a tin—round or square

1. Cut a single or double piece of greaseproof paper as required to fit the bottom—be careful that it is not bigger than the bottom or it will spoil the shape of the cake.

2. Measure the circumference of the tin and cut a strip, single or double, long enough to line the sides of the tin, allowing for an overwrap. Make the strip 2 in. deeper than the height of the tin.
3. Fold up 1 in. along the bottom of the strip and cut this 1 in. fold with diagonal cuts so that it will "give" and shape well into the roundness of the tin. Paper for a square tin does not require to be snipped; it should be mitred at the corners—two pieces are easier to fit than one.
4. Place the strip round the sides of the tin with the cut edge on the bottom of the tin. Fit in the bottom piece. Grease the lined tin with clarified fat if necessary.

To line a Swiss Roll tin

Cut a piece of greaseproof paper large enough to fit the tin, base and sides. If the paper is made higher than the sides of the tin it may prevent the heat from browning the top of the roll. Bisect each corner by cutting down 1½ in. Fit the paper into the tin and grease it carefully.

INGREDIENTS USED IN CAKE-MAKING

Flour: In cake-making a less glutinous (viscid protein) flour can be used than that which is required for bread-making. For large solid rich cakes where a close texture is desired, it is always advisable to use plain flour plus baking-powder or bicarbonate of soda, as required. The richer the cake and the more eggs used, the less baking-powder will be needed, probably none at all.

Self-raising flour: This may be utilized for some of the smaller cakes, and cakes of the sandwich and spongy types where the texture of the finished article is more "open" than for large fruit cakes. As the raising agent content varies in different brands of flour, it is sometimes necessary to add extra baking-powder, an average quantity being one rounded teaspoonful to each pound of flour.

For cake-making, flour should always be sifted.

Rice-flour: Is used, e.g. in the making of shortbread, macaroons, etc.

Cornflour: Sometimes called cornstarch, is another type of flour used generally in conjunction with plain flour. Its addition tends to produce a cake which is rather short and dry, crumbles easily and "melts" in the mouth.

Fats: *Butter* gives the best flavour, particularly in the case of large rich cakes and shortbreads. Its cost, however, may make it prohibitive and *margarine* proves a very good substitute; it is easily creamed. *Lard* is flavourless and should only be used alone where there are highly flavoured ingredients introduced, e.g. spices and black treacle. Lard is 100% fat and this must be taken into account when considering proportions. A point to note is that it does not hold air well when creamed, and for this reason also, is unsuitable for the making of many cakes. Lard is particularly good, combined with margarine, in the making of pastry.

There are on the market fats which are sometimes described as "all purpose" fats. These fats have air finely dispersed through them, which helps to give a quick start when creaming. When using these "all purpose" fats the "fork mix" method is advocated by the manufacturers as being speedy and economical of utensils—it means that a fork is used to distribute the fat and mix to required consistency. Because of the fact that both margarine and butter contain water, it is claimed that these "all purpose" shortenings are more economical, e.g. where 4 oz. margarine or butter is given in a recipe, 3–3½ oz. of the shortening will be sufficient. Butter or margarine has been suggested for most of the recipes in this book, but it is for the cook to substitute other fats as she thinks fit, so long as the proportions are kept adequate, i.e. that the quantity of fat in the recipe, when replaced by "all purpose" fat should be reduced by about one fifth.

Sugar: *Castor sugar* is best for most cakes; *granulated sugar* is apt to give a speckled appearance. *Moist brown sugar* is satisfactory for gingerbread and cakes where a good dark brown colour is required. *Loaf sugar* crushed down to suitable small-sized pieces is effective when sprinkled on the top of yeast mixtures such as "S" buns, bath buns, etc.

Icing sugar, being very fine, is used mostly for icings—glacé, royal, almond paste etc; it can be introduced successfully into shortcrust pastry and some mixtures.

Eggs: All eggs should be very fresh or an unpleasant flavour will be imparted to the cake. New-laid eggs are best for sponge cakes and meringues. Eggs may be whisked with a fork, small whisk or wheel whisk. It is usually enough to whisk till the liquid flows freely and is well frothed. In making large cakes the eggs may be added whole one at a time, each being beaten in very thoroughly to the creamed fat and sugar. The housewife who possesses an electric mixer will find the work much simplified and expenditure of time and energy greatly reduced.

Fruits: The methodical housewife will wash her purchased fruit as soon as possible and after drying it *slowly* in a warm place (otherwise it becomes hard), will store it in suitable jars until required for use. It is best to buy *dried fruit* when the grocer gets in his fresh stock. Dry-cleaning of fruit with flour is not to be advocated. No adverse results should arise from washing the fruit immediately before use, so long as it is very thoroughly dried on a clean cloth to remove as much moisture as possible otherwise it will be heavy and will tend to sink to the bottom of the cake. Wet fruit would alter the consistency of the cake. Stones must always be removed from *raisins*; drop the stones into a basin of hot water to prevent the sticky stones from adhering to the fingers.

The sugar is removed from *peel* before shredding and chopping. Citron peel is best for putting on top of a madeira cake.

Glacé cherries are very heavy and for most cakes it is advisable to cut them into pieces.

Angelica (a candied stem) is used more as decoration but it can be chopped as peel and used in the cake.

Caraway Seeds: These should be used with care; they make a delicious cake but are not universally popular.

Nuts: *Almonds* require to be blanched to remove the skins. Put the nuts into cold water and bring almost to boiling point; pour away the water and run plenty of cold water over them. Pinch off the skins and rub the nuts dry in a soft cloth. They are usually either chopped or shredded but if for the top of a Dundee cake, etc., they are generally split into halves and distributed over the top of the cake with the rounded side up.

To brown almonds: Blanch, skin, shred and place on an oven tray, put in a moderate oven till a good golden colour. Turn frequently; allow to cool and store in a jar.

To make almonds shine: Brush them over with egg white and dry off in the oven.

Coconut—desiccated or shredded. Desiccated coconut may be included in cake mixtures or used to coat a cake already brushed with jam or spread with butter or glacé icing. Shredded, it may be used for decoration.

Pistachio nuts: Skin by immersing in hot water for a minute or two, then cut or chop. Thin cross-sections, three together, can be used as shamrock in decoration, or the finely chopped nuts can be sprinkled for green decoration.

1

PLATE 23
Making Puff Pastry

1 Sift the flour and salt into a bowl, then well rub in about 2 oz. of butter.

2 Add the lemon juice to the flour and mix to a smooth dough with cold water.

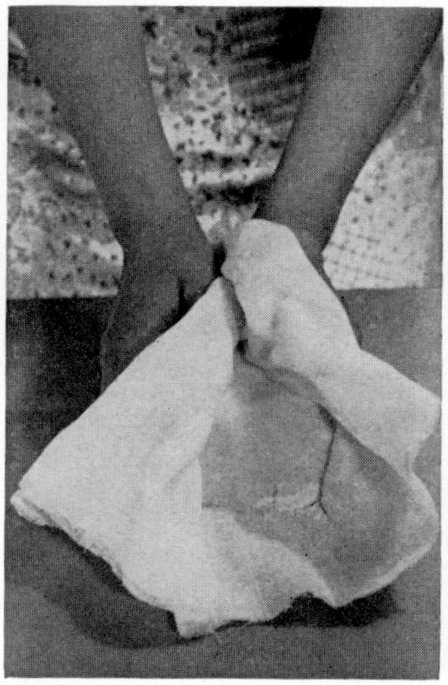

3

4

3 Press the remaining butter in a floured cloth to remove all the surplus moisture.

4 Knead the dough well. Roll it into a strip large enough to enclose the butter. Place the butter on one half of pastry.

5 Fold the other half over, press the two edges together firmly with a rolling pin.

6 Roll into a strip three times the original length, but the same width. Fold the bottom $\frac{1}{3}$ up and top $\frac{1}{3}$ down, press the edges together and give the pastry a half-turn. Roll and fold seven times, leaving the pastry in a cool place for about 15 minutes between each rolling.

5

6

PLATE 24

Apple Dumplings

Making apple dumplings (see page 423) is one way of using up that bumper apple crop.

Walnuts are not blanched; they may be chopped up to go into the mixture or left whole for decorating an iced cake. In their chopped state they are used, e.g. to coat the sides of an iced sandwich cake, sieved apricot jam being used to make the nuts adhere to the sides.

Manufactured decorations: These include silver or coloured balls (dragees), crystallized violets, mimosa, rose petals, etc., chocolate shreds and flakes, "hundreds and thousands", marzipan fruits and flowers, glacé fruits, etc., and jellies and other confectionery can be used.

AIDS TO SUCCESS IN CAKE-MAKING

1. Always have necessary utensils and ingredients collected before beginning to make a cake.
2. Line tins carefully.
3. Prepare the oven so that it is at the correct temperature when required.
4. Follow instructions implicitly.
5. Measure accurately.
6. Cream fat and sugar very thoroughly with a wooden spoon or with the hand, until light and fluffy and white in colour. Warm the fat slightly to facilitate creaming—do not melt it, melted fat does not hold air.
7. Make sure that the proper consistency is obtained.
8. Place cake in correct position in oven.
9. Do not let anxiety override good judgment so that the oven door is opened unnecessarily.
10. Remember that temperature is maintained in an electric oven for much longer than in a gas one—this is an important consideration in baking a cake.
11. Test carefully for readiness.
12. Allow cake to cool on a rack where there is circulation of air—if laid on a solid board it will become damp and sodden underneath.

POINTS TO REMEMBER WHEN MAKING CAKES

1. Have correct proportions. Fat and sugar are liquefying ingredients, therefore the richer the cake, the less liquid, such as milk, is required; in some cases, none. It is better to add water instead of milk in the sandwich cake type of mixture.
2. For cakes of the sponge variety, e.g. sandwich cake, as much as possible of the egg should be added to the creamed fat without the addition of

flour, unless the mixture appears to be curdling. For fruit cakes, where a close texture is required, add egg and flour alternately.

3. For rich cakes add the fruit at the end, mixed with some of the flour to help to keep the fruit suspended in the cake.
4. Generally speaking, the plainer the cake, the hotter the oven; the richer the cake, the cooler the oven. Bake small cakes in the top or the hottest part of the oven, larger cakes in the middle, and very large cakes in the lower part of the oven. Cakes must not be placed over the flame at the sides of a gas oven or too near the element in an electric oven. Never bake a cake on a browning sheet.
5. Avoid opening the oven door before a cake has begun to set. Do not slam the door—especially is this important with sponge mixtures and gingerbreads.

TESTS FOR READINESS OF CAKES

The time given for baking cakes is approximate.

1. Open door carefully and just enough to test cake quickly.
2. The cake should be well risen and evenly browned.
3. Touch the surface lightly and, if it seems firm to the touch, the cake is done. If the impression of the finger remains the cake is not ready.
4. Insert a warm skewer into the cake; if it comes out dry the cake is ready.
5. If the cake is shrinking from the sides of the tin it is probably over-baked.

REASONS FOR SOME COMMON FAILURES IN CAKE-MAKING

1. *A coarse textured cake* results from the use of too much raising agent.
2. *A damp and heavy cake* may be due to:
   (*a*) incorrect proportion of ingredients
   (*b*) too much orange or lemon juice added to the mixture
   (*c*) the oven has been too cool
   (*d*) the cake has been cooled too rapidly, making it damp
   (*e*) the cake may have been packed into a tin before it has cooled sufficiently, so causing dampness.
3. *Fruit sunk to the bottom of a cake*, may be due to:
   (*a*) incorrect proportions of ingredients—too much liquefying material, e.g. sugar
   (*b*) too much baking-powder
   (*c*) oven too slow
   (*d*) the use of wet fruit

(*e*) fruit not mixed with some of the flour before adding
(*f*) a sudden draught or shake given to the tin.

4. *A cake which has fallen in the middle*, may be due to:
(*a*) wrong proportion of liquefying material
(*b*) sudden draught caused by opening the oven door too soon
(*c*) too hot an oven at first or too much baking-powder, which causes overstretching of the gluten of the flour, with consequent collapse.

5. *A cake with a peaked top* may be due to:
(*a*) insufficient liquid
(*b*) a depression not being made in the centre of the mixture in the tin
(*c*) too hot an oven
(*d*) cake baked too high in oven.

MEASURING OF RAISING AGENTS AND SPICES

1 teasp. bicarbonate of soda	=	1 rounded teaspoonful
1 teasp. cream of tartar	=	1 rounded teaspoonful
1 teasp. baking powder	=	1 rounded teaspoonful

For accuracy it is wise to measure in level teaspoons so that 1 rounded teaspoonful of bicarbonate of soda will be 2 level ones. The addition of too much soda gives an unpleasant taste, smell and colour.

PLAIN BUNS AND CAKES

(Fat added by rubbing or melting)

Foundation Proportions

Base	—1 lb. flour
	—$\frac{1}{2}$–1 teasp. salt
Shortening	—4–8 oz. fat
Sweetening	—4–8 oz. sugar
Raising Agents	—2–4 teasp. baking-powder
	—1 teasp. bicarbonate of soda and 2 teasp. cream of tartar
	—1 teasp. bicarbonate of soda and 1–2 tablesp. vinegar
	—1–2 teasp. bicarbonate of soda without cream of tartar for brown cakes and gingerbreads
	—2–4 eggs

Flavouring, etc.—4–16 oz. fruit
—1–2 rounded teasp. mixed spice *or* cinnamon *or* ginger
—Grated rind of 2–3 lemons *or* oranges
—3–4 oz. desiccated coconut
—1 teasp. vanilla *or* lemon *or* almond essence

Liquid —Milk *or* water to mix to required consistency

It is best to line the bottom of all cake-tins with paper to ensure that the cakes will not stick.

PLAIN BUNS or COOKIES

Basic Recipe

(Self-raising flour can be used for any of the following, in which case omit the raising agent.)

1 lb. plain flour	**3 teasp. baking-powder**
¼ teasp. salt	**2 eggs**
2–6 oz. margarine *or* lard *or* dripping	**1–1½ gills milk *or* enough to make a stiff consistency**
4–6 oz. sugar	

Sift flour and salt into bowl, cut in fat with round-bladed knife, then rub with finger tips till quite fine. Add sugar and baking-powder. Mix with egg and milk to a stiff consistency. (The fork with which the buns are mixed should stand up in the mixture.) Divide into pieces and form into rocky heaps on a greased baking-sheet. Bake in a hot oven (**450°–425° F., Gas 8–7**).

24–32 buns
Cooking time—10–15 min.

Variations of Basic Recipe

Chocolate Buns

Add 1–1½ oz. cocoa to the flour and 1 teasp. vanilla essence with the milk.

Coconut Buns

Mix in 4 oz. desiccated coconut with the sugar.

Ginger Buns

Add 2 small teasp. ground ginger to the flour and add 4 oz. chopped or grated crystallized ginger with the sugar.

Lemon Buns

Add 1 teasp. lemon essence with the milk. Turn mixture on to floured board and make into a roll. Divide into 24 pieces, form into balls, brush with egg *or* milk and sprinkle with coarse sugar.

London Buns

Add 2 oz. chopped peel and 2 teasp. grated lemon rind when adding the sugar and form mixture into balls as for lemon buns. Glaze and sprinkle with coarse sugar. Place 2 pieces of lemon *or* orange peel on top of each bun.

Nut Buns

Add 4 oz. chopped nuts when adding the sugar.

Raspberry Buns

Form basic mixture into 24 balls, make a hole in each bun and place a little raspberry jam in the hole. Close the opening, brush with milk *or* egg and sprinkle with coarse sugar.

Rock Buns (**Plate 20**)

Add 4–6 oz. currants and 2 oz. chopped peel when adding the sugar.

Seed Buns

Add 2 dessertsp. caraway seeds with the sugar.

COFFEE BUNS

8 oz. plain flour	**3 oz. brown sugar**
1/8 teasp. salt	**2 level teasp. mixed spice**
4 oz. butter *or* margarine	**1 tablesp. milk**
2 level teasp. baking-powder	**1 egg**
1 oz. ground rice	**2 tablesp. coffee essence**

Sift flour and salt and rub in the fat. Add baking-powder and other dry ingredients. Mix to a rather stiff dough with milk, egg and coffee essence. Place in heaps or balls on a greased tray and brush with egg. Bake in a fairly hot oven (**400° F., Gas 6**).

12–16 buns
Cooking time—15–20 min.

DOUGHNUTS WITHOUT YEAST

8 oz. plain flour	**1½ teasp. baking-powder**
1/8 teasp. salt	**1 egg**
1½ oz. butter *or* margarine	**3/4 gill milk *or* enough to make a light dough**
1½ oz. sugar	
A little grated lemon rind	

Mix flour and salt, rub in fat. Add other dry ingredients and mix to a light dough with egg and milk. Roll out on a floured board ½ in. thick, cut out and fry as for yeast doughnuts (p. 499).

NOTE: 2 small level teasp. cream of tartar may be used and 1 small level teasp. bicarbonate of soda instead of baking-powder.

12–16 doughnuts

OATEN BUNS

4 oz. rolled oats	**1 teasp. baking-powder**
4 oz. wheaten flour	**3 tablesp. chopped stoned raisins**
1/8 teasp. salt	**1 egg**
1½–2 oz. butter *or* margarine	**Milk as required**
1½–2 oz. sugar	

Mix the flour, oats and salt, and rub in the fat. Add the other dry ingredients and mix with egg and enough milk to make a fairly stiff dough. Divide into 12–14 pieces and shape into buns. Place on a greased baking-sheet and bake in a fairly hot oven (**400° F., Gas 6**).

12–14 buns
Cooking time—15–20 min.

ORANGE BUNS

8 oz. plain flour	**1 egg**
1/8 teasp. salt	**3/4 gill milk *or* enough to make a fairly soft dough**
2 oz. butter *or* margarine and lard	**Marmalade**
1½ oz. sugar	
3 level teasp. baking-powder	

Mix the flour and salt and rub in the fat. Add the other dry ingredients and mix to a fairly soft dough with the egg and milk. Roll out about ⅜ in. thick and cut into rounds with a 2½–3 in. cutter. Put 1 teasp. of marmalade in the centre of each, gather up the dough round the marmalade and pinch the edges together. Place on a greased baking-sheet, pinched side down, mark lightly with a cross, brush with milk *or* egg, and sprinkle with coarse sugar as for lemon buns (p. 516). Bake in a fairly hot oven (**400° F., Gas 6**).

12–16 buns
Cooking time—15–20 min.

VICTORIA BUNS

10 oz. plain flour	**2 teasp. golden syrup**
1/4 teasp. salt	**2 teasp. treacle**
3–4 oz. sugar	**4 oz. butter *or* margarine**
2 small teasp. ground cinnamon	**2 eggs**
1/8 teasp. grated nutmeg	**Enough warm milk to make a pouring consistency**
1 level teasp. bicarbonate of soda	

DECORATION
Blanched almonds

Grease queen cake or deep patty tins and place a half blanched almond in the bottom of each. Mix all dry ingredients in a bowl, heat the fat, syrup and treacle and add to dry ingredients with the beaten eggs. Add enough warm milk to make a pouring consistency. Half-fill the prepared tins and bake in a moderate oven (**350° F., Gas 4**).

26–30 buns **Cooking time—20–30 min.**

PLAIN CAKES

Line the bottom of all cake-tins with greaseproof paper.

DATE AND WALNUT CAKE

Gâteau aux Dattes et aux Noix

¾ lb. plain flour	**2 level teasp. cream of tartar**
¼ teasp. salt	**4 oz. chopped dates**
4½ oz. butter *or* margarine	**1½ oz. chopped walnuts**
5 oz. sugar	**2 eggs**
A little grated nutmeg	**1½–2 gills milk (approx.)**
1½ level teasp. bicarbonate of soda	

Sift flour and salt and rub in the fat. Add the other dry ingredients and mix with the eggs and milk to a dropping consistency. Put into a greased 8-in. tin and bake in a fairly hot oven **(375° F., Gas 5)**. Reduce heat to moderate **(350° F., Gas 4)** after 15 min.

Cooking time—1¼–1½ hr.

DOODLE CAKE

8 oz. plain flour	**1 level teasp. bicarbonate of soda**
⅛ teasp. salt	**8 oz. sultanas *or* raisins**
4 oz. butter *or* margarine	**1 egg**
4 oz. moist sugar	**1½ gills milk (approx.)**

Grease a 6-in. cake-tin and line the bottom with greased greaseproof paper.

Sift flour and salt and rub in the fat. Add the sugar, soda and fruit and mix to a soft dropping consistency with the egg and milk. Put into the cake-tin and bake in a fairly hot oven **(400°–375° F., Gas 6–5)**.

Cooking time—1½ hr.

ECONOMICAL SULTANA CAKE

Gâteau aux Raisins, Economique

8 oz. plain flour	**4 oz. moist sugar**
⅛ teasp. salt	**½ lb. sultanas**
3 oz. beef dripping	**2 oz. mixed shredded peel**
2 level teasp. cream of tartar	**1 egg**
1 level teasp. bicarbonate of soda	**1¼ gills milk (approx.)**

Sift flour and salt and rub in the fat. Mix raising agents thoroughly with the flour and add other dry ingredients. Beat egg and add with milk to make a soft dropping consistency. Place in a greased 7-in. cake-tin and bake in a fairly hot oven **(375° F., Gas 5)**. Reduce heat after 15 min. to moderate **(350° F., Gas 4)**.

Cooking time—1½ hr.

HOLIDAY CAKE

Gâteau de Fête

1 lb. plain flour	**4 oz. stoned raisins**
¼ teasp. salt	**2 oz. chopped candied peel**
6 oz. butter *or* margarine and lard	**1 oz. baking-powder**
6 oz. sugar	**1½ eggs *or* 2 small eggs**
8 oz. currants	**2–2½ gills milk**

Sift the flour and salt and rub in the fat. Add the other dry ingredients—cut the raisins into small pieces; do not chop them. Mix the beaten eggs and milk with the dry ingredients to make a rather soft mixture, beat well. Put the mixture into a prepared greased cake-tin (two 6-in. tins *or* one 8-in. *or* 9-in. tin). Bake in a fairly hot oven **(375° F., Gas 5)**. Reduce heat to moderate **(350° F., Gas 4)** after 15 min.

Cooking time—2 hr. for a large cake, 1–1¼ hr. for 2 small cakes

LUNCH CAKE

8 oz. plain flour	**1 level teasp. bicarbonate of soda**
⅛ teasp. salt	**¾ teasp. ground cinnamon**
3 oz. butter *or* lard and margarine	**¾ teasp. mixed spice**
4 oz. sugar	**3 oz. currants**
½ level teasp. cream of tartar	**2 oz. raisins**
Small ¼ teasp. ground cloves	**1½ oz. shredded peel**
	2 eggs
	Milk to mix

Sift flour and salt; rub the fat into the flour. Add other dry ingredients to flour. Beat eggs and add with milk to make a dropping consistency. Place in a greased 7-in. tin and bake in the middle of a fairly hot oven **(375° F., Gas 5)** for 15 min., then reduce heat to moderate (350° F., Gas 4).

Cooking time—1½ hr.

PATRIOTIC CAKE

Gâteau Patriotique

10 oz. plain flour
⅛ teasp. salt
4 oz. butter *or* margarine
6 oz. sugar
1 level teasp. bicarbonate of soda
2 level teasp. cream of tartar
2 eggs
1½ gills milk *or* enough to mix to a thick batter

GLAZE

2 tablesp. milk
1 tablesp. sugar

DECORATION

Dessicated coconut *or* crushed cornflakes

Grease a dripping-tin and line the bottom with greaseproof paper.

Sift flour and salt and rub in the fat. Add the other dry ingredients and mix to a very thick batter with the eggs and milk. Pour into the tin and bake in the top middle of a fairly hot oven (**375° F., Gas 5**) for 15 min. then reduce heat to **350° F., Gas 4**, till firm and well browned.

Boil together the milk and sugar for the glaze for 2 min.; brush the top of the cake with this and sprinkle with coconut or cornflakes.

NOTE: The cake may be spread with glacé icing (p. 547) *or* with flavoured and coloured butter icing (p. 550) and cut into fancy shapes.

Cooking time—about 40 min.

SODA CAKE

8 oz. plain flour
⅛ teasp. salt
4 oz. butter *or* margarine
4 oz. sugar
½ teasp. mixed spice *or* nutmeg
2 oz. currants
2 oz. sultanas
2 oz. raisins
2 oz. peel
1 level teasp. bicarbonate of soda
1 egg
1½ gills milk (approx.)

Sift flour and salt and rub in the fat. Add all the dry ingredients except soda. Slightly beat the egg and dissolve soda in a little milk. Add both to dry ingredients, using enough milk to make a soft dropping consistency. Beat well. Place in a greased 7-in. tin and bake on the middle shelf of a fairly hot oven (**375° F., Gas 5**), reduce heat to **350° F., Gas 4** after 15 min. about 1–1½ hr. in all.

SPICE CAKE

Gâteau aux Quatre Épices

8 oz. plain flour
⅛ teasp. salt
3 oz. margarine
1 teasp. mixed spice
3 oz. sugar
1½ teasp. baking-powder
1 egg
1–1½ gills milk *or* enough to make a soft dropping consistency

Grease a 6-in. cake-tin and line the bottom with greaseproof paper.

Sift flour, salt and spice into a bowl, cut in fat with a round-bladed knife, then rub with finger tips till quite fine. Add sugar and baking-powder. Mix with egg and milk to a soft dropping consistency. Put into the cake-tin and bake in a fairly hot oven (**375° F., Gas 5**).

NOTE: Self-raising flour may be used with advantage in the above recipe, in which case omit the baking-powder.

Cooking time—1¼ hr.

SPINSTER'S CAKE

¾ lb. plain flour
¼ teasp. salt
3 oz. butter *or* margarine
8 oz. sugar
4 oz. stoned raisins
8 oz. currants
2 oz. almonds
1 oz. caraway seeds
¾ oz. chopped orange peel
1 oz. chopped citron peel
½ oz. ground cinnamon
½ oz. allspice *or* mixed spice
½ oz. ground ginger
2 level teasp. bicarbonate of soda
2 gills sour milk *or* buttermilk (approx.)

Grease a 8-in. cake-tin, line the bottom with greased greaseproof paper. Sift flour and salt and rub in the fat. Add all other dry ingredients, and mix to a fairly soft consistency—do not make too soft. Put into cake-tin and bake in the middle of a fairly hot oven (**375° F., Gas 5**), reduce heat to moderate (**350° F., Gas 4**) after 15 min.

Cooking time—1¾–2 hr.

GINGERBREAD

Foundation Proportions

Base —1 lb. flour *or* flour and oatmeal
—¼ teasp. salt
Shortening —4–8 oz. fat
Sweetening —4–6 oz. sugar
—Syrup *or* treacle up to 8 oz.
Raising agent—1–2 teasp. bicarbonate of soda
—2–6 eggs
Flavouring —2–4 teasp. ground ginger
—2–4 teasp. cinnamon *or* mixed spice
—½ lb. crystallized ginger, sultanas, dates, almonds
Liquid —Milk *or* water—usually to make a thick pouring consistency, but this depends on the amount of liquefying ingredients such as treacle, syrup and fat.

ANDREW'S GINGERBREAD

¾ lb. plain flour
¼ teasp. salt
1 small dessertsp. ground ginger
3 oz. butter *or* margarine
2 oz. sugar
3 oz. golden syrup
1½–2 eggs

Sift the flour, salt and ginger. Cream the fat, sugar and syrup, and beat in the eggs, one at a time. Add the flour to make a mixture which will roll out on the board. Roll out ⅛–¼ in. thick and cut into squares or into rounds, using a plain 2½–3 in. cutter. Bake on greased baking-sheets in a moderate oven **(350°–335° F., Gas 4–3)**.

Cooking time—20–25 min.

GINGERBREAD

Pain d'Épice

¾ lb. plain flour
¼ teasp. salt
¼ oz. ground ginger
3 oz. sugar
3 oz. lard
½ lb. black treacle
4–6 tablesp. milk
1 level teasp. bicarbonate of soda
1 egg

Sift the flour, salt and ginger into a bowl, add the sugar. Put the fat, treacle and most of the milk into a pan and warm them. Dissolve the soda in the rest of the milk. Pour the warm liquid into the flour, add the beaten egg and the dissolved soda and beat well—the mixture should be soft enough to run easily from the spoon. Pour into a greased 7–8-in. tin, or into a bread-tin and bake in a moderate oven **(350°–335° F., Gas 4–3)**, reduce heat to the lower temperature after 20 min.

Cooking time—about 1¼–1½ hr.

GOOD GINGERBREAD

8 oz. plain flour
⅛ teasp. salt
1–2 level teasp. ground cinnamon
1–2 level teasp. mixed spice
2 level teasp. ground ginger
2 oz. dates *or* raisins, *or* sultanas
1 level teasp. bicarbonate of soda
2–4 oz. crystallized ginger
2 oz. blanched and chopped almonds
4 oz. butter *or* margarine
4 oz. sugar
4 oz. treacle
2 eggs
A little warm milk, if required

Grease a 7-in. tin and line the bottom with greased greaseproof paper.

Mix flour and salt and other dry ingredients with prepared fruit, crystallized ginger—cut into pieces, and almonds—chopped roughly. Melt fat, sugar and treacle, add to dry ingredients with beaten eggs. If the mixture seems stiff, add a little warm milk but do not make it too soft. Pour into the tin, and bake in a warm to cool oven (335°–310° F., Gas 3–2).

Cooking time—1¾–2 hr.

MOIST GINGERBREAD

10 oz. plain flour
½ level teasp. bicarbonate of soda
¼ teasp. salt
4 oz. brown sugar
2 level teasp. ground cinnamon
2 level teasp. ground ginger
4 oz. sultanas
1–2 oz. shredded almonds
2 oz. treacle
2 oz. golden syrup
6 oz. butter *or* margarine
2 eggs
Warm milk to mix

Grease a 7-in. tin and line the bottom with greased greaseproof paper.

Mix sifted flour and soda with other dry ingredients. Cream treacle, syrup and fat together. Add dry ingredients, beaten eggs and enough warm milk to make a stiff consistency. Put into the tin and bake in a moderate oven (350°–335° F., Gas 4–3), reduce heat to the lower temperature after 20 min.

Cooking time—1¼–1½ hr.

NORTHERN GINGERBREAD

6 oz. plain flour
¼ teasp. salt
6 oz. oatmeal
2 oz. butter *or* margarine
2 level teasp. ground ginger
A good level teasp. bicarbonate of soda
3 oz. moist sugar
2 tablesp. treacle
1 egg
1½ gills milk (approx.) (sour milk, if possible)

Sift flour and salt, add oatmeal and rub in the fat; add other dry ingredients. Melt the treacle and add to dry ingredients, with beaten egg and sufficient sour milk to make a very soft dropping consistency. Pour into a greased 7-in. cake-tin and bake in a moderate oven (375°–350° F., Gas 5–4).

Cooking time—1½ hr.

PLAIN GINGERBREAD

8 oz. plain flour
⅛ teasp. salt
2 oz. butter *or* margarine
2 level teasp. ground ginger
1 level teasp. ground cinnamon *or* mixed spice
2 oz. sugar
1 level teasp. bicarbonate of soda
1 tablesp. treacle
2 tablesp. golden syrup
1 egg
3–4 tablesp. boiling water

Grease a 6-in. cake-tin and line the bottom with greased greaseproof paper.

Sift flour and salt and rub in fat; add other dry ingredients. Melt syrup and treacle and add to beaten egg, pour into dry ingredients and add boiling water to mix to a thick coating consistency. Pour into the cake-tin and bake in a fairly hot to moderate oven (375°–350° F., Gas 5–4).

Cooking time—about 1 hr.

RUSSIAN GINGERBREAD

Pain d'Épice Russe

8 oz. plain flour
⅛ teasp. salt
3 oz. butter *or* margarine
2 oz. sugar
1 level teasp. bicarbonate of soda
1 level teasp. ground cloves
1 level teasp. mixed spice
½ level teasp. ground ginger
2 oz. chopped crystallized ginger
2 tablesp. golden syrup
1 egg
Milk—about ¾ gill
1 oz. shredded almonds

Sift flour and salt, rub in the fat and add all other dry ingredients, including the ginger cut into pieces. Mix with syrup, egg and milk to make a soft consistency, and beat well. Pour into a greased 6–7-in. cake-tin and sprinkle the almonds (blanched and shredded) on top. Bake in a moderate reducing to cool oven (350°–310° F., Gas 4–2).

Cooking time—1–1¼ hr.

RICH CAKES—LARGE

The fat is usually creamed with the sugar

Foundation Proportions

Base	—1 lb. plain flour
	—¼ teasp. salt
Shortening	—½–1 lb. fat
Sweetening	—½–1 lb. sugar
Raising agents	—2–4 level teasp. baking-powder (less as the number of eggs is increased.) Self-raising flour may be used alone or with 1 teasp. baking-powder for small rich cakes and sandwich cakes.
	—4–12 eggs
Fruit	—½–3 lb.
Other flavouring	—grated rind 3–4 oranges *or* lemons
	—1–2 teasp. vanilla essence
	—3 oz. cocoa (flour reduced by 1 oz.)
	—3 tablesp. coffee essence, etc.
Liquid	—Milk *or* water to mix to required consistency. The more "melting ingredients", e.g. fat, sugar etc., the stiffer the consistency.

RICH CAKE

Basic Recipe

6 oz. butter *or* margarine
6 oz. sugar
3 eggs
8 oz. plain flour
⅛ teasp. salt
1½–2 level teasp. baking-powder
Milk *or* water to mix

Line a 7-in. cake-tin with greaseproof paper (p. 509). Cream fat and sugar till white, whisk eggs and add to the fat a little at a time, beating well between each addition. If mixture shows signs of curdling, add a little flour. Sift the flour and salt. Add the flour to the mixture, stirring in lightly with the baking-powder. (The eggs may be added whole and the egg and flour may be added alternately for a close-textured cake, e.g. fruit cake.) Add milk or water to make a fairly soft consistency. Turn into the cake-tin and bake in a moderate oven **(350° F., Gas 4).**

Cooking time—1¼–1½ hr.

Variations of Basic Recipe

Cherry Cake (1)

Gâteau aux Cerises

Add 4 oz. chopped glacé cherries when adding the flour.

Cornflour Cake (1)

Gâteau à la Crème de maïs

Use 6 oz. cornflour and 2 oz. flour in the basic mixture. Dredge top of the cake with castor sugar before baking. The tin may be prepared by greasing and dusting with equal quantities of sugar and flour.

Fruit Cake

Gâteau anglais

Add 6–8 oz. sultanas, currants, raisins or dates to basic mixture. For fruit cake add eggs and flour alternately. Stir in fruit mixed with some of the flour *after* eggs have been added.

Ginger Cake

Gâteau au Gingembre

Sift ½ teasp. ground ginger with the flour, add 2–4 oz. coarsely chopped crystallized ginger with the flour.

Ground Rice Cake

Gâteau de Riz

Use 6 oz. flour and 2 oz. ground rice in basic mixture.

Lemon Cake

Gâteau au Citron

Add the grated rind of 2 lemons with the flour. The cake may be iced when cold with lemon glacé icing.

Madeira Cake

Gâteau de Savoie

Add the grated rind of 1 lemon with the flour. Place 2 strips of citron peel on top of the cake when mixture has begun to set (after about 30 min.).

Seed Cake

Gâteau parfumé au carvi

Add 2 teasp. caraway seeds with the flour.

AMERICAN WALNUT CAKE

2½ oz. butter *or* margarine	**5 oz. plain flour**
3 oz. castor sugar	**2 level teasp. baking-powder**
2 eggs	**Pinch of salt**
1 oz. roughly-chopped walnuts	**American frosting using 8 oz. sugar, etc.**
½ teasp. vanilla essence	**Some walnut halves**

Line a 6-in. cake-tin with greaseproof paper (p. 509). Cream the fat and sugar till light and white, add the beaten eggs gradually, beating well between each addition. Add the walnuts, essence and the sifted flour, baking-powder and salt. Put the mixture into the cake-tin and bake in a moderate oven (**350° F., Gas 4**).

When cold cut the cake through the middle, spread with a small amount of American frosting and sandwich together again. Coat with American frosting and decorate immediately with the walnuts.

Cooking time—1–1¼ hr.

BELFAST PLUM CAKE

6 oz. butter *or* margarine	**1 lb. raisins**
8 oz. brown sugar	**1 lb. currants**
5 eggs	**¼ lb. peel**
14 oz. plain flour	**4 oz. ground almonds**
½ teasp. salt	**⅛ teasp. nutmeg**
1 level teasp. bicarbonate of soda	**½ teacup milk**

Line an 8-in. cake-tin with greaseproof paper. Cream fat and sugar, add beaten eggs one at a time, beat well. Sift flour, salt and soda. Stir the flour, fruit and other dry ingredients into the mixture. Add milk. Put into the cake-tin, cover with greased paper and steam 1½–2 hr. Bake in a moderate oven (**350° F., Gas 4**) for 1½ hr.

Cooking time—(steaming 1½–2 hr.) (baking 1½ hr.) } about 3–3½ hr.

BIRTHDAY CAKE

Gâteau de Fête

4 oz. butter *or* margarine	**1 level teasp. mixed spice**
4 oz. moist brown sugar	**11 oz. mixed fruit—sultanas, currants, glacé cherries**
1½ oz. golden syrup	
2 eggs	
6 oz. plain flour	**2 oz. candied peel *or* marmalade**
⅛ teasp. salt	
1 level teasp. baking-powder	**½ gill milk (approx.)**

Line a 6–7-in. cake-tin with greaseproof paper. Cream fat, sugar and syrup thoroughly. Whisk eggs and add alternately with the sifted flour, salt and baking-powder, beating well with each addition. Add remaining ingredients and fruit, which has been mixed with a little of the flour. Mix to a fairly soft consistency with milk and place in the cake-tin. Bake for ½ hr. in a moderate oven (**350° F., Gas 4**) and a further 2–2½ hr. in a cool oven (**310°–290° F., Gas 2–1**).

NOTE: This cake can be coated with almond paste (p. 548) and decorated with royal icing (p. 549).

Cooking time—about 3 hr.

CHERRY CAKE (2)

Gâteau aux Cerises

9 oz. butter *or* margarine
9 oz. sugar
3 eggs
¾ lb. plain flour
¼ teasp. salt
1 level teasp. baking-powder
4 oz. glacé cherries
½ teasp. vanilla essence
Milk to mix

Line a 7-in. cake-tin with greaseproof paper. Cream the fat and sugar until light and creamy and gradually beat in the eggs, one at a time. Add a little flour if curdling takes place. Sift together flour, salt and baking-powder. Chop cherries into pieces (leaving a few whole for decorating the top) and mix with a little of the flour. Stir into the creamed fat the flour, cherries, essence and enough milk to make a dropping consistency. Put into the cake-tin and place a few cherries lightly on the top. Bake in a moderate oven (**350°–335° F., Gas 4–3**). Avoid making mixture too soft.

Cooking time—1½–1¾ hr.

CHERRY CAKE (3)

8 oz. butter *or* margarine
6 oz. castor sugar
3 eggs
¾ lb. plain flour
¼ teasp. salt
2 level teasp. baking-powder
Grated rind of 1 lemon
4 oz. glacé cherries
Milk to mix

Line a 7-in. cake-tin with greaseproof paper (p. 509). Cream the fat and sugar; add the beaten eggs a little at a time. Sift together flour, salt and baking-powder and grate in lemon rind. Cut the cherries in halves and mix with a little of the flour. Stir the flour lightly into the creamed fat and eggs. Add the cherries and enough milk to make a fairly soft consistency. Put into the cake-tin; bake in a moderate oven (**350°–335° F., Gas 4–3**).

Cooking time—1½–1¾ hr.

CHRISTMAS CAKE (1)

Gâteau de Noël

8 oz. butter *or* margarine
8 oz. castor sugar
½ teasp. gravy browning
8 oz. plain flour
⅛ teasp. salt
1 level teasp. mixed spice
½ level teasp. baking-powder
5–6 eggs
1 lb. currants
8 oz. raisins
4 oz. glacé cherries
2 oz. chopped peel
4 oz. blanched, chopped almonds
Milk, if necessary
4–5 tablesp. brandy (optional)

Line an 8-in cake-tin with greaseproof paper. Cream fat and sugar until white; add gravy browning. Sift together flour, salt, mixed spice and baking-powder. Add egg and flour alternately to the creamed fat, beating well between each addition. Stir in the prepared fruit, almonds and if necessary, add a little milk to make a heavy dropping consistency. Place the mixture in the cake-tin and tie a piece of paper round the outside of the tin. Smooth the mixture and make a depression in the centre. Bake in a warm oven (**335° F., Gas 3**) for ½ hr. then reduce heat to **290° F., Gas 1** for a further 3–3½ hr. Allow to firm before removing from tin and when cold remove paper. Prick bottom of cake well and sprinkle brandy over. Leave for a few days before icing.

Cooking time—4 hr.

CHRISTMAS CAKE (2)

4 oz. butter
12 oz. plain flour
6 oz. moist sugar
¼ oz. ground ginger
½ lb. raisins
¼ pt. cream
5 tablesp. treacle
2 eggs
1 tablesp. vinegar
2 level teasp. bicarbonate of soda

Grease and line a 7-in. cake-tin.

Warm the butter but do not allow it to oil. Sift the flour into a bowl, add the sugar, ginger and chopped raisins. Mix well, then stir in the butter, cream, treacle and well-beaten eggs. Beat for a few minutes. Pour the vinegar on to the soda and stir into the mixture. Put into the prepared cake-tin and place immediately in a warm oven (**335° F., Gas 3**). Reduce heat to (**310° F., Gas 2**).

Cooking time—2¼ hr.

NELL'S CHRISTMAS CAKE (3)

8 oz. butter *or* margarine
8 oz. soft brown sugar
1 level teasp. black treacle
4 eggs
10 oz. plain flour
¼ teasp. salt
1 level teasp. soluble coffee powder *or* essence
1 level teasp. mixed spice
½ level teasp. ground ginger
1 teasp. vanilla essence
2 teasp. rum *or* lemon juice
1 teasp. almond essence
1 level teasp. baking-powder
8 oz. currants
8 oz. sultanas
1 oz. chopped mixed peel
1 oz. chopped glacé cherries
8 oz. chopped valencia raisins
1 oz. blanched chopped almonds

Line a 7–8-in. cake-tin with greaseproof paper (p. 509). Cream the fat and sugar well and add the treacle. Beat the eggs and add a small amount to the fat, beat well. Sift the flour, salt, coffee powder and spices. Stir into the creamed fat a tablespoonful of the spiced flour, add some more egg, beat well and add a second tablespoonful of the spiced flour. Add the rest of the egg gradually, beating well between each addition. Add vanilla, rum or lemon juice, almond essence and coffee essence if used. Stir in the rest of the flour and baking-powder and lastly add the dried fruits and almonds. Put the mixture into the prepared cake-tin and bake in the middle of a warm oven (**335° F., Gas 3**) for 1 hr.; reduce to very cool (**290° F., Gas 1**), for last 2 hr.

When cool remove paper and store in a tin for 2–3 weeks. Cover with almond paste and royal icing.

NOTE: One pouring coating of royal icing will be sufficient, using 1¼ lb. icing sugar.

Cooking time—3 hr.

CORNFLOUR CAKE (2)

3 oz. butter *or* margarine
3 oz. sugar
2 eggs
3 oz. plain flour
2 oz. cornflour
Pinch of salt
½ teasp. vanilla essence
½ level teasp. cream of tartar
½ level teasp. bicarbonate of soda
3–4 tablesp. milk

Grease and flour a 6-in. cake-tin, line the bottom with greaseproof paper. Cream the fat and sugar. Beat the eggs very lightly. Sift flour, cornflour and salt and add flour and egg alternately to the creamed fat, beating well between each addition. Add vanilla, tartar, soda and milk. Put into the prepared tin and bake in a moderate oven (**350°–335° F., Gas 4–3**).

Cooking time—40–50 min.

DUNDEE CAKE (1)

7 oz. butter *or* margarine
7 oz. castor sugar
¾ lb. plain flour
¼ teasp. salt
12–16 oz. mixed fruit—currants, raisins sultanas
3–4 eggs
1 level teasp. baking-powder
Milk *or* water as required
Blanched almonds

Line a 7–8-in. cake-tin with greaseproof paper (p. 509). Cream the fat and sugar till light. Sift together flour and salt and mix the fruit with a small amount of the flour. Add the eggs and flour alternately to the creamed fat, beating well between each addition. Mix baking-powder with the last lot of flour, stir in the fruit and if necessary add a little milk *or* water to make a heavy dropping consistency. Put into the cake-tin, make a slight depression in the centre and spread some split blanched almonds over the surface. Bake in a moderate oven (**350° F., Gas 4**), reduce heat after ¾ hr. to warm to cool (**335°–310° F., Gas 3–2**).

Cooking time—2½ hr.

DUNDEE CAKE (2)

6 oz. butter *or* margarine
6 oz. castor sugar
3 eggs
¼ gill brandy (optional)
8 oz. plain flour
⅛ teasp. salt
1 level teasp. baking-powder
½ teasp. ground cinnamon
⅛ teasp. grated nutmeg
Grated rind of 1 lemon
6 oz. currants
3 oz. stoned, chopped raisins
4 oz. sultanas
2 oz. chopped mixed peel
2 oz. chopped and blanched almonds
Milk, if necessary

Line a 7-in. cake-tin with greaseproof paper (p. 509). Cream the fat and sugar; add the well-beaten eggs one at a time, beating between each addition (add a little flour if any sign of curdling), and stir in the brandy, if used. Sift flour, salt and baking-powder, mix prepared fruit with a small amount of the flour. Mix in the flour, fruit and lemon rind and half of the chopped almonds. If necessary add a little milk but do not make too moist. Place the mixture in the cake-tin; sprinkle over the remainder of the almonds and bake in a moderate oven (**350° F., Gas 4**), reduce heat after ¾ hr. to warm to cool (**335°–310° F., Gas 3–2**).

Cooking time—2–2¼ hr.

HAZELNUT CAKE

Gâteau aux Noisettes

3 oz. butter *or* **margarine**
5 oz. sugar
2 eggs
12 oz. self-raising flour
¼ teasp. salt
4 oz. hazelnuts
Milk as required

Line a 7-in. cake-tin with greaseproof paper (p. 509). Cream the fat, add the sugar and beat well till light and white. Beat in each egg very thoroughly. Sift together the flour and salt; pass the nuts through a nut mill. Add to the mixture the flour, nuts and enough milk to make a fairly soft dough. Put the mixture into the cake-tin and bake in a fairly hot oven (**375° F., Gas 5**), reduce heat to warm (**335° F., Gas 3**) after 30 min.

Cooking time—1¼–1½ hr.

MOTHER'S CAKE

To be served on Mothering Sunday

Mixture: as for Birthday Cake (p. 523) baked in a 6-in. tin.
Almond paste (p. 548) using 6 oz. ground almonds, etc.
Royal icing (p. 549) using 12 oz. icing sugar, etc.

Cover cake with almond paste (*see* p. 549) and allow to dry. Pour over royal icing of coating consistency—make as smooth as possible and remove blisters by means of a hat pin or skewer; allow to firm before decorating. Place the cake on a cake-board 1 in. larger than the cake. Pipe a circle round the top rim of the cake with a ¼ in. plain pipe. Leave to set, then pipe a second circle on top of the first, repeat a third time (but use a small plain pipe) and a fourth, if fancied. Pipe in the same way on the base. Make some yellow or red roses and some green leaves from coloured almond paste and use to decorate the top; pipe on the words "Mother's Day".

ORANGE CAKE

Gâteau à l'Orange

6 oz. butter *or* **margarine**
6 oz. castor sugar
3 eggs
8 oz. plain flour
¼ teasp. salt
1½ level teasp. baking-powder
1 orange

Line a 7-in. cake-tin with greaseproof paper (p. 509). Cream the fat and sugar till white; add the beaten eggs gradually, beating well between each addition. Sift flour, salt and baking-powder and add with the grated rind and juice of the orange to the creamed fat; mix well. Place in the cake-tin and bake in a moderate oven (**350° F., Gas 4**) for 1–1¼ hr.

PLUM CAKE

8 oz. butter *or* **margarine**
Grated rind of 1 lemon
8 oz. castor sugar
4 eggs
2 teasp. glycerine
¼ teasp. almond essence
10 oz. plain flour
¼ teasp. salt
2 oz. mixed peel
12–16 oz. cherries, raisins and currants
2 oz. ground almonds
2 tablesp. brandy

Line a 7–8 in. cake-tin with greaseproof paper (p. 509). Cream fat with grated lemon rind, add sugar and cream again. Add the well-beaten eggs a little at a time and continue beating. Add the glycerine and almond essence. Sift the flour and salt and fold in ⅓ of the flour. Add mixed fruit and almonds and the remainder of the flour. Put into the cake-tin and bake in a warm oven (**335° F., Gas 3**), reduce to cool (**310° F., Gas 2**) after 30 min. When cold turn the cake over, make some holes in the bottom with a skewer, and pour the brandy in. Wrap in paper and store for 2 or 3 weeks before cutting.

Cooking time—2½–3 hr.

POPULAR CAKE

Gâteau, Populaire

2 oz. butter *or* margarine
2 oz. sugar
2 eggs
8 oz. plain flour
⅛ teasp. salt
2 level teasp. baking-powder
3 oz. currants
½ oz. shredded peel
1 oz. blanched, shredded almonds
½ teacup milk

Line a 6–7-in cake-tin with greaseproof paper (p. 509). Cream fat and sugar well, add eggs gradually, beating thoroughly after each addition. Sift flour, salt and baking-powder and add with the fruit, nuts and milk to the mixture. Put into the cake-tin. Bake in a fairly hot oven (**375° F., Gas 5**). Reduce to warm (**335° F., Gas 3**) after 30 min.

Cooking time—about 1–1¼ hr.

SAND CAKE

Gâteau sablé

4 oz. butter *or* margarine
Grated rind of 1 lemon
4 oz. castor sugar
2 large eggs
4 oz. cornflour
½ oz. ground rice
Pinch of salt
½ level teasp. baking-powder
Ratafia crumbs (optional)

Grease a border mould or 6 in. cake-tin and if liked, coat with ratafia biscuit crumbs *or* with equal quantities of castor sugar and flour.

Cream the fat with the lemon rind; add the sugar and cream again. Beat the eggs and add them gradually, beating well between each addition. Sift together the cornflour, ground rice, salt and baking-powder. Add the flour lightly to the creamed fat, ⅓ at a time, and put the mixture into the mould. Bake in a moderate oven (**350°–335° F., Gas 4–3**).

Cooking time—about 1 hr.

SIMNEL CAKE

Gâteau de la mi-carême

Mixture: as for Birthday Cake (p. 523) or any other fruit cake.
Almond paste: 6 oz. ground almonds, etc. (p. 548).
Glacé icing: 2 oz. icing sugar, etc. (p. 547).

Line a 6–7-in. cake-tin with greaseproof paper (p. 509). Cut off about ⅓ of the almond paste and roll out into a round slightly less than the diameter of the tin to be used. Place ½ the cake mixture in the tin, cover with a round of almond paste and place the remaining cake mixture on top. Bake in a moderate oven (**350° F., Gas 4**) for ½ hr., reduce heat to cool (**310°–290° F., Gas 2–1**) for 2–2½ hr. Leave for 24 hr. Using about ½ the remaining almond paste, cover the top of the cake. With the remainder, make small balls and place these at even intervals round top edge of the cake. Brush them over with egg wash. Tie a band of greaseproof paper tightly round the top of the cake. Place in a hot oven until balls are nicely browned. When cool, pour glacé icing into the centre of the cake and decorate as required with almond paste eggs, small chicks, etc.

Cooking time—about 3 hr.

NOTE: This cake used to be served only on Mother's Day but is now often served on Easter Sunday.

SQUARE WALNUT CAKE

Gâteau carré aux Noix

4 oz. butter *or* margarine
4 oz. sugar
3 eggs
5 oz. self-raising flour
1 level teasp. baking-powder
Pinch of salt
1½ oz. chopped walnuts

FILLING

3 tablesp. ground almonds
1 teasp. vanilla essence
1 tablesp. chopped walnuts
2–3 tablesp. sieved apricot jam

DECORATION

Glacé icing (p. 547) using 10 oz. icing sugar
Halved walnuts
Glacé cherries

Grease an 8-in. square sandwich tin and line the bottom with greaseproof paper.

Cream the fat and sugar till light and white, add beaten egg gradually, beating well between each addition. Sift flour, baking-powder and salt and stir into the mixture with the walnuts. Put into the sandwich tin. Bake in a moderate oven (**350° F., Gas 4**).

Beat together all ingredients for the filling. When cake is cold, cut through the middle, spread with the filling and sandwich together again. Ice with white glacé icing; use some of the icing to pipe squares on the top and place a walnut and a glacé cherry alternately in the squares.

NOTE: The sides may be brushed with apricot glaze (p. 547) and coated with chopped walnuts, the top only being iced with glacé icing.

Cooking time—40–50 min.

TWELFTH NIGHT CAKE

Gâteau des Rois

6 oz. butter *or* margarine	**4 oz. sultanas**
3 oz. brown sugar	**4 oz. mixed peel**
3 eggs	**½ level teasp. ground cinnamon**
½ gill milk	**½ level teasp. mixed spice**
1 level teasp. bicarbonate of soda	**¾ lb. plain flour**
2 oz. treacle	**¼ teasp. salt**
4 oz. currants	

Line a 7-in. cake-tin with greaseproof paper (p. 509). Cream the fat and sugar and beat in the eggs gradually. Add the milk in which the soda is dissolved; stir in the treacle and beat well. Add the prepared fruit and spices. Sift in the flour and salt and mix lightly. Put into the tin and bake in a warm oven (**335° F., Gas 3**). Silver charms should be baked in the cake; wrap in greaseproof paper.

Cooking time—2–2½ hr.

WALNUT LAYER CAKE

Gâteau aux Noix

6 oz. butter *or* margarine	**Pinch of salt**
6 oz. castor sugar	**2 teasp. coffee essence**
3 eggs	**1 level teasp. baking-powder**
6 oz. plain flour	

FILLING

2 oz. butter *or* margarine	**1–2 teasp. coffee essence**
4 oz. icing sugar	**2 oz. chopped walnuts**

DECORATION

American frosting (p. 547), **using 8 oz. sugar etc.**

Cream fat and sugar; beat in the eggs one at a time. Fold in the sifted flour, baking-powder and salt and add coffee essence. Put mixture into a 6-in. lined cake-tin (or it may be baked in 2 or 3 sandwich cake-tins) and bake in a moderate oven (**350° F., Gas 4**) for 1 hr.

Cut the cake into three sections when cold. Make the filling: cream together the fat and sugar, and add the coffee essence and chopped walnuts. Spread each section with filling and sandwich together again.

Make the American frosting and quickly pour over the cake to cover it completely.

To finish the cake put a few half walnuts on top before the icing has set.

WEDDING CAKE

Gâteau de Noce

NOTE: These quantities are sufficient for a 3-tier cake.

3–3¼ lb. flour	**24 large eggs**
¼ teasp. salt	**5½ lb. currants**
3 level teasp. ground cinnamon	**2 lb. sultanas**
3 level teasp. ground mace	**1–1½ lb. glacé cherries**
1 nutmeg (grated)	**1–1¼ lb. mixed chopped peel**
1½ teasp. baking-powder	**Rind and juice of 1 lemon**
3 lb. butter	**½–1 lb. blanched chopped almonds**
3 lb. castor sugar	**1½ gills rum *or* brandy *or* rum and brandy**
1½ teasp. parisian essence *or* other gravy browning	

Prepare and line 3 cake-tins (p. 509), one 12 in. diameter, one 8 in., and one 4 in. diameter.

Sift together flour, salt, spices and baking-powder. Mix together all the fruit with a little of the measured flour. Cream the butter and sugar very well, add browning. Add egg and flour alternately to the creamed fat beating well between each addition. Stir in the prepared fruit, almonds and brandy. Divide ½ of the mixture between the 2 smaller tins, and put the remaining ½ of the mixture in the biggest tin. Tie a thick band of brown paper round the outside of each tin. Smooth the mixture and make a depression in the centre of each cake. Bake the 4-in. cake for 2–3 hr., the 8-in. cake for 3½–4 hr., and the 12-in. cake for 5–6 hr. Put in a cool oven **(310° F., Gas 2)** for the first ½ hr. then reduce heat to very cool **(290°–240° F., Gas 1–½)** for the remainder of the time.

To finish the cakes see pp. 549–50.

To cover the 4-in. cake with almond paste (p. 548) 1 lb. ground almonds etc. will be required; 2 lb. ground almonds etc. for the 8-in. cake and 3 lb. ground almonds, etc., for the 12-in. cake.

For the royal icing (p. 549) use 1 lb. icing sugar, etc., for the 4-in. cake, 2 lb. for the 8-in. cake and 3 lb. sugar, etc., for the 12-in. cake.

Transparent icing (p. 548) may be poured over as a last layer, if liked. For the 4-in. cake use 1–1½ lb. loaf sugar, etc., for the 8-in. cake use 3 lb. sugar, etc., and for the 12-in. cake 4 lb. sugar, etc.

Decoration of each cake is then completed upon silver boards (of correct size) covered with a lace d'oyley. The cake is then assembled by placing one cake on top of the other with pillars supporting them. The pillars for the bottom tier should be 3 in. in height and for the top the pillars should be 4 in. high. Place a silver vase containing white flowers and smilax on top.

SANDWICH CAKES

NOTE: Sandwich cakes differ from true sponges in that they contain fat; sponges are generally fatless.

In each case the tin is greased and the bottom lined with paper

Basic Recipes

SANDWICH CAKE

3 oz. butter *or* margarine
4 oz. sugar
2 eggs
5 oz. plain flour
1 level teasp. baking-powder
Pinch of salt

Cream fat and sugar well; add egg yolks and continue beating. Sift flour, baking-powder and salt and stir into the mixture. Fold in the stiffly-whisked egg whites; add a little tepid water if necessary to make the mixture "easy". Place in a prepared 7-in. sandwich cake-tin and bake in a moderate oven **(350° F., Gas 4)**.

NOTE: Self-raising flour may be used with satisfactory results, in which case no baking-powder is required.

Cooking time—30–40 min.

LARGE SANDWICH CAKE

3 oz. butter *or* margarine
4½ oz. sugar
3 eggs
4½ oz. plain flour
Pinch of salt
2 level teasp. baking-powder

As for Victoria sandwich cake (below) using an 8-in. sandwich cake-tin. Bake in a moderate oven **(350° F., Gas 4)**.

Cooking time—50–60 min.

SMALL SANDWICH CAKE

(useful for icing variations)

2 oz. butter *or* margarine
3 oz. castor sugar
2 eggs
3 oz. self-raising flour
Pinch of salt
½ level teasp. baking-powder
Cold water as required —1–2 dessertsp.

As for Victoria sandwich (below), using a 6-in. sandwich tin. Bake in a moderate oven **(350° F., Gas 4)**.

Cooking time—40 min.

VICTORIA SANDWICH

4 oz. butter *or* margarine
4 oz. castor sugar
2 eggs
4 oz. plain flour
Pinch of salt
1½ level teasp. baking-powder

SANDWICH CAKES

Cream fat and sugar very thoroughly. Add well-whisked eggs gradually, beating well between each addition—if sign of curdling, add some flour. Sift flour, salt and baking-powder and stir lightly into the creamed fat and eggs. Mix to a soft dropping consistency, adding a little water if necessary. Place the mixture in a prepared 7-in. sandwich tin and bake in a moderate oven (**350° F., Gas 4**).

Cooking time—40–45 min.

Variations

BATTENBURG CAKE

Gâteau Battenbourg

2 Victoria sandwich cakes made in oblong tins, one white and the other coloured pink *or* Patriotic cake (p. 519) **may be used**
1 tablesp. apricot glaze
Almond paste (p. 548), **using 3 oz. ground almonds etc.**

DECORATION

Glacé cherries | **Angelica**

Cut the cake into strips 8–9-in. long and 1½ in. square at ends—2 pink and 2 white pieces will be needed. Join these together with apricot glaze to make a square end having pink and white pieces alternately. Roll almond paste into an oblong, wide enough and long enough to wrap round the cake leaving the ends open. Trim edges of almond paste. Spread top of cake with apricot glaze and invert on to almond paste. Spread the remaining three sides with glaze, roll up firmly and join almond paste neatly. To decorate, pinch the two top edges between thumb and forefinger. Mark the top of the cake lattice fashion with a knife and decorate with cherries and angelica.

FEATHER-ICED SANDWICH CAKE

Coat the sides of a sandwich cake with butter icing and browned crumbs as in Iced Sandwich Cake (2)

GLACÉ ICING (1)

3–4 oz. icing sugar
Warm water to mix to coating consistency
A delicate shade of colouring, e.g. pale pink

GLACÉ ICING (2)

1 oz. icing sugar
Warm water to mix
A darker shade of colouring, e.g. dark chocolate

Place dark icing in an icing bag or syringe with a fine writing pipe. Spread top of cake with pale icing. Before it starts to set, pipe parallel lines of the contrasting colour across the cake about ½ in. apart. Lightly run a pin or fine skewer across the cake in lines, back and forward at right angles to the piping. Allow icing to set. Pipe round the edge of the cake with remaining butter icing.

ICED SANDWICH CAKE (1)

Gâteau Sandwich glacé

1 small sandwich cake

FILLING

Butter icing (p. 550) **using 2 oz. butter, etc.**

DECORATION

Glacé icing (p. 547) **using 7 oz. icing sugar**

Colour and flavour the butter icing as desired. Cut the sandwich cake through the middle and spread with just over half of the butter icing. Sandwich together again and remove any loose crumbs with a clean pastry brush. Place cake on a cooling tray over a plate. Mix glacé icing to coating consistency, colour and flavour carefully. Pour icing on to centre of cake and allow to run over top and down sides. Try to avoid touching the top with a knife—a knife will be necessary for completing the sides. Allow to set.

Decorate, if desired, by piping with remaining butter icing.

ICED SANDWICH CAKE (2)

1 sandwich cake

DECORATION

Butter icing (p. 550), **using 1½ oz. butter, etc.**
Glacé icing (p. 547), **using 4 oz. icing sugar**
2–3 tablesp. sifted, dried, lightly browned, cake-crumbs *or* browned coconut *or* chopped walnuts

Spread sides of cake evenly with butter icing. Have crumbs in a paper, roll sides of cake in them and press the crumbs into position. Remove any loose crumbs. Mix glacé icing to a stiff coating consistency, pour on to top of cake and spread to edges. Allow to set and trim off any icing which has run down the sides of the cake. Decorate top of cake by piping on butter icing.

ORANGE SANDWICH CAKE (Plate 20)

1 large sandwich cake (p. 529)
Orange-flavoured butter icing (p. 550)
Crystallized orange slices

Cut cake through centre and spread with orange-flavoured butter icing, sandwich together again. Spread the top of the cake with icing, smooth with a knife and decorate with slices of crystallized orange.

NOTE: A more pronounced flavour may be obtained by adding the finely-grated rind of 1 orange when mixing the cake.

Lemon may be substituted for orange if liked.

PINEAPPLE CAKE

Gâteau d'Ananas

1 large sandwich cake (p. 529)

FILLING

4 tablesp. whipped *or* mock cream
1 oz. chopped glacé pineapple
3 drops pineapple essence
½ oz. castor sugar

PINEAPPLE ICING

1 pt. water
12 oz. loaf sugar
6 drops pineapple essence
Pieces of pineapple
Apricot jam
3–4 oz. finely-chopped walnuts

Cut cake through centre and spread with the filling, sandwich together again. Put water and sugar for icing into a strong pan. Allow to dissolve, then bring to boiling-point; skim well. Boil quickly without stirring until a pale brown colour and the syrup threads like caramel. Add pineapple essence. Place some pieces of pineapple neatly on the cake, pour syrup over. When set, coat sides with apricot jam, and chopped walnuts pressed well in.

CHOCOLATE SANDWICH CAKE —EGGLESS

1 oz. butter *or* margarine
2 oz. sugar
2 tablesp. golden syrup
1 level teasp. bicarbonate of soda
1–1½ gills milk
6 oz. self-raising flour
1 oz. cocoa
Pinch of salt
Chocolate butter icing

Cream together the fat, sugar, and syrup, and dissolve the soda in the milk. Sift together flour, salt and cocoa. Add flour and milk alternately to the creamed fat mixture—the consistency should be that of a thick batter. Place the mixture in a prepared 8-in. sandwich cake-tin and bake in a fairly hot oven (**375°–350° F., Gas 5–4**). When cool spread the top of the cake with butter icing, smooth with a knife and decorate by marking with circles or lines.

Cooking time—40 min.

COBURG SPONGE

Madeleine de Cobourg

8 oz. plain flour
Pinch of salt
1 level teasp. bicarbonate of soda
4 oz. butter *or* margarine
4 oz. castor sugar
2 eggs
2 small level teasp. ground ginger
½ level teasp. ground cloves
½ level teasp. mixed spice
½ level teasp. ground cinnamon
1 tablesp. golden syrup
2 tablesp. warm water

DECORATION

Butter icing (p.550), **using 1 oz. butter etc., flavoured with ground cinnamon**

Sift the flour, salt and bicarbonate of soda. Cream fat and sugar; add eggs gradually, beating well between each addition. Add syrup and stir in the dry ingredients with sufficient warm water to make a dropping consistency. Place in two greased 6–7-in. sandwich tins and bake in a moderate oven (**375°–350° F., Gas 5–4**).

When the cakes are cold, spread with butter icing and sandwich together. Dust the top with icing sugar.

Cooking time—30–40 min.

COFFEE SPONGE

Madeleine au Café

3 oz. butter *or* **margarine**
3 oz. castor sugar
2 eggs
3½ oz. self-raising flour
Pinch of salt
½ level teasp. baking-powder
2 teasp. soluble coffee powder
1 tablesp. water

Cream the fat and sugar, add beaten eggs gradually, beating well between each addition. Sift the flour, salt, baking-powder and coffee and stir into the creamed mixture, add enough water to make a dropping consistency. Place in a greased 6-in. sandwich tin and bake in a moderate oven (**350° F., Gas 4**). When the cake is cold, split and spread with coffee butter icing (p. 550), sandwich together and coat with coffee glacé icing (p. 547). Decorate with halved walnuts or chopped pistachios or green crumbs.

Cooking time—20–30 min.

COFFEE LAYER CAKE

4 oz. butter *or* **margarine**
4 oz. castor sugar
2 eggs
8 oz. plain flour
1 teasp. baking-powder
2 teasp. soluble coffee powder
3 tablesp. milk

MOCHA ICING

2 teasp. soluble coffee powder
2 oz. chocolate
4 tablesp. water
3 oz. butter *or* **margarine**
1 lb. icing sugar

DECORATION

Almonds

Cream the fat and sugar until very light and add the eggs one at a time with a dessertsp. of flour—beat well. Sift the flour, baking-powder and coffee powder and fold lightly into the mixture with the milk. Pour into 2 greased sandwich tins and spread evenly. Bake in a fairly hot oven (**375° F., Gas 5**) for 35-40 min. until firm. Cool.

To make the mocha icing: dissolve coffee powder and grated chocolate in the almost boiling water. Cream the margarine and 2 tablesp. of the sugar. Beat well. Add the rest of the sugar and liquid alternately, beating until it is smooth and easy to spread.

Cut the two cakes across in half, and sandwich the halves together with some of the icing, spreading the rest of the icing on the top and sides and frost or "rough up" with a fork. Decorate with blanched almonds.

VANCOUVER SPONGE

4 oz. butter
4 oz. sugar
2 eggs
8 oz. plain flour
Pinch of salt
2½ level teasp. ground ginger
2 level teasp. ground cinnamon
1 level teasp. ground cloves
1 level teasp. mixed spice
4 oz. treacle
½–¾ gill boiling water
1 level teasp. bicarbonate of soda

Grease and line the bottom of a Yorkshire pudding tin, approximately 6 in. wide by 10 in. long.

Cream fat and sugar, beat in eggs, beating well between each addition. Sift flour, salt and spices, and lightly stir into the creamed fat mixture. Warm the treacle, add to it half of the water, and stir in. Lastly, add the bicarbonate of soda dissolved in the rest of the water.

Put the mixture into the tin and bake in a fairly hot to moderate oven (**375°–350° F., Gas 5–4**).

Cut into squares when cold.

Cooking time—1–1¼ hr.

RICH CAKES—SMALL

THE following is a suitable mixture for small cakes; it can be varied in many ways.

Basic Recipe

2 oz. butter *or* margarine
2 oz. castor sugar
1 egg
3 oz. self-raising flour *or* 3 oz. plain flour and 1 level teasp. baking-powder
Pinch of salt
Water *or* milk as required

Beat the fat and sugar until creamy and white. Whisk the egg and add gradually; beat well between each addition. Sift together the flour, salt and baking-powder. Gently stir flour, etc., into creamed fat; add milk *or* water to make a soft dropping consistency (water is considered best). Half-fill greased bun tins with the mixture and bake in a fairly hot to moderate oven (**375°–350° F., Gas 5–4**).

NOTE: This mixture may be baked in paper cases and decorated with glacé icing or cherries.

10–12 cakes
Cooking time—15–20 min.

Variations of Basic Recipe

Cherry Cakes

Add 1–2 oz. coarsely chopped glacé cherries with the flour.

Chocolate Cakes

Sift ½ oz. cocoa with the flour, and add a few drops of vanilla essence with the water or milk. The cakes may be iced with chocolate glacé icing.

Coconut Cakes

Add ½ oz. coconut with the flour and add ¼ teasp. vanilla essence with the milk or water.

Lemon Cakes

Add the grated rind of 1 lemon with the flour, and ice with lemon glacé icing.

Madeleines

Bake the basic mixture in greased dariole moulds. Turn out when baked; cool. Spread all round top and side with warmed apricot jam. Roll in desiccated coconut, decorate with ½ glacé cherry.

Nut Cakes

Add 1–2 oz. coarsely chopped walnuts, almonds, etc., with the flour.

Queen Cakes

Add 1–2 oz. currants *or* sultanas with the flour or a few currants may be placed in the bottom of each queen cake tin and the mixture placed on top.

APRICOT BASKETS (Plate 20)

The basic mixture baked in small bun tins
1 small can apricots
¼ pt. packet lemon jelly
A little whipped sweetened cream
Piece of angelica 6 in. long

Whilst the buns are cooling, drain the apricots from the syrup. Make up the syrup to just under ½ pt. with water, bring to the boil and pour on to the jelly. Stir until dissolved and leave to cool until it is just starting to thicken. *To make the baskets:* Put an apricot, round side uppermost, on each bun, coat with the jelly, which must be just starting to thicken. Pipe small stars of whipped cream around the apricots. Soak the angelica in warm water, cut into strips ¼ in. wide and long enough to arch over the buns to form a "handle". Make two small holes in each bun with a skewer to keep the handle in place.

BUTTERFLY CAKES

The basic mixture (above) **cooked in greased bouché (small) tins**
1 gill sweetened and flavoured cream
A little jam

Cut a thin slice from the top of each cake, cut each slice in 2 to make wings; dredge with icing sugar. Spread cut top of cake with a little red jam, pipe a large rosette of beaten cream on this and place wings in position.

CORK CAKES

The basic mixture cooked in greased bouché tins
Apricot glaze
Pistachio nuts *or* green cake crumbs
1 gill sweetened and flavoured cream

With a small cutter or apple corer remove a small piece, about ½ in. in depth, from the centre of each cake. Brush the top of these small "corks" with apricot glaze (p. 547) and dip into chopped pistachio nuts or green cake crumbs. Dredge the cakes with icing sugar. Place a little jam in the centre of each cake and pipe a rosette of beaten cream on top. Place the corks on top of the rosettes, pressing very lightly into the cream.

BRUNSWICK CAKES

3 oz. butter *or* margarine	**1 level teasp. ground cloves**
6 oz. castor sugar	**1 level teasp. ground cinnamon**
2 eggs	**1 level teasp. ground nutmeg**
8 oz. plain flour	**¾ teacup milk**
Pinch of salt	
3 level teasp. baking-powder	

DECORATION

Glacé icing (p. 547), using 8 oz. icing sugar flavoured with ginger *or* 1–2 drops essence of cloves

Cream the fat and sugar and add the beaten eggs gradually, beating well between each addition. Sift together the flour, salt, baking-powder and spices; stir into the creamed fat mixture adding enough milk to make a dropping consistency. Put the mixture into queen cake, or other small greased tins, half filling the tins, and bake in a fairly hot to moderate oven **(375°–350° F., Gas 5–4)** for 20–30 min. When cold, ice the tops with glacé icing.

22–24 cakes

GENOESE PASTRY

Génoise

(Base for small cakes)

Basic Recipe

4 oz. flour	**4 eggs**
Pinch of salt	**4 oz. castor sugar**
	3 oz. butter *or* margarine

Sift flour and salt. Beat eggs and sugar in a basin over a pan of hot water till thick. Clarify the fat and fold lightly into egg mixture, then fold in salted flour. Pour into lined Swiss roll tin and bake in a moderate oven **(350° F., Gas 4)**. When cold (after 24 hr.) cut and use as desired for small iced cakes, etc.

Cooking time—30–40 min.

Variations

CAULIFLOWER CAKES

Rounds of Genoese pastry 1½ in. in diameter
Green colouring
Almond paste
Apricot glaze
Cream (flavoured and sweetened)

Add a few drops of green colouring to the almond paste and work it well in—roll out paste very thinly. Cut out five circles of almond paste for each cake using 1½-in. cutter. Brush the sides of the cake with apricot glaze, press the pieces of almond paste round so that they overlap slightly, shape top of almond paste pieces slightly. Pipe cream into centre of cakes using a small rose pipe.

20–24 cakes

CONTINENTAL CAKES

Gâteaux à la Continentale

Genoese pastry
Butter icing (p. 550), using 1½ oz. butter, etc. flavoured with vanilla and coloured pink
Glacé icing (p. 547), using 12 oz. icing sugar

Cut genoese pastry into rounds 1½ in. in diameter or into diamond shapes 1 in. by 1¾ in. Pile some butter icing on to the top of each cake and smooth off with a knife to shape of cake. Allow icing to harden and stand cakes on wire cooling tray over a large dish. Make glacé icing and coat cakes; the butter icing should just show through. When set decorate by piping lines or spirals of coloured glacé icing on cakes.

20–26 cakes

FRENCH CAKES

Gâteaux français

Genoese pastry—1–1½ in. thick

Filling as desired: jam *or* lemon curd *or* butter icing (p. 550), etc.
Glacé icing
Decoration: chopped nuts, crystallized violets, rose leaves, silver balls, glacé fruits, angelica, piping, etc.

Cut cake through centre, spread thinly with filling and sandwich together again. If necessary, trim off the brown part from the top of the cake, and cut the cake into rounds, triangles, squares, etc. Brush off any loose crumbs and put the pieces of cake on an icing rack over a large flat dish. Make the icing of a good coating consistency, to flow easily over without being too thin. Dip each cake in and under the icing and return the pieces to the icing rack, being careful not to leave marks on the icing with the fingers or dip with a fork or skewer. Another method is to place the cakes on the icing rack, and pour the icing from a teaspoon over each piece of genoese. Arrange a small quantity of decoration on the top of each cake, and when firm serve the cakes in paper cases.

28 cakes

MARZIPAN POTATO CAKES

Genoese pastry	**Apricot glaze**
Rum	**Cinnamon *or* chocolate powder**
Almond paste	

Cut out pastry with a small oval cutter 1 in. by 1½ in. and sprinkle the pastry with the rum. Roll out almond paste about ⅛ in. thick. Brush pastry with apricot glaze and wrap enough almond paste round to make a well shaped potato. Mark with skewer for eyes and roll in cinnamon or chocolate powder. Serve in paper cases.

MAYFAIR CAKES

Genoese pastry
Sweetened and flavoured cream *or* mock cream
Chocolate vermicelli

Cut pastry into rounds, 1½ in. in diameter. Spread top and sides of pastry rounds thinly with cream. Coat with chocolate vermicelli and press this well on with a knife. Pipe a large rose of cream on top.

20–24 cakes

MOCHA FINGERS

Genoese pastry
Shredded browned almonds
Coffee butter icing (p.550) using 2–3 oz. butter, etc.

When genoese pastry is cold, spread top with coffee butter icing, rather roughly. Press shredded browned almonds over and dredge with icing sugar. Cut into fingers 3 in. by 1 in.

SPONGES

NOTE: True sponges contain no fat.

SAVOY FINGERS

Biscuits à la Cuiller de Savoie

5 oz. plain flour	**4 eggs**
1 oz. cornflour	**5 oz. sugar**
Pinch of salt	

Sift together flour, cornflour and salt. Beat the whites of the eggs stiffly, add the sugar and beat well again. Stir in the beaten yolks and fold in the sifted flour. Place the mixture into a bag with a plain ½-in. pipe and pipe on to a greased baking-sheet in 3-in. lengths. Dust the biscuits with castor sugar. Bake in a moderate oven (**350° F., Gas 4**).

NOTE: These biscuits are particularly useful for making such sweets as Charlotte Russe (p. 452).

28 fingers **Cooking time—10–20 min.**

SPONGES

SPONGE CAKE (Plate 20)

Gâteau mousseline

4 oz. plain flour
Pinch of salt
3 eggs
4½ oz. castor sugar
Grated lemon rind

Grease and dust a 6-in tin with 1 teasp. flour and 1 teasp. castor sugar mixed together. Sift the flour and salt. Beat the eggs and sugar over a pan of hot water till thick and creamy. Fold flour, salt and lemon lightly into the egg and turn the mixture into the tin. Bake in a warm oven (**335° F., Gas 3**). When cold, split the sponge and spread with jam. Dust with icing sugar.

This may be cooked in a border or other mould if to be used as the base of a sweet.

Cooking time—45 min.

SPONGE CAKES—SMALL

3 oz. plain flour
Pinch of salt
3 eggs
3 oz. sugar
1 level teasp. baking-powder
½ teasp. vanilla essence

As for Sponge Cake. Put the mixture into oblong sponge cake-tins prepared by greasing and dusting with equal quantities of flour and castor sugar. Half-fill the tins and dredge the tops with castor sugar. Bake in a moderate oven (**350°–335° F., Gas 4–3**) until well risen, firm and a pale fawn colour.

10–12 cakes **Cooking time—20 min.**

SPONGE DROPS

4 oz. plain flour
Pinch of salt
1 level teasp. baking-powder
2 eggs
4 oz. castor sugar
Jam
¼ pt. sweetened and flavoured whipped cream *or* mock cream

Sift together flour, salt and baking-powder. Whisk eggs and sugar together over hot water till thick and creamy; fold the flour in lightly. Force out into drops or put teaspoonfuls on a greased, floured baking-sheet. Dredge thickly with castor sugar and bake in a moderate oven (**375°–350° F., Gas 5–4**).

When cold, spread half of the drops with jam, and force a rose of cream on the remaining half. Sandwich them together.

6–7 doubles
Cooking time—10–15 min.

SWISS ROLL

Bûche

3 oz. plain flour
Pinch of salt
1 level teasp. baking-powder
3 fresh eggs
3 oz. castor sugar
¼ teasp. vanilla essence
2 tablesp. raspberry jam

Line and grease a Swiss roll tin.

Sift flour, salt and baking-powder. Beat eggs and sugar in a bowl over a pan of hot water till thick and pale in colour. Do not let the bottom of the bowl touch the water. Lightly fold in flour etc. and add the vanilla essence. Spread on the tin and bake in a hot oven (**425° F., Gas 7**). Quick cooking is essential to keep the roll moist. Sprinkle castor sugar on to a sheet of kitchen paper, turn the roll on to this and cut half-way through the roll about 1 in. from the bottom end. Spread the roll with warm jam to within ½ in. of edge. Turn in the 1 in. at the bottom to make the initial roll and continue to roll up firmly with the aid of the kitchen paper. Press gently to keep in place. Remove paper and dust with castor sugar. (A very *lightly* damped clean tea cloth may be used instead of paper.)

NOTE: If the edges are very crisp it is advisable to trim them before rolling or the roll may crack.

Cooking time—7 min.

CHOCOLATE SWISS ROLL (Plate 20)

Bûche au Chocolat

As for Swiss roll, with the addition of 2–3 teasp. cocoa sifted with the flour.

When the roll is cooked, turn on to sugared paper, place a piece of greaseproof paper on top and roll up. When the roll has cooled, unroll it gently and spread with vanilla butter icing (p. 550). Roll up again. Dust with castor sugar.

MISCELLANEOUS CAKES

ALMOND FINGERS

Tranches d'Amandes

PASTRY

6 oz. margarine	**2 oz. cake-crumbs**
8 oz. plain flour	**2 oz. ground almonds**
Pinch of salt	**1 egg yolk**
4 oz. sugar	**Raspberry jam**

TOPPING

3 egg whites	**¼–½ teasp. almond essence**
8 oz. castor sugar	
3 oz. blanched chopped almonds	

Make the pastry: rub fat into sifted flour and salt; add sugar, crumbs and ground almonds. Mix with egg yolk and enough water to make a stiff consistency. Roll out to ¼ in. thickness and line a shallow baking-tin 13 in. by 9 in. Bake lightly in a moderate oven (**350° F., Gas 4**). When nearly cooked spread with raspberry jam.

Make the topping: whisk egg whites stiffly, fold in sugar, chopped almonds and essence, put into a saucepan and stir lightly till mixture boils. Spread on to pastry, return to oven and bake in a moderate-warm oven at (**350°–335° F., Gas 4–3**), until set and lightly browned. When cold cut into fingers about 3 in. long and 1 in. wide.

18 fingers
Cooking time—about 30–40 min.

ANGEL CAKE

2 oz. flour	**½ teasp. cream of tartar**
4½ oz. castor sugar	
¼ pt. egg whites	**½ teasp. vanilla essence**
Pinch of salt	

Use a 6-in. sandwich cake tin or a funnel tin which is not greased. Sift the flour and sugar separately three times, then sift the flour with ¼ of the sugar. Put the egg white and salt in a large, clean, dry bowl and whisk until frothy. Sprinkle on the cream of tartar and continue whisking till the white stands up in peaks. Avoid overwhisking so that the white has lost flavouring, then using a tablespoon fold in the sifted flour and sugar carefully and gradually. Pour into tin and gently cut through mixture with a knife to release air bubbles. Bake for 40–45 min. in a very cool oven (**290° F., Gas 1**) increasing the heat to (**335° F., Gas 3**) for the last 10–15 min. Allow the cake to stand in the inverted tin for 30 min. then turn out on to a cooling tray.

NOTE: When top springs back on finger pressure the cake is considered ready.

CALIFORNIAN JUMBLES

8 oz. butter *or* margarine	**2 egg whites**
8 oz. castor sugar	**10 oz. plain flour**
Finely-grated rind of 1 lemon	**Pinch of salt**

Cream the fat and sugar, add the lemon rind and lightly beaten egg whites, and stir in the sifted flour and salt. Turn the dough on to a pastry board and knead lightly, divide into 2 or 3 pieces and roll each out into lengths the thickness of the little finger. Cut off 4-in. pieces and turn the ends in scroll fashion; place on greased baking-sheets allowing room for spreading and bake in a moderate oven (**350° F., Gas 4**).

35–40 jumbles **Cooking time—20 min.**

CHOCOLATE FINGERS

Biscuits à la cuiller au Chocolat

2 oz. unsweetened chocolate	**Pinch of salt**
1 gill milk	**2 level teasp. cream of tartar**
Vanilla essence	**1 level teasp. bicarbonate of soda**
3 oz. butter *or* margarine	**Chocolate glacé icing** (p. 547)
4 oz. castor sugar	**Almonds (optional)**
2 eggs	
6 oz. plain flour	

Line with greased paper a shallow baking-tin such as is used for Genoese or Swiss roll. Melt the chocolate in a pan with ½ gill milk;

stir till boiling, add a few drops of vanilla essence and allow to cool. Cream the fat and sugar, add the egg yolks and beat well. Sift together the flour, salt and tartar. Dissolve the bicarbonate of soda in the remaining ½ gill milk, add to the creamed fat, then stir in the chocolate, flour and, lastly, the stiffly-whisked egg whites. Put mixture into the prepared tin, spread evenly over the tin about ¾ in. thick. Bake in a fairly hot oven (**400° F., Gas 6**).

Turn carefully on to a sugared paper and when cool ice with chocolate icing. Cut in fingers and decorate to taste with icing, almonds, etc.

24 fingers **Cooking time—15 min.**

COCONUT CONES

2 egg whites
5 oz. castor sugar
5–6 oz. desiccated coconut
1 teasp. ground rice *or* semolina

Beat the egg whites stiffly, stir in the other ingredients. Make into small cone shapes or, if desired, pack the mixture into wet egg-cups and turn out on to a greased baking-sheet. Bake in a cool oven (**310° F., Gas 2**) until fawn colour.

NOTE: If desired, cones may be coloured pink by adding carmine to egg whites while whisking.

12–14 cones

COCONUT PYRAMIDS

3 egg whites
1½ oz. rice flour
4–5 oz. castor sugar
8 oz. desiccated coconut
½ teasp. vanilla essence
Rice paper

Whisk the egg whites very stiffly, stir in lightly the rice flour, castor sugar, coconut and essence. Put the mixture in small close heaps on rice paper; bake in a cool oven (**310° F., Gas 2**) till they are light brown.

18 pyramids

COCONUT ROCKS

8 oz. butter *or* margarine
8 oz. castor sugar
10 oz. flour
Pinch of salt
6 oz. desiccated coconut
2 eggs *or* 3 small ones

Cream the fat and sugar. Sift the flour and salt, and add gradually with the coconut, to the creamed fat. Add the eggs, still beating the mixture. Drop small spoonfuls on to a greased baking-sheet or into paper cases and bake in a hot oven (**425° F., Gas 7**).

30 cakes
Cooking time—8–10 min.

COCONUT ROUNDS

2 oz. plain flour
1 oz. rice flour
Pinch of salt
4 oz. sugar
2 oz. butter *or* margarine
1 egg
3 oz. desiccated coconut
1 oz. glacé cherries

Sift the flour, rice flour, salt and 2 oz. sugar into a bowl. Add the fat and rub in with the finger tips. Mix to a stiff dough with the yolk of the egg. Sprinkle the board with rice flour and knead dough lightly on it. Roll out ¼ in. thick and cut into 2-in. or 2½-in. rounds. Beat the egg white very stiffly and add to it the remaining 2 oz. of sugar and the coconut. Pile the mixture on top of the pastry rounds, put a half cherry on each and bake in a warm oven (**335° F., Gas 3**) till biscuits are pale brown and coconut mixture firm.

10–12 cakes
Cooking time—30–40 min.

FRUIT CHEWS

4 oz. plain flour
1 level teasp. baking-powder
4–6 oz. castor sugar
3 oz. shelled walnuts
8 oz. stoned dates
2 eggs
½ teasp. vanilla essence (optional)
Milk to mix
Icing sugar

Grease, and line the bottom of a Yorkshire pudding tin with greased paper.

Sift the flour, baking-powder and sugar; add the chopped walnuts and dates. Mix with the eggs, vanilla if used, and milk as necessary, to make a soft dropping consistency. Put the mixture in the tin and bake till firm and brown in a fairly hot oven (**400° F., Gas 6**). Turn out, cut into fingers and roll in icing sugar.

18–20 chews
Cooking time—20–30 min.

JAP CAKES

2 egg whites
4 oz. castor sugar
4 oz. ground almonds
A few drops almond essence
Glacé icing
Butter icing (p. 550), using 1½ oz. butter, etc., flavoured with coffee

Grease and flour a small baking-tray. Whisk egg whites—not too stiffly. Whisk in ½ of the castor sugar, then fold in ground almonds, essence and remaining sugar, lightly. Spread the mixture evenly over the prepared tray. Bake in a moderate oven (**350° F., Gas 4**) until almost set, then cut at once into rounds 1½ in. in diameter, return them to the oven with the trimmings, until quite firm, and place on a cooling tray. Allow trimmings to continue cooking till a good golden colour and when cold crush with a rolling-pin and pass through a fine sieve. Sandwich rounds together in pairs with butter icing, spread top and sides smoothly with butter icing and coat with the sieved crumbs.

Re-shape the cakes, using a knife, and decorate the top of each with a little pink glacé icing dropped in the centre.

12–14 cakes
Cooking time—20–30 min.

MERINGUE BATON

SHORTBREAD

3 oz. flour
½ oz. sugar
2 oz. butter *or* margarine
Jam

MERINGUE

2 egg whites
4 oz. castor sugar

Sift the flour, add the sugar, knead it into the fat. Roll out ¼ in. thick and cut into fingers 3 in. by 1 in. Prick well and cook in a moderate oven (**350° F., Gas 4**).

Whisk egg whites stiffly and gradually whisk in the castor sugar. Spread biscuits with a very little jam, pipe meringue on top using a vegetable pipe and dredge with sugar. Finish in a slow oven (**310° F., Gas 2**) until meringue is crisp and light fawn.

8 batons
Cooking time—40 min.

MERINGUES (Plate 13)

2 egg whites
Pinch of salt
4 oz. castor sugar
¼ pt. sweetened and flavoured cream

Place egg whites and salt in a clean dry bowl and whisk until whites stand up in points. Beat in 2–3 teasp. of sugar, then lightly fold in remainder. Using a bag and plain vegetable pipe, force the mixture in shell shapes on to greaseproof paper on a baking-sheet. Alternatively, use 2 dessertsp. to shape oval meringues, dip the spoons in cold water. Dredge with castor sugar and bake in a very cool oven (**265° F., Gas ½**). When meringues are firm, loosen from paper and press-in the soft centre; return to oven till dry and crisp. When cool, sandwich 2 meringue shells together with whipped cream. Decorate with glacé cherries and angelica.

12 shells *or* 6 doubles **Cooking time—3–4 hr.**

NEAPOLITAN CAKES

4 oz. plain flour
Pinch of salt
4 oz. butter or margarine
4 oz. sugar
4 oz. ground almonds
1 egg
Apricot jam

DECORATION

A few glacé cherries
Glacé icing (p. 547), using 6–8 oz. icing sugar

Sift flour and salt and rub in the fat. Add the sugar and ground almonds and mix to a stiff paste with the egg. Roll the paste a good ⅛ in. thick and cut into rounds with a 2½-in. or 3-in. cutter. Bake on a greased baking-sheet in a fairly hot oven (**375° F., Gas 5**) till golden brown. When cold, spread half of the rounds with jam and place the other rounds evenly on top. Ice the top with glacé icing and place half a cherry in centre of each cake.

12 cakes
Cooking time—20 min.

NUTTY MERINGUES

Méringues aux Noix

2 egg whites
4 oz. castor sugar
2 oz. chopped blanched almonds *or* walnuts

Whisk egg whites and sugar in a basin over a pan of hot water until stiff enough to pile up; stir in chopped nuts. Put in rough heaps on to a tray covered with greased paper. Cook in a warm oven (**335°–310° F., Gas 3–2**) until firm 30–40 min. The meringues may be coloured.

8 meringues

PITCAITHLY BANNOCK

8 oz. plain flour
2 oz. castor sugar
4 oz. butter
1 oz. blanched chopped almonds
1 oz. candied orange peel

Mix the sifted flour and sugar and rub in the butter until a dough is formed. Add the almonds and chopped peel. Form into a round thick cake and prick with a fork. Decorate edge.

Pin a band of paper round and bake in a warm to cool oven (**335°–310° F., Gas 3–2**).

Cooking time—¾–1 hr.

PRINCESS CAKES

7 oz. butter *or* margarine
1–2 oz. castor sugar
8 oz. self-raising flour
Pinch of salt
Grated rind of ½ orange
Orange butter icing (p. 550)
Chocolate glacé icing (p. 547)

Beat fat and sugar till very creamy and soft, stir in the sifted flour and salt. Stir in the orange rind. Using a vegetable star pipe, pipe out the mixture in 3½-4 in. lengths on greased baking-sheets. Bake in a moderate oven (**375°–350° F., Gas 5–4**), then sandwich 2 together with butter icing and dip the ends in chocolate glacé icing.

NOTE: ½ an egg may be added to the creamed fat and sugar.

16–20 cakes **Cooking time—15–20 min.**

QUEEN'S FINGERS

4–5 oz. butter *or* margarine
2½ oz. castor sugar
4 oz. plain flour
4 oz. ground rice *or* semolina
1 oz. ground almonds
A few drops almond essence
Jam
Glacé icing (p. 547) **using 3 oz. icing sugar, etc., coloured pink**

DECORATION

A few chopped blanched almonds

Cream fat and sugar thoroughly; add the sifted flour and other dry ingredients and the almond essence. Knead until smooth, but mixture should be stiff. Roll out into a square or oblong shape ¼ in. thick, cut into 3 equal sized pieces and sandwich these together with jam. Bake in a fairly hot oven (**375°–350° F., Gas 5–4**) until firm and pale brown. When cool spread with glacé icing and sprinkle with chopped almonds. When set, cut into fingers.

12 fingers
Cooking time—20–30 min.

RING CAKES

2 oz. butter *or* margarine
1 oz. castor sugar
¼ of an egg
4 oz. plain flour
Pinch of salt
½ level teasp. baking-powder
Redcurrant jelly
Green cake crumbs *or* chopped pistachio nuts

ALMOND MIXTURE

1½ egg whites
4 oz. ground almonds
2 oz. castor sugar
Few drops of almond *or* ratafia essence

Cream the fat and sugar, add the egg and work in the sifted flour, salt and baking-powder. Knead till smooth then roll out and cut into rounds with a 2½–3-in. fluted cutter. Put the almond mixture into a piping bag with a star pipe and pipe some of the mixture in a circle round each biscuit. Bake in a moderate oven (**350° F., Gas 4**) and when cool put ½ teasp. redcurrant jelly in the centre of each cake and sprinkle with chopped nuts *or* green crumbs.

10 cakes
Cooking time—15–20 min.

SHORTBREAD (SCOTTISH)

Sablé

8 oz. flour
2 oz. castor sugar
4 oz. butter

Put the flour and sugar in a pile on a pastry-board. Gradually knead the sugared flour into the butter with the hand. It is important not to let the butter become broken up. When a firm dough is formed, roll out and shape into a cake about 1 in. high. Decorate the edges by marking with a fork or fluting with finger and thumb, or make in a shortbread mould, and prick a pattern on top with a fork or skewer. Fasten a narrow band of paper round to keep the cake in shape. Bake in a warm to cool oven (**335°–310° F., Gas 3–2**). Dredge with castor sugar when cooked.

Cooking time—about 1 hr.

SHORTBREAD ROLLS

3 oz. plain *or* self-raising flour
1½ oz. butter *or* margarine
¾ oz. sugar
Raspberry *or* apricot jam

Sift the flour and rub in the fat. Add the sugar and work all together into a smooth paste. Divide into lumps, place on a greased baking-sheet and dent the centre of each with the thumb. Bake in a moderate–warm oven (**350°–335° F., Gas 4–3**) till lightly browned. When cool, fill each hollow with jam.

NOTE: Self-raising flour gives a more open texture to the rolls.

8–10 rolls
Cooking time—15–20 min.

ALMOND SHORTCAKE

4 oz. butter *or* margarine
2 oz. Barbados sugar
½ egg yolk
8 oz. wholemeal flour
Pinch of salt
1 oz. ground almonds

Cream fat and sugar; add egg yolk, sifted flour and salt. Add the almonds. Knead all together to a stiff dough. Make into a cake as for Shortbread (Scottish) (p. 540)and bake in a warm to cool oven (**335°–310° F., Gas 3–2**).

The dough may be cut into fingers or other fancy shapes and baked as biscuits.

Cooking time—50–60 min.

STRAWBERRY SHORTCAKE

Gâteau de Fraises

8 oz. plain flour
⅛ teasp. salt
Pinch of baking-powder
½ oz. ground almonds
4½ oz. margarine
2 oz. sugar
1 egg yolk

FILLING

1 pt. strawberries
Sugar to taste
1–2 gills whipped cream

Sift flour, salt and baking-powder and mix with the ground almonds. Cream the fat and sugar and add egg yolk. Work in the flour mixture as for a cake of shortbread. Divide into three pieces and roll into rounds a good ¼ in. thick. Bake in a moderate oven (**350° F., Gas 4**) until golden brown, then allow to become cold. Crush strawberries slightly with sugar to taste and add a little whipped cream. Spread this on to the first round of shortcake, cover with the second round and so on finishing with a layer of strawberries. Pipe whipped cream on top and round edges. Decorate as desired.

Cooking time—30–40 min.

NOTE: Self-raising flour may be used if liked.

APPLE SHORTCAKE

Make the cake as above but use apples for the filling. Peel the apples, cut into neat pieces and stew in sugar syrup—keep some nice pieces for the top. Alternatively mix some grated raw apple with whipped sweetened cream and use for filling.

SWISS SHORTCAKES

3 oz. butter *or* margarine
1½ oz. castor sugar
3 oz. self-raising flour
1 oz. cornflour
Pinch of salt
¼ teasp. vanilla essence
1½ tablesp. cold water
Jam

Cream fat and sugar. Sift the flour, cornflour and salt, and add with the vanilla, to the creamed fat. Add a little cold water, if necessary. Using a large vegetable star pipe, force the mixture into paper cases and bake in a moderate oven (**350° F., Gas 4**). When cold, dust with icing sugar and place a small amount of red jam in the centre of each.

9 cakes **Cooking time—30–40 min.**

BISCUITS

ALMOND CIRCLES

Cercles d'Amandes

5½ oz. plain flour
Pinch of salt
2 oz. butter *or* margarine
2½ oz. sugar
½ teasp. almond essence
½ teasp. baking-powder
Egg *or* milk to mix
Glacé icing using 4 oz. icing sugar

Sift flour and salt, and rub in the fat. Add sugar, essence and baking-powder and mix to stiff dough with egg or milk. Roll out ¼ in. thick and cut into rings using 2½–1½-in. cutters. Place on a greased baking-sheet and bake in a moderate oven (**350° F., Gas 4**) until lightly browned. When cool spread tops of biscuits with glacé icing and if desired decorate with a sprinkling of "hundreds and thousands".

40 circles
Cooking time—20 min.

NOTE: Self-raising flour may be used if liked.

ALMOND SHORTBREAD BISCUITS

Biscuits d'Amandes

5 oz. butter *or* margarine
1 oz. ground almonds
8 oz. plain flour
1 oz. cornflour
3 oz. sugar

Cream the fat in a bowl, add the almonds. Sift flour and cornflour. Gradually work them into the creamed fat with the sugar, using the hand. Knead on board, roll out ¼ in. thick and cut into rounds or fancy shapes. Allow to firm for 1 hr. then bake in a moderate oven (**350° F., Gas 4**).

30–36 biscuits
Cooking time—20–30 min.

AUSTRALIAN BISCUITS

3 oz. plain flour
2 oz. coconut
2 oz. rolled oats
1½ oz. sugar
1 level teasp. bicarbonate of soda
3 oz. lard *or* margarine
1 tablesp. golden syrup
1 teasp. water

Sift flour and mix with other dry ingredients. Melt fat and syrup with water, pour into dry ingredients and mix well. Allow to set. Form into small balls and place well apart on a greased baking-sheet. Bake in a moderate oven (**350° F., Gas 4**).

20 biscuits
Cooking time—10–15 min.

BRANDY SNAPS

2½ oz. sugar
1 oz. butter *or* margarine
1 oz. golden syrup
1 oz. plain flour
1 level teasp. ground ginger

Cream sugar, fat and syrup, and stir in the sifted flour and ginger. Make into 12–16 small balls and place well apart on greased baking-sheets. Bake in a cool oven (**310° F., Gas 2**) until rich brown colour. Allow to cool slightly, remove from sheet with a knife and, while soft enough, roll round the handle of a wooden spoon, remove when set. The snaps may be filled with sweetened and flavoured cream.

12–16 Brandy snaps
Cooking time—10–15 min.

CHOCOLATE JUMBLE BISCUITS

4 oz. margarine
4 oz. sugar
1 small egg
¼ teasp. vanilla essence
8 oz. self-raising flour
1–2 dessertsp. cocoa
Milk, as required

Cream margarine and sugar, add the well beaten egg and vanilla. Sift the flour and cocoa, and stir into the cream mixture, and if necessary add a little milk to make a fairly stiff consistency—not sticky. Using a forcing bag and a rose vegetable pipe, pipe the mixture on to a greased baking-sheet. Bake in a fairly hot-moderate oven (**375°–350° F., Gas 5–4**). If liked, they may when cool, be sandwiched in pairs with butter icing.

NOTE: The cocoa may be omitted and a piece of glacé cherry and angelica put on each biscuit before baking.

16 doubles, 32 singles
Cooking time—15–20 min.

COCONUT RINGS

5 oz. self-raising flour
3 oz. butter *or* margarine
2 oz. castor sugar
2 oz. desiccated coconut
½ egg
Milk, if necessary
Additional castor sugar and coconut for top

Rub fat into flour; add sugar and coconut. Mix with some of the beaten egg, adding a little milk, if necessary, to make a stiff consistency. Roll out ⅛–¼ in. thick, cut into 2½-in. rounds and cut the centre out of each with 1¼-in. cutter. Brush the rings with the remaining egg and sprinkle with equal parts of castor sugar and coconut. Bake in a moderate oven (**350° F., Gas 4**).

36 rings
Cooking time—10–15 min.

CREAM BISCUITS

2 oz. margarine
2 oz. sugar
½ teasp. vanilla essence
2½ oz. plain flour
1½ oz. custard powder *or* cornflour
½ egg (approx.)
Vanilla butter icing (p. 550), using 3 oz. icing sugar, etc.

Cream the margarine, sugar and flavouring. Sift flour and custard powder, and add to the creamed margarine. Mix with enough egg to make a stiff but pliable dough. Roll out thinly on a floured board and cut into fingers 1 in. by 3 in. Bake in a moderate oven (**350° F., Gas 4**) until crisp but still cream in colour. When cold, sandwich pairs together with vanilla butter icing.

NOTE: The use of a ridged roller gives an attractive and more unusual surface to the biscuits.

12–16 doubles
Cooking time—20 min.

DOVER BISCUITS

3 oz. butter *or* margarine
3½ oz. castor sugar
2 *or* 3 egg yolks
1 level tablesp. currants
8 oz. plain flour
Pinch of salt
½ level teasp. mixed spice
Egg white and castor sugar

Cream the fat, add sugar and cream again. Beat in the yolks thoroughly, add the currants and sifted flour, salt and spice and knead well —the dough should be stiff. Roll out ¼ in. thick and cut into rounds with 2–2½-in. cutter. Decorate by scoring the biscuits with a knife, and bake in a moderate oven (**350° F., Gas 4**) till golden brown. When nearly cooked, brush with slightly beaten egg white and sprinkle with castor sugar.

20 biscuits
Cooking time—20 min.

GERMAN BISCUITS

2 oz. margarine
1½ oz. sugar
¼ egg
4 oz. plain flour
Pinch of salt
½ level teasp. powdered cinnamon
¼ level teasp. baking-powder
A little jam

DECORATION

Glacé cherries
Glacé icing using 3 oz. icing sugar

Cream fat and sugar, add egg. Sift dry ingredients and work into the fat mixture. Mix to a stiff consistency and roll out thinly. Cut into 2–2½-in. rounds and bake in a moderate oven (**350° F., Gas 4**). When cold, put 2 together with jam, coat with the icing and decorate with pieces of cherry or a spot of red colouring.

12–16 biscuits
Cooking time—20 min.

GINGER SNAPS

6 oz. self-raising flour
Pinch of salt
1 level teasp. bicarbonate of soda
2 level teasp. ground ginger
3–4 oz. sugar
2 oz. lard *or* shortening
1½ oz. golden syrup
1 egg

NOTE: Take small measure of bicarbonate and ginger.

Sift flour, salt, soda and ginger; add sugar. Melt lard and syrup, cool slightly, then add to dry ingredients; add the egg. Divide into 24 pieces and make into balls, place well apart on greased baking-sheets. Bake in a fairly hot to moderate oven (**375°–350° F., Gas 5–4**) till a good rich brown colour.

24 Ginger Snaps **Cooking time—20 min.**

JEWEL BISCUITS

Shortbread mixture | **Jam** | **Icing sugar**

Roll shortbread out thinly and cut into 2-in rounds. From half the number of rounds remove the centre with a 1-in. cutter. Bake as for Shortbread Biscuits. When cold, spread the uncut biscuits with jam, dredge cut-out biscuits with icing sugar and place on top.

12–14 biscuits

LAKELAND FINGERS

8 oz. plain flour
Pinch of salt
1½–2 level teasp. ground ginger
½ level teasp. bicarbonate of soda
1 level teasp. cream of tartar
4 oz. brown sugar
4 oz. butter *or* margarine

Sift dry ingredients into a bowl. Rub in fat till quite fine. Put into a shallow tin and press lightly making the mixture ½–¾ in. thick. Bake in a moderate oven (**350° F., Gas 4**). Cut into fingers while still warm.

12 fingers **Cooking time—20–30 min.**

MACAROONS

Macarons

2 egg whites
4 oz. castor sugar
3 oz. ground almonds
1 teasp. rice flour
½ teasp. vanilla essence
Rice paper *or* greaseproof paper
Shredded almonds for top

Beat egg whites stiffly in a large bowl. Mix the sugar, almonds and rice flour together and fold into the beaten whites, add vanilla essence. Place the rice paper or greaseproof paper on a baking-sheet. Put the mixture into a large bag with a ½–1-in. plain pipe and pipe on to the rice paper in rounds about 1½ in. diameter. Decorate with the shredded almonds and bake in a moderate oven (**350° F., Gas 4**).

20 macaroons **Cooking time—20–30 min.**

MELTING MOMENTS

2 oz. lard *or* other all-purpose shortening
2 oz. margarine
3 oz. sugar
½ egg
½ teasp. vanilla essence
5 oz. self-raising flour
Cornflakes

Cream fat and sugar and beat in egg. Add flavouring, stir in the sifted flour and with wet hands make into balls the size of marbles and roll in crushed cornflakes. Bake in a fairly hot to moderate oven (**375°–350° F., Gas 5–4**).

24 biscuits **Cooking time—15 min.**

MUNCHIES

2 oz. sweetened chocolate
½ oz. butter *or* margarine
Wheat flakes
1 level tablesp. chopped stoned raisins
1 level tablesp. chopped walnuts
A few drops of vanilla essence

Grate the chocolate and put it in a basin over a pan of hot water till melted. Stir in the fat and enough lightly toasted wheat flakes to thicken. Add the raisins, nuts and vanilla. Drop the mixture in teaspoonfuls into small paper cases or on to greaseproof paper and leave to firm.

OATCAKES—Rich

3 oz. plain flour
½ teasp. salt
2 level teasp. bicarbonate of soda
2 level teasp. cream of tartar
1 lb. oatmeal
1 oz. sugar
4 oz. butter and lard *or* margarine and lard
Milk

Sift the flour, salt, soda and cream of tartar; add the oatmeal and sugar and rub in the fat. Add the milk, and mix to a stiff but not hard dough. Dust the baking-board with a mixture of flour and oatmeal, and roll out thinly. Rub the surface with oatmeal and cut out with a 3½-4-in. cutter *or* cut into triangles. Place on a baking-sheet and cook in a warm to cool oven (**335°–310° F., Gas 3–2**).

About 40 oatcakes—depending on size
Cooking time—20–30 min.

PANAMA BISCUITS

4 oz. self-raising flour
Pinch of salt
1–2 dessertsp. cocoa
1 level teasp. baking-powder
2 oz. butter *or* margarine *or* lard
1½ oz. sugar
1 teasp. syrup
¼–½ egg
Water, if necessary
Chocolate butter icing (p. 550), **using 2 oz. icing sugar etc.**

Sift flour, salt, cocoa and baking-powder. Cream the fat and sugar, add syrup and egg and work in the flour, etc. to make a stiff consistency; add a very little water if necessary. Roll out fairly thinly, cut into fingers 1 in. by 3 in., and prick slightly. Dust with castor sugar and bake in a moderate oven (**350°–335° F., Gas 4–3**) until firm.

When cold sandwich together with chocolate butter icing.

NOTE: The amount of cocoa depends on the kind used, and whether or not a strong flavouring of cocoa is desired.

10–12 biscuits
Cooking time—20 min.

PARKIN BISCUITS

2 oz. plain flour
2 oz. oatmeal
1½ oz. sugar
½ level teasp. ground ginger
½ level teasp. powdered cinnamon
¼ level teasp. mixed spice
1 oz. lard *or* all-purpose shortening
1 level teasp. bicarbonate of soda
1½ oz. golden syrup
¼ egg

DECORATION

Blanched almonds

Sift and mix flour, oatmeal, sugar and spices, and rub in the fat. Add soda, syrup and egg. Mix well to a fairly stiff consistency. Form into balls and place a little apart on greased baking-sheets; put ½ a blanched almond on top of each. Bake in a moderate to warm oven (**350°–335° F., Gas 4-3**). Allow to cool slightly before removing from sheet.

12–14 biscuits
Cooking time—15–20 min.

PETITS FOURS (1) (Plate 32)

2 egg whites
4 oz. ground almonds
2 oz. castor sugar
A few drops almond essence
Rice paper

DECORATION

Glacé cherries
Angelica

Whisk egg whites very stiffly and fold in mixed almonds and sugar very lightly, with the almond essence. Place the mixture in a forcing bag fitted with a large rose vegetable pipe and force it on to rice paper in rosettes or oblongs. Decorate with small pieces of cherry and angelica and bake in a moderate to warm oven (**350°–335° F., Gas 4–3**) till golden brown.

20–30 petits fours **Cooking time—20–30 min.**

PETITS FOURS (2) (Plate 32)

Genoese pastry (p. 534)
Apricot marmalade *or* glaze
Butter icing (p. 550) **and cake-crumbs**
Almond paste
Glacé icing *or* royal icing

Cut neat shapes of genoese pastry squares, rings, triangles, etc. Using apricot marmalade fasten a small piece of almond paste *or* some butter icing mixed with cake-crumbs and flavoured with vanilla, kirsch, rum, etc., neatly on top of each piece of genoese. Coat with glacé or royal icing and decorate with fine piping, scrolls, etc.

RATAFIA BISCUITS

Biscuits au Ratafia

1½ egg whites
1 oz. butter
6 oz. castor sugar
4 oz. ground almonds
Rice paper *or* greaseproof paper

Beat the egg whites stiffly in a large bowl. Cream the butter and sugar. Add the ground almonds and mix well together. Fold into the egg whites and mix to a smooth paste. When the mixture begins to get stiff put it into a large bag with a plain pipe. Place the rice paper or greaseproof paper on a baking-sheet and pipe small drops about 2 in. apart. Bake in a moderate oven (**350° F., Gas 4**).

24–30 ratafias **Cooking time—about 15 min.**

SCOTTISH OATCAKES

8 oz. medium oatmeal
½ teasp. salt
Pinch of bicarbonate of soda
1 tablesp. melted dripping
Boiling water

Mix oatmeal, salt and bicarbonate of soda in a bowl; add melted fat and enough boiling water to make a pliable but not wet dough. Knead well. Sprinkle board with oatmeal and roll mixture out thinly. Cut into 3½-in. rounds or alternatively cut into 6-in. rounds and divide into 4 triangles. Rub with oatmeal to whiten. Cook on *one side* on a moderately hot girdle, then place in oven or before fire to crisp through and till ends curl up.

12 oatcakes depending on size

SHERRY BISCUITS

5 oz. plain flour	**1 egg**
4 oz. butter *or* margarine	**1 tablesp. sherry**
3 oz. castor sugar	**Chopped almonds**

Sift the flour and rub in the fat. Add the sugar and mix stiffly with the egg yolk and sherry. Roll out the dough to ⅛ in. thickness. Prick all over and cut into fancy shapes, using 2–2½-in. cutter. Brush the biscuits with lightly beaten egg white and sprinkle with chopped almonds. Bake in a moderate oven (**350° F., Gas 4**).

30–32 biscuits **Cooking time—15–20 min.**

SHORTBREAD BISCUITS

4 oz. butter *or* margarine	**2 oz. castor sugar**
	8 oz. plain flour

Cream fat and sugar and work in the sifted flour with the hand; knead well. Roll out a good ¼ in. thick and cut into fancy shapes or fingers (for fingers a more effective result is obtained if shortbread is rolled from ¼ in. to ½ in. thick). Prick neatly and bake in a moderate–warm oven (**350°–335° F., Gas 4–3**) till pale fawn in colour and crisp. Dredge with castor sugar while still warm.

16–20 fingers *or* 24–30 biscuits
Cooking time—20–30 min.

SHREWSBURY BISCUITS

Basic Recipe

4 oz. butter *or* margarine	**½ level teasp. ground cinnamon *or* 1 teasp. grated lemon rind**
4 oz. castor sugar	**Milk as required**
1 small egg	
8 oz. plain flour	

Cream the fat and sugar and beat in the egg. Sift flour with cinnamon, *or* add grated rind, and add to the creamed fat mixture. Mix to a stiff consistency, using milk if required. Roll out fairly thinly and cut out with a 2½-in. cutter. Place on a greased baking-sheet and bake in a moderate oven (**350° F., Gas 4**) till light fawn colour.

30–32 biscuits **Cooking time—15–20 min.**

Variations of Basic Recipe

EASTERTIDE BISCUITS

Add ½ level teasp. mixed spice and 2 oz. currants to the basic recipe for Shrewsbury Biscuits. Roll out mixture to ¼ in. thickness and cut into 4-in. rounds. If desired, brush with egg white and dredge with sugar. Bake in a moderate oven (**350° F., Gas 4**) until golden brown.

12–16 biscuits **Cooking time—20–30 min.**

SULTANA, CURRANT or DATE FINGERS

Add 4–6 oz. sultanas or currants or chopped dates to the basic recipe for Shrewsbury Biscuits. Divide mixture into 2 pieces. Roll each into an oblong and spread one with the fruit. Cover with second piece. Roll lightly till about ¼ in. thick, trim edges and decorate top with a knife, cutting diamond shapes. Brush with egg-wash and cut into fingers 1 in. by 3 in. long. Put on a greased baking-sheet and bake in a fairly hot to moderate oven (**375°–350° F., Gas 5–4**) till golden brown.

24 fingers **Cooking time—15–20 min.**

YORK BISCUITS

2 oz. lard *or* margarine	**½ level teasp. bicarbonate of soda (good measure)**
3 oz. sugar	**2 level teasp. ground ginger**
¼ egg	**Milk as required**
4 oz. plain flour	
1 level teasp. cream of tartar	

Cream the fat and sugar, add the egg. Sift the dry ingredients and work into the fat mixture, adding milk as necessary. The consistency should be such that it can be handled; not too soft but not stiff. Make into about 20 balls and place well apart on greased baking-sheets, press very lightly if necessary. Bake in a moderate to warm oven (**350°–335° F., Gas 4–3**) till fawn colour.

20 biscuits **Cooking time—20 min.**

ICINGS AND CAKE DECORATION

AMERICAN FROSTING

8 oz. granulated sugar **1 egg white**
4 tablesp. water

Put the sugar and water into a pan, dissolve the sugar slowly in the water and when quite dissolved bring to boiling-point. Boil to 240° F. without stirring. Brush down the sides of the pan with a brush dipped in cold water and remove scum as it rises. Pour on to the stiffly beaten egg white, beating all the time. Continue beating until the icing begins to thicken and coats the back of a spoon thickly. Pour quickly over the cake, spread with a palette knife and work up the icing in swirls.

NOTE: ½ teasp. vanilla essence or lemon juice and a pinch of cream of tartar may be added if liked. The frosting may be used either as a covering or as a filling.

APRICOT GLAZE

2 tablesp. apricot jam **1 tablesp. water**

Sieve apricot jam and water and bring to boiling-point. Use to glaze the top of small cakes, e.g. nougatines, and to stick almond paste to Christmas cakes, etc.

FONDANT ICING

1 lb. loaf *or* granulated sugar **1½ teasp. glucose *or* a good pinch of cream of tartar**
¼ pt. water

Dissolve the sugar in the water over a low heat, add the glucose or cream of tartar, bring to the boil quickly, and boil to a temperature of 237° F. Pour on to an oiled or wetted slab, let it cool slightly (if worked when too hot it will grain), and work well with a palette knife, keeping the mass together as much as possible. When the paste is sufficiently cool, knead well with the hands. Wrap in paper and store in an airtight tin.

When required put into a basin over a saucepan containing sufficient hot water to come half-way up the sides of the basin. Stir over a very low heat until icing has the consistency of thick cream. Flavour and colour as required. Allow to cool slightly before using.

FLAVOURINGS

Chocolate: Add 3 dessertsp. grated chocolate, *or* 2 dessertsp. cocoa, or to taste.

Coffee: Stir in 2 dessertsp. coffee essence or to taste.

GLACÉ ICING

Glacé icing or water icing (soft icing) is made from sifted icing sugar moistened with warm water to make a thin coating consistency. It is used for icing sponges, sandwich and layer cakes, small cakes, biscuits and petits fours.

Basic Recipe

4 oz. icing sugar **Flavouring**
1 tablesp. warm water **Colouring**

If the sugar is lumpy, break up the lumps by rolling the sugar with a rolling-pin before sieving. Sieve the icing sugar and put into a small bowl over hot water. Add the 1 tablesp. warm water gradually. Stir until all the sugar is dissolved and the icing is smooth and warm. Do not allow to get too hot or the icing will lose its gloss. Add the flavouring and the colouring a drop at a time until the required shade is obtained. The icing should be thick enough to coat the back of the spoon; if too thin add more sugar, if too thick add more water. When of the correct consistency, cool slightly, then use at once.

This quantity will coat the top of a 6–8 in. cake.

Coffee icing: Add ½ teasp. coffee essence to the basic recipe, omitting ½ teasp. of the water.

Lemon icing: Substitute strained lemon juice for all or part of the water in the basic recipe. Add a few drops of colouring.

Orange icing: Substitute strained orange juice for all or part of the water in the basic recipe. Add a few drops of colouring.

CHOCOLATE ICING

3 oz. chocolate (preferably couverture *or* plain chocolate)	**8 oz. icing sugar**
	½ gill water

Break the chocolate into small pieces, put into a small bowl over a bowl of warm water and allow to dissolve. Add the sieved icing sugar and water, stir until well mixed and smooth. Use as required.

PINEAPPLE ICING

1 pt. water	**3 drops pineapple essence**
12 oz. loaf sugar	

Put the water and sugar into a strong pan. Allow to dissolve, then bring to boiling-point; skim well. Boil quickly without stirring until a pale brown colour and the syrup threads like caramel. Add the pineapple essence.

To Apply Glacé Icing

Place cakes on a wire cooling tray over a large flat dish or clean table-top. Petits fours and other small cakes that have to be coated all over are best dipped into the icing on a fork or skewer, then drained. For large cakes the cake top should be fairly level. Brush off any loose crumbs. When the icing is the desired consistency pour quickly into the centre of the cake and allow to run down the sides. Avoid using a knife if possible, but if this is necessary use a palette knife dipped in hot water and dried.

If the top only is to be iced, a smooth flat surface can be easily obtained by pinning a double thickness of greaseproof paper round the sides of the cake so that the paper stands 1 in. higher than the cake. Pour on the icing which will find its own level, and allow to set. When the icing has set remove the paper with the aid of a knife dipped in hot water.

Put any ready-made decorations on to the icing while it is still soft, but piped icing should be added after the surface is dry and firm.

TRANSPARENT ICING

1 lb. loaf sugar	**Lemon juice to flavour**
½ gill warm water	

Put the sugar and water into a strong saucepan, let it dissolve, then bring to the boil and simmer for about 5 min., or until a thick syrup is formed (**230° F.** on a saccharometer), brushing down the sides of the pan with a damp brush to remove the sugar. Stir in the lemon juice, and beat until the icing thickens and becomes opaque, then use as required.

ALMOND PASTE (ICING) (1)

Almond paste—often called almond icing or marzipan—is used to cover rich cakes before applying royal or glacé icing. (It is also used alone to decorate cakes, e.g. Simnel Cake and Battenburg Cake.) It is often coloured and flavoured and then moulded into various shapes to be used for cake decoration.

6 oz. icing sugar and 6 oz. castor sugar *or* 12 oz. icing sugar	**¾ teasp. orange flower water**
12 oz. ground almonds	**¾ teasp. vanilla essence**
Juice of ½ lemon	**1–2 egg yolks**

Sieve the icing sugar into a bowl and mix with the ground almonds and castor sugar. Add the lemon juice, essences and enough egg yolk to bind the ingredients into a pliable but dry paste. Knead thoroughly with the hand until smooth.

NOTE: A whole egg *or* egg whites may be used instead of egg yolks. Egg yolk gives a richer and yellower paste, whilst egg white gives a whiter, more brittle paste. (Economically the yolks can be used for almond paste and the whites used for royal icing.)

This quantity of paste is sufficient to cover the top and sides of an 8-in. cake.

ALMOND PASTE (2) Boiled

1 lb. loaf sugar	**12 oz. ground almonds**
¼ pt. water	**2 egg whites**

Dissolve the sugar in the water slowly, over a low heat. When the sugar has dissolved, bring to the boil, skim well, and boil to 240° F. Remove from heat and stir briskly until the syrup becomes cloudy. When slightly cooled, add the almonds and then the egg whites. Stir well and then turn on to a marble or enamel slab. Work with a palette knife

until the mixture is cool enough to handle. Knead with the hands until smooth.

NOTE: This paste can be coloured and flavoured to taste and is useful for moulding into sweets.

To Apply Almond Paste (Plate 28)

To cover the top and sides of a rich fruit cake, the cake top should be fairly level and the surface free from loose crumbs.

Brush the top and sides with warm apricot glaze, using a pastry brush. Dredge a little castor sugar on to a clean board and roll out the almond paste to a round which is 4 in. wider than the diameter of the cake. Place the cake in the centre of this with its glazed top downwards and work the paste upwards round the sides of the cake with the hands until it is within ¼ in. of the top edge, i.e. the cake bottom. Using a straight-sided jar or thick tumbler, roll firmly round the sides, pressing slightly with the other hand on the upturned bottom of the cake and turning the cake round on the sugared board when necessary.

Continue rolling and turning until the sides are straight and smoothly covered and the top edges of the cake are sharp and smooth, when the process is completed and the cake is turned upright.

NOTE: Allow a few days for the almond paste to dry, before putting on the royal icing, or the oil from the almond paste will discolour it. Cover with a clean cloth to protect from dust whilst drying.

ROYAL ICING

Glace Royal

1 lb. icing sugar (approx.)
2 egg whites
1 teasp. lemon juice

If the sugar is lumpy, roll with a rolling-pin before sieving. Put the egg whites into a bowl, beat slightly with a wooden spoon. Add 2 tablesp. sieved sugar and beat again. Gradually add the remainder of the sugar, beating well until a thick, smooth consistency and a good white colour are obtained. Add the lemon **juice** and beat again.

NOTE: If a softer icing is required 1 teasp. glycerine may be stirred in after the sugar; this prevents the icing becoming brittle and facilitates cutting.

If the icing is not to be used immediately, cover the bowl with a damp cloth to keep the icing soft.

Some cooks add 1 or 2 drops of confectioner's blue to make the icing white, but if the eggs are fresh and the icing is sufficiently well beaten, no blue colouring is necessary.

To Ice a Cake with Royal Icing

NOTE: These quantities are sufficient to coat a cake of 8 in. diameter.

Place the cake already covered with almond paste on a cake-board or inverted plate. Place the cake-board on a turntable if available.

AMOUNTS REQUIRED

First coating: Royal icing, using 1¼ lb. icing sugar, etc., mixed to a stiff consistency.

Second coating: ¾–1 lb. icing sugar, etc., consistency to coat the back of a spoon.

Decorative piping: ½ lb. icing sugar, etc., mixed to a stiff consistency, i.e. that will stand up in points when the back of the spoon is drawn away from the side of the bowl.

TO APPLY FIRST COATING

With a tablespoon take enough icing to cover the top, and place it in the centre of the cake. Spread evenly over top, smoothing the surface with a hot, wet palette knife (shake or dry the knife after dipping it in hot water as too much water softens the icing). Take up small portions of the icing with the end of the palette knife blade, spread it smoothly round the side until the cake is completely covered and the surface smooth.

Allow to set for a few days before applying the second coat. Whilst the icing is drying and as soon as it is hard enough, place a thin sheet of paper lightly over the top to protect it from dust.

TO APPLY SECOND COATING

Mix icing to a thin coating consistency and pour over the cake. Prick any bubbles with a fine skewer or pin; allow to firm before decorating.

TO DECORATE THE CAKE WITH PIPED ICING

Cut pieces of greaseproof paper the same sizes as the top and sides of the cake. Sketch on to these the patterns to be used for the decoration. Pin papers firmly into position on cake and prick pattern through. Mix icing to a stiff consistency and pipe design on to cake, starting at centre and working outwards, and finishing with the sides and the base.

Using a forcing bag: Decorative icing can be piped from a forcing bag and pipe. Fold an oblong of greaseproof paper in half diagonally and cut along the fold. Form one half into a cone-shaped bag. Cut off the pointed end of the cone and slip a forcing pipe into the bag so that it protrudes halfway through the cut point. Make a bag for each pipe to be used. Fill the bags ⅔ full with icing and fold over the top edges. Holding the pipe between the first and second fingers force the icing through the pipe by exerting pressure with the thumbs on the top of the bag.

Icing syringes are made of metal or plastic and can be bought in sets complete with decorative pipes and a turntable. If coloured icings are being used the syringe must be washed before filling with another colour.

All pipes must be kept clean. Always keep the bowl containing the icing covered with a damp cloth whilst decorating, to prevent the icing drying out.

The beginner should practise on an upturned cake tin or plate before starting on the cake, and the icing may be removed if scraped off immediately and returned to the covered bowl.

For Christmas cakes other decorations may be made with coloured marzipan, e.g. holly, mistletoe, etc., and the smooth icing surface roughened into points with a palette knife to form "snow drifts". For this one coat only is needed.

FILLINGS

ALMOND AND WALNUT FILLING

3 tablesp. ground almonds
1 teasp. vanilla essence
1 tablesp. chopped walnuts
2–3 tablesp. sieved apricot jam

Work all the ingredients well together.

BUTTER ICING (BUTTER CREAM)

2 oz. butter *or* margarine
3 oz. icing sugar
Flavouring
Colouring

Cream the butter or margarine. Add the sugar gradually and cream together. Beat until smooth, creamy and pale. Add flavouring and colouring to taste.

NOTE: In cold weather the butter may be warmed slightly to facilitate creaming but do not allow it to oil.

FLAVOURINGS

Almond: Beat in ¼ teasp. almond essence.

Chocolate: Dissolve 1 oz. chocolate in 1 tablesp. water and beat in, *or* beat in 1 dessertsp. cocoa and a few drops of vanilla essence.

Coffee: Beat in 1 dessertsp. coffee essence.

Jam: Add 1 tablesp. strong flavoured jam, e.g. plum, raspberry.

Lemon: Beat in 1 dessertsp. strained lemon juice.

Orange: Beat in 1 teasp. strained orange juice.

Vanilla: Beat in ½ teasp. vanilla essence.

Walnut: Add 2 oz. chopped walnuts and 1–2 teasp. coffee essence.

CHOCOLATE FILLING (1)

2 oz. butter *or* margarine
2 oz. grated plain chocolate
2 oz. ground almonds
2 oz. castor sugar

Cream the fat, work in the grated chocolate, add ground almonds and sugar.

CHOCOLATE FILLING (2)

3 oz. butter
5 oz. icing sugar
½ oz. plain chocolate
2 teasp. milk

Cream the butter and gradually work in the

sugar. Heat the chocolate in the milk until dissolved. Cool slightly then stir into the creamed butter and sugar. Mix well.

COCONUT FILLING

2 oz. icing sugar
1 egg yolk
1 tablesp. lemon juice
1 oz. desiccated coconut

Sift the sugar into a basin and mix to a smooth paste with the egg yolk and lemon juice. Place the basin over a pan of hot water over a low heat and cook until thick—about 5 min., stirring all the time. Remove from heat and stir in coconut, allow to cool before using.

COFFEE FILLING

2 oz. butter *or* margarine
1 tablesp. castor sugar
1 tablesp. cold water
1 tablesp. hot water
Few drops of coffee essence

Cream together the fat and sugar. Gradually beat in the cold water, then the hot (not boiling) water. Add coffee essence to taste.

CONFECTIONERS' CUSTARD

½ pt. milk
¾ oz. cornflour
2 yolks *or* 1 whole egg
1 oz. sugar
½ teasp. vanilla essence

Blend the cornflour with the milk, stir in the egg yolks and sugar, and cook over a gentle heat until thick. Beat in the vanilla. Allow to cool.

MINCEMEAT (1)

1 lb. cooking apples (prepared weight) finely chopped
1 lb. currants, cleaned and picked
1 lb. beef suet, finely chopped
1 lb. large raisins, stoned and quartered
½ lb. sultanas, halved
1 lb. demerara sugar
2 oz. almonds, blanched and finely chopped
½ gill rum
2 oz. each candied lemon, orange and citron peel, all finely chopped
Grated rind and juice of 2 large lemons
½ nutmeg, finely grated
¼ level teasp. each ground cloves and cinnamon
⅛ teasp. each ground mace and ginger
½ level teasp. salt
¼ pt. brandy

Mix all the prepared ingredients together, stirring well, and cover closely in clean dry jars. Keep for 2 or 3 weeks to allow to mellow before using.

MINCEMEAT (2)

1¼ lb. cooking apples (prepared weight)
1 lb. currants
1 lb. seedless raisins
½ lb. sultanas
¼ lb. candied peel
1 lb. beef suet
1 lb. sugar
Grated rind and juice of 2 lemons
1 level teasp. ground nutmeg
¼ level teasp. ground cloves
¼ level teasp. ground cinnamon
½ level teasp. salt
⅛ pt. brandy (*see note below*)

Peel and core the apples. Put these with the fruit, candied peel and suet through the mincer. Add the other ingredients and mix well. Cover in jars and use as required.

NOTE: If the mincemeat is to be used within a few days the brandy may be omitted.

MOCHA FILLING

½ oz. cornflour
1 gill milk
1 oz. loaf sugar
½ oz. butter
1 teasp. coffee essence
A few drops of vanilla essence
1 egg

Blend the cornflour in a little cold milk. Put the remaining milk and sugar in a saucepan and bring to boiling-point. Pour the boiling milk on to the blended cornflour, stirring all the time, return the mixture to the saucepan and boil for 3 min. Add the butter and flavourings and lastly the beaten egg. Stir till the mixture thickens then allow to cool.

MOCK CREAM

½ oz. cornflour
¼ pt. milk
1 oz. margarine
1 oz. sugar
A few drops of vanilla essence

Blend the cornflour with a little of the milk, and put the rest of the milk on to boil. Pour the boiling milk on to the blended cornflour, stirring well. Return mixture to pan and cook for 2–3 min. Cool. Cream together the margarine and sugar. Gradually beat the cornflour mixture into the creamed fat a little at a time, beat well. Stir in the vanilla essence.

RUM AND WALNUT FILLING

2 oz. butter
3 oz. brown sugar
1–2 dessertsp. rum
2 oz. chopped walnuts

Cream together the butter and sugar. Add the rum a few drops at a time, beating well between each addition. Beat in the walnuts.

PASTRY-MAKING

THE AIM in pastry-making is to make the pastry as light as possible and this depends on the amount of cold air incorporated in the mixture during the making. The cold air expands on heating, thus making the pastry light.

When making puff, flaky or rough puff pastry, the air is incorporated in the pastry in thin layers, while in short crust and suet pastry the air fills the cavities all through the pastry. Self-raising flour is only suitable for suet crust pastry and plain short crust pastry, and should not be used for rich pastries.

Butter, or butter and lard in equal quantities, should be used for pastry-making if possible, but in all the following recipes margarine may be substituted for butter.

When the amount of fat is less than $\frac{1}{2}$ the amount of flour a little baking-powder (1 level teasp. to $\frac{1}{2}$ lb. flour) may be added.

GENERAL HINTS

1. Keep everything for pastry-making cool.
2. Work in a cool place and if possible, on a marble slab or enamelled surface.
3. Always sift the flour.
4. When rubbing the fat into the flour use the finger-tips, and lift the hands up from the bowl so that air is caught as the flour falls back into the bowl.
5. Use freshly drawn cold water for mixing and mix with a round-bladed knife. Do not use too much water or the pastry will be hard.
6. Lemon juice tends to make pastry lighter.
7. Handle the pastry as little and as lightly as possible. Work quickly.
8. Allow the pastry to stand for a short time in a cool place after making, particularly in hot weather.
9. Roll the pastry lightly, quickly and evenly with short strokes, lifting the rolling-pin between each stroke. Do not roll off the edge of the pastry or the air will be pressed out.
10. Always roll away from oneself and never from side to side.

11. Use very little flour for rolling out and remove any surplus flour with a pastry brush.
12. Use the rolled side of the pastry for the outside.
13. When making puff, flaky or rough puff pastry allow the pastry to relax, if possible, for 15 min. between every two rollings.
14. Most pastries are baked in a fairly hot oven, but the richer the pastry the hotter the oven required for cooking. A high temperature is necessary to expand the air or gas, thus making the pastry light. The starch grains swell with the moisture thereby enabling the fat globules to intermingle more easily with the starch. Unless the heat is sufficiently great to act upon the flour in this way, the melted fat runs out and leaves the pastry less rich, and also, probably, heavy and tough.

NOTE: Hot Water Crust, Choux Pastry and Genoese Pastry are exceptions to these rules.

TO GLAZE PASTRY

Meat pies, patties, sausage-rolls, etc., are usually brushed over with well-beaten egg before, or during baking. When a deeper tone is desired the yolk alone is used, or if the egg white is being used in the preparation of a dish, a little milk may be added to the egg yolk to increase the quantity.

Fruit tarts, puffs, etc., may be brushed lightly with cold water, and dredged with castor sugar before baking. If a thin coating of icing is desired, they can be brushed over with well-beaten egg white and well-dredged with castor sugar, when nearly baked.

TO KEEP PASTRY

Pastry not intended for immediate use should be folded in greaseproof paper and kept in a refrigerator or cool place.

BUTTER CRUST

For boiled puddings

1 lb. plain flour	**6 oz. butter**
Pinch of salt	**Cold water to mix**

Sift the flour and salt and, using a knife, mix to a smooth paste with cold water, adding the water gradually. Roll out thinly. Place the butter over it in small pieces and dredge lightly with flour. Fold the pastry over, roll out again.

Use as required.

CHEESE PASTRY

For savoury pies and canapés

4 oz. flour	**3 oz. butter**
Pinch of dry mustard	**3 oz. Parmesan cheese**
Pinch of salt	**1 egg yolk**
Cayenne pepper	**2 teasp. cold water**

Sift flour, mustard and seasonings. Cream butter till very soft and white. Add flour, grated cheese and enough egg yolk and water to mix to a stiff dough. Bake in a fairly hot oven **(400° F., Gas 6)**.

PASTRY

CHOUX PASTRY

Pâte à choux

For Cream buns, Cream puffs and Éclairs

4 oz. plain flour
½ pt. water
⅛ teasp. salt
2 oz. butter *or* margarine
½ teasp. vanilla essence
1 egg yolk
2 eggs

Sift and warm the flour. Place water, salt and fat in a pan, and bring to boiling-point. Remove from heat, add flour all at once and beat well (using a wooden spoon) over the heat again, until it becomes a smooth soft paste and leaves the sides of the pan clean. Remove from the heat, add vanilla and egg yolk immediately and beat well. Add the other two eggs one at a time, beating thoroughly between each addition. (It is important to get the first of the egg in while the mixture is hot enough to cook it slightly, otherwise it becomes too soft.) Use as required.

Bake in a fairly hot oven (**400°–425° F., Gas 6–7**).

DRIPPING CRUST

For Plain Pies and Puddings

1 lb. plain flour
Pinch of salt
Cold water to mix
6 oz. clarified dripping

Using a knife, mix the flour and salt to a smooth paste with cold water added gradually. Roll out the pastry thinly, place ⅓ of the dripping over it in small pieces and fold over. Repeat this process twice, using ⅓ of the fat each time and use as required.

FLAKY PASTRY

Pâte feuilletée

For Pies, Tarts and Tartlets

1 lb. plain flour
Pinch of salt
10 oz. butter *or* butter and lard
Cold water to mix
½ teasp. lemon juice

Sift the flour and salt into a basin. Divide the butter into 4 equal portions and lightly rub ¼ of the butter into the flour. (If a mixture of butter and lard is used, blend them together with a round-bladed knife to get an even consistency, before dividing into 4.) Mix to a soft dough with cold water and lemon juice. The dough should be of the same consistency as the butter.

Roll out into an oblong strip, keeping the ends square and place ¼ of the butter in small pieces on the top ⅔ of the pastry. Dredge lightly with flour, fold up the bottom third of pastry on to the fat and fold down the top third. Using the rolling-pin, press the edges lightly together to prevent the air escaping. Half-turn the pastry so that the folded edges are left and right when rolling. With the rolling-pin press ridges in the pastry to distribute the air evenly. Roll out as before. Always roll carefully, do not allow the butter to break through the dough. If possible, allow the pastry to relax in a cool place.

Repeat the process with the other two portions of butter and again allow the pastry to relax. Roll out once more and use as required.

Flaky pastry should be put into a very hot oven (**450° F., Gas 8**) until set, then the heat should be reduced to fairly hot (**375° F., Gas 5**).

FRENCH CRUST

Pâte brisée

1 lb. plain flour
½ teasp. salt
6 oz. butter
2 eggs
Cold water to mix

Sift the flour and salt. Lightly rub in the butter. Mix to a smooth firm paste with the eggs and cold water added gradually. Use as required.

OATMEAL PASTRY

½ lb. plain flour
¼ lb. oatmeal
Pinch of salt
¼ lb. butter and lard
Cold water to mix

Mix the flour, oatmeal and salt together. Rub in the butter and lard. Mix to a stiff dough with cold water.

Use as required.

PÂTE SUCRÉE

8 oz. plain flour
Pinch of salt
5 oz. butter
2 oz. sugar
1 egg yolk
Cold water to mix

Sift together the flour and salt. Cut the butter into small pieces and rub it lightly into the flour using the finger tips. Add the sugar and mix with egg yolk and sufficient cold water to make a stiff paste.

Use as required.

NOTE In warm weather only a very small quantity of water will be required.

POTATO PASTRY

For covering meat or vegetable pies

1 lb. dry floury potatoes	**Pinch of salt**
1 lb. plain flour	**2 teasp. baking-powder**
2 oz. lard	**1 egg**
2 oz. dripping	**Warm milk to mix**

Bake sufficient potatoes (in their skins) to give 1 lb. potatoes. Remove skins and either mash the potatoes or rub them through a fine wire sieve. Rub the fat lightly into the flour and add the potatoes, salt and baking-powder. Add the beaten egg and enough milk to mix to a smooth paste.

Use as required.

PUFF PASTRY (Plate 23)

Feuilletage

For Pies, Tarts, Tartlets, Bouchées, Vol-au-Vents, Patties, etc.

1 lb. plain flour	**1 teasp. lemon juice**
Pinch of salt	**⅓ pt. cold water**
1 lb. butter	**(approx.)**

Sift the flour and salt and rub in about 2 oz. of butter. Press the remaining butter firmly in a floured cloth to remove the moisture, and shape into a flat cake. Add the lemon juice to the flour and mix to a smooth dough with cold water. The consistency of the dough must be the same as that of the butter. Knead the dough well and roll it out into a strip a little wider than the butter and rather more than twice its length. Place the butter on one half of the pastry, fold the other half over and press the edges together with the rolling-pin to form a neat parcel. Leave in a cool place for 15 min. to allow the butter to harden.

Roll out into a long strip 3 times the original length but the original width, keeping the corners square and the sides straight to ensure an even thickness when the pastry is folded. Do not let the butter break through the dough. Fold the bottom third up and the top third down, press the edges together with a rolling-pin and half turn the pastry so that the folded edges are on the right and left. Roll and fold again and lay aside in a cool place for 15 min. Repeat this process until the pastry has been rolled out 6 times. The rolling should be done as evenly as possible and the pastry kept in a long narrow shape which, when folded, forms a square. Roll out as required and leave in a cool place before cooking.

Bake in a very hot oven (**450° F., Gas 8**)—the oven door should not be opened until the pastry has risen and become partially baked, as a current of cold air may cause the pastry to collapse.

TO MAKE A VOL-AU-VENT CASE

Roll out the puff pastry to about ¾ in. thickness, and with a cutter previously dipped in flour, cut into a round or oval shape as desired. Cut cleanly without dragging or twisting the pastry. Place on a baking-sheet, brush over the top of the pastry with beaten egg. With a smaller, floured cutter cut an inner ring, cutting the pastry to about ½ its depth. Bake in a very hot oven (**450° F., Gas 8**). When baked, remove the lid and scoop out the soft inside.

TO MAKE PATTY CASES

Roll out the puff or flaky pastry to a thickness of ⅛ in. and cut into rounds with a 2½-in. or 3-in. cutter. Remove the centres from half of these rounds with a 1¼-in. or 1½-in. cutter. Turn the pastry upside down after cutting. Moisten the plain halves and place the ringed halves evenly on top. Prick the centres. Place on a baking-tray and allow to stand for at least 10 min. in a cold place. Glaze the ringed halves and the small lids and bake in a very hot oven (**450° F., Gas 8**). When baked, remove and scoop out any soft inside part. If liked the cases can be made as vol-au-vent cases (above), using smaller cutters.

TO MAKE HORN OR CORNET CASES

Roll out pastry thinly, then cut into strips ½ in. wide and 12–14 in. long. Moisten strips with water and wind round cornet mould from the point upwards with moist surface on outside. Finish final overlap on underside of tin and trim neatly. Brush with milk and bake in the middle of a very hot oven (**450° F., Gas 8**).

Cooking time—10–15 min.

RAISED PIE CRUST *or* HOT WATER CRUST PASTRY

For Pork, Veal and Ham or Raised Game Pies

10 oz. plain flour	**3 oz. lard**
½ teasp. salt	**¼ pt. milk *or* water**

Sift the flour and salt into a warm bowl, make a well in the centre, and keep in a warm place. Heat the lard and milk *or* water together gently until boiling then add them to the flour, mixing well with a wooden spoon, until cool enough to knead with the hands. Knead thoroughly, use as required. Leave covered for ½ hr.

Throughout the processes of mixing, kneading and moulding, the pastry must be kept warm, otherwise moulding will be extremely difficult. On the other hand, if the pastry is too warm it will be so soft and pliable that it cannot retain its shape, or support its own weight.

Bake in a hot oven (**425° F., Gas 7**), reduce heat to moderate (**350° F., Gas 4**) as soon as pastry is set.

TO RAISE A PIE

The pastry must be raised or moulded whilst still warm. Reserve ¼ for the lid and leave in the bowl in a warm place covered with a cloth. Roll out the remainder to about ¼ in. thickness in a round or oval shape as preferred. Gently mould the pie with the hands; if this proves too difficult mould it over a jam jar. Grease and flour the jar, invert it, place the pastry over and mould the pastry round the sides, taking care not to stretch the pastry and ensuring that the sides and base are of an even thickness. Leave to cool.

When cold, remove the pastry case from the jar, put in the filling. Roll the ¼ of pastry reserved for the lid, damp the rim of the case, put on the lid and press edges firmly together.

Three or four folds of greased paper should be pinned round the pie to preserve its shape during baking and to prevent it becoming too brown.

NOTE: If the pie is raised without using a jar, when the lower part of the pie has been raised to the required shape and thinness, moulding can be facilitated by pressing in firmly some of the filling to support the lower part of the pie. If liked the pie can be baked in a pie mould, cake-tin or a small loaf-tin; grease well before lining with the pastry.

RICH SHORT CRUST PASTRY

For Pies, Tarts, etc.

1 lb. plain flour	**2 teasp. castor sugar**
Pinch of salt	**2 egg yolks**
10–12 oz. butter	**Cold water to mix**

Sift the flour and salt together. Cut the butter into small pieces and rub it lightly into the flour using the finger tips. Add the sugar and mix to a stiff paste with the egg yolks and 1 tablesp. cold water, using more water if necessary. Use as required.

ROUGH PUFF PASTRY

½ lb. plain flour	**½ teasp. lemon juice**
Pinch of salt	**Cold water to mix**
6 oz. butter *or* butter and lard	

Sift the flour and salt. Add the butter cut up into pieces the size of a walnut and mix lightly with the flour. Make a well in the centre, put in the lemon juice and gradually add sufficient water to mix to an elastic dough. Roll into a long strip, keeping the corners square, fold into three. With the rolling-pin seal the edges and give the pastry a half-turn, so that the folded edges are on the right and left. Repeat until the pastry has been rolled and folded 4 times, if possible leaving for 15 min. in a cool place between the second and third rollings.

Use as required. Bake in a very hot oven (**450° F., Gas 8**).

SHORT CRUST PASTRY

For Pies, Tarts, etc.

½ lb. plain flour
Pinch of salt
2 oz. butter
2 oz. lard
Cold water to mix

Sift together the flour and salt. Rub the butter and lard lightly into the flour using the fingertips. Mix to a stiff paste with cold water.

Use as required.

SUET CRUST PASTRY

For Meat puddings, Fruit puddings, Jam Roly Poly, Suet Puddings, etc.

3–4 oz. suet
½ lb. plain flour
¼ teasp. salt
1 teasp. baking-powder
Cold water to mix

Chop the suet finely with a little flour or use shredded suet. Sift the flour, salt and baking-powder, and mix in the suet. Mix to a firm dough with cold water. Use as required.

SUET CRUST PASTRY—RICH

½ lb. plain flour
3 oz. breadcrumbs
¼ teasp. salt
6 oz. suet
1 teasp. baking-powder
Cold water to mix

Sift the flour and salt and add the breadcrumbs. Chop the suet finely or use shredded suet, add to the flour and breadcrumbs. Add the baking-powder and mix with cold water to a firm dough—soft enough to roll out easily, but not so moist that it sticks to the board and rolling-pin. Use as required.

NOTE: This pastry makes a very light, easily digested pudding but is liable to break if turned out of the basin.

SWEET PASTRY FOR TARTLETS

1 lb. plain flour
Pinch of salt
5 oz. butter
Rind of ½ lemon
8 oz. castor sugar
1 egg
Cold water, if necessary

Sift the flour and salt. Rub in the butter, add the sugar and finely grated lemon rind and mix to a stiff dough with beaten egg and a little cold water, if necessary.

Use as required.

TRANSPARENT PASTRY

For certain pies

¾ lb. butter
1 lb. plain flour
Pinch of salt
1 egg

Remove as much moisture as possible from the butter, using a dry cloth. Melt the butter over a very low heat; allow to cool. When almost cold stir in the sifted flour, salt and beaten egg. Knead lightly until smooth and use as required.

FLANS

TO LINE A FLAN RING

TO LINE a 7-in. flan ring about 4 oz. pastry (i.e. 4 oz. flour plus the other ingredients made into pastry) will be required. Grease a baking-sheet and the flan ring; place the flan ring on the baking-sheet. Roll the pastry into a circle about 1 in. larger than the flan ring and $\frac{1}{8}$ in. thick. Lift the pastry with the rolling-pin to prevent stretching and line the ring carefully with the pastry. Press to fit the bottom and sides so that no air bubbles form underneath the crust. Trim off the surplus pastry with a sharp knife or roll across the top of the ring with the rolling-pin.

"BAKING BLIND"

If a flan is to be cooked without filling it must be baked "blind". Prick the bottom of the flan, cover with a piece of greaseproof paper and fill with rice, beans, etc. (this prevents the flan from losing its shape during cooking). Bake according to the kind of pastry. When the pastry is cooked remove the paper and rice, beans, etc., and replace the flan case in the oven for 5 min. to dry the bottom. The rice or beans can be used over and over again—cool, store in a tin and keep them for this purpose.

See Plate 19

OPEN TARTS

OPEN TARTS are usually baked on fire-proof glass or enamel plates. The tarts may be filled with jam, syrup, treacle, custard, fruit etc. For a 7-in. plate about 4 oz. of pastry will be required.

Knead the dough into a round shape then roll into a round about $\frac{1}{8}$ in. thick and a little larger than the plate. Fold the pastry over the rolling-pin and gently lift it on to the plate. Smooth it over carefully with the fingers so that no air is trapped between the pastry and the plate—but take care that the pastry is not stretched in the process, as it will only shrink back later.

If the tart is being baked without a filling prick the base well or bake it "blind" (*see* above). When baking stand the plate on a baking-sheet.

The tart may be given a lattice top or the edge may be decorated with fancy shapes, see Plate 15.

APPLE MERINGUE FLAN

Flan aux Pommes meringué

Short crust pastry (p. 557), using 4 oz. flour, etc.
1½ lb. cooking apples
2 tablesp. water
Rind of ½ lemon
2 oz. butter *or* **margarine**
3 oz. brown sugar
2 eggs
2-3 oz. castor sugar for the meringue

Peel, core and slice the apples; put them in a saucepan and stew with the water and the finely-grated lemon rind. When soft, pass through a nylon sieve. Return the apple pulp to the pan and re-heat slightly, add the butter, brown sugar and egg yolks. Meanwhile line a 7-in. flan ring with the pastry. Put the apple mixture into the uncooked lined flan ring and bake gently in a moderate oven (**350° F., Gas 4**) for about 30 min., until the apple mixture is set. Stiffly whisk the egg whites and fold in 2–3 oz. castor sugar. Pile on top of the apple mixture, dredge lightly with castor sugar and decorate, if liked, with pieces of angelica and glacé cherry. Bake in a very cool oven (**290° F., Gas 1**) until the meringue is golden brown; about 30-40 min.

NOTE: A good pinch of ground cinnamon and ground cloves can be added to the apples before the butter, sugar and egg yolks, if liked.

6–7 helpings

BAKEWELL TART

Short crust pastry (p. 557), using 4 oz. flour, etc.	**1 egg**
Raspberry jam	**2 oz. ground almonds**
2 oz. butter	**2 oz. cake-crumbs**
2 oz. sugar	**Almond essence**
	Icing sugar

Line a 7-in. flan ring or a pie-plate with the pastry. Place a good layer of raspberry jam on the bottom. Cream together the butter and sugar till thick and white. Beat in the egg and add the ground almonds and cake-crumbs and a few drops of almond essence. Spread the mixture on top of the jam and bake in a fairly hot oven (**400° F., Gas 6**) for about ½ hr.

Sprinkle icing sugar on top and serve hot or cold.

5–6 helpings

BANANA FLAN

Flan de Bananes

Short crust pastry (p. 557), using 4 oz. flour, etc.	**½ pt. confectioner's custard**
	3 bananas
	Apricot glaze

Line a 7-in. flan ring with the pastry and bake it "blind" (p. 558). When cool, pour in the confectioner's custard and cover the custard with overlapping rings of banana arranged neatly on top. Glaze immediately with hot apricot glaze, allow to set and serve cold.

CUSTARD FLAN

Flan de Crème Custard

Short crust pastry (p. 557) using 4 oz. flour, etc.	**1 egg yolk**
1 egg	**¾ oz. sugar**
	½ pt. milk
	Grated nutmeg

Line a 7-in. flan ring with short crust pastry. Bake "blind". Beat the eggs and add to them the sugar and warmed milk. Strain into the flan case, sprinkle with grated nutmeg and bake in a warm oven till set (**335° F., Gas 3**).

5–6 helpings

Cooking time—30–40 min.

FRANGIPANE TART

Tourte à la Frangipane

Rich short crust pastry (p. 556), using 4 oz. flour, etc.	**2 oz. butter**
2 oz. sugar	**1 egg**
	2 oz. ground almonds
	1 teasp. flour

Line a 7-in. flan ring or pie-plate with the pastry. Cream the butter and sugar till thick and white. Add the egg, beating well, and then mix in the ground almonds and flour. Place the mixture in the pastry case and bake in a moderate oven (**350° F., Gas 4**) for 25–30 min.

When cool, dredge with icing sugar.

6 helpings

FRUIT FLAN

Flan de Fruits

Rich short crust pastry (p. 557), using 4 oz. flour, etc.

FILLING

1 medium sized can of fruit *or* **¾ lb. fresh fruit, e.g. strawberries, pears, pineapple, cherries, apricots, peaches, etc.**

COATING GLAZE

¼ pt. syrup from canned fruit, *or* **fruit juice** *or* **water**	**Sugar (if necessary)**
	1 teasp. arrowroot
	Lemon juice to taste

DECORATION (optional)

Whipped sweetened cream

Line a 7-in. flan ring with the pastry. Prick the bottom of the flan, and bake it "blind". Bake for about 30 min. first in a fairly hot oven (**400° F., Gas 6**) reducing the heat as the pastry sets to moderate (**350° F., Gas 4**). When the pastry is cooked remove the paper and dummy used for blind baking and replace the case in the oven for 5 min. to dry the bottom. Allow to cool.

If fresh fruit is used, stew gently till tender, if necessary. Drain the fruit. Place the sugar if used and liquid in a pan and boil for 10 min. Blend the arrowroot with some lemon juice and add it to the syrup, stirring all the time. Continue stirring, cook for 3 min. then cool slightly. Arrange the fruit attractively in the flan case and coat it with fruit syrup.

If liked, the flan may be decorated with piped whipped, sweetened cream.

JAM TART

Tarte à la Confiture

Trimmings of puff pastry (p. 555)
Any kind of jam

Grease a fireproof plate or tart pan. Roll out the pastry to a thickness of ⅛ in. and line the plate with it. Spread with jam and decorate the edges. Bake the tart in a hot oven (**425° F., Gas 7**) for 10–15 min.

LEMON MERINGUE FLAN

Flan au Citron meringué

Short crust pastry (p. 557), **using 4 oz. flour, etc.**
1 oz. cornflour
Rind and juice of 2 lemons
1–2 oz. granulated sugar
1 oz. butter
2 eggs
3 oz. castor sugar

Line a 7-in. flan ring with the pastry and bake it "blind" (*see* p. 558) Make the lemon juice up to ½ pt. with water. Blend the cornflour in a little of the lemon liquid, boil the remaining liquid and pour it over the blended cornflour stirring all the time. Put the mixture back in the pan, boil for 3 min. and add the granulated sugar, grated lemon rind and butter. Allow to cool slightly, add the egg yolks and pour the mixture into the flan case. Bake in a moderate oven (**350° F., Gas 4**) till set. Whisk the egg whites stiffly, fold in the castor sugar and pile on top of the flan. Decorate with cherries and angelica. Dredge with castor-sugar, return to the oven (**290° F., gas 1**) till the meringue is set and lightly browned.

6 helpings **Cooking time—45–50 min.**

TREACLE JELLY TART

Short crust pastry (p. 557), **using 4 oz. flour, etc.**
3 tablesp. golden syrup
1 egg

Line a deep sandwich tin with the pastry. Slightly warm the syrup and beat it up with the egg. Pour over the pastry, and bake in a moderate oven (**350° F., Gas 4**) till golden brown. When cold the filling sets like jelly.

6 helpings **Cooking time—about 30 min.**

TREACLE TART

Short crust pastry (p. 557), **using 6 oz. flour, etc.**
3 tablesp. golden syrup
Lemon juice ***or*** **ginger**
2 oz. fresh breadcrumbs

Slightly warm the syrup, flavour with a pinch of ginger or a little lemon juice, then stir in the breadcrumbs.

Line a 9-in. fireproof plate with the pastry, trim and decorate the edge. Spread over the syrup mixture, decorate with cross strips of pastry, and bake in a fairly hot oven (**400° F., Gas 6**) for about 30 min.

NOTE: If preferred the tart may be baked as a double crust tart, increase the amount of pastry and bake for 50 min. Crushed cornflakes may be substituted for the breadcrumbs if liked.

6 helpings

PUDDINGS USING PASTRY

TO LINE THE SIDES OF A PIE-DISH

FOR a 1½-pt. pie-dish 4 oz. pastry will be required (i.e. 4 oz. flour etc.).

Wet the pie-dish with cold water. Roll out the pastry thinly, cut a strip 3–4 in. wide and lay it round the sides of the dish so that it lies slightly over the outer rim (to allow for shrinkage during baking). Press the pastry well on to the pie-dish, joining the strip neatly by wetting the edges with cold water and pressing firmly together. Wet the rim of pastry and decorate the edge with small fancy shapes of pastry laid round it.

ALMOND PUDDING

Short crust pastry (p. 557) using 4 oz. flour, etc.
3 oz. butter
2 oz. castor sugar
2 eggs
2 oz. cake *or* white breadcrumbs
½ lemon
4 oz. ground almonds
1 pt. milk

Line the sides of a 1½-pt. pie-dish with pastry. Cream the butter and sugar together; beat in the eggs gradually. Add the crumbs, lemon rind, juice and almonds. Boil the milk, pour it over the rest of the ingredients, stirring all the time. Pour the mixture into the lined pie-dish. Bake in a moderate to fairly hot oven **(350°–375° F., Gas 4–5)** until the pastry is cooked and the filling is golden brown and set, about 20–30 min.

6–7 helpings

APPLE AMBER *Tarte à la Gelée de Pommes*

Short crust pastry (p. 557,) using 4 oz. flour, etc.
1½ lb. cooking apples
2 tablesp. water
Rind of 1 lemon
2 oz. butter *or* margarine
3 oz. brown sugar
2 eggs
2–3 oz. castor sugar for the meringue

Line the sides of a 1½-pt. pie-dish with the pastry and decorate the edge.

Peel, core and slice the apples; put them in a saucepan and stew with the water and the lemon rind. When soft, pass through a nylon sieve. Return the apple pulp to the pan and re-heat slightly, add the butter, brown sugar and egg yolks. Put the mixture into the lined pie-dish and bake gently in a moderate oven **(350° F., Gas 4)** for about 30 min., until the apple mixture is set. Stiffly whisk the egg whites and fold in 2–3 oz. of castor sugar. Pile on top of the apple mixture, dredge lightly with castor sugar and decorate, if liked, with pieces of angelica and glacé cherry. Bake in a very cool oven **(290° F., Gas 1)** until the meringue is golden brown; about 30–40 min. Serve hot or cold.

NOTE: A good pinch of ground cinnamon and ground cloves can be added to the apples before the butter, sugar and egg yolks, if liked.

6–7 helpings

APRICOT PUDDING *Pouding d'Abricots*

¾ pt. milk
¾ pt. fresh breadcrumbs *or* cakecrumbs
Short crust pastry (p. 557), using 5–6 oz. flour, etc.
One 12 oz. can *or* 1 bottle of apricots
2 oz. castor sugar
2 eggs
1 glass sherry
2–4 oz. castor sugar for the meringue

Boil the milk, pour it over the breadcrumbs and let them soak for ½ hr. Line the sides of a 2-pt. pie-dish with the pastry.

Strain the apricots, pass them through a fine sieve and add to them 2 oz. sugar, egg yolks, sherry and soaked crumbs. Pour into the pie-dish. Bake in a fairly hot oven **(400° F., Gas 6)** until the pastry is cooked and the filling is set —25–30 min. Whisk the egg whites stiffly, stir in lightly the 2–4 oz. castor sugar and spread this meringue over the top of the pudding. Dredge well with castor sugar and decorate with strips of angelica and cut glacé cherry, if liked. Bake in a very cool oven **(290° F., Gas 1)** until the meringue is crisp and golden, about 30 min.

6 helpings

CHESTER PUDDING *Pouding à la Chester*

Short crust pastry (p. 557), using 5–6 oz. flour, etc.
3 eggs
6 oz. castor sugar
1½ tablesp. ground almonds
3 oz. warmed butter *or* margarine
½ lemon

Line the sides of a 2-pt. pie-dish *or* pie-plate with the pastry. Separate the eggs. Whisk together the egg yolks and 3 oz. of the sugar until thick and smooth. Add the ground almonds, melted fat and fine-grated rind and juice of ½ lemon. Pour the mixture into the lined pie-dish or pie-plate. Bake in a moderate oven **(350° F., Gas 4)** for about 20–25 min. until the filling is set and the pastry cooked. Whisk the egg whites until stiff, and stir in lightly the remaining 3 oz. sugar. Pile on top. Bake in a very cool oven **(290° F., Gas 1)** until the meringue is just coloured and set; about 30 min.

4–5 helpings

CHESTNUT AMBER

Tarte à la Gelée de Marrons

Short crust pastry (p. 557), using 4 oz. flour, etc.
½ pt. chestnuts
1 lemon
½ pt. milk
2 oz. breadcrumbs
1 oz. butter
4 oz. castor sugar
2 eggs
Vanilla essence

Bake the chestnuts for about 20 min. and remove the skins. Put them in a pan with sufficient water to cover the bottom of the pan, simmer gently till tender and rub through a fine sieve. Cut the rind from the lemon in thin strips and put it in a pan with the milk. Simmer very gently for 15–20 min. then strain it over the breadcrumbs. Cream the butter with 1 oz. of the sugar till thick and white. Add the egg yolks, lemon juice and vanilla essence. Stir in the chestnuts, breadcrumbs and milk.

Line the sides of a 1½-pt. pie-dish with the pastry (p. 560). Pour in the mixture and bake in a fairly hot oven (**400° F., Gas 6**) for 25–30 min. till set and lightly browned. Whisk the egg whites stiffly, fold in the remaining 3 oz. sugar and pile on top of the pudding. Dredge with castor sugar and return to a very cool oven (**290° F., Gas 1**) till firm and lightly browned.

6 helpings
Cooking time—1 hr. approx.

COCONUT PUDDING

Pouding à la noix de coco

Short crust pastry (p. 557), using 5–6 oz. flour, etc.
6 oz. desiccated coconut
¾ pt. milk
1½ oz. butter
1½ oz. sugar
3 eggs
1½ oz. cake-crumbs
¼ pt. cream *or* milk
Vanilla essence
2 oz. castor sugar

Line the sides of a 2-pt. pie-dish with the pastry. Simmer the coconut in the ¾ pt. milk until tender—about 10–15 min. ; allow to cool. Cream together the butter and the 1½ oz. sugar until soft, work in the egg yolks one at a time and add the cake-crumbs, cream *or* milk, the prepared coconut and the vanilla essence. Pour the mixture into the pie-dish and bake in a fairly hot oven (**375° F., Gas 5**) until the pastry is cooked and the mixture set—about ½ hr. Stiffly whisk the egg whites and fold in the 2 oz. castor sugar; pile on top of the pudding. Reduce oven heat to very cool (**290° F., Gas 1**) and put the pudding back into oven until the meringue is golden—30–40 min.

6 helpings

GOOSEBERRY PUDDING

Pouding aux groseilles

1 lb. gooseberries
1 gill water
Short crust pastry (p. 557), using 5–6 oz. flour, etc.
3–4 oz. castor sugar
½ pt. breadcrumbs
2 oz. butter *or* margarine
2 eggs

Top and tail the gooseberries and cook them in the water until tender. Line the sides of a 2-pt. pie-dish with the pastry. Rub the gooseberries through a fine sieve and add sugar to sweeten. This should give about 1 pt. of purée. Add to the purée the breadcrumbs, butter and well-beaten eggs. Pour the mixture into the lined pie-dish. Bake in a moderate oven (**350° F., Gas 4**) for about 40 min., until set.

4 helpings

LEMON PUDDING

Pouding au citron

Short crust pastry (p. 557), using 4 oz. flour, etc.
½ pt. milk
1 oz. butter
4 oz. castor sugar
2 lemons
2 eggs
3 individual sponge cakes

Line the sides of a 2-pt. pie-dish with the pastry. Put the milk, butter, 2 oz. of the sugar and the grated rind of the lemons into a saucepan, boil up, let it infuse for about 15 min. Separate the eggs and beat the yolks. Pour the infusion over the beaten egg yolks, then add the crumbled sponge-cakes and lemon juice. Stir well and pour into the lined pie-dish. Bake in a fairly hot oven (about **375°–400° F., Gas 5–6**) until the pastry is cooked and the filling set, about 30–35 min. Stiffly whip the egg whites and fold in lightly the remaining 2 oz. of sugar. Pile on top of the pudding, dredge with castor sugar and bake in a very cool oven (**290° F., Gas 1**) for 30–40 min., until the meringue is set and golden brown.

ORANGE PUDDING

Short crust pastry (p. 557), using 5-6 oz. flour, etc.
4 oranges
½ pt. milk
3 oz. sugar
3 oz. cake-crumbs *or* sponge cakes
Pinch of grated nutmeg
2 eggs

Line the sides of a 2-pt. pie-dish with the pastry.

Thinly cut the rind from one orange and infuse this in the milk for about 20 min. then remove it. Add to the milk, the sugar, cake-crumbs, nutmeg and well beaten eggs and lastly the juice of all the oranges. Pour into the lined pie-dish and bake in a fairly hot oven (**375° F., Gas 5**) until the pastry is cooked and the mixture is set; about 30–35 min.

WEST RIDING PUDDING

Short crust pastry (p. 557), using 5-6 oz. flour, etc.
4 oz. butter *or* margarine
4 oz. castor sugar
2 eggs
6 oz. plain flour
1 teasp. baking-powder
Milk to mix
2 tablesp. jam

Line and decorate the sides of a 2-pt. pie-dish with the pastry.

Cream the fat and sugar together until white and creamy. Beat in the eggs gradually. Beat thoroughly. Sift in the flour and baking-powder. Stir in lightly, adding milk until the mixture drops easily from the spoon. Cover the bottom of the pie-dish with the jam; then spread on the mixture. Bake in a fairly hot oven (**375° F., Gas 5**) for about 1 hr., until the pudding is cooked and nicely brown.

PIES OR TARTS

TO MAKE A FRUIT PIE OR TART

A 1½-pt. pie-dish will require about 6 oz. pastry (i.e. 6 oz. flour plus the other ingredients made into pastry) and 1½–2 lb. fruit.

Place ½ the amount of fruit in the dish, sprinkle over the sugar and flavouring (if used) and pile the remaining fruit on top, piling it high in the centre. The sugar should not be sprinkled on top as it would go into the pastry and make it soggy. If the fruit is likely to shrink during cooking or if there is insufficient fruit to fill the dish, place a pie funnel or inverted egg-cup in the centre.

Roll out the pastry a little larger than the pie-dish. Cut off a strip of pastry the width and length of the rim of the dish, wet the edge of the pie-dish with cold water and place the strip on the pie-dish cut edge inwards, without stretching it. Join the strip by wetting the cut ends and pressing them firmly together.

Wet the strip of pastry; lift the remaining pastry with the rolling-pin and place it gently over the dish, taking care not to stretch it. Press the strip and the cover together and trim off the surplus with a sharp knife. Knock up the edge of the pastry with the back of a knife and decorate as desired (*see* plate 15).

To allow the steam to escape either cut a slit in the centre of the crust before placing pie in the oven (if a pie funnel has been used the slit should come over it); *or* leave a few gaps under the pastry cover at the edge; *or* raise the pastry slightly at one corner immediately after cooking.

DOUBLE CRUST PIES OR TARTS

DOUBLE CRUST PIES or tarts may be made in fireproof glass or enamel plates or dishes.

About 8 oz. pastry (i.e. 8 oz. flour plus the other ingredients made up into pastry) will be required for an 8–9 in. plate.

Divide the dough into 2 portions, form each into a round shape and roll one portion into a round about $\frac{1}{8}$ in. thick and a little larger than the plate. Fold over the rolling-pin and lift on to the plate; smooth to fit the plate without stretching the pastry. Cut off the surplus pastry with a sharp knife or scissors. Put in a layer of filling, sprinkle with sugar if required and cover with another layer of filling. This prevents the sugar getting into the pastry and making it soggy.

Roll the remaining piece of pastry into a round a little larger than the plate. Wet with cold water the edge of the pastry lining the plate; lift on the cover and ease into position without stretching—if stretched it will only shrink back later. Press the 2 edges together firmly, knock up the edge and decorate.

Bake according to the type of pastry, and to ensure that the bottom crust cooks through stand the plate on a baking-sheet.

APPLE PIE or TART

Tourte aux Pommes

Short crust pastry (p. 557), using 6 oz. flour, etc.
1½–2 lb. apples
4 oz. moist sugar
6 cloves *or* ½ teasp. grated lemon rind

Peel, quarter and core the apples and cut in thick slices. Place half the apples in a 1½-pt. pie-dish, add the sugar and flavouring and pile the remaining fruit on top, piling it high in the centre. Line the edge of the pie-dish with pastry and cover the pie with pastry. Knock up the edges of the pastry with the back of a knife. Bake for 40 min., first in a fairly hot oven (**400° F., Gas 6**), reducing the heat to moderate (**350° F., Gas 4**) when the pastry is set.

Dredge with castor sugar and serve hot or cold.

NOTE: If liked, the pastry may be brushed with egg white and sprinkled with sugar before cooking.

6 helpings

APRICOT TART

Tourte aux Abricots

Short crust pastry (p. 557), using 6 oz. flour, etc.
1 large can of apricots
Sugar to taste

Place the apricots in a 1½-pt. pie-dish;

sprinkle with sugar and half fill the dish with the syrup from the can. Line the edge of the dish with pastry, cover with the remaining pastry (*see* p. 564) and bake in a fairly hot oven (**400° F., Gas 6**) for 30–40 min. When the pastry has set brush it over lightly with water and dredge well with castor sugar. Return to oven quickly and finish cooking.

6 helpings

DAMSON TART

Tourte aux Prunes de Damas

Short crust pastry (p. 557), using 6 oz. flour, etc.
1½ lb. damsons
4 oz. demerara sugar

Half-fill a 1½-pt. pie-dish with damsons, sprinkle on the sugar, pile the remaining damsons on top, piling them high in the centre. Line the edge of the dish with pastry and cover it with pastry, brush lightly over with cold water, dredge with castor sugar, and bake in a fairly hot oven (**400° F., Gas 6**).

5–6 helpings
Cooking time—about 1 hr.

GOOSEBERRY TART

Tourte aux Groseilles

Short crust pastry (p. 557), using 6 oz. flour, etc.
1½ lb. gooseberries
2 tablesp. water
4 oz. demerara sugar

Top and tail the gooseberries with a pair of scissors, wash the gooseberries well. Place half of them in a 1½-pt. pie-dish, add the sugar and water and then the remaining gooseberries, piling them high in the centre. Line the edge of the dish with pastry, cover with the remaining pastry (*see* p. 564). Bake in a fairly hot oven (**400° F., Gas 6**) reducing the heat to moderate (**350° F., Gas 4**) when the pastry is set. Continue cooking till the fruit is tender—about 45 min. altogether.

Dredge with castor sugar and serve.

6 helpings

PRUNE TART

Tourte aux Pruneaux

Short crust pastry (p. 557), using 6 oz. flour, etc.
¾ lb. prunes
2 tablesp. cranberry juice
Sugar to taste

Soak the prunes, remove the stones and take out the kernels. Put the fruit and kernels in the cranberry juice, add sugar, and simmer for 10 min. Allow to cool, place in a 1½-pt. pie-dish. Line the edge of the dish with pastry and cover with remaining pastry (*see* p. 564). Bake for about 45 min. in a fairly hot oven (**400° F., Gas 6**). Dredge with sugar and serve.

6 helpings

REDCURRANT AND RASPBERRY TART

Short crust pastry (p. 557), using 6 oz. flour, etc.
1½ lb. redcurrants
½ lb. raspberries
2–3 tablesp. sugar

Strip the currants from the stalks, rinse and place half of the currants in a 1½-pt. pie-dish. Add the sugar, the hulled raspberries, then the remaining redcurrants, piling them high in the centre. Line the edge of the dish with pastry. Cover with pastry (*see* p. 564), brush lightly with water and dredge well with castor sugar. Bake in a fairly hot oven (**400° F., Gas 6**) for about ¾ hr.

6 helpings
Cooking time—about 45 min.

RHUBARB TART

Tourte à la Rhubarbe

Short crust pastry (p. 557), using 6 oz. flour, etc.
1½ lb. rhubarb
4 oz. sugar

Wipe the rhubarb, remove the skin, if it is coarse, and cut into lengths of 1 in. Make as for Apple Tart (p. 564).

6 helpings
Cooking time—40 min.

TARTLETS AND PASTRY BASE CAKES

ALMOND CHEESECAKES

Tartelettes aux amandes

Short crust pastry (p. 557), using 6 oz. flour, etc.
1–2 dessertsp. jam
4 oz. castor sugar
2 oz. ground almonds
¼ teasp. almond essence
2 egg whites
1 dessertsp. water

Roll pastry out thinly, cut into rounds and line patty or bouché tins. Place a little jam in the bottom of each. Mix castor sugar and ground almonds, add essence to egg whites and whisk stiffly. Fold almond mixture into egg white and add water. Half-fill pastry cases with mixture. If desired, place pastry crosses on top of the mixture. Bake in a fairly hot to moderate oven (**375°–350° F., Gas 5–4**).

16–18 cheesecakes
Cooking time—15–20 min.

ALMOND TARTLETS

Tartelettes aux Amandes

Short crust pastry (p. 557), using 4 oz. flour, etc.
Raspberry jam
2 oz. butter
2 oz. sugar
1 egg
4 oz. ground almonds
½ teasp. lemon juice

Roll the pastry thinly, cut out 12 rounds and line 12 patty tins. Place a little raspberry jam in the bottom of each. Cream the butter and sugar till thick and white. Beat in the egg and add the ground almonds and lemon juice. Half fill the tins with the mixture. Roll out the trimmings of pastry and cut into strips ¼ in. wide. Place a cross on top of each tartlet and bake in a fairly hot oven (**400°–375° F., Gas 6–5**) for 20–25 min.

12 tartlets

APPLE CHEESECAKES

Short crust pastry (p. 557), using 4 oz. flour, etc.
1 lb. apples
2 oz. granulated sugar
1 tablesp. water
1 oz. butter
1 lemon
2 eggs
3 oz. castor sugar

Line 12 patty tins with the pastry and partially bake. Peel, core and slice the apples and place in a saucepan with the granulated sugar and water. Simmer gently till tender then rub through a hair or nylon sieve. Return the pulp to the pan, add the butter, lemon juice, finely-grated rind and the egg yolks. Re-heat and cook until the mixture thickens. Fill the pastry cases with the apple mixture and bake in a moderate oven (**350° F., Gas 4**) till set. Whisk the egg whites stiffly and fold in the castor sugar.

Cover the apple mixture with the meringue and bake in a very cool oven (**290° F., Gas 1**) till light brown and crisp.

12 cheesecakes
Cooking time—45–55 min.

APPLE TURNOVERS

See Fruit or Jam Turnovers (p. 571).

APRICOT BOUCHÉES

Bouchées d'Abricots

Puff pastry (p. 555), using 8 oz. flour, etc.
1 can apricots
¼ pt. double cream
Sugar to sweeten

Roll out the pastry to rather less than ½ in. thickness. Cut into rounds 2½ in. diameter with a cutter dipped in hot water. Make an incision half-way through the rounds with a smaller cutter. Bake in a hot oven (**450° F., Gas 8**) for about 12 min. When cool, scoop out the paste within the ring. Drain the apricots from the syrup, and place ½ an apricot, rounded side down, in each case. Pipe a rosette of stiffly-whipped sweetened cream in each hollow.

14–12 bouchées

BALMORAL TARTLETS

Tartelettes à la Balmoral

Short crust pastry (p. 557), using 4 oz. flour, etc.	**½ oz. chopped glacé cherries**
2 oz. butter	**½ oz. shredded candied peel**
2 oz. sugar	**1 teasp. cornflour**
1 egg	**Icing sugar**
1 oz. cake-crumbs	

Line 12 patty tins with pastry. Cream the butter and sugar until thick and white and beat in the egg yolk. Add the cake-crumbs, cherries, peel and cornflour and mix well. Whisk the egg white till stiff and fold lightly into the mixture. Fill the patty tins with the mixture, and bake in a fairly hot oven (**400°–375° F., Gas 6–5**) for about 20 min.

Dredge with icing sugar and serve cold.

12 tartlets

BANBURY CAKES

Petits gâteaux à la Banbury

Rough puff pastry (p. 556) using 8 oz. flour, etc. *or* **puff** *or* **flaky pastry may be used**

FILLING

Small 1 oz. butter *or* **margarine**	**4 oz. currants**
½ oz. plain flour	**½ oz. chopped candied peel**
¼ nutmeg (grated) *or* **¼ teasp. ground cinnamon**	**2 oz. brown sugar**
	2 tablesp. rum

GLAZE

Egg white	**Castor sugar**

To make the filling: melt the fat, stir in the flour and spice and cook for a minute or two. Remove from the heat, add the fruit, sugar and rum.

Roll the pastry out ¼ in. thick and cut into 3-in. rounds. Place a spoonful of filling in the centre of each, damp the edges and gather them together to form a ball; turn over so that the smooth side is uppermost. Roll each out and shape into an oval shape 4 in. by 2½ in.; make 3 cuts in the centre. Put the cakes on a greased tin and bake in a hot oven (**425° F., Gas 7**).

Brush with the egg white and dust immediately with castor sugar. Return to the oven for a few minutes, to frost the glaze.

14 cakes
Cooking time—20 min.

BEATRICE TARTLETS

Tartelettes Béatrice

Pate sucrée (p. 554), using 6 oz. flour, etc.	**1 oz. chopped walnuts**
3 bananas	**¼ pt. double cream**
Juice of 1 lemon	**1 oz. finely-grated chocolate**
½ oz. castor sugar	

Line 12 patty tins with pâte sucrée and bake them "blind" (*see* p. 558) in a moderate oven (**350° F., Gas 4**). Allow to cool. Chop the bananas with the lemon juice and add sugar and walnuts. Pile the mixture into the tartlet cases. Pipe a large rosette of whipped sweetened cream on top and dredge with grated chocolate.

12 tartlets
Cooking time—15 min.

BLACK BUN

Gâteau noir

PASTRY

1 lb. plain flour	**5 oz. butter** *or* **margarine**
¼ teasp. salt	**Water to mix**
¾ level teasp. baking-powder	

FILLING

2 lb. currants	**1 teasp. ground ginger**
1½ lb. valencia raisins	**1 teasp. allspice**
2 oz. glacé cherries	**1 teasp. black pepper**
½ lb. sultanas	**2 level teasp. bicarbonate of soda**
2 oz. chopped peel	**2 level teasp. cream of tartar**
6 oz. blanched, chopped almonds	**1 egg**
½ lb. sugar	**Milk to bind**
¾ lb. plain flour	
2 level teasp. ground cinnamon	

Make the pastry: sift flour, salt and baking-powder, rub in the margarine and mix with water to a stiff dough.

Mix prepared fruit and nuts with flour, sugar, spices and raising agents for the filling, add the egg and enough milk to mix stiffly.

Line a greased 7-in. or 8-in. cake-tin with

⅔ of the pastry, put in the mixture and make level, wet the edges. Roll out the remaining ⅓ of pastry, place on top and neaten the edges. Prick well all over the top, brush with egg and bake in a very cool oven (**310°–290° F., Gas 2–1**).

Cooking time—4–5 hr.

BLACKCURRANT TARTLETS

Tartelettes de Cassis

Short crust pastry (p. 557), using 4 oz. flour, etc.	**4 tablesp. sugar**
1 lb. blackcurrants	**2 tablesp. water**
	¼ pt. cream (optional)

Top and tail the blackcurrants and cook gently with the sugar and water. Line 12 patty tins with the pastry, and bake them "blind" (*see* p. 558) in a fairly hot oven (**400° F., Gas 6**) for about 15 min. When cool fill with the cold fruit and syrup and decorate with stiffly-whipped, sweetened cream (if used).

12 tartlets

CANADIAN CAKES

Short crust pastry (p. 557), using 6 oz. flour, etc.	**4 oz. currants (washed)**
1 egg	**4 oz. sugar**
	½ oz. melted butter

Line 15 patty tins with the pastry. Beat the egg and add the currants, sugar and melted butter and mix well. Place the mixture in the patty tins and bake in a fairly hot oven (**400° F., Gas 6**) for 15–20 min.

NOTE: These cakes may be decorated with whipped sweetened cream when cold.

15 cakes

CHERRY TARTLETS

Tartelettes de Cerises

Rich short crust pastry (p. 556), using 6 oz. flour, etc.	**Lemon juice to flavour**
1 can bright red cherries	**1 teasp. arrowroot**
¼ pt. fruit syrup	**Carmine**
1½ oz. loaf sugar	**Sweetened, whipped cream**

Line 15 patty tins or boat-shaped moulds with the pastry. Bake them "blind" (*see* p. 558) in a fairly hot oven (**400° F., Gas 6**) until set. Remove the weighted paper and return the tartlet cases to the oven for 2–3 min. to dry the pastry. Drain the juice from the cherries and remove the stones. Place a layer of cherries in the tartlet cases. Dissolve the sugar in the fruit syrup and boil for 5 min. Blend the arrowroot with the lemon juice, add to the syrup stirring all the time and boil for 2 min. till the syrup is clear. Add a few drops of carmine to colour. Pour a little syrup over the cherries and allow to set. Decorate with piped, sweetened whipped cream.

NOTE: The syrup must be stirred and boiled gently.

15 tartlets

CHOCOLATE NUT TARTLETS

Tartelettes de Noisettes au Chocolat

PASTRY

2½ oz. margarine	**Pinch of salt**
1 oz. icing sugar	**1 oz. cornflour**
3 oz. flour	**Egg to bind**

FILLING

2 oz. butter *or* margarine	**2 oz. ground almonds**
2 oz. grated plain chocolate	**2 oz. castor sugar**
	1 egg

DECORATION

Chocolate glacé icing	**Walnuts**

Make the pastry: cream the margarine and sugar. Sift together the flour, salt and cornflour. Add the flour to the creamed margarine and bind with egg to form a stiff dough. Roll very thinly and line greased patty tins.

Make the filling: cream the fat, work in the grated chocolate, add ground almonds and sugar. Mix with egg to a dropping consistency.

Place the mixture in the tins and bake in a fairly hot oven (**400°–375° F., Gas 6–5**). When cold decorate with chocolate glacé icing and walnut halves.

16 tartlets **Cooking time—15 min.**

CHOCOLATE TARTLETS (1)

Tartelettes au Chocolat

Pâté sucrée using 2 oz. flour, etc.

FILLING

½ teasp. cornflour	**2 small egg yolks**
½ teasp. cocoa	**Few drops vanilla essence**
½ gill milk	**Pinch of ground cinnamon**
¼ oz. butter *or* margarine	
¼ oz. sugar	

MERINGUE

2 small egg whites — **3 oz. castor sugar**

DECORATION

Glacé cherries — **Angelica**

Roll the pastry out thinly and line eight tartlet tins. Mix together the cornflour and cocoa and blend with the milk. Pour into a saucepan and boil 2–3 min., stirring briskly. Cool slightly, stir in fat, sugar, egg yolks and flavouring, and half-fill tins with mixture. Bake in a fairly hot oven (**375°–350° F., Gas 5–4**), 10–15 min. Whisk the egg whites stiffly, beat in 2 teasp. sugar and fold in the remainder. Using a vegetable star pipe, pipe the meringue in a spiral on top of tartlets. Dredge with castor sugar, and decorate with cherry and angelica. Place in a cool oven (**310° F., Gas 2**) till meringue is crisp and very lightly browned, about 15–20 min.

8 tartlets

CHOCOLATE TARTLETS (2)

Short crust pastry (p. 557), **using 6 oz. flour, etc.**	**2 oz. grated chocolate**
3 oz. castor sugar	**½ oz. cornflour**
2 eggs	**2 oz. butter**
4 oz. cake-crumbs	**Chocolate glacé icing**

Line 15 patty tins with the pastry. Cream the sugar and egg yolks well together till thick and white, and add the cake-crumbs, chocolate, cornflour and melted butter. Whisk the egg whites till stiff and fold them carefully into the mixture. Fill the patty tins and bake in a fairly hot oven (**400° F., Gas 6**) for 20–25 min. When cold spread with chocolate glacé icing.

15 tartlets

CHOCOLATE TARTLETS (3)

Short crust pastry (p. 557), **using 6 oz. flour, etc.**	**Chocolate glacé icing** (p. 547)
Genoese pastry (p. 534)	**Desiccated coconut**

Line 15 patty tins with short crust pastry and fill with Genoese pastry. Bake in a fairly hot oven (**400° F., Gas 6**) for 20–25 min. When cold, ice with chocolate icing and sprinkle with coconut.

NOTE: Orange glacé icing (p. 547) or transparent icing (p. 548) may be used to give variety and the tartlets may be decorated with chopped pistachio nuts.

15 tartlets

COVENTRY TURNOVERS

Fresh puff, rough puff *or* flaky pastry (pp. 554–7), ***or* pastry trimmings**

Roll pastry out to a good ⅛ in. in thickness and cut into 4-in. or 5-in. rounds with a plain cutter. Wet the edges and place a small quantity (¾ teasp.) of raspberry jam slightly off the centre. Enclose the jam by folding over the edge of the paste to form one side of a triangle, fold the other sides over to complete the equilateral triangle. Reverse the pastry and brush with water, dust well with castor sugar and place on baking-tray. Allow to firm for 1 hr. then bake in a hot oven (**425° F., Gas 7**).

Cooking time—20 min.

CREAM BUNS

Petits Choux à la Crème

Choux pastry (p. 554), **using 4 oz. flour, etc.**
Icing sugar

FILLING

½ pt. sweetened double cream flavoured with vanilla essence *or* confectioner's custard *or* mock cream may be used

(1) Put the pastry into a forcing bag and pipe balls on to a greased baking-sheet using a 1-in. vegetable pipe, or shape the mixture with a spoon into piles and bake in a fairly hot oven (**425°–400° F., Gas 7–6**) for 30 min. (do not open the door), then move to a cooler part of the oven for about 10 min. until dried inside. Split the buns and remove any damp mixture. When cold fill with whipped cream and dust with icing sugar.

12 buns
Cooking time—40 min.

(2) Put the pastry in 12 spoonfuls on to a damp Yorkshire pudding tin, cover with a tin of the same size and seal the edges with a thick paste of flour and water (make sure that the edges of the tins are joined securely). Bake in a hot oven (**425°–400° F., Gas 7–6**), for 35 min., by which time the pastry on the edges of the tin should be a rich dark colour—not burned. Remove the buns and place on a cooling tray, split at once to allow steam to escape. Remove any damp mixture. When cold fill with whipped cream and dust with icing sugar.

NOTE: Do not remove the lid too soon or the buns will collapse.

12 buns
Cooking time—35 min.

CREAM HORNS

Cornets de Crème

Puff *or* flaky pastry (p. 555), using 4 oz. flour, etc.
Raspberry jam
1 gill sweetened and flavoured cream
Chopped pistachio nuts

Roll pastry out ⅛ in. thick and cut into strips ½ in. wide and 12–14 in. long. Moisten strip with water and wind round the cornet mould from the point upwards keeping moist surface on the outside. Finish final overlap on under side of tin and trim neatly. Allow to stand for 1 hr. Place horns on baking-sheet, brush over with egg and milk and place in a hot oven (**425° F., Gas 7**) until nicely browned and cooked through. Remove tins and return horns to oven to dry for a few minutes. When cool, place a little jam in each horn, pipe a rosette of cream on top and sprinkle with nuts.

7–8 horns
Cooking time—15–20 min.

CREAM SLICES

Tartes à la Crème

Puff pastry using 3 oz. flour, etc.
A little royal icing (p. 549)
¼ pt. sweetened, flavoured cream

Roll pastry ½ in. thick and cut into fingers 4 in. by 1 in. Spread top thinly with royal icing. Bake in a hot oven (**425°–450° F., Gas 7–8**) until pastry is well risen and icing lightly browned. Allow to cool. Slit carefully through the centre, spread bottom half with jam. Pipe or spread whipped cream over the jam and sandwich the two halves together again.

NOTE: If liked, glacé icing may be spread on top *after* the slices have been baked.

8 slices
Cooking time—20 min.

CREAM TARTLETS

Tartelettes à la Crème

Short crust pastry (p. 557), using 4 oz. flour, etc.
Apricot jam
⅓ pt. double cream
Castor sugar
Pistachio nuts

Line 12 patty tins with pastry and bake them "blind" (*see* p. 558) in a fairly hot oven (**400° F., Gas 6**). When cool, half fill the cases with jam and pipe the stiffly-whipped, sweetened cream on top. Decorate with finely-chopped pistachio nuts.

12 tartlets
Cooking time—15–20 min.

CUSTARD TARTLETS

Tartelettes à la Crème cuite

Short crust pastry (p. 557), using 6 oz. flour, etc.
2 eggs
¾ pt. milk
1 tablesp. granulated sugar

MERINGUE

2 egg whites
3 oz. castor sugar

Line 12 deep patty tins with pastry and partially bake. Beat the 2 eggs and add the granulated sugar and warm milk. Strain into the pastry-lined patty tins and bake in a warm oven (**335° F., Gas 3**) for 15–20 min. until the custard sets. Whisk the egg whites stiffly and fold in the castor sugar. Pile lightly on the tarts and bake in a very cool oven (**290° F., Gas 1**) until the meringue hardens and becomes lightly coloured. Serve cold.

12 tartlets
Cooking time—45–55 min.

ECCLES CAKES

Flaky *or* rough puff pastry (p. 556), **using 6 oz. flour, etc. *or* trimmings may be used**
½ oz. butter *or* margarine
¼ oz. sugar
2 oz. currants
¾ oz. chopped peel
¼ teasp. mixed spice
A little grated nutmeg

Roll out pastry ¼ in. thick, cut into 4-in. rounds. Cream fat and sugar, add currants, peel and spice and place a good teasp. of the mixture in the centre of each round of pastry. Gather the edges together, pinch firmly, and form into a flat cake; reverse the cake and roll gently till the fruit begins to show through. Make two cuts on top of each, brush with water and dust with castor sugar. Bake in a hot oven (**425° F., Gas 7**).

12–14 cakes
Cooking time—20 min.

ÉCLAIRS

Choux pastry
½ pt. double cream *or* confectioner's custard *or* mock cream
Sugar to sweeten
Vanilla essence
Chocolate *or* coffee glacé icing

Grease a baking-sheet. Place the pastry in a forcing bag with a large plain pipe (¾ in. to 1 in.), and pipe mixture out on to the greased sheet in 4-in. lengths, cutting off each length with a knife dipped in hot water. Bake in a hot oven (**425°–400° F., Gas 7–6**) until risen and crisp (do not open the door during this time). Reduce heat and move to a cooler part of the oven, until éclairs are light and dry inside, about 30 min. altogether. Place on a cooling tray and slit open. When cold fill the cavities with stiffly-whipped, sweetened cream flavoured with vanilla. Spread tops with chocolate or coffee glacé icing (p. 547). Put the icing on in a straight line, using a teaspoon—hold the éclair in a slanting position when doing so.

9–10 éclairs **Cooking time—30 min.**

FRANGIPANE TARTLETS

Tartelettes à la Frangipane

Rich short crust pastry (p. 556), **using 2–3 oz. flour, etc.**

FILLING

1 teasp. cornflour
½ gill milk
1 teasp. chopped peel
Grated lemon rind
1 dessertsp. sherry
1 dessertsp. brandy
2 egg yolks
½ oz. sugar

MERINGUE

2 egg whites
2 oz. castor sugar

DECORATION

Glacé cherries
Angelica

Blend the cornflour with the milk, bring to boiling-point and cook 1–2 min.; add the other filling ingredients. Roll out pastry thinly, cut out rounds with fluted cutter and line greased tartlet tins. Half fill them with the mixture and bake in a fairly hot oven (**375° F., Gas 5**) till mixture is firm. Beat the egg whites stiffly, then beat in 2 teasp. of sugar and fold in the remainder. Pipe or pile on top of tartlets and dredge with sugar. Decorate with cherry and angelica and place in a cool oven (**310° F., Gas 2**) till meringue is crisp.

8–10 tartlets

FRUIT or JAM TURNOVERS

Short crust, flaky, rough puff *or* puff pastry (pp. 554–7)
Stewed fruit *or* jam
Castor sugar

Roll the pastry thinly and cut into rounds of about 4 in. diameter. Place some jam *or* fruit in the centre of each round and moisten the edges with cold water. Fold the pastry over and press the edges together. Knock up the edges with the back of a knife and place on a baking-sheet. Brush the top with water, sprinkle with sugar and bake in a fairly hot or hot oven (**400°–425° F., Gas 6–7**)—depending on the type of pastry—for 20 min.

FRUIT TARTLETS

Tartelettes aux Fruits

Short crust pastry (p. 557), **using 3–4 oz. flour, etc.**

FILLING

Fresh fruit, e.g. strawberries, raspberries, etc., *or* canned fruit, e.g. cherries, peaches, etc.

COATING GLAZE

1 teasp. arrowroot
A few drops of colouring
¼ pt. fruit syrup

or if no fruit syrup:

1 teasp. arrowroot
½–1 oz. sugar
¼ pt. water
A few drops of colouring
Lemon juice to taste

DECORATION

1 gill whipped, sweetened and flavoured cream

Roll pastry thinly, cut out with fluted cutter and line small tartlet tins. Bake them "blind" (*see* p. 558) in a fairly hot oven (**425°–400° F., Gas 7–6**) for 15 min. Remove weighted paper and return cases to oven for 2–3 min. or till dry. When cool arrange fruit neatly in the cases. Blend the arrowroot with a little syrup, boil remainder of syrup and pour on to blended mixture, stirring gently. Return to pan and bring to boil again, stirring *very* gently, otherwise the mixture loses its clear colour because of bubbles of air introduced in stirring or boiling syrup. Pour the glaze gently over the fruit and allow to cool. Pipe the cream neatly round the edge.

8–10 tartlets

GRANVILLE TARTLETS

Tartelettes à la Granville

Short crust pastry (p. 557), using 6 oz. flour, etc.
2 oz. butter
3 oz. sugar
2 oz. currants (cleaned)
1 oz. ground rice
1 oz. candied peel
3 oz. cake-crumbs
1 tablesp. cream (optional)
4–5 drops lemon essence
2 egg whites
Transparent icing (p. 548)
1 oz. desiccated coconut

Line 15 patty tins with pastry. Cream the butter and sugar till soft and white. Add the currants, ground rice, finely shredded peel, cake-crumbs, cream (if used) and lemon essence. Fold in the stiffly whisked egg whites. Fill the patty tins with the mixture and bake in a fairly hot oven (**400° F., Gas 6**) for 15–20 min. When cool, coat the tartlets with transparent icing and sprinkle with coconut.

15 tartlets

JAM TARTLETS

Tartelettes à la Confiture

Short crust *or* rich short crust, flaky *or* rough puff pastry (pp 554–7), using 4 oz. flour, etc.
3–4 tablesp. jam

Roll pastry out thinly, cut into rounds with fluted cutter (a little larger than patty tin to allow for depth of tin). Line the tins with the pastry and press in well with the fingers. About half-fill with jam and bake in a hot oven (**425° F., Gas 7**).

10–12 tartlets
Cooking time—15 min.

LEMON CHEESECAKES

Tartelettes à la Frangipane au Citron

Short crust pastry (p.557), using 12 oz. flour, etc.
1 lb. loaf sugar
4 oz. butter
3 lemons
3 eggs
Finely-shredded candied peel

Line about 30 patty tins with the pastry. Put the sugar, butter, juice of 3 lemons and the grated rind of 2 lemons in a pan and stir till the sugar is dissolved. Add the beaten eggs and stir over a gentle heat until the mixture becomes thick. Allow to cool then ¾ fill the patty tins with the mixture. Place a few strips of candied peel on top and bake in a fairly hot oven (**400° F., Gas 6**) for about 20 min.

NOTE: The above filling (lemon curd), if closely covered and stored in a cool, dry place, will keep for several weeks and may be used as required.

30 cheesecakes

LEMON TARTLETS

Tartelettes au Citron

4 oz. butter
4 oz. sugar
2 eggs
1 lemon
Short crust pastry (p.557), using 6 oz. flour, etc.
Icing sugar

Cream the butter and sugar till thick and white; beat in each egg separately. Add the finely-grated lemon rind and the lemon juice.

Allow the mixture to stand in a cool dry place for 24 hr. Line 16–18 patty tins with pastry. Place the mixture in the patty tins and bake in a fairly hot oven (**400° F., Gas 6**) for 15–20 min.

When cool, dredge with icing sugar.

16–18 tartlets

MAIDS OF HONOUR

Dâmes d'Honneur

Puff pastry (p. 555), **using 4 oz. flour, etc.**
4 oz. ground almonds
2 oz. castor sugar
1 egg
½ oz. flour
2 tablesp. cream
1 tablesp. orange-flower water

Roll out the pastry thinly and line 12 patty tins. Mix the ground almonds and sugar together, add the beaten egg and mix in the flour, cream and orange-flower water. Put a little mixture in each patty tin and bake in a fairly hot oven (**400° F., Gas 6**) till set and golden brown.

10–12 tartlets
Cooking time—25–30 min.

MASERINES

4 oz. plain flour
2 oz. butter *or* **margarine**
½ oz. castor sugar
1 oz. ground almonds
1 egg yolk

FILLING

4 oz. granulated sugar
Small ½ teasp. ground cinnamon
1 tablesp. grated plain chocolate
2 oz. blanched chopped almonds
1 egg white

Sift the flour. Cream the fat and sugar, add flour and almonds and mix to a stiff paste with the egg yolk. Roll the paste 4–5 in. wide and 9–10 in. long. From the width at each side, cut off a strip ½ in. wide, damp it and turn it on to the main piece making a wall. Partly cook the paste in a fairly hot oven (**375° F., Gas 5**); remove from oven spread with jam. Make the filling: beat the egg white slightly, put all ingredients into a pan, stir till boiling and spread at once on top of the jam. Complete the cooking in a moderate oven (**350° F., Gas 4**) 15–20 min. and cut into fingers while warm.

16 cakes
Cooking time—about 30–40 min. (altogether)

MINCE PIES

Short crust, rich short crust, flaky, rough puff *or* **puff pastry** (pp. 554–7), **using 6 oz. flour, etc.**
10–12 oz. mincemeat
Castor *or* **icing sugar**

Roll the pastry out to about ⅛ in. thickness. Cut half of it into rounds of about 2½ in. diameter and reserve these for lids. (Use a plain cutter for flaky, rough puff or puff pastry.) Cut the remaining pastry into rounds of about 3 in. diameter and line some patty tins. Place some mincemeat in the tins, brush the edge of the pastry with water and place a lid on top of each. Press the edges well together; if a plain cutter has been used knock up the edges. Brush the tops with water and sprinkle with sugar. Make a hole or 2 small cuts in the top of each. Bake in a hot oven (**450°–425° F., Gas 8–7**) depending on the type of pastry, for 25–30 min.

Dredge tops with castor sugar *or* icing sugar. Serve hot or cold.

8–10 pies

NOUGATINES

Short crust pastry (p. 557), **using 3 oz. flour, etc.**
1 dessertsp. apricot jam

FILLING

1½ oz. butter *or* **margarine**
1½ oz. sugar
1 egg
1 tablesp. cake-crumbs
1 tablesp. ground almonds
A few drops of almond essence
A few chopped almonds

DECORATION

1 tablesp. apricot glaze
Chopped pistachio nuts *or* **coloured cake-crumbs**

Roll pastry thinly, cut into rounds to fit small bouché tins. Put a little jam in each.

Cream fat and sugar, and add egg gradually,

beating well between each addition. Stir in crumbs, ground almonds and essence. Half fill each tin with mixture, smooth the surface and sprinkle with chopped almonds. Bake in a fairly hot oven (**375° F., Gas 5**) until quite firm on top. Allow to cool, brush over top with apricot glaze and decorate round edge with chopped pistachio nuts or coloured crumbs.

12–15 cakes
Cooking time—20–30 min.

ORANGE BOATS

Tartelettes aux Oranges

PASTRY

6 oz. plain flour	**3 oz. butter**
Pinch of salt	**1 egg yolk**
½ oz. ground almonds	**Water to mix**

FILLING

3 oz. ground almonds	**Grated rind of 1 orange**
4 oz. castor sugar	**1 egg white**

ORANGE GLACÉ ICING

2 oz. icing sugar mixed with 1½ tablesp. orange juice and water

Sift flour and salt, add the ½ oz. ground almonds and rub in the butter. Mix to a stiff paste with egg and water, roll out thinly and line greased boat-shaped moulds.

Mix the 3 oz. almonds, sugar and orange rind and fold into the stiffly beaten egg white. Two-thirds fill the lined tins and bake in a fairly hot oven (**375°–350° F., Gas 5–4**). When cold put a little glacé icing down the centre of each.

20 cakes
Cooking time—20–30 min.

ORANGE TARTLETS (1)

Tartelettes aux Oranges

Short crust pastry (p. 557), using 6 oz. flour, etc.	**3 oz. sugar**
	1 egg
	1 egg yolk
2 oranges	**½ teasp. vanilla essence**
3 oz. butter	

Line 15 patty tins with the pastry. Grate orange rind finely. Cream butter and sugar well together. Separate the egg yolk from the white and beat both egg yolks into the mixture, one at a time. Add 2 tablesp. orange juice, the orange rind and vanilla essence. Whisk the egg white stiffly and fold it into the mixture. Place the mixture in the patty tins and bake in a fairly hot oven (**400° F., Gas 6**) for 15–20 min. When ¾ baked, dredge with castor sugar.

15 tartlets

ORANGE TARTLETS (2)

Short crust pastry (p. 557), using 6 oz. flour, etc.	**3 oz. castor sugar**
	2 eggs
	1 teasp. cornflour
2 oranges	**1½ oz. cake-crumbs**
3 oz. butter	

Line 15 patty tins with pastry. Grate orange rind finely. Cream butter and sugar well together. Separate the egg yolks from the whites and beat the yolks into the mixture, one at a time. Mix the juice of one orange with the cornflour and orange rind. Add this to the mixture with the cake-crumbs and fold in the stiffly whisked egg whites. Place the mixture in the patty tins and bake in a fairly hot oven (**400° F., Gas 6**) for about 20 min. When cold decorate with glacé icing.

15 tartlets

PARISIAN TARTLETS

Tartelettes à la Parisienne

Short crust pastry (p. 557), using 6 oz. flour, etc.	**1 oz. cornflour**
	1 oz. ground almonds
	2 oz. cake-crumbs
3 oz. butter	**1 teasp. cinnamon**
3 oz. castor sugar	**1 dessertsp. lemon juice**
2 small eggs	
2 tablesp. cream *or* milk	

Line 15 patty tins with pastry. Cream the butter and sugar till soft and white; add the eggs separately and beat well. Blend the cornflour with the cream *or* milk, stir this into the mixture and add the ground almonds, cake-crumbs, cinnamon and lemon juice. Fill the patty tins with the mixture and bake in a fairly hot oven (**400° F., Gas 6**) for 15–20 min. When ¾ baked dredge well with castor sugar.

15 tartlets

POLISH TARTLETS

Puff pastry trimmings
Raspberry jam
Apricot jam
Chopped pistachio nuts
Desiccated coconut

Roll the pastry out thinly and cut into 3½-in. squares. Moisten each corner, fold them over to meet in the centre and cover the join with a small round of pastry. Bake in a fairly hot oven (**400° F., Gas 6**) for about 15 min. When cool, place a little jam at each corner. Sprinkle coconut on the raspberry jam and finely-chopped pistachio nuts on the apricot jam.

SAINT DENIS TARTLETS

Short crust pastry (p. 557), using 6 oz. flour, etc.
2 oz. butter
2 oz. castor sugar
1 egg
1 egg yolk
2 oz. ground almonds
1 level tablesp. cornflour
Vanilla essence
Raspberry jam
Icing sugar

Roll out the pastry and line 15 patty tins. Cream the butter and sugar together until thick; beat in the egg yolks one at a time. Add the ground almonds, cornflour and vanilla essence and lastly fold in the stiffly whisked egg white. Place a small teasp. of jam at the bottom of each tin and fill with the mixture. Place two narrow strips of pastry across the top. Bake in a fairly hot oven (**400° F., Gas 6**) for 15–20 min.

When cool, dust with icing sugar.

15 tartlets

"SLY" CAKES

Rough puff pastry (p. 556), using 8 oz. flour, etc, *or* trimmings may be used
8 oz. currants
1 apple
1 oz. chopped peel
2 oz. sugar
2 level teasp. mixed spice
1 oz. melted margarine *or* butter

Divide pastry into 2 pieces and roll out each piece into a square of the same size and about ⅛ in. thick. Mix the currants, chopped apple and peel with the other ingredients and spread on one piece of pastry. Lay the other half on top, mark with a knife, brush with egg and bake in a hot oven (**425° F., Gas 7**). Cut into squares or fingers and dust with icing or castor sugar.

16–20 fingers **Cooking time—20–30 min.**

VANILLA SLICES

Tartes à la Vanille

Puff pastry (p. 555), using 3 oz. flour, etc.
A little glacé icing

FILLING

½ pt. milk
¾ oz. cornflour
2 egg yolks *or* 1 whole egg
1 oz. sugar
½ teasp. vanilla essence

Roll pastry ½ in. thick and cut into fingers 4 in. by 1 in. Bake in a fairly hot oven (**425° F., Gas 7**) until pastry is well risen. Allow to cool.

Blend the cornflour with the milk, beat in the egg yolks and sugar, and cook over a gentle heat until thick. Beat in the vanilla. Allow to cool.

Slit carefully through the centre of the pastry fingers, spread the custard over one half and sandwich the halves together again. Spread tops thinly with glacé icing.

8 slices
Cooking time—20 min.

WELSH CHEESECAKES

Tartes à la Galloise

Short crust pastry (p. 557), using 4 oz. flour
2 oz. butter *or* margarine
2 oz. sugar
3 oz. plain flour
½ level teasp. baking-powder
Grated rind of ½ lemon
1 egg
Milk *or* water, if necessary
Raspberry jam

Roll out pastry thinly, cut into rounds using a cutter a little larger than the tins, and line 12 patty tins. Cream the fat and sugar. Sift flour and baking-powder, add the grated lemon rind. Whisk the egg, and add a little at a time to the creamed fat. Stir in the flour and add milk or water to make a soft dropping consistency. Half-fill the pastry cases with the mixture, after putting a small amount of jam in the bottom of each. Place on top 2 strips of pastry in the form of a cross and bake in a fairly hot oven (**400° F., Gas 6**).

12 cheesecakes
Cooking time—15–20 min.

SAVOURIES & APPETIZERS

IN THIS SECTION are included a number of different kinds of savoury dishes. First a collection of easy to make recipes that form a fitting end to a good lunch or dinner—some people omit the sweet preferring a savoury to a sweet at the end of the meal. On the other hand these recipes will be found very useful for a light lunch or supper dish—served in a somewhat larger quantity.

The rest of the section deals with savouries for cocktail parties, for buffet parties, and for the evenings when the family and friends are watching television.

Some of the recipes for hors d'œuvres—if put on rounds of toast, etc., are very suitable for these occasions.

A selection of interesting, easy to make, yet delicious tasting snacks will be appreciated in these days of informal entertaining.

SAVOURIES FOR FORMAL MEALS AND LIGHT LUNCHES

"ANGELS ON HORSEBACK"

Les Anges à Cheval

12 oysters
12 small thin slices of bacon
Paprika *or* cayenne pepper
½ teasp. chopped shallot *or* onion
½ teasp. chopped parsley
Lemon juice
12 small rounds of fried bread *or* 4 slices of toast

Beard the oysters, trim the bacon, cutting each piece just large enough to roll round an oyster, season with paprika or cayenne pepper, sprinkle on a little shallot and parsley. Lay an oyster on each, add a few drops of lemon juice, roll up tightly and secure the bacon in position with a fine skewer. Cook in a frying-pan, under the grill or in a hot oven (**425° F., Gas 7**), *just long enough* to crisp the bacon (further cooking would harden the oysters), remove the skewers and serve on the croûtes.

4 helpings *or* 12 small savouries
Cooking time—5–10 min.

BLOATER TOAST

Croûtes à la Yarmouth

2 bloaters with soft roes
1½ oz. butter
1 egg
Salt
Cayenne pepper
8 squares of buttered toast *or* 2 large pieces of toast

Remove the roes, grill the bloaters, free them from skin and bone, then chop or rub them through a fine sieve. Heat 1 oz. of butter in a small saucepan, add the fish, and when

PLATE 25

Making a Decorative Pie Rose

1 Roll out left-overs of pastry into a thin round shape, and cut it with a knife into quarters.

1

2 Arrange pieces one on top of the other, overlapping at angles.

3 Put the thumb into the centre of the pastry and push into a tube.

2

3

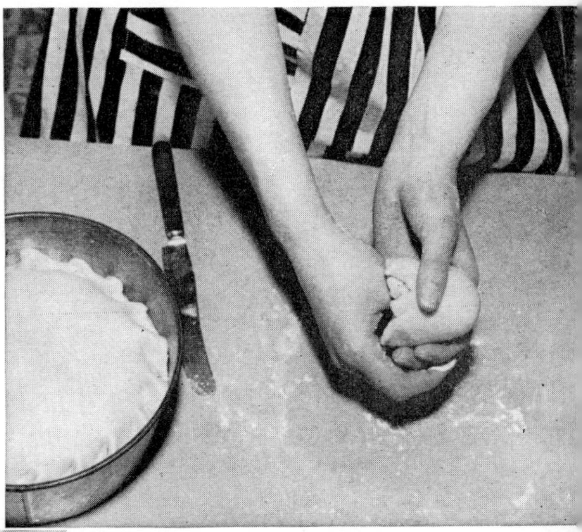

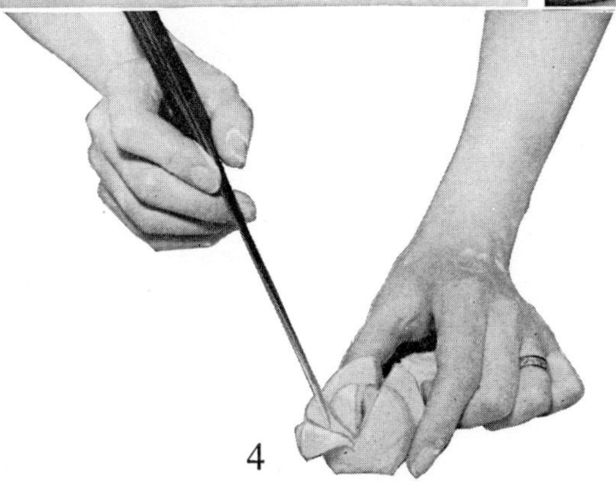

4

4 Cut off the uneven ends, and at the rounded end make two cuts at right angles forming a cross. Open the pastry to form petals.

PLATE 26

Making a Small Raised Pie

1 Reserve approximately ¼ of the hot water crust pastry for the lid and mould the remainder to the shape of the pie. Put in the filling.

2 Roll out the pastry reserved for the lid; damp the rim of the case and carefully put on the lid.

3 Press the edges firmly together.

4 Pin three or four folds of greased greaseproof paper round the pie to preserve its shape during baking, and make a hole in the top of the pastry with a skewer.

5 When the pie is baked remove the greaseproof paper surrounding it.

6 Make a cone of greaseproof paper, and use to fill pie with the stock.

1

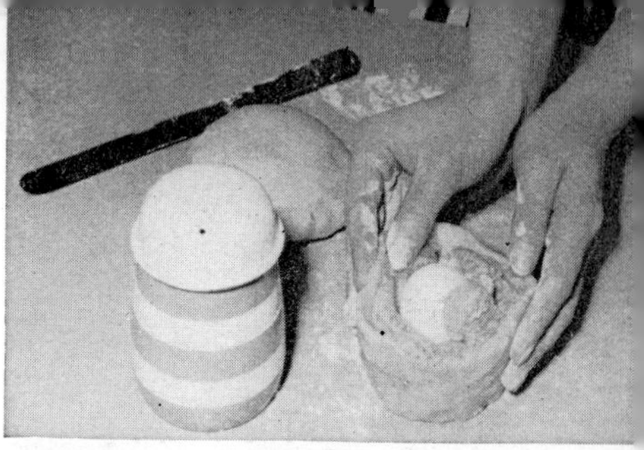

2

3

4

6

5

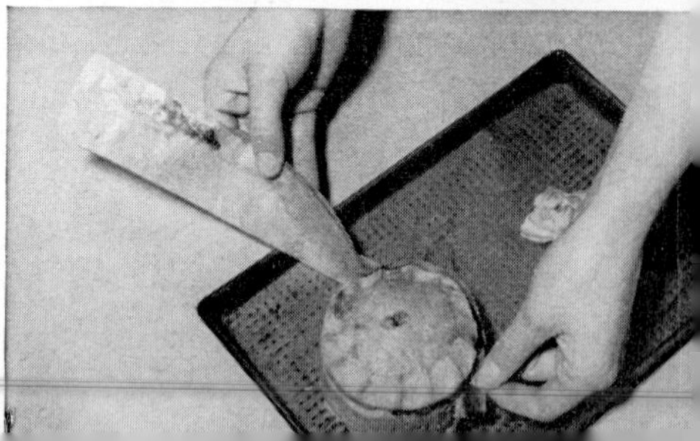

hot put in the egg, season to taste, and stir over a low heat until the mixture thickens. Meanwhile divide the roes into 8 pieces, and fry them in the remainder of the butter. Spread the fish mixture on the toast, place the roe on the top, and serve as hot as possible.

2 helpings *or* 8 small savouries
Cooking time—5 min.

Cheese Savouries

CHEESE AIGRETTES

Aigrettes au Parmesan

2 oz. butter	**2 eggs**
½ pt. water	**Pinch of salt**
4 oz. flour (plain *or* self-raising)	**Pinch of pepper**
	Deep fat for frying
3 oz. grated cheese (preferably Parmesan)	**Grated cheese**
	Cayenne pepper

Put the butter and water into a small saucepan; when boiling add the sifted flour, and stir vigorously over heat until the panada leaves the sides of the pan quite clean. Remove from heat and mix in the cheese, egg yolks, beating each one in separately, add seasoning to taste, and lastly stir in the stiffly whisked egg whites. Turn the mixture on to a plate, and when cold drop small rough pieces of it into hot fat, do not allow to fry too quickly or the outside will become too brown before the inside is sufficiently cooked. On the other hand, if the fat is too cold it soaks into the paste and the aigrettes are greasy. As the success of this dish depends chiefly on the frying, the greatest possible care should be taken. Drain well, then arrange the aigrettes in pyramid form on a savoury d'oyley and sprinkle with Parmesan cheese and cayenne pepper.

About 24 savouries
Cooking time—about 4 min. for each batch

CHEESE AND SARDINE FINGERS

1 small can sardines in oil	**2 oz. grated Cheddar cheese**
½ teacup breadcrumbs	**A little margarine *or* butter if necessary**
Seasoning	
½ teasp. mixed mustard	**4 slices buttered toast**
	1 tomato
1 teasp. Worcester sauce	

Mash the sardines very well, and season. Mix the oil from the can of sardines with the breadcrumbs, seasoning, mustard, Worcester sauce and cheese. If there is not sufficient oil to give a soft mixture then add a little margarine or butter and cream well. Spread the mashed sardines on the slices of toast, and cover with the crumb mixture. Put under a hot grill for a few minutes until crisp and golden brown. Garnish with a small piece of tomato.

4 helpings *or* 8 small savouries
Cooking time—4 min.

CHEESE CREAM—COLD

Crème au Fromage froid

1 oz. grated Parmesan cheese	**Cayenne pepper**
	Pinch of salt
1–2 oz. grated Cheddar *or* Gruyère cheese	**½ gill aspic jelly**
	1 gill cream
Mixed mustard	**Watercress**

Season the cheese with the mustard, a good pinch of salt and cayenne pepper. Stir the aspic jelly—which should be quite cold, and just beginning to stiffen slightly—into the cheese. Add the lightly whipped cream. Put the mixture into a glass dish, or individual soufflé dishes and allow to set. Garnish with a light dusting of cayenne or paprika pepper and watercress. If preferred the mixture can be put into small dariole moulds, previously coated with aspic jelly and decorated with tiny pieces of tomato, gherkin, etc.

This dish can be served either as a cold hors d'œuvres or a savoury.

4 helpings

CHEESE CREAM CROÛTES

Croûtes de Fromage

Ingredients for cheese mixture as in Cheese cream	**Cayenne *or* paprika pepper**
	Chopped aspic jelly
10–12 croûtes of fried bread (approx.)	**Watercress**

Spread the cheese cream mixture over the bottom of a shallow baking-tin, and when set cut into rounds the same size as the croûtes of fried bread—i.e. 1–1½ in. in diameter. Lift the jellied cheese mixture on to the croûtes with a palette knife dipped in hot water.

Dust with cayenne or paprika pepper and garnish with chopped aspic jelly and watercress.

10–12 savouries

CHEESE D'ARTOIS *D'Artois au Parmesan*

1 egg	**Puff pastry using 4 oz. flour, etc.**
4 oz. grated cheese	**Egg yolk**
1 oz. butter	**Parsley**
Salt and pepper	

Beat the yolk and white of the whole egg slightly, add 3 oz. of cheese, butter (melted), and season rather highly with salt and pepper. Roll the pastry out thinly, cut it in 2, spread the mixture over one ½, and cover with the other ½. Place carefully on a greased baking-sheet, score it in 1 in. deep strips, brush over with egg yolk, sprinkle with remainder of grated cheese, and bake for about 10 min. in a hot oven (**425° F., Gas 7**). When ready cut through the scores, pile on a hot dish, and serve. Garnish with parsley.

CHEESE MERINGUES

Meringues au Parmesan

2 egg whites	**2 oz. grated Parmesan cheese**
Pinch of cayenne pepper	**Deep fat for frying**
Pinch of salt	**A little Parmesan cheese for garnish**

Whisk the egg whites to a very stiff froth. Add a good seasoning of cayenne and a little salt to the cheese, then stir it lightly into the whisked egg whites. Have ready a deep pan of hot fat, drop in the mixture in small teaspoonfuls, and fry until nicely browned. Drain well, and serve sprinkled with Parmesan cheese and more cayenne pepper.

About 14 savouries **Cooking time—5 min.**

CHEESE PUDDING *Pouding au Fromage*

2 eggs	**Pinch of pepper**
4 oz. grated cheese	**½ pt. milk**
1 teasp. mixed mustard	**1 oz. breadcrumbs**
Pinch of salt	

Beat the eggs slightly, add to them the cheese, mustard, salt and pepper. Boil the milk, pour over the eggs then add the breadcrumbs. Pour into a pie-dish or soufflé dish and bake for 25–30 min. in the centre of a fairly hot oven (**375° F., Gas 5**). Serve at once. If baked in 4 or 5 individual dishes allow approximately 15 min.

4–5 helpings

CHEESE SOUFFLÉ (Plate 13)

Soufflé au Fromage

A little butter for greasing	**3 oz. grated cheese**
1 oz. butter	**Pinch of salt**
1 oz. flour	**Pinch of cayenne pepper**
¼ pt. milk	**1–2 egg whites**
2 eggs	

Coat a soufflé dish well with butter and tie round it a well-buttered, thickly folded piece of paper to support the soufflé when it rises above the level of the dish. Melt the 1 oz. butter in a pan, stir in the flour, add the milk, and boil well. Remove from heat, and mix in the 2 egg yolks, beat well, then stir in the cheese and add seasoning to taste. Whisk all the egg whites to a stiff froth, add them lightly to the rest of the ingredients, pour the mixture into the soufflé dish, and bake in a moderate oven (**350° F., Gas 4**) for 30–35 min. Serve in the dish in which it is baked. Serve immediately.

5–6 helpings **Cooking time—35 min.**

COLD CHEESE SOUFFLÉ

¼ pt. cream	**2 egg whites**
1 oz. grated Parmesan cheese	**Good pinch of salt**
1 oz. grated Cheddar *or* Gruyère cheese	**Good pinch of cayenne pepper**
½ gill aspic jelly	**Tomato**
	Gherkin

Whip the cream *lightly*, fold in all the cheese, the cold but not set aspic jelly, the stiffly-beaten egg whites and the seasoning. Pour into a small prepared soufflé dish and when set, garnish with tiny pieces of tomato and gherkin.

4 helpings

GOLDEN BUCK

4 oz. Cheshire *or* Cheddar cheese	**2 eggs**
½ oz. butter	**Pinch of celery salt**
3 tablesp. ale	**Pinch of cayenne pepper**
½ teasp. Worcester sauce	**2 large slices buttered toast**
½ teasp. lemon juice *or* vinegar	

Grate the cheese finely. Put it into a pan with the butter and ale and stir vigorously until creamy. Then add the Worcester sauce, lemon juice or vinegar and the eggs previously beaten. Season to taste with celery salt and cayenne pepper, and continue stirring briskly until the mixture thickens. Trim the toast, and cover with cheese mixture. Garnish with parsley. Serve as hot as possible.

4 small *or* 2 large helpings
Cooking time—10 min.

IRISH RABBIT or RAREBIT

3 tablesp. milk	**1 teasp. mixed mustard**
1 oz. margarine *or* butter	**Salt and pepper**
4 oz. grated Cheddar *or* Cheshire cheese	**1 dessertsp. chopped gherkin**
1 teasp. vinegar	**Buttered toast**

Put the milk, butter and cheese into a saucepan, and stir over a LOW heat until the cheese melts and the mixture becomes creamy. Add the vinegar, mustard, a good pinch of salt and pepper and lastly the gherkin. Put on to hot buttered toast and either serve at once, or brown for a few minutes under a hot grill.

2 helpings *or* 4–5 small savouries
Cooking time—8 min. (approx.)

WELSH RAREBIT

1 oz. butter *or* margarine	**Few drops of Worcester sauce**
1 level tablesp. flour	**4–6 oz. grated Cheddar cheese**
5 tablesp. milk; *or* 3 tablesp. milk and 2 tablesp. ale *or* beer	**Salt and pepper**
1 teasp. mixed mustard	**4 slices of buttered toast**

Heat the fat in a pan and stir in the flour. Cook for several minutes, stirring well. Add the milk and stir well over the heat until a smooth thick mixture, then add the ale, mustard, Worcester sauce, cheese and a good pinch of salt and pepper. Do not overcook the mixture otherwise the cheese will become "oily". Spread on the slices of buttered toast and put under a hot grill until golden brown. Serve at once.

NOTE: A larger quantity of Welsh Rarebit mixture can be made and stored in the refrigerator being used as required.

4 helpings *or* 8 small savouries
Cooking time—10 min. (approx.)

BUCK RAREBIT

As for Welsh Rarebit, but top each slice of cooked Welsh Rarebit with a poached egg and serve at once.

YORKSHIRE RAREBIT

As for Welsh Rarebit, but add 2 oz. cooked ham.

The ham can either be cut into 4 thin slices, put on the toast and warmed for a minute under the grill before putting the cheese mixture on top or it can be diced and mixed with the cheese, etc.

ZEPHIRES OF CHEESE

Zephires au Parmesan

1 oz. gelatine	**¼ pt. cream**
½ gill water	**Seasoning**
2½ gills milk	**½ pt. aspic jelly**
2 oz. grated Parmesan cheese	**Watercress**
2 oz. grated Cheddar cheese	**Red pepper (capsicum)**

Dissolve the gelatine in the very hot $\frac{1}{2}$ gill of water, cool slightly, add milk and when quite cold, but not set, stir in all the cheese, lightly whipped cream and seasoning. Turn into individual fluted moulds or 1 large mould, allow to set. Turn out and garnish with chopped set aspic jelly, watercress and strips of red pepper.

4–5 helpings

Egg Savouries

EGGS STUFFED WITH PRAWNS

Œufs farcis aux Crevettes

4 hard-boiled eggs
12 large *or* 18 small prawns
1½ oz. butter
1 tablesp. mayonnaise
Pinch of salt
Pinch of pepper
Pinch of cayenne pepper
1 tablesp. grated Parmesan cheese

Cut the shelled eggs across in halves, cut off their extreme ends so that they stand firmly and remove the yolks. Put the prawns into a basin, add the egg yolks, pound until smooth; add the butter and mayonnaise, season to taste, then fill the egg cases. Sprinkle the surface with Parmesan cheese, place a prawn head in the centre of each.

8 savouries

SWISS EGGS

1½ oz. butter *or* margarine
2 tablesp. grated cheese
4 eggs
Good pinch of salt
Pinch of pepper
Cayenne *or* paprika pepper

Well grease 4 small dishes. Put ½ the cheese at the bottom of the dishes. Carefully break the eggs and put one into each dish on top of the cheese. Cover with seasoning, cheese and butter. Bake for about 10 min. in a fairly hot oven (**400° F., Gas 6**). Garnish with pepper and serve at once with hot rolls or crisp toast.

4 helpings

Fish Savouries

HELFORD ANGELS

Thin slices of brown bread
Butter
Oysters
Pepper
Nutmeg

Thickly spread the slices of brown bread with butter and trim into neat 2 in. squares. Place a raw oyster on each, sprinkle with a shake of pepper and grated nutmeg, and roll up corner wise. Place in a greased fireproof dish and bake in a fairly hot oven (**375° F., Gas 5**) about 10 min. until the bread is crisp. Spear with cocktail sticks and serve immediately.

Serve as a savoury, allowing 2 per helping; or as "hot" individual savouries for a cocktail party.

SARDINES WITH TOMATOES

Sardines à la Napolitaine

8 large sardines
8 finger-shaped pieces of toast
A little butter
2 large tomatoes
1 level teasp. cornflour
Salt and pepper
2 teasp. grated Parmesan cheese *or* 4 teasp. grated Cheddar cheese

Bone the sardines, but keep them a good shape. Spread the toast with butter and keep it hot. Sieve the tomatoes, and put the pulp with the cornflour and a good pinch of salt and pepper into a pan and cook for several minutes, adding the grated cheese. Spread ½ the tomato mixture on the pieces of toast, put the sardines on top, spread with the last of the tomato mixture and heat through for a few minutes in a hot oven (**425° F., Gas 7**), taking care the tomato mixture does not dry.

4 helpings **Cooking time—10 min.**

SMOKED HADDOCK SOUFFLÉ

Soufflé de Merluche fumée

1 small cooked smoked haddock
1½ oz. butter
2 eggs
1 egg white
Pinch of pepper
Cayenne pepper

Flake the fish while still hot, and when quite smooth beat in most of the butter and the yolks of the eggs. Use the rest of the butter to grease a soufflé dish. Add all the stiffly-beaten egg whites and pepper and cayenne pepper. It should not be necessary to add salt, but it is advisable to taste the mixture, since the saltiness of smoked haddock varies a great deal. Put the mixture into the soufflé dish and bake for approximately 15–20 min. in the centre of a moderate oven (**350° F., Gas 4**).

Serve at once.

NOTE: For a softer texture add 2–3 tablesp. white sauce *or* cream to the haddock before putting in the egg yolks.

An excellent flavour is given to this dish if 1 tablesp. grated Parmesan cheese is added with the egg yolks.

4-5 helpings

Miscellaneous Savouries

DEVILLED CHICKENS' LIVERS

Foie de Volaille à la Diable

4 chickens' livers
1 shallot *or* small onion
½ teasp. chopped parsley
Pinch of cayenne pepper
Pinch of salt
8 small rashers of bacon
4 croûtes of fried bread

Wash and dry the livers, cut them in halves. Finely chop the shallot or onion and mix with the parsley, cayenne pepper and salt. Sprinkle this mixture over the livers. Wrap the rashers of bacon round the livers, and fasten them in position with skewers. Bake in a moderate oven (**350° F., Gas 4**) for 7–8 min., or cook under the grill. Remove the skewers, put 2 bacon rolls on each croûte of bread, and serve as hot as possible.

4 helpings

DEVILS ON HORSEBACK

1–2 chicken livers *or* equivalent of calf's liver
Butter
Salt and pepper
Cayenne pepper
8 well-drained canned prunes
8 short thin rindless rashers streaky bacon
4 small bread squares
Olives stuffed with pimento

Gently cook the liver in a little butter, then cut it into 8 pieces. Season well and dust with a few grains of cayenne pepper. Stone the prunes and stuff with the liver. Stretch the bacon to double its size with the flat of a knife. Encircle each prune in a piece of bacon and secure with a cocktail stick. Grill all over or bake in a very hot oven. Fry the bread in shallow bacon fat and drain well. Remove sticks and place the "devils" on the bread. Garnish with a pimento-stuffed olive.

4 helpings

MARROW TOAST

Marrow from 2 beef bones
Buttered toast
Salt and pepper

Soak the marrow in tepid water for about 2 hr. About 15 min. before the dish is needed, cut the marrow into small pieces, put into cold water, bring rapidly to the boil, add a good pinch of salt and cook for 1 min. only. Drain the marrow thoroughly then put on to the hot buttered toast, season well. Either cook for several minutes in a hot oven, until the marrow is well melted, or put under a hot grill—taking care the marrow does not dry. Serve at once. When **savoury marrow** is preferred sprinkle with chopped parsley, chopped chives and lemon juice before serving.

6–7 helpings **Cooking time—20 min. (approx.)**

MUSHROOM SOUFFLÉ

1 oz. butter *or* margarine
1 oz. flour
¼ pt. milk
4 oz. mushrooms
3 eggs
Seasoning
1 egg white

Melt the butter or margarine in a saucepan, stir in the flour and cook for several minutes, stirring well. Gradually add the milk, bring to the boil and cook until thickened. Add the very finely chopped or minced mushrooms—the stalks can be used in this recipe—the yolks of the eggs and seasoning. Lastly fold in all the stiffly-beaten egg whites. Put into a well greased soufflé dish. Bake for approximately 30 min. in the centre of a fairly hot oven (**375° F., Gas 5**).

Serve at once.

4 helpings

SCOTCH WOODCOCK

4 slices of toast
Butter
4 eggs
2 tablesp. milk
Good pinch of salt
Good pinch of pepper
1 small can anchovy fillets

Cover the hot toast with butter and keep warm. Beat the eggs with the milk and seasoning. Put a good knob of butter (about 1 oz.) into a saucepan, heat gently, then add the eggs and milk. Cook gently until the mixture thickens. Spread on toast and garnish with anchovy fillets—arranged in a lattice design.

4 helpings *or* 8 small savouries
Cooking time—6 min. (approx.)

SAVOURIES FOR COCKTAIL, BUFFET AND T.V. PARTIES

ANCHOVIES—PORTUGUESE

12 rounds of fried bread *or* small biscuits
2 oz. anchovy butter
12 anchovy fillets
12 stuffed olives
Watercress

Spread the biscuits or fried bread with anchovy butter. Wrap the anchovy fillets round the olives and stand on the biscuits. With a small rose pipe make a tiny rosette of anchovy butter on top of each olive. Garnish with single watercress leaves.

12 savouries

ANCHOVIES—RUTLAND STYLE

Anchois à la Rutland

Cheese pastry using 3 oz. flour, etc.
1 small can anchovy fillets (well drained) *or* 4 whole anchovies (boned and filleted)
1 tablesp. cream *or* white sauce
1 hard-boiled egg
Pinch of cayenne pepper
Anchovy essence
Cochineal
Watercress

Roll out the cheese pastry thinly, cut into $1\frac{1}{2}$–$1\frac{3}{4}$ in. squares, bake in a fairly hot oven (**400° F., Gas 6**) until crisp, and use when cool. Chop the anchovies and mix with the white sauce or cream and the finely-sieved yolk of the egg. Season with cayenne, add a few drops of anchovy essence and cochineal, drop by drop, until a pale pink colour is obtained. Pile the mixture on the biscuits, garnish with fine strips of egg white and watercress.

12 savouries
Cooking time—12 min. (approx.)

ANCHOVY CROÛTES

Croûtes d'Anchois

1 hard-boiled egg
½ teasp. curry paste *or* powder
2 oz. butter
Toast
12 anchovy fillets
Paprika pepper
Lemon juice
Parsley

Chop the white of the egg finely. Rub the yolk through a fine sieve and combine with the curry paste and butter. Mix to a soft paste. Make the toast thin and crisp, cut it into rounds or triangles and spread on the mixture. Lay on each an anchovy fillet, and season with paprika pepper. Add 2–3 drops of lemon juice, decorate with egg white and parsley. Place them in a hot oven for 3–4 min., then serve.

12 savouries
Cooking time—3–4 min.

ANCHOVY FINGERS

Canapés d'Anchois

Buttered toast
1 shallot
Chopped parsley
8–10 anchovy fillets
Lemon juice
Cayenne pepper *or* paprika pepper
½ oz. butter

Cut the toast into fingers, sprinkle them with finely-chopped shallot and parsley, and place on each an anchovy fillet. Add a few drops of lemon juice and a seasoning of pepper. Sprinkle on a little paprika or cayenne pepper, place a little butter on each.

Heat for a few minutes in a fairly hot oven (**400° F., Gas 6**).

8–10 savouries
Cooking time 5–10 min.

ANCHOVY TARTLETS

Tartlettes d'Anchôis

Anchovy pastry (see Royal Anchovy Biscuits)
Anchovy cream
Lobster coral *or* paprika pepper
Capers

Line 12 very small patty-pans with the pastry, prick them all over. Bake in a fairly hot oven (**400° F., Gas 6**) until crisp, and when cold fill with anchovy cream. Pile the mixture high in the centre and sprinkle with lobster coral or paprika pepper. Garnish with capers.

About 12 tarts **Cooking time—10–12 min.**

ANCHOVY TOAST *Croûtes d'Anchois*

1 small can of anchovies
1 *small* shallot *or* onion
1 oz. butter
½ teasp. chopped parsley
4 eggs
Cayenne pepper
4 slices buttered toast

Drain the anchovy fillets, chop them coarsely. Chop the shallot or onion. Heat the butter in a small saucepan, fry the shallot or onion until lightly browned, then add the anchovies, parsley and eggs and season with cayenne pepper. Stir over low heat until the mixture thickens, then pour it on the buttered toast.

4 helpings *or* 8–10 small savouries
Cooking time—3–4 min.

ROYAL ANCHOVY BISCUITS

ANCHOVY PASTRY

1½ oz. butter *or* margarine
3 oz. flour (preferably plain)
1 egg yolk
Few drops of anchovy essence

ANCHOVY CREAM

1 small can anchovy fillets (well drained)
1 hard-boiled egg
1 oz. butter
Pinch of cayenne pepper
3 tablesp. cream
Few drops of cochineal

Rub the fat into the flour, add the egg yolk, anchovy essence and sufficient water to mix to a stiff paste. Roll out thinly, stamp into rounds 1½–1¾ in. in diameter, bake in a fairly hot oven **(400° F., Gas 6)** until crisp, and use when cool. Pound the anchovies with the yolk of the egg and the butter until smooth, season with a little cayenne pepper. Whip the cream stiffly, stir the fish mixture in lightly, and add the colouring drop by drop until a pale pink colour is obtained. Pipe the mixture on to the biscuits in the form of rosettes.

About 12 savouries
Cooking time—12 min. (approx.)

ASPARAGUS ROLLS

Thin slices of FRESH brown bread and butter
Cooked *or* canned asparagus tips
Mayonnaise if wished *or* Hollandaise sauce
Seasoning

Remove the crusts from the bread and butter. Put a well-drained asparagus tip on each piece of bread and butter, adding a little mayonnaise or Hollandaise sauce and seasoning. Roll up firmly. Keep under a damp cloth or cover with aluminium foil until required.

NOTE: If wished the bread and butter can also be spread with demi-sel or soft cream cheese.

ASPIC FINGERS

To about 6 slices of bread allow ½ pt. aspic jelly

SELECTION OF TOPPINGS FOR THE BREAD

Sardines
Anchovies
Tiny pieces of smoked salmon
Prawns
Shrimps
Cooked peas and diced carrots
Asparagus tips

GARNISH

Anchovy butter *or* Savoury butter *or* Tomato butter (*see below*)

Making aspic fingers is a troublesome rather than difficult task. Either butter the bread, or toast and spread with butter or one of the flavoured butters used for piping.

Arrange the topping on the toast or bread. Make the aspic jelly and allow it to become quite cold and just beginning to thicken, then either spread this over the topping with a knife dipped in hot water or brush it over. It is better to have several thin coatings—allowing each one to set before adding the next than to try and give too thick a coating.

The piping in the flavoured butter can either be put on top of the set aspic jelly or put on the topping and then coated with a thin layer of aspic jelly. The latter method is best since it prevents the butter from drying. When the jelly is quite set, cut the slices of bread into tiny fingers with a sharp knife dipped in hot water.

It is advisable to stand the slices of bread on a tray or pastry-board, when coating with jelly so that any jelly that "drips off" the bread can be picked up and used again.

Anchovy butter

To each 2 oz. butter add 1–2 teasp. anchovy essence.

Savoury butter

Add salt, cayenne pepper, a little celery salt and mixed mustard to creamed butter. Tint a pale green or pink as wished.

Tomato butter

To each 2 oz. butter add 1 teasp. tomato purée or tomato ketchup and a squeeze of lemon juice or a few drops of vinegar.

BEETROOT CROÛTES

Betterave à l'Orientale

Brown bread
Butter
1 small beetroot
2 hard-boiled eggs
1 shallot
1 tablesp. capers
Lemon juice
Anchovy essence
Cayenne pepper
Pinch of salt

Prepare thin slices of bread and butter, cut from them 8–9 rounds about 1¾ in. in diameter, and cover them with slices of beetroot of corresponding size and thickness. Cut the eggs across in thin slices, select 8–9 of suitable size, remove the yolk, and place the rings of egg white on the croûtes, leaving visible a narrow margin of beetroot. Chop the shallot very finely. Pass the egg yolks through a sieve, mix with them the capers and shallot, add a few drops of lemon juice and sufficient anchovy essence to form a moist paste. Season to taste, pile the mixture in the centre of the croûtes.

8–9 savouries

BURLINGTON CROÛTES

4 oz. finely-chopped *or* minced chicken; *or* a jar of chicken paste
2 tablesp. thick mayonnaise
2 tomatoes
Seasoning
12 rounds of fried bread *or* crisp biscuits
Butter
12 stuffed olives

Mix the chicken with the mayonnaise. Cut the tomatoes into 12 very thin slices; season. Butter the biscuits or drain the fried bread well. Top with sliced tomatoes and the chicken mixture. Press a stuffed olive on top of each.

12 savouries

CANAPÉS

Canapés for savouries can be neat shapes of bread and butter, toast or fried bread; or crisp biscuits of cheese, short or flaky pastry. Tiny round firm pancakes are a good base for savoury mixtures too.

Toast is the most usual but it does become soft if prepared too far ahead. Fried bread should be very well drained on kitchen or crumpled tissue paper so that it is dry and no longer greasy.

CAVIARE CROUSTADES

Croustades au Caviar

2 oz. butter
1 teasp. anchovy essence
Stale bread
Clarified butter
1 shallot
1 dessertsp. lemon juice
1 small pot of caviare

Make anchovy butter by creaming together the butter and anchovy essence. From slices of stale bread about ½–¾ in. thick, cut or stamp out about 12 rounds, ovals, or squares 2 in. in diameter. With a smaller cutter cut the shapes to ½ their depth and hollow out the centres. Fry the cases carefully in clarified butter until lightly browned, drain and cool. Add the finely-chopped shallot and lemon juice to the caviare, stir well with a wooden skewer, and put the mixture in the crisp shapes. Put the anchovy butter into a forcing bag and decorate each croustade. Serve cold.

About 12 savouries

Cooking time—3–4 min.

FOIE GRAS CROÛTES

Foie gras
Cream *or* white sauce
Salt and pepper
Croûtes of fried *or* toasted bread

Pound the foie gras, adding a little cream or white sauce until the right consistency is obtained. Pass through a fine sieve, season to taste, and arrange on the croûtes, using a piping bag if available.

HADDOCK BOATS

Short crust pastry (p. 557), using 4 oz. flour, etc.	**4 oz. cooked smoked haddock (approx.)**
1 teasp. chutney	**1 oz. butter**
2 teasp. mustard	**1 tablesp. cream**
Few drops Worcester sauce	**6–8 anchovy fillets**
	Pinch of pepper
	1–2 gherkins

Line about 12–14 small boat-shaped tins with thin short crust pastry and bake "blind" (*see* p. 558) for approximately 10 min. in a hot oven (**425° F., Gas 7**). Allow to cool. Mix the chutney, mixed mustard and Worcester sauce together. Spread a thin layer at the bottom of each boat shape. Flake the haddock flesh very finely, add the creamed butter and cream. Mix well and put into the boats. Top with half an anchovy fillet and sliced gherkins.

12–14 savouries

HADDOCK CROUSTADES

1 small dried haddock (smoked)	**Grating of nutmeg**
1 oz. butter	**Croustades of bread**
2 eggs	**Bread**
2 tablesp. milk	**Butter**
Good pinch of pepper	**Cayenne pepper**

Cook the haddock in boiling water until just tender. Flake all the fish away from the bones. Heat the butter in a pan, and when hot add the eggs, beaten with the milk, and pepper, flaked haddock, and nutmeg. Cook very gently until lightly set. Fill croustades of bread—for directions on preparing these see recipe for Sardine Croustades—or put the mixture on to crisp fingers of buttered toast. Garnish with cayenne pepper.

4 helpings *or* 12 small savouries
Cooking time—12 min. (approx.)

HAM CROÛTES

Croûtes au Jambon

2 teasp. chopped shallots *or* onion	**1 tablesp. cream**
1 oz. butter	**Pinch of pepper**
6 oz. cooked ham	**4 round croûtes of fried bread *or* toast**
2 egg yolks *or* 1 whole egg	**Chopped parsley**

Fry the shallot or onion in the butter until slightly browned, then add the ham and stir over the heat until hot. Put in the egg yolks or egg and cream and season with pepper. Stir until the mixture thickens, then dish on the croûtes and serve sprinkled with parsley.

6–7 helpings
Cooking time—5 min.

HAM FINGERS

Jambon sur croûtes

4 oz. lean ham	**1 teasp. chopped parsley**
1 sliced onion	**Fingers of baked cheese pastry *or* toast**
1 oz. butter *or* fat	
2 eggs	
Salt and pepper	
Mixed mustard	

Finely chop the ham. Chop the onion finely and fry in the fat without browning. Add the ham and beaten eggs. Stir over a gentle heat until eggs begin to thicken. Add seasoning, mustard to taste and ½ the parsley. Cover the pastry or toast fingers thickly with the mixture, sprinkle with the remainder of the parsley, and serve very hot or quite cold.

Cooking time—about 10 min.

HAM ROLLS

4 thin slices of cooked ham	**1–2 tablesp. sweet chutney**
2 oz. cream cheese	**Crisp lettuce**

Spread each slice of ham on a board, trim off surplus fat. Mix the cream cheese and chutney together, spread over the ham and roll. Put on to lettuce leaves. If wished cut the slices into 1 in. lengths and instead of putting on to lettuce leaves put on small buttered biscuits and garnish with watercress leaves.

4 helpings *or* 12 small savouries

HERRING ROE TIT-BITS

Bonnes Bouches de Laitance de Harengs

6 large soft herring roes	**12 small rounds of toast *or* fried bread**
Salt and pepper	**Anchovy paste**
6 rashers of bacon	**2–3 small gherkins**
A little lemon juice	

Cut the roes into halves, season lightly with salt and pepper. Divide the rashers of bacon into halves, remove the rinds and wrap each piece of roe in the bacon. Sprinkle lemon juice on the bacon and secure the rolls on a skewer. Cook for about 15 min. in a fairly hot oven (**375° F., Gas 5**) or under a moderately hot grill—reducing the heat after crisping the bacon, to make sure the roes are cooked. Spread the rounds of toast or fried bread with anchovy paste and thin slices of gherkin. Put the roes on top—serve hot or cold.

12 savouries
Cooking time—15 min. in the oven
6 min. (approx.) under the grill

LOBSTER CROÛTES

Croûtes de Homard à la Diable

1 small lobster (cooked)
1 tablesp. breadcrumbs
1 oz. butter
1–2 teasp. vinegar
Pinch of cayenne pepper
Pinch of pepper
½–1 teasp. mixed mustard
Grating of nutmeg
Pinch of curry powder
8–10 rounds of toast *or* **fried bread**
Lemon juice

Remove the flesh of the lobster from the body and claws, mix with the crumbs, butter, 1 teasp. vinegar and all the seasonings. Beat well to give a smooth mixture, and if necessary add the rest of the vinegar. Put on to the rounds of toast or fried bread, squeeze over a little lemon juice and garnish with cayenne pepper.

NOTE: If wished a slightly larger quantity of breadcrumbs may be used to give a more economical mixture—add a very little milk as well as vinegar to moisten.

Canned lobster could be substituted in this dish.

8–10 small savouries

MUSHROOMS—PRINCESS

12 small mushrooms
2 oz. butter
3 oz. demi-sel *or* **cream cheese**
Paprika pepper
12 rounds of toast *or* **fried bread** *or* **4 larger slices of toast**

Cook the mushrooms in the butter, removing the stalks before cooking, but using these as well. Drain thoroughly and cool. Pipe a rosette of the soft cheese in the centre of each mushroom. Dust with paprika pepper and put the stalk into position. Serve on toast or fried bread.

NOTE: If preferred the mushrooms could be cooked in a little water and vinegar.

4 helpings *or* **12 savouries**
Cooking time—5 min.

OYSTER TIT-BITS

Bonnes Bouches aux Huîtres

9 small oysters
1 oz. butter
9 round croûtes of bread
Anchovy paste
3 small rashers of bacon
Lemon juice
Cayenne pepper
Watercress

Beard the oysters and place between 2 plates with their own liquid and the butter. Warm thoroughly in the oven, or over a saucepan of boiling water. Spread the croûtes of bread—which can be toasted or fried if wished—with anchovy paste. Cut each rasher of bacon into 3 pieces, grill or fry, put on the croûtes of bread and top with a hot oyster. Sprinkle with lemon juice and cayenne pepper, and garnish with watercress.

Can be served cold, but nicer hot.

9 small savouries
Cooking time—12–15 min. (approx.)

PASTRY CASES

Vol-au-Vent shapes or cornet shapes—filled with savoury mixtures are excellent for buffet parties. They can be served hot or cold. If the mixture is being put into the cold pastry cases make sure it is quite cold. If on the other hand it is being put into hot pastry cases heat the filling and the pastry separately, and put together at the last minute, so that the filling does not make the pastry soft.

Directions for making vol-au-vent shapes and cornet shapes are given in the Pastry section.

SUGGESTED FILLINGS

Quantities given are enough to fill 12 medium sized vol-au-vent cases or about

16 cornet cases (allowing a liberal amount of filling).

Chicken

½ pt. thick sauce made with ½ milk and ½ chicken stock
¾–1 lb. diced cooked chicken (approx.)
Seasoning

Mix together well, and if possible add just 1 tablesp. cream.

Mushroom

¾ lb. mushrooms
2 oz. butter *or* margarine
2½ gills milk
1½ oz. flour
Seasoning
Cayenne pepper

Chop the mushrooms into small pieces and toss in the hot butter for a few minutes. Add ½ pt. of milk and cook gently for about 10 min. Blend the flour with the other ½ gill milk, add to the mushroom mixture. Season well and boil until smooth and thick. Stir as the mixture cools. If wished add 1 tablesp. thick cream. Dust with cayenne pepper when the cases are filled.

Sardine

1 small can of sardines
1 tablesp. white *or* tomato sauce
Salt and pepper
Few drops of lemon juice
2 teasp. grated Parmesan cheese *or* 1 tablesp. grated Cheddar cheese

Remove the bones and mash the sardines. Mix with the white or tomato sauce (if using white sauce, add a few drops of anchovy essence). Season, blend with a few drops of lemon juice and the cheese.

Savoury Egg

5 eggs
3 tablesp. cream *or* mayonnaise
1 oz. butter
Seasoning
2 oz. finely-diced lean tongue

Beat the eggs and cream or mayonnaise together. Heat the butter, add the eggs, season well and cook gently until commencing to thicken. If serving the mixture hot add the diced tongue—but if serving cold do not add this until the eggs are cold. Take care the mixture does not become too stiff—if it appears rather dry beat in more cream or mayonnaise.

Shell Fish

½ pt. thick sauce—made with ½ milk and ½ stock made by simmering prawn *or* lobster shells
1 large flaked lobster *or* about 1¼ pt. picked prawns
2 tablesp. thick mayonnaise
Seasoning

Mix well together, and if wished add 1–2 chopped gherkins and capers. Garnish with whole prawns.

PRAWNS À LA TARTARE

4 small round dinner rolls
18 large prawns (picked)
1 large gherkin *or* 4 small gherkins
6 anchovy fillets
1 hard-boiled egg
Mustard and cress

Cut the rolls in equal halves, scoop out the crumbs and allow the crusts to dry in the oven. Chop together 10 of the prawns, gherkins, anchovy fillets and white of the egg. Put a little mustard and cress at the bottom of each crust and fill with the mixture. Garnish with egg yolk and whole prawns.

8 savouries

SARDINE AND EGG FINGERS

Canapés d'Œufs et Sardines

8–10 sardines
2 hard-boiled eggs
Bread
Butter *or* fat
1 tablesp. chopped gherkin
Cayenne pepper
Anchovy essence

Lift the sardines out of the tin, and drain them well. Rub the yolks of the eggs through a fine sieve, or mash them, and chop the whites finely. Cut thin slices of stale bread into fingers, fry in clarified butter or fat, and drain well. Chop the gherkin finely. Add a pinch of cayenne pepper and a few drops anchovy essence to a little butter, mix well and spread it on the fingers. Put a sardine on each. Decorate in 3 sections—covering the centre lightly with the chopped gherkin, one end with egg white and the other end with the egg yolk.

8–10 savouries

COCKTAIL SAVOURIES

SARDINE CROUSTADES

Croustades de Sardines

3 large slices of stale bread (approx.)
Butter *or* fat for frying
1 small can of sardines
1 tablesp. white *or* tomato sauce
Salt and pepper
Few drops of lemon juice
2 teasp. grated Parmesan cheese *or* 1 tablesp. Cheddar cheese
Watercress

Cut slices of stale bread about ¾ in. in thickness, stamp out 8–10 rounds or oval shapes of about 2 in. diameter. With a smaller cutter make an inner circle or oval about ⅓ in. from the outer edge of the croustade. Fry these bread shapes in hot fat until lightly browned, drain, then with the point of a small knife lift out the inner ring, remove any moist crumb—and if wished place the cases in a moderate oven for a short time to crisp the inside. Cool before using. Mash the sardines—removing bones first—mix with the white or tomato sauce; if using white sauce add a few drops of anchovy essence. Season, blend with a few drops of lemon juice and the cheese. Put into the crisp cases and garnish with watercress.

10 savouries
Cooking time—5 min.

SARDINE RISSOLETTES

Rissolettes des Sardines

8–10 sardines
2 hard-boiled eggs
1 tablesp. grated cheese
Shortcrust pastry (p. 557)using 6 oz. flour, etc.
1 egg *or* egg yolk
2–3 tablesp. breadcrumbs
Fat for frying
Grated Parmesan *or* Cheddar cheese
Chopped parsley

Mix the sardines with the finely-chopped hard-boiled eggs and cheese. Roll out the pastry until it is wafer thin. Cut it into 1½–2 in. rounds, put a spoonful of the sardine mixture on ½ the rounds, wet the edges, then cover with a pastry round. Alternatively put a little sardine mixture in the centre of each round and fold over into a crescent shape. Brush with beaten egg or egg yolk, coat with breadcrumbs, fry in hot fat until crisp and brown, then drain well. Dish in a pyramid shape, sprinkle with grated Parmesan or Cheddar cheese and chopped parsley and serve hot or cold.

12–14 savouries

SHELL FISH COCKTAIL

4–6 oz. picked shrimps or prawns *or* 6 oz. lobster *or* crawfish meat, diced
Shredded lettuce

COCKTAIL SAUCE

2 medium-sized ripe tomatoes
Juice of ½ lemon
1 teasp. Worcester sauce
Salt
¼ pt. thin cream *or* evaporated milk

Sieve the tomatoes, add the lemon juice and seasonings and stir in the cream or milk. Mix the shell fish with the sauce. Place shredded lettuce at the bottom of four glasses and pile the shellfish on top. Sprinkle with paprika and serve as an appetizer.

4 helpings

TOMATO JUICE COCKTAIL

1 pt. tomato juice (canned *or* bottled)
2 teasp. lemon juice
1–2 teasp. Worcester sauce
Good pinch of celery salt
Good pinch of paprika pepper

Mix all the ingredients together. Serve very cold.

Sufficient for 4–5 people

TOMATO RAREBIT

As for Welsh Rarebit(p. 579), but instead of the milk and ale use tomato purée (made by sieving fresh tomatoes) or tomato ketchup—or use ½ tomato ketchup and ½ milk.

UGLI COCKTAIL

2 uglis
Juice of 1 lemon
Few drops of Maraschino

Cut the uglis in half and remove the pulp. Sprinkle the pulp with lemon juice and add Maraschino to taste. Put into cocktail glasses or return to the skins, and serve very cold.

6 helpings

SUPPER DISHES

WE GIVE HERE a selection of dishes suitable for serving at high teas, suppers and supper parties. Recipes for other dishes which may be served at such meals will be found in the sections on Savouries, p. 576; Vegetables, p. 320; Cereals, p. 594; Eggs, p. 679; Cheese, p. 678; Réchauffés, p. 601; and for cold supper dishes *see also* Salads, p. 362.

CHEESE AND ONION PIE

Short crust pastry (p. 557), using 8 oz. flour, etc.
3 small onions
½ oz. flour
Salt and pepper
4 oz. cheese
2 tablesp. milk

Parboil the onions whilst making the pastry. Line an 8-in. fireproof plate with half the pastry. Mix the salt and pepper with the flour. Slice the onions and dip in the seasoned flour, spread them over the bottom of the lined plate. Grate the cheese and sprinkle it over the onion, add the milk. Wet the edge of the pastry, put on the cover and press the edges firmly together. Knock up the edges, decorate as desired and brush over with milk. Bake in a hot oven (**425° F., Gas 7**) for about 40 min.

NOTE: This can be made as an open tart if liked, use 4 oz. flour, etc., for the pastry.

6–8 helpings

CORNISH PASTIES

¼ lb. raw meat
¼ lb. potatoes
½ teasp. finely-chopped onion
Mixed herbs to taste
Salt and pepper
2 tablesp. gravy *or* water
Short crust pastry, using 8 oz. flour, etc.

Mince the meat finely. Dice the potatoes. Add the onion, herbs, salt, pepper and gravy to the meat and potatoes, and mix well together. Divide the pastry into 8 equal portions and roll them out ¼ in. thick, keeping the portions as round as possible. Pile the mixture in the centre of each piece of pastry, wet the edges and join them together on the top to form an upstanding frill, prick them with a fork. Bake in a hot oven (**425° F., Gas 7**) for 10 min., then reduce heat to moderate (**350° F., Gas 4**) and cook for about 50 min. longer.

5–6 helpings

CREAMED HAM ON TOAST

6 oz. cooked ham
½ pt. white sauce (p. 115)
3 hard-boiled eggs
¼ teasp. dry mustard
Salt and pepper
6 slices buttered toast

Dice the ham. Add to the white sauce, the chopped ham, sliced eggs, mustard and seasoning to taste. Serve hot on toast with stuffed olives.

6 helpings

HAM AND EGG PIE

4 oz. mushrooms
4 tablesp. milk
Salt and pepper
6–8 oz. cooked ham
3 oz. cooked peas
2 hard-boiled eggs
1 teasp. mixed mustard
Flaky pastry (p. 554), using 8 oz. flour, etc.
Egg *or* milk

Prepare the mushrooms and simmer them for 10 min. in milk seasoned with salt and pepper. Chop the ham roughly and mix with the peas, hard-boiled eggs, mushrooms, mustard and seasoning. Divide the pastry into 2 unequal portions. Roll out the larger piece and cover a fireproof dish or plate and trim the edges. Put in the prepared filling. Roll out the remaining pastry and cover the pie.

Flake and scallop the edges and decorate as desired. Glaze top with beaten egg or milk. Bake in a very hot oven (**450° F., Gas 8**) until set and then reduce heat to warm (**335° F., Gas 3**) for the remainder of the time. Cook for about 45 min. in all.

HAM AND TONGUE SOUFFLÉ

3 oz. cooked ham	**1½ gills stock**
3 oz. cooked tongue	**2 teasp. chopped parsley**
1½ gills tomato purée	**Salt and pepper**
1½ oz. butter *or* fat	**3 eggs**
1½ oz. flour	

Remove all the skin and bone then mince the meat. Rub either fresh or canned tomatoes through a sieve to make the purée. Melt the fat in a saucepan, add the flour and cook a little, then add the stock, tomato purée and parsley and cook until boiling. Lightly sprinkle in the meat, season to taste and cook together for a few minutes. Cool slightly then add the egg yolks one at a time. Whisk the egg whites to a stiff froth and fold them lightly in. Pour the mixture into a well greased soufflé dish, leaving room for it to rise. Bake in a moderate oven (**350° F., Gas 4**) for about 30–45 min. until well risen and firm.

HAM MOUSSE

Mousse de Jambon Espagnole

½ lb. cooked ham	**2 tablesp. white stock**
Salt and pepper	**1 drop of carmine**
Grated nutmeg	**1½ gills cream *or* milk**
½ pt. Espagnole sauce (p. 130)	**1 tablesp. chopped truffles**
½ oz. gelatine	**½ gill pale aspic jelly**
¼ pt. aspic jelly	

Tie a band of stiff paper round a china soufflé dish of about 5 in. diameter so that it stands about 2 in. higher than the dish.

Pass the ham twice through a mincer and sieve it. Season with salt, pepper and nutmeg. Add the Espagnole sauce which is well coloured and flavoured with tomato. Dissolve the gelatine in the aspic, together with the stock; colour with carmine and add to the ham. Whip the cream very lightly and fold lightly into the mixture. When it is beginning to set creamily, pour into the prepared soufflé case and allow to set. Add the chopped truffle to the pale aspic and pour on the top of the mould, when the jelly is cold, but not set. When set remove paper and serve with green salad.

JELLIED HAM SLICES

¼ lb. cooked ham	**1 gill aspic jelly**
1 oz. cooked macaroni	**2 hard-boiled eggs**
1 medium-sized tomato	**½ oz. gelatine**
Salt and pepper	**½ gill good white stock**
1 teasp. chopped parsley	

Chop or mince the ham; chop the macaroni; skin and slice the tomato. Mix together and add seasoning and a little chopped parsley. Line a small, flat meat tin, with half the aspic jelly. Decorate with slices of hard-boiled egg and chopped parsley and leave to set. Dissolve the gelatine in the stock with the rest of the aspic jelly, and when cool, add to the mixed ingredients. Pour into the prepared tin when cold and leave until set. When set unmould and cut in strips. Garnish with green salad.

POTATO, ONION AND CHEESE SAVOURY

½ oz. fat	**6–8 oz. mashed potatoes**
4 oz. finely-chopped onion	**Salt and pepper**
2 oz. grated cheese	
2 tablesp. chopped parsley	

Melt the fat in a saucepan and fry the onion till golden brown. Add most of the cheese, all the parsley and mashed potatoes, and season to taste. Stir over the heat until the mixture is well mixed and warmed through. Then put into a fireproof dish, sprinkle the remaining cheese on top and brown under the grill. If liked the mixture can be divided between 4 slices of toast, the cheese sprinkled over and browned under the grill.

4 helpings

POTATO PASTY

Pâté de Pommes de Terre

4 oz. lean beef	**Salt and pepper**
1 oz. finely-chopped onion	**A little gravy *or* stock**
4 oz. raw diced potato	**Short crust pastry, using 8 oz. flour, etc.**

Dice the meat and mix with the onion and potato. Season well, moisten with 2–3 tablesp. of gravy or stock. Roll out the pastry ¼ in. thick keeping it as round as possible. Place the mixture on one half of the pastry round and wet the edges. Then fold over the other half forming a semicircle, press and crimp the edges. Bake in a hot oven (**425° F., Gas 7**) and reduce after 10 min. to moderate (**350° F., Gas 4**). Bake for about 45 min. testing to see if the filling is cooked with a skewer. If preferred, after rolling out the pastry, it can be cut into rounds about the size of a saucer and individual pasties made.

4 helpings

SAUSAGE ROLLS

Rough puff pastry (p. 556), **using 4 oz. flour, etc.**	**½ lb. sausages**
	Egg yolk to glaze

Roll out the pastry and cut into 8 even-sized squares. Skin the sausages. Divide the sausage meat into 8 portions and make each piece into a roll the same length as the pastry. Place the sausage meat on the pastry, wet the edge and fold over leaving the ends open. Knock up the edges with the back of a knife. Make three incisions on top. Brush over with beaten egg and place on a baking-sheet. Bake in a hot oven (**425° F., Gas 7**) until the pastry is well risen and brown. Reduce the heat and continue baking till the pastry is cooked.

NOTE: Small sausage rolls can be quickly made by rolling the pastry into an oblong. Form the sausage meat into long rolls the length of the pastry, place the meat on the pastry then divide the pastry into strips wide enough to encircle the meat. Damp one edge of each strip, fold over and press together firmly. Cut into rolls of the desired length, finish as above.

8 sausage rolls **Cooking time—about ½ hr.**

SAVOURY BATTER

4 oz. flour	**1 teasp. finely-chopped parsley**
1 egg	**½ teasp. mixed herbs**
½ pt. milk	
Salt and pepper	
4 tablesp. finely-chopped beef *or* mutton	

Mix the flour, egg, milk, salt and pepper into a smooth batter, let it stand for ½ hr. Then add the meat, parsley and herbs. Melt a little dripping in a Yorkshire pudding-tin, pour in the batter, and bake in a fairly hot oven (**375° F., Gas 5**) until set.

2–3 helpings
Cooking time—20–30 min.

SAVOURY SANDWICH LOAF

1 day-old loaf	**Salt and pepper**
Butter *or* margarine	**6 tablesp. crushed sardines**
6 tablesp. lean cooked ham (minced)	**1 small tomato**
Mayonnaise	**2 green olives**
6–8 oz. cream cheese	**Green colouring (optional)**
2 hard-boiled eggs	

Remove crusts from loaf and cut loaf lengthwise in five equal slices. Butter each slice and spread the lower one with the ham mixed with enough mayonnaise to make an easy spreading consistency. Spread the next slice with 2 oz. cream cheese and place on top of the ham slice. Spread the third slice with crushed eggs, seasoned and mixed to a spreading consistency with mayonnaise; place on top of the cheese slice. Spread the fourth slice with sardines, place on top of the egg slice. Put the fifth slice on top, so that it has the form of the original loaf. Soften the remaining cream cheese with a little milk if necessary, colour if liked, and coat the top and sides of the loaf.

Decorate with slices of tomato and olives. The loaf can be wrapped in damp greaseproof paper and a cloth and stored in the refrigerator until required.

TOAD IN THE HOLE

4 oz. plain flour	**1 lb. sausages**
¼ teasp. salt	**1 tablesp. cooking fat**
1 egg	
½ pt. milk *or* milk and water	

Make a batter with the flour, salt, egg and milk, and leave to stand for ½ hr. Heat the fat in a Yorkshire pudding-tin, skin the sausages, put the sausages in the hot fat, pour the batter over and bake in a hot oven (**425° F., Gas 7**) for about 30 min.

BREAKFAST DISHES

ALL SUCH FAMILIAR standard breakfast dishes as bacon, eggs, sausages, kidneys, cutlets, rissoles, etc., are fully dealt with under their respective headings of Beef, Lamb, Mutton, Pork and Eggs. Those who prefer cereals to more solid food should refer to the section on Cereals.

BACON—to fry

Cut the rind off the rashers of bacon. Heat the frying-pan for a few minutes. Place the bacon in the hot pan, reduce the heat and cook for a few minutes. Turn the rashers over and continue cooking until the fat is transparent or crisp, as preferred.

BACON—to grill

Cut the rind off the bacon rashers. Place the rashers on the grill rack below the hot grill. After a few minutes' grilling, turn and finish cooking.

BLOATERS—GRILLED

Split the bloaters open and remove the backbone, then either fold each bloater back into shape, or leave them opened out flat and place 2 together with their insides facing. Rub over with a little oil or fat and grill as for kippers.

HAM AND EGG TARTLETS

Tartlettes au Jambon et aux Œufs

6 oz. finely-chopped cooked ham
2 oz. white breadcrumbs
Nutmeg
Salt and pepper
½ gill milk
Browned breadcrumbs
6 eggs
½ oz. butter

Mix together the ham and breadcrumbs, add a good pinch of nutmeg, season well with salt and pepper, and moisten gradually with milk until a stiff paste is obtained. Grease 6 patty tins, coat them thickly with browned breadcrumbs, and line them with the meat mixture. Break an egg carefully into each, sprinkle lightly with browned breadcrumbs, and add a few bits of butter. Bake in a moderate oven (**350° F., Gas 4**) until the eggs are set. Remove carefully from the tins and serve hot.

6 helpings

SAUTÉD KIDNEYS

Rognons sautés

2 sheep's *or* 1 pork kidney
1 shallot *or* small onion
1 oz. butter
½ teasp. finely-chopped parsley
Salt and pepper
3–4 tablesp. good brown sauce

Skin the kidneys, cut them across into very thin slices and remove the core. Chop the shallot or onion finely. Heat the butter and fry the shallot until golden brown, then put in the kidney and parsley. Season with salt and pepper, and toss over heat for 5–6 min., Add the brown sauce, mix it well with the kidneys and when thoroughly hot, serve.

NOTE: More recipes for cooking kidneys will be found on pp. 222–3 and 243.

2 helpings

GRILLED KIPPERS

1–2 kippers per person
Butter *or* margarine

Remove the heads and lay the kippers flat, skin side up, on the grid. Cook for about 3 min. each side, adding a dab of butter or margarine when they are turned over.

Serve alone or on a slice of toast. Alternatively, place a pair of kippers, flesh sides together, and grill under medium heat first on one side then on the other; to serve, separate and top each with a nut of butter.

JUGGED KIPPERS

Simply place the kippers in a tall jug and cover with boiling water. Cover the jug and stand it in a warm place for 5–10 min. Drain, and serve with a knob of butter or margarine on each kipper.

NOTE: This method produces plump, juicy kippers, though some say a little flavour is lost.

MUSHROOMS

Recipes for cooking mushrooms will be found on p. 342.

ROES ON TOAST

3/4 lb. herring roes	**1 bacon rasher**
Seasoned flour	**4 rounds of toast**

Wash and dry the roes, dip in seasoned flour and fry in a little hot fat. Chop the bacon and add it to the roes when they are almost cooked.

Serve piled on rounds of buttered toast.

4 helpings

SAUSAGE CROQUETTES

Croquettes de Saucisse

1 lb. pork sausages	**Salt and pepper**
1/2 oz. butter	**Nutmeg**
1/2 lb. mashed potatoes	**1 egg yolk**
1 dessertsp. cream *or* milk	**Egg and breadcrumbs**
	Frying fat

Prick the sausages, put them into boiling water, cook them for 10 min. and when cold remove the skins and cut them across in half. Melt the butter in a saucepan, add the potatoes and cream, season well with salt, pepper and nutmeg. Stir until hot, then add the egg yolk and continue the cooking and stirring for about 5 min. longer. Let the potato cool, then spread a thin layer over each piece of sausage. Coat with egg and breadcrumbs and fry in hot fat until golden brown.

Garnish with fried parsley.

4 helpings

SAVOURY MEAT TOAST

1/2 oz. butter	**2 tablesp. gravy *or* milk**
2 tablesp. finely-chopped *or* minced cold meat	**Salt and pepper**
1 egg	**2 rounds of buttered toast**

Warm the butter and meat in a saucepan. Beat the egg slightly, add the gravy or milk, season to taste, pour the mixture into the saucepan, and stir until the egg begins to set. Trim the toast, spread with the mixture and serve.

NOTE: This may be varied by adding parsley, onion, herbs or ketchup, Worcester sauce, etc.

1–2 helpings

SAVOURY PANCAKES (1)

Batter as for Batter Pudding (p. 396)	**4 bacon rashers**
	Dripping

Whilst the batter is standing for ½ hr., remove the rind from the bacon, cut the bacon into small pieces and fry gently. Remove from frying-pan and stir into the batter. Put a little dripping into the frying-pan and heat until smoking hot. Quickly pour in enough batter to coat the bottom of the pan evenly. Cook until brown underneath, turn and brown on the other side.

Serve immediately.

4 helpings

SAVOURY PANCAKES (2)

1 small onion	**2 tablesp. milk**
2 oz. cheese	**Salt and pepper**
1/2 oz. butter *or* margarine	**Batter as for Batter Pudding (p. 396)**

Grate the onion and cheese. Put into a saucepan, add the butter or margarine and stir in the milk. Season to taste. Heat gently until thoroughly hot.

Make the pancakes, spread with the hot filling and roll up. Serve immediately.

4 helpings

TOMATOES

Recipes for cooking tomatoes will be found on p. 357.

CEREALS, RISOTTOS AND PASTA

THE SUCCESS OF THIS TYPE of cooking depends largely upon giving the cereal, which is normally rather tasteless, a pleasant texture and a full, appetizing flavour when cooked. The dishes can be used for economical meals and are most useful for providing filling meals cheaply, where these are required. They are also easily varied in flavour and can provide a wide range of dishes from the same basic method.

Dishes containing starchy substances should be made fresh as required and not kept hot or reheated where it can be avoided, as this spoils the flavour and the texture; and they are easily contaminated by bacteria if left uncovered.

Macaroni is best cooked until it is just tender but can still be felt between the teeth when bitten, i.e. not too soft.

Colourful garnishing is important as these dishes may tend to be colourless. For garnishing, choose foods for their colour and shape to add interest, e.g. shrimps, croûtons, parsley, paprika, cayenne, browned onion rings, etc., and where the dish is browned before serving, cook to an appetizing golden brown and serve very hot indeed.

GNOCCHI AU GRATIN

½ pt. water
2 oz. butter
Salt
3 oz. flour *or* 2 oz. semolina
2 eggs
3 oz. chopped ham
3 oz. grated cheese
½ pt. Béchamel sauce
Paprika pepper

Put the water, butter and a good pinch of salt into a saucepan over heat. When boiling stir in the flour or semolina, and work vigorously over the heat until the dough leaves the sides of the pan clear. Allow to cool slightly, then beat in the eggs separately, and add the ham and 2 oz. of the cheese. Shape the mixture into quenelles, poach them for about 10 min. in salted boiling water, and drain well. When cool, arrange in a buttered fireproof dish, pour over the Béchamel sauce, sprinkle on the remainder of the cheese, and season well with paprika pepper. Bake in a hot oven **(425° F., Gas 7)** for about 10 min., and serve.

4–5 helpings

ITALIAN RISOTTO

½ lb. Patna rice
2 oz. butter
1 small onion, finely chopped
½ teasp. saffron
Nutmeg
1 teasp. salt
¼ teasp. pepper
Stock
1 pt. tomato sauce
2 oz. grated Parmesan cheese

Wash, drain and dry the rice thoroughly in a clean cloth. Heat the butter in a saucepan, put in the onion, and when lightly browned add the rice, and shake the pan over the heat for about 10 min. Then sprinkle in the saffron, a good pinch of nutmeg, salt and pepper. Cover with stock, and cook gently for about 1 hr., adding meanwhile the tomato sauce and as much stock as the rice will absorb, the sauce being added when the rice is about half cooked. Just before serving stir in the cheese.

NOTE: This savoury rice is frequently used for borders instead of plainly-boiled rice or mashed potatoes.

MACARONI À LA NAPOLITAINE

½ lb. macaroni	**1 tablesp. finely-chopped ham *or* tongue**
½ shallot, finely-chopped	**2 oz. grated cheese**
1 oz. butter	**Salt and pepper**
¼ pt. Béchamel sauce	**Fried croûtons**
¼ pt. tomato sauce	

Break the macaroni into short pieces, put them into rapidly-boiling salted water, and cook until tender. Fry the shallot in the butter without browning, add the Béchamel and tomato sauces, ham or tongue, macaroni and cheese. Season to taste and stir over the heat until thoroughly hot. Serve heaped on a hot dish with the croûtons arranged round the base.

4–5 helpings

MACARONI AND TOMATOES

Macaroni aux Tomates

4 oz. macaroni	**1 oz. flour**
½ pt. tomato purée	**Good pinch of sugar**
1 oz. butter	**Salt and pepper**

Break the macaroni into short lengths, put it into rapidly-boiling salted water and cook until tender. Melt the butter in a saucepan, add the flour and cook for a few minutes. Put in the tomato purée, sugar and season to taste. Let it boil for a few minutes, then add the macaroni, and when thoroughly hot turn on to a dish and serve.

2–3 helpings

MACARONI AU GRATIN

4 oz. macaroni	**Salt and pepper**
1 pt. white sauce	**Brown breadcrumbs**
4 oz. grated cheese	**Butter**

Break the macaroni into pieces about 1½ in. long, put them into rapidly-boiling salted water and boil for about 20 min., or until the macaroni is tender. (If not required for immediate use, cover the macaroni with cold water to prevent the pieces sticking together.) Cover the bottom of a well-buttered baking-dish with white sauce, sprinkle liberally with cheese, seasoning to taste, and add a layer of macaroni. Repeat the layers, cover the last layer of macaroni thickly with sauce, sprinkle the surface lightly with breadcrumbs and add a few small pieces of butter. Bake in a hot oven (**425° F., Gas 7**) for about 20 min., then serve in the dish in which it is cooked.

6–7 helpings

NOUILLE or NOODLE PASTE (also called Ribbon Macaroni)

Pâte à Nouilles

1 lb. flour	**Salt**
1½ oz. butter	**A little milk *or* water**
3 egg yolks *or* 2 small whole eggs	

Sift the flour into a basin, make a well in the centre, and put in the butter, eggs and a good pinch of salt. Mix thoroughly and add a little milk or water if necessary, but the paste should be rather stiff. Knead well for about 15 min., or until the paste is perfectly smooth and elastic, then use as required.

8 helpings

NOUILLES AND EGGS

Œufs aux Nouilles

½ lb. nouille paste	**Pepper and nutmeg**
½ lb. mushrooms	**2–3 tablesp. grated cheese**
Butter	**¼ pt. white sauce**
4 hard-boiled eggs	

Let the nouille paste stand for at least 1 hr. before rolling out as thinly as possible. Cut it into long strips 2–3 in. wide, place them on top of each other and cut them into filaments not more than ⅛ in. wide. Shake them well in a little flour to separate and slightly coat them. Put them into rapidly-boiling salted water, boil for 10 min., drain well, then toss them over heat in a little butter. Prepare the mushrooms and cook them for 8–10 min. in hot butter. Cut the eggs into slices. Place a layer of nouilles in the bottom of a well-buttered fireproof dish, season with pepper and a little nutmeg and sprinkle thickly with cheese. Cover with slices of egg, add seasoning, then another layer of nouilles and finally the mushrooms. Spread the white sauce over the surface, sprinkle well with cheese, add a few small pieces of butter and bake in a hot oven (**425° F., Gas 7**) for 10–15 min. Serve in the dish in which it was baked.

6–7 helpings

NOUILLES AU GRATIN

½ lb. nouille paste	**Butter**
White sauce	**Salt and pepper**
Grated cheese	**Breadcrumbs**

Prepare and cook the nouilles as in the preceding recipe. After draining well let them cool. Spread 1–2 tablesp. white sauce on the bottom of a fireproof dish, cover with a layer of nouilles, sprinkle thickly with grated cheese, add a few drops of liquid butter and a little seasoning. Repeat until the nouilles are used, cover the last layer thickly with white sauce, sprinkle with breadcrumbs and add a few bits of butter. Bake in a hot oven (**425° F., Gas 7**) for about 10 min.

5–6 helpings

RICE

To boil rice for curry and savoury dishes, *see* p. 37.

RICE AND TOMATOES

Riz aux Tomates

4 oz. rice	**2 oz. butter**
1 onion stuck with a clove	**Salt and pepper**
	Cayenne pepper
Bouquet garni	**Mace**
1 gill stock	**1 oz. grated cheese**
2 gills tomato sauce	**3 small, firm tomatoes**
2 shallots, finely-chopped	

Pick over, wash, and blanch the rice in salted water. Drain well, replace in the stewpan with the onion, bouquet garni, stock and tomato sauce, and cook gently until tender, adding more sauce or stock, if necessary, to prevent the rice becoming too dry. Fry the shallots in 1 oz of butter until brown, then add both to the contents of the pan. Remove the onion and bouquet garni, season to taste with salt, pepper, cayenne and mace, and stir in the cheese. Meanwhile the tomatoes should have been thinly sliced and fried in the remaining 1 oz. of butter; now pile the rice on a hot dish, garnish with the tomatoes and serve hot.

3–4 helpings

RICE—CURRIED

Riz à l'Indienne

4 oz. Patna rice	**1 tablesp. cream**
2 shallots, finely-chopped	**1 gill brown sauce**
	Salt and pepper
1½ oz. butter	**Mace**
1 teasp. curry powder	**Nutmeg**
1 tomato	**1 hard-boiled egg**
1 gill stock	**Watercress**

Pick over, wash, drain and dry the rice thoroughly. Fry the shallots slightly in hot butter, sprinkle in the curry powder, cook for a few minutes, then add the rice and cook and shake well over the heat. Now add the tomato skinned and cut into dice, the stock, cream and sauce, season to taste with salt, pepper, mace and nutmeg, and cook gently until the rice is tender, adding more stock or sauce, if necessary, to prevent the rice becoming too dry. When ready, pile on a hot dish, garnish with slices of hard boiled egg and tufts of watercress.

RICE, FLORENTINE STYLE

Riz à la Florentine

4 oz. Patna rice	**Cayenne pepper**
1 medium size Spanish onion	**1 tablesp. grated Parmesan cheese**
1½ oz. butter	**¼ pt. picked shrimps**
1¼ pt. stock (approx.)	**Krona pepper**
1 teasp. curry paste	**Finely-chopped parsley**
Salt and pepper	

Pick over, wash, blanch and drain the rice. Chop the onion finely. Melt the butter in a saucepan, put in the rice and onion, cook and stir for a few minutes. Then cover with stock, add curry paste, salt, pepper and cayenne to taste. Simmer until tender. Add more stock when necessary, and when the rice is nearly tender let it cook uncovered to allow some of the moisture to escape. As it becomes dry, frequent stirring will be necessary to prevent the rice sticking to the bottom of the pan. A few minutes before serving add the cheese, shrimps cut in halves, salt and pepper if necessary, and stir gently until thoroughly hot. Serve piled on a hot dish, garnished with Krona pepper and parsley.

RICE, POLISH STYLE

Riz à la Polonaise

4 oz. Patna rice
1¼ pt. stock (approx.)
1½ oz. butter
4 small mild onions
2 tablesp. finely-shredded cooked ham
Salt and pepper
Cayenne pepper
1 tablesp. grated Parmesan cheese
Finely-chopped parsley

Pick over, wash, blanch and drain the rice, replace it in the pan, cover with stock and simmer gently until tender, adding more stock as that in the pan boils away. When the rice is nearly ready heat the butter in a saucepan, put in the onions thinly sliced, fry for a few minutes without browning, then add the ham and the rice. Season to taste, as soon as the rice is sufficiently dry stir in the cheese, let it cook for 2–3 min., then pile on a hot dish, sprinkle with parsley and serve.

3–4 helpings

SEMOLINA CROQUETTES

Croquettes de Semoule

1 pt. milk
1 oz. butter
1 lb. semolina
3 egg yolks
1 oz. grated Parmesan cheese
Salt and pepper
Egg and breadcrumbs
Fat for frying

Put the milk and butter into a pan, when boiling stir in the semolina and cook slowly for about 10 min. Then add the 3 egg yolks, cheese and seasoning. Continue the cooking and stirring for a few minutes longer, then spread the mixture on a large dish. When cold, cut into rounds or other shapes, coat them with egg and breadcrumbs and fry in hot fat until nicely browned. Drain well, dish in a pyramid.

5–6 helpings

SMALL FLORADOR ROLLS

1 pt. milk
1 oz. butter
3 oz. semolina
2 oz. grated cheese
Salt and pepper
½ lb. nouille paste
2 slices cooked ham *or* tongue
Egg and breadcrumbs
Fat for frying

Put the milk and butter into a pan; when boiling sprinkle in the semolina, stir and cook gently for 10 min., then add the cheese, salt and pepper to taste, and spread the mixture on a large dish. Roll the nouille paste out thinly, and cut it into strips 3 in. long and about 1 in. wide. Spread the centre of each strip thickly with the semolina mixture, put a narrow strip of ham or tongue in the centre, wet the edges and roll up lightly, taking care that the paste completely encloses the mixture. Dip the rolls in egg and roll in breadcrumbs. Repeat the egg and breadcrumbing process, then fry them in hot butter or fat until golden brown. Drain well, and serve garnished with parsley.

6–7 helpings

VERMICELLI CROQUETTES

Croquettes de Vermicelle au Fromage

2 oz. vermicelli
¾ pt. milk
2 oz. grated cheese
1 oz. butter
½ teasp. mixed mustard
Cayenne pepper
Salt and pepper
Egg and breadcrumbs *or* extra vermicelli
Parsley

Break the vermicelli into short pieces; put it into the milk when boiling, and cook until tender. Add the cheese, butter, mustard, a few grains of cayenne and salt and pepper to taste. Stir over heat until well mixed, then spread to about ½ in. thick on a large dish. When cold, cut into circles, ovals or crescents. Dip in beaten egg, coat with breadcrumbs or crushed vermicelli and fry in hot fat until lightly browned. Garnish with fried parsley.

3–4 helpings

SANDWICHES

THE TERM SANDWICH HAS today a much wider meaning than when it was first introduced by the Earl of Sandwich, and applied only to slices of meat placed between bread and butter. We have now "Open" or Continental sandwiches, Club or Two-decker sandwiches, Toasted sandwiches and the charming, attractively-shaped Party sandwiches. The fillings of sandwiches now consist of an endless variety of preparations—savoury or sweet—minced and shredded and mixed with various butters, sauces and seasonings. It requires little skill just plenty of imagination and an eye for colour to produce sandwiches which are appetizing, wholesome and decorative.

For sandwiches the bread should be fresh but not too new; French rolls, Vienna rolls, wholemeal or milk bread make an interesting change from ordinary loaves. Creamed butter (*see* p. 675) is more easily spread than ordinary butter, but when ordinary butter is used it should first be beaten to a cream (add 1 teasp. hot water to ½ lb. butter) to facilitate spreading. Savoury butters (*see* p. 675) give piquancy and variety to other fillings, and can be used alone for rolled sandwiches.

Sandwiches help to simplify entertaining, for they can be prepared well in advance and they can be served buffet-style, leaving the hostess free to mix with her guests. If prepared some time before required, sandwiches will keep fresh and moist if they are wrapped in greaseproof then in a damp cloth, or put into a polythene bag, or wrapped in waxed paper or aluminium foil, and kept in the refrigerator or cool place. Sandwiches with different fillings should be wrapped separately to prevent the flavours mixing.

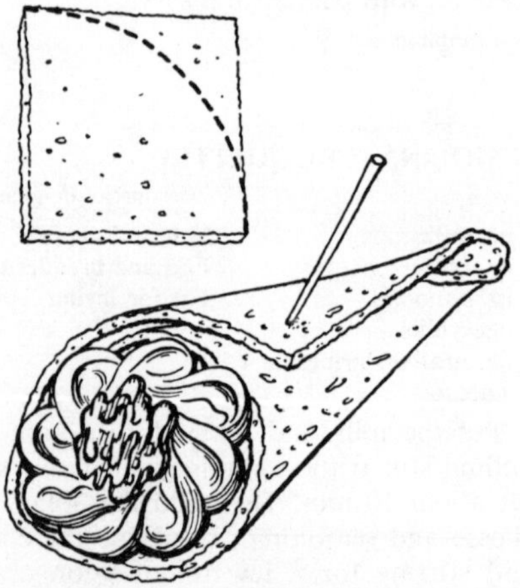

Making a horn-shaped sandwich

CLUB or DOUBLE DECKER SANDWICHES

Either brown or white bread may be used for club or double-decker sandwiches. Cut the slices thinly—three slices for each sandwich. Butter the slices thickly—the middle slice should be buttered on both sides—spread with 2 fillings and sandwich together. Press together firmly so that the layers stick to each other. These sandwiches may be served plain or toasted, hot or cold, and knives and forks should be provided.

Fillings

1. *1st layer:* Slices of cold roast beef, seasoned and spread with horseradish sauce.
   2nd layer: Watercress with thin slices of drained, pickled beetroot.
2. *1st layer:* A slice of Cheddar cheese spread with mango chutney.
   2nd layer: A mixture of grated raw apple and mayonnaise.
3. *1st layer:* Cooked skinned pork sausage split lengthwise.
   2nd layer: Grilled mushrooms.

OPEN SANDWICHES

Use $\frac{1}{4}$-in. thick slices of white or brown bread, cut into fancy shapes, triangles, diamonds, hearts, etc. Spread with creamed butter and any of the party sandwich fillings. Garnish with stuffed olives, slices of hard-boiled egg, small pieces of tomato, watercress, piped cream cheese, etc. The appeal of these sandwiches, of course, lies in the artistic way in which the garnish is arranged; the sandwiches should look colourful and tempting.

PARTY SANDWICHES

Bread for party sandwiches must be cut very thin, and the crusts be removed; amusing and unusual shapes can be cut with pastry or biscuit cutters. Attractive results can be achieved by alternating 3 thinly-cut slices of white and brown bread when making up the sandwiches, before cutting them into fingers, triangles or squares.

To make rolled sandwiches: Take single slices of thinly-cut bread and butter, remove the crusts; spread with a savoury butter or with creamed butter and the selected filling, then roll up lightly, skewer with a cocktail stick and chill. Remove the sticks before serving.

To make horn shapes: Use thinly-cut slices of bread preferably 24 hours old, remove the crusts, trim as shown in diag. opposite. Spread the bread with a creamed filling or savoury butter, then roll into cones. Hold in shape with a cocktail stick and chill. Remove sticks before serving and decorate to taste.

Savoury party sandwiches may be decorated with parsley, cress, fancily-cut shapes of hard boiled egg, tomato, pickled gherkin, stuffed olives, etc., or swirls and rosettes of piped savoury butters. Sweet-filled sandwiches can be garnished with glacé cherry, angelica, halved grapes, etc.

Savoury fillings

1. Anchovies mixed with hard-boiled egg yolk, cheese and butter, with a sprinkling of cayenne. Spread the bread with curry butter.
2. Canned tuna fish mixed with salad cream and chopped parsley, with a dash of cayenne.
3. Canned salmon, mashed with lemon juice and chopped chives, spread on a bed of cucumber slices.
4. Minced cooked smoked haddock, seasoned and mixed to a smooth paste with butter and anchovy paste.
5. Very thin slices of cooked chicken and ham, seasoned and placed between bread spread with curry butter.
6. Very finely shredded celery, moistened slightly with canned or double cream, seasoned to taste.
7. Finely-grated cheese, mixed to a smooth paste with a little seasoning, anchovy essence or paste, and butter.
8. A layer of finely-chopped gherkin, olives and capers, mixed with mayonnaise sauce, covered with a layer of cream cheese.
9. Mashed sardines, a little lemon juice and seasoning, mixed to a smooth paste with butter.

10. Sardines mashed with an equal amount of grated cheese until smooth; seasoned to taste, with a little lemon juice or vinegar added and sufficient cream or milk to moisten.

11. Minced cooked chicken and ham or tongue, combined with cream cheese and egg yolk, seasoned and moistened with oil.

12. Finely-shredded lettuce and watercress, seasoned with salt and mixed with mayonnaise.

13. Thin slices of Gruyère cheese on slices of bread and butter, spread with French mustard, seasoned with pepper.

14. Slices of hard-boiled egg, seasoned, covered with watercress or mustard and cress, sprinkled with equal quantities of oil and vinegar.

15. Canned foie gras.

16. Minced cooked chicken and ham or tongue, moistened with a little liquid butter and mayonnaise.

17. Lightly spread caviare, sprinkled with lemon juice and a little cayenne. (The bread may be spread with lobster, or shrimp butter, *see* p. 677).

Sweet fillings

1. Bananas mashed with lemon juice and ground almonds and sprinkled with sugar.

2. A layer of cream or cottage cheese, covered with a layer of fresh strawberries or raspberries sprinkled with castor sugar.

3. Softened creamed cheese, mixed with canned crushed pineapple and finely-chopped preserved ginger.

4. Chocolate spread, mixed with chopped walnuts.

5. Chopped pears, dates and walnuts, mixed with golden syrup.

6. Thick slices of banana sprinkled with coarsely-grated chocolate.

PICNIC or PACKED LUNCH SANDWICHES

For picnic or packed lunch sandwiches use brown or white bread which is 24 hours old to facilitate cutting. Cut even slices or use fresh sliced bread, small baps, barm cakes, tea cakes or rolls.

Fillings

1. A slice of Cheddar or Cheshire cheese, topped with thin slices of tomato and chopped fresh mint.

2. A slice of boiled ham with tomato sauce or chutney.

3. Scrambled egg sprinkled with chopped parsley.

4. Chopped hard-boiled egg mixed with anchovies.

5. Thin slices of skinned tomatoes, seasoned and sprinkled with lemon juice or vinegar to taste.

6. Minced cooked chicken and ham, moistened with mayonnaise if liked, sprinkled with watercress.

7. Thin slices of cold roast beef, topped with slices of tomato and cucumber, or a thin layer of horseradish sauce.

8. Smoked cod's roe, sprinkled with lemon juice and topped with slices of cucumber.

9. Flaked cold, cooked white fish, mixed with mayonnaise and chopped parsley.

10. Minced turkey or chicken, mixed with peanut butter and a little ordinary butter.

11. Cooked veal or lean pork with sliced pickled gherkins.

TOAST SANDWICHES

Toast made from either white or brown bread may be used for toast sandwiches and the sandwiches may be single, double or triple decker (the toast should of course be very thin for double or triple-decker sandwiches). The bread may be toasted on one side only or on both sides; the sandwiches may be eaten hot or cold. Spread the toast with butter and one of the suggested fillings, sandwich together and cut into triangles.

Fillings

1. Cooked skinned sausages split lengthwise and covered with a layer of apple sauce.

2. A rasher of fried bacon covered with sautéd mushrooms.

3. A thick slice of fried canned meat, topped with slices of grilled or fried tomato.

4. Cooked skinned sausages split lengthwise and spread with scrambled egg.

5. Lettuce leaf with a slice of Cheddar or Cheshire cheese and slices of tomato on top.

RÉCHAUFFÉS

EVERY HOUSEWIFE AT SOME time is faced with left-over food, and with a little skill and ingenuity, the economical wife will turn this into tempting, palatable dishes to be served at another meal. We suggest here some ways in which left-over food may be used; *see also* cold meats in the Meat Section, p. 272; and also Supper Dishes, p. 589.

FISH

AMERICAN FISH PIE

½ lb. cooked turbot, cod *or* other white fish
1½ oz. butter
½ pt. white sauce
1 oz. grated Parmesan cheese
Salt and pepper
Cayenne pepper
¾ lb. mashed potatoes
1 egg
Nutmeg

Free the fish from skin and bones, divide it into large flakes and put them into a saucepan with ½ oz. butter, the sauce and some of the cheese. Season with salt and pepper, and a few grains of cayenne, and heat gradually over a low heat. Melt the remaining 1 oz. butter in another pan, add the potatoes and most of the egg, season well with salt and pepper and a little nutmeg. Stir vigorously over the heat until thoroughly hot. Have ready a well-buttered pie-dish, line the bottom and sides thinly with potato purée, using about ½ of it, put in the prepared fish, and cover with the remaining potatoes. Smooth the surface and notch the edges with a knife, giving it the appearance of pastry crust, brush over with egg, sprinkle liberally with grated cheese. Bake in a fairly hot oven (**375° F., Gas 5**) until well browned. Serve hot.

4–5 helpings

FISH CAKES

1 lb. cooked fish
1 oz. butter *or* margarine
½ lb. mashed potatoes
2 eggs
Salt and pepper
Breadcrumbs

Remove skin and bones and chop fish coarsely. Heat the butter in a saucepan, add the fish, potatoes, yolk of 1 egg, salt and pepper. Stir over heat for a few minutes, then turn on to a plate and allow to cool. When cold, shape into round flat cakes, brush over with beaten egg, coat with breadcrumbs and fry in hot fat. The fish may be made into one large cake instead of several small ones, in which case grease a fish mould or flat tin and shape the mixture as much like a fish as possible. Brush over with egg, cover with slightly browned breadcrumbs and bake for about 20 min. in a fairly hot oven (**375° F., Gas 5**).

3–7 helpings

KEDGEREE

1 lb. cold fish (smoked haddock is generally preferred)
¼ lb. rice
2 hard-boiled eggs
2 oz. butter
Salt and pepper
Cayenne pepper

Boil and dry the rice. Divide the fish into small flakes. Cut the whites of the eggs into slices and sieve the yolks. Melt the butter in a saucepan, add to it the fish, rice, egg whites, salt, pepper and cayenne and stir until hot. Turn the mixture on to a hot dish. Press into the shape of a pyramid with a fork, decorate with egg yolk and serve as hot as possible.

5–6 helpings **Cooking time—40–50 min.**

SCALLOPS OF FISH

Escalopes de Poisson

½ lb. cold fish of any kind
1½ oz. butter
2 oz. flour
½ pt. milk
1 teasp. anchovy essence
1 teasp. walnut ketchup
½ teasp. mixed mustard
Salt and pepper
Cayenne pepper
Breadcrumbs

Melt the butter in a saucepan, add the flour and cook for 3–4 min.; then pour in the milk, stir until boiling, then simmer slowly for 10 min. Meanwhile separate the fish into large flakes. When the sauce is ready, put the fish into the saucepan with the anchovy essence, ketchup, mustard, a liberal seasoning of salt and pepper and a small pinch of cayenne. Stir until the mixture is thoroughly hot, then fill 3–4 escallop-shells (previously well buttered), cover lightly with breadcrumbs and place small pieces of butter on top of each. Bake in a hot oven until nicely browned, or brown under a hot grill.

3–4 helpings

MEAT

BUBBLE AND SQUEAK

Thin slices of cold roast *or* boiled meat
Dripping
1 shredded onion
Cold mashed potatoes
Cold greens of any kind
Salt and pepper
Vinegar (optional)

Heat some fat in a frying-pan and put in the meat and fry quickly on both sides until lightly browned. Remove and keep hot. Fry the onion until browned, add the potatoes and greens which have been mixed together and well seasoned. Stir until thoroughly hot, add a little vinegar if liked, and turn on to a hot dish. Place the meat on top and serve.

NOTE: The name Bubble and Squeak is now often given to a dish of re-heated vegetables without meat.

Cooking time—about 20 min.

MEAT CROQUETTES

½ lb. cold, cooked beef *or* mutton
½ oz. fat
½ oz. flour
1 gill stock *or* gravy
Salt and pepper
1 teasp. chopped parsley
1 teasp. of any savoury sauce
Egg and breadcrumbs
Deep fat
Fresh *or* fried parsley

Remove all the fat, skin and gristle from the meat and mince or chop the meat finely. Melt the ½ oz. fat in a saucepan, add the flour and cook for a few minutes. Add the stock, stir and bring to the boil; cook for 3 min. Add the meat, salt, pepper, chopped parsley and sauce, and stir over heat for 2–3 min. Then turn the mixture on to a plate, smooth over and mark into 6–8 equal-sized sections. Allow to become quite cold and firm before forming into 6–8 croquettes. Coat well with egg and breadcrumbs and press the coating firmly on. Fry in hot, deep fat until crisp and a good brown colour, then drain well. Serve piled on a hot dish garnished with fresh or fried parsley.

6 helpings

MINCED MEAT

1½ lb. cold cooked meat
3 oz. butter *or* margarine
1 onion
½ oz. flour
¾ pt. stock
1 tablesp. of pickled walnut liquor *or* a sharp sauce
Salt and pepper
Sippets of toast

Mince the meat or cut into very small dice. Melt the fat in a saucepan and fry the finely-chopped onion carefully until lightly browned. Add the flour and brown. Stir in the stock, add the walnut liquor or sauce and seasoning and boil for 5 min. Put in the meat, bring just to simmering point and keep at this temperature for about ½ hr. Arrange in the centre of a hot dish and place neat sippets of toast all round.

Macaroni or mashed potatoes may be served with this dish.

6 helpings

SAVOURY FRITTERS

Cold meat
Mashed potatoes
Salt and pepper
Milk
Coating batter *or* egg and breadcrumbs
Frying-fat

This dish can be varied in many ways: thin slices of veal and ham put together; underdone beef seasoned with ketchup or Worcester sauce; mutton with slices of tomato, etc. Whatever meat is used, it must be cut into rounds of 1½–1¾ in. diameter. Season the potatoes liberally with salt and pepper, and stir over heat, adding a little milk gradually until moist enough to be easily spread. Cover both sides of the meat with potato, smoothing it with a hot wet knife. Dip in batter or coat with egg and breadcrumbs and fry in hot fat.

SHEPHERD'S PIE

1 lb. cold cooked beef *or* mutton
1 small onion
½ pt. gravy
2 lb. cooked mashed potatoes
Egg *or* milk
Salt and pepper

Remove any skin, gristle or bone and cut the meat into small dice. Parboil and finely chop the onion and place in a pie-dish with the meat and the gravy. Season well. Cover with mashed potatoes and smooth and decorate the top to look like pie-crust. Glaze with beaten egg or milk if liked. Bake in a moderate oven (**350° F., Gas 4**) for about ½ hr. until thoroughly warmed and the surface is well browned.

6 helpings

Beef

BEEF AU GRATIN

1¼ lb. cold cooked beef
1 oz. butter *or* fat
1 small Spanish onion
1 oz. flour
¾ pt. well flavoured stock
Salt and pepper
Breadcrumbs

Mince the beef very finely. Melt the fat in a saucepan and fry the sliced onion until lightly browned. Add the flour and cook, stirring, until nut-brown. Then add the stock and stir until boiling. Season to taste and simmer gently for 20 min. Strain and add to the meat. Fill well-greased scallop shells with the mixture, cover thickly with breadcrumbs and dot with butter or fat. Put in a fairly hot oven (**375° F., Gas 5**) until browned. Garnish with sprigs of parsley and serve immediately.

6 helpings **Cooking time—about 35 min.**

BEEF CAKE *Gâteau de Bœuf*

1 lb. cold roast beef
2 oz. bread raspings
2 oz. cooked ham *or* bacon
1 oz. butter *or* fat
1 small onion
4 oz. breadcrumbs
1 teasp. chopped parsley
Salt and pepper
1 egg
1 gill stock
Gravy *or* brown sauce
Parsley

Grease a plain mould or shallow cake-tin and put in the bread raspings. Shake the mould until it is well covered with raspings. Mince the beef and bacon or ham finely. Melt the fat and fry the finely-chopped onion until slightly brown and add to the minced meats. Then mix together with the breadcrumbs, chopped parsley, seasoning, egg and stock. Use more stock if the mixture is very dry. Place the mixture in the prepared mould, pressing down well. Cover with greased paper and bake in a fairly hot oven (**375° F., Gas 5**) for about 45 min. Turn out carefully on to a hot dish and pour a little sauce or gravy around. Garnish with parsley sprigs.

6 helpings

BEEF HASH *Hachis de Bœuf*

1 lb. cold roast beef
2–3 oz. streaky bacon
2 onions
1 oz. butter *or* fat
¾ pt. mixed Spanish and tomato sauce

GARNISH

Croûtes of fried *or* toasted bread
Parsley

Trim and cut the meat into thin slices. Dice the bacon, slice the onions; melt the fat and fry them until light brown. Add the sliced meat and pour the mixed sauces over. Heat thoroughly without boiling for about ½ hr. If liked this dish can be prepared and served in a casserole and heated in the oven.

Serve neatly garnished with croûtes and parsley.

6 helpings

BEEF POLANTINE

8 oz. cold roast beef
1 gill brown sauce (p. 119)
Salt and pepper
Nutmeg
2 medium-sized onions
Milk
Flour
2 ripe, firm tomatoes
1 oz. butter
¼ pt. gravy

Cut the meat into short fine shreds, or mince it, put into a saucepan with the sauce, a good seasoning of salt and pepper, nutmeg to taste, and warm gradually. Peel the onions, cut them across in slices, divide the slices into rings. Dip the rings in milk and then in flour, fry in hot fat and keep them warm. Slice the tomatoes and fry them in butter, add salt and pepper, and arrange on a hot dish. Place the meat on top of the tomatoes, and garnish with the onion rings. Pour the gravy round and serve.

2–3 helpings

CANNELON OF BEEF

Cannelon de Bœuf

1 lb. cold cooked beef	**1 cup cooked, chopped potatoes (optional)**
½ lb. cooked *or* raw ham *or* bacon	**Salt and pepper**
½ teasp. powdered mixed herbs	**1 egg**
Rind of ½ a lemon	**1 oz. butter *or* fat**
Pinch of grated nutmeg	**¼ pt. stock**
	Brown *or* tomato sauce

Finely chop the beef and the ham or bacon and mix well together with the herbs, finely-grated lemon rind, nutmeg, potatoes (if used) and season well. Bind this mixture with the beaten egg. Form into a short thick roll and wrap in well-greased paper. Place in a baking-tin with the fat and stock and bake in a fairly hot oven (**400° F., Gas 6**) for nearly 1 hr., basting occasionally with the liquid. When ready, remove the paper, place the roll on a hot dish and pour a little brown or tomato sauce over it.

6 helpings

CURRY OF COLD BEEF

Réchauffé de Bœuf en Kari

1½ lb. cold cooked beef	**1 pt. stock *or* coconut infusion**
1 oz. butter *or* fat	**1 teasp. curry paste**
1 onion	**Salt and pepper**
1 sour apple	**4–6 oz. Patna rice**
1–2 teasp. curry powder	**2 teasp. lemon juice**
1 oz. flour	**1 teasp. jam *or* jelly**

GARNISH

Parsley	**Gherkins**
Paprika	

Trim the meat and cut into small neat pieces. Heat the fat and fry the finely-chopped onion and apple for about 7 min. without browning too much. Add the curry powder and flour and cook for at least 5 min. Add the stock or coconut infusion, curry paste and salt, and whilst stirring bring slowly to the boil. Put in the meat and simmer very gently for 20–30 min. until the meat is thoroughly heated and blended with the curry. Cook the rice and arrange as a border on a hot dish and keep hot. Add the lemon juice and jelly to the curry, season if required. Pour into the centre of the rice border, garnish with chopped parsley, paprika and slices of gherkin.

6 helpings
Cooking time—45 min. (approx.)

FRIZZLED BEEF

Slices of cold, cooked beef	**Cold mashed potatoes**
Fat	**Salt and pepper**
Finely-chopped onions	**Gravy**

Heat some fat in a frying-pan or trim the meat and cook the pieces of fat very slowly, until as much liquid fat as is required is obtained. Then strain and return to the pan. Heat the fat and fry the meat until lightly browned. Remove and keep hot. Fry the onions until brown, add the potatoes and season with salt and pepper. Press well down in the pan and fry both sides until well browned. Arrange on a hot dish, place the meat on top and serve with gravy.

MINCED BEEF AND POACHED EGGS

Emince de Bœuf aux Œufs poches

½ lb. under-done roast beef	**½ teasp. mushroom ketchup, Worcester sauce *or* vinegar**
½ oz. butter	**Salt and pepper**
1 small onion	**2 eggs**
½ oz. flour	**Toast**
¼ pt. gravy *or* stock	

Mince or cut the meat into dice. Melt the butter in a saucepan and fry the finely-chopped onion until lightly browned. Sprinkle in the flour and brown slightly, then add the gravy or stock and boil for 2–3 min. Add the meat, ketchup, sauce or vinegar, season with salt and pepper, and keep hot without boiling for 10–15 min. Meanwhile poach the eggs and cut the toast into small triangles. Turn the mince on to a hot dish, place the eggs on top and place the pieces of toast round the base.

2 helpings

RAGOÛT OF BEEF

Ragoût de Bœuf

1½ lb. cold under-done roast beef	**1 pt. stock**
2 onions	**Salt and pepper**
2 oz. fat	**1 tablesp. mushroom ketchup *or* vinegar**
1½ oz. flour	

GARNISH

2 diced carrots	**Parsley**
2 diced turnips	

Cut the meat into neat slices. Chop the onions coarsely. Melt the fat in a saucepan, add the onions and fry until brown. Sprinkle in the flour, stir and cook slowly until well browned. Add the stock, stir and bring to the boil. Season to taste, add the carrot and turnip trimmings from the garnish, mushroom ketchup or vinegar, and simmer for 15 min. Put in the slices of meat and heat thoroughly without boiling for about 1 hr. When nearly ready, cook the diced vegetables. Place the meat on a hot dish and pour the strained sauce over it. Garnish with the diced vegetables and chopped parsley.

6 helpings

ROAST BEEF PUDDING

1 lb. cold cooked roast beef	**½–1 teasp. powdered herbs**
¾ pt. batter	**¾ oz. dripping**
Salt and pepper	**Parsley**

Chop the meat finely. Season the batter with salt and pepper and add the herbs and meat. Melt the dripping in a deep baking-tin and when smoking hot put in the meat batter. Bake for 40 min., first in a very hot oven (**450° F., Gas 8**) for 10 min. and then reduce to moderate (**350° F., Gas 4**) for the remainder of the time. Serve on a hot dish and garnish with parsley.

6 helpings

Lamb and Mutton

COLLOPS OF LAMB AND ASPARAGUS

Escalopes d'Agneau aux Asperges

1½ lb. cold under-cooked lean lamb	**¼ teasp. mixed herbs**
1 tablesp. flour	**About 50 asparagus tips**
¼ teasp. salt	**1½ oz. butter *or* fat**
⅛ teasp. pepper	**½ oz. flour**
Pinch of grated lemon rind	**½ pt. good gravy, stock *or* water**

Cut the meat into neat fillets about 2½ in. in diameter. Mix the flour, salt, pepper, lemon rind and mixed herbs together and sprinkle on both sides of each fillet. Leave to stand for about 1 hr. Cut the asparagus tips about 2 in. long and cook gently in salted water for about 20 min. or until tender. (The stems can be used for soup.) Heat the fat in a frying-pan and cook the collops lightly and quickly until just browned on both sides. Arrange the collops in a close circle on a hot dish. Keep hot. Sprinkle the flour into the pan, cook until brown, then add the gravy, stock or water. Place the drained asparagus tips in the centre of the circle of collops. Carefully season the gravy, strain and pour round the dish.

6 helpings

NEST OF MINCED LAMB

Réchauffé de Mouton

1¼ lb. cold cooked lamb	**Egg *or* milk**
2 lb. potatoes	**¼ pt. gravy *or* stock**
½ oz. butter	**1 tablesp. ketchup**
1 egg yolk	**2 tablesp finely-chopped parsley**
Salt and pepper	**½ pt. brown gravy**
Brown breadcrumbs	

Cook the potatoes and drain well. Mash them with the butter, egg yolk, pepper and salt. Well grease a loose-bottomed cake-tin and cover well with fine brown breadcrumbs. Carefully and evenly line the sides and the bottom with the mashed potato, leaving a hole in the centre (the nest). Smooth the top edge of the potato with a knife, then rough up with a fork and brush with egg or milk. Bake in a hot oven (**425° F., Gas 7**) until set and brown on top. Meanwhile mince the lamb and heat with the ¼ pt. gravy or stock and ketchup, seasonings and parsley. Season well. When the potato nest is set, stand the tin on a jam-jar and push off the side of the cake-tin, leaving the nest intact on the loose bottom. Place the nest on a hot dish, fill with hot mince and serve with brown gravy.

6 helpings

RÉCHAUFFÉ OF LAMB

Réchauffé d'Agneau

1½ lb. cold cooked lamb
1 small onion
¾ oz. butter *or* margarine
½ oz. flour
¾ pt. gravy *or* stock
1 tablesp. mushroom ketchup
Salt and pepper
Mashed potatoes *or* boiled rice
Sippets of toast

Cut the meat into neat dice and boil the bones and trimmings for stock. Finely chop the onion, melt the fat in a saucepan and fry the onion lightly. Add the flour and brown. Stir in the stock, add the ketchup and season to taste. Simmer for 10 min. Put in the meat and bring to simmering point. Keep just below simmering for about ½ hr.

Serve the meat surrounded by a border of mashed potatoes or boiled rice and garnished with sippets of toast.

6 helpings

BAKED MINCED MUTTON

Hachis de Mouton, cuit au Four

1¼ lb. cold cooked mutton
2 tablesp. browned breadcrumbs
8 tablesp. white bread-crumbs
3 teasp. finely-chopped parsley
3 shallots
Salt and pepper
2 eggs
2 tablesp. mushroom ketchup
A little gravy
Baked tomatoes

Finely dice or mince the mutton. Well grease a plain mould or cake-tin and cover with browned breadcrumbs. Mix together the meat, white breadcrumbs, parsley, the finely-chopped shallots and the salt, pepper, beaten eggs, mushroom ketchup and just enough gravy to slightly moisten. Put the mixture into the prepared tin and bake gently in a cool oven (**310° F., Gas 2**) for 1½ hr. until firm and set. Unmould carefully on to a hot dish. Garnish with baked tomatoes and serve with gravy.

6 helpings

FRENCH HASH

Hachis de Mouton à la Française

1¼ lb. cold shoulder *or* leg of mutton
3 oz. Patna rice
¾ pt. Espagnole sauce
4 oz. stewed prunes
6 oz. preserved cherries
Paprika
Salt

Boil the rice in plenty of seasoned water for about 20 min. or until tender, then drain and dry well. Cut the meat into neat pieces. Heat the sauce and put in the meat. Simmer very gently for about ¾ hr. Then add the prunes, previously stewed and stoned, and also the cherries and rice. Season carefully with paprika and salt.

6 helpings

MUTTON AND POTATO PIE

Pâté de Mouton à l'Anglaise

2 lb. cold cooked lean mutton
2 lb. potatoes
2 onions
Salt and pepper
¾ pt. gravy

Cut the meat into neat thin pieces. Make the gravy from the meat trimmings. Parboil and slice the potatoes and onions. Line a pie-dish with slices of potato and cover with layers of meat, onions and potatoes, seasoning each layer. Repeat in layers, until all the ingredients are used, the top layer should consist of potato. Add the gravy, cover with greaseproof paper and bake in a moderate oven (**350° F., Gas 4**) for 1 hr. For the last 15 min. remove the greaseproof paper to allow the potatoes to brown.

6 helpings

MUTTON HASH

Hachis de Mouton

1½ lb. cooked mutton (approx.)
Breadcrumbs
Gherkins
Salt and pepper
¾ pt. good brown sauce

Cut the meat into neat slices (the bones and trimmings may be boiled for stock for the brown sauce). Grease a 1-pt. pie-dish and sprinkle with breadcrumbs. Arrange a layer of slices of meat slightly overlapping each other. Sprinkle with finely-chopped gherkins, salt and pepper and 2–3 tablesp. brown sauce. Repeat until all the ingredients are used, making the top layer a rather thicker one of breadcrumbs. Cover with greaseproof paper and bake gently, for about ½ hr. in a moderate oven (350° F., Gas 4). Serve in the pie-dish.

6 helpings

RÉCHAUFFÉ OF MUTTON

Réchauffé de Mouton

1½ lb. slices of cold mutton
1 turnip
1 small carrot
Salt and pepper
1 onion
1½ oz. butter *or* good dripping
1½ oz. flour
1 tablesp. mushroom ketchup

To make stock: put the bones, meat trimmings, sliced turnip and carrot in a saucepan and just cover with water. Simmer for at least 1 hr. Strain and season to taste.

Finely chop the onion. Heat the fat in a saucepan and fry the onion until lightly browned. Then add the flour, stir and cook slowly until brown. Add ¾ pt. stock and stir until boiling. Season to taste and add the mushroom ketchup. Place the slices of meat in the prepared sauce and simmer for at least ½ hr. Then arrange the meat neatly on a hot dish and strain the sauce over.

6 helpings

Ham and Pork

HAM CROQUETTES

Croquettes de Jambon

½ lb. cooked ham
4 oz. fresh breadcrumbs
2 tablesp. mashed potatoes
½ egg
4 tablesp. white sauce
Salt and pepper
1 egg
Breadcrumbs
Deep fat
Paprika pepper
Parsley

Mince the ham and mix with the breadcrumbs and potatoes. Place in a small pan and, heating gently, bind with the beaten egg and white sauce. Season well and spread on a plate. Divide into 12 equal portions and leave until cool. Shape into croquettes, coat with egg and breadcrumbs, and fry until golden brown in deep fat. Drain, sprinkle with paprika pepper and garnish with parsley.

Serve with tomato sauce.

6 helpings

HAM FRICASSÉE

12 oz. grilled ham
6 oz. mushrooms
1¼ pt. milk (approx.)
1½ oz. butter *or* fat
1½ oz. flour
Salt and pepper
¼ teasp. dry mustard
2 egg yolks
1 tablesp. chopped parsley
Sprigs of parsley
Croûtons of fried bread

Prepare the mushrooms and chop roughly. Simmer for 5 min. in about ¼ pt. milk. Remove the mushrooms, drain off the milk in the saucepan and make up to 1 pt. with more milk. Cut the ham into dice. Melt the fat in the saucepan, add the flour and cook for 3 min. Add the milk, stirring carefully and boil for 3 min. until cooked. Allow to cool, then add the seasoning, mustard and lightly beaten egg yolks. Add the ham and mushrooms and correct the seasoning. Heat thoroughly but do *not* boil. Add the chopped parsley just before serving. Garnish with parsley sprigs and fried croûtons.

6 helpings

MINCED PORK

1¼ lb. cold roast pork
2 onions
2 apples
2 oz. butter *or* fat
1 dessertsp. flour
A pinch of dry mustard
⅓ pt. stock
Salt and pepper
1 teasp. lemon juice

Cut the meat into neat dice—any bones and trimmings may be boiled (for at least 1 hr.) to make the stock. Finely chop the onions and coarsely chop the apples. Melt the fat in a saucepan and fry the onions until lightly browned. Add the apple and cook with lid on until tender but not pulped. Sprinkle in the flour and mustard and stir and cook gently for 3–4 min. Add the strained stock, bring to the boil and correct the seasoning. Put in the meat and lemon juice and simmer for about ½ hr. Do not allow to boil. The meat may be served on a border of rice or mashed potato, or garnished with sippets of toast.

6 helpings

PORK CROQUETTES

Croquettes de Porc

½ lb. cold cooked lean pork	**¼ pt. good stock**
½ oz. butter *or* fat	**A pinch of marjoram**
½ teasp. finely-chopped onion	**¼ teasp. powdered sage**
¾ oz. flour	**Salt and pepper**
	Egg and breadcrumbs
	Deep fat

Finely chop the pork. Melt the butter in a saucepan and fry the onion lightly. Stir in the flour, add the stock, and boil gently for 10–12 min., stirring continually. Add the meat, marjoram, sage and seasoning. Stir until well mixed then turn out on to a plate to cool. Form into croquettes and coat with egg and breadcrumbs. Fry in hot deep fat until golden brown.

6 helpings

PORK HASH

Ragoût de Porc

1½ lb. cold roast *or* boiled pork	**1 dessertsp. Worcester sauce**
Salt	**1 level teasp. mixed mustard**
Cayenne pepper	**1 teasp. lemon juice**
2 oz. butter *or* dripping	

Cut the meat into small neat pieces and sprinkle with salt and a little cayenne. Melt the fat in a pan and add the sauce, mustard and lemon juice. When hot, add the meat and toss over the heat for about 15–20 min. until thoroughly hot and impregnated with the flavours.

6 helpings **Cooking time—about 20 min.**

PORK MOULD

1 lb. cold roast pork	**Salt and pepper**
1 teasp. parboiled finely-chopped onion	**¼ pt. cream *or* milk (approx.)**
2 tablesp. mashed potato	**Brown breadcrumbs**
	½ pt. gravy

Remove all the skin, fat and bone and mince or chop the pork very finely. Add the onion to the minced pork with mashed potato, seasoning and sufficient milk or cream just to bind the mixture together. Well grease a mould or pie-dish and coat it thickly with brown breadcrumbs. Put in the mixture carefully and bake for ¾ hr. in a moderate oven (350° F., Gas 4). The gravy which may be made from the bones and trimmings should be served separately.

NOTE: If liked, this mixture may be shaped into small cakes, coated with egg and breadcrumbs and fried.

6 helpings

Veal

MINCED VEAL WITH POACHED EGGS

Hachis aux Œufs Pochés

1 lb. cold roast veal	**1 teasp. lemon juice**
1½ oz. butter *or* fat	**Salt and pepper**
1½ oz. flour	**6 eggs**
1 pt. well-flavoured stock	

GARNISH

Sippets of toast **Parsley**

Mince the meat very finely. Melt the fat, add the flour and make a brown roux. Add the stock, stir until boiling and simmer for 5 min. Keep half the sauce to serve separately with the finished dish. Put the prepared meat into the remainder of the sauce, add the lemon juice and seasoning and simmer very gently for ½ hr. When nearly ready, prepare the toast, then place the meat in the centre of a hot dish and keep hot. Poach the eggs and arrange round the meat. Garnish with sippets of toast and parsley and serve the remainder of the sauce separately.

6 helpings

MIROTON OF VEAL

Miroton de Veau

1¼ lb. cold roast veal	**½ teasp. finely-grated lemon rind**
1 onion	**½ teasp. finely-chopped parsley**
¾ oz. butter *or* fat	**Browned breadcrumbs**
¾ oz. flour	
¾ pt. stock	
Salt and pepper	

Remove any fat and gristle and cut the meat into thin slices. Slice the onion, melt the fat in a saucepan and fry the onion lightly. Add the flour and cook slowly until well browned. Add the stock, stir until boiling, season to taste and simmer gently for 10 min. Cover the

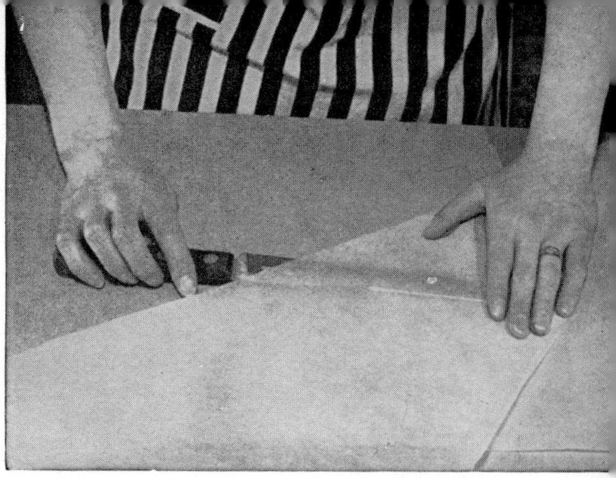

1

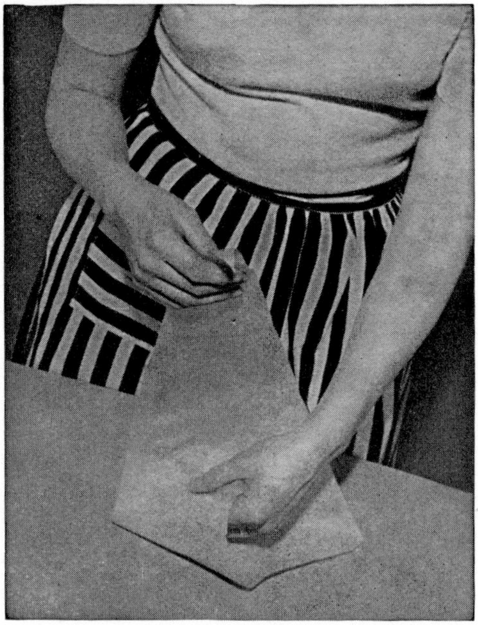

2

PLATE 27

Folding an Icing Bag

1 Fold an oblong-shaped piece of greaseproof paper in half diagonally and cut carefully along the fold.

2 Using one half take it by the longest side in the left and right hands. Fold over the left hand.

3 Form into a cone shape and fold over at the top to seal the join.

4 Cut off the pointed end of the cone and slip a forcing pipe into the bag so that the pipe protrudes half-way through the cut point.

3

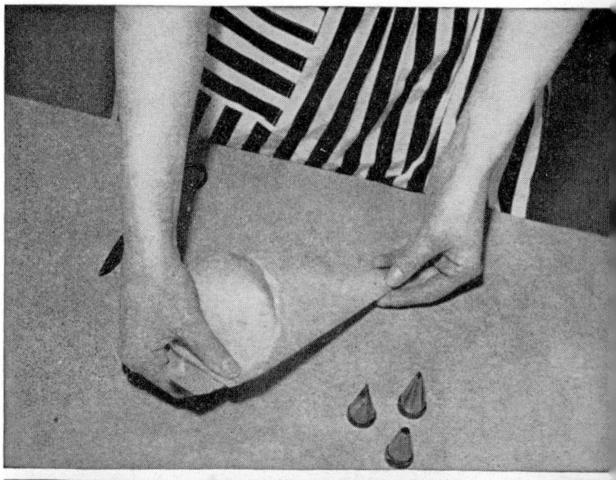

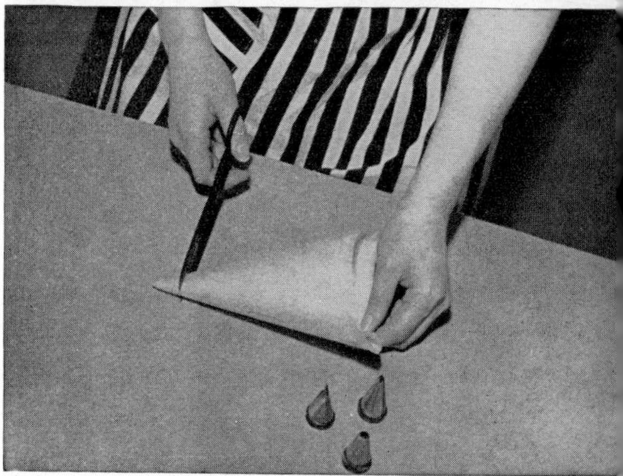

4

PLATE 28

Icing a Cake

1 Using a pastry brush, brush top and side of cake with apricot glaze. Roll out the almond paste to a round shape about 4 inches wider than the diameter of the cake.

2 Place the cake in the centre of the almond paste with the topside downwards.

3 With the hands work the paste up side of the cake until it is within ½ inch of the top edge (i.e. the bottom of the cake).

4 Using a straight-sided jar roll round the side, holding the cake firm with the other hand and pressing down only very slightly.

5 Take a spoonful of icing and smooth with a palette knife, do the top first, then side.

6 Decorate, using a forcing bag and pipe. Draw design first on greaseproof paper, cut to fit top and side of cake. Prick the lines of the design through with a pin. Decorate top, then side, then base.

1

2

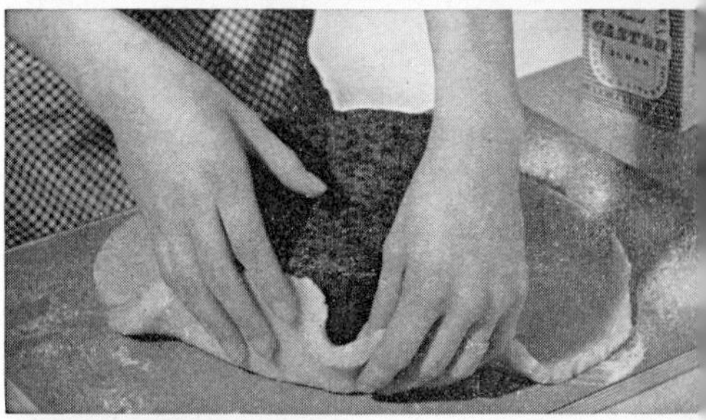

3

4

5

6

bottom of a fireproof dish with some of the sauce. Add some slices of meat, season, and add a little of the lemon rind and parsley. Continue to add all ingredients in layers. Cover the top layer thickly with the browned breadcrumbs and bake in a hot oven (**425° F., Gas 7**) for 15 min.

6 helpings

RÉCHAUFFÉ OF VEAL

Réchauffé de Veau

1¼ lb. cold roast veal	**¾ oz. flour**
1 onion	**1–2 tablesp. lemon juice**
Pinch of mace	**Salt and pepper**
¾ oz. butter *or* fat	**1 tablesp. chopped gherkins *or* capers**

Slice the meat thinly. Make stock from the bones and trimmings of meat, sliced onion and mace; cover with cold water and simmer gently for at least 1 hr. Strain and make up to ¾ pt. with water. Melt the fat, add the flour and brown slightly. Then add the stock and stir until boiling. Add the lemon juice, seasoning and the meat. Heat thoroughly without boiling for about ¾ hr. stirring occasionally. Place the meat on a hot dish, strain the sauce, re-season if necessary, and add the gherkins or capers. Pour over the meat.

Garnish with forcemeat balls and sippets of toast, if liked.

6 helpings

SCOTCH COLLOPS

Réchauffé de Veau à l'Ecossaise

1¼ lb. cold roast veal (approx.)	**¾ oz. flour**
Salt and pepper	**½ pt. good stock**
Powdered mace *or* nutmeg	**Seasoned flour**
¾ oz. butter *or* fat	**Fat for frying**
	1 teasp. lemon juice

Cut the veal into slices ½ in. thick and trim into rounds about 2–3 in. across. Score them on both sides with a sharp knife, sprinkle well with salt, pepper, powdered mace or nutmeg, and put aside. Melt the ¾ oz. fat in a saucepan, add the flour and cook until nut brown, then add the stock. Stir until boiling, season to taste and simmer gently for 20 min. Meanwhile dip the collops in a little seasoned flour, fry them in a little hot fat, drain well and arrange on a hot dish. Add the lemon juice to the sauce, strain and pour some round the collops. Serve the rest separately.

If liked, garnish the meat with parsley and crisply fried bacon rolls.

6 helpings

VEAL CROQUETTES

Croquettes de Veau

1 lb. cooked veal	**Grated rind of ½–1 lemon**
1 oz. butter *or* margarine	**Good pinch of nutmeg**
1 oz. flour	**Salt and pepper**
½ pt. stock	**Egg and breadcrumbs**
2 teasp. finely-chopped parsley	**Deep fat**

GARNISH

Slices of lemon	**Parsley**

Remove any fat, skin or gristle and mince the meat finely. Melt the fat in a saucepan, add the flour and cook slightly without browning. Add the stock slowly, stirring all the time and cook well until thick. Chop the parsley finely and grate the lemon and add to the pan with the minced meat, nutmeg, salt and pepper. Mix well, spread the mixture evenly on a wet plate and leave to cool. When cool, cut into 12 sections and shape into croquettes. Coat with egg and breadcrumbs, twice if necessary. Fry in deep fat until golden brown, then drain well.

Arrange neatly on a dish and garnish with fried parsley or sprigs of fresh parsley and lemon.

6 helpings

VEAL FINGERS

Tranchettes de Veau

6 oz. cold roast veal	**Pinch of mace *or* nutmeg**
½ oz. butter	**6 fingers of toast *or* fried bread**
½ oz. flour	**Chopped parsley**
⅓ pt. stock	
½ teasp. lemon juice	
Salt and pepper	

Mince the veal finely. Make a sauce as follows: melt the butter in a small saucepan, add the flour and cook slowly until light brown.

Then add the strained stock and stir until boiling. Add the lemon juice, seasoning to taste, and simmer gently for 20 min. Mix the veal, sauce, mace or nutmeg well together and season if necessary. Spread on fingers of toast or fried bread and put in a very hot oven (**450° F., Gas 8**) for about 5 min. Sprinkle with parsley and serve.

Cooking time—about ½ hr.

VEAL LOAF

1 lb. cold roast veal	**Gravy *or* stock**
½ lb. sausage meat	**Flour *or* egg and breadcrumbs**
1 oz. breadcrumbs	**Fat for basting**
Salt and pepper	**Sauce *or* gravy *or* salad**
1 egg	

Finely chop the veal and mix with the sausage meat and breadcrumbs. Season well and add the beaten egg. Mix thoroughly, adding gravy or stock until the whole mixture is well moistened, but not wet. Form into a short thick roll and coat lightly with flour or egg and breadcrumbs. Heat some fat in a saucepan, put in the meat roll and baste. Bake in a fairly hot oven (**400° F., Gas 6**) for about 1 hr., basting occasionally.

Serve either hot with a good gravy or sauce, or cold with salad.

6 helpings

VEAL PATTIES

Bouchées de Veau

8 oz. lean cooked veal	**1 teasp. lemon juice**
2 oz. lean cooked ham	**1 tablesp. stock**
Salt and pepper	**4–5 tablesp. good white sauce**
Pinch of nutmeg	**8 patty cases**
Finely-grated rind of ½ lemon	**Parsley**

Chop the veal and ham very finely, and if liked rub through a sieve. Add the salt, pepper, nutmeg, lemon rind, lemon juice and a little stock to moisten. Add the white sauce and more seasoning if necessary. Fill the cases with the mixture, replace the lids and garnish with sprigs of parsley.

Serve hot or cold.

POULTRY

CHICKEN AU GRATIN

Volaille au Gratin

½ lb. cold cooked chicken	**1 teasp. lemon juice**
½ pt. white sauce	**1 teasp. chopped parsley**
	1 tablesp. breadcrumbs
	1 tablesp. grated cheese

Dice the chicken; add to the sauce and heat thoroughly. Add lemon juice and parsley. Turn into a shallow fireproof dish. Mix together the breadcrumbs and cheese, and sprinkle over the sauce. Brown under a hot grill.

Serve from the dish with fingers of toast *or* (to make a main course) with potatoes baked in their jackets.

If liked, the dish may be lined or piped with creamed or duchess potato mixture (p. 350) before the chicken is put in. Green peas *or* French beans may be used up with the chicken in this dish.

CHICKEN CREAMS (Cold)

Crèmes de Volaille à la Gelée

½ lb. cooked chicken	**Salt and pepper**
2 tablesp. white sauce	**½ oz. gelatine**
1 tablesp. sherry (optional)	**½ pt. aspic jelly**
	½ gill cream

FOR COATING MOULDS:

Aspic jelly	**Selection of: peas, truffle, red pepper, tomato, hard-boiled egg, cucumber**
Cream	

Prepare 1 large mould (approx. 5 in. diameter, 3–4 in. deep) *or* 8 individual moulds:

(1) Coat moulds thinly with aspic jelly, decorate with the chosen garnish, and set with a little more aspic (*see* p. 442).

(2) If liked, the moulds may now be lined with aspic cream, i.e. equal quantities cream and aspic jelly mixed together—about ¼ pt. of each.

Chop and pound chicken until smooth; add sauce and sherry (if used) gradually. Season, and sieve if required very smooth. Dissolve gelatine in aspic jelly, cool, add to chicken. Fold in stiffly-beaten cream, pour mixture into mould. When set, dip mould a few times in warm water, wipe, and unmould the cream.

Serve with a dressed salad, *or* in a border mould of salad. (*See Dutch or Flemish Salad*, p. 375).

6 helpings
Setting time—2–3 hr.

CHICKEN CROQUETTES

Croquettes de Volaille

8 oz. cold chicken *or* fowl (boned)	**2 oz. cooked ham *or* tongue**
1 truffle (optional)	**1 oz. butter**
1 tablesp. cream *or* milk	**1 oz. flour**
1 teasp. lemon juice	**¼ pt. stock**
Salt and pepper	**Egg and fresh bread-crumbs**
6 button mushrooms	

Chop the chicken and ham *or* tongue finely. Melt the butter in a saucepan, stir in flour stir in stock slowly, boil 3–5 min. Add all other ingredients, chopping the mushrooms and truffle, turn on to a plate to cool. Form into cork-shapes, coat with egg and fresh breadcrumbs, fry until golden brown in hot deep fat. Drain and serve on a dish-paper.

6 helpings **Cooking time—15 min.**

CHICKEN CUTLETS

Côtelettes de Volaille

½ lb. cold cooked chicken	**¼ pt. white sauce**
½ shallot, chopped	**Nutmeg**
½ oz. flour	**Salt and pepper**
1 oz. butter	**1 egg**
	Egg and breadcrumbs

GARNISH

Fried parsley

Chop the chicken finely. Fry shallot and flour in the butter without browning, add sauce, boil well. Put in the chicken, add nutmeg, season to taste. Stir over low heat until thoroughly heated, add egg, cook 3 min. longer. Cool. When firm, divide into 6 or 8 equal pieces, shape into cutlets, egg and crumb, fry in deep fat.

Drain, arrange in a circle on dish-paper, garnish with the parsley, serve hot.

4 helpings

Cooking time—25 min.

CHICKEN FRIED IN BATTER

Fricandelles de Volaille

Chicken croquettes mixture
Egg and fresh breadcrumbs **Frying fat**

BATTER

4 oz. flour	**1 egg**
1 saltsp. salt	**½ pt. milk**

Make the chicken mixture. Sift flour and salt, add egg and half of milk, beat until smooth. Add remainder of milk, and allow to stand for ½ hr. Make very thin pancakes, and when each is cooked, spread it with the chicken mixture, roll up tightly and leave to become cold. Cut the rolls in 1½ in. pieces, coat with egg and fresh breadcrumbs, fry in deep fat until golden brown. Drain well.

Serve very hot, garnished with fried parsley.

6 helpings

CHICKEN LEGS IN BATTER

Cuisses de Volaille en Pâte lisse

2 legs of cold roast chicken	**Frying fat**

BATTER

3 oz. flour	**3 tablesp. warm water**
Salt and pepper	**1 egg**
1 dessertsp. salad oil	

GARNISH

Fried parsley **Tomatoes**

Remove skin from chicken, cut each leg in half. Mix together flour, salt, pepper, salad oil, warm water and egg yolk. Whisk egg white stiffly and fold into batter. Dip pieces of chicken in batter, fry in deep fat, drain.

Serve at once, piled on a dish paper and garnished with the parsley and tomatoes.

2 helpings **Cooking time—about 5 min.**

CHICKEN PATTIES

Bouchées à la Reine

½ lb. cold cooked chicken	**1 truffle (optional)**
12 puff-pastry cases (p. 555)	**¼ pt. Béchamel sauce** (p. 128)
2 oz. boiled ham	**1 teasp. lemon juice**
6 small mushrooms	**Salt and pepper**

GARNISH

Sprigs of fresh *or* fried parsley

Warm the puff-pastry cases. Chop the chicken and ham, dice the mushrooms and truffle, mix with chicken. Add the mixture to the Béchamel sauce, season, add lemon, stir over a low heat until mushrooms are cooked. Fill the cases with the mixture and put on the lids.

Garnish with parsley and serve.

6 helpings
Cooking time—about 15 min.

MINCED CHICKEN

Émincé de Poulet

1 lb. cold cooked chicken
1 pt. white coating sauce
Salt and pepper
4 poached eggs

Boil chicken bones and trimmings about 1½ hr., use this stock to make the sauce. When sauce is cooked, add minced chicken, season well, and heat thoroughly.

Serve in a shallow dish, very hot, with poached eggs on top.

NOTE: The sauce may be made with ½ pt. stock and ½ pt. milk.

4 helpings

MINCED CHICKEN—WITH BREADCRUMBS

Poulet au Gratin

½ lb. cooked chicken
¼ lb. cooked ham
½ pt. Béchamel sauce (p. 128)
Salt and pepper
Nutmeg
1 oz. butter
3 tablesp. fine breadcrumbs

Remove skin and bone from chicken, chop meat coarsely. Chop ham finely, add to chicken, moisten the mixture well with sauce, season well, and add a little nutmeg. Butter 6 deep scallop shells (or an entrée dish), fill with the mixture, sprinkle evenly with breadcrumbs and place remainder of butter in shavings on the top. Bake in a fairly hot oven (**375°–400° F., Gas 5–6**) until golden brown. Serve hot.

4–6 helpings
Cooking time—about 20 min.

DUCK AND RED CABBAGE

Canard au Chou rouge

Trimmings of 2 cold roast ducks
½ red cabbage
2 oz. butter
Good gravy *or* stock
Salt and pepper
1 tablesp. vinegar

Wash and drain cabbage, shred it finely and cook gently for 1 hr. with the butter, in a tightly-covered pan, adding gravy *or* stock if necessary to prevent burning; season well. Divide duck into neat joints and heat the pieces in a little gravy. Add vinegar to the cabbage—turn on to hot dish.

Arrange the duck on top, and serve with good gravy.

DUCK WITH CARROTS

Canard aux Carottes

Trimmings of 2 cold cooked ducks
3 or 4 large carrots
Sugar
Salt and pepper
1 oz. butter
½ pt. Espagnole sauce

Slice and boil carrots in a little water, with sugar. Strain, sieve or chop them, season and re-heat in the butter. Cut the ducks into pieces convenient for serving. Thoroughly heat the pieces of duck in the sauce. Place the purée of carrots on a hot dish, pile pieces of duck on top, and pour the sauce round.

Cooking time— ½ hr. to re-heat duck

STEWED DUCK—WITH GREEN PEAS

Canard aux Petits Pois

Trimmings of 2 cold roast ducks
1 pt. shelled peas
1 sprig mint
1 lump sugar
½ – ¾ pt. brown sauce (p. 119)
Lemon juice

Parboil peas with mint and sugar; drain well. Divide duck into neat pieces, put into the hot brown sauce, add peas, correct seasoning and simmer ½ hr. Add a little lemon juice, just before serving.

Cooking time—about ½ hr.

FRIED FOWL—WITH PEAS

Poulet frit aux Petits Pois

Trimmings of 2 cold roast fowls
2 oz. butter
1 oz. flour
¾ pt. stock
Salt and pepper

GARNISH
Boiled garden peas

Cut fowl into pieces convenient for serving. Boil fowl bones for stock. Heat the butter in a saucepan. Fry pieces of fowl in butter until brown. Remove fowl from butter, add flour to butter and brown lightly; stir in stock, simmer 5 min. and season. Replace fowl in sauce, cover and cook gently until thoroughly hot.

Serve with sauce strained over and garnished with peas.

Cooking time—about 40 min.

HASHED FOWL

Hachis de Volaille

Trimmings of 2 cold roast fowls
1 bay leaf
1 blade mace
1 carrot
1 onion
A little celery
Piece of turnip
Salt and pepper
1½ oz. butter
1½ oz. flour
1 pt. stock

Divide fowl into neat pieces. Boil fowl bones, bay leaf, mace and sliced vegetables in 1 pt. water for good stock. Melt butter in a saucepan, stir in flour, and lightly brown the roux; stir in the stock, boil well and season to taste. Add the trimmed pieces of fowl to sauce and heat thoroughly.

Dish the fowl, and strain the sauce over.

Cooking time—1½ hr., including making stock

INDIAN DISH OF FOWL

Poulet à la Diable

Trimmings of 2 cold roast fowls
2–3 oz. butter
1 tablesp. curry powder and paste
Salt and pepper
2–3 small onions
1 lemon

Score the pieces of fowl with a sharp knife and spread with a mixture of ½ the butter, curry powder and paste, and seasoning. Allow to stand about 1 hr. Slice the onions, fry until golden brown in remainder of butter, remove onions, drain and keep them hot. Fry the pieces of fowl until well browned.

Serve the fowl piled on the onions and garnished with quarters of lemon.

4 helpings

HASHED GOOSE

Hachis d'Oie

Trimmings of roast goose
2 onions
2 oz. butter
1 oz. flour
1 pt. stock
6 small mushrooms
2 cloves
1 blade of mace
6 allspice
Salt and pepper
Apple sauce

GARNISH
Croûtes of fried bread

Cut the goose meat into neat pieces. Chop onions finely, put in a saucepan and fry in butter until lightly browned, stir in flour and cook slowly until nut-brown. Stir in stock and boil 10 min. Add goose, mushrooms, and spices wrapped in muslin. Season, simmer gently ¾ hr. Arrange the pieces of meat neatly on a hot dish, remove spices from sauce, correct seasoning and pour over meat.

Garnish; serve sauce separately.

BLANQUETTE OF TURKEY

Blanquette de Dinde

¾–1 lb. cold turkey
1 small onion
1 blade of mace
Salt and pepper
1½ oz. butter
1 oz. flour
¾ pt. stock *or* water
Pinch of nutmeg
2 tablesp. cream *or* milk
1 egg yolk

Cut turkey into neat pieces. Place some turkey bones, the sliced onion, mace and seasoning in a pan, cover with stock or water, simmer at least 1 hr. Melt butter in a saucepan, stir in flour, cook 3 min. without browning, stir in hot strained stock. Simmer 10 min., season to taste, add nutmeg and pieces of turkey, allow to heat thoroughly—about 20 min. Mix cream *or* milk with egg yolk, stir in a little of the hot liquid, return all to pan, heat gently without boiling for about 5 min.

Serve hot.

4 helpings

DEVILLED TURKEY

Dinde à la Diable

3/4 lb. cold roast turkey	**1/2 pt. piquant sauce** (p. 121)

DEVILLED BUTTER

1 oz. butter	**1/2 saltsp. curry paste**
1/2 saltsp. cayenne	**Pinch of ground ginger**
1/2 saltsp. black pepper	

Mix together all the ingredients for the devilled butter. Divide the turkey into portions convenient for serving, remove all skin, score the flesh deeply, spread lightly with the devilled butter and leave 1 hr. (Leave longer if a highly-seasoned dish is desired.) Grill meat about 8 min. Serve sauce separately.

3–4 helpings

FRIED TURKEY

Dinde frite

Slices of cold turkey	**2–3 oz. fresh breadcrumbs**
1 egg	**2 oz. minced ham**
1 teasp. olive oil	**2 teasp. chopped parsley**

Cut the cold turkey into neat portions, brush well with lightly-beaten egg, to which the olive oil has been added. Mix together the breadcrumbs, finely minced ham and chopped parsley. Coat the prepared turkey with the mixture, pressing it well into the egg. Fry in deep fat, drain, serve immediately.

Serve with Tartare sauce (p. 130) handed separately.

Cooking time—about 5 min.

HASHED TURKEY

Hachis de Dinde

3/4 lb.– 1 lb. cold roast turkey	**1 1/2 oz. flour**
3/4 pt. turkey stock	**Salt and pepper**
1 1/2 oz. butter	**Toasted bread *or* mashed potato**

Cut the turkey into neat pieces. Make turkey stock with water, turkey bones, vegetables, bouquet garni, seasoning. Melt butter in a saucepan, stir in flour, cook without browning for 3 min., stir in strained stock, boil 10 min., correct seasoning. Add pieces of turkey, allow to heat thoroughly—15–20 min.

Serve on hot buttered toast, *or* in a border of mashed potato.

4–6 helpings

Cooking time—about 2 hr., including stock

ANDOUILLETTES OF GAME

Andouillettes de Gibier

4 oz. cooked game	**1/4 teasp. lemon juice**
1/2 oz. butter	**Nutmeg**
1 chopped shallot	**Salt and pepper**
1 dessertsp. flour	**1 egg yolk**
1/8 pt. stock	**Egg and fresh breadcrumbs**
2 oz. cooked ham	
3 mushrooms	**Frying fat**
1 teasp. chopped parsley	**Fried parsley**

Melt butter, in a saucepan, add shallot, and fry slightly. Stir in flour and when lightly browned, stir in stock and boil 3–5 min. Add to this the finely chopped game, ham, mushrooms, the parsley, lemon juice, nutmeg, seasoning and egg yolk. Stir over low heat until thoroughly mixed and hot, then spread on a plate to cool. When cold form the mixture into cork-shapes, coat with egg and breadcrumbs, repeating the process if the mixture is very soft. Fry in deep fat until golden brown and dish on a bed of fried parsley.

NOTE: The shaped Andouillettes may be wrapped in pieces of pig's caul, brushed with egg white, fried in butter, glazed, and served in paper cases, if desired.

2 helpings

Cooking time—about 30 min.

GAME MOULD

Moule de Gibier

8 oz. cold cooked game	**2 shallots**
4 oz. boiled ham	**Salt and pepper**
4 oz. breadcrumbs	**1/4 teasp. mixed herbs**
	1 egg

Mince the game and boiled ham; mix with breadcrumbs. Slice and fry shallots, chop finely, add to meat, season well, add the mixed herbs. Add the lightly-beaten egg, and if the mixture is dry, some stock *or* milk. Turn mixture into a greased basin, cover, steam 2 hr. Cool, turn out and serve cold with salad.

6 helpings

GAME RISSOLETTES À L'HORLY

Rissolettes de Gibier

6 tablesp. cooked game
¼ pt. thick brown sauce
1 egg
Salt and pepper

BATTER

2 oz. flour
1 tablesp. milk
Salt
½ teasp. salad oil
1 egg

GARNISH

Fried Parsley

Heat the sauce, add minced game, egg and seasoning. Stir over a low heat until mixture thickens, turn on to a plate to cool. Mix flour, milk, salt, salad oil and egg yolk smoothly together for batter. Allow to stand ½ hr., then fold in stiffly-beaten egg white. Divide game mixture into pieces about the size of a large walnut, dip in batter, fry in deep fat until golden brown. Drain well.

Serve immediately, piled on a dish paper and garnished with crisp fried parsley.

3 helpings

PURÉE OF GAME

Purée de Gibier

4 oz. cold cooked game
⅛ pt. gravy *or* stock
1 oz. butter
Salt and pepper
1 tablesp. cream *or* milk

Remove skin and bones from meat, and use carcase to make stock if no gravy is available. Mince meat very finely, and sieve if a very smooth purée is desired. Add melted butter and sufficient stock *or* gravy to make a moist mixture, season well and add cream *or* milk. Press mixture into well-buttered scallop shells, cover with a greased paper and heat thoroughly in a fairly hot oven **(375°–400° F., Gas 5–6)**.

Alternatively, this may be used cold as a spread for sandwiches or on toast.

4 scallop shells
Cooking time—20 min. for heating

SALMI OF WILD DUCK

Canards sauvages en Salmis

Cold roast duck
1 small onion
2 or 3 sprigs thyme
1 bay leaf
1½ oz. butter
1 oz. flour
1 pt. stock
1 teasp. orange juice
1 teasp. lemon juice
1 glass port *or* claret (optional)
Salt and cayenne pepper
Thin strips of orange rind

GARNISH

Orange *or* lemon sections

Cut the remains of 2 cold roast wild ducks into neat pieces. Place bones, trimmings, onion, thyme and bay leaf into a pan with 1 pt. stock *or* water and simmer at least 1½ hr. Meanwhile, melt butter in a saucepan, stir in flour and brown roux very slowly. Stir in the strained stock, stir until boiling, boil 5 min. Add duck, fruit juices, wine (if used), orange rind and seasoning to taste. Allow to become thoroughly hot but do not boil again.

Serve garnished with sections of orange or lemon.

TO PREPARE ORANGE OR LEMON SECTIONS: Scrub fruit, cut into 4, 6 or 8 sections, lengthways; cut off any white pith or skin from the inner edge so that the juice may be pressed out of the fruit easily.

A salmi may be made from any cold cooked game, and makes an excellent dish if the sauce is good. Other garnishes may be used, e.g. croûtes of fried bread *or* fleurons of puff paste, braised olives, button mushrooms *or* truffles.

Cooking time—about 2 hr.

QUICK-FROZEN FOOD

QUICK-FROZEN FOODS ARE an important factor in modern housekeeping; their use means that almost any menu or recipe can be used all the year round. Garden vegetables, sea-fresh fish fillets, fruit and poultry are all available independent of the seasons, and there is absolutely no waste. What you buy you can eat. Tedious preparation is cut out, and the time saved can be devoted to "finishing touches".

Quick-frozen food can be kept up to 36 hours in the ice-making compartment of a refrigerator. Although below freezing-point, it is only a "shallow" freeze, and therefore foods cannot be kept there indefinitely. If a refrigerator is not available, provided quick-frozen foods are placed in a cool place, they will keep up to 24 hours. Some people take the added precaution of wrapping the cartons in newspaper.

In general, once quick-frozen foods have thawed, they should be eaten as soon as possible, *and not under any circumstances be refrozen.*

To preserve the maximum flavour and nutritive value, quick-frozen vegetables should be cooked as soon after purchase as possible, preferably while still frozen. The cooking time required is only a fraction of that necessary for market-bought vegetables, therefore the instructions on the cartons should be followed and care taken not to overcook. Drain well, and serve as usual.

Quick-frozen fish fillets on the other hand should be partially thawed—sufficiently to separate the fillets—before cooking. Thawing is best done naturally by leaving the unopened carton at room temperature for 2–3 hours, but if it is necessary to hasten the operation, place the unopened carton under running cold water. The only occasion when complete thawing is necessary is when the fish is to be fried in deep fat. Quick-frozen fish would reduce the temperature too greatly and could cause severe spluttering. Cooking times vary with the thickness of the fish and the degree of thaw, but average times for *partially thawed* fish are as follows: to fry—8–15 minutes; to grill—8–16 minutes; to bake—15–30 minutes; to steam—8–20 minutes.

Quick-frozen fruits need no preparation other than thawing, and they are packaged with a natural sweetening of cane sugar or syrup. Always thaw in the unopened carton and as slowly as possible; 3–4 hours at room temperature is an average time to allow for this. These fruits are at their best if served as soon as they are completely thawed, as they will still be slightly chilled. The most popular way of eating dessert fruit is in its natural state with either cream or ice cream. They can, however, be used for flans, tarts and shortcakes, in jellies, fruit creams, salads, or served in any of the numerous ways in which fruits are used. One 10 oz. carton of fruit will fill a 7-in. flan case or 6 large tartlet cases.

Quick-frozen young chicken should be completely thawed before cooking. They are ready then for roasting, frying or grilling, according to individual taste, and all the familiar chicken recipes can be adapted for their use. Cooking times depend on the recipe selected.

CREAM OF SPINACH SOUP

One 11-oz. carton chopped spinach
¾ oz. margarine
1 level teasp. grated onion
¾ oz. flour
1 pt. milk
Salt and pepper

Cook the spinach according to the directions on the carton, then pass the spinach and liquor through a sieve. Melt the margarine and add the onion, fry gently without browning until soft, add the flour and cook for 2 min. Add the milk and bring to the boil, stirring all the time. Boil gently for 5 min. Add the spinach purée, adjusting to the correct consistency with a little more milk if necessary; add seasoning to taste and reheat.

NOTE: ¼ level teasp. grated nutmeg may be added to the soup as an alternative flavouring to the onion.

4–5 helpings

BAKED HADDOCK WITH CUCUMBER SAUCE

One 14-oz. carton fillets of haddock
½ pt. milk
1 oz. margarine
1 oz. flour
¼ cucumber
Salt and pepper

Partially thaw and separate the fillets and divide into suitable portions for serving. Place in a baking-tin, cover with the milk and bake for 20 min. in a fairly hot oven (**375° F., Gas 5**). When cooked, remove the fillets on to a serving dish and keep hot. Make a sauce, using the margarine, flour and the milk in which the fish was cooked. Just before serving add the diced cucumber and season to taste. Pour over the fish and serve at once.

3–4 helpings

CREAMED SCAMPI

1 carton scampi
½ pt. very rich white sauce

Thaw the scampi sufficiently to separate the tails. Heat the sauce, add the scampi and simmer for 4–5 min. Serve hot.

FILLETS OF PLAICE CAPRICE

One 14 oz. carton plaice fillets
A little lemon juice
Seasoned flour
2 oz. clarified margarine
Bananas (half for each plaice fillet)
Chopped parsley

Partially thaw the fillets and separate them. Sprinkle each with a little lemon juice and then coat with seasoned flour. Fry the fish in the clarified margarine until golden brown and cooked through, about 7 min., then drain and keep hot. Cut the bananas in half lengthwise, rub with lemon juice and sauté in the remainder of the margarine until soft but not broken. Place a half banana on each plaice fillet, sprinkle with parsley and serve at once.

CORN FRITTERS

One 5-oz. carton sweet corn	**1 egg**
2 oz. self-raising flour	**4 tablesp. milk**
Pinch of salt	**Fat for frying**

Cook the corn according to the directions on the carton, drain and cool. Make a batter with flour, salt, well-beaten egg and milk and stir in the cooled corn. Fry tablespoonfuls of the mixture in a little hot fat until crisp and golden brown on both sides, drain, serve hot.

Serve plain as an accompaniment to fried or grilled chicken, or sausages and bacon; serve with lemon juice and sugar, or with jam or syrup for a sweet.

12 fritters

GARDEN PEAS AND CELERY

One 12-oz. carton peas	**½ pt. boiling water**
½ oz. margarine	**½ teasp. salt**
2–3 sticks celery—cut crosswise	

Melt the fat and gently sauté the celery pieces until soft but not browned. Add the boiling water, salt and then the peas. Cook for 3–6 min. until tender. Drain and serve.

GREEN PEA AND PEPPER SALAD

4 oz. rice	**One 10-oz. carton green peas**
Salt	
1 large *or* 2 small peppers (red *or* green)	

DRESSING

1 tablesp. oil	**¼ level teasp. sugar**
2 tablesp. vinegar	**½ level teasp. mustard**
¼ level teasp. salt	**Shake of pepper**

GARNISH

Lettuce	**Watercress**
Tomatoes	

Cook the rice in plenty of fast boiling, salted water until tender, approximately 12–15 min., then drain and dry well in a cool oven. Meanwhile blanch the peppers then remove pips and pith, and shred finely. Cook the peas according to the directions on the packet, strain and leave until cold. Make up the dressing, then add the rice, peas and peppers, mixing all carefully together.

Arrange the lettuce around the edge of a flat dish and pile the rice mixture in the centre. Decorate with quarters of tomatoes and watercress.

NOTE: This is an ideal salad to serve with chicken or cold skinless pork sausages.

4–6 helpings

HARICOTS VERTS A LA NIÇOISE

One 10-oz. carton sliced green beans	**¼ pt. thick fresh tomato purée**
½ oz. butter	**A little chopped parsley**
Pepper	

Cook the beans as directed on the packet and then drain thoroughly. Place the butter in the pan and add the beans, pepper and tomato purée. Toss over a gentle heat until piping hot and serve in a shallow dish sprinkled with chopped parsley.

3–4 helpings

PISELLI AL PROSCIUTTO

1 small onion	**One 10 oz. carton green peas**
½ oz. butter	
3 oz. cooked ham	**Salt and pepper**

Chop the onion finely. Melt the butter and sauté the onion until soft but not brown. Cut the ham into thin strips, add to the onion and toss for a few minutes in the fat. Add the peas (breaking them up with a fork if still frozen) and the seasoning to taste. Cover the pan and cook over a gentle heat for 12–15 min., shaking the pan occasionally.

4 helpings

THATCHED BROAD BEANS

One 10-oz. carton broad beans	**Salt and pepper**
½ pt. white sauce (coating consistency)	**4 rashers streaky bacon**
	Parsley

Cook the beans according to the directions on the carton. While the beans are cooking, make the white sauce and when cooked, add the strained beans. Season to taste and turn into a shallow fireproof dish. Cut the bacon into strips and use to "thatch" the top of the beans. Place under a fairly hot grill and grill slowly until the bacon is crisp.

3–4 helpings

PRINCESS TRIFLES

One 10-oz. carton raspberries (just thawed)
4 trifle sponge cakes
1 tablesp. orange liqueur *or* to taste
¼ pt. double cream
2 meringue shells
Angelica

Crumble the sponge cakes and divide between 4 shallow glasses. Strain the syrup from the raspberries and flavour to taste with the orange liqueur. Pour over the sponge in each glass, add a layer of raspberries and leave to soak in. *Just before serving* whisk the cream until slightly stiff and fold in the roughly crumbled meringues. Completely cover the soaked sponge with this cream and stud thickly with the remaining whole raspberries. Decorate with angelica leaves.

RASPBERRY KISSEL

One 11 oz. carton raspberries in sugar (just thawed)
¼ pt. water
½ cinnamon stick
1 orange
2 level teasp. arrowroot
A little castor sugar

Strain the syrup from the raspberries, add any undissolved sugar and place both in a small pan with the water, cinnamon and thin strips of orange rind. Bring slowly to the boil, remove from the heat and allow to stand for 5 min., then strain. Blend the arrowroot with a little cold water, add the strained syrup and bring to the boil, stirring all the time. Stir in the juice from the orange and then the raspberries. Pour into individual glasses and sprinkle each with a little castor sugar to prevent a skin from forming. If possible chill before serving.

4 helpings

STRAWBERRY MERINGUE PIE

One 10-oz. carton whole strawberries (just thawed)
One 7-in. baked short crust pastry case
2 level teasp. arrowroot
1 egg white
2 level tablesp. castor sugar

Strain the strawberries from the syrup and arrange them in the baked pastry case. Make up the syrup to ¼ pt. with water. In a small saucepan blend the arrowroot with the syrup, bring to the boil, stirring constantly, and cook for 2–3 min. until clear. Cool slightly, then pour it over the strawberries to form a glaze. Whisk the egg white until stiff and dry, whisk in 1 tablesp. of the sugar, then lightly fold in the remainder. Pipe or spoon this meringue around the edge of the pastry case and place in a fairly hot oven (**400° F., Gas 6**) for 5 min.

Serve hot or cold.

STRAWBERRY TORTONI

One 10-oz. carton whole strawberries (just thawed)
3–4 macaroons
¼ pt. double cream
1 egg white
Flavouring of kirsch *or* 1 teasp. lemon juice

Crumble the macaroons coarsely, strain the syrup from the strawberries. Whip the cream until thick and fold in the stiffly-beaten egg white. Then fold in the kirsch or lemon juice, the syrup from the strawberries and finally the crumbled macaroons. Divide between 4 sundae dishes and stud the top with whole strawberries. This sweet should be prepared not longer than 1 hr. before serving.

VACHERIN DE FRAMBOISES

3 egg whites
Pinch of salt
6 oz. castor sugar
One 11-oz. carton raspberries (just thawed)
½ pt. double cream
Orange flavoured liqueur
A few angelica leaves

Prepare a meringue from the egg-whites, salt and sugar, and place in a piping bag fitted with a ½-in. plain tube. Pipe two round bases of 6 in. diameter on to a prepared baking-sheet and, with the remaining mixture, pipe small meringues of about 1½ in. length. Bake in a very cool oven until dry.

Strain the sugar syrup from the raspberries. Whip the cream till thick, then stir in the fruit syrup and sufficient liqueur to flavour to taste. Place one of the meringue rounds on a serving plate and spread with a little of the cream and half of the raspberries; place the second meringue round on top, arrange the remaining raspberries in the centre and pipe cream around the berries. Decorate the sides with the small meringue shells and angelica leaves.

PRESERVES

JAM–MAKING (See plate 29)

BECAUSE OF VARIATIONS in utensils or ingredients, even a well-tried jam recipe may differ from household to household. The following recipes have been thoroughly tested, but, according to utensils used, yields may vary slightly.

The fruits from which jams are made vary in their content of sugar, acid and pectin (a natural gum-like substance). All three of these make an essential contribution to the set and finished result. Generally speaking, fruits can be divided into three main categories:

(1) Fruits which are easy to make into a well set jam, e.g. apples, blackcurrants, damsons, gooseberries, plums, redcurrants.

(2) Fruits of medium setting quality, e.g. apricots, blackberries, raspberries and loganberries.

(3) Fruits of poor setting quality, e.g. cherries and strawberries.

If there is any doubt about the pectin content of the fruit in any particular season the housewife can perform a simple test on the juice (see Pectin Test, p. 632). But it is generally sufficient to realize that in the following recipes pectin has been added to medium or poor-setting fruits (*a*) by adding another fruit which contains plenty of pectin (e.g. blackberry and *apple* jam, *gooseberry* and strawberry), or (*b*) by adding a commercial pectin (e.g. whole strawberry jam), or (*c*) by adding fruit juice rich in pectin, e.g. redcurrant, apple, gooseberry or lemon juice. Fruits deficient in pectin are generally those which are also deficient in acid. Fortunately (*a*) and (*c*) above both help to add acid to the recipe.

CHOICE OF FRUIT FOR JAMS

Choose firm-ripe fruit. Alternatively, use a mixture of just ripe and slightly under-ripe fruits. Never use over-ripe fruit or the jam will not set. One exception to the above notes: gooseberries should be hard and under-ripe.

CHOICE OF A PRESERVING-PAN FOR JAMS

Choose a pan which is large enough. It should not be more than half-full when the fruit and sugar are in because they must boil together rapidly without risk of boiling over. A pressure pan must never be more than half filled when ready for pressure cooking jams.

Use a preserving-pan, or a large pan of aluminium, stainless steel or unchipped enamel (it should be unchipped, otherwise the jam may stick and burn, or the iron may spoil its colour). Copper or brass preserving pans can be used—so long as any metal polish used for cleaning is thoroughly removed—but jam made in these pans may contain less vitamin C. Do not use iron or zinc pans—the fruit acid will attack the metal, and the colour and flavour of the jam will be spoiled.

To prevent the jam sticking and to help to avoid scum, the inside of the pan can be rubbed before use with glycerine or a small piece of butter or margarine.

TESTING FOR SETTING POINT

There are several tests for setting point including these simple methods given below. Unless otherwise stated in the recipe, jams are usually tested when high frothing ceases and boiling becomes noisy, with heavy plopping bubbles. If the jam is not set then, continue testing at frequent intervals.

1. *Cold Plate Test*

Remove the pan from the heat (otherwise setting point may be missed while this test is being made). Spoon a little jam on to a cold plate or saucer, and allow it to cool. If the setting point has been reached, the surface will set and will wrinkle when pushed with the finger.

2. *Temperature Test*

For this an accurate thermometer marked in degrees up to and above 220° F. is required:

Put the thermometer in hot water before and after use. Stir the jam thoroughly so that it is all of an even temperature. Transfer the thermometer into the jam, holding it well in. Provided a reliable recipe which gives sufficient acid and sugar is being used, a good set should be obtained when the jam reaches 220° F. Occasionally a temperature of 221° F. or 222° F. will give better results. Use this test in conjunction with the Flake Test on p. 622.

3. *Flake Test*

Dip a clean wooden spoon into the jam, remove it and twirl it around until the jam on it has cooled slightly. Then tilt the spoon to allow the jam to drop from it; if it has been boiled sufficiently, the jam will partially set on the spoon and the drops will run together to form flakes which will fall cleanly and sharply.

4. *Volume Test*

In a good recipe it is generally reckoned that 5 lb. of jam should be obtained for every 3 lb. of sugar used. To test the volume of the jam:

(*a*) Fill a 1 lb. jam jar with water five times, pouring the water into the preserving pan. See that the pan is perfectly level.

(*b*) Carefully hold the handle of a wooden spoon upright in the centre of the pan, and mark on it the level of the water. Then empty the pan and make the jam.

(*c*) When the jam is to be tested, remove it from the heat so that the bubbling will subside, then hold upright in it the handle of the wooden spoon. A good setting jam should be obtained when the level has been boiled down to the mark on the spoon handle. (It follows that, when making 10 lb. of jam, the level of 10 filled jam jars should be marked on the spoon.)

NOTE: It is an excellent plan to have another wooden spoon marked off in this way permanently, to give the level in the centre of your pan *for each pint* of liquid it contains. This means that if, for example, a recipe calls for the addition of 1 lb. sugar to every 1 pint jam or marmalade, you do not have to pour the preserve out to measure it. Use a pint measure in place of the jam jar, to pour the water in.

If you intend to put jam pot covers on when jam is cold, cover the hot jars with a clean cloth, keeping the cloth from the jam with a spoon.

APPLE GINGER JAM

3 lb. apples
1 oz. bruised root ginger
1 pt. water
Juice of 1 lemon
3 lb. sugar
4 oz. crystallized ginger

Peel, core and cut up the apples, tying the peel, cores and bruised root ginger in muslin. Place the apples, water and bag of peel in the preserving-pan with the lemon juice and cook slowly until tender. Remove the bag of peel after squeezing. Add the sugar, and the crystallized ginger cut into neat pieces. Allow the sugar to dissolve over a low heat and then boil rapidly until setting point is reached. Pot and cover immediately.

Yield—approx. 5 lb.

APRICOT JAM (Fresh Fruit)

3 lb. fresh apricots
½ pt. water
3 lb. sugar

Wash, halve and stone the fruit and put into the preserving-pan with the water. If desired, crack a few of the stones, remove the kernels and blanch them by dipping in boiling water. Add the halved kernels to the pan. Simmer till tender and the contents of the pan are reduced. Add the sugar and stir over a low heat till dissolved. Bring to the boil and boil rapidly until setting point is reached. Skim, pot and cover.

Yield—5 lb.

APRICOT JAM—(Fresh Fruit) (with added pectin)

2 lb. ripe apricots
¼ pt. water
3 tablesp. lemon juice
3 lb. sugar
½ bottle pectin

Use only ripe fruit. Wash, stone and cut the apricots into slices. Do not peel. Place the fruit in a preserving-pan with the water and lemon juice. Cover and simmer for 20 min. until the fruit is tender. Add the sugar, stir over a low heat until it has dissolved. Bring to a rolling boil and boil rapidly for 1 min., stirring occasionally. Remove from the heat. Stir in the pectin. Cool 5 min. Pot and put on waxed discs immediately. Cover and label.

A few blanched kernels may be added whilst the fruit is cooking if desired.

Yield—5 lb.

APRICOT or PEACH JAM (Dried Fruit)

This is a popular jam for making in the winter when most other fruits are scarce.

1 lb. dried apricots *or* peaches
2–3 pt. water (2 pt. for peaches, 3 pt. for apricots)
Juice of 1 lemon
3 lb. sugar
2–3 oz. blanched and finely shredded almonds (optional)

Wash the fruit and put in a basin with the water. Soak for 24–48 hr. Transfer the fruit and water to the preserving-pan and simmer for 30 min., stirring occasionally. Add the sugar, lemon juice and the shredded almonds. Stir over a low heat until the sugar is dissolved. Boil rapidly until setting point is reached. Skim, pot and cover.

Yield—approx. 5 lb.

BANANA JAM

This jam has been found to be popular with children, but is generally too sweet for their elders.

3½ lb. bananas
Rind, pith and pips of 4 lemons, and the juice from 2
¼ pt. water
3 lb. sugar

Put the rind, pith and pips from the 4 lemons into a muslin bag. Peel and slice the bananas into ¼-in. slices and put into a bowl, pour over the juice from 2 of the lemons and the water. Add the bag of pith and pips, cover all with the sugar and allow to stand for 24 hr. Put all into the preserving-pan, warm over a gentle heat until the sugar is dissolved, bring to the boil and boil until setting point is reached. Remove bag. Pour into hot, dry jars. Cover.

Yield—approx. 5 lb.

BLACKBERRY JAM

3 lb. blackberries
2 tablesp. lemon juice
3 lb. sugar

Pick over the blackberries, wash gently but

thoroughly. Place the berries in the pan with the lemon juice and simmer gently until the fruit is cooked and well softened. Add the sugar and stir over a low heat till dissolved. Bring to the boil and boil rapidly until setting point is reached. Skim. Pour into hot, dry jars. Cover.

Yield—5 lb.

BLACKBERRY AND APPLE JAM

¾ lb. sour apples (weighed when peeled and cored)	**½ pt. water**
	2 lb. blackberries
	3 lb. sugar

Slice the apples and stew them till soft in ¼ pt. of the water. Pick over the blackberries, add the other ¼ pt. of water and stew slowly in another pan till tender. Mix the 2 cooked fruits together. Add the sugar, heat gently until dissolved, then boil rapidly until setting point is reached. Skim, pour into warm, dry jars and cover.

Yield—5 lb.

SEEDLESS BLACKBERRY AND APPLE JAM

2 lb. blackberries	**¼–½ pt. water**
¾ lb. prepared cooking apples	**Sugar**

Place the blackberries in a pan with half the water and stew over a very low heat till tender. Rub through a hair or nylon sieve to remove the seeds (at least 1 lb. of pulp should be obtained). Cook the peeled, cored apples in the rest of the water until soft. Mix the apple pulp with the blackberry pulp and weigh. Weigh out an equal quantity of sugar. Simmer the pulp until thick, stir in the sugar till dissolved, then boil rapidly till setting point is reached. Skim. Pour into hot, dry jars, put on the waxed circles and cover immediately.

Yield—5 lb. of jam for every 3 lb. of sugar used.

BLACKCURRANT JAM

2 lb. blackcurrants	**3 lb. sugar**
1½ pt. water	

Remove currants from the stalks. If the fruit is dirty, wash it thoroughly and drain. Put into the preserving pan with the water, and stew slowly till the skins are soft. *This will take at least ½ hr., probably more.* As the pulp thickens, stir frequently to prevent burning. Add the sugar, stir over a low heat until dissolved, then boil rapidly till setting point is reached. (Test for set at intervals after about 10 min. rapid boiling). Skim, pour into dry, warm jars and cover.

NOTE: This is a good jam for beginners—it sets very easily. But beware of adding the sugar too soon, otherwise hard, "boot-button" currants will result. Try adding 1 tablesp. blackcurrant jam when cooking curry; it helps to darken the curry and gives a good flavour.

Yield—5 lb.

CHERRY (BLACK) JAM
(with added pectin)

2½ lb. black cherries (after stoning)	**6 tablesp. lemon juice**
	3 lb. sugar
¼ pt. water	**1 bottle pectin**

Place the washed and stoned cherries in a preserving-pan with the water and lemon juice. Cook gently with the lid on for 15 min. Remove lid. Add the sugar and stir over gentle heat until it has dissolved. Bring to a full rolling boil and boil rapidly for 3 min. Remove from heat, stir in the pectin, return to heat, bring to boil and boil 1 min. only. Cool for 15 min. to prevent fruit rising. Pot and put on waxed discs immediately. Cover and label.

Yield—5 lb.

CHERRY (MORELLO) JAM
(with added pectin)

2½ lb. Morello cherries (after stoning)	**3 tablesp. lemon juice**
	3 lb. sugar
	1 bottle pectin
¼ pt. water	

Place the washed and stoned cherries in a preserving-pan with the water and lemon juice. Simmer with the lid on for 15 min. Remove lid. Add the sugar and stir over a low heat until it has dissolved. Bring to a rolling boil and boil rapidly for 3 min. Remove from heat, add the pectin and stir well. Cool for 15 min. Pot and put on waxed discs immediately. Cover and label when cold.

Yield—5 lb.

CHERRY (MORELLO) JAM (with redcurrant juice)

3 lb. Morello cherries | **3 lb. sugar**
½ pt. redcurrant juice

To obtain the redcurrant juice, cook about 1½ lb. redcurrants in enough water barely to cover until quite tender (1 hr.). Strain without squeezing. Return the juice to the pan and reduce by heating until ½ pt. remains. Wash the cherries and remove the stones. Put the stones in a loose muslin bag. Put the cherries, redcurrant juice and bag of stones into the preserving-pan and cook all gently until the cherries are very tender. Add the sugar and allow to dissolve away from the heat. When the sugar has dissolved, return to heat, bring to the boil and boil rapidly until a set is obtained. Cool for 7–10 min. to prevent the fruit from rising in the jars. Stir very gently, then pour into hot, dry jars. Put on waxed circles immediately. Cover and tie down when cold.

Yield—approx. 5 lb.

DAMSON JAM

2½ lb. damsons | **3 lb. sugar**
¾–1 pt. water

Remove the stalks, wash the damsons and put into the pan with the water. Stew slowly until the damsons are well broken down. Add the sugar, stir over a low heat till dissolved, bring to the boil, then boil rapidly. Remove stones as they rise to the surface (a stone-basket clipped to the side of the pan is useful for holding the stones, and allows any liquid to drip back into the pan). Continue boiling rapidly until setting point is reached. (Test for set after about 10 min. boiling.) Skim, pour into dry, warm jars and cover.

Yield—5 lb.

GOOSEBERRY JAM—GREEN or RED

2¼ lb. gooseberries | **3 lb. sugar**
¾–1 pt. water

Pick or buy the gooseberries at the green stage, before they have ripened or turned colour. Top and tail and wash them, and put in a pan with the water. Simmer gently until the fruit is soft (this may take ½ hr. or longer). Then add the sugar and stir over a low heat until dissolved. Bring to the boil and boil rapidly until setting point is reached (remove from the heat after 10 min. rapid boiling to test for the set). Skim, pour into dry, warm jars and cover.

NOTE: This is a good jam for beginners, because it is a notoriously good setter. It is specially good served on scones with whipped cream.

GREEN GOOSEBERRY JAM—looks decorative in cakes and biscuits.

Most gooseberry jam turns a reddish colour as it cooks. If preferred gooseberry jam can be kept green by taking the following steps:

1. Choose a variety of gooseberry which is green when ripe, e.g. "Careless", "Green Gem", "Keepsake".
2. Use a copper or brass preserving-pan.
3. Give the jam the shortest possible boil in which it will set once the sugar has been dissolved.

"MUSCAT FLAVOURED" GOOSEBERRY JAM

For another variation to gooseberry jam, put the flowers from 8 heads of elder flowers in a muslin bag and cook with the gooseberries. Squeeze out the juice and remove the bag before the sugar is added.

GOOSEBERRY AND STRAWBERRY JAM

1½ lb. gooseberries, weighed after they have been topped and tailed
1½ lb. strawberries, weighed after they have been hulled
¼ pt. water
3 lb. sugar

Simmer the gooseberries in the water until they are tender. Add the strawberries and simmer a further 3–4 min. Add the sugar, stir over a low heat till dissolved, then boil rapidly until setting point is reached. Skim, pour into warm, dry jars and cover.

Yield—5 lb.

GREENGAGE JAM

3 lb. greengages | **3 lb. sugar**
¼–½ pt. water

Remove stalks and put the washed greengages into the pan with the water. Stew slowly until the fruit is well broken down. Ripe fruit or very juicy varieties will need only a small quantity of water and will be cooked in a few minutes. Firmer varieties may take about 20 min. to break down, and will need the larger quantity of water. Add the sugar, stir over a low heat till dissolved, then boil rapidly, removing the stones as they rise to the surface (a stone basket clipped to the side of the pan is useful for holding the stones, and allows any liquid to drip back into the pan). Keep testing for setting point after about 10 min. rapid boiling. Skim, pot and cover.

Yield—5 lb.

LEMON CURD

3 eggs
3 oz. butter
8 oz. sugar
Rind and juice of 2 lemons

Whisk the eggs and put into a basin with the butter, sugar, finely-grated lemon rind and the juice. Place the basin over a pan of boiling water, stir until the mixture is thick and smooth. Pour into clean, warm jars and cover.

LOGANBERRY JAM

3 lb. loganberries
3 lb. granulated sugar

Cook the loganberries very gently—without any added water—until the centre core of the fruit is tender. Add the sugar, stir over a gentle heat until it is thoroughly dissolved. Boil rapidly until setting point is reached. Skim, pour into dry, warm jars and cover.

Yield—5 lb.

MARROW JAM—PULPED

3 lb. marrow (peeled and cut up)
2 lemons
¼ lb. crystallized ginger
3 lb. sugar

Steam the marrow until it is tender. Drain thoroughly and mash to a pulp. Grate the rind from the lemons and squeeze out the juice. Add rind, juice and the cut-up ginger to the marrow. Bring to the boil, add the sugar and stir over a low heat till the sugar is dissolved. Continue boiling, with frequent stirring, for about 20 min. or until thick. Pour into warm, dry jars and cover.

Yield—approx. 5½ lb.

MARROW AND GINGER PRESERVE

4 lb. marrow (weighed after preparation)
3 lb. sugar
2 oz. root ginger
3 tablesp. lemon juice

Peel the marrow and cut into cubes, removing the seeds. Place the cubes in a colander over a pan of boiling water, put the pan lid on top of the marrow and steam until just cooked and tender. Place in a basin, cover with the sugar and leave overnight. Next day, bruise the root ginger (bang it with a hammer or weight) and tie it in muslin. Put the bag of ginger into a preserving pan with the marrow and lemon juice. Cook slowly for about 1 hr. until the marrow is clear and transparent. This jam does not give a firm set, so do not hopefully go on cooking it. Stop cooking when the correct yield (5 lb.) is obtained (*see* p. 622). By this time the marrow should be transparent and the syrup thick. Remove the bag of ginger just before the end. Pour into dry, warm jars and cover.

Yield—5 lb.

MELON AND LEMON JAM

4 lb. melon (weighed when prepared)
4 lemons
3 lb. sugar

Peel the melon and remove the centre pith, reserving the pips. Cut the flesh into cubes. Wash the lemons, wipe dry and peel with a vegetable peeler to remove only the yellow rind. Cut the fruit in halves and squeeze out the juice. Strain off the juice into a small bowl. Put the lemon peel (yellow part only) and the pips and pulp from the squeezer and the pips from the melon into a loose muslin bag and add this to the melon in the preserving-pan. Heat gently until the juice runs and then cook gently until the melon is tender and transparent (30–45 min). Remove the muslin bag. Add the lemon juice and sugar and stir without further heating until the sugar is completely dissolved. Bring to the boil and boil as rapidly as possible until a set is obtained. Pour into hot, dry jars and cover.

Yield—approx. 5 lb.

MULBERRY AND APPLE JAM—SIEVED

2½ lb. mulberries	**1 lb. apples (peeled and cored)**
½ pt. water	**3 lb. sugar**

Stew the mulberries in some of the water till soft. Rub through a sieve. Stew the apples in the rest of the water. When soft, stir in the sieved mulberries and the sugar. Stir over a low heat till the sugar is dissolved. Bring to the boil and boil till 5 lb. jam are obtained (*see* volume test, p. 622).

Yield—5 lb.

ORANGE CURD

Rind and juice of 2 oranges	**4 eggs**
Juice of 1 lemon	**2 oz. butter**
	8 oz. loaf sugar

Finely grate the orange rind. Squeeze the juice from the oranges and lemon and remove the pips. Thoroughly whisk the eggs. Place the butter in a double saucepan, or in a basin over boiling water, and when the butter has melted add the orange rind, juices, sugar and eggs. Cook gently until the curd thickens, stirring frequently to obtain an even consistency.

Yield—1½ lb. (approx.)

PEACH (FRESH) JAM
(with added pectin)

2 lb. yellow flesh peaches	**6 tablesp. lemon juice**
¼ pt. water	**3 lb. sugar**
	½ bottle pectin

Stone and skin the peaches and cut into slices. Place in a large preserving-pan with the water and lemon juice. Cover the pan and simmer gently for 15–20 min. until the fruit is tender. Add the sugar and stir over a low heat until the sugar has dissolved. Bring to a rolling boil and boil rapidly for 1 min. stirring occasionally. Remove from the heat and stir in the pectin. Cool 5 min. Pot and put on waxed discs immediately. Cover and label.

Yield—5 lb.

PECTIN STOCK

(To add to fruit deficient in pectin when making jams.)

Prepare apples, redcurrants or gooseberries, cook and strain through a scalded jelly bag as for jelly making. Bring the juice to the boil but do not add any sugar. Pour into hot preserving jars, sterilize in a pan of hot water, raised to boiling-point and boiled for 5 min. (*See Fruit Pulps*, p. 649).

PINEAPPLE CONSERVE

1 lb. pineapple (weighed after preparation)	**4 lemons**
	¼ pt. water
	1 lb. sugar

Peel the pineapple and cut the flesh into small neat cubes. Strain the juice of the lemons into a bowl, put the rind, pith and pips into a muslin bag. Put the cubes of pineapple, 4 tablesp. juice from lemons and the muslin bag with the water into a pan. Allow to simmer gently until the cubes are completely tender. Remove the muslin bag and the pineapple cubes. Add the sugar and allow to dissolve. Return the pineapple to the syrup and cook until clear and the syrup thick. Pour into hot jars and cover as for jam.

Yield—approx. 2 lb.

PLUM JAM

3 lb. plums	**¼–¾ pt. water (¼ pt. for ripe, juicy dessert plums, ¾ pt. for cooking varieties)**
3 lb. sugar	

Proceed as for Greengage Jam (p. 625) If desired, a few of the raw plums may be stoned; crack the stones, remove the kernels, blanch them by dipping in boiling water and add the halved kernels to the pan.

Yield—approx. 5 lb.

PLUM AND APPLE JAM

1½ lb. plums	**¾ pt. water**
1½ lb. apples (prepared weight)	**3 lb. sugar**

Wash the plums. Peel and core the apples. Stew the fruit slowly in the water until the skins of the plums are softened. Add the sugar, stir over a low heat till dissolved, bring to the boil and boil rapidly till setting point is reached.

Pour into warm dry jars and cover.

NOTE: As many stones as possible should be removed during cooking. Alternatively, the plums may be stoned before cooking.

Yield—5 lb.

RASPBERRY JAM—Quick Method

This jam does not set very firmly, but it has a delicious fresh flavour. Do not wash the raspberries unless absolutely necessary; if they have to be washed, drain very thoroughly.

2½ lb. raspberries	**3 lb. granulated sugar**

Bring the fruit gently to the boil, then boil rapidly for 5 min. Remove from the heat, add the warmed sugar and stir well over a low heat until all the sugar has dissolved. Bring to the boil and boil rapidly *for* 1 *min.* Skim quickly, pour the jam at once into dry, warm jars and cover.

Yield—5 lb.

RASPBERRY (or LOGANBERRY) AND RHUBARB JAM

2 lb. rhubarb	**¼ pt. water**
1 lb. raspberries *or* **loganberries**	**3 lb. sugar**

Wash and cut up the rhubarb and stew it gently in the water until it is reduced to a thick pulp. Meanwhile pick over the loganberries, add them to the rhubarb and simmer 5–10 min. till tender. Add the sugar. If raspberries are being used, there is no need to cook them first—just add them with the sugar. Stir over a low heat till the sugar is dissolved. Bring to the boil and boil rapidly till setting point is reached. Skim. Pour into hot, dry jars and cover.

Yield—5 lb.

RHUBARB AND GINGER JAM

3 lb. rhubarb	**1 oz. bruised root ginger**
3 lb. sugar	
Juice of 3 lemons	

Wipe the rhubarb and cut it into chunks. Place it in a basin, sprinkling on the sugar in layers. Add the lemon juice and leave to stand overnight. Next day put the contents of the basin into a preserving-pan and add the ginger, tied in muslin. Bring to the boil and boil briskly till the correct yield is obtained (*see* volume test, p. 622).

Yield—5 lb.

STRAWBERRY JAM

3½ lb. hulled strawberries	**Juice of 1 large lemon**
	3 lb. sugar

Heat the strawberries and lemon juice gently in the pan, stirring constantly to reduce the volume. Add the sugar, stir till dissolved and boil until setting point is reached. Remove the scum. Leave the jam undisturbed to cool until a skin forms on the surface and the fruit sinks (about 20 min.). Stir gently to distribute the strawberries. Pour into warm, dry jars and cover immediately with waxed discs. Tie down when cold.

Yield—5 lb.

WHOLE STRAWBERRY JAM (with added pectin)

2¼ lb. small strawberries	**A little butter** *or* **margarine**
3 lb. sugar	**½ bottle pectin**
3 tablesp. lemon juice	

Hull the strawberries and put in a preserving-pan with the sugar and lemon juice. Stand for 1 hr., giving the contents of the pan an occasional stir. Place over a low heat and, when the sugar has dissolved, add a small piece of butter or margarine to reduce foaming. Bring to a rolling boil and boil rapidly for 4 min. Remove from the heat and add the pectin. Stir well. Allow to cool for at least 20 min. to prevent the fruit rising. Stir gently, then pour into clean, warm, dry jars. Put on waxed discs immediately. Cover and label when cold.

Yield—5 lb.

JAM—USING A PRESSURE COOKER

APPLE GINGER JAM

3 lb. green apples	**½ pt. water**
1 large lemon	**3 lb. sugar**
3 level teasp. ground ginger	**4 dessertsp. crystallized ginger**

Peel, core and cut the apples into quarters; tie the cores and peel in a muslin bag. Remove the trivet from the pressure cooker: put in the apples, rind and juice of the lemon, muslin bag, ground ginger and water. Cover the cooker, bring to 10 lb. pressure over a LOW heat; cook for 5 min. Reduce pressure at room temperature. Remove the muslin bag. Return the cooker to the heat; add the sugar and stir until the sugar has dissolved. Add the finely-chopped crystallized ginger; bring to boil and boil rapidly in the open cooker until setting point is reached. Pot and tie down immediately.

Yield—approx. 4 lb.

APRICOT (DRIED) or DRIED PEACH JAM

1 lb. dried apricots *or* dried peaches	**3 lb. sugar**
1½ pt. water	**Juice of 1 large lemon**

Wash the apricots or peaches; put the water to boil; put the sugar to warm. Remove the trivet from the pressure cooker. Put in the fruit, pour over the 1½ pt. BOILING water and allow to soak for 10 min. Bring to 15 lb. pressure in the usual way and pressure cook for 10 min. Reduce pressure immediately with cold water, add lemon juice and warmed sugar and stir, away from the heat, until the sugar is dissolved. Return the cooker to the heat and boil rapidly in the open cooker until setting point is reached. Skim, pot and tie down immediately. A few blanched, halved almonds may be added with the sugar.

Yield—approx. 5 lb.

BLACKBERRY AND APPLE JAM

2 lb. blackberries	**Juice of 1 lemon**
1½ lb. green apples	**3 lb. sugar**
½ pt. water	

Prepare and wash the blackberries. Peel and core the apples and tie peel and cores loosely in a muslin bag. Remove the trivet from the pressure cooker, then put in the blackberries, roughly sliced apples, the muslin bag and the water. Bring to 10 lb. pressure in the usual way and pressure cook for 7 min. Reduce pressure at room temperature. Lift out the muslin bag, add the lemon juice and warmed sugar. Stir over a low heat until sugar is dissolved, then boil rapidly in the open cooker until setting point is reached. Pour into warm jars and cover in the usual way.

Yield—approx. 5 lb.

BLACKCURRANT JAM

2 lb. blackcurrants	**2 lb. sugar**
½ pt. water	

Remove the stalks and wash the fruit. Remove the trivet from the pressure cooker. Pour the water into the cooker and add the blackcurrants. Cover, bring to 10 lb. pressure and pressure cook for 3 min. Reduce pressure at room temperature. Remove cover and add sugar, stir until sugar has dissolved. Bring to the boil without the cover, and boil rapidly until a little will jell when tested on a cold plate. Pour into warmed jars and cover in the usual way.

NOTE: This needs only 3 min. pressure cooking instead of the usual long simmer necessary to soften the skins in an ordinary pan.

Yield—approx. 3 lb.

BLACKCURRANT PURÉE

Wash and string the currants. Remove the trivet from the cooker and put in ½ pt. water for every 2 lb. of prepared fruit. Do not more than half-fill the cooker. Bring to 15 lb. pressure in the usual way and cook for 3 min. Allow the pressure to reduce at room temperature. Put the fruit through a fine sieve—a hair sieve will give the smoothest purée. Return the purée to the cooker, add sufficient sugar for sweetening, stir over a low heat until the sugar is dissolved, then bring to the boil.

NOTE: This purée can be used when cold for trifles, as a sauce over ice cream, with breakfast cereals, or with steamed sponge or suet puddings.

If plenty of fruit is available, or if it is a family favourite, larger quantities can be made and bottled for use in the winter.

BOTTLING PURÉE

Pour the hot purée into hot bottling jars, leaving at least 1 in. headspace. Fix the sealing rings and sterilize in the pressure cooker (following the instructions given on p. 648) for 1 min. at 5 lb. pressure.

Pressure Cooking Time—3 min. at 15 lb. pressure
Sterilizing—1 min. at 5 lb. pressure

DAMSON, PLUM or GREENGAGE JAM

3 lb. fruit
3½ lb. sugar
¼ pt. water

Wash, halve and stone the fruit. Remove kernels from some of the stones and blanch them. Remove the trivet from the pressure cooker, then add the fruit, water and kernels. Bring to 10 lb. pressure in the usual way and pressure cook for 5 min. Reduce pressure at room temperature, add the warmed sugar. Return the cooker to the heat and stir until sugar is dissolved. Boil rapidly in the open cooker until setting point is reached (approx. 10 min.). Skim, pot and tie down immediately.

Yield—approx. 5½ lb.

FRUIT SALAD PRESERVE

NOTE: This is an excellent recipe to keep in mind when doing a mixed batch of fruit bottling or jam-making. Some fruits are certain to be left over; keep them aside, and with very little extra expense or time a few more pounds of jam for winter store can be made.

Fruit Salad Preserve is a new jam, ideal to make in a pressure cooker, as it is important that all the fruits should be thoroughly softened and lose their identity, to give the delicate taste of a mixed fruit salad.

This jam can be made at any time in the summer, with a selection of any fruits which happen to be in season. Care must be taken that not too much of any particular fruit is included, otherwise its particular flavour will predominate, and in the same way the colours of the fruit should be considered so that the result does not look too definitely the colour of any particular jam.

Remember too, that fruits rich in pectin such as gooseberries and redcurrants should always be included with others such as strawberries and cherries, so that an easy and good set is obtained.

The sample Fruit Salad jam, which was tested and tasted refreshing and delicious was made up as follows:

5 oz. redcurrants
4 oz. strawberries
5 oz. gooseberries
5 oz. greengages
5 oz. raspberries
5 oz. cherries
3 oz. blackcurrants

32 oz. = 2 lb. fruit: to this amount allow 2 lb. sugar and ½ pt. water

Prepare, stone and wash the fruit. Remove the trivet from the pressure cooker and put in the fruit. Add water in the proportion given above, cook for 5 min. at 10 lb. pressure. Reduce pressure at room temperature, add the warmed sugar. Stir over a low heat until the sugar is dissolved, then boil rapidly in the open cooker until setting point is reached (approx. 20 min.).

Yield—3⅓ lb.

LEMON CURD

2 eggs
½ lb. granulated sugar
2 oz. butter *or* margarine
2 lemons

Beat the eggs well in a heatproof glass or china bowl. Add the sugar and the fat cut into small pieces. Add the grated rind and strained juice of the lemons. Stir all well together. Put ½ pt. water in the pressure cooker, plus 1 tablesp. vinegar (the vinegar prevents discolouration of the inside of the cooker). Cover the basin with 2 layers of greaseproof paper, tied on with string. Stand the basin on the trivet in the cooker. Bring to 15 lb. pressure in the usual way and pressure cook for 10 min. Allow the pressure to reduce gradually at room temperature. Stir the curd very thoroughly, pour into a warm, dry jar, cover with a waxed disc and tie down immediately.

Yield—1 lb.

MARROW GINGER JAM

4 lb. marrow	**4 lemons**
½ pt. water	**2 oz. root ginger**
4 lb. sugar	

Peel the marrow and cut flesh into cubes Put the water in the pressure cooker, then the trivet and the prepared marrow. Bring to 15 lb. pressure in the usual way and pressure cook 1–2 min. according to the ripeness of the marrow. Reduce pressure immediately with cold water and transfer the marrow to a large bowl, adding the sugar, grated rind and juice of the lemons and the ginger, banged with a hammer to "bruise" it, and tied in a muslin bag. Allow to soak for 24 hr. Next day, remove the trivet from the cooker, take out the ginger, return all other ingredients to the open cooker and bring slowly to boiling point, stirring well. Continue to boil until marrow is transparent and the syrup thick. Pot and tie down immediately.

Yield—approx. 4 lb.

MELON AND PINEAPPLE JAM

2 lb. melon (weighed after preparation)	**Juice of 3 lemons**
½ lb. pineapple (weighed after preparation)	**3 lb. sugar**

Peel, core, cut the melon into small cubes and weigh out 2 lb. Peel, core and cut the pineapple into small cubes and weigh out ½ lb. Remove the trivet from the pressure cooker, then add the melon, pineapple and lemon juice. Bring to 10 lb. pressure in the usual way and pressure cook 10 min. Reduce pressure at room temperature, then add the warmed sugar. Return the cooker to the heat and stir until the sugar is dissolved. Boil rapidly in the open cooker until setting-point is reached. Pot and tie down immediately.

Yield—4–4½ lb.

PEACH (FRESH) JAM

3 lb. fresh peaches	**3 lb. sugar**
½ pt. water	

Wash, halve and stone the fruit. Remove the kernels from some of the stones, blanch and halve. Remove trivet from the cooker, then add the fruit, kernels and water. Bring to 10 lb. pressure in the usual way and pressure cook for 4 min. Reduce pressure at room temperature and add the warmed sugar. Return the cooker to the heat and stir until the sugar is dissolved. Boil rapidly in the open cooker until setting point is reached, 10–15 min. approx. Allow the jam to stand until a skin forms, stir well, pot and tie down immediately.

Yield—approx. 5 lb.

PINEAPPLE AND APRICOT PRESERVE

NOTE: This is a useful—and delicious—jam to make during the times when there is little or no fresh fruit available.

1 pt. water	**Pinch of salt**
1 lb. dried apricots	**2 lb. sugar**
1 lb. canned pineapple (crushed)	**Juice of 1 lemon**

Boil the water and pour over the washed apricots. Leave to soak for 15 min. Weigh out 1 lb. of crushed pineapple. Remove the trivet from the pressure cooker and put in the soaked apricots and water, the pineapple and the salt. Bring to 10 lb. pressure in the usual way and pressure cook for 10 min. Reduce pressure at room temperature. Return the cooker to the heat, without the lid, add the sugar and lemon juice and stir over a low heat until the sugar is dissolved. Boil rapidly until setting point is reached. Pot and tie down immediately.

Yield—approx. 3½ lb.

QUINCE JAM

2 lb. quinces (weighed after peeling and coring)	**1½ pt. water**
	2½ lb. sugar
	Juice of 1 lemon

Peel, core and slice the quinces. Boil the skins and cores in a small saucepan with

½ pt. of the water for 10 min. Strain off and keep the liquid. Remove the trivet from the pressure cooker, then add the sliced fruit and the remaining 1 pt. water. Bring to 10 lb. pressure in the usual way and pressure cook for 6 min. Reduce pressure at room temperature, add the sugar, strained liquid and lemon juice. Return the cooker to the heat and stir until the sugar is dissolved. Boil rapidly in the open cooker until setting point is reached. Skim, pot and tie down immediately.

Yield—approx. 4½ lb.

RED TOMATO JAM

1¾ lb. tomatoes	**1 lemon**
¼ lb. apples (sharp)	**1 lb. sugar**

Scald the tomatoes, skin and cut them up. Peel, core and cut up apples. Put peel and core into a muslin bag. Remove the trivet from the pressure cooker. Put the tomatoes and apples into the cooker with the muslin bag and rind of the lemon and bring SLOWLY to the boil without lid of cooker, stirring to prevent burning or sticking to bottom of cooker. Cover, bring to pressure, pressure cook for 5 min. Reduce pressure at room temperature. Lift out muslin bag and lemon rind. Return to heat, add warmed sugar and lemon juice, stir over low heat till sugar is dissolved and boil without the lid on the cooker, until a little will jell when tested on a cold plate.

Yield—approx. 2 lb.

JELLY–MAKING

IMPORTANT POINTS IN THE MAKING OF JELLIES:

1. Use fresh fruit, not over-ripe.

2. Simmer gently in water (the amount varies with the recipe) till the fruit is tender and thoroughly broken down (usually about ¾–1 hour). *If in any doubt about its setting properties, test for pectin at this stage*, as a good set depends upon the amount of acid, pectin and sugar present.

Test for pectin

After the fruit has cooked till tender, squeeze from it a teaspoon of juice. Place to cool in a cup or glass. Then add 3 teaspoons methylated spirits. Shake gently and leave 1 minute. If there is plenty of pectin in the fruit, a transparent jelly-like lump will form. If there is only a moderate amount of pectin there may be two or three lumps, not very firm. If there is insufficient pectin, the lump will break into many small pieces and the fruit should be simmered for a little longer before another pectin test is made. It is a waste of effort to strain the juice and attempt to make jelly if there is only a poor amount of pectin. It is preferable to mix with another fruit which is known to be a good setter (e.g. apple—*see Blackberry and Apple Jelly*, p. 634).

3. After cooking, strain the fruit through a jelly bag, first scalding the bag by pouring boiling water through it. Hang the bag on a special frame, or

suspend it from the legs of an upturned stool *or* chair with a basin below to catch the drips.

4. Never hurry the straining of the juice by squeezing the bag—this might make the jelly cloudy. Some people leave it to drip overnight, but do not leave the juice too long before completing the jelly—certainly not more than 24 hours. Fruit which is very rich in pectin can be extracted twice (*see Black-currant Jelly*, p. 634). The two juices can be mixed together, or two grades of jelly can be made, one from the first and another from the second.

5. Measure the juice into a preserving-pan, bring to the boil. Add the sugar. Strained juice rich in pectin needs 1 lb. sugar to each pint of juice. Juice with only a fair pectin content needs only $\frac{3}{4}$ lb. sugar to each pint. A thick, sticky juice is almost certain to contain plenty of pectin, but many people prefer to be sure by using the Pectin Test described in paragraph 2.

6. After dissolving the sugar, boil rapidly till setting point is reached (about 10 minutes—test by any of the methods for Jam on p. 621). The Flake Test, used with the Temperature Test, is probably the most satisfactory).

7. Skim, removing the last traces of scum from the surface with the torn edge of a piece of kitchen paper. Pour into warm jars (1 lb. size or smaller) at once, before it has time to begin setting in the pan. Put on waxed circles (waxed side down) immediately. Cover when hot or cold. Do not tilt the jars until the jelly has set. Store in a cool, dry, dark place.

NOTE: *Exact yield of jelly from each recipe cannot be given because of varying losses in straining the juice, but usually 10 lb. of jelly should be made from each 6 lb. sugar used.*

APPLE JELLY

4 lb. well-flavoured crabapples, *or* cooking apples (windfalls can be used)
Flavouring: lemon peel *or* root ginger
Sugar

Wash the apples and cut up without peeling or coring—just remove any bad portions. Barely cover with water (about 2–3 pt.) and simmer with the chosen flavouring till tender and well mashed (about 1 hr.). Strain through a scalded jelly bag. Bring the strained juice to the boil and test for pectin. Add the sugar (usually 1 lb. sugar to every pint of juice). Stir to dissolve. Boil briskly till setting point is reached.

APPLE AND ROWANBERRY JELLY

3 lb. rowanberries (Mountain Ash berries)
3 lb. of apples
3 pt. water
Sugar

Remove rowanberry stalks, wash and drain the berries. Wash and slice the apples and cook them with the rowanberries and water till soft and broken up. Strain the juice through a scalded jelly bag. Return the juice to the pan, heat and add 1 lb. sugar to each pint of juice. Stir till dissolved. Boil rapidly till setting point is reached.

NOTE: This jelly has the characteristic bitterness of the rowanberry. It is excellent with meat dishes as a change from Redcurrant Jelly.

BLACKBERRY AND APPLE JELLY

4 lb. blackberries — **2 pt. water**
4 lb. cooking apples — **Sugar**

Rinse the fruit. Cut up the apples without peeling or coring. Simmer the blackberries and apples separately with the water for about 1 hr., until the fruits are tender. Mash well and allow to drip through a jelly bag. Measure the juice. Bring to the boil, then stir in the sugar (usually 1 lb. to each 1 pt. of juice). Boil briskly till set.

BLACKCURRANT JELLY

4 lb. ripe blackcurrants — **Sugar**
2½ pt. water

Remove the leaves and only the larger stems and wash the blackcurrants. Place in the preserving-pan, add 1½ pt. water, and simmer gently till thoroughly tender. Mash well, then strain the pulp through a scalded jelly bag, leaving it to drip undisturbed for at least 15 min. Return the pulp left in the jelly bag to the pan, add another pint of water and simmer for ½ hr. Tip this pulp back into the bag and allow to drip for 1 hr. Mix the first and second extracts together. Measure the juice into the cleaned pan, bring to the boil. Then add 1 lb. sugar to each pint of juice and stir till dissolved. Boil briskly, without stirring, until setting point is reached. Remove the scum, then immediately pour the jelly into warm jars.

CRANBERRY AND APPLE JELLY

3 lb. apples — **Water**
2 lb. cranberries — **Sugar**

Rinse the fruit. Slice the apples, without peeling or coring, and place in a pan with the cranberries and sufficient water to cover. Simmer gently till thoroughly mashed. Test for pectin. Allow to drip through a jelly bag. Measure the juice. Allow usually 1 lb. sugar to each pint of juice, but this depends on the pectin test. Bring the juice to the boil. Add the sugar and stir till dissolved, then boil briskly till setting point is reached.

DAMSON AND APPLE JELLY

6 lb. apples — **4 pt. water**
3 lb. damsons — **Sugar**

Slice the apples, without peeling or coring, and add to the damsons and water. Simmer gently until the fruit is thoroughly mashed. Strain through a scalded jelly bag, allowing it to drip undisturbed. Return the juice to the pan, bring to the boil. Allow usually 1 lb. sugar for each 1 pt. of juice, stir till dissolved, then boil briskly till setting point is reached.

ELDERBERRY AND APPLE JELLY

Equal weights of elderberries and sliced apples (not peeled or cored) — **Sugar**

Cook the elderberries and apples separately, with enough water just to cover the fruit. Simmer till tender and broken up. Test for pectin and if the set is poor reduce further. Strain the fruit through a scalded jelly bag. Measure the juices, mix, return to the pan and heat. Add ¾ lb. sugar for every pint of juice. Stir till dissolved. Boil rapidly till setting point is reached.

GOOSEBERRY JELLY

4 lb. green gooseberries — **Sugar**
2–3 pt. water

Wash the gooseberries and place them in the pan without topping and tailing. Add the water, cook till thoroughly tender and broken. Test for pectin (*see* p. 632). Strain through a scalded jelly bag and add ¾–1 lb. of sugar to each pint of cold juice. (The amount depends on the results of the pectin test.) Bring to the boil, stirring to dissolve the sugar, and boil rapidly till setting point is reached.

NOTE: The addition of sugar to the cold juice allows it a longer boiling time and gives a darker, pleasanter colour to the jelly.

MINT JELLY

3 lb. green apples — **Sugar**
1⅛ pt. water — **3 level tablesp. chopped mint**
A small bunch of fresh mint — **A few drops of green colouring**
1⅛ pt. vinegar

Wash the apples, cut in quarters and place in a preserving-pan with the water and the bunch of mint. Simmer until the apples are soft and pulpy, then add the vinegar and boil for 5 min. Strain overnight through a cloth, measure the juice and to each pint, allow 1 lb. sugar. Put the juice and sugar into the pan and bring to the boil, stirring until the sugar is dissolved. Boil rapidly until setting point is nearly reached, add the chopped mint and colouring, then boil until setting point is reached. Pour into hot jars and cover immediately with waxed discs. When quite cold, tie down with parchment or transparent covers, label and store.

ORANGE SHRED (APPLE) JELLY

(Rather mild in flavour, but a clear jelly with a delightful colour.)

3 lb. apples (crab-apples *or* windfall apples)	**Peel and juice of 3 oranges**
	Sugar

Wash the apples and cut into rough pieces, discarding any bad portions. Place in a preserving-pan with water barely to cover. Simmer gently until the fruit is quite tender (approx. 1 hr.). Strain through a scalded jelly bag. Meanwhile, wash the oranges and remove the peel in quarters. Cook the peel in $\frac{1}{4}$ pt. water in a small covered saucepan for about 1 hr., or until tender. Measure the apple juice, remaining water from the cooked peel, and the strained juice of the oranges, and put into the preserving-pan with 1 lb. sugar to each pint of liquid. Put over a low heat to dissolve the sugar and then boil fast until setting point is reached. Skim *quickly*. Meanwhile, dry the cooked peel in a cloth, and cut into fine shreds. Add these to the jelly immediately after skimming. Allow to cool slightly until a skin is formed on the surface of the jelly and then pour into hot, dry jars.

QUINCE JELLY

Quinces	**Sugar**
Water	

Wipe fruit carefully. Do not peel but cut into quarters and put into the preserving pan with sufficient cold water to cover. Bring slowly to the boil and simmer gently until the quinces are quite tender. Strain through a scalded jelly bag—do not squeeze or the jelly will not be clear. Add 1 lb. of sugar to each pint of juice and boil till setting point is reached.

RASPBERRY JELLY

8 lb. raspberries	**Sugar**

Put the raspberries in the pan without any added water and heat gently until they are quite soft. Crush the fruit well. Strain through a scalded jelly bag. Return the measured juice to the clean pan, bring it to the boil and add 1 lb. sugar to each pint of juice. Stir until the sugar is dissolved, then boil rapidly till setting point is reached.

REDCURRANT JELLY—RICH

6 lb. large, juicy red-currants *or* red-currants and white-currants mixed	**Sugar**

Remove the leaves and only the larger stems. Place the cleaned fruit in the preserving-pan, without any water, and heat very gently until the currants are softened and well cooked (about $\frac{3}{4}$ hr.). Mash, then strain the pulp through a scalded jelly bag, leaving it to drip undisturbed. Measure the juice into the cleaned pan. Add $1\frac{1}{4}$ lb. of sugar to each pint of juice. Bring to the boil, stirring constantly, and boil, without stirring, for 1 min. Swiftly skim the jelly and immediately pour it into the warmed jars, before it has a chance to set in the pan.

SLOE AND APPLE JELLY

4 lb. apples	**Sugar**
2 lb. sloes	

Wash and cut up the apples but do not peel or core. Place in a pan with the sloes, just cover with water and simmer to a pulp. Strain through a scalded jelly bag. Allow 1 lb. sugar to each pint of juice. Boil till setting point is reached.

JELLIES—USING A PRESSURE COOKER

BLACKBERRY JELLY

2 lb. blackberries | **Sugar**
½ pt. water | **Juice of 1 lemon**

Wash the fruit. Remove trivet from the cooker and pressure cook the blackberries and water at 10 lb. pressure for 5 min. Allow pressure to reduce at room temperature. Mash the fruit and strain through a fine jelly bag, allowing to drip undisturbed overnight. Allow 1 lb. warmed sugar to each pint of juice. Add the strained lemon juice with the sugar. Stir over a low heat *in the open cooker* till the sugar is dissolved. Boil briskly till setting point is reached.

MEDLAR JELLY

4 lb. medlars | **4 lemons**
1½ pt. water | **Sugar**

Cut the washed fruit up roughly, peel the lemons thinly and squeeze out the juice. Remove the trivet from the pressure cooker. Put in the medlars, lemon rinds and water. Bring to 10 lb. pressure in the usual way and cook for 30 min. Allow the pressure to reduce at room temperature. Strain the contents through a cloth, allowing to drip overnight if possible. Do not squeeze the cloth as this will cloud the jelly. Next day, measure the juice, return to the pan and add ¾ lb. sugar to each pint of juice and the strained lemon juice. Stir over a low heat until the sugar is dissolved, then boil rapidly in the open cooker until setting point is reached.

MINT JELLY

2 lb. sour green apples | **1 pt. water**
Large bunch of mint | **1 dessertsp. vinegar**
1 lemon | **Sugar**

Wash, peel and core the apples and cut in quarters. Wash the mint well. Remove the trivet from the pressure cooker and put in the apples, the mint (stalks as well), the thinly-grated rind and juice of lemon, the water and the vinegar. Bring to 10 lb. pressure over a medium heat and pressure cook for 8 min. Reduce pressure at room temperature and strain through a scalded fine muslin bag, leaving overnight if possible. Measure the juice, add 1 lb. of warmed sugar to each pint. Stir over a low heat until the sugar is dissolved, bring to the boil and boil rapidly in the open cooker until setting point is reached. Pot and tie down immediately.

NOTE: A little very finely-chopped mint may be added just before setting point is reached.

REDCURRANT JELLY

3 lb. redcurrants | **Sugar**
½ pt. water

Wash the redcurrants and string them. Remove trivet from the cooker and pressure cook the fruit and water for 4 min at 10 lb. pressure. Allow pressure to reduce at room temperature. Mash the fruit and allow to drip overnight through a scalded jelly bag. To every pint of juice add 1¼ lb. of warmed sugar. Stir over low heat till the sugar has dissolved. Bring to the boil, and boil rapidly in the open cooker till setting point is reached.

ROSE HIP JELLY

2 lb. rose hips | **Sugar**
1½ pt. water | **Tartaric acid**

Choose firm but well ripened fruit. Wash and top and tail. Remove the trivet from the pressure cooker. Put in the fruit and water. Bring to 10 lb. pressure over a medium heat and pressure cook for 30 min. Reduce pressure at room temperature and stir well with a wooden spoon through a wire sieve. Strain the pulp again through a scalded jelly bag. Add 1 lb. sugar and ½ teasp. of tartaric acid to each pint of juice. Return to heat in open cooker. Stir over low heat until sugar is dissolved. Bring to boil and boil until setting point is reached.

MARMALADE–MAKING

MARMALADE-MAKING IS similar to jam-making and nearly all the same rules apply. As in jam-making, the fruit is first simmered gently, usually in an open pan, until it is thoroughly softened. During this long, slow cooking, in the presence of acid, the jellying substance—pectin—is brought into solution. After this, the sugar is added and stirred over a gentle heat till dissolved. Then the marmalade is boiled rapidly, with a full, rolling boil, until setting point is reached. The tests for setting point are the same as for jam-making (*see* p. 621).

These are the essential differences:

(*a*) The peel of citrus fruit takes longer to soften than the fruit used for jams. For this reason, a number of pressure cooker recipes—which cut down the cooking time—are included.

(*b*) Because most of the pectin is present in the pips and the pith—rather than in the fruit pulp or fruit juice—these are important ingredients of marmalade recipes. The pips and pith should not be discarded (unless they are being replaced by commercial pectin) but should be tied loosely in muslin and cooked with the fruit until the pectin has been extracted. If the muslin bag is tied to the handle of the pan, it can easily be removed before adding the sugar.

FURTHER POINTS TO NOTE FOR MARMALADE-MAKING

1. Remember that all citrus fruits should be just ripe, and must be used as soon as possible; so it is advisable, if possible, to order the fruit in advance and ask the greengrocer to tell you as soon as it comes into his shop.

2. It is not usually easy for the layman to distinguish between the true Seville orange and other imported bitter oranges. Sevilles are considered to have a superior flavour, but ordinary bitter oranges can replace them in the recipes.

3. If the recipe tells you to peel the citrus fruit, try soaking the fruit in boiling water first for 1–2 min. This helps the skin to peel off easily.

4. It is necessary to use a very sharp stainless knife to cut the peel into shreds. Remember that the peel will swell slightly during the cooking. If large quantities of marmalade are made, it might be worthwhile to buy a special machine which cuts the peel swiftly and easily.

If a coarse-cut marmalade is preferred, usc thc method on p. 641 (Seville

Orange Marmalade 2). Alternatively, with some other methods the uncooked fruit can be put through a coarse mincer, but it does not look so attractive.

Many recipes recommend soaking the peel, etc., for 24–48 hr. to soften it before continuing with the cooking. If time is limited, this is not essential. But if the soaking is omitted, it may be necessary to cook a little longer to make sure that the peel is sufficiently softened.

The sugar should not be added until the pulp is considerably reduced and the peel will disintegrate when squeezed (about 1½–2 hr.). If this is faithfully observed, setting point is generally reached after about 15–20 min. rapid boiling but this depends on the recipe.

HOW TO POT AND COVER MARMALADES

Always remove the scum from marmalade as soon as the setting point is reached. Use a hot metal spoon. If the scum is not removed immediately, it subsides gently on the peel and is then extremely difficult to skim off.

To prevent the peel rising to the top of the pots, leave the skimmed marmalade to cool undisturbed in the pan until a thin skin begins to form on the surface. Then stir it to distribute the peel (but do this gently to avoid air bubbles, and do not stir clear jelly marmalades).

Pour into the pots, using a small jug or cup to pour easily.

Waxed discs should be placed on the marmalade immediately, taking care to avoid air bubbles under the disc. Some recipes advise putting on the outer cover when the marmalade is quite cold. Alternatively, the outer covers can be put on while the marmalade is still very hot. But do not put them on when it is only warm, as the warm marmalade would make moisture condense on the underside of the cover and the heat from the marmalade would not be sufficient to dry it. Moulds would readily grow in this damp atmosphere.

CLEAR SHRED ORANGE MARMALADE

3 lb. Seville oranges
2 lemons
1 sweet orange
6 pt. water
Sugar

Wash the fruit, dry and cut in half. Squeeze out the juice and strain, keeping back pulp and pips. Scrape all the white pith from the skins, using a spoon, and put pips, pulp and white pith into a bowl with 2 pt. water. Shred the peel finely with a sharp knife and put this into another bowl with 4 pt. water and the juice. Leave all to stand 24 hr. Strain the pips, etc., through a muslin bag and tie loosely. Put the bag and strained liquor, the peel and juice into the preserving-pan and bring to simmering point. Simmer for 1½ hr. until the peel is tender. Remove from the heat and squeeze out the muslin bag gently. For a very clear jelly, allow to drip only. Measure 1 lb. sugar to each pint juice and allow the sugar to dissolve completely over a low heat. Bring to the boil and boil rapidly until a set is obtained (20–25 min.). Remove from the heat and cool until a skin forms on the surface. Pour into hot jars and cover immediately.

Yield—approx. 10 lb.

DARK COARSE-CUT MARMALADE

2 lb. Seville oranges
1 lemon
7 pt. water
6 lb. sugar
1 tablesp. black treacle

Wash the fruit, cut in half and squeeze the juice. Tie the pips loosely in a muslin bag. Slice the skins into medium-thick shreds. Put the juice, muslin bag, sliced peel and water into a preserving-pan and simmer until the peel is tender and the liquid reduced by *at least* ⅓ (approx. 1½–2 hr.). Remove the bag of pips, after squeezing the juice out gently. Remove from the heat then add the sugar and the treacle, return to heat and stir over a low heat till the sugar is dissolved. Then boil rapidly till setting point is reached.

Yield—10 lb.

FIVE FRUIT MARMALADE

2 lb. fruit: 1 orange, 1 grapefruit, 1 lemon, 1 large apple, 1 pear
3 pt. water
3 lb. sugar

Wash and skin orange, grapefruit and lemon and shred the peel finely. Cut this fruit coarsely. Put the pips and coarse tissue in a basin with ½ pt. water. Place the peel and cut citrus fruit in a bowl with 2½ pt. water. Soak for 24 hr. Strain the pips and tissue, tie in a muslin bag and place in a preserving-pan with the fruit, the peel and all the liquid. Peel and dice the apple and pear and add to the rest of the fruit. Bring to the boil, simmer for 1¼ hr. and until reduced by ⅓. Remove muslin bag. Add the sugar, stir over low heat until dissolved. Bring to the boil and boil rapidly until set (about 30 min.). Cool slightly then pot into clean warm jars. Seal and label in the usual way.

Yield—5 lb.

GRAPEFRUIT MARMALADE

1½ lb. grapefruit
2 lemons
3 pt. water
3 lb. sugar

Wash the fruit, cut in half and squeeze out the juice. Remove some of the pith if it is thick, cut it up coarsely and put it with the pips in a muslin bag. Slice the peel finely. Put all the fruit and juice into a bowl, cover with the water and leave overnight. Next day put it all into a preserving-pan and cook gently for 2 hr. or until the peel is soft. Remove the bag of pips, add the sugar, stir until it is dissolved, then boil rapidly until setting point is reached. Pot and cover in the usual way.

Yield—5 lb.

GRAPEFRUIT AND PINEAPPLE MARMALADE (1)

1¼ lb. grapefruit (fruit, juice and shreds = 1 pt.)
1 small pineapple and juice of 1 lemon = ½ pt. after preparation
3 pt. water
3 lb. sugar

Wash the grapefruit and remove the skins. Put the white pith to one side and cut the skins into fine shreds. Cut up the peeled grapefruit, putting the pips and coarse tissue to one side. Put the fruit and skins into a bowl with 2½ pt. water. Put the pips, tissue and a little of the pith into a basin with ½ pt. water. Soak for 24 hr. Next day, cut the pineapple into slices, removing skin, eyes and hard centre; chop the flesh into small pieces and place in a preserving-pan with the lemon juice, the other fruit and all the liquid, and the tissue and pips tied in a muslin bag. Bring to the boil, reduce heat and simmer gently until contents of pan are reduced by ⅓. Remove the muslin bag. Add sugar, stir over low heat till dissolved. Bring to the boil and boil rapidly for 25–30 min. until a little tested on a saucer will wrinkle. Cool 15–20 min. Pot and cover in the usual way.

Yield—5 lb.

GRAPEFRUIT AND PINEAPPLE MARMALADE (2) (with added pectin)

2 large grapefruit
2 lemons
¾ pt. water
⅛ teasp. bicarbonate of soda
1 can crushed pineapple
4 lb. sugar
1 bottle pectin

MARMALADE

Wash the fruit and remove the skins in quarters. Shave off and discard the thick white part. Slice the rind very finely with a sharp knife and place in a preserving-pan with the water and the bicarbonate of soda. Bring to the boil and simmer, covered, for 10 min., stirring occasionally. Meantime, cut up the peeled fruit, discarding the pips and coarse tissue. Add the juice, pulp and the can of crushed pineapple and juice and simmer, covered, for 15 min. Add the sugar, stir over low heat until the sugar is dissolved. Bring to a full rolling boil and keep it boiling fast for 3 min., stirring. Remove from the heat, stir in the pectin. Bring to the boil and boil 1 min. Cool for 10–15 min. Pour into clean, warm jars and seal at once.

Yield—6 lb.

LEMON MARMALADE

1½ lb. lemons **3 lb. sugar**
3 pt. water

Wash the lemons and shred the peel finely (removing some of the pith if very thick). Cut up the fruit, putting aside the pips and coarse tissue. Put the fruit and shredded peel in a large bowl with 2½ pt. water. Put the pips, pith and coarse tissue in a basin covered with ½ pt. water. Leave all to soak for 24 hr. Next day transfer all to the preserving-pan tying the pips, etc. in a muslin bag, bring to the boil and simmer gently for about 1½ hr., until the peel is tender and the contents of the pan are reduced by at least ⅓. Remove the muslin bag. Add the sugar, stir until dissolved, then bring to the boil and boil rapidly till setting point is reached (approx. 15–20 min.).

Yield—5 lb. approx.

LEMON AND GINGER MARMALADE

1½ lb. lemons **3 lb. sugar**
3 pt. water **8 oz. crystallized ginger**
2 oz. root ginger

Wash and peel the lemons in quarters, cut the peel in fine shreds and place in a large bowl. Cut the fruit finely, putting aside the pips and coarse tissue. Put the fruit with the cut peel and cover with 2½ pt. water. Put the pips and coarse tissue into a basin with ½ pt. water. Soak for 24 hr.

Drain the liquid from the pips and tissue and place in a preserving-pan with the rest of the fruit and liquid. Tie the tissue, pips and root ginger in a muslin bag and add to the pan. Bring to the boil, reduce the heat and simmer gently for 1¼–1½ hr. and until reduced by ⅓. Remove muslin bag. Add the sugar and finely-chopped crystallized ginger and place over low heat, stirring until sugar has dissolved. Bring to the boil and boil rapidly until setting point is reached, approx. 20 min. Cool 5–10 min. Pot into clean jars. Cover and label.

Yield—5 lb.

LEMON JELLY MARMALADE

2 lb. lemons **3 lb. sugar**
3¼ pt. water

Scrub the lemons and wipe dry. Peel off the outer yellow skin, using a vegetable peeler or sharp knife, and cut the peelings into fine shreds. Tie these in a muslin bag. (N.B. If a marmalade with fewer shreds is preferred, add the shredded peel from only half the lemons.) Cook the shreds in 1½ pt. of water, in a covered pan, until tender. Meanwhile, roughly cut up the fruit and cook with the remaining water in a preserving-pan for 2 hr., with the lid on the pan. Pour off the liquid from the shreds, add it to the cooked fruit and strain it all through a scalded jelly bag. Pour the strained liquid into the rinsed preserving pan, simmer a little if it seems rather thin, then add the sugar and stir over a low heat till dissolved. Add the shreds and boil hard until setting point is reached.

LEMON SHRED JELLY MARMALADE (with added pectin)

1 tablesp. very finely-shredded lemon peel **¾ cup lemon juice (4–5 lemons)**
1 pt. water **2 lb. 10 oz. sugar**
⅛ level teasp. bicarbonate of soda **1 bottle pectin**

Cook the peel in the water and bi-carbonate of soda for 10 min. Add the lemon juice and sugar and heat gently until the sugar has dis-

PLATE 29

Jam-Making

Wash and dry jars and heat them on the rack over the cooker or in a cool oven. Prepare the fruit (1). Add water and acid if called for in the recipe (2). Simmer very slowly with the lid off the pan unless otherwise stated. The fruit must be thoroughly broken down and the skins softened and, if water has been added, contents of pan should be boiled down by about ⅓ before addition of sugar. Use preserving, granulated or lump sugar. Stir to dissolve before bringing to the boil. Boil rapidly, with a good rolling boil, to setting point. This should take 1–20 min. according to kind of jam, size of pan and quantity being made. For details of various methods of testing for setting point, see page 621, and pictures 3a and 3b. After setting point has been reached, remove jam from heat. Use a metal spoon to remove any scum from the surface of the jam. Allow jam to cool and thicken slightly in the pan until fruit ceases to rise; then stir gently to distribute the fruit. With the aid of a cup or jug fill the jars right to the top (4). Place on waxed circles immediately, waxed side to jam, making sure that there are no air bubbles left between the circles and the jam. Wipe jars with a clean cloth wrung out in hot water. Either cover jars with a clean cloth until jam is cold (not warm), see page 622; then put on outer covers. Or put on outer covers at once whilst jam is hot (5). Label; when cold store in a dark airy cupboard at ordinary room temperature.

1

2

4

5

3a Flake test

3*a*

3b Cold plate test

3*b*

PLATE 30

Making Marmalade in a Pressure Cooker

1 Wash fruit, remove peel and pips. Cut fruit up roughly, shred peel (coarse or fine according to taste).

2 The trivet is removed from the pressure cooker and the chopped fruit, pips, peel and the measured water are put in the pan together.

3 After pressure cooking and reducing pressure, add sugar, allow to dissolve, then boil in the OPEN pan until the setting point is reached.

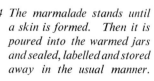

4 The marmalade stands until a skin is formed. Then it is poured into the warmed jars and sealed, labelled and stored away in the usual manner.

1

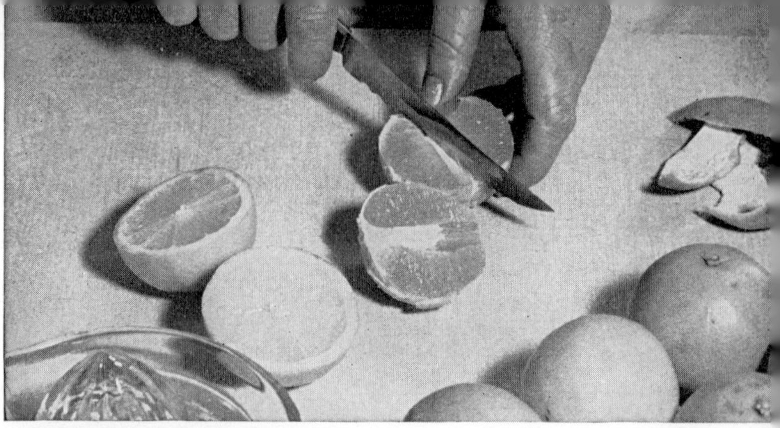

2

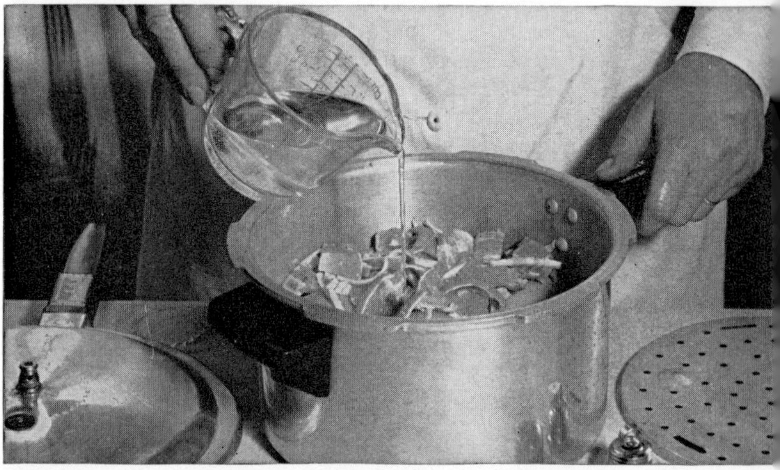

3

4

solved, stirring occasionally. Bring to a full rolling boil and boil rapidly for ½ min. Remove from the heat and add the pectin. Reboil for ½ min. Allow to cool slightly to prevent the fruit floating and skim if necessary. Pot and cover.

Yield–about 4½ lb.

MELON AND LEMON MARMALADE

Juice and rind of 1¼ lb. lemons	**1 lb. melon, prepared and cut in cubes**
¼ pt. water	**3 lb. sugar**
⅛ teasp. bicarbonate of soda	**1 bottle pectin**

Wash the fruit. Squeeze the juice from the lemons, remove most of the pith and shred the rinds very finely. Measure ¼ pt. water into pan, add juice, rinds and the bicarbonate of soda. Simmer, covered, for 10 min. Add cubed melon, simmer till tender and transparent. Add sugar, heat gently till dissolved, stirring occasionally. Bring to full rolling boil quickly and boil for 2 min. Remove from heat, stir in pectin. Leave to cool for a few minutes to prevent fruit rising. Skim if necessary. Stir, pot and cover.

Yield—about 4½ lb.

ORANGE JELLY MARMALADE

2 lb. Seville oranges	**Juice of 2 lemons**
4½ pt. water	**3 lb. sugar**

Peel the oranges, remove the thick pith and shred finely 4 oz. of the rind. Cook the shreds in 1 pt. water, in a covered pan, until tender (approx. 1½ hr.). Meanwhile, roughly cut up the fruit and put it with the lemon juice and 2½ pt. water in a pan. Simmer for 2 hr., with the lid on the pan. Drain the liquid from the shreds, add it to the cooked fruit and strain it all through a scalded jelly bag. After it has dripped for ¼ hr., return the pulp to the preserving pan and add 1 pt. water. Simmer for 20 min. then strain again through the jelly bag, allowing it to drip undisturbed. Pour the strained liquid into the rinsed preserving-pan, simmer a little if it seems rather thin, then add the sugar and stir over a low heat till dissolved. Add the shreds and boil hard until setting point is reached.

Yield—5 lb.

SEVILLE ORANGE MARMALADE (1)

1½ lb. Seville oranges	**Juice of 1 lemon**
4 pt. water	**Sugar**

Wash the fruit and cut it in half. Squeeze out the juice and the pips. Cut the peel into shreds. Tie the pips in a muslin bag and put into a bowl with the orange and lemon juice, water and peel. Soak for 24–48 hr., covered to keep it clean. Transfer to the pan and cook gently until the peel is soft (approx. 1½ hr.). Remove the bag of pips, squeezing it gently. Take the pan from the heat, add 1 lb. sugar to each pint (see volume test p. 622). and stir till dissolved. Return pan to heat, bring to the boil, and boil rapidly until setting point is reached.

Yield: about 6½ lb.

SEVILLE ORANGE MARMALADE (2)

1½ lb. Seville oranges	**Juice of 1 lemon**
2 pt. water	**3 lb. sugar**

Wash the fruit and put it whole and unpeeled into a saucepan. Pour on 2 pt. boiling water and simmer gently *with the lid on the pan* until the fruit is tender enough to be pierced easily with a fork (approx. 2 hr.). (*Alternatively, the whole fruit and water can be baked in a covered casserole in a cool oven until the fruit is soft; this will take about* 4–5 *hr.*) When the fruit is tender, cut it in half and remove pips then cut up the fruit with a knife and fork, carefully retaining all the juice. Return the pips to the water in which the fruit was cooked, and boil for 5 min. to extract more pectin. Put the sliced fruit with the liquid (strained free from pips) and lemon juice in the preserving-pan. Reduce the heat, add the sugar and stir till dissolved. Bring to the boil and boil rapidly till setting point is reached.

NOTE: This method is simple to do and is recommended if a fairly coarse-cut marmalade is liked.

Yield—5 lb.

SEVILLE ORANGE MARMALADE (3)

1½ lb. Seville oranges	**Juice of 1 lemon**
3 pt. water	**3 lb. sugar**

Wash the oranges and, with a sharp knife,

shred finely. Tie the pips and pieces of coarse tissue in a muslin bag. Put fruit, muslin bag and water in a basin and leave overnight. Next day transfer to the preserving-pan, bring to the boil, add the lemon juice, and simmer gently till the peel is soft and the contents of the pan are reduced by at least $\frac{1}{3}$ (approx. $1\frac{1}{2}$–2 hr.). Remove the muslin bag, after squeezing gently. Add the sugar, stir over low heat till dissolved, then bring to the boil and boil rapidly till setting point is reached. Skim. Allow to cool for about 10 min. before potting.

Yield—5 lb.

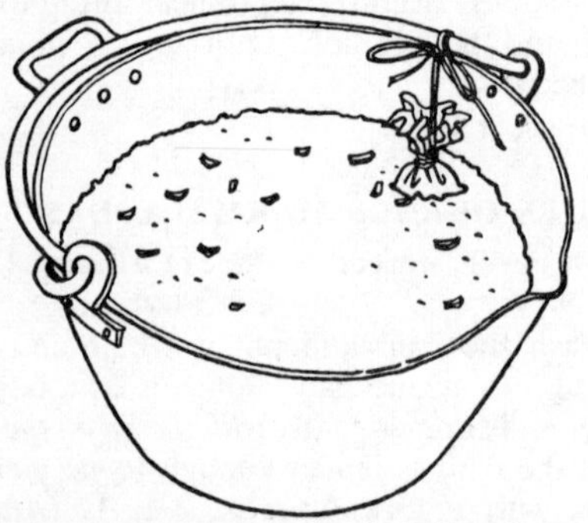

A bag containing pips and pith tied to the handle of the pan is easily removed before adding sugar.

SEVILLE ORANGE AND GINGER MARMALADE

1¼ lb. Seville oranges	**3½ pt. water**
1 lemon	**8 oz. crystallized ginger**
1 oz. root ginger	**Sugar**

Wash the oranges and lemon, cut in halves and squeeze out the juice and pips. Strain the juice into a bowl and tie the pips with the root ginger in a muslin bag. Cut the peel into shreds, thickness according to preference, and put with the juice, water and bag of pips in the bowl. Leave to soak overnight. Next day, put into a preserving-pan, bring to the boil and simmer gently until the peel is quite soft (about $1\frac{1}{2}$–2 hr.). Remove the bag of pips after squeezing gently. Cut the crystallized ginger into $\frac{1}{4}$-in. cubes and add to the cooked peel. Remove from the heat and measure. Add 1 lb. of sugar to each pint of fruit (see volume test p. 622). Stir over a gentle heat until the sugar is dissolved and then boil rapidly until setting point is reached.

Yield—6½ lb. (approx.)

TANGERINE MARMALADE (with added pectin)

3 lb. tangerines	**5 lb. sugar**
2 pt. water	**1 bottle pectin**
Juice of 3 lemons	

Wash the tangerines and put into a preserving-pan with the water. Simmer gently, covered, for 40 min. When cool enough to handle, remove peel and cut up fruit, taking out the pips and the very coarse tissue. Return the pips and tissue to the liquid and boil hard for 5 min. Shred half the peel, discard the rest. Strain the liquid, discarding the pips and tissue, and put back in the preserving-pan with the pulp, peel, lemon juice and sugar. Stir over gentle heat until the sugar has dissolved and then bring to a full rolling boil. Boil hard for 3 min. Remove from heat, stir in pectin, boil for 1 min. Skim if necessary. Cool slightly and pot in the usual way.

NOTE: Tangerine Marmalade is normally a difficult one to set; the addition of pectin gives an easy method.

Yield—about 7 lb.

THREE FRUIT MARMALADE

About 1½ lb. fruit— 1 grapefruit, 2 lemons and 1 sweet orange	**3 pt. water**
	3 lb. sugar

Wash and peel the fruit, and shred the peel coarsely or finely according to taste. (Remove some of the pith if it is very thick.) Cut up the fruit, tying the pips and any pith or coarse tissue in a muslin bag. Soak the fruit, peel and muslin bag in the water in a bowl for 24 hr. Next day, transfer to the preserving-pan and simmer gently for $1\frac{1}{2}$ hr. or until the peel is tender and the contents of the pan are reduced by about $\frac{1}{3}$. Remove the muslin bag, after squeezing gently. Add the sugar, stir over a low heat till dissolved. Bring to the boil and boil rapidly till setting point is reached.

Yield—5 lb.

MARMALADE—USING A PRESSURE COOKER

In order to soften the peel sufficiently, marmalade making has to be a lengthy process; the cooking time (which may normally be about $1\frac{1}{2}$–2 hr.) can be shortened to about 7–10 min. if a pressure cooker is used. The preliminary cooking to soften the peel is done in the closed pan. The sugar is then added and the cooking finished in the open pan.

NOTE: Some types of pressure cooker will not make more than 5 lb. of marmalade at a time. The pressure cooker must not be more than $\frac{1}{2}$ filled when ready for pressure cooking.

GRAPEFRUIT MARMALADE

2 lb. fruit (approx.)— 4 lemons and 2 grapefruit
1½ pt. water
3 lb. sugar

Scrub the lemons, shred finely and put the pips on one side. Scrub the grapefruit and peel; remove the thick white pith and the pips, and tie with the lemon pips in a muslin bag. Shred the grapefruit peel finely. Shred the grapefruit coarsely. Remove the trivet from the pressure cooker. Put into the cooker the water, all the prepared fruit, the peel and the muslin bag. Bring to 10 lb. pressure in the usual way and pressure cook for 10 min. Reduce pressure at room temperature, remove the muslin bag and add the sugar. Return the open cooker to the heat, stir over low heat until the sugar is completely dissolved. Bring to the boil and boil rapidly until setting point is reached.

Yield—approx. 5 lb.

LEMON MARMALADE

1 lb. lemons
2½ lb. sugar
1 pt. water

Wash the fruit and shred, but not too finely. Remove pips and tie in a muslin bag. Remove the trivet from the pressure cooker and put in the fruit, water and the muslin bag. Bring to 10 lb. pressure in the usual way, and pressure cook for 7 min. Reduce pressure at room temperature, remove the bag of pips and add the sugar. Return cooker to the heat and stir until sugar is dissolved. Boil rapidly in the open cooker until setting point is reached.

Yield—4–4½ lb.

LEMON JELLY MARMALADE

2 lb. lemons
3 lb. sugar
2½ pt. water

Make as for Orange Jelly Marmalade (p. 644), substituting lemons for oranges.

NOTE: No soaking of the fruit is necessary, and it is softened in 20 min. (compared with about 2 hr. by ordinary cooking). In spite of the quick cooking, the jelly is full of flavour.

LIME MARMALADE

IMPORTANT: The limes should not be used whilst they are still bright green and obviously unripe. They will only give a bitter marmalade, very difficult to set. Put them on one side and leave till they turn yellowish and very slightly shrivelled.

1 lb. limes
1⅓ lb. sugar
1¼ pt. water

Take the peel off half the fruit. Remove the pith from the peel, shred the peel finely and tie loosely in a small piece of muslin. Cut the limes up roughly. Remove trivet from the cooker, put in fruit, pith, water and muslin bag. Bring to 10 lb. pressure and cook for 20 min. Allow pressure to reduce at room temperature. Strain through a fine sieve or jelly bag. Return the strained liquid to the cooker, add the sugar, stir over a low heat till dissolved. Boil rapidly for 3–5 min. Skim. Wash shreds from muslin bag in a sieve with plenty of water to separate them. Add to the marmalade. Continue boiling until setting point is reached.

Yield—2–2⅓ lb.

This recipe can be doubled exactly, but if trebled the amount of water required is only $3\frac{1}{2}$ pt. not $3\frac{3}{4}$ pt.

ORANGE JELLY MARMALADE

NOTE: No soaking of the fruit is necessary, and it is softened in 20 min. (compared with about 2 hr. by ordinary cooking). In spite of the quick cooking, the jelly is full of flavour.

2 lb. Seville *or* sweet oranges	**2½ pt. water**
Juice and pips from 3 lemons	**3 lb. sugar**

Wash the fruit; peel 2 of the oranges very thinly, carefully removing all the pith; shred the peel very finely and tie it loosely in a muslin bag. Roughly chop the 2 peeled oranges, together with the unpeeled oranges and put into the pressure cooker (from which the trivet has been removed). Add the lemon pips, the orange pips and pith, the muslin bag and the water. Bring to 10 lb. pressure in the usual way, and pressure cook for 20 min. Allow the pressure to reduce at room temperature. Remove the muslin bag and wash the shreds thoroughly in a strainer under cold water. Strain all the rest through a scalded jelly bag or double thickness of linen tea towel, waiting until all the liquid has dripped through (do not hurry the straining by squeezing as this will cloud the jelly). Rinse out the pressure cooker. Return to it the strained liquid, and heat slightly. Add the warmed sugar and strained lemon juice, stir over a low heat until dissolved. Bring to boil and boil rapidly in the open cooker for 5–10 min. Skim thoroughly. Add shreds and boil till setting point is reached.

Yield—about 4 lb.

SEVILLE ORANGE MARMALADE

2 lb. Seville oranges	**4 lb. sugar**
2 pt. water	**Juice of 2 lemons**

Wash the oranges and remove the peel and pips. Cut the fruit up roughly. Shred the peel according to taste. Tie the pips in a muslin bag. Remove the trivet from the pressure cooker, then add the prepared oranges, peel, muslin bag and water. Bring to 10 lb. pressure in the usual way and pressure cook for 10 min. Reduce pressure at room temperature, remove the bag of pips, and add warmed sugar and strained lemon juice. Return cooker to heat and stir until sugar is dissolved. Boil in the open cooker until setting point is reached (approx. 7 min.).

Yield—approx. 6½ lb.

TANGERINE JELLY MARMALADE

3 lb. tangerines *or* mandarins	**3 lemons**
	3 pt. water
1 grapefruit	**4 lb. sugar**

Wash all the fruit. Peel 8 of the tangerines or mandarins and be sure that all the pith is removed. Shred this peel finely, and tie loosely in a muslin bag. Chop up the 8 tangerines and the rest of the unpeeled, unpipped fruit and put together with the muslin bag and the water into a pressure cooker, from which the trivet has been removed. Bring to 10 lb. pressure in the usual way and cook for 12 min. Allow the pressure to reduce at room temperature then continue as for Orange Jelly Marmalade.

Yield—approx. 5½ lb.

THREE FRUIT MARMALADE

Approx. 2 lb. fruit—2 oranges, 1 grapefruit and 2 lemons	**1½ pt. water**
	4 lb. sugar

Cut the washed fruit in quarters. Remove pips and tie loosely in a muslin bag. (Note: do not use "seedless" fruit, otherwise a good set will not be obtained.) Remove the trivet from the pressure cooker; add the prepared fruit and the water and muslin bag. Bring to 10 lb. pressure in the usual way and pressure cook for 7 min. Reduce pressure at room temperature. Remove the muslin bag and chop the fruit, either coarsely or finely according to taste. Return the fruit to the cooker, replace on the heat and add the sugar, stirring over low heat until it is dissolved. Boil rapidly in the open cooker until setting point is reached.

Yield—approx. 6½ lb.

BOTTLING

FRUIT BOTTLING

FROM many successful bottling methods, we have chosen four to give in detail. The *Quick Deep Pan* method is probably the most useful for a busy housewife who wishes to complete a large amount of bottling in the shortest possible time. The *Slow Deep Pan* method is recommended for those who wish to display for exhibitions—this method is more likely to produce jars which are perfect in appearance.

If you want to buy only small quantities of fruit, or if you possess a garden and wish to process only two or three jars at a time, as the fruit ripens, the *Pressure Pan* method is speedy and ideal.

Oven methods are not really recommended. Oven temperatures are not always uniform and factors such as the size of the jars and the numbers being processed may affect the success of the finished result. But one Oven method is included for those housewives who do not possess a pressure pan or a large enough sterilizing pan for the "Deep Pan" methods.

PREPARING AND TESTING THE JARS

There are two main types of preserving jar—one which fastens with a screwband and the other fastening with clips or grips. Some are straight-sided, for easy packing, others have a "shoulder". Jam jars can also be used—fastened with special covers.

Always examine jars before use to see that they are unchipped. If the lid or the rim of the jar is chipped, discard it, because it would prevent an air-tight seal. Do not use metal covers a second time if they are bent or if the lacquer has been attacked by the fruit acid. It is not advisable to use rubber rings a second time. Test unused rubber rings by stretching them: if they are good, they feel elastic and should return to normal size.

Before filling the jars, wash them thoroughly and drain—do not wipe dry.

PREPARING THE SYRUP OR BRINE

Fruit can be preserved in plain water, but a sugar syrup gives a better flavour and colour. The quantity of sugar used for a sugar syrup may be varied according to taste, but the usual quantity for most fruits is *8 oz. granulated or loaf sugar to each 1 pt. of water*. Heat together and, when dissolved, bring to boiling-point and boil for 1 min. (If the syrup is to be used cold, save cooling time by heating the sugar with half the water and then adding the rest of the water cold.) If it is to be kept hot for long, put the lid on the pan to prevent evaporation.

If preferred, substitute equal weights of *golden syrup* or *honey* for sugar.

To prepare brine for bottling tomatoes—add ½ oz. salt to each 1 qt. of water. Bring to the boil and boil for 1 min.

CHOOSING, PREPARING AND PACKING THE FRUIT

Choose fresh, firm, ripe fruit (except gooseberries, which should be green and hard). It is a waste of time and labour to bottle damaged or over-ripe fruit. Grade according to size, so that fruit of the same size is packed into each jar. If necessary, use the handle of a wooden spoon to help to place firm fruit in position. To ensure a tight pack for soft fruit, tap the filled jars on a folded cloth or on the palm of the hand.

FRUIT

Apples: Peel, core, cut into slices, or rings ¼ in. thick. To prevent discoloration drop them into brine (1 oz. salt to 4 pt. water), keeping under surface with a plate. Drain, rinse and pack immediately.

Apples—(Solid Pack): After draining from brine (as above), scald in boiling water 2–3 min. This shrinks the fruit so that the jar can be tightly filled, with no air-spaces and little or no added liquid. A mixed pack of alternate layers of apples (solid pack) and blackberries (unscalded) is recommended.

Apricots: Choose fully ripe fruit, not too soft. Stalk and rinse. Pack whole, *or* halve by slitting and twisting the fruit; stone and pack quickly to avoid browning. A few cracked kernels can be added to each jar.

Blackberries: Choose large, juicy, fully ripe berries. Remove stalks, leaves and unsound fruit. For pressure pan, *see* p. 649.

Cherries: Should have small stones and plump flesh (Morello, for choice). Stalk and rinse. Can be stoned, but take care not to lose the juice.

Currants (Black, Red, White): Choose large, firm, juicy and well-flavoured currants. They should be evenly ripened and unbroken. Remove stalks, rinse. Red and white currants have large seeds and are best mixed with raspberries.

Damsons: Choose ripe, firm, purple fruit. Stalk and rinse.

Gooseberries: Choose green, hard and unripe berries. Top and tail and, if preserving in syrup, cut off a small slice at either end with a stainless-steel knife (this prevents shrivelling and toughening, but is not necessary with preserving by pressure pan).

Greengages: Choose firm, ripe fruit. Remove stalks. After processing, the fruit will turn greenish-brown and the syrup may be cloudy. But if a pressure pan is used the fruit should keep a good colour due to the short cooking time.

Loganberries: Choose firm, deep-red fruit. Handle as little as possible. Remove stalks, leaves and any fruit attacked by maggots. *See* p. 649 for pressure cooking.

Mulberries: Choose slightly under-ripe and use really freshly picked fruit. Handle as little as possible. Remove over-ripe and misshapen fruit.

Peaches: Choose a free-stone variety (e.g. Hale) just fully ripe. Halve and stone by slitting and twisting the fruit. Dip in a pan of boiling water for 1 min., then put into cold water: the skin should then peel off easily. Pack quickly.

Pears: Choose one of the best dessert varieties, e.g. Williams' Bon Chrétien, Conference, Doyenné du Comice, just fully ripened. Peel, halve and scoop out cores and fibres with a sharp-pointed teaspoon. Place in an acid brine (4 pt. water; 1 oz. salt; ½ oz. citric acid), keeping below surface with a plate. Rinse when ready for packing. Pack quickly.

Pears—cooking: Prepare like the dessert varieties. Then stew till tender in a sugar syrup (4–6 oz. sugar to 1 pt. water). Drain, pack and cover with the syrup in which they were cooked. Sterilize as for other pears. These cooking pears will be darker in colour than the dessert varieties.

Pineapples: Remove both ends, the peel, eyes and centre core from pineapples. Cut the fruit into rings or cubes. If using pressure pan, pressure cook in thick syrup (1 cup sugar; 2 cups water) for 7 min. before bottling.

Plums: Choose Victoria plums when they are fully grown but firm and just turning pink. Choose purple varieties before the colour has developed, when they are bright red. Choose yellow varieties when they are firm and lemon-yellow. Remove stalks, and rinse in cold water. Wipe to remove the bloom. Free-stone varieties can be halved, others must be packed whole. Prick whole plums before preserving by Pressure Pan method.

Raspberries: Choose large, firm, bright red and fully flavoured berries. Pick carefully, putting the fruit gently in shallow baskets to prevent squashing. Remove plugs and damaged fruit. Preserve as soon as possible—it is not usually necessary to rinse the fruit first. For pressure pan *see* p. 649.

Rhubarb: Choose Champagne or Linnaeus rhubarb and bottle it in the spring when it is tender and needs no peeling. Wipe the stalks and cut in short lengths. Pack straightaway (in water or syrup) *or* after soaking. *To soak* pour a hot syrup (8 oz. sugar to 1 pt. water) over the prepared rhubarb. Leave to soak and shrink for 8–12 hr. Pack, cover with the syrup.

To avoid a white deposit (unsightly but harmless) use previously boiled or softened water.

Strawberries: Hull the berries. Rinse fruit in cold water. Good preserved by pressure pan (*see* p. 649).

Tight Pack for small soft fruit, e.g. elderberries, blackberries, raspberries, strawberries, mulberries: Roll the fruit in castor sugar, then pack into the jars tightly, without any added liquid. Process as for Deep Pan methods.

Tomatoes: *Tomatoes in their own juice:* Dip into boiling water for up to 30 seconds (according to ripeness) then into cold water; the skins should then peel off easily. Leave whole, or pack in halves or quarters if large. Press tightly into the jars, sprinkling the layers with sugar and salt—use 1 teasp. sugar and 2 teasp. salt to each 2 lb. tomatoes. No additional liquid is needed.

Whole, unskinned tomatoes (best for Oven method). Remove stalks, rinse tomatoes and pack into jars. Use a brine (½ oz. salt to 1 qt. water) in place of syrup or water. *See* p. 650 for recipes for Tomato Purée and Tomato Juice.

Whortleberries: Prepare as for blackcurrants.

METHODS OF BOTTLING

QUICK DEEP PAN METHOD

1. Pack prepared fruit tightly into tested jars. Put rubber rings to soak in warm water.
2. Fill jars to overflowing with *HOT* (about 140° F.) syrup or water. For tomatoes use hot brine.
3. Dip the rubber rings in boiling water and put them on the jars, with the lids. Fasten with screwbands, clips or other grips.
4. If using screwbands, tighten them, *then unscrew ¼ turn to allow for expansion.*
5. Stand jars in the pan on wooden slats or on a thick piece of towelling or cardboard. See that they do not touch each other or the side of the pan. Cover completely with *WARM* (about 100° F.) water. Put on the lid of the pan.
6. Bring up to SIMMERING POINT (190° F.) in 25–30 min. Simmer for time indicated below. Then remove jars one at a time on to a wooden surface (use tongs to lift jars *or*, using a cup, empty out sufficient water to enable jars to be lifted with a cloth).
7. Tighten screwbands. Cool 24 hr., tightening screwbands further if necessary. Clips should hold properly without attention.
8. Next day, remove screwband or clip. Lift each jar by lid. If properly sealed the lid will stay on securely. Label with date and other details and store in a cool, dark, dry place. Wash, dry and grease screwbands and clips and store till next year.

PROCESSING TIMES FOR QUICK DEEP PAN METHOD

Simmer for time indicated below:

2 min. Apple rings, Blackberries, Currants (Black, Red, White), Gooseberries (for pies), Loganberries, Mulberries, Raspberries, Rhubarb (for pies), Strawberries, Whortleberries.

10 min. Apricots, Cherries, Damsons, Gooseberries (for dessert), Greengages, Plums (whole), Rhubarb (for dessert), Tight pack of soft Fruit (except Strawberries).

20 min. Apples (solid pack), Nectarines, Peaches, Pineapples, Plums (halved), Tight pack of Strawberries.

40 min. Pears, Tomatoes (whole).

50 min. Tomatoes (in own juice).

SLOW DEEP PAN METHOD

This is the same as the Quick Deep Pan method, with the following exceptions:

FRUIT BOTTLING

At Step 2, the jars are filled with *COLD* syrup, water or brine.

At Step 5, the fastened jars are covered with *COLD* water.

At Step 6, the water is raised gradually (i.e. in 90 min.) to the temperature indicated below, and is maintained at that temperature for the time stated below.

PROCESSING TIMES FOR SLOW DEEP PAN METHOD

Raise to 165° F. and maintain at that temperature for 10 min.

Apple rings, Blackberries, Currants (Black, Red, White), Gooseberries (for pies), Loganberries, Mulberries, Raspberries, Rhubarb (for pies), Strawberries, Whortleberries.

Raise to 180° F. and maintain at that temperature for 15 min.

Apples (solid pack), Apricots, Cherries, Damsons, Gooseberries (for dessert), Greengages, Nectarines, Plums (whole or halved), Peaches, Pineapples, Rhubarb (for dessert), Tight pack of soft Fruit.

Raise to 190° F. and maintain at that temperature for 30 min.

Pears, Tomatoes (whole).

Raise to 190° F. and maintain at that temperature for 40 min.

Tomatoes (in own juice).

PRESSURE PAN METHOD

(These instructions apply to most suitable-sized pressure pans with a gauge or weight control to maintain a steady pressure. But as different makes of pressure pan vary, consult also the manufacturer's handbook for your particular make).

1. Place clean, warm, tested preserving jars (*see* p. 645) into a large bowl of very hot water.

2. Remove jars one at a time and pack tightly to the top with prepared fruit (*see* pp. 646–647). Fill with *BOILING* syrup or water to within ¼ in. of the top.

3. Dip the rubber rings in boiling water and put them on the jars with the lids. Fasten with screwbands, clips or grips. *If using screwbands, tighten them, then unscrew them ¼ turn to allow for expansion.* Put jars back into the bowl of hot water until all are packed and fastened.

4. Meanwhile, put the trivet (inverted) and about 1½ pt. water into the pressure pan (water should be 1 in. deep in the pan). Add 1 tablesp. of vinegar or a little lemon juice to prevent the pan from staining. Bring to the boil.

5. Lift the prepared jars of fruit on to the trivet, making sure they do not touch each other or the sides of the pan.

6. Fix on the lid. Allow steam to escape from the centre vent until it will form drops of moisture on a knife blade passed through it.

7. *BRING UP TO 5 LB. PRESSURE*, adjusting the heat so that it takes about 3 min. to bring to pressure (i.e. on a MEDIUM heat if using an electric cooker).

8. Process according to the times given below. Lower the heat sufficiently at this stage to maintain a steady pressure. Fluctuations in pressure must be avoided because they cause loss of liquid from the jars and the fruit may be under-processed.

9. Remove the pan gently away from the heat. *Allow the pressure to drop at room temperature for 10 min.*

10. Lift out the jars one at a time on to a wooden surface, tightening screwbands immediately. Cool 24 hr., tightening screwbands further if necessary. Clips should hold properly without attention.

11. Test, label and store—see Step 8, "Quick Deep Pan method".

PROCESSING TIMES USING A PRESSURE PAN

Process at 5 lb. pressure for 1 min.

Apples (quarters), Apricots, Cherries, Currants (Black, Red, White), Damsons, Fruit Pulp, Fruit Salad, Gooseberries, Plums, Rhubarb (not soaked).

Process at 5 lb. pressure for 3 min.

Blackberries, Greengages, Loganberries, Raspberries, Strawberries.

Process at 5 lb. pressure for 3–4 min.

Peaches, Pineapples (for pineapples, *see* method of preparation, p. 646).

Process at 5 lb. pressure for 5 min.

Pears, Tomatoes (whole or halved).

Process at 5 lb. pressure for 15 min.

Tomatoes (solid pack).

SPECIAL PREPARATIONS FOR BOTTLING BY PRESSURE PAN

(*a*) SOFT FRUIT, e.g. blackberries, loganberries, raspberries, strawberries.

1. Lay the prepared fruit in a single layer in the bottom of a large enamel, glass or china bowl (not metal).
2. Prepare a syrup with 6 oz. sugar to 1 pt. water and pour, boiling, over the fruit. Leave to soak overnight.
3. Next morning, drain off the syrup (using this syrup to cover the fruit in the jars). Continue as from No. 1 of the directions on p. 648. The pressure cooking time for a solid pack of soft fruit like this is *3 min. at 5 lb. pressure.*

(*b*) FRUIT PULP, e.g. apples, cranberries, tomatoes.

1. Wash and cut up, without coring or peeling.
2. Remove the trivet from the pressure pan, and pressure cook the fruit or tomatoes in $\frac{1}{4}$ pt. water at 15 lb. pressure for 2–3 min. (NOTE: The pan must not be more than half full.)
3. Reduce pressure at room temperature. Sieve.
4. *While still hot* (re-heat if necessary), pour into the prepared warm jars, leaving 1 in. headspace.
5. Continue from No. 3–7 of the directions on p. 648.
6. Process at *5 lb. pressure for 1 min.* and continue with the directions.

(*c*) FRUIT SALAD: Any fruit may be used, but care should be taken not to use too large a proportion of red fruits, such as raspberries, blackcurrants, cherries, etc., or the syrup will be so dark in colour that it will spoil the appearance of fruits such as apricots, gooseberries, greengages, peaches, pears, pineapples.

Each fruit should be prepared in the usual way and the general instructions for bottling by pressure cooker should be followed. But as *only 1 min. at 5 lb. pressure* is necessary for processing, if hard fruits (such as pineapples or cooking pears) are used, they should be pre-cooked for 7 min. under pressure.

A good syrup should be used for the bottling —at least 8 oz. sugar to 1 pt. water to allow for the less sweet fruits which may be included.

OVEN METHOD

In the time-honoured Oven method, the fruit is packed into the jars, cooked in the oven, and then removed and boiling liquid added; but the dry heat of the oven causes the fruit to shrink. The Moderate Oven method given below is a newer and more successful adaptation.

1. Fill the warmed jars tightly with the prepared fruit (*see* pp. 646–7).
2. Fill to within 1 in. of the top with boiling syrup or water.
3. Put on the rubber rings and lids (both first dipped in boiling water). Both clips and screwbands should not be put on until after the processing.
4. Line a baking-sheet with newspaper, to catch any liquid should it boil over during heating. Stand the jars, 2 in. apart, on the paper.
5. Put in the central part of the oven, preheated for 15 min., to 300° F. Process for the times given below.
6. Remove on to a wooden surface. Fasten clips and screwbands and tighten screwbands further as the jars cool. Next day, test for set (see Step 8, "Quick Deep Pan method"), label and store.

NOTE: Four 1-lb. jars require the same processing time as two 2-lb. jars.

PROCESSING TIMES USING A MODERATE OVEN

30–40 min. (*if processing 1 lb.–4 lb.*)
45–60 min. (*if processing 5 lb.–10 lb.*)

Apple rings, Blackberries, Currants (Red,

Black. White), Gooseberries (for pies), Loganberries, Mulberries, Raspberries, Rhubarb (for pies), Whortleberries.

40–50 min. (*if processing 1 lb.–4 lb.*)
55–70 min. (*if processing 5 lb.–10 lb.*)
Apricots, Cherries, Damsons, Gooseberries (for dessert), Greengages, Plums (whole), Rhubarb (for dessert).

50–60 min. (*if processing 1 lb.–4 lb.*)
65–80 min. (*if processing 5 lb.–10 lb.*)
Apples (solid pack), Nectarines, Peaches, Pineapples, Plums (halved).

60–70 min. (*if processing 1 lb.–4 lb.*)
75–90 min. (*if processing 5 lb.–10 lb.*)
Pears, Tomatoes (whole).

70–80 min. (*if processing 1 lb.–4 lb.*)
85–100 min. (*if processing 5 lb.–10 lb.*)
Tomatoes (in own juice).

SPECIAL RECIPES FOR BOTTLING PULPED OR PURÉE FRUIT AND TOMATO JUICE

Fruit: Pulped soft and stone fruit, e.g. blackcurrants, apples, tomatoes, plums. (*See* p. 649 for bottling fruit pulp by Pressure Pan method). Avoid copper or iron utensils. Remove skins if necessary, stems and diseased or bruised portions. Peel and core apples. Stone plums. Stew with just sufficient water to prevent burning. When cooked right through, pour quickly (while still boiling) into hot, clean preserving jars. Seal *immediately* with hot lids and rubber rings dipped in boiling water. Process, using a pan with a false bottom.

To process: Cover the jars with hot water, raise to boiling-point and boil for 5 min. Remove from water. Test for seal next day.

Apple purée: Cut unpeeled apples into slices, removing bruised or diseased portions. Stew apples till soft in just sufficient water to prevent burning. Rub through a sieve. Add a paring of lemon rind and sugar to taste. Immediately return the pulp and rind to the pan, bring to the boil, stirring to dissolve the sugar, pour into hot preserving jars and seal at once. Process as for pulp above.

Tomato purée: Rinse the ripe tomatoes. Heat in a covered pan with a little salt and water. When soft, rub through a hair or nylon sieve. Reheat, and fill quickly into hot preserving jars. Fasten and process, using a pan with a false bottom.

To process: Cover the jars with hot water, raise to boiling-point, and boil for 10 min. Remove from water. Test for seal next day.

Tomato juice: Rinse and heat the ripe tomatoes in a covered pan till they are soft. Sieve through a hair or nylon sieve. To each quart of pulp add: $\frac{1}{2}$ pt. water, 1 teasp. salt, 1 oz. sugar and a pinch of pepper. Reheat, fasten and process as for Tomato Purée above.

PICKLES, CHUTNEYS AND SAUCES

POINTS TO WATCH

1. It is often economical to cut up mis-shapen vegetables and fruits for pickles, chutneys and sauces. But they should, nevertheless, be fresh—not over-ripe or in poor condition.

2. When making vegetable pickles, it is usual either to soak the vegetables in brine or to cover them with layers of salt. This draws some of the water from the vegetables. When they are covered with the spiced vinegar, they should be covered by at least ½ in. and the jars should be covered tightly so that none of the vegetables are left out of the vinegar by subsequent evaporation.

3. When making chutneys, it is advisable to make a trial lot first because tastes vary and it may be necessary to adjust the spices in the recipe. But remember when tasting that chutneys are always spicier when first made—they mellow on keeping.

4. Use aluminium, unchipped enamel-lined or monel metal pans, NOT brass, copper or iron.

5. If sieving is necessary, use a hair, nylon or fine-meshed monel metal sieve —other metals may give an unpleasant taste.

6. Cover the jars with one of the following:

(*a*) A cork, boiled to be thoroughly clean, and covered with greaseproof paper.

(*b*) Synthetic skin.

(*c*) A well-lacquered metal cap, lined with a layer of cork, waxed cardboard or vinegarproof paper. The vinegar must not come in contact with the metal otherwise it may cause corrosion and rusting.

(*d*) Greaseproof paper, covered with a circle of cotton material dipped in melted paraffin wax.

SPICED VINEGAR

Buy only the best bottled vinegar for pickling; this should have an acetic acid content of at least 5 per cent. It is false economy to buy cheap barrelled vinegar: if—as is often the case—the percentage of acetic acid is too low the pickles will not keep.

For exhibition, white vinegar is often recommended because it shows off the colour and texture of the pickle, but for home use, the flavour of malt vinegar is generally preferred.

To make spiced vinegar, add to 1 qt. of vinegar: ½ oz. cloves, ½ oz. allspice, ½ oz. ginger, ½ oz. cinnamon, ½ oz. white pepper.

NOTE: All the above spices should be whole, not ground. Buy them fresh. If you find this spice too strong, the quantities can be reduced—even halved.

Steep the spices in the unheated vinegar for 1–2 months. Shake the bottle occasionally. Then strain and re-cork the bottle until needed.

Quick method: If the spiced vinegar is wanted immediately, put the spices and vinegar into a basin. Cover the basin with a plate and stand it in a saucepan of cold water. Bring the water to the boil, remove the pan from the heat, and allow the spices to remain in the warm vinegar for about 2 hr. Keep the plate on top of the basin so that no flavour is lost. Strain the vinegar and it will be ready to use, either cold or hot according to the recipe.

TARRAGON VINEGAR

This can be bought ready-made, but if you grow tarragon it is cheaper to make the vinegar at home. Pick the leaves just before the herb flowers. Half-fill a wide-mouthed jar or bottle with the freshly gathered leaves (bang them lightly to bruise them). Fill the jar with best quality malt vinegar and cover. Leave for 2 weeks or longer before removing the leaves. Put a cork or stopper on the jar before storing.

PICKLES

MIXED PICKLE

Make a selection of available vegetables. Any of the following are suitable: small cucumbers, cauliflower, small onions, French beans. Prepare the vegetables: only the onions need be peeled, the rest should merely be cut into suitably sized pieces.

Put all into a large bowl, sprinkle with salt, and leave for 24 hr. Drain thoroughly and pack into jars. Cover with cold spiced vinegar, seal, and leave for at least a month before using.

PICCALILLI

2 lb. mixed vegetables (*see below*)
2 oz. cooking salt
1 pt. vinegar
15 chillies
½ lb. granulated sugar
2 oz. mustard
½ oz. turmeric
2 level tablesp. cornflour

Cut into small pieces a variety of vegetables such as cauliflower, cucumber, shallots and young kidney beans, weighing about 2 lb. in all when prepared. Place in a large earthenware bowl and sprinkle with the cooking salt.

Leave to stand for 24 hr. and then drain well. Boil the vinegar and chillies for 2 min., allow to stand for ½ hr. and then strain the vinegar.

Mix together the sugar, mustard, turmeric and cornflour. Blend with a little of the cooled vinegar, bring the remainder of the vinegar back to the boil, pour over the blend, return to the saucepan and boil for 3 min. Remove from the heat and fold in the strained vegetables. Pack into prepared jars and cover at once with vinegar-proof covers.

PICKLED APPLES AND ONIONS

Equal quantities of onions and sour apples	**Spiced vinegar**
	½ oz. salt to every 2 pt. spiced vinegar

Slice the peeled onions and the peeled, cored apples. Mix well together and fill into jars. Pour on sufficient HOT salted spiced vinegar to cover. Seal. This pickle is ready to use when cold.

PICKLED BEETROOT

Beetroots are obtainable most of the year and, like all the root crops, require cooking before pickling. Wash off any soil still clinging to the roots, taking care not to break the skin, for beetroot bleeds easily. If pickling for immediate use, simmer for 1½–2 hr. When cold, skin and cut into squares or slices, and cover with unspiced or spiced vinegar, whichever is preferred.

If pickling for storage, bake the roots in a moderate oven **(350° F., Gas 4)** until tender and, when cold, skin and cut into squares—it packs better that way for keeping; cover with spiced vinegar to which has been added ½ oz. salt to each pint.

Beetroot contains a good deal of sugar, and fermentation is more likely than with other vegetables, so seal thoroughly well to exclude air.

PICKLED CAULIFLOWER

Cauliflower must not be too mature for pickling, and close-packed heads are best. Break into even-sized pieces, but don't use a knife at all (the stalk of cauliflower stains easily, and this is less likely to occur when broken and not cut). Steep in a brine (½ lb. salt to 3 pt. water) for 24 hr., drain really well, pack into jars and cover with cold spiced vinegar. If pickling for use later in other mixed pickles, unspiced vinegar can be used for the temporary pickling.

As a straight pickle, cauliflower is best sweet, and sweetening can most easily be done by adding anything from 1 teasp. to 1 tablesp. sugar (according to size of jar) a couple of days before the pickle is wanted. Turn the jar up 2–3 times till the sugar is dissolved.

This is much simpler than putting down in a sweet pickle and less likely to develop fermentation.

PICKLED CUCUMBER

The easiest way to pickle cucumbers is to quarter them lengthwise, cut into smaller pieces, brine with dry salt for 24 hr., then pack and cover with spiced vinegar. Like most of the vegetables they are best mixed with others.

PICKLED GHERKINS

The small immature cucumbers that are known as dills or gherkins require a longer process, especially if their deep green colour is to be fixed, and they need partial cooking.

Method 1: Select gherkins of a uniform size, place in a saucepan and cover with standard brine (½ lb. salt to 3 pt. water). Bring to nearly boiling-point, do not actually boil, but simmer for 10 min.

Drain until cold, then pack into jars and cover with spiced vinegar, preferably aromatic.

Method 2: Brine the gherkins for 3 days in standard brine. Drain off the brine and repeat for another 3 days. Drain and soak in water to which alum has been added in the proportion of 1 dessertsp. to 2 qt. for 6 hr., then drain well and simmer for 10 min. in spiced vinegar, pack into warmed jars and cover with the still hot vinegar.

NOTE: The first method is the simplest, but No. 2 gives rather a better colour.

A great many people prefer gherkins sweet; they are particularly popular at cocktail parties. These are quite easy to prepare from the ordinary pickled fruit.

A spoonful of sugar added to the jar and

shaken up, then allowed to stand for 24 hr., is all that is necessary. It is not advisable to do this too long in advance as sugar added to a cold pickle in this way may very easily start to ferment. Another way is to turn the gherkins out on to a shallow dish, the one in which they will be served, and sprinkle with sugar. They can be done this way with a few hours' notice.

PICKLED ONIONS

Use small even-sized pickling onions. Peel with a stainless knife and drop them into a basin of salted water until all have been peeled. Remove from water and allow to drain thoroughly before packing into jars or bottles. Cover with cold spiced vinegar and keep for at least 1 month before using.

PICKLED FRESH PEACHES

6 lb. fresh peaches
1 oz. cloves
1 oz. allspice
1 oz. cinnamon
3 lb. granulated sugar
1½ pt. distilled malt vinegar

Peel the peaches (dipping them first into boiling water then into cold makes peeling easy). Halve, remove the stones and crack some to take out the kernels. Tie the spices in muslin and place with the sugar and vinegar into a pan; bring to the boil to dissolve the sugar. Add the peaches and simmer till just tender but not overcooked or broken. Lift out and pack into clean, warm jars with a few of the blanched kernels. Meanwhile, continue to boil the liquid until it thickens, then pour it over the peaches. Tie down whilst hot and store for at least a week.

PEACHES PRESERVED IN BRANDY

Peaches
Sugar
Water
Brandy

Dip peaches in hot water, one at a time, and rub off "fur" with clean towel. Weigh. For each lb. fruit, allow ¾ lb. sugar and 8 oz. (in a measuring jug) water. Boil sugar and water together for 10 min. without stirring. Add peaches to syrup and cook (only a few at a time to prevent bruising) for about 5 min. until tender. Remove peaches from syrup with strainer and pack firmly into hot sterilized jars. Continue cooking syrup, after removing peaches, until thick. Cool and measure. Add equal quantity of brandy. Bring to boiling point and fill jars of peaches to overflowing. Seal.

PICKLED PEARS

2 lb. hard cooking pears
2 level teasp. whole cloves
2 level teasp. allspice
1 level teasp. crushed cinnamon stick
A small piece of root ginger
8 oz. sugar
½ pt. vinegar

Crush the spices together and tie in a piece of muslin. Add the muslin bag and the sugar to the vinegar and heat gently until the sugar is dissolved. Peel and core the pears, cut into quarters or eighths and simmer gently in the sweetened spiced vinegar until they are tender but not overcooked or broken. Lift out and pack into clean, warm jars. Meanwhile, continue to boil the vinegar until it thickens slightly, then pour it over the pears, filling each jar. Tie down and seal securely when cold.

NOTE: These are best kept for 2–3 months before use.

PICKLED RED CABBAGE

Choose a firm, fresh cabbage. After removing any discoloured outer leaves, cut the cabbage into quarters and then into shreds. Put layers of the shreds into a large basin or dish, sprinkling each layer with salt. Leave overnight. Next day, drain very thoroughly in a colander, pressing out all the surplus liquor.

Pack layers of the shreds into large jars; pack about 3 in. of cabbage, cover with a layer of very thinly sliced onion, and sprinkle with 1 teasp. brown sugar. Then add another 3 in. of cabbage, another layer of onion and another teaspoon of sugar. Continue until the jars are filled, ending with the onion and sugar.

Cover with cold spiced vinegar, tie down and leave for at least 5 days to a week before opening the jar.

NOTE: Do not make too much of this pickle at a time, because it will lose its essential crispness after 2 or 3 months' storage.

PICKLED SHALLOTS

Use even-sized shallots. Do not skin them, place straight in a brine (1 lb. salt to 1 gallon water), leave for 12 hr.

Remove from brine and peel, using a stainless knife. Cover with fresh brine, making sure that all are kept below surface and leave for a further 24–36 hr. Drain thoroughly. Pack tightly in the jars. Cover with cold spiced vinegar so that the vinegar comes ½ in. above onions and keep for 3 months before use.

PICKLED WALNUTS

Use walnuts whose shells have not begun to form. Prick well with a silver fork; if the shell can be felt, do not use the walnut. The shell begins to form opposite the stalk, about ¼ in. from the end.

Cover with a brine (1 lb. salt to 1 gal. water) and leave to soak for about 6 days. Drain, make fresh brine, and leave to soak for a further 7 days.

Drain, and spread in a single layer on dishes, leaving them exposed to the air, preferably in sunshine, until they blacken (1–2 days). Pack into jars and cover with hot spiced vinegar. Tie down when cold and leave for at least a month before using.

NOTE: To help to prevent stained hands, wear gloves when handling the walnuts.

CHUTNEYS AND KETCHUPS

APPLE CHUTNEY

6 lb. apples
2 lb. sultanas
¾ lb. preserved ginger
3 pt. vinegar
3½ lb. sugar
1 oz. salt
1 teasp. allspice

Peel, core and chop the apples into small pieces and chop up the sultanas and ginger. Mix the vinegar, sugar, salt and spice together and bring to the boil, then add the apples and simmer for 10 min. before adding the ginger and sultanas. Simmer until the mixture becomes fairly thick, then pour into the jars.

CHINESE GOOSEBERRY CHUTNEY

12 Chinese gooseberries peeled and cut up
1 large banana, cut up
1 small cup sultanas *or* raisins
¼ lb. preserved ginger
1 dessertsp. *or* a little less of salt
3 medium-sized grated onions
2 lemons, peeled and cut into chunks
1 teasp. ground ginger
1 large cup brown sugar
½ teasp. pepper
1 large cup vinegar

Put all into a saucepan, add the vinegar—it should just cover, so add more if necessary—and simmer about 1½ hr. Mash with the potato masher—do not strain through a colander. When cool, bottle and cork well.

GOOSEBERRY CHUTNEY

4 lb. gooseberries
¼ lb. mustard seed
1 lb. moist sugar
1 qt. vinegar
1 lb. onions
1½ lb. stoned raisins
2 oz. allspice
¼ lb. salt

Bruise the mustard seed gently. Mix the sugar with 1 pt. of the vinegar and boil until a syrup forms, then add the finely-chopped onions, raisins and spice.

Boil the gooseberries in the rest of the vinegar until tender, then mix both lots together and cook until it thickens. Bottle and tie down tightly.

NOTE: The longer kept the better.

GREEN TOMATO CHUTNEY

5 lb. green tomatoes
1 lb. onions
½ oz. peppercorns
1 oz. salt
1 lb. sugar
1 qt. vinegar
½ lb. raisins
½ lb. sultanas

Slice the tomatoes and chop the onions and mix together in a basin with the peppercorns and salt. Allow this to stand overnight. Next day boil up the sugar in the vinegar, then add the raisins (which may be chopped) and the sultanas. Simmer for 5 min., then add the tomatoes and onions, and simmer till thick.

TOMATO KETCHUP (1)

6 lb. ripe tomatoes	**½ teasp. cloves**
1 pt. vinegar	**½ teasp. cinnamon**
½ lb. sugar	**½ teasp. cayenne pepper**
1 oz. salt	
½ teasp. allspice	

Cut the tomatoes into quarters, place them in a preserving-pan with the salt and vinegar and simmer until the tomatoes are quite soft and broken up. Strain the mixture through coarse muslin or a nylon sieve, then return the purée to the preserving-pan and add the sugar. Continue to simmer till the ketchup starts to thicken, and then add the spices a little at a time, stirring thoroughly until the flavour is to taste.

When the ketchup is reasonably thick, fill into hot bottles and seal immediately, or allow it to cool slightly, then fill the bottles and sterilize at 170° F. for 30 min.

Remember it will be thicker when cold than hot, so don't reduce it too far.

TOMATO KETCHUP (2)

12 ripe tomatoes	**2 teasp. cinnamon**
2 onions	**2 teasp. allspice**
1 pt. vinegar	**2 teasp. grated nutmeg**
3 tablesp. sugar	**½ teasp. cayenne pepper**
1 tablesp. salt	
2 teasp. cloves	

Cut the tomatoes into quarters and chop the onions finely. Put all the ingredients into a preserving-pan, bring to the boil and cook slowly for 2½ hr. Through very coarse muslin strain out the tomato skins, fill into bottles, sterilize at 170° F. for 30 min., and close whilst hot.

TOMATO KETCHUP (3)

¼ pt. malt vinegar	**6 oz. sugar**
1 flat teasp. pickling spice	**Pinch of cayenne pepper**
3½ lb. tomatoes	**½ oz. salt**
¼ lb. onions, peeled	**1 tablesp. tarragon vinegar**
½ lb. apples	

Bring the pickling spice to the boil with the malt vinegar and leave to infuse for 2 hr. before straining. Meanwhile, cut up the tomatoes, onions and apples (the onions should be peeled, but there is no need to peel or core the tomatoes and apples). Simmer these cut-up fruits and vegetables very slowly in a covered pan—the juice from the tomatoes should be sufficient to prevent burning. When they are thoroughly softened, rub through a hair or nylon sieve. Return the pulp to the pan; add the sugar, pepper and salt, and boil—with the lid off the pan—till the sauce begins to thicken, stirring occasionally with a wooden spoon. Add the strained malt vinegar and the tarragon vinegar. Boil—with the lid off the pan—till thick and creamy. Pour into hot bottles and seal. Sterilize in a simmering water bath for 30 min.

CHUTNEYS AND SAUCES—USING A PRESSURE COOKER

APPLE CHUTNEY

3 lb. apples	**¼ teasp. cayenne pepper**
1 lb. onions	**¼ lb. preserved ginger**
½ pt. vinegar	**½ lb. sultanas**
1 dessertsp. salt	**1½ lb. sugar**

Peel, core and cut up apples. Peel onions and slice finely. Remove trivet. Put the apples and onions into the pressure cooker, together with vinegar and all ingredients, except sugar. Stir well, cover cooker and bring to 15 lb. pressure in usual way. Pressure cook 10 min. and allow pressure to reduce at room temperature. Remove cover, add sugar, stir until dissolved, then boil steadily until the chutney is the consistency of thick jam. Pour into hot jars and seal immediately.

GREEN TOMATO CHUTNEY

3 lb. green tomatoes	**½ oz. root ginger**
1 lb. sour apples	**1 teasp. salt**
¾ lb. dates	**¼ pt. vinegar**
¼ lb. onions	**¼ lb. sugar**

Skin the tomatoes. Peel and core the apples and cut into very small pieces with the dates. Chop the onions. Tie the ginger in a muslin bag. Remove the trivet from the pressure cooker. Put all the ingredients, except the sugar, into the pressure cooker. Stir well, cover, bring to 15 lb. pressure and pressure cook for 10 min. Reduce pressure at room temperature. Add the sugar and simmer with the lid off the cooker until the chutney is of a thick consistency. Remove the ginger. Put the chutney into warm jars and seal.

PLUM CHUTNEY

3 lb. plums	**4 tablesp. cinnamon**
2 medium onions	**4 tablesp. allspice**
2 medium apples	**1½ tablesp. salt**
4 tablesp. ground ginger	**1 pt. vinegar (approx.)**
	¾ lb. sugar

Peel and chop the onions; peel, core and chop the apples; stone the plums and cut the plums in quarters. Remove the trivet from the pressure cooker. Put into the cooker the plums, onions and apples, the spices and salt and half the vinegar. Bring to the boil slowly in the open cooker, then cover, bring to 15 lb. pressure in the usual way, and cook for 10 min. Reduce pressure at room temperature. Return the cooker to the heat and, stirring all the time, add some of the vinegar gradually until the mixture is thick and smooth. Add the sugar and if necessary a little more of the vinegar, then boil rapidly until the chutney is the consistency of thick jam. Pour into hot jars and seal immediately.

RED TOMATO CHUTNEY

2 lb. tomatoes	**3 teasp. mixed whole spice**
1 apple	
1 onion	**1 oz. salt**
6 oz. sultanas	**½ pt. vinegar**
3 oz. dates	**½ lb. brown sugar**

Skin the tomatoes. Peel, core and slice the apple. Peel and slice the onion. Wash the sultanas and dates in hot water before chopping. Remove the trivet from the pressure cooker, then put in these ingredients. Add the spices, tied in a muslin bag, the salt and ¼ pt. of the vinegar. Bring to 15 lb. pressure and cook for 10 min. Allow pressure to reduce at room temperature. Add the rest of the vinegar and the sugar and stir until the sugar is dissolved. Bring to the boil and simmer gently, in the open cooker, until thick. Pour into hot jars and seal immediately.

TOMATO SAUCE

6 lb. tomatoes	**Pinch of cayenne pepper**
¼ pt. water	
½ teasp. ground ginger	**1 oz. salt**
½ teasp. ground mace	**½ lb. sugar**
½ teasp. ground cloves	**1 gill vinegar**

Slice the tomatoes; remove the trivet from the pressure cooker and put the tomatoes in the cooker together with the water. Bring to 15 lb. pressure over a medium heat, and pressure cook for 3 min. Reduce pressure immediately with cold water, and rub the pulp through a hair or nylon sieve. Dissolve the spices, salt and sugar in the vinegar and return, together with the sieved tomatoes, to the open cooker. Stir over a medium heat until the consistency of thick cream—this takes ½ hr. or longer.

With a pressure cooker, it is easy to sterilize this sauce so that it can be kept.

(*a*) Pour the sauce immediately into hot, prepared bottling jars, leaving 1 in. head space; adjust rings and lids; if using screw-top jars, screw bands tight, unscrewing ¼ turn.

(*b*) Rinse out the cooker and return it to the stove with 1½ pt. boiling water, to which 1 tablesp. vinegar has been added, and put in the inverted trivet.

(*c*) Lift in the prepared jars, and bring cooker to 5 lb. pressure over a medium heat. This process should take approximately 5 min.

(*d*) Pressure cook for 2 min.

(*e*) Remove the cooker from the heat and reduce pressure at room temperature for 10 min.

(*f*) Lift out jars; tighten screwbands and leave for 24 hr.

(*g*) Test seal and store in a cool dark place.

Yield—2 pt. of sauce

DRYING AND SALTING

DRYING—Points to Note

1. Use fresh fruits and young, tender vegetables. They usually need to be dried on trays. Special trays can be bought or they can be improvised, e.g. by covering a wire cake rack or oven rack with a loose piece of muslin.

2. In good weather it is sometimes possible to dry fruits and vegetables in the sunshine or in a current of warm air by an open window. But it is generally better to rely on artificial heat, using a temperature of 120°–150° F. A cool oven can be used, or—on several successive days—the residual heat from the oven; alternatively, use a rack over a hot water cistern, or a rack over a coal range, provided there is some protection from the dust.

3. The drying can either take several hours or, if intermittent, 2 or 3 days.

4. It is important to heat very slowly at first to prevent the outside of fruit from hardening or skins from bursting.

5. To store dried fruit and vegetables: leave for 12 hr. to cool at ordinary room temperature, then pack in wooden or cardboard boxes lined with greaseproof paper. Keep in a dry place.

DRIED APPLE RINGS

Peel and core the apples and, after removing all blemishes, cut into rings ¼ in. thick. Place immediately into salt water (2 oz. salt to 1 gal. water). After a few minutes, shake off superfluous water and thread the rings on sticks. Balance them across a baking-tin and put to dry at a temperature of not more than 140° F. If they are dried in continuous heat this may take about 6 hr. When they are dry enough, they should resemble chamois leather in texture. If the centre is pressed with the thumb-nail it should resist the pressure and no juice should ooze out of the apple ring.

DRIED PLUMS

Use a dark-skinned, fleshy variety, e.g. Pond's Seedling. Wash, if necessary, halve and stone, then put to dry. The temperature must be low at first (120° F.) till the skins begin to shrivel. It can then be raised gradually to 150° F. When it is dry enough, gentle squeezing will not break the skin of the plum or squeeze out any juice from it.

DRIED MUSHROOMS

Use fresh-picked mushrooms. Remove the stems. If the skins are clean and white, it is not necessary to peel the mushrooms. Spread them on trays to dry. Alternatively, thread them on a string, tying a knot between each, and hang up to dry, in a temperature not more than 120° F., until they are crisp.

DRIED PARSLEY

Wash the parsley and dry in a cloth to remove surplus moisture. Spread on muslin on an oven shelf or tray. Put at the top of a hot oven **(450° F.)** until dried—about 1 min. Crush between the fingers, then sieve to a coarse powder.

DRIED THYME AND SAGE

Wash, shake the herbs and dry in a cloth to remove surplus moisture. Put the bunches on paper in a warm place. As soon as the leaves can be shaken off the stalks, remove them all and store the thyme in a jar with a tight fitting lid.

NOTE: Sage takes longer to dry than thyme and needs to be rubbed through the fingers and sieved.

DRIED MINT AND OTHER HERBS

Wash and dry on a cloth to remove surplus moisture. Tie in a bundle, then put into a paper bag, binding the top of the bag with string so that the herbs are encased with only the stalks projecting. The paper protects them from dust. Hang in a warm place to dry.

SALTING BEANS

Choose fresh, young, tender French beans or runner beans. Wash and dry them and top-and-tail to remove strings. Slice runner beans but leave French beans whole. To every 3 lb. beans weigh out 1 lb. kitchen salt—NOT free-running salt. (Weigh accurately and do not use less than this quantity otherwise the beans will become slimy and will not keep.) Pack the salt and beans into a large glass or stoneware jar in the following manner: pack a layer of salt into the bottom of the jar; on top of this, press down very firmly a layer of beans; add another layer of salt, another layer of beans, and continue until the jar is full, finishing with a layer of salt, each layer to be about ½ in. thick. Cover, and leave for 3 or 4 days. At the end of this time, you will find that the salt is drawing moisture from the beans and forming a brine, and that there will be room to fill up with more beans and salt, again pressing down very firmly and finishing with a layer of salt. When full to the top, cover the jar securely with several layers of greaseproof paper.

To cook salted beans: Take out as many as required, wash them thoroughly in cold water, then soak them for a couple of hours in warm water—don't soak them overnight or they will toughen. Boil in unsalted water till tender.

QUICK FREEZING IN THE HOME

QUICK FREEZING, often referred to as Deep Freezing, is one of the simplest methods of preserving fruits and vegetables, meat, poultry and game—as well as fish and other foods—and it is a method which is becoming increasingly popular.

Many refrigerators now provide large frozen-food compartments which will store packets of frozen foods for several weeks, but they should not be confused with the quick-freeze units which are provided on very few refrigerators. Usually a special freezer cabinet has to be bought.

Temperatures in the ordinary domestic refrigerator (34°–50° F. is reckoned as the "safety zone") are not low enough for deep freezing. The fresh food has to be frozen between 0° F. and minus 10° F. or colder, and has to be stored at a temperature of about 0° F. When frozen at the lower temperatures, food keeps for longer periods in the prime condition in which it was picked or bought. Fruits and vegetables should keep for 9 months to a year; meat, poultry and game *can* be kept longer, but it is generally uneconomic. In the process of freezing, the growth of bacteria, yeasts and moulds is arrested, so keeping the food safe from deterioration provided the storage temperature is maintained at approximately 0° F. and not allowed to fluctuate too much.

Careful use of a freezer will fairly soon offset the capital outlay on the machine. Large quantities of home-grown and home-reared produce can be preserved, at their prime, in glut periods. Moreover, when cooking meals "make two and freeze one" saves time, labour and fuel, and prevents wastage of ingredients and money. So the great advantage of preserving food by freezing is its long-term economy.

CHOICE OF FOOD

Many varieties of fruits and vegetables have been found excellent for freezing. But see that they are near ripe, firm, in perfect condition and freshly picked. Vegetables should be picked when they are young, barely mature. Freezing cannot improve poor food, so avoid any which is over-ripe, damaged or tasteless. Try to freeze the produce as soon as it is picked but, if this is not possible, keep it in a cool place, preferably a refrigerator—but not longer than 12–24 hours.

CHOICE OF CONTAINERS

Foods to be frozen must be suitably wrapped or packed to avoid drying out in the freezer. If even-sized containers are carefully stacked, it should be possible to pack about 28 lb. of prepared fruit or vegetables into 1 cubic foot of storage space. Make up packages of a size most suitable to serve the family for one meal; this avoids left-over defrosted food. IT MUST NOT BE RE-FROZEN ONCE IT HAS THAWED.

The manufacturers of the Deep Freeze Cabinets generally sell suitable containers and wrapping materials. If possible, choose square or rectangular cartons rather than irregular-shaped containers which take up more space. They should be air-tight (*see* SEALING, p. 665). Foil dishes and plastic boxes are not cheap but they can be washed and used again. Wrapping materials must be moisture-vapour-proof, such as polythene, aluminium foil and cling film. These will not go brittle at low-temperatures. Polythene bags can be heat-sealed with a warm iron or curling tongs, or twisted and tied with a plastic bag fastener to close. Large articles such as chicken, turkeys, joints, etc. can be over-wrapped with mutton cloth or paper after they have been sealed in a moisture-vapour-proof wrap. This is to protect the wrap from being torn by another package in the freezer.

Avoid glass preserving jars—they might crack and they slow down the time of freezing. Specially avoid any jar with a "shoulder" which makes it narrower at the top than the base—this makes it impossible to turn out the food in its frozen state.

Fruits

Fruits may be frozen plain, unsweetened. But for the best flavour, colour and texture, it is advisable to:

(*a*) freeze them with granulated sugar. (Sprinkle the recommended amount of sugar over the fruit in a basin and stir lightly when the sugar begins to melt in the juice.)

or (*b*) cover them with a syrup.

Recipes for Syrup

Note: prepare this in advance and use when quite cold. It can be stored for a week or so in a refrigerator.

The amount of sugar used can be varied according to taste, the recommended strengths are:

2 oz. sugar dissolved in water and made up to 1 pt.	= 10%
4 oz. sugar dissolved in water and made up to 1 pt.	= 20%
6 oz. sugar dissolved in water and made up to 1 pt.	= 30%
8 oz. sugar dissolved in water and made up to 1 pt.	= 40%
10 oz. sugar dissolved in water and made up to 1 pt.	= 50%

Method: Bring the sugar and water just to the boil. Cover to prevent evaporation and put to one side until quite cold. Allow about 1 pt. of syrup to each 2 lb. fruit. This should be sufficient to cover the fruit.

Vegetables

In order to keep the colour, flavour and nutrient value during storage, it is essential to scald vegetables before packing and freezing.

To scald

Do not scald more than 1–2 lb. of vegetables at a time. After preparing the vegetables, bring some water to a rolling boil in a large saucepan (allow 8 pt. of water for 1–2 lb. of non-leafy vegetables; for leafy vegetables, allow 12 pt. of water).

Place the vegetables in a wire basket or in a muslin bag. Immerse them in the boiling water, note the time, and bring the water rapidly to the boil again. Move the vegetables around in the water for the time given in the table below. Remove *immediately* the time is up, and chill thoroughly in ice-cold water. Drain, pack into a moisture-vapour-proof container and seal. A polythene bag is an easy container to use in freezing vegetables.

The same water may be used for successive batches of the same vegetable. Do not add any salt to the water—salt should not be added until the frozen vegetables are removed from their packets for cooking.

FILLING THE CONTAINERS FOR FRUITS AND VEGETABLES

(1) Just as water expands when turning into ice, so fruit purée or fruit in syrup expand when frozen. Therefore, the container should never be filled to capacity. Leave $\frac{1}{2}$–$\frac{3}{4}$ in. head space, according to the size of the carton.

(2) If the fruit is packed plain or in dry sugar, there is no need to leave space. It is the water which expands, not the fruit.

(3) Vegetables are packed without added liquid, so they can come almost to the brim of the container, or can be wrapped tightly in suitable material.

(4) Avoid wetting the seal edges of packets. A wide-mouthed funnel is useful for filling neatly.

Fruit	*Method of Preparation*	*Type of Pack*
Apple slices (good cooking variety)	Peel, core and slice. Scald for 3 min. (Work quickly to prevent discoloration. If cutting up large quantities, scald them in batches.)	Pack plain *or* cover completely with 20% syrup.
Apple purée (good cooking variety)	Stew, then rub through a sieve.	Mix 1 lb. granulated sugar with 4–5 lb. pulped apple, *or* freeze without sugar.
Apricots	Wash, cut in halves, stone (not necessary to peel).	Cover with 40% syrup.
Blackberries Cranberries	Sort and stem. If really necessary, rinse gently in ice-cold water and drain well.	Pack plain (sugar can be added at the cooking stage) *or* cover with 50% syrup *or* mix 1 lb. granulated sugar with 3–4 lb. fruit.
Blackberry and Apple	Clean the blackberries, Peel, core and slice the apples, working quickly to avoid browning. Mix in required quantities.	Mix 1 lb. granulated sugar with 4–5 lb. fruit.
Cherries (a well-flavoured black variety)	Stem. Rinse gently in ice-cold water. Stone if desired.	Cover with 30% syrup.
Currants (black or red)	Stem. If really necessary, rinse gently in ice-cold water and drain well.	Cover with 30% syrup, *or* mix 1 lb. granulated sugar with 3 lb. currants.
Gooseberries	Pick just before fully ripened. Top and tail. Wash in ice-cold water. Drain.	Pack plain if for cooking, or with sugar if desired.
Grapes (delicate flavour, tender skins)	Stem. Wash in ice-cold water. Drain. Cut in half and take the pips out. Grapes need careful defrosting.	Cover with 40% syrup.
Grapefruit, oranges, tangerines	Chill. Wash, peel and remove all pith. Remove segments by cutting along membrane (or halve and remove the fruit pulp with a grapefruit spoon). Remove pips. (Work quickly, pre-	Pack in own juice without sugar *or* mix 1 part granulated sugar with 4 parts fruit segments by weight *or*

Fruit	*Method of Preparation*	*Type of Pack*
	paring one or two packages at a time.)	cover with 50% syrup.
Juice of grapefruit, oranges, tangerines, lemons	Extract the juice and strain it through a double thickness of muslin. Fill into the containers to within ½ in. of the lid.	Freeze plain, immediately.
Loganberries, raspberries	Look over carefully. Do not wash them unless necessary. If essential, rinse a few at a time in ice-cold water. Drain.	Cover with 40% syrup *or* mix 1 lb. granulated sugar with 3–4 lb. fruit.
Loganberry *or* raspberry purée	After sorting and rinsing if necessary, rub fruit through a sieve.	Mix 1 part sugar with 4–5 parts sieved fruit.
Peaches	Peel, stone and slice.	Cover with 40% syrup.†
Plums (dark variety)	Stem. Rinse in ice-cold water. Drain.	Pack plain *or* cover with 40% syrup.
Rhubarb	Wash, trim and cut stalks into 1 in. lengths.	Pack plain *or* cover with 30% syrup *or* mix 1 lb. granulated sugar with 5 lb. rhubarb.
Strawberries (firm, ripe, well-coloured)	Remove calyx. Rinse a few at a time in ice-cold water. Drain. Slice or leave whole. Weigh.	Mix 1 lb. granulated sugar with 4–5 lb. fruit *or* cover with 40% syrup.
Strawberry purée	Remove calyx. See Loganberry, raspberry purée.	

† To help preserve the natural colour, slice the peaches into a citric acid solution (¼ teasp. citric acid dissolved in 1 qt. water. Leave 1–2 min., drain and pack with syrup.) *Or* add ¼ teasp. ascorbic acid to each teacup of syrup before pouring it over the sliced fruit.

Vegetable	*Method of Preparation*	*Scalding Time*
Asparagus	Grade into thick and thin stems. Wash, scrape off bracts, cut so that stems measure 6 in. from the tips.	Thin stems: 2 min. Thick stems: 4 min.
Broad beans (young, tender)	Remove pods.	3 min.
Beans—French *or* Runner (small, tender)	Wash, top and tail, string if necessary. Leave small beans whole; slice larger ones.	2–3 min.

Vegetable	*Method of Preparation*	*Scalding Time*
Broccoli, Purple Sprouting	Cut into even lengths, about 2–3 in. long. Wash carefully.	4 min.
Brussels Sprouts (small, tight "button" sprouts)	Wash carefully.	4 min.
Carrots (young, even sizes)	Wash, scald, then cool and rub off the skins. Leave whole or slice or dice before packing for freezing.	5 min.
Cauliflower and Broccoli (Winter Cauliflower)	Break into florets 2 in. across.	3 min.
Corn-on-the-cob (just mature)	Cut off tough skin, strip off the outer green leaves and the silky threads, and cut off any immature grains. Wash.	Small: 4 min. Large: 6 min.
Whole grain sweet corn	Prepare as for corn-on-the-cob, cut off the grain with a sharp knife. After scalding and cooling, pack into containers for freezing.	
Peas (good cooking variety, just mature)	Remove pods.	1–2 min.
Potatoes (new—avoid potatoes which tend to blacken when cleaned)	Wash, scrape.	2 min.
Spinach	Wash very thoroughly in several changes of water until free of dirt. Remove tough stems. Divide into batches each weighing about 3 oz.	$2\frac{1}{2}$ min.
Vegetable Purées (asparagus, beetroot, carrots, parsnips, peas, spinach *or* turnips)	Cook in boiling water or steam till tender. Mash with a potato ricer so that the purée is smooth without having air whipped into it, or use a kitchen utensil made specially for puréeing foods. Pack into the container, heat-seal if necessary, label and freeze.	

Poultry

Choose only the best-quality, healthy, well-formed birds for quick freezing. Clean and wash well in running water and drain.

For freezing, truss the bird as for the table. Wrap the well-washed giblets in foil or plastic material and pack separately.

Package the bird in a moisture-vapour-proof container, a bag being the most suitable for quick handling. If the bones of the legs are sharp and pointed, wrap small pieces of paper round them so that they do not pierce the bag. Label, mark weight of bird and date frozen.

The bag should now be carefully sealed either by heat-sealing or with a bag fastener, or with special sealing tape, see SEALING.

Jointed birds. If the bird is to be cut up prior to freezing, the same method of preparation applies; proceed by cutting up the bird. Wrap each piece separately in foil, cling film, or polythene, and pack together in either a waxed carton, a polythene bag or plastic box.

The giblets must be wrapped in the same way and then packed separately.

Meat

Choose only the best-quality, young, tender meat for quick freezing. All meats must be protected from drying out through loss of moisture during the freezing and storing process and so it must be properly packaged in moisture-vapour-proof containers prior to quick freezing.

When preparing roasts, joints, etc., for quick freezing, each piece of meat must be wrapped individually, eliminating as much air as possible from the package by pressing and wrapping material close to the meat. Meat can be wrapped in a variety of ways, the easiest way being to use a bag which can be filled, sealed by heat, or with a bag fastener, or special sealing tape. When emptied it can be washed thoroughly and put away, in a sterile condition, for future use.

When preparing chops or fillets of steak, etc., first trim off excess fat. When packing two or more pieces of meat in one container, each portion must be separated by placing two small pieces of greaseproof or waxed paper between them to keep them from freezing together (By doing this it is quite easy to take out any piece of meat while still solidly frozen.) The meat should then be packed in a suitable container for quick freezing and storing.

Each package should be marked with the date, weight of meat or any other remarks required.

When meat is packed in bags or sheets of polythene, it is advisable to over-wrap it with strong paper or mutton cloth.

When meat is quick frozen, it is essential to freeze it in small joints to ensure that it freezes quickly right through.

SEALING

It is essential that the container should be air-tight before freezing.

Special waxed containers should be sealed with adhesive tape sold for this purpose. Tubs have lids which seal into a groove, or screw tops.

When using bags made of moisture-proof materials they need to be heat-sealed with a warm iron, curling tongs or a bag fastener; squeeze out as much air as possible before sealing. Some materials need to be protected from direct contact with the iron by a piece of paper.

Before wrapping meat, poultry or game, cover all sharp ends of bone with several thicknesses of clean kitchen paper, to avoid piercing the wrapper.

LABELLING AND STACKING

Do not attempt to use stick-on labels in the freezer, or to write in ink. It is best to mark the container with a chinagraph pencil. Note the variety, quantity and the amount of sugar or syrup (if used) and the date, e.g. "Whole strawberries, 15 oz.; in 40% syrup; July 20, 19——".

Stack the containers closely (once the food

is frozen, the closer it is stacked the better. It is in the freezing process that they must not touch). Tubs are most economically stacked with every other one upside down. DO NOT OVER-LOAD THE FREEZER at the actual time of freezing fresh produce. Manufacturers should state the maximum load to be frozen at any one time.

STORING

(1) Once frozen, it is a good idea to keep similar varieties together, either with coloured paper or tapes, or in string nets, or cardboard boxes or special baskets provided with some freezers. (These can be purchased separately and used in other models.) Keep a plan showing where the produce is stored—this saves keeping the freezer open while you search for a particular packet.

(2) It is best not to store frozen food for longer than a year. Plan to have a quick turn-over of stock, with as much variety as possible.

(3) If there is a short power-cut, do not open the cabinet unless it is really necessary. It should then remain at a temperature sufficiently low not to harm the food. If the food has to be kept like this for more than a day it should be all right provided it does not thaw completely. This depends mainly on the type, size and insulation of the freezer. If you are moving house and the freezer has to be emptied, most Distributors can arrange to provide insulated containers for transport, but the food must be packed with dry ice for transport or the Distributors may store the food until it can be replaced in your freezer.

(4) To defrost, follow the manufacturers' instructions carefully. With careful handling defrosting will probably only be necessary about twice a year. But do not leave it too long because too much ice round the inside of the compartment takes up space and impairs the efficiency of the freezer.

TO USE FROZEN FOODS

Fruits: To preserve the best appearance allow the fruit to thaw gradually when required for dessert use. Do not open the packet while the food is thawing; merely leave it at room temperature for 3–4 hr. per 1 lb. weight, or leave it—still unopened—in a domestic refrigerator for 5–6 hr. per 1 lb. weight.

If you are in a hurry for the fruit, place an unopened pack in cold water, allowing the tap to run slightly, so changing the water.

Fruit to be used for cooking need not be defrosted first.

Vegetables: Corn on the cob should be thawed before it is cooked, or the outside will be over-cooked before the heat can penetrate properly to the inside.

It is unnecessary to thaw any other deep-frozen vegetables before cooking. As a general rule, allow about ½ pt. water and ½ teasp. salt to a 1-lb. pack, adding any other seasoning to taste. Bring the salted water to the boil, add the frozen vegetables, and as they heat, break up the block with a fork to help it to thaw quickly. Boil for only about half the time needed to cook fresh vegetables. Cooking time is counted from the time the water begins to boil again.

Meat or **poultry:** Joints of meat or poultry should be thawed before cooking to ensure even cooking right through. Allow 5–6 hr. per lb. if thawed in a domestic refrigerator or 2–3 hr. per lb. if thawed at room temperature. If more rapid thawing is necessary, place the sealed package in a warm place or in the draught from an electric fan, allowing about 45 min. per lb. in weight. The meat should be left in the unopened package while thawing. Cook the food as soon as possible after it has been completely thawed, as at this stage it will not keep as well as fresh food; once it has been cooked, however, it will keep for the same time as similarly cooked fresh meat.

Chops, sausages and thin portions of meat can be cooked without thawing, but will take longer to cook than normally.

DAIRY PRODUCE

MILK

MILK as a food needs no introduction to either the housewife or the nutrition scientist. It has often been described as the only substance created by Nature solely for use as a food, and its value for babies is without question.

Not all milk comes from a cow but, because it is the kind most widely known and used in this country, it is the one considered here.

A cow's milk is, of course, intended for feeding the young calf until it has developed sufficiently to care for itself. For this reason it must contain some quantity of all those nutrients which the growing animal needs—high-quality protein, vitamins and minerals for body-building and repair as well as the energy-giving fats and carbohydrates.

However, just as the young calf is not exactly like a young human being, so their requirements vary. For example, milk contains very little iron at any time and its vitamin C content is gradually destroyed after leaving the cow. It is not, therefore, a *perfect* food—but there is no such thing. It is, on the other hand, an excellent foundation on which to build the diet because it is just about the best food one can obtain.

Because milk is the principal source of calcium in the diet, medical authorities recommend certain daily quantities for various age-groups—1 pint for adults, 1–1½ pints for young children, while for teenagers, whose needs are greatest, 1½ pints or more.

In addition to its nutritional qualities, milk contains a number of non-pathogenic, or harmless, bacteria. These include those which bring about souring due to the formation of lactic acid and are of great value in cheese-making—even though they may cause some inconvenience in the home. Although bacteria will multiply under warm conditions, they are destroyed by heat. Heat-treatment, therefore, will delay souring and is one of the advantages of pasteurization. Boiling is the more usual method used by the housewife.

GRADES OF MILK

There are a number of grades of milk and their retail prices are fixed by the Government. The designation depends on two factors—the butterfat content and the hygienic quality. The former must be at least 3% for most grades.

Pasteurized Milk has been heated in order to destroy all harmful germs without affecting the flavour. This is the most usual grade supplied.

Homogenized Milk has been heat-treated and processed so as to break up the fat into such tiny particles that they do not rise to the top to form a creamline. It has a richer, creamier taste all the way through and is very good for milk puddings.

Sterilized Milk is simply homogenized milk which has been bottled and heat-treated at a higher temperature to ensure that it will keep (while still sealed) for at least seven days.

U.H.T. Milk is treated by heating to a very high temperature and will keep in the unopened pack for several months.

T.T. Milk comes from cows of any breed

which have passed the tuberculin test. It is not now marked, or considered separately from other tested milk.

Channel Islands T.T. Milk comes from cows of the Channel Islands breeds (Jerseys and Guernseys) which have passed the tuberculin test. It is of superior hygienic quality and must have a butterfat content of at least 4%.

South Devon T.T. Milk is similar to Channel Islands T.T. Milk but comes from cows of the South Devon breed.

Channel Islands Milk and **South Devon Milk** are similar to their T.T. counterparts but do not necessarily come from cows which have passed the tuberculin test. Their hygienic quality is superior and butterfat content at least 4%.

Farm-Bottled Milk, as its name implies, is milk from the above grades which has been bottled at the place of production.

Buttermilk is the by-product from the churning of sour cream into butter. It is usually pasteurized and has a similar "solids not fat" content to that of whole milk. Its fat content however is between 0·1 and 1·5%.

Skim Milk is milk from which the cream has been removed—thus reducing its butterfat content to somewhere in the region of 0·1%.

Kosher or **Kedassiah Milk** is specially prepared in accordance with Jewish practice.

Evaporated Milk is milk from which approximately half the water has been removed by heat. After evaporation it is homogenized, canned and sterilized.

Condensed Milk is also heat-treated to remove much of the water but sugar is added so that the finished product contains about 42% sugar. This acts as a preservative and it is not necessary to apply heat-treatment after canning.

Dried Milk has been so treated that practically all the moisture (about 95–98%) has been removed and the milk becomes a powder. It may be made from whole or skimmed milk. It will keep for a much longer time but, once it has been opened, care should be taken to see that the lid is always replaced.

After reconstitution, evaporated, condensed and dried milks require the same care as fresh milk.

Frozen Milk is not now very widely used. Whole milk is homogenized, pasteurized and quickly frozen. It must be kept at a temperature between −10° and −20° F. but, once it has been defrosted, it requires the same care as fresh milk.

Yoghourt, though described in some dictionaries as "a thick fermented liquor made by the Turks from milk", is what is known as a cultured milk. Often prescribed for special diets, it is healthy for everyone. It is slightly tart in flavour and makes an excellent dessert, either flavoured or with fruit.

CARE OF MILK IN THE HOME

All the efforts taken to ensure the delivery of safe milk to the home would be wasted if the housewife herself failed to take care also. Milk should be kept "cool, clean and covered".

Never let milk stay outside. Its quality can be affected in a short time if it is left in a warm, sunny spot. Put it in a refrigerator, or a cool part of the larder, as soon as possible after it is delivered. If you have no refrigerator, it is a good idea to stand the bottles in a basin of cold water, covered with a damp piece of muslin.

Milk should be kept in the dark because sunlight destroys some of the important vitamins and will tend to spoil the flavour. It should also be kept covered, because an open bottle or jug will soon pick up dust and germs and because milk has a tendency to absorb flavours and odours from other food.

The best place to keep milk is in the bottle but, once it has been poured into a glass or jug, for table use, it should not be returned to the bottle. One day's milk should not be mixed with milk from the day before and milk jugs should have wide tops so that they are easy to clean.

It is not often realized that it is illegal to use milk bottles for anything but milk. They belong to the dairy and should be rinsed in cold water as soon as they are empty and put out for collection by the milkman.

USE OF MILK

Milk in any form is very easily digested but sour milk and junket are most readily assimilated by the body.

Apart from its nutritional importance, one of the chief values of milk is in the infinite number of ways in which it can be used and served by the cook. Furthermore, there is no waste, because every drop can be utilized in both sweet and savoury dishes as well as for drinking purposes.

CREAM

CREAM is a concentration of the fat globules of milk and the standards of butterfat content are laid down as follows:

Single Cream (sometimes known as pouring or coffee cream): not less than 18% (usually homogenized); **Double Cream** (sometimes known as thick cream): not less than 48%; **Whipping cream:** approx. 35%; and **Canned Cream:** 23% (usually sterilized). **Clotted Cream** has been heat-treated so that the liquid in it is reduced and the butterfat content is a minimum of 48%—though it is often nearer 60%.

Provided the bacteriological condition of the cream is good, and heat treatment has been given, chilled cream can be stored for up to five days in perfect safety. It is illegal to add preservatives, and fresh cream means, literally, fresh cream.

Single cream will not whip unless helped by the addition of a stiffly whisked egg-white. Really fresh cream will not whip as well as that which is 24 hours old. It is best to use it straight from a refrigerator for whipping, although it should not be too cold when served.

Cream as a food has a high energy value and its easy digestibility makes it useful in a sick-room diet.

BUTTER

BUTTER is a conglomeration of fat globules in large clusters and is made from the cream of milk. It usually consists of 80% fat but also contains some protein and milk sugar adhering in the buttermilk together with minerals and vitamins A and D. Its main purpose in the diet is to provide energy.

Butter can be made from either "sweet" (i.e. fresh) cream or "sour" (ripened) cream. In the latter case, a "starter" is added which develops the flavour but shortens the keeping quality.

The main butter-producing and exporting countries are Australia, Denmark, the Netherlands and New Zealand. Considerable quantities are also made in Great Britain, Eire, Canada, Sweden, Finland and the United States. Local factors such as types of grass and breeds of cattle cause the colour and texture of butter to vary from country to country—as well as affecting the flavour.

TO CHOOSE BUTTER

The main considerations in buying butter are matters of personal taste, price and, to some extent, the way in which it will be used. Butters imported from New Zealand and Australia are mostly "sweet", whilst Danish and Dutch are generally "ripened". The former have a firm, cold texture and tend to be brighter in colour than the latter, which are soft and fine-textured. Both kinds of butter are made in other countries and may be salted or unsalted according to taste.

All butter is good for frying but a firm butter is better for all but very rich pastries, whilst soft butter is easier to cream. Ripened butters are best for sweets—toffees, fudge, etc.—because of their strong flavour. Unsalted butter is the most suitable for butter icing and butter cream.

STORING BUTTER

Butter is best kept in its wrapper and, like milk, should be in a cool, dark place, away from strong flavours or odours. If you have no refrigerator, an earthenware dish or butter-cooler is useful.

MARGARINE

AT one time, margarine was made entirely

from the fat of animals, chiefly the ox, the fluid components of which, after being melted down and clarified, were churned up with milk to reproduce orthodox flavours. Nowadays, vegetable fats have virtually superseded animal fats with this advantage, that the slightly lower price enables the manufacturer to use much larger quantities of milk in their preparation than was formerly the case with the use of animal fats.

In many ways, margarine today is vastly superior to that of earlier days. The manufacturing processes have improved and the product is clean and wholesome. The proportion of fat is the same as the average specimen of butter and the keeping quality is superior. Margarine is absorbed almost as completely as butter, the difference being only 2%.

In recent years, the flavour of most margarines has been greatly improved and prejudice against it has almost completely disappeared. Some manufacturers add about 10% butter to improve the flavour and texture still further.

Margarine is a useful adjunct for culinary purposes, such as cake or pastry-making, and forms a valuable medium for supplying fat in the diet or for spreading on bread.

CHEESE

CHEESE is the natural way of preserving milk's nourishment. It is like making a junket, or "curds and whey", by adding a small amount of rennet to fresh milk. The most valuable part of the milk becomes solid (the curd) and the watery part (the whey) readily separates. This is similar to the method whereby milk is allowed to become sour naturally but, in the former case, the curd contains a higher proportion of fat. In souring, much of the fat remains in the whey and the resulting cheese has a lower calorific value.

Like butter and cream, most cheese is now made in creameries, but the principles remain basically the same as those used in farmhouses. Production in creameries makes it possible to ensure the same rigid controls with regard to standards and hygiene that exist in other branches of the dairy industry.

NUTRITIONAL VALUE OF CHEESE

All classes of cheese contain a high proportion of protein. An ordinary fat cheese consists of one-third protein, one-third fat and one-third water with large amounts of calcium and riboflavin (one of the B vitamins) and worthwhile quantities of vitamins A and D. Cheese, therefore, has an extremely high nutritional value.

This nutritional value varies with the proportion of milk and cream used in the manufacture of the different cheeses. The higher the proportion of cream, the greater the fat content, while cheeses made from skimmed milk have little fat but a large amount of protein.

DIGESTIBILITY

There has been much discussion as to the digestibility of cheese and this has led to differences of opinion. However, it is generally agreed that if certain rules are followed in the preparation and cooking, cheese will be easily digested. Owing to its high nutritive value, it is most important that it should be included in the diet.

Before cooking, cheese should be finely divided by grating or chopping. It should be very well chewed if eaten raw. The eating of some form of starch will aid the digestion, and, as starch is usually accompanied by some vegetable protein, it is particularly recommended by nutritionists. (If animal and vegetable protein are eaten together, more value is obtained from both than if they are taken separately.)

HARD AND SOFT CHEESES

Generally speaking, the cheeses made from skimmed milk are hard and those made from full-cream are soft. There is one notable exception to this—Cottage Cheese (made from soured, skimmed milk) is soft. Soft cheeses contain more water than hard cheeses, partly because the latter are subjected to higher temperatures and pressures during their manufacture.

It is almost impossible to classify cheeses beyond this stage, because so many factors can affect the finished product and local variations are innumerable. The type of soil in the district; the fat content of the milk; the acidity of the curd at various stages of cheesemaking; the amount of pressure and the length of time for which it is applied; as well as other factors, all contribute to the individuality of each cheese. Therefore, although the principles are the same, no two types of cheese are made in exactly the same way.

TO CHOOSE CHEESE

The taste and smell are the best indications of quality and there is so much difference of taste that the old saying "taste and try before you buy" is still to be recommended where possible. However, the opportunity does not often arise and the next wisest course is to consult your grocer. He can usually give helpful advice.

Cheese has almost every virtue for the housewife. It is cheap, portable, easy to store and palatable.

STORAGE HINTS

Cheese will keep well if wrapped in a polythene bag to prevent drying and then stored in a cool larder (50°–60° F.) or in a refrigerator. In the latter case the cheese should be tightly wrapped and brought to room temperature half an hour before serving.

Many grocers now sell cheese in pre-packed portions, which means that the cheese reaches you in excellent condition. Although cheese packed in this way will keep longer at home, the storage method mentioned above is still recommended.

SERVING CHEESE

Cheese is often served as a separate course and, where possible, a variety of types should be offered. They should be attractively arranged on a cheeseboard or large plate and accompanied by bread rolls or a choice of biscuits. Vegetables such as watercress, radishes, small onions or celery go very well with cheese and make an attractive addition to the course. Many people like a little butter with cheese. Stilton Cheese deserves special mention because it is so often incorrectly served. It should be cut horizontally—not scooped from the centre. Port may be served *with* it but should not be poured *into* it.

KINDS OF CHEESE

There are well over 400 different kinds of cheese but those in the following list are among the best-known.

English cheeses

Caerphilly Cheese is the small white cheese which originated in a small Glamorgan village but is now made in the West of England. It has a mild, creamy taste and a smooth, springy texture. Welsh miners like it because it is moist and salty. This cheese is 3 in. high, 9 in. across and weighs 8–9 lb. It is also possible to obtain 1-lb. midgets.

Cheddar Cheese is the best-known of all English cheese, but is now made all over the world. A good Cheddar is solid and firm, pale yellow in colour with a succulent, "nutty" taste. The usual size is 11 in. high and 12 in. across, weighing 50–60 lb., but it is also produced in 35 lb., 10–12-lb. truckles and 1-lb midgets.

Cheshire Cheese has a keen, tangy flavour and an open texture. There are red, white and blue varieties, "Old Blue" being the richest and rarest. It has been produced in England since the twelfth century. The large cheese is 13 in. high and 11 in. across with a weight of about 50 lb. Smaller ones of 40 lb., 20 lb. and 1-lb. midgets are also made.

Cream Cheese is always very mild in flavour. It must be eaten fresh as it will not keep for very long and is therefore normally made up in small quantities.

Derby Cheese is another mild, creamy cheese with a smooth texture. If allowed to mature for 4–6 months, it develops a fuller flavour. The rare **Sage Derby** is given extra flavour with layers of finely-chopped sage leaves. The size is approximately 5 in. high by 14 in. across and the weight, 30 lb.

Dorset Blue or **Blue Vinny** is an unusual, strong-tasting cheese. It is straw-coloured with deep blue veins and a stiff, crumbly texture. It is the only English cheese made from partly skimmed milk. It measures 6 in. high by 8 in. across and weighs 10–12 lb.

Double Gloucester Cheese is a pungent, smooth-textured cheese somewhat similar to Cheddar, but fuller in flavour. Straw-coloured or light red, it is usually 4 in. high and 15 in. across and weighs 35 lb. There is also a smaller one weighing 8–10 lb. and a 1-lb. midget.

Lancashire Cheese is especially famous for its toasting qualities. It has a crumbly and fairly soft texture which makes it easy to spread, while its flavour is clean and mild. 8 in. high and 13 in. across, a Lancashire cheese weighs about 45 lb., although there are also 20-lb. and 1-lb. sizes made.

Leicester Cheese is a fine dessert cheese with a mild flavour which becomes more piquant with maturity. It is rich red in colour and has a soft, crumbly texture. Shaped like a large millstone, it weighs 40 lb. and measures 4 in. high by 18 in. across.

Stilton Cheese is famous the world over. The rich, mellow, strong-flavoured Blue Stilton is creamy white in colour with plenty of blue veins and a wrinkled brown coat. The texture should be open and flaky and the body soft and slightly moist. A creamy, young White Stilton has a mild flavour and is popular in the North Country. Both varieties measure 9 in. high by 8 in. across and weigh 14 lb.

Wensleydale Cheese has a unique lingering, sweet flavour. Its texture is velvety and, when mature, is creamy enough to spread. The White Wensleydale is most common, but small quantities of Blue Wensleydale are also made. These cheeses weigh about 10–12 lb. and measure 6 in. high by 8 in. across.

Scottish cheese

Dunlop Cheese is the principal Scottish cheese. Its flavour is not unlike that of Cheddar but it has a closer texture and is more moist.

Danish cheeses

Danish Blue Cheese is a semi-hard cheese made from whole milk. It is ripened by blue-green mould which gives it a mottled appearance. The texture is creamy and the flavour mellow.

Samsoe Cheese is another Danish cheese made from whole milk. It is mild and creamy with a nutty flavour. Like some Swiss cheese, it has a number of holes, or eyes.

French cheeses

Camembert Cheese is a rich cream cheese from Brittany. It is small and flat, pale yellow in colour and has a dark rind. Weighing about 10 oz., the size is usually about 4½ in. across by 1–1½ in. high.

Roquefort Cheese is another very rich French cheese. Strictly speaking it should be made from ewe's milk but similar types are made in other countries from other kinds of milk. The flavour is sharp and peppery while the appearance is of white curd with mottled blue veins. It has to be kept a considerable time before ripening and is similar in size to Stilton or Dorset Blue.

Tôme au Raisin Cheese is a rich cream cheese which also comes from France. The outside is coated with grape pips which impart a unique flavour to the cheese.

Italian cheeses

Bel Paese is the name given to the best-known of a group of Italian table cheeses. They are uncooked, soft, sweet and mild. The ripening period is short—about 6 weeks. Bel Paese is made from whole milk and the finished product is wrapped in tinfoil. Measuring about 5¼ to 6 in. in diameter, their weight is in the region of 4½ lb.

Gorgonzola Cheese is the principal blue-veined cheese from Italy. It now has counterparts in many other countries. The interior has blue-green veins mottling the creamy cheese and its coat resembles a form of clay. The ripening period is at least 3 months and sometimes extends to a year. The cheeses are cylindrical and flat and vary between 8½ in.

1

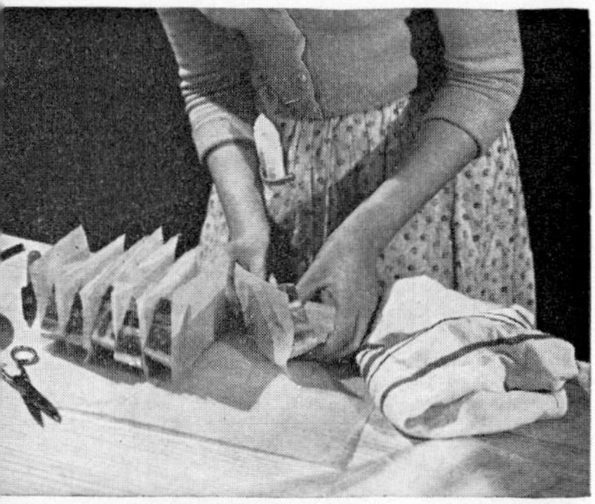

2

3

4

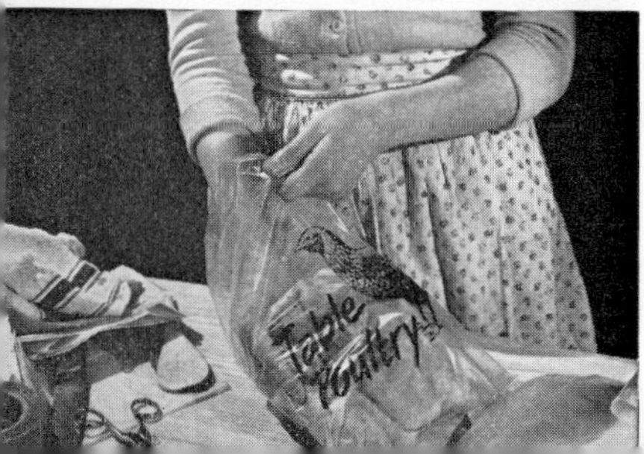

5

6

7

PLATE 31

Preparing Food for Quick Freezing

1 Meat is cut into portions suitable for use. Wrap large pieces of meat in moisture-vapour-proof covers. Turn in the edges and seal with special sealing tape or by heat.

2 Separate small cuts by 2 pieces of greaseproof paper so that number needed can be removed without defrosting rest.

3 After sealing, over-wrap with a mutton cloth or similar wrapping to protect them from damage in the home freezer.

4 Before freezing, prepare poultry ready for cooking. Wrap sharp ends to protect container. Wrap giblets separately.

5 Place the bird in a suitable container, e.g. plastic bag. Place the giblets by the side, expel the air and seal.

6 Blanched and cooled vegetables may be packed in various types of container—polythene bag, box with grooved lid.

7 Shows how peas blanched, drained and cooled, are placed in a bag, then the air is expelled and the bag sealed.

8 Fruits—in this case strawberries, packed in a polythene bag, covered with syrup, the air expelled and bag sealed.

8

Boxes of home-made sweets make unusual presents. Also illustrated are toffee apples (page 489); coconut ice (page 480); peppermint creams dipped in chocolate (page 483).

1 2

Petits fours (1) consist of almond paste piped on to rice paper. Some glacé icing and a little butter cream are all that are required to turn small fancy-cut shapes of genoese pastry into petit fours (2) (page 545).

PLATE 32
Home-Made
Sweets and Petits Fours

to 11 in. across, 6½ in. to 8 in. high and 14 to 17 lb. in weight.

Mozzarella Cheese is a soft plastic-curd cheese that was originally made from buffalo's milk. Made mainly in Southern Italy, it is now produced from cow's milk as well. Used mainly in cooking, this cheese has little or no ripening period and is shaped into rather irregular spheres—each weighing about 8 to 16 oz.

Parmesan Cheese is the name given to a group of very hard cheeses which originated in Italy but are now made in some other countries. Made entirely from skimmed cow's milk, their high flavour is largely due to the pasturage but also to the long maturing period—from 6 months to 4 years. This cheese is very hard and therefore grates easily. It is often sold in the powder form and keeps almost indefinitely.

Provolone Cheese is made in many parts of Italy as well as in the United States. It is light in colour, mellow and smooth, cuts without crumbling and has a delightful flavour. This cheese is made in many shapes and sizes—each one having a special name.

Dutch cheeses

Edam Cheese originated in the Netherlands and is a semi-soft to hard, sweet-curd cheese made from cow's milk in which the fat content has been slightly reduced. It has a mild, clean flavour with a rather firm but crumbly texture. Usually shaped like a flattened ball, this cheese is made in a variety of weights from 3½ to 14 lb. Those which are exported have a bright red coat, but when consumed in their home country this is omitted.

Gouda Cheese is very similar to Edam but contains more fat. Its shape is almost spherical and it usually weighs between 10 and 25 lb.

Swiss cheeses

Emmenthaler Cheese is a famous Swiss cheese similar to Gruyère in that it has an elastic body in which holes develop. However, its nut-like, sweetish flavour is more mild. These cheeses are usually about 6 in. high and sometimes as much as 36 in. across. The weight varies from 160 to 230 lb.

Gruyère Cheese takes its name from a Swiss village, although much of it is in fact produced in France. Made from whole milk, it has a sharp flavour. The body is elastic in texture and, as the cheese ripens, holes, or eyes, develop in it.

Processed Cheeses are usually sold in tinfoil or plastic wrapping, in separate portions or slices. The cheese has been specially treated to avoid any further ripening or deterioration during storage.

EGGS

FOOD VALUE

Eggs are rich in protein, including the ten amino acids considered indispensable for growth and tissue repair; they contain vitamins A, B, D and E, as well as the minerals iron and calcium. In fact, a single egg contains some of all the essential nutrients of our daily diet, except vitamin C (mainly found in fruit and vegetables).

What is more, the egg supplies these nutrients in an easily assimilable form.

BUYING AND KEEPING EGGS

The vast majority of British hens' eggs in retail shops have been quality tested and graded by weight at Packing Stations. These eggs are stamped according to their weight (Large, Standard, Medium or Small); the number of the Packing Station; and the lion mark of the British Egg Marketing Board.

Some retail shops sell eggs they have obtained direct from producers; these eggs are stamped "B", together with the producer's licence number.

It is also possible, on occasion, to buy eggs marked "second" (perfectly fit for quick consumption), and "chilled" (cold-stored at times of plenty, and sold when eggs are in shorter supply).

Ducks' eggs are larger and richer than hens' eggs. They can be used for most egg dishes, but it is advisable always to cook them well.

Although the pattern of egg production is changing, in that the number produced in the Autumn is now much nearer the production total in the Spring, Spring is still the "flush" season when eggs are at their cheapest and best. If eggs are to be preserved, do so then.

In buying eggs, avoid those that have been kept for days in sunny shop-windows: glass attracts heat, and heat is bad for eggs. Avoid, too, buying dirty eggs: an eggshell is porous and dirt and germs are quickly absorbed. For the same reason, do not keep eggs next to onions, cheese, fish or other strong-smelling foods.

Shell colour varies according to the breed of chicken and does not affect the egg's flavour or nutritional value. Neither does the size. Weight for weight, a small egg is of equal value to that of a large.

Keep eggs pointed-end downwards, in an egg-box, in the cool. In a refrigerator, well away from the ice-box or freezer is ideal; but do take them out some time before use to give them time to reach room temperature, otherwise they often crack on being boiled, and are difficult to whip.

COOKING AND SERVING EGGS

There are limitless ways in which eggs can be used. Served alone they can be fried, boiled, baked, poached or scrambled. They are the essentials of omelets and soufflés. As cooking aids, they have a leavening effect in cakes, they help to prevent the formation of ice-crystals in ice-cream, they thicken sauces and custards; their fat properties are essential to good mayonnaise; they serve as a binding agent in meat loaves; with breadcrumbs, they make a coating for fish and meat to be fried.

It is generally accepted that anyone can cook an egg. This is probably true. But many cooks rob eggs of their delicate flavour and attractiveness by cooking them badly. The important thing to remember is that, whether cooked alone, or combined with other foods, an egg should be cooked slowly at a low to moderate temperature; extreme heat is a major enemy.

PRESERVING EGGS

Hens' eggs only should be preserved; it is unwise to preserve ducks' eggs even when newly laid. When buying eggs for preserving tell your shopkeeper why you want them and make sure he sells you those from his latest delivery. Preserve them straightaway. Even if you have the opportunity of doing so, do *not* preserve eggs taken straight from the nest. Time must be allowed (say 24–48 hr.) for the internal temperature and air pressure to drop.

Do not preserve dirty eggs, or those with rough or mis-shapen shells. If the eggs are soiled, dry-clean them with a stiff brush or wipe clean with a damp cloth.

Make sure the eggs are cool before you start; the material used in preserving must be cool, and the eggs must be stored in a cool place.

Whichever method of preserving is used, follow the manufacturer's instructions implicitly.

The Waterglass Method

Use a pail, galvanized iron bath or stone jar, and sufficient waterglass (sodium silicate) to fill it about three-quarters full.

Place the eggs, if possible pointed-end downwards, in the solution. More eggs can be placed in the solution as they become available, but always be sure they are completely covered by the liquid. Keep the receptacle covered to avoid dust and evaporation. Should evaporation take place, leaving the top layer of eggs exposed, add cold water until the original level is reached. A fall in the level due to removal of eggs should not be made good except by the addition of more solution of the same strength.

Dry Preserving

This consists of applying a protective coating of fat on the shell; there are two ways of doing this:

(*a*) The eggs may be treated with a special liquid preparation, consisting of fat dissolved in a suitable solvent. This evaporates, leaving a coating of fat over the egg.

(*b*) The eggs may be rubbed over with white

Vaseline or other odourless, greasy preparation, using the palms of the hands. Care must be taken to cover the shell completely.

Preserving in Lime Water

This involves rather more work but is a method sometimes preferred. A solution of slaked lime is made—four parts lime to twenty parts of cold water. This is stirred each day for a week, one part of common salt being added on the 4th or 5th day. Avoiding all sediment the clear solution is poured over the eggs in a clear glass or glazed earthenware vessel. In time a crust forms on the surface. This checks evaporation.

PICKLING EGGS

For every 6 eggs allow 1 pint of white wine or cider vinegar, 6 cloves of garlic, 1 oz. pickling spice, a small piece of orange peel and a piece of whole mace. Boil together all the ingredients (except the eggs) for ½ hour. When the liquid is cool, strain into a wide-mouthed earthen or glass jar with a screw lid, or tight cork. Put the whole, shelled eggs that have been hard boiled, into the liquid. They can be added to as convenient, but must always be covered by the liquid. The eggs should be left for 6 weeks before eating.

Cream

DEVONSHIRE CREAM

Before starting to make Devonshire Cream at home, fresh milk should be allowed to stand for some hours. In very cold weather, this period should be 12 hours but about half that time is sufficient if the weather is warm.

The milk should be heated, in a milk pan, until it is quite hot but not boiling. Boiling coagulates the protein and a skin will form on the surface. The more slowly the milk is heated. the better will be the result. The time required depends upon the size and shape of the pan and the amount of heat applied but slight movement on the surface of the milk indicates that it is sufficiently scalded.

When scalding is completed, the pan should at once be transferred to a cold place and left there until the following day. The cream can then be skimmed off the surface.

Butters

CREAMED BUTTER (for sandwiches)

8 oz. butter
1 gill double cream
Mustard
Salt and pepper
Cayenne pepper

Beat the butter to a cream. Whip the cream stiffly and add it lightly to the butter. Season to taste with mustard, salt and pepper or cayenne.

SAVOURY BUTTERS

Beurres Composés

General Method:

Roughly chop the ingredients to be mixed with butter. Crush and pound the additions. Pound the butter and additions together. Usually the compound butter is sieved and chilled.

NOTE: Herbs are best scalded in boiling water and dried in a cloth before being chopped and pounded.

Uses of Savoury Butters:

1. Used in place of sauce, e.g. Maître d'hôtel butter, with any grill.
2. As a thickening and flavouring combined, e.g. Lobster Butter in Cardinal Sauce.

ANCHOVY BUTTER

Beurre d'Anchois

6 bottled anchovies
2 oz. butter
Lemon juice
Pepper

Crush the anchovies, rub through a sieve. Mix them smoothly with the butter, add pepper and lemon juice to taste. Sieve and chill.

"BLACK" BUTTER

Beurre Noir

Butter
Vinegar

Heat the required amount of butter till brown but not burnt, strain, add a dash of vinegar. Use hot.

BUTTERS

CHUTNEY BUTTER

1 oz. mango chutney
2 oz. butter
1 teasp. French mustard
Lemon juice

Pound the chutney, cream the butter, mix the two smoothly together. Mix in the mustard, add a drop or two of lemon juice to taste. Sieve.

CURRY BUTTER

4 oz. butter
1 heaped teasp. curry powder
½ teasp. lemon juice
Salt to taste

Cream the butter then stir in the curry powder and lemon juice. Beat well and add salt to taste.

DEVILLED BUTTER

Beurre à la Diable

2 oz. butter
¼ teasp. cayenne
⅛ teasp. pepper
¼ teasp. curry powder
¼ teasp. ground ginger

Pound all the ingredients together, then rub through a fine sieve.

FISH ROE BUTTER

Beurre d' Œufs ou de Laite

Equal quantities of butter and cooked *or* raw, soft *or* hard, fish roe, according to use and taste
Salt and pepper
Lemon juice

Pound the fish roe, cream the butter, pound the two together. Add the lemon juice a drop at a time. Season to taste. Sieve.

GARLIC BUTTER

Beurre d'Ail

2 oz. butter
1 clove of garlic

Crush the garlic, pound it with the butter, pass through a fine sieve. Spread in a layer ½ in. thick on a plate, chill.

GREEN BUTTER

4 oz. butter
1½ tablesp. finely-chopped, washed parsley
Anchovy essence *or* paste
1 tablesp. lemon juice
Salt and pepper

Cream the butter, add the parsley, lemon juice, and anchovy essence or paste to taste. Season with salt and pepper and, when thoroughly mixed, use as required.

GREEN HERB BUTTER

See Ravigote Sauce (p. 134).

HAM BUTTER

4 oz. finely-chopped, lean, cooked ham
1 tablesp. double cream
2 oz. butter
Pepper

Pound the ham until smooth and mix in a little of the butter. Pass through a fine sieve and work in the cream and the rest of the butter. Season to taste and use as required.

HERB BUTTER

2 oz. butter
Pinch of dried thyme
¼ teasp. salt
Pinch dried parsley

Cream the butter and work in the herbs and salt. Use as required.

HORSERADISH BUTTER

Beurre de Raifort

2 oz. butter
1 tablesp. grated horseradish
Lemon juice

Pound the butter with the horseradish, beat in the lemon juice a drop at a time. This butter need not be sieved.

LOBSTER BUTTER

Beurre de Homard

Coral and spawn of lobster (raw if to be used in sauce or bisque); double this quantity of butter.
Salt and pepper

Dry the coral thoroughly then pound until smooth. Season to taste, add butter gradually until twice as much butter as coral has been added. Pass through a sieve.

NOTE: If this butter is to be used in Cardinal Sauce or Lobster Bisque; the *raw* spawn should be pounded then creamed with butter.

MAÎTRE D'HÔTEL BUTTER

2 teasp. finely-chopped parsley
½ teasp. chopped chervil and tarragon (optional)
2 oz. butter
1 teasp. lemon juice
Salt and pepper

Scald the parsley, chervil and tarragon, if used, in boiling water and dry in a cloth before chopping. Cream the butter, mix in the herbs gradually, add the lemon juice a drop at a time, season to taste. Do not sieve but spread on a plate and chill until firm.

MEUNIÈRE BUTTER or NOISETTE BUTTER

Butter | **Lemon juice**

Heat the required amount of butter till it just turns golden-fawn, add a dash of lemon juice. Use hot.

MONTPELIER BUTTER

Beurre Montpelier

½ bunch watercress | **Salt and pepper**
2 oz. butter

Wash the watercress and dry it thoroughly. Chop very finely and squeeze it in a piece of muslin to dry still further. Cream the butter and knead in the watercress until it is sufficiently green. Add salt and pepper to taste and use as required.

MUSTARD BUTTER

2 oz. butter | **1–2 teasp. French mustard**

Cream the butter, then mix in the mustard.

PAPRIKA BUTTER

2 oz. butter | **1 teasp. paprika pepper**

Cream the butter, then mix in the pepper.

SARDINE BUTTER

2 oz. butter | **1½ oz. sardines**

Sieve the sardines (including the bones) and cream the butter. Blend the two together and use as required.

SHALLOT BUTTER

Beurre d'Échalote

2 oz. butter | **½ oz. shallot**

Cream the butter, chop and pound the shallot. Mix smoothly together.

SHRIMP BUTTER

Beurre de Crevettes

2 oz. butter | **Lemon juice**
¼ pt. picked shrimps free from salt

Roughly chop, then pound the shrimps. Pound the butter, pound in the shrimps. Beat in lemon juice to taste a drop at a time.

TARRAGON BUTTER

Beurre d'Estragon

2 oz. butter | **Lemon juice**
1 teasp. chopped tarragon

Scald the tarragon in boiling water and dry in a cloth before chopping. Pound the chopped tarragon with the butter, add lemon juice to taste, pass through a sieve.

WATERCRESS BUTTER

2 oz. butter | **Salt**
2 tablesp. watercress leaves

Scald the watercress in boiling water and dry in a cloth. Chop finely and pound into the butter. Add salt to taste. Do not sieve.

Sweet Butters

BRANDY BUTTER (Hard sauce)

3 oz. butter | **1 teasp.–1 tablesp. brandy**
6 oz. icing sugar *or* 4½ oz. icing sugar and 1 oz. ground almonds | **1 whipped egg white (optional)**

Cream the butter till soft. Sift the icing sugar and cream it with the butter till white and light in texture. Mix in the almonds if used. Work the brandy carefully into the mixture. Fold the stiffly-whipped egg white into the sauce.

Serve with Christmas or other steamed puddings.

NOTE: This sauce may be stored for several weeks in an airtight jar. It makes an excellent filling for sweet sandwiches.

RUM BUTTER

4 oz. butter | **1 sherryglass rum**
8 oz. soft brown sugar

Beat the butter to a cream and beat in the sugar. When light and creamy, add the rum gradually. Transfer to a serving dish and chill thoroughly before using.

SHERRY BUTTER

As for Rum Butter using sherry in place of

rum and castor sugar in place of soft brown sugar.

Cheese Dishes

CAYENNE CHEESE FINGERS

4 oz. finely-grated cheese
4 oz. butter
4 oz. flour
½ saltsp. salt
½ saltsp. cayenne pepper

Rub the butter into the flour and add grated cheese, salt and cayenne pepper. Mix well together and add sufficient water to make a stiff paste. Roll out to about ¼ in. thick and cut into fingers 3½ in. long by ¾ in. wide. Transfer to a greased baking-sheet and bake in a warm oven (**335° F., Gas 3**) until crisp and lightly browned. Serve either hot or cold.

10 helpings
Cooking time—30–45 min.

CHEESE BUTTERFLIES

Cheese pastry using 3 oz. flour, etc.
3 oz. cream cheese
Few drops anchovy essence *or* cochineal

Roll out the pastry thinly, and cut into rounds about 1½ in. in diameter. Cut ½ the rounds across the centre—the "butterfly wings". Bake for about 10 min. in a fairly hot oven (**400° F., Gas 6**), then cool on the baking-sheets. When quite cold lift off. Colour the cream cheese a delicate pink. Pipe a line of this across each biscuit circle and press the wing-shaped biscuits on top.

15–16 savouries
Cooking time—10 min.

CHEESE FONDUE

Fondue de Fromage

4 oz. grated Gruyère *or* Swiss cheese
1 oz. butter
1 oz. flour
¼ pt. milk
A pinch of salt
A small pinch white pepper
2 eggs

Melt the butter in a saucepan and mix in the flour. Stir in the milk and simmer gently until smooth and thick. Add the cheese, salt and pepper. When well mixed, pour the mixture on to the well-beaten egg yolks. Whisk the egg whites and stir them lightly into the mixture. Grease a fondue dish or tin which is large enough for the mixture to ½ fill it. Pour in the mixture and bake in a fairly hot oven (**375° F., Gas 5**) for about 20 min. This dish should be served the moment it is ready.

4 helpings
Cooking time—20 min.

CHEESE RAMAKINS

Ramequins de Fromage

1 tablesp. breadcrumbs
Milk
1 oz. grated Parmesan cheese
1 oz. grated Cheshire cheese
1 oz. butter
1 egg
Salt and pepper
Mace

Barely cover the breadcrumbs with boiling milk and leave to stand for 10 min. Stir well. Add cheeses, butter, egg yolk and seasoning to taste. Beat until the mixture is quite smooth. Whisk the egg white to a stiff froth and fold it into the mixture. Pour into well-greased ramakin dishes and bake in a hot oven (**425° F., Gas 7**) until set.

4–6 helpings
Cooking time—15 min.

CHEESE STRAWS

Cheese pastry using 3 oz. flour, etc.

Roll out pastry thinly, cut into strips about 4 in. long and about ⅛ in. wide, and from the trimmings cut out some rings of about 1¼ in. diameter. Bake in a fairly hot oven (**400° F., Gas 6**) until crisp. Cool on the baking-sheet. Fill each ring with straws and arrange neatly on a dish.

18 straws **Cooking time—10 min.**

CREAM CHEESE

Although not regarded as a true cheese, cream cheese is often made at home. It is usually ready to eat after 2 days, but it should be made only in small quantities as it will not keep as long as other types of cheese.

Double Cream Cheese. The fat content of the cream should be high—between 50% and 60%—and, after cooling to 50° F., add 1½ oz. salt for every 4 pt. double cream. The cream may then be left to sour naturally or starter may be added to hasten this process. Leave to stand in a cool place for 12 hr. Place a strong linen cloth over a large basin and pour the cream into the cloth. Gather the four corners and tie a piece of string round them (using a slip knot) to form a "bag". Hang the bag over the basin in a cool place (*not* a refrigerator) with a good draught. Every 4 or 5 hr., open the bag and scrape the sides. When drainage is complete, the cheese may be shaped into small portions (usually about 1–2 oz.), wrapped and stored in a refrigerator.

Single Cream Cheese. The fat content of the cream should be between 20% and 40%. Heat the cream to 80° F. and add ¼ teasp. cheese-making rennet (to which 1 teasp. cold water has been added) to every 4 pt. single cream. Leave for about 3 hr. until a curd has formed. Transfer the mixture to a strong linen cloth placed over a basin and hang it up to drain, keeping it at a temperature of about 60° F. Leave for 24 hr. and then scrape the sides of the cloth. Transfer the bag and basin to a cool place (*not* a refrigerator) and leave to hang until drainage is complete. Make up in small portions, wrap and store in a refrigerator.

For more recipes for Cheese Dishes see the Savouries Section (pp. 576–588).

Baked Eggs

Œufs en Cocotte

Heat one cocotte (a special little dish manufactured for this purpose) for each person. Add a little butter or cream, break an egg into each, season to taste, and place the cocottes in a pan of boiling water to come half way up their sides. Cover the pan and place in a moderate oven (**350° F., Gas 4**). Cooking time when the eggs are in thin china dishes will be 6–7 min.; allow 8–9 min. with thicker dishes.

Œufs sur le Plat

These are usually cooked in small dishes, one for each person, but the dish can be larger provided that the egg whites do not spread out too much when broken in, otherwise they will cook before the yolks. Heat the dish, add butter, eggs and seasonings as for Œufs en Cocotte. Place the dish in a moderate oven (**350° F., Gas 4**) and cook until the white is set but soft, and the yolk shows through a film of white. This will take about 5 min.; time will vary according to the thickness of the eggs and dish.

ALPINE EGGS

Œufs à la Suisse

4 eggs
2 oz. butter
6 oz. cheese
Finely-chopped parsley
Salt and pepper

Butter a fireproof baking-dish thickly, line it with most of the cheese cut into thin slices and break the eggs over this, keeping the yolks whole. Grate the remainder of the cheese and mix it with the parsley. Season the eggs liberally, sprinkle the grated cheese on top and add the remainder of the butter broken into small pieces. Bake till set.

4 helpings **Cooking time—10 min. (approx.)**

BAKED EGGS—COQUETTE STYLE

Œufs à la Coquette

6 eggs
1 oz. butter
6 dessertsp. cream
Nutmeg
Salt and pepper
Cayenne pepper
2 oz. finely-chopped ham *or* tongue

Liberally butter 6 ramekin cases, divide the remainder of the butter into 6 portions and place a portion in each case. To each add 1 dessertsp. cream, a pinch of nutmeg and salt and pepper, and place on a baking-sheet in the oven. When the contents begin to simmer, break an egg into each case, add a pinch of cayenne to the centre of each yolk and replace in an oven set at a low heat. When cooked, sprinkle the ham or tongue lightly on the white of each egg, taking care to keep the yolk uncovered. Serve hot.

6 helpings
Cooking time—15 min. (approx.)

BUTTERED EGGS—INDIAN STYLE

3 hard-boiled eggs
½ oz. butter
½ teasp. curry powder
Cayenne pepper
2 raw eggs
Salt and pepper
Browned breadcrumbs

BOILED EGGS

Cut the hard-boiled eggs, crosswise, in rather thick slices. Place them in a well buttered gratin dish or baking-dish, in which they may be served, and sprinkle the curry powder and a few grains of cayenne over them. Slightly beat the raw eggs, season with salt and pepper, and pour them into the dish. Cover the surface lightly with browned breadcrumbs, add a few pieces of butter, then bake in a moderate oven (**350° F., Gas 4**) for about 10 min. Serve as hot as possible.

4–5 helpings

EGGS IN CASES

Œufs en Caisses

6 eggs	**1 teasp. chopped parsley**
Butter	**Salt and pepper**
1 shallot	**2 tablesp. cream (optional)**
2 tablesp. breadcrumbs	
1 tablesp. grated Parmesan cheese	

Brush 6 ramekin cases with melted butter, and place them on a baking-tin in the oven for a few minutes. Chop the shallot finely and fry in a little butter, then drain and divide it equally in the ramekin cases. To the breadcrumbs add ½ the cheese and parsley, and seasonings. Put an equal amount into each case. Add a very small piece of butter. Then break and put one egg in each case, sprinkle with seasonings. Pour a little cream (if used) over each egg, add the remainder of the cheese, bake in a moderate oven (**350° F., Gas 4**) until set, then sprinkle with parsley.

6 helpings **Cooking time—8 min. (approx.**

EGGS WITH HAM

Œufs au Jambon

6 eggs	**2 tablesp. brown** *or* **white sauce** (*see* pp. 119, 115), *or* **gravy**
Butter	**1 tablesp. browned breadcrumbs**
2 tablesp. finely-chopped cooked ham	
Salt and pepper	
Mushroom ketchup *or* **similar sauce**	

Butter 6 individual soufflé cases. Season the ham with salt and pepper, add a few drops of ketchup, moisten with the sauce or gravy, and put the mixture into the cases. Break an egg into each case, keeping the yolks whole, and sprinkle with a little salt and pepper. Cover with a thin layer of breadcrumbs, place small pieces of butter on top and bake in a moderate oven (**350° F., Gas 4**) until the eggs are set. Serve in the cases in which they were cooked.

6 helpings
Cooking time—15 min. (approx.)

OX EYES

6 eggs	**Butter**
6 slices stale bread	**Milk**
Sour cream	

Cut the bread in slices about ¾ in. thick. Toast and trim them into rounds of about 3 in. in diameter then take out the middle of each round with a 1½-in. diameter pastry cutter. Place the rings in a well-buttered fireproof dish and pour over them, gradually, as much sour cream as they will absorb without becoming sodden. Then break 1 egg into each ring. Season lightly, cover each egg with a teasp. milk and bake gently until the eggs are done.

6 helpings **Cooking time—10 min. (approx.)**

Boiled Eggs

Boiling eggs is a simple job, but not everyone does it perfectly. There are three ways of doing it; a good cook finds the method that suits her best, and sticks to it.

Method 1. Bring sufficient water to cover the eggs to the boil. Gently place the eggs in the water, set the egg-timer, or make a note of the time, and cook from 3–4½ min., according to taste. Take out the eggs, tap each lightly, once, with the back of a spoon, and serve.

Method 2. Put the eggs into a pan containing cold water and bring to the boil. When boiling point is reached, start timing. Cooking will take a little less time than with Method 1.

Method 3. This method is, in effect, "coddling", and it produces an egg with a softer white than if actually boiled. Have a pan of boiling water ready, put in the eggs, cover the pan and turn off the heat. Let the pan stand for 6–8 min., according to the degree of softness required.

Hard-Boiled Eggs

For a really hard-boiled egg, cook by either Method 1 or 2, boiling for about 12 min. Then take out the eggs and put them under cold running water to cool them as quickly as possible. This prevents discolouration around the yolk.

CURRIED EGGS

Œufs au Kari

4 hard-boiled eggs	**1 teasp. curry powder**
4 oz. cooked rice	**1/3 pt. stock *or* milk**
1 small onion	**Salt**
1 oz. butter	**Lemon juice**
1 teasp. flour	

Prepare the rice (*see* p. 37), shell the eggs and cut them into quarters. Chop the onion finely and fry lightly in the butter, sprinkle in the flour and curry powder, and cook slowly for 5–6 min. Add the stock or milk, season with salt and lemon juice and simmer gently for ½ hr. Then add the eggs and let them remain until thoroughly heated and serve. The rice may be arranged as a border, or served separately.

4 helpings
Cooking time—45 min. (approx.)

EGG MORNAY

Œufs à la Mornay

4–5 hard-boiled eggs	**1½ oz. grated cheese**
1 oz. butter	**¼ pt. white sauce (*see* p. 115)**
Nutmeg	
Salt and pepper	

Cut the eggs into thick slices, place them on a well-buttered fireproof dish, sprinkle them lightly with nutmeg and more liberally with salt and pepper. Add 1 oz. cheese to the sauce and pour it over the eggs. Sprinkle thickly with cheese, and add a few tiny pieces of butter. Brown the surface in a hot oven or under the grill and serve.

4–5 helpings
Cooking time—5 min. (approx.)

EGGS À LA MAÎTRE D'HÔTEL

3 eggs	**Salt and pepper**
2 oz. butter	**1 teasp. chopped parsley**
1 dessertsp. flour	**1 teasp. lemon juice**
¼ pt. milk	

Melt 1 oz. butter in a saucepan, stir in the flour, add the milk and boil for 2 min. Have ready the eggs boiled hard, remove the shells, cut each egg in 4 or 8 pieces, and arrange them neatly on a dish. Season the sauce to taste, whisk in the remainder of the butter, add it gradually in small pieces, stir in the parsley and the lemon juice, then pour the sauce over the eggs.

Serve as quickly as possible.

2–3 helpings
Cooking time—20 min. (approx.)

EGGS IN ASPIC

3 hard-boiled eggs	**Chervil**
1 pt. aspic jelly (*see* p. 40)	**Cress**

Coat the bottom of 6 dariole moulds with jelly, decorate them with chervil; when set, put in slices of egg and aspic jelly alternately, taking care that each layer of jelly is firmly set before adding the egg. When the whole is firmly set, unmould and decorate with chopped aspic and cress.

6 helpings
Time (including setting)—2 hr. (approx.)

FRICASSÉE OF EGGS

Fricassée d'Œufs

4 hard-boiled eggs	**Chopped parsley**
½ pt. white sauce (*see* p. 115)	**Fried *or* toasted croûtons of bread**
Salt and pepper	

Reserve 1 egg yolk for garnishing; slice the other eggs. Well season the sauce, put in the sliced eggs and heat through thoroughly. Arrange on a hot dish, sprinkle with parsley and the egg yolk passed through a sieve, garnish with croûtons and serve.

2–3 helpings
Cooking time—30 min. (approx.)

SCOTCH EGGS

Œufs Écossaises

3 hard-boiled eggs	**Egg and breadcrumbs**
½ lb. sausage meat	**Frying fat**

FRIED EGGS

Shell the eggs and cover each egg with sausage meat. If liked, a little finely-chopped onion can be mixed with the sausage meat before using. Coat carefully with beaten egg and breadcrumbs, fry in hot fat until nicely browned. Cut each egg in half. Scotch eggs can be served either hot or cold.

3 helpings
Cooking time—40 min. (approx.)

Fried Eggs

Œufs à la Poêle

These are eggs fried on one side only. Melt a little bacon fat or butter in a frying-pan, break the eggs and slip them carefully into the pan. Cook over a gentle heat, basting the eggs with some of the hot fat, until the white is no longer transparent and the yolk is set. Season with pepper and salt.

Œufs Frits

Only one egg can be cooked at a time, but each takes less than one minute. Put a teacupful of oil into a small pan so that the egg will actually swim in the oil. Heat until the oil begins to smoke lightly, then maintain this temperature. Break the egg into a cup or saucer and season the yolk with salt and pepper. Slip it quickly into the oil, putting the edge of the cup to the surface of the oil. Dip a smooth wooden spoon into the hot oil, then pull the white over the yolk so as to cover it completely. Then turn the egg over in the oil and leave for a second only. It will then be done.

EGG CROQUETTES

Croquettes aux Œufs

4 hard-boiled eggs
6 mushrooms
1 oz. butter
½ oz. flour
½ gill milk
Salt and pepper
Pinch of nutmeg
A little flour and milk for coating
Breadcrumbs
Fried parsley

Chop the eggs finely. Chop the mushrooms roughly and fry them lightly in the butter, stir in the flour, add the milk and boil well. Now put in the eggs, add seasoning and nutmeg, mix well over heat, then spread on a plate to cool. When ready to use, shape into balls, coat carefully with a batter (milk and flour mixed to the consistency of cream), cover with breadcrumbs and fry in hot fat until golden brown. Drain well and serve garnished with fried parsley.

4 helpings

EGG FRITTERS—MILANAISE STYLE

Beignets d'Œufs à la Milanaise

4 hard-boiled eggs
½ oz. butter
½ oz. flour
⅛ pt. milk
1 oz. finely-chopped ham *or* tongue
1 teasp. finely-chopped parsley
1 small shallot, chopped and fried in butter
Lemon juice
Salt and pepper
Egg and breadcrumbs
Frying fat
Parsley

Halve the eggs lengthwise, and remove the yolks. Melt butter in a saucepan, stir in the flour, add the milk and boil gently for 2–3 min. Add chopped ham or tongue, parsley, shallot, chopped yolks, a little lemon juice and seasonings. Mix well. Fill egg whites with the mixture, coat carefully with egg and breadcrumbs and fry in hot fat until nicely browned. Drain well and serve garnished with parsley.

4 helpings
Cooking time—30 min.

EGG FRITTERS—ROYAL STYLE

Beignets d'Œufs à la Royale

4 eggs
1 tablesp. cream
Salt and pepper
Coating batter (*see* p. 399)
Frying fat

Beat the eggs, add the cream and season to taste. Pour the mixture into a well-buttered plain mould. Steam gently until set, let it cool, then turn out and cut into strips about 2½ in. long and ½ in. thick. Make batter as directed, dip in the egg strips and fry in hot fat until crisp and lightly browned. Drain well and serve.

4 helpings
Cooking time—30 min. (approx.)

EGG KROMESKIS

Cromesquis d'Œufs

3 hard-boiled eggs
1/8 pt. white sauce
1 tablesp. chopped tongue *or* ham
1/2 teasp. finely-chopped truffles
Salt and pepper
5 thin pancakes (*see* p. 397)
Frying fat
Coating batter

Chop the eggs coarsely, add the sauce, tongue, truffles and seasoning. Stir over heat for a few minutes. Let the mixture cool, then divide it into pieces the size and shape of a cork, and enfold in squares of pancake. Dip separately into batter, fry in hot fat until nicely browned, drain well and serve.

3–4 helpings
Cooking time—40 min. (approx.)

EGGS WITH BLACK BUTTER

Œufs frits au beurre noir

4 eggs
2 oz. butter
Buttered toast
Anchovy paste
1 dessertsp. tarragon vinegar
Chopped parsley

Melt the butter in a frying-pan, then fry the eggs taking care to keep the yolks whole. Have ready some well-buttered toast cut into small rounds, spread them lightly with anchovy paste, then place the eggs on them. Re-heat the butter with the vinegar, cook until dark brown, then pour over the eggs. Serve garnished with parsley.

2–4 helpings
Cooking time—15 min. (approx.)

Poached Eggs

Œufs pochés

To poach well, eggs must be fresh. They should be broken into a cup or saucer and then slipped into boiling salted water to which 1 tablesp. vinegar has been added. The water will cease to boil when the eggs are added: do not let it boil again. An average egg will take about 3 min. to poach: it is ready when the white has enveloped the yolk and may be touched without breaking. Remove with a perforated spoon.

If you like poached eggs round in shape, boil them for ½ min. before breaking into the poaching pan.

POACHED EGGS WITH POTATO AND ONION PURÉE

5 eggs
1 lb. potatoes
1 lb. onions
1 oz. butter
1 dessertsp. cream
Salt and pepper
Nutmeg

Boil the potatoes and onions in salted water. When soft put through a fine sieve, then mash with the butter and cream. Season with salt and pepper, and nutmeg. Separate one egg and add the yolk to the potato mixture. Mix well. Serve with 4 poached eggs on top.

4 helpings
Cooking time—30 min. (approx.)

POACHED EGGS WITH SPINACH

Œufs pochés aux Epinards

6 eggs
1 pt. spinach purée (fresh *or* canned)
1 oz. butter
Nutmeg
Salt and pepper
1 tablesp. brown sauce (*see* p. 119)
Croûtons of toast

Prepare the spinach purée (*see* p. 355), place it in a saucepan, add the butter, a good pinch of nutmeg, salt and pepper, and the brown sauce. Heat through thoroughly. Meanwhile, poach the eggs and trim them neatly. Turn the spinach on to a hot dish, flatten the surface slightly and on it place the eggs. Garnish with croûtons and serve a good gravy or brown sauce separately.

6 helpings
Cooking time—30 min. (approx.)

POACHED EGGS WITH TOMATO SAUCE

Œufs pochés à la Tomate

6 eggs
4 oz. rice
1/2 pt. stock
1 oz. butter
Salt and pepper
1/4 pt. tomato sauce

Wash and drain the rice, add it to the boiling stock. When cooked and the stock has been absorbed, stir in the butter and season to taste. Poach the eggs and trim them neatly. Arrange rice lightly on a hot dish, place the eggs on it, pour the hot sauce around and serve.

6 helpings
Cooking time—30 min. (approx.)

POACHED EGGS WITH TONGUE

Langue de Bœuf aux Œufs

4 eggs
4 slices cooked tongue
2–3 tablesp. good gravy
Small piece of meat glaze
Salt and pepper
Lemon juice

Put the slices of tongue into a shallow pan, with the gravy and glaze. Heat thoroughly and season to taste. Poach the eggs in salted water flavoured with lemon juice, trim them to a round shape. Place the tongue on a hot dish with an egg on top of each slice, then strain the gravy over and serve.

4 helpings
Cooking time—15 min. (approx.)

Scrambled Eggs

Œufs brouillés

The secret of serving good scrambled eggs lies in slow cooking over a very low heat (a double saucepan is useful for this), continuous stirring, and immediate service as the eggs go on cooking in their own heat. It is helpful to add a little butter, or cream, when the scrambling is almost finished: this stops the cooking and improves the flavour.

4 eggs
Salt and pepper
1 tablesp. butter
½ tablesp. butter *or* cream

Break the eggs into a bowl, add seasonings and beat eggs lightly. Meanwhile melt the 1 tablesp. butter in the bottom of a pan and roll it around. Before it begins to sizzle pour the eggs into the pan. Reduce the heat to very low, and stir the mixture evenly and constantly with a wooden spoon. When almost ready add about ½ tablesp. butter or cream. Remove from the heat as soon as the eggs are set to a soft creamy consistency. Serve immediately.

2 helpings
Cooking time—10 min. (approx.)

CURRIED SCRAMBLED EGGS

4 eggs
1 small onion
½ oz. butter
1 teasp. curry powder
Salt
¼ pt. milk
Buttered toast
Lemon juice

Chop the onion finely. Melt the butter in a stewpan, add the onion and fry for 2–3 min.; sprinkle in the curry powder, let this cook for a few minutes, stirring meanwhile. Beat the eggs slightly, season with salt, add the milk, pour the mixture into the stewpan and stir until the eggs begin to set. Have ready squares of well-buttered toast, pile the egg mixture lightly on them, sprinkle with lemon juice and serve at once.

4 helpings
Cooking time—15 min. (approx.)

EGGS À LA COURTET

2 eggs
1½ oz. butter
Salt and pepper
4 tomatoes
1 gill aspic jelly
Salad
2 tablesp. mayonnaise

Scramble the eggs with the butter and seasonings. Cut the tomatoes in halves and scoop out the centres. Fill the tomato cups with the eggs and set aside until quite cold. Coat with cool aspic jelly; when set, serve garnished with salad dressed with mayonnaise.

4 helpings **Cooking time—30 min. (approx.)**

PIPERADE BASQUE

6 eggs
2 red peppers
2 green peppers
1½ lb. tomatoes
1 clove garlic
Salt
Olive oil
Pinch of sugar
Black pepper
Croûtons

Cut the peppers in half, remove the seeds and pith, chop finely and plunge into boiling salted water. Simmer for about 10 min. Reserve 3 tomatoes, skin and quarter the rest. Crush garlic with a pinch of salt and add to 4 tablesp. olive oil in a sauté pan. Heat, add the strained peppers and cook slowly for 3–4 min. Then add the quartered tomatoes, salt and pepper, and sugar. Cover pan and simmer for 15 min. Skin and slice the 3 tomatoes and fry gently in oil. When the pepper mixture is mushy, beat the eggs lightly and add to the pan. Cook, stirring constantly, over a low heat, then pile on a dish and serve with the sliced tomatoes and croûtons arranged around.

8 helpings **Cooking time—40 min. (approx.)**

SCRAMBLED EGGS AND HAM

Œufs brouillés au Jambon

2 eggs
1 oz. butter
2 tablesp. finely-chopped ham
1 tablesp. milk
Salt and pepper
2 rounds buttered toast

Melt the butter in a pan, add the ham and let it heat gradually in the butter. Beat the eggs, add the milk and season to taste, pour into the pan and stir until the eggs begin to set. Have the toast ready and pile the egg mixture on it. Serve at once. Tongue, or other cold meat may be substituted for ham.

2 helpings
Cooking time—15 min. (approx.)

SCRAMBLED EGGS WITH MUSHROOMS

Œufs brouillés aux Champignons

4 eggs
6 small mushrooms
1 oz. butter
2 slices buttered toast
Salt and pepper
2 tablesp. cream *or* milk

Prepare the mushrooms, chop them and fry lightly in the butter. Meanwhile, trim the toast and divide each slice into 4 squares. Beat the eggs lightly, season to taste, add the cream and scramble in the usual way. Pile on the toast, serve immediately.

4 helpings
Cooking time—15 min. (approx.)

Separated Eggs

Recipes often call for the use of egg yolks or whites alone, resulting in one or the other remaining unused.

Egg Yolks

Whole yolks will keep for 2–3 days if covered with cold water and placed in a screw-top jar in a refrigerator.

To use them: add an extra egg yolk or two to scrambled eggs and custards, it will make them more creamy. Or add them to a cream sauce or soup, but do not let the liquid boil after adding the yolks. Or poach them hard and put through a sieve, then use the "mimosa balls" to garnish salads, rice dishes and soups.

Egg Whites

Place in a covered bowl in a refrigerator (well away from the ice-box), and they will keep for 5–6 days.

To use them: add an extra egg white to a mousse, meringue or soufflé. Or whisk the white and fold it into a jelly just before it sets. Or give a meringue top to plain milk puddings or tarts; a few minutes in a hot oven, just long enough to set the meringue is sufficient.

Mousses

Mousse is a French word meaning froth or foam. Whether savoury or sweet; whether hot, cold or frozen, a mousse is always frothy, light and creamy.

CHICKEN MOUSSE

3 egg yolks
1 tablesp. gelatine
1 teacup chicken broth
Salt and pepper
1 teacup cooked chicken, minced finely
1 teacup double cream lightly whipped
¼ teacup mayonnaise

Soak the gelatine for 5 min. in ½ cup broth. Beat the egg yolks and stir lightly in the remaining broth, add salt and pepper, cook in top of a double boiler, stirring constantly until thickened to custard consistency. Stir in the dissolved gelatine. Pour this over the chicken until the mousse begins to set. (This operation is speeded up if the chicken is put in a basin stood in cold water or cracked ice.) Then fold in the cream and mayonnaise. Turn into a mould which has been moistened with cold water. Chill until set.

To serve, turn out and garnish with watercress and lettuce.

4 helpings
Cooking time—45 min. (approx.)

CHOCOLATE MOUSSE

4 eggs
4 oz. plain *or* vanilla chocolate (sweetened)

Melt the chocolate with 1 tablesp. water (*or* black coffee) in a pan over a very low heat. Stir until smooth. Meanwhile separate the eggs and beat the yolks. Stir the melted chocolate into the yolks. Whip the whites very stiff and fold them into the chocolate. Make sure they are perfectly blended. Turn into a serving dish, or 4 individual dishes and leave to cool. Unless in a hurry, it is best not to put chocolate mousse in a refrigerator.

4 helpings
Cooking time—15 min. (approx.)

EGG MOUSSE

4–5 hard-boiled eggs	**½ pt. (bare) double cream**
1 dash Worcester *or* Anchovy sauce	**Salt and pepper**
4 tablesp. aspic jelly	**½ teasp. paprika**

Chop the egg whites finely and sieve the yolks. Mix the yolks with the sauce and aspic, let the mixture start to set, then add the lightly whipped cream and seasonings; fold together. Add the chopped whites and leave to set, preferably in a refrigerator. Turn out to serve.

4 helpings
Cooking time—45 min. (approx.)

FISH MOUSSE

2 eggs	**Salt and pepper**
1 lb. canned *or* cooked fish (canned salmon is excellent)	**1 dessertsp. lemon juice**
½ teacup milk	**1 tablesp. chopped parsley**
1 teacup breadcrumbs	

Drain the fish, remove the skin and bone and flake. Put the milk and breadcrumbs into a pan and add the juice from the canned fish (or ½ teacup liquid in which the fish was cooked). Put this over a low heat for 5 min., stirring occasionally. Then add the fish, salt and pepper, lemon juice and parsley. Mix, leave to cool slightly.

Separate the eggs; add the lightly beaten yolks to the fish mixture and stir well, beat the whites until stiff and fold them in thoroughly. Pour into a well-greased mould, cover with greaseproof paper and place in a tin of hot water reaching quarter-way up the side of the mould. Bake in a cool oven (**310° F., Gas 2**) for 40–45 min. During the last 10 minutes' cooking have the mould uncovered.

When cold, turn out and serve garnished with hard-boiled egg and cucumber.

4 generous helpings
Cooking time—1 hr. (approx.)

FROZEN ORANGE MOUSSE

3 egg yolks	**Pinch of salt**
⅔ teacup fresh orange juice	**¼ pt. cream lightly whipped**
⅔ teacup castor sugar	

Heat the orange juice, sugar and salt in the top of a double boiler. Beat the egg yolks until thick and lemon coloured. Add them to the orange mixture and slowly cook until thick, stirring constantly. Cool thoroughly and fold in the cream. Pour into individual cups and put into the freezing compartment of the refrigerator (or the coldest place available) until set.

4 helpings
Cooking time—25 min. (approx.)

Savoury Omelets

There are two types of omelet; the French which is flat and generally served folded into three, and the English which is fluffy and more like a soufflé. The essentials in making either type are a thick, clean and dry omelet pan of the right size, i.e. 6–7 in. in diameter for a 2 or 3 egg omelet; butter; eggs; and seasonings.

For recipes for sweet omelets, see pp. 407–8.

FRENCH OMELETTE (Plate 13)

2–3 eggs	**½ oz. butter**
Salt and pepper	

Break the eggs into a basin. Add salt and pepper to taste. Beat the eggs with a fork until they are lightly mixed. Heat the butter in the pan and slowly let it get hot, but not so hot that the butter browns. Without drawing the pan off the heat, pour in the egg mixture. It will cover the pan and start cooking at once.

Shake the pan and stir the eggs with a fork away from the side to the middle. Shake again. In about 1 min. the omelette will be soft but no longer runny. Let it stand for 4 or 5 seconds for the bottom to brown slightly. Then remove from the heat.

Using a palette knife, fold the omelette from two sides over the middle. Then slip on to a hot dish, or turn it upside down on to the dish.

This omelette can be eaten plain, or it can be filled. There are two methods of filling; flavouring such as herbs, cheese can be added to the eggs after they are beaten, or added to the cmelette just before it is folded.

Suggested savoury fillings (quantities given are for 2 egg omelettes)

Cheese: Grate 2 oz. hard cheese finely. Add most of it to the mixed eggs, saving a little to top the finished omelette.

Fines Herbes: Finely chop 1 tablesp. parsley and a few chives, and add this to the mixed eggs before cooking.

Onion: Sauté a large onion in a little butter but do not get it too greasy. When cool, add to the egg mixture, saving a few hot morsels for garnishing the omelette.

Kidney: Peel, core and cut 2 lamb's kidneys into smallish pieces, and sauté them in a little butter with a small chopped onion or shallot. Pile this mixture along the centre of the omelette after cooking but before folding.

Mushroom: Wash and chop 2 oz. mushrooms, sauté them in a little butter until tender. Put them along the centre of the cooked omelette.

Shellfish: Shrimps, prawns, crayfish, lobster or crab, fresh or canned, can be used. Chop if necessary and warm slowly through in a little white sauce (*see* p. 115) so they are hot when the omelette is cooked. Then pile the mixture along the centre.

Spanish: Make a mixture of chopped ham, tomato, sweet pepper, a few raisins, 1 or 2 mushrooms, and sauté in a little butter or olive oil. Add this to the egg before cooking; serve this omelette flat.

ENGLISH OMELET (Plate 13)

Separate the eggs. Add half an egg-shell of water for each egg, to the yolks: beat them with a wooden spoon until creamy. Whisk the whites until they stay in the basin when turned upside down. Gently fold the whites into the yolks. Have the butter ready in the pan as for the French Omelette. Pour in the egg mixture, and cook until it is golden brown on the underside. Then put the pan under the grill and lightly brown the top. Fillings are usually spread over the cooked omelet. Now run a palette knife round the edge of the pan. Fold the omelet over and slip on to a hot dish.

PRESSURE COOKERY

As cooking in a pressure cooker means that the food is cooked in steam it is essential always to have in the cooker a liquid which, when it boils, will give steam. This may be water, stock, gravy, fruit juice, milk or cooking wine but can never be fat, of any kind, on its own.

As pressure-cooking times are very much shorter than ordinary ones and as evaporation is almost completely eliminated, only a very small quantity of liquid is necessary and, wherever possible, this should be kept to the minimum. This amount must nevertheless be sufficient to completely cover the bottom of the cooker and to last the required cooking time. The actual quantities for each recipe will be shown in the manufacturer's booklet. When cooking soups, stews, milk puddings, etc., the amount of liquid is increased, however. to that required per person, regardless of the cooking time.

When cooking solids, a pressure cooker should not be more than two-thirds full. There must be room for the steam to circulate and do its work and there should always be sufficient space between the food and the cover to prevent the steam vent getting blocked. With a flat cover this is two-thirds of the base; with a domed cover the base can be filled to the top. When cooking liquids, the maximum quantity is one-half of the base. In this case, space must be left to allow for the liquid boiling up. Stock, milk, soup could easily fill the pan, and boil over or block the steam outlet.

To adjust recipes to cook for varying numbers of people a simple guide is to remember that, where the food is being timed by the pound, e.g. a joint of meat, the cooking time increases with the weight and so does the amount of liquid required. If only the quantity of food is being increased, e.g. 4 lb. potatoes, instead of 1 lb., no addition need be made to the cooking time or the liquid.

There is really no hard and fast rule for changing one's own favourite dishes over to pressure cooking but usually a basic recipe containing similar ingredients can be found in the instruction booklet. Working from this, method—together with the necessary amount of liquid and time required—

can often be worked out. Otherwise, it is best to make one's first experiment taking one-third of the normal cooking-time and then an adjustment of more or less time can be made as necessary.

Because of the effect of atmospheric pressure on the pressure—and therefore the temperature—inside a pressure cooker, allowance must be made when one is used at considerable altitudes above sea-level. As the altitude increases, the boiling-point of liquids decreases and extra cooking time or pressure is necessary. If 15 lb. pressure is indicated, increase the cooking time by 1 min. for every 1,000 ft. above 2,000 ft. above sea-level. Where 10 lb. pressure is required use 15 lb., for 5 lb. use 10 lb., then in neither case will it be necessary to increase the cooking time.

Domestic pressure cookers may also be used for actual sterilization purposes. Instructions are available for the preparation and sterilization of baby foods, feeding bottles, teats, etc., so that everything necessary for a 24 hr.'s feeding schedule may be done at the same time, requiring 10 min. only, at 10 lb. pressure; surgical or household rubber gloves require 20 min. at 15 lb. pressure.

INVALID COOKERY

AT NO TIME IS THE CAREFUL selection of food more important than when cooking for an invalid.

First of all the kind of foods or diet to follow must be ascertained from the Doctor, and *at all times* work within the scope of his instructions.

Consult the patient as little as possible, for a sick person should not be bothered about selecting dishes, although it is wise to avoid serving the food in a manner which is known to be disliked by the patient—a substitute food can generally be found, or it can be "disguised" in some way. Many people dislike milk but will eat a junket or enjoy a soup or savoury drink made from milk, and the nutritive value of the milk is as good.

Obviously the tray and the food should look as attractive as possible. Make individual moulds, etc., wherever possible, rather than serve a portion of a large mould. Take out bones of meat or skin from fish and check carefully that salt, etc., are on the tray. Use a gay cloth, decorative china and perhaps put a flower on the tray to help to create an interest in food.

Before a meal make sure the patient is quite comfortable (he might enjoy a cool wash)—see the bed is straightened and that the tray is firmly in position. Never leave half-eaten food in the sick room. Remove it at once for the patient will not "eat it later", and it looks most unappetising as well as being unhygienic.

On the other hand ensure that there is a good supply of drinks available—either iced water, lemonade, etc., or hot drinks. Cold drinks can be kept very cold in a thermos flask in the same way that a flask keeps liquids hot. Rinse out the flask with cold water before filling.

Soups—while the patient is very ill it may be found advisable to give soup as an evening meal rather than the first course of a meal. Many people like soup rather than milk as a "snack" between meals. See pages 74–113 for recipes for soups.

Fish is an ideal food for invalids—for it is easily digested and nutritious. It can become monotonous unless care is taken to prepare it in attractive ways. See pages 145–196 for recipes for cooking fish.

Meat dishes—avoid fatty or rich meat such as pork or sausages—concentrate on the ways of cooking that are attractive yet easy to digest. Do not ignore foods such as tripe, liver or sweetbreads, for they are admirable for an invalid.

In hot weather the invalid will appreciate the cool refreshing flavour of sweet or savoury jellies. *Do not use too much gelatine*, for an over-stiff jelly is difficult to eat.

Most milk puddings are suitable for an invalid. In *most* cases a certain amount of fruit is essential, so do not disregard the importance of fresh fruit and particularly citrus fruits in an invalid diet.

At supper-time an attractive savoury, made perhaps with egg or vegetables, is more suitable for an invalid than a heavier meal. See pages 576–588 for recipes for savouries.

BEVERAGES

APPLE JUICE

1 lb. cooking apples
Rind of 1 lemon
1 pt. boiling water
Sugar to taste

Peel and slice the apples *very thinly*. Put them into a basin or jug with the lemon rind; add the boiling water. Cover jug and allow to cool. Strain—add sugar to taste.

1 pt. liquid

APPLE AND LEMON JUICE

As above using rind and juice of 2 lemons. Serve with slices of lemon.

ARROWROOT

1 small dessertsp. arrowroot
½ pt. milk *or* water
1 teasp. castor sugar

Mix the arrowroot smoothly with a little cold milk. Boil the remainder of the milk and pour it on the arrowroot paste, stirring briskly meanwhile. Return to saucepan. Boil for 5 min., stirring all the time. Add the sugar and serve. If preferred, an equal quantity of water may be substituted for the milk.

1 good helping **Cooking time—8 min.**

ARROWROOT AND BLACKCURRANT TEA

2 rounded tablesp. blackcurrant jam
1 pt. water
1 dessertsp. arrowroot

Put the jam and water into a saucepan. Bring to the boil. Strain, return the liquid to the saucepan, and bring again to boiling point. Mix the arrowroot smoothly with a little cold water, pour it into the saucepan and boil gently for about 10 min. Pour into a jug, stir from time to time until cold.

1 generous helping
Cooking time—15 min.

BARLEY GRUEL

1 tablesp. patent barley
A little cold water
A pinch of salt
½ pt. boiling water *or* milk
Sugar

Mix the barley well with cold water until a smooth paste about the thickness of cream is formed. Add salt, the boiling water (or milk, which is preferable) put into an enamelled saucepan, add sugar to taste. Simmer for 10 min., stirring all the time with a silver or wooden spoon.

1 generous helping
Cooking time—10 min.

BARLEY WATER

2 oz. pearl barley
2–3 lumps of sugar
Thinly-peeled rind of ½ a small lemon
1 pt. boiling water

Cover the barley with cold water. Boil for 2 min. to blanch, then strain. Place the barley, sugar, and lemon rind in a jug. Pour in the 1 pt. boiling water. Cover closely. When cold, strain and use.

NOTE: This forms a nutritious, agreeable drink, and it is also largely used to dilute milk, making it easier to digest.

1 generous helping
Cooking time—5 min.

BEEF ESSENCE

1 lb. lean juicy beef | **Salt and pepper**

Trim off all fat and skin from the beef; put the beef into a basin or jar without water. Cover with a lid or several thicknesses of paper, and stand the jar in a pan of boiling water. Cook slowly for approximately 3 hr. Strain, pressing all the liquid from the meat. Season. Store in a cool place and serve with crisp fingers of toast.

NOTE: Lean mutton or veal could be used instead.

Cooking time—3 hr. (approx.)

BEEF TEA (1)

1 lb. gravy beef (flank *or* skirt of beef)
1 pt. water
½ teasp. salt

Cut all fat from the meat. Put the meat into a jar, basin or top of a double saucepan, add the water and salt. Stand in or over a pan of water and allow to simmer for 2–3 hr. Put through fine strainer or muslin. Allow to cool; remove any fat on top of beef tea. Re-heat *without boiling*—serve with biscuits or toast.

NOTE: This must be stored in a cool place. If this is not possible, then make freshly each time.

2–3 helpings
Cooking time—2–3 hr.

BEEF TEA (2)

Ingredients as Beef Tea (1) but add :

1 small carrot, sliced
½ small turnip, sliced
1 small onion, sliced
Small bunch parsley
2 bay leaves

Prepare as Beef Tea (1) adding the vegetables. Either cook over water as before *or* cook for 2–3 hr. in a very cool oven (**265°–290° F., Gas ½–1**). The liquid should never boil. Strain and serve as in Recipe (1).

NOTE: Particular care must be taken in storing this beef tea when vegetables have been added.

2–3 helpings
Cooking time—2–3 hr.

BEEF TEA (3)

Where the patient *must* avoid every trace of fats, the cooked beef tea should first be strained then blotting or tissue paper repeatedly drawn over the surface to absorb the very tiny particles of fat.

Reheat without boiling and serve as before.

BEEF TEA (4)

1 egg yolk
Salt
¼ pt. beef tea
Thin strips of toast

NOTE: Beef tea, veal tea, mutton tea, or diluted beef essence may be used in this preparation.

Beat the egg yolk in a teacup. Season lightly with salt, and if allowed, add a little pepper. Heat the beef tea, but do not allow it to boil. Pour it over the egg yolk, stirring briskly meanwhile. Serve with thin strips of toast.

1 helping
Cooking time—10 min.

BEEF TEA (5) — RAW

2 oz. lean juicy beef
2 tablesp. cold water
Pinch of salt

Cut off all skin and fat from the meat; shred the meat finely. Pour over it the water, add the salt, cover and let it stand for at least 2 hr. When ready to use, strain into an attractive cup or glass. Season to taste.

NOTE: This variety of beef tea is more easily digested than any other, in consequence of the albumen being contained in an uncooked and therefore soluble condition.

1 helping **Time—2 hr.**

BEEF TEA CUSTARD

1 egg | **¼ pt. beef tea**
1 egg yolk | **Salt**

Beat the egg and egg yolk thoroughly together. Pour on to it the beef tea and season to taste. Have ready a well-buttered cup, and pour in the mixture. Cover with a buttered paper and stand the cup in a saucepan containing a little boiling water. Steam very gently for about 20 min. Turn out carefully. Serve either hot or cold, or cut into dice, and serve in broth or soup.

1 generous helping | **Cooking time—20 min.**

BLACKCURRANT TEA

1 tablesp. blackcurrant jam
1 teasp. castor sugar
1 teasp. lemon juice
½ pt. boiling water

Put the jam, sugar and lemon juice into a jug. Pour on the boiling water; stir well. Cover with a plate or saucer. Stand the jug in a warm place for 15 min. Strain and use as a remedy for a cold. Alternatively allow it to become cold, and use as a beverage to quench thirst or relieve hoarseness.

½ pt. tea | **Cooking time—a few minutes**

BRANDY AND EGG MIXTURE

1 egg yolk
¼ oz. loaf sugar
2 oz. cinnamon water
1 tablesp. brandy

Beat together the egg yolk and sugar; add the cinnamon water and brandy.

This is a palatable restorative.

EGG AND BRANDY (or WINE)

1 egg
Castor sugar to taste
1 tablesp. hot *or* cold water
1 tablesp. brandy *or* a small glass port *or* sherry

Beat the egg well in a cup, add a little sugar, and the water, brandy, port or sherry, and mix well. Strain into a tumbler and serve.

1 helping

EGG FLIP

1 tablesp. brandy *or* sherry
¼ pt. milk
A little castor sugar (optional)
1 egg white

Mix the brandy or wine and the milk together in a tumbler. If liked, add a little castor sugar. Beat the egg white to a stiff froth, stir it lightly into the flavoured milk and serve.

1 helping

EGG NOG

1 tablesp. sherry *or* brandy
1 tablesp. cream
Castor sugar to taste
1 egg white

Put the wine or brandy in a tumbler, add the cream and a little sugar and mix well. Whisk the egg white to a stiff froth, stir it lightly into the contents of the tumbler, and serve.

1 helping

EGG NOG—HOT

1 egg yolk
1 tablesp. castor sugar
1 tablesp. brandy *or* whisky
Just under ½ pt. milk

Beat the egg yolk and sugar well together. Stir in the brandy or whisky. Bring the milk to boiling-point and pour it over the mixed ingredients. Stir well, and serve.

1 large helping

HONEY AND LEMON DRINK (for sore throats)

1 heaped tablesp. honey
Juice of ½ large *or* 1 small lemon
Boiling water
½ teasp. glycerine if wished

Mix the honey and lemon in a tumbler. Pour on the boiling water. Stir well, adding glycerine if desired.

LEMON SQUASH

Juice of 1 lemon
1 teasp. castor sugar
1 small bottle of soda water

Squeeze and strain the lemon juice into a tumbler. Add the sugar, pour in the soda water and serve at once.

LEMON WHEY

1 pt. milk
Juice of 1 lemon
Castor sugar to taste

Heat the milk in a double saucepan, or in a jug placed in a saucepan of boiling water. Add the lemon juice, sweeten to taste. Continue cooking until the curd separates, then drain off the whey. Serve either hot or cold.

(A very light and refreshing drink.)

About ¾ pt.
Cooking time—20 min. (approx.)

MILK AND BEEF TEA

½ tumbler Beef Tea
½ tumbler milk

Heat together and serve piping hot or serve very cold.

NOTE: This combination will be enjoyed by people who find milk insipid. Also try flavouring milk with any of the well-known beef or vegetable extracts.

MILK POSSET or SPICED BREAD AND MILK

2 moderately thin slices of stale bread
Salt
Nutmeg to taste
1 dessertsp. castor sugar
1 pt. milk
1 tablesp. brandy *or* sherry

Cut the bread into small dice. Put it into a bowl. Sprinkle over a pinch of salt, pinch of nutmeg, and the sugar. Bring the milk nearly to boiling point. Pour it over the bread. Stir in the brandy or sherry, and serve.

1 generous helping
Cooking time—a few minutes

MUTTON TEA

½ lb. lean mutton
¼ teasp. salt
½ pt. water

Mutton tea is used less than beef tea, but it is a good means of varying the diet. It is both light and easily digested. For invalids it should be prepared as directed for Beef Tea, using any of the given recipes.

MEAT DISHES

BEEF JELLY

1 teasp. powdered gelatine
2 tablesp. cold water
¼ pt. strong beef tea
Salt and pepper (if necessary)

Soften gelatine in 2 tablesp. cold water; pour on to it the very hot beef tea. Stir until gelatine is dissolved; season to taste. Pour into rinsed mould, allow to set.

NOTE: In cases where all nourishment must be given cold or iced, the above recipe will be found useful.

1 individual jelly

CALF'S FOOT JELLY

1 calf's foot
2 pt. water
Salt and pepper
1 large lemon
1 egg white and shell
Pinch of powdered cinnamon
2 cloves
½ wineglass sherry (optional)

Wash and blanch the calf's foot; cut into pieces. Put in a pan with the 2 pt. water and seasoning. Simmer for 3–4 hr., removing scum if necessary. Strain and measure stock. If more than 1 pt., boil until reduced to this quantity. Allow to cool, remove fat. Return to pan with rind and juice of the lemon, egg white and shell, cinnamon, cloves and sherry (if used). Simmer for 10 min. Strain or put through a jelly bag. Store in a cool place.

3–4 helpings
Cooking time—4 hr. (approx.)

RAW BEEF BALLS

3–4 oz. raw juicy fillet *or* rump steak
½ teasp. cream *or* strong beef-tea
Butter

Scrape the meat into tiny fragments with a sharp knife. Press it through a wire sieve. Mix with it the cream or beef-tea. Form into balls the size of a very small Spanish nut. Rub the bottom of a sauté pan or saucepan slightly with butter. Make the pan hot. Put in the balls, and move them about for a few seconds with a spoon until the colour is slightly changed, but leaving the inside absolutely raw. Serve with beef-tea or soup.

1–2 helpings
Cooking time—½ hr.

RAW BEEF SANDWICHES

2–3 oz. raw juicy steak
Salt and pepper
Thin slices of bread and butter
Castor sugar (optional)

Scrape the meat finely. Rub it through a wire sieve and season lightly with salt and pepper. Spread it on thin bread and butter, and place another piece on top. Cut into dainty squares and serve. If preferred, the pepper and salt may be omitted, and the meat, when spread on the bread, thickly dredged with castor sugar. This entirely masks the flavour of the meat.

1–2 helpings

STEWED TRIPE

4–6 oz. tripe
1½ gills milk
1 finely-chopped onion
Salt and pepper
½ oz. flour

Cover the tripe with cold water, bring to the boil. Drain well, and cut tripe into 1 in. squares. Replace it in the pan, add the milk, onion and a seasoning of salt and pepper, bring to the boil and simmer very gently for 2 hr. Ten min. before serving add the flour mixed smoothly with a little cold milk, stir until boiling, simmer for 5 min. longer, and serve.

1 helping **Cooking time—2¼ hr.**

SWEETS

CARAGHEEN MOSS BLANCMANGE

¼ oz. caragheen (Irish sea-moss)
1 dessertsp. sugar
1½ gills milk
Few drops of vanilla essence

Wash the caragheen moss well. Put into a saucepan with all the ingredients and simmer for 10 min. Strain through muslin into 2 rinsed small moulds or glasses—adding a little extra sugar if necessary. Leave to set.

NOTE: Irish moss possesses medicinal properties, but the flavour is somewhat unpalatable, hence the necessity of disguising it with flavouring.

2 small helpings

INVALID TRIFLE

1 sponge cake
1 dessertsp. redcurrant jelly
2 tablesp. hot fruit purée (if allowed)
¼ pt. egg custard sauce

DECORATION

A very little whipped cream or fat-less mock cream

Split the sponge cake and spread with jelly. Put into dish and cover with hot fruit purée. Allow to cool then pour over the warm custard. When set decorate with cream.

NOTE: As the patient becomes stronger more colourful decorations could be used, i.e. glacé cherries, angelica, whole fruit.

1 helping

IRISH MOSS JELLY

Many people prefer Agar-Agar or Irish (Caragheen) moss instead of gelatine.

¼ oz. Agar-Agar *or* Caragheen moss
Good ½ pt. water
¼ wineglass sherry
1 teasp. lemon juice
Sugar to taste

Wash the moss carefully. Soak overnight in a little cold water. Put in a pan with ½ pt. water and simmer for 8 min. Strain through muslin. Add sherry, lemon juice and sugar to taste. Pour into 2 sundae glasses or rinsed individual moulds. Leave to set.

NOTE: Irish moss possesses medicinal properties, but the flavour is somewhat unpalatable, hence the necessity of disguising it with sherry, lemon juice, or other flavouring.

2 individual jellies **Cooking time—8 min.**

JUNKETS

½ pt. milk
½–1 teasp. rennet (see directions on bottle)
Sugar to taste

Heat milk to blood heat; stir in rennet and sugar. Pour into 2 small glasses. Leave in a warm place to "clot".

NOTE: With pasteurized milk it is advisable to use double quantities of rennet.

Never put the junket into a refrigerator until firm.

2 small helpings
Cooking time—2–3 min.

FLAVOURINGS

Chocolate: Dissolve 1 tablesp. grated chocolate in warm milk.

Coffee: Dissolve 1 dessertsp. coffee essence in warm milk.

Caramel: Heat 1 oz. brown sugar with 1 tablesp. water until golden caramel. Add milk slowly. Warm.

MOCK CREAM or EGG WHITE CREAM (suitable for fat free diet)

1 egg white
1 level dessertsp. warmed golden syrup *or* clear honey

Whisk egg white until very firm. Gradually whisk in the warmed syrup or honey. Serve cold.

2–3 helpings

MILK JELLY (1)

½ pt. milk
Thinly-cut rind of ½ lemon
1 oz. sugar
1 level dessertsp. powdered gelatine
½ gill water

Simmer milk with the lemon rind and sugar for a few minutes, then cool. Soften gelatine in 1 tablesp. cold water. Add rest of water (*boiling*). Stir until gelatine is dissolved then cool slightly. Strain milk over gelatine. Stir until dissolved. Pour into 2 sundae glasses or rinsed moulds and allow to set.

This method entirely prevents milk curdling.

2 individual jellies
Cooking time—5 min. (approx.)

MILK JELLY (2)

½ packet fruit flavoured jelly crystals *or* cubes
½ gill water
1½ gills cold milk

Put jelly crystals or cubes into a basin or top of double saucepan; add ½ gill water. Stir over boiling water until jelly is dissolved. Cool. Add cold milk. Pour into 2 sundae glasses or rinsed moulds and allow to set.

2 individual jellies
Cooking time—5–10 min. (approx.)

EGG DISHES

CODDLED EGG

1 new-laid egg

Place the egg in boiling water, put on the lid, and let the saucepan stand for 7–8 min. where the water will keep hot without simmering.

An egg cooked in this manner is more easily digested than when boiled in the ordinary way.

1 helping

ONE EGG OMELET

This is generally sufficient for a sick person.

¼–½ oz. butter
1 egg
Seasoning

Heat the butter in an omelet pan. Add the seasoned and beaten egg. When just beginning to set, push back egg mixture so only ½ pan is covered. Cook quickly allowing liquid egg to flow down sides of pan. Put in filling—if the omelet is not to be served plain, fold away from pan-handle and tip on to a hot plate.

Serve at once—garnished with parsley.

All plain omelets are eminently suitable for invalids. The following fillings are to be recommended:

Creamed spinach: Cook a small quantity of spinach, sieve, then reheat with a little butter and milk. Season well.

Creamed fish: Heat cooked flaked fish in a white sauce.

Creamed chicken: Heat cooked chopped breast of chicken in a white sauce.

Cheese: where allowed by the doctor, fill with grated or cream cheese before folding.

DIABETIC FOODS

This section gives general recipes and ideas for the Diabetic sufferer. One must of course always be guided by one's diet sheet, and by the Doctor's instructions. The amount of carbohydrates is given against each recipe in order that the patient may check with his or her diet.

If in any doubt regarding recipes the Diabetic Association will be found most helpful.

Most egg dishes are excellent for a diabetic diet and can be included wherever possible—milk, cheese, fish, meat are also valuable foods.

The carbohydrate value of most leafy green vegetables is negligible so the patient may enjoy salads, cooked green vegetables and many vegetable soups, as one pleases.

The following may be useful in planning a diet sheet:

1 pint of milk contains 30 grams carbohydrate, 24 grams protein, 24 grams fats, so the moment one drinks or adds ¼ pint milk to a soup then 7½ grams carbohydrate, 6 grams protein and 4 grams fat are added.

¼ oz. flour (¾ level tablespoonful) used in thickening a soup or stew gives 5 grams carbohydrate and 1 gram protein but no fat.

⅙th oz. sugar (1 good teaspoonful) gives 5 grams carbohydrate but no added protein or fat.

SOUPS WHICH CAN BE SERVED AT ANY TIME

(their food value is negligible)

CELERY SOUP

1 teacup diced celery
½ pt. vegetable stock *or* water
½ small onion
Yeast extract to flavour
Seasoning

Put the celery with the other ingredients into a pan. Simmer until tender. Sieve, re-heat adding extra seasoning if desired.

1 helping
Cooking time—15 min. (approx.)

ASPARAGUS SOUP

1 small bundle asparagus
¼ pt. vegetable stock
Seasoning

Clean and trim the asparagus stalks. Put into a saucepan with the liquid and seasoning. Simmer until asparagus is tender. Lift out of liquid—cut off extreme tips—keep for garnish. Rub rest of asparagus through a sieve. Return to pan with liquid—re-heat. Add tips and extra seasoning if wished.

NOTE: Other vegetables which may be used in this way: spinach, runner beans, cauliflower, greens. These have sufficient flavour to make an appetising soup without the addition of milk, flour, etc.

2 helpings
Cooking time—15–20 min. (approx.)

SOUPS THAT MUST BE COUNTED IN DIET

Other vegetables contain sufficient carbohydrates etc., to affect the diet.

CARROT SOUP

—this would contain 5 grams of carbohydrate but no protein or fat.

4 oz. carrots
½ pt. stock
Seasoning
A little meat extract to flavour
Chopped parsley

Put the carrots with stock, seasoning and meat extract into a saucepan. Simmer until carrots are soft. Sieve, then re-heat. Add parsley and serve.

NOTE: Other vegetables to watch and count the calories would be: artichokes, broad beans, potatoes, peas, turnips, swedes.

1 generous helping
Cooking time—15 min. (approx.)

SOUPS CONTAINING MILK

CREAMED CELERY SOUP

—7 grams carbohydrate, 6 grams protein, 4 grams fat.

As for Celery Soup, but use only ¼ pt. water *or* stock. Add ¼ pt. milk after sieving soup.

CREAMED POTATO SOUP

—17 grams carbohydrate, 8 grams protein and 4 grams fat.

2 oz. potatoes
¼ pt. stock *or* water
Seasoning
1 small onion
A little meat extract to flavour
¼ pt. milk

GARNISH
Chopped watercress

Cut potatoes into small pieces. Simmer them with the stock, seasoning and onion until soft. Put through a sieve. Add the meat extract, milk and more seasoning, then re-heat. Garnish with freshly-chopped watercress.

1 generous helping
Cooking time—15 min. (approx.)

FISH, MEAT and POULTRY DISHES

Neither fish, meat or poultry contain carbohydrates by themselves, but the moment other foods, i.e., breadcrumbs, certain vegetables, are added then one must check against one's diet.

For example, the average sausage mixture contains *approximately* 5 grams carbohydrates in a sausage.

1 tablespoonful breadcrumbs used in coating fish for frying contains 5 grams carbohydrates.

FRUITS AND SWEETS

All fruits contain a certain amount of carbohydrates—so this must be checked when serving raw or cooked. The amount of carbohydrates present varies considerably—dried fruits are rich in this, sweet fruits less so, but very acid fruits—under-ripe gooseberries, rhubarb, etc. contain so little that it is unimportant.

To sweeten fruit use crushed saccharine tablets. Simmer the fruit until just soft. Dissolve saccharine in warm but NOT boiling water. Stir into warm fruit.

GELATINE is a useful addition to give interest to fruit, for it contains no carbohydrates.

Allow 1 level teaspoonful powdered gelatine to each teacup fruit purée (sweetened with saccharine).

Follow the recipes for milk jellies and junkets in the Invalid Section—using the milk from the daily allowance but sweetening with crushed saccharine, dissolved in warm water instead of sugar.

CAKES AND BISCUITS

When making cakes for the family a careful check must be made as to quantities used, so one has a clear idea of the carbohydrates, etc., present in the slice one takes or gives to the patient for tea.

In time the food value of kinds of biscuits, etc., will easily be assessed and it is possible to obtain carbohydrate-free flour.

PRESERVES

It is possible to make diabetic preserves at home, and these will assist in providing variety for tea.

Fruits should be *bottled* in water, then crushed saccharine, dissolved in warm water added to the fruit when the jars are opened.

DIABETIC LEMON CURD

2 oz. butter
Grated rind and juice 2 lemons
3 large eggs
3 (0·3 gram) saccharine tablets
1 teasp. warm water

Put the butter, lemon juice and rind (take care to grate only top yellow from lemons) into a double saucepan. Heat until butter is melted; add beaten eggs. Cook, without boiling, until thick. Cool slightly—then add saccharine dissolved in water. *Taste* and if desired more saccharine can be added.

Store in a cool place—this keeps for some days.

SUGARLESS JAM

1 lb. fruit
A little water
8–10 (0·3 gram) saccharine tablets
1 tablesp. hot water
½ oz. powdered gelatine
½ gill water

Simmer fruit with a little water until soft. Crush saccharine tablets dissolved in the hot water, add to *hot* but not boiling fruit. Add the gelatine dissolved in the ½ gill hot water. Stir briskly for several minutes, pour into small jars with firmly fitting tops and seal down. Stand in a cool place. This will keep for some days.

To make jam that keeps, pour very hot jam into hot bottling jar. Seal down, giving screw band half turn back. Stand in a pan of boiling water and boil briskly for 5 min. Lift out and tighten screw band. Test for seal next day by seeing if lid is tight.

SUGARLESS MARMALADE

SEVILLE ORANGE MARMALADE

1 lb. Seville oranges (3 medium sized)
2 pt. water
1 oz. powdered gelatine
¼ pt. hot water
18–20 (0·3 gram) saccharine tablets
2 tablesp. hot water

Shred the orange peel—discarding *some* of the white pith. Tie pips in a muslin bag. Put juice in a separate container. Soak peel and pips in the 2 pt. water for 12–24 hr. Simmer gently until peel is very soft, adding the pips and juice. Remove bag of pips. Dissolve gelatine in the ¼ pt. hot water, and the saccharine in the 2 tablesp. hot water. Add to the fruit. Stir from time to time—to distribute the peel then put into jars and seal down. This should keep for some days in a cool place.

To preserve for a longer period, pour into bottling jars, seal, giving screw band half turn back, stand in a pan of boiling water and sterilize for 5–10 min. Lift out, tighten screw band. Test for seal next day by seeing if lid is tight.

LEMON MARMALADE

As for Seville Orange Marmalade, substituting lemons for oranges.

SWEET ORANGE MARMALADE

As for Seville Orange Marmalade, but allow only 15 (0·3 gram) saccharine tablets, and to 1 lb. sweet oranges add 1 lemon.

VEGETARIAN COOKERY

VEGETARIANS CAN BE DIVIDED into two classes, the strict vegetarians (known as vegans) who eat no food of animal origin whatsoever; and those who do not eat meat or fish, but will include eggs, milk and milk products in their diet. This second group do not present much difficulty to the cook, for a varied and pleasant diet can be achieved using these foods. The strict vegetarians are, however, more of a problem.

For healthy life and growth it is necessary that one should have an adequate supply of proteins, fats, carbohydrates, mineral matter and vitamins in the diet. In a normal mixed diet most of the protein is obtained from meat, fish, eggs, cheese and milk, so that on this score a vegan would be sadly lacking. However, there are of course vegetable proteins, though they have not such a high biological value as animal ones. The chief sources of vegetable proteins are cereals, pulses (lentils, peas and beans) and nuts, and in order to safeguard the health of those who adopt this very restricted form of diet it is essential that a wide variety of all types of vegetable proteins should be regularly included in the dishes. For instance, it is not advisable to use just one variety of nut kernel or, in fact, to restrict oneself to nuts alone or to any one type of such foods, but to include, as far as possible, all varieties in each group. The biological value of pulse dishes is improved considerably if some form of cereal and green leaf protein is added to them.

Soya-bean protein is valuable and is now available in many different forms, some of which can be cooked and used in the same way as meat.

The sweet course does not present any considerable difficulty as most vegetarians (of both categories) prefer fruit in some form or other and, except in the case of the vegans, are quite willing to partake of foods incorporating eggs and milk, though without the use of animal gelatine. An acceptable substitute for the latter is *agar-agar* which is of vegetable origin.

There is on the market a large variety of ready-to-eat savouries in cans; rissole and fritter mixtures available in packets; several savoury spreads and canned vegetarian sausages, which the housewife will find are a great help in preparing a quick vegetarian meal. These can be obtained from Health Food Stores.

More recipes suitable for vegetarians will be found in the sections on Vegetables, p. 320; Salads, p. 362; Sweets, p. 381; Cereals, p. 594; Dairy Produce, p. 667.

BANANAS—FRIED

Bananas
Flour
Oil *or* butter to fry
Poached eggs

Peel the bananas and cut them in half lengthwise. Flour each and fry in butter or oil until light brown. Drain well and serve with poached eggs, just as bacon and eggs would be served.

CARROT PUDDING

Boiled carrots
Half the bulk of carrots in breadcrumbs
2 oz. butter
1–2 eggs
Salt and pepper
Béchamel sauce

Boil some carrots until soft, chop them small or rub them through a sieve, add the breadcrumbs and butter, and sufficient egg to bind the whole together, with seasoning to taste. Butter a pudding basin, put in the mixture and steam for 1–1½ hr., according to size. Turn out the pudding and serve hot with Béchamel sauce poured round.

NOTE: This pudding can be made with other vegetables. Chopped turnips or cauliflowers mixed with the carrot are excellent.

2 helpings

NUT MINCE

½ lb. of any kind of nut *or* mixed nuts
1 oz. butter
6 oz. dry breadcrumbs
1 onion
1 tablesp. mushroom ketchup *or* any sauce
Salt and pepper
¾ pt. vegetable stock (approx.)
Mashed potatoes
Croûtons of bread

Pass the nuts through a nut-mill or chop finely. Melt the butter in a frying-pan and fry the nuts, breadcrumbs, and grated onion until pale brown, then add the ketchup, seasoning and sufficient stock, and cook for a few minutes. Make a border with the potato on a hot dish, put the mince in the centre and garnish with croûtons of bread. Serve very hot.

6–7 helpings
Cooking time—20 min.

OATMEAL PORRIDGE

Oatmeal
Salt
Water

1. There are several ways of making porridge. The one generally adopted is to sprinkle the oatmeal into boiling, slightly salted water with the left hand, meanwhile stirring briskly with a wooden spoon. When the porridge is thick enough the heat is reduced and the porridge slowly cooked for 20–30 min., being occasionally stirred to prevent it sticking to the bottom of the pan.

2. Probably the best method is to use a double saucepan for making porridge, for it is always desirable to have oatmeal thoroughly cooked, and as the water in the outer pan obviates the necessity of frequent stirring, the porridge may, with little trouble, be cooked thoroughly on the previous day and re-heated when required; a pinch of salt should always be added to the porridge.

Fully and partially cooked oatmeals can be prepared in a few minutes. Full instructions are given on the packages.

WALNUT ROAST

½ lb. milled walnuts
½ lb. fresh, wholemeal breadcrumbs
Salt and pepper
1 large onion
2 oz. vegetable margarine
¼ teasp. powdered sage
6 tablesp. thick gravy

FILLING

4 oz. fresh, wholemeal breadcrumbs
2 oz. melted margarine
½ teasp. thyme
2 tablesp. chopped parsley
Rind of ½ lemon (grated)
Salt and pepper

Mix the nuts, breadcrumbs and seasoning together. Chop the onion finely and fry until golden brown in the margarine, mix in the powdered sage. Place the onion on top of the nut mixture and pour over the gravy. Mix to a stiff dough and form into a roll. Cut through the centre of the roll lengthwise. Mix together all the ingredients for the filling and spread over one half of the roll, sandwich the two halves together and smooth with a knife. Place on a greased baking-sheet and bake for 30 min.

BEVERAGES

COFFEE

TO MAKE COFFEE

To make perfect coffee the beans should be roasted and ground just before they are to be used. As this is impracticable it is better to buy the beans and grind only as many as are required for immediate use. The beans should be stored in an airtight container. If a coffee mill is not available, it is better to buy only a small quantity of ground coffee at a time to avoid loss of flavour, and to store it in an airtight container.

Allow 2 heaped dessertsp. coffee (or 2 of the coffee-measuring spoons sponsored by the Coffee Publicity Association) and ½ pt. freshly boiled water for each person. Some people also add a pinch of salt.

Method 1: Warm an ordinary china jug, put in the coarsely ground coffee, pour on to it the boiling water, and stir vigorously. Allow the jug to stand for 1 min., then skim off any floating coffee grains, stand for a further 4 min., closely covered, where the contents will remain just below boiling-point. The coffee can then be poured slowly or strained into another warmed china jug and used at once.

Method 2: Put the coffee (coarsely ground) with the water into an enamel saucepan and bring almost to the boil. Reduce the heat and simmer very gently for 3 min. Dash in 1 teasp. cold water to help the grounds to settle. Strain into a warmed coffee-pot or jug.

Method 3: Use a percolator and fine- or medium-ground coffee. Into the percolator put as much fresh, cold water as is required and bring to the boil. Put the coffee into the basket and insert it in the percolator, cover, and return to heat. Allow to percolate *gently* for 6–8 min.

Method 4: The vacuum method. The equipment for this method consists of 2 containers plus a source of heat. Put the required amount of cold water into the lower container and place on the heat. Put the filter in the upper container and the required amount of fine- or medium-ground coffee in the upper container. Allow the water in the lower container to boil, then reduce heat—if electric switch off—then insert upper bowl with a slight twist to ensure a tight fit. Some vacuum models can be assembled completely before placing on the heat. When the water has risen into the upper container (some water will always remain in the lower container) stir well. In 1–3 min. (fine-ground coffee will require the shorter time) turn off heat; remove electric models from unit. When all the coffee has been drawn into the lower container, remove upper container and serve.

Method 5: Café filtre. Heat a coffee-pot or individual cups, place the finely ground coffee in the strainer over the coffee-pot and slowly pour over freshly boiled water and allow to drip through. When the water has dripped through remove strainer—if the coffee is not strong enough filter again.

Equipment for making coffee should always be kept scrupulously clean.

Coffee may be served black (*Café Noir*) or with milk (*Café au Lait*) or with cream (*Café Crème*). When serving *Café au Lait* it is usual to pour the 2 liquids into the cup at the same time, *the milk should be hot but not boiled.*

To make iced coffee: Make the coffee in the usual way, put into a closely covered, nonmetal container, then chill for not more than 3 hr. in a refrigerator. Chill the milk separately. Just before serving add milk to coffee, sweeten to taste, mix in a shaker or beat with a whisk.

To make burnt coffee: Allow 3 good teasp. coffee to each ½ pt. water, and prepare according to any of the preceding methods. Sweeten it rather more than ordinarily, and strain into small cups. Pour a little brandy into each over a spoon, set fire to it, and when the spirit is partly consumed the flame should be blown out, and the coffee drunk immediately.

TEA

The most popular non-alcoholic beverage is tea, now considered almost a necessity of life.

It is a pleasant beverage which has an exhilarating and refreshing effect.

TO MAKE TEA

To make good tea it is necessary that the water should be quite boiling and freshly boiled. It is a good plan to empty the kettle and refill it with fresh, cold water, and make the tea the moment the water reaches boiling-point.

The tea-pot should be thoroughly warmed before making the tea. The boiling water should be poured on the tea then left to stand for 3–4 min.; it should never be allowed to stand for longer. Some people like to stir the tea before pouring it out.

MISCELLANEOUS DRINKS

BACCHUS CUP

½ bottle of champagne
½ pt. sherry
⅛ pt. brandy
1 liqueur glass noyeau
1 tablesp. castor sugar
A few balm leaves
Ice
1 bottle of soda water

Put the champagne, sherry, brandy, noyeau, sugar and balm leaves into a jug, let it stand for a few minutes, then add a few pieces of ice and the soda water.

Serve at once.

CIDER CUP

1 bottle of cider
1 bottle of soda water
1 liqueur glass brandy
A few thin strips of cucumber rind
A few thin strips of lemon rind
1 dessertsp. lemon juice
1 dessertsp. castor sugar *or* to taste

Chill the cider and soda water for ½ hr. Put the brandy, cucumber and lemon rind, lemon juice and sugar into a large jug, add the chilled cider and soda water. Serve at once.

CLARET CUP

1 bottle of claret
Thinly-cut rind of 1 lemon
1–2 tablesp. castor sugar
1 wineglass sherry
1 liqueur glass brandy
1 liqueur glass noyeau
1 liqueur glass Maraschino
A few strips of cucumber rind *or* 2–3 sprigs balm, borage *or* verbena
1 large bottle of soda water

Put the claret, lemon rind and the sugar into a large jug, cover and chill for 1 hr. Add the rest of the ingredients and serve.

HOT PUNCH

1 large lemon
2–3 oz. loaf sugar
Pinch of ground cinnamon
Pinch of grated nutmeg
Pinch of cloves
½ pt. brandy
½ pt. rum
1 pt. boiling water

Remove the rind of the lemon by rubbing it with some of the sugar. Put all the sugar, the cinnamon, nutmeg, cloves, brandy, rum and boiling water into a stewpan, heat gently on the side of the stove, but do not let it boil. Strain the lemon juice into a punch bowl, add the hot liquid, serve at once.

MILK PUNCH

1 qt. milk
1 lemon
6 sweet almonds
2 bitter almonds
2 oz. sugar
1 egg white
1 gill cream
1 gill brandy
1 gill rum

Put the milk into an enamel saucepan together with the thinly-peeled rind of the lemon and the almonds and heat gently but do not boil. Stir in the sugar and when dissolved strain off the liquid into a basin and mix in the stiffly-whisked egg white, the cream, brandy and rum. Serve hot.

MULLED ALE

1 qt. ale
1 tablesp. castor sugar
Pinch of ground cloves
Pinch of ground nutmeg
Good pinch of ground ginger
1 glass rum *or* brandy

Put the ale, sugar, cloves, nutmeg and ginger into a stewpan, and bring nearly to boiling-point. Add the brandy and more sugar and flavouring if necessary; serve at once.

MULLED WINE

½ pt. water
6 cloves
¼ oz. bruised cinnamon
Nutmeg
½ lemon
1½ pt. port *or* claret
Sugar

Put the water in an enamel saucepan and heat gently, stir in the cloves, cinnamon, a grate of nutmeg and the thinly-peeled rind of the lemon. Bring to the boil and cook for 10 min. Strain off the liquid into a basin and add the wine. Sweeten to taste. Return the liquid to the pan and make hot without boiling. Serve at once with fingers of dry toast or wine biscuits.

TEA PUNCH

4 oz. loaf sugar
1 lemon
1 qt. tea
1 gill rum
1 gill brandy

Rub the sugar on the rind of the lemon to extract all the zest. Crush it in a basin and pour over it the tea. Stir in the strained lemon juice and add the rum and brandy. Stir until the sugar has dissolved, then stand in the refrigerator or on ice for 3 hr. Serve in wineglasses.

RASPBERRY VINEGAR

2 qt. raspberries
2 qt. white wine vinegar
1 lb. loaf *or* preserving sugar to every pt. of liquid

Put the raspberries into a wide-necked glass bottle, or an unglazed jar; pour over them the vinegar; cover, and let the liquid stand for 10 days, stirring it once or twice daily. Strain and measure the vinegar: add sugar in the proportion stated above and stir occasionally till the sugar is dissolved. Pour into a jar, place the jar in a saucepan of boiling water, and simmer gently for 1¼ hr., skimming when necessary. When quite cold, rack off into bottles and store in a cool, dry place, for use.

ROSE HIP SYRUP

6 pt. water
3 lb. ripe, wild, rose hips
2 lb. preserving sugar

Boil 4 pt. of the water. Mince the hips coarsely and put immediately into the boiling water. Heat until the water boils again, skim off the scum as it rises and boil for a few minutes. Then allow to cool for about 15 min. Pass the pulp through fine linen or muslin twice to ensure that all the hairs are removed. Put the liquid obtained to one side. Boil the pulp again with the remaining 2 pt. water, leave to cool for 15 min., and strain twice as before. Return both extracted liquids to the pan and boil until the juice is reduced to about 3 pt. Sweeten, stirring well. Pour into warmed bottles, seal; store in a dark cupboard until required.

WINE CUP

1 pt. champagne (iced)
1 pt. claret
1 pt. Apollinaris
1 wineglass brandy
1 wineglass Curaçao
1 orange, sliced
1 lemon, sliced
2 pieces of cucumber rind
Mint
2–3 tablesp. crushed ice

Put all the ingredients into a large glass jug, adding the crushed ice. If liked, a little castor sugar may be added. The cup is served with small sprigs of mint floating on its surface.

TABLE WINES

TO SERVE WINE with a meal at once enhances the value of the food and turns what might be an "everyday" meal into an "occasion". Many people think that wine-drinking in the home with meals is a rather expensive pleasure, for a fallacy concerning wine is that a cheap wine is necessarily a poor wine, but there are many good reasonably-priced wines on the market.

STORING WINE

The majority of people buy wine as they need it, very often only a few hours before it is going to be consumed. This practice has definite disadvantages; (*a*) it is not always possible to obtain the wine that is most wanted, and one has to make do with second best; (*b*) there is insufficient time to acclimatize the wine to room temperature and it is therefore not drunk at its prime; *and* (*c*) you often pay more for a good wine than you need. The reason for this last is that a good wine bought when it is young and laid down for a number of years may well cost only half of what it does when purchased from a merchant at the height of its maturity.

HOW TO STORE WINE

The ideal, of course, is to have a proper cellar, but in these days of flats and small houses the word "cellar" is receding from the vocabulary of wine. It is still used, however, to suggest a stock of wine, however small, and one may be said to have "built up a cellar" even though there be no cellar at all.

Wine should always be kept lying on its side; otherwise the cork will become dry and possibly allow the entry of air. The contrary, however, prevails in the case of spirits, where the action of the spirit may eat into the cork. Therefore spirits must be kept upright, the others arising from the bottle's contents having the effect of keeping the cork moist. If a proper place is available for keeping wine, even though it may only be under the stairs, it is well to have a simple wine-rack placed there. One advantage of a rack is that it saves the wine from being disturbed domestically, as it would be if lying loose beside the vacuum cleaner. Moreover, there is something satisfactory in seeing your bottles resting neatly in a rack.

Wine should be kept in the dark, or as nearly as possible. Otherwise, a cloth covering or even a sheet of brown paper may be found effective.

A NOTE ON TEMPERATURE

Wherever wine is kept one should keep an eye on the temperature. The accepted temperature is from 55° to 60° F.

It is advisable to store wine with the label uppermost so that, if the bottles must necessarily be moved, they can be relaid in the same position, thus avoiding any serious disturbance of the sediment, if any.

WHEN TO DECANT WINE

Speaking generally, the only wines one needs to decant are those red wines which throw a heavy sediment as they age. Both Clarets and Burgundies do this in varying degrees.

First, the decanter must be absolutely clean, for it is surprising how the mustiness left behind by its previous occupant persists in lingering. The decanter must also be absolutely dry.

An essential to decanting is a handled basket in which the bottle to be decanted is placed. The angle of the "cradle", as the basket is called, gives the bottle just sufficient tilt to ensure that no wine is spilt when the cork is withdrawn. This is the true function of the cradle, and it is *not* considered the right thing to use it to serve wine. Nor is it used in the actual decanting process, as it would be almost impossible to see when the sediment was approaching the neck.

THE ART OF DECANTING

To decant: having placed the bottle in the cradle and withdrawn the cork, the next step is to clean the neck inside and out. The bottle is now lifted carefully from the cradle, still tilted, and the transference of its contents into the decanter is begun. There should be a light behind the shoulder of the bottle—preferably a candle—so that the sediment can be seen as soon as it approaches the neck. This is the signal to stop decanting. On no account should the wine have been allowed to flow back during the pouring.

One can, of course, decant without a cradle, in this way: place the bottle to be decanted in an upright position and leave it so for at least 24 hours—the longer the better. This will allow the looser of the sediment, as distinct from crust, to sink to the bottom. Extract the cork while the bottle is still vertical, then gradually tilt it and proceed as before.

To be on the safe side, especially in the case of a Crusted Port, one may pour the wine into the decanter by way of a plastic or enamel funnel, in which has been placed a lining of fine muslin, or, better still, a chemist's filter paper.

Sherry *Wine* *Champagne* *Brandy* *Port* *Claret*

WINE AND FOOD

MEALS	WINES BEST SUITED TO ACCOMPANY THEM			
Aperitifs, to stimulate the appetite	Sherry Fino *or* Amontillado	Vermouth French *or* Italian (chilled)	White Port	Dry Madeira
Soup, hors d'œuvres	Sherry Fino *or* Amontillado	Dry Madeira		
Shellfish, oysters, fish, cold chicken	A dry white wine such as Hock, Moselle, White Burgundy *or* Dry Graves. Dry white Portuguese, Spanish *or* Italian wines are also very suitable.			
Meat dishes, roast chicken, goose, duck, game	A red wine, usually a light claret, with white meats and a heavier wine, like a Burgundy, with the stronger flavours. The lovers Hock *or* Traminer. Spanish, Portuguese *or* Italian dry *or* fuller wines.			
Sweets, ices	Sweets with the sweet is the rule. Here a sweet white wine, a Sauterne, a sweet Graves, Barsac, Cerons, from Bordeaux, a rich sweet Hock *or* any sweet white wine from Spain, Portugal, Italy, Cyprus, Australia, South Africa.			
Nuts, coffee	A fine old Tawny Port *or* a vintage Port *or* Madeira.			

INDEX